Birth Card and Planetary Ruling Card Chart

JULY

	BC	PRC		BC	PRC
1	A♠	3♦	17	J♣	Q♠
2	K♦	K♥	18	10♣	Q♥
3	Q♦	A♦	19	9♣	J♥
4	J♦	K♣	20	8♣	J♠
5	10♦	10♥	21	7♣	9♥
6	9♦	J♣	22	6♣	8♥
7	8♦	10♣	23	5♣	10♠ or 5♣*
8	7♦	7♥	24	4♣	4♠
9	6♦	8♣	25	3♣	3♠
10	5♦	7♣	26	2♣	2♣
11	4♦	4♥	27	A♣	A♣
12	3♦	5♣	28	K♥	K♥
13	2♦	4♣	29	Q♥	Q♥
14	A♦	A♥	30	J♥	J♥
15	K♣	2♣	31	10♥	10♥
16	Q♣	A♣			

[AUGUST]

	BC	PRC		BC	PRC
1	Q♦	Q♦			
2	J♦	J♦			
3	10♦	10♦			
4	9♦	9♦	20	6♣	6♣
5	8♦	8♦	21	5♣	5♣
6	7♦	7♦	22	4♣	4♣ or 2♦*
7	6♦	6♦	23	3♣	3♣ or 3♠*
8	5♦	5♦	24	2♣	K♣
9	4♦	4♦	25	A♣	Q♣
10	3♦	3♦	26	K♥	K♦
11	2♦	2♦	27	Q♥	10♣
12	A♦	A♦	28	J♥	9♣
13	K♣	K♣	29	10♥	10♦
14	Q♣	Q♣	30	9♥	7♣
15	J♣	J♣	31	8♥	6♣
16	10♣	10♣			

SEPTEMBER

	BC	PRC		BC	PRC
1	10♦	8♠	16	8♣	6♦
2	9♦	7♠	17	7♣	5♦
3	8♦	K♠	18	6♣	6♠
4	7♦	5♠	19	5♣	3♦
5	6♦	4♠	20	4♣	2♦
6	5♦	Q♠	21	3♣	3♠
7	4♦	2♠	22	2♣	K♣ or J♦*
8	3♦	A♠	23	A♣	Q♣ or 10♠*
9	2♦	J♠	24	K♥	6♥
10	A♦	Q♦	25	Q♥	8♦
11	K♣	J♦	26	J♥	9♠
12	Q♣	10♠	27	10♥	8♣
13	J♣	9♦	28	9♥	5♦
14	10♣	8♦	29	8♥	6♣
15	9♣	9♠	30	7♥	5♠

OCTOBER

	BC	PRC		BC	PRC
1	8♦	3♥	18	4♣	J♠
2	7♦	J♥	19	3♣	9♥
3	6♦	10♥	20	2♣	J♦
4	5♦	J♣	21	A♣	10♠
5	4♦	8♥	22	K♥	6♥
6	3♦	7♥	23	Q♥	8♦, or K♠ & 5♣*
7	2♦	8♣			
8	A♦	5♥	24	J♥	9♥, or 2♥ & 2♦*
9	K♣	4♥			
10	Q♣	5♣	25	10♥	A♥ & 3♠
11	J♣	7♠	26	9♥	Q♠ & K♠
12	10♣	K♠	27	8♥	Q♥ & A♣
13	9♣	2♥	28	7♥	J♥ & K♠
14	8♣	4♠	29	6♥	J♠ & 10♦
15	7♣	Q♠	30	5♥	9♥ & 9♦
16	6♣	Q♥	31	4♥	8♥ & 8♦
17	5♣	A♠			

NOVEMBER

	BC	PRC		BC	PRC
1	6♦	10♦ & 5♥	16	4♣	8♣ & 8♠
2	5♦	9♦ & 4♥	17	3♣	7♣ & 7♠
3	4♦	6♣ & K♠	18	2♣	4♥ & 6♠
4	3♦	7♦ & 2♥	19	A♣	5♣ & 5♠
5	2♦	6♦ & A♥	20	K♥	4♣ & 4♠
6	A♦	3♣ & Q♠	21	Q♥	K♠ & 5♣
7	K♣	4♦ & Q♥	22	J♥	2♥ & 2♦
8	Q♣	3♦ & J♥	23	10♥	A♦
9	J♣	2♣ & 2♠	24	9♥	J♣
10	10♣	3♥ & 3♦	25	8♥	10♣
11	9♣	K♥ & J♠	26	7♥	9♣
12	8♣	10♥ & Q♦	27	6♥	8♣
13	7♣	J♣ & J♦	28	5♥	7♣
14	6♣	10♣ & Q♣	29	4♥	6♣
15	5♣	7♥ & 9♠	30	3♥	5♣

DECEMBER

	BC	PRC		BC	PRC
1	4♦	6♠	17	A♣	3♦
2	3♦	5♠	18	K♥	2♦
3	2♦	4♠	19	Q♥	3♥
4	A♦	3♠	20	J♥	K♥
5	K♣	2♠	21	10♥	A♦ or Q♦*
6	Q♣	A♠	22	9♥	J♣ or 9♦*
7	J♣	K♣	23	8♥	8♦
8	10♣	A♣	24	7♥	9♠
9	9♣	K♦	25	6♥	6♦
10	8♣	10♦	26	5♥	5♦
11	7♣	9♦	27	4♥	6♠
12	6♣	8♦	28	3♥	3♦
13	5♣	7♦	29	2♥	2♦
14	4♣	6♦	30	A♥	3♠
15	3♣	5♦	31	Joker	
16	2♣	4♦			

*denotes cusp birth dates—see page 109 for full explanation.

CARDS

What
Your Birthday
Reveals About You
and Your Past,
Present, and
Future

Of
YOUR
DESTINY

ROBERT LEE CAMP

 sourcebooks

This publication is designed to provide accurate and authoritative information in regard to the subject matter covered. It is sold with the understanding that the publisher is not engaged in rendering legal, accounting, or other professional service. If legal advice or other expert assistance is required, the services of a competent professional person should be sought.
—*From a Declaration of Principles Jointly Adopted by a Committee of the American Bar Association and a Committee of Publishers and Associations*

Published by Sourcebooks, Inc.
P.O. Box 4410, Naperville, Illinois 60566
(630) 961-3900
Fax: (630) 961-2168
www.sourcebooks.com

Originally published in 1998 as *Destiny Cards*.

Library of Congress Cataloging-in-Publication data is on file with the publisher.

Printed and bound in the United States of America.
BB 10 9 8 7 6 5 4 3 2 1

This book is dedicated to all seekers of truth who are willing to look where others fear to tread. May this book deepen your connection to yourself and to life here on this beautiful planet as it really is.

Contents

Introduction

In 1973, a man by the name of Arne Lein made an amazing and startling prediction. Arne Lein studied astrology, numerology, and the science of the cards and had many television and motion picture personalities among his clients. By chance, he was asked by *Tennis Illustrated* magazine to test his system of prediction by deciding who would be the winners of the Wimbledon tennis matches for that year. As Arne began his study of all the contenders, he discovered a fascinating pattern emerging. He noticed that the cards of all the American contenders were showing very bad results for the date of the matches. Their cards showed frustration and disappointment, usually associated with losing matches. Trusting in his system, Arne told *Tennis Illustrated* that none of the Americans would win those matches or even do well. This was unusual since so many of the top contenders were American. As the date of the matches drew near, a political issue came up whereby none of the Americans were allowed to compete in the matches that year. *Tennis Illustrated* was stunned that Arne's prediction had come true. So much so, in fact, that they asked him to write a monthly astrology column, which, as you can imagine, is unusual for a tennis magazine. The techniques that Arne Lein used to make his predictions are the very same that you are about to learn while reading this book. Arne Lein was one of my first teachers in the cards, and I pass on to you this ancient and amazing science of forecasting that I have used successfully in my reading practice for the past eight years. It is the most accurate and easy to learn system I have ever found. Prepare yourself to be amazed at the information you will obtain from it. I certainly was and still am.

What you are about to learn is part of an ancient esoteric science that has been kept secret for centuries. Mystical orders that have been in existence since before ancient Egypt have carefully preserved its secrets totally intact to be released to the public when the time was right. This is the first book to completely unveil these secrets and to show you, in great detail, how to use this fortune-telling system to learn everything about your past, present, or future. You are among the first to discover and use the power of this ancient system, which is the original science associated with our common playing cards.

Inside, you will first discover what your Birth Card is. Once you know what this card is, you will be able to look up any year of your life and read the cards of your Yearly Spreads, which give specific and detailed information about every important area of your life. You will be able to know, in advance, what will be happening in the areas of love, romance, family, work, finances, health, travel, legal matters, and your spiritual life. You will know what are the best times for marriage, business expansion, changing jobs or lines of work, travel, and the sale of real estate. You will be able to see what is going to happen between you and anyone else that you know. People you know will be mentioned in your cards by their exact birthday. The essential nature of all your relationships will be fully explained, both on a lifelong basis and for the year ahead.

This book will guide you through the simple steps of doing a complete one-year reading for yourself. This one-year reading has specific information concerning each month of the year. In addition to this, you will learn how to do a weekly reading that shows you the influences present for every day of the week. With these two tools, you will have a valuable guide to help you make all your important decisions. Again, you can also use what you learn to do readings for anyone you choose. Many people have turned this science into a full-time career. Just as Arne Lein did, you will be able to make predictions about anyone for any purpose. Its knowledge can be applied to business or personal matters with great success.

This system is unique. Though it involves our common playing cards, you do not need a deck of cards to do a yearly reading, nor will you need any psychic power. All the cards that represent the events and relationships of every month and year of your life are already chosen for you and ready to be looked up in this book. It is like the fabled and mysterious book of destiny that so many ancient myths allude to. You will actually find a record of your entire life within this book. Whether you care to look into the future or the past, the information is here. All you have to learn is where to look it up and how to interpret the language of the cards. The meanings of all the cards are included so that you can easily translate your cards into information you can use.

To do a reading for yourself or anyone else you only need know three bits of information—1) birth date, 2) sex, and 3) occupation. With this information alone, you will be able to access information that is both pertinent and practical. Unlike astrology, you do not need the place or time of birth.

Anyone can learn and use this method to advantage—both novices and professionals. If you are new to forecasting techniques, this system will give you some basics of astrology and numerology that will expand your overall comprehension of those subjects. This system is a magical combination of the cards, astrology, and numerology that can be learned quickly and easily. If you have tried other systems, you will find this technique easy to understand and apply. The average person can begin doing readings within hours of beginning this book. Compare that to the years it takes most people to learn the art of astrological predictions. If you have studied numerology or astrology, you will find that your previous studies will add to your comprehension of this "science" and accelerate your mastery of it.

But how specific and accurate is the information? Most people who learn it are surprised by its uncanny accuracy—how it names specific people and dates for events, often pinpointing exactly what will happen and with whom. I have found that this system is 100 percent accurate. This I have discovered after years

of using and studying it. The more you use it, the more accurate it becomes because your comprehension of it increases. In the beginning, you will find it pinpointing specific events in an amazing way. Later, as you become more experienced at using it, you will see that it also shows you the hidden influences that are behind the external manifestations in your life. Its value as a guide for life decisions increases each time you use it.

After using this method for a while, you will find that it offers other benefits you probably were not expecting. Because this system has its roots in some of our oldest mystical orders, the information it provides can be a spiritual guide to help you better understand how and why you create your life the way you do. In a way, this book is a gateway to an entire philosophy of material and spiritual attainment, a philosophy sustained by one of the oldest spiritual fellowships in existence—The Order of the Magi. As you study the meanings of your cards each year, you will find that you have opportunities to alter the course of your destiny. The card meanings will provide you with alternative approaches to the situations that arise in your life and will suggest how to get the greatest good from them. Difficulties can often be avoided through approaching the situation with the right attitude. For example, knowing in advance when the influences are favorable for expansion of your finances and business interests will give you the green light to move forward with confidence. The same principle will increase your successes in your romantic life. Using this system is sort of like driving at night with your headlights on. With your lights on, you can see in advance what is ahead of you and make the proper adjustments in your course to arrive quickly and safely at your destination.

In the next chapters, you will begin your study by learning about the cards which represent you—your Birth Card, Planetary Ruling Card, and Personality Cards. Next, using the charts provided, you will learn how to use and interpret the Yearly Spreads of yourself and your friends. Later, this book will teach you how to do weekly readings using a simple but advanced technique of interpreting the spreads. Both beginners and experts will benefit from the detailed interpretations of every card found within.

I hope you enjoy using this system and discover for yourself just how amazing and fun it is to use. We offer many forms of support and instruction for those who are interested. There are audio and video tapes, computer software packages, and classes you can take if you decide you want or need further clarification or instruction. Look in the back of the book for more information on these products and services. In the meantime, enjoy using a system that was once only used by the high priests in ancient mystical orders. The truth is for all to share and use, especially now, in our awakening Age of Aquarius.

Best wishes,

Robert Lee Camp

Chapter One
Our Fascinating Playing Cards

Most people have never stopped to wonder about the many interesting things associated with our common playing cards. Why, for instance, are there fifty-two cards in a deck? Why four suits? What do these suits represent, if anything? Where did the playing cards come from? I would like to share with you some interesting connections that our cards have with our world and reveal to you why they are actually a calendar system that is intimately connected to our life here on Earth.

The Deck of Cards Is Our Calendar

Let's examine some of the things our little deck and calendar have in common. First of all, as I just mentioned there are four suits of thirteen cards each, totaling fifty-two cards, plus a Joker. Let's begin with the number 52. What else is there fifty-two of that is common knowledge? Well, there are fifty-two weeks in a year. Now, in numerology we reduce numbers by adding their digits. If we reduce the number 52 we get 5 + 2 = 7 — the number of days in a week, and the number of visible planets. Seven is a very magical number in many ways and is considered the most spiritual number. It is also used extensively in many mystical traditions, including the Bible. Fascinating, isn't it? We can imagine that sometime in our ancient past, man discovered that a full year comprised something in the neighborhood of 365 days and nights. Looking into the heavens, they also noticed the sun, moon, and five other visible 'objects' that we now know are planets circling our sun. Taking their combined number, 7, and dividing the number of days in a year by it, they came up with fifty-two cycles in a year that we now call weeks. The wise ones realized that this number had much more significance and used these simple facts as a springboard for more advanced study.

Once again, taking the numerology of the cards, we assign numeric values to each of the cards. The Aces are 1, the Twos, 2, and so forth until we get to the Jack. The Jack is given the value of 11, the Queen, 12, and the King 13. Now, if we add up all the number values of every card in the deck, what do you guess will be the result? This means four times thirteen for the four Kings plus four times twelve for the four Queens, etc. What would be the resulting total of every card in the deck? Did you guess 365? Well, that's pretty close. The total actually comes to 364. We know that there are 365 and 1/4 days in a year, so what happened to the other day and a quarter? There is also another card in the deck that we haven't counted yet, and that is the Joker. And guess what? The Joker's value is exactly that of one and one quarter, which brings the total value of the deck of cards to exactly equal the number of days in a year. The twelve court cards in the deck represent the twelve months in the year. The Joker's value of one and one quarter comes from the fact that he is 'all the four suits plus himself.' He stands apart as a unique balancing element in the scheme of the cards and the many card personalities.

These numeric values alone should convince the average person that there is more to a deck of cards than meets the eye. In fact, our deck of cards originated as a tool used to make calculations and estimations of time and the movements of Earth and the other planets surrounding our sun. Using the most advanced techniques, a deck of cards has been used to calculate the exact movement of the planets in our solar system. The closer we look at a deck of cards, the more fascinating they become. Every aspect of their construction and design has significance and pertains to the world we live in.

THE JOKER

There is one birthday of the year that cannot be read by this system. That is December 31st, the birthday of the Joker Card. Since the person born a Joker can choose to be any card in the deck, it is impossible to read them. In the days of Kings and courts, New Year's Eve was considered "Fool's Day." On that day, the court jester would ascend to the throne and make jest of the King and Queen and all the citizens of the court and country. He would imitate them all, showing them the folly of their ways and how absurd some of their pompous drama was. Perhaps this is why the Joker Card is an enigma.

The Seasons and Their Corresponding Suits

Let's look now at the four suits. Our cards are symbols, and everything about them symbolizes something. What do you imagine they represent? The numbers have meanings as well as the suits. Well, if you guessed that the suits represent the four seasons and the four elements (water, air, earth, and fire), you are right again. All these sets of four things are connected, as anyone who studies the Tarot or astrology will tell you. There is a suit for each season and element. Before we examine the suits and their meanings more closely, I suggest you look up your Birth Card in the chart at the end of the book. Just see which card is listed for your birthday, that is your Birth Card. The suit of your Birth Card will reveal something about your life and personality.

The first season of the year is spring. Animals are bearing their young, April showers are bringing a riot of colorful flowers, love is in the air, and life is erupting everywhere. In the first season of our life, we are surrounded by the love and caring of our parents and family. This season, so filled with love and life-giving rain, is represented by the suit of Hearts, which is the element of water and would be the suit of cups in the Tarot. In the Book of Destiny system, Heart Cards represent love and relationships. If your personal Birth Card is of the Hearts suit, you are a person whose main form of expression and whose personal karma is worked out through the vehicle of relationships. In addition, if you are a Heart, you are essentially childlike in your nature, and you relate well to children—you may even work with them. Hearts are the children of the deck, regardless of their physical age. No matter what your Birth Card is, when any of the Heart Cards appear in your Yearly Spreads they will be referring to the status or quality of your relationships, or will tell you of changes to that status or quality. All of the Marriage Cards and most of the Divorce Cards are Hearts.

The next season is summer, and during the summer season of life, love and family no longer surround us. Instead, we find ourselves occupied by school, books, and knowledge. In this season, we leave the love and tears of childhood behind and turn our attention to more educational pursuits. The suit that corresponds to summer is Clubs, which is of the air element. This is the same as the swords suit in the Tarot. Clubs represent the status of our mind and mental pursuits, acquisition of knowledge, and communications. Those who are born in the suit of Clubs work with ideas, points of view, and the ability to communicate. For them, the idea and concept of a person or thing is often just as important as the thing itself. Clubs are the eternal college students, usually eager to learn new things and interested in the details of life. When you find Club Cards in your yearly readings, these will tell you about the status of your mind, your ability to communicate, or the success or failure of your mental pursuits and interests. These pursuits would include publishing, teaching, writing, public speaking, or going to school.

In the autumn season, we are harvesting the fruits or our efforts, reaping the riches we have sown in the soil of our lives. It is in the autumn season of life that we generally accumulate wealth and property. Diamonds represent this third season, and they coincide with the element of earth and the suit of Pentacles in the Tarot. The most common meaning of Diamonds is money, though on a deeper level, they represent what we most value in life. Those born as a Diamond Card work out their karma with money and values. Diamonds are the adults of the deck, and Diamond children do not like being treated as anything other than adults. When Diamonds appear in your Yearly Spread, they are usually referring to the status of or changes to your money supply. All of the Money Cards are Diamond Cards, though some of them point to the status of your basic value system.

It is in the winter season that death and transformation reign supreme. After the harvest, winter sets in, and much of what was born in the spring dies away. In the winter season of life, we prepare for, and eventually experience, our own death. Health concerns become more prominent, as well as our interest in our spiritual life. Though the shadow of the gravedigger's spade is ever present on our minds, so too, is the promise of a new spiritual life. This promise, like a phoenix rising from the ashes, makes the winter suit, the suit of Spades, the most powerful suit. This transformative quality of the last period of our life connects Spades to the element of fire and the suit of wands in the Tarot. Spades are a more complicated suit in some ways. They represent work and health on a basic, material level, but on a deeper level, they represent spirituality and the condition of our inner 'fire.' All of the traditional Death Cards are Spades. Those born as Spade Cards usually have a very strong materialistic nature or a very spiritual nature, sometimes both. In any case, they are very hard-working people. Spades are the old people of the deck, often showing more wisdom and maturity at an early age. They usually focus much of their attention on the perfection of their work. When Spade Cards are found in your Yearly Spreads, they will be telling you about the status of or changes in your work or health. On a deeper level, Spades can tell you about the status of your spiritual endeavors.

THE FASCINATING ACE OF SPADES

If you get out a deck of cards right now and look through them, you will notice that the Ace of Spades is much different than the other Aces in the deck. First of all, it has a much larger symbol in the center of the card. Secondly, on many decks, you will find that the center Spade symbol has been ornately decorated, often very beautifully. Usually manufacturers will place their company name on this card somewhere. Do you know why the Ace of Spades is so different? Most of the manufacturers don't even know, but it is because the Ace of Spades is the card that represents The Order of the Magi and the secret societies of old. It is the one card, above all others, that represents the secrets that are there to be discovered by studying the cards in-depth. In our system, the Ace of Spades represents secrets as well. It is the card that represents the science of the cards.

The Ace of Spades has always been a symbol of death as well. It is likened to a single bullet that ends our life. Many cultures have used this card in film and literature as a death

symbol. It holds true here as well. The Ace of Spades is one of the more powerful symbols for personal transformation, and in some cases, physical death.

The Little Book of the Seven Thunders

Now that we have learned a little about the fascinating links that the cards have to our world, let's look a bit at the history of our cards. First consider this verse from the Bible:

> And when the Seven Thunders had uttered their voices, I was about to write; but I heard a voice from heaven saying unto me, "Seal up those things, uttered by the Seven Thunders, and write them not."
>
> And I took the little book out of the Angel's hand and devoured it; and to my taste it was sweet as honey; but as soon as I had devoured it, it became bitter unto my inside.
>
> And he said unto me, "You must prophecy again before many peoples and nations and tongues and kings."
>
> *Revelations, 10:4, 10, and 11*

The first-known book ever published about this system of divination and self-understanding is *The Mystic Test Book*, by Olney Richmond, originally published in 1893. Mr. Richmond was at that time the Grand Master of a secret society known as The Order of the Magi. He claims that his order was instructed, since the days of Egypt, to keep the secrets of the cards alive and protected until the proper time for their revelation to the world. Olney Richmond claims that the above passage from Revelations, if translated with awareness of the subtleties of spiritual discernment, reveals that the 'little book' mentioned is the book of our same fifty-two cards. According to Mr. Richmond, these passages clearly indicate their mission to keep their secrets hidden from the reach of the common man until the time was right. Whether this is true or not, it is interesting to note that his book was the first book to reveal any of these secrets. No other books have been found with any similar materials prior to that time.

Richmond goes on to explain how the cards must have originated in Atlantis, since all major civilizations claim their invention, and then goes on to explore many other facets of the cards that are both fascinating and amazing. Having read his book several times and used the cards as long as I have, I still haven't begun to understand some of the topics in that book. I will say, however, that based on what I have learned so far, it is clear to me that if we were to completely understand their numbers and meanings, we would have a tool that could easily give us specific information about almost any area of life or science. His is a fascinating book that can still be purchased at some metaphysical bookstores.

One other interesting fact he discusses that I would like to mention is that over the years, card manufacturers have tried unsuccessfully to print cards with different faces on the Queens, Kings, and Jacks. Even today, if you go into some of the larger game stores, you will find a host of other kinds of playing cards. Some will have oriental characters, some will have the faces of famous people on them and the like. At any rate, if you ask any card manufacturer, they will tell you that these variations of cards never sell that well. Richmond claims that the reason the other variations of cards do not sell is that the decks of cards have a mystical potency, which maintains the integrity of their original design. For this reason, he says, the other cards never sell. Olney says that the members of their order were instructed never to deface, alter, or otherwise change the cards in any way. For this reason, I personally recommend that when you choose cards to use to do your weekly readings, choose cards that are of the original design, and avoid cards that are different. This includes cards that have the large numbers and the reduced faces. Stick with the old standbys, and your chances of obtaining an accurate reading are increased.

I hope that I've stimulated your interest in our not so common deck of cards. Now, we will begin to learn more about you and your place in the cards. As we uncover more of its secrets, keep in mind that the science you are now learning has been around a long time and has many connections to our past heritage.

Chapter Two

Your Place among the Cards

All of the information you will need to do a reading can be found in the cards. The most important card, the specific card that represents each of us, is our Birth Card. However, there are other cards that represent us and other people. There are also cards that tell us what the events will be in our lives. In this chapter, we will begin by looking at the cards that represent you and the people you know. We call this group of cards the *personal significators*.

What Is Your Birth Card?

If you haven't looked up your birthday yet, do so now by finding the card that corresponds to your birthday in the Birth and Planetary Ruling Card Chart, located in the back of this book. This chart is a valuable tool, because it will be important to know your Birth Card, as well as the Birth Cards of all your friends and associates. As we begin looking at the cards that make up your yearly readings, we will want to know if any of the cards we find are either your Birth Card or the Birth Cards of people you know. This will become clearer as we look at your Yearly Spreads of cards. You can learn much about yourself and your friends and family by studying Birth Cards and knowing more about their meanings. Although this book does not go into much detail about the personality of each card, there is a wealth of information about your life and personality available in my book, *Love Cards*, which is available where you purchased this book. The purpose of *Cards of Your Destiny* is to teach you the predictive aspects of this wonderful science, so for now, we'll talk about these cards just enough to help you learn how to do your own readings. It is important to know that your Birth Card is the single most important of your personal significators. When we begin looking up your Yearly Spreads, we will always pay more attention to the Yearly Spread of your Birth Card than any other. If you only had time to read the cards for one of your significators, you would always choose the Birth Card.

What Is Your Planetary Ruling Card?

Though the Birth Card is the most important of the personal significators, the Planetary Ruling Card is close behind. It acts as a secondary symbol of your life and personality, essentially another card that we act like. Some people even act more like their Planetary Ruling Card than their Birth Card. When we do a personal reading, we will use the Yearly Spreads for both the Birth Card and Planetary Ruling Card, giving us two Yearly Spreads to consider.

We find our Planetary Ruling Card in the same way as the Birth Card, by using the table in the back of the book. It is listed just after the Birth Card. Pay special attention if your Planetary Ruling Card has an asterisk (*) beside it. This means you were born on one of the cusp birthdays. Since the Planetary Ruling Card is determined from our sun sign, astrologically speaking, people born on the cusp have to first identify their exact sun sign before they determine which card is their Planetary Ruling Card. See chapter nine if you want to learn more about where the Planetary Ruling Card comes from and how to determine what yours is if you are born on a cusp birthday.

A quick note about Leos and Scorpios: the Planetary Ruling Card for Leos is the same as their Birth Card, so we don't use them or do a separate Yearly Spread for them. On the other hand, Scorpios have two Planetary Ruling Cards, and they have a choice whether to do Yearly Spreads for both, or one. Again, see chapter nine for more specifics about these topics.

What Are Your Personality Cards?

In some cases, you will want to do Yearly Spreads for one or more of your Personality Cards. The Personality Cards are the Jacks, Queens, and Kings of the same suit as your Birth Card. They are much like hats that we wear for different roles that we play at different times in our life. Unlike the Birth Card and Planetary Ruling Card, the Personality Cards are not really a strong symbol of who we are. They are roles that we can choose to play or not over the course of our lives. You can start and stop operating as your Personality Card at any time, but you can never stop being either your Birth Card or Planetary Ruling Card.

Your age, sex, and occupation determine many Personality Cards you have available to use, and what they are. The following section explains how to determine which Personality Cards are available to you.

The Personality Cards for Women

If you are a female of any age, you always have the **Queen** of your suit as one of your Personality Cards. For example, if your Birth Card is the 9♥, then one of your Personality Cards is the Q♥. If your Birth Card is already a Queen, such as the Q♦, then you wouldn't have the Q♦ as a Personality Card also. In this case, you are already a Queen in personality by birth. If you do have a Queen as a Personality Card, the Queen represents your feminine, romantic, and motherly side, and the part of you that is service-oriented.

To give a couple examples, if your birthday was May 19th and you are a female, then your Birth Card would be the K♣. In this case, you would have the Q♣ as a Personality Card as well. If your birthday were March 17th, your Birth Card is the 6♦, and at least one of your Personality Cards is the Q♦.

I say at least one of your Personality Cards, because women can have up to three Personality Cards. Any woman who is self-employed as the owner of a business establishment or who manages others at her job also has the **King** of her suit as a Personality Card. However, for this to be true, that business must employ at least one other person. In this case, the King represents her role as the head of that business or the head of whatever group she is managing.

A woman who is employed as an actress, creative writer, or a professional artist can also consider the **Jack** of her suit as another Personality Card. From this, you can see that a woman may have three Personality Cards by being an actress, artist, or writer who also has a business of her own. Remember that if a woman's Birth Card is already a King or Jack, then you do not consider them as Personality Cards also. Please study the following examples closely until you fully grasp this concept.

Examples:

Let's take the example of a woman born on November 7th. We look up and see that her Birth Card is the K♣. We discover that she is not self-employed or working as an actress or artist, so her only Personality Card is the Q♣.

How about the woman born on September 26th who has her own business? Well, her Birth Card is the J♥. Her first Personality Card would be the Q♥, since she is a woman, and she would also have the K♥ as a second Personality Card that represents her role in her business.

The Personality Cards for Men

Every man, regardless of his age, has the **Jack** of the same suit as his Birth Card as one of his Personality Cards. This is, of course, unless his Birth Card is already a Jack. The Jack represents that aspect of a man's personality that is more youthful, playful, and creative. Salesmen, actors, and creative occupations are also associated with Jacks, so if a man is a salesman, inventor, or actor, the Jack would represent those parts of his life.

When a man becomes thirty-six years of age, regardless of his occupation, he acquires the **King** of his suit as an additional Personality Card. Also, just as in the case of women, a man of any age who owns and runs a business with at least one employee has the **King** as one of his Personality Cards. The King represents a man's more mature side or his role as the provider, the business owner, and the king of his castle or household.

Examples:

A man who is born on June 19th, who is twenty-eight years old and going to school has no Personality Cards. His Birth Card is the J♣ and he is not self-employed or old enough to be a King.

A man born on January 15th is a Q♦. If he is over thirty-six years old, then he has two Personality Cards, the K♦, as well as the J♦.

Exceptions

I have recently noted that young women can often be considered as the Jack of their suit until they reach an age where they fully develop and move into their roles as women. Jacks are often considered as being neither male nor female, as they are the undeveloped, undetermined cards, equivalent to the Pages in the Tarot. I suggest that you use Jacks for women under the age of twenty unless they exhibit full maturity in their feminine role.

I have also seen that women and men who are in actuality not the owners of businesses, but who, instead, are managers of groups of people, also act as Kings and should be given the King as a Personality Card for readings. Since the concept of a King is that of a ruler, anyone in a position of power in management would qualify in fitting this description.

From this, you can see that these rules are not completely hard and fast. Much will depend upon the personality of the person you are reading for.

The Personality Cards for Homosexuals and Bisexuals

In today's world, gender is not a fixed quality that can be ascribed to anyone completely. Some people, such as men who are Queens by Birth Card or women who are Kings, will act a lot like the opposite sex. Homosexual roles and personalities can be any number of combinations of male and female. Below are the general rules for determination, but in the end, let your judgment be the guide.

Since much of the determination of the Personality Cards is based upon gender, those who behave opposite their natural gender roles can often be considered to have the opposite Personality Cards than usual. For example, any woman who is decidedly masculine in a gay relationship can be considered to have the **Jack** or **King** of her suit as a Personality Card. In fact, most masculine and aggressive women usually have a Jack or King as their Birth Card or Planetary Ruling Card. But if you are, or meet one who doesn't have a Jack or King already, you can certainly consider these Personality Cards here.

In a similar fashion, any man who is in a gay relationship and decidedly feminine can be considered to have the **Queen** of his suit as a Personality Card. In this case, you would look under the Queen to find out about the events for that part of his personality and life.

The Cards I Use in Doing Yearly Spreads

If we use too many personal significators and end up with too many Yearly Spreads, interpreting our cards can become very confusing. It is a very bad idea to try and do as many of the personal significators as you can. In both my personal and professional readings, I usually focus on the Yearly Spreads for just two cards—the Birth Card and Planetary Ruling Card. If the person I am reading for is a Leo, who has no separate Planetary Ruling Card, I will use their Jack or Queen, depending upon their sex. The only other case when I use a Jack or Queen is when the person I am reading for is currently involved in an important romantic involvement or when they have important marriage or relationship issues that did not get addressed in the Yearly Spreads for their Birth Card or Planetary Ruling Card. I find that the Personality Cards are rarely necessary, because I generally get information about my clients' love lives from the Yearly Spreads of their Birth Card and Planetary Ruling Card. So, for most people, it's just two Yearly Spreads I concern myself with. If they have relationship and romantic issues, I usually find cards pertaining to these in the spreads for their Birth Card and Planetary Ruling Card. If I don't, then, and then only, do I look at the Personality Card Spreads. I rarely use the King for anyone. People who are operating in a kingly position are usually already a King by Birth Card or Planetary Ruling Card.

You may want to come back and reread this section later after you have learned more about the system. This one little bit of information can save you hours and hours of needless work.

Exercise:

These are the rules for determining the cards that represent you and others that you know. It is very important that you fully understand these rules before you go on, so I would like you to complete the table in the back of the book on page 361 called Friends and Associates. For now, write down the names and birth dates of the ten most important people in your life. Then, look up their Birth Card and Planetary Ruling Cards, and write them in at the appropriate spot. Finally, apply the rules you just learned to determine their Personality Cards, and write them in as well. When you are done, you will have a list that you will be using very soon as you do your very first personal reading.

Chapter Three
The Cards of Your Yearly Spreads

Now that you know the personal significators of you and your friends, you are ready to read the *Cards of Your Destiny* for this year of your life. The Yearly Spreads contain the actual cards of your destiny—the cards that tell you what is going to happen to you, when it is going to happen, and who it is going to happen with. There is at least one Yearly Spread for every year of your life already recorded in this book. If you have a Planetary Ruling Card or plan to use one or more of your Personality Cards, there is a Yearly Spread for each of them as well. So, there will be one Yearly Spread for your Birth Card, one for your Planetary Ruling Card, and one for each Personality Card that you choose to use for your reading. Each of your Yearly Spreads, whether you use one or four or five, will have some specific information about your life this year, so you will need to look at all of them to get the total picture of what is going on for you. Let's begin by looking at your Yearly Spreads and see how the cards in them are organized.

To see your Yearly Spread for your Birth Card this year, turn to the section of the book that begins on page 249, The Yearly Spreads, and find the two pages that have your *Birth Card* at the top of the page. It is organized with all the cards of each suit together, beginning with the Hearts from Ace to King and then going to the Clubs, Diamonds, and Spades. Go ahead and find your two pages now.

Once you have found the correct pages, find the group of cards next to the number of your current age. For example, if your Birth Card is the 9♦, and you are thirty-one years old, your Yearly Spread would look like this:

	AGE	MER	VEN	MAR	JUP	SAT	URA	NEP	LR	PLU/RES	ENV	DISP
9♦ BIRTH CARD	31	7♠	K♦	Q♥	J♠	3♠	3♥	7♦	10♥	9♠/6♦	9♣	8♠
		3♣	A♦	10♣	K♠	5♦	5♥					

These cards represent specific periods of the year → | These cards govern the entire year

Once you have found your Yearly Spread for this year, look carefully at how the cards are arranged. You do not yet know what any of the cards mean, but you may have noticed some of the Birth Cards or Personality Cards of people you know among the cards of your spread. Look carefully, and follow the next section closely.

Before you begin to interpret your Yearly Spread, read this next section carefully so that you understand the significance of the *position* of each card in your spread and how the various cards in the spread relate to each other. Every card in your Yearly Spread is representing either something that will happen to you or someone playing a role in your life this year. In this manner, the cards in your spread tell us what is going to happen to you this year, when it is going to happen, and with whom it is going to happen.

The headings at the top of the columns in the spread tell us what the cards under them represent. Look carefully at the headings above each of the cards in your Yearly Spread as we discuss this next section. We will begin with the most important cards of the year, the ones that describe the entire year, from one birthday to the next.

The Yearlong Influence Cards

There are five cards that will influence your entire year. They are the Long-Range, Pluto, Result, Environment, and Displacement. These are the most powerful cards in your Yearly Spread, because their influence lasts the entire year. Because they are so important, it is a good idea to study this next section carefully, looking up your Yearlong Cards as you do so. Pay special attention to the specific messages that each of these cards tells you.

THE LONG-RANGE CARD

Want to know the most important card of the year? Each year of your life you have one card that represents the major focus of the year, called the Long-Range Card. Your Long-Range Card can be found under the column entitled "LR" in your Yearly Spread. This is the first card you look up in any reading, because it gives you an up-front look at the entire year you are in at a glance.

The Long-Range Card can be a person you know (by birthday or Personality Card) or a mental state or type of experience that seems to come up over and over throughout the year and takes up much of your attention. The Long-Range Card usually indicates the single most important focus of the year in question, and this alone can give you a lot of valuable information about any year of your life. Being the Long-Range Card doesn't mean it is a good influence or a bad influence, it means it is *important*. This card could be a card of success and

happiness or a card of challenge and hard work, but whatever it is, it will be important to you. Sometimes the meaning of the Long-Range Card relates only to internal events or things that are going on inside of you that no one knows anything about except you.

I am sure you are anxious to know the meaning of your Long-Range Card. If it is the card of someone you know, you already know most of the meaning of it—simply that this person will be an important focus of your attention this year. However, every card has a meaning of its own that you can look up and read right now. To do this, look in The Card Interpretations section following chapter nine, and find the page with your Long-Range Card's interpretation. This section is organized by card, beginning with the Aces and ending with the Kings. First find the section that has all the meanings for the card that is your Long-Range Card, and then find the specific section that tells you what that card means when it is the Long-Range Card. For example, if your Long-Range Card this year were the 10♦, you would first find that card in the Interpretations section. Then you would locate the section that's entitled: Ten of Diamonds as the Long-Range Card. That's how you find the specific interpretation you are looking for.

Note: Each card in the deck has a different meaning, depending upon where it fell in the Yearly Spread. That is why there is a separate interpretation for each of these twelve different placements. However, you can also read the Basic Keywords and Basic Meaning for any card you are studying to get some additional information about it.

THE PLUTO AND RESULT CARDS

Want to know the biggest challenge you have put before yourself for the upcoming or present year, as well as what will be the outcome of your efforts at personal transformation? Well, the next two 'yearlong' influence cards are going to give you this vital information. These are called the Pluto and Result Cards, found under the "Plu/Res" columns respectively.

The Pluto Card and Result Card are interpreted as a pair of cards. They represent something or someone that you have decided you want something from, something you likely did not have at the beginning of this year and something that you are willing to make changes in your life to acquire or master. This is your major area of challenge and change for this year. You might call these cards your objective for the year.

To properly interpret these two cards, you must learn how to interpret pairs of cards together, something that we will cover in-depth in chapter seven on the Art of Interpretation. Chapter seven also has a lot more information on the importance of these two cards and how to get more understanding of their meanings, both combined and separately. For now, notice if either one of these two cards is the Birth Card or Personality Card of anyone you know. This alone may give you some valuable information. Beyond that, you are welcome to look up the meanings of these two cards in the same way you did the Long-Range Card. Once you find them, read the sections for Pluto and Result respectively to understand the influences present for you this year. Are you beginning to see the power of this system? You will be able to enhance the reading and interpretation of your spread as you learn more about the entire system, but even the novice can gain insight with just this small amount of information.

In addition to being part of the challenge or objective, the Result Card tells you who or what you may end up with by the end of this year. This may be a person, an event such as marriage or divorce, or a state of being such as success in work or money. In either case, the Result Card is always a blessing in our life that comes towards the end of the year. So, when you read the meanings of your Pluto and Result Cards, keep in mind that you may end up with the Result Card, whatever or whomever that may be.

The Environment and Displacement Cards

These next two cards have some unique characteristics and can be extremely important. In some cases, either one of these could be the most important card of your entire year. The first represents an area where you will receive easily and the second, an area where you must give freely. There is one important consideration you should be aware of as you start to use them.

There is a special family of seven cards that have no Environment and Displacement Cards each year. We will not go into the specific reasons why this is so in this book, but just know that this is the case, and be aware of it. These seven cards are the 2♥, A♣, 7♦, 8♣, 9♥, J♥, and K♠. If your Birth Card or Planetary Ruling Card is one of these cards, you will not find an Environment or Displacement Card in the Yearly Spreads for those cards. Even if your Birth Card is one of these cards, chances are that your Planetary Ruling Card is not, so most people will usually have an Environment and Displacement Card for at least one of their personal significators. The only exception to this would be the Leo birthdays of the A♣, 8♣, and J♥. For these few birthdays, there will be no Environment or Displacement Cards unless they do a Yearly Spread for one of their Personality Cards.

The Environment Card

Among the yearlong influence cards, two of them are always blessings. The first is the Result Card, which we just discussed. The next is the Environment Card, which in some ways is even better than the Result Card. This is because you get the blessings of the Environment Card all year long instead of just at the end of the year, as in the case of the Result Card. The Result Card is like the little gift waiting for you at the end of a year of hard work, while the Environment Card's blessings begin immediately on your birthday and extend the entire year. It is an area or person in your life that is a fairly constant source of good things. It can be an area where everything seems to come easily to you, or where you reap many rewards with little effort. This is a good card to focus on, one of the pure blessing cards of the year. The way to maximize the beneficial influence of this card is to just be open to receiving as much as you can and consciously affirm your appreciation for what you are receiving.

The Displacement Card

The Displacement Card is in some ways the reverse of the Environment Card, but it often has an even greater significance as well. First, it represents an area or person in your life, that will require some effort on your part. Some would say this is where you must give more of yourself this year in order to achieve success. It may represent an area that you are currently weak in, either personally or professionally, or in other cases, a person to whom you must give more than you receive in order to fulfill some unspoken obligation. It can actually be a very constructive influence if we merely recognize that we must put more of ourselves into this area and just do it. It is an area where hard work can really pay off in the year in question.

But beyond that basic meaning, many times the Displacement Card can indicate a year of your life that has a very auspicious meaning for you personally. It could indicate a year that you make an important change in your life, a year that you will get a special wish fulfilled, and other interesting cycles of life. So, don't think the Displacement Card is a card of bad news. It can often represent a turning point in your life or a year that is destined to be the most important of your entire life. Displacement Cards and their special significance is discussed in detail in chapter eight.

The Fifty-Two-Day Planetary Periods and Their Cards

While studying your Yearly Spread, you probably noticed that the rest of the cards are found under headings Mer, for Mercury, Ven for Venus, Mar for Mars, Jup for Jupiter, Sat for Saturn, Ura for Uranus, and Nep for Neptune. These headings represent the seven Planetary Periods of your year, and the cards under each period are the ones that will be in effect during each particular period. Most periods have two cards under the heading, though the Neptune Period will often have only one.

Right now, you are in one of the Planetary Periods of the year. To find out which one you are in, look at the table called The Planetary Period Dates that begins on page 363 and find the page that has your birth month as the heading at the top of the page. Once you have found your birth month page, look up your birthday in the left-hand column. Moving across the page from left to right you will see seven dates that are the beginning dates of your Planetary Periods. These seven dates apply to every year of your life, and the first period, the Mercury Period, always begins on your birthday. Each of these periods is fifty-two days long, and their names appear at the top of the columns. Knowing the dates of these periods tells you when certain cards are in effect for you each year. If you are not sure you understand this, follow this next example closely:

Example:

Let's say that your birthday is July 17th, and you are a J♣ card. Your Mercury Period begins each year on July 17th and ends on September 6th, the day before your Venus Period begins. To take this a step further, if today's date is January 24th, which period would you be in if you were this J♣? Well, since January 24th falls after the Jupiter Period begins on December 20th and before the Saturn Period begins on February 11th, we would know that you are currently in your Jupiter Period.

Now let's say that you are thirty-nine years old. If we look up the Yearly Spreads for the J♣ and find the one for age thirty-nine, we see that the Mercury Cards for that year are the 9♠ and J♥, while the Venus Cards are the 3♥ and 8♦. So, in this example, the 9♠ and J♥ cards will tell you what is going to happen during your Mercury Period, from July 17th until September 7th, and the 3♥ and 8♦ will be in effect during your Venus Period, which lasts from September 7th until October 29th.

Exercises:

1. Which Planetary Period are you in right now? Knowing that, which card or cards are present for you at this time? In other words, if you are currently in your Mars Period, what two cards are in your Mars Period? These two cards are the ones that are in effect for this period, and they remain in effect until the beginning of your next period.

2. Which period will you be in every year at Christmas? On Independence Day? If you have any trouble with this,

go back to the example and read it carefully before you proceed any further.

We are not yet ready to go into the art of interpreting the cards, though I am sure that you may have been tempted to jump ahead and begin to read the interpretations for your cards. Well, you already know what period you are in, and if you look back, you will know what two cards (or perhaps one card in case you are currently in your Neptune Period) are currently affecting you. I am sure you are curious to know what your cards mean, and although it would be easy to skip ahead and delve into the interpretation section, I encourage you to stay with the steps we are covering now. There are some important topics we need to cover first so you will be well-acquainted with this incredible system before you try to interpret the cards.

The Direct and Vertical Cards of Each Period

If you look in The Yearly Spreads table, you will notice that most of the Planetary Periods have two cards under them. The upper card of these pairs is called the **direct card** and the one under it is called the **vertical card**. It is important to know that the direct card has a different significance than the vertical card by virtue of its position. The direct card is always considered the strongest influence and indicator of what is going to happen to you in any given period. This is especially true for the *direct card found in the spread of your Birth Card*. This card represents an event, experience, or person that is a major focus for that period of your year. I often refer to that one card as the *headline* for the period it sits in.

Example:

Looking at our example spread on page 9, we see that our 9♦ person has a 3♠ as the direct card during his or her Saturn Period. This 3♠ will be the strongest influence in effect for that time period, the headline, if you will, for that fifty-two-day period. This 3♠ may represent a person whose Birth Card is the 3♠ playing a role during that period, or it could represent the subjective experience indicated by the interpretation of the 3♠ in the Saturn Period. In fact, this 3♠ could mean both things at the same time.

The **vertical card** is a slightly less important influence, often supporting or elaborating on the meaning of the direct card in some way. Often the direct card will be an experience of some kind, and the vertical card will be a person who is involved somehow in that experience, maybe as its cause, or somehow related to it in an important way. In other cases, the vertical card *further explains* the event or experience indicated by the direct card. Much like the Pluto and Result Cards, they are interpreted as a pair, always being closely related to each other. Since the direct card is more significant, the vertical card is usually interpreted as supporting the direct card in some manner. The reason for calling these cards direct and vertical involves understanding many other aspects of this system that are covered in the advanced book, *Exploring the Little Book of the Seven Thunders*.

Note: If you look through The Yearly Spreads table, you will notice under the Neptune column that sometimes there is only a direct card and no vertical card. When this is the case, the card that is found is the only influence of that period and has a strong, unified influence.

Looking up the Yearly Spreads of Your Planetary Ruling and Personality Cards

Up until now, we have only dealt with the Yearly Spreads of your Birth Card. As I mentioned earlier, there are spreads for each of your Personality Cards and your Planetary Ruling Card as well. If you have followed my advice in the previous chapter, you will be looking up the Yearly Spreads for at least one more of your personal significators, probably your Planetary Ruling Card.

You can look up these other Yearly Spreads in exactly the same way you did for your Birth Card. For example, if you are a Gemini 6♦ Birth Card, like Joe Montana, you would be looking up the Yearly Spreads for your 4♠ Planetary Ruling Card. You would first locate the page with all of the 4♠ Yearly Spreads on it. Once you find that page, you look up the spread by the age that you are reading for and read them in the same way as the ones for your Birth Card. The Yearly Spreads for any other significator look the same as the ones for your Birth Card. They will contain different cards, but they are read in the same fashion. Each of the spreads has cards that represent things that will happen, and to you they might be very important. My research has shown, however, that the Birth

Card's Spread is generally the most important, followed by the Planetary Ruling Card's Spread.

In the next chapter, we will learn how to distinguish between the different spreads and how to interpret them. For now, I would like you to do the following exercise:

Exercise:

In the back of the book you will find several copies of *Cards of Your Destiny* Reading Worksheet forms. Photocopy one of these so that you can use it to write down all the cards of your Yearly Spreads this year.

1. Write in your name, birth date, Birth Card, Planetary Ruling Card, Personality Cards, etc., in the spaces provided.

2. Write in your current age in the Age for Reading spot.

3. Then, fill in all the cards for each of your Yearly Spreads in the spaces provided. This means the Yearly Spreads for your Birth Card, Planetary Ruling Card, and each Personality Card you have decided to use as well. You will find an example form filled out on page 357. Refer to it if you have any questions. There is room for four Yearly Spreads, though you will most likely have only two or three. Put the spread for your Birth Card in the top group of boxes and the spreads for your Planetary Ruling Cards and Personality Cards underneath.

4. Look up the dates of your Planetary Periods and write them in on the worksheet where it says "Planetary Period Begin Dates."

When you are finished with this exercise you will be well on your way to doing your first complete reading. Have this completed form filled out and handy when you begin the next chapter.

Chapter Four
Doing a Yearly Reading

Congratulations! You have already completed the first four steps for doing a yearly reading. You have learned the mechanics of finding all the cards for your Yearly Spreads and looking up the Planetary Period dates. That was the easy part, but also the most necessary part to learn first. Until you have those spreads written down, you will not be able to begin interpreting them. Throughout this chapter, we will be referring to your spread of cards and to the example spread on page 9. If there is ever something that you don't understand, refer back to the example.

There are several things we are going to cover in this chapter. First of all, I will lead you through doing your first reading of your cards and teach you a recommended flow to follow that you can use for readings you do for others as well. Next, we are going to talk about combining card influences together and interpreting them as a pair since most cards in this system show up as pairs and must be interpreted together. Finally, we are going to cover some other important considerations about doing readings and interpreting the cards that will help you fine tune readings. I am going to share many of the things that I have learned while using this system professionally and teaching thousands of students how to use it. When you are done with this chapter, you will have a good understanding of the art of doing readings and will have completed your current yearly reading.

The Eight Steps in Doing a Reading

So, to begin with, what are the steps to do a reading? Well, here they are in outline form. You have already completed the first four steps, but I want to list them so that you know where you are in the flow of things.

Already Completed Steps (see previous chapters):

1. Determine the Birth Card, Planetary Ruling Card, and Personality Cards for the subject of the reading.

2. Determine the Birth Card, Planetary Ruling Card, and Personality Cards for all the important friends and associates of the subject. (This part you have completed, see your 'Friends and Associates' list on page 361.)

3. Decide which year you are going to read for, and look up the Yearly Spreads for each personal significator, writing them into the worksheet.

4. Look up and fill in the Planetary Period dates on the worksheet.

New Steps

5. Locate the cards of the friends and associates in the Yearly Spreads first to get an overview of the subject's relationships for the upcoming year. (This is so important that I have devoted the entire next chapter to it.)

6. Read the Long-Range, Pluto, Result, Environment, and Displacement Cards' meanings to give the big picture about the whole next year.

7. Read the direct cards in the Birth Card's Yearly Spread to get the overall nature of the year in the seven different departments.

8. Read the cards for each period as they come up.

This is all there is to it. When you have completed these eight steps, you will have a very detailed picture of what the upcoming year is about and some very specific information about certain aspects of it. It is impossible to know everything about the year before it unfolds, since many of the cards may represent people you haven't met yet. Also, the cards can have many levels of meaning, and you may not know just which of the many different meanings it will be. The more readings you do, the better you will be at making predictions. When I do readings, I focus more on the yearlong influences and less on trying to determine what will happen specifically in each period. I have gotten much better at doing the Planetary Period readings but only because I took a 'wait and see' attitude with them until I got a better feel for the meanings of the cards.

Let's now go through the steps we haven't covered yet in more detail so you fully understand what to do.

Locating the Cards of Your Friends and Associates in Your Yearly Spreads

Step 5: Locate the cards of the friends and associates in the Yearly Spreads first to get an overview of the subject's relationships for the upcoming year.

Looking at your Yearly Spreads and comparing them with your list of friends and associates, note where the Birth Cards, Planetary Ruling Cards, and Personality Cards of your friends and associates fall in your spreads. Knowing where their cards are located will tell you quite a bit about your relationship with them this year. It is highly likely that more than one of your friends share the same Personality Cards, some may even have the same Birth Card. When this is the case, the cards that fall in your Yearly Spreads may represent one or both of them. It is also likely that you will find the card or cards of someone you know in several different positions this year.

The next chapter goes into great detail on the subject of relationships. There is a lot you need to understand about this before you do your first reading. There are cards that represent your current marriage or committed relationship, other than the Birth Card of your other half, and there are cards that represent love affairs, love triangles, marriage, divorce, and hidden love affairs. If you are ready to learn everything about your relationships, turn to the next chapter right now. Otherwise, circle the cards in your Yearly Spread that belong to people you know, and write their names in small letters next to their cards, as I have done in the example spreads, so that when you begin to synthesize the reading, you will know immediately where they are located.

Interpreting the Yearlong Influence Cards

Step 6: Read the Long-Range, Pluto, Result, Environment, and Displacement Cards' meanings to give the big picture about the whole next year.

All of the above-mentioned cards are yearlong influences. That is, they describe the most important things about the entire year, as opposed to the Planetary Period Cards and their influence of fifty-two days. However, it is important that you know the distinctions between them because each has a different use and meaning.

LONG-RANGE CARD

Read your Long-Range Card or Cards first to get the bigger picture of what this year is about for you. Of course you may have as many as four Long-Range Cards to consider, since there is one for each of your Personality Cards you have chosen, your Planetary Ruling Card, and your Birth Card. But hopefully, you only have two or three at most. Look upon each of your Long-Range Cards as being a separate but important yearlong influence.

The Long-Range Card describes something or someone that is a major focus of your attention this year. It could be something that you are thinking about all the time, having to deal with all the time, or someone who has become an important part of your life. The Long-Range Card is neither good nor bad, merely important.

Example:

A good example of the neutral quality of the Long-Range Card occurred to me about seven years ago when I had the 7♦ Long-Range. This card can indicate financial problems or financial success, but it always indicates a focusing of one's attention on values and money. That particular year, I reached an extremely low point, financially, only to become quite wealthy practically overnight after I had an inner breakthrough about money. At that point, I began to access the 'Millionaire's Card' aspect of the 7♦. The 7♦ itself as Long-Range Card doesn't tell you if you are going to be rich or poor, only that your values and inner state of prosperity will be tested. If you pass the test, great abundance is available. Remember that the Long-Range Card, regardless of what it is, is always powerful in its effect upon us in any given year.

PLUTO AND RESULT CARDS

Now, look up the interpretations for your Pluto and Result Cards. Remember that the Pluto and Result Cards indicate something that you are striving to achieve this year. Often these qualities may be hidden in another person or someone else may be reminding you of what you are trying to achieve this year. This is often the case when either the Pluto or Result Card is the card of someone you know. As in the case of the Long-Range Cards, each set of Pluto and Result Cards will represent separate but important areas that you are working on this year. Look at each set of Pluto and Result Cards as a separate area that you are working on. For every spread, there are a variety of interpretations. Let's take a look at an example so we can take an in-depth look at a possible avenue of interpretation:

Example:

In our first sample reading, in chapter seven, we have a woman who has the 3♠ and Ace♠ combination for her Pluto and Result Cards. The fact that both of these cards are Spades points to a strong possibility that there would

be some major issues this year with either her health or her work. The challenging influence, the 3♠, points to either great uncertainty in these areas or a division of one's self in such a way that great stress is manifested in one's life. The Result Card, the Ace♠, tells us that regardless of what particular challenging influences are there, the net result of the year's issues will be a nearly total transformation on a fundamental level for this person. Anyone having this powerful combination of influence is sure to have a very challenging time of it at the beginning to middle of the year. Spades is the most powerful suit, the one that effects us the most. A 3♠ Pluto Card could make us feel that we are being literally torn in two. Anyone who has the powerful Ace of Spades in any of the yearlong influence positions probably has a need for a fundamental change of lifestyle. We just cannot underestimate the power or importance of this card. It often occurs in the life of someone who is just way off track and needs a helping push to get going in the right direction.

Another message these cards could deliver is that we must move from a position of being varied and split in our energies (3♠) to one in which we are moving forward in one (Ace♠) direction.

The Pluto and Result Cards represent things we don't feel we have at the beginning of the year.

PLUTO, THE GOD OF DEATH AND TRANSFORMATION

The planet Pluto is considered by many astrologers to be the most powerful planet of all. Its discovery coincided with some of the first tests of nuclear bombs on earth. Pluto often represents an unrelenting and destructive power, one that clears away all debris and wipes the slate clean for a new beginning. Pluto is the planet that governs the sign of Scorpio, and as many of us have discovered, Scorpio people can be unrelenting at times as well. Our Pluto Card each year will present us with opportunities for self-transformation or personal change. Some personality types can adapt to new circumstances easily, while others tend to resist change. Whether we acknowledge the change implied by our Pluto Card and take it on as a personal challenge, or whether we perceive it as some outside force that is trying to destroy us, the change will occur nonetheless.

One of the beauties of this system is that, knowing ahead of time what this change might be, we can consciously choose to take a positive attitude regarding it and, in doing so, relieve ourselves of what could be a very painful situation. Our point of view is more responsible for our happiness than what is occurring around us. Death occurs to us all, and psychological deaths occur many times over the course of our lives. Our Pluto Card tells us that we have at least one little death each year, but in this case, we can turn this death into a triumphant transformation. These little deaths each year are like steps on a staircase. Each one lifts us a little higher to a place where we can see and understand more about life and our place in this beautiful universe. To Pluto, we should be grateful for the clearing away of the old and outworn so that we can be made anew and refreshed to start a new cycle.

THE ENVIRONMENT AND DISPLACEMENT CARDS

There is one significant piece of information that is very important to know before reading the next section. That is that there are seven cards in the deck that have no Environment and Displacement Cards. It goes beyond the scope of this book to explain why this is so, but it is good to get familiar with these seven cards because they account for most of the exceptions in this system. These cards collectively are called the Mystical Family of Seven and comprise the three Fixed Cards (8♣, J♥, and K♠) and the four Semi-fixed Cards (A♣, 2♥, 7♦, and 9♥). For a complete discussion of these cards and their unique place in the grand scheme, read my book *Love Cards*.

The Environment Card is one of the most significant blessing cards each year. Whether it is the card of someone you know or a quality that comes easily to you, it will act as a protective and beneficial influence throughout the year. In some cases, the help it brings can be quite dramatic. In any case, we can always benefit by keeping this card in mind and consciously taking advantage of its influence in our lives. For example, if you happened to have a 4♦ as an Environment Card one year, you could be assured that your finances would be stable all year regardless of what other cards were found in your Yearly Spreads.

Example:

If a man has a 3♣ Environment Card in his Birth Card's Yearly Spread, this gives him a special creative gift for the year that could bring many rewards, financial and otherwise. The 3♣ is often called the 'writer's card.' If this man pursued any creative writing projects, he would find that success in these areas would come easily. He could even win songwriting or other contests. If he were not involved in any particularly creative professions, he would still reap benefits from speaking to others and expressing himself verbally and in writing. He would also have the ability to carry on two or more lines of work successfully, especially if these lines of work involved communications in some way.

If this same man has a 10♥ Environment Card in his Planetary Ruling Card Spread, it will bring many pleasant and gratifying experiences where the public is involved or where groups of people are found. If he attended or hosted any large gatherings, these would be very successful for him. If he decided to advertise his business or services, these would also tend to be successful under this card of social success. Combining this with the influence of the 3♣, we can see a huge potential for success if he was a performing literary or musical artist. Though we don't actually combine these two cards and create a combined interpretation, both of them individually would contribute to success in that area.

WHO OWES WHO?
THE ENVIRONMENT AND DISPLACEMENT CARDS

The best way to understand the Environment and Displacement Cards is to use the following analogy. Imagine that you own a home, but for whatever reason, you decide to move around each year to different locations. While you are gone, you rent your house out to other people who are also moving around from year to year. Wherever you move to, you have to pay rent, and whoever lives in your house while you are away pays rent to you. The Displacement Card is the card whose house you are living in each year as you travel around. And that is the card you pay rent to. The Environment Card is the card who is occupying your house each year and who pays you rent. On the year of your birth, and again at ages forty-five and ninety you return to your birthplace and neither collect or pay rent. But every other year, you are occupying some other card's place and thus having this exchange. This concept will become completely clear if and when you study some of our advanced material on this system. Look in the back of the book for more information.

THE DISPLACEMENT CARD

Though not fully understood, the Displacement Card is one of the most powerful of the year. In some cases, it is an indicator of life-changing events for the year in question. In chapter eight, we will discuss some of the particularly powerful Displacement Cards and what they mean. For now, we will focus on the usual meaning of the Displacement Cards and give some examples to illustrate them. The general meaning of the Displacement Card is pretty much the opposite of the Environment Card. Where the Environment Card represents things that come easily to us, the Displacement Card represents things that come with effort and struggle. Usually we have to put extra effort into that area, or the things pointed to by that card will be a drain on our energy or resources. It can, just as with any other card in the deck, be the card of someone we know who requires us to make payment to them throughout the year in one form or another.

That concludes our basic discussion of the Yearlong Cards.

Now we will talk about how the cards in the individual periods can also cast a yearlong influence of their own. Read this section carefully, because there are exceptions to note and special circumstances that can alter their meanings.

The Yearlong Influences of the Direct Cards in the Birth Card Spread

Step 7: Read the direct cards in the Birth Card Spreads to get the overall nature of the year in the seven different departments.

Taking the direct cards from the Planetary Periods of the Birth Card Spread, we can often derive some additional yearlong trends. Each period of the year governs a certain department of life. The direct card in these periods can often represent a general indication of how things will go in each of those departments for the year in question. These yearly planetary rulers, as we might call them, are general indicators. Often other cards in the Yearly Spreads will indicate otherwise. For example, though you may have a wonderful card in Venus, such as an 8♥ or 2♥, a difficult card later in the year, such as a 7♥ in the Saturn Period would tell you that though things were going wonderfully in the relationship department earlier in the year, during the Saturn Period, the situation was practically reversed. Another thing that may reverse the meaning of one of these general indicators would be a Yearlong Card such as the Pluto or Displacement Card. So, as we use these general indicators, also look for contra-indicators before making any final assessment.

The Direct Mercury Card tells us what the status of your mind and mental occupations will be for the year. It also details how your communications will go. In our first example spread of the 9♦, age thirty-one, there is a 7♠ direct Mercury Card. This tells us that he or she will have many challenges mentally and will have to work on developing a positive attitude in regards to communication for the year. This could also indicate an interest in metaphysical subjects.

The Direct Venus Card tells us how things will go in your home, with your family and loved ones and how your romantic life will favor for the year. It also tells us how your romantic relationships will be this year. In our same example, there is a K♦ as the direct Venus Card. This tells us that there is financial power in the home, perhaps running a business out of the home. This also tells us that this person will be more attracted to those of wealth this year.

The Direct Mars Card tells us how your aggressive energies will manifest this year, the outcome of legal matters, and how you will relate to men in general for the year. The Q♥ direct Mars Card in our example tells us that there will be good relations with men. This is a Marriage Card and so could indicate a marriage that is very aggressive or passionate.

The Direct Jupiter Card tells us the nature of business for the year or something important about how to get the most out of your business this year. It is also the card of the most blessings for the year. In our example, there is a J♠. This tells us that this person could make more money in the creative fields, even as an actor or actress. This also tells us that there would be many benefits stemming from a spiritual initiation this year.

The Direct Saturn Card tells us where there will be the most difficulties and the status of our health. The 3♠ in our example points to physical stress as being the major area of challenge for the year, at least health-wise.

The Direct Uranus Card tells us where there will be unexpected changes this year, the status of friendships and associations, and the status of relationships with co-workers and real estate matters. The 3♥ in our example tells us that there will be some uncertainty in friendships throughout the year for this person.

The Direct Neptune Card has been called the 'hopes and fears' card of the year. It often tells us what we are dreaming about or wanting secretly. Sometimes it also represents the status of foreign or distant affairs, both personal and professional. It can also be the contents of our subconscious mind. In our example, the 7♦ tells us that there may be some worry about money that is in the subconscious of this person and also that there could be some financial challenges related to distant interests this year. In another example, an associate of mine reported to me that he had an 8♦ in Neptune during a period when he made a great deal of money with people in foreign countries after he had returned from a trip overseas.

Interpreting the Direct and Vertical Cards for Each Period

Step 8: Read the cards for each period as they come up.

Until you have used this system for a while, it will be difficult to make accurate predictions for each period until that period approaches. So many of the cards will turn out to be people that you do not know yet, and so many things will develop as the year progresses, which you are not aware of now, that may make many of your predictions inaccurate. However, as each period approaches, you will know what the cards mean because you will be aware of what is happening in your life and who is involved in your life. I recommend that you do Step 7 for a quick scan of the year, and then wait until about fifteen to thirty days before each period to take a close look at the cards coming up.

In most periods, there are two cards. It is important to know that these two cards are always interpreted as a pair. In other words, you have to combine their influences together and arrive at the combined interpretation of the two cards. They each support and elaborate on the other. In general, we look at the top or direct card to be the headline of the period, while the vertical card provides the details of the story. If either one of the cards is that of someone you know, then it will probably represent them taking some action in your life during that period, while the other card may describe what they do or how the things they do will affect you at that time.

Combining two cards' meanings together is one of the most challenging aspects of learning the cards, so I have given you some examples to study. Read these carefully, and see how I have taken two separate cards and combined them together. There are more examples of this in chapter seven, so study them all.

Example:

Continuing with our first example spread, in the Saturn column, the vertical card under the 3♠ is the 5♦. To demonstrate how these two may be related, we can look up their interpretations. First look up the page that has all the interpretations for the 3♠ in The Card Interpretations section. Look down until you find the section under the title The Three of Spades in the Saturn Period and read what it says. The 3♠ under Saturn's influence can represent indecision about work or health, or a state of worry, stress, and anxiety. Looking for The Five of Diamonds in the Saturn Period, we see that the 5♦ under the influence of the Saturn Period represents a loss of money related to ill health or a difficult change in one's business or financial matters. Put these two interpretations together, remembering that the direct card is the strongest, and we could predict a very trying and difficult period for this person, one in which ill health interferes with work and causes outlays of money in trying to get better. This may be a prolonged illness and may cause much worry and anxiety about work, money, and health.

Sometimes, the vertical card will be just the opposite of the direct card in meaning. In many of these cases, it is a contrary influence to the direct card and cancels out the influence of it. One example would be a 5♠ direct card with a 6♠ vertical card in the same period. This could mean a trip or move (5♠) that is planned but gets postponed or canceled (6♠). Another example would be having a 9♠ as a direct card in the Saturn Period and an 8♠ as the vertical card underneath it. In this case, there would be some sort of health difficulty that is overcome or resolved by the recuperative powers of the 8♠. It may not completely erase the influence of the 9♠, but it certainly will lessen that influence and give good chances for recovery. *Whenever you have a supposedly 'bad' card such as a Seven or Nine and you also have a very good card (Four, Eight) with it in any period, the good card will mitigate the effects of the bad card. The bad card will point to some problem that arises and the good card guarantees a successful resolution to that problem.*

Once you have read and looked up the cards for the Planetary Periods in your Birth Card's Yearly Spreads, go ahead and do the same thing for your Planetary Ruling Card's Yearly Spreads and those for any Personality Cards you have decided to use. In chapter seven, I will show you how to distinguish between the different spreads and how to combine the meanings of the different Long-Range and other cards to put together an accurate description of the year ahead.

Now you really have the 'mechanics' of this system down. You know how to find a person's Birth Card and Personality Cards, how to look up their Yearly Spreads, how to find out the dates of their planetary periods, and how to look up the individual meanings of each card in the Yearly Spread. You are well on your way to understanding the *Cards of Your Destiny* system. There are many details and considerations that will help you get more information and help you fine-tune your readings. We will begin in the next chapter, where I will I present you with everything you need to get information about all your important relationships.

Chapter Five

Your Relationships Are in the Cards

Marriages, divorce, love affairs, secret love involvements, and love triangles. There are cards that represent each of these kinds of relationship events, and more. Not only that, but the occurrence of the personal significators of people you know can tell you, ahead of time, how you will be getting along with each person in your life for the upcoming year. Since everyone you know has a Birth Card, and usually a Planetary Ruling Card and some Personality Cards, you will often find them in your Weekly or Yearly Spreads or your cards in their weekly or Yearly Spreads. This chapter will tell you the meaning of each position that a card can be found in. This information is easy to memorize also, so that soon you will not have to look it up. A quick look-up table is provided so that you can get the meanings at a glance.

The bottom line is that you can really know what roles the important people in your life will be playing in the year ahead. All you need to know to get this information is where someone's card is found. Is it the Long-Range Card, or is it under the Mercury Period? Is it found under Saturn or Venus? First look under your spreads carefully and find out where the cards of people you know are found. Be sure to look for their Planetary Ruling and Personality Cards, as well as the Birth Card. Look in all of the Yearly Spreads that you have chosen for this year. Once you know where they are found, you can use the following information to translate what that means to you.

Which of Your Spreads Are Their Cards Found In?

Each Yearly Spread in your reading for this year has its own special significance. For example, the Birth Card Spread is the most important, and the cards there may pertain to most any part of your life. Contrast this with a Personality Card Spread, which is much less important and where the cards will only pertain to specific roles that you are playing this year. These distinctions carry through into the relationship area as well. If you see someone's card falling under the spread of your Birth Card, you know that they are likely to be playing a major role in your life during that Planetary Period, especially if their card is the direct card of that period. A personal significator of someone you know falling in your Birth Card's Yearly Spread will have more importance than one found in a Personality Card Spread. Finding others' cards in your Planetary Ruling Card's Yearly Spread is very much the same as the Birth Card. The Planetary Ruling Card is in many ways equal to the Birth Card. A personal significator of someone you know found there could also pertain to any area of your life. Cards found under the spreads of one or more of your Personality Cards relate more specifically to those parts of your life. For example, if you were the owner of a business, people's cards found in the spread for your King would be more likely to have something to do with your business. A woman who finds a man's cards under her Queen usually indicates that he is relating to her as a lover or somehow connected to her in her role as a wife or mother.

While interpreting the cards in your spread, always keep in mind that the cards you find might be people that you haven't met yet, someone new coming into your life. You can never have the final say on any card until that period arrives.

Are Their Cards in the Direct or Vertical Position?

Remember that direct cards are the strongest influence. When someone's card is the direct card for that period, they are definitely playing a major role. The vertical card underneath will tell you something about their role in your life. If their card shows up as the vertical card, they are somehow contributing to the experience represented by the direct card they fall under. But, in either case, they will tend to affect you in the same way. For example, anyone's card found in a Venus Period, regardless of whether it is the direct or vertical card, will be a friendly influence in your life. However, if their card is the direct card, it is likely that their role in your life will be more important during that period than if it were the vertical card.

The Significance of the Location of Their Cards in Your Spread

Exactly where their cards show up in your spreads tells you many important things:

1. It tells you how they will be relating to you during the time period that their card falls under yours and also, how they will appear to you. Will they be friendly or hostile? Will they be a love interest or a business partner? How they relate to you, from your point of view, is indicated by the location of their card, either in a Planetary Period, or as the Long-Range, Pluto, or Pluto Result Card. In this

chapter, you will find sections on each of the possible locations and what that means to you. Once you know which location you find someone's card(s), read the section under that heading to know how they will affect you during that period or for that year.

Remember that this will tell you what the relationship will be like from your point of view, not theirs. To find out how they are experiencing relating to you, you will have to look at their Yearly Spread and find where your cards show up.

2. The position also tells you when they will be playing a direct role in your life. Each Planetary Period gives you a space of fifty-two days within which this person will be a part of some event or experience of yours. The periods that their card or cards fall under will be the ones where they play a direct role and where you notice them most.

3. The position also tells you what department of your life they will be affecting this entire year. As discussed in the last chapter, each period has an influence over a certain department of your life for the entire year. Mars, for example, has a focus on dealings with men and legal affairs. Jupiter focuses on money and business and Venus on love, etc. Look in the previous chapter and chapter seven for more on which department of your life each period rules. As an example, if someone you know has their card in your Venus Period, you can assume that they will be affecting your heart or your home and family in some way because those are the areas ruled by Venus in this system. This influence lasts the entire year to some extent, though it is predominant during the period their card shows up.

Finally, their position tells you in a more specific way how they will influence you for the entire year. Though they play a direct role in your life during the period or periods that their cards fall under, their position by Planetary Period also gives a long-range influence for the year. For example, someone found in your Mars Period will be someone that you have either have passion for all year or that you will be fighting and competing with all year.

It is possible for relationships to change during a year and your cards may indicate such a change. It is also possible for one person to play multiple roles in your life during one year. They may be a love interest (Venus Period position) and a business partner (Jupiter Period position). They may be a source of uncertainty (Uranus Period position) and someone with whom you can communicate easily (Mercury Period position).

A little warning—don't be upset if the cards of someone important to you are not in your Yearly Spreads. Often, I have seen that people who are married or in a relationship will not find their mate or spouse's cards in their Yearly Spreads. This does not mean that they are not there. It usually indicates that the relationship will continue as before without any major changes, which can be a welcome sign.

After you have studied the following paragraphs about the influence of the location of their cards on you, you will begin to understand the subtle influences of the planets, much in the same way as an astrologer does. Before long, you will not have to read these interpretations in order to see what relationships will be like in the upcoming year. But for now, study them carefully and strive to understand the basic essence of these planetary influences.

Their Card Is Your Long-Range Card

When someone's Birth Card, Planetary Ruling Card, or Personality Card shows up as your Long-Range Card, either for the year or for the week, it means they will play an important role in your life either that year or that week. They will likely be a major focus for you. Either you will be thinking about them a lot, seeing them a lot, or doing things with them a lot. This location does not tell you whether they will be challenging to you or loving you or anything else. It only means important, a major focus of your attention. If their card shows up somewhere else, it may reveal more details about their involvement in your life.

Their Card Is Your Pluto Card

When someone's Birth Card, Planetary Ruling Card, or Personality Card shows up as your Pluto Card, you can bet that they will in some way be involved in changing you this year. They may not be doing this intentionally, but you will probably feel challenged by their presence in some way. Often, someone who is your Pluto Card is a source of difficulty for you. There can be many reasons for this difficulty, and your Result Card may help to further define how they are a part of your transformation this year. If you look at the way that you relate to this person a little closer, you may become aware that there is something about them that you want to master in yourself. Either they have something you want, or they bring out a weakness in you that you want to overcome. If you take this person as a mirror for your own personal challenge, you will be able to get the maximum benefits from this relationship. They are somehow reminding you of something that you want to achieve personally.

Their Card Is Your Result Card

If someone's Birth Card, Planetary Ruling Card, or Personality Card is your Result Card this year, they are likely to be some-

one that you want something from in some way. Often, I have seen people marry people who are their Result Card. It can be someone that you end up with by year's end in one of many ways. A new baby can be the Result Card as well.

In as much as the Result Card is closely related to the Pluto Card, the person who shows up here can also have a role in some major changes you are making in your life this year. They can be a source of difficulty for you in one of many ways. You may feel challenged by them, either by their behavior or just by what they have or do. There could be something about them that you want for yourself, either a quality of theirs or something that they do that reminds you of what you would like to have for yourself. As the Result Card, it is highly likely that you will achieve whatever it is in them or about them that you want for yourself. Use this person as a guide to something or some quality that you want to possess and then work hard to get it. In this way, you will get the most out of the relationship.

Their Card Is Your Environment Card

When someone's Birth Card or other significator is your Environment Card, you can bet that they will be a helpful influence in your life for the year in question. I have noted that people in the Environment position will help out financially, emotionally, or just about in any way that you can imagine. But the influence is always a positive one and one that you will perceive as a blessing in your life. Simply being consciously grateful for what is received can magnify the blessings that come from an Environment Card person. This is a little 'trick' that few people know about, but it can produce powerful results.

Their Card Is Your Displacement Card

When someone is your Displacement Card it means that you will have to help them, much in the same way as people who are your Environment Card will help you in any given year. You may perceive a Displacement Card person as a drain on you, but usually you will just recognize that you have to give things to them and be done with it. Look at your Displacement Card people as those to whom you must pay some dues this year. It is interesting sometimes when our spouse or lover is our Displacement Card. I have seen a woman, for example, whose husband was her Displacement Card for a particular year. The woman wanted to leave her husband because the relationship had run its course. But because of the Displacement Card influence, she stayed with him another year and essentially did whatever he wanted for that time.

In looking at relationships in the cards it is also valuable to check and see if any of your personal significators are found to be the Environment or Displacement Cards in the Yearly Spreads of the people you associate with. This information can help explain their actions and the ways you relate to them for that year.

Their Card Is in Your Mercury Period

When someone's Birth Card, Planetary Ruling Card, or Personality Card shows up in your Mercury Period, you are given the gift of communication with them this year. The Mercury connection is basically a good one. You two have a good mental connection. This may be someone with whom you are involved in a mental pursuit, such as school or classes of some kind. You probably have much in common and much to talk about. This ability to communicate is very good for intimate relationships such as a marriage or a love affair because communication is an important ingredient to long-term success. If the person you find in a Mercury position to you is not a lover or marriage partner, then you should at least be good friends and have something in common to talk about. One word of caution should be mentioned also. A new person that you meet during a Mercury Period should not be counted on in any long-term, committed way. New Mercury relationships are often short-lived affairs, pleasant and sweet, but over just as quickly as they start.

I have also seen times when someone who is Mercury to a person is someone that they are not communicating with. One time, a client of mine's father was her Mercury Card. She told me that they were not speaking at all and were very mad at each other for the past five years. I reminded her that the Mercury connection is there, but she would have to take advantage of it. Later, she did call her father, and they had a breakthrough in their relationship. So, when you see this Mercury connection, use it to your best advantage.

Their Card Is in Your Venus Period

Anyone you find in your Venus Period or position is someone you love or have a lot of affection for. This can range from a dear friend or relative to someone you would spend the rest of your life with. The people you find here will be friendly and helpful to you this year and possibly a source of financial help as well. Venus is the planet of love, the ruler of the signs of Taurus (earthly love, gifts, material objects) and Libra (marriage and relationships). With Venus's help, this could be someone special in many ways. Often a Venus person is someone in your home. A marriage during this period is considered blessed by favorable influences, and any love affairs will also be very fulfilling. Keep in mind that though you love the person you find in this position, there is no guarantee that the feeling is totally mutual. Again, you must look into their

spread to get this information. The bottom line is that you will probably get along very well with anyone who is in your Venus Period.

Their Card Is in Your Mars Period

The Mars relationship can manifest in several ways, most of them dramatic and stimulating. Since Mars rules the aggressive and sexual sides of our natures, we find one or both of these elements operating in Mars-ruled relationships. The person or persons you find in this position will be either a source of passion for you or a source of competitive or aggressive energies. It is either making love or making war. There seems to be no in between for Mars relationships unless they are your lawyer or your physical trainer. For women, a man in the Mars Period could be a lover or husband. It is considered a good sign for women to find someone you are attracted to in their Mars Period. Other women in their Mars Period are invariably those with whom anger, jealousy, and animosity are felt. For men, we find the women they desire in this position and often other men with whom they are either competing or having difficulty.

One of the best ways to channel Mars energy is to work together. So, for working relationships Mars connections can be very good. It stimulates you both to be more productive. But it is important that you are working for the same goals. If you are competing, the good effects may be wasted in trying to outdo each other.

Their Card Is in Your Jupiter Period

People who are Jupiter to you in any given year are those from whom you might receive a great deal of support, both financially and spiritually. This is considered to be one of the better positions to find someone's card in. Jupiter people are expansive and have for the most part what is termed "abundance consciousness," at least in their attitude toward you. Their positive attitude will be an expansive influence, affecting your decisions, which in turn may help you expand your financial or business dealings. They may even give you money or help your business in some other direct manner. Doing business with a Jupiter person will invariably prove to be profitable unless other cards in the same period say otherwise. To take advantage of their influence, prepare yourself to go beyond the normal boundaries you have set for yourself, especially those relating to your business. A love relationship or marriage during the Jupiter Period is considered blessed in many ways.

Relationship Quick Reference Table

Name	Keywords—Description
Mercury	Good communications, love to talk, share ideas
Venus	Love, either close friendship, family, or intimate
Mars	Aggression and Competition/Anger or Passion
Jupiter	Spiritual and financial/material benefits
Saturn	Restriction, burden, challenges, learning lessons, illness, karma, good for career
Uranus	Spiritual, needs freedom, leaves you feeling uncertain, friendship without attachments
Neptune	Projecting your fantasies onto people or situations, illusion, self-deception or secret deceptions, can be spiritual in a profound way
Long-Range	An important focus of your attention for the entire year. Neither positive nor negative in itself.
Pluto	Things you want to accomplish or learn to deal with, challenging! Interpret with Result Card.
Result	Same as Pluto Card but you also might end up with this person in some way. Interpret in conjunction with the Pluto Card.
Environment	The person is a helpful and protective influence for the entire year—a blessing in your life.
Displacement	The person is someone that you must give to throughout the year, oftentimes they seem to be a burden or you must repay them some debt.

Their Card Is in Your Saturn Period

When you find someone's Birth Card, Planetary Ruling Card, or Personality Card in your Saturn Period, it tells you that this will be a challenging relationship for you in one or more ways. Saturn is the great teacher, and he usually teaches by showing us parts of ourselves that need improving. He usually brings a certain amount of pain or hard work to the picture as well, so the person that is Saturn to you will place a burden or limitation upon you in some way. They may not do it intentionally, but in some way, you will feel restricted or burdened by their association. Often, there is an element of hardship or physical illness between the two of you. One of you may be ill, and one of you may be the healer. Family doctors are often found under Saturn. Sometimes under Saturn, we find a teacher who is an authority figure of some kind. Because Saturn rules the tenth house of career and social aspirations in astrology, Saturn-ruled relationships could have a direct bearing upon your reputation or career advancement.

The major gift of the Saturn relationship is learning. Anyone who is Saturn to us can make an excellent teacher. It is highly recommended to choose a Saturn relationship if there was something that you want to learn and learn well. You may learn discipline and hard work, and it may be that you don't appreciate it until later. Saturn is also associated with "karma," so here we find destined relationships that arise to pay off debts that were created sometime in the past, perhaps in a past life. Though you may feel restricted and burdened by this relationship, you may also sense that this relationship is something you must put up with for a while until the debt is paid or collected or until you have learned and mastered the lesson at hand. With the proper attitude, a Saturn relationship will bring you to an entirely new level of maturity and strength.

Their Card Is in Your Uranus Period

The planet Uranus has several unique qualities that you will find reflected in the persons found during this period. First of all, Uranus people are your friends. Some of my best lifetime friends are my Uranus Cards. There has to be a lot of freedom in the Uranus relationship. Neither of you can place heavy expectations on the other. This is why the Uranus relationship is also considered a person who leaves you feeling uncertain in some way. There can be an element of the unexpected change about them. People you find here may be those that leave you feeling a bit uneasy and unsettled. You just don't know what they might do next. They can be very independent and rebellious, demanding freedom at all costs, and they may have come into your life and upset your stability in some way.

The nature of Uranus is such that you will be unable to control, change, or hold onto any of these people. It is likely that the changes they bring into your life are ones that have been long overdue. If you can let go of your past structures, you may find a new perspective dawning in your consciousness that rejuvenates you spiritually. You may discover how joyful it can be to love another person without trying to change them. This is called unconditional love, which is a real possibility in a Uranian relationship.

Uranian relationships may also be very unusual in some way, such as a bisexual or homosexual relationship, or it could have some other sort of difference about it. An element of stark individuality or unexpectedness is found in these people that can carry over into your relationship. The Uranian relationship may also have the common bond of some kind of service to humanity, dealings with real estate, psychic development, or service to some large organization. This electrifying planet also rules mental pursuits that are futuristic or high-tech, such as television and computers.

Their Card Is in Your Neptune Period

Associated with Neptune are: travel over water or to foreign countries, drugs, alcohol, deception, hidden things, dreaminess, and illusion. Look for one or more of these elements in your Neptune-ruled relationships. It may be that you meet this person on a vacation or journey of some sort. Here we find those that you see through rose-colored glasses. You choose to see them the way you want to see them, instead of for who they are. Perhaps they seem to be the answer to a prayer or dream of yours. Just as likely is that they may be deceiving you. Though a Neptune relationship can sometimes be a dream come true, in most cases, it is full of illusion and deception. The Neptune relationship can be one that involves alcohol, drug addiction, or co-dependency. It is commonly an addictive relationship of one kind or another. Either you are trying to save the other, or you want to be saved by them.

Be careful that you are not being deceived by this person in love or business and also be just as mindful of the possibility that you are fooling yourself. If someone you find in this position seems to good to be true, there is a good chance that they are. Though it could be very romantic and a feel-good type encounter, it is advisable that you not make important decisions about the people you find in this position until after the Neptune Period is over. Then, you will be able to be more objective about them and better able to assess their value in your life.

The chart on the next page gives you a quick reference for all your relationships. Just look up where someone falls in your spread, and read the quick description given.

Indicators of Marriage, Divorce, and Love Affairs

There are cards in certain positions that are strong influences of marriage and divorce. The occurrence of these cards does not guarantee that you will definitely have a marriage or divorce, but the influence does support these experiences

strongly. I have found that most people I have known were married or engaged under the influence of a Marriage Card. However, the Marriage Cards come up very often in a person's life and obviously one does not get married each time a Marriage Card appears. Even so, the appearance of a Marriage Card does indicate that your current relationships are doing better than average. The love influence is strong.

The Traditional Marriage Cards

The 4♥ is one of the two Marriage Cards. The Threes of Hearts signifies a foundation of love in one's life and protection in marriage. A 4♥ day is one of the best to get married on if you want the marriage to last. It indicates happiness within the home and marriage and other intimate relationships. The 4♥ also represents a plentiful supply of love in one's life and satisfaction in love. A marriage during a period with this influence is considered auspicious and fruitful, especially if you see this marriage as the foundation of a home and family existence. The strongest marriage influence is when the 4♥ falls in the Venus Period as the direct card, since the Venus Period also rules marriage and the home. The next strongest position is 4♥ as the vertical Venus Card. The 4♥ as the Long-Range or Result Card of your year is also a strong indicator of marriage.

The Q♥ is the other Marriage Card and is just as strong of a marriage indicator. The Q♥ is the card of the wife and mother, a servant of love and the creator of the family. Just as with the 4♥, the Q♥ in Venus, direct, is the strongest influence, followed by the Q♥ in vertical Venus and then as the Long-Range or Result Card of the year.

Though the above examples are the strongest indicators of marriage, I have noted many people get married with the 4♥ or the Q♥ in other periods as well. The occurrence of either the 4♥ or the Q♥ in any period of your Yearly Spread can indicate marriage. However, the marriage will have a different flavor to it depending upon which Planetary Period it falls under. Let's take a closer look.

Other Marriage Cards

After using this system a while you are likely to discover that there are other cards that can mean marriage, and sometimes they are surprising. One thing to keep in mind in all card readings is that whatever card appears in a person's reading represents how they are experiencing their life. In other words, it is a very subjective experience. A marriage can mean many things to many different people. To some, the wedding itself is the main focus. This is often the case when a 10♥ appears during the time of the marriage. 10♥ means a large gathering of people, and a wedding often qualifies for just that. The same could apply to the

Years (ages 12 to 90) with a Strong Marriage Influence

(4♥ or Q♥ in Venus, Vertical Venus, Long-Range, or Result)

CARD	YEARS (REPRESENTED BY AGE)	CARD	YEARS (REPRESENTED BY AGE)
A♥	19, 23, 24, 25, 41, 51, 54, 64, 68, 69, 70, 86	A♦	16, 19, 32, 40, 42, 49, 51, 64, 77, 87
2♥	46, 48, 70, 72, 83, 85, 88, 89, 90	2♦	21, 23, 26, 32, 37, 46, 66, 68, 71, 77, 83
3♥	15, 21, 24, 25, 30, 44, 54, 60, 62, 66, 70, 89	3♦	12, 29, 31, 41, 49, 74, 82
4♥	23	4♦	16, 18, 20, 26, 37, 48, 61, 63, 65, 71, 81, 82
5♥	33, 38, 39, 43, 45, 47, 50, 51, 66, 78, 83, 84, 87	5♦	18, 35, 36, 37, 39, 50, 63, 72, 80, 82, 84
6♥	33, 36, 46, 74, 78, 81	6♦	14, 25, 34, 53, 54, 57, 64, 70, 79
7♥	14, 17, 24, 27, 30, 34, 35, 41, 43, 45, 55, 59, 79, 80, 86, 88, 90	7♦	27, 29, 32, 34, 39, 41, 57, 59, 80, 82
		8♦	19, 43, 47, 54, 55, 64, 88
8♥	14, 17, 28, 46, 48, 53, 59, 62, 69, 73	9♦	22, 23, 26, 40, 45, 47, 55, 56, 63, 67, 85
9♥	14, 28, 35, 37, 42, 44, 58, 72, 74, 77, 79, 84, 86	10♦	17, 27, 33, 35, 41, 62, 72, 76, 86, 87
10♥	14, 16, 18, 35, 42, 44, 46, 54, 61, 63, 64, 74, 80, 87, 89	J♦	27, 28, 40, 42, 50, 52, 56, 60, 67, 72, 78, 85, 87, 90
J♥	18, 20, 48, 50, 52, 63, 65	Q♦	16, 22, 25, 33, 38, 48, 61, 78, 83, 88
Q♥	20, 43, 51	K♦	15, 32, 39, 41, 55, 60, 84, 86
K♥	12, 22, 25, 28, 29, 31, 56, 57, 67, 70, 73, 74, 85		
A♣	25, 26, 27, 38, 40, 43, 44, 45, 46, 56, 70	A♠	16, 17, 23, 30, 42, 55, 61, 62, 68, 75
2♣	12, 13, 33, 36, 38, 43, 44, 45, 46, 47, 57, 58, 78, 81, 84, 88	2♠	25, 27, 29, 32, 38, 40, 53, 54, 72, 74, 77, 83, 85
		3♠	12, 31, 49, 57, 73, 76, 85
3♣	13, 18, 21, 24, 29, 37, 39, 42, 54, 58, 61, 63, 66, 69, 74, 80, 84, 87	4♠	12, 13, 15, 17, 28, 34, 36, 48, 51, 53, 56, 57, 58, 60, 62, 73, 79, 81
4♣	27, 40, 49, 52, 59, 65, 72, 80, 85	5♠	19, 29, 31, 34, 37, 49, 50, 52, 73, 76, 79, 82
5♣	18, 19, 28, 31, 44, 63, 73, 75, 76, 89	6♠	14, 24, 30, 31, 42, 52, 59, 69, 75, 76, 87, 90
6♣	15, 17, 25, 29, 30, 41, 45, 47, 49, 55, 60, 62, 70, 73, 75, 86, 90	7♠	12, 13, 20, 23, 26, 31, 33, 41, 56, 57, 65, 68, 71, 76, 78, 86
7♣	16, 19, 20, 22, 35, 37, 42, 45, 48, 51, 61, 64, 67, 68, 70, 80, 82, 87, 90	8♠	18, 24, 29, 30, 31, 39, 44, 69, 74, 75, 76, 89
8♣	21, 22, 23, 34, 36, 46, 48, 52, 66, 68, 75, 79, 81, 83, 89	9♠	15, 16, 30, 35, 36, 38, 39, 52, 60, 75, 80, 81, 83
9♣	13, 21, 35, 55, 56, 59, 71	10♠	13, 19, 30, 36, 38, 50, 55, 58, 64, 71, 75, 77, 81, 83
10♣	37, 39, 47, 53, 82, 84	J♠	12, 13, 26, 49, 51, 56, 57, 58, 68, 71, 78
J♣	21, 32, 33, 36, 50, 65, 76, 77, 78	Q♠	14, 17, 20, 22, 24, 34, 40, 52, 59, 62, 65, 67, 69, 79, 81, 85, 89
Q♣	20, 21, 22, 26, 32, 38, 43, 56, 65, 66, 67, 71, 77, 88	K♠	20, 22, 58, 63, 65, 67, 72, 77
K♣	13, 15, 16, 23, 26, 27, 43, 44, 45, 47, 53, 54, 58, 60, 61, 68, 71, 88, 89, 90		

8♥ card, which in meaning is very close to the 10♥ and can also represent groups of people.

I have seen people get married with a 5♥ Long-Range Card. If we look at the essential meaning of the 5♥, we see that it only implies a change in the area of relationships. Though it is often called one of the classic Divorce Cards, the change it implies can easily be a change from being single to being married. This same 5♥ could indicate marriage if it is the Result Card or found anywhere in the Yearly Spreads.

To some people, the marriage is of little importance com-

pared to the idea that they are now with someone who is the ideal lover and partner. For these people, a 2♥ could indicate a marriage. Many cards, such as the 9♣ Birth Card, are more concerned with the love relationship with their spouse than the whole concept of marriage. It is the perfect love affair that they seek, not necessarily the marriage. But they will get married in order to have this important love union. So, keep your eyes open for 2♥ as a marriage influence in some cases.

For women, the K♥ card is an archetypal symbol of the perfect lover, just as the Q♥ is for men. So, it comes as no surprise that a K♥ Result Card can be an indicator of a marriage. It invariably indicates meeting a man and having some form of intimate relationship. In a way, the K♥ is like the 2♥ in that it is the love affair that is valued more than the contract of marriage. But you will find this K♥ to be found commonly in the spreads of women who are getting married anyway.

Marriage Influence by Planetary Period

The period of year in which we get married often has a great impact on how that marriage is perceived by us. As we all know, not all marriages are easy and fun, and more of them end up in divorce than not. The general tone of the marriage may be revealed by this influence. Keep in mind that it is usually different for each partner. For example, you may have gotten married in your Venus Period, but it may have been your husband's Uranus Period.

When I am consulted for good days to get married, I first try to find a range of days in which both partners are in either Venus or Jupiter, which are traditionally the best times. If I can't find days that match both partners during those periods, I will then search the Uranus Periods as well. Mars could go either way and is better to avoid if possible.

During the **Mercury Period**, a marriage could be unexpected, quick, and also has the possibility of being short-lived. In general, it is not advised to marry in Mercury's Period for this reason.

During the **Venus Period**, a marriage is considered the most fortunate, being full of love and promise.

During the **Mars Period**, a marriage could be one marked by much stimulation and sexuality. Also, the possibility of much aggressiveness and perhaps fighting and arguing is present under this influence. This is a better marriage influence for women than for men.

During the **Jupiter Period**, a marriage could be one associated with a large sum of money. One or both of the partners will be bringing much wealth to the partnership. There are spiritual blessings as well under Jupiter's influence, so this is considered a fortunate influence for marriage.

During the **Saturn Period**, a marriage could be one that is marked by burden, responsibility, restriction, and hardship. There could be major lessons to learn in this relationship, and it will probably last a long time. This could be a karmic marriage, destined perhaps, but one where one of the partners has a debt to repay to the other or where one of the partners must endure hardship in some form. Also during this period

would be a marriage for money, status, career, or any other reason other than love. There could be a large age difference between the partners.

During the **Uranus Period**, we find a marriage for spiritual reasons, one that is unusual, unexpected, and sudden. These two people are likely to be very good friends and are able to give each other a lot of freedom in the relationship. This marriage may be to further their spiritual self-development, and this could be quite an honorable and loving bonding.

During the **Neptune Period** the marriage could be one where one or both of the partners would be holding illusions about the other. Though quite romantic, beautiful, and full of promise, the marriage could be an addictive relationship, where one of the partners is needing a "caretaker" and the other is needing someone to demonstrate his or her healing love powers. One of the partners could be in for a huge sacrifice. Also possible is a marriage while on a journey that takes one over water. In general, caution is advised since the illusory power of Neptune tends to block perceptions of reality to the extent that the relationship later turns into a nightmare instead of a dream come true.

Occurrences of the Marriage Cards

The following page contains a list of the times when Marriage Cards show up for the various cards. This list gives the strongest indicators of marriage, namely the Q♥ and 4♥ in Venus, direct and vertical, and the Q♥ and 4♥ as the Long-Range or Result Cards. Of course, you can get married with the Q♥ or 4♥ in any position, but these placements are the strongest.

Don't be alarmed if you do not see many good marriage years under your card. The 3♦ for example has very few occurrences of the Marriage Cards, but I know several 3♦ who have been married at least once and often twice. Use this list to find good years to get married, years and periods when the planetary influences are in your favor. Marriages occurring under these influences have a good chance of being favored by the 'powers that be.' When looking for the occurrences of Marriage Cards, look them up for both your Birth Card and Planetary Ruling Cards.

Also bear in mind that these charts do not report on any of the other Marriage Cards discussed earlier. You will have to scour your own Yearly Spreads to see when those cards appear and make your own predictions. These charts are just giving you some of the strongest occurrences of the two traditional Marriage Cards.

The Traditional Divorce Cards

The 5♥ means "a change of heart." It has several possible meanings in a Yearly Spread, one of which is that of a divorce from a current relationship. Under Venus, it is a powerful divorce influence, indicating that you leave one person for another or that in your heart you change your mind and feelings for the other. However, it can also mean a journey or trip that takes you away from someone you love or your family, such as a business trip. Never immediately assume that the 5♥ means a divorce. Just like the Marriage Cards, the 5♥ comes up often in life and does not always mark the time of a change in the relationship. You must combine the meaning of the card with your life situation to make the best possible interpretation. Of course, if you are seriously considering a rupture in your current relationship, this card could signal the time when it will occur. The 5♥ as the Long-Range or Result Card can also indicate divorce or endings of certain relationships. The 5♥ in any position is an influence of a change of heart, so be aware of this whenever you see its appearance.

The 9♥ signifies a disappointment about love or friendship. Nines also signify completions and endings, and since Hearts mean "of the heart," we have an excellent indicator for the ending of a love relationship or friendship. Under Venus, the 9♥ can indicate the ending of a marriage since Venus rules marriage and family. In the case of the 9♥, you might be the one who is being "left" for someone else. The 9♥ under Saturn can bring a very disappointing and karmic breakup of a relationship.

Other Divorce Cards and Positions

There are lots of other combinations of cards and positions that can indicate divorce. As I write this, I do so realizing that some who read this will become panicked when they see these cards appearing, fearing that their marriage is going to end. But this happens no matter what I say, so I don't let it stop me. Just wait until the worrywarts read about the Death Cards later in this book! I remember a woman called me one day in a panic, telling me that she found a Divorce Card in her Yearly Spreads. It turned out that the Divorce Card was ten years in the future, but that didn't stop her from getting all upset about it right now. So, having said that, here are the other possible divorce combinations.

The A♠ in Venus, 9♠ in Venus, or any Nine card in Venus, for that matter, can be an indication of the ending of the marriage. Since our Venus Period represents our home and family and all Nines represent completions, this is an easy one to figure out. The A♠ is one of the traditional Death Cards, and putting that in the period of home and family…well, you get the picture.

If you have one of the Death Cards, such as the A♠ or 9♠, in a given period along with the 4♥ or Q♥, this can mean a divorce. This is a case where the two cards in a period combine together to give us the whole story. The Death Card represents the ending of something, and the Marriage Card there with it tells us that it is our marriage that is ending.

The Cards of Love Affairs and Love Triangles

As a professional reader, I am often asked by my clients "when will I meet someone new?" or "when will I have a new relationship and get married?" *Cards of Your Destiny* provides this information with ease. Either the A♥, 2♥, 3♥, or 4♥ can indicate the timing of a new relationship. The 4♥ you already know about since we already discussed the Marriage Cards, so let's take a look at the rest of them.

The best indicator of a love meeting is the 2♥ in any period, but especially in Venus. The 2♥ indicates a meeting of two people for love or a get-together of two close friends or relatives. It doesn't always indicate a love affair, but it usually does. A 2♥ under Mercury could mean a short-lived affair, something like a one night stand. Under Venus, it is one of the best influences for love. Under Mars, the affair could be marked by sexuality, aggression, or stimulation. Under Jupiter, one that has business or money connections as well as love and some spiritual overtones. Under Saturn, not recommended, since Saturn brings hardships, restrictions, or burdens. Under Uranus, one that is perhaps bizarre, unusual, unexpected, or it could be one that has spiritual overtones. Under Neptune, it could be wonderful until Neptune's influence melts away to the Mercury Period. At that time, you will know whether the person you chose is who you think they are.

The A♥ is the card of "desire for affection," and this card can also indicate the beginning of a new relationship, especially in the Venus Period. Under Saturn, this card represents an unfulfilled or a thwarted desire for love. Under other cards, it has various other possible meanings in addition to the possibility of a new relationship.

The 3♥ is the card of emotional indecision or variety. Usually this is the result of having two or more loves at the same time, and here we have the love triangle. This can be a welcome occurrence to someone who has not had any relationships in some time and who has a strong desire for one, especially if you find the 3♥ in Venus or Jupiter. However, if this card falls in the spread of someone who is married or in a relationship already, it can signal a time of indecision and difficulty with love, especially if the card comes up in the Saturn Period.

The Secret or Hidden Love Affair Cards

There are several indicators of secret or clandestine love involvements. First of all there is the A♥ or 2♥ sitting in the Neptune Period. Neptune has the element of secrets and deceptions and therefore, this can be one indicator of a secret love involvement. If you remember, Neptune represents our hopes and fears for the year. The A♥ or 2♥ could mean a hope for a new love, one that may or may not actually manifest itself. However, in many cases, it does actually come to pass. If you look up these cards in the interpretations, you will note that there are other, more common meanings for these cards as well.

The other indicators of secret relationships are the A♠ cards falling in either the Venus Period or the Mars Period. The A♠ means secrets. Under Venus, it is a secret love, under Mars, a secret passion. Once again, these cards have other meanings as well, so it would not be wise to tell someone that they are having a secret affair just because you find these cards in their Venus or Mars Period.

Relationships on a Lifelong Level

So far, we have dealt with relationship influences on a yearly or weekly basis. However, everyone that you know or meet is likely to have an influence on you from a lifelong level, and this is often more important than the yearly influence, especially when considering a marriage or business partnership. The lifelong influence is one that is always there and is usually the strongest influence for any relationship. This is where you can look up members of your family and important love relationships to understand their deeper meanings. You would naturally want to check this relationship influence for any new and important people that come into your life, especially if you are considering being with them for an extended period of time. This is such an important topic that I have devoted practically an entire book to it—my book called *Love Cards*. In that book, you can go into great detail about the lifelong connections between any two Birth Cards to discover the real inner workings of any relationship. In this book, we will touch upon the subject just enough to give you some tools to work with to begin your exploration.

The place you can look to determine this lifelong influence is in the Ages 89 and 90 Spreads. The Age 89 Spread has another name. So does the Age 90 Spread. These two spreads are called the Spiritual Spread and the Life Spread respectively. Besides being the spreads for the years 89 and 90, they both cast a lifelong influence on your personality and life experiences. They are the *spreads for your whole life*. My book, *Love Cards*, goes into great detail to describe who you are and what your life will be like based on these two spreads. We will

not get into this here except to show you how to find the most important lifelong relationship influences.

If you look at these two spreads of yours and search for the Birth, Planetary Ruling, and Personality Cards of people you know, you will likely find some interesting connections here. The same interpretations apply for these relationships as they did earlier. It is the position that the cards fall in that matters. For example, if someone is your Mercury Card in your Age 90 Spread, then they are a Mercury relationship to you for your whole life. This is someone that you will have good communication with for your whole life, quite a good relationship by most measures. Anyone whose cards you find in these two spreads are fairly important, and your connections to them are more powerful than others. Look carefully for members of your family in these spreads, and you will learn a lot about your most important relationships.

If you are considering a marriage with someone, it would be advisable to check these two Lifelong Spreads for their cards to tell what the relationship with them will be like for you long term. Likewise, you can check in their Natural and Life Spreads for your Birth Cards and Personality Cards to know how you will be affecting them on a long-term basis. This process will reveal to you the true connection that you have to another person. Knowing this information may not change your mind about marrying them, but it will provide you with the knowledge of how to make the relationship work better. People do not always marry people who are their Venus or Jupiter Cards, even though these are the two most blessed. There are many reasons for relationships in this coming Age of Aquarius, most of them having to do with our personal development.

There Is No Long-Range Card for Life

Though the Age 89 and 90 Spreads have Long-Range Cards in them, these Long-Range Cards do not also apply to us on a lifelong basis. If there were a Long-Range Card for life, it would have to be our Birth Card. There is a tremendous amount of information that can be derived from these two spreads, but one must fully understand them in order to get this information. Practically this entire system is derived from those two spreads. If you are sincerely interested in learning more about them, my book, *Love Cards*, gives a fairly complete introduction to their purpose and use.

Remember that these connections are from your point of view if you are looking at your Life and Spiritual Spreads. You must look at their spreads for your cards to see how you fit into their life.

To use these two spreads most effectively, first check your Spiritual (Age 89) and Life (Age 90) Spreads for their Birth Cards, Planetary Ruling Cards, and Personality Cards. Next look for their cards in the 89 and 90 age years of your

Planetary Ruling Card's Yearly Spreads. These are also just as valid, though they are slightly less powerful than the spreads under your Birth Card.

Each time you find one of their cards in one of your spreads, note what position it falls in and read about its significance as indicated by that position.

Next, reverse the process and check their Spiritual and Life Spreads of their Birth Card and Planetary Ruling Card for your personal significators. This shows you how you are affecting them. Then, finally, check the same two spreads under each of their Personality Cards for your cards. Now you have the complete picture of your relationships on a long-term basis, which is really the most important if you plan to be with someone for a long time.

Let's take an example just so you are clear on how to do this.

Who	Sex	Birthday	Birth Card	Planetary Ruling Card
Person One	female	July 16, 1945	Q♣	A♣
Person Two	male	May 30, 1940	2♣	K♣

This is an interesting combination. Glancing at the Age 90 Spreads for both people's Birth Cards and Planetary Ruling

Your Karma Cards

Your Card	Karma Cards		Your Card	Karma Cards
A♥ -	A♦, 3♥		A♦ -	2♦, A♥
2♥ -	A♣ (9♥, 7♦, K♠, J♥, 8♣)*		2♦ -	6♣, A♦
3♥ -	A♥, Q♣		3♦ -	6♥, Q♦
4♥ -	4♦, 10♠		4♦ -	5♠, 5♥
5♥ -	4♦, 5♣		5♦ -	9♥, 3♣
6♥ -	4♣, 3♦		6♦ -	9♣, 3♠
7♥ -	8♥, A♠		7♦ -	9♥ (A♣, 2♥, K♠, J♥, 8♣)*
8♥ -	7♥, 7♠		8♦ -	Q♠, 7♣
9♥ -	7♦ (A♣, 2♥, K♠, J♥, 8♣)*		9♦ -	Q♦, 5♦
10♥ -	J♣, 5♠		10♦ -	Q♣, Q♠
J♥ -	K♠, 8♣ (A♣, 2♥, 7♦, 9♥)*		J♦ -	3♠, J♣
Q♥ -	10♠, 9♣		Q♦ -	3♦, 9♦
K♥ -	2♣, 9♠		K♦ -	3♣, 7♠
A♣ -	2♥ (9♥, 7♦, K♠, J♥, 8♣)*		A♠ -	7♥, 2♣
2♣ -	A♠, K♥		2♠ -	6♠, K♣
3♣ -	5♦, K♦		3♠ -	6♦, J♦
4♣ -	5♣, 6♥		4♠ -	10♣, 4♥
5♣ -	5♥, 4♣		5♠ -	10♥, 4♦
6♣ -	8♠, 2♦		6♠ -	9♠, 2♠
7♣ -	8♦, J♠		7♠ -	K♦, 8♥
8♣ -	J♥, K♠ (A♣, 2♥, 7♦, 9♥)*		8♠ -	K♣, 6♣
9♣ -	Q♥, 6♦		9♠ -	K♥, 6♠
10♣ -	J♠, 4♠		10♠ -	4♥, Q♥
J♣ -	J♦, 10♥		J♠ -	7♣, 10♣
Q♣ -	3♥, 10♦		Q♠ -	10♦, 8♦
K♣ -	2♠, 8♠		K♠ -	8♣, J♥ (A♣, 2♥, 7♦, 9♥)*

*These seven cards belong to a special family of cards that have different rules as far as their karmic relationships.

Cards, we find no connections whatsoever. However, if we look in the Age 89 or Spiritual Spreads, we find some significant connections—namely that both people are past life cards to each other. This also translates as being the Mercury Card in the Age 89 Spread. The K♣, Person Two's Planetary Ruling Card, is the Mercury Card to the Q♣. Likewise, the 2♣, Person Two's Birth Card, is the Mercury Card to Person One's Planetary Ruling Card, the A♣. This double, past-life, Mercury connection is unusual and rare. But it does translate to one of the strongest marriage bonds that exist. See the *Love Cards* book for more information on the past-life/Mercury connection, which is called the moon connection.

The Past Life Relationship Connection

In my experience as a reader of both the cards and astrology, I have come to appreciate that many, if not most of the people we know in this lifetime are those that we have been with before. Many people can feel these connections intuitively, and others can relate to it when you mention that as a possibility. There is a certain connection between cards that is one of the strongest indicators of a past life together. My research has shown this to be a consistent indicator, even though those people with whom you share this connection in the cards are not the only ones that you may have had past lives with. For a complete list of all the past life connections, read my *Love Cards* book. For now, here's how you determine who you have this first and most important past life connection with:

The *natural order* of the cards is from the A♥ to the K♠ as follows:

THE NATURAL ORDER OF THE CARDS
A♥– 2♥– 3♥– 4♥– 5♥– 6♥– 7♥– 8♥– 9♥– 10♥– J♥– Q♥– K♥–
A♣– 2♣– 3♣– 4♣– 5♣– 6♣– 7♣– 8♣– 9♣– 10♣– J♣– Q♣– K♣–
A♦– 2♦– 3♦– 4♦– 5♦– 6♦– 7♦– 8♦– 9♦– 10♦– J♦– Q♦– K♦–
A♠– 2♠– 3♠– 4♠– 5♠– 6♠– 7♠– 8♠– 9♠– 10♠– J♠– Q♠– K♠
A♥– 2♥–...

The two cards that are likely to be past life influences for you are the cards *just before* and *just after* your Birth Card in this natural order. This means that if your Birth Card is the 5♥, your two Past Life Cards are the 4♥ and the 6♥. If your card is the A♦, your two Past Life Cards are the K♣ and the 2♦. Likewise, if your Birth Card is the A♥, your two Past Life Cards are the K♠ and the 2♥.

Those people that are Past Life Cards to you are those with whom you will feel a sense of familiarity, even when you first meet them. You may even sense that there is some past history between you, even though you cannot remember what it is. Usually past life people are friendly to you, and the two of you have an easy time getting along.

Past Life Cards have the greatest potential for marriage of all of the possible connections. When two people meet who have this connection, there is a strong pull towards being together and making a lasting commitment. In my research of couples, it is the single most often found connection among married couples.

In truth, any connection found in the Spiritual Spread is a past life connection. When we meet someone who is our Venus or Mars Card in the Age 89 Spread, we often get this instant recognition feeling associated with having been together before.

Your Karma Cards

Most people have two Karma Cards. The people that are your Karma Cards are those with whom there is a strong karmic bond of one kind or another. This means that one of you likely owes something to the other. Your reason for being attracted together is often to settle this debt from some past life. The Karma Cards are also strong mirrors of who you are, they are like other sides of your own personality. For this reason, you will either love them or feel some distaste for them. You can actually look at your Karma Cards as being different parts of your own personality reflected back to you. I always tell people that when you meet someone who is one of your Karma Cards, you should be prepared to either give to them or receive from them. There is no way to really know which you will have to do with them until you get to know them a little. You will either feel an urge to give to them, or they will feel an urge to give to you. Exactly what is supposed to be given is not apparent either. Since I am a Diamond, for example, it seems that all the Karma Card people I meet either owe me money, or I owe them money in some form. You will have to see how it works for you. On the last page of this chapter is a list of each Birth Card and their Karma Cards. Keep in mind that these Karma Cards only apply to your Birth Card and not your Personality Cards.

The Special Family of Seven and Their Karmic Relationships

If you look at the list of Karma Cards on the next page, you will note that seven of the Birth Cards listed have six Karma Cards beside them. If you look a little closer, you will realize that among these seven, their Karma Cards are themselves and no others. This unique family of cards has no official title, but they do hold a different place among the Birth Cards and have different kinds of karmic bonds than the remaining forty-five cards. These seven are actually comprised of two groups. The first are the three Fixed Cards (the 8♣, J♥, and K♠) and the two pairs of Semi-Fixed Cards, the A♣ and 2♥, and the 7♦ and 9♥. I'll discuss these two sub-groups separately since they each have distinctive characteristics.

The Fixed Cards—The 8♣, J♥, and K♠

These three cards only have one thing in common, and that is that they have a strong fixed nature to their personality. Some would call them stubborn, while others would call them dependable. In any case, these three cards actually have no Karma Cards to whom they owe something or receive something. Usually they will have one or more family members or loved ones who are one of the other six special cards, but it is difficult to say exactly why they are drawn together without a closer study of the relationship. They are rarely found together with other members of their fixed family of three, probably because of their inability to adapt or yield, which is often a requirement in personal relationships.

The Semi-Fixed Pairs— the A♣ and 2♥, and the 7♦ and 9♥

I have named these two pairs of cards the Cosmic Soul Twins. No other cards in the deck have a special relationship like these cards do with their partners. The A♣ and 2♥ are very much mirrors of each other, each one sharing the exact same qualities as the other. The same applies to the 7♦ and 9♥. And these cards are often found together in families or marriages. Though somehow related to all of the other cards of the family of Seven, these Soul Twins find the strongest connection with their other half. It is a strong bond that has the highest potential for intimacy of most any relationships found in the cards.

Now you have many tools with which to use this card system to explore your personal relationships. And there are more available in my other book, *Love Cards*. A little research can uncover many enlightening bits of information that could make a difference in your love life and family.

In the next chapter, you will learn how to do a weekly reading, which will give you cards for each day of the week and more.

Chapter Six

How to Do the Weekly Reading

The Weekly Reading is your personal tool. It gives you important information about your life on a weekly basis that can help you make decisions and make better sense of the things going on in your life. But what is actually more important is that the Weekly Reading is the technique that will teach you the meanings of the cards faster than most anything else you could do. Because you will have direct experiences each week that you can compare with the cards that you draw, you will increase your learning rate many times. I have found that people learn things much more quickly by experience than by memorization. As you watch what happens each week and interpret the meanings of the cards in your reading, you will begin to understand the 'essence of the cards' by your personal experience. You will know when you have truly learned something about the cards, because you will have a definite feeling that goes with that knowing.

To insure that your weekly readings are accurate, you must follow the instructions carefully. The timing of the shuffle and the cuts are of particular importance. This is a technique that has been passed down from Olney Richmond himself. The one-minute shuffle and three, twenty-second cuts were always performed at the beginning of any important reading or demonstration of the power of the cards. These shuffles and cuts are necessary to instill your personal magnetism into an otherwise randomly ordered deck of cards. Done correctly in the manner prescribed, you can rest assured that all of your readings will be accurate and pertinent.

There are specific instructions and rules for this reading that you must follow if you are to get the most out of it. Read them carefully so that you understand. First, the rules that you must follow:

Rules for the Weekly Reading

1. The reading is done every Sunday and covers one week beginning the following day, Monday.

2. You only do the reading once. If you do not like the cards you drew, take a closer look at how you are interpreting them. Every card has a positive side.

3. Always use the Poker sized playing cards (2½ inches by 3½ inches) whenever possible, and never use any decks that have different faces on the Jacks, Queens, and Kings than the standard faces. This rule is very important according to the Order of the Magi who were the original keepers of this science. Never use the Jumbo Index cards or any larger sized deck, as all of these constitute changes to the original deck of cards.

4. Find a place in your home where you can leave these cards laying out for the week if possible, such as a table top or dresser top. In this way, you can observe them day by day as the week unfolds and learn much more about the cards as you go through the week.

5. Remove the Jokers from the deck before doing this reading. This is important according to the Order of the Magi, as the Jokers will spoil and make invalid the reading if left in the deck. I usually just throw them away.

6. One final thought is that we never perform the weekly reading on December 31st, which is the Joker's day. On that day, which really has no card for its significator, no accurate readings may be obtained. Olney Richmond was able to perform hundreds of mystical 'tests' with the cards, but never on the day of the Joker.

Preparation

1. Find a quiet place in your home where you can be alone for five to ten minutes.

2. Light a candle, put on some soft music, and burn some incense. Do whatever you like to create an atmosphere of reverence for what you are about to do.

3. Make sure that you have a watch handy in order to time your reading. A watch with a second hand is essential.

The One-Minute Shuffle and Three, Twenty-Second Cuts of the Deck

1. Keeping an eye on your watch, wait until the second hand reaches the "12", and begin shuffling the deck. There is no right or wrong way to shuffle the deck, just be sure that you are handling and moving the cards around for exactly one minute.

2. When the second hand reaches the "12" again, cease your shuffling of the deck, and perform your first cut. A cut consists of removing some of the cards from the top of the deck with one hand, placing them to the side, and then picking up the remaining cards and placing them on top of the cards you removed.

Note: You have a plus or minus 2½ second margin for error on each of these timed actions, so don't fret if you miss the mark by a second or two. However, if you miss the mark by 3 seconds or more, stop, and then start the shuffle and cuts over from the beginning.

3. Wait another 20 seconds, until the second hand reaches the "4", and then perform your second cut of the deck.

Note: You may use either hand for the cut, though traditionally the left hand was preferred because it is the feminine or receptive hand.

4. Finally, when the second hand reaches the "8", you may perform your third and final cut of the deck.

5. At this point, your deck of cards has your personal magnetism instilled in it, and you need not have any concern about how soon you perform the reading. You can wait a few minutes or even hours as long as the deck is not disturbed. This is your deck now and every card in it is exactly where it should be as a reflection of your personal magnetism combined with the magnetism of the current day, hour, and minute. These combinations of energies are what will guarantee an accurate reading for you.

Laying Out the Cards

Before laying out my cards each week, I like to close my eyes and say a small prayer. I don't pray for good cards or that I will win the lottery. Instead, I pray that I may understand my reading and gain some insight into myself and the Science of the Cards by its use. Then I open my eyes and lay out the cards.

1. Following the diagram, you lay out the cards, as numbered, face up. This means that your first card goes where the number one box is, the second on the number two box, and so forth until all twenty-four cards are on the table, face up. The last three cards that you lay down should be numbers twenty-two, twenty-three, and twenty-four, which correspond to the Long-Range, Pluto, and Result for the week.

Note: I like to lap the third row of cards (numbers fifteen to twenty-one) on top of the second row (numbers eight to fourteen). These cards being lapped over each other, while the top row is completely open, helps denote the special significance of the top row. The bottom two rows are called the Underlying Cards, which we will discuss more later.

2. To get the Environment Card, simply turn the remaining cards in the deck over. The card that was on the very bottom of the deck is the Environment Card and should be placed at the very top of the layout as pictured.

Understanding the Structure of the Layout

All the cards except for the last four fall under one of the planetary headings. For example, the fourth card you laid down falls under Jupiter. So do cards number eleven and eighteen. These twenty-one cards are also associated with a certain time of the week, as they fall under the heading of Monday through Sunday. For this reason, we might call these the *Daily Cards*.

The remaining four cards are all *Weeklong* influences and are governed by different forces than the Daily Cards.

Interpreting the Meanings of the Cards

Now you are ready to look up the meanings of the cards. If you follow this suggested order, the process will be simple and complete. After you have done it for a while, you may choose to adopt your own order or technique. Essentially, you will look up the meanings of the cards in the Weekly Reading the same way you look up the cards in your Yearly Spreads. You will even use the same interpretations that you used for your Yearly Spreads. The only difference is that as you read them, you will translate their meanings to adjust for the time difference.

For example, as you look up the Environment Card for the week and read the meaning of it, you will adjust for the fact that this Environment Card only governs seven days of your life, not an entire year. The interpretation in the book will say 'this year,' but you will translate this to 'this week.'

I suggest you do this final part of the reading in the following order.

1. Look for relationship connections with people you know for the week.

2. Read the Weeklong Cards, and look up their meanings. This includes the Long-Range, Pluto, Result, and Environment Cards.

3. Read the Top Row of Daily Cards, and look up their meanings.

4. Study the Underlying Rows of Daily Cards for how they may contribute to the meaning of the Top Row to get additional information about them.

That final step is more of an advanced technique, which I will discuss more about later. Let's take them one at a time.

1. LOOK FOR RELATIONSHIP CONNECTIONS WITH PEOPLE YOU KNOW FOR THE WEEK.

The first thing you can do with your Weekly Reading is look for cards in it that are the same as the Birth Cards or Planetary Ruling Cards as people you know. For example, if card eleven, found in the Underlying Position of the Jupiter column, was a Q♥ and your best friend was a Q♥, this would tell you that your friend would be Jupiter to you for this week. Look for their Birth Cards and Planetary Ruling Cards first. Then you can scan for Personality Cards as well. However, if you find a Q♣ in your Weekly Spread, for example, you may have several women who are Clubs and may have to decide or determine which one of them it applies to. It could apply to them all, if they are actually interacting with you that week. For example, a Q♣ in Venus would mean that virtually all of your Clubs female friends and associates would be a Venus influence in your life for that week. However, if you find their Birth or Planetary Ruling Card somewhere else in the layout, that card will be more significant than their Personality Card. Given the previous example, if one of your female friends was a 7♣ and you found her Birth Card in your Pluto position this week, she would be much more of a Pluto influence than a Venus one.

Use the Relationship Quick Reference Table in chapter five to interpret the influences of the various positions. Or, read more about those positions in that chapter. If the card falls in an Underlying Card position, it still has the same influence of that planetary column. For example, a card falling in position thirteen or twenty will have a Uranus influence just as strong as the first Uranus Card in position six.

2. READ THE WEEKLONG CARDS AND LOOK UP THEIR MEANINGS. THIS INCLUDES THE LONG-RANGE, PLUTO, RESULT, AND ENVIRONMENT CARDS.

In a Weekly Reading, the cards governing each day are somewhat inconsequential. Daily influences often pass us by without our notice. But the weeklong influences will definitely be felt and experienced by most people. Keep this in mind as you read the interpretations of their meanings, once again bearing in mind that these only govern one week of time, not the entire year, as the interpretations were written in this book.

I suggest you pay particular attention to the Pluto and Result Cards each week. I have found these two to always have a special message for me about what I am learning or trying to achieve in any given week. I cannot tell you how many important and good lessons I have learned from paying attention to these two cards. Later in this chapter, I will give you some pointers and suggestions of ways that I get the most out of my readings each week.

3. Read the Top Row of Daily Cards and Look Up Their Meanings.

Once you have studied the weeklong cards in detail, you will want to turn your attention to the first seven cards that you drew from the deck. These cards are the ones that govern each day of the week individually. The first card, the Mercury Card, governs Monday. The next, Venus, governs Tuesday and so forth. As you look up these cards' meanings, you will do so just as you did the Mercury–Neptune Period Cards in your Yearly Spreads. For example, if you have a 8♥ in the Venus (two) Card position, you would look up the interpretation for the 8♥ in the Venus Period. The only difference is that now the card only affects one day, instead of an entire fifty-two-day period. Experience has shown that events that relate to these seven cards do not always occur exactly on the specified day. Sometimes they are off by a day or two. However, they do occur at the same general time of the week. So the Mercury–Mars Cards tell of things that happen toward the beginning of the week, the Mars–Saturn Cards affect the middle of the week, and the Saturn–Neptune Cards cover events towards the ending of the week.

4. Study the Underlying Rows of Daily Cards for How They May Contribute to the Meaning of the Top Row to Get Additional Information about Them.

This final step is more advanced and is not necessary until you feel ready for it. We always use the Underlying Cards to perform step one about the relationships, but to interpret their meanings for the week and to integrate these into the meanings of the Top Row of Daily Cards is a somewhat advanced concept. Essentially, these cards are underlying influences that contribute to the meaning of the card they fall under. So, card numbers eight and fifteen contribute to card number one. Card numbers nine and sixteen to number two and so forth. They act much like the vertical cards in the Yearly Spreads in that they often provide background information about the event or person that is described by the Top Row Card. They may tell you who is involved in that event or experience. Or, if the Top Card is one of someone you know, they may tell you

more specifically what that person will do that will affect you this week at that time. Or, as in most cases, they simply give you some specifics about the event or experience represented by the Top Card for that particular day.

To interpret these cards well, you will need to know more about combining card influences together. That topic is covered in-depth in the next chapter, among other important topics that will hone your interpretation skills.

Other Considerations and Ideas

I suggest that you copy the layout diagram at the end of this chapter and make a record of each week's reading. I have left enough room in the boxes for you to write in the cards that you pulled for that week. Then, you can make notes on the page as to what happened as you went through the week. This exercise will teach you more about the cards in a short period of time than anything else you could do.

I also suggest that you do these weekly readings for your friends and family. I have never met anyone that would refuse a free reading. This provides you with more experience and more fun too.

I caution you not to take the cards in your weekly reading too seriously. Many beginners make the mistake of interpreting these cards just as they would a Yearly Spread. The fact is that these cards are very minor influences and very transitory. As you do these readings for yourself and others and see how things turn out, you will realize that you really cannot interpret them just the same as you would the same card found in a Yearly Spread. They just don't have the same strength.

How to Get the Most Out of Your Weekly Reading

The weekly readings fulfill a vital purpose, both for beginners and for the advanced student of the cards. For beginners, they are able to get cards every day and every week that can be compared with the experiences and relationships in their lives, so they learn the meanings of the cards by experience. This is important, as the true meanings of the cards only reveal themselves to those who are sincerely interested in using this system for themselves. Once we have experienced what happens in our lives and have compared that to the cards we see in our weekly reading, we learn in a way that sinks in and becomes a part of our understanding. Later, when we share this understanding with others, whether we are giving them a reading or simply telling them about this system, we speak with power and conviction.

Once the language of the cards becomes part of our vocabulary, the weekly readings serve as a useful guide that reflect back to us what we are doing, saying, and thinking. It becomes

Weekly Reading Card Layout

Reading Begins on Monday, _____/_____/_____

		Env 25		

LR 22	Plu 23	Res 24

Mer 1	Ven 2	Mar 3	Jup 4	Sat 5	Ura 6	Nep 7
Und 8	Und 9	Und 10	Und 11	Und 12	Und 13	Und 14
Und 15	Und 16	Und 17	Und 18	Und 19	Und 20	Und 21
Monday	**Tuesday**	**Wednesday**	**Thursday**	**Friday**	**Saturday**	**Sunday**

almost like a friend that reflects different parts of ourselves, often challenging us to rise up to higher standards of behavior and relating. One week, for example, I had a 3♣ as my Long-Range Card. Sometimes I look at this card and tell myself, 'Oh great, another week of worry and indecision.' But that week, I consciously chose to look at it and tell myself, 'Oh great, now I will have all the creativity I need to get some writing done!' Well, I got into my writing, and it flowed very well. I programmed myself a long time ago to think "creativity" whenever the 3♣ appears. In a way, I have created a positive association with that card that always inspires me to write. This is what each of us can do with the weekly readings. But there is more. I want to share with you exactly how I do a weekly reading, how I look at it, and what I think about it so I get the most results possible for my life and use it as a tool to bring me more happiness and fulfillment.

First of all, I always light a candle and say a prayer just before lay out the cards for my weekly reading. I pray to my spirit guides and masters to teach me, and I ask them to use these cards to give me messages that will lead me to the light. Then, I drop any desire for the cards to turn out in any certain way and promise that I will be open to what the cards are for the week and that I will learn from them. This, in itself, increases the chances that I will get positive results from these cards. Keep in mind that I want to use this reading to lift myself up to a higher level. It has become a ritual for me that keeps me connected to my spiritual path.

After I have laid the cards out, I first look for all the signs of success, power, and good fortune. First, I look for the obvious. I look at the Jupiter Card in the first row as representing what or whom will be a major source of blessings for me this week. Remember that every card manifests positively under Jupiter's influence. Next, I look for power, satisfaction, and accomplishment cards. These are the Fours, Eights, Tens and the Face Cards in either the first row or the top row (Long-Range, Pluto, Result, and Environment). All of these cards represent success and satisfaction in one or more areas. Just having one of these cards in my reading is enough to give me a happy expectation of the week ahead and to feel safe and prosperous. Last week, I had some pretty tough cards. As I laid them out, there were none of the "good" cards anywhere in the top row or the Long-Range, Pluto, or Result. Then I turned the deck over to see the

Environment Card for the week, and it was an 8♠. I sighed with relief and knew that nothing negative could possibly happen to me that week, as the 8♠ is a powerful card of overcoming any and all problems. In the Environment position, it acts as a 'protective umbrella.' There was really nothing to worry about.

The next thing I do is look at the top row of cards (numbers one through seven) and see what the week has in store. I look at them like this:

Mercury Card—tells me what I will be thinking about this week.

Venus Card—tells me who I will be having affection for or what I will love this week.

Mars Card—tells me what will inspire me to action or what will anger me this week.

Jupiter Card—tells me where my biggest source of blessings are for the week.

Saturn Card—tells me what this week's biggest lessons will be about.

Uranus Card—tells me what will surprise me this week or what spiritual things will be occurring.

Neptune Card—tells me what I will be dreaming about this week. Who or what is in my dreams, hopes, secret desires or fears, etc.

Of course, there are other meanings for the cards, but these are the general ones that I attach to the first seven cards.

The last thing I do is look for cards that I don't understand at all. I watch carefully as the week progresses for signs that would indicate the true meaning of the cards. There is usually a secret message hidden for me in these cards. I keep an open mind and let the events of the week be my teacher. I am still learning new things about the cards every week, and I hope you do too.

Chapter Seven
The Art of Interpretation

In this chapter, you will be learning the fine art of card interpretation. Now that you have mastered the techniques of locating all the cards for your Yearly or Weekly Spreads, the last thing that you need to work on is how to combine card meanings to get the most precise interpretation for the cards. There are many other little hints and suggestions that I want to share with you that will help you get the best interpretations as well. In this chapter, we will learn:

1. Important rules for interpretation that will help you make better predictions

2. The individual components of a card's meaning that go into a complete interpretation

3. How to combine two cards together to get a singular story line from them

4. The importance of our attitude and life context in the meaning of the cards we have

5. How the position of a card affects its meaning

We will also have some sample readings, several yearly readings and a weekly reading. When you see how I put the meanings of cards together, you will begin to understand the fine art of interpretation and be able to do powerful readings for yourself and others.

Read the Basic Meanings of the Cards

Generally speaking, to understand the meanings of the individual cards in your spreads, all you have to do is look up the meanings of the cards in the interpretations section of this book. A different meaning is given for each card in each possible position. All possibilities are covered. However, to get even more out of these interpretations, I suggest that you do the following:

Before you read the interpretation given for the card in the exact position you find it in the spread, first read the Basic Meaning for that card. There are many possible meanings for each card, and it was not practical to list every single one under each location. However, under the Basic Meaning heading, I have given you the root meanings and possible ways the card can manifest, and sometimes there are possibilities given that are not listed under the specific location you are reading for. Always strive to understand the origins of the card meaning. Try to get to the root of it. Once you understand its basic meaning, it will be easy to translate that into the planetary position it occupies. The planetary position sheds a certain influence on each card in their period as follows:

The Cards Are Subjective in Their Interpretation, Not Objective

It is very helpful to understand how the cards end up reflecting things in our life. And this is one of the first rules of interpretation. If you don't get this, it could take you a long time to understand how to be accurate with the cards. The cards in your reading tell you what the events and experiences in your life will be to you. And this is not necessarily what they would be to someone else. One good example relates to the Death Cards. Traditionally, the A♠ and 9♠ are Death Cards. However, if you do some research, you will find many different cards showing up at the time of someone's death. I have seen 5♥, 9♥, 8♠, and 9♦ just to mention a few. Each of these cards could tell us what that person's death was for them. The 5♥ death means a voyage to somewhere new, leaving loved ones behind. The 9♥ death means the ending of important personal relationships. The 8♠ means a death that was desired, an accomplishment. The 9♦ death would occur to someone whose death meant the loss of many material possessions. In each case, the cards revealed what their death was to them, not what we usually associate with death. When you study the Yearly Spreads, both your own and others, keep in mind that whatever cards you see there will accurately reflect how they are interpreting and experiencing life and not necessarily what is actually happening to them in the usual sense of the word.

The Different Levels of Meaning for Each Card

The next thing that you must realize about doing interpretations of the cards is that each card has several levels of meaning. One card can represent a variety of experiences, and to be good at doing readings, you must first be familiar with all the ways that a certain card can manifest. Once your mind is aware of all the possibilities present for a certain card, your

intuition or "knowing-ness" will tell you which meaning is the most appropriate. Sometimes a card will represent many of its possible meanings at the same time. For most of the cards, the way it manifests in our lives is determined by our attitudes. Remember that this is a purely subjective reading that the cards give you.

For example, a 9♦ in Mercury can represent a loss or expenditure of money from many different sources. Since Mercury rules automobile travel or short trips, education, and all the mental fields, the loss or outgo of money will be related to one or more of these subjects. Because Mercury represents things that happen quickly and are quickly over, this loss will not be a big one, nor will it prove to be a major disappointment, such as the 9♦ in Mars or Saturn would. Any Nine can mean an ending of something that was going on for a long time. A 9♦ could mean the ending of a job, the loss (or ending) of something valued, or the ending of plans (Mercury) to make some money in the future.

Card Meanings Can Be Changed by Our Attitude

If you had a 9♦ in your Mercury Period, much of the way it affects you would be determined by your attitude. A 9♦ can either be a disappointment financially or a release that allows the universal flow of wealth to later come back to you. On its highest level of manifestation, a 9♦ would give you a spiritual experience of cosmic understanding about the laws of money and finances. This would be a very pleasurable and mind-expanding experience that would broaden your outlook on money and values. This understanding would likely even bring more money into your life, and often it prompts us to give money away. How you personally would experience a 9♦ or how anyone else would experience it is determined by their mind-set, their attitudes, their beliefs, and their relationship to wealth and money.

The Sevens and Nines are the cards that can give us the most problems and the greatest release and freedom. They are the most dramatic examples of how our attitude and point of view can alter our perception of events and experiences in our life. You yourself will someday experience 'turning a negative into a positive' if you use this system for long.

As you read the interpretations for your cards, remember this point. Try to see that you can actually change the meaning of the card by adjusting your attitude. Each card in your reading will challenge you to take it to its highest level of manifestation. Make that your goal, and you will lead a life full of magic and mystery.

Also keep in mind that when you read for others, their attitude has more power over their destiny than the cards they have. I have met several people who, through a truly pessimistic and gloomy attitude, have had continually problematic and troublesome lives in spite of all sorts of positive cycles and cards. If I am reading for such a person nowadays, I address their attitude problem first. Without some awareness in that area, anything else I tell them will have little effect.

To those who have some energy and a half-way positive approach to life, the cards provide a blueprint for success. Since I first learned this system, I have followed my cards closely and endeavored to transform negative influences wherever I could. Though I have lost a few battles in doing this, overall, I have become very successful and happy using them for guidance. But I do know that it is not the cards that make me successful. It is my own determination and efforts that are the real key to my success. Without them, no cards could help me.

The Components of a Card's Interpretation

It is helpful for beginners to take a moment to examine what the basic components are that contribute to a card's meaning. If you just take a look at this and reflect on it, you will get a handle on this system that much sooner. The components of a card's meaning are:

1. The Card's Number

2. The Card's Suit

3. The Card's Position—generally a Planetary Influence

4. The Context of the Person you are reading for

The *number* of a card is the first element of its meaning. There is an exact meaning to every number that can be not only memorized, but understood. Numbers are an integral part of the world we live in. We find their meanings reflected in our lives everywhere we look. But most of us never really looked at number meanings that carefully. For example, if you look at the number four and look around you at everything that has a four associated with it, the meaning becomes instantly recognizable. Most of our homes have four sides, boxes have four sides, bricks and things we build with have four sides. Fours mean protection, foundation, and good supply. For those who want to explore this further, I have written a book called *The Science of Numbers*. In it, I begin with the number zero and go from all of the card numbers to explain how and why numbers have to be the meanings that they are. This can help you not just memorize their meanings, but truly understand the origin the cards' interpretations based upon the essential qualities of the numeric evolution of numbers.

The *suit* of a card is its next component. The suit tells us generally what the subject of the card's meaning will refer to. It is fairly simple really. You can just memorize the following, and you will be right most of the time:

1. Hearts are relationship and emotional conditions.

2. Clubs are mental condition and communications with others.

3. Diamonds are values and financial conditions.

4. Spades are work and health conditions.

That's really all you need to remember.

The *position* of a card is very important, because it tells us another delineation of the specific area that a card influences or what sort of influence it will have upon us. Much of this meaning can be derived from the information I presented in chapter five. Here is a quick description about how the periods that the cards fall under influence them:

The Mercury Period tends to make the influences of the cards in it to be more quick-acting and transitory. It tends to relate to things that happen while you are driving a car, making communications, and it has a lot to do with intellectual pursuits that you may be involved in. For example, a 10♠ in Mercury would bring a quick or sudden success, or a success related to a mental endeavor, such as school.

The Venus Period tends to relate the cards in it to the home, family, women, social occasions, or your love life. They also talk about your relationships with women. For those involved in work with the arts, beauty products, performing, and the public, the Venus Cards will often tell you the success or challenges in these lines of work. For example, a K♥ in Venus is a great success card for performers and artists, aside from its usual meanings.

The Mars Period colors the cards in it to refer to legal matters, your passions, or relationships with men in some manner. Whatever you are aggressively pursuing this period will be referred to by the cards in this period. They are often indicators of success or difficulties in your legal matters, be it a lawsuit or just meetings with attorneys. Any competitive enterprises are governed by Mars. Competitive sports or business endeavors and their outcomes are often revealed by our Mars Cards.

The Jupiter Period always brings out the most positive sides of the cards in it, emphasizing the spiritually and financially beneficial aspects of the cards. Even the most challenging cards will have more likelihood of manifesting their positive sides because of Jupiter's influence. Jupiter is primarily related to money and business success. For most of us, our Jupiter Cards each year tell us how we can make the most money. Don't underestimate the value of that last statement.

The Saturn Period is almost the opposite of Jupiter. It tends to bring out the most difficult aspects of cards. It combines the meanings of the cards with health issues, hard work, and challenging lessons about how to be mature and responsible. It also brings the element of karma into the cards under it. Often, we have to deal with situations that we left unresolved earlier in our life during the Saturn Period. And if we didn't handle it right the first time, we get a second chance to straighten things out. Saturn is very much concerned with justice and fairness, along with proper consideration for how our actions and words affect those around us.

The Uranus Period brings an element of spirituality, intuition, unexpectedness, or unusualness to the cards in its period. Real estate and labor relations are also covered by Uranus, so often, the cards here will speak of the success or difficulties in these areas. Unexpected things happen during Uranus. Sometimes they take us completely by surprise and upset the status quo of our lives in a way that has a positive effect in the end.

The Neptune Period adds the elements of fantasy, illusion, spirituality, hidden matters, foreign matters, travel, and possibly deception to the cards under it. Look here for the success or failure of foreign interests, travel, or of your dreams coming true. The Neptune Cards are often the things you are dreaming about this year. It is also called the 'secrets' period and the 'hopes and fears' period. The cards there may reveal your secret desires, fears, or hopes.

The final element, and one of the least understood in our interpretations of the cards, is the *context* of the person we are reading for. This is where you have to become somewhat of a detective or prosecuting attorney when you do readings for others. I usually put my clients on the witness stand for a while—just long enough for me to get a fairly good understanding of how their life is, their overall attitudes and beliefs, and of course to find out some of the background circumstances that are currently affecting their lives.

This is a crucial part of the reading. Without this information, any predictions I make would be a stab in the dark at best—an educated guess. With some background information, I can become nearly 100 percent accurate. After using the cards for as long as I have, I have come to appreciate how important knowing the person a little is. If I see a 7♠ Long-

Range Card in a reading, I know there are some challenges present. But unless I get more information about them, I will not know if it is about their work or their health, whether or not they are taking it as a personal challenge or as a big problem, and what the overall effect of it will be. Will they learn from it or will they just try and avoid it as much as possible? These sorts of answers only come from getting to know the person I am reading for. Never be afraid to ask a few questions.

Combining Card Influences to Get the Whole Story

Most of the time, when you are interpreting the cards in a Yearly or Weekly Spread, there are two cards to consider, not just one. You have the direct and vertical card for each period, and then you have the Pluto and Result Cards for each year or week. These cards have to be interpreted as pairs, not singly, because they always relate to each other and give more information about each other. It is almost like they tell a story together.

Often, one of the cards will be the Birth, Planetary Ruling, or Personality Card of someone you know, while the other will tell you how or what they are involved in as related to you. For example, if your best friend is a male 2♠ and you find a J♠ direct with a 7♦ vertical in your Venus Period, you could assume that this friend of yours would somehow be involved in a situation that is going to test you or cost you financially. He might cause you to spend some money that you were not planning on spending. Perhaps you paid his way on a date or—just as likely under Venus—he accidentally breaks something in your home and can't afford to replace it or fix it. This shows you how you take those two cards, knowing that one is the card of your friend, and combine them together. I am going to list some examples of pairs of cards in certain periods to show you some of the possible ways to put the interpretations together. Read these carefully, and you will learn a lot about this important aspect of doing readings.

What to Do When You Find One of Your Own Cards in Your Reading

Whenever your own Birth, Planetary Ruling, or Personality Card is found in your yearly or weekly readings, the cards are foretelling an event that will involve you personally. For this reason, it is important to analyze the surrounding cards carefully. After all, this is happening to you, and you'll want the complete picture. For example, if your Birth Card is the 9♥ and you are a man, and you found a J♥ and a 10♠ in the Saturn Period, you could assume that you would be working very hard during that period. You would be successful, but it would be hard work, as well as probably being involved in some sort of creative work (because it is your Jack).

Cards	Position	Possible Interpretation
Q♣, 6♥	Saturn	You get involved with a Clubs woman in a karmic and difficult relationship. You learn a lot through this relationship about the laws of give and take in love.
10♠, 4♦	Mars	You are very successful, working very hard and making money during this period.
A♥, 2♣	Venus	You have a sudden infatuation for someone you meet at a class where you are sharing ideas.
10♦, 3♠	Jupiter	You make a lot of money working two different businesses or jobs at the same time.
9♦, J♥	Venus	You give some money to a younger relative in need, sacrificing some plans you had to use the money to improve your home or buy some furniture.
2♥, 8♠	Plu/Res	You are working hard this year to have successful friendships or love relationships.
5♦, 5♣	Plu/Res	You have a year of major changes in your values and philosophy of life. You move to a new house, get a new job, and change relationships.
8♣, J♠	Plu/Res	You are initiated into a new spiritual understanding that is causing you to do a lot of mental work and to develop mental power this year.
9♦, 7♦	Saturn	Your health will cost you a lot of money this year, or you will be worrying about money so much that you will get sick over it.
5♣, 8♦	Neptune	You take a long trip and have ample money to enjoy it, or you actually make money on the journey.
5♥, J♦	Venus	You have a break up with a Diamond man.
5♠, 3♠	Plu/Res	You want to change jobs but are quite undecided about it. You decide to work two jobs at the same time before your next birthday.
3♥, 2♥	Venus	You meet someone new and are undecided between him (or her) and someone you are already dating.
A♥, A♦	Plu/Res	Your desire for love and your career interests are competing for your attention.
9♠, 7♥	Plu/Res	You finally end, or let go of, a situation in which you felt betrayed (7♥) by another.
9♠, 7♠	Saturn	You go through an important death of a part of your personality that prevented you from leading a happy life in the past.
A♦, K♥	Jupiter	You begin a new business enterprise that involves your being an artist of some kind.
A♠, J♣	Venus	You have a secret love affair with a J♣ person, who could be any male of the Club suit.
7♠, 8♠	Plu/Res	You learn how to have faith in your work and how to proceed ahead with what you know you should do, in spite of challenging circumstances.
5♥, A♥	Venus	While on vacation, you meet someone and fall in love.
6♥, K♣	Jupiter	A Clubs man comes into your life offering many good things. It is a relationship from a past life to repay your good deeds at that time.
8♦, K♠	Plu/Res	Your desire to have more money to spend causes you to develop more power and authority in your life and work.
2♣, 8♥	Plu/Res	You overcome your fear of being alone and become very social and popular by getting clear about what you want in personal relationships.
K♥, 9♥	Jupiter	A divorce from a K♥ person proves to be financially beneficial for you.
10♣, 10♥	Plu/Res	Your efforts to publicize your work results in great success and more visibility.
6♠, 6♦	Uranus	This represents a period in which nothing new occurs, but one in which you have great opportunities to contact your inner guidance and find some true direction for your life.

Keep in mind that when you find one of your Personality Cards in your reading, it is most likely referring to that side of your personality. Chapter two tells you in detail what sides of your personality the various cards represent.

More on the Pluto and Result Cards

In chapter four you learned about the Pluto and Result Cards and how to interpret them. Because these two cards are so important,

I thought I might spend some more time on them to make sure you realize how to understand the ways they fit together.

First of all, these two cards are always read as a pair. They are never separate. Then again, you may have more than one set of them since there are a pair of them for each of your personal significators. When you have more than one pair, each pair is read separately as referring to a different area of your life.

These two cards are telling you what one of your major objectives or goals is for the year. This may be a goal that is forced upon you in some way or one that you take on consciously. A lot of it depends on how you take it or how you approach it. You can always turn a Pluto and Result Card pair into a major victory for yourself if you choose. To do this, you must decide that there is something there that is good for you, something that will improve your life or give you something that you want.

As we begin our year, both the Pluto and Result Cards represent challenges to us. Together, these two cards combine to describe what it is that we want so much that we are willing to make some big changes to get, or what things will cause us to change in spite of ourselves. However, as we move toward the end of the year, by which time we have pretty much made the necessary changes implied by these cards, we start to perceive the blessing aspect of the Result Card. In truth, the Result Card has a very strong Jupiter influence to it. But until we have crossed the bridge of Pluto's transformation, we are only able to see it as a challenge of some kind.

The Result Card is always what we will end up with by the end of the year that we will consider to be a blessing. And as we end each year, we are usually grateful for what it has brought into our life.

Often, the Pluto or the Result Card is that of someone you know. Usually when this is the case, that person shows up as a source of difficulty for you. In this situation, it is wise to look closer at that relationship and ask yourself what it is about that person that is most difficult for you. An honest self-evaluation will usually reveal that there is something about them that reminds you of a place where you are lacking in some way. If this is the case, you can turn this whole situation around by making a goal of taking on the challenge of acquiring the things that you want or need that the other person reminds you of.

How to Get the Most Out of Your Readings

Whenever I look at the cards of my yearly or weekly reading for the first time, I am immediately aware of my state of mind and emotions. Am I reading the Sevens and Nines as problems or opportunities? Am I worrying about my Saturn Cards or my Pluto Cards for the week? It is important to keep in mind that the meanings of all the cards in the deck depend upon our attitude. We can make them positive by having a positive attitude about them. Here are some suggestions, some things that I do to get more out of my readings, both weekly and yearly:

1. I always look for the best cards first. Are there any Kings, Queens, or Jacks? These always represent success and power in the areas they sit. How about Fours, Eights, and Tens? These are the success and satisfaction cards. I especially like the 10♠, 8♠, and 4♠. If I find any of them, I immediately focus on the benefits of those cards. Often those benefits will be enough to help me feel that this will be a good week or year, regardless of the other cards present.

2. Next, I look at the Jupiter, Environment, and Result Cards. These cards are always good, no matter what their suit and number. They point to areas in my life where a lot of blessings will come from this year or week. These positions always bring out the more positive aspects of the cards found in them. If I focus on the benefits I will be getting from these cards, it changes my attitude significantly.

3. Remember to interpret the Sevens and Nines as spiritual influences. I am involved full time in spiritually-related work. So, I always remember the possibility of interpreting any Seven or Nine I find in my reading as a spiritual victory or as spiritual work accomplished. These two cards mean letting go of attachments and letting the higher powers take care of us. If I am giving of myself to others, I can always see these cards as potentials for happy experiences of helping others and as experiences of higher consciousness.

4. Last, but not least, I remember that negative influences are only temporary. Every period is either one day long, as in the case of the weekly reading or fifty-two days, as in the case of the yearly readings. Fifty-two days is not that long. Even the worst cards in Saturn will only last for a while.

Getting the Most Out of the Face Cards

Each of the face cards, the Jacks, Queens, and Kings, have the ability to bestow upon you certain power or success when they show up. It is likely that you will always have at least one or two of them in every yearly or weekly reading. You can choose to see these cards as gifts to you—gifts of power, love, strength, wisdom, or experience. On page 360, you will find a brief description of the gifts that each member of the royal

Sample Weekly Reading

	Q♣	
	Env	
	25	

3♦	10♠	2♥
LR	Plu	Res
22	23	24

3♥	K♥	7♠	5♦	6♥	7♣	A♠
Mer	Ven	Mar	Jup	Sat	Ura	Nep
1	2	3	4	5	6	7

Q♥	J♣	10♦	Q♦	9♣	7♦	8♦
Und	Und	Und	Und	Und	Und	Und
8	9	10	11	12	13	14

5♠	6♦	10♣	8♠	8♥	A♣	2♣
Und	Und	Und	Und	Und	Und	Und
15	16	17	18	19	20	21

| Monday | Tuesday | Wednesday | Thursday | Friday | Saturday | Sunday |

family brings to you when they show up in your reading. By acknowledging and using these gifts, you can actually create more success and accomplishment, joy and happiness in your life. All you need to do is realize what is being offered and take it.

Sample Readings

The sample readings that follow will give you some good experience of how a person well-versed in this system would interpret an actual reading. The first is a weekly reading of someone I know and what happened to them that week. After that, I will give you several Yearly Spreads of some of my clients with the real things they were going through, the questions that were most on their minds, and what I told them based upon their cards. I think you will learn a lot if you read these carefully and try to interpret them yourself first. Then, when you see what I said and did, you will see the different possibilities that you may not have noticed before. Good luck.

THE WEEKLY READING EXAMPLE

This was a weekly reading for a woman named Jane. Jane was, at that time, dating one guy who was a May 14th birthday. That makes him a 5♦ with a J♣ Planetary Ruling Card. Jane herself is a Cancer 2♣ (June 28th) with a K♣ Planetary Ruling Card. However, she just met another man born on July 28th, a K♥. She really likes both men for different reasons, and this is how her week went.

The uncertainty about her love life is reflected in both her 3♦ Long-Range Card and the 3♥ card in Mercury. The 3♥ in Mercury can mean a preoccupation with matters of the heart, trying to use our minds to make decisions related to the heart. Jane has a best friend born on October 13th (9♣, 2♥) who she talks to. Jane's friend gave her a lot of advice and support while she went through this week of uncertainty. You can see her represented by the Q♣ Environment Card. Her friend's Birth Card is also located in Saturn, telling her that she could receive some useful guidance from her now. Of course, the 6♥ on top indicates that some of her guidance may be directing Jane to be more responsible in her love life, which may seem harsh from Jane's point of view. This is because we don't always like the things that Saturn people tell us. But Jane's friend is also the 2♥ (her Ruling Card), and this falls in the Result position. It looks like she is a blessing this week, but also an integral part of the changes that Jane has to make to come to terms with her indecision.

However, this Q♣ is also Jane's Personality Card, the one she becomes when she falls in love or is involved romantically. Even though she is experiencing a lot of uncertainty and indecisiveness about her love life, she is also reaping many rewards

from her love life this week. That is further supported by the fact that her boyfriend is her Jupiter Card this week. She has both her boyfriend, the J♣, and her new interest, the K♥, in her Venus position, telling us that she has affection for both of them and that with either one of them she will basically have a good time.

Jane saw each of these men once early in the week. Wednesday was a sort of tough day at work, but she received a wonderful gift from her 5♦ boyfriend on Thursday, who found out that she had a tough day at work on Wednesday. After many talks with her best friend, Jane realized that there were some aspects of her relationship with the 5♦ that just were not working for her, but she had been afraid to bring them up. This is why she began looking around and finally connected with the K♥ guy. She got together the courage to bring these things up with her 5♦ boyfriend and as a result, they became even closer and more in love with each other. It was very scary, and he did get mad when he found out she had seen the K♥ guy, but once they communicated their feelings more, they both felt better. Jane stopped seeing the K♥ and felt like she was back into the relationship that she had always wanted (2♥ Result).

The last two days of the week were ones in which Jane experienced a lot of freedom internally and happiness. She meditated and felt very connected to her spiritual self.

EXAMPLES OF YEARLY READINGS

JOY'S READING

This first reading is for a woman that we will call Joy. Joy has never been married, a classic A♦ pattern, and had been without a relationship for a long time. She had just met someone, we'll call him Bill, who is born on 7/10/57, making him a 5♦, with a 7♣ Planetary Ruling Card. She wanted a general reading, but also wanted to know how things would work out between her and Bill. Here are her spreads for the year. This reading occurred just after her birthday at age forty.

The most significant indicators for Joy's questions are the 4♥ Long-Range Card combined with the 6♥ Environment Card. The 4♥ Long-Range can indicate marriage, but it always indicates happiness and satisfaction in one's love life. Because of Joy's history of having never been married and because Bill is a card that is known to be noncommittal (see *Love Cards* for more about the individual card personalities). I wouldn't bet that this 4♥ is a Marriage Card. The 6♥ Environment Card, found in her Planetary Ruling Card's Spread, means we have a fated sort of relationship, one that was destined to occur in this lifetime, with someone that we knew and helped before. When a 6♥ is the Environment Card, it often brings a good relationship into our lives, and one that comes with many blessings. They come

Planetary Periods	Mercury	Venus	Mars	Jupiter	Saturn	Uranus	Neptune
Period Dates	3/22/97	5/13/97	7/4/97	8/25/97	10/16/97	12/7/97	1/29/98
Birth Card — Direct	Q♥	5♣	Q♦	K♦	2♣	10♠	8♦
Birth Card — Vertical	5♥	4♠	7♠	5♦	8♠	8♦	

Long-Range: 4♥	Pluto: 3♠	Result: A♠	Environment: 2♠	Displacement: Q♠

Planetary Periods	Mercury	Venus	Mars	Jupiter	Saturn	Uranus	Neptune
Planet Ruling Card — Direct	5♦	7♦	6♣	J♥	10♣	8♥	2♥
Planet Ruling Card — Vertical	J♠	10♠	4♣	2♠	8♣	2♥	

Long-Range: 6♦	Pluto: 7♠	Result: 3♦	Environment: 6♥	Displacement: A♠

Name: Joy Birthday: 3/22/57 Birth Card: A♦ Planetary Ruling Card: 3♣
Age for Reading: 40 Personality Cards Used: None

back, so to speak, to repay us for the good deeds we did before. So, though I don't think these two would get married, I did see a lot of potential for love and happiness for however long it lasted. We notice that Bill's Birth Card also shows up in Jupiter along with the K♦. This is still another indicator that he would be a blessing in her life, perhaps on a financial level, this year.

Notice that Joy's Result Card in her Birth Card Spread is the A♠ and so is the Displacement Card in her Planetary Ruling Card's Spread. These two A♠ cards in such powerful positions for this year tell me that this year will be one of big changes for her. As we talked, it became apparent that she was feeling like she was embarking on a new phase of her life. The 3♠ Pluto is an indicator that she would be having questions and considerations about which job to take and even that she may be working a second job at certain times this year, but the A♠ Result shows her starting an entirely new job or direction by her next birthday. This 3♠/A♠ combination could have many other meanings for her or for someone else. For example, it could have meant a health problem that was hard to diagnose or just an overall uncertainty about one's life direction. In either of these cases, the A♠ promises a singular direction by year's end and a new start on life.

What is also very significant and doesn't show in these spreads is that she just completed her Pinnacle Year at age thirty-nine. This time of her life, from age thirty-six to forty-five, is the most significant cycle for all A♦ people. Big changes and great success in work are very possible for them. As I consulted with her, I advised her to also pay attention to her career, which was likely to have some big changes and success this year. Looking at her cards in the Uranus and Neptune Periods, we see great potential at those times. As part of this cycle, the age forty-one years, which for Joy is the next year, is one of the most significant. If you casually take a glance at the A♦ for age forty-one, you will

see two outstanding things. First of all, they have the K♠ Long-Range, and secondly, they are displacing the 10♦, which is called the Most Blessed Spot. This powerful combination occurs only for the A♦ Birth Card and only at age forty-one. These are both extremely fortunate influences that combine together to present a once in a lifetime opportunity for career advancement and fulfillment of heart-felt dreams, desires, and wishes. I mentioned all of this to Joy so that she would know this was coming ahead of time and could be prepared to take full advantage of this influence, which only occurs once in a lifetime.

Honestly, I didn't think this relationship with Bill would last very long, and I told her so. But I did heartily recommend that she explore it and take from it everything that it had to offer her. If you have the *Love Cards* book, you will discover that Bill is actually Neptune to Joy twice. This powerful Neptune influence can make us feel as though we have found the person of our dreams. There is a lot we can learn from these kinds of relationships, and though they rarely end up bringing long-term happiness, I often see great value in them for certain people at certain times. This was one of these times, though I usually admonish a client to be very wary of such a relationship.

You will notice that there are no cards here indicating divorce or splitting up with Bill. For this reason, it appeared to me that these two would be together all year. However, the 8♥ and 2♥ cards found in Uranus and Neptune are interesting. Could they mean that Joy meets someone new then? That is entirely possible and only time will tell.

DINA'S READING

Dina is a client I have been consulting with for over five years. It is very interesting when you get to see what happens in someone's life over that period of time—what sorts of things

		Mercury	Venus	Mars	Jupiter	Saturn	Uranus	Neptune
Planetary Periods **Period Dates**		6/18/97	8/9/97	9/30/97	11/21/97	1/13/98	3/6/98	4/27/98
Birth Card	Direct	8♠	K♣	3♠	6♥	8♣	7♠	Q♦
	Vertical	7♦	A♣	9♠	A♠	6♠	Q♦	
Long-Range: K♠	Pluto: 2♣	Result: 4♦		Environment: 5♠		Displacement: K♦		
Planet Ruling Card	Direct	Q♠	6♦	4♥	3♣	3♦	5♣	K♠
	Vertical	A♦	3♥	2♣	8♠	K♥	5♠	3♦
Long-Range: 4♣	Pluto: 10♥	Result: A♣		Environment: 5♦		Displacement: 2♦		

they get involved in, who they meet and hang out with, and what challenges present themselves on a more or less regular basis. Most of us have certain patterns that our lives follow to some degree. There are certain themes that keep reoccurring on a more or less regular basis. Over the five years that I have been consulting with Dina, she has been through two significant deaths, one of a close friend and another of a child that she voluntarily took up to help. This is a pattern that is not uncommon for a Q♣. In the Life Spread of a Q♣, they have a J♥ as their Pluto Card. It is through sacrifices made on the behalf of others, often younger children, that they learn their most important lessons. It is also interesting to note that the close friend of hers who died of AIDS was a J♥. The same thing happened to my mother, another Q♣. We had a younger brother who was a 10♥ Birth Card who died when he was four years old. That death changed my mother's life forever.

At any rate, when Dina called this year, she had just discovered that she had a brain tumor. She confided that exactly fourteen years ago, she had the very same condition and had an operation that supposedly removed it. Now, here it was again, exactly two, seven-year cycles later. Of course, what was most prominent on her mind was what was going to happen. She wanted to know the best times to plan her operation and things like that. Her spreads are shown above.

I am a firm believer that most everything that happens to us in life has an important message or meaning for us. I have found that if we explore these things closely, we often find that we ourselves are the cause of the events in our life, or that there is some very important message for us. In most cases, the things that we usually label as 'bad' are just important messages coming to us from areas where we have been largely unconscious. If we pay attention to those messages, often the

problems themselves disappear. Dina felt that the fact that this tumor reappeared after fourteen years was significant, and she was searching for the deeper meaning of the situation as we talked. She also said that her intuition told her that she was going to come through this whole thing just fine. Being one of the most psychically attuned cards in the deck, I didn't doubt her. And when I looked at her cards, it only confirmed her intuition.

Our Saturn Cards each year are usually the strongest indicators of health matters. The best possible cards you can have for health matters are Fours and Eights. Anytime we have the K♦ as a Displacement Card, we have the 8♣ in Saturn that year because the 8♣ is one of the three Fixed Cards. The 8♣ in Saturn promises success in health matters, but particularly success when one uses the power of their mind to assist the healing process. Another very strong indication of success in health matters for Dina is the K♠ Long-Range Card. This card can bring success in any area that it is directed and health has long been under the domain of the Spades suit. So, I told Dina that success would be hers if she applied herself with diligence. The fact is that she has many difficult Health Cards this year. Look at the cards in her Mars and Uranus Periods. Her operation was planned for her Mercury Period where she has the fortunate 8♠ ruling it. So, I saw success for the operation. However, the cards in Mars and Uranus could indicate further aspects of health challenges occurring later in the year. For this reason, I suggested that even though the operation would be good, that other aspects of health issues would be cropping up throughout the year. But I also told her that no matter what came up, she would overcome them with the power of her Saturn and Long-Range Cards.

Dina has two Fives as her Environment Cards this year. I told her that this year would be a lot about making some

Planetary Periods Period Dates		Mercury 1/29/97	Venus 3/22/97	Mars 5/13/97	Jupiter 7/4/97	Saturn 8/25/97	Uranus 10/16/97	Neptune 12/7/97
Birth Card	Direct	9♦	7♠	2♣	K♣	J♦	4♥	4♦
	Vertical	5♥	4♠	K♦	9♥	2♥	4♦	

Long-Range: 2♠   Pluto: 2♠   Result: 8♥   Environment: J♣   Displacement: J♣ (Rebirth Year)

		Mercury	Venus	Mars	Jupiter	Saturn	Uranus	Neptune
Planet Ruling Card	Direct	4♦	2♠	8♥	6♣	6♠	Q♥	10♣
	Vertical	Q♠	Q♦	6♦	K♥	7♥	3♥	

Long-Range: 8♠   Pluto: 8♦   Result: K♠   Environment: 4♥   Displacement: 4♥

favorable changes in her life. She might even move to a different place, and if she did, it would be something that would bring blessings into her life. She told me she had been considering such a move lately.

The 2♣/4♦ Pluto and Result Cards point to some fears (2♣) about having enough money (4♦), and indeed, that was something that Dina mentioned in the course of the reading. The 3♦ in Saturn in her Planetary Ruling Card Spread also says the same thing. I told her that these cards were mostly financial problems in the mind, not in form. The work for her this year was to just deal with her fears. The 4♦ Result Card always means we end up with plenty of money when it is all said and done. So, part of her work this year was to keep her fears in check as part of focusing her mind (8♣) to overcome all her problems.

One last issue for Dina is that she is writing a book and wanted to know if it would be published or completed this year. Again, with such powerful cards in Saturn and Long-Range, I told her to set her goals clearly and watch what happens. The K♣/A♣ in Venus and 10♥/A♣ Pluto and Result found in her Planetary Ruling Card Spread are both very favorable indicators for success in publishing.

You just cannot underestimate the power and potential of a K♠ Long-Range Card. Dina, or anyone with this card, can accomplish practically anything they desire for that year. However, it does require that one be willing to set clear goals and to take full responsibility for one's success. It does nothing for those who are waiting for good things to come to them.

CAROL'S READING

Carol is also a client of many years, and again, I have seen her progress through several important chapters of her life. This reading occurred at her Rebirth Year, age forty-five. Having gone through the death of her husband two years prior and having started a new life for herself since then, it was interesting that her Rebirth Year occurred at this juncture in her life. The Rebirth Year always points to a new beginning. The question was, what would this new beginning be in light of the fact that she had already been through so many changes? As we got into the reading, these new areas for change became apparent.

Carol had been married once for over ten years to a man who completely adored her and took care of her financially. He then became ill with cancer and died (illness of the mate is a common J♣ trait—see *Love Cards*) shortly thereafter, leaving Carol with a new life to make for herself. As it turned out, there were several issues in life that she had never addressed yet, important ones that never came up because of her marriage, which overshadowed her life for so long.

The first issue Carol had to deal with is common to many women who have a spouse that dies. That is that they have never had to hold a job and take care of themselves financially. Though her husband had left her some money, it was only enough to last for a couple of years. She had to create some financial security for herself in that time.

The next issue was a deeper one that came out in the reading and had come out in a two-year relationship that Carol had entered into just after her husband's death. Carol had a deep-seated belief that she wasn't good enough to be loved or lovable. Even during her marriage, which was to a man who completely idolized her, she confided that she was always insecure and felt that she didn't measure up. So, even in the face of all the praise and security that he provided, she was inwardly afraid and uncertain. Then, in the relationship that followed her husband's death, she attracted a man, a 6♣

Libra, that though being single, was still attached to his former spouse and was always comparing Carol to her. The bottom line was that Carol always came up short in the comparison. In addition, this man always told Carol from the beginning of the relationship that he was certain that she was not the woman of his dreams and that he would not marry her. Though this may seem like cruel behavior from an outside point of view, his actions exactly reflected how Carol felt about herself. When she came to me for this reading, she had broken up with this 6♣ guy for good and was considering a relationship with a married man (a 9♣) who had propositioned her recently. However, she confided that even though she hadn't even given this man any indication of whether or not she would be interested, she was already inwardly comparing herself to his wife and coming up short in her own mind. Her spreads are listed in the chart on the preceding page.

As far as Carol's work and career were concerned, there is no question that she would be successful. She had already began a new business which was showing signs of success. The J♣ Birth Card is a successful card for work already. The fact that she has such good cards in her Planetary Ruling Card's Spreads highlighted the fact that she was going in the right direction—one that would become more successful as the year progressed, bringing her financial security along the way (8♦/K♠ Pluto and Result). The 2♠ Long-Range and Pluto Cards point to a possibility of a working partnership, and Carol mentioned there was someone that she was considering for a partner on a limited basis in her business.

Carol has a lot of Heart Cards in her reading, but mostly in the second half of the year, beginning in her Jupiter Period. Interestingly enough, the K♣ and 6♣ found in both her spreads could point to a return of her previous 6♣ boyfriend whom she had broken up with. If he did return, I told her, he would come bearing gifts of some kind (Jupiter). However, I felt that with the 9♥ there, this could signal the real end of that relationship. As we all know, the actual end of a relationship can occur much later than the physical separation. This 9♥ in Jupiter pointed to the possibility of a good ending, one that was easy and rewarding at the same time.

It was her Saturn and Uranus Periods that most interested me. Saturn in both spreads held important Heart Cards. The J♦/2♥ combination in her Birth Card Spread was a strong indicator of a romantic relationship with some Diamond male who would teach her many things. Though relationships in Saturn are often difficult, the lessons they teach can alter our lives in a very positive way if we approach them with the right attitude. The other thing is that Saturn relationships are often destined. Just like the 6♥ in the example reading for Joy, any relationship beginning in Saturn often has karmic or past-life reasons for happening. The 6♠ and 7♥ in Saturn under her Planetary Ruling Card's Spread underscore that this is very

likely to occur. Six is very closely connected to Saturn, being a number of karma, just as Saturn is the planet of karma. Put a Six in Saturn and you have a very powerful combination of karmic influences. The 7♥ there with the 6♠ says that this karmic experience will be related to letting go of attachments and fears in personal relationships. After Carol and I discussed her insecurity and self-esteem issues, I felt for sure that these would come to a head during that period in the form of a new relationship. Since none of the men that she was currently entertaining were Diamonds, I told her that this man would be someone that she didn't know yet or at least someone that she wasn't thinking about in romantic terms at this time.

The cards in her Uranus Periods in both spreads are cards of happiness and satisfaction in love matters. This told me that after this challenging Saturn Period would be happiness and emotional healing. The 3♥ that lies below the Q♥ may even suggest that at that time she has two boyfriends at the same time.

The 2♠ and 8♥ Pluto and Result Cards, besides talking about her work and success there, are subtle indicators of her working on her self-esteem issues. The 2♠ is the partnership card of partnership cards. Within that card are all the forms of partnership one can imagine and all of our desire for a perfect mate. When we have an inward lack of something, we often look to fill this lack with a person, as Carol had tried many times. The 8♥ Result is like getting the power to heal ourselves. I told Carol that the work for her this year was to learn to love herself and get her fixation off of trying to find the right person to fill her inner need for self-love. This is good advice for anyone, but for Carol, this is the most important issue in her life at this time. The 8♥ Result is also a great indicator that she would be successful in this area and that by the end of the year she would possess a lot of emotional power and charm that could help her attract a better partner.

The J♣ has the 7♠ as a lifetime Venus Card. This 7♠ often points to mates who have health problems of one sort or another, but also of an inner fear that must be dealt with. Because it is a Spade, this fear is more likely to be one that is deep within the person, one that runs closer to the core of their being. For Carol, it was a basic feeling that she was inadequate in some way. I gave her several suggestions on ways she could explore this part of her personality and begin to make some changes in that area. If there is one thing I have learned from doing so many readings, it is that we must make these inner changes first. Otherwise, our life is like a repeating story line. We just keep doing the same things over and over again, and it doesn't matter who we fall in love with, where we live, or what kind of work we do. We take our emotional baggage with us wherever we go.

I have performed thousands of readings as of this time. I think I have seen pretty much every possible scenario that

Cards of Your Destiny Reading Worksheet

Name: _____   Birthday: _____   Birth Card:____   Ruling Card: ____

Age for Reading: ____   Personality Cards Used: ____   ____

Planetary Periods	Mercury	Venus	Mars	Jupiter	Saturn	Uranus	Neptune
Period Dates							

Birth Card		Mercury	Venus	Mars	Jupiter	Saturn	Uranus	Neptune
	Direct							
	Vertical							

Long-Range: Pluto: Result: Environment: Displacement:

Planet Ruling Card		Mercury	Venus	Mars	Jupiter	Saturn	Uranus	Neptune
	Direct							
	Vertical							

Long-Range: Pluto: Result: Environment: Displacement:

Personality Card 1		Mercury	Venus	Mars	Jupiter	Saturn	Uranus	Neptune
	Direct							
	Vertical							

Long-Range: Pluto: Result: Environment: Displacement:

Personality Card 2		Mercury	Venus	Mars	Jupiter	Saturn	Uranus	Neptune
	Direct							
	Vertical							

Long-Range: Pluto: Result: Environment: Displacement:

NOTES

exists in interpersonal relationships, and I use this card science to help others uncover the deeper reasons for their lives the way they are. I hope these example readings help you get a taste for how this system can be used in this way. I may one day publish an entire book of actual readings I have done and how this information can be used to transform people's lives. I hope that you will use it to penetrate into the deeper levels of causality in our lives, for which this system was intended.

Chapter Eight
The Life Map for Your Birth and Planetary Ruling Cards

In one manner of speaking, every year of our life is auspicious in one way or another. It would be hard to find any year of someone's life where there was nothing of importance occurring. However, there are years in which more dramatic things occur, and there are cycles during the lifetime in which we often make significant changes and progress. Sometimes these are very positive and uplifting times, and at other times, we are faced with personal challenges and endings of a more difficult nature. It is very helpful to know, at a glance, just when these auspicious years are and what are the probable events that we are likely to experience at those times.

This chapter presents a list of fourteen of the most significant auspicious occurrences for each card and tells exactly when they will occur. As you study these eventful years for both your Birth Card and Planetary Ruling Card, study the meanings that I give you here carefully so that you understand the full potential, either positive or negative for the probable events that are scheduled to occur. In most cases, you have a great deal of choice as to just how these cards will play out in your life. Every card has a high side expression and can give good results if we approach it carefully and with conscious awareness.

Be certain that you check these positions for both your Birth Card and Planetary Ruling Card. Both will apply, though the Planetary Ruling Card's events will have slightly less impact in most situations. It actually varies from person to person. For some people, the Planetary Ruling Card is such a strong expression that the auspicious events for that card seem more significant than those for the Birth Card. However, this is the exception rather than the rule.

One thing you may note is that some of the cards, namely the Fixed and Semi-Fixed Cards, do not have many of these auspicious events listed. This is because these cards do not have Displacement Cards each year, which cause many of the events. If your Birth or Planetary Ruling Card is one of these seven cards, you will have fewer of these events to keep track of. Chances are at least one of your personal significators is not one of these cards, and in that case, you will have occurrences of all those events that depend upon the Displacement Card. A vast majority of people have both Birth and Planetary Ruling Cards that are not of the family of seven.

You will also find some notes about each card on the page with their auspicious years that

What Is a Displacement Card?

Most of the special influences discussed in this chapter are derived from the Displacement Card. Our Displacement Card is literally the card our Birth or Planetary Ruling Card is displacing each year in the Grand Solar Spread. The illustration below shows the Grand Solar Spread, from which all of the Yearly Spreads used in this book come. If you compare your Displacement Card this year to the picture, you can see where your Birth Card (or ruling card) is sitting this year. For example, during the Pinnacle Year, we are displacing the 8♦, which sits in the top center, also called the Sun position.

Many of the positions in the Grand Solar Spread have special significance. Each row and column in this special array of cards is influenced by a planetary energy. In addition, the cards surrounding any one card also influence it. And that is what many of these auspicious events are all about—special events that occur as a result of the unique positioning of one of our personal significators. Notice where the three Fixed and four Semi-Fixed Cards sit. If you are not one of these cards, your card will never sit in any of their positions. Likewise, these seven never move about and enjoy the experiences of sitting in the remaining 45 positions.

There is a lot more to learn about these special positions and the movement of our cards each year about this spread. As we study this system, we are studying the very fabric and mathematical basis of the world we live in.

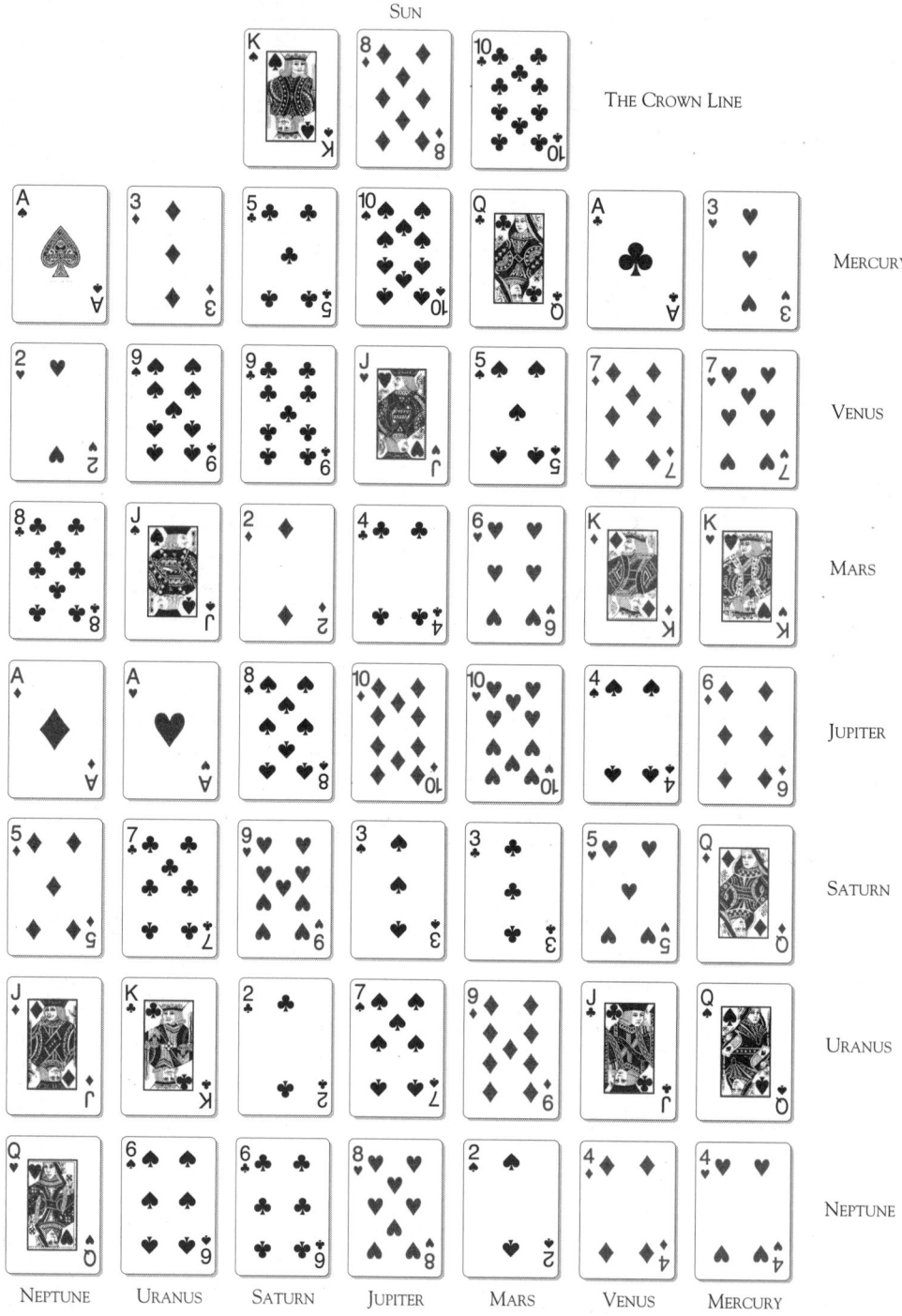

clue you into some unique characteristics for the life cycle of that person. In some cases, there is information that even goes beyond the scope of these fifteen different events and reveals some special situations for certain cards that are very significant at different times of life.

First, we need to fully explain these fifteen events so that you have a place to refer to when you begin looking up your personal years of major importance.

Cycles We All Go through at the Same Age

AGES 44 AND 45, 89 AND 90— THE PREBIRTH AND REBIRTH YEARS

If you study your Yearly Spreads carefully, you may notice that for most Birth Cards, the Age 0, 45, and 90 Spreads are identical or nearly identical. The same applies for any two Yearly Spreads that are forty-five years apart, such as the spreads for ages 3 and 48, or ages 23 and 68. The only exceptions to this are the Semi-Fixed Birth Cards that actually exchange places with each other for the second forty-five years. This can be confirmed by comparing the Age 20 Spread for the A♣ with the Age 65 Spread for its cosmic soul twin, the 2♥.

This phenomena implies a forty-five-year cycle that we each go through that is repeated after we turn 45 and again at age 90. The only cards that are not repeated are the Long-Range Cards. Because we have the same cards, essentially, at age 45 that we have when we are born, we experience a rebirth of sorts. This can be a very powerful year if one is aware of its potential and significance. Those familiar with the concept of rebirthing will tell you that it represents an opportunity to remake ourselves in a higher fashion by re-experiencing our physical birth. The physical process of rebirthing involves a guided experience that includes specific breathing techniques designed to get us in touch with what we went through as we entered this world for the first time. It is quite dramatic and effective, as it offers us an opportunity to reprogram ourselves with more positive thoughts.

The same principle applies to our Prebirth and Rebirth Years of life. During the age 44 year, we are back in the womb, metaphorically speaking. We are experiencing our life as a journey through our own Spiritual Spread. Many people find the age 44 year to be very confusing on a mundane level. But the potential for spiritual development and increased self-awareness is great. On one hand, the Prebirth Year is like being an expectant mother. We are pregnant, in a sense, with a child that is to be ourselves. There is often some sense of confusion or anxiety about an uncertain future, just like the would-be parent who doesn't really have any way of knowing just what their child is going to be like. During the Prebirth Year, you may find that you don't have a clear direction, and there is some uncertainty about your life that causes some apprehension in certain areas. But it is a very powerful time to meditate and explore your inner self. The more soul-searching we do at age 44, the more powerful and positive will be our Rebirth at age 45.

At age 45 we have, in almost every sense of the word, all of the cards that we were born with. We get a chance to experience who we are and what made us the way we are. In some ways, the experiences at age 45 mirror our experiences during the first year of our life, though few of us can actually remember what happened in that first year. But it was that first year, and actually the first seven years of our life, that molded our character. Did you ever notice that the Long-Range Cards for the first seven years of your life are the same cards (from Mercury to Neptune) that are in your Age 0 Yearly Spread? Realizing this, it is easy to see just how significant our age 45 year is. Here again, we have those same cards, all in one year. They present us with an opportunity to remake ourselves. Here we are again, presented with many of the same kinds of experiences that molded our character earlier in life. But now we are more conscious, more mature, and much more able to translate these experiences into a positive meaning for our life. Just as in the rebirthing process, we can elevate our character by choosing to take a higher path as each of these experiences present themselves to us for re-evaluation. If we handle this age 45 year with care, we can use it to alter the course of the rest of our life. Take any card in your age 0 Yearly Spread, which is also your Life Spread, and you have an element of your character personified in its symbol and suit. Now, think of how that card can be expressed in its most positive fashion. Then, during your age 45 year, make a commitment to express each of those seven cards in the highest light possible, and honor yourself and your life and the ways that you have already developed those higher qualities. In all these ways, the Rebirth Year can be quite significant and powerful.

Cycles We Go through at Different Ages—All Cards

THE FATED YEARS AND YEARS IN WHICH WE CAN DEEPEN OUR SENSE OF LIFE PURPOSE

Any Six Displaced, Long-Range, Result, or Environment

This event occurs when there is at least one occurrence of a Six card in your Yearly Spread in a prominent position (Long-Range, Result, Environment, or Displacement). This gives you a special opportunity, but one that is only taken advantage of by those who are aware of it. Sixes give us an opportunity to discover what our true purpose is for our life. Most people search their entire life to discover what their life is about and whether or not they have some special purpose or goal that they are to achieve during their time here on the planet. Many never find this purpose at all. Because of the presence of a Six card in a powerful position this year, you will have a special opportunity to discover what your purpose is. Of course, this only applies to you if you have the desire to know. If you are not that interested in knowing more about your life's direction, this will probably manifest itself as a year of steady progress towards existing goals.

Sixes can be frustrating as well, because they often represent static and unchanging conditions in our life. However, they also bestow upon us a special ability to perceive that which is usually hidden from our conscious minds. By listening to our inner voice, we can receive great inspiration and direction when these cards are present and you have at least one of them for this entire year. If you have more than one Six in a prominent position in either your Birth Card or Planetary Ruling Card Spreads, then this message becomes even more significant.

Another important aspect of having a Six card that governs the entire year is that there is a good possibility that fated events will occur that year. Though there are many things in our life that come by our choice in the here and now, there are also some events that are destined to happen because of things that we did or said in lifetimes past. During a year with a Six influence, it is entirely possible for some life-altering events to occur.

A Six as the Result or Environment Card is more likely to have a positive influence and create good things in your life. A Six Displacement Card will require some work and effort to actualize or may have a troublesome effect overall. A Long-Range Six Card will be neutral.

Study any and all Sixes that you find in these prominent positions this year, along with other Sixes that appear in your Yearly Spreads. They will reveal much about the special destiny that is coming your way. Good luck on your path to inner discovery.

Note: Years that display a '+' and a number after it are years in which there was more than one occurrence of a Six. During these years, fated events and the realization of your personal destiny are heightened.

BLESSED ENDING YEARS

Any Nine in Jupiter, Result, or Environment

Nines are generally regarded by most people as experiences to avoid and ones that will bring heart-breaking situations and circumstances. In general, we as humans grieve somewhat over anything that comes to an end in our life, and we have a

tendency to avoid Nines because they signal an ending. It is part of being human and not necessarily a bad thing. However, when a Nine appears in a favorable position, it brings many blessings and rewards along with the completion of some relationship, job, phase of life, plans, or lifestyle. These Nines come bearing gifts of many kinds. So, during these years, you can still expect some endings to occur, but they will usually be painless or at least accompanied by some wonderful blessings that will ease in the transition to the next phase.

Note: As before, when you see a '+' and some number next to the year, it indicates a more powerful influence for that particular year. The higher the number, the more powerful the influence.

DIFFICULT ENDING YEARS

Any Nine in Saturn, Long-Range, Displacement, or Pluto

Quite the opposite of the previous section, other occurrences of Nines are often more difficult for the average person to deal with. Of the four possible positions listed above, the Long-Range is the least inherently difficult one, but even a Long-Range Nine can be difficult for some people. It is a good idea to get a complete understanding of what a Nine means. Once it is fully understood, we can greatly minimize the fear and disappointment aspects of it and use it to propel us into our next phase of life. In chapter nine, there is an section on the 9♠ that applies to all Nines and gives a good foundation of information on how Nines work in our lives. If you see a Nine coming and have some concerns, read this article and any others you can find. The true meaning of a Nine is completion, simple and clear. It signifies that something you have engaged yourself in for many years is now complete and coming to a close. It doesn't have to be a loss or disappointment to those who understand their own cycles of life. It can be a cause for celebration, with eyes turned toward a bright future.

Note: As before, when you see a '+' and some number next to the year, it indicates a more powerful influence for that particular year. The higher the number, the more pronounced is that influence for that year of life.

CAUTION YEARS

Displacing the 4♥ or 7♥; A♠ Long-Range, Saturn, Pluto, or Displacement; 6♠ in Saturn

There are certain combinations of influences that present themselves from time to time that can have very dramatic and negative effects in certain circumstances. None of these positions by itself is a guarantee that something bad will occur. But given a certain set of circumstances, life-altering events could occur with these combinations. It really depends upon the individual and what their approach to life has been up until that point. For example, a 6♠ in Saturn can bring a very heavy payment of karma. People have actually died under this influence. But only those whose life was so out of line with the truth that they actually had earned their own death by their own ill actions towards others. If you have lived a life conscious of how the things you do and say affect those around you, you need not fear any Six in Saturn.

A '+' and a number next to the year numbers denote years in which there are either more than one of these cautionary influences or certain ones that are stronger. The higher the number, the more important it is to take a cautious approach that year. When the 4♥ or 7♥ is the Displacement Card for the year, for example, I give it a double influence rating. The reason the 4♥ and 7♥ Displacement Cards beget a higher rating is that each of these cards has what we call an underlying influence in the Saturn Period of the 9♠. The 4♥ Displacement Card has an underlying Saturn influence of both the 9♠ and 6♠, giving it the potential for a quite dramatic experience. For example, though O. J. Simpson had wonderful cards of success during the year or so of his first trial, he lost the civil suit while displacing the 4♥. Not only that, but he actually lost the verdict during the Saturn Period itself, where these two powerful Karmic Debt Cards have their influence. The potentially negative effect of either of these Displacement Cards can be mitigated by a good card in Saturn. For example, if you were displacing the 4♥ this year but your Saturn Card was an 8♠, 4♠, 10♠ or any Four or Eight, you are very unlikely to have any negative consequences at that time. The same applies when you are displacing the 7♥.

The A♠ has always been considered a powerful card of transformation, or death and rebirth. When this powerful 'bullet' is located in a not so favorable position or any very powerful positions, it is wise to be aware and act carefully. Long-Range A♠ is more neutral in its meaning but still could mean a year of powerful changes in your life.

CHALLENGE YEARS

Any Seven in Saturn, Pluto, Long-Range, or Displacement

Seven cards always present us with a challenge and a way out of it. Unlike the Nine, which portends an ending that cannot be reversed, the situations indicated by a Seven have a resolution within our reach. However, that resolution always comes from inside of us, not from trying to change or manipulate the circumstances outside of us. And this is the catch for most of us, because our society teaches us nothing about how to go within for our answers. All of our training and direction is towards developing what I call external skills. Self-knowledge is rarely mentioned, if at all, as a solution to our problems in life.

So Sevens are almost always challenging in some respects, but in these particular positions, they exert a stronger nature, usually causing us to face directly the issue at hand. In every case, that issue will reflect some area of our life where we have given our power away to others or to things beyond our control and where we are blaming our problems on other things or people. For example, under a 7♦ Long-Range one year, I went completely broke financially. And then, when I was the most down and out I could get, I had a spiritual breakthrough about my relationship with money that caused an immediate and dramatic turn around in my financial condition, all without making even one effort to change my external situation. The change occurred within myself.

In these positions, a Seven will cause events to occur that are nearly impossible to avoid. They will have to be dealt with or there will usually be losses of one kind or another. When there are two or more occurrences of these positions in any given year, there will be a plus sign(+) followed by a number that represents the number of instances, and therefore, the intensity of the influence. Be sure to check both your Birth and Planetary Ruling Card listings to see if there are years when you get challenging influences from both significators at the same time.

Cycles We Go through at Different Ages

Family of 45 Cards only

The events in this category will apply only to the Birth and Planetary Ruling Cards that are not one of the Fixed (8♣, J♥, and K♠) or the Semi-Fixed (A♣, 2♥, 7♦, and 9♥) Cards. The reason these seven cards do not have Displacement (and Environment Cards) each year is that they do not move about the Grand Solar Spread the way the other forty-five cards do. For a complete explanation of this, check out *The Advanced Oracle Workbook*, available in the back of this book. For now, just accept this, and realize that the seven cards that are excluded from this section have a different sort of life experience than the other forty-five.

AGE 52—THE CRITICAL YEAR

The Age 52 year is one of great significance. In one manner of speaking, it represents an important decision that is made in our lives—the decision to truly live or not. To truly live means to make choices from that part of us that loves our life and is glad for the opportunity to be here on the planet. The opposite of this is to live our lives always from our fear side, always sacrificing that which would make us happy by doing everything in our power to avoid that which we are afraid of. All of us have fears and all that separates those who are 'alive' from those who are 'dead' is the ability to face these fears and to make conscious choices in spite of them. It is only those who never question their fear-based decisions that end up in lives that are going nowhere, lives that have little happiness or joy.

A good example of this would be someone whose fear of abandonment in personal relationships causes them to stay with a partner who is abusive in some way. Because the person has such a great fear of being 'left alone,' they will stay with such an abusive partner even though they are not happy or enjoying the relationship. This is an example of making decisions based upon fear instead of love. If we are making our most important choices in life based upon fear and avoiding negative things, we are literally dead even though we may still be breathing.

During this year, you will be given an opportunity to deal with several of the most important fear-based challenges of your life in a very loving and positive way. To a large extent, these challenges are signified by your Environment Card in your Birth Card's Age 52 Spread. It would be a good idea to study the significance of this card carefully. In some way, it represents one of your most important lifetime challenges. What's so important this year is that though this card represents a lifetime challenge, because it falls in the Environment position, it is literally given to you as a blessing without effort this year. It will be very easy to deal with the experiences represented by this card and to access it on its most positive and powerful side. You might say that, in an area that you usually have great difficulty, everything will be handed to you on a silver platter. It will come easily and require little effort. Therefore, it can represent the last opportunity in this lifetime to overcome this challenge. It seems to be true that those who do not 'get it' during this year, never do. It represents a final and loving call from our soul to rise up and claim our birthright of happiness and joy.

THE ASCENT TO THE PINNACLE YEAR

Displacing the 10♣

Because of the position of your Birth or Planetary Ruling Card this year, you are beginning a particularly significant five-year cycle of your life. We call this the Ascent to the Pinnacle Cycle. This cycle's effect on you will depend largely on what the direction of your life is to this point, so read carefully to determine its significance for you.

If you are aware of your personal goals and purpose to a large degree, this year and the next three years together will mark

a rising up to a position of accomplishment and recognition. This year will see significant advancements in your career interests, marking the first step up a ladder that culminates in three years when your Birth Card displaces the 8♦. At that time, you could reach the very top of your profession and end up on a new level of work and attainment. Many people have achieved great goals and dreams during this three-year period. If you are career oriented, this is the time to press forward with any plans to advance yourself. Many people get promoted or in some way recognized for their contributions during this year.

If, on the other hand, you are not so certain about your life's direction or purpose, the next three years will mark a culmination for you of your life as you know it. These next three years will be the last three that you will spend in your current mode of life. What is actually happening is that you are reaping the best that this cycle of life has to offer you right now. Whatever your life direction at this time, the next three years will give you as much as that direction has that is good for you. Allow yourself to enjoy it as much as possible, because it is slowly coming to its fruition and end. Be prepared during the Pinnacle Year to make a big change, to depart from a significant chapter of your life, and to move on to a new and better cycle.

In either case, personal relationships should go smoothly this year. You actually have a great deal of power at your disposal. Use it for your best advantage. Also read about the 10♣ Displacement for additional information.

THE PINNACLE YEAR

Displacing the 8♦

The Pinnacle Year is much like it sounds. We reach the highest point in some way related to our life during this year, often stepping off into an entirely new direction at that time. People have become president of the United States during their Pinnacle Year, while others lost the race during their Pinnacle Year. One associate of mine had his company reach the highest point possible during that year, and yet another person, born on his same birthday, was murdered during that year. I myself reached a high point in my musical profession when I was in my Pinnacle Year at age 21. In every case, the individual involved reached the final destination of a cycle of their life and in most cases began a new cycle. Those who are career minded usually achieve some amount of fame or recognition this year. Some become notoriously famous, as did Nicole Simpson and Ron Goldman, who were both in their Pinnacle Year when they were murdered (incidentally, O. J. Simpson's Birth Card, the 6♦, was Ron's Pluto Card that year). Just how your Pinnacle Year will play out for you will depend largely on your lifestyle, your direction in life, and what arena you are playing out the dramas of your life at that time.

Some people reach the Pinnacle Year quite unaware of what is happening in their life, and the year goes by with little or no meaning. But even in their cases, if we examine the circumstances and events of the year, we see the effect of this powerful position playing itself out. At its essence, the Pinnacle Year is one of transformation. Something dies to make way for something new to come in. The reason it is often so dramatic is because of its position in the very top center of the Grand Solar Spread. This position often brings some sort of fame or recognition, whether we like it or not. People notice us and what we are doing. This can result in great success for those who have clear goals, dreams, and direction for their life that include recognition by the public in some way. But sometimes during this year, we don't reach our goals, or we do but not in the way we planned. George Bush was in his Pinnacle Year when he lost the election to Bill Clinton. Likewise, Bob Dole had just completed his Pinnacle Year when he lost to Clinton. In both these cases, we still see the playing out of the theme of the great ending, which at its essence is what the Pinnacle Year is all about.

The Pinnacle Year comes every forty-five years and many people experience it twice in the course of their lifetime. If you also include the Planetary Ruling Card, a person could experience four or more of these pinnacles before they leave this earth plane.

THE MOST BLESSED YEAR

Displacing the 10♦

The Most Blessed Year marks the end of the five-year cycle started by the Ascent to Pinnacle Year. After all of the rising up and transformation associated with those two years, this year seems mild by comparison. However, many good things are possible this year because our card is displacing the 10♦ in the very center of the Grand Solar Spread. This position is governed by the most beneficial planet, Jupiter, both vertically and horizontally. It is the wish-fulfilling year of wish-fulfilling years. I have noted that most people receive that thing that they truly want the most during that year. And many times that gift turns out to be one of the most significant blessings of their life. The gift that is received can be mundane, such as money or a relationship, or it can be a very spiritual thing such as inner transformation or the resolution of a lifelong problem on an emotional level. It makes an interesting study to talk to people about what exactly happened to them during one of these years.

If you have one of these years coming soon, you have a special opportunity. Ask yourself just what it is that would be the greatest gift you could receive now. The chances are good that you will receive it over the course of this year. Be honest with yourself about this. Don't just dream up some big wish for the fun of it. It doesn't work that way. This is something that you want in your heart of hearts—something that will truly bring you happiness and peace of mind. Be open to all possibilities, and see what happens. You are blessed now and nothing can really hurt you. Trust that you can proceed ahead in most any direction you choose, knowing that you are protected by divine forces.

THE WISH FULFILLMENT YEARS

Displacing the 10♠, 4♣, 3♠, 7♠, 8♥

When displacing one of the cards listed above, you are located in the Jupiter column of the Grand Solar Spread. For this reason, you will get one or more of your wishes fulfilled during this year. Though it would be incorrect to say that all of your affairs will go without a hitch, Jupiter's influence guarantees that some of them will definitely work out in beneficial ways. This indicates a prosperous time for you in general. Think about some of the things on your wish list, and see if you don't get some of them during this year. Of the ones listed, the 8♥ Displacement is perhaps the most beneficial for those involved in business, because it also has other benefits in terms of popularity, recognition, and success (see the next section for more about this).

YEARS OF RECOGNITION

Displacing the 4♥, 4♦, 2♠, 8♥, 6♣, 6♠, or Q♥; Long-Range Card in the Crown Line

If you look at the illustration of the Grand Solar Spread on page 56, notice the three cards at the very top of the spread. These are the 10♣, 8♦, and K♠. These three cards collectively are called the Crown Line, and anyone who has one of these cards as a Birth or Planetary Ruling Card will have kingly qualities such as leadership and a desire for recognition. The King of Spades never moves from its spot there, and no one except those with that card will ever get to experience being in that most powerful position. However, many times the cards in our Yearly Spread and Long-Range Cards will fall in this Crown Line, and we will have the opportunity to experience some of the power and recognition associated with that most high of places.

When someone displaces the 4♦, for example, the cards of their Uranus and Neptune Periods are displacing the 10♣ and 8♦ respectively. This means that for those two periods of the year, the opportunities for recognition and fame are increased. Any period of the year in which you have the K♠ as the direct card will be one in which you are likely to make great progress in your work, provided that you are willing to take a leadership or responsible position in that regard. Kingly cards and influences only bring kingly results to those who act as kings.

Oftentimes, a person will have a string of three years in which their Long-Range Card will be in the Crown Line. These years are usually marked by a +2 or +3 next to them. One of those three years will be the one that you have the K♠ Long-Range. In this situation, the effects are more powerful, since the influence is for an entire year, or in some cases, for three years in succession. Study your Yearly Spreads to see if and when you have the K♠ Long-Range. This is one of the most powerful influences that exists for success on the material level.

During the years listed, you are much more likely to receive promotions or job advancements, to be recognized for your contributions by those in high places, and to become well-known among your peers. Younger people will experience success and popularity at school. Some cards have especially fortunate experiences in childhood and during their school years due to these influences. During these years, anyone in business would be wise to promote and advertise their products and services, seeking to expand the scope of their influence. Many people have received titles and other forms of honor and recognition during these years.

YEARS WITH GOOD MONEY CARDS

Displacing the 5♣ (gives the 7♦/9♥ or 9♥/7♦ in Jupiter); 8♦ or 10♦ in Jupiter, Long-Range, Environment, or Result

The 5♣ person has a peculiar good karma when it comes to money. Though it doesn't manifest in every single 5♣ person you meet, many of them receive an abundance of money at one or more points in their life. This money usually comes easily and is not usually the result of some work that they did. When your Birth or Planetary Ruling Card displaces the 5♣ some year, you inherit some of the 5♣ good money karma for a time. Many people receive a lot of money during those years. The actual interpretation of a 7♦ in Jupiter, which has been called the Millionaire's Card, says that there will be a tremendous outlay of money. This huge spending spree is generally the result of a lot of money coming in from somewhere and thus it represents some windfall.

Don't make the mistake of making plans for this money before you get it. This is not a guarantee of riches by any means. However, if you have a generally positive attitude about your finances, you may be surprised by a gift from the abundance of the universe.

The 8♦ and 10♦ in Jupiter are the best indicators of financial success. However, it must be stated here that this good fortune only comes to those who are engaged in activities that can actually make good money. A person on a fixed income,

working a menial job, or who is retired is unlikely to experience any increase financially when these cards are present. However, if you are in a business or occupation where you have opportunities to expand the nature of your goods and services, these cards can indicate huge financial gains.

The other instances of the 8♦ and 10♦ are likewise good and can indicate financial prosperity to most anyone. But again, it would be foolish to expect these cards to bring you wealth when you are not engaged in any form of business or work that has the potential to increase dramatically.

THE KING OF SPADES LONG-RANGE CARD

One of the most powerful and potentially rewarding Long-Range Cards to have is the K♠, which, on a material plane, is considered to be the most powerful card in the deck. With a K♠ Long-Range Card, virtually anything is possible for someone who is willing to assume the responsibility for their actions. A K♠ Long-Range Card may not do much for a person who believes that they have no personal power and that they are not responsible for what happens in their life. But for a person who is willing to take it on, this card can act as a magic genie that will grant all of your wishes. Some cards never have the K♠ Long-Range over the course of their lifetime. Most cards do, and some cards have it as many as four times. Whenever a certain card has the K♠ more than once in their lifetime, I mention it along with the years that this occurs. These are years of special opportunity for those who are ready to take advantage of it.

The Life Path and the Thirteen-Year Cycles and Their Ruling Cards

Under each card in this chapter is a table of the thirteen-year cycles and the cards that rule them. Those familiar with this system will recognize these are the first seven cards from the Life Spread that we also call the Life Path Cards. These are essentially the same cards as those found in the first year of life, the forty-fifth year of life and the ninetieth year of life and each also governs thirteen years of our life. So, for example, the Mercury Card in our Life Spread governs the first thirteen years of life and the Venus Card the next thirteen years, and so on. These ruling cards give an overall influence for the period that many people can relate to. For example, anyone who as any of the Five cards governing a particular thirteen-year cycle will probably experience a lot of travel or moves to new places during that time.

Seven thirteen-year periods give us eighty-nine years, quite close to the exact number of quadrations of the Grand Solar Spreads that makes up the Yearly Spreads that we use in this book. It seems that the life span was figured in somehow to be around 90 years old.

Of course not everybody lives to be 90 years of old. Some live longer and most live fewer years. This is why we cannot hold these ninety-year cycles to be exact in length. Especially after the Saturn Period, from ages 52–64, we find it more difficult to determine just which stage we are in and what card is governing our lives. I generally look at the Uranus and Neptune Cards together and just ascribe those to the 'last years of life.' In your own research, I believe you will find that there are many variations among different people. Some will have changes in life at exactly the time when they move from one period to the next, such as from the Mars to the Jupiter Period of life while others will find the transitions from one period to the next to occur a year or two early or late.

Sometimes the transitions between periods are quite profound. Many people find that they make life changes around the ages of 13, 26, 39, etc. This is especially the case when the card of the new period is quite different from the one of the preceding one. In my own life, for example, the transition from my Mars Period ruled by the 3♠ to the Jupiter Period ruled by the 9♥ was quite a big event. The 3♠ can be such a scattered force in our lives while the 9♥, which is one of the Semi-Fixed Cards, is quite the opposite. The same could be said for someone transitioning from a period ruled by a Five card to one governed by a more stable card such as a Four, Six, Eight, etc.

You are welcome to study these thirteen-year cycles in more depth. To derive some meaning for them, just use the meanings given in the book for the same card in the appropriate yearly period. For example, if your Jupiter Period of life is ruled by the A♠, you would read the interpretation for the A♠ in the Jupiter Period found in this book and merely translate it to a thirteen-year period instead of a fifty-two-day period. I would also suggest that you read the basic meaning of those cards, as they will offer additional insight.

Auspicious Years for the A♥

Prebirth Years: Ages 44 and 89

Rebirth Years: Ages 45 and 90

Critical Year: Age 52

Purpose-Finding and Fated Years: Ages 3+2, 7, 14, 21, 24, 26, 31, 38, 42+2, 46, 48+2, 52, 58, 59, 66, 69, 71, 75, 76, 81, 83, 87, 93+2, 97+2

Years of Blessed Endings: Ages 5, 9, 13, 17, 23, 27, 31, 33, 37, 50, 54, 58, 62, 64, 72+2, 76, 78, 82, 95, 99

Years of Difficult Endings: Ages 5+3, 7, 8+2, 17+2, 18+2, 25+2, 29+2, 32+2, 34, 38+2, 39, 42+2, 46+2, 50+2, 53+2, 62+2, 63+2, 70+2, 74+2, 77+2, 78, 79+2, 83+2, 89+2, 95+2, 98+2

Years of Caution: Ages 11+2, 12+2, 14, 35+2, 56+2, 57+2, 59, 80+2

Years of Personal Challenge: Ages 1, 4, 6, 8, 11, 12, 14, 15, 22, 24, 31, 32, 34, 39, 40, 43, 44, 49, 53, 57, 59, 60+2, 61, 64, 67, 69, 76, 84+2, 85+2, 87, 88, 91, 92, 94, 98

Ascent to Pinnacle Years: Ages 37, 82

Pinnacle Years: Ages 40, 85

Most Blessed Years: Ages 42, 87

Years of Wish Fulfillment: Ages 13, 14, 22, 34, 58, 59, 67, 79

Years of Recognition, Fame, and Business Success: Ages 3, 6, 7, 13, 23+2, 24+2, 25+3, 33, 35, 46+2, 47+2, 48+3, 50+2, 51+3, 52+3, 58, 70, 78, 80, 93, 94+2, 95+2, 96+3, 97

Years with Good Money Cards: Ages 3, 5, 17, 19, 23, 29, 42, 43, 48, 50, 62, 68, 70, 82, 87, 90, 93, 95

LIFE PATH AND THE THIRTEEN-YEAR CYCLE RULING CARDS FOR THE A♥

MERCURY	VENUS	MARS	JUPITER	SATURN	URANUS	NEPTUNE
Ages 0–12	Ages 13–25	Ages 26–38	Ages 39–51	Ages 52–64	Ages 65–77	Ages 78–90
A♦	Q♦	5♥	3♣	3♠	9♥	7♣

Notes:

The A♥ has an especially fortunate cycle for ages 23, 24, and 25, where their Long-Range Cards sit in the Crown Line. However, since all A♠ have the 3♠ as their Planetary Ruling Card, this is actually part of an even longer cycle of success that begins at 21. So, for ages 21–25 there are great possibilities for promotion and advancement along career lines. Age 23 is particularly highlighted since both their Birth and Planetary Ruling Cards have a Long-Range Card in the Crown Line at that time. Ages 46–48 and 50–53 have similar powerful influence for success.

Age 53 is a year of special caution where they are displacing the 9♠ and have the 7♠ in Saturn. Health and work issues could be challenging that year. Ages 14, 49, 50, and 59 have a very similar influences and are ones to pay close attention to.

The A♥ is fortunate to have four years with the K♠ as the Long-Range Card. They are ages 25, 48, 52, and 96.

Auspicious Years for the 2♥

Prebirth Years: Ages 44 and 89
Rebirth Years: Ages 45 and 90
Purpose-Finding and Fated Years: Ages 2, 14, 22, 40, 42, 50, 57, 60, 68, 74, 78, 85, 92, 94, 100
Years of Blessed Endings: Ages 4+2, 14, 18, 28, 33, 47, 57, 80, 94+2
Years of Difficult Endings: Ages 3+2, 13, 25, 27, 31, 37, 39+2, 41, 44+2, 47, 53+2, 55, 58+2, 60+2, 63+2, 68+2, 69+3, 74+2, 77, 83+3, 84+2, 93+2, 97
Years of Caution: Ages 12, 15, 20, 29, 36, 40, 45, 49, 66, 72
Years of Personal Challenge: Ages 8, 17, 57, 59+2, 60, 62, 64, 65, 73, 77, 78, 79, 80, 82, 87, 89, 98
Years with Good Money Cards: Ages 7, 21, 23, 25, 70, 72, 84+2, 86, 98

LIFE PATH AND THE THIRTEEN-YEAR CYCLE RULING CARDS FOR THE 2♥

MERCURY	VENUS	MARS	JUPITER	SATURN	URANUS	NEPTUNE
Ages 0–12 K♥	Ages 13–25 K♦	Ages 26–38 6♥	Ages 39–51 4♣	Ages 52–64 2♦	Ages 65–77 J♠	Ages 78–90 8♣

Notes:

All 2♥, like the A♥, have the same Planetary Ruling Card, in this case the 2♦, so we can consider both cards when we look at their special years. However, keep in mind that the Planetary Ruling Card's cycles are slightly less significant than the ones for the Birth Card. Being one half of the cosmic pairing with the A♣, they share much of the same life in many ways. One theory is that any 2♥ person could also read the Yearly Spreads for the A♣ each year, and they would be relevant since these two cards merely switch places with each other every year in the Grand Solar Spread. The 2♦ card has its best career and recognition influences in their thirties, and this seems to be a time of great advancement for 2♥ people as well. On the other hand, the sixties seem to be the time that both cards have their share of personal challenges of one sort or another. Age 84 is a year with particularly challenging health aspects where they have both the 9♠ and 6♠ in Saturn.

Both the 2♥ and 2♦ have fairly good, if not excellent, karma for material matters. So, the life is one that is fortunate in many regards. Years when there exist multiple combinations of challenging influences include those at age 25, 40, 49, 57, 84, and 93.

Auspicious Years for the 3♥

Prebirth Years: Ages 44 and 89

Rebirth Years: Ages 45 and 90

Critical Year: Age 52

Purpose-Finding and Fated Years: Ages 4, 6, 8, 12, 13, 18, 22, 23, 28, 32, 34, 37, 41, 46, 49, 51, 53, 57, 58, 63, 67, 68, 76, 77, 79, 82, 86, 94, 96, 98

Years of Blessed Endings: Ages 12, 13, 20, 23, 26+2, 28+2, 35, 36, 37, 38, 57, 58, 68, 69, 71+2, 73, 80, 81, 82, 83

Years of Difficult Endings: Ages 2+2, 8, 9+2, 18, 19+2, 20+2, 30+2, 33+2, 35+2, 42+2, 45+2, 54+2, 58, 64+2, 65+2, 75+2, 78+3, 87+2, 88+2, 91, 92+2, 99+2

Years of Caution: Ages 5+2, 6, 12+2, 13+2, 16, 26, 36+2, 39, 50, 51, 57+2, 58+2, 61, 71+2, 81+2, 95, 96

Years of Personal Challenge: Ages 0, 2, 4, 6, 12, 13, 15, 16, 19, 26, 37, 40, 41, 43, 47+2, 49, 58, 60, 64, 66, 72, 77, 80+2, 85+2, 86, 90, 92, 94

Ascent to Pinnacle Years: Ages 38, 83

Pinnacle Years: Ages 41, 86

Most Blessed Years: Ages 43, 88

Years of Wish Fulfillment: Ages 14, 15, 23, 35, 59, 60, 68, 80

Years of Recognition, Fame, and Business Success: Ages 4, 7, 8, 14, 26, 30+2, 31+2, 32+2, 34, 36, 49, 52, 53+3, 54+2, 55+2, 57+2, 58+2, 59+3, 71, 79, 81, 94, 97, 98

Years with Good Money Cards: Ages 1, 2, 4, 24, 33, 35, 40, 46, 47+2, 49, 69, 81, 85, 91, 92, 94, 95

LIFE PATH AND THE THIRTEEN-YEAR CYCLE RULING CARDS FOR THE 3♥

MERCURY	VENUS	MARS	JUPITER	SATURN	URANUS	NEPTUNE
Ages 0–12	Ages 13–25	Ages 26–38	Ages 39–51	Ages 52–64	Ages 65–77	Ages 78–90
A♣	Q♣	10♠	5♣	3♦	A♠	7♥

Notes:

The 3♥ comes in two flavors—the Sagitarrians with their 5♣ Planetary Ruling Card and the Capricorns and their 3♦ Planetary Ruling Card. Of the two, the first is generally more successful in a worldly sense. The 5♣ has that 7♦ in Jupiter Millionaire's Card in their Life Spread, which often brings wealth at some point in the lifetime.

For either birthday, the years between ages 21–27 are fortunate financially, and especially so for the Capricorn birthdays. Though the tables above do not reflect it, that seven-year cycle has some very good financial and business influences that last the entire period. The years from 57–59 are probably the best of the entire life, where either Planetary Ruling Card also has good influences for financial success. Age 59 is the peak. The 3♥ is also fortunate to have three years with a K♠ Long-Range, ages 32, 55, and 59.

Auspicious Years for the 4♥

Prebirth Years: Ages 44 and 89

Rebirth Years: Ages 45 and 90

Critical Year: Age 52

Purpose-Finding and Fated Years: Ages 3, 4+3, 5, 9, 10, 13+2, 14+2, 17, 20, 28, 31, 32, 41, 49+2, 50, 55, 58+2, 59+3, 62, 69, 73, 76, 77, 86, 94+2, 95, 96, 98, 100

Years of Blessed Endings: Ages 3, 7, 17, 19, 27+2, 31, 33, 41, 42, 48, 52, 62, 64, 72+2, 74, 76, 82, 86, 87, 93, 97

Years of Difficult Endings: Ages 2+2, 9+2, 12, 15+2, 18+2, 19, 20+2, 27+2, 28+2, 36+2, 40, 42+2, 44, 47+2, 52+2, 56+2, 60+2, 62, 63+2, 65+2, 72+2, 73+2, 75, 77, 81+2, 87+2, 89+2, 92+2, 99+3

Years of Caution: Ages 0+3, 9, 21+3, 22+2, 28, 31, 45+3, 54, 66+3, 67+3, 73, 76, 90+3, 99

Years of Personal Challenge: Ages 3, 4, 7, 11, 22, 24, 25, 31, 36, 43, 44, 48, 49, 51, 52, 54, 58, 61, 66, 67, 69, 72, 81, 91, 93, 94, 97

Ascent to Pinnacle Years: Ages 2, 47, 92

Pinnacle Years: Ages 5, 50, 95

Most Blessed Years: Ages 7, 52, 97

Years of Wish Fulfillment: Ages 23, 24, 32, 44, 68, 69, 77, 89

Years of Recognition, Fame, and Business Success: Ages 0, 6+2, 13, 14+2, 15+2, 16, 17, 23, 35+3, 43, 45, 58, 61, 62, 68, 80, 88, 90, 93+2, 94+2, 95+2

Years with Good Money Cards: Ages 16, 27, 33, 38, 40, 49, 78, 83, 85

LIFE PATH AND THE THIRTEEN-YEAR CYCLE RULING CARDS FOR THE 4♥

MERCURY	VENUS	MARS	JUPITER	SATURN	URANUS	NEPTUNE
Ages 0–12	Ages 13–25	Ages 26–38	Ages 39–51	Ages 52–64	Ages 65–77	Ages 78–90
4♦	2♠	8♥	6♣	6♠	Q♥	10♣

Notes:

Health is an ongoing issue for most 4♥, and it often begins in the first year and again at age 4 when influences point to possible health problems. The Rebirth Year at age 45 provides another visitation of this same influence and a chance to remake their relationship with their health concerns in a higher light.

The 4♥ often experiences some success in school and has a generally fun time from ages 14–20. Then, at ages 35–41 their Birth Card spends seven years in the Pinnacle position displacing the 8♦. This can often bring great success to those who have career ambitions. This is especially true of the Scorpio 4♥ who has the 8♦ as a Planetary Ruling Card. The 4♥ is fortunate to have three years in life in which the K♠ is their Long-Range Card. These are at ages 15, 35, and 95.

Ages 21 and 66 are ones to be especially watchful of. In those years, they have an A♠ as both their Saturn and Displacement Cards.

Auspicious Years for the 5♥

Prebirth Years: Ages 44 and 89

Rebirth Years: Ages 45 and 90

Critical Year: Age 52

Purpose-Finding and Fated Years: Ages 3, 7, 17, 18+2, 21, 24, 26, 28, 33, 34, 38, 42+2, 48, 52, 59, 62, 63, 64, 66, 69, 73, 83, 87+2, 89, 93+2, 96, 97

Years of Blessed Endings: Ages 5, 6, 12, 16, 22, 37+2, 38, 40, 48, 50, 51, 57, 61, 67, 82+2, 83, 89, 95, 96

Years of Difficult Endings: Ages 0+2, 1+2, 2, 5+2, 8+2, 11, 14+2, 16+2, 17+2, 18+2, 22+2, 26+2, 29+2, 30+2, 38, 39+2, 42, 45+2, 46+2, 48, 50+2, 53+2, 55+2, 59+2, 61+2, 62+2, 65+2, 71+2, 74+2, 75+2, 84+2, 90+2, 91+2, 95+2, 98

Years of Caution: Ages 2, 11+2, 32+2, 33+2, 44, 47, 56+2, 77+2, 78+2, 92

Years of Personal Challenge: Ages 3, 8, 9, 10, 13, 15+2, 20, 21, 25, 28, 33, 35, 47, 54+2, 55, 60+2, 61, 62, 63, 67, 70, 74, 77, 78, 80, 90, 99, 100

Ascent to Pinnacle Years: Ages 13, 58

Pinnacle Years: Ages 16, 61

Most Blessed Years: Ages 18, 63

Years of Wish Fulfillment: Ages 10, 34, 35, 43, 55, 79, 80, 88, 100

Years of Recognition, Fame, and Business Success: Ages 1, 9, 11, 12+2, 13+2, 24, 27, 28, 34, 46, 54, 56, 63+2, 64+2, 65+2, 69, 72, 73, 79, 83+2, 91+3, 92+2, 99

Years with Good Money Cards: Ages 7, 21, 23, 27, 28, 29, 30, 44, 52+2, 66, 72, 73, 74, 75, 78, 89, 97

LIFE PATH AND THE THIRTEEN-YEAR CYCLE RULING CARDS FOR THE 5♥

MERCURY	VENUS	MARS	JUPITER	SATURN	URANUS	NEPTUNE
Ages 0–12	Ages 13–25	Ages 26–38	Ages 39–51	Ages 52–64	Ages 65–77	Ages 78–90
3♣	3♠	9♥	7♣	5♦	Q♠	J♣

Notes:

Due to the arrangement of their Yearly and Seven-Year Spreads, combined with the fact that their Birth Card sits in the Saturn line of the Grand Solar Spread, the 5♥ person often experiences some traumatic experiences related to moves and changes in the early part of their life from birth to age 21. Not all of those experiences are bad, but key events contribute a lot towards the forming of their personalities as adults. Many of these traits relate to travel and personal freedom.

From approximately ages 26–52, their lives settle down and there is less traveling and fewer changes in most cases. However, after that, changes again ensue for another thirteen years or so.

Ages 47 and 55 have particularly challenging aspects, mostly in regards to their health and personal relationships at the same time. Age 58 may also be one to be careful in health matters.

Auspicious Years for the 6♥

Prebirth Years: Ages 44 and 89

Rebirth Years: Ages 45 and 90

Critical Year: Age 52

Purpose-Finding and Fated Years: Ages 0+2, 4, 10, 14, 18, 20, 23, 25, 27+2, 31+2, 35, 37, 39, 45+2, 50, 51, 55, 59, 63, 65, 68, 70, 72+2, 76, 80, 84, 89, 90+2, 92, 100

Years of Blessed Endings: Ages 3, 6, 8, 9, 12+2, 13, 21, 29, 34, 41, 42, 47, 48, 53, 54, 57+2, 58, 66, 74, 79, 86, 87, 88, 93, 96, 98, 99

Years of Difficult Endings: Ages 11+2, 13+2, 14, 23+2, 32+2, 34+2, 38+2, 42+2, 47, 55, 56+2, 65, 66+3, 70+2, 72, 77+2, 79+2, 83+2, 87+3, 95

Years of Caution: Ages 12, 14+2, 18, 28, 30, 35+2, 36+2, 49, 57, 59+2, 63, 73, 75, 80+2, 81+2, 82, 98

Years of Personal Challenge: Ages 3, 10, 17, 18, 21, 23, 25+2, 30, 36, 38, 41+2, 44, 48, 55, 58, 63+2, 68, 73, 75, 81, 83, 86+2, 93, 100

Ascent to Pinnacle Years: Ages 16, 61

Pinnacle Years: Ages 19, 64

Most Blessed Years: Ages 21, 66

Years of Wish Fulfillment: Ages 1, 13, 37, 38, 46, 58, 82, 83, 91

Years of Recognition, Fame, and Business Success: Ages 4, 12, 14, 27, 30, 31, 33+2, 34+2, 37, 49, 57, 59, 72, 75, 76, 82, 84+2, 85+2, 86+2, 94

Years with Good Money Cards: Ages 2, 4, 5, 6, 13, 16, 24, 26, 38, 45, 47, 49, 50, 51, 58, 60, 61, 69, 71, 77, 83, 92, 94, 95, 96

LIFE PATH AND THE THIRTEEN-YEAR CYCLE RULING CARDS FOR THE 6♥

MERCURY	VENUS	MARS	JUPITER	SATURN	URANUS	NEPTUNE
Ages 0–12	Ages 13–25	Ages 26–38	Ages 39–51	Ages 52–64	Ages 65–77	Ages 78–90
4♣	2♦	J♠	8♣	6♦	4♠	10♥

Notes:

The 6♥ has quite a few good money years, more than any other Heart Card, giving them more than the usual amount of good fortune financially. In addition, they have overall good fortune with money, as denoted by all the even-numbered cards in their Life Spread (which are the same as the thirteen-year cycle cards).

They often do quite well in school and reach the Pinnacle Year at age 19—right in the middle of those years. Overall, they get off to a much better start than other cards because of the favorable influences in childhood. After age 22, they begin learning some of life's lessons where they encounter changes and challenges as part of their maturing process. At ages 30 and 31, they often go through a process of searching for a deeper meaning and purpose in their life. With a sincere effort, they are put on the right path for more happiness and fulfillment in their work and life.

Ages 65 and 66 are often years of some health and other challenges that lead to an entirely new change of life. The endings then, though difficult, open up many new possibilities for a happy future.

Auspicious Years for the 7♥

Prebirth Years: Ages 44 and 89
Rebirth Years: Ages 45 and 90
Critical Year: Age 52
Purpose-Finding and Fated Years: Ages 0, 5, 9+2, 13, 15, 19, 22, 25, 26, 36+2, 40, 45, 50, 54+2, 56, 58, 64, 67, 70, 71, 73, 81+2, 83, 85, 90, 95, 99+2
Years of Blessed Endings: Ages 0, 4, 8, 11, 18, 25, 27, 33, 37, 39, 45, 49, 52, 53, 60, 63, 70, 72, 78, 82, 84, 90, 94, 98
Years of Difficult Endings: Ages 0+2, 3, 4, 6+2, 7+2, 9, 14+3, 20+4, 21, 25+2, 27+2, 29, 30+2, 34+2, 41+2, 42, 43+2, 45+2, 51+2, 52+2, 53, 59+3, 65+4, 67+2, 69, 70+2, 72+2, 76, 77+2, 80, 85, 86+3, 88+2, 90+2, 96+2, 97+2, 99
Years of Caution: Ages 0+2, 20, 23+2, 44+2, 45+2, 68+2, 89+2, 90+2
Years of Personal Challenge: Ages 0+2, 1, 2, 10, 11, 22, 27, 30, 32, 34, 40, 42, 45, 46, 47, 52, 55, 58, 72, 75+2, 79, 85, 87, 90, 91, 92, 94, 100+2
Ascent to Pinnacle Years: Ages 25, 70
Pinnacle Years: Ages 28, 73
Most Blessed Years: Ages 30, 75
Years of Wish Fulfillment: Ages 1, 2, 10, 22, 46, 47, 55, 67, 91, 92, 100
Years of Recognition, Fame, and Business Success: Ages 1, 10+2, 11+2, 12+2, 13, 21, 23, 36, 39, 40, 46, 58, 66, 68, 81, 84, 85, 91, 96+2, 97+2
Years with Good Money Cards: Ages 1, 6, 9, 11, 15, 16, 17, 19, 20, 46, 51, 54, 56, 60, 61, 62, 64, 65, 91, 96, 99

LIFE PATH AND THE THIRTEEN-YEAR CYCLE RULING CARDS FOR THE 7♥

MERCURY	VENUS	MARS	JUPITER	SATURN	URANUS	NEPTUNE
Ages 0–12 7♦	Ages 13–25 5♠	Ages 26–38 J♥	Ages 39–51 9♣	Ages 52–64 9♠	Ages 65–77 2♥	Ages 78–90 K♥

Notes:

The transition from the first thirteen-year cycle to the next is often dramatic, going from a fairly stable lifestyle to one of a lot of changes and traveling. Then, in the third period, from ages 26–38, things settle down again. Ages 3 and 4 are ones to be careful of for health matters in the 7♥ child. Even if the health is fine, there will always be some situations in their life that leave a lasting impression upon them. These can be losses on the emotional or mental level. The 7♥ has a very spiritually-oriented Life Path, reflected by the two Nines and the J♥. For this reason, there can be disappointments and discouragement or success and reward through giving.

Ages 7–13, and particularly 10–12, are a lot of fun. The 7♥ often has great successes in school, and popularity to match. This continues on into the college years if they go that far, though many of them opt for a business career by that age. Ages 14 and 20 are ones to watch out for, where some endings in life could be more or less difficult to deal with. The 7♥ often has trouble with personal attachments, and this is where endings have the most impact.

Auspicious Years for the 8♥

Prebirth Years: Ages 44 and 89

Rebirth Years: Ages 45 and 90

Critical Year: Age 52

Purpose-Finding and Fated Years: Ages 0, 1, 3, 4, 6, 8, 10, 11, 18, 23, 27, 35, 37, 39, 41, 48, 49, 51, 53, 55, 56, 63, 68, 72, 80, 82, 84, 86, 88, 93, 94, 96, 98, 100+2

Years of Blessed Endings: Ages 5, 6, 12, 14+2, 21, 24, 26, 40, 50, 55, 57, 59, 66, 69, 71, 85, 95, 96

Years of Difficult Endings: Ages 5+4, 16+2, 19+2, 21+2, 22+2, 31+2, 33+2, 35+2, 40+2, 42, 45, 50+4, 51, 61+2, 64+2, 67+2, 68, 74+2, 78+4, 80+2, 85+2, 95+4, 97

Years of Caution: Ages 3, 17, 21, 22+2, 27, 34, 43+3, 44+2, 47, 48, 62, 66, 67+2, 72, 79, 88+3, 89+2, 93

Years of Personal Challenge: Ages 1, 13, 15, 22, 24, 26, 29, 30, 33, 44, 46, 56, 57, 60, 66, 71, 73, 76, 79, 84, 89, 91

Ascent to Pinnacle Years: Ages 24, 69

Pinnacle Years: Ages 27, 72

Most Blessed Years: Ages 29, 74

Years of Wish Fulfillment: Ages 0, 1, 9, 21, 45, 46, 54, 66, 90, 91, 99

Years of Recognition, Fame, and Business Success: Ages 0, 3+2, 4+2, 5+2, 12, 20, 22, 35, 38, 39, 45, 57, 65, 67, 80, 83, 84, 89+2, 90+3

Years with Good Money Cards: Ages 2, 4, 10, 12, 16+2, 18, 31, 33+2, 38, 47, 55, 57, 61+2, 63, 76, 78+2, 83, 87, 92, 93, 100

LIFE PATH AND THE THIRTEEN-YEAR CYCLE RULING CARDS FOR THE 8♥

MERCURY	VENUS	MARS	JUPITER	SATURN	URANUS	NEPTUNE
Ages 0–12	Ages 13–25	Ages 26–38	Ages 39–51	Ages 52–64	Ages 65–77	Ages 78–90
6♣	6♠	Q♥	10♣	8♦	K♠	3♥

Notes:

All 8♥ have great potential for success in their careers if they decide to go that path. Every year from ages 39–77 has the Crown Line influence, which contributes to success, fame, and notoriety. A generally good childhood that brings them a lot of attention and recognition gives them a boost that carries many of them throughout life on a more positive note. The third year of life should be watched for health matters, but the rest of the childhood usually passes without incident.

The 8♥ has potentially negative health influences at ages 17 and 62 where they have an A♠ in Saturn, combined with a 3♠ Displacement Card. But overall, their life is much more blessed than other cards, and they have a lot to be grateful for.

Auspicious Years for the 9♥

Prebirth Years: Ages 44 and 89

Rebirth Years: Ages 45 and 90

Purpose-Finding and Fated Years: Ages 1, 8, 9, 10, 15, 19, 22, 26, 35, 38, 56, 71, 72, 79, 81, 88, 91, 98, 99

Years of Blessed Endings: Ages 10, 20, 21, 35+2, 42, 45, 49, 56, 59, 66, 86, 100

Years of Difficult Endings: Ages 0+2, 3+2, 4, 10+2, 12, 13+2, 18+2, 20, 32+2, 42+2, 47, 55, 73, 74, 76+2, 79+2, 90+2, 93+2, 100+2

Years of Caution: Ages 43, 52, 55, 56, 84

Years of Personal Challenge: Ages 0, 4, 5, 6, 7, 9, 13, 16, 19, 24, 27+2, 32, 36, 38, 46, 56, 94, 96, 97, 99

Years with Good Money Cards: Ages 11, 13, 25, 27, 32, 34, 76, 78, 80, 94

LIFE PATH AND THE THIRTEEN-YEAR CYCLE RULING CARDS FOR THE 9♥

MERCURY	VENUS	MARS	JUPITER	SATURN	URANUS	NEPTUNE
Ages 0–12	Ages 13–25	Ages 26–38	Ages 39–51	Ages 52–64	Ages 65–77	Ages 78–90
7♣	5♦	Q♠	J♣	9♦	7♠	2♣

Notes:

A close examination of the Yearly Spreads for the 9♥ reveals that every year in the first cycle of seven has a strong Nine influence or a Seven in Saturn, etc. This tells us that many of the developmental years in the life of a 9♥ person are marked by challenges, losses, or in some cases, tragedies. These may be dramatic events or simply emotional interpretations of regular events, but in either case, the 9♥ personality is formed in these early years, and the leaning is towards feeling somewhat victimized by life.

However, being one of the Semi-Fixed Cards, the 9♥ has the strength to deal with such experiences. They are closely linked with their Cosmic Soul Twin, the 7♦, with whom they share many traits and life cycles. The main difference between them is that at Birth the 7♦ occupies the Venus/Venus line/column position, while the 9♥ occupies the Saturn/Saturn. For all intents and purposes, the Saturn/Saturn position can be regarded as the one most difficult and full of karmic obligations. Saturn positions in the Grand Solar Spread represent past lives in which there was ignorance of the law of cause and effect and in which we had little awareness of how our deeds and words affected those around us. If the karma is so great and so many negative experiences must be gone through to rectify it, the person going through all of these can easily feel as though they have been singled out for punishment at an early age or that they are the victims of some cruel cosmic joke. This contributes to the victim/savior personality that is common with 9♥ people but also accounts for their dedication to service and to helping the world. This can happen to any of those in the Saturn line, but perhaps the most to the 9♥.

Not that the 9♥ is any less capable of success or recognition. Many of them achieve great prominence in their work and life and accomplish great deeds in service to the world. For specific indicators of this, remember to look up the success cycles for their Planetary Ruling Card.

Auspicious Years for the 10♥

Prebirth Years: Ages 44 and 89

Rebirth Years: Ages 45 and 90

Critical Year: Age 52

Purpose-Finding and Fated Years: Ages 4, 6, 9, 20+2, 21, 24, 25, 29, 34, 35, 39, 41, 42, 44, 49, 51, 54, 65, 66, 69, 70, 74, 79, 81, 84, 86, 89, 92, 94, 95, 96, 97, 99

Years of Blessed Endings: Ages 0, 9, 11, 19, 40, 41, 54, 56, 64, 82, 85, 90, 99

Years of Difficult Endings: Ages 5+2, 7+2, 8+2, 17+2, 26+2, 28, 36+2, 50+2, 53+3, 60+2, 63, 64+2, 71+2, 81+2, 95+2, 97+2, 98+2

Years of Caution: Ages 8+2, 14, 17, 20, 27+2, 29+2, 30+2, 34, 53+2, 59, 65, 72, 74+2, 75+2, 79, 98+2

Years of Personal Challenge: Ages 12, 15, 18, 19, 21, 22, 23, 30, 32, 33, 41, 52, 57, 62, 63, 67, 75, 77, 78, 86, 98

Ascent to Pinnacle Years: Ages 10, 55, 100

Pinnacle Years: Ages 13, 58

Most Blessed Years: Ages 15, 60

Years of Wish Fulfillment: Ages 7, 31, 32, 40, 52, 76, 77, 85, 97

Years of Recognition, Fame, and Business Success: Ages 6, 8, 21, 24, 25, 31, 42+2, 43+3, 44+2, 51, 53, 62+2, 66, 69, 70+3, 71+2, 76, 88, 91+2, 96, 98

Years with Good Money Cards: Ages 0, 8, 16, 22, 26, 28, 30, 32, 33, 41+2, 42, 53, 59, 61, 65, 67, 71, 73, 75, 77, 86, 87, 98

LIFE PATH AND THE THIRTEEN-YEAR CYCLE RULING CARDS FOR THE 10♥

MERCURY	VENUS	MARS	JUPITER	SATURN	URANUS	NEPTUNE
Ages 0–12	Ages 13–25	Ages 26–38	Ages 39–51	Ages 52–64	Ages 65–77	Ages 78–90
10♦	8♠	A♥	A♦	Q♦	5♥	3♣

Notes:

The 10♥ has a particularly fortunate childhood and adolescence that gets them off to a good start and helps form a strong and healthy personality. However, ages 14 and 17 have fairly strong influences of challenge or loss. Care should be taken those years in regards health and other matters.

The seven-year cycle that begins at age 28 is a very fortunate one because each of the Long-Range Cards of that cycle sit in the Jupiter row. There should be a lot of success, both financially and otherwise at that time. Ages 42–44 are usually some of the greatest for business success and recognition.

The 10♥ is fortunate to have three years in life in which the K♠ is the Long-Range Card. These are at ages 44, 71, and 91.

Auspicious Years for the J♥

Prebirth Years: Ages 44 and 89
Rebirth Years: Ages 45 and 90
Purpose-Finding and Fated Years: Ages 5, 7+2, 8, 13, 17+2, 31, 35, 36, 45, 52, 60, 62, 76, 77, 80, 88, 97
Years of Blessed Endings: Ages 1, 6, 20, 22, 30, 36, 46, 51, 65, 67, 75, 81, 91, 96
Years of Difficult Endings: Ages 0, 1, 7+2, 10, 15+2, 26, 28+2, 29+2, 34, 39+2, 42+2, 52+2, 53, 60+2, 73+2, 74+2, 84+2, 87+2, 96, 97+2, 98
Years of Caution: Ages 4, 8, 32, 36, 49, 53, 75, 81, 83, 94, 98
Years of Personal Challenge: Ages 1, 3, 8, 11, 21, 25, 33, 35, 46, 48, 53, 54, 62, 66, 68, 76, 78, 80, 91, 93, 98, 99
Years with Good Money Cards: Ages 12, 14, 41, 43, 57, 59, 78, 86, 87, 88, 92

LIFE PATH AND THE THIRTEEN-YEAR CYCLE RULING CARDS FOR THE J♥

MERCURY	VENUS	MARS	JUPITER	SATURN	URANUS	NEPTUNE
Ages 0–12	Ages 13–25	Ages 26–38	Ages 39–51	Ages 52–64	Ages 65–77	Ages 78–90
9♣	9♠	2♥	K♥	K♦	6♥	4♣

Notes:

As you can see above, the cards ruling the first twenty-six years of life for the J♥ are Nines, and Nines usually represent losses and disappointments. However, the J♥ sits, for their entire life, in the Jupiter column (since they are one of the Fixed Cards and never move to a different location). This Jupiter influence provides a protection for them and the ability to translate seemingly negative experiences into more positive ones. Thus, the giving nature of the J♥ personality is born of personal tragedies seen in the light of love and truth. The two Kings later in life point to success and leadership in their work. Look to the Planetary Ruling Card cycles for specific years of success and recognition.

Age 53 is one to be watchful for with both a 6♠ in Saturn and 9♠ Long-Range. Age 75 has particularly challenging health aspects.

Auspicious Years for the Q♥

Prebirth Years: Ages 44 and 89

Rebirth Years: Ages 45 and 90

Critical Year: Age 52

Purpose-Finding and Fated Years: Ages 1, 2, 4, 12, 15, 19+2, 26, 27, 30, 33, 37+2, 43, 46, 47, 49, 57, 60, 61, 64, 68, 69, 71, 75, 78, 82, 85, 88, 91, 92, 93, 94

Years of Blessed Endings: Ages 1, 14, 15, 16, 24, 25+2, 30, 31, 35, 40, 42, 43, 46, 59, 60, 61, 69, 70+2, 75, 76+2, 84, 85, 87, 88, 91

Years of Difficult Endings: Ages 1+2, 6+2, 11+3, 12+2, 20+2, 30+2, 31+2, 35+2, 44+2, 46, 51+2, 54+2, 57+2, 58+2, 65+2, 75+2, 76+2, 78, 80+2, 88, 89+3, 91+2, 96+2

Years of Caution: Ages 2+2, 10, 16, 23+2, 24+2, 40, 41, 42, 47+2, 68+2, 69+2, 85, 86, 92+3

Years of Personal Challenge: Ages 4, 6, 9, 13, 22, 24, 26, 32, 44, 45, 46, 49, 51, 56, 69, 71, 75, 80, 86, 89, 94, 95, 96, 99

Ascent to Pinnacle Years: Ages 4, 49, 94

Pinnacle Years: Ages 7, 52, 97

Most Blessed Years: Ages 9, 54, 99

Years of Wish Fulfillment: Ages 1, 25, 26, 34, 46, 70, 71, 79, 91

Years of Recognition, Fame, and Business Success: Ages 0+3, 1+2, 2+3, 15, 18, 19, 20+2, 25, 28+2, 29+2, 37, 45, 47, 49+2, 60, 63, 64, 70, 82, 90, 92

Years with Good Money Cards: Ages 1, 3, 24+2, 30, 34, 35, 36, 38, 41, 48, 60, 63, 69, 79, 80, 81, 83, 93

LIFE PATH AND THE THIRTEEN-YEAR CYCLE RULING CARDS FOR THE Q♥

MERCURY	VENUS	MARS	JUPITER	SATURN	URANUS	NEPTUNE
Ages 0–12 10♣	Ages 13–25 8♦	Ages 26–38 K♠	Ages 39–51 3♥	Ages 52–64 A♣	Ages 65–77 Q♣	Ages 78–90 10♠

Notes:

The Q♥ has one of the most fortunate beginnings in life of all the cards, and often, there is an emphasis in their childhood on their great potential and the specialness of their life. Many of them do go right into a successful career, and they can excel in most any area they choose. The seven-year cycle that begins at age 7 is particularly fortunate, because their Birth Card sits in the Jupiter column displacing the 10♠ that entire cycle. The 9♥ Long-Range at age 11 could be difficult, but these are just lessons along their path of success. They are again in the Jupiter column for seven years at ages 21–27, though the good fortune of this cycle depends a lot on how much work they are willing to put into their careers. Finally they sit in the Crown Line from ages 28–34 and again at ages 49–55, giving the Q♥ some of the best potential of any card in the deck for success, fame, recognition, and happiness. The career-minded Q♥ people should have no problem achieving all of their goals. The seven-year cycle beginning at age 63 brings them a wealth of spiritual and other blessings. The Q♥ is fortunate to have three years in life in which the K♠ is their Long-Range Card. These are at ages 2, 29, and 49.

The Q♥ has very few years in which there is a particularly powerful configuration of negative cards, which is another reason their life is so blessed. Age 68 is the only one that stands out as having two challenging influences of importance at the same time.

Auspicious Years for the K♥

Prebirth Years: Ages 44 and 89

Rebirth Years: Ages 45 and 90

Critical Year: Age 52

Purpose-Finding and Fated Years: Ages 1, 2, 6+2, 7, 12, 22, 23, 27, 29, 33, 39, 43, 47, 51, 52, 54, 57, 62, 67, 68, 72, 75, 76, 78, 82, 84, 88, 92, 96, 97

Years of Blessed Endings: Ages 1+2, 3, 6, 10+2, 13+2, 18, 22, 25, 27, 36, 38, 44, 46+2, 48, 51, 55, 58+2, 59, 67, 70, 72, 81, 83, 89, 91+2, 93, 96, 100+2

Years of Difficult Endings: Ages 9+2, 10+2, 19+2, 21, 23+2, 25+2, 32+2, 35+2, 41, 44+2, 45, 51, 54+2, 55+2, 64+2, 68+2, 73, 77+2, 78+2, 79, 82+2, 89+2, 94, 99+2, 100+2

Years of Caution: Ages 2+2, 3+2, 21, 26+2, 47+2, 48+2, 55, 66, 71+2, 92+2, 93+2

Years of Personal Challenge: Ages 3+2, 5, 12, 14+2, 15, 18, 26, 30, 33, 36, 37, 48+2, 50+2, 59+2, 63, 70+2, 71, 75, 80, 81, 93+2, 95, 96

Ascent to Pinnacle Years: Ages 28, 73

Pinnacle Years: Ages 31, 76

Most Blessed Years: Ages 33, 78

Years of Wish Fulfillment: Ages 4, 5, 13, 25, 49, 50, 58, 70, 94, 95

Years of Recognition, Fame, and Business Success: Ages 4, 16, 24, 26, 31+2, 32+2, 33+2, 39, 42, 43, 49, 61, 69, 71, 84, 87, 88, 94

Years with Good Money Cards: Ages 12, 14+2, 34, 39, 57, 59+2, 61, 69, 83, 84, 99

LIFE PATH AND THE THIRTEEN-YEAR CYCLE RULING CARDS FOR THE K♥

MERCURY	VENUS	MARS	JUPITER	SATURN	URANUS	NEPTUNE
Ages 0–12 K♦	Ages 13–25 6♥	Ages 26–38 4♣	Ages 39–51 2♦	Ages 52–64 J♠	Ages 65–77 8♣	Ages 78–90 6♦

Notes:

The K♥ has a relatively fortunate childhood with mostly good Long-Range Cards in the formative years. Then, at ages 28–34 they sit in a particularly good position that often brings great success in their chosen career. However, some of them get married at age 31, which becomes the object of their goals and dreams. Ages 21, 41, 47, 52, and 66 are ones in which health matters may become prominent, though this is by no means a lifelong issue for most of them. The seven years beginning at age 70 are generally the most difficult, as most of that time their Long-Range Cards fall in the Saturn line in the Grand Solar Spread. In addition, there is a seven-year Pluto/Result of the 9♦ and 9♠ respectively.

Years in which the K♥ has combinations of challenging influences occur at ages 2, 21, 25, 38, 47, 55, 70, 83, and 92.

Auspicious Years for the A♣

Prebirth Years: Ages 44 and 89

Rebirth Years: Ages 45 and 90

Purpose-Finding and Fated Years: Ages 5, 10, 15, 16, 29, 32, 33, 54, 60, 84, 95

Years of Blessed Endings: Ages 2, 12, 35, 49+2, 59, 63, 73, 78, 92

Years of Difficult Endings: Ages 7, 8+2, 13+2, 15+3, 17, 18+2, 23+3, 24+2, 29+2, 33, 38+2, 39+2, 48+2, 50, 84+2, 87, 89+2, 93, 98+2

Years of Caution: Ages 0, 4+2, 60, 65, 80, 81, 85, 86, 90, 94

Years of Personal Challenge: Ages 5, 6, 8, 12, 14, 17, 19, 20, 22, 28, 32, 33, 34, 35, 37, 42, 44, 45, 48, 51, 53, 59, 62+2, 65, 76, 90

Years with Good Money Cards: Ages 25, 27, 39+2, 41, 53, 68, 70

LIFE PATH AND THE THIRTEEN-YEAR CYCLE RULING CARDS FOR THE A♣

MERCURY	VENUS	MARS	JUPITER	SATURN	URANUS	NEPTUNE
Ages 0–12	Ages 13–25	Ages 26–38	Ages 39–51	Ages 52–64	Ages 65–77	Ages 78–90
Q♣	10♠	5♣	3♦	A♠	7♥	7♦

Notes:

The Q♣, which governs the first thirteen years of the life of the A♣, usually represents their mother, who is a more or less dominating influence at that time. She is usually a very powerful woman as well. Since the A♣ is one of the Semi-Fixed Cards, it would be wise to study the yearly influences for their Planetary Ruling Card to get a better idea of the years for business and other success and recognition. However, overall, this is a successful card.

The last years of life, governed by the two Sevens are either going to be challenging or uplifting, depending upon whether or not the A♣ has developed any spiritual meaning and purpose to their life.

Years with notable cautions are ages 4, 32, 33, and 39 where combinations of challenging cards exist.

Auspicious Years for the 2♣

Prebirth Years: Ages 44 and 89

Rebirth Years: Ages 45 and 90

Critical Year: Age 52

Purpose-Finding and Fated Years: Ages 3, 4, 6, 7, 11+2, 12, 16, 19, 20, 21, 24, 31, 32+2, 34, 38, 41, 42, 48, 49, 50, 52+2, 53, 56, 59, 61, 64+2, 65, 66, 69, 77, 79, 83, 87, 91, 93, 94, 97

Years of Blessed Endings: Ages 2, 7, 13, 18, 23, 32, 37, 47, 52, 54, 62, 63, 68, 77, 82, 92, 97

Years of Difficult Endings: Ages 1+2, 6+2, 8+3, 15+2, 19+2, 20+2, 22+2, 24+2, 28+2, 32+2, 36+2, 37+2, 40+2, 43+3, 46+2, 51+2, 53+2, 60+2, 64+2, 65+2, 67+2, 68, 69+5, 73+2, 79+2, 82+2, 85+2, 88+2, 91+2, 94, 96+2, 98+2, 100

Years of Caution: Ages 1+2, 2+2, 7, 18, 25+2, 45, 46+2, 47+2, 51, 63, 70+2, 77, 91+2, 92+2

Years of Personal Challenge: Ages 2, 4, 14, 24, 28, 29, 31, 34, 44, 47, 48, 49, 66, 72, 73, 74, 76, 77, 81, 89, 92, 94

Ascent to Pinnacle Years: Ages 27, 72

Pinnacle Years: Ages 30, 75

Most Blessed Years: Ages 32, 77

Years of Wish Fulfillment: Ages 3, 4, 12, 24, 48, 49, 57, 69, 93, 94

Years of Recognition, Fame, and Business Success: Ages 3, 15, 23, 24+2, 25+3, 26+2, 38, 41, 42, 48, 60, 68, 70, 83, 86, 87, 93

Years with Good Money Cards: Ages 3, 8, 13+2, 15, 18, 21, 23, 37, 40, 48, 53, 58+3, 60, 63, 66, 68, 85, 93, 98

LIFE PATH AND THE THIRTEEN-YEAR CYCLE RULING CARDS FOR THE 2♣

MERCURY	VENUS	MARS	JUPITER	SATURN	URANUS	NEPTUNE
Ages 0–12 K♣	Ages 13–25 J♦	Ages 26–38 4♥	Ages 39–51 4♦	Ages 52–64 2♠	Ages 65–77 8♥	Ages 78–90 6♣

Notes:

The 2♣ has lifelong connections to the A♠, their first Karma Card, and it often shows up in their Yearly and Seven-Year Spreads in one fashion or another. This becomes very apparent in the second seven-year cycle where their Birth Card displaces the A♠ for the entire cycle. The A♠ governs the first year of that cycle at age 7. Overall, that second cycle is one that impacts them the most in childhood. It has the A♠, 9♥, 6♦, and 6♠ all as Long-Range Cards in that cycle, and some of these are in more challenging positions. This is more likely in the seven years that the 2♣ develop some of the fear syndromes that many are noted for. There is a healing influence of the K♥ in the cycle that helps mitigate the other influences. This is usually the influence of their father or some male figure that is helpful and loving.

Years in which the 2♣ has combinations of challenging influences occur at ages 1, 20, 45, 46, 51, 65, 69, and 91. The actual life path of the 2♣ is very fortunate. It's just that their concerns often seem greater than their successes.

The seven years from ages 21–27 stand out as being particularly fortunate for work, finances, career, and recognition. Many 2♣ do achieve great success in their lives, and this is a notable time for their rise to the top. This rise continues until age 30 when they reach the Pinnacle and usually move into a new position or take up a new direction. All in all, they get a wonderful start in their work at just the right time to guarantee future success.

Auspicious Years for the 3♣

Prebirth Years: Ages 44 and 89

Rebirth Years: Ages 45 and 90

Critical Year: Age 52

Purpose-Finding and Fated Years: Ages 5, 9, 13, 15, 16, 17, 21, 28, 30, 32, 34, 36, 40+2, 47, 50, 54, 58, 59, 60, 62, 69, 75, 77+2, 79, 81, 85, 95, 99, 100

Years of Blessed Endings: Ages 7, 8, 29+2, 32, 36, 43, 48, 53, 56, 74+2, 77, 81, 88, 97, 98

Years of Difficult Endings: Ages 1, 2+2, 6, 11+2, 15, 16+2, 24+2, 26+2, 29, 30+2, 36+2, 37+2, 43, 47+2, 52, 56+3, 58, 61+2, 63+2, 69+2, 73+2, 81+3, 82+2, 92+2, 98

Years of Caution: Ages 2, 19+2, 30, 32, 40+2, 41+2, 47, 64+2, 75, 76, 77, 85+2, 86+2, 92

Years of Personal Challenge: Ages 0, 2, 10, 12, 14+2, 18+2, 23, 24, 26, 28, 30, 31, 39, 40, 41+2, 43, 45, 55, 57, 59, 63, 65, 68, 71, 75, 76, 84, 85, 86+2, 88, 90, 92, 96, 100

Ascent to Pinnacle Years: Ages 21, 66

Pinnacle Years: Ages 24, 69

Most Blessed Years: Ages 26, 71

Years of Wish Fulfillment: Ages 6, 18, 42, 43, 51, 63, 87, 88, 96

Years of Recognition, Fame, and Business Success: Ages 9, 17, 19, 32, 35, 36, 42, 54, 62, 64, 68+2, 69+2, 77, 80, 81, 87, 99

Years with Good Money Cards: Ages 7+2, 19, 21, 22, 23, 28, 36, 42, 52, 63, 64, 66, 67, 68, 73, 87, 97

LIFE PATH AND THE THIRTEEN-YEAR CYCLE RULING CARDS FOR THE 3♣

MERCURY	VENUS	MARS	JUPITER	SATURN	URANUS	NEPTUNE
Ages 0–12	Ages 13–25	Ages 26–38	Ages 39–51	Ages 52–64	Ages 65–77	Ages 78–90
3♠	9♥	7♣	5♦	Q♠	J♣	9♦

Notes:

The 3♣ is often subjected to a lot of changes in childhood that cause them to develop an equally changeable personality in adulthood. Travel is something that most of them do a lot, and often, they change professions frequently until they get the money they desire from their line of work. The thirteen-year period from ages 13–25 does allow them to settle down more, but overall, they are very restless. They reach their first Pinnacle Year rather early in life (age 24) but soon enough to show them that they have special potential and that they can achieve high goals when they set their mind to it. The second Pinnacle Year is the most dramatic of their life because it coincides with another very fortunate seven-year cycle. Age 69 often stands out as a year of crowning achievement and recognition for them. Both Pinnacle years are ones in which they have a 9♣ as their Pluto Card. Their successes come along with a challenging ending or loss in most cases.

Notable years with combinations of cautionary influences are at ages 2, 15, 30, 36, 37, 40, 47, 56, 76, and 81, with age 81 being the most outstanding of all of these.

Auspicious Years for the 4♣

Prebirth Years: Ages 44 and 89

Rebirth Years: Ages 45 and 90

Critical Year: Age 52

Purpose-Finding and Fated Years: Ages 1, 3, 6, 9+2, 13, 15, 16, 19, 21, 25, 26, 30, 35, 36+2, 41, 42, 44, 46, 51, 54+2, 57, 60, 61, 64, 70, 71, 75, 80, 81+2, 86, 87, 89, 91, 96, 99+2

Years of Blessed Endings: Ages 1, 4, 14, 17, 19, 23, 26, 35, 42, 49, 50, 59, 62, 64, 68, 71, 80, 91, 94

Years of Difficult Endings: Ages 4+2, 10+3, 14+2, 16, 20+2, 24+2, 29+2, 31+2, 33+2, 35+2, 41+2, 43, 44+2, 49+2, 50, 55+2, 56, 57+2, 59+2, 64, 67+2, 74+2, 76+2, 78+2, 80+2, 82, 85, 86+2, 89+2, 94+2, 100+2

Years of Caution: Ages 9, 10, 13+2, 23, 33, 34+2, 35+2, 37, 41, 55, 58+2, 68, 74, 79+2, 80+2, 82, 84, 100

Years of Personal Challenge: Ages 5, 11, 12, 13, 14, 17+2, 19, 22, 23, 27, 30, 35, 37, 39, 41, 42, 50, 56, 58, 62+2, 65, 68, 69, 72, 75+2, 80, 82, 86, 88, 89, 91, 95+2

Ascent to Pinnacle Years: Ages 15, 60

Pinnacle Years: Ages 18, 63

Most Blessed Years: Ages 20, 65

Years of Wish Fulfillment: Ages 0, 12, 36, 37, 45, 57, 81, 82, 90

Years of Recognition, Fame, and Business Success: Ages 3, 11, 13, 26+3, 27+2, 29, 30, 36, 48, 56, 58, 71, 74, 75, 77+2, 78+2, 79+2, 81, 93, 97+2

Years with Good Money Cards: Ages 1, 6, 8, 9, 25, 27+2, 32, 35, 37, 46, 53, 54, 66, 70, 72+2, 77, 80, 91, 98, 99

LIFE PATH AND THE THIRTEEN-YEAR CYCLE RULING CARDS FOR THE 4♣

MERCURY	VENUS	MARS	JUPITER	SATURN	URANUS	NEPTUNE
Ages 0–12	Ages 13–25	Ages 26–38	Ages 39–51	Ages 52–64	Ages 65–77	Ages 78–90
2♦	J♠	8♣	6♦	4♠	10♥	10♦

Notes:

The 4♣ has one of the more fortunate Life Paths. Most of the Life Spread Cards are even numbers, their Birth Card sits in the blessed Jupiter column, and the cards from the Jupiter Period on all sit in the Jupiter line. They get off to a good start in life and have much more to be grateful for than the average person. From ages 7–20, their life has many changes, and it is these years that contribute to the restless side of the adult 4♣ personality. At ages 26 and 27, they get a taste of recognition, and that period usually directs them into a field where they can make a good living and enjoy continued successes. If they live long enough, they can enjoy a similar period at ages 77–79.

The 4♣ has fewer combinations of truly challenging cards than most other cards. But the years they should take extra care are at ages 30, 36, 41, 55, 74, 75, and 82.

Auspicious Years for the 5♣

Prebirth Years: Ages 44 and 89

Rebirth Years: Ages 45 and 90

Critical Year: Age 52

Purpose-Finding and Fated Years: Ages 2, 8, 16, 18, 20, 25, 29, 37, 39, 43, 45, 47, 53+2, 55, 61, 65, 70, 74, 82, 84, 88, 89, 92, 98

Years of Blessed Endings: Ages 4, 5+2, 8, 13, 15, 34, 35, 36, 40, 44, 45, 50+2, 53, 58, 60, 79, 80, 81, 85, 86, 89, 94, 95+2, 98

Years of Difficult Endings: Ages 0+2, 6, 9+2, 11+2, 18+2, 21+2, 22+2, 23+2, 25+2, 27, 30+2, 40+4, 41+2, 45+2, 50, 54+2, 63+2, 64+2, 67+2, 68+4, 70+2, 75+2, 81, 85+4, 86+2, 90+2, 94, 99+2

Years of Caution: Ages 1, 12+2, 15, 31, 33+2, 34+2, 54, 57+2, 62, 76, 78+2, 79+2, 97

Years of Personal Challenge: Ages 2, 3, 9+2, 16, 17, 19, 23, 26, 34+2, 36+2, 49, 54, 56, 61, 62, 66, 67, 77, 79, 81+2, 85, 91, 99

Ascent to Pinnacle Years: Ages 14, 59

Pinnacle Years: Ages 17, 62

Most Blessed Years: Ages 19, 64

Years of Wish Fulfillment: Ages 11, 35, 36, 44, 56, 80, 81, 89

Years of Recognition, Fame, and Business Success: Ages 2, 10, 12, 19+2, 20+2, 25, 28, 29, 35, 47, 55, 57, 70+3, 71+2, 72+2, 73, 74, 80, 90+2, 92, 98+2, 99+2, 100

Years with Good Money Cards: Ages 0, 2, 4, 11, 12, 14, 17, 26, 28, 31, 45, 46, 47, 49, 56, 59, 62, 71, 73, 88, 90, 92, 94

LIFE PATH AND THE THIRTEEN-YEAR CYCLE RULING CARDS FOR THE 5♣

MERCURY	VENUS	MARS	JUPITER	SATURN	URANUS	NEPTUNE
Ages 0–12	Ages 13–25	Ages 26–38	Ages 39–51	Ages 52–64	Ages 65–77	Ages 78–90
3♦	A♠	7♥	7♦	5♠	J♥	9♣

Notes:

The restless 5♣ begins life on a changeable note, displacing the 5♥ (Spiritual Spread) and having a 5♠ Long-Range in the Saturn year for the 5th year of life. In addition, there are losses or challenges at ages 5 and 6 that make an indelible mark on their personalities. Losses in childhood are one of the major causes of restlessness and avoidance of commitments in adulthood. This changeable period extends again for seven more years as they displace the 5♥, this time in the Life Spread. What this adds up to is fourteen years of changes that makes the 5♣ so prone to travel and taking on new adventures.

Ages 19 and 20 bring some early successes in work that inspires the 5♣ to take a more active role in their careers. Remember that the 5♣ has the 7♦ in Jupiter for life, which often brings financial opulence in their thirties or forties.

Years of particular caution for 5♣ are at ages 18, 45, 54, 63, and 97, with age 45 being the strongest of these.

Auspicious Years for the 6♣

Prebirth Years: Ages 44 and 89

Rebirth Years: Ages 45 and 90

Critical Year: Age 52

Purpose-Finding and Fated Years: Ages 0+3, 4, 6, 8, 17, 18+2, 27, 28, 41, 45+2, 49, 51, 53, 62, 63+2, 72, 73, 86, 90+2, 94, 96, 98

Years of Blessed Endings: Ages 7, 16+2, 21, 24, 26, 30, 40, 43, 52, 61, 65, 66, 71, 75, 85, 88, 97

Years of Difficult Endings: Ages 5+2, 6+2, 9, 15+2, 29+2, 31+2, 32+2, 38+2, 41+2, 46, 50+2, 51+2, 52, 58, 60+2, 63, 74+2, 77+2, 79, 83+2, 84+2, 88+2, 95+2, 96+2

Years of Caution: Ages 2, 8+2, 9+2, 18, 22, 26, 32+2, 35+2, 47, 53+2, 54+2, 67, 71, 77+2, 80+2, 92, 98+2, 99+2

Years of Personal Challenge: Ages 9, 11+2, 13, 16, 34, 36, 38, 39, 43, 54, 56+2, 57, 61, 76, 78, 81+2, 83, 86, 92, 99+2

Ascent to Pinnacle Years: Ages 34, 79

Pinnacle Years: Ages 37, 82

Most Blessed Years: Ages 39, 84

Years of Wish Fulfillment: Ages 10, 11, 19, 31, 55, 56, 64, 76, 100

Years of Recognition, Fame, and Business Success: Ages 0, 2+2, 3+3, 4+3, 10, 22, 25+2, 26+2, 27+2, 29+2, 30+3, 31+2, 32, 45, 48, 49, 55, 67, 73+2, 74+2, 75+3, 77, 90, 93, 94, 100

Years with Good Money Cards: Ages 0, 3, 6, 8, 13, 20, 32, 33, 40, 45, 51, 53, 58, 65, 71, 78, 82, 90, 96, 98

LIFE PATH AND THE THIRTEEN-YEAR CYCLE RULING CARDS FOR THE 6♣

MERCURY	VENUS	MARS	JUPITER	SATURN	URANUS	NEPTUNE
Ages 0–12	Ages 13–25	Ages 26–38	Ages 39–51	Ages 52–64	Ages 65–77	Ages 78–90
6♠	Q♥	10♣	8♦	K♠	3♥	A♣

Notes:

Career-wise, the 6♣ is one of the most fortunate cards in the deck. The cards that govern the thirteen-year cycles from ages 26–64 are all located in the Crown Line where great recognition and success are possible. When they do get involved in work matters, most 6♣ do it in a big way or play in the higher levels of business. In addition to these influences, the 6♣ person has fortuitous cycles from ages 25–27 and again from ages 29–31. They are also very fortunate to have four years in life in which the K♠ is their Long-Range Card. These are at ages 4, 27, 31, and 75. Combining all of these influences gives the 6♣ no reason, but perhaps their own inertia, to fail in any career they choose. However, the crowning years of their life could be the best, because ages 70–76 are in a very auspicious influence that can be both fun, as well as highly successful and overflowing with recognition on a grand scale.

Years of particular caution include those at ages 4, 35, 49, and 80.

Auspicious Years for the 7♣

Prebirth Years: Ages 44 and 89

Rebirth Years: Ages 45 and 90

Critical Year: Age 52

Purpose-Finding and Fated Years: Ages 5, 7, 8, 9, 10, 13, 18+3, 21, 25, 27, 31, 32, 36, 37, 41, 50, 52, 53, 54, 55, 58, 63+2, 66+2, 72, 77, 81, 82, 87, 95+2, 97, 98, 99, 100

Years of Blessed Endings: Ages 0, 2, 5, 7, 15, 19, 20, 21, 29, 31, 45, 47, 50, 52, 60, 64, 65, 66, 70, 76, 78, 90, 92, 95, 97

Years of Difficult Endings: Ages 3, 4+2, 5+2, 12+2, 14+4, 17, 23+2, 24+2, 28+2, 30+2, 32, 37+4, 38+3, 44, 47, 48+2, 49+2, 52+2, 54, 57+2, 59+4, 68+2, 69+2, 73+2, 75+2, 76, 77, 82+4, 83+2, 85+2, 94+2, 95+2

Years of Caution: Ages 6, 17+2, 18+2, 24, 41+3, 51, 62+2, 63+2, 69, 86+3, 96

Years of Personal Challenge: Ages 0+2, 3, 4, 7, 16, 18, 20, 23, 25, 33, 40, 45+2, 49, 50, 53, 63, 65, 68, 70, 73, 79, 90+2, 93, 97

Ascent to Pinnacle Years: Ages 43, 88

Pinnacle Years: Ages 1, 46, 91

Most Blessed Years: Ages 3, 48, 93

Years of Wish Fulfillment: Ages 19, 20, 28, 40, 64, 65, 73, 85

Years of Recognition, Fame, and Business Success: Ages 7+2, 9, 12, 13, 19, 31, 39, 41, 54, 57, 58, 64, 65+2, 66+2, 67+2, 76, 84, 86, 88+2, 89+2, 90+2, 92+2, 93+2, 94+2, 99

Years with Good Money Cards: Ages 1, 10, 11, 22+2, 29, 42+2, 44, 46, 56, 67, 74, 80, 86, 87, 89, 91, 99

LIFE PATH AND THE THIRTEEN-YEAR CYCLE RULING CARDS FOR THE 7♣

MERCURY	VENUS	MARS	JUPITER	SATURN	URANUS	NEPTUNE
Ages 0–12	Ages 13–25	Ages 26–38	Ages 39–51	Ages 52–64	Ages 65–77	Ages 78–90
5♦	Q♠	J♣	9♦	7♠	2♣	K♣

Notes:

Being the Karma Card of the 8♦, the 7♣ goes right up to the Crown Line for seven years beginning on their 7th birthday. For many of them, the positive experiences of that period whets their appetite for recognition and being noticed, which proves a compelling motivation throughout life. And, at ages 21–27, they spend another seven years in a highly blessed position displacing the 10♦. This period serves to strengthen their faith and opens up some spiritual channels for their minds to explore. They often have a good bit of success in this period as well. Their Ascent to Pinnacle and Pinnacle Year come in mid-life, the time for some further success and recognition and the opportunity to step up to a new level in their work.

The 7♣ is very fortunate to have four years in life in which the K♠ is their Long-Range Card, though the last two occur in their nineties. These are at ages 7, 67, 90, and 94.

Caution years include ages 4, 17, 24, 41, 59, 62, and 73, with age 41 being the strongest of these.

Auspicious Years for the 8♣

Prebirth Years: Ages 44 and 89

Rebirth Years: Ages 45 and 90

Purpose-Finding and Fated Years: Ages 0, 3, 11, 17, 21, 36, 38, 44, 48, 62, 66, 70, 80, 83, 93

Years of Blessed Endings: Ages 6, 10, 16, 24, 34, 37, 51, 55, 61, 69, 79, 82, 96, 100

Years of Difficult Endings: Ages 1+2, 11+2, 17+2, 29, 31+2, 32+2, 41+2, 46+2, 56+2, 62+2, 65, 73, 76+2, 77+2, 86+2, 91+3, 96

Years of Caution: Ages 8, 38, 42, 53, 83, 87, 98

Years of Personal Challenge: Ages 5, 7, 10, 24, 25, 35, 37, 47, 50, 52, 55+2, 70, 74, 80, 82, 93, 95, 97, 100

Years with Good Money Cards: Ages 0, 2, 3, 17, 26, 27, 29, 34, 40, 45, 47, 48, 53, 67, 72, 74, 90, 92

LIFE PATH AND THE THIRTEEN-YEAR CYCLE RULING CARDS FOR THE 8♣

MERCURY	VENUS	MARS	JUPITER	SATURN	URANUS	NEPTUNE
Ages 0–12 6♦	Ages 13–25 4♠	Ages 26–38 10♥	Ages 39–51 10♦	Ages 52–64 8♠	Ages 65–77 A♥	Ages 78–90 A♦

Notes:

The 8♣ has one of the most fortunate life paths of any card in the deck, especially along the lines of money and career. All the thirteen-year periods from ages 13–64 are cards of success, protection, and security. The power of their 8♣ Birth Card just adds to this success. Being one of the three Fixed Cards, you will have to look at the cycles of their Planetary Ruling Card for specific times of recognition and reward, but it is easy to see that they can have as much success as they want in the most important of the work years. The cycle from ages 39–51 can be their most fortunate of all. The 10♦ Card found in that cycle is in the Most Blessed Spot. Huge financial rewards are entirely possible then.

Years in which the 8♣ has combinations of challenging influences are rare and not nearly as strong as those of other cards. They occur at ages 12, 57, and 87.

Auspicious Years for the 9♣

Prebirth Years: Ages 44 and 89

Rebirth Years: Ages 45 and 90

Critical Year: Age 52

Purpose-Finding and Fated Years: Ages 1, 4, 11+2, 14, 15, 16, 20+2, 22, 25, 29, 32, 33, 34, 43, 44, 45, 46, 51, 53, 54, 56+2, 60, 61, 65+2, 70, 74, 77, 78, 79, 85, 88, 89, 91, 94

Years of Blessed Endings: Ages 0, 14, 16, 24, 27, 32, 39, 40, 45, 59, 61, 69, 72, 81, 84, 90

Years of Difficult Endings: Ages 0+3, 10+2, 12+2, 14+2, 15, 19+2, 21+2, 24+2, 31+2, 34+2, 41, 45+2, 47+2, 57+4, 64+2, 66+2, 69+2, 76+2, 79+2, 82, 88, 90+2, 100+2

Years of Caution: Ages 3+2, 7, 24+2, 25+2, 32, 48+2, 52+2, 69+2, 70+2, 77, 87, 93+3, 97

Years of Personal Challenge: Ages 2, 4, 7, 8, 10, 12, 15, 18, 20, 22, 25, 26, 27, 29, 35, 37, 43, 48, 49, 52, 55+2, 59, 60, 62, 65, 67, 70+2, 71, 72, 74+2, 78, 80, 88, 92, 94, 96, 97, 100

Ascent to Pinnacle Years: Ages 5, 50, 95

Pinnacle Years: Ages 8, 53, 98

Most Blessed Years: Ages 10, 55, 100

Years of Wish Fulfillment: Ages 2, 26, 27, 35, 47, 71, 72, 80, 92

Years of Recognition, Fame, and Business Success: Ages 1, 3, 7+2, 8+2, 9+2, 16, 19, 20, 26, 27+2, 35+2, 36+2, 38, 46, 48, 56+2, 61, 64, 65, 71, 83, 91, 93

Years with Good Money Cards: Ages 9, 12, 30, 32, 35, 36, 37, 54, 75, 80, 81, 82, 99

LIFE PATH AND THE THIRTEEN-YEAR CYCLE RULING CARDS FOR THE 9♣

MERCURY	VENUS	MARS	JUPITER	SATURN	URANUS	NEPTUNE
Ages 0–12	Ages 13–25	Ages 26–38	Ages 39–51	Ages 52–64	Ages 65–77	Ages 78–90
9♠	2♥	K♥	K♦	6♥	4♣	2♦

Notes:

The 9♣ person often has many losses in the first years of their life, as denoted by the 9♠ card governing their first thirteen years. After these losses, either physically or emotionally, the next thirteen years are spent exploring love relationships, which becomes more or less a driving force for the rest of their life. Some recognition in school as they reach their first Pinnacle Year at age 8 gives them the drive and courage to achieve more in their adult lives. Additional success often occurs at age 27.

The 9♣ is fortunate to have three years in life in which the K♠ is their Long-Range Card. These are at ages 9, 36, and 56.

Years with especially cautionary influences include those at age 20, 24, 52, 53, 57, 65, 69, and 88.

Auspicious Years for the 10♣

Prebirth Years: Ages 44 and 89

Rebirth Years: Ages 45 and 90

Critical Year: Age 52

Purpose-Finding and Fated Years: Ages 6, 11, 12, 15, 16, 20, 24, 25, 29, 30, 34+2, 37, 39, 44, 51, 56, 60, 61, 62, 65, 66, 69, 72, 74, 75, 79, 82, 84, 86, 89, 96

Years of Blessed Endings: Ages 1, 5, 8, 15, 19, 29, 31, 46, 50, 53, 60, 64, 72, 74, 80, 91, 95, 98

Years of Difficult Endings: Ages 3+2, 7+2, 9+2, 11+2, 16+2, 19, 26+4, 40+2, 48+2, 50+2, 54+4, 56+2, 59, 61+3, 69, 71+4, 75, 85+2, 87+2, 89, 90, 93+2, 97+2, 99+2

Years of Caution: Ages 19+2, 20+2, 37, 40, 43+2, 57, 64+2, 65+2, 82, 88+2

Years of Personal Challenge: Ages 2+2, 5, 9, 15, 18, 20, 22, 27, 29, 38, 42, 44, 47+3, 52, 65, 67+2, 72, 76, 87, 92+2, 93, 95, 97, 99

Ascent to Pinnacle Years: Ages 0, 45, 90

Pinnacle Years: Ages 3, 48, 93

Most Blessed Years: Ages 5, 50, 95

Years of Wish Fulfillment: Ages 21, 22, 30, 42, 66, 67, 75, 87

Years of Recognition, Fame, and Business Success: Ages 0+2, 1+2, 11, 14, 15, 21+3, 33, 41, 43, 56, 59, 60, 66, 78, 79+2, 80+2, 81+2, 86, 88

Years with Good Money Cards: Ages 0, 3, 24, 31, 36, 40, 42, 48, 76, 85, 87, 93

LIFE PATH AND THE THIRTEEN-YEAR CYCLE RULING CARDS FOR THE 10♣

MERCURY	VENUS	MARS	JUPITER	SATURN	URANUS	NEPTUNE
Ages 0–12	Ages 13–25	Ages 26–38	Ages 39–51	Ages 52–64	Ages 65–77	Ages 78–90
8♦	K♠	3♥	A♣	Q♣	10♠	5♣

Notes:

For all intents and purposes, the 10♣ person lives their entire life in the Crown Line since that is where their Birth Card sits in the Grand Solar Spread. This brings tremendous opportunities for success and recognition by the public. Most of them are driven by their careers and a desire to become known in some way. They start out life with a bang, often getting a lot of success and recognition in childhood and school years. Then at age 21, they begin a seven-year period where their Birth Card sits in the Crown Line again, this time in the Sun position, displacing the 8♦. Success again is practically guaranteed in whatever field or work or study they choose to follow. The 10♣ is also fortunate to have three years in life in which the K♠ is their Long-Range Card. These are at ages 1, 21, and 81. At the Rebirth Year, age 45, they again return to the Crown Line for their Ascent to Pinnacle for another visitation to the higher realms of their circle. With all of this going for them, it is only their indecision that stands between them and any sort of success they desire.

Years of special caution in both work and health matters include those at ages 19, 40, 59, and 61.

Auspicious Years for the J♣

Prebirth Years: Ages 44 and 89

Rebirth Years: Ages 45 and 90

Critical Year: Age 52

Purpose-Finding and Fated Years: Ages 2, 3, 7, 20, 21, 24, 25, 31, 38, 42, 47, 48, 52, 63, 65, 66, 69, 70, 71, 76, 80, 81, 83, 87+2, 92, 93, 97, 99

Years of Blessed Endings: Ages 10, 20, 28, 36, 41+2, 44, 55, 65, 73, 85, 86+2, 100

Years of Difficult Endings: Ages 0, 2+2, 4+2, 5+2, 8+2, 10+2, 11+2, 13, 14+3, 18+2, 19+2, 21+2, 25+2, 33+3, 35+3, 47+2, 49+3, 50+2, 51+2, 53+2, 55+2, 56+2, 61+2, 64+2, 66+2, 70+2, 74, 78+2, 80+2, 85, 90, 92+2, 94+2, 95+2, 98+2, 100+3

Years of Caution: Ages 7+2, 9, 22, 28+2, 29+2, 31, 43, 52+2, 54, 61, 67, 73+2, 74+2, 88, 89, 97+2, 99

Years of Personal Challenge: Ages 1, 6, 10, 11, 13, 16, 17, 20, 23+2, 26, 29, 31+2, 38, 43, 46, 56, 58, 59, 63, 68, 69, 71, 74, 75, 76+2, 83, 96

Ascent to Pinnacle Years: Ages 9, 54, 99

Pinnacle Years: Ages 12, 57

Most Blessed Years: Ages 14, 59

Years of Wish Fulfillment: Ages 6, 30, 31, 39, 51, 75, 76, 84, 96

Years of Recognition, Fame, and Business Success: Ages 5, 7, 20, 23, 24, 30, 35+2, 36+2, 37+2, 42, 50, 52, 55+2, 63+2, 64+2, 65, 68, 69, 75, 84+2, 87, 95, 97

Years with Good Money Cards: Ages 13, 25, 31, 33, 40, 58, 76, 78, 85, 94

Life Path and the Thirteen-Year Cycle Ruling Cards for the J♣

Mercury	Venus	Mars	Jupiter	Saturn	Uranus	Neptune
Ages 0–12	Ages 13–25	Ages 26–38	Ages 39–51	Ages 52–64	Ages 65–77	Ages 78–90
9♦	7♠	2♣	K♣	J♦	4♥	4♦

Notes:

The J♣ has a fortunate Life Path by most standards, with many good cards ruling the thirteen-year periods of their life. But it is during the Jupiter and Saturn Periods that they really reach their potential, often becoming leaders in some field of study or work. The six years beginning at 21 are fairly fortunate, because each of the Long-Range Cards those years fall in the Jupiter row, with the age 23 7♠ Long-Range being particularly highlighted for blessings of many kinds. The next cycle, from ages 28–34, is more trying and has some challenges to deal with. Ages 28 and 31 stand out as being the most challenging of that seven-year period. The seven-year cycle beginning at age 42 is another fortunate one, though one that is also filled with hard work and some challenges. At age 63, the J♣ begins a seven-year cycle in which their Birth Card displaces the 10♣ in the Crown Line. For those with career ambitions, this is often a time of great reward and recognition, particularly ages 63 and 64.

Some of the most trying personal challenges for the J♣ revolve around their intimate relationships and friendships. Years when these issues are confronted head-on occur at ages 7, 29, 52, and 74. Years when health/lifestyle and work matters have particularly challenging influences occur at ages 2, 31, 33, 43, 61, 69, 78, 80, 88, and 92.

The J♣ is fortunate to have three years in life in which the K♠ is their Long-Range Card. These are at ages 37, 64, and 84.

Auspicious Years for the Q♣

Prebirth Years: Ages 44 and 89

Rebirth Years: Ages 45 and 90

Critical Year: Age 52

Purpose-Finding and Fated Years: Ages 5, 9, 10, 12+2, 14, 22+2, 23, 24, 33, 36, 40, 50, 54, 55, 57+2, 59, 65, 67, 68, 69, 78, 81, 85, 95, 99, 100

Years of Blessed Endings: Ages 0, 4, 6, 11, 14, 22, 25+2, 32, 35, 40, 43, 45, 49, 51, 56, 59, 66, 67, 70, 74, 77, 80, 85, 88, 90, 94, 96

Years of Difficult Endings: Ages 1+2, 10+2, 16+2, 19, 20+2, 21+2, 23+2, 31, 34+4, 37, 38+2, 41+2, 44+2, 45, 48+3, 51, 55+2, 61+3, 65+2, 66+2, 68+2, 79+4, 81+2, 83+2, 86+2, 91+2, 92, 100+2

Years of Caution: Ages 3, 13+3, 14+2, 37+2, 43, 58+2, 59+2, 73, 79, 82+2, 88

Years of Personal Challenge: Ages 0, 3, 4, 5, 10, 12, 14+2, 16, 17, 24, 25, 27, 28, 33, 36, 40, 41, 42+2, 45, 46, 55, 57, 59+2, 61, 69, 73, 74, 78, 86, 87, 88, 89, 90, 93, 98, 99, 100

Ascent to Pinnacle Years: Ages 39, 84

Pinnacle Years: Ages 42, 87

Most Blessed Years: Ages 44, 89

Years of Wish Fulfillment: Ages 15, 16, 24, 36, 60, 61, 69, 81

Years of Recognition, Fame, and Business Success: Ages 5, 8, 9, 15, 27, 35, 37+3, 38+2, 39+2, 50, 53, 54, 60+3, 61+2, 62+2, 64+2, 65+2, 66+2, 72, 80, 82, 95, 98, 99

Years with Good Money Cards: Ages 1, 3, 4, 8, 19, 21, 25, 43, 44, 46, 48, 49, 57, 64, 66, 70, 89, 91, 93, 94, 96

LIFE PATH AND THE THIRTEEN-YEAR CYCLE RULING CARDS FOR THE Q♣

MERCURY	VENUS	MARS	JUPITER	SATURN	URANUS	NEPTUNE
Ages 0–12	Ages 13–25	Ages 26–38	Ages 39–51	Ages 52–64	Ages 65–77	Ages 78–90
10♠	5♣	3♦	A♠	7♥	7♦	5♠

Notes:

The Q♣ is one of the cards that has a particularly difficult life in emotional terms. The first fourteen years of life are filled with experiences at ages 3 and 4 that often cause them to retreat from trusting others completely. The second seven years are better than the first, but still a sense of insecurity on the emotional level persists in the background as they develop into teenagers. It is the overall sense of goodness from past incarnations that serves to mitigate these circumstances and give them a positive outlook. But in the emotional and relationship arena, there is often great karma to be dealt with. There is often a sense of financial limitation as well in the developmental years, which colors their attitude and adult life. The real blessings of the Q♣ are spiritual, and those who have made a strong connection can breeze through all of this unscathed. At ages 37–39 the ones who are career-minded experience good success and realize their great potential, if they have not already. A marriage at age 38 would be especially auspicious. Another important and good seven-year cycle begins at age 56, with the last three years of this bringing some crowning achievements. The Q♣ is fortunate to have three years in life in which the K♠ is their Long-Range Card. These are at ages 39, 62, and 66.

If the Q♣ has not taken good care of their bodies, and many of them do not for some reason, ages 63–69 will see them having health problems that take away much of the luster of an otherwise very powerful and beneficial cycle. Great success and recognition can be achieved then, but health problems could dampen their enjoyment of it. Other particularly challenging years occur at ages 13, 14, 21, 66, 73, 79, and 88.

Auspicious Years for the K♣

Prebirth Years: Ages 44 and 89

Rebirth Years: Ages 45 and 90

Critical Year: Age 52

Purpose-Finding and Fated Years: Ages 2+3, 5, 6, 14, 16, 19, 26, 29, 33, 43+2, 47+3, 61, 64, 71, 74, 75, 78, 83, 88+2, 92+3

Years of Blessed Endings: Ages 1, 3, 10, 14, 18, 20, 22, 30, 32, 35, 38, 39, 41, 42, 44, 46, 48, 55, 63+2, 65, 75, 77, 80, 83, 84, 86, 87, 89, 91, 93, 100

Years of Difficult Endings: Ages 2+2, 3+2, 4+2, 7+2, 8+2, 10, 13+2, 17+2, 18+2, 22+2, 24, 27+2, 29+2, 30, 37+2, 39+2, 40, 47+2, 48+2, 49+3, 52+2, 53+2, 58+2, 60, 62+2, 63+2, 67+2, 72+2, 82+4, 86+2, 92+2, 93+2, 94+2, 97+2, 98

Years of Caution: Ages 6+2, 7+2, 27, 28, 30+2, 32, 51+2, 52+2, 70, 72, 75+2, 77, 96+2, 97+2

Years of Personal Challenge: Ages 7+2, 9+2, 12, 14, 23, 27, 34, 36, 37, 41, 43, 52, 54+2, 59, 71, 72, 74, 78, 79, 81, 84, 96, 97, 99+2

Ascent to Pinnacle Years: Ages 32, 77

Pinnacle Years: Ages 35, 80

Most Blessed Years: Ages 37, 82

Years of Wish Fulfillment: Ages 8, 9, 17, 29, 53, 54, 62, 74, 98, 99

Years of Recognition, Fame, and Business Success: Ages 1, 2, 8, 11+2, 12+2, 13+2, 15+2, 16+2, 17+2, 20, 28, 30, 43, 46, 47, 53, 59+2, 60+2, 61+2, 65, 73, 75, 88, 91, 92, 98

Years with Good Money Cards: Ages 8, 10, 18+2, 19, 43, 53, 55, 56, 63, 64, 68, 88, 92, 98, 100

LIFE PATH AND THE THIRTEEN-YEAR CYCLE RULING CARDS FOR THE K♣

MERCURY	VENUS	MARS	JUPITER	SATURN	URANUS	NEPTUNE
Ages 0–12	Ages 13–25	Ages 26–38	Ages 39–51	Ages 52–64	Ages 65–77	Ages 78–90
J♦	4♥	4♦	2♠	8♥	6♣	6♠

Notes:

The K♣ has a fortunate Life Path in most respects, and their childhood has many good elements that give them a solid foundation upon which to build a good life. As they get into high school, their potential reveals itself, and many of them achieve a lot of success at ages 11–13 and then again from ages 15–17, which shows them that they are a cut above the average person in terms of intelligence and ability. They often discover their leadership potential during this same time. The seven-year period beginning at age 21 is a bit more difficult in some respects, many of them discovering that their health is something they must attend to with care. During this time, their Birth Card displaces the 9♠ in the Grand Solar Spread. However, they still achieve a lot of success in this period. Another similar cycle begins at age 42 when their Birth Card displaces the A♠. The seven years beginning at age 56 are perhaps the best of the entire life in terms of success and recognition. The K♣ is fortunate to have three years in life in which the K♠ is their Long-Range Card. These are at ages 13, 17, and 61.

Particularly challenging years include those at ages 2, 6, 7, 27, 47, 52, 70, 72, 96, and 97.

Auspicious Years for the A♦

Prebirth Years: Ages 44 and 89

Rebirth Years: Ages 45 and 90

Critical Year: Age 52

Purpose-Finding and Fated Years: Ages 2, 6, 12, 13, 15+2, 17, 20, 24, 25, 27, 29+2, 30+3, 34, 39, 43+2, 47, 51, 55, 56, 57, 60, 62, 65, 70, 72, 74, 75+2, 80, 84, 86, 88, 92, 96, 98

Years of Blessed Endings: Ages 2, 14, 18, 26, 28, 38, 39, 47, 59, 67, 73, 83, 84, 92

Years of Difficult Endings: Ages 0+2, 4, 5+2, 7+2, 17+4, 31+2, 33+2, 34+2, 35, 39, 43+2, 44+2, 50+2, 51, 52+2, 62+4, 76+2, 77, 79+2, 86+2, 89+2, 90+3, 95+2, 97+2, 99

Years of Caution: Ages 10+2, 11+2, 20, 34+2, 35, 36, 55+2, 56+2, 65, 79+2, 80, 81, 100+2

Years of Personal Challenge: Ages 5+2, 11, 13+2, 16, 23, 27, 30, 38, 41, 45, 50, 52, 56, 58+3, 59, 61, 68, 69, 71, 75, 78, 83, 88, 95+2

Ascent to Pinnacle Years: Ages 36, 81

Pinnacle Years: Ages 39, 84

Most Blessed Years: Ages 41, 86

Years of Wish Fulfillment: Ages 12, 13, 21, 33, 57, 58, 66, 78

Years of Recognition, Fame, and Business Success: Ages 2, 5, 6, 12, 16+2, 17+2, 18+2, 24, 32, 34, 39+2, 40+2, 41+2, 43+2, 44+2, 45+2, 47, 50, 51, 57, 69, 77, 79, 87+2, 88+2, 89+2, 92,

Years with Good Money Cards: Ages 4, 6, 15, 19, 21, 22, 35, 38, 44, 49, 51, 54, 60, 67+2, 80, 81, 83, 85, 89, 91, 94, 96

LIFE PATH AND THE THIRTEEN-YEAR CYCLE RULING CARDS FOR THE A♦

MERCURY	VENUS	MARS	JUPITER	SATURN	URANUS	NEPTUNE
Ages 0–12	Ages 13–25	Ages 26–38	Ages 39–51	Ages 52–64	Ages 65–77	Ages 78–90
Q♦	5♥	3♣	3♠	9♥	7♣	5♦

Notes:

Though every card in the Life Path of the A♦ falls in the Saturn line, the position of their Birth Card as the Jupiter/Neptune Card in the Grand Solar Spread gives them the optimism to overcome the negative influences that surround them, both in childhood and later as adults. There are challenging years in childhood to be sure, but they have the knack of re-interpreting these in light of a higher good. These people have strong work and career drives and a good bit of luck and good fortune in these areas that elevates many of them to great achievement. Ages 14–20 are particularly good in these areas. Whatever happens then often shows them that they know how to and can make money, which is a chief drive in their lives. But the best period of their life begins at age 35 and extends till age 48. During this time, they often rise up to great heights in their chosen field and achieve financial success as well. They reach the Pinnacle during this time as well, making them one of the few cards that gets a double influence of the Crown line at the same time (both yearly and in the Seven-Year Spread). A glance at age 41 reveals a particularly wonderful combination. It is a Most-Blessed Year combined with a K♠ Long-Range. No other card gets this sort of preferred treatment. Of course, the measure of their success in this cycle will depend largely on how clear they are about their goals and directions. The A♦ is also very fortunate to have four years in life in which the K♠ is their Long-Range Card. These are at ages 18, 41, 45, and 89.

Years of particular caution are relatively few and occur at ages 31, 35, 51, 56, 52, and 76.

Auspicious Years for the 2♦

Prebirth Years: Ages 44 and 89

Rebirth Years: Ages 45 and 90

Critical Year: Age 52

Purpose-Finding and Fated Years: Ages 1, 2, 5, 16, 19, 23, 24, 26, 29, 30, 32, 35, 40, 43, 44, 46, 50, 53, 57, 61, 63, 64, 68, 71, 74, 77, 80, 85, 89, 91, 95

Years of Blessed Endings: Ages 5, 11, 15, 16, 18, 21, 26, 29+2, 39, 43, 50, 56, 60, 61, 62, 63, 70, 71, 74+2, 84, 88, 95

Years of Difficult Endings: Ages 6+2, 8, 16+2, 20, 21+2, 22, 30+4, 35+2, 36, 38+2, 40+2, 43+2, 44+2, 48, 49, 51+2, 61+2, 64, 66+2, 75+4, 77+2, 80+2, 83+2, 87+2, 88+2, 91, 96+3, 99

Years of Caution: Ages 9+2, 10+2, 17, 33+2, 39, 54+2, 55+2, 62, 78+2, 84, 99+2, 100+2

Years of Personal Challenge: Ages 2, 5, 10+2, 12, 13, 18, 19, 25, 32, 34, 37, 39, 42, 47, 50+2, 55, 57, 58, 64, 70+2, 79, 82, 85, 89+2, 92, 95, 100

Ascent to Pinnacle Years: Ages 35, 80

Pinnacle Years: Ages 38, 83

Most Blessed Years: Ages 40, 85

Years of Wish Fulfillment: Ages 11, 12, 20, 32, 56, 57, 65, 77

Years of Recognition, Fame, and Business Success: Ages 1, 4, 5, 9+2, 10+2, 11+3, 23, 31, 32+2, 33+3, 34+2, 36+2, 37+2, 38+2, 46, 49, 50, 56, 68, 76, 78, 80+2, 81+2, 82+2, 91, 94, 95

Years with Good Money Cards: Ages 5+2, 7+2, 12, 21, 50, 52+3, 56, 57, 62, 66, 95, 97+2

LIFE PATH AND THE THIRTEEN-YEAR CYCLE RULING CARDS FOR THE 2♦

MERCURY	VENUS	MARS	JUPITER	SATURN	URANUS	NEPTUNE
Ages 0–12	Ages 13–25	Ages 26–38	Ages 39–51	Ages 52–64	Ages 65–77	Ages 78–90
J♠	8♣	6♦	4♠	10♥	10♦	8♠

Notes:

The 2♦ has one of the best Life Paths that exist in terms of material success. Most of them achieve great financial success in life and are very enterprising. Many success cycles in early life are attributable to a sense of their own ability to achieve whatever they set their mind to. Years of particular success are at ages 9–11, 32–34, and 36–38. The power cards in the last two thirteen-year cycles insure that most 2♦ will retire with a lot of money and live to an old age. The 2♦ is also very fortunate to have four years in life in which the K♠ is their Long-Range Card. These are at ages 11, 34, 38, and 82.

Years that are particularly challenging occur at ages 5, 30, 35, 39, 50, 75, 80, 96, and 99.

Auspicious Years for the 3♦

Prebirth Years: Ages 44 and 89

Rebirth Years: Ages 45 and 90

Critical Year: Age 52

Purpose-Finding and Fated Years: Ages 1+2, 7, 9, 11, 13+2, 17, 28, 30, 32, 34, 44, 46+3, 54, 56, 58+2, 60, 62, 72, 73+2, 75, 77, 79+2, 87, 89, 91+2, 94, 97, 99

Years of Blessed Endings: Ages 2, 3, 12, 33, 44, 47, 52, 57, 78, 92, 93

Years of Difficult Endings: Ages 5, 6, 10+2, 12+2, 14+2, 22+3, 24, 26+2, 27+2, 29+2, 30, 33+2, 36+3, 40+3, 41+2, 43+2, 55+2, 57+2, 59+4, 69+2, 70, 72+2, 74+3, 75, 78+2, 81+2, 83, 85+2, 86+2, 88+2, 100+2

Years of Caution: Ages 0, 15+2, 36+2, 37+2, 60+2, 81+2, 82+2

Years of Personal Challenge: Ages 1, 2, 4, 7, 9, 14, 19, 20, 24, 28, 32, 37, 39, 49, 52+2, 53, 54, 64, 65, 67+2, 71, 77, 82, 84, 94, 97, 99

Ascent to Pinnacle Years: Ages 17, 62

Pinnacle Years: Ages 20, 65

Most Blessed Years: Ages 22, 67

Years of Wish Fulfillment: Ages 2, 14, 38, 39, 47, 59, 83, 84, 92

Years of Recognition, Fame, and Business Success: Ages 5, 13, 15, 28, 31, 32, 38, 40+2, 41+2, 50, 58, 60, 73, 76, 77, 83, 91+2, 92+2, 93+2, 95

Years with Good Money Cards: Ages 3, 8, 10, 20, 22, 23, 25, 29, 37, 48, 50, 53, 55, 59, 65, 67, 68, 70, 74, 82, 86, 93, 98, 100+2

LIFE PATH AND THE THIRTEEN-YEAR CYCLE RULING CARDS FOR THE 3♦

MERCURY	VENUS	MARS	JUPITER	SATURN	URANUS	NEPTUNE
Ages 0–12 A♠	Ages 13–25 7♥	Ages 26–38 7♦	Ages 39–51 5♠	Ages 52–64 J♥	Ages 65–77 9♣	Ages 78–90 9♠

Notes:

The 3♦ has one of the more challenging Life Paths. A glance at the cards above reveals mostly odd-numbered cards with two Sevens and two Nines, both considered to be the most difficult on the mundane and material level. The 3♦ person gets a taste of all these cards the first seven years of life, which molds their character for better or worse. Many tribulations of different sorts are common for them these first seven years. The period from ages 14–20 is much better and has a healing influence on their lives. They discover during this time that they have some qualities that they can be proud of. Age 17 begins their Ascent to the Pinnacle, and age 20 is their Pinnacle Year, all contributing to success and recognition by their peers. Ages 21–27 bring another host of challenges, but this time they have their past successes to help them get through it. Ages 35–41 ends on a high note again for them and brings additional success and recognition at ages 40 and 41. All in all, it is the degree of their spiritual inclinations that determines their success in life. This is one of the cards that must adopt a spiritual lifestyle to have any sort of happiness or accomplishment.

Particularly challenging years occur at ages 0, 22, 32, 36, 77, and 81.

Auspicious Years for the 4♦

Prebirth Years: Ages 44 and 89

Rebirth Years: Ages 45 and 90

Critical Year: Age 52

Purpose-Finding and Fated Years: Ages 2, 3, 4, 6, 8, 9, 14, 18, 19, 20, 21, 22, 23+2, 27, 28+2, 29, 30, 33, 35, 39, 41, 42, 43, 49, 51, 59, 63, 64, 65, 66+2, 67, 68, 72+2, 73, 75, 78, 80, 84, 86, 87, 88, 94, 96, 98

Years of Blessed Endings: Ages 2, 7+2, 17, 29, 34, 38, 41, 43, 52+2, 62, 74, 79, 83, 84, 86, 92, 97+2

Years of Difficult Endings: Ages 1+2, 6+2, 7+2, 9+2, 11, 12+2, 19+2, 25+2, 26+3, 28+2, 37+2, 38+2, 44+2, 46+2, 51+2, 52+3, 57+3, 62+2, 66+2, 67, 70+2, 71+2, 73+2, 82+3, 83+2, 86, 89+2, 91+2, 92, 96+2, 97+3, 99+2

Years of Caution: Ages 10+2, 17, 22, 26, 31+2, 32+2, 33, 55+2, 62, 64, 71, 76+2, 77+2, 78, 90, 100+2

Years of Personal Challenge: Ages 6, 7, 12, 14, 17, 18, 20, 21, 28, 32, 34+2, 35, 37, 42, 46, 51, 52, 53, 54, 59, 63+2, 64, 73, 77, 79+2, 87, 94, 96, 97, 100

Ascent to Pinnacle Years: Ages 12, 57

Pinnacle Years: Ages 15, 60

Most Blessed Years: Ages 17, 62

Years of Wish Fulfillment: Ages 9, 33, 34, 42, 54, 78, 79, 87, 99

Years of Recognition, Fame, and Business Success: Ages 0, 5+2, 6+2, 8, 10, 23, 26, 27, 33, 45, 53, 55, 56+2, 57+2, 58+2, 68, 71, 72, 76+2, 78, 84+2, 85+2, 90, 98, 100

Years with Good Money Cards: Ages 6, 14, 15, 28, 30+2, 43, 44, 47, 55, 60, 73, 74, 75+2, 88, 89

LIFE PATH AND THE THIRTEEN-YEAR CYCLE RULING CARDS FOR THE 4♦

MERCURY	VENUS	MARS	JUPITER	SATURN	URANUS	NEPTUNE
Ages 0–12	Ages 13–25	Ages 26–38	Ages 39–51	Ages 52–64	Ages 65–77	Ages 78–90
2♠	8♥	6♣	6♠	Q♥	10♣	8♦

Notes:

The 4♦ has a fairly fortunate Life Path in most respects, but it is the nature of their Birth Card to become mired in struggle to some extent in their life. Perhaps it is the 6♣ in Mars, which can represent the repression of aggressive energies. Whatever the case, they seem to attract situations that pile up the amount of work they must do day in and day out. Their card is somewhat well-situated with the last two cards in their Life Path ending up in the Crown Line. This speaks of some freedom in the later years of their life—freedom to travel and the money to do it. They often end up very independent at this stage of life. Ages 5 and 6 bring some form of attention or recognition, which contributes to their feeling that there is something important they can accomplish in this lifetime. Ages 7–13 bring many changes that contribute to their overall restlessness as adults. Age 29 can be a key year for them, as they have the opportunity to realize a higher purpose for their lives. Many of them step off the struggle cycle at that age and take up a career that brings more satisfaction. The seven years beginning at age 35 can be very productive and successful, provided they are willing to put in the hard work required. Finally, their second Pinnacle at ages 57–60, is accompanied by Seven-Year Cards in the Crown Line as well, making this perhaps the most successful time of life.

Years of particular caution for the 4♦ occur at ages 12, 26, 27, 28, 42, 52, 57, 62, 71, 72, 73, 82, and 87.

Auspicious Years for the 5♦

Prebirth Years: Ages 44 and 89

Rebirth Years: Ages 45 and 90

Critical Year: Age 52

Purpose-Finding and Fated Years: Ages 4, 7, 10, 14+2, 31+3, 35, 39+2, 41, 49, 52, 55+2, 59+2, 76+3, 77, 78, 80, 84, 86, 90, 94, 97, 100

Years of Blessed Endings: Ages 2, 7, 9, 10, 30, 33, 38, 44+2, 51, 52, 54, 75, 78, 83, 89+2, 92, 97, 99, 100

Years of Difficult Endings: Ages 1+2, 2, 11+2, 15+2, 17+3, 21, 23, 27+2, 28, 33, 36+2, 46+2, 52, 56+2, 60+2, 62, 70+3, 74+2, 81+3, 91+2

Years of Caution: Ages 7, 18+2, 23, 39+2, 40+2, 52, 63+2, 68, 84+2, 85+2, 97

Years of Personal Challenge: Ages 1, 3, 15, 20, 22, 25, 29+2, 31, 38, 40, 42+2, 45, 46, 51, 62, 67, 69, 71, 72, 74, 75, 76, 80, 83+2, 85, 86, 87, 91+2

Ascent to Pinnacle Years: Ages 20, 65

Pinnacle Years: Ages 23, 68

Most Blessed Years: Ages 25, 70

Years of Wish Fulfillment: Ages 5, 17, 41, 42, 50, 62, 86, 87, 95

Years of Recognition, Fame, and Business Success: Ages 8, 16, 18, 31, 34, 35, 41, 53, 61+3, 62+2, 63, 76, 79, 80, 86, 98

Years with Good Money Cards: Ages 5, 6, 17, 20, 22, 35, 36, 38, 43, 50, 51, 58, 62, 65, 67, 81, 83, 88, 89, 95, 96

LIFE PATH AND THE THIRTEEN-YEAR CYCLE RULING CARDS FOR THE 5♦

MERCURY	VENUS	MARS	JUPITER	SATURN	URANUS	NEPTUNE
Ages 0–12	Ages 13–25	Ages 26–38	Ages 39–51	Ages 52–64	Ages 65–77	Ages 78–90
Q♠	J♣	9♦	7♠	2♣	K♣	J♦

Notes:

With all of the Life Path Cards in the Uranus line of the Grand Solar Spread, most of the 5♦ issues in life are associated with their need for personal freedom and individuality. Some of these cards are challenging, but overall, they have much to be grateful for. The Mars thirteen-year cycle is particularly challenging, because the 9♦ that rules it is also their first Karma Card, which represents some of their lifetime challenges. During that period, there seem to be many losses as they let go of past life patterns that are holding them back. This pattern began in childhood where most of their expressions of aggressiveness and competitiveness met with defeat or disappointment. During the ages 7–13, their Birth Card displaces this same 9♦ causing some challenging situations in the same area, but with more or less fortunate cards overall. In other words, they have many successes at this time, as well as challenges. At ages 35–41, their prosperity increases and they often find a niche for themselves that fits as well as provides a stable income. Ages 42–55 are a particularly restless period where moves and changes are more common. At age 56, they enter a seven-year period that often ends with some degree of recognition and reward. Much in the way of self-mastery is achieved at this time as well.

Years of significant challenges for the 5♦ include those at ages 7, 21, 22, 23, 52, 67, 77, 80, and 81.

Auspicious Years for the 6♦

Prebirth Years: Ages 44 and 89

Rebirth Years: Ages 45 and 90

Critical Year: Age 52

Purpose-Finding and Fated Years: Ages 0+2, 7, 9, 10, 12, 17, 21, 24, 28+2, 32, 35, 38, 40, 45+2, 54, 55, 62, 66, 69, 73, 80, 83, 85, 90+2, 93, 95, 99, 100

Years of Blessed Endings: Ages 2, 11, 13, 19+2, 23, 30, 37, 42, 44, 47, 56, 58, 64+2, 68, 75, 78, 86, 87, 89, 92

Years of Difficult Endings: Ages 1+2, 3+2, 9, 13+2, 20, 22+2, 23, 25, 32+2, 42+2, 46+2, 56+2, 60+2, 67+2, 70, 71, 77+2, 80, 86, 87+2, 91+2, 93+2, 98

Years of Caution: Ages 4+2, 5, 13, 16, 25+3, 26+2, 30, 44, 49+2, 50, 58, 61, 69, 70+3, 71+2, 75, 85, 89, 94+2, 95

Years of Personal Challenge: Ages 6, 7, 8, 10, 11, 15, 19+2, 26, 28, 39, 40+2, 43, 48, 51, 52, 53, 58, 64+2, 68, 71, 73, 84, 85, 88, 89, 90, 96, 97, 98

Ascent to Pinnacle Years: Ages 6, 51, 96

Pinnacle Years: Ages 9, 54, 99

Most Blessed Years: Ages 11, 56

Years of Wish Fulfillment: Ages 3, 27, 28, 36, 48, 72, 73, 81, 93

Years of Recognition, Fame, and Business Success: Ages 2, 4, 14+2, 15+2, 16+2, 17, 20, 21, 27, 34+2, 39, 42+2, 43+2, 47, 49, 62, 63+2, 65, 66, 72, 84, 92, 94

Years with Good Money Cards: Ages 2+2, 5, 17, 26, 32, 34, 36+2, 37, 38, 43, 44, 47, 50, 54, 62, 71, 74, 77, 79, 81+2, 82, 88, 89, 92, 95

LIFE PATH AND THE THIRTEEN-YEAR CYCLE RULING CARDS FOR THE 6♦

MERCURY	VENUS	MARS	JUPITER	SATURN	URANUS	NEPTUNE
Ages 0–12	Ages 13–25	Ages 26–38	Ages 39–51	Ages 52–64	Ages 65–77	Ages 78–90
4♠	10♥	10♦	8♠	A♥	A♦	Q♦

Notes:

The 6♦ have one of the more fortunate Life Paths tempered by their willingness to put in the necessary work to achieve their goals and dreams. There are many opportunities and good things to be grateful for, as seen by the cards governing their first four thirteen-year cycles. The Mars cycle is particularly blessed since the 10♦ sits in the Most Blessed Spot in the Grand Solar Spread. There is protection and the possibility of many of their dreams coming to pass. The first seven years of life are pretty good, but the years from ages 7–13 can often be somewhat traumatic. The 6♠, 7♠, and 9♠ governing ages 8, 10, and 11 respectively can indicate challenging experiences and events that can dampen the 6♦ enthusiasm. Some develop a sense of powerlessness during this period, while others engage their strong competitive drive to help deal with it in a more constructive way. Ages 14–16 provide a welcome boost of success and recognition that help mitigate the earlier experiences. The period from ages 21–27 is often fortunate as well, though many of them have to work very hard at this time. Age 32 is a significantly powerful year when their life may undergo a large-scale change. Similar influences exist at ages 4 and 49. Care should be taken those years, as events can go to extremes for good or bad. At the end of the seven-year cycle that begins at age 28, the 6♦ often achieves some measure of success and recognition. The 6♦ is also fortunate to have three years in life in which the K♠ is their Long-Range Card. These are at ages 16, 43, and 63.

Years of stronger influences of a challenging nature include those at ages 7, 23, 25, 44, 70, 71, 80, 85, 89, and 95.

Auspicious Years for the 7♦

Prebirth Years: Ages 44 and 89

Rebirth Years: Ages 45 and 90

Purpose-Finding and Fated Years: Ages 19, 27, 36, 43, 46, 47, 52, 53, 54, 55, 60, 62, 64, 67, 71, 81, 82, 90

Years of Blessed Endings: Ages 0, 4, 11, 14, 21, 41, 55, 65, 66, 80+2, 87, 90, 94

Years of Difficult Endings: Ages 2, 3, 31+2, 34+2, 45+2, 48+2, 49, 55+2, 56, 58+2, 63+2, 64, 65, 77+2, 87+2, 100

Years of Caution: Ages 7, 10, 11, 26, 34, 39, 53, 97, 100

Years of Personal Challenge: Ages 11, 22, 36, 49, 51, 52, 54, 69, 72, 81, 83, 84, 98

Years with Good Money Cards: Ages 9, 31, 33, 56, 58, 70, 72, 77, 79, 89, 97

LIFE PATH AND THE THIRTEEN-YEAR CYCLE RULING CARDS FOR THE 7♦

MERCURY	VENUS	MARS	JUPITER	SATURN	URANUS	NEPTUNE
Ages 0–12	Ages 13–25	Ages 26–38	Ages 39–51	Ages 52–64	Ages 65–77	Ages 78–90
5♠	J♥	9♣	9♠	2♥	K♥	K♦

Notes:

7♦ people usually come in two varieties—one that is very successful and one that isn't. Those in the second group worry about money a great deal, while the first group know that their needs are always provided if they just attend to their work. The two Nines in the Life Path, along with the J♥ in Venus, give them many experiences from early childhood that teach them the importance of giving to others and letting go. This is a spiritual card, and only those who take up a spiritual approach to life succeed happily. They also share some of the karma of their sibling, the 9♥, with whom they are intimately connected. Every other year they move back and forth between the Venus/Venus to the Saturn/Saturn positions in the Grand Solar Spread. This is like going to extreme ends of the pendulum every year, and often their life reflects this. Look at the cycles and movements of their Planetary Ruling Card for specific times when success and recognition may appear in their lives.

Every other year, the 7♦ has the 2♥ in Saturn. This occurs because of the nature of its semi-fixed movement. Every sixteen years, beginning at age 4, the 7♦ person falls in a Saturn year with the 2♥ Long-Range as well. This unusual pattern is found in no other card except the 9♥ who does essentially the same thing with the A♣ (see Age Eleven Spread). For the 7♦, this speaks to often repeated trials in intimate relationships.

Years with very significant challenging influence combinations include those at ages 11, 34, 87, and 100.

Auspicious Years for the 8♦

Prebirth Years: Ages 44 and 89

Rebirth Years: Ages 45 and 90

Critical Year: Age 52

Purpose-Finding and Fated Years: Ages 8, 9, 12, 19, 21, 22, 26, 33+2, 36, 37, 43, 49, 53, 54, 57, 64, 67+2, 68, 71, 74, 78, 81, 82, 84, 88, 90, 98, 99+2

Years of Blessed Endings: Ages 3, 8+2, 9, 13+2, 15, 20, 22, 24, 27, 32+2, 39, 40, 48, 53+2, 54, 58+2, 60, 65, 67, 72, 73, 77, 84, 85, 93, 98+2, 99

Years of Difficult Endings: Ages 2+2, 6+2, 12+2, 13+2, 23+2, 24, 26, 32+2, 33+2, 34, 37+2, 39+2, 43, 46, 49+2, 57+2, 58+2, 59, 68+2, 77+2, 78+2, 82+2, 88, 92+2, 94, 96+2, 100

Years of Caution: Ages 0, 9, 16+2, 17+2, 38, 40+2, 45, 48, 54, 61+2, 62+2, 85+2, 90, 99

Years of Personal Challenge: Ages 4, 5, 17, 19+2, 23, 29, 34, 36, 40+2, 44, 47, 50, 51, 62, 64, 68, 69, 79, 84, 85, 89, 94, 95

Ascent to Pinnacle Years: Ages 42, 87

Pinnacle Years: Ages 0, 45, 90

Most Blessed Years: Ages 2, 47, 92

Years of Wish Fulfillment: Ages 18, 19, 27, 39, 63, 64, 72, 84

Years of Recognition, Fame, and Business Success: Ages 0+2, 8, 11, 12, 18, 30, 38, 40, 53, 56, 57, 58+2, 59+2, 60+2, 63, 75, 81+2, 82+2, 83+3, 85+3, 86+2, 87+2, 98

Years with Good Money Cards: Ages 0, 28, 43, 45, 55, 73, 76, 88, 90

LIFE PATH AND THE THIRTEEN-YEAR CYCLE RULING CARDS FOR THE 8♦

MERCURY	VENUS	MARS	JUPITER	SATURN	URANUS	NEPTUNE
Ages 0–12 K♠	Ages 13–25 3♥	Ages 26–38 A♣	Ages 39–51 Q♣	Ages 52–64 10♠	Ages 65–77 5♣	Ages 78–90 3♦

Notes:

Being the 'Sun Card,' the 8♦ person sits in the Crown Line their entire life in a manner of speaking. The first seven years are under that influence, and this embeds a feeling of 'specialness' to each 8♦ person that stays with them throughout life. There are few challenging influences the first twenty-one years of life, and the third seven-year cycle finds them sitting in the Most Blessed Spot the entire time from ages 14–20. Age 19 is the first occurrence of a combination of challenging influences in their life. With this good foundation, the 8♦ person is well-equipped to deal with whatever challenges may occur for the rest of their life. But let's not forget their lifetime Pluto Card, the A♠. This tells us that all of them must undergo one or more challenging personal transformations during the lifetime. Occurrences of the A♠ and 9♠ in the Yearly Spreads may indicate the particular times. At age 24, for example, their 9♠ Long-Range Card displaces the A♠ in the Grand Solar Spread. This is one year where such a transformation is highly possible.

The 8♦ is very fortunate to have four years in life in which the K♠ is their Long-Range Card. These are at ages 0, 60, 83, and 87.

Auspicious Years for the 9♦

Prebirth Years: Ages 44 and 89

Rebirth Years: Ages 45 and 90

Critical Year: Age 52

Purpose-Finding and Fated Years: Ages 0, 2, 3, 10, 11, 13+2, 15, 25, 30, 31, 32, 34, 37, 39, 40, 42, 45, 47, 48, 55, 56, 58+2, 60, 61, 69, 70, 75, 76, 77, 79, 85, 87, 90, 92, 93, 100

Years of Blessed Endings: Ages 0, 5, 6, 10, 23, 31, 45, 46, 51, 54, 55, 68, 76, 90, 95, 96, 100

Years of Difficult Endings: Ages 0+2, 4+2, 13+2, 14+2, 15+2, 21+2, 24+2, 25+2, 28+2, 31+2, 32, 35+4, 38, 44, 45+2, 49+2, 58+2, 59+2, 60+2, 61+2, 66+2, 70+3, 71+2, 76+2, 80+4, 84, 90+2, 94+2, 95

Years of Caution: Ages 6, 13, 14, 17+2, 33, 38+2, 39+2, 44, 46, 51, 58, 59, 62+2, 78, 83+2, 84+2, 89, 96

Years of Personal Challenge: Ages 0, 3, 6, 8, 10, 16+2, 21, 22, 26+2, 37, 38, 39+2, 41, 48, 51, 53, 66, 67, 69, 71, 73, 78, 82, 83, 84+2, 86, 92, 93, 96, 98+2

Ascent to Pinnacle Years: Ages 19, 64

Pinnacle Years: Ages 22, 67

Most Blessed Years: Ages 24, 69

Years of Wish Fulfillment: Ages 4, 16, 40, 41, 49, 61, 85, 86, 94

Years of Recognition, Fame, and Business Success: Ages 7, 15, 17, 30, 33, 34, 40, 52, 54+2, 55+2, 60, 62, 75, 78, 79, 85, 97

Years with Good Money Cards: Ages 5, 10, 13, 21+2, 23, 24, 26, 40, 50, 55, 64, 66+2, 68, 69, 71, 73, 79, 85, 95, 100+2

LIFE PATH AND THE THIRTEEN-YEAR CYCLE RULING CARDS FOR THE 9♦

MERCURY	VENUS	MARS	JUPITER	SATURN	URANUS	NEPTUNE
Ages 0–12	Ages 13–25	Ages 26–38	Ages 39–51	Ages 52–64	Ages 65–77	Ages 78–90
7♠	2♣	K♣	J♦	4♥	4♦	2♠

Notes:

The 9♦ has a fairly fortunate Life Path in normal terms. But being a Nine Birth Card has inherent challenges along personal lines—the need to let go of certain things. This often results in losses and disappointments in life regardless of the seeming good fortune of the cards present in the time periods. Ages 0 and 6 have combinations of challenging influences that can affect the developing personality of the 9♦ child. However, they end up with special gifts and abilities along mental and material lines that carry them through life on a more or less high note. The seven-year cycle that begins at age 28 is one of the more fortunate, having Jupiterian protection and blessings influencing it. The first Pinnacle year, at age 22, shows many of them that they do have the potential to achieve something of measure in their life. Another brush with the Crown Line occurs at ages 54 and 55 and often comes with a measure of recognition and reward. But the 9♦ has less interaction with the Crown Line than most cards, and many of these people prefer to work behind the scenes instead of in front of the public eye.

Their families are often the source of some of their most important challenges because of the 4♥ in Saturn in their Life Path. Ages 17 and 62 are years when these issues come to a head. Other years of significantly challenging influence combinations include those at ages 6, 13, 14, 21, 31, 35, 38, 39, 41, 44, 58, 59, 66, 70, 76, 80, 83, 84, 86, and 96, many more than most cards in the deck.

Auspicious Years for the 10♦

Prebirth Years: Ages 44 and 89

Rebirth Years: Ages 45 and 90

Critical Year: Age 52

Purpose-Finding and Fated Years: Ages 1, 6, 10, 11, 17, 21, 23+2, 24, 34, 35, 38, 39, 44+2, 46, 51, 55, 56+2, 66, 68+2, 69, 79, 80, 84+2, 89, 91, 96, 100

Years of Blessed Endings: Ages 10, 17, 21, 22, 24, 27, 29, 30, 32, 33, 34, 36, 55, 62, 66, 69, 71, 72, 74, 77, 78, 79, 81, 100

Years of Difficult Endings: Ages 0+2, 2+2, 4+2, 7+2, 11+2, 12, 14+2, 16, 17+2, 18, 21+2, 24+2, 32, 35+2, 36+2, 37+2, 42+2, 47+4, 52+2, 56+2, 59+2, 62+2, 66+2, 69+2, 80+2, 81+2, 87+2, 90+2, 92+2, 94+2, 97+2

Years of Caution: Ages 1, 11+2, 14+2, 15+2, 24, 25, 34, 38+2, 39, 46, 56, 59+2, 60+2, 69, 70, 79, 81, 83+2, 84, 91

Years of Personal Challenge: Ages 2, 3, 13, 15, 17, 21, 26, 30, 38, 42, 45, 48, 49, 50, 51, 55, 58, 60, 62, 64, 66, 82, 83, 87, 92, 93, 94, 99, 100

Ascent to Pinnacle Years: Ages 40, 85

Pinnacle Years: Ages 43, 88

Most Blessed Years: Ages 0, 45, 90

Years of Wish Fulfillment: Ages 16, 17, 25, 37, 61, 62, 70, 82

Years of Recognition, Fame, and Business Success: Ages 6, 9, 10, 16, 28, 36, 38, 44+2, 45+2, 46+2, 51, 54, 55, 61, 67+2, 68+2, 69+2, 71+2, 72+2, 73+3, 81, 83, 96, 99, 100

Years with Good Money Cards: Ages 0, 2, 26, 45, 47, 61, 71, 90, 92

LIFE PATH AND THE THIRTEEN-YEAR CYCLE RULING CARDS FOR THE 10♦

MERCURY	VENUS	MARS	JUPITER	SATURN	URANUS	NEPTUNE
Ages 0–12	Ages 13–25	Ages 26–38	Ages 39–51	Ages 52–64	Ages 65–77	Ages 78–90
8♠	A♥	A♦	Q♦	5♥	3♣	3♠

Notes:

The 10♦ spends their entire life in the Most Blessed Spot, surrounded on all sides by Jupiter's blessings. It is no wonder that they seem to pull through the most difficult situations without a scratch. It is no guarantee of happiness, but they do have a lot more than most to be grateful for. It is inherently a past life spiritual blessing that protects them, and those who realize the importance of the spiritual side of life will reap those benefits the most. The protection begins at birth even though they do have some challenging influences in that first seven years. With the double Aces and the 5♥ in Saturn, they begin their quest for self-fulfillment that becomes a dominant theme in their lives. That theme becomes much more prominent from ages 21–34 when they displace the two Aces for seven years each. Some success and recognition is realized at ages 43–46 with cards of popularity and fame from the Crown Line's influence. Another very fortunate period begins in this same regard at age 63 and lasts until age 74. If they live that long, these could be their crowning years. The 10♦ is also fortunate to have three years in life in which the K♠ is their Long-Range Card. These are at ages 46, 69, and 73.

Years with notable combinations of challenging influences include those at ages 11, 14, 17, 24, 55, 56, 59, 62, 69, and 81.

Auspicious Years for the J♦

Prebirth Years: Ages 44 and 89

Rebirth Years: Ages 45 and 90

Critical Year: Age 52

Purpose-Finding and Fated Years: Ages 2, 4, 5+2, 8+2, 19, 22, 23, 24, 26+2, 37, 38+2, 40, 41, 43, 44, 47, 48, 50, 53+2, 64, 67, 68, 69, 70, 71+3, 82, 83, 86, 88, 92, 95, 96, 98+2

Years of Blessed Endings: Ages 9, 10, 11+2, 14, 15, 18, 21, 29, 36, 39, 42, 54, 55, 56+2, 59, 60, 63, 66, 74, 80, 81, 87, 88, 99, 100

Years of Difficult Endings: Ages 3+4, 5+2, 15+2, 24+2, 25, 28+2, 30+2, 34+2, 35, 39+3, 43+2, 48+4, 56, 58+2, 62+2, 66, 69+2, 72, 73+3, 75+2, 79+2, 80, 84+2, 88+2, 92, 93+4, 95+2

Years of Caution: Ages 6+2, 13, 23, 25, 27+2, 28+2, 29, 38, 51+2, 58, 68, 70, 72+2, 73+2, 74, 83, 95, 96+2

Years of Personal Challenge: Ages 7+2, 8, 10, 13, 16, 17, 21, 24, 28, 30, 33, 37, 39, 42, 50, 52, 53+2, 54, 55, 60, 61, 66, 73, 75, 82+2, 84, 87, 97, 98, 100

Ascent to Pinnacle Years: Ages 8, 53, 98

Pinnacle Years: Ages 11, 56

Most Blessed Years: Ages 13, 58

Years of Wish Fulfillment: Ages 5, 29, 30, 38, 50, 74, 75, 83, 95

Years of Recognition, Fame, and Business Success: Ages 4, 6, 19, 22, 23, 28+2, 29+3, 30+2, 41, 48+2, 49, 51, 56+2, 57+2, 64, 67, 68, 74, 77+2, 86, 94, 96

Years with Good Money Cards: Ages 0, 1, 4, 6, 10, 14, 16, 20, 24, 31, 32, 34+2, 39, 45+2, 46, 49, 51+2, 59, 65, 68, 69, 76, 77, 79+2, 84, 90, 91, 94, 96

LIFE PATH AND THE THIRTEEN-YEAR CYCLE RULING CARDS FOR THE J♦

MERCURY	VENUS	MARS	JUPITER	SATURN	URANUS	NEPTUNE
Ages 0–12	Ages 13–25	Ages 26–38	Ages 39–51	Ages 52–64	Ages 65–77	Ages 78–90
4♥	4♦	2♠	8♥	6♣	6♠	Q♥

Notes:

The J♦ has a fortunate Life Path overall, but the double Sixes can indicate stagnation at certain points in life. Moreover, every card falls in the Neptune line of the Grand Solar Spread making the issues of ideals, dreams, illusions, and caretaking common for these people. Their life is based upon these factors for better or worse. The childhood is one of protection and security overall, though events at ages 5 and 7 may be difficult. The J♦ reaches the first Pinnacle Year at age 11. This can mean that they excel at school for a while and have a lot of popularity or merely that they go through a big change at that age. The cycle from ages 21–27 can be trying, especially those years at ages 23–26 where a host of losses and challenges present themselves in succession. But immediately following that cycle, we have four years, from ages 28–31 that are especially good, often bringing rewards and recognition of various kinds. This leads them into another hard-working but successful cycle from ages 35–41. However, the J♦ has its best years in the latter stages of life. Ages 56–72 are especially good and if they live long enough, ages 77–83 bring the highest rewards. The J♦ is also fortunate to have three years in life in which the K♠ is their Long-Range Card. These are at ages 30, 57, and 77. Age 38 can be a year of major realization and positive transformation.

Years of particularly challenging combinations of influences include those at ages 13, 23, 24, 25, 44, 58, 68, 69, 72, 73, 89, and 95.

Auspicious Years for the Q♦

Prebirth Years: Ages 44 and 89

Rebirth Years: Ages 45 and 90

Critical Year: Age 52

Purpose-Finding and Fated Years: Ages 2, 12+3, 13, 16, 29+2, 33+2, 43+2, 47+2, 57+2, 61, 73, 74, 78+2, 82, 83, 88, 90, 92

Years of Blessed Endings: Ages 0+2, 1+2, 8, 11, 16, 19, 24+2, 28+2, 30, 32, 34, 45, 46+2, 49, 56, 61, 64, 69+2, 73+2, 75, 77, 79, 90+2, 91+2, 98

Years of Difficult Endings: Ages 3, 9, 13+4, 15+2, 25+2, 30, 34+2, 40+2, 44+2, 54, 58+4, 62, 68+2, 72+2, 79+2, 85+2, 89+2, 95

Years of Caution: Ages 8+2, 16+2, 33, 35, 37+2, 38+2, 53, 60, 61+2, 78, 82+2, 83+2, 98

Years of Personal Challenge: Ages 0, 4, 5, 12, 20+2, 23, 27+3, 29, 31, 32, 37, 38, 39, 40, 43, 44, 45, 50, 55, 57, 60, 65+2, 70, 72, 74, 77+2, 83, 85, 88, 89, 90, 95

Ascent to Pinnacle Years: Ages 18, 63

Pinnacle Years: Ages 21, 66

Most Blessed Years: Ages 23, 68

Years of Wish Fulfillment: Ages 3, 15, 39, 40, 48, 60, 84, 85, 93

Years of Recognition, Fame, and Business Success: Ages 6, 14, 16, 29, 32, 33, 39, 47+2, 48+2, 51, 59, 61, 74, 77, 78, 84, 96, 98+2, 99+2, 100+2

Years with Good Money Cards: Ages 3, 4, 7, 15, 22, 24, 34, 36, 40, 41, 44, 48, 49, 52, 60, 67, 69, 75, 79, 81, 85, 86, 91, 93, 94, 97

LIFE PATH AND THE THIRTEEN-YEAR CYCLE RULING CARDS FOR THE Q♦

MERCURY	VENUS	MARS	JUPITER	SATURN	URANUS	NEPTUNE
Ages 0–12 5♥	Ages 13–25 3♣	Ages 26–38 3♠	Ages 39–51 9♥	Ages 52–64 7♣	Ages 65–77 5♦	Ages 78–90 Q♠

Notes:

The Q♦ has a Life Path with great potential but also an abundance of challenges and negative karma to deal with. All but one of the Life Path Cards falls in the Saturn line, promising one challenge after another and the necessity to learn the laws of life in most every department. There is generally much traveling or many moves in childhood that contribute to a similar restless nature as an adult. There is often financial limitation in childhood, especially in the second seven years of life, which is why most Q♦ have a sense of lack that must be dealt with. Life is very changeable and presents much variety until around age 39 when they enter the Jupiter thirteen-year period governed by the 9♥. Since the 9♥ is more of a stable influence, their lives often settle down at that point. The Q♦ reaches the first Pinnacle Year at age 21, demonstrating that they have immense potential. This first Pinnacle often represents a big change in life as well that sets them on a higher path. Ages 28–41 bring many changes of residence and relationships, but as mentioned earlier, they often settle down at the end of that cycle, which also brings some financial rewards at ages 40 and 41 that are quite outstanding in some cases. The cycle at ages 42–48 can bring additional recognition and reward. Many of their dreams are realized during their second Ascent to the Pinnacle and Pinnacle at ages 63–66.

Years with challenging combinations of influences include those at ages 8, 13, 33, 37, 40, 58, 78, 85, and 95.

Auspicious Years for the K♦

Prebirth Years: Ages 44 and 89

Rebirth Years: Ages 45 and 90

Critical Year: Age 52

Purpose-Finding and Fated Years: Ages 0, 5, 6, 8, 12, 16, 19, 22, 27, 29, 33, 36, 37+2, 38, 39, 41, 48, 50, 51, 53, 57+2, 61, 63, 64, 71, 74, 78+2, 82+2, 84, 88, 96, 98+2

Years of Blessed Endings: Ages 4, 7, 12, 25+2, 28, 39, 42, 44, 52, 53, 70+2, 73, 84, 87, 89, 94, 97

Years of Difficult Endings: Ages 2+2, 3+4, 8+2, 9+2, 12+2, 16+2, 17+2, 18, 19+2, 20+2, 25, 29+2, 30+2, 31, 36+2, 37, 38+2, 42+2, 44, 47+2, 48+4, 53+2, 54+2, 57+2, 60, 61+2, 62+2, 65+2, 67, 68, 72+2, 75+2, 76+2, 81+2, 83+2, 87+2, 92+2, 93+4, 98

Years of Caution: Ages 11, 12, 20+2, 21, 37, 40, 41+2, 42+3, 56, 57, 65+2, 82, 85, 86+2, 87+3, 99

Years of Personal Challenge: Ages 8, 14, 17, 24, 27, 29, 31, 40, 42, 44, 56, 59, 64, 65, 69, 74, 85, 87, 89+2, 97

Ascent to Pinnacle Years: Ages 22, 67

Pinnacle Years: Ages 25, 70

Most Blessed Years: Ages 27, 72

Years of Wish Fulfillment: Ages 7, 19, 43, 44, 52, 64, 88, 89, 97

Years of Recognition, Fame, and Business Success: Ages 10, 18, 20, 33, 36, 37, 43, 55, 63, 65, 75+2, 76+2, 78, 81, 82, 88, 100

Years with Good Money Cards: Ages 0, 8, 10, 11, 18, 20, 29, 31, 36, 45, 49, 53, 55, 63, 65, 73, 74, 76, 79, 81, 90, 93, 98, 100

LIFE PATH AND THE THIRTEEN-YEAR CYCLE RULING CARDS FOR THE K♦

MERCURY	VENUS	MARS	JUPITER	SATURN	URANUS	NEPTUNE
Ages 0–12	Ages 13–25	Ages 26–38	Ages 39–51	Ages 52–64	Ages 65–77	Ages 78–90
6♥	4♣	2♦	J♠	8♣	6♦	4♠

Notes:

The K♦ has one of the more fortunate Life Paths. All of the cards are even numbers, numerologically, and even the Saturn Card is one of power and success. Success on the material plane is indicated coming from a fairly good childhood and karma. The first seven years are generally stable, and while the next fourteen years present some changes and insecurities, they are not that severe. There are often losses and disappointments from ages 20–27. This is also when the K♦ reaches their first Pinnacle, so they may also expect some success and recognition to accompany the challenges they go through. Ages 20, 42, 65, and 87 are ones with very strong influences of endings that do not come easily. Caution should be exercised in those years more than any others. The first Pinnacle Year is often one of big transition for them, having a 9♣ Long-Range and Result. The second Pinnacle Year is usually the best for recognition and reward, as it is accompanied by Crown Line influences from the Long-Range Cards as well.

Other years with challenging combinations of influences for the K♦ person include those at ages 12, 37, 40, 56, 57, 82, 85, and 99.

Auspicious Years for the A♠

Prebirth Years: Ages 44 and 89

Rebirth Years: Ages 45 and 90

Critical Year: Age 52

Purpose-Finding and Fated Years: Ages 4, 8, 10+2, 11, 16, 19, 20, 21, 25, 26, 28, 30, 34, 35, 37, 41, 49+2, 50, 53, 55, 60, 64+2, 65, 70, 73, 74, 75, 79, 80, 82, 83, 86, 91, 94, 98, 100

Years of Blessed Endings: Ages 3+2, 6, 8, 15, 16, 24, 31, 38, 48+2, 51, 57, 60, 69, 76, 83, 93+2, 96, 98

Years of Difficult Endings: Ages 0+2, 4, 5, 7+3, 10+2, 13, 21+2, 23+2, 24, 29, 33+4, 34, 42+2, 44+2, 45+3, 52+2, 54, 55+2, 57, 59, 65, 66+2, 76+2, 78+2, 80+2, 84, 87+2, 89+2, 90+2, 97+2, 100+2

Years of Caution: Ages 0+2, 1+3, 24+2, 44, 45+2, 46+3, 69+2, 89, 90+2, 91+3

Years of Personal Challenge: Ages 0, 1+3, 3, 12, 15, 16, 17, 26, 28, 31, 35, 36, 38, 39, 44, 46+2, 48, 57, 60, 61, 62, 68, 70, 71, 73, 78, 84, 87, 88, 91+2, 93+2

Ascent to Pinnacle Years: Ages 26, 71

Pinnacle Years: Ages 29, 74

Most Blessed Years: Ages 31, 76

Years of Wish Fulfillment: Ages 2, 3, 11, 23, 47, 48, 56, 68, 92, 93

Years of Recognition, Fame, and Business Success: Ages 2, 14, 17+2, 18+2, 19+2, 22, 24, 37, 40, 41, 47, 59, 67, 69, 82, 85, 86, 92

Years with Good Money Cards: Ages 12, 14, 16, 18, 20, 35, 37, 57, 59, 61, 63, 80, 82

LIFE PATH AND THE THIRTEEN-YEAR CYCLE RULING CARDS FOR THE A♠

MERCURY	VENUS	MARS	JUPITER	SATURN	URANUS	NEPTUNE
Ages 0–12	Ages 13–25	Ages 26–38	Ages 39–51	Ages 52–64	Ages 65–77	Ages 78–90
7♥	7♦	5♠	J♥	9♣	9♠	2♥

Notes:

A quick glance at the A♠ Life Path reveals two Sevens and two Nines—spiritual challenges throughout life that begin at an early age. Remember that we experience all of the cards in our Life Path both in the first year of life where each one governs a fifty-two-day period and in the first seven years of life where each card is the Long-Range Card. These Sevens and Nines produce challenges and losses that mold the character of the A♠ early on, often producing a sense of tragedy about their personal lives that they carry with them into adulthood. Only spiritual understanding can conquer these apparent losses, and many of them are drawn to spiritual study at an early age. The first fourteen years are often very difficult. Though there are some successes too, some form of personal tragedy is bound to occur. Ages 4, 5, 10, and 11 stand out for the intensity of the challenging aspects presented. Then, at age 14, they enter a very fortunate cycle that brings success and recognition. Since this occurs in the high school and college years, they often associate success with academic accomplishment from then on. They have a generally successful life until they reach their first Pinnacle (age 29) where they often undergo a dramatic change in life. At this point, some of their childhood issues may resurface to be dealt with or worked on. However, that seven-year cycle, which extends from age 28–34 is a good one overall, and more successes can be expected. From ages 35–48 there can be many changes and a measure of uncertainty with it. The first set of Prebirth and Rebirth Years are ones in which significant endings and challenges present themselves. Once the A♠ adopts a spiritual lifestyle, all of the materially challenging cards that seem to follow them around turn into blessings and valuable lessons that lead them to self-fulfillment and peace of mind. They are, at heart, one of the most spiritual cards in the deck.

Years that present the A♠ with strong combinations of challenging influences include those at ages 0, 1, 15, 44, 45, 46, 57, 60, 84, 86, 87, 89, 90, and 91.

Auspicious Years for the 2♠

Prebirth Years: Ages 44 and 89

Rebirth Years: Ages 45 and 90

Critical Year: Age 52

Purpose-Finding and Fated Years: Ages 1+2, 2, 3, 15+2, 20, 25, 30+2, 31, 35, 36, 37, 40, 42, 44, 46, 48+2, 58, 60, 65, 70, 73, 74, 75, 79, 80, 81, 87, 89, 91, 92, 93

Years of Blessed Endings: Ages 17, 19, 32, 33, 43, 58, 64, 66, 77, 78, 88

Years of Difficult Endings: Ages 2+2, 7, 9+2, 12+2, 22, 26+2, 36+3, 40+2, 43+2, 47+2, 54+2, 57+2, 71+3, 73+2, 75, 76, 83+3, 88+2, 92+2, 99+2

Years of Caution: Ages 5+2, 6+2, 22, 29+3, 50+2, 51+2, 67, 74+3, 91, 95+2, 96+2

Years of Personal Challenge: Ages 6, 8, 9, 19, 21, 23, 26, 28, 31, 32, 33, 38, 42, 44, 51, 53, 63, 64, 68, 71, 76, 77, 78, 81, 82, 85, 89, 90, 94, 96, 98, 100

Ascent to Pinnacle Years: Ages 31, 76

Pinnacle Years: Ages 34, 79

Most Blessed Years: Ages 36, 81

Years of Wish Fulfillment: Ages 7, 8, 16, 28, 52, 53, 61, 73, 97, 98

Years of Recognition, Fame, and Business Success: Ages 0, 1, 4+2, 5+2, 6+2, 7, 8+2, 9+2, 10+2, 19, 27, 29, 42, 45, 46, 52+3, 53+2, 54+2, 64, 72, 74, 87, 90, 91, 97

Years with Good Money Cards: Ages 5, 9, 11, 13, 14, 17, 32, 37, 41, 54, 56, 57, 59, 62, 77, 82, 86, 98, 99

Life Path and the Thirteen-Year Cycle Ruling Cards for the 2♠

Mercury	Venus	Mars	Jupiter	Saturn	Uranus	Neptune
Ages 0–12	Ages 13–25	Ages 26–38	Ages 39–51	Ages 52–64	Ages 65–77	Ages 78–90
8♥	6♣	6♠	Q♥	10♣	8♦	K♠

Notes:

The 2♠ has a fortunate Life Path in most respects, and it is only their own inertia that stands between them and any sort of success they choose. Materially speaking, there is no real excuse for any problems. The childhood is often one with a lot of success and popularity among school mates and friends. They often excel in school and thus guarantee themselves a good position in adult life. There are cautions with this card, especially in the areas of health where they do not get away with any abuse of their bodies. But on the mundane level, they have most everything they could want. The two seven-year cycles at ages 14–20 and 35–41 bring some challenging endings or losses in their life and upset their normally steady lifestyle. But these are meant to broaden their understanding of life and help them let go of aspects of their life that they don't really need. The period between ages 49–62 is often their best, and many of them can achieve great goals and accomplishments at that time. The 2♠ is also fortunate to have three years in life in which the K♠ is their Long-Range Card. These are at ages 6, 10, and 54.

Years that the 2♠ faces combinations of challenging influences are the fewest of any card in the deck and include those at ages 22, 76, and 91.

Auspicious Years for the 3♠

Prebirth Years: Ages 44 and 89

Rebirth Years: Ages 45 and 90

Critical Year: Age 52

Purpose-Finding and Fated Years: Ages 1, 9, 10, 16, 18, 22, 23, 24, 27+2, 30, 36, 42, 44, 46, 54, 63, 67, 68, 69, 72, 78, 79, 81, 87, 89, 91+2, 93, 99

Years of Blessed Endings: Ages 4, 12, 22, 23, 25, 30, 34, 37, 42, 43, 49, 57, 67, 68, 70, 75, 82, 83, 88, 94

Years of Difficult Endings: Ages 0, 2+2, 5, 12+2, 13, 16+2, 23+2, 31, 33+2, 37, 41, 43+2, 47+2, 48, 49+2, 59+2, 63, 64, 68+2, 78+2, 82, 88+2, 90, 92+2, 96

Years of Caution: Ages 5+2, 26+2, 27+2, 50+2, 71+2, 72+2, 95+2

Years of Personal Challenge: Ages 1, 4, 6, 9, 11+2, 12, 14, 22, 24+2, 27, 28, 29, 32, 34, 37, 45, 54, 56+2, 57+2, 61, 67, 69+2, 72, 73, 74, 79, 81, 82, 88, 94, 99

Ascent to Pinnacle Years: Ages 7, 52, 97

Pinnacle Years: Ages 10, 55, 100

Most Blessed Years: Ages 12, 57

Years of Wish Fulfillment: Ages 4, 28, 29, 37, 49, 73, 74, 82, 94

Years of Recognition, Fame, and Business Success: Ages 3, 5, 18, 21+3, 22+3, 23+2, 28, 40, 41+2, 48, 49+2, 50+3, 63, 66, 67, 70+2, 73, 85, 93, 95

Years with Good Money Cards: Ages 11, 26, 33, 35, 38, 46, 56, 78, 80, 83

LIFE PATH AND THE THIRTEEN-YEAR CYCLE RULING CARDS FOR THE 3♠

MERCURY	VENUS	MARS	JUPITER	SATURN	URANUS	NEPTUNE
Ages 0–12	Ages 13–25	Ages 26–38	Ages 39–51	Ages 52–64	Ages 65–77	Ages 78–90
9♥	7♣	5♦	Q♠	J♣	9♦	7♠

Notes:

The 3♠ sits in the Jupiter column and Saturn row of the Grand Solar Spread. Success and benefits are there, but only through hard work and discipline. There is also some negative karma that must be dispelled, but nothing strong enough to prevent them from achieving happiness and success. The first seven years have two Sevens and two Nines as Long-Range Cards, bringing a host of challenging experiences that embed certain qualities into the 3♠ personality. In the second seven-year cycle, they reach their first Pinnacle, which can bring success in school but also a big change or transition. The cycle from ages 14–20 also has an influence of endings or losses that can dampen the otherwise successful cards of that period. But ages 21–23 are very good and show them some of their potential for success. If they add the ingredient of hard work, they can achieve many of their dreams from ages 28–34. Around age 39, they enter their Jupiter cycle and leave the Saturn line influence of the previous years. Their lives often lighten up quite a bit at that point, and they achieve some recognition in the process. The 3♠ is one of those cards that can have the greatest success in the later years of life. From ages 49–55 and again from ages 70–76 they sit in the Crown Line. Those among them that are career minded will have their greatest successes at this time. The 3♠ is fortunate to have three years in life in which the K♠ is their Long-Range Card. These are at ages 23, 50, and 70.

Years in which the 3♠ has particularly challenging combinations of influences are very few, occurring at ages 37, 67, and 88.

Auspicious Years for the 4♠

Prebirth Years: Ages 44 and 89

Rebirth Years: Ages 45 and 90

Critical Year: Age 52

Purpose-Finding and Fated Years: Ages 5, 12, 15, 16+2, 22, 26, 27, 29, 30, 33, 37, 40+2, 50, 57, 60, 61+3, 66, 67+2, 72, 74, 75, 76, 78, 82+2, 85+3, 95+2, 99

Years of Blessed Endings: Ages 3, 4+2, 8, 9, 10, 15, 18, 24, 28+2, 34, 36, 48, 49+2, 53, 54, 55, 60, 63, 69, 73, 77, 79, 93, 94+2, 98, 99, 100

Years of Difficult Endings: Ages 6+4, 9+2, 10+2, 16+2, 17+2, 18+2, 19+2, 21+2, 22+2, 27+4, 31+2, 35+2, 41+2, 43+2, 44+2, 46, 51+2, 53+2, 54+3, 61+2, 62+2, 63+2, 64+2, 66+2, 67+2, 72+4, 74, 76+2, 80+2, 86+2, 89+3, 91, 96+4, 99+2, 100+2

Years of Caution: Ages 3, 20+2, 21+2, 25, 28, 44+2, 48, 65+2, 66+2, 73, 89+2, 93, 94, 100

Years of Personal Challenge: Ages 3, 7, 8+2, 20, 21+3, 23, 30, 31, 32, 36, 37, 43, 48, 51, 53, 55, 60, 65, 66+2, 68+2, 71, 75, 77, 81, 82, 88, 93, 97, 98+2

Ascent to Pinnacle Years: Ages 1, 46, 91

Pinnacle Years: Ages 4, 49, 94

Most Blessed Years: Ages 6, 51, 96

Years of Wish Fulfillment: Ages 22, 23, 31, 43, 67, 68, 76, 88

Years of Recognition, Fame, and Business Success: Ages 7+2, 8+2, 12, 15, 16, 22, 28+2, 34, 42, 44, 57, 60, 61, 67, 79, 86+2, 87+3, 88+2, 89

Years with Good Money Cards: Ages 1, 11, 18, 20, 29+2, 32, 39, 41, 44, 65, 74, 77, 84+2, 86

LIFE PATH AND THE THIRTEEN-YEAR CYCLE RULING CARDS FOR THE 4♠

MERCURY	VENUS	MARS	JUPITER	SATURN	URANUS	NEPTUNE
Ages 0–12 10♥	Ages 13–25 10♦	Ages 26–38 8♠	Ages 39–51 A♥	Ages 52–64 A♦	Ages 65–77 Q♦	Ages 78–90 5♥

Notes:

The 4♠ has a fortunate Life Path overall, where success comes with hard work and attention to the creation of stability and security. They do achieve much success in childhood, giving them a better than average start in life. It is their pervading sense of financial lack that both motivates them and sometimes limits their success. The entire period from ages 7–13 is spent in the Crown Line, as are ages 28–34. Both these periods bring great success and recognition. They usually excel in school and derive great satisfaction from their mental accomplishments. Then they spend seven years in the Most Blessed Spot, displacing the 10♦ from ages 42–48, something that few cards in the deck do. During this period, they really can achieve or have most anything they desire. Again, their success is only limited by their inner state of poverty, which is something they can work on and overcome if they put their minds to it. Overall, they have so much good fortune that there is no reason for any of them to fail or be without. The 4♠ is also fortunate to have three years in life in which the K♠ is their Long-Range Card. These are at ages 8, 28, and 88. Ages 21, 44, 66, and 89 have an unusual combination of cautionary influences. Great care should be exercised during those years if possible.

   Other years in which the 4♠ experiences combinations of challenging influences include those at ages 3, 4, 9, 16, 20, 27, 48, 49, 54, 61, 65, 66, 72, 76, 89, 93, and 94.

Auspicious Years for the 5♠

Prebirth Years: Ages 44 and 89

Rebirth Years: Ages 45 and 90

Critical Year: Age 52

Purpose-Finding and Fated Years: Ages 5+2, 6, 8, 12, 17, 19, 22, 23+2, 26, 35, 40+2, 44, 50+2, 57, 58, 64, 67, 68, 71, 85+2, 95+2

Years of Blessed Endings: Ages 8, 18+2, 20, 22, 25, 34, 38, 39+2, 44, 46, 53, 63+2, 65, 67, 70, 79, 84+2, 87, 89, 98

Years of Difficult Endings: Ages 1+3, 2, 6+4, 11+3, 16+5, 20+2, 21, 26+4, 27+2, 28+3, 32+2, 37+2, 41+2, 46+2, 51+4, 53+2, 56+2, 61+3, 63+2, 71+5, 72+2, 73+2, 77+2, 81, 82+2, 86+2, 91+2, 96+4

Years of Caution: Ages 9+2, 19, 30+2, 31+2, 42, 54+2, 64, 75+2, 76+2, 87, 99+2

Years of Personal Challenge: Ages 8, 13, 15, 18, 25, 31, 33+2, 41, 57, 58, 60, 61, 65, 66, 70, 72, 76+2, 78, 83, 98

Ascent to Pinnacle Years: Ages 11, 56

Pinnacle Years: Ages 14, 59

Most Blessed Years: Ages 16, 61

Years of Wish Fulfillment: Ages 8, 32, 33, 41, 53, 77, 78, 86, 98

Years of Recognition, Fame, and Business Success: Ages 7, 9, 22, 25, 26, 32, 44, 49+2, 50+2, 51+2, 52, 54, 67, 69+2, 70, 71, 77+3, 78+2, 89, 97, 98+2, 99

Years with Good Money Cards: Ages 15, 19, 26, 29, 31, 39, 42, 60, 64+2, 71, 74, 76, 87, 96

LIFE PATH AND THE THIRTEEN-YEAR CYCLE RULING CARDS FOR THE 5♠

MERCURY	VENUS	MARS	JUPITER	SATURN	URANUS	NEPTUNE
Ages 0–12	Ages 13–25	Ages 26–38	Ages 39–51	Ages 52–64	Ages 65–77	Ages 78–90
J♥	9♣	9♠	2♥	K♥	K♦	6♥

Notes:

The two Nines in the Life Path of the 5♠ can bring losses and disappointments. However, they begin under the J♥ influence, which often gives them a good spiritual foundation that leads them through the troubling periods with understanding and wisdom to make the path easier. All the years past Mars are relatively good, and we see the possibility for great success in the last two thirds of life. They reach their first Pinnacle at age 14, which gives them a taste of their potential. Much of their success is related to people and especially groups of people. The school years bring success in that area that they bring with them into their adult life and work arena. The cycle from ages 21–27 usually ends with some recognition and accomplishment carrying them into another seven years where hard work brings more rewards and success. The cycle from ages 42–48 brings additional success but also an important ending or completion that opens them up to a new beginning with more success from ages 49–52. Overall, they are slated to have much success throughout their life if they just keep going. The 5♠ is also fortunate to have three years in life in which the K♠ is their Long-Range Card. These are at ages 51, 78, and 98.

Years that the 5♠ has particularly challenging combinations of influences occur at ages 16, 26, 28, 41, 61, 71, and 72.

Auspicious Years for the 6♠

Prebirth Years: Ages 44 and 89

Rebirth Years: Ages 45 and 90

Critical Year: Age 52

Purpose-Finding and Fated Years: Ages 0+2, 4, 11, 14, 21, 24, 25, 31, 32, 36, 38, 39, 41, 45+3, 49+2, 59, 63, 66, 69, 70, 76, 77+2, 83, 86, 90+2, 94

Years of Blessed Endings: Ages 9, 11, 12, 20+2, 22, 23, 26, 34, 43, 44, 54, 56, 61, 65, 67, 68, 71, 79, 88, 89, 99

Years of Difficult Endings: Ages 1+2, 7+2, 8, 9+2, 11+2, 21+2, 23+3, 25+2, 27+2, 28, 29+2, 35, 37+2, 40+2, 46+2, 52+2, 53, 54+2, 56+2, 66+3, 67, 68+2, 70+2, 71, 72, 74+2, 80+3, 84+2, 85+2, 86, 87, 91+2, 93, 97+2, 98, 99+2

Years of Caution: Ages 4+2, 5+2, 28+2, 31, 49+2, 50+2, 73+2, 76, 94+2, 95+2

Years of Personal Challenge: Ages 5, 7, 9, 28, 29, 32, 35, 39, 50, 52, 57, 58, 64, 72, 73, 77, 79, 82+2, 84, 95, 97

Ascent to Pinnacle Years: Ages 30, 75

Pinnacle Years: Ages 33, 78

Most Blessed Years: Ages 35, 80

Years of Wish Fulfillment: Ages 6, 7, 15, 27, 51, 52, 60, 72, 96, 97

Years of Recognition, Fame, and Business Success: Ages 0, 1+2, 2+2, 3+2, 6, 18, 26, 28, 41, 44, 45+3, 46+2, 47+2, 51, 63, 71, 73, 86, 89, 90, 96

Years with Good Money Cards: Ages 2, 10, 12, 16, 17, 42, 55, 57, 61, 62, 75, 83, 97, 100

LIFE PATH AND THE THIRTEEN-YEAR CYCLE RULING CARDS FOR THE 6♠

MERCURY	VENUS	MARS	JUPITER	SATURN	URANUS	NEPTUNE
Ages 0–12 Q♥	Ages 13–25 10♣	Ages 26–38 8♦	Ages 39–51 K♠	Ages 52–64 3♥	Ages 65–77 A♣	Ages 78–90 Q♣

Notes:

The 6♠ gets off to a good start the first seven years, but their association with the 9♠, which is their first Karma Card and the card that they displace the second seven years of life, brings some losses or disappointments that often color their personalities with a sense of tragedy. They often become toughened by these early life challenges, but sometimes they close themselves off from opportunities that present themselves later. Still, the great potential is there, and many of them reach out to take the brass ring that is presented to them by the winds of fate. One glance at the Venus, Mars, and Jupiter Periods will tell you that these people can achieve greatness if they choose. All three of these cards sit in the Crown Line of the Grand Solar Spread. The period from ages 28–34 is often very significant and brings about a complete change of life. Those with high ambitions often achieve them and are led to a new level of recognition as a reward then. The seven-year period that follows often has a lot of challenges in the areas of personal relationships, ages 35 and 39 being the most significant of these. That period is followed by one that could be one of the most successful and fortuitous of their life. During ages 42–48, great success and recognition can come. Those who aspire to great heights often reach it during this period, which also coincides with their fortunate Jupiter thirteen-year cycle governed by the K♠. The potential is there for all 6♠, but only those who are willing to take charge ever realize it.

Years in which the 6♠ has particularly challenging combinations of influences occur at ages 21, 28, 66, and 72.

Auspicious Years for the 7♠

Prebirth Years: Ages 44 and 89

Rebirth Years: Ages 45 and 90

Critical Year: Age 52

Purpose-Finding and Fated Years: Ages 0, 6, 7+2, 8, 11, 17, 25, 26, 28, 29, 32, 33, 34, 38+2, 45, 51+2, 52+2, 56, 62, 65, 71, 73, 74+2, 75, 79, 83+2, 89, 90, 96, 97+3

Years of Blessed Endings: Ages 2, 6, 9, 17, 22, 27, 40, 41, 42, 47, 50, 51, 58, 62, 67, 72, 85, 86, 87, 92, 96, 99

Years of Difficult Endings: Ages 3+2, 4+2, 10+2, 15, 18+2, 24+2, 26+2, 28+2, 32+2, 39+2, 48+2, 49+2, 55+2, 63+2, 65+2, 66, 69+2, 71+2, 72, 75+2, 76, 84+2, 93+3, 94+2, 100+2

Years of Caution: Ages 3, 10, 21+2, 24, 36, 41, 42+2, 43+2, 48, 55, 63, 66+2, 86, 87+2, 88+2, 93, 96, 100

Years of Personal Challenge: Ages 0, 2+2, 16+2, 18, 20+2, 22, 25, 30, 33+2, 38, 40, 42, 43, 44, 45, 47+2, 56, 61+2, 65, 67, 70, 73, 77, 78+2, 87, 88, 90, 92+2

Ascent to Pinnacle Years: Ages 23, 68

Pinnacle Years: Ages 26, 71

Most Blessed Years: Ages 28, 73

Years of Wish Fulfillment: Ages 0, 8, 20, 44, 45, 53, 65, 89, 90, 98

Years of Recognition, Fame, and Business Success: Ages 11, 19, 21, 34, 37, 38, 44, 56, 64, 66, 79, 82+3, 83+3, 89

Years with Good Money Cards: Ages 7, 9, 17, 18, 19, 24, 50, 52, 54, 62, 63, 64, 69, 77, 88, 97, 99

LIFE PATH AND THE THIRTEEN-YEAR CYCLE RULING CARDS FOR THE 7♠

MERCURY	VENUS	MARS	JUPITER	SATURN	URANUS	NEPTUNE
Ages 0–12	Ages 13–25	Ages 26–38	Ages 39–51	Ages 52–64	Ages 65–77	Ages 78–90
2♣	K♣	J♦	4♥	4♦	2♠	8♥

Notes:

The 7♠ sits in the fortunate Jupiter column of the Grand Solar Spread, but being the 'Seven of Sevens,' their blessings come from spiritual avenues more than the mundane ones. Health and work challenges are part of their life until they learn the lessons concerning freedom from personal attachments. However, their Life Path is fortunate, and they do have successes frequently. All in all, they have little to complain about. The childhood is relatively good, with mostly good influences the entire first fourteen years. They go into a fourteen-year cycle (14–27) of changes and some uncertainty after that, but still we have years of good influences throughout it all. Many of them develop their business and financial skills at this time, which is usually a major part of every 7♠ karmic destiny. The first Pinnacle also occurs during this cycle, which brings a successful rise followed by a challenging ending at age 28. It all comes back to their Birth Card and the need to walk the spiritual path. Any successes they have must come from a place of non-attachment to results. Overall, the cards of their life give them continual opportunities to let go of negative past life tendencies. When they get the message and make the internal change, all of these cards transform into success and peace of mind in a higher spiritual light.

Years that the 7♠ has particularly challenging combinations of influences occur at ages 3, 10, 24, 26, 38, 42, 48, 55, 71, 87, 93, and 100.

Auspicious Years for the 8♠

Prebirth Years: Ages 44 and 89

Rebirth Years: Ages 45 and 90

Critical Year: Age 52

Purpose-Finding and Fated Years: Ages 1, 3, 11, 15, 17+2, 18, 27, 28, 36, 40, 42+2, 43, 44, 46, 47, 48, 56, 60, 62, 63, 67, 72, 73, 76, 81, 85, 87+2, 88, 89, 91, 93

Years of Blessed Endings: Ages 7, 17+2, 19, 28, 31, 37, 41, 52, 60, 62+2, 68, 73, 76, 82, 86, 97

Years of Difficult Endings: Ages 1+2, 4+4, 6, 14+2, 18+2, 22+2, 27+2, 28+2, 32, 33+2, 34+2, 38+2, 39+2, 42+2, 46+2, 49+4, 50, 57, 59+2, 63+2, 67+2, 72+2, 73+2, 75+2, 78+2, 79+2, 84+3, 85+3, 91+2, 94+4

Years of Caution: Ages 7+2, 8+2, 14, 19, 30, 31+2, 52+2, 53+2, 64, 76+2, 78, 97+2, 98+2

Years of Personal Challenge: Ages 0, 1, 8, 10, 11, 17, 21, 25, 29, 30, 32, 34, 35+2, 40, 45, 46, 53, 55, 56, 62, 63, 66, 70, 74, 77, 79, 80+2, 83, 87, 90, 91, 98, 100

Ascent to Pinnacle Years: Ages 33, 78

Pinnacle Years: Ages 36, 81

Most Blessed Years: Ages 38, 83

Years of Wish Fulfillment: Ages 9, 10, 18, 30, 54, 55, 63, 75, 99, 100

Years of Recognition, Fame, and Business Success: Ages 2, 3, 9, 18+2, 19+2, 20+2, 21, 22+2, 23+2, 24+2, 29, 31, 44, 47, 48, 54, 66+3, 67+2, 68+2, 74, 76, 89, 92, 93, 99

Years with Good Money Cards: Ages 5, 7, 9, 10, 19, 27, 38, 48, 50, 52, 54, 55, 64, 71, 95+2, 97, 99, 100

LIFE PATH AND THE THIRTEEN-YEAR CYCLE RULING CARDS FOR THE 8♠

MERCURY	VENUS	MARS	JUPITER	SATURN	URANUS	NEPTUNE
Ages 0–12	Ages 13–25	Ages 26–38	Ages 39–51	Ages 52–64	Ages 65–77	Ages 78–90
A♥	A♦	Q♦	5♥	3♣	3♠	9♥

Notes:

The two Aces that govern the first twenty-six years of the 8♠ life concern themselves with self-exploration. This can either produce a person who is self-aware and at peace or one who is very selfish and thoughtless of others. At age 26 the 8♠ enters the Saturn line with the Q♦ card, which is where all the remaining cards in the Life Path are. Saturn promises that they will act with awareness of others' needs or pay the consequences. With all odd-numbered cards in the Life Path, there are challenges to be sure. But the inherent power in their Birth Card can overcome them as long as they operate within the law of cause and effect. Though the first seven years are somewhat difficult, the next are much better, and the 8♠ often does well in school. They end up standing out among their classmates, especially at ages 16, 18, 19, and 20 when they have especially good influences. This fortunate influence continues into the next seven-year cycle that begins at age 21, where they again end up in the Crown Line with their Long-Range Cards. Notice how the 8♠ is fortunate to have three years in life in which the K♠ is their Long-Range Card. These are at ages 20, 24, and 68. Early successes give a great boost to the spirit and often lead them to even greater accomplishments as adults. The cycle from ages 28–34 presents them with some of the strongest challenges in life, ages 30 and 32 being the highlighted years of that cycle where endings must occur. A similar cycle of spiritual challenges occurs at ages 49–55. Possibly the best cycle of life occurs at ages 63–69, which affords much success, recognition, and reward to those with high ambitions.

Years that the 8♠ has particularly challenging combinations of influences occur at ages 4, 8, 14, 30, 34, 49, 52, 53, 78, 79, 94, and 98.

Auspicious Years for the 9♠

Prebirth Years: Ages 44 and 89

Rebirth Years: Ages 45 and 90

Critical Year: Age 52

Purpose-Finding and Fated Years: Ages 0, 1, 2, 3, 5, 9, 11, 13, 14+2, 22, 23, 32, 39, 40, 41, 44, 45, 46, 47, 48, 50, 52, 56, 58+2, 59, 67, 68, 77, 84, 85, 86, 89, 90, 91, 92, 95

Years of Blessed Endings: Ages 0, 5, 15, 21, 31, 33, 35, 36, 45, 50, 56, 64, 66, 76, 78, 80, 81, 90, 95

Years of Difficult Endings: Ages 0+2, 10+2, 13+2, 22, 24+2, 28+2, 34+2, 38+3, 45+2, 55+2, 57, 58+2, 63, 69+2, 71+2, 73+2, 81+2, 90+2, 95, 100+2

Years of Caution: Ages 3+2, 4+3, 15, 19+2, 27+2, 48+2, 49+3, 60, 64, 72+2, 93+2, 94+3

Years of Personal Challenge: Ages 4, 6, 7, 24, 26, 28, 29, 30, 31, 36, 41, 43, 49+2, 51, 69, 74, 75, 76, 79, 80, 83, 86, 87, 88, 94, 96, 97

Ascent to Pinnacle Years: Ages 29, 74

Pinnacle Years: Ages 32, 77

Most Blessed Years: Ages 34, 79

Years of Wish Fulfillment: Ages 5, 6, 14, 26, 50, 51, 59, 71, 95, 96

Years of Recognition, Fame, and Business Success: Ages 5, 17, 25, 27, 38+2, 39+2, 40+3, 43, 44, 50, 62, 70, 72, 85, 88, 89, 95

Years with Good Money Cards: Ages 11, 12, 13, 15, 25, 30, 35, 39, 42, 51, 56, 57, 58, 60, 70, 72, 75, 80, 84, 87

LIFE PATH AND THE THIRTEEN-YEAR CYCLE RULING CARDS FOR THE 9♠

MERCURY	VENUS	MARS	JUPITER	SATURN	URANUS	NEPTUNE
Ages 0–12	Ages 13–25	Ages 26–38	Ages 39–51	Ages 52–64	Ages 65–77	Ages 78–90
2♥	K♥	K♦	6♥	4♣	2♦	J♠

Notes:

The 9♠ has one of the better Life Paths, which often brings material success to them. However, there is no escaping the strength of their Birth Card's potential for loss or disappointment, so some of them have personal tragedy, as well as the success that comes in their Life Path. There is generally protection in childhood overall, though in some cases there are losses in the family. Most 9♠ have some talent, usually musical or one to do with entertaining. This often reveals itself in the second seven-year cycle from ages 7–13. The period from ages 21–27 can bring a big change in life that sets them on a new path that culminates at their first Pinnacle Year at age 32. Then, at the Pinnacle, they make another major change. Perhaps the most successful and fun cycle is the one that begins at age 35 and extends to age 41. Many get married in that cycle as well.

Years in which the 9♠ has powerful combinations of challenging influences occur at ages 4, 19, 49, 64, and 94.

Auspicious Years for the 10♠

Prebirth Years: Ages 44 and 89

Rebirth Years: Ages 45 and 90

Critical Year: Age 52

Purpose-Finding and Fated Years: Ages 3, 8, 13, 14, 16, 18, 20, 26, 27, 31, 32, 42, 44, 48, 49, 51, 52, 53, 58, 59, 61, 63, 65, 67, 72, 76, 77, 84, 87, 89, 93, 98

Years of Blessed Endings: Ages 0, 2, 3, 12, 16, 26, 30, 36, 38+2, 40, 45, 47, 48, 57, 61, 71, 79, 81, 83, 85, 90, 92, 93

Years of Difficult Endings: Ages 0+2, 7+2, 8+2, 12+3, 13+2, 19+2, 20+2, 22+2, 27+2, 29+2, 30, 40+2, 41+2, 43+2, 45+4, 52+2, 55+2, 58+2, 61, 64+2, 65+2, 67+2, 68, 72+2, 74+2, 78, 85+2, 86+2, 87, 88+3, 90+2, 93, 97+2, 98+2

Years of Caution: Ages 1+2, 2, 22+2, 23+2, 46+2, 50, 59, 65, 67+2, 68+2, 91+2

Years of Personal Challenge: Ages 0, 1, 2, 3, 4, 5, 9, 10, 13, 23, 25, 27, 35, 39, 41, 46, 47, 48, 50, 53, 57, 58, 64, 68, 70, 72, 82, 84, 85, 86, 90, 91, 92, 95+2, 100

Ascent to Pinnacle Years: Ages 3, 48, 93

Pinnacle Years: Ages 6, 51, 96

Most Blessed Years: Ages 8, 53, 98

Years of Wish Fulfillment: Ages 0, 24, 25, 33, 45, 69, 70, 78, 90

Years of Recognition, Fame, and Business Success: Ages 1, 13+2, 14, 17, 18, 21+2, 22+2, 24, 36, 42+2, 44, 46, 59, 62, 63, 69, 81, 89, 91, 100+2

Years with Good Money Cards: Ages 15, 25, 28, 31, 34, 37, 39, 73, 76, 79, 82, 84

LIFE PATH AND THE THIRTEEN-YEAR CYCLE RULING CARDS FOR THE 10♠

MERCURY	VENUS	MARS	JUPITER	SATURN	URANUS	NEPTUNE
Ages 0–12	Ages 13–25	Ages 26–38	Ages 39–51	Ages 52–64	Ages 65–77	Ages 78–90
5♣	3♦	A♠	7♥	7♦	5♠	J♥

Notes:

The 10♠ sits in the fortunate Jupiter column in the Grand Solar Spread. This guarantees a certain amount of protection and success in life that most cards do not have. The two Sevens in the Life Path can be difficult but can always be surmounted with hard work, which is one of their strongest qualities. The first seven years is a mixed bag. With so many odd-numbered cards for the Long-Range each year, there are bound to be some changes and challenging situations in their life. The second seven years are often much better, and as they get into school, they often find they excel and get some recognition there. Beginning at age 21, they spend an entire seven years in the Crown Line. Those who are career-oriented often have great success at this time, while having a lot of freedom as well to do whatever they wish. This cycle is repeated, but in an even grander way from ages 42–48, where they spend seven years displacing the 8♦ in the Sun position of the Crown Line. This is the most fortuitous cycle for them, the one that can raise them up to the heights of their profession, which then culminates at their second Pinnacle Year at age 51. Then, from ages 56–62, they sit in the Most Blessed Spot, where Jupiter's blessings surround them. If they are spiritually inclined, this can be a time when they make their deepest connections while receiving many material blessings at the same time. Few cards have such a life path with so many wonderful possibilities.

Years in which the 10♠ person has strong combinations of challenging influences occur at ages 2, 22, 50, 64, 65, 67, and 85.

Auspicious Years for the J♠

Prebirth Years: Ages 44 and 89

Rebirth Years: Ages 45 and 90

Critical Year: Age 52

Purpose-Finding and Fated Years: Ages 1, 3, 7, 10, 14, 17, 19, 21, 24, 28+2, 31, 35, 38, 39, 41, 48, 52, 55, 59, 61, 62, 66, 73+2, 76, 80, 83, 93, 97, 100

Years of Blessed Endings: Ages 6, 17, 20, 23, 26, 30, 31, 34, 43, 51, 62, 65, 68, 75+2, 76, 88, 96

Years of Difficult Endings: Ages 2+2, 4+2, 8+2, 9+2, 15+2, 18, 20, 23+2, 25+2, 27, 31+2, 36, 37+2, 39+2, 40, 41+2, 43+2, 47+2, 51+2, 54+2, 55, 58, 60+3, 67, 68+2, 70+2, 76+2, 79, 82+2, 84+2, 88+2, 92+2, 94+2, 98+2, 99+2

Years of Caution: Ages 5, 15, 18+2, 19+2, 23, 24, 29, 38, 42+2, 50, 56, 60, 63+2, 64+2, 69, 74, 83, 87+2, 95

Years of Personal Challenge: Ages 1, 6+2, 18, 19, 21, 28, 33, 35, 36, 46+2, 49+2, 50, 51, 53, 54, 63, 64, 66, 73, 80, 81, 83, 86, 87, 91, 93, 96+2

Ascent to Pinnacle Years: Ages 44, 89

Pinnacle Years: Ages 2, 47, 92

Most Blessed Years: Ages 4, 49, 94

Years of Wish Fulfillment: Ages 20, 21, 29, 41, 65, 66, 74, 86

Years of Recognition, Fame, and Business Success: Ages 10, 13, 14+3, 20, 32, 40, 42, 55, 58, 59, 65, 72+2, 73+2, 74+2, 77, 85, 87, 95+2, 96+2, 97+2, 99+2, 100+3

Years with Good Money Cards: Ages 4, 8, 15, 18, 30+2, 41, 43, 63, 69, 70, 75, 86, 88, 90

LIFE PATH AND THE THIRTEEN-YEAR CYCLE RULING CARDS FOR THE J♠

MERCURY	VENUS	MARS	JUPITER	SATURN	URANUS	NEPTUNE
Ages 0–12	Ages 13–25	Ages 26–38	Ages 39–51	Ages 52–64	Ages 65–77	Ages 78–90
8♣	6♦	4♠	10♥	10♦	8♠	A♥

Notes:

The J♠ has a very fortunate Life Path, one in which most of the cards are even-numbered and which every card after Mercury falls in the Jupiter row. For all intents and purposes, these people can excel at most anything and are given more than most cards in the way of success and recognition. Being the Jack of Jacks, though, can make it difficult for them to harness all of this good fortune. They may just want to play and avoid responsibility, which will lessen their achievements quite a bit. Nearly every card in their Life Path is one of success or power. They spend an entire seven years in the Crown Line from ages 14–20 and another seven years in the Most Blessed Spot from ages 28–34. Based on the foundation they get from those fortunate years, the challenges that follow those periods can be seen more as new experiences than bad luck or difficulties. The J♠ is also fortunate to have three years in life in which the K♠ is their Long-Range Card. These are at ages 14, 74, and 97.

Years in which the J♠ has combinations of challenging influences occur at ages 14, 15, 18, 23, 24, 38, 50, 59, 60, 63, and 79. Ages 38 and 83 are unusual years in which there are four Sixes in challenging positions. Those could represent a heavy karmic payback years for them and should be watched carefully.

Auspicious Years for the Q♠

Prebirth Years: Ages 44 and 89

Rebirth Years: Ages 45 and 90

Critical Year: Age 52

Purpose-Finding and Fated Years: Ages 7+2, 10, 11, 15, 20, 23, 25, 28, 33, 34, 35, 38, 46, 52, 55, 56, 65, 70+2, 73, 78, 79, 80, 83, 86, 97, 100+2

Years of Blessed Endings: Ages 1, 9, 23, 27, 32, 33, 46, 54, 68+2, 76, 77, 78, 91, 99

Years of Difficult Endings: Ages 1, 3+2, 8+2, 10, 12+2, 14, 16, 19+2, 22+2, 26, 33, 36+2, 42, 46+2, 50+2, 53+2, 57+2, 60, 62, 64+2, 67+2, 81+2, 83+3, 92, 93+2, 97, 98+2

Years of Caution: Ages 15+2, 16+2, 18, 37, 39+2, 58, 60+2, 61+2, 63, 84+2

Years of Personal Challenge: Ages 1, 2, 5, 6, 15, 16, 18, 19, 20, 21, 31, 34, 35, 38+2, 39, 41, 43, 44, 48, 51, 60, 61, 63, 65, 66, 68, 79, 83, 88, 89, 91, 95, 96

Ascent to Pinnacle Years: Ages 41, 86

Pinnacle Years: Ages 44, 89

Most Blessed Years: Ages 1, 46, 91

Years of Wish Fulfillment: Ages 17, 18, 26, 38, 62, 63, 71, 83

Years of Recognition, Fame, and Business Success: Ages 7, 10, 11, 17, 29, 37, 39, 51+2, 52+3, 53+2, 55, 56, 62, 74+3, 75+2, 76+2, 78+2, 79+2, 80+2, 82, 84, 97, 100

Years with Good Money Cards: Ages 1, 6, 9, 20, 22, 23, 27, 28, 44, 46, 51, 54, 65, 66, 68, 72+2, 85, 89, 91, 96, 99

LIFE PATH AND THE THIRTEEN-YEAR CYCLE RULING CARDS FOR THE Q♠

MERCURY	VENUS	MARS	JUPITER	SATURN	URANUS	NEPTUNE
Ages 0–12	Ages 13–25	Ages 26–38	Ages 39–51	Ages 52–64	Ages 65–77	Ages 78–90
J♣	9♦	7♠	2♣	K♣	J♦	4♥

Notes:

The Life Path of the Q♠ has a mixture of spiritual and materially good cards. This affords them the opportunity to have success in both areas at the same time if they choose. Otherwise, the 9♦ and 7♠ could represent many challenges on the material plane, especially during the years they govern from ages 13–38. Except for a possible health challenge at age 2, the first seven years go pretty smoothly. The second seven years are spent in the Most Blessed Spot. Though there are challenges during that time, there is a pervading protective and helpful influence that helps many things go well for them. Age 26 is one in which their 9♠ Long-Range Card displaces the powerful A♠. This could be a significant ending year for them, perhaps one in which some key personal relationship comes to an end. The cycle from ages 42–48 is fairly fortunate and usually brings financial blessings. It is during this cycle that they go to the Pinnacle for the first time as well. This often brings a change in life at age 44, which is also the Prebirth Year. All in all, that is an important time for them. Then at ages 52–54, they move into the Crown Line where they can have some recognition and reward. The Q♠ is also fortunate to have three years in life in which the K♠ is their Long-Range Card. These are at ages 53, 76, and 80.

Years in which the Q♠ has combinations of challenging influences occur at ages 15, 18, 19, 60, and 63.

Auspicious Years for the K♠

Prebirth Years: Ages 44 and 89

Rebirth Years: Ages 45 and 90

Purpose-Finding and Fated Years: Ages 18, 24, 34, 62, 86, 91, 94, 96

Years of Blessed Endings: Ages 1, 2, 3, 5, 7, 9, 11, 13, 15, 16, 17, 19, 21, 23, 25, 26, 27, 29, 31, 33, 35, 37, 39, 41, 43, 45, 47+2, 49, 51, 53, 55, 57, 59, 61+2, 63, 65, 67, 69, 71+2, 73, 75, 77, 79, 81, 83, 85, 87, 89, 91, 92, 93, 95, 97, 99

Years of Difficult Endings: Ages 4+2, 5+2, 15+2, 17, 19, 25+2, 27, 36+2, 39+3, 49+2, 50+2, 60+2, 70+2, 79, 81+2, 84+3, 89, 94+2, 95+2

Years of Caution: Ages 1, 6, 12, 16, 46, 57, 61, 68, 88, 91

Years of Personal Challenge: Ages 0, 9, 11, 18, 29, 30, 35, 43, 45, 47, 54, 56, 61, 63, 67, 74, 81, 88, 90, 99

Years with Good Money Cards: Ages 9, 14, 23, 28, 37, 39, 82, 84

LIFE PATH AND THE THIRTEEN-YEAR CYCLE RULING CARDS FOR THE K♠

MERCURY	VENUS	MARS	JUPITER	SATURN	URANUS	NEPTUNE
Ages 0–12	Ages 13–25	Ages 26–38	Ages 39–51	Ages 52–64	Ages 65–77	Ages 78–90
3♥	A♣	Q♣	10♠	5♣	3♦	A♠

Notes:

The K♠ is the only card in the deck who spends the entire life in the Crown Line. This tends to make them independent and strong-willed, but also affords them the opportunity to achieve great success provided they supply the necessary ingredients. The chief ingredient necessary is that of being willing to assume great responsibility. Because all K♠ have the 5♣ as their Planetary Ruling Card, responsibility often represents imprisonment, and perhaps this is why so few of them actually achieve the greatness that is available to them. The Life Path itself is a mixture, but strong overall. It is the last two periods of life that are the most challenging. Happiness at those stages will require a spiritual outlook on life. Otherwise, there may be financial worries and losses. To learn more about the particular cycles of success and challenge, read the same for the 5♣, their Planetary Ruler. The first thirteen-year cycle, governed by the 3♥, often contains experiences that color the emotional makeup of the K♠ person adversely. That card can represent uncertainty in love and a fear of not getting enough affection. In some cases it represents uncertainty about sex or sexual roles. The most significant challenge for the K♠ is in the relationship area, even though every other year they have the 2♥ in Venus, which by any measure would indicate a happy and wonderful love bond with another. Another interesting aspect of their Yearly Spreads is that every other year they have either the 7♦ or 9♥ as their Result Card. These cards both produce challenging situations that can turn to blessings at the end of the year. The 9♥ Result means good things that come from ending certain relationships, while the 7♦ Result can indicate financial abundance after dealing with some sort of challenge implied by their Pluto Card that year.

Years in which the K♠ has particularly strong combinations of challenging influences include those occurring at ages 5, 15, 16, 50, 60, 61, and 95.

Chapter Nine
Articles for Advanced Study

The Significance of the Planetary Ruling Card

The Birth Card and Planetary Ruling Card are the two most important symbols of your life and personality. Unlike the Personality Cards, which we can assume or discard at will, we always have the characteristics of these two main personal significators. The Birth Card you have is determined by a complex formula that assigns the correct card for each day of the year. This disbursement of cards is not random, and it is not even. There are significantly more birthdays for some cards than others. However, it is the way is has to be, and there are underlying reasons for each and every thing in this system. The more you study it, the more you will uncover these reasons.

    The Planetary Ruling Card is derived from your Birth Card, its Life Spread Cards, and your Sun Sign, astrologically speaking. The table in the back of the book is the easy way to just look up your Planetary Ruling Card, but it is also helpful to know where it comes from.

    First of all, you need to know what the Life Spread Cards are. The Life Spread is essentially the one spread that governs our entire life. It is discussed at length in my book, *Love Cards*, but

Planetary Rulers of the Sun Signs

Sun Sign	Ruling Planet	Sun Sign	Ruling Planet
Aries	Mars	Libra	Venus
Taurus	Venus	Scorpio	Pluto, Mars*
Gemini	Mercury	Sagittarius	Jupiter
Cancer	Moon	Capricorn	Saturn
Leo	The Sun	Aquarius	Uranus
Virgo	Mercury	Pisces	Neptune

* Mars is the secondary ruler of Scorpio

The Life Spreads of the Birth Cards

MOON	BIRTH CARD	MER	VEN	MAR	JUP	SAT	URA	NEP	PLU	RES	LESSON
8♠	A♥	A♦	Q♦	5♥	3♣	3♠	9♥	7♣	5♦	Q♠	J♣
9♠	2♥	K♥	K♦	6♥	4♣	2♦	J♠	8♣	6♦	4♠	10♥
K♠	3♥	A♣	Q♣	10♠	5♣	3♦	A♠	7♥	7♦	5♠	J♥
J♦	4♥	4♦	2♠	8♥	6♣	6♠	Q♥	10♣	8♦	K♠	3♥
Q♦	5♥	3♣	3♠	9♥	7♣	5♦	Q♠	J♣	9♦	7♠	2♣
K♦	6♥	4♣	2♦	J♠	8♣	6♦	4♠	10♥	10♦	8♠	A♥
A♠	7♥	7♦	5♠	J♥	9♣	9♠	2♥	K♥	K♦	6♥	4♣
2♠	8♥	6♣	6♠	Q♥	10♣	8♦	K♠	3♥	A♣	Q♣	10♠
3♠	9♥	7♣	5♦	Q♠	J♣	9♦	7♠	2♣	K♣	J♦	4♥
4♠	10♥	10♦	8♠	A♥	A♦	Q♦	5♥	3♣	3♠	9♦	7♣
5♠	J♥	9♣	9♠	2♥	K♥	K♦	6♥	4♣	2♦	J♠	8♣
6♠	Q♥	10♣	8♦	K♠	3♥	A♣	Q♣	10♠	5♣	3♦	A♠
2♥	K♥	K♦	6♥	4♣	2♦	J♠	8♣	6♦	4♠	10♥	10♦
3♥	A♣	Q♣	10♠	5♣	3♦	A♠	7♥	7♦	5♠	J♥	9♣
7♠	2♣	K♣	J♦	4♥	4♦	2♠	8♥	6♣	6♠	Q♥	10♣
5♥	3♣	3♠	9♥	7♣	5♦	Q♠	J♣	9♦	7♠	2♣	K♣
6♥	4♣	2♦	J♠	8♣	6♦	4♠	10♥	10♦	8♠	A♥	A♦
10♠	5♣	3♦	A♠	7♥	7♦	5♠	J♥	9♣	9♠	2♥	K♥
8♥	6♣	6♠	Q♥	10♣	8♦	K♠	3♥	A♣	Q♣	10♠	5♣
9♥	7♣	5♦	Q♠	J♣	9♦	7♠	2♣	K♣	J♦	4♥	4♦
J♠	8♣	6♦	4♠	10♥	10♦	8♠	A♥	A♦	Q♦	5♥	3♣
J♥	9♣	9♠	2♥	K♥	K♦	6♥	4♣	2♦	J♠	8♣	6♦
Q♥	10♣	8♦	K♠	3♥	A♣	Q♣	10♠	5♣	3♦	A♠	7♥
Q♠	J♣	9♦	7♠	2♣	K♣	J♦	4♥	4♦	2♠	8♥	6♣
A♣	Q♣	10♠	5♣	3♦	A♠	7♥	7♦	5♠	J♥	9♣	9♠
2♣	K♣	J♦	4♥	4♦	2♠	8♥	6♣	6♠	Q♥	10♣	8♦
A♥	A♦	Q♦	5♥	3♣	3♠	9♥	7♣	5♦	Q♠	J♣	9♦
4♣	2♦	J♠	8♣	6♦	4♠	10♥	10♦	8♠	A♥	A♦	Q♦
5♣	3♦	A♠	7♥	7♦	5♠	J♥	9♣	9♠	2♥	K♥	K♦
4♥	4♦	2♠	8♥	6♣	6♠	Q♥	10♣	8♦	K♠	3♥	A♣
7♣	5♦	Q♠	J♣	9♦	7♠	2♣	K♣	J♦	4♥	4♦	2♠
8♣	6♦	4♠	10♥	10♦	8♠	A♥	A♦	Q♦	5♥	3♣	3♠
7♥	7♦	5♠	J♥	9♣	9♠	2♥	K♥	K♦	6♥	4♣	2♦
10♣	8♦	K♠	3♥	A♣	Q♣	10♠	5♣	3♦	A♠	7♥	7♦
J♣	9♦	7♠	2♣	K♣	J♦	4♥	4♦	2♠	8♥	6♣	6♠
10♥	10♦	8♠	A♥	A♦	Q♦	5♥	3♣	3♠	9♥	7♣	5♦
K♣	J♦	4♥	4♦	2♠	8♥	6♣	6♠	Q♥	10♣	8♦	K♠
A♦	Q♦	5♥	3♣	3♠	9♥	7♣	5♦	Q♠	J♣	9♦	7♠
K♥	K♦	6♥	4♣	2♦	J♠	8♣	6♦	4♠	10♥	10♦	8♠
3♦	A♠	7♥	7♦	5♠	J♥	9♣	9♠	2♥	K♥	K♦	6♥
4♦	2♠	8♥	6♣	6♠	Q♥	10♣	8♦	K♠	3♥	A♣	Q♣
3♣	3♠	9♥	7♣	5♦	Q♠	J♣	9♦	7♠	2♣	K♣	J♦
6♠	4♠	10♥	10♦	8♠	A♥	A♦	Q♦	5♥	3♣	3♠	9♥
7♦	5♠	J♥	9♣	9♠	2♥	K♥	K♦	6♥	4♣	2♦	J♠
6♣	6♠	Q♥	10♣	8♦	K♠	3♥	A♣	Q♣	10♠	5♣	3♦
9♦	7♠	2♣	K♣	J♦	4♥	4♦	2♠	8♥	6♣	6♠	Q♥
10♦	8♠	A♥	A♦	Q♦	5♥	3♣	3♠	9♥	7♣	5♦	Q♠
9♣	9♠	2♥	K♥	K♦	6♥	4♣	2♦	J♠	8♣	6♦	4♠
Q♣	10♠	5♣	3♦	A♠	7♥	7♦	5♠	J♥	9♣	9♠	2♥
2♦	J♠	8♣	6♦	4♠	10♥	10♦	8♠	A♥	A♦	Q♦	5♥
5♦	Q♠	J♣	9♦	7♠	2♣	K♣	J♦	4♥	4♦	2♠	8♥
8♦	K♠	3♥	A♣	Q♣	10♠	5♣	3♦	A♠	7♥	7♦	5♠

for our purposes here, you may refer to the table on the facing page. It lists all of the Life Spread Cards for each of the Birth Cards. Now, find your Sun Sign in the table on page 117 and see what planet governs that sign. Then find the card in your Birth Card's Life Spread that matches your ruling planet, and you have it.

As an example, if your birthday is December 12th, your Birth Card is the 6♣, and you are a Sagittarius. Since Sagittarius is governed by Jupiter, you would look on the previous page to see what your Jupiter card is in your Life Spread. Looking there, you see that it is the 8♦. Therefore, your Planetary Ruling Card is the 8♦. Remember that Leos' Planetary Ruling Card is the same as their Birth Card and that Scorpios have two rulers, thus two Planetary Ruling Cards. I generally consider the Pluto Card for Scorpios to be the most significant, though I have noticed that they all use both of them from time to time.

For Those Born on the Cusps

The Planetary Ruling Card is based upon your Birth Card and your Sun Sign, so you must be absolutely sure of your Sun Sign in order to know what your Planetary Ruling Card is. Many people are born on what we call a 'cusp date' in which they could one of two signs. Each month of the year, there are a couple of days, usually 2–4, where the Sun changes from one sign to the next. Because of leap year and other considerations, this can occur within a 3–4 day range each year. When you are born on one of these cusp days, you will probably need to have a professional astrological chart in order to determine exactly which sign you are. If you are born on a cusp day, you will find an OR statement between which two Planetary Ruling Cards you may be, depending upon your Sun Sign. It is up to you to settle the question of your Sun Sign. This is very important, and you will want to be accurate about this if at all possible.

The Seven-Year Cycles

You may not have gathered this yet from reading this book, but your Long-Range Card each year is part of a seven-year cycle. These seven-year cycles begin the day you are born. Your Long-Range Card for the first year of life is also the same as your Mercury Card in that first year and, of course, the same as the Mercury Card in your Life Spread. If you haven't realized it yet, the Age 0 Spread has a lot of significance. In essence, that spread is all of the following and more:

1. The spread for the first year of your life

2. The spread for your entire life

3. The spread for the forty-fifth and ninetieth years of your life

4. The spread for the first seven years of your life

5. The spread for the first seven weeks of your life

6. The spread for the first seven days of your life

That is a lot of spreads. To understand the significance of this is one of the most advanced areas of this science, but as you begin studying your Yearly Spreads, much of this will become apparent to you.

I invite you now to compare your Long-Range Cards for the first forty-nine years of your life with the Planetary Period Cards for the first seven years of your life. You will find that they are identical. For example, the Long-Range Card for age 19 is the same as your Uranus Period Card in the third year of your life (Age Two Spread) and the Long-Range Card for age 20 is the Neptune Card in that Age 2 Spread that follows the Uranus Period.

What this can reveal to you is that the Long-Range Cards are part of a seven-year cycle in the same way as the seven Planetary Period Cards are part of a yearly cycle. But here is where the subject gets more interesting.

Each seven years has a Long-Range, Pluto, Result, Environment, and Displacement Card too. Now, this is important information that you can explore to derive even more information from this system. Before I explain how you can find these, in case you haven't already figured it out, let me tell you more about these seven-year cycles.

Just as you have cards that govern each fifty-two-day period of the year and other cards that govern each year, you

YEARLY SPREAD FOR AGE	GOVERNS SEVEN YEARS FOR AGES
0	0-6
1	7-13
2	14-20
3	21-27
4	28-34
5	35-41
6	42-48
7	49-55
8	56-62
9	63-69
10	70-76
11	77-83
12	84-90
13	91-97
14	98-104

have cards that govern each seven-year period of your life as well. These influences are broader to be sure. You have to think in longer terms in order to understand their meanings. For example, if you have a seven-year Long-Range Card of the 5♣, you will probably find that for the entire seven years that you are experiencing a lot of changes and a general sense of dissatisfaction that causes you to travel and make important changes. Over the course of that seven years, you may move three or four times, perhaps even get divorced or otherwise change relationships once or more. The seven-year Long-Range Card doesn't tell you specifically which year you will experience these changes in anymore than the Long-Range Card tells you in which period you can expect its influences to be more predominant. However, it does foretell the changes themselves as being a dominant theme of that period of time. So, when you think about the seven-year influence cards, think in broader terms as you interpret them. You can use the same interpretations given here in the book to get you started, just lengthen the time of their influence to match the appropriate time period, just as you shortened them for the Weekly Reading.

We can use our Yearly Spreads to derive our Seven-Year Spreads, and some of you have already figured out how to do this. In essence, the spread for the first year of your life is also the spread for the first seven years, and the spread for age 1 (the second year) is the Seven-Year Spread for the next seven years. Just to clarify this, I have provided you with the table on page 119 to use to make sure you have the correct years matched up with the seven-year cycle.

Often, the information from these spreads can answer questions about events that occur over a longer period than one year. One particular thing to look for is the Seven-Year Result Card for each cycle. What is significant about that card is that it represents a person or experience that will definitely affect you as you end that cycle. Using that information, I was able to predict the birth of my second son, even though my yearly readings had no indication of his birth. My Seven-Year Result Card was the K♥, the father card. Just as I ended that cycle, my wife became pregnant with a son who was born later that same year.

Don't get these seven-year cycles confused with the thirteen-year influence of the Life Path Cards that we discussed in the previous chapter. Those are also in effect, but work in a different way. That is one reason why these are advanced subjects. It can become a bit confusing to work with so many cards and cycles at the same time. One must find a way to keep them all distinguished from each other and keep a clear record of what they are.

Now, if you have a clear view of the system to this point, you can use this same principle to determine seven-week, weekly, and daily cards. Remember, the Yearly Spread also governs the first seven weeks of your life and the first seven days of your life. The professional software programs listed in the back of this book contain a feature to do this. You can also visit our website to get a daily card reading based upon this same principle.

Are You in a Spiritual or Material Cycle Right Now?

At any given time in our life, we are in either a spiritual or a material cycle. These cycles last anywhere from one to seven years in length and will go back and forth over the course of our lives. If we understand the benefits of each cycle, we can know how to best take advantage of them and the gifts they bring us. Every cycle has something to offer us, if we know where to look.

During a material cycle, we will have more prosperity and success in our work. Things will come easier to us, and we will witness ourselves growing in relationships, finances, popularity, and recognition. Many of our wishes will come true. During a material cycle, we will go along for a while and gather up a certain amount of success.

However, a great material cycle may not enhance our spirituality at all. As a matter of fact, it could decrease our spirituality and our awareness of ourselves. We could take all the good fortune we have for granted and begin to expect that life should be a certain way. If we are inwardly afraid of certain things, we could use the money and power we gain to avoid facing the truth about ourselves. This happens a lot to those of us who experience great success and ease of life in our younger years. We begin to place demands and expectations on life that are based upon avoiding some of our deepest fears. When this happens, we become ripe for a "pruning" time. We reach a plateau in our life and must enter a spiritual cycle to progress in our lives. At this point, we often feel dead in a sense. We often have lost the ability to really enjoy our life and have lost touch with who we really are.

A friend of mine did a dramatic shift from a material to a spiritual cycle. She had received a lot of money through a legal matter that turned out in her favor. This money gave her about a year of time in which she did not have to work and in which she didn't have to look closely at how or where she was spending her money. She had just gotten divorced from a ten-year marriage as well and had never really had to learn to budget or even how to earn her own money. As a result, she spent her money quickly and foolishly. However, at the time, she thought that she was in the midst of a very prosperous period of her life.

Then, about a year later, the money ran out and reality set in. Without money, she had to work, and she discovered that work wasn't something that she had ever learned how to do or to enjoy. She had to stop eating out at restaurants and stop spending money on her credit cards. The illusion of wealth took almost six months to wear off, but eventually, she realized that she was in big trouble and had to do something about it. This realization marked her initiation into her spiritual cycle.

When a spiritual cycle comes along, material concerns will be troublesome and difficult. Finances could be a major problem. Relationships could be extremely difficult, and we could have other challenges such as health or work concerns. We will have problems in the areas in which we need the most growth. People or things that we are attached to are pulled right out from under us. Actually, we experience the greatest difficulty in those areas where we have erected big attachments and have little self-awareness. The pain we suffer during these times serves to wake us up to our own truth and shake us up to what living is really about. However, at the time, we usually complain bitterly about our experiences and go through the whole process of anger and blame until we arrive at the truth, which can take many years in some cases. The harder we resist what is happening and try to avoid the pain we are feeling, the worse it gets.

When I was twenty-one years old, I was at such a place in my life. I had accomplished what I wanted, and yet, I was most unhappy. I had many lovers, success in music, and financial success, but I found that I was miserable inside. I was even thinking about suicide, because I could see no other option that could help me. After two years of much prayer, I met my first real spiritual teacher and moved in to his ashram to study yoga. This was the beginning of a major spiritual cycle in my life.

My first years at my master's ashram were some of the most difficult of my life. It was only knowing that I had no alternatives and believing that I could improve myself by being there that kept me going. It was so difficult that I had to make one-day commitments to be there. I would wake up and just tell myself, "I'll stay here one more day and see if I can handle it." I hated it. And yet I trusted that if I just kept doing the things I hated, my life would improve.

Spiritual cycles are the ones that we think of as being the most difficult, and yet, they are the ones in which we mature and develop true wisdom. They always usher in a new cycle of material prosperity as we rise up to a life with expanded awareness of ourselves. The spiritual cycle is the one that brings us in touch with our inner self. This is the time that we really develop inner wisdom and self-acceptance. For example, in a material cycle, we can go along having success even though we hate ourselves on the inside. During the spiritual cycle, this inner self hate will come to the surface and will have to be dealt with. Without the wisdom that we gain in the spiritual cycle, we would not be able to go forth into the next material cycle.

If we think of a child as an example, we can see the cycles at work more clearly. A child is basically happy in the arms of his or her mother, but as it grows, it must face the challenges of learning to walk, expressing its needs, and integrating into society with all of the rules that make up living in our world. There are many trying times for a child as it grows and encounters new situations to which it must adjust and learn. The challenges are synonymous to the spiritual cycles that adults go through, just on simpler terms.

Some cards in the deck, such as the Sevens and Nines and my own, the Queen of Diamonds, will have many spiritual cycles early on in their life. The early life will seem to be full of trials and great tragedy in some cases. For us, the material cycles seem to be few and far between. However, these same cards develop a lot of wisdom early on in life as a result of all the hardships. Thus, when they reach their thirties and forties, they usually have a lot of life experience that helps them to have good fortune as adults and even more as they get older. The classic Horatio Alger story is an example of this dynamic at work. It can be seen from this that adversity in life usually breeds strength and determination. This goes contrary to the belief held by many parents that they should do everything in their power to protect their children from the hardships of life.

People who do not experience spiritual cycles in their early life will usually do so later. These are the ones that rise up to great heights early in life but seem to fall down to tremendous lows as adults. Going to a twenty-year high school reunion should convince you of this, as you will notice that many of the people who were the most popular and successful as high school students ended up having tragic lives as adults.

We tend to avoid spiritual cycles at all cost, but in truth, it is the hardships and challenges of life that bring us the precious gift of wisdom. This wisdom, in turn, reduces the number and frequency of the spiritual cycles in our adult life. Once we have learned the lessons of the spiritual cycles, we have no need to experience the pain and suffering that goes with being so out of line with our inner self. I have found that spiritual awareness is something that, once developed, continues to be my guide and friend regardless of which cycle I am a part of. Less and less do I feel the great difference between a spiritual and a mundane cycle. Spiritual challenges seem to be more or less constant now, as do material successes.

A person who has reached a point in their life where they have discontinued any self-exploration and self-analysis will live a life that is at the mercy of things called "luck" and "fate." Those are the ones with the "Shit Happens" bumper stickers. For these people, there will always be a nagging feeling in the back of their minds that something bad could happen any moment. They know that those spiritual cycles, which they consider to be bad luck cycles, are bound to occur at any time.

I do believe that all of us have the ability, through our spiritual and personal development, to reach a point where we have basically an unending flow of material success, along with daily, weekly, and yearly spiritual challenges. I don't believe that anyone ever grows beyond any challenges, but we progress into more subtle and less gross/material challenges as our spiritual development unfolds. However, as the challenges become more subtle, we are also enjoying our life more in general and tasting experiences that we have never had before. Life becomes a true adventure with more wonder unfolding every day. We become 'wonder-full,' full of wonder at the mystery and beauty of life.

The Ace of Spades and the Hidden Truth

"Let those with eyes see."

PART ONE

The Ace of Spades is a direct symbol of some of the deepest of spiritual truths. As many of you know, this card has many meanings. First of all, it is one of the most ancient symbols for death and transformation. The appearance of an A♠ has always instilled fear in the hearts of men for ages, especially those of us who are afraid of change. Next, the A♠ is the most ancient symbol for The Order of the Magi, the fellowship of esoteric scientists, sages, astrologers, and teachers that is responsible for the preservation and dissemination of this valuable system of self- understanding. One must ask, 'Why would the Order of the Magi choose the A♠ as their symbol?' and 'What is the true meaning of this powerful card and its implications for our life?'

The A♠ on a very basic level means 'secrets.' The appearance of an A♠ in your reading could indicate a secret of some kind in your life. It is also the most powerful of the Aces, and Aces mean 'desire' and 'passion.' Aces are beginnings, and as such, the A♠ can mean a new beginning in our lives on a profound level. Every new beginning in life happens just after a death of some kind. Thus, the association of the A♠ is with death.

But on a deeper level, the A♠ has a much more profound and valuable message for us. The A♠ is the one card in the deck that represents the hidden truth that lies behind the veil of illusion in the world. To understand this, we must see first of all that there is a difference between what we perceive and what the truth is.

Take, for example, the act of reading a newspaper. We sit and read a certain story, an article, which is essentially some person's report of something that has happened. So, we have this report, and in this report, certain conclusions are drawn about what happened, the motives of the people involved, the reason why it happened, and the outcome of the action. So, basically we have an evaluation of what has occurred, and now comes the test. Are we going to believe what that article has told us? Do

we take that article to be the truth? What is the real truth of that situation?

The O. J. Simpson case is a perfect example of this dynamic. Do you really know the truth about this case, or are you drawing conclusions based on what you have heard and read? We must be honest with ourselves and admit that we do not know. In this example, even the facts of the case seem to be questionable. We really don't know who to believe.

The true master of life is the person who can see through the veil of illusion into the heart of each matter that crosses their path. When we look at a certain person and see them doing the things they do in their life, is there any way for us to know their true reasons for doing what they are doing? Is there any way we can know if what they are doing is making them happy or not? I say that most of us draw quick conclusions about other people and other things in life but that in the majority of cases, we are wrong, and in some cases, seriously wrong.

As an example, let's say that you notice a person who has achieved great financial wealth in their life. This person is admired by others, and you look at him or her and you say to yourself, 'Wow, I would love to be that person! He (or she) must be very happy!' This is a very common thing that most of us do most every day in some fashion. However, do you have any idea why that person worked so hard to achieve that accumulation of financial power, and do you have any idea of what that person went through to get it? If we believe what the media tells us, we might fall into the classic Horatio Alger story of the young person who grows up in a home of poverty and strikes out to make it on their own, the classical American success story. However, it is entirely possible that this person's entire motivation for being successful is a deep-seated belief that he or she is not worthy of love. In this person's rise to fame or financial success, he or she could have committed many injustices to his or her family and friends. Many could have been hurt in the process, and that person could be one of the most miserable people you have ever met, constantly having to protect themselves against imagined attackers on all sides.

Only someone who knows their own weaknesses can see the weaknesses of others. Only someone who is courageous enough to look at their own faults, errors, and mistakes can see those of others without judgment. And this is just what it takes to see through the veil of illusion. What is really going on around us is in reality much different than most of us perceive. Many of the dreams and fantasies that we hold about life were based on false evidence presented to us by the media, books, magazines, and people of low consciousness and integrity. And that is the reason that those dreams never come true. That is the reason for so many suicides and other deaths among those that we hold in such high esteem.

We are going to examine this 'Truth Behind the Veil' more in upcoming sections. If we can begin to see the world as it really is, we can discover and tap into our unlimited power. Once we see the hidden truth behind our own actions, we will understand the actions of others more completely and will not be fooled by anyone or anything. Let's end this first section by simply saying, 'Begin to distrust what you know.' It is not what we don't know that hurts us, it is what we don't know that we don't know. Begin to distrust what you think is the truth, and be open to seeing things differently. Create some mental and perceptive flexibility. It could lead to some profound discoveries and revelations.

PART TWO

In this section, we examine more of the common misconceptions about life and discover how to look life in the eye, as the Ace of Spades suggests we do.

When we look at someone who is held in high esteem in the eyes of the world, what do we see? When you see a famous actor or actress, someone who has risen to the very heights of fame and fortune, do you think they are a wonderful, evolved person who must be full of goodness and good qualities? Does it seem that God must love them because they have achieved such success? In other words, are successful people happy, adjusted, and loving people? Or, on the other hand, are they so successful because they have such tremendous needs for approval that they would stop at nothing to avoid facing their inner self-rejection? Perhaps the people we hold in such high regard are actually those whose emotional problems are so great that even the approval and admiration of a million people does nothing to help them feel good about themselves.

When we see a man or woman in office, such as a senator or a president, do we see a person who has the public's interest at heart, someone dedicated to helping those that he or she has been elected to govern? Or is this elected official only interested in power and fame at all costs, stopping at nothing, even murder, to stay in power, as long as they don't get caught? Perhaps many of those whom we have elected have deep emotional problems, problems that began in childhood, like you and I, problems that have never been addressed to any extent at all. So, in this light, I would like to present some other situations for you to ponder on.

1. Is the man who falls madly in love an example of the beauty of love OR is he an example of someone with such a low self-esteem that he needs someone else to make his life okay?

2. Is a rich person rich because of a healthy sense of prosperity OR because the fear of poverty is so great that it completely dominates her life? In other words, is the rich person rich because it takes a million dollars to make her feel safe and okay?

3. Is that woman a loving and caring mother OR is she a woman who will do anything to keep her kids from leaving her because she is afraid of finding out that she is nothing without someone to sacrifice herself for?

4. Is that man 'the world's greatest lover' because he has a gift from God in the sexual sense OR is he hopelessly addicted to sex and so makes it the most important thing in his life because deep down inside he hates who he is?

5. Is television a great source of information and entertainment OR is it a vehicle for some of the richest corporations in this country to use subtle psychological manipulation on the masses in order to increase their profits?

6. Is that woman a great spiritual teacher OR is she using her God-given charisma and spiritual power to use her followers for money and sex?

7. Is insurance (life, health, car, house, etc.) a wonderful institution that helps us in time of need OR is it a calculated gamble that we use in order to not have to take financial responsibility for our actions? From the insurance company's point of view, is it a bet against us that they can collect more money than they pay out (with them usually winning)?

8. Is that story we read in the newspaper or see on television a true account of what happened OR is it a story that was fabricated and fed to the press in order to achieve some other goal, such as free publicity to sell some product or service? In another sense, is the story a true account OR is it an account that is tremendously biased by the beliefs and emotional problems of the reporter who wrote it?

These are just a few of the misconceptions that occur commonly in today's society. I am not saying that all of them are true all the time, but I think that most of us would be surprised if we knew the truth. If we pay close attention, however, we can know the truth, but only when we have developed the habit of being truthful with ourselves first.

PART THREE

One of the most important things I have learned about truth is that it is relative. The other important thing I have learned about truth is that truth without love is untruth. No matter how much we know or understand about life, this knowledge will be useless to us if it is not used with love and compassion. Truth can be used like a hammer to hit someone in the head or like a healing massage to help someone in time of need. Just how we use the truth we have will determine whether or not it is real truth or truth being turned around to meet our purposes.

Today, our media is exploding in its impact on our society. We see people in power using this as a tool to attempt to shape our beliefs and opinions. If I am a lazy person, which most people are, I might grow to depend upon the media or some certain television show to provide me with the things that I believe. If I give all of my beliefs over to anyone outside of myself, I am opening myself up to be very wrong about certain aspects of life. More and more, I see the need for me to take the initiative and explore things for myself and not believe what I read or hear without making it true for myself.

I now believe that everything is essentially good from some point of view. I see life as a grand evolutionary play of energy and each of us a being somewhere in this vast cosmic soup of evolution. Each of us is heading up stream like the salmon at breeding time, striving to improve our lives in every way we can.

At some points, we think that we need more money to be happy and, we strive like crazy to make more. Is this wrong? Someone who has already tried it and found that money did not bring them happiness may tell you that striving for money is wrong or bad. But when they say this, they are not considering who they are talking to. They themselves needed to make money an obsession for a while in order to learn about it.

You may say that the Jehovah's Witnesses are a bunch of looneys or that the Hare Krishnas are out of their minds. Did you know that I was a Jehovah's Witness for a year and lived in an ashram chanting Hare Krishna for ten years? Is it bad or wrong to do these things? Or are they steps on a particular path to the highest truth?

Lately, when I have counseled people, I have come to realize that some of the truths that I may have in me from my years of experience may not be appropriate for certain people at a certain stage in their development. They may need to make mistakes and go through certain painful experiences, just as I did. Pain has been my greatest teacher in my entire life. Who am I to deprive others of getting the valuable lessons that I myself have gotten? Do I think I can help them by shielding them from the pain?

In keeping with the new Age of Aquarius, I must allow each individual the freedom to pursue whatever path they choose, unless their actions prove harmful to others in some way. I must allow them to get the lessons they are learning from whatever position of truth they are at. I must believe that they are doing what they are doing because that is the best thing for them at their current stage of development. This applies not only to their religious beliefs, but also to their choices of lifestyle, music, relationships, and other areas. This is the Aquarian Age, where everyone is to be allowed their own unique expression.

Today, we are more aware of the diversity of this world than at any other time in history. Because of the tremendous growth and development of communications, ruled by Aquarius, we are now in touch with everything in this world as if it were in our own backyards. We now see and feel what is going on everywhere and are forced to decide what we make of it all and how we fit into all of it. It is frightening at times, as we are constantly bombarded with so many cultures, beliefs,

and points of view. Everything is being intensified, especially our fears and judgments of others. It is now, more than ever, that we must be aware of the relative quality of truth and not use our own truth to try and force others to conform to our personal place in the evolutionary stream.

Otherwise, we may kill each other in the name of our own personal beliefs, as we have for so many centuries. There have been more wars and wrongful deaths done in the name of God than anything else. Killing, for any reason other than pure survival or defense, is still killing. No philosophy, religion, or reason will make it okay, or protect you from the laws of karma that will cause you to reap what you sow.

So let's begin to see everyone in our world as doing the best they can. Whatever their goals and dreams, beliefs and ideas, let's see them as finding their own highest expression among the diversity of life. In this way, we will allow ourselves to be less than perfect and to fully explore all that this life has to offer.

Consider the table on page 125 as we discuss the qualities of the suits and how they apply to our lives. The four suits can be seen as an evolutionary process that we go through in the course of the development of our soul and personality. We have the four seasons of life in which we have these four predominating influences for certain periods. If we examine the lives of ten thousand people, we will see a pattern emerging that fits these suit-phases exactly. I believe that these phases are also a part of our spiritual and personal growth, whether it takes one lifetime or a thousand. I have listed these suits in reverse order just to illustrate the powers of the suits—that the higher the suit is, the more power it has.

Hearts are the first and least powerful of the suits. This is not to imply that any suit is better than any other. In fact, we need mastery of all four suits if we are to achieve complete mastery of the self and of our external lives. Hearts is childhood, home and family, love, relationships, feelings, and emotions. It is during our childhood that we develop our self-esteem. Our feeling and emotional habits are formed and set through the influence of our parents and our life at home. Our childhood influences us, for better or worse, for the rest of our life. Childhood is the time in which we develop our basic sense of lovability and self-esteem. If we have challenging events at this time, it can affect us in profound ways, and may take years of therapy and self-analysis to change those feeling patterns that we created then. Many of us try and try to change the way we feel about life and the way in which we respond emotionally to situations. Just think of yourself. How many emotional habits, such as fear or anger, have you been working on? How successful have you been in changing these patterns? The task is enormous. But this feeling of self-love is the very foundation of the rest of our lives and thus is the importance of this first stage of development. Without self-love, all of our actions are fruitless, because they stem from this belief that we are not lovable or worthy of others' love either. Even though people may achieve great accomplishments in their life, they will end up feeling like a personal failure if they have not learned to love themselves and give themselves the credit.

One of the keys that psychologists and others have discovered is that our emotions come from our beliefs about ourselves. Negative emotional patterns can always be traced to a deep-seated belief. For example, if I believe that I am basically unlovable, every time someone says something that I think is unloving, I may respond in anger or in shame. It may not be true that they were actually being unloving or even expressing disapproval of me, but my perceptions are colored by my internal beliefs. Thus, for me, the truth doesn't really matter. I am stuck with my personal interpretation.

If I believe that they were unloving or uncaring, I am already responding emotionally to what they said before my mind has a chance to intervene. These underlying beliefs are where the Clubs come in. If we can alter our beliefs about life and ourselves, we can watch our emotional patterns change instantly. Clubs have that power over the Hearts, and if we learn how to access it, we can cure ourselves of childhood wounds. If you have a specific emotional problem, you can bet that it is because on some level you have a negative belief about yourself. The trick is that in order to find and identify that negative belief, one must be willing to experience the negative feelings that arise out of it. A good exercise is to just allow yourself to really feel some negative feeling. It will eventually lead you to the thought, belief, or idea that it sprang from. It may lead you, for example, to an event in your childhood where one of your parents said something that you took, at that moment, to be completely true about you, even though that wasn't what they intended. Exploring these sorts of beliefs can lead us to emotional freedom. Ultimately, truth will overcome any and all negative emotional patterns. There is an ultimate truth that most Clubs are searching for. It could be a truth that encompasses all things and situations. One of those truths is that the universe is a loving universe. If we could adopt just this one truth in our lives, it has the potential to heal countless emotional wounds. Many people believe the world to be a basically unloving world that is out to get them.

Beliefs are very powerful things. They influence our lives in countless ways, especially our feelings. They act like filters through which we see life. We interpret most every incoming signal, whether it is something we see, hear, taste, touch, or smell, through our beliefs before deciding what it means to us. But did you know that our beliefs are also very transitory things? Beliefs are influenced to a great extent by our values. To put it simply, what we want is more powerful than what we believe.

When we want something, we can create reasons for having it, we can justify it. This process of justification is belief-making in action. When someone asks us "why?," about anything in our life, we can tell them our reason, and it all sounds very real and believable. The real and only reason, so often, is just that we wanted it. This can be a hard concept to grasp. Do you really know why you like the things that you like? Really?

Take a closer look, and I think that you will discover as I did, that I like them because I like them. Once I like or want something, my mind will come up with an appropriate set of beliefs, reasons, and opinions to justify my having that particular thing or person. We often acquire beliefs that will go along with the things we are creating in our life. If I want to smoke cigarettes, I can believe that cigarettes are okay, and I can cite many examples of people who have lived to one hundred while smoking a pack a day to prove my point. Then, when I am quitting smoking, I can prove that cigarettes are not good for me with all of the cancer research and believe that cigarettes are the worse thing. So, what is really true about cigarettes and what changed in me or in cigarettes to make them good at one moment and not so good the next? This is the thing about beliefs. They are tools of a sort that we use to accomplish things that we desire. They are like suits of clothing that we wear for different occasions. When we are done with a certain occasion, we just take them off and put on something different.

Now, let's get back to those desires of yours. Where do they come from? Are they immutable and fixed, or do they change from time to time? If they change, who or what changes them? There is this thing call the 'Will of God' that must be reckoned with in this equation of ours. You see, no matter what we feel, think, or want, in the end, it will meet with conflict and problems if it is out of sync with universal will. We might call this

The Evolution of the Soul as Seen in the Cards

Suit	Season	Quality	Cycle of Life
Spades	Winter	Will (ours verses the Divine)	Last Years of Life
Diamonds	Fall	Values, Desires (self-worth)	Adulthood/Money-Making Years
Clubs	Summer	Truth, Beliefs, Attitudes (self-truth)	Adolescence/School Years
Hearts	Spring	Feelings, Emotions (self-love)	Childhood

will the Tao, or as a guy on my pool team calls it, "the zone." When we are in the zone, we are flowing with things, and everything proceeds smoothly and successfully. Regardless of what we want, it seems to harmonize with the rest of our life, and it meshes in nicely, becoming a part of our unique expression. When we are out of the zone, we have one failure after another, in spite of our best efforts. This is where the Spades come in.

Spade people as a group may not necessarily be masters of will, but as a rule, they are more preoccupied with it than the other suits. They know, from experience, how the Will of God is flowing. Many of their personal battles occur with others and themselves in the area of their will, which usually translates to work and health issues. They appreciate others who have experience in something more than those who just have a feeling or desire about something. Experience is a key word for Spades. Wisdom is too, and wisdom comes to us only through experience. It is by trial and error that we learn about the Will of God. It is by going through our mistakes and feeling the pain and paying the prices for them that we really learn about life on its deepest levels. We may have dreams, desires, feelings, and ideas about things, but if they are out of sync with reality, they will not manifest. It is when we have become totally aligned with the Universal Will that we find peace and enlightenment. This may be the stepping off place or the beginning of an entirely new cycle in a new existence. All that we know is that, in our current reality, these are the cycles that we know.

So, our path on the road to life begins with the Hearts and ends with the Spades. Along the way, we learn many important lessons from each of these suits as we experience the many levels of experience that each has to offer. But the secret to ultimate success may be just the opposite. By aligning ourselves with the divine will, we get in sync with the universe that gives us the desires (Diamonds) that are fruitful and for which we provide justification (Clubs) that also works well and gives us a sense of self-esteem (Hearts). It is interesting how life can flow in two directions at once and how many approaches can take us to the same ultimate goal.

The Cards Versus Our Personal Power

After doing literally thousands of readings, I have seen practically everything that we humans get into. In each reading I do, I strive to give my client information that will really make a difference in their life. The cards often provide such information, as does astrology, but I know for certain that without the personal efforts of my client, nothing will change in their life.

Just recently, I was doing a reading for a client, and in the middle of the reading, he stopped me with a disappointed look on his face. I asked him what was going on. He told me that he was a little disappointed in my reading. I asked him why, but sensing what he was thinking, I asked him to elaborate on what his expectations were of the reading. I said to him, "If this reading could be just exactly the best reading you ever had, what would it look like?" He responded by asking, "In a perfect world?" I said, "Yes, if this reading could be everything you would like it to be, how would it be?" He then said, "Well, you would look into my future and tell me exactly what I would do, and my life would be better. You would say something like I would read the paper, see this incredible job offer, and then go and apply. I would make millions of dollars and live happily ever after." I really appreciated him describing this for me, and I told him so. Then I told him that I would never give him a reading like that. I told him that I knew that even if I did tell him exactly what to do that would really work and make him happy, he wouldn't do it. What good would it be if I were to tell him what would be the best thing to do if he had no interest in doing it? Then I told him that if I were to make an honest prediction about his future, I would be willing to bet that his life would be pretty much the same from now on, but getting a little worse each year. Now that's a shocking thing to tell a client! Your life is going to stay the same but worse now on. But anyone who sincerely looks at people's lives and their patterns will tell you that this is the norm of our society.

After I let that statement sink in for a few moments, I began to explain how he could have a better life and just what it would take for this to happen. It is never my intention to just give my clients bad news. In fact, I really believe in my heart of hearts that all of us are going to 'make it' someday. It's just that for some of us it's going to take a long time. We have to go through tremendous pain before we are usually willing to let go of the patterns that we have that are in conflict with reality.

So, in any reading I do, I always get to know my client a little first. I know what all the cards and all of the astrological transits and planets mean. But how these will actually show up in someone's life is completely dependent upon their personal intention and the ways they are currently using their personal power. One of my teachers, Arne Lein, once told me how people's attitudes can completely change their destinies. He mentioned several of his clients who had the greatest cards and transits but whose negative attitude blocked any good fortune they may have experienced. Contrast this to someone who let's say becomes a millionaire one year when they have the 10♦ in Jupiter.

I often appear as a guest on radio shows around the country where people call in for a mini-reading. It always intrigues me when I get calls from people in their seventies who are on fixed incomes and who are asking me about their finances. I know what is going to happen to them—essentially their financial fortunes are fixed. It will not matter what their cards or astrology transits are, their finances are just not going to change that much. Every card in the deck has many meanings. Our cards always reflect what is going on in our lives, but we cannot pick a meaning for a card that we want if we are unwilling or unable in some cases to do what it takes to take advantage of that influence.

This leads me to the main point of this article, and that is just what the cards and astrology are and what they are not. Everyone likes the cards a lot, especially when they look into their past and see just how accurately their cards describe what happened to them. But it is when we begin playing with the future that most people get it all wrong. Essentially people tend to do two things that are wrong. First, they really worry about the bad cards they see in their future. They get all upset when they see a 9♠ or an A♠ in their future. I remember when my oldest sister called me up one day shortly after learning how to read her destiny. She said, "Robert I am going to die." "What?" I said. "Well I looked into my cards, and in seven years, I have the death card." I then went on to explain how the cards have several meanings and how death cards come up frequently in life. Only one of those many death cards will actually represent our physical death. Anyway, this is a common mistake that people make using the cards in reference to their future.

The other mistake is that they get all worked up about good cards, thinking that the good cards will do for them what they refuse to do for themselves. I have many single, female clients who just cannot seem to get a relationship going. They are attractive and successful but just cannot seem to find a partner. I have gotten calls from them that go something like this: "Robert, I had this great card for a love affair this year and nothing happened." The implication is that the cards are all wrong and undependable. But I can tell you that the cards are 100 percent accurate. So, what is going on here? In each individual case, these women are internally blocking the possibility of love coming into their life. Though they profess wanting a relationship badly, none of them are actually doing the things that people who really want a relationship do. This is evidence of an powerful struggle going on inside of them. Part of them really wants to have a relationship, while another, more powerful part of them doesn't. Unfortunately, in these cases the part that doesn't want the relationship is far stronger than the part that does, even though these women are largely unconscious of that other part. This particular pattern is fairly commonplace these days and is found in a lot of career women's lives.

So, how are we supposed to use our cards in relationship to our future? If we are to access them in the highest way possible, what must we do? This information is so important that I hope everyone using the cards will read this and understand it. The cards, and astrology for that matter, are guideposts for us. Each year there are challenging influences and beneficial influences. A person who is conscious of their internal state can always get the very best from every card they have. All that it takes is self-awareness. I use my cards to plan my future, knowing my own limitations and being aware of my own inner conflicts at the same time. I know now that nothing will manifest itself in my life if part of me is rejecting it. I continually strive to pay attention to my feelings, my fears in particular. It is these fears, by and large, that represent the often subconscious elements that affect my destiny. If one does not know their own fears and internal conflicts, little is possible in terms of having the power to shape their destiny.

Some of you may have read my articles on following the planet Jupiter's transits for continual success. I have personally used this for the past seven years with great success and plan to continue using it for the rest of my life. But I have also seen areas in my own life where my own internal struggles have blocked what Jupiter may have brought me. The same goes for the cards. There are really great cards each and every year of our life. The Jupiter, Result, and Environment Cards are always good. But do we have an opening within our consciousness to allow these good things to come in? That is real question. The question is not 'How good are my cards this year?' but 'How much good can I allow to manifest in my life this year?' Once we become aware of how powerful we really are, we will be able to use the cards to write our own success story. What's first in your script of the future? Only you hold that key.

The Nine of Spades and the Stages of Life

The 9♠ is one of the most powerful cards in the deck in terms of how much it can affect our lives. To study this card and its effects on us brings a lot of information that can better our lives. All of us will have the 9♠ in our Yearly Spreads at one time or another. And some of us have the 9♠ as our Birth Card or Planetary Ruling Card. Or perhaps we know someone that does. In any case, the 9♠ affects us all in one way or another, and this card can teach us a lot about life and the cycles that govern it. Many people have a big fear of Nines in general and the 9♠ in particular, and perhaps this article may serve to replace that fear with a deeper understanding of life.

Those familiar with my writings will know by now that the number Nine represents the ending of a cycle. To understand this more fully, we first have to realize that everything in our life has a cycle. Everything has a beginning, and everything has an ending. Let's say you get a new idea today for a new way to improve your health. This idea stage is the first stage of the cycle. You begin a new diet or exercise that helps improve your health. You go out and find and purchase the right equipment or resources needed and initiate the new plan. You follow the plan for a while and watch to see what happens. Each of these steps are steps of the life cycle of that plan that began with the original idea. The original idea can be thought of as the Ace in this cycle. The acquisition of necessary materials might be the Two stage. The Three stage might be reading books about it or talking to others about your new phase. We continue on in this cycle until we reach the Eight stage, the stage of fullness and power. When we reach the Eight stage in our life in regards to anything, whether it be a new health regime or a relationship, we are reaping the rewards of that thing to its fullest potential. It is important to stop for a moment here and really understand the importance of the Eight stage in order to fully understand and appreciate the Nine stage. At the stage of the Eight, this thing or person or idea or way of communicating, whatever, is at it very peak for us. You may liken it to the fruit on the tree that has reached its peak ripeness. When it is picked at this moment, it will be the sweetest and have the most flavor. Any earlier than this, and it will not be as sweet or flavorful. Any later than this, and it may be too sweet or have a flavor that is undesirable. It could even begin to decompose after this. So at the Eight stage, we harvest the very best and the most from whatever it is that we are doing.

Following the Eight comes the Nine, which says, "Okay, it's over now. Time to clean up and prepare for the next cycle." So, one of the most important things to understand about the Nine is that whatever is coming to an end right now is something that we have had for a considerable length of time, and it is something from which we have already harvested all of the good it had for us. Whatever that thing is, the good it held for us has come and gone, and anyone who has consciously gone through a Nine experience will agree with this. If everyone who had a Nine in their Yearly Spreads would just stop and think about this for a moment, much of their fear and trepidation about what they may lose would disappear. It is only our lack of awareness about the true nature of what is going on that makes us afraid. Many people see a Nine coming and immediately think "Something bad is going to happen to me." This is exactly the opposite of what is really true, but because they are not looking closer at their life and what is going on, this is the best they can come up with. The Nine is actually a very important blessing. It is the cleanup stage that prepares us to receive the next blessing that is about to come into our lives. "Only an empty cup can be filled." How can we expect anything new and good to come into our life when we are clutching onto things in our past? Not only do we cling to things in our past, but these are the things that are not doing us any good at all. But this is exactly what we do when, in our ignorance, we do not see that this thing that is ending is something that has already served us to its fullest capacity.

So the Nine can be seen as a liberating experience or as a tragic loss. It is actually neither of these. It is just the last stage in the life cycle of something in our life. The liberation and tragic loss labels are creations of our point of view. The only question that remains about Nines is which of these points of view will you choose? One way that you and I can use Nines is that when we see one or more coming in our spreads, we can let them remind us to stop and examine the situation for a moment and ask ourselves some questions. We can ask ourselves first of all, "Am I afraid of this Nine?" If so, then ask "What am I afraid of losing?" followed by "Is this thing that I am afraid of losing already lost (or over)?" The point is to identify exactly what is coming to an end and then take a closer look at it and see if is not actually over already.

Many times what is over is not over the way we imagine it. For example a 9♥ can indicate a divorce or ending of a significant relationship, but it also can merely indicate that the relationship, in its present form, ends. The two people could actually stay together but sort of restart their relationship based upon new realizations that they have come to in their quest to perfect their being together. The same could apply to a 9♠ work situation. You may not actually lose your job, but instead get transferred or even promoted into a different position where what you do would be drastically different. So here we have another reason to stop and think before we get really scared about the coming of a Nine.

With all this in mind, we come to the Spades version of the Nine, which is the most potent of all the Nines and is one of the three classic 'death cards'. On February 4, 1997, O. J. Simpson received a guilty verdict in his civil trial. He was just two days into his Saturn cycle. What cards did he have in his Saturn Period? : the 6♣ and 9♠. Did he die? No. Was there an ending in his life? Yes, that stage of his civil trial ended on that date. Did he like the ending? Probably not since the verdict went against what he was working for and ended up costing him most of his wealth. In this version of the 9♠, it fell in his Saturn Period. The 9♠ occurring in Saturn is usually going to be a difficult ending for us, one that we would generally describe as a loss. It is often a karmic ending as well. The 6♣ in O. J.'s cards were indications that his ending had karmic implications, but Saturn is a karmic influence as well. This would make his ending a double-karmic one, which means that the events that transpired were a result of his words and deeds from the past more than they were from his actions at the immediate time of the current events. The 9♠ in Saturn is often, though not always, perceived as a tragic loss by the individual. But again, this would only be the case when this person is completely unaware of their own role in the events that transpired.

A 9♠ in Jupiter could bring a very beneficial ending or even one that is financially lucrative. It still may scare you, but there will be some obvious benefits from it. One client of mine was looking at a 9♠ coming in her Jupiter Period. She confided in me that she was very afraid that she would lose her job. There had been many layoffs lately, and she feared that she would be next. Sure enough, she was laid off during her Jupiter Period. However, the Jupiter part of it was that she was given an entire year's pay as a send-off bonus. Because she had a very well-paying job, it turned out to be quite a nice sum of money.

What the 9♠ is essentially is the 'ending of a lifestyle.' Spades represent the things that we actually spend time doing in our life each day. When a 9♠ appears, the ending that it signifies will alter our lifestyle or schedule in some meaningful way. Now that O. J.'s civil trial is over, he will not have to spend as much time in court. This represents a change in his doing. I imagine he will initiate appeals to the verdict, but it is likely that he will not have to appear in court often to do this—that can be handled by his lawyers. Other examples of a 9♠ experience could be someone who quits smoking, takes up jogging, changes professions, has a child, becomes crippled, loses their eyesight, starts a new job—really anything that causes what we were spending our time doing each day to come to an end. The 9♠ itself is neither positive or negative. It merely signifies that something we have been doing for some time has now reached that stage where, for us, it is over and no longer can bring us any good. If we acknowledge it and release it, we can remain happy and prepare for the new cycle that is about to begin. If we fight it or are simply unaware of the ending that is taking place, we can suffer more under the 9♠ than with most any other card. It can, in some cases, represent the ending of our life. In Saturn, it is a near certainty that the 9♠ ending will not come easily to us. It is probably an area that we have avoided for a long time or refused to acknowledge for some reason. But even there, the blow can be greatly lessened by a spiritual approach to the situation, keeping an open mind, and so forth.

So this pretty well describes the 9♠ as a card found in our Yearly, Weekly, Seven-Year, or whatever spreads for some time period. By taking the position of any 9♠ that shows up and keeping in mind the cards that are found with it, one can derive a better interpretation for its meaning using the information that I have presented here. The last thing to talk about are people who have the 9♠ as a Birth Card or Planetary Ruling Card. In this case, we have a 9♠ experience that is in some ways destined to last an entire lifetime. That is a fairly hard concept for most people to grasp. How could an ending take an entire lifetime to complete? What kind of person would require an entire lifetime to finish up some aspect of their life? To understand this, we have to take a broader approach to the interpretation of the 9♠ and expand our view of it to include some new concepts. Every 9♠ person is different, but all have one thing in common. Something about their life or lifestyle is in need of completion. But here we are talking about things that are much more deeply ingrained and

often harder for the individual to see. Earlier, I talked about how we suffer with an ending when we are unaware of how something in our life had already run its course and brought us everything that it had to bring us. This same principle applies to people whose Birth Card or Planetary Ruling Card is the 9♠. Usually this person has, for whatever reasons, chosen to ignore the need for this ending and has perpetuated the thing or pattern longer than the average person.

Perhaps in a past life, many 9♠ people were Eights who abused their power and reinforced this negative behavior with years of experiences of doing it. Remember that the Nine follows the Eight and that the Eight represents power. It could stand to reason that some 9♠ people are Eights that abused power before, especially when one looks at their current patterns. The 9♠ has a K♥ first Karma Card. Keeping in mind that the first Karma Card represents negative traits carried over from previous lives and that Kings represent power and authority, it is easy to imagine that many 9♠ people have issues around control or power. Another possibility is that a 9♠ person had some other habitual way of approaching life that had become so ingrained in a previous lifetime that it now takes an entire lifetime to undo it. There are other possibilities as well, but if you study the 9♠ people you meet carefully, you will sooner or later discover a negative pattern (Nine), often one connected to their health, use of will power, or their work (all governed by Spades), that has been an issue for them as long as they can remember. In some cases, it is prominent and easy to spot, while with other 9♠ people, it is kept secret from others and is only known by those who are closest to them. I know one 9♠ person who lost his entire family, through various tragedies, before he was sixteen. He has had an ongoing struggle with his belief that he will fail at anything he does. Another 9♠ woman has had an ongoing struggle with a tendency to overeat and overindulge in other sensual pleasures. The variations are as endless as the personalities of different people but carry a common underlying theme.

On the positive side, all 9♠ people have many opportunities in life to experience things that are usually denied the average person. These experiences will be of the spiritual kind. In their struggle to make the completions that are their destiny, they will have moments of revelation and clarity of understanding, in some cases experiences of what is called 'universal consciousness.' At these moments, their understanding of their life and the lives of others will become crystal clear. They get the chance to glimpse the divine plan for all people and see their individual roles from this universal point of view. These moments become the inspiration for many of them to become involved in work that is of a spiritual nature—helping others and becoming someone who is available to others for compassionate support during times of need. These moments also give them the much-needed understanding that helps them continue on their quest for freedom through what are surely to be difficult experiences at times. And, in some cases, these experiences become the catalyst for them to finally let go of the major negative pattern that they are working on in this lifetime. 9♠ people are not fated to have an entire lifetime of pain and suffering and struggle. Their destined transformation may occur at any age. When it does, their lives are generally transformed to great happiness and contentment. As Nines they are all naturally givers to others, but they become even greater givers once they have given away that which was hardest to give. I am referring here to that particular pattern that is the main one they are here to let go of in this lifetime. The joy they experience can be likened to a person who has just completed college and is on the stage to receive their diploma. There is a sense of accomplishment and freedom from the old that comes with a conscious completion in this manner. The transformed 9♠ may dedicate his or her life to giving something important to the world. They no longer are concerned with their own personal losses but are now focused on the needs of others and how they can make a valuable contribution.

The Cards of Moves and Changes

It is most appropriate that I write this article now since our family is moving across the country within a month. This being such a big move for us would surely prove to be helpful in showing what cards may be present during such a change. Typically we associate Fives with moves and travel, but when it comes to actually leaving one's home and moving to another, many other factors come into play, all of which can show up in the cards in many ways. We are actually moving from one end of the country to the other, so this qualifies as being a move of major significance for all of us.

As in all other cases, the cards that do show up during a person's life at the time of a major event will tell you what that event is to them, not necessarily what it appears to be on the external level. For example, at the time of the murder of Nicole Simpson and Ron Goldman, O. J. Simpson had no cards indicating a personal tragedy or loss. Instead, he had cards of success and accomplishment, which indicated to me the successful completion of a plot to get back at Nicole for the supposed injustices she had caused him. Another example is when someone dies. Whatever cards you find at that time will tell you what that death was to them—not what you or I might imagine death to be. For some, death may be a 9♥— the ending of key relationships, while for others it may be a 9♦—loss of personal possessions. And in some cases, a death may appear as a Five, indicating that for that person it is just a new adventure and experience. So, I wasn't surprised when I discovered that Katherine and my son, Michael, both had such different cards for the time of our big move.

Before we had a definite date for the move, I guessed when the move would take place by looking at my cards. This particular year, I had an A♠ in Venus and a 5♠ in Uranus. I figured it would happen in one of these periods. Venus rules the home and family, and Uranus rules real estate in general. The A♠ in Venus would mean a rebirth in the home, which could possibly translate as a move to a new home. The 5♠ in Uranus is a classic move card, probably one of the strongest, though it does have other possible meanings as well. The 5♠ is the strongest of all the Fives and generally indicates a long trip or a complete change of job or lifestyle. In Uranus, it generally indicates property changing hands or a move. It turns out that this move is occurring during my Venus Period, where I have the A♠. Knowing this now, I can predict that this move will have a profound effect on me because the A♠ is such a card of transformation.

For my wife Katherine, this move occurs in her Uranus Period, which as I have said is the period generally associated with changes of real estate. But the card she has for this period in her Birth Card's yearly spread is the 9♥. For her, this move is more about all of the relationships that are ending. It is a major thing for her to let go of nearly every relationship she has cultivated here and start over again. Even though the move is a month away, she has already cried a couple of times realizing how some of her key relationships are ending. In her Planetary Ruling Card spread, she has an 8♦, which displaces the 4♥ in the Life Spread this year. The 8♦ in Uranus is an indicator of the purchase of a house or real estate. This move has quite a lot of financial details and does involve the largest purchase we have ever made. It is interesting that Katherine's Long-Range Card in her Birth Card Spread is the 9♠. She and I both felt that it was time to leave California, though we don't have any particular reason for it. The 9♠ as the Long-Range Card always indicates that some significant chapter of life is coming to a close. Though I don't have a Nine Long-Range this year, I am displacing the 9♦, which is just as potent. This just feels like a Nine year for our whole family, which is a year of major endings and completions.

My fifteen-month old son, Michael, will have the move in his Mars Period where he has a J♠. The J♠ can always indicate a change of lifestyle and usually a change for the better. Though you wouldn't normally associate it with a move, we have to consider the fact that Michael is only a year old. Whatever changes he perceives will in some way represent a new lifestyle for him, hopefully a better one.

Venus represents our home and family, and any card in that period could represent some change or events occurring in relation to our home or house. That is why any Nine in Venus could represent a move to a new home. The A♠ carries much the same meaning as a Nine. And of course, any Five in Venus could represent a change of residence.

Successfully Predicting Presidential Elections and Other Contests

Probably one of the most difficult predictions you will ever make will be those involving sports or political contests. Both are basically competitive events, and it is relatively easy to see if a contestant has strong cards for competition. One would look at their Mars cards. Sevens and Nines in Mars indicate problems or failures, while Fours, Eights, Tens, Queens, and Kings are indicators of success. And also, you might want to look for overall indicators of success for that particular year in the Long-Range, Pluto, Result, Environment, and Displacement cards. Unfortunately, it is never that simple. I myself have about a 60 percent success rate with presidential elections, and I will explain the main reason for my failures below. Some elections are really easy. But most of them are not. For many of the elections of the past twenty years, there have not been clear-cut winners in the yearly spreads. If you compare both candidates' cards, you don't get a definite win. That happened recently with the Barack Obama/Mitt Romney match up. Judging by their cards, Romney had an edge. It wasn't a really big advantage, but his cards were just better than Obama's. You can compare them yourself. Obama was born August 4, 1961 (9♦), and Mitt Romney was born March 12, 1947 (J♦/Q♥). The election took place on Tuesday, November 6, 2012. Just look at Obama's Age 51 spread and Romney's Age 65 spreads. Romney clearly has better cards for the year, and yet, he lost.

In any competitive event, we usually make the assumption that each contestant wants to win. In fact, though this is usually the case, it is not always true. And it is hard to know the true intentions of contestants in any contest. I have seen contests where it is clear that one of the contestants is not really in it to win. They, in fact, want to lose. This happened when Bill Clinton ran against George H. W. Bush in 1988. I could tell Bush's heart was not in the race just by his demeanor in public. I do not know the reasons for this, but the cards give us a clue. During that race, both he and Clinton were having a Pinnacle Year. It is very rare for this to occur. Bush was already at the top when this election and Pinnacle Year came along. So, the big change we usually associate with the Pinnacle Year had to mean his stepping down. On the other hand, Bill Clinton had not reached the pinnacle of his career yet, so the big change of his Pinnacle Year was a step up. Most people would not think to look for things like the Pinnacle Year, but it is a definite item to add to the checklist for presidential elections. One could assume, and usually be right, that any candidate who is having a Pinnacle Year at the time of the election, and who is not currently in office, is going to win. And that is regardless of what their other yearly cards may say. That is the power of the Pinnacle Year, one of the most important auspicious

events discussed in chapter eight of this book. When I do predictions for contests of these sorts, I first ask myself, "Do both contestants appear to really want to win?"

Another technique I have used in presidential elections is to look for Fives and sometimes Nines in the president's cards or in his wife's cards. If a man is running for president and is not currently in office, a win would mean moving into the White House. This could be quite a significant move for any family, and moves show up as Fives or Nines. Of course, you would look for those move cards after the election, probably in January of the following year. It is harder when looking at the president himself because you would imagine that getting elected the first time would focus his or her attention on many factors, and the move might not even show up in his or her cards.

I faced this same issue recently making a prediction for the 2012 Olympics. It was for Liu Xiang, a famous Chinese athlete. Born July 13, 1983, he is the first Chinese athlete to achieve the "triple crown" of athletics: World Record Holder, World Champion, and Olympic Champion. All eyes in China were upon him at the 110-meter hurdles at the Beijing Olympics. When I looked at his cards, I saw mediocre cards. Nothing bad, but nothing great. As I read more about him, I learned that he had dropped out of the 2008 Olympics at the last moment, disappointing all his fans greatly. I had to wonder if his heart was truly in the Olympics. I could not predict a win, but I did predict that he would be okay with whatever happened. What happened was that he lost, very badly. He tripped on the very first hurdle in round one and did not finish. Later, I realized I should have looked at his coach's cards. His coach, Haiping Sun, was born on January 13, 1955. The contest was held on August 7 and 8, 2012. In Haiping's cards, he had the 7♠ and 9♠ in his Saturn period right at that time. If I had looked there, I would have seen Liu Xiang's loss. So, one of the other really important things to add to your checklist is to look for cards of success or disappointment in other people related to the contestant who you know that contest will affect.

Another really important factor in any contest, if you know the birthdays of the two contestants, is whether either one has a Moon connection to the other or a Saturn connection. This factor has a strength much like the Pinnacle Year and usually will determine the outcome. Whoever is Moon to the other will lose. Now this may not occur in 100 percent of cases, but so far, I have never seen it fail. Mitt Romney is Moon to Barack Obama (J♣ Karma card to 9♦ Birth Card). Even though his yearly cards were stronger, I believe the Moon connection did it. If someone is Moon to you and you compete with them, they subconsciously do things to help you win. They do not even know they are doing it. I saw this happening during the final days of the campaign as Mitt Romney made some big mistakes, which many think turned the tide on his chances. I have seen this Sun/Moon connection be responsible for many events of competition, including legal matters. So, add this also to your checklist if you are seeking to make an accurate prediction.

Likewise, the Saturn connection is very important, and usually this needs to be Life Spread Saturn connection (see my book *Love Cards* for more about this). When you are Saturn to someone, you are their teacher, their critic, and the one who limits them. Because of this, you would usually win against them in any contest. Barack Obama is Hillary Clinton's direct Saturn card in her Life Spread. This is the strongest of all Saturn connections. She lost in the primaries to him and then later became his Secretary of State. So, look for any strong Saturn connections in any contest. Often these will determine the winner.

The final element of your checklist I saved for last. It is the most important factor as far as your accuracy goes. This factor is about you, not the contestants. Simply put, you must be completely unbiased if you are to make an accurate prediction. If you consciously or unconsciously want either party in the contest to win, you will not be able to make an objective evaluation. This happened to me in the 2012 elections. I really didn't want to write about who would win, but I ended up adding it into my newsletter. I wanted Romney to win for reasons I will not go into here. And because of this, I completely missed that Romney was Moon to Obama. I just focused my attention on what I wanted to see, the good cards in the yearly spreads that gave Romney better chances. And this is what happens when we have any interest at all in the outcome. We lose our objectivity and make mistakes or slant what we see to match what we want.

As another example, when I watched the Super Bowl XLVII (even though I rarely watch professional football), I recognized that I went into the game rooting for the Ravens. I reflected on that a bit and realized that most of us go into watching any game by choosing one side we want to win. Even if we have no real connection to either team, we pick a team to identify with. This is a subconscious process. I watched myself pick the Ravens and so was elated when they scored and disappointed when the San Francisco 49ers made good plays. I saw that I would be unable to really predict an outcome for that game as long as I was on one team's side. It made the game a lot more interesting to me to step back and just observe. But what was really interesting for me was what I learned about how we identify with someone or something in every competitive event we watch. If you are to make successful predictions about any event, you will have to undo this process for yourself. You will have to be aware of yourself enough to know whether you are biased toward one side or the other. My suggestion is to put this item first on your checklist. If you do not, you will slant your research for the rest of your examination and usually get it wrong.

Here is the complete checklist, in the order of priority:

1. Check if you are biased in any way as to the outcome of the contest. If you are, stop here unless and until you can become unbiased.
2. Check the relationship connections between the rivals using the *Love Cards* book. Look for Moon and Saturn connections. A strong Moon or Saturn connection will determine the winner.
3. Check for Pinnacle Years. Use the Birth cards and Planetary Ruling cards for this.
4. Check the cards of that year and period for indications of success. Check the Mars card of that year in particular, since Mars rules competitive activities.
5. Check the cards of other people in the lives of the contestants who would have a strong interest in the outcome of the contest. This includes spouses, trainers, etc.

With a little practice, and keeping these items in mind, you can make amazing predictions about upcoming contests.

The Golden Rule of Interpretation that Will Help You Be More Accurate

Have you ever felt that your ability to predict using the cards could be better? Or that you could be more accurate in identifying people's traits based upon their cards? I think if you gain an understanding of the principle of this article, you will do much better in both areas, and in using the cards in general.

I love the card system. It will always tell us the truth. People will tell you all kinds of things. But the cards never lie. They tell what is really going on, if you know where to look and how to interpret them correctly. The number-one golden rule of card interpretation that really is the key that we all need to get to be good at it is this:

The cards are subjective, not objective. Put in other words, the cards will tell you how a certain person is experiencing his or her life, not what that experience is. This begs further explanation.

First of all, there is no card that absolutely means a certain event will happen. There is no "death card," "divorce card," or "millionaire card" that will always show up in just that way. There are cards we label as such, for sure. However, all these cards can show up in many different ways for a certain person. For example, the A♠ is often called the Death card. But that card can mean so many different things. For example, it could mean getting a new job or having a secret about something. The 5♥ and 9♥ are commonly known as divorce cards. However, did you know that these same cards can also indicate marriage? In case you can't see this, let me explain. The 5♥ really means a change in relationship status or a change of residence. Both divorce and marriage constitute a change. And marriage often involves a change of residence. The 9♥ really means an ending of something related to another person or relationships in general. It can also mean the fulfillment of something important, connected to relationship. Therefore, a 9♥ can mean the ending of being single and the fulfillment of the desire to have a marriage, just as much as it can mean the ending of a current marriage or relationship.

So, the first thing we must consider whenever we are reading someone's cards is "how much do we know about this person?" We absolutely need some reference information about someone to make an accurate assessment of what the cards tell us. If you see a 9♥ or 5♥, wouldn't it be nice to know if the person you are reading for is currently married or single? It makes all the difference in the world.

The more we know about someone, the more accurate we can be with their card readings. But there is another side to this, one that is equally important. If you see cards in a person's spread that seem to contradict what you see happening to them, you will benefit by taking a closer look. Often people will tell you that such and such is going on in their life. And what they say may contradict what you see in the cards. I have had clients, for example, who come to me for a reading telling me that their main questions are about work. Then, when I look into their cards, all I see are Heart cards for the year. A predominance of any one suit in a yearly spread tells you that the affairs of that suit are really the most important. So, I then spoke to the clients asking them about their love life. Sure enough, every time, it was their love life that was really the important focus of that year.

A really good exercise is to study the obituaries. Or, read about famous people in the news who have died. Study their cards at the time of their death. You will be amazed at what you find. Traditionally, death cards are the A♠ and 9♠ in Saturn or in other key placements. But you will see that these are found only rarely in the cards of someone who has passed away. When the space shuttle Challenger blew up in 1986, killing all aboard, I looked up the birthdays of the seven astronauts who perished and didn't find any traditional death cards in their spreads. What I found most was a lot of Fives. Death can certainly be regarded as an adventure, a journey, or a grand change. I have studied the cards of many people who died, and it can show up in many ways. To some, death is a 9♦, or loss of material things. I advise never to predict anyone's death. How could you know anyway? The cards that show up for any person at any given time only tell us one thing—what is going on for them personally. We may see success externally, but if the cards they have are one of trouble or challenge, we know this is what is going on for them on a personal level. This is what I mean when I say the cards are subjective, not objective. And if we are to truly know what someone's cards are saying, we have to at least attempt to get inside their heads.

The other side of this is that the cards often will tell you what the person involved will not. People have many reasons for not sharing the whole truth about a situation. Usually, it is because they do not want to look bad or because they are afraid of what will happen if the truth were revealed. Or perhaps someone doesn't tell the truth because he or she is afraid of the consequences of others knowing. This is true for most of us. Even if we are telling the truth, we may withhold parts, parts that we don't want to share for one of the above reasons. The cards can reveal things like secret affairs, unhappiness in some area, health and work problems, dissatisfaction with a job or relationship, and other important information that may be withheld.

Whenever I meet someone, be that a client or just an acquaintance, as soon as I know their birthday, I begin to know them better. For example, I recently had a client who was a J♣. During the reading I asked him who, among the three to four women he gave me to look at, he was actually sleeping with. He said one of them and told me which. But knowing he was a Jack and seeing also in his astrology chart a propensity to stretch or misdirect the truth, I held reservations. It wasn't necessarily important to me that he be honest about this. I told him what I needed to tell him anyway, and I think we had a great reading. A little voice told me, however, that there were things he wasn't sharing with me. I would be likely to doubt things that most Jacks would say, and a few other cards as well. I myself have been a consummate liar at different points in my life, and I am familiar with how it works from my direct experience.

It is comforting to know that the cards can be such a source of truth, especially in a world today where the truth is so undervalued.

When You Find Life Spread Cards in Your Yearly Spreads—Pay Attention!

When I was in my Neptune period at age 54, I had a 3♣ in Neptune in my Birth Card spread and a 7♣ in Neptune in my Planetary Ruling Card spread. As a Q♦ Birth Card, both of these cards are found in my Life Spread. The 3♣ is my Venus card, and the 7♣ is my Saturn card. I didn't pay too much attention to this until I was nearly done with my Neptune period, but then I realized just how significant these two cards were to me. What dawned on me was just how powerful these two cards were because they came from my Life Spread! First of all, the 7♣ is my Saturn card, and every Q♦ has issues with negativity on the mental level. Pessimism and even meanness are part of the Q♦ pattern. But in the Neptune position, this natural inclination toward pessimism and negativity was transferred to the realm of the hidden (Neptune) and illusion. Basically, this manifested negatively as vague fears and worries.

However, it did also manifest positively as a strong interest in spiritual studies (Eckhart Tolle's work mainly) and more time spent in meditation.

The 3♣ is my Venus card, and all Q♦ must contend with a certain amount of desire for romantic variety, plus worries about not having enough love and affection. This one card causes many Q♦ to be unmarriageable. And I have certainly experienced the negative and positive influences of this card over the course of my life. In Neptune, this card caused me to fantasize a lot about romance and relationships and to have a desire for variety that was above and beyond normal. Fortunately for me, it did not manifest on the material plane; it was certainly a distraction on the mental plane for the whole period. And that's often the way with Neptune cards. Remember that Neptune is the period of hopes and fears. It is anything we secretly hope for or are secretly afraid will come to pass.

This one experience really drove home the impact that our Life Spread cards have on us when they show up in our yearly readings. And now I will always recommend that one of the first things we do when looking at our yearly spreads is to check for the occurrences of our Life Spread cards and Karma cards. The way to use this information is as follows:

- Examine your Birth Card's yearly spread and your Planetary Ruling Card's yearly spread. Look to see if either of your Karma cards appears in the spreads. The first Karma card points to the possibility of difficulties and the second card to positive experiences. The period in which either of these appears will mark a time when you will receive either positive or negative karma from them.
- Now look for the cards in your Life Spread. Focus mainly on just the direct cards in your Birth Card's Life Spread. The vertical cards may be important too, but from my experience, it is the direct cards that play the most important role. The direct cards are the only ones mentioned in the *Love Cards* book, so that is the best place to look.
- For now, I would probably ignore the Cosmic Lesson and Cosmic Reward cards and any other cards beyond them that are mentioned in *Exploring the Little Book of the Seven Thunders*. Why, you ask? Well, these cards are fairly hard to interpret and often do not have any personal relevance when they appear. I would focus on the cards we can relate to the most.
- As you look at your Life Spread cards, see if you can identify which personal issues and character traits correspond to each of your Life Spread cards. You need to identify these before you can really interpret what they will mean when they show up in your yearly spreads.
- As you find occurrences of your Life Spread cards in

your yearly spreads, be aware of the issues that each card represents for you personally and see how that is or will be expressed in the time period where it shows up.

Here are a couple of examples of what you might find:

What if your Life Spread Saturn card appears as your Long-Range card for the year? This would tell you that you will be dealing with this Saturn issue of yours in a big way in the current year. If I had my 7♣ as a Long-Range card, it would tell me that this year I will be dealing with my tendency toward pessimism and negativity. Essentially, this could be a year in which I really handle that part of myself.

What if your Planetary Ruling Card is your Long-Range card in your Birth Card's yearly spread for the current year? This would tell you that your focus is going to be on that part of your personality that is represented by your Planetary Ruling Card. This happens frequently, and even the reverse can happen. You can have your Birth Card be the Long-Range card in your Planetary Ruling Card's yearly spread. These sorts of events point to a certain focus on a specific part of your overall personality makeup. You will have to get familiar with which parts of your overall personality are described by your Birth Card and Planetary Ruling Card individually to use this. But it is extremely useful when you do that.

Your Life Spread Jupiter card is your Environment card this year. This would be a pretty powerful culmination of positive forces in your favor, something to take advantage of, for sure.

Your Life Spread Pluto card is found in your spread somewhere this year. If it is a yearlong influence such as Long-Range or Displacement, you can bet that this will be a transformative year for you, one in which you really deal with the issues suggested by your Pluto card. If it falls into a certain period, the same applies, but it will be just a limited duration.

Your first Karma card is your Saturn card in this year's spread. This could be a particularly challenging time period and year. Here you will be faced with the issues represented by your first Karma card, but in a more challenging way because of Saturn's pressure. This may not bother you at all if you have already made peace with your first Karma card. But if not, this could be a very difficult period.

I hope these examples give you something to work with and explore. I think the yearly spreads take on a lot more meaning when you find your Life Spread cards located there. You find out that your life has a certain schedule, one in which you know ahead of time when you will be experiencing the various elements of your birth pattern for your spiritual development.

Your Decanate Ruling Cards

The cards and astrology are intimately connected in many wonderful ways. One important way is that our Planetary

Ruling cards are derived from our astrological Sun Sign. Take a look, for a minute, at the Planetary Ruling Card of several people you know. First of all, if you look carefully, you will see that each Planetary Ruling Card is a card from the person's Life Spread, always. Furthermore, it is the card in their Life Spread that corresponds to the planet that governs their Sun Sign, as shown in the list here. A planet rules each sign, and the card in the Life Spread that corresponds to that planet is emphasized, thus the term Planetary Ruling Card. If you were to memorize the table displayed here, you could actually know what a person's Planetary Ruling Card is without having to look it up.

This Sign:	Is Ruled by:
Aries	Mars
Taurus	Venus
Gemini	Mercury
Cancer	Moon
Leo	Sun
Virgo	Mercury
Libra	Venus
Scorpio	Mars/Pluto
Sagittarius	Jupiter
Capricorn	Saturn
Aquarius	Uranus
Pisces	Neptune

There is another ruling card that I do not discuss much, though I am finding that it holds a lot of significance. The more I look at it, the more I see that it is important, especially in the area of relationships. This is called the Decanate Ruling (DR) card. Like the Planetary Ruling Card, the Decanate Ruling card is found among the cards in your Life Spread. However, it comes instead from the planetary card that governs the sign of the Decanate you were born under. Which Decanate were you born under? The first thing you need to understand is how Decanates of signs are derived.

Each sign of the zodiac is 30 degrees in size. Twelve signs give us the total 360 degrees of the circle that surrounds our planet. But each 30-degree sign can be broken down into three Decanates, each 10 degrees. The first of these three Decanates is governed by the planet that rules that sign naturally. For example, if your birthday is June 24, the Sun was in Cancer at around 2 degrees of that sign at that time of the year and will be reflected as such in your natal chart. This would make you the first Decanate of Cancer, which is also governed by Cancer. The second Decanate of each sign is governed by the

next sign of the same element when progressing through the zodiac in natural order. Below is a table that lists the Decanates of each sign. In order to use this, you must know exactly how many degrees your Sun Sign is. If you do not know this, go to www.astro.com and do one of their free natal charts and look to see just how many degrees your Sun is in its particular Sun Sign. Once you know how many degrees your Sun is in its sign, you can use the table below to determine which Decanate your Sun is in and which planet governs that Decanate.

If your birthday is December 6, for example, your Sun sign would be approximately 16 degrees of Sagittarius, making you the second Decanate of Sagittarius—in this case, governed by Aries, which in turn is governed by the planet Mars. For this birthday, the Decanate Ruling card will be the Mars card in their Life Spread. December 6 is a Q♣ and the Mars card in the Life Spread of the Q♣ is the 3♦. Therefore, a Sagittarius Q♣ will have a DR card of the 3♦, even though their PR card is the A♠. I invite all of you Sagittarius Q♣ people out there to look at your 3♦ card as a secondary ruler and see if you can identify with it and its characteristics. If a person was born on December 18, however, the Sun would be more than 20 degrees in Sagittarius, making it the third Decanate ruled by the sign of Leo, governed by the Sun. Since the Birth Card is the Sun card, a person in the third Decanate of Sagittarius would have a DR card that is the same as their Birth Card.

Sign	First Decanate (0-9.59 deg.)	Second Decanate (10–19.59 deg)	Third Decanate (20–29.59 deg)
Aries	Aries	Leo	Sagittarius
Taurus	Taurus	Virgo	Capricorn
Gemini	Gemini	Libra	Aquarius
Cancer	Cancer	Scorpio	Pisces
Leo	Leo	Sagittarius	Aries
Virgo	Virgo	Capricorn	Taurus
Libra	Libra	Aquarius	Gemini
Scorpio	Scorpio	Pisces	Cancer
Sagittarius	Sagittarius	Aries	Leo
Capricorn	Capricorn	Taurus	Virgo
Aquarius	Aquarius	Gemini	Libra
Pisces	Pisces	Cancer	Scorpio

If your birthday falls in the first Decanate of your Sun Sign, your DR card will be the same as your Planetary Ruling Card, making you a "double-ruler" birthday. This may explain why people in this first Decanate are more extreme examples of their card. I have always found this to be true. People in the first Decanate of their Sun Sign are what I call the "early degree" people of the zodiac. They are often more dramatic versions of their card, much in the same way that a Leo person, because of their double Sun/Planetary Ruling Card mix, are dramatic versions of their Birth cards. There are actually a couple of other Decanates that will act in this manner. Those would be the ones who yield a Decanate governed by the sign of Leo. These include the second Decanate of Aries Sun Sign and the third Decanate of the sign of Sagittarius. Though not normally considered to stand out in any particular way, you will notice that these people exhibit this same dramatic flair in their personalities. Russell Crowe (April 7) and Brad Pitt (December 18) are good examples of this. There are a lot of folks born on December 18 who have ended up in Hollywood or in very Leo-like roles, including Steven Spielberg, Katie Holmes, Keith Richards, Christine Aguilera, DMX, and Ray Liotta. You know this birthday, being a K♥, is going to be even more Kingly with that Leo Decanate behind it.

The Decanate Rulers and Relationships

I have a double DR card, because I am in the second Decanate of Cancer, governed by Scorpio, which has a double ruler (Mars and Pluto). This makes my DR cards the 3♠ and J♣. The more I look, the more I see, especially when I see how I connect with people I meet. My wife Desiree is a K♣/2♠. Since I am a Q♦/A♦, we already have one Moon connection between my A♦ and her K♣. But with the addition of the 3♠ DR card, we have another Moon connection between her 2♠ and my 3♠. Her DR card is the 4♦, which yields another Moon connection between her 4♦ and my 3♦ first Karma card.

I have also noticed that even though there are no direct connections between my Birth Card or Planetary Ruling Card and the 10♣, I always have a great connection with 10♣ people. Seeing my J♣ DR card explains just why that works so well and the fact that they show up as Moon to me. I always know that when I meet a 10♣ that we will get along well and they will appreciate a reading or the information in my books for this reason.

The 3♠ and J♣ DR cards of mine also point to how I have gotten more involved with creative aspects in my life. I have been a professional musician and artist. I have designed jewelry and played in many music groups. All in all, the DR cards make a lot of sense for me and play themselves out over and over.

As another example, Ben Affleck is a Leo J♣ (August 15), married to Jennifer Garner (April 17), a 4♦/6♣. His DR card, being in the third Decanate of his sign, is his Mars card, the 2♣. I have spoken often about how I see so many 4♣ being happily married to 4♦, which occurs far more often than one would think based on averages. I attribute it to two things—

the fact that it is a Neptune connection and the fact that the J♣ has such a fixed notion of what the perfect wife is (7♠ in Venus, underlied by the K♦). Because of this fixed notion, it takes a Neptune connection to override it. In the case of Ben and Jennifer, they get two direct Neptune connections when you add the fact that her 6♣ Planetary Ruling Card is Neptune to the 2♣ DR card of Ben's. This is a double-whammy for him. Her DR card is the 6♠, which ends up being double Pluto to him if you look carefully. Though this relationship is highly idealized by him, I am sure she can be very difficult for him at times. And if I were to size this relationship up in a sentence, I would say that it is easy for her and challenging for him. But in spite of that, she is a 4♦ and life is never easy for a 4♦, regardless of their circumstances or who they are married to.

David Beckham (May 2, 1975) is a 4♠ with a 10♦ Planetary Ruling Card. He is married to Victoria, who is the same birthday as Jennifer Garner (4♦/6♣ with a 6♠ DR card). Because David's DR card is the 10♥ and because that 10♥ has a J♣ first Karma card, we see the same Neptune connection apply as with Ben and Jennifer, just not as strong. However, when you hear about David and Victoria's romance, you get the sense that these two were destined to be together. Interesting that they are both Fours, and Fours tend to have to work for everything.

If you haven't already done so, I would highly recommend figuring out your DR card(s). Also, take some time to look up those cards for any people in your life who are really close to you. I am sure you will be surprised at what you discover. If you are doing readings for others, look up their DR cards. Often, the connections you seek are located there. Be aware of who is Moon to your DR card(s) and who your DR cards are Moon to, or karmically connected to. I believe you will discover that you make many connections with others through those cards, both yours and theirs.

It is possible that there are undiscovered distinctions between the Birth Card, Planetary Ruling Card, and Decanate Ruling cards. Perhaps each of them represents a particular part of our personality or our lifetime Karma. I have yet to see these distinctions, though I have an intuition that they exist. For now, however, I see that they are very important. So important that I plan to include them in the next revision of my software. I hope you enjoy discovering yours and seeing how they contribute to the way you are in the world and who you connect with.

The O. J. Simpson Saga

There is a lot we can learn about the cards by watching our lives and the lives of others unfold. The O. J. Simpson story, with its cast of supporting actors, has many valuable lessons hidden within it. For those who can't remember, here are some of the facts of the initial murder and trial (according to Wikipedia):

First the players:

- O. J. Simpson, born July 9, 1947—6♦/8♣
- Nicole Brown Simpson, born May 19, 1959—K♣/4♥
- Ronald Goldman, born July 2, 1968—K♦/K♥
- Fred Goldman, born December 6, 1940—Q♣/A♠ (Ronald's father)
- Robert Shapiro, born September 2, 1942—9♦/7♠ (O. J.'s attorney)
- Johnnie Cochran, born October 2, 1937—7♦/J♥ (O. J.'s attorney)
- F. Lee Bailey, born June 10, 1933—7♦/5♠ (O. J.'s attorney)

Dates:

- Murder of Nicole Simpson and Ronald Goldman—June 12, 1994
- O. J.'s trial for that murder—jury sworn in November 2, 1994; opening statements January 24, 1995; verdict October 3, 1995
- O. J.'s civil trial—verdict handed down February 5, 1997
- O. J.'s trial for robbery—September 15, 2008

O. J.'s Murder Trial

As a 6♦, O. J. was very successful in professional football. He set records that still have not been broken today, more than thirty years later. Sixes are known to excel in competitive sports and endeavors. They are also known to start fights over what others might consider insignificant matters. And, they usually win. In the Super Bowl of 2013, both quarterbacks had a 6♣ as their Planetary Ruling cards. The list of the best sports figures of all time is comprised of men and women who are mostly Sixes. So, we see this competitive, but also vindictive, quality in Sixes. Add to that O. J.'s 8♣ PR card, and you get a mixture that could result in violence. Eights are known to press matters to the limit, and once they have decided upon a course of action, this can result in violent outbursts. Though O. J. and Nicole had been divorced for about two years at the time of the murders, they had not been getting along well. There had been several occasions where the police had been called for domestic violence disputes between them. Nicole, a K♣ herself, is someone who would not tolerate injustice. It is a little strange that these two even got married, because their cards do not have many connections, and the ones they have are not good. When this is the case, it is usually because there was some past-life karma involved. In other words, these two were destined to be together to act out some drama that had

started earlier. In any event, rumor was that Nicole and Ron were lovers. It was all fateful. Ron went to Nicole's house to return a pair of glasses she had left at the restaurant where he worked. He arrived just as she was being murdered and was murdered as well.

At the time of the murders, I was living in Los Angeles. It was all over the news. I immediately looked into the cards of O. J., Ron, and Nicole, searching for answers. What surprised me at first were O. J.'s cards.

Sun	Mercury 7/9/1993	Venus 8/30/1993	Mars 10/21/1993	Jupiter 12/12/1993	Saturn 2/3/1994	Uranus 3/27/1994	Neptune 5/18/1994	Pluto	CReward	CLesson	CMoon	TransSelf
6◇	6♠	2♡	9♠	7♠	3◇	6♡	A◇	10♣	8♣	3♠	4♡	5♠
	4♣	K♠	2◇	K♡	9♡	6♣	A◇		LR: 10♣	Env: 3♠	Dis: 9♣	
8♣	3♠	4♡	5♠	Q♠	6♣	3♡	A♡		9◇	5♣	K◇	J◇	9♡
	2♡	2♣	9♣	J♣	3♠	A♡			LR: Q♣	Env: 8♣	Dis: 8♣	

FIGURE 1: O. J.'s CARDS AT THE TIME OF THE MURDERS.

The murders of Nicole and Ron occurred in O. J.'s Neptune period, just prior to his forty-seventh birthday. When an event happens near the end of a period, I always look at the Result Card for that year to see what was coming in. I was surprised when I did not see any cards of loss or disappointment. What I did see was his 8♣ Result Card, shown here as the Reward card. That 8♣ means success. It means the successful conclusion of a plan. And, as hinted earlier, it can mean the use of force to accomplish one's goals. This caused me to suspect that O. J. had actually murdered his wife.

As for Ron and Nicole, they shared a very unusual connection at that time in their life. Both of them were in their Pinnacle Year, where they displaced the Sun card, the 8♦. The Pinnacle year has two keywords that stand out the most: change and fame. It is large-scale change for most of us. The Pinnacle Year is a year in which our life often changes complete direction. The Pluto card of the Pinnacle Year is very significant that year. It usually tells us something about the change that will occur. And the Result Card that goes with it contributes. Both Nicole and Ron had a Six as a Pluto card in 1994. Sixes are the number of karma. Nicole had a 6♥, which could refer to the escalating karma of fighting between her and O. J. Ron had the 6♦, O. J.'s Birth Card.

Sun	Mercury 5/19/1994	Venus 7/10/1994	Mars 8/31/1994	Jupiter 10/22/1994	Saturn 12/13/1994	Uranus 2/4/1995	Neptune 3/28/1995	Pluto	CReward	CLesson	CMoon	TransSelf
K♣	K♠	K♡	2♡	9♠	3◇	Q♡	3♠	6♡	4♣	9♡	4♠	J♡
	5♠	5♡	8◇	6♠	9♠	J♠	3♡		LR: A♡	Env: K◇	Dis: 8◇	
4♡	3♣	5♣	8♡	5◇	Q♣	2◇	K♣	K♠	K♡	2♡	9♠	3♡
	J♠	10♠	A◇	4◇	9♡	2♡			LR: K♠	Env: A♡	Dis: 4◇	

FIGURE 2: NICOLE SIMPSON'S CARDS AT THE TIME OF HER MURDER.

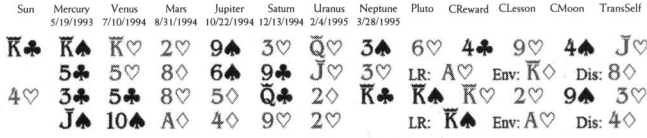

Sun	Mercury 7/2/1993	Venus 8/23/1993	Mars 10/14/1993	Jupiter 12/5/1993	Saturn 1/27/1994	Uranus 3/20/1994	Neptune 5/11/1994	Pluto	CReward	CLesson	CMoon	TransSelf
K◇	K♠	Q♡	2♡	9◇	K◇	Q♣	8◇	6◇	9♣	9♡	A◇	J♡
	Q♡	10♠	K♣	5◇	10◇	J◇	K♡		LR: 9♣	Env: 4♡	Dis: 8◇	
K♡	Q♣	8◇	6◇	9♣	9◇	A◇	J♡	6♠	J♣	A♣	J◇	4♡
	K◇	Q♡	10♠	K♣	5◇	10◇			LR: K♣	Env: J◇	Dis: 10♠	

FIGURE 3: RON GOLDMAN'S CARDS AT THE TIME OF HIS MURDER.

O. J.'s trial started and occurred mostly in his Age 47 year, depicted here. What is most significant about this spread is that O. J. displaced the Q♥. The Q♥ is not significant, but whenever anyone displaces the Q♥, they will have the K♠ in their Mars period. The K♠ in Mars is the strongest and best card you can possibly have for any kind of legal matter. The Q♥ has the K♠ in Mars in their Life Spread and so, they rarely, if ever, lose in any legal matter.

Sun	Mercury	Venus	Mars	Jupiter	Saturn	Uranus	Neptune	Pluto	CReward	CLesson	CMoon	TransSelf
	7/9/1994	8/30/1994	10/21/1994	12/12/1994	2/3/1995	3/27/1995	5/18/1995					
6◇	4♥	J♠	K♠	10◇	2♥	Q♠	9♣	6♥	9◇	K♥	2♣	9♥
	10♥	K◇	3♥	8♣	A♣	K♥			LR: J♠	Env: J◇	Dis: Q♥	
8♣	J◇	10♠	4◇	8◇	2◇	Q♣	3♥	5◇	4♣	7♠	J♣	7♥
	A♣	K♥	6◇	10♥	K◇	3♥			LR: 7♠	Env: 8♣	Dis: 8♠	

FIGURE 4: O. J.'S CARDS AT THE TIME OF HIS MURDER TRIAL.

Two of O. J.'s attorneys, Johnnie Cochran and F. Lee Bailey, were 7♦ Birth cards. Since O. J. is a 6♦, he would be Moon to them. The Moon connection is extremely important here. First of all, the 7♦ has the ability to lead and guide the 6♦, which is exactly what O. J. needed. In return, since O. J. was Moon to them, he furthered their careers immensely, making them both key players in one of the trials of the century. As we know, O. J. was found not guilty, in what seemed a miracle at the time.

O. J.'s Civil Trial

Thanks mostly to Fred Goldman, O. J. had to face trial again, this time for the wrongful deaths of Ron and Nicole. This time, O. J. was not in that most fortunate position with the K♠ in Mars. Instead, he was displacing the 4♥ and his trial verdict was handed down in his Saturn period.

Sun	Mercury	Venus	Mars	Jupiter	Saturn	Uranus	Neptune	Pluto	CReward	CLesson	CMoon	TransSelf
	7/9/1996	8/30/1996	10/21/1996	12/12/1996	2/3/1997	3/27/1997	5/18/1997					
6◇	6♥	2◇	K♠	3♥	6♣	J◇	Q♥	4♠	K♠	8◇	2♥	7♣
10♠	K◇	10♥	K♠	9♠	8◇			LR: 8♠	Env: 10♥	Dis: 4♥		
8♣	10♥	9♣	5♠	J♠	A♥	Q♠	10◇	K◇	3◇	7♥	5♠	7◇
	A♣	6♠	J◇	4◇	8♥	10◇			LR: 5♥	Env: 8♣	Dis: 8♣	

FIGURE 5: O. J.'S CARDS AT THE TIME OF HIS CIVIL

TRIAL FOR WRONGFUL DEATHS.

What is significant about displacing the 4♥ is that you have the 6♠ and 9♠ as underlying cards in your Saturn period. I have included the underlying cards in the illustration here so you can see them. Notice that when you include the underlying cards, O. J. has the 9♠ twice and two Sixes, the 6♣ and 6♠. I knew before the trial ended back then that he would lose that trial. Any Six in Saturn tells us that some negative karma from our past will come due and need to be reckoned with. And the 9♠ also in Saturn is typically the most challenging card you can have, resulting in some form of large-scale loss. His loss of that trial resulted in a $33 million judgment against him. But

if you look at the Result Card for the year, another K♠, you can see that though this loss may have been devastating at the time, his year ended on a positive note. It is true that very little of that $33 million has ever been paid.

O. J.'s Robbery Trial

According to Wikipedia: "On the night of September 13, 2007, a group of men led by Simpson entered a room in the Palace Station Hotel in Las Vegas, Nevada. Bruce Fromong, a sports memorabilia dealer, testified that the group of men broke into his hotel room and stole various sports memorabilia at gunpoint. Three days later, on September 16, 2007, Simpson was arrested for his involvement in the robbery and held without bail. He admitted taking the items, which he said had been stolen from him, but denied breaking into the room. Simpson also denied the allegation that he or the people with him carried weapons."

He was tried on ten counts, ranging from conspiracy to rob and kidnap, to first-degree kidnapping with the use of a deadly weapon and assault with a deadly weapon.

According to Wikipedia: "On October 3, 2008—exactly thirteen years to the day after he was acquitted of the murders of his wife, Nicole Brown, and Ronald Goldman—Simpson was found guilty of all ten charges. On December 5, 2008, Simpson was sentenced to thirty-three years in prison with eligibility for parole in nine years." Simpson's cards at the time of this third trial were likewise not so good.

Sun	Mercury	Venus	Mars	Jupiter	Saturn	Uranus	Neptune	Pluto	CReward	CLesson	CMoon	TransSelf
	7/9/2008	8/30/2008	10/21/2008	12/12/2008	2/3/2009	3/27/2009	5/18/2009					
6◇	4♠	8♣	K◇	3◇	A♠	5♠	Q◇	J◇	3♠	6♣	9♠	A♥
	3♣	6♠	K♠	9♣	7♣	7◇	Q♥		LR: 2◇	Env: K◇	Dis: 2◇	
8♣	K◇	3◇	A♠	5♠	Q♥	J◇	3♠	6♣	9♠	A♥	7♠	7◇
	A♣	8◇	5◇	8♥	A◇	3♠			LR: 10♣	Env: 8♣	Dis: 8♣	

FIGURE 6: O. J.'S CARDS AT THE TIME OF HIS TRIAL FOR ROBBERY.

In this case, it was not so much the cards of the year or even the cards at the time of the crime itself. It was the cards at the time of his sentencing that told the story. The A♠ in Saturn, considered a traditional death card, reigned at that time. O. J. will be eligible for parole in 2017: he will be seventy years old.

The Neptune Cards

There is a host of Birth cards that have a strong Neptune influence. And this influence manifests in many positive and negative ways for the individuals who possess them. Here I will explain more about the Neptune influence itself and how it can have a profound impact on people whose Birth or Planetary Ruling cards happen to be one of these Neptune cards.

In the Life Spread pictured on page 56, there is both a Neptune row and a Neptune column. The Neptune row is the bottom row, in which you see the Q♥, 6♠, 6♣, 8♥, 2♠, 4♦, and 4♥. The Neptune column is the leftmost column, and in that column you have the A♠, 2♥, 8♣, A♦, 5♦, J♦, and Q♥. Notice that the Q♥ is Neptune in both row and column. As you might guess, this gives them a double Neptune influence. All these cards are Neptune cards. But in addition to these, we need to add all the Nines. Nine is the number associated with Neptune, and all Nine Birth Card and Planetary Ruling Card people display Neptune/Piscean traits. The planet Neptune is the lord of the sign of Pisces, so we can also add to this list anyone who is a Pisces Sun Sign. When you add all of these together, you get quite a list of people born each year who are under a powerful Neptune influence, and it plays out in many ways that are definable and specific.

The number Nine is the last number in the cycle. The sign of Pisces governs the last house in a natal chart, the twelfth house. Thus, Nine and Pisces and twelfth house are all pretty much synonymous. In the cycle of birth, life, and death, Neptune represents that point where we are dissolving our individuality and returning to the oneness of all things. We become universal instead of individual. We merge with the infinite instead of being a singular individual struggling in his or her own private world.

When you think about it, this is why so many Neptune card people are so caring of others. They feel your pain. They are very psychic and make good counselors. They can be empathetic and consoling and accepting. You will feel understood and accepted by a Neptune person. This is the good side of this planet's expression.

The Nines

The Neptune energy causes us to think more about others than ourselves, though some Neptune card people struggle with this. Many people who are Nines, for example, have come from a past life pattern of being fairly selfish and full of self-importance, arrogance and a tendency to dominate others. This was their "eighth" stage of evolution, reaching the fullness of their power. But that stage ended in that lifetime, and now they must let it all go. This is the main reason a person is born as a Nine Birth or Planetary Ruling Card. They need nearly a lifetime to let go of these past patterns. And this "letting go" process is often experienced by them as disappointment, reversals in fate, tragedy, and difficulties. They are not really these things; this is just their interpretation of the events of their life, and if you examine them and their situations carefully, you will see that much of their tragedies are really just their interpretation of what happened. Whether something in our lives is a tragedy or a blessing largely depends upon our point of view. And Nines just tend to have higher expectations of how things should be. These expectations are unconscious, having been set in

those previous lives. Therefore, the Nine person is generally unaware that the real problem is in their point of view. The same could be said for all of us, but it is much more apparent in the Nine cards.

The positive side of Nines is that they get to experience moments of true cosmic bliss and the feeling of being one with everyone and everything. All Nines will have these experiences, which serve as reminders of where they are going. Their destination is to become much greater than the little person who was powerful, controlling, and dominating. So, this is the Nine struggle, just one of the many aspects of the Neptune energy.

The cards in the Neptune rows and columns, along with all the Pisces Sun Sign people, usually express other manifestations of the Neptune energy. This includes the following cards: 4♥, 4♦, 2♠, 8♥, 6♣, 6♠, Q♥, J♦, 5♦, A♦, 8♣, 2♥, and the A♠. I have studied the charts of many people whose cards fall in these Neptune positions, and I always find strong Neptune influences in their natal charts. Among these, I find:

1. Sun or the ascendant's ruling planet in the twelfth house.
2. Sun or the ascendant's ruling planet heavily aspected by Neptune, such as conjunction, square, opposition, or trine.
3. Many planets either in the sign of Pisces or located in the twelfth house.

My wife is a perfect example. She is a Sagittarius K♣/2♠. You would not normally associate Neptune with a K♣, but you might with the 2♠ since it is one of the cards in the Neptune row of the Grand Solar Spread. And sure enough, she has both Sun and Mercury in the twelfth house, making her literally as much Pisces as she is Sagittarius.

I find that most 2♠ women act a lot like Pisces Sun Sign people. They have that somewhat spacey expression to them and often make very strange conversation and choices in life. As smart as the 2♠ is, there is a part that seems to misconnect on many important levels. And this, I believe, comes from the heavy Neptune influence.

Neptune, you see, can be an influence of confusion and, in many cases, deception. The twelfth house is the hidden house, or so it is called. People with heavy Neptune can be lost in their own house. Keep in mind also that Pisces is the sign opposite to Virgo. If Virgos are neat freaks and orderly, Pisces are their opposite. So, having a heavy Neptune influence as in the cards we have discusses here can mean a lot of confusion in life and sometimes deception, both perpetrated by the individual and to them as well.

There are some birthdays in particular that have the highest concentration of this Neptune energy. First of all, any of the aforementioned cards that are also a Pisces Sun Sign are going to be rather dramatic in their Neptune-ness. Some examples of this are February 24 (A♦), March 4 (6♠), March 8 (2♠), March 9 (A♠), March 12 (J♦), March 18 (5♦), and March 19 (4♦). But we need to add to that the one double Nine birthday, December 22 (9♥/9♦) and any Q♥ birthday, since they are the one and only double Neptune card in the deck. These birthdays could be considered more or less extreme examples of the Neptune effect and thus are worthy of study.

In its highest expression, a Neptune person will dedicate their life for the benefit of mankind, achieve cosmic consciousness, or both. Eckhart Tolle, a 9♦ spiritual teacher, is a perfect example of this. In achieving the highest that Neptune can bring, one must completely lose the sense of "me" (also called the "little me" by Eckhart). In losing the "me," we become more identified as "we," and we become universal in all ways. We don't realize it in our normal state of consciousness, but losing the "me" is the answer to all of our problems. No problems can exist once we have let go of our identity with our little self. And this is Neptune's message to us all. Like the other twelve houses in our zodiac, it has its message for us. But this is the last of all the houses, pointing to our ultimate destination—oneness with all.

Your Second Saturn Card

One Saturn card is enough, don't you think? Most of us would agree. But there are two Saturn cards, and the second one can often yield significant information about your life or about your current year. This second Saturn card is what I call the Cosmic Lesson card. I haven't written much about it over the years. And I honestly haven't used it that much either. But recently I had a realization about it that has caused me to take a closer look.

Let me start by saying that in the Life Spread, pictured on page 56, many cards that are five spaces apart are the same number: The A♣/A♠, the 2♥/2♦, the 2♣/2♠, the 3♥/3♦, the 4♣/4♠, the 5♥/5♦, the 5♣/5♠, the 6♥/6♦, the 7♣/7♠, the 8♣/8♠, the 8♥/8♦, the 9♥/9♦, and the J♣/J♦. Interesting to note that there are thirteen pairs and that the Fives and Eights have all four cards of a number in the five-space arrangement. It is also interesting that only the two Jacks are different colors. All the other pairs are cards of the same color.

When there are five spaces between cards, it makes a Saturn connection. And Mars and Pluto are five spaces apart, which makes both Capricorns ruled by Saturn and Scorpios ruled by Mars and Pluto Saturn unto themselves. And this is true in life. So it is not surprising that many Cosmic Lesson cards are the same number as someone's Saturn card, just a different suit. However, it is rare to find a Cosmic Lesson card with the same number as your Saturn card in a yearly spread. Only the Life Spread has this particular feature. Even so, the Cosmic Lesson is the Super Saturn card. I have called it the Cosmic

Lesson card because I believe it to represent a responsibility we have to the world around us, rather than a personal responsibility. I see it as a role we must play in life to fulfill an obligation to our fellow men and women. In a yearly spread, I think the Cosmic Lesson card gives us additional information about our Saturn period cards, sometimes revealing the key lesson found in that period.

This hit home for me in 2013 when I had a 9♠ in my Saturn period. The same day I started Saturn, I realized that I was going to owe the IRS a lot of money, a lot more than I ever had in my life. But I was surprised when I could not find any Diamond cards in either of my spreads in my Saturn period. It wasn't until a week or two later that I realized that my Cosmic Lesson card in that same spread was the 9♦. That is when it clicked for me. I saw that my Cosmic Lesson card was giving me information about my Saturn period; it was connected to that period. Once I realized the message of the 9♦, I was able to align myself to letting money flow out of my life and the difficulty of Saturn ended. I was back in alignment with the place I was meant to be, and for now, that meant letting money go out.

So now I really look at the Cosmic Lesson card and compare it to the Saturn period card of anyone I am looking at. It has opened up a world of understanding. Usually, the Saturn period cards themselves tell most of the story. But every so often, like in my own case, there is information not found in the Saturn period cards that is found in the Cosmic Lesson cards.

How to Find Your Yearly Cosmic Lesson Card

The yearly Cosmic Lesson card does not appear in the *Cards of Your Destiny* book. The cards stop at the Result, or Cosmic Reward card. But there is a way to find it, if you want. Just follow these instructions.

1. Look at your Mercury card this year. Note which card it is.
2. Now look up the yearly spread for that Mercury card for the same year you are in now, the same age.
3. The Result Card or Cosmic Reward card for that card this year is your Cosmic Lesson card this year.

Example: I am a 10♦, age 42. My Mercury card in 2013 is the 3♦. When I look in the age 42 yearly spread for the 3♦, I see that it has the a Result Card of the J♣. Therefore, the J♣ is my (10♦) Cosmic Lesson card at age 42.

When you look at your Cosmic Lesson card, first look at your Saturn card. See if you can project or imagine what that Saturn period might be about, judging by the direct and vertical cards in your Saturn period. Once you have done that, then look at the Cosmic Lesson card and see how that might offer additional information about your Saturn period. See if any of these cards are the Birth or Planetary Ruling Card of anyone you know. If so, they might play a key role in your Saturn period.

I held a special class shortly after discovering the significance of the Cosmic Lesson card. As people in the class began studying their yearly spreads, many found significant information about their Saturn periods in those Cosmic Lesson cards. Now, for me at least, it has become a regular part of my reading checklist. If difficult cards appear in Saturn, check the Cosmic Lesson card for more details about that Saturn period.

I would be interested to hear from you if you discover any significant connections using this method. Look at any past Saturn periods that were important in your life and see if the Cosmic Lesson card offers any new information that told more about what happened at that time.

The Card Interpretations

I have endeavored to make the interpretations in this book as complete as possible. Still, if you keep in mind a few tips presented here, you can get even more out of it and use it to your advantage in doing your personal or professional readings. The ways that cards can manifest themselves in our lives is not endless. But there can be quite a variety, and I don't believe that any book could possibly list every one.

1. When you look up the meaning of a card, don't forget to read the Basic Meaning of that card as well. You may find additional information that could apply in the reading you are doing. For example, let's say that you are looking up the meaning of a Nine of Clubs in the Mars Period. You look there and notice that it talks about disappointments or problems with a legal matter. The problem is that you are not involved in some legal matter. However, you read the Basic Meaning and discover that this card means the 'completion of ideas and plans.' This Basic Meaning may clue you in to the meaning that this card will have for you during this period. Perhaps you finish some job or project that you are working on, or some other sort of ending occurs in your life.

2. Remember that a card has more power when it is the top card in that particular period. As the top card, any card becomes the 'headline' of that period. The interpretations in this book do not distinguish whether the card is in the top (direct) or bottom (vertical) position. It is up to you to give greater weight to top cards.

3. When two cards seem to contradict each other in the same period remember that:

    A. Cards of success mean successful conclusions of matters represented by cards of problems, whether they fall in the top or bottom position. The success cards are generally the Fours, Eights, Tens, Jacks, Queens, and Kings. However, the face cards can represent people who are involved in some situation rather than success with it. For example a Seven of Spades on top of a Jack of Diamonds in Mars would more likely mean difficulties in some legal matter with a tricky Diamond male than it would a successful outcome to some legal problem by use of financial creativity.

    B. The changes represented by Fives are usually negated by the presence of a Six in the same period.

4. Remember to keep the readings for the Planetary Ruling and Personality Card Spreads separate from the Birth Card Spread. The Birth Card Spread is the most important of all, and information about any important life topic may be found among its cards. The Planetary Ruling Card's Yearly Spread will also pertain to any department of life, but it is still not as potent as the Birth Card Spread. However, the cards under the Yearly Spreads of the Personality Cards (your Jack, Queen, or King) will only pertain to the areas of life they govern. In general, the Queen for women and Jack for men deal with romantic and personal issues, while the King usually deals with work issues only. There are exceptions, but it is better to look at them this way at the outset.

Ace of Hearts

The desire for love or the beginning of a new love

The Basic Meaning of the Ace of Hearts

The Ace of Hearts represents a desire for affection or love that is the stimulus that causes new relationships to be created. For this reason, it can indicate a new love affair or the birth of a child. Though influenced by each planetary period in a specific and unique way, this creative love energy always represents an awakening of love or passion in one's heart.

On a deeper level, the Ace of Hearts, being the very first card in the deck, represents a search for something inside of our self. It is the card of 'soul-searching' and often introspection. Perhaps it is the search for self-identity or for those things that help us to love who we are unconditionally. In order to love ourselves, we often find someone to love who reflects back to us what we are seeking within. This is why the Ace of Hearts can represent a new relationship beginning.

THE ACE OF HEARTS IN THE MERCURY PERIOD

At this time, you may experience a sudden infatuation for someone. This time period could also bring an unexpected letter, telephone call, or offering of love from someone you were not thinking about. This period may also see you being very fickle with your affections and getting very dramatic about your love life, while being primarily preoccupied with your own interests. You are more attracted to those of wit and intelligence during this period and the whole year.

THE ACE OF HEARTS IN THE VENUS PERIOD

This period could bring a letter of love or friendship from someone very dear to you. Another possibility is that you begin a new relationship under this auspicious influence. All kinds of relationships will be important to you now. This card can also indicate the birth of a child if that is something you are contemplating. If so, the child is likely to be a girl. This is one of the best influences for a new love affair.

THE ACE OF HEARTS IN THE MARS PERIOD

Mars's aggressive nature will cause you to be energetically pursuing friendships and/or lovers during this period. Men may be more stimulating at this time, but in any case, you will be the initiator of relationships. This stimulating influence could help you make new friends, but guard against emotional impatience and an over-sensitive ego that may thwart your own desires to be with another. A child born under this influence would likely be a boy.

THE ACE OF HEARTS IN THE JUPITER PERIOD

During this period you may find yourself feeling and acting upon a desire for money for the purpose of helping others unselfishly. Jupiter's expansive and beneficial influence brings a humanitarian or spiritual ideal into your heart that seeks completion. You may also receive a letter or communication about money or about this unselfish purpose. Relationships you initiate now will bring good results, financially, romantically, and spiritually.

THE ACE OF HEARTS IN THE SATURN PERIOD

Saturn's karmic influence says that you are now dealing with some experiences that were created in the past. If you have a frustrated or unsuccessful attempt to gain another's affection, it could be the result of your actions from the past, even a previous life. Another possibility of this influence is a letter from a friend in need or having some kind of illness or burden. A birth occurring during this period is likely to be difficult and problematic.

This influence often represents a desire for affection and attention that is difficult, if not impossible, to fulfill. It can represent loneliness and an aching heart. This influence can prompt us to even become somewhat desperate about our need for love, but its purpose is to direct our attention within so that we learn how to fulfill ourselves from inside and depend less on others for our sense of being loved. Whatever happens during this period, it is likely to help you get your attention back on to your inner needs and feelings, and the end result will be your having more ability to love yourself.

THE ACE OF HEARTS IN THE URANUS PERIOD

Uranus's influence here brings an element of the unusual to your social and romantic attractions. You may be the recipient of an unusual romantic proposition. In both these cases, unusual can also mean spiritual, 'New Age,' Aquarian, sudden, or ahead of its time in some way. This influence can also bring about a desire to work, or to acquire occult, mystical, or futuristic knowledge. You could meet many different and exciting people during this period.

THE ACE OF HEARTS IN THE NEPTUNE PERIOD

During this period and perhaps for the entire year, you may find yourself dreaming about an idealistic love affair or birth of a child. If traveling, you may meet someone. Any affairs during this period will be marked by strong idealism and fantasy. You are cautioned not to make any serious commitments until after your birthday. However, the mystical feelings that come up around such a person may be hints to your past and bring you significant self-knowledge.

This card can also represent the beginning of a new relationship that takes you in new directions. It is also common for women to conceive or even give birth under this influence.

THE ACE OF HEARTS IS YOUR PLUTO CARD

Getting your affectional needs met will be a major issue for you this year, one that motivates you to make adjustments in your life to create new relationships. There is a strong desire for affection present. Whether it is directed towards one person, who might be your Result Card, or just towards finding a special person you can share your love with, it is certain that you will be making some changes in your life this year in order to see some results in this area.

This is an important year for you emotionally. You may have just ended a time where your love life was unsatisfactory in one or more ways. You now realize that you have to do something if you are to create new or better relationships in your life. In all your zest for love and friendships, be careful not to overdo it or expect too much from others. Remember that everyone does not have the exact same needs that you do and is not in the exact same situation. Their needs may be different, and their level of desire for love may not be at the same level of intensity as yours. Whatever the case, your own desire will guide you to make the best decisions. Look at the meaning of the Result Card for this year to get more information about this passion for love or to find out who may be involved in it.

Another important note for those who might be working on having a baby. This year could be challenging for you in this regard but don't give up. Look at your Result Card's meaning to get more information about what adjustments you may need to make to accomplish your goal or to deal with the situation best. Your Result Card could also represent the Birth Card of a baby that will arrive by your next birthday. Good luck!

AFFIRMATION:

I reach inside of myself for the love that makes me the most happy and fulfilled. Then, I manifest that love as new people or relationships in my life.

THE ACE OF HEARTS IS YOUR RESULT CARD

Somehow connected with your Pluto Card will be the element of desire for affection, a new love interest, or the birth of a child. This highly motivating influence tells us that your creative impulses are directed towards love, home, and romance this year. Your pursuit will either cause you to complete this year with a new love or a child. This is one of the strongest indicators of childbirth for women. Your Pluto Card will tell you more about this desire or the object of your desire.

AFFIRMATION:

I complete this year with a new love, which could be a lover, friend, child, or something else that brings me great joy.

THE ACE OF HEARTS IS YOUR LONG-RANGE CARD

This will be a year of much love activity for you. The Ace of Hearts as your Long-Range Card could indicate the beginning of one or more important personal relationships. This card is also the card of childbirth and could indicate that a new member of the family is about to arrive or that the topic of childbirth assumes a much greater importance this year. Often, the Ace of Hearts indicates a motivation for love and affection that gets you out of your social complacency.

It is a very stimulating influence, one that makes you the initiator of relationships. It may be that you have been a long time without a close relationship and this is the year you begin to explore having an important someone in your life. In any event, this powerful card usually indicates one or more new relationships forming, and among them, at least one very important one.

KEYWORDS:

A desire for love and affection; initiating new love relationships and love affairs; the birth of a child.

THE ACE OF HEARTS IS YOUR ENVIRONMENT CARD

This is a year when new beginnings in the area of personal relationships will bring many rewards and blessings to you. Whether you will start a new love affair or help bring a new child into this world, this is the time for you to discover just what helps you love yourself the most. This is likely to be a year of joy and pleasure, and the focus will be on you, your needs, and attracting to you other people that will fulfill you on the deepest levels.

THE ACE OF HEARTS IS YOUR DISPLACEMENT CARD

This is a year when your own personal satisfaction in love matters will assume a greater importance in your life. Just what will best satisfy your yearning for affection will come into focus. You also have a restlessness on the emotional level, one probably due to some dissatisfaction with your current emotional environment. This may precipitate new love affairs or even the birth of a child; for in many ways this year marks the beginning of a new way of loving yourself. Our relationships always reflect how we love ourselves, so expect some new experiences in this area. You will probably need more time to yourself this year to sort out your feelings and inner drives and motivations. Self-expression can play a key role in allowing you to find the answers you seek from inside.

Ace of Clubs

The desire for knowledge or beginning of some new mental occupation

The Basic Meaning of the Ace of Clubs

The Ace of Clubs means a strong desire for knowledge of some kind or the birth of a new idea, plan, or way of communicating with the world around you. This could also mean a desire for some specific information, for an education, or to pursue some new plans you make.

The Ace of Clubs always means a new beginning of some sort. This could be a new job idea or just embarking on a new way of thinking and communicating with others. The exact nature of the beginning will depend on the position of the card and the circumstances in your life at the time, but in general, this is a good time to plan to start something new.

THE ACE OF CLUBS IN THE MERCURY PERIOD

This is an influence of great interest and curiosity about something, arising quickly. It could be the desire for news about something at a short distance or about one of your relatives. There is something that you want to know *right now!* This could also mean a secret letter containing valuable information. In general, you will have a curiosity at this time that could motivate you to pursue educational goals or to increase your knowledge in many areas.

THE ACE OF CLUBS IN THE VENUS PERIOD

During this period you receive benefits from intellectual pursuits and sharing these pursuits with loved ones. Your wish for certain knowledge or information could be gratified, or you may receive a welcome letter or communication, perhaps from someone you love dearly. You will have a love of learning and things dealing with the mind and communications now. Many good things will come from this. Your communications with women and those you love will be better than usual.

THE ACE OF CLUBS IN THE MARS PERIOD

This influence bestows an aggressive quest for knowledge or self-improvement. Seeking knowledge for power, aggressive communications, and communications with men are in focus. Metaphysical knowledge can bring valuable rewards now. There is a possibility of you needing specific information to help you in some sort of legal proceeding during this period. Overall, you will be more aggressive and passionate in your pursuit of knowledge, whether it be specific information or knowledge in general.

This influence can also mean the beginning of a new job or project, especially if they are associated with communications, publishing, or teaching in some way.

THE ACE OF CLUBS IN THE JUPITER PERIOD

During this period, you will find that knowledge is your greatest asset. Your desire for knowledge can lead to professional and material success with this influence. A new idea or plan for business or financial success will have good consequences now. Follow your impulses to start something new and see what happens. You probably have a wealth of good ideas now, especially related to business ventures.

Watch out for over-ambitiousness, which could place too much value on reaching a high social status. This could undermine your success. This influence could also cause you to be impatient with those who are not as quick as you are to grasp the concepts and meanings of things. Be careful your mind doesn't get out of hand now. It is in high gear and needs to be directed into practical pursuits as much as possible.

THE ACE OF CLUBS IN THE SATURN PERIOD

This period may bring an unwelcome letter or news, perhaps from or about a sick person. Unfulfilled desires for knowledge or unrealized goals are also possible now. Projects, plans, or ideas that begin now will be challenging and require more work than imagined. Success requires a serious and determined education; doing things halfway or sporadically will not work. To realize your educational goals, you will have to be self-disciplined and focused. Distractions and a lack of focused effort could bring disappointments in this regard.

THE ACE OF CLUBS IN THE URANUS PERIOD

This card often represents the beginning of a new job or a new way of communicating. People often purchase computers or upgrade their computers under this influence. Aces are beginnings, and Uranus can relate to real estate, your job, or something Uranian like computers or other high-tech items.

Under this influence, your answers come from unusual sources, such as your own intuition. Unusual knowledge is desired, such as occult knowledge or information about work matters. You may receive a letter about work or about a real estate transaction. Your intuition is strong now and can bring you invaluable information that benefits you in many areas. Listen carefully, and trust what you hear from the voice within.

THE ACE OF CLUBS IN THE NEPTUNE PERIOD

This card indicates a desire for knowledge about something distant or the kind of education that comes from traveling. You may find yourself traveling in a quest for the answers to life during this period. This is a good influence for that. Yearnings for information beyond this realm of reality or from past lives are common with this influence. Your own intuition can lead you to secret or invaluable information about yourself and others now.

This card can also represent the beginning of a new job or an idea that takes you in new directions.

THE ACE OF CLUBS IS YOUR PLUTO CARD

Having the Ace of Clubs in this powerful position tells us that many of your goals and changes this year will be related to knowledge and communications. One of your important goals for this year will be to launch yourself into an entirely new mental direction. Perhaps you desire a new course of study or to understand a new philosophy of life. Your exposure to some new ideas and beliefs could cause many changes in your life this year, and at times, you may feel a little overwhelmed by these same new ideas and concepts.

The Ace of Clubs also represents computers as new sources of information, so this change could involve something related to them as well. Your curiosity about things will be at an all-time high this year, and you will likely find yourself reading many books and attending classes of different sorts to satisfy this thirst for knowledge.

This will be a year of important new beginnings on many levels, but especially in relationship to your mind, your thinking and your communications with others. You have arrived at a place where you are ready to look at life with an entirely new perspective. Look at the Result Card to see what is related to this new information or philosophy that makes it so stimulating and challenging to you.

AFFIRMATION:

I am transformed by knowledge, new information, and ways of communicating. I create a new beginning for myself that takes me in new directions.

THE ACE OF CLUBS IS YOUR RESULT CARD

One of the net results of this year's activities will be an entirely new way of thinking or radically different plans for your future. This year may see you having contact with some advanced methods of communication that alter the way you think or increase your knowledge. You will end this year with a new beginning along mental lines. Your Pluto Card will tell you more about this change in your ideas, philosophy, or thinking or who is involved in it.

AFFIRMATION:

I am transformed by some new plans, ideas, knowledge, or form of communication. I end this year with new plans and new things to do.

THE ACE OF CLUBS IS YOUR LONG-RANGE CARD

The Ace of Clubs tells us that you will have a strong desire for knowledge of some kind this year and that new plans, ideas, and forms of communication could have a major impact on you. You may throw yourself into some new educational pursuit or some other Mercury-ruled activity such as writing, speaking, or teaching. You may purchase a new computer or be exposed to some advanced system of knowledge. This will probably mean that you begin some new job as well. This is a powerful indicator of new beginnings in many areas of your life.

Your natural curiosity is heightened this year, and this could lead you into many new ideas, concepts, beliefs, and ways of communicating. With all the passion of this 'one' energy, try to stay relaxed.

KEYWORDS:

I am thinking new ideas and thoughts, launching new plans, ideas, and new forms of work for my future. I am exposed to new forms of knowledge.

THE ACE OF CLUBS IS YOUR ENVIRONMENT CARD

The Ace of Clubs will never be anyone's Environment Card due to the fact that it is one of the Semi-Fixed Cards.

THE ACE OF CLUBS IS YOUR DISPLACEMENT CARD

The Ace of Clubs will never be anyone's Displacement Card due to the fact that it is one of the Semi-Fixed Cards.

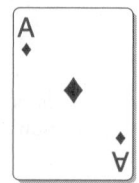

Ace of Diamonds

The desire for money and the beginning of new ways to make money

The Basic Meaning of the Ace of Diamonds

The Ace of Diamonds means the desire for money or the birth of a new way of earning money. All Aces represent new beginnings, a desire for something that starts a new cycle of creating. Aces are the representatives of pure creative energy.

Diamonds represent our value systems, the things that we like or dislike, treasure or discard. So, the Ace of Diamonds means that we experience the birth of a new value or that we suddenly like or want something that we didn't before.

Because diamonds are commonly associated with money and our work, the Ace of Diamonds can mean the beginning of a new financial enterprise or the desire to obtain money for a specific purpose.

THE ACE OF DIAMONDS IN THE MERCURY PERIOD

This influence brings a sudden desire to have more money or a desire to make money quickly. This can also represent a letter or phone call regarding money matters. This influence is one of impatience about money that might cause you to get involved in get rich quick schemes of one kind or another. Just be sure that what you get involved in doesn't cost you more than it's worth. Oftentimes hurry and impatience can cause mistakes.

THE ACE OF DIAMONDS IN THE VENUS PERIOD

This card brings a desire for money to help others in some way or a desire to live in a more luxurious manner. Basically, as an indication of charity or sharing of wealth, you will work hard for those you love during this period. During this period, you may choose to spend time with friends that further your financial plans or with those of strong financial backgrounds. Be careful that the love of money doesn't come before the love of your friends and family.

THE ACE OF DIAMONDS IN THE MARS PERIOD

This influence brings an aggressive desire for money that, when controlled, can be very effective in increasing your net worth. As a result of this, this card often represents the beginning of a new job or enterprise. This desire for money could be related to some male friend or a legal proceeding. This could also represent a letter or phone call regarding a money or legal venture that you are currently involved in. During this period, you may look upon the acquisition of money as a sport. Just be careful that you do not bend the rules too much.

THE ACE OF DIAMONDS IN THE JUPITER PERIOD

During this period, you may have a strong desire to maintain status and financial standing that motivates you into much work and action. Under this influence, it is highly likely that you will begin a new job, line of work, or find a new way to make money. Things that begin during this period are destined for success. This could also represent an important communication regarding your business or financial investments. The effects of this influence will probably be an increase in hard work and perseverance that brings financial success.

THE ACE OF DIAMONDS IN THE SATURN PERIOD

During this period, you may experience a thwarted desire for money or a desire for money (fear of poverty) that brings problems or ill health. Any new businesses or money-making enterprises that begin now will demand a lot of hard work to get them to pay off. This could also represent a desire for money to help someone who is in need or ill. This is a karmic influence, that is, a payment for past actions. It may well be that some of the problems you are experiencing now stem from your actions in the past, especially if you have been overly attached to material status or possessions.

This influence leads to a general state of feeling impoverished, and it tends to affect the entire year to some extent. It is interesting that our state of abundance is more about how we feel inside than the state of our external affairs. See if you are actually doing fine financially and simply worrying about it more than you need to.

THE ACE OF DIAMONDS IN THE URANUS PERIOD

You are likely to begin a new job or new way of making money during this period. This card represents an ambition for money that is in some way unusual or meant to be used for some public service project, but it can just mean starting a new job as well. This can also mean a desire for prominence in labor or service groups. During this time, you may spend much energy and time communicating about these ambitions. This card can also represent a letter or phone call about any of the above. If you combine your spiritual or philosophic interests with your financial ones, you can achieve success.

THE ACE OF DIAMONDS IN THE NEPTUNE PERIOD

This period may bring ambition that encourages travel or is in some way related to travel or foreign interests. This could be a desire for money to take a business trip or to be used in some distant business deal. Caution is advised under Neptune's illusory influence, so be sure that all business communications and activities are clear. Also, you should question your own motives and desires, lest you fall prey to deception along these lines.

This card can also represent the beginning of a new job or money-making project that takes you in new directions.

THE ACE OF DIAMONDS IS YOUR PLUTO CARD

This will be a year when you make some major changes in the way you relate to money and finances. You may have just had a change in your values or your philosophy about money that leaves you clear that you definitely want to obtain more prosperity and abundance. A strong impetus is present that will most likely motivate you into action to create more prosperity in your life. It is likely that you will make entirely new plans for creating more wealth, perhaps launching a new business or financial enterprise.

To achieve your new financial goals, you will have to make many changes in the way you do things. This will not always be easy. This year could very well be the dawning of material success as one of your new enterprises could prove to be quite lucrative in a long-term sense. Look at the Result Card for more specifics about this new desire for prosperity and how you mean to achieve it.

My strong desires for financial prosperity transform me and my actions. I create new beginnings for me, my work, and life.

THE ACE OF DIAMONDS IS YOUR RESULT CARD

One of your major goals this year, noted by your Pluto Card, will somehow include or cause you to end up with an entirely new way of making money. Perhaps this is the year that you set definite financial goals for yourself and decide that you deserve to have more money to spend. At any rate, this highly motivating influence promises that by year's end you will be off in a new direction heading towards the realization of your financial dreams.

AFFIRMATION:

I end up this year with a new way of thinking about and making money. I have a new career or job.

THE ACE OF DIAMONDS IS YOUR LONG-RANGE CARD

A strong desire for money will be one of the major influences in your life this year. For some reason, you have decided that this is the year you get serious about your financial condition and do something about it. This desire could signal the beginning of a new financial enterprise or a new job.

While this desire may help to get you out of a financial rut, be careful that you don't lose sight of the other important areas in your life. Keep this in balance with the rest of your life for best results. Look for other cards in your yearly reading for indications of the success or failure of your money-making endeavors.

Essentially, this card means the birth of new values in your life. It is as though some new things have come into your awareness that you think are important enough to attain. This could actually be many kinds of things, money, possessions, relationships, or new kinds of work. Now a desire to attain them will motivate you into new actions of many kinds.

KEYWORDS:

A year motivated by the desire for money or new business and financial endeavors.

THE ACE OF DIAMONDS IS YOUR ENVIRONMENT CARD

This will be a year when new beginnings, both in your work and in other financial enterprises, will bring many blessings and good fortune to you. This would be an ideal influence for starting a new business or even a new personal relationship. Because this is a year of beginnings as far as your values are concerned, you may find that you are starting over in many important areas of your life, areas that will ultimately bring you more joy and contentment. Rest assured that any opportunities for new money-making enterprises, new jobs, or financial deals will be good for you and bring you greater success.

THE ACE OF DIAMONDS IS YOUR DISPLACEMENT CARD

This year could be one in which you experience some amount of financial limitation, whether real or imagined. A desire for more on the material plane could motivate you into new enterprises or directions, or it could just prove to be a nagging feeling of not having enough. New jobs or money-making ventures may take more effort than you expected and you may feel that all you do is work, work, work. A restless urge may overtake you and inspire you to take a trip or even move to a new location. All in all, you will need to pay more attention to your work or financial situation and put in a little extra effort to guarantee that everything works right in your life.

Ace of Spades

Secrets, the desire for work, transformation of the lifestyle, the Magi Card

The Basic Meaning of the Ace of Spades

The Ace of Spades means a SECRET of some kind. This card was the emblem for many of the secret societies of old, being the 'key to the mysteries.' As such, it represents the 'truth that lies behind the veil of illusion.' So, it has often been the symbol for the study and pursuit of esoteric knowledge and mystical wisdoms.

The Ace of Spades is also one of the traditional cards for death, change, and transformation. With this mystical card in your spread, it is certain that you will go through some sort of death and rebirth, or at the least some important and powerful changes.

Another facet of the Ace of Spades is the desire for work. Since all Aces represent new beginnings, the Ace of Spades can come up when we are preparing to launch a new job or occupation.

THE ACE OF SPADES IN THE MERCURY PERIOD

This card represents secret activities, communications, or short trips. This can be a secret about a brother or sister. This can also be a desire for secret knowledge, either mundane or spiritual or an unexpected and secret desire for somebody or something. This card can signal an unexpected change or even a death in the family, though this is not a strong possibility. It can also represent a powerful spiritual experience that changes your life.

THE ACE OF SPADES IN THE VENUS PERIOD

During this period, you may have a secret lover or close friend who relieves the boredom of your current relationship. This could also be secret plans, hopes, friends, a gift, or a secret desire or wish for money and luxury. This can represent a close friend with whom you share secrets or a desire for work in the arts or dealing in some way with women. This card also holds the promise of spiritual resolutions to some of your mundane problems.

The Ace of Spades means 'transformation,' the process of death and rebirth. Regardless of the particulars of this period, you will probably experience an ending and a beginning somehow related to your love life or your family.

THE ACE OF SPADES IN THE MARS PERIOD

This card can represent a secret love affair or marriage, especially for women. There could be involvement in secret work or investigative work. This can also mean a secret shared with a male or a desire to delve into the 'inner mysteries' of life. The Ace of Spades in Mars is probably the most passionate and aggressive combination of influences possible. With this powerful card in this position, you have all the drive and ambition you need to excel at anything you do. You might find many answers to your problems by applying a spiritual approach. Just be careful not to overdo things during this period. Excessiveness can be dangerous at times.

THE ACE OF SPADES IN THE JUPITER PERIOD

During this period, you may be involved in a secret business deal or have a strong desire for work that brings in much success and money. This card can mean a drastic change in your business or financial picture or the beginning of an entirely new business. Large sums of money could change hands during this period. The basic meaning of this card is a new beginning in your work or a new way of making money. Because it falls in this, the most beneficial period, any new businesses or jobs that begin now will be destined for success.

Also possible is your having a strong desire for occult manifestations or receiving much benefit from the use of secret or mystical information. The *Cards of Your Destiny* system is represented by the Ace of Spades card, so often people make money doing some sort of esoteric or spiritual work when this card falls in this position. At any rate, many blessings will come from any involvement with the metaphysical sciences.

THE ACE OF SPADES IN THE SATURN PERIOD

This period could hold some kind of concealed trouble, such as a disease or illness, either yours or someone else's, and perhaps a secret kept from you. Something kept hidden could be hindering you. This is a good influence for healers and physicians. This card can bring a recovery from illness or some kind of reversal in your health picture. A desire to uncover the underlying causes of illness could lead to your recovery or that of someone else's.

As much as the Ace of Spades means a beginning, it can also mean an ending. It is the card of transformation, and transformation means death of the old and the beginning of the new. If there are parts of yourself or your lifestyle that are due for a change, this is probably the time when it will happen. Your other Saturn Card could tell you more about this change or tell you what area of your life it will affect. Though most of us fear changes, they always lead us to something new and better.

THE ACE OF SPADES IN THE URANUS PERIOD

This period may bring a secret real estate transaction, labor-related issue, or some secret about your job. This card is a card of ambition and desire. Thus, people often begin new jobs or careers under its influence. However, for those on the spiritual path, this card holds a deep and mystical meaning that may also apply at the same time.

This can also mean a strong desire for occult knowledge or secret knowledge. A card that represents psychic gifts, you may even be motivated to join a secret society or organization during this period. This card can represent a powerful religious or psychic experience or a strong desire for some specific work or project.

THE ACE OF SPADES IN THE NEPTUNE PERIOD

This period may bring a secret journey, a secret uncovered on a journey, or secret information about a distant interest. You have strong intuition at this time and perhaps a desire to uncover things about the past or past lives. This card represents a desire to uncover secrets about your inner self and the mysteries of the universe and can be a motivating factor in getting you involved in meaningful study or practice.

This card can also represent the beginning of a job that takes you in new directions. On the spiritual level, this is one of the most powerful influences that exist. A desire to delve into the deepest parts of yourself are likely to be well-rewarded.

THE ACE OF SPADES IS YOUR PLUTO CARD

The powerful Ace of Spades signifies that this year will see you go through some major changes, internal and external. You may have to face the loss of one or more close relationships, or other facets of your life may come to an end, leaving you changed as nothing else could. You may be ending a major chapter of your life. The Ace of Spades is one of the most powerful cards for personal transformation, and this year it is challenging you to let go of the past and start over.

This is also a year for you where you have a strong desire to make a definite and fundamental change in your life and/or work. You realize that a change is due now, and you are ready to pursue the best means to achieve it.

On a mundane level, you may be wanting to begin a totally new line of work or effect a total change in the way you approach your work. You may be looking for something that will really motivate you to put yourself totally into your work.

On a deeper level, you may be overdue for a totally new way of living your life, and you are making a concerted effort at self-exploration to uncover the deeper mysteries of yourself. This quest may lead you to the study of metaphysical sciences, such as this Science of the Cards or Astrology, or it may get you involved with some ancient mystical or occult order. All of these are possibilities with this influence.

On the other hand, the passing of someone near to you may be something that is very challenging this year. Since the Ace of Spades is the card for transformation, this passing would radically change you as well.

Look to the Result Card to get more information about this change you are wanting in your life this year. If the Result Card is that of someone you know, then this change will be directly related to that person. If not, study the meaning of the Result Card, and combine it with the basic theme of radical change to get the whole picture of the challenge you have put before yourself this year.

AFFIRMATION:

I create a powerful transformation in my life this year. I am manifesting new beginnings in many important areas and letting go of the past.

THE ACE OF SPADES IS YOUR RESULT CARD

Whatever the nature of your Pluto Card this year, it is certain that the result of dealing with it will be a major change in your life that could be the death of the old and the beginning of the new. Whether this change comes about through the departure of current friends or family or whether your own health or work plays a significant role, you will emerge at the end of this year with a totally new direction that is more alive, healthy, and loving.

AFFIRMATION:

I am making major changes in my life, work, health, and spirituality. I end this year transformed and starting over.

THE ACE OF SPADES IS YOUR LONG-RANGE CARD

This is likely to be a year of great change for you. You will likely go through a large scale transformation as this year progresses and this change could affect many important areas of your life. There is a fundamental change due for you at this time. This could be about your attitudes or relationships, but it is likely to be deeper than that.

This change is more likely to pertain to how you live your life, your approach to work and health, and how you maintain your sense of alive-ness and vitality.

During this change and new beginning, you may get a firsthand experience of the intimate relationship of death and rebirth. It is even possible that someone you know will pass on. If this happens, it is likely to be someone that is close enough to you to put you more in touch with your own mortality. Your job may also undergo a radical change this year. You may enter a totally new line of work, ending a chapter of your life in the old line. This change may not be comfortable, but the end result will be a more alive and vital you.

On a mundane level, the Ace of Spades means 'desire for work.' Thus you may have an overwhelming desire to work and initiate a new profession. It is also possible that involvement in secret work or work that uncovers your own secrets may take on a major role this year. The Ace of Spades is the card that represents the Science of the Cards, the Order of the Magi, and other secret organizations that help man to understand the deeper mysteries of life so you might find yourself involved in one of these this year as well.

KEYWORDS:

I am surrounded by death and transformation this year. I am exploring the deeper mysteries of life.

THE ACE OF SPADES IS YOUR ENVIRONMENT CARD

This is a year when new beginnings in your health, work, or other important lifestyle areas will bring you much in the way of blessings and happiness. This is one of the best influences under which to start a new business or job. However, the beginnings that you experience this year could be on even deeper levels for you. Your very lifestyle could be undergoing a transformation. Rest assured that any changes will be extremely positive in nature.

THE ACE OF SPADES IS YOUR DISPLACEMENT CARD

This could be a significant year for you in many ways, and one in which you make a major change in your lifestyle. It is time for a fundamental change in your life or lifestyle. If you recognize this and make some changes intentionally and consciously, this could be a life-changing year that sets you upon a brand new path and direction. For those who are either completely unaware of their need to change, or those who have great fears surrounding this change, this card could prove to be quite a problem. Unexpected or unwanted events could bring some dramatic shifts in your life or lifestyle. Sometimes this card brings the death of a relative, but what is really happening is that some part of yourself is passing away—a part that is no longer serving you or those around you in any meaningful way. This card is like the surgeon's knife that cuts deeply, but removes a poisonous tumor that threatens your very life. Expect to pay more attention to the inner part of your life this year.

On a mundane level, new jobs or projects begun during this year will consume more energy than usual and tend to produce fewer results. However, sometimes this card can indicate a 'fated beginning,' a new undertaking that will eventually lead you to something you were meant to do from the day you were born.

Two of Hearts

A union in love

The Basic Meaning of the Two of Hearts

The Two of Hearts literally means a 'union of hearts.' This card speaks of your close relationships, including lovers, marriage partner, or closest friends. For someone desiring a relationship, this could be the best possible card to have since it is one of the strongest love affair cards. It can also mean time spent with dear friends or family members.

Even the birth of a child can show up as a Two of Hearts, since the pairing of a mother or father with a baby can be much like a love affair. Whenever the Two of Hearts appears, you can be certain that you will be spending some time with someone you love.

THE TWO OF HEARTS IN THE MERCURY PERIOD

This time period could bring a sudden or unexpected relationship, passion for someone, or meeting of lovers or dear friends. This is a good influence for getting together with a close friend to share intellectual pursuits. Mercury's influence brings a flirtatious and flighty nature into your life, and you may be learning about love through experimentation and variety now. Relationships may not last long during this period, but they will be enjoyable.

THE TWO OF HEARTS IN THE VENUS PERIOD

This time period should bring you a very satisfying love relationship. This is one of the best indicators of love and happiness in relationships of all sorts. In particular, you may have a satisfying reunion with a dear friend or lover. This could also be the time that you meet someone new and get off on the right foot for a long-term love affair, friendship, or marriage. Relationships now are somewhat blessed and bring positive energy into your life.

THE TWO OF HEARTS IN THE MARS PERIOD

This time period brings relationships that are aggressive, stimulating, and intense. Over-aggressiveness could lead to quarreling and disruptions, though this is a good influence for sexual pleasure. Control this energy, and you could reap its more positive aspects. Just be aware that this Martian aggressiveness can result in anger or quarreling if not handled carefully. Use this energy to expand your circle of male friends.

THE TWO OF HEARTS IN THE JUPITER PERIOD

During this period, you can expect financial and spiritual gains through partnerships and close personal relationships of all kinds. This is a good influence for a personal relationship with a business partner, which is not usually recommended. Jupiter's beneficial influence casts a warm and healthy light on all your personal relationships during this period. Any friendships or love affairs now will likely be blessings in your life in more ways than one.

In some situations, this card can also represent a successful childbirth.

THE TWO OF HEARTS IN THE SATURN PERIOD

This period may bring a karmic relationship into your life. You may have a close friend or lover who needs your help to battle an illness or burden. They may, in turn, become a burden for you. Any intimate affairs begun now will likely have a fated quality about them and are likely to be challenging in one or more ways. You may be learning about the responsibilities that go along with love or your personal sexual expression. The net result of such 'lessons in love' will be a more mature you, capable of acting with integrity and fairness in your most intimate relationships.

THE TWO OF HEARTS IN THE URANUS PERIOD

The planetary influence of Uranus will bring about an element of the unusual and unexpected to your close relationships and partnerships during this period. Your status quo may be disrupted by a partnership or friendship, or you may find yourself in an unusual romantic affair. There may be time spent with a close friend at work or one that you meet in some community affair. This is a good time to make good friends who will love you for yourself.

THE TWO OF HEARTS IN THE NEPTUNE PERIOD

This period may bring a very romantic and idealistic love affair or friendship. You may meet someone while traveling, or it could also be a secret or mystical affair. Neptune's glamour may prevent you from being objective. The person you meet may seem to be the one of your dreams, but caution is advised. Postpone any important decisions about love until after your birthday. Also, be watchful for miscommunications that could stir up trouble between you.

This card will actually affect you for the entire year, causing you to yearn for some sort of perfect love or lover. You are dreaming about your soul mate, but only time will tell if this person actually shows up.

THE TWO OF HEARTS IS YOUR PLUTO CARD

A major goal for you this year will be to have a successful love relationship or friendship. For this reason, this is the year that you will make many changes within your self in the name of love, friendship, or romance. Whether you are interested in the partner of your dreams or just good, close friendships, you will have to take a different approach in your life if you are to be successful in these areas. Love and intimacy require compromise and cooperation, two of the keynotes for this card of the 'love union.' Your intense desire for this closeness will cause you to confront some of the parts of yourself that tend to keep this intimacy from you. At times, this may seem very challenging or difficult, but it helps to keep in mind your reasons for facing these situations—to have more intimacy in your life.

There may be a certain person, indicated by the Result Card, who is the main challenge for you this year and shows you, whether intentionally or not, the changes you need to make to have the love you want. If not a person, the Result Card will point to other aspects of this goal or challenge that you have put before yourself this year. It is clear that you want successful relationships and are willing to work for them.

AFFIRMATION:

I create the ideal love partner. Satisfaction in my love life, my friendships, and lovers are mine to embrace.

THE TWO OF HEARTS IS YOUR RESULT CARD

The result of many of your efforts this year will be a satisfactory love partnership, or at the very least, a deep friendship. The Two of Hearts is the 'Union of Hearts,' the 'Love Affair Card,' and it is obvious that this is one of your major goals for the year. Though you may have to make changes in your life or behavior, be assured that you will achieve your desired wish. Your Pluto Card will tell you more about this union of hearts or describe the person you are pursuing.

AFFIRMATION:

I will have an intimate relationship or close friendship by year's end. I am developing successful love relationships.

THE TWO OF HEARTS IS YOUR LONG-RANGE CARD

The Two of Hearts literally means a 'union of hearts.' With the card of the lovers in such a prominent position this year, you can bet that relationships of all kinds are one of the most important issues for you. If you are single, it is likely that you will be experiencing important relationships this year. You may even have more than one romantic involvement.

What this year is about for you is to learn what your needs are for a partnership, what kind of partner is best for you, and just where you stand on the whole issue of love and romance. It may be that you are just getting back into the dating scene and are looking for that special person to complete your picture of a happy home and social life.

If you are married, the same could apply between you and your spouse, but it is more likely that your close friends would take on a level of prominence for you and that you will go through the same process of finding out where you stand in the area of friendships. In some cases, a love affair comes along to rekindle those fires of passion. In any case, love and feelings are important and will be a big part of your life.

KEYWORDS:

Relationships are important to me. I am learning everything about love and relationships this year.

THE TWO OF HEARTS IS YOUR ENVIRONMENT CARD

The Two of Hearts will never be anyone's Environment Card because it is one of the Semi-Fixed Cards.

THE TWO OF HEARTS IS YOUR DISPLACEMENT CARD

The Two of Hearts will never be anyone's Displacement Card because it is one of the Semi-Fixed Cards.

Two of Clubs
Communications, fear, and arguing

The Basic Meaning of the Two of Clubs

The Two of Clubs means conversation, communication, sharing ideas, and cooperation on a communication level. However, it is also known as the card of fear and arguing. When it is present you may feel compelled to talk to others and to establish lines of communication.

Look deeper into yourself and you may discover an inner conflict between your desire to be alone and to be with others. Talking to others may shed more light on who you are. Just make sure that you are being honest with yourself.

The Two of Clubs in the Mercury Period

This period could bring intellectual arguments or arguments with someone who is quick-witted and hot-headed. Your desire to learn something very quickly brings on impatience and a quick temper that may cause a heated discussion. This provocation will soon be over, so it shouldn't cause any lasting damage. This period could also see one or more sudden and unexpected meetings with friends or family. There is also the possibility of joint studies of some kind.

The Two of Clubs in the Venus Period

You are most likely to be attracted to those with whom you can share intellectual pursuits, and this may stimulate you to join a group with this sort of focus in mind. You don't want to be alone now, and this will motivate you to be more socially involved. In your love relationships, you will be attracted to those with whom you can communicate as well as share common interests of the mind.

The Two of Clubs in the Mars Period

A meeting with a man in relation to a lawsuit or a business deal could be a major event of this period. With Mars's influence, it would be wise to hold your tongue in check, as a quarrelsome attitude could do a lot of damage now. This is a very strong influence for arguments, especially with men, or in connection with a legal proceeding, so take care in those areas. This period could also see you aggressively pursuing some specific information for a specific desire.

The Two of Clubs in the Jupiter Period

This influence is one of successful meetings of business interests or partnerships. Emphasize cooperation and avoid quarreling to get best results and the financial rewards could be great. In general, sharing your quest for knowledge could bring material and personal benefits during this period. This influence promotes harmony and wisdom in all meetings and intellectual partnerships and gives financial rewards through these avenues.

The Two of Clubs in the Saturn Period

Avoid all arguments and quarreling during this period, as they will have pronounced negative results now. If you have been harboring negative attitudes about anything or anyone, you will now be confronted with the results of such attitudes. Your own health could suffer now at the hands of your belief systems. This period could also see a meeting with a doctor or lawyer for some reason. Power and success are gained through cooperation and a positive attitude.

The Two of Clubs is also known as the 'Fear Card,' and under Saturn's influence, it is very likely that you will experience some of this more or less negative influence. It is usually a fear of being alone or the fear of death, and it may not have any basis in reality. The best remedy for this fear is patience and doing things that relax you and make you happy. Any attempts to change your external situation now, if motivated by this fear, will likely backfire. Before trying to change any part of the world outside you, be with your inner feelings, and your chances for success will be much greater.

The Two of Clubs in the Uranus Period

During this period, benefits come through sharing your personal quest for knowledge and cooperative efforts involving labor or some kind of community service project. An unexpected meeting of the minds may arise also. This is not a good influence for real estate deals or speculation, as the argumentative nature of the Two of Clubs could mean problems there. In addition, you must guard against a quarrelsome disposition with those you work with. Common goals help.

The Two of Clubs in the Neptune Period

If you are traveling at this time, you may meet one or more people with whom you have much in common intellectually. You may also meet one who is well traveled with whom you share many interests and have one or more pleasant meetings. In general, this is a good influence for the sharing of intellectual pursuits and making new friends, especially if that is something you have been dreaming about.

This card can often indicate some secret fears you may be having about things that affect you off and on for the entire year. If so, the things you are afraid of will probably never happen, but you will have to keep a positive attitude to compensate for these negative psychic impressions.

The Two of Clubs Is Your Pluto Card

Successful communication is one of your important goals this year and one that challenges you to watch the ways in which you communicate and share your ideas with others. This year you will likely be forced into having more conversations and communications than you have had for a while, the purpose of which may be to develop and hone your communication skills.

The Two of Clubs has been known as the 'Arguing and Fear Card.' If you find yourself in many debates or arguments, watch closely to see what the results are of 'being right.' Many of your debates and arguments may be based in some deep fears of yours that are surfacing this year more than ever. You could experience a lot of fear of being alone this year, something that many Two of Clubs people have to face throughout their life.

You love to keep in touch with others, and for this year, you may feel like you are at the center of a communications hub. There are likely to be many short trips and meetings of all kinds as you develop your ability to express and share yourself with others. Look to the Result Card to either know more about your desire to communicate effectively or to know about a special person in your life that will reflect back to you the way you communicate.

I communicate clearly and effectively. I am learning to face my deepest fears.

THE TWO OF CLUBS IS YOUR RESULT CARD

The Two of Clubs in this position means that you are working on your ability to communicate with others. You have a strong desire to communicate your ideas, thoughts, and opinions with others this year. There may be a special message you want to convey. A tendency to argue may be brought to your attention by those around you. Whatever the case may be, you must make changes in the way you communicate if you are to achieve harmony with others.

AFFIRMATION:

I attain successful communications and transform arguing into cooperative mental relations.

THE TWO OF CLUBS IS YOUR LONG-RANGE CARD

The Two of Clubs tells us that a partnership involved in some Mercury-ruled activity will play a major role for you this year. Mercury rules the written and spoken word and all kinds of mental activities. Studying, teaching, writing, publishing, and advertising all fall under his jurisdiction. This also indicates that meetings or discussions and arguments could be major themes this year as well. Watch out for impatience and a quick temper to get the best results.

You will be wanting to share your thoughts and ideas with others and thus will probably attract a lot of other people into your life this year. The Two of Clubs can even represent your being somewhat afraid of being alone, but this might be just what you need to motivate you into seeking others to be with.

Just how you communicate with others will be brought to your attention this year in a big way. You will most likely find yourself in one or more situations that require you to develop harmonious lines of communication with others. There may be one special person with whom you share many ideas and thoughts who becomes the focus of this year for you. In any event, your ability to share what you know with those around you without arousing their opposition will be in focus.

Arguing is always a possibility with this card, but it will show you the areas where you can improve the quality and content of your communications with others.

KEYWORDS:

I am learning to have harmonious communications with others. I am transforming arguing into smooth communication.

THE TWO OF CLUBS IS YOUR ENVIRONMENT CARD

During the upcoming year, much will be gained by communicating with those in your life and establishing mutual friendships based on common intellectual pursuits and interests. You are likely to find many people with whom you have much in common on an intellectual and philosophical basis, people you can talk to and share your ideas with. These same people will definitely be a source of blessings for you throughout this year. Close relationships of all kinds are favored by this auspicious influence.

THE TWO OF CLUBS IS YOUR DISPLACEMENT CARD

A fear of being alone and tendency to be argumentative could cause a few problems for you this year. However, if you handle yourself with care, nothing of any importance will actually materialize into an actual problem. Fears of all kinds may seem to just follow you around and you will need to watch a tendency to overreact to things that happen. To counter the effects of this card, it is recommended that you meditate or just take some time to get inside yourself and explore your feelings.

On the other hand, this is a fairly fortunate position for work and financial success. This means that even though you may be fearing the worst, your actual experiences will be positive and successful.

Two of Diamonds
Wheeling and dealing

The Basic Meaning of the Two of Diamonds

The Two of Diamonds signifies that a money partnership of some kind will be playing a role in your life. This could be a standard business partnership or something out of the ordinary, but it will certainly have something related to money as the end result.

Whether this 'joining of financial interests' becomes an asset or a liability depends largely upon the surrounding circumstances and the position of this card.

We often need the association of others in order to achieve our financial goals. The Two of Diamonds will encourage us to develop relationships that are mutually beneficial between ourselves and others in our business and financial life. The most success comes with this card when we adopt a "win-win" attitude towards all our business dealings.

THE TWO OF DIAMONDS IN THE MERCURY PERIOD

Here we have a business communication or meeting that comes and goes quickly. This could be an unexpected or fleeting money deal or partnership or a sudden business deal that requires some short trips. Also possible is a financial arrangement with a relative such as a brother or sister. Under Mercury this partnership may happen suddenly and last a short time only. It may be a quick investment that pays quick returns. Be ready for the unexpected.

THE TWO OF DIAMONDS IN THE VENUS PERIOD

This represents a business partnership with a friend, lover, spouse, or a woman. This partnership is bound to be profitable. This also promotes a love of partnerships and a desire to associate with those of means, perhaps out of a fear of not having enough yourself. Just be careful when you mix love and money. There is always the possibility of deception when your heart rules your head.

THE TWO OF DIAMONDS IN THE MARS PERIOD

This represents a partnership for money with a male or a lawyer, or one that is aggressively pursued. This could also be a meeting with a male regarding money and possibly about some legal matter. Watch out for too much aggression and bossiness in business deals, especially with friends. This is a great influence for finding venture capital and for using your wits to make successful financial deals.

THE TWO OF DIAMONDS IN THE JUPITER PERIOD

This represents a profitable business partnership or deal, perhaps with a large organization or involving a large sum of money. This placement suggests much success in financial partnerships at this time, so take advantage of it. Jupiter's expansive and beneficial influence suggests that expansion of your business interests will bring success.

THE TWO OF DIAMONDS IN THE SATURN PERIOD

During this period, you may have a money deal or partnership that goes sour, or one that causes burdens or restrictions. This could be a partnership with an older authority figure. Success comes through sustained effort in this union of interests. Under Saturn, your partnerships may have an element of fate, karma, or illness about them. They may not be agreeable, but with effort, you will be able to learn a lot and make steady progress towards your goals.

THE TWO OF DIAMONDS IN THE URANUS PERIOD

During this period, you may enter into a real estate partnership or have a meeting about labor issues. This could represent the signing of a real estate contract. Let others attend to the details, and don't let financial fears bother you so much at this time. Partnerships can be the source of both spiritual and material benefits under Uranus and may have an element of the unusual or unexpected about them. The focus may now be more on business deals and relations. Sometimes we have to make arrangements with others in order to further our own financial future.

THE TWO OF DIAMONDS IN THE NEPTUNE PERIOD

During this period, you may begin a money partnership regarding travel or interests at a distance. This could also represent a meeting about a business trip or foreign interests. You may even be able to apply some of your psychic ability in your business affairs for success now. Under Neptune's illusory influence, there is always the possibility of being deceived, by yourself or by others. Be clear and extra careful in your communications.

THE TWO OF DIAMONDS IS YOUR PLUTO CARD

An area that will need much of your attention this year and cause you to make some important changes in your life is the area of financial partnerships, arrangements, and investments. The Two of Diamonds means financial arrangements and agreements, meetings and contracts. By adopting a 'Win-Win' philosophy in all your deals, you insure your own success and future prosperity, but you may have to work at it till you get the hang of it. You will likely have many meetings and make many deals this year, perhaps with many different people to achieve your goals. You need others' cooperation and input to achieve your own goals, and you may have to make concessions and changes in order to get their cooperation. Look to the Result Card to find out more about these deals or to see which person in your life is the focus of many of these deals in the upcoming year.

AFFIRMATION:

I find ways to increase my wealth with the help and assistance of others. I create cooperation in financial partnerships.

THE TWO OF DIAMONDS IS YOUR RESULT CARD

The net result of one of your important goals this year is likely to be successful financial partnerships and arrangements. Your Pluto Card will tell you more about this or tell you who, in particular, you are joining forces with. Taking advantage of other people's help may cause you to go through some changes this year. However, cooperation is the key to your success and all business deals will have to be a "win-win" so that you and all others profit from them.

AFFIRMATION:

I create successful financial deals and partnerships. I end up this year connected to others in a financial way.

THE TWO OF DIAMONDS IS YOUR LONG-RANGE CARD

The Two of Diamonds signifies that money partnerships and deals will be playing a major role in your life this year. This could be a standard business partnership or something out of the ordinary. Your financial success requires the assistance of others this year, so you can expect to have many phone calls, meetings and business deals to achieve working and successful financial arrangements. By letting others guide you and share in the risk, you can increase your finances. This card usually brings a great deal of phone calls, letters, emails, and other communications about money or business, and it is usually considered favorable for making more money.

KEYWORDS:

A year of business deals, communications, financial arrangements with others, and money meetings.

THE TWO OF DIAMONDS IS YOUR ENVIRONMENT CARD

This will be a year in which you will receive blessings from financial deals and business agreements. This card could indicate some success through a financial broker or partner in business. All in all, most of your business arrangements should go well and help your prosperity level. Look for specific individuals who hold the keys to your success. Reach out and make the contact, and you won't be disappointed. Success with people is especially good now.

THE TWO OF DIAMONDS IS YOUR DISPLACEMENT CARD

This can be a year of significant financial success, especially through your connections with other people. However, these same relationships may require a lot of your attention this year to maintain and keep in a healthy condition. Partners in business and work will have more demands and needs of you than usual. At the same time, you may find yourself torn between your personal relationships and your work. Just which one you will place the most importance on will determine to a large extent just how successful you will be. This will likely be a very productive year, but you will have to work hard for the success you get.

Two of Spades
Friendships and working partnerships

The Basic Meaning of the Two of Spades

The Two of Spades means a union or partnership in work or friendship. Since this is a Spade, the partnerships that it may foretell will be ones where you and the other person actually spend time doing things together, whether it be work or things such as hiking, exercising, camping, biking, or another sport.

When the Two of Spades occurs in your reading, you will be feeling the need for others in your life and as such will likely attract someone with whom you can have a pleasant friendship or working relationship. The key to success with this card is cooperation. Close relationships always require a bit of give and take for success.

THE TWO OF SPADES IN THE MERCURY PERIOD

This card brings an unexpected or sudden partnership, one that doesn't last long or one that is initiated for a quick return or fast results. This partnership could involve writing, speaking, communicating, telephone calls, or letters, and it could be with a younger person or a brother or sister. Your desire for partnerships may stem from a fear of taking all the responsibility in a certain work or project.

THE TWO OF SPADES IN THE VENUS PERIOD

This period could bring a partnership with a friend, relative, or spouse, possibly a woman. This could be a partnership to make money or to buy or sell luxury items, and this partnership could combine business and romance. Your partner could be wealthy, and this 'business' could be centered in your home. This can also mean a meeting in your home for some work-related topic. You might join a class to learn one of the arts during this period.

THE TWO OF SPADES IN THE MARS PERIOD

This card means a partnership with a man or men. This could also indicate a meeting with an attorney about a legal matter. This is an excellent influence for attorneys or anyone involved in negotiating work. Under this influence, you will work best in a partnership and have the ability to keep the peace among those at odds with each other. Though it may be a challenge, your honest efforts and hard work could bring much progress towards your work goals now.

THE TWO OF SPADES IN THE JUPITER PERIOD

This period could bring you a very beneficial business partnership or one that involves large amounts of money. Look to the underlying cards and other cards nearby to determine who this partner will be. This card guarantees that your most financially successful areas will be in partnerships, not only in this period, but for the entire year to some extent. This card can also indicate successful business meetings. Get consultation on all important money decisions.

THE TWO OF SPADES IN THE SATURN PERIOD

This period could bring a work partnership that is a burden or source of restriction. This could also be a meeting with a doctor or sick friend. Any partnerships now, especially business and work related, may require hard work and discipline to be successful.

This card can also indicate fears about the status of your health or wealth, and these fears may get you involved in a dubious partnership or prompt you to see the doctor. It will take more than the usual amount of patience to be successful now.

THE TWO OF SPADES IN THE URANUS PERIOD

This card brings a partnership involving land, real estate, humanitarian work, some sort of futuristic technology, or some 'New Age' type work. This also includes computers and other forms of high technology. It is bound to be innovative or unusual in some way, and it may happen unexpectedly. This partnership may cause you a bit of uncertainty or happen too fast for you. This is one of the best influences for spending quality time with a friend or group of friends.

THE TWO OF SPADES IN THE NEPTUNE PERIOD

This influence brings a partnership related to foreign interests, travel, the movies, or drugs. This could also indicate a meeting about any of the above or a joining together for spiritual or religious study. This partnership may have an element of idealism or even deception to it, and this influence is best for spiritual or religious work. Otherwise, caution is advised since there could be a strong element of deception or self-delusion.

THE TWO OF SPADES IS YOUR PLUTO CARD

It is likely that you will be learning lessons of cooperation and compromise this year, perhaps in the context of a working partnership, a live-in partner, or a friend. There may be someone who has skills, abilities, or other assets that you need to pull off a successful business or project. Cooperation should be written across your chest as you endeavor to successfully live, work, and create with others in a big way this year. If not cooperation, try the 'Win-Win' philosophy. You have challenged yourself to create harmonious working relationships this year, and this extends into all your relationships to some extent. You are likely to see this as the next rung on the ladder to your dreams, a quality that you must master.

You need others' cooperation and support. It helps you to multiply your own efforts and to integrate your work into the fabric of your business and social community. To achieve this goal, you will have to make some changes in your behavior or communications. Look to the Result Card for more details on this effort, or to discover the card of someone that you know or will meet that you will have to integrate into your life this year.

AFFIRMATION:

I create harmonious friendships and working relationships by learning to give and receive.

THE TWO OF SPADES IS YOUR RESULT CARD

You have set before you a great task and one that requires the assistance and cooperation of other people, or at least one key person, to accomplish. Now, you must learn the ways to get the benefits of others' support without the friction that partnerships create. Though this may cause you to go through many changes this year, you are sure to pull it off successfully. Your Pluto Card will give more details about this or tell you who is involved in this union of interests.

AFFIRMATION:

The results of my efforts this year will be a successful working relationship or partnership. I learn to cooperate.

THE TWO OF SPADES IS YOUR LONG-RANGE CARD

The Two of Spades means a union or partnership in work. It is the card of the 'Aquarian Age' of cooperation and mutual respect. For you, this card signifies that these elements will take on more importance this year and you will be learning the value of cooperation, either at work or in some other endeavor. We can achieve much more in groups than by ourselves, and often others hold the keys to our own success. See how you can achieve more with others than by yourself this year. This card also bestows the gift of a keen logical mind. You probably won't want to put up with much untruth from your friends and associates this year, and you could excel at occupations that require detailed and precise thinking and evaluation of facts and situations.

KEYWORDS:

A year of work partnerships and learning the value of cooperation and compromise to get desired results.

THE TWO OF SPADES IS YOUR ENVIRONMENT CARD

Many blessings can come this year through working partnerships or through people in your life that you do things with. This is the friendship card, and it will bring many good things from most everyone that you spend time with this year. This would be an especially good year to begin or expand a business-related working partnership or to make the contacts that will help you expand the scope of what you are doing. Cooperation is the key to success.

THE TWO OF SPADES IS YOUR DISPLACEMENT CARD

This will likely be a year when you grow to appreciate the friendships in your life and those you may consider working partners in your life. You will find that these relationships require a lot more of your energy and attention and that you may be less comfortable just being by yourself a lot. However, a certain amount of popularity goes along with this card, and this will help you make new friends if that is what you decide to do. It is also possible to have some health challenges with this card, but this is not certain by any means. One of the really good aspects of this card is in regards to your work and career. If you have any goals of becoming better known in your field, this is the year that you will realize them. This could translate as a raise or promotion or as just becoming more recognized for the work that you are doing.

The Card Int

Three of Hearts

Indecision or variety in love and relationships, expression of feelings

The Basic Meaning of the Three of Hearts

The Three of Hearts signifies creativity or indecision in affection that can manifest in different ways. This could indicate having two or more love interests at the same time or simply that we are unsure of where to place our affections. This indecision can lead to either more fun or worry and fear, depending upon how we handle it. This card's influence usually occurs at a time when we are wanting to learn about love through experimentation and variety. Its presence usually means that we will not be making any hard and fast relationship commitments until later.

On a positive note, the Three of Hearts is a card of self-expression, and its presence can indicate that we are talking more, expressing our feelings, and meeting new people.

The Three of Hearts in the Mercury Period

Don't be surprised if some situation comes up unexpectedly during this period that leaves you perplexed about love or friendship. You may receive two offers at once, or someone new may come in who you find immensely attractive and gives you some cause to doubt your existing relationship. This is also an influence that means immaturity in love and fickleness of the affections. Don't let your mind run away with your heart now. It may be hard to catch later.

Your other Mercury Card may indicate the person or situation you are feeling indecisive about. The good side of this card is that you have the desire and motivation to meet new people and to express your feelings, especially feelings of love and affection. This is a great influence for getting socially involved and making new contacts in either work or pleasure areas.

The Three of Hearts in the Venus Period

You may find yourself with two lovers or close friends at once, resulting in indecision about where to invest your time or open up your heart. Your own popularity, and perhaps emotional indecision, may get you into trouble now, so take care. If your loved ones seem unstable now, they may only be a reflection of yourself. Perhaps your indecision has gotten you into this predicament. Maybe it would be better to just learn from this experience and make commitments later.

The Three of Hearts in the Mars Period

During this period, much of your aggressive energy are directed towards love. This is a highly creative influence that could help you create more friends or lovers, if that is what you desire. It can be a 'love triangle' card too. You may find that you are impatient in love, but this energy can help you go out and meet many new people for work or business. This is an influence of creative self-expression. Let others know who you are and what you think.

Your other Mars Card may tell you who or what you are either feeling indecisive or creative about. It will also tell you the outcome of any creative pursuits during this period. Remember that a Four, Eight, or Ten as your other Mars Card will foretell very good results and a happy outcome during this period of active and aggressive creativity.

The Three of Hearts in the Jupiter Period

An overabundance of charm and magnetism could lead to social or romantic problems during this period. Overdoing it romantically or scattering your interests could lead to relationships of questionable value and could even cost you money if you mix love and money together.

On the positive side, this energy is best used for success in social and business situations, as you apply your charm to groups. The people you meet now could be very helpful in these areas. Sometimes this can also represent having two love interests at the same time. If so, the challenge could be just handling so much attention at the same time.

The Three of Hearts in the Saturn Period

Indecision over love or friendship could make you ill during this period. Any love triangles that you may be involved in will be more difficult than ever. The situation at hand may be one that you created in the past and are now having to contend with. Your indecisiveness is probably at the root of it, and now you may have no choice but to wait it out and see how the cards fall. This card could also mean someone you love is in poor health and taxing your peace of mind. Try not to worry so much, and take care of your body until this is over.

This card can indicate chronic worry about love and about not getting enough affection. Often it's our own indecision and refusal to stay with one relationship that threatens our security in love, which we all need in one form or another.

Also, the difficulties indicated by this card could be offset by a strong card in the other position; for example, any of the Fours, Eights, or Tens.

The Three of Hearts in the Uranus Period

A unexpected situation may arise during this period that has you feeling very undecided about where your heart lies in terms of romance or work. Your own versatility and many social interests can bring unexpected problems in love and friendships or in your work. There could even be indecision about some real estate-related activity. Expect some unusual romantic or social occurrences that will show you where you have some inner, unresolved issue about love.

However, this is also a wonderful and beneficial influence for creative work, writing, or self-expression. You can do a lot towards relieving any mental worry and anxiety by getting yourself involved in some creative project. This is also a good influence for meeting new people and opening up your social life.

The Three of Hearts in the Neptune Period

Many of your fantasies and perhaps confusions this year revolve around either a romantic triangle or expanding your circle of friends and associates. This highly creative love influence stimulates you to meet new people and try out new romantic experiences. You want to learn about love through experimentation. Make a special effort to keep all your communications clear, as others will tend to misunderstand you and your intentions. Don't leave assumptions to chance.

The Three of Hearts Is Your Pluto Card

This year is likely to be a time of variety and experimentation in your love life and social life. It may be that you are just getting back into dating again and want to rediscover what kind of relationship is best for you. This might mean dating many different people, and this could be something that is challenging and new for you. On the other hand, you may already be in some sort of situation romantically or socially where your interests are divided between two or more people. Coming to some sort of decision as to how to handle this would then be the major challenge for you this year.

This card often occurs in the spreads of those who are having an affair, or having doubts about their existing relationship or marriage. It can predict a divorce or separation. To access the most positive levels of this influence, see yourself meeting new and interesting people and learning to express your feelings more clearly to everyone that is special to you. Your Result Card will give you more details about this situation or tell you who, in your life, is the one that you are feeling some uncertainty about.

AFFIRMATION:

I am learning about what I really want in love and romance by expressing my feelings and being open to new relationships.

The Three of Hearts Is Your Result Card

Somehow, the result of your efforts this year will be that of having more friends and perhaps lovers in your life. You have been developing your ability to meet others, to communicate and share yourself. The three is a number of expression. Put that three in Hearts and you are developing your ability to express your feelings and emotional and romantic needs.

As you complete this year, you will find that your efforts have paid off. However, if you cannot handle having so many people in your life, you may experience indecision and worry over love. Look at your Pluto Card to give you more details about this.

AFFIRMATION:

I am getting clearer about what I want in relationships through experimentation. I end up with two love interests and a better ability to express my feelings to others.

The Three of Hearts Is Your Long-Range Card

This year you will have a strong desire to learn about love and intimate relationships and friendships, mostly through experimentation. Your mind is involved with your heart matters, thus you may expect many changes in romantic areas. This will likely be the cause of many different experiences with love and friendships.

If you are in a position to be wanting a new relationship, this will be a year filled with variety. This means you are likely to have more than one person to love at different times of the year. This card often

comes up in people's spreads who are just getting back into relationships after a time of being without one. They often need a year or so to get familiar with who is available and to discover what they are truly looking for. There can be times of confusion and indecision, but these are merely part of the process of getting enough information to make an informed decision.

If you are not looking for a new relationship, this card could indicate meeting many new and interesting people in the year or of having some prolonged element of indecision in your existing love situation. Sometimes the Three of Hearts can mean fears about not getting enough love. If that is the case, you may be able to see that it is your own indecision or uncertainty about commitment that is at the root of your worries.

KEYWORDS:

A year of experimentation in love and friendships, and indecision in these areas. I am learning about love or sex.

The Three of Hearts Is Your Environment Card

Benefits will come this year through broadening the scope of your personal or social relationships. A desire to express yourself and your feelings will bring many good things into your life. This could be the year that you successfully add to your list of personal contacts. You could meet a new lover or two or merely make some new friends who bring more fun and diversity into your romantic or social life. Remember to say what you feel.

The Three of Hearts Is Your Displacement Card

Emotional uncertainties and indecision may become a drain on your energy this year. If you are involved in two relationships at the same time, or feeling dissatisfied with your current relationship, you may find that the answer to your dilemma is to learn to provide your own emotional security and not seek it from external sources. There could be a certain relationship with two or more friends or relatives that you are caught up in and divided by that is requiring a lot of your attention to maintain. Artistic expression, while a good tool for self-exploration, may also seemed more burdened this year and require more effort and struggle to accomplish. The Three of Hearts often makes us very intellectual when it comes to matters of the heart. We tend to have our concerns rolling around and around in our head and attempt to apply all sorts of concepts to our situation when what we really need is to feel our feelings and trust our experiences. You may find that you are doing a lot of soul-searching this year, a process of turning your attention within to find the real answers.

Three of Clubs

Creativity, worry, expression of ideas orally or through writing

The Basic Meaning of the Three of Clubs

The Three of Clubs is the card of mental creativity, so much so that it is called the 'Writer's Card.' On the other hand, it can be the card of worry, indecision, and mental stress. Whenever this card appears in your reading, you will have an opportunity to either get the benefits of heightened creativity of mind, or suffer the liability of more stress and indecision.

Use this influence for writing, either personally or professionally. Express yourself to all you meet, and you will reap positive rewards.

THE THREE OF CLUBS IN THE MERCURY PERIOD

This card in this position means indecision about a short trip, where to work, or what to study. Two opportunities or two responsibilities at one time could bring uncertainty and worry. Your own restlessness and changeability could be the underlying causes of your indecision now. If you can see how you have created this situation, you may discover a way to resolve it successfully. Your other Mercury Card may point to an area where your indecision or worry lies. This could be a person or a situation in your life.

This is also a very creative influence and could bring you success in either writing, talking, or some form of verbal or written expression. You will be getting many good ideas during this period. Write them down, you may be glad you did later.

THE THREE OF CLUBS IN THE VENUS PERIOD

Indecision about love and friendship is the major influence of this card. There may be some uncertainty in choosing friends and some disappointments as well. Making sacrifices for loved ones could also confuse you in some way. Too many social or personal love interests could prove to be draining or burdensome during this period. See if it isn't your own fickleness and indecision that is the root cause of any disappointments with friendships.

THE THREE OF CLUBS IN THE MARS PERIOD

This period could bring a considerable amount of indecision in matters dealing with men, lawsuits, or work. Difficulty in thinking clearly or making decisions under pressure could cause the loss of one or more opportunities. In general, an overactive mind fueled by worry could be the main source of problems. Exercise care in all written and spoken agreements, and do things to relieve tension and anxiety to help you make better decisions.

Your other Mars Card may tell you who or what you are either feeling indecisive or creative about. It will also tell you the outcome of any creative pursuits during this period. Remember that a Four, Eight, or Ten as the other Mars Card will foretell very good results and a happy outcome during this period of active and aggressive creativity.

THE THREE OF CLUBS IN THE JUPITER PERIOD

This period will bring financial success by applying creativity or by doing creative work. The Three of Clubs is the 'Writer's Card.' Under Jupiter's influence, success is assured in any of the creative pursuits. This can also indicate success in more than one area at the same time. You are learning how to juggle two things at the same time and keep your creative juices flowing.

Under Jupiter, this card could also bring some indecision about business or money. Which job? Which investment? Now your mind is somewhat keen and versatile and could profit by utilizing more than one opportunity at once. It may be that you need two things to do because you get bored with doing just one. Don't worry, just do them both and see what happens.

THE THREE OF CLUBS IN THE SATURN PERIOD

Worry and fear of the future could be your major concerns this year, especially in this period. This worry could be related somehow to an illness of a family member or yourself. Either you are worrying about this illness or the worry reaches the point of causing illness. Saturn has a karmic implication, which means that this could be a repayment of one of your past actions. Take extra special care of your health and diet now.

You have a lot of creative energy now, and in order to stay in a positive frame of mind, you would be better off if you found some way to express this creativity in a positive way. Though creative projects may be difficult now, it is in your best interest to pursue them and to keep these creative juices flowing into constructive projects and goals. Also, the difficulties indicated by this card could be offset by a strong card in the other position, for example any of the Fours, Eights, or Tens.

THE THREE OF CLUBS IN THE URANUS PERIOD

This is a very creative influence that can either bring you a lot of good ideas or cause you to do a lot of worrying or fretting about certain situations in your life. It can be a card of indecision about something, and this something may be your work, people you work with, or some real estate matter. On the other hand, this could also bring you success in doing some sort of creative work, especially writing or speaking. Knowing that this influence is coming, you can gear up for some creative work and get a lot out of it.

Your other Uranus Card may tell you something about this creative expression, or what you may be feeling undecided about.

THE THREE OF CLUBS IN THE NEPTUNE PERIOD

This card means indecision, doubt, or worry related to travel or something important to you that is at a distance. This can also indicate just plain old vague worries about a host of things, most of them trivial. This is not a good influence for travel, as there could be problems or uncertainties that take away from the joy of it. You may be feeling somewhat confused now, as some long cherished beliefs are eroding under Neptune's powerful elixir. Drugs and alcohol could cause even more confusion now. This is a good influence for musical or artistic expression, because it generates variety and many new ideas.

THE THREE OF CLUBS IS YOUR PLUTO CARD

This is a year when you will be striving for more creativity and more forms of personal or professional expression. Whether this means working two jobs at once or being more creative and expressive in your current line of work, you will have to make some effort to achieve the results you desire. In your quest for more creativity you will also have to contend with the limitations of the mind—too much mental activity can cause indecision and worry, and these can lead to stress and lack of focus.

The Three of Clubs can be a card of extreme worry and indecision, but this is only the case when the creative aspects of the energy are not being properly expressed. Keeping a balance between the positive and negative manifestations of this card will be a challenge for you this year. Your Result Card for this year will point to either a person who is involved in this division of yourself or to more information about the specific content of your creative urges and desire to do two things at once.

AFFIRMATION:

I am developing my creativity. Dividing my interests and energies transforms me. I strive to be a writer and to fully express my thoughts and feelings.

THE THREE OF CLUBS IS YOUR RESULT CARD

You will probably have a lot on your mind this year. You may be involved in creative writing or advertising, or you may be working two jobs at once. Creative energies are flowing, and you will need a constructive outlet to keep them from turning into worry and indecision. By your next birthday, you are likely to be successfully involved in some form of writing or other creative endeavor. Your Pluto Card will give more details about this or reveal who is involved.

AFFIRMATION:

I am harnessing my creativity and overcoming my worry and indecision. I become a successful writer.

THE THREE OF CLUBS IS YOUR LONG-RANGE CARD

It is likely that you will have a lot on your mind this year. The Three of Clubs promises an active mind, full of new ideas and ways of doing things. This may stimulate you to branch out in more than one direction at the same time. You may, for example, be learning two or more things at the same time, going to different schools for each, and possibly working two jobs at the same time. You have many good ideas, and you will be able to come up with some unique and valuable ways of doing things and looking at things.

If this mental creativity is harnessed, you could experience much success in writing or in other creative pursuits. If this creativity and versatility gets carried to extremes, you could find yourself manifesting the lower vibrations of this powerful influence in your life this year—that is worry and indecision.

Most people are not well equipped to handle so many things at once and yet some are; it all depends on you. To get the most from this card, write down all the great ideas you get this year. You may not be able to do them all right away, but they are valuable just the same and could be saved for later when your natural creativity is not running so high.

KEYWORDS:

A year of mental creativity, such as writing, and generating ideas, or a year of dealing with worry and indecision.

THE THREE OF CLUBS IS YOUR ENVIRONMENT CARD

Rewards and blessings this year will be available to you from creative expression, writing, and talking. This is the year to get your ideas across to others with the confidence that they will be well received. This would also be a great year to write that book you have been thinking about. Any form of creative expression will benefit from this influence. Diversifying your work efforts, such as working at more than one job or project at a time, will also benefit you.

THE THREE OF CLUBS IS YOUR DISPLACEMENT CARD

An over-stimulated mind, coupled with some minor concerns about many things, could become a problem that must be dealt with in an ongoing way this year. Financial concerns may be at the top of the list, even though they may be more imagined than real. You may have gotten yourself involved in just too many projects or plans. So much so that you feel torn in many directions and cannot give much real attention to any one area. A creative writing project, in particular, may seem somewhat of a burden this year or require a lot more of your energy than you had planned.

This year, you are likely going to be in a wrestling match with your own mind—a mind that may have gotten out of hand a little too much lately and must be reeled in. Our minds, while a valuable tool to help us get things done, can also become a burden and problem when given the responsibility for our personal happiness. A mind that is out of hand has difficulty focusing on one thing at a time. In this state, the things that we do are not done that well, which can reduce the rewards we seek from them and add to our uncertainty.

Three of Diamonds

Diversity in values, financial creativity, or worry about finances

The Basic Meaning of the Three of Diamonds

The Three of Diamonds signifies that indecision or worry about some money matter may be a large part of your experience when this card is present. This card has such a strong creative energy associated with it that if we don't find some productive, creative outlet for its energies, we will inevitably feel afraid and indecisive. The key is to find ways to express ourselves when this card shows up.

It could also mean getting two opportunities for work at one time or having to split our time between two projects or money-making deals. Often variety can be a blessing allowing us to explore other areas. Usually, however, lack of focus brings lack of achievement or lack of detail in one project or the other. Knowing this may help you avoid wasting this invaluable creative force.

THE THREE OF DIAMONDS IN THE MERCURY PERIOD

This period could bring about a situation that arises suddenly and causes some indecision about money or your work. This is a card of mental unrest over money matters and concerns over material limitations. This is a good influence for social charm and also of getting and communicating new ideas about ways to make money. However it is also an influence of worry brought about by an overactive mind and lack of focus on one singular path to success.

Look to your other Mercury Card to tell you what or whom your indecision and worry OR creativity may be about. Also, keep in mind that this influence can be channeled into creative outlets for great success.

THE THREE OF DIAMONDS IN THE VENUS PERIOD

This card represents financial worries that can cause problems in your relationships. At this time, you may be choosing friends and lovers out of your worry over money or choosing a job in a hurry that meets your immediate money needs but doesn't suit you in the long run. In any event, it is unwise to mix love and money during this period. It is also advised to do things that will relax you so you can make better decisions about your work and money.

THE THREE OF DIAMONDS IN THE MARS PERIOD

This is a good influence for creativity and for getting new money-making ideas. However, an aggressive impulsive nature could lead to financial or legal problems at this time. Stay focused and organized as much as possible to reach your goals. Tension combined with insecurity over money limitations could lead to many problematic situations now. You may have to wait until after this period to implement them because of an underlying impatience and lack of focus.

Your other Mars Card may tell you who or what you are either feeling indecisive or creative about. It will also tell you the outcome of any creative pursuits during this period. Remember that a Four, Eight, or Ten as your other Mars Card will foretell very good results and a happy outcome during this period of active and aggressive creativity.

THE THREE OF DIAMONDS IN THE JUPITER PERIOD

Here you have the possibility of financial success in two or more areas at once, or by expressing your creative energies. This is a great influence for those in the creative fields, whether that be artistic or financially creative work. Your involvement in two or more money schemes at once may also create some indecision and worry. The Jupiter period usually brings out the best of any cards found there, especially financially. Use this influence to make more money doing creative work or by diversifying what you are already doing into various channels.

THE THREE OF DIAMONDS IN THE SATURN PERIOD

This influence brings excessive worry about money that bothers you a lot, perhaps to the point of illness. Or, someone else's death or ill health causes some financial problems or worry. Under Saturn, your current money fears are probably karmic in nature, that is, a payment for past deeds or actions. Keep a low profile now, and take care of your health and nerves. Any kind of speculation is not supported by this influence.

On a deeper level, you are being given a jolt of creative energy now, and this energy could be used to help you find more and better ways to make money. However, it will be a challenge to see if you can utilize this energy without letting it turn into worry about money, which is the negative side of this card. Also, the difficulties indicated by this card could be offset by a strong card in the other position, for example any of the Fours, Eights, or Tens.

THE THREE OF DIAMONDS IN THE URANUS PERIOD

This influence can bring indecisiveness and insecurity over labor relations, a real estate deal, or your job. On the other hand, you could get a lot of great ideas for how to make more money and actually branch out in new directions for greater success. You may not be sure that the work you have been doing is the best for you. Your hunches and intuitions relating to money matters may have you somewhat confused at this time, though you do have a lot of good ideas. Whenever there is a strong creative energy present like this one, it is up to us to use it to our advantage by accentuating the creative side of it and not allowing ourselves to get too worried.

THE THREE OF DIAMONDS IN THE NEPTUNE PERIOD

This influence brings worry over some money matter, perhaps connected with travel or distant interests. Indecision and confusion over financial matters can dissipate your energies, and vague fears and worry may interfere with your desire to achieve financial success. Also, miscommunications are a distinct possibility now, and clarity should be stressed here. It is best to postpone any important financial decisions until after this period.

The best way to handle this influence is to direct it into creative expression. This is one of the better cards for ideas that can both make you money and also allow you to express yourself.

THE THREE OF DIAMONDS IS YOUR PLUTO CARD

This powerful influence tells us that you are striking out in one or more new directions this year. You have an urge to be creative and to explore new ways of making money. You are in the midst of a period of exploration of new values that could have you trying more new things than you ever have before. This could manifest as working two jobs or businesses at once or simply diversifying your current activities creatively. You are challenging yourself to be more creative, versatile, and perhaps even more romantic, and this will have a strong impact on every area of your life.

With such a strong, creative force present this year, it is unlikely that you will be able to make any definite decisions about your future until later. This can lead to some uncertainty and even worry in some cases. Financial worries are a common manifestation of this card. To best utilize this year's influences, get creative and come up with some new ideas for making money, while at the same time allowing yourself a more complete form of self-expression. The more you express yourself this year, the less you will worry. After your next birthday, you will be better able to settle into one direction and make a success of it.

Look to your Result Card to get more details about this exploration or to determine who, among your friends and associates, is involved in this exploration.

AFFIRMATION:

I am exploring different values and ways of making money this year, and this is transforming me.

THE THREE OF DIAMONDS IS YOUR RESULT CARD

This is a year for you to express some of your latent creative energies and to try new things, meet new people, and explore new ways of making money. Somehow, the energies of your Pluto Card are stimulating you into new directions. It may be that you are in a major transition time, moving from the stability (and sameness) of the past into an uncertain future, and at times, this may be scary. However, your inner creativity is being awakened, and for this, you will be very happy and fulfilled.

AFFIRMATION:

I am learning about what I want through experimentation and diversity. I am broadening my perspective on values. I complete this year with two or more ways of earning money.

THE THREE OF DIAMONDS IS YOUR LONG-RANGE CARD

You are somehow at a fork in the road this year in terms of your values. Do you want this or do you want that? What is your relationship to money and love? What is most important to you? These questions and more are likely to be uppermost in your mind as you progress through the year, experimenting with new avenues for satisfaction in work, love, and finances. When we allow ourselves to explore alternatives, we often lose the momentum of our present focus, and this can result in less success financially. We have scattered our forces and have less to devote to any one project or endeavor.

If this is the case, remember that it is important to you to make these experiments, and don't let your lack of success turn to worry. This is a highly creative influence that must be put to work in constructive ways. Otherwise, it may cause too much preoccupation with money and indecision. You need to experiment and express your creativity this year. Later, you will decide which avenue is the best for your long-term satisfaction. You can find several avenues of income this year and learn how diversity can be more profitable in these changing times.

KEYWORDS:

A year of creative money pursuits, or worry and indecision about money. I will focus on diversifying my sources of income.

THE THREE OF DIAMONDS IS YOUR ENVIRONMENT CARD

Creative financial or business ideas could bring you many blessings this year, as well as afford you a certain amount of protection. You could take on more than one job at a time successfully as well. Highlighted for success are any types of work that allow you to express your creativity. Art, music, promotions, and advertising are a few of the activities that will benefit most from this card's influence. Diversify, and you will gain in many ways.

THE THREE OF DIAMONDS IS YOUR DISPLACEMENT CARD

This year you will experience the liabilities associated with creativity and an active mind. Artistic endeavors, creative business deals, and other creative enterprises will seem burdened this year and require more energy than planned. Your own worrisome nature will be something that you must deal with this year while you go about your work and life. Worries about money, in particular, may come to the forefront, even though your actual financial situation is fine. Any Three as a Displacement Card is a signal that our mind is a little overactive or overworked and that our many interests have led us to a place of uncertainty and indecision. Settling on one plan, one idea, or one job and finishing it may help relieve some of the doubts and fears that could come up. Try and find a way to weave in the variety you seek in your work or life without sacrificing your security at the same time.

Three of Spades

Creativity, stress, working two jobs at once

The Basic Meaning of the Three of Spades

The Three of Spades is one of the most creative cards in the deck. It is known as the 'Artist's Card.' It is so creative that if not channeled properly, it can represent indecision, fear, and physical stress.

The Three of Spades can mean literally splitting ourselves in two so that we are working two jobs at the same time or are somehow pursuing two lifestyles at the same time. Whether we are successful at doing this will depend upon the position of the card (Jupiter is best, Saturn is worst) and how well we are able to direct its energies into creative enterprises.

THE THREE OF SPADES IN THE MERCURY PERIOD

This period could bring some insecurity arising from indecision over two choices of some kind. This could be about work, health, travel, home, or friends. There could be many short trips during this period, and you may be working two jobs at once. You may unexpectedly receive two offers for work at the same time. Under this influence, variety and changes may cause more anxiety than usual, and your own indecisive nature could be the underlying cause.

The Three of Spades is called the 'Artist's Card' because it brings so much creativity. Use this influence to create new ideas and plans for your future. Your other Mercury Card may tell you what you are creative or indecisive about or indicate the outcome of your creative endeavors during this fifty-two-day period.

THE THREE OF SPADES IN THE VENUS PERIOD

This influence brings many fluctuations and indecision about romantic involvements and work. This could be about your job, money, a woman, or even your health. You may dread monotony and sameness now, especially in romance. During this period, you may be fickle and aloof with your close friends and family, and you can expect many changes in your attractions and friendships. Be careful that your indecisiveness doesn't leave you feeling insecure.

THE THREE OF SPADES IN THE MARS PERIOD

This indicates an undecided business or work matter, possibly the result of having two jobs at once or getting two offers of work at once. This is not a good aspect for legal matters, as there could be some doubts or unsettled issues in this regard. With this influence, your own aggressive pursuit of all that you desire may get you involved in more projects or jobs than you can handle. This could be more draining than helpful for you at this time.

Your other Mars Card may tell you who or what you are either feeling indecisive or creative about. It will also tell you the outcome of any creative pursuits during this period. Remember that a Four, Eight, or Ten as the other Mars Card will foretell very good results and a happy outcome during this period of active and aggressive creativity.

THE THREE OF SPADES IN THE JUPITER PERIOD

This is a time when diversity usually brings many blessings. This influence is actually favorable for many things, such as gambling and short-term speculation, if you can handle the risk. With this Three of Spades influence, success is also possible in two areas at once or in businesses that involve artistic or creative expression. This is called the 'Artist's Card' and thus is very favorable for any sort of art or expression of ideas. In Jupiter, it could bring great financial success if channeled into positive creative work.

THE THREE OF SPADES IN THE SATURN PERIOD

Under this influence, indecision about work or money problems can affect your health. Doubt or worry about your health or someone else's health could affect your business dealings. This card can indicate an undecided health matter, as well as extra sensitivity to negative vibrations of others and the environment. Extra precautions are advisable in health matters and in choosing who you work and play with. This card can indicate chronic indecision.

Creative projects that you are involved in during this period will be more difficult to achieve, but not impossible. If you are either working two jobs at once or doing something artistic, musical, or in any other way creative, just keep working and letting your ideas flow. Though there are likely to be hurdles and some indecisiveness on your part, you will make definite progress. Also, the difficulties indicated by this card could be offset by a strong card in the other position, for example any of the Fours, Eights, or Tens.

THE THREE OF SPADES IN THE URANUS PERIOD

This influence indicates indecision about a real estate deal, your work, affairs of employees, or psychic experiments. During this period, you may find yourself either working two jobs at the same time or finding a creative outlet in which to invest yourself. Whether this is a positive or stressful influence will depend upon how you decide to use this strong creative influence.

The Three of Spades is called the 'Artist's Card,' and for this reason, this is a wonderful and beneficial influence for self-expression and creative work of all kinds. You can do a lot towards relieving any mental worry and anxiety by getting yourself involved in some creative project.

THE THREE OF SPADES IN THE NEPTUNE PERIOD

This period can bring doubts and uncertainty about a journey, your health, your work, or foreign interests of all kinds. Keep all work arrangements clear and concise during this time. This is basically an influence of doubts about anything foreign or at a great distance from you. This could be religious beliefs or psychic phenomena, but it also extends to work and health because spades rule these as well. Be certain that any work you do has a foundation of planning and reality, or you may have regrets later.

On the positive sides, this is one of the best cards for success in artistic expression. You will probably get a lot of wonderful ideas, along with a desire to express yourself. By taking up some form of expression, you can greatly minimize any of the worrisome effects of this card.

THE THREE OF SPADES IS YOUR PLUTO CARD

A major goal for you this year is to achieve mastery over a situation where your basic energies are divided into two or more important directions. This could manifest as working two jobs at once or dealing with a long-term health issue that points to a deep division within yourself. At times, you may feel literally torn in two this year, and this could create a lot of physical and emotional stress for you. Can you overcome all the stress in your life? That may be a major goal for you this year as well. Sometimes we have made decisions to divide ourselves and then must master the actual doing of them without sacrificing our health and well-being.

The Three of Spades is also known as the 'Artist's Card,' and for this reason, you may find much relief and satisfaction in different forms of self-expression. If you have artistic goals this year, it is likely that success in this area will require some fundamental changes in the way you are approaching these goals and directions.

Look to the Result Card for more information about this division of yourself, this desire to find a successful form of self-expression, or to see who would be directly connected to this situation that may be helping you learn from it.

AFFIRMATION:

I am learning how to express my creative energies without becoming stressed or unhealthy in the process.

THE THREE OF SPADES IS YOUR RESULT CARD

The powerful creative nature of this card must be handled carefully to access its healthy, positive side, because it can easily turn into stress and poor health. Take the meaning of your Pluto Card combined with the influence of this creative energy to give you the total picture of one of your major goals and challenges for the year. This is not the year to make major life decisions but to simply experience different avenues to see what you like.

AFFIRMATION:

I create myself to be a successful artist. I end up this year with two jobs or an undecided health matter.

THE THREE OF SPADES IS YOUR LONG-RANGE CARD

You will somehow be 'divided' this year, either in your work or your health. The Three of Spades is one of the most creative cards in the deck, and as with all threes, it may be challenging to keep the energy of this card from turning into worry, indecision, and stress, the low sides of this card. It all depends on how you use the energies of this powerful card.

Somehow you are facing a crossroads in your life. You may be trying to do or be too many things at the same time. You are feeling an urge to be creative and explore many avenues at the same time. If handled successfully, you could be more productive than ever. The trick is in keeping your energy high and being clear

that you are doing two or more things at once. Don't expect yourself to settle into one path now. Flow with the energies of this powerful card, and do things to stay relaxed and at peace with yourself.

Sometimes things that happen 'in spades' are things that we cannot escape from though it is likely that you will be successful in this division. Just keep an awareness on your health and see that any problems in that area are likely the result of a deep conflict or division inside your being. Resolve the conflict, and you resolve the problems.

This card, in its highest expression is the 'Artist's Card,' and thus it could bestow upon you much success in one or more of the artistic lines of work. Self-expression is essential to achieve success with this powerful creative influence.

KEYWORDS:

A year of high creativity, which must be handled carefully to keep it from turning to stress and health problems.

THE THREE OF SPADES IS YOUR ENVIRONMENT CARD

Many benefits will come to you this year through creative self-expression. This is an especially good influence for any sort of artistic pursuit such as painting, design, music, or acting. You can also receive many blessings by diversifying your work situation. Working two jobs or projects at the same time will tend to bring you more success and less stress. Look for ways to express yourself and to diversify to take the best advantage of this card.

THE THREE OF SPADES IS YOUR DISPLACEMENT CARD

This will be a fortunate year in some respects, and you should see some things in your life come to pass in just the way you would want them to. However, a tendency to scatter your energies in too many directions could result in physical stress or health problems that are difficult to diagnose. You can make some substantial progress this year and reap many rewards if you are willing to put in some real work towards your goals. At the same time, be aware of your body and peace of mind so that you do not stress yourself too much, which would decrease your ability to enjoy the fruits of these efforts.

Even though you may not necessarily want to, you may find yourself torn between two jobs or essentially two separate lives that you lead. As you do this, you will learn just how difficult that can be. In that regard, this year will bring you a real appreciation for having a more peaceful lifestyle and may motivate you to take a different path in the future rather than scatter yourself in so many directions.

Four of Hearts
Stability in love and home

The Basic Meaning of the Four of Hearts

The Four of Hearts is a sign of protection in love, marriage, and family. It represents one's marriage and the foundation of love upon which a family and life can be built. The Four of Hearts is usually considered a good influence, especially for a happy family and social life. You may even turn down offers of love at those times when you are feeling so fulfilled in the areas of friendship and romance. If you are single, the Four of Hearts, as the Result or Venus Card, is a strong indicator of marriage.

The Four of Hearts can also speak about your home and family and things going on in these areas. It represents, at its most basic level, the foundation of love upon which all of our other relationships are built. It is the home of the heart.

THE FOUR OF HEARTS IN THE MERCURY PERIOD

This card usually brings a short-lived, but happy time in love and romance. A sudden happiness or pleasure, at home or while on a short trip, perhaps a good book or a new friend. Don't look for lasting relationships now, as Mercury is a fleeting influence. Any marriage under this influence may not have staying power unless the two of you share many intellectual pursuits. Generally a great card for sharing the enjoyment of mentally stimulating activities.

This is such a powerful and stabilizing influence that it will produce very good results during this period, even if your other Mercury Card is one of challenge or adversity.

THE FOUR OF HEARTS IN THE VENUS PERIOD

This card bestows much happiness in love or marriage or friendships in general. A card of overall contentment with many blessings, both material and spiritual, this is one of the best influences for marriage and starting a family. Under this influence, your closest relationships will be very satisfying. This card could represent your current marriage, and chances are that now you are enjoying it more than ever.

This is such a powerful and stabilizing influence that it will produce very good results during this period, even if your other Venus Card is one of challenge or adversity.

THE FOUR OF HEARTS IN THE MARS PERIOD

The influence brings happy relations with men and aggressive women. Combine aggressiveness with love for maximum benefits during this period. Aggressive pursuit of social popularity can bring success now. This card could also be the sign of success in a legal matter or any endeavor where men are concerned. This is a good influence for actors or actresses or anyone interacting with the public, particularly with men.

This stabilizing influence of this card is powerful and will bring a happy period for you, even if the indications of your other Mars Card are more challenging. Even if your other Mars card indicated a challenge or problem, this card guarantees that you will overcome it and that the result will be a positive one. A successful card in the other position will further strengthen the influence of this card and could tell you who or what you will experience such satisfaction with during this fifty-two-day period.

THE FOUR OF HEARTS IN THE JUPITER PERIOD

This influence combines love with money for success in many areas. Social success can bring financial gains and promotions. You could have much pleasure in making and spending money now. You may even marry into money under this influence. Your own marriage could be bringing you many benefits, both spiritual and material, at this time. Jupiter's beneficial and expansive influence will help you see the bigger picture of just how wonderful life can be.

For married people, this influence usually means that your spouse is making more money than usual (and giving you some to spend).

THE FOUR OF HEARTS IN THE SATURN PERIOD

This period could see you or someone you love recovering from illness or other troubles that have been present. Marriage is also a possibility now. You may marry someone older, younger, or who is marked by burdens or restrictions. Your own marriage could be a source of burden or responsibility now and may not seem as happy or light as in other times. Marriage for status or money is also a possibility with this influence.

This card tells us that whatever your other Saturn Card represents, it will have something to do with your marriage, family, or home life. This is a good card that can bring good results, though it will take some effort. If you are prepared to work hard during this period and keep your relationship and family goals forefront in your mind, this card could indicate a favorable outcome to whatever situations arise.

THE FOUR OF HEARTS IN THE URANUS PERIOD

Somehow, the affairs indicated by your other Uranus Card will have something to do with marriage, a home, a house, or the attainment of satisfaction in your love life.

THE FOUR OF HEARTS IN THE NEPTUNE PERIOD

This period could see you taking a pleasurable journey, probably over water. Your marriage or closest relationship will probably take on an idealistic tone that may seem quite wonderful and romantic now. Indeed there is the possibility of experiencing a 'divine' love now with real spiritual overtones. Just be careful under the Neptune influence, as you may tend to see others as you want them to be, rather than as they truly are.

This card can also affect you for the entire year, causing you to dream about a perfect marriage or house that you want.

THE FOUR OF HEARTS IS YOUR PLUTO CARD

This year will bring a major focus on the concept of marriage or on your own family and closest relationships. If you are already married, there may be some new stimuli that you will need to digest in order to maintain a balance in your relationship with your spouse. There could likely be aspects of your marriage that are causing problems for you. This could be challenging at times, as these are issues that you haven't dealt with lately.

If you are single, you may be just considering the concept of marriage. This may be challenging to integrate these new energies and ideas into your life. Often when the Four of Hearts is the Pluto Card, the Result Card will be the Birthday Card of someone that you want to get married to. If so, it is likely that the two of you will end up together, though not necessarily married, by your next birthday.

This is not a strong influence for actually getting married unless you have other marriage cards elsewhere in your yearly spread, but it may be the year that prepares you for an eventual marriage. This card can also mean that you are striving to have more success in your family life, in general, which would include your children, if you have any, and your home, all represented by the Four of Hearts.

In general, the Four of Hearts means that you are desiring to have more stability and security in terms of affection and friendships this year. In this position, it also implies that to have this stability, you will have to take some new avenues of approach in these key areas of your life. Look to the Result Card for more details about how the concept of marriage fits into the picture this year or to see who may be involved in this transformation process you are experiencing.

AFFIRMATION:

Marriage, home, and family stability transforms me. I am creating a successful marriage or family life. I create love, satisfaction, and security.

THE FOUR OF HEARTS IS YOUR RESULT CARD

This is a strong indicator of marriage before your next birthday. At the least, you should find yourself in a satisfying love partnership before year's end. Stability in love and just having an abundant supply of love will be some of the results of your efforts this year. You may even find yourself refusing love at times because you are full. Your Pluto Card will further specify the changes you must make to achieve this stability or tell you who you will marry.

No matter just how challenging your Pluto Card may be this year, this card guarantees that everything will come to a happy and satisfactory conclusion and that you will end up this year feeling emotionally sound and secure, and probably in a very good relationship.

AFFIRMATION:

I develop stability in my closest relationships. I am creating family or marriage. I end up married this year.

THE FOUR OF HEARTS IS YOUR LONG-RANGE CARD

The Four of Hearts is a sign of protection in love and friendship. This could likely be a year of satisfaction in your emotional, romantic, and family life. If you are currently married or in a committed relationship, your marriage and family take on an important role, regardless of the circumstances. You will have to devote more than the usual attention to them this year for whatever reason. If you are single and unattached, the concept of marriage is becoming the focus for you in a big way. It is likely that you will have one or more very satisfying relationships this year. This is one of the stronger influences for getting married, though other cards in the yearly spread would have to be examined to make a more definite determination.

KEYWORDS:

Stability in love, family, and marriage are major areas of interest for me this year. I am surrounded by love.

THE FOUR OF HEARTS IS YOUR ENVIRONMENT CARD

Home, family, and your closest circle of friends will provide a certain amount of protection and blessings this year. This is a year to enjoy the security in love that these things bring to your life. If you were to get married, rest assured that this would be a wonderful and healing experience for you. If you are married, many blessings will come through your partner this year. If you are single, you will find that your circle of closest friends will be there for you, a source of many good things. This would be a wonderful year to purchase a home or to move into a better living environment. Your knowing what you want in love matters has gotten you what you want. So enjoy!

THE FOUR OF HEARTS IS YOUR DISPLACEMENT CARD

This card offers a mixture of success potential along with a cautionary influence that should be taken with some discrimination. There are several things going on here that may help you understand how to best deal with this influence. First of all the Four of Hearts represents either our marriage, our family, our closest circle of friends, or our home. As the Displacement Card, it is a sure thing that these areas of your life will require more of your attention this year, even though you yourself may not want to put your attention into these areas.

The nature of being in this card's position this year tells us that you may have some career ambitions that are dominating your attention. Perhaps you are striving to get more recognition for what you do. Since you have the King of Spades as your Result Card this year, there is undoubtedly something with which you want more mastery, and perhaps recognition and responsibility as well. This is likely just what you will achieve by year's end, but along the way, you must pass through your Saturn period. And during that period, there are some matters that must be dealt with, matters of great importance as far as you are concerned. The underlying influences of that period are such that some long-standing issue in your life will come to judgment day and be reckoned with. This reckoning may be quite dramatic, and it may not seem to go in your favor or direction. But in fact, it will represent an equal and just settlement of those affairs in your life up to this point. Because of the Four of Hearts, these matters often have something to do with marriage, home, and family or your circle of friends. Study the basic meanings of the Six of Spades and Nine of Spades cards, as well as their meanings in Saturn, to get a better idea of what this period and this year have in store for you. With conscious awareness, the events this year can be less dramatic and can have a favorable outcome as far as you are concerned.

Four of Clubs

Organization and clarity of mind brings peace of mind

The Basic Meaning of the Four of Clubs

The Four of Clubs is the card of mental satisfaction and stability. Whenever this card appears, you can bet that you will experience some mental peace for a while. Any sort of mental occupation you may be involved in will benefit from this stabilizing and practical influence.

This is a good time to make plans for the future since you are thinking clearer than ever. This card brings organizational ability and the ability to achieve a solid foundation of knowledge about a particular subject. Just watch out for a tendency towards fixed mental attitudes that might alienate you from others.

THE FOUR OF CLUBS IN THE MERCURY PERIOD

This period will bring a pleasant but brief experience of contentment, such as a book or a new companion. This is also a good influence for learning new things, in gaining knowledge, and in all things related to the mind, such as writing, speaking, or teaching. Your studies will be a source of joy to you now, and in general, you should be enjoying life.

This is such a powerful and stabilizing influence that it will produce very good results during this period, even if your other Mercury Card is one of challenge or adversity.

THE FOUR OF CLUBS IN THE VENUS PERIOD

This is a very good influence, indicating satisfaction and happiness in the home and marriage or in your personal life if you are single. Having knowledge of a comforting nature is also a possibility and happiness in the company of others who share similar intellectual tastes as yourself. Most of your friendships will be going smoothly now, and the only possible negative aspect of this influence is a tendency toward mental stubbornness and fixedness.

This is such a powerful and stabilizing influence that it will produce very good results during this period, even if your other Venus Card is one of challenge or adversity.

THE FOUR OF CLUBS IN THE MARS PERIOD

This is a good influence for satisfying emotional and intellectual relationships, especially with men. For women this is an indicator of happiness in marriage and home or good news from home. Aggressive pursuits of education and friendships will bring rewards during this period. Mental activity can be successfully applied in work, especially in the areas of organization, efficiency, and practicality.

The stabilizing influence of this card is powerful and will bring a happy period for you, even if the indications of your other Mars Card are more challenging. Even if your other Mars card indicated a challenge or problem, this card guarantees that you will overcome it and that the result will be a positive one. A successful card in the other position will further strengthen the influence of this card and could tell you who or what you will experience such satisfaction with during this fifty-two-day period.

THE FOUR OF CLUBS IN THE JUPITER PERIOD

This is a good indicator of satisfaction in finances and business, one of the best indicators of a good year. Though much comes through being steady and one-pointed, you can also benefit from expansive changes in your business or profession. You can use your mind to your advantage, perhaps in planning or bargaining. Most of your relationships should be flowing smoothly now. Everything should be going well now and according to plan. You can get more organized and productive, which should lead to greater financial success.

THE FOUR OF CLUBS IN THE SATURN PERIOD

This is a card of overcoming illness and unfavorable influences. This could take the form of good news from someone who is ill or happy in spite of ill health. You have great power in positive thinking now, power of the mind that can be used constructively in many ways. Use this power to heal yourself or someone else or to remove obstacles from your path. Any skepticism you display now is not in harmony with your inner beliefs.

This card is such a strong influence that it will override any negative influences present during this period. Even if your other Saturn Card were one of challenge or problem, this card guarantees that you will have a successful outcome and will overcome difficulties.

THE FOUR OF CLUBS IN THE URANUS PERIOD

This period brings contentment in labor, service, or in some real estate related activity. Success in humanitarian or spiritually related activities is also indicated by this card of contentment and peace. With this influence, your greatest satisfaction will come through helping others. This may happen in the context of some larger organization. Your positive thoughts and prayers can be an effective healing agent now, even for those at a distance.

This influence is a strongly grounding force that will bring satisfaction in this period, regardless of what card may appear as your other Uranus Card. The net and overall result of this period will be satisfaction and contentment.

THE FOUR OF CLUBS IN THE NEPTUNE PERIOD

Happiness and satisfaction can come through traveling or in something connected to a distant affair or one who travels. Also indicated is contentment in some role as a healer or in being the 'nurse' for someone. The contentment you feel now may have deep spiritual overtones to it and thus may resonate some deeper parts of yourself. This influence can also indicate contact with the unseen realms or other forms of psychic phenomena.

THE FOUR OF CLUBS IS YOUR PLUTO CARD

This year you are working to achieve strength, stability, and satisfaction in one or more areas of your life that will help your whole life to settle down and be more contented. You might be learning a new subject or trying to focus your energies into more of a single direction. Possibly you are learning how to get organized and take a more practical attitude toward your personal and professional affairs. Satisfaction of mind is one of your goals this year, and whatever contributes to this will take a higher priority in your life.

You need a lot of strength of mind to accomplish this goal, and it is likely that you will have to make some changes in the way you think or do things in order to accomplish it. At times, this may seem very difficult. At other times, other people in your life may see you as stubborn or being too fixed on your purpose for their liking, but all of this is part of the process of achieving what is most important to you. Just who this peace of mind is related to specifically might be revealed by your Result Card, along with more details about what aspects of your life are the ones that you really want to be peaceful and organized about.

AFFIRMATION:

I create stability and satisfaction in my life. Achieving peace of mind and contentment transforms me.

THE FOUR OF CLUBS IS YOUR RESULT CARD

Somehow, in conjunction with your Pluto Card, you are achieving strength and satisfaction in your mind. You will make important and necessary changes to achieve this goal and you will be successful. You may desire more knowledge or simply more peace of mind. At times, others may see you as stubborn and narrow-minded in this pursuit. However, keep your goals in sight, realizing that focus, determination, and clarity of purpose build strength of mind.

No matter just how challenging your Pluto Card may be this year, this card guarantees that everything will come to a happy and satisfactory conclusion and that you will end up this year feeling solid and well-organized.

AFFIRMATION:

I achieve stability and satisfaction in my mind and in my life this year.

THE FOUR OF CLUBS IS YOUR LONG-RANGE CARD

This will be a year for you of mental stability and general satisfaction in all affairs. Regardless of your occupation and interests, you will find that you are able to maintain an inner peace that tends to allow things to go the best for you time after time. This is a very positive influence since the mind is usually the source of our problems. This influence can be applied with great success to any intellectual endeavor, such as writing, teaching, or learning new subjects. You should have satisfaction in any of those areas by virtue of this card. The only negative side of this card is a tendency to be mentally fixed and often narrow-minded. But if things are going so well for us, why should we change anyway? As they say, 'Why fix it if it isn't broken?'

KEYWORDS:

A year of satisfaction in all affairs, mental stability, organizational ability, and sometimes, stubbornness.

THE FOUR OF CLUBS IS YOUR ENVIRONMENT CARD

This will be a year in which you are basically protected from any real serious problems by a solid and organized mental outlook. You will have success in anything that is associated with learning or getting organized, and you will feel a sense of mental peace and stability that will aid most areas of your life. It's not often that we can have such a clear picture of our life and keep everything in its proper perspective, so enjoy this year of protection and stability.

THE FOUR OF CLUBS IS YOUR DISPLACEMENT CARD

This will be a good year in many ways and one in which your mind is more relaxed and balanced than usual. In addition, this will be a year in which you get one or more important wishes fulfilled. Much success will come from focusing your objectives and being willing to work for what you want. You have considerable power available to you this year, especially mental power. And you are likely to wield this power to meet your goals with success. However, watch out for a tendency to be short-sighted mentally and to overemphasize your own point of view to the exclusion of others. Though you have a formula that works well for you, it may not be the formula that works for everyone. In addition, stubbornness on your part will only tend to alienate others from you, which is probably not your true intention.

Four of Diamonds

Sound values bring financial stability

The Basic Meaning of the Four of Diamonds

The Four of Diamonds means a solid sense of values that attracts enough money to meet our security needs and then some. When we know exactly what it is we want, we tend to attract those things to us more quickly. Thus, when this card shows up, it usually means that we have become clear on what we want and then we get it. Satisfaction and prosperity are indicated here, and you may have a good foundation upon which you can begin building a financial future. Managing your resources could come into focus in a greater way when this card is present, and this card can give you the ability to handle financial matters with a clear mind.

THE FOUR OF DIAMONDS IN THE MERCURY PERIOD

During this period, you could find that some money comes in suddenly or that your desire for money is unexpectedly realized. This could be a quick turnover or return on an investment or business deal. This is a good influence for investing money in furthering your education or buying equipment for your business. In general, this card means satisfaction about money, one that is short-lived and perhaps unexpected.

This is such a powerful and stabilizing influence that it will produce very good results during this period, even if your other Mercury Card is one of challenge or adversity.

THE FOUR OF DIAMONDS IN THE VENUS PERIOD

During this period, you will most likely have money to spend on luxury items to beautify your home or yourself, such as clothing. During this period, you are also likely to associate with successful people of financial means. With this influence, you can make money in businesses related to the home, clothing, artistic, or beauty products, as well as have much financial success with women. This generally indicates contentment in all financial matters.

This is such a powerful and stabilizing influence that it will produce very good results during this period, even if your other Venus Card is one of challenge or adversity.

THE FOUR OF DIAMONDS IN THE MARS PERIOD

This influence brings an aggressive capacity to make money. This can also indicate satisfaction in a legal or tax matter or one involving a male associate. This is a card of overcoming other ill influences and can counteract any negative cards during this same period. An aggressive pursuit of your financial goals now could bring in huge returns. You will want to work hard to earn your money. Make a wish list and pursue it.

This stabilizing influence of this card is powerful and will bring a happy period for you, even if the indications of your other Mars Card are more challenging. Even if your other Mars card indicated a challenge or problem, this card guarantees that you will overcome it and that the result will be a positive one. A successful card in the other position will further strengthen the influence of this card and could tell you who or what you will experience such satisfaction with during this fifty-two-day period.

THE FOUR OF DIAMONDS IN THE JUPITER PERIOD

This is one of the best money cards that you can have. It indicates success and prosperity in all business affairs or satisfaction in a large investment. Business expansion is favored by this influence, as you should see good returns from all your past efforts at this time. You will make more through steady progress and sticking with your original plans now. This is a card of financial protection against any other influences, so don't worry.

THE FOUR OF DIAMONDS IN THE SATURN PERIOD

This influence can bring in money made through another's misfortune or death. It indicates a satisfactory ending to a financial problem since it is a card of overcoming difficulties. Success is achieved through hard work, patience, and discipline. This card assures you that you will have good health care in the case of any illness. You may have to work harder now for results, but they will come and will be long lasting.

This card is such a strong influence that it will override any negative influences present during this period. Even if your other Saturn Card were one of challenge or problem, this card guarantees that you will have a successful outcome and an overcoming of difficulties.

THE FOUR OF DIAMONDS IN THE URANUS PERIOD

This is a good money card, indicating money made through labor, real estate, humanitarian efforts, or in futuristic technology. This can also represent an unusual or unexpected income of money. Your efforts will bring gains at this time. This influence brings good relations with coworkers and any large institutions, which may also be a source of financial gains for you now. In general, you will be feeling satisfied with your financial situation.

This influence is a strong grounding force that will bring satisfaction in this period, regardless of what card may appear as your other Uranus Card. The net and overall result of this period will be satisfaction and contentment.

THE FOUR OF DIAMONDS IN THE NEPTUNE PERIOD

This is a good card for money and indicates money made related to travel or foreign interests, in the care of others, or in some secret way. You are somewhat protected in all your business dealings under this influence. This is a card of satisfaction in financial affairs and one where you can take time to enjoy the fruits of your labor as well. This can also mean money made through an inheritance, taxes, insurance, or in some secret way.

THE FOUR OF DIAMONDS IS YOUR PLUTO CARD

Achieving financial stability is likely to be a major priority this year and one that will require you to make some changes. Deciding what you want out of life and what is most important to you will be a major theme in accomplishing this goal. You may also have to focus your interests in a more singular direction in order to reap the success you desire, and this may prove to be a challenge at times as well. All we need to do to attract more money and prosperity is to become very clear about what we want and why we want it. This, in essence, is what you will be focusing on this year. Look to your Result Card to get more information about this goal of satisfaction in your financial affairs or to see who or what may be affecting it in some important way.

AFFIRMATION:

Creating a sound financial condition transforms me this year. I am getting very clear about my values and goals.

THE FOUR OF DIAMONDS IS YOUR RESULT CARD

Many of your efforts will be directed towards the end result of financial stability. To acquire this foundation of money, it is likely that you will have to get clear about what is most important to you as you progress this year. Sound and unchanging values attract prosperity. To achieve this, you may have to go through many changes in the way you think and communicate your needs and wishes. However, you will be rewarded for your efforts in kind.

No matter just how challenging your Pluto Card may be this year, this card guarantees that everything will come to a happy and satisfactory conclusion and that you will end up this year feeling financially sound and well-organized.

AFFIRMATION:

I achieve financial satisfaction and stability by the end of the year.

THE FOUR OF DIAMONDS IS YOUR LONG-RANGE CARD

Regardless of your actual financial situation as you enter this year, you are sure to be feeling contented and satisfied with money and finances for the majority of the year. A sound sense of what you want seems to attract everything you need without much effort. Perhaps you are laying the foundation for long-term prosperity. This is not a card of overwhelming success with money. It means that you will have enough to meet your needs and a little extra. This can be a very welcome card, especially if things have not been up to par lately.

What's really happening is that you are getting clear about your values, that is, what things are most important to you in life, and what things are not. You know, at least for this year, where and how

money fits into your life among the other things you hold important. This knowledge tends to attract abundance and prosperity as you have everything in its best place. This is really an inner process that you are bound to develop successfully this year. Share your wealth, both materially and knowledge-wise with others and you multiply your blessings.

KEYWORDS:

My soundness and firmness in values solidifies my financial resources and creates financial protection and satisfaction.

THE FOUR OF DIAMONDS IS YOUR ENVIRONMENT CARD

Financial concerns, a common problem in today's culture, should not be a problem for you this year. You have a certain amount of protection around money this year. This is partly due to the fact that you have gotten clear about just what it is that you want and don't want. As a result, you tend to attract more prosperity to you. You are protected this year. You will not have tremendous success, but all your needs will be provided for and more.

THE FOUR OF DIAMONDS IS YOUR DISPLACEMENT CARD

You may have to work a lot harder than you expected this year, but in many ways, this hard work could pay off in more success in your work or business. What you are being called upon to do this year is get really clear about what you want in your life and then to be willing to put in the proper amount of work in order to achieve it. If either of these two ingredients is lacking, the results will diminish significantly. The Four of Diamonds requires that we narrow down our focus and invest ourselves into just one or two directions so we may achieve more success. Once we have this focus, all that is needed is some hard work to make some pretty spectacular things happen. Essentially, you will get what you work for this year. The more you put in, the more you get back. It is very likely that you will receive more recognition for your efforts, especially towards the end of this year. You could get promoted or in some way become better known or more popular.

Four of Spades
Hard work brings stability and protection

The Basic Meaning of the Four of Spades

The Four of Spades is a card of satisfaction and stability in health, work, and all affairs in general. Recovery from illness and any work-related problems can be expected under this influence. It can mean working hard and steadily, but usually this is a welcome situation, making us feel more secure and stable in our lives.

Essentially, the Four of Spades is the strongest card of security and foundation in our life. When it shows up in our reading, we will always achieve this kind of satisfaction.

THE FOUR OF SPADES IN THE MERCURY PERIOD

This period may bring an unexpected or sudden satisfaction or resolution of some matter, perhaps related to your work or health. This satisfaction could also be related to a short trip, a communication, education, or a relative of yours. It may also be a somewhat short-lived satisfaction. This basically indicates a settling of affairs in the areas indicated. The only negative effect of this influence would be a stubbornness of the mind.

This is such a powerful and stabilizing influence that it will produce very good results during this period, even if your bottom Mercury Card is one of challenge or adversity.

THE FOUR OF SPADES IN THE VENUS PERIOD

This should be a very good period, one marked by success in work and love. There can be satisfaction in conjunction with a woman, romance, or money. A wonderful card of contentment in marriage, home life, and your work. You may do work that helps others emotionally in some way. This is a time when problems and illness will be overcome by love and prosperity. You will value being with those who are mentally and emotionally stimulating and compatible.

This is such a powerful and stabilizing influence that it will produce very good results during this period, even if your other Venus Card is one of challenge or adversity.

THE FOUR OF SPADES IN THE MARS PERIOD

This card represents success in work, with men, or in any work where drive, industriousness, and ambition are exerted. This is an indicator of a happy married life for females and an indication of organizational and executive ability that can be applied for great success. This card represents a successful outcome to a legal or tax matter and is good for lawyers and executives. You can overcome any ill influences now with determination and action.

This stabilizing influence of this card is powerful and will bring a happy period for you, even if the indications of your other Mars Card are more challenging. Even if your other Mars card indicated a challenge or problem, this card guarantees that you will overcome it and that the result will be a positive one. A successful card in the other position will further strengthen the influence of this card and could tell you who or what you will experience such satisfaction with during this fifty-two-day period.

THE FOUR OF SPADES IN THE JUPITER PERIOD

This card indicates that success and satisfaction in business and money matters can be yours now. Laborious efforts bring many good returns. Your greatest success comes through established businesses and not through risky investments, speculation, or gambling. This is one of the best influences for your hard work paying off in a big way. Expansion along established lines and association with established businesses and professionals is highlighted.

THE FOUR OF SPADES IN THE SATURN PERIOD

This period can bring a recovery from illness and other problems. Success comes now through determination, discipline, hard work, or working with the sick. This can also bring success related to someone's misfortune or illness, i.e., inheritance. Success will not come easy now, but with effort, you can achieve much. Watch out for a tendency to be very stubborn, as this may cause problems in close relationships.

This card is such a strong influence that it will override any negative influences present during this period. Even if your other Saturn Card were one of challenge or problem, this card guarantees that you will have a successful outcome and will overcome difficulties.

THE FOUR OF SPADES IN THE URANUS PERIOD

This period brings success in your work, real estate, land or farming, labor groups, or service organizations. This can also mean satisfaction in gaining wisdom or in some form of intuitive development. This is a strong influence for getting a home or house. You have strong intuitive powers now and can use them profitably. This is a great influence for professional psychics or those using their intuitive gifts. Relations with coworkers are good now and contribute to your success.

This influence is a strong grounding force that will bring satisfaction in this period regardless of what card may appear as your other Uranus Card. The net and overall result of this period will be satisfaction and contentment.

THE FOUR OF SPADES IN THE NEPTUNE PERIOD

This card indicates satisfaction in a business journey or in some distant or foreign business or work. This can indicate a happy vacation or trip, and travel is particularly favored now. This period can bring the realization of a desired professional goal. Your health is good now and productivity is the order of the day. Intellectual work and putting ideas to work is also favored by this influence.

THE FOUR OF SPADES IS YOUR PLUTO CARD

One important aspect of your aspirations this year will be to create strength and stability in either your work, health, or living situation. You have made a decision to work hard and overcome a host of difficulties through developing inner strength and fortitude. To accomplish this goal, you must make many changes. Perhaps you have decided to take full responsibility for your health and will begin a comprehensive program of diet and fitness. Or just as likely, you may want to develop more efficient and organized work habits.

On a deep level, you are wanting more peace of mind, stability, and security in your life. This may not be easy, but you can do it. Perhaps things have not been going as well as you would like at work. Whatever your specific goals for the year, it will require inner strength and determination and the willingness to try new approaches. Your Result Card will either describe this goal better or tell you who, in your life, is closely related to the work you have set before yourself.

AFFIRMATION:

I create stability and security in my life, a foundation of good health and satisfaction at work. I enjoy learning the value of hard and consistent work.

THE FOUR OF SPADES IS YOUR RESULT CARD

As the 'Four of Fours,' the Four of Spades card tells us that you will end this year in a much more solid and stabilized state, related to either your health, work, or living situation. The changes you are making, represented by your Pluto Card, tell us why you are wanting this stability or who it may be associated with. Rest assured that though the changes may at times seem difficult, you will succeed in accomplishing the stability and freedom from problems that you desire.

No matter just how challenging your Pluto Card may be this year, this card guarantees that everything will come to a happy and satisfactory conclusion and that you will end up this year feeling sound and secure in most every department of your life.

AFFIRMATION:

I create stability, security, and satisfaction in my life, health, and work. I create a foundation for myself that nurtures me.

THE FOUR OF SPADES IS YOUR LONG-RANGE CARD

The Four of Spades tells us that this will be a year of satisfaction in matters of work and health. Recovery from illness and any work-related problems can be expected under this influence. You will feel like getting 'solid' in most areas of your life. The words foundation, structure, and security become more important, along with the ability to create these in your life.

Your work and health should be good. This card actually can indicate recovery from some kind of health problem. The only possible negative effect of this influence would be a resistance to change and stubbornness. However, this same resistance is the strength that is bringing you so much satisfaction now. This year is a blessing in many ways, as well as a time to lay a secure foundation for the future.

KEYWORDS:

A year of good health, solid home and work situations. A year of strength and satisfaction in almost all matters. Hard work brings me many rewards.

THE FOUR OF SPADES IS YOUR ENVIRONMENT CARD

This year you will find that hard work and stability are the main source of blessings and protection. This card will help you overcome any health or work problems you may have and will also provide a certain amount of protection from any legal problems that may arise. Your will is strong this year, along with your desire to create some foundation in your life. The Four of Spades brings security and stability, but don't forget that you may have to work for it.

THE FOUR OF SPADES IS YOUR DISPLACEMENT CARD

This could be a year when you feel that all you do is work, work, and more work. And in fact, that may be just what you are being called upon to do in order to create the secure lifestyle that you desire. Your focus will more than likely revolve around security issues and having a stable home and family life. It is really your security or the security of your family that is on the line here. Are you willing to do what it takes to have this foundation in your life? On the other hand, there could be health issues that need to be tended to, ones that you have neglected in the past. Finally, there could be some things at your job that need more of your attention this year. Spades represent primarily work and health. The Four of Spades says that having security and stability in these areas is where you will have to put in some effort this year, and that may require some focus and consistency on your part.

Five of Hearts

Changes of heart, move to a new home

The Basic Meaning of the Five of Hearts

The Five of Hearts speaks of changes and restlessness in your heart that can manifest in many ways. At the deepest level, you will probably be feeling a dissatisfaction with your current relationship or home situation and desire some sort of change.

This same dissatisfaction may extend to your living situation. Many people move to a new home or living environment under the influence of this card. Hearts represents home and family just as much as it does our romantic relationships. The Five of Hearts in any period could indicate this sort of move.

When this card appears, there is always the chance of a separation or divorce with someone you love, but there is an equal possibility that you will be taking a trip or moving to a new home. The highest manifestation of this card is that of going out and meeting new people, telling others about what you are doing and who you are. You can make important contacts when this card is around.

The Five of Hearts in the Mercury Period

This period could be marked by sudden changes in feelings or a sudden move away from loved ones. Travel, separations, and changes could bring emotional turmoil and insecurity during this period. Watch out for a tendency towards fickleness that goes along with this influence. At the same time, you may be able to meet a lot of new and interesting people during this period, and some of them could end up as romantic partners.

The Five of Hearts in the Venus Period

This is one of the divorce cards, and it is very likely that you will have some sort of separation from loved ones during this period. It may be that your own emotional restlessness and love of travel and adventure end up competing with your own desire for a stable relationship. This card can indicate a trip of some sort that takes you away from your family for a while. This is an excellent time to go out and meet new and interesting people.

The Five of Hearts in the Mars Period

In Mars, the Five of Hearts promises many changes and a certain restlessness within you. These may jeopardize love and work relationships. Connected with a man or your work are possible changes in feelings or location. Men provide stimulation but also stimulate restlessness. In general, you will be more restless than usual and this could inspire changes in work or love. Be careful with this energy as breakups can often be devastating and expensive, especially if you end up in a legal battle.

The Five of Hearts in the Jupiter Period

Change in business personnel or location, travel, and changes of all kinds can bring rewards at this time and should not be resisted. A very good influence for traveling or making changes in your business. Social and business contacts should bring in more than the usual good fortune though you may find some of your close relationships suffering from your travels and mood changes. A business trip now could be very successful.

In certain situations, this card can represent a divorce that is financially successful for you. If you are planning a divorce or separation, this is a guarantee that financially, at least, things will go in your favor and that you have much to be grateful for.

The Five of Hearts in the Saturn Period

You may find yourself taking a trip caused by someone's ill health at this time, maybe even your own. Take extra care while traveling. Separations from lovers or friends are more traumatic under this influence.

Under Saturn, you may experience a difficult separation or divorce. If so, keep in mind that Saturn brings challenges of a karmic nature. There are debts to be paid, even from past lives. See if your own restlessness has not played a role in this.

This would not be a good time to take a vacation or travel, so try to schedule any trips either before or after this period. The only exception to this would be if you have a very strong card as the other Saturn Card, such as a Four or Eight, which could bring satisfactory results with minimal struggle.

The Five of Hearts in the Uranus Period

During this period, you may take an unexpected trip or have a sudden change of feelings or even a separation from a loved one. This may result from your own need for personal freedom combined with some restlessness of the heart. This influence may also see you making a trip somehow connected to labor, work, or real estate. This is one of the stronger influences for a move to a new home or for the sale of property.

The Five of Hearts in the Neptune Period

This influence is a strong indicator of taking a journey to distant places, perhaps in a quest for love. Under Neptune's influence, you must guard yourself against decisions based upon some fantasy you are having. Also, a lack of clarity or miscommunication could cause problems in important relationships now, even a separation. Take extra care that you are clearly understood in all your communications until this influence passes.

If you have been dreaming all year of either social or romantic freedom, this is the time when it is very likely to materialize.

The Five of Hearts Is Your Pluto Card

This is likely to be a major change in your relationships or marriage this year that is causing you to make other major changes in your life. As one of the divorce cards, this could indicate an actual separation from a long-term relationship. Whether you are getting divorced or not, you will be desiring to meet new people and have different experiences socially or romantically. This is probably something that you really want or need on a deep level, but it is not always an easy process to go through.

On a deep level, you are going through a change in what you want and need in terms of affection and partners. This may have created a restlessness in you that initiated either a lot of travel or looking for someone new in your life. Often the very act of ending a relationship can be a very arduous and drawn out affair. It is sometimes difficult to end something that we have spent so much time creating.

If you are single, this card probably means a strong restlessness in your affectional life that could cause a lot of changes and new experiences emotionally. You may have several involvements this year in your quest for the perfect partner, but it wouldn't be wise to assume that you will settle down until after your next birthday. Look at your Result Card to discover more about these changes or to see who is involved in these changes of heart.

AFFIRMATION:

I attract new people and love experiences into my life. I am challenged to change my relationships and discard the past.

THE FIVE OF HEARTS IS YOUR RESULT CARD

One of your major goals this year involves making changes in either your friendships or intimate relationships. These important changes may even result in a divorce from one or more current long-term relationships. You are changing what you want emotionally and are wanting to experience new and different people and pleasures. This may be a big transition year for you. Your Pluto Card may specify a person who is central to this change or further describe it.

A change is coming. It will be a good one that leads you in new directions and provides more and much needed personal freedom.

AFFIRMATION:

I achieve new freedom in my choice of friends or lovers. I successfully broaden the scope of my friends and associates.

THE FIVE OF HEARTS IS YOUR LONG-RANGE CARD

This will be a year of many changes of the heart for you. It may be that you are in the process of a separation or divorce and that this will take a lot of your time, energy, and attention to handle. It could also be a year when you are just restless emotionally and want to break out of your current relationship or explore new ones. This may involve travel, which could take you away from your loved one or ones at different times of the year. One last and common occurrence under this card is that of moving to a new home.

At the same time, you will find that you are seeking many new emotional experiences and that you are meeting many new people as you progress. There is likely to be a basic change in the way you view relationships, marriage, and friendships. This is a year of transition from one way of being in relationship to another, and it deserves to be acknowledged as being the place where your path is leading you.

KEYWORDS:

A year of changes in affection, travel, or one of meeting many new people. Perhaps a major focus on divorce or moving to a new home.

THE FIVE OF HEARTS IS YOUR ENVIRONMENT CARD

Travel, moves, changes of residence, and even changes in your relationship status will tend to have a very positive effect this year and could be the source of many blessings. If you are planning a divorce or change of location, this is the year you can proceed ahead with assurance of a happy outcome. You will likely feel somewhat restless emotionally or otherwise this year, which will in turn lead to an expansion of your current situation.

THE FIVE OF HEARTS IS YOUR DISPLACEMENT CARD

Dissatisfaction with your love life or family/home situation could prompt some changes during this period. You may even get the urge to travel or move to a new home. However, changes do not come easily this year. Your personal or romantic freedom may be desired but hard to achieve. This is a card of change but also of dissatisfaction with what you already have. Any separations or divorces from loved ones will likely be a drain on your energy. It would be wise to plan such a change after this year is over if possible. It could very well be that your personal freedom is at stake this year and that you must pay closer attention to the things that make you happy in order to achieve it.

Five of Clubs
Changes in plans or thinking

The Basic Meaning of the Five of Clubs

'Change of mind and plans' is the basic meaning of the Five of Clubs. However, any five can mean change in residence or travel opportunities. Five of Clubs can also mean a restlessness that brings up a desire to explore new realms, at least on the mental level.

Whenever this card appears, it may be a signal for a change in your life. You will likely feel a dissatisfaction with things as they are and want to progress into new areas. Be open to new plans, new ideas, new places to go, etc. The only negative side of this card is an unwillingness to commit one's self to any particular belief or philosophy.

THE FIVE OF CLUBS IN THE MERCURY PERIOD

During this period, a sudden change of mind brought about by a short trip or some unexpected news is likely. You may take many short trips or make an unexpected journey or move, possibly due to your own impatience. Don't let restlessness drive you crazy; it may just be that some change is overdo and will bring about many improvements in your present situation. Advice from friends may be helpful now.

THE FIVE OF CLUBS IN THE VENUS PERIOD

Your inner uncertainty or fickleness in affections can bring changes in relationships during this period. You might even have a change in the family or your place of residence during this period. Be careful that your own restlessness doesn't threaten your need for security now. You desire intellectually stimulating relationships, as well as personal freedom. You need to balance these with your need for some security to get the best of this influence.

THE FIVE OF CLUBS IN THE MARS PERIOD

Your own changeability may be a bit out of control during this period. This could precipitate arguments with some male that could force some unwanted changes. Your opinions regarding some male may change many times during this period. Your restlessness will be stronger than usual and cause you to make decisions that threaten either your relationships or your security in some way.

THE FIVE OF CLUBS IN THE JUPITER PERIOD

Now is the time to make a change in your work or profession. You may want to make a change that allows you more freedom and better financial returns. This could take the form of taking a profitable business trip or of changing the nature of your business or location. This is also a very good influence for sales and marketing of products and services. Get the word out about what you are doing, and you may be surprised at the results you get.

Even if your plans need to change unexpectedly, this influence promises that any changes will lead you to something better and more rewarding financially.

THE FIVE OF CLUBS IN THE SATURN PERIOD

During this period, you may feel discontent with yourself, and these feelings may motivate some of the changes you make now. This could also indicate travel to see a sick friend or travel because of your own illness. More than usual, changes now will not leave you with a feeling of satisfaction, or they may be forced upon you in some manner that is not agreeable to you. This influence could be a motivator of constructive changes in your life.

This would not be a good time to take a vacation or travel, so try to schedule any trips either before or after this period. The only exception to this would be if you have a very strong card as the other Saturn Card, such as a Four or Eight, which could bring satisfactory results with minimal struggle.

THE FIVE OF CLUBS IN THE URANUS PERIOD

The Five of Clubs in Uranus is a very strong influence for a change in residence or the sale of real estate. Change related to your work is also possible. This is a progressive influence that prompts necessary changes in one's life, sometimes quite radical and unexpected. Work requiring travel or new and progressive methods is highly favored during this period, as well as humanitarian work with large organizations.

THE FIVE OF CLUBS IN THE NEPTUNE PERIOD

This is one of the stronger indicators of a long journey over water or to foreign countries. This trip could be most enjoyable and bring new friends and learning opportunities. This period could also bring about many opportunities to help others in some way that could bring much contentment. This influence may make it difficult for you to focus your energies on any one thing—you may even lose some things by being too scattered—but it is excellent for travel.

THE FIVE OF CLUBS IS YOUR PLUTO CARD

This will be a year of many important changes for you. Inside, there is a change of your basic philosophy of life that is causing you to be restless and desiring to branch out in new directions. Circumstances may appear suddenly in your life to upset you and your plans, and if you are not careful, you may feel somewhat victimized by them. You may be running into many new ideas or forms of communications, and these are challenging you to branch out in new directions. Perhaps you want to do some travel or maybe move to a new location. Perhaps you desire a new occupation or more favorable health conditions. Whatever changes you desire, they are sure to require extra amounts of energy and determination to accomplish.

Whatever the specifics of the changes coming your way this year, on a deep level, they are merely a mirror of some internal changes in your basic philosophy of life. This change in your philosophy could cause you to abandon much of what you have known for the past five to ten years, even many of your friendships. You are in the midst of a transition that could affect your whole life or important aspects of your life. This transition will only be difficult to the degree that you resist these changes.

Combine this change influence with the meaning of your Result Card to get the complete picture of the major goal for you this year on an internal and external level. If the Result Card is the Birth Card of someone you know, it is likely that they are a major stimulus in this process you are going through.

I am challenged to change my philosophies, ideas, or plans. This is a major transition year for me and my thinking in which I am expanding my view of the world and myself. I am limitless possibilities.

THE FIVE OF CLUBS IS YOUR RESULT CARD

The Five of Clubs as the Result Card signals change and transition is in store for you. You may move to a new location or start a new job by your next birthday. A sense of restlessness and unsettledness is driving you to explore new areas. You may experience a fundamental change in your philosophy of life or in the way you think or communicate. This could be a result of new technology. Your Pluto Card will tell you who or what is involved in this change of plans or thinking.

A change is coming, and it will be a good one that leads you in new directions and provides more and much-needed personal freedom.

AFFIRMATION:

I end this year with a new philosophy or way of communicating. I change my life plans in a major way.

THE FIVE OF CLUBS IS YOUR LONG-RANGE CARD

This will be a year of important changes for you, both within and without your mind, and in your external environment. On a deep level, you are undergoing a shift in your belief structures or in your philosophy of life, or in the way you have been thinking about your future. These changes could be the result of many new influences in your life and possibly from things you learn while traveling. Often, this card shows up in people's spreads who are taking on new ideas through school or new jobs.

Often, this card manifests as curiosity and restlessness. Many people move to a new location under this influence, so if you are thinking of moving, this could be the year. However it manifests externally, it will reflect a change in your mental pattern. Traveling is also a common experience when this card is present and is probably one of the easier ways to manifest its energies.

The negative possibilities of this card are that of being skeptical to other's ideas and of not having any commitment to any philosophy or ideology. You could feel like a leaf blowing in the wind of other's opinions and ideas. If so, rest assured that it is only part of the process. Your point of view is changing and probably won't settle down until the year is over.

KEYWORDS:

I change my thinking or I change my basic philosophy. I travel a lot this year. My plans change a lot this year.

THE FIVE OF CLUBS IS YOUR ENVIRONMENT CARD

Travel, moves, and other changes will bring benefits into your life this year. You are experiencing a broadening of your mental boundaries and perspectives that will alter the way you see yourself and your life. Let these changes happen, because they are a necessary part of your own progress and development. Welcome opportunities to travel this year. They will bring blessings. At the same time, be open to new points of view, beliefs, and perspectives.

THE FIVE OF CLUBS IS YOUR DISPLACEMENT CARD

This could be a year of great dissatisfaction for you, one in which you reach out for some changes in your life on many levels in order to fulfill an inner desire to expand your life in meaningful ways. At the same time, this same dissatisfaction could prove to be a source of problems for you if not kept in perspective with the rest of your life. Your own urge for freedom or adventure could cost you more than you think it is worth. On the other hand, sometimes this card indicates a need for changes in one's life even when we are resisting them. In all likelihood, there will be a significant change or move this year, and in some ways, that change will be difficult. Your Saturn period is one of the times when that change is most likely to occur. One of the side benefits of this Displacement Card is that oftentimes a person in this position can come into a great deal of money during the course of the year. However, the main theme of this year is changes of mind, plans, or even work or living situations.

Five of Diamonds

Changes in values, occupation, business travel

The Basic Meaning of the Five of Diamonds

The Five of Diamonds indicates a change in your financial condition, up or down, money coming in or going out. This card can also indicate changes within your present business, such as changing locations or the way in which you do business. Another possible manifestation of this card would be taking one or more business trips.

At its deepest level, the Five of Diamonds signals a time when you will undergo a change in values. If our values, or what we really want from life, changes, it is likely that many other changes will occur at the same time. We could move to a new location, get a new job, or even change relationships. In other words, all things valued are susceptible to a big change when this card appears, especially if it appears as the Long-Range, Pluto, or Result Card.

Discontentment with what we have is a common occurrence when any Five card is present. The Five of Diamonds can bring dissatisfaction with one's work or occupation, along with the areas mentioned above. Out of that discontent arises the changes commonly associated with this card. On a deeper level, the Five represents an evolution from security to adventure (from Four to Five), a branching out in new directions to claim more territory and gather new experiences.

THE FIVE OF DIAMONDS IN THE MERCURY PERIOD

This card indicates a sudden and unexpected change in employment, material circumstances, or the family financial situation. This is possibly an unexpected loss of money. It can also indicate a short journey undertaken for your work or a money deal. Change is in the air under this influence, and it could be up or down and possibly related to education or brothers and sisters.

THE FIVE OF DIAMONDS IN THE VENUS PERIOD

During this period, you may find that your friends or lovers somehow become expensive. You should not do business with friends under this influence. Your desire for love or luxury could deplete your resources. An overemphasis on money could affect the status of your friendships during this period, especially related to some woman in your life. This is an influence of emotional instability and restlessness, and this could be the cause of changes now.

THE FIVE OF DIAMONDS IN THE MARS PERIOD

Under this influence, impulsive actions or competing with others could cause a loss of money. This could also represent a business journey or changes in your business. There may be interference from some male in a business deal. This is not necessarily a negative influence, as it could provide the impetus for positive changes. However, under Mars, you must guard against too much aggressiveness or impatience, as these could produce negative results.

THE FIVE OF DIAMONDS IN THE JUPITER PERIOD

Changes in business and traveling are financially beneficial under this influence. This is one of the best influences for a successful business trip, doing selling and promoting, or making a change of occupation. Honesty and repayment of debts are also promoted by this influence. Your own extravagance could deplete your resources now, so be care-

ful. The Five of Diamonds in this period may indicate large sums of money changing hands, changing your job, or changing the way that you make money. If so, flow with the changes, as they are leading you to greater success and satisfaction.

THE FIVE OF DIAMONDS IN THE SATURN PERIOD

Under Saturn, this card brings a restlessness that contributes to a loss of money and financial insecurity. This could also bring a change in business due to the ill health of yourself or someone else. You may find a lot of money being spent on health care or many short trips for the same reason. Many remedies may be tried in the pursuit of healing.

This would not be a good time to take a vacation or travel, so try to schedule any trips either before or after this period. The only exception to this would be if you have a very strong card as the other Saturn Card, such as a Four or Eight, which could bring satisfactory results with minimal struggle.

THE FIVE OF DIAMONDS IN THE URANUS PERIOD

This is a strong influence for a change of residence or business, perhaps unexpected. This can indicate the purchase or sale of real estate. This also indicates a journey over land for business. Making changes in the way you do business, in personnel, or location are beneficial now but keep a cautious eye on all transactions. The unexpected is bound to happen.

THE FIVE OF DIAMONDS IN THE NEPTUNE PERIOD

This card represents a long business trip or business interests that are at some distance. Be extra cautious in all communications and contracts under this influence, and you may do much of what you dreamed you wanted to do. This is one of the strongest indicators of a long business trip or change in location of the business, and that could be profitable. However, under Neptune you must be watchful for deception or misunderstandings.

This card can also represent either the sale or purchase of something important, perhaps something that lies far away from where you live.

THE FIVE OF DIAMONDS IS YOUR PLUTO CARD

This year you will be challenged by a major internal change in your basic value system that will result in many important external changes in your life. You may feel that changes are forced upon you at times, but if you look closer, you may notice that you have been wanting these changes for a long time. Now your desires are being fulfilled. But still, it is not easy to flow all the time during this big transition.

You could change jobs, the location of your business, your place of residence, or even your primary relationship status under this powerful card's influence. You don't want the same things you wanted earlier. Your priorities have shifted, and you will be challenged to follow your inner truth. To the extent that you are the one who wants and needs these changes, this process will be easier. To get the complete picture of this change, look at the meaning of your Result Card, and combine it with this basic change in values.

AFFIRMATION:

I am challenged and transformed in making necessary and important changes in my life. My values are changing in order for me to make personal and professional progress.

The Five of Diamonds Is Your Result Card

This will be a year of many changes for you, and as a result of dealing with your Pluto Card, you may find that by year's end you are in a much different place than when the year started. There may be a new relationship, living location, and a new career on the horizon. Behind these changes, you are undergoing a shift in your basic values. At times, there may be some challenges as people and situations seem to confront you. But it seems that change is inevitable.

A change is coming, and it will be a good one that leads you in new directions and provides more and much-needed personal freedom.

Affirmation:

I complete this year with an entirely new set of values that sets me free to explore new areas in my life.

The Five of Diamonds Is Your Long-Range Card

This will be an important year of transition for you that will leave you in an entirely new place by your next birthday. A fundamental change in what is most important to you will be likely to cause major changes in your job, approach to money, and even relationships. You could even move to a new location during this powerful transition. Since our lives are basically structured to provide us with the things that we deem most important, when this inner picture of what is important to us changes, our exterior world has no choice but to follow suit.

To get the most out of this year, allow the changes to flow in your life without trying to know exactly what lies ahead. When you are in transition, you must change and depart from what has been, and the future is not always clear. But there are always clear skies ahead just beyond what we can see. It would be wise to expect changes and to not make big commitments until after your next birthday.

Keywords:

I experience a major change in my values, which affects every important area of my life this year.

The Five of Diamonds Is Your Environment Card

Favorable changes in your work or business will bring blessings this year. Any travel connected to work or making money will also be a source of benefits. It would be wise to think about ways that you can expand or change your current money-making enterprises with this influence. In addition, any travel, moves, or changes will tend to have a positive result. A change in your values toward greater expansion is bringing rewards and blessings.

The Five of Diamonds Is Your Displacement Card

Discontentment with your financial situation and restlessness may motivate some important changes in your life this year. However, most changes, whether in your work or personal life, will carry a higher price than usual in terms of your time and energy. Your dissatisfaction may prove bothersome and a source of irritation during the course of this year, as though there is something more that you need from life, but you are having a hard time putting your finger on it. It is highly likely that you will change occupations this year to some degree or that at the least you will try some new ways of making money. Just take care that the changes you make do not contribute to a sense of insecurity and instability. Try to maintain some areas of stability that you can draw upon when you need it.

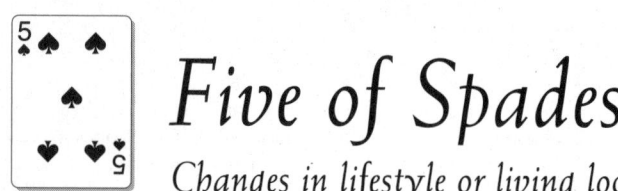

Five of Spades

Changes in lifestyle or living location, a long trip, change of job

The Basic Meaning of the Five of Spades

The Five of Spades is one of the strongest indicators of travel or moving your home or your business. It could indicate a change in your health as well. At its most basic level, the Five of Spades means a change in your lifestyle or the things that you do day in and day out. When this card appears, something will change that affects the way you live or the things that you do each day.

This card usually brings with it a certain amount of restlessness and the desire for changes or travel. It can result in a dissatisfaction with the way your life has been that motivates you to want new things, lifestyles, and experiences. This card has a strong Sagittarian influence to it.

THE FIVE OF SPADES IN THE MERCURY PERIOD

This period could bring a sudden or unexpected move of your home or business to a new location. You might also experience a sudden change of health, either for better or worse. A change of employment or business methods is another possibility, even a new job. You may be feeling very restless now, and this might be the cause of some of the changes during this period. You will gravitate more towards versatility in your work.

THE FIVE OF SPADES IN THE VENUS PERIOD

This period may bring a trip for love, or one that takes you away from a loved one. You might have a change in your love life or a visit from a female. Business travel or changes are favored and bring money. You may be more fickle than usual now, and this may be the cause of changes in your relationships. This is an excellent time to move to a new home or better living conditions. You may even remodel or redecorate your home now.

THE FIVE OF SPADES IN THE MARS PERIOD

This indicates changes and travel related to work or some male person. This can be a move to a new location. You may find work with males stimulating at this time and these may be a catalyst for productive changes. This influence can bring a change regarding taxes, insurance, or legal matters. You may have a lot of restlessness now that stimulates you to travel and perhaps even move or change jobs. However, personal relationships may suffer.

THE FIVE OF SPADES IN THE JUPITER PERIOD

This indicates a change for the better, either to a new home or to a new job. Any moves or travel at this time will be rewarding in many ways. A lot of money could be made on a business trip now as well. This can also indicate a large sum of money changing hands. Almost all changes in your work methods or location will be beneficial during this period. It may be that changes are long overdue in this area of your life. Follow the hunch of your own inner restlessness, and pursue those things that give you more variety now.

This is also an excellent influence for promoting and selling your products and services.

THE FIVE OF SPADES IN THE SATURN PERIOD

Health issues or a journey caused by someone's illness may cause a change in your job or home during this period. A change in career or work will involve more work and some problems, though it may be unavoidable. Changes tend to bring more harm than good now, though you may not be able to avoid them, as they may be necessary for other reasons. This card can also represent a change in your health condition (for the worse) or a visit to a doctor.

This would not be a good time to take a vacation or travel, so try to schedule any trips either before or after this period. The only exception to this would be if you have a very strong card as the other Saturn Card, such as a Four or Eight, which could bring satisfactory results with minimal struggle.

THE FIVE OF SPADES IN THE URANUS PERIOD

During this period, you will have a change of some importance. This could be a change of profession or a change in the labor force of a business. This is also a strong indicator of a sale of real estate or a change of residence, both of which might be unexpected. Changes or travel that happen now may happen unexpectedly and may leave you feeling somewhat insecure or unsettled. These changes are most likely overdue and beneficial in many ways.

THE FIVE OF SPADES IN THE NEPTUNE PERIOD

This is the strongest indicator of a long journey for business or for pleasure. Also, this influence could see change in the location of your business or home. Be cautious in all business dealings under this influence, and avoid drugs and alcohol. The possibility of deception and confusion is very high during this period, and there is a possibility of getting involved in some 'pie in the sky' scheme. This card can also indicate a change in occupation.

THE FIVE OF SPADES IS YOUR PLUTO CARD

There are some challenging and powerful changes in front of you this year. You may feel as though these are forced upon you, but it is more likely that you have been wanting them and asking for them for a while before now. However, now they are upon you, and change you must. These changes may involve your job or business, your place of residence, or your health condition. This would be a good time to get involved in some health improvement program if the latter is the case. Travel may also prove challenging this year in some way. You may want to take a certain trip or vacation and end up with a lot more problems than you imagined just to get it going.

These changes likely reflect a major transition in your lifestyle, and this transition will not always be easy. The time is now to effect some different approaches to the way you live, work, or approach your health. Everything will settle back down next year after these changes have been made. In the meantime, do things that help you stay relaxed. Combine this card with your Result Card to get the whole picture of what this change is about or who is involved in it.

AFFIRMATION:

I am transformed by changes in my health, work, lifestyle, or residence. I make important changes in one or more of these areas.

THE FIVE OF SPADES IS YOUR RESULT CARD

Somehow connected to your Pluto Card, you are making some important changes this year that will leave you in an entirely new situation in many respects by your next birthday. You may change jobs, residence, or have a totally new health picture by year's end. The Five of Spades usually appears when one is ready to make a major life transition, and because it is the Result Card, you can rest assured that though it may be tough at times, you will make it through successfully. If you have been desiring a major change in your lifestyle, your wish is about to come true.

A change is coming, and it will be a good one that leads you in new directions and provides more and much-needed personal freedom.

AFFIRMATION:

I complete this year with a new job, new health picture, new residence, or new lifestyle. I make a major transition.

THE FIVE OF SPADES IS YOUR LONG-RANGE CARD

The Five of Spades is the strongest indicator of travel or moving your home or your business, but on a deeper level, it means a change that will somehow affect what you do every day, a change of 'lifestyle.' It can indicate changes in your work or health as well. You may be faced with the need to make basic changes in your lifestyle that could affect every area of your life. In some cases, this card simply reflects changes in one's work environment or the way one conducts business. But usually it indicates much more fundamental changes, either in one's residence, lifestyle, or health.

Underneath all the changes is likely to be an inner restlessness. The time has come for you to move in new directions. These new directions could be in the area of work or the location of your home. You could have a strong desire to travel that sets you off on a great adventure this year. Hopefully, these changes will be for the better.

KEYWORDS:

A year of changes in work or health, travel, lifestyle, or one or more changes in residence. My life is changing in important ways.

THE FIVE OF SPADES IS YOUR ENVIRONMENT CARD

Most all changes and opportunities to travel will bring blessings of one sort or another this year. This includes changes in business, lifestyle, living situation, work, or residence. Accept changes and look for opportunities to travel as indicators of where to go for more benefits in your life. This could be an important transition year for you and one that leads you up one step towards a more expansive and freer lifestyle.

THE FIVE OF SPADES IS YOUR DISPLACEMENT CARD

It is very likely that you will either move to a new home this year or change jobs. You could even do both under this powerful card of changes. Expect some significant changes in your lifestyle, ones that will lead to a fuller expression of your life force in the current cycle. The actual changes may entail a lot of work and energy on your part, and at times, you may feel burdened by them. But this is your time to make the move. Make your adjustments and get on with it. Spades represent our lifestyle—the things that we actually do each and every day. This powerful Five tells you that somehow your lifestyle will change this year in a significant way. Flow with these changes as best you can, and you will be led to a better place for yourself and those you love.

Six of Hearts

Making the peace, the return of love or friendship karma, a karmic relationship begins

The Basic Meaning of the Six of Hearts

The Six of Hearts is a powerful influence of balance and peace in personal relationships. How it affects you will largely depend upon your current status in your love life and how responsible you have been in that area. This card will demand that all outstanding love debts be settled and will encourage you to take responsibility for your actions and words in your closest relationships. You may find that you have to make compromises and adjustments to accomplish this as well.

On a more universal level, the Six of Hearts may also reveal to you a special purpose in your life, one of helping others by sharing love with them. You may become aware of a special mission that you are to perform when this card appears. It is the card of peace and of intuitively knowing how to love others in a spiritual sense. Sometimes we have a fated meeting when the Six of Hearts is present. There are some relationships that we are destined to experience due to our actions in previous lives. The Six of Hearts can indicate the timing of the beginning of such a relationship. Its actual position may tell just what sort of relationship it will be or how you will experience it.

THE SIX OF HEARTS IN THE MERCURY PERIOD

During this period, you will be faced with the results of your past communications with those you love most. If you have been responsible and have been willing to give and take, this will likely be a period of peace and happiness. If there are unsettled emotional debts incurred by you in the past, you may be faced with payment of these, and the opportunity to take more responsibility in this important area. Practice the 'law of love' in your mind and heart.

THE SIX OF HEARTS IN THE VENUS PERIOD

This should be a period of contentment, stability, and happiness in your personal relationships. You can use the 'law of love' and the willingness to make compromises to overcome any hurdles or obstacles in your family and romantic areas. By acting with responsibility and fairness in all matters of the heart, you will ensure that peace reigns in your house and heart. Any love affairs begun during this period will be for the settling of karmic debts.

THE SIX OF HEARTS IN THE MARS PERIOD

During this period, the steadying influence of the Six of Hearts will cause relationship issues to be dealt with and settled. Though you might be impatient at this time, you may be forced to slow down and act responsibly in all your personal affairs. You will get exactly what you give to others now, so be especially careful in what you are putting out. Rest assured that any matters, whether legal or romantic, will result in a fair and equal settlement for all concerned.

THE SIX OF HEARTS IN THE JUPITER PERIOD

During this period, it is likely that you will be receiving some good 'Love Karma' for having done good for others in the past. Past efforts to take responsibility and willingness to make compromises in love and friendship are now bearing fruit as others come into your life to repay you in some fashion. Maintaining your composure and resting in the knowledge that 'as you give, so shall you receive,' you are in the happy harvest time of peace and domestic harmony.

THE SIX OF HEARTS IN THE SATURN PERIOD

During this period, you will be face to face with the results of your words and deeds, especially in the areas of love and friendship. This card often brings one or more karmic relationships throughout the year, as well as many lessons about taking responsibility for our actions and sexual expression. The net result of this period will be more maturity, knowing that what you give is what you receive. This will lead to more success in relationships later.

We often are unaware of how we are acting or how our acts and speech are affecting those around us. The Six of Hearts in Saturn will serve to increase your awareness in these areas.

Your other Saturn Card may define who you could have a karmic relationship with or tell you more about the relationship challenges that may occur during this period.

THE SIX OF HEARTS IN THE URANUS PERIOD

This is an influence of success in humanitarian pursuits and affairs of labor and coworkers. This is also good for steady progress in these areas and sticking to one chosen path and working it through. Watch out that you don't allow this steadiness to become an excuse for being stubborn and inflexible in your work and friendships. You may have to make compromises now to maintain peace and harmony with friends or on the job but it will be worth the cooperation.

By tuning in to your most subtle thoughts and feelings now, you can make a strong connection to exactly what your life's purpose is, especially as it relates to your work with people and your own circle of friends and family.

THE SIX OF HEARTS IN THE NEPTUNE PERIOD

You are not likely to travel under this influence, even if you have made plans to do so. Relax and enjoy the peace and tranquility. Your home, family, and close relationships should be a source of satisfaction now, so enjoy them. This influence does not support any travel or changes of any kind. Things at a distance will go smoothly now without changes. This influence can bring profound spiritual revelations if you tune in to your subconscious.

One of the possible benefits of this card in Neptune is that you could discover or deepen your life's purpose. All that is required is for you to tune in to your thoughts and feelings, especially when you are alone or meditating.

THE SIX OF HEARTS IS YOUR PLUTO CARD

Some of the major keywords for this year are compromise and responsibility in love. It is likely that you will be confronted with many situations where you see clearly how you behave in relationships and how that behavior affects others in your life. This can be with friends or associates, but usually it is with someone with whom we are intimately involved. You may find yourself involved in one or more challenging relationships that don't seem to go the way you want them to until you expend a lot of energy to work things out. These 'destined' relationships will often be strong mirrors of ourselves that help us see how we are behaving in our most intimate relationships. The lessons they teach us are often difficult, but the value of what we learn is immeasurable.

This powerful karma card will challenge you to make adjustments and compromises in order to be fair and just in all your relationships.

If you are not getting the love you want or think you deserve, check out how much love you are giving. Your current or new relationships could have an element of fate about them, and it is certain that you will learn much about love this year. Your Result Card will either represent a particular person that you will be karmically connected to as you work out your love issues or will describe more about this challenge you are facing this year.

One of the greatest potentials of this card is that you could actually discover or deepen your connection to an important and meaningful purpose in your life. This card's appearance in this important spot could be the signal of the time in your life when you find something of greater meaning to stand for.

AFFIRMATION:

I am learning to make compromises and to take complete responsibility in my personal relationships. I am discovering my true life's purpose.

THE SIX OF HEARTS IS YOUR RESULT CARD

At this time in your life, the challenges you face will have a lot to do with showing you the results of your past actions among those who are and have been closest to you. This karmic influence tells us that you will be taught much about the law of love. 'As you sow, so shall you reap' captures it in a nutshell. There may be one or more relationships where affectional debts from the past are settled. The Pluto Card may be the birth card of one of these people.

This card can also bring you a special gift by your next birthday. You could discover, by turning your attention within, to a special purpose for your life, one that involves loving others in a specific way. This purpose could transform your life, giving it more meaningful direction.

AFFIRMATION:

By listening to my inner voice, I find my special purpose in life that will direct me to the highest occupation. I strengthen my sense of responsibility in all relationship and romantic matters.

THE SIX OF HEARTS IS YOUR LONG-RANGE CARD

The Six of Hearts is a symbol of stability and perhaps monotony in love and affections. For those who seek a secure foundation in love, this could be a welcome situation, though there will likely be compromises and lessons. At the same time, the karmic nature of the six indicates the possibility of relationships that are in some way paying off old debts, even from past lives. If a significant new relationship does enter your life this year, you can bet that this will bring with it the balancing of the karmic scales in terms of love and affection. This year will show you the value of giving as you 'reap what you sow' in the areas of love.

Whatever the specific nature of the events in your relationships this year, it is sure that what you will be experiencing will help you develop an appreciation for being responsible for yourself as far as your romantic and friendship connections are concerned.

KEYWORDS:

I learn about responsibility in love and how to make compromises to maintain balance in my closest relationships. I open myself up to discovering a special and higher purpose for my life's work.

THE SIX OF HEARTS IS YOUR ENVIRONMENT CARD

Having the 'peacemaker's card' as your Environment Card, this year will bring many blessings from helping others and from being responsible in all your love relationships. You could actually receive some good karmic pay-backs from loving others in the past. There is an outside possibility that you could meet a new lover who is actually someone you have known in a past life, but it is more likely that there will be little change, if any, in your romantic life.

THE SIX OF HEARTS IS YOUR DISPLACEMENT CARD

Sixes denote the law of karma, which states that as someone sows, so shall they reap. In the suit of Hearts, the Six represents becoming more conscious of our actions in the area of personal relationships. While sitting in this position this year, it is highly likely that you will be learning lessons in this area. It is entirely possible that some fated events occur in your life this year as a result of some of your actions in the past in your personal relationships. These events may not be to your liking. They may even seem unfair as far as you are concerned, as if what is happening is something that you do not deserve. These are likely to be difficult situations, especially during your Saturn period of the year, and they will involve some key relationships. However, these events are fair and just, the result of something you did in the past, be it in this lifetime or one prior to now.

Sometimes this card has been known to attract a karmic relationship into our lives. This would usually be a past-life relationship that returns for us to settle some unfinished business. If someone new and significant comes into your life this year, this is likely the cause. Be attentive to what is going on between you—what are the real issues that you are dealing with in this relationship?

Issues will revolve around fairness and having an awareness of our personal responsibility in matters of love and family. It is up to you to explore any situations that come up and to be open to learning more about fairness. You may have always thought that your actions in certain areas were good and just when in fact they were not. Keep an open mind, and be willing to give whatever is asked of you if you wish to get the most from this powerful influence.

On the brighter side, this card gives you extraordinary powers of mental concentration this year, which should bring you a lot more success in your business or job.

Six of Clubs

Awareness of our personal destiny, intuition, paying for things said in the past

The Basic Meaning of the Six of Clubs

The Six of Clubs is *the* card of intuition. Its presence in your cards can indicate a time when your intuition will be stronger than usual. It is also the card of responsibility in speech and communications and of making compromises to maintain a peaceful surrounding. When this card shows up, situations will arise that promote bringing your life into balance and stability. Whatever is out of balance will have to be adjusted, so there may be karmic debts to pay.

Because the six is a karmic influence, people often receive the fruits of things they said in the past when the Six of Clubs is present. This karma can be good or bad, depending on what the individual had said, or in many cases, promised, in the past. You should be ready to make good on your promises when this card appears and be willing to pay up for things you have said to others in the past.

On a more universal level, the presence of the Six of Clubs can indicate a time when we can become aware of a special purpose in our life, something to do with sharing higher knowledge with others. It has also been called the 'John the Baptist Card' and the 'Way-Shower's Card.' Thus it can be a harbinger of an important mission for you, one which will lead you to a higher purpose and lifestyle in the spiritual sense.

THE SIX OF CLUBS IN THE MERCURY PERIOD

This can mean a period of relative quiet and harmony that lasts but a few days. This is a card of intuitive potential but an inclination to laziness now may prevent you from doing anything with it. Your life can be harmonious now if you take steps towards being responsible for the ways in which you communicate with others and be willing to make compromises and adjustments as well. This could be a very peaceful and enjoyable period.

THE SIX OF CLUBS IN THE VENUS PERIOD

This card represents a lack of change in the status of your personal relationships. This can be good or bad depending on your current situation and just what you desire at this time. Peace and tranquility are possible now if you are able to make compromises and are willing to assume responsibility for the ways in which you communicate with those you love.

THE SIX OF CLUBS IN THE MARS PERIOD

This card represents harmony in relations with men and steadiness regarding any legal matters you may be currently involved in. You can rest assured that the outcome of any legal matters will be resolved in fairness. Your intuition is strong now and can be used to help you achieve your goals and desires. With effort and sensitivity you could make some real progress now, but if you get too comfortable you may fall into a rut and not make the effort.

THE SIX OF CLUBS IN THE JUPITER PERIOD

A heightened sense of intuition and sensitivity are the keys to much success in all areas at this time, particularly financial and business related. At the same time, your complacency could be your greatest obstacle. Overcome your complacency and contentment now and make the extra effort during this auspicious influence. Every effort will pay off in a big way. Of course, if you already have everything you want, you can just sit back and enjoy it.

It is a good idea to stay with the things and projects you have already initiated. That is where your financial gains lie during this period unless other indicators are present.

THE SIX OF CLUBS IN THE SATURN PERIOD

Health conditions, whether good or bad, will not change under this influence. Intuition is present for you, but you may find it hard to follow, or fears prevent you from using it. You may feel that you are being forced by circumstances into making compromises and adjustments with others. Be aware of how you talk to others, because what you give, you will get in return.

Be open to others' ideas and plans in order to get the most out of this powerful influence. If you have told untruths in the past or made promises that you haven't kept, this may be the time that you have to pay up or come clean. Otherwise, this influence could indicate a time when you become much more aware of your life's purpose. You are being brought in line with the will of God.

THE SIX OF CLUBS IN THE URANUS PERIOD

This could be a period of heightened intuition and sensitivity. If you choose to, you could apply these gifts to your work with good results. However, this period may also be one where you are feeling so content with yourself that you choose not to do much with these available gifts. In any event, this will be a period of steadiness in your work and life, especially if you are willing to make a few compromises with friends and associates to keep the peace.

By tuning in to your most subtle thoughts and feelings now, you can make a strong connection to exactly what your life's purpose is.

THE SIX OF CLUBS IN THE NEPTUNE PERIOD

This will most likely be a pleasant period. However, if you were planning a trip for this period, it may not happen. Your intuition is strong and available for the pursuit of knowledge or spiritual goals and may bring you some valuable self-knowledge and understanding. This is a good time for inner development and simply enjoying the things you have worked for and acquired. This is not a good time to plan or execute any major changes in your life.

One of the possible benefits of this card in Neptune is that you could discover or deepen your life's purpose. All that is required is for you to tune in to your thoughts and feelings, especially when you are alone or meditating.

THE SIX OF CLUBS IS YOUR PLUTO CARD

Key situations in your life will resist change, and this may prove challenging for you this year. You will feel as though you have to make many compromises to keep the peace and to make the best of a static situation. Involved with your transformation this year will be either the element of your intuition and psychic ability or having to get the most out of a situation that seems to be static and unchanging.

Compromises and taking responsibility on a communication level will be necessary this year in order to maintain harmony and openness in your personal and professional relationships, and this could be challenging for you this year. You may feel as though you are in a rut, which can be the cause of anger and resentment at the world.

On a deeper level, try and see how you have created this situation and what you hope to achieve by experiencing it and working with it. Whether or not you acknowledge your own intuitive ability, it could play an important role in understanding and mastering the situations and circumstances that are coming into your life this year.

This will be a year in which you strive to understand just what your main purpose in life is. Though some situations in your life may seem static and immovable, this is your opportunity to listen to your inner voice to receive the important message that is coming your way. Many people live their entire life without knowing what their real purpose is. With some attention to your inner thoughts, you can find yours.

Check out your Result Card for more information about what or who is transforming you this year in conjunction with the stability of the Six of Clubs.

AFFIRMATION:

I learn the value of truthfulness and keeping my word. I am discovering my true life's purpose.

THE SIX OF CLUBS IS YOUR RESULT CARD

One result of many of your efforts this year will be either to develop heightened intuition or to create peaceful and effective communications with those around you. The six is a powerful steadying influence and demands responsibility and the willingness to compromise to be handled effectively. Your Pluto Card will tell you who is involved in these situations or give you more details about the steps you are taking towards intuitive and responsible communications.

This card also can signal a year in which you discover a special purpose or destiny for yourself. This purpose could have something to do with sharing truth or a higher form of knowledge with the world. Listen to the voice within and much will be revealed to you.

AFFIRMATION:

By listening to my inner voice, I find my special purpose in life that will direct me to the highest path.

THE SIX OF CLUBS IS YOUR LONG-RANGE CARD

The Six of Clubs is the card of intuition and of finding one's personal or professional path or destiny. If you are inclined towards development of your psychic ability or if you use it professionally, this could be a year of much progress in those areas. Your natural intuitive abilities are heightened for this year, and they become more the focus of your attention. Overall, this should be a year of relative stability for you. Peace and harmony with respect to all your communications are the order of the day. To maintain this harmony, one often has to make compromises and be willing to see things from other people's points of view.

Another aspect of this card is that of dealing with honesty and responsibility in communications. Under this powerful influence, you may have experiences that help you appreciate the value of these qualities, both in yourself and in others.

Many with this card have discovered a special purpose in their life in the year that it appeared, a purpose that was very meaningful and fulfilling. If you listen to the voice within, you may discover such a destiny for yourself too.

KEYWORDS:

A year of learning responsibility in communications and work, and a year of having enhanced intuitive abilities. I discover a special purpose for my life by tuning in to my inner self.

THE SIX OF CLUBS IS YOUR ENVIRONMENT CARD

This could be an important year for you in many ways that are more subtle and spiritual in nature. This is a year when you can listen to your inner voice and get important messages from your higher self. If you have always wanted to know what your life's purpose is, this is the year that you can make that discovery. This card often occurs at a key time in life when we realize our purpose. And for you, this purpose could entail bringing knowledge or wisdom to others.

THE SIX OF CLUBS IS YOUR DISPLACEMENT CARD

With this powerful card of karma and equality, it is highly likely that you will have to come to terms with some things you have done in your past and make amends. This card also has some other equally important influences that can affect you on many levels, so read carefully to understand what is happening.

First of all, you could have some experiences this year that occur as a result of things that you have been telling others that were either untrue or unjust in their application. For example, someone who has proclaimed to the world about their innocence in a certain manner, but who in fact is guilty, may get caught under this powerful karmic influence. The Six of Clubs can mean the settlement of an old score, and when this is the case, the effect of the settlement is equal to how long the misrepresentation has been going on and how many people were affected by it. However, if you have been truthful in your dealings and have not been using any specific philosophy that has been causing harm or pain to others, you have nothing to worry about. The negative aspects of this card only affect those who have been misusing the power of their spoken or written word. It is amazing though, how secrets can come out under this influence.

On the other hand, this card can have a powerful and positive effect on your work and career. This could be a year when you become much better known and recognized for your contributions. Someone employed in a regular job situation may get a raise or promotion. Others who are self-employed will find that their business takes off as the public becomes more conscious of what they are doing. This would be an ideal time to devote some of your resources to advertising or to getting into the media, because success in these areas is almost certain. All in all, this should be a hallmark year where work is concerned.

Finally, this card points to a need for more focus on one's purpose in life. Those people whose actions, plans, and work are part of some mission or purpose always achieve more than those whose life has no direction or meaning. This could be a year when circumstances cause you to reflect on your life and make a sincere effort to finding the path that is best for you. Once that path is found, you are obligated on a spiritual level to follow it to the best of your ability, regardless of external circumstances. Following the path you have set for yourself, or just finding the path that is meant for you, may be one of the significant challenges of this year.

Six of Diamonds

Peace at work, financial responsibility and karma, discovering one's special purpose

The Basic Meaning of the Six of Diamonds

Whenever this powerful stabilizing influence is present in your cards, you can bet there will be some sort of settling of accounts. Though this usually takes the form of financial debts being paid or repaid, it can manifest in payments of other forms of 'value.' The Six of Diamonds will also encourage you to make compromises where money is concerned and to take full responsibility for all your debts and actions that involve exchange of value.

When this card occurs in a prominent position, it could represent a time when we have an opportunity to discover a special purpose for our life that will lead us into a special destiny. If you feel drawn to a certain occupation or mission when this card is present, it could be one that opens up an entirely new and powerful direction for your life.

The Six of Diamonds in the Mercury Period

This card indicates a lack of change in business affairs and a smoothing out in this area. Under a Six of Diamonds, there is no escape from debts and obligations. So if you owe money, you may have to pay now. This works both ways. This influence does not support changes in business, and you may find any travel plans or business changes get postponed until later. Be prepared to settle up financially with anyone that you owe money to, especially if they are related to education or your vehicle.

The Six of Diamonds in the Venus Period

This card indicates that financial and social affairs are running smoothly and without changes, but be careful about falling into a comfortable rut at this time. There may be a settlement of a financial matter with a family member or loved one and this may just be the key to keeping the love flowing between you. Acting responsibly with all your money affairs will only bring you greater happiness and prosperity at this time.

The Six of Diamonds in the Mars Period

You may run into your own debts at this time. What happens is a reflection of your value system, so take heed. Honesty is the best policy now. Settlements of legal and business debts and difficulties will happen now, and you will get just what you deserve. You may have to make good on all promises you make now, so watch what you say and do. Don't let a fear of failure cause you to procrastinate on financial deals that you started earlier, as they are your best bet.

The Six of Diamonds in the Jupiter Period

During this period, you may receive payments owed to you by others that will contribute to your financial success. Allow yourself to receive. At the same time, your best success comes from remaining constant and from being open to compromise and adjustments within the context of your existing business agreements. Avoid speculation and gambling during this period. Just keep giving to others, and watch the returns keep coming in.

The Six of Diamonds in the Saturn Period

This card indicates a lack of change in money, health, or business, even when it is desired. Financial debts and obligations will be paid during this period, and they could be expensive, depending upon how you have handled matters in the past. Any deviations from strict honesty and fairness in your financial dealings could be very expensive in more ways than one. Though compromises and honesty may be difficult now, they are the only route to freedom.

You may be confronted with the results of things you did in the past now, and you may not like what you see or appreciate the timing. of having to pay for such actions now. But this is how karma works, and if you face it squarely and honestly, you will learn and grow from this experience.

The Six of Diamonds in the Uranus Period

This card can indicate a lack of change in location or type of work or the lack of sale or purchase of real estate. Everything will tend to remain static during this period, but your financial sixth sense may give you some invaluable insights into ways of making more money. Remember that you always receive exactly what you give to others, and during this period, you may have to unexpectedly pay off some outstanding obligations. Give more to receive more.

By tuning in to your most subtle thoughts and feelings now, you can make a strong connection to exactly what your life's purpose is, especially as it relates to your work and money-making enterprises.

The Six of Diamonds in the Neptune Period

This card represents either the delay of a long journey or one that is monotonous and disappointing. This is most likely a business-related journey. There may not be changes in any distant business interests either. However, you may intuitively realize new and perhaps secret ways to make money that could be profitable later. Just be as honest and clear in all your financial affairs as possible. Past debts may come into focus at this time.

One of the possible benefits of this card in Neptune is that you could discover or deepen your life's purpose. All that is required is for you to tune in to your thoughts and feelings, especially when you are alone or meditating.

The Six of Diamonds Is Your Pluto Card

The Six of Diamonds is a very strong influence for the settling out of financial matters and repayment of debts. Somehow, you are either dealing with these in a very big way this year or you are working on developing a definite sense of good values about your money and debts. Perhaps you are very much in debt and are facing the situation squarely and honestly, doing everything you can to meet your obligations. Or perhaps you are very restless by nature, and this year you want to acquire the benefits of working consistently in one vein. Sometimes, the Six of Diamonds creates a situation whereby financial matters remain somewhat static, and this can be challenging when a change is desired.

One of the greatest potentials of this card is that you could actually discover or deepen your connection to an important and meaningful purpose in your life. This card's appearance in this important spot could be the signal of the time in your life when you find something of greater meaning to stand for.

Whatever the case, you will be challenged to be successful with this Six of Diamonds influence, especially its meaning combined with the meaning of your Result Card for this year.

AFFIRMATION:

I learn the value of truthfulness and fairness in all of my financial dealings. I am discovering my true life's purpose.

THE SIX OF DIAMONDS IS YOUR RESULT CARD

As a result of dealing with your Pluto Card this year, you will end up settling some outstanding financial obligations that are either owed to you or by you. Challenging situations this year will show you the way to total fairness in your money and business dealings, resulting in a more mature and healthy attitude about money and debts. This will naturally lead to a stable financial condition as all past debts are settled and brought into balance.

The Six of Diamonds has another special significance as the Result Card of this year. That is, it could signal the time when you actually discover or deepen your connection to a special mission or purpose for your life. Since so many people are searching for their special purpose, you are extremely fortunate to have this opportunity happen at this time.

AFFIRMATION:

By listening to my inner voice, I find my special purpose in life that will direct me to the highest occupation. I strengthen my sense of responsibility in all financial matters.

THE SIX OF DIAMONDS IS YOUR LONG-RANGE CARD

The Six of Diamonds is a very steadying influence, and when it shows up as the Long-Range card, this influence extends strongly for an entire year. This can be good if you are in good financial shape when the year begins, because this card will tend to sustain whatever conditions were in effect when the year began. However it can be difficult if you enter the year lacking financially in some way. You could find yourself in a financial rut this year, struggling to get ahead and constantly beset with unpaid bills that sap your accounts.

This powerful 'karma card' insures that any imbalances in your financial picture will be evened out during this year. This may mean you pay off existing debts or you are repaid money you loaned earlier. It is wise to be totally responsible under this influence, as dishonest dealings are likely to receive immediate pay-back. On the other hand, if you recognize the inherent potential in this powerful card, you could get well ahead by always doing more than you were paid for in all your business and financial dealings. This is surely going to bring you additional returns, especially under the karmic money card. As you sow, so shall you reap.

In any event, many of your experiences this year will prove to

demonstrate the need for personal integrity and responsibility in all of your financial concerns.

In another vein, this card can mark a year in which you find a deeper purpose for your life and work. Any six in such a prominent position can signal a time when we discover something that we are fated to do. In this case, it would involve helping others to find a more meaningful set of values to base their life upon.

KEYWORDS:

A year of focus on financial responsibility, balancing of accounts, and compromise for balance in financial affairs. I open myself up to discovering a special and higher purpose for my life's work.

THE SIX OF DIAMONDS IS YOUR ENVIRONMENT CARD

This is a year when the most benefits come from sticking to whatever it is that you have been doing in your work. Though you may receive some financial pay-backs from others, don't expect many changes in your work or business. Instead, find ways to improve or to get more out of what you are already doing if you want the most success. Also, being honest and responsible with all your financial debts and dealings will bring additional blessings. The Mars period, in particular, should be very successful.

THE SIX OF DIAMONDS IS YOUR DISPLACEMENT CARD

Outstanding financial obligations, incurred by you in the past, may need to be settled this year, whether or not you may think they are fair or just. The truth is that whatever happens on a financial level will be just, but it may not appear that way from your personal perspective. As humans, our personal perspective is rarely complete or entirely accurate, and that is the reason we often rebel at things that we do not completely understand. As such, financial situations surrounding debts of any kind may surface this year, perhaps ones which have been outstanding for some time or at least kept in the background.

Another possible manifestation of this influence is that your current employment status, regardless of what it is, remains pretty much the same all year long. You may desire some changes in this area, and this card often indicates that things will remain as they are. In most cases, the best way to get the most from this card is to develop what we are already doing instead of seeking something new.

Finally, this card can often represent a year in which we do some soul-searching to find out more about our purpose and personal destiny. One becomes much more powerful when he or she has a definite sense of purpose in life. Finding that purpose or staying with it may be a significant issue for you this year.

Six of Spades

Fate and karma in action, paybacks from the past in many forms

The Basic Meaning of the Six of Spades

The Six of Spades is the strongest of the karma cards. When this card is present, you can expect a smoothing out of affairs in the realms of work and health. However, if you have had bad or negative habits in these areas or if your lifestyle has included any activities which have intentionally or inadvertently hurt others, you may have to settle your accounts when this powerful card appears. Whatever happens when this card appears, see that as a guidepost to make corrections in your path.

Sometimes events happen under this card's influence that are things which we were destined to do at some time in our life. Often, these events change the course of our life, always for the better, even though at the time the events may not seem so good or life-enhancing.

The Six of Spades will cause a settling of all affairs and at the same time bring some much-needed peace into your life. If, during that time, you take some time to tune in to your deepest thoughts and feelings, you may become aware of a special message for you that comes from inside. This message may lead you to perform a special mission in your life, one that uplifts others in some important way. The Six of Spades is the card of FATE.

THE SIX OF SPADES IN THE MERCURY PERIOD

During this period, you can expect steady employment, steady health, and the steady pursuit of educational goals. However, you could stay unemployed if you already are when you begin this period. At the same time, you will be encouraged to be responsible in your communications with others at this time and to make compromises to maintain peace and achieve your goals. Be aware of what you say and how you say it, or others may have to point it out for you.

THE SIX OF SPADES IN THE VENUS PERIOD

This period should be one of steadiness in areas of finances, love life, and work. You will want to create peace in your home and most intimate relationships. To do this, you may have to make adjustments on behalf of those you love and learn the art of responsibility in love. The other possibility of this powerful card would be that of starting a 'karmic' relationship. This would be a 'fated' or destined relationship where one of you owes the other and have returned to pay or collect a debt.

THE SIX OF SPADES IN THE MARS PERIOD

This period may bring the settlement of a lawsuit or of some dealings with men. This card indicates steady employment and steady health and neutralizes any influence that promotes change. If you are involved in a legal matter, rest assured that the outcome will be strictly just in all ways. You should be careful of all aggressive actions and expressions now, as this powerful karmic influence promises that you will get back exactly what you put out.

THE SIX OF SPADES IN THE JUPITER PERIOD

During this period, your business and financial interests should be running smoothly and steadily. Staying in your current business brings the most rewards now, and it may be difficult to effect any changes now. Look for ways that you can get more out of what you are doing with whom you are currently involved. It is likely that there are some favors or rewards owed you that will come your way before this period ends. The more you give, the more you will receive.

THE SIX OF SPADES IN THE SATURN PERIOD

Any physical problems you face now are likely to be the result of an accumulation of bad health habits from the past. As this is a 'triple karmic' influence, most any area of your life could be the one where you are receiving payment for past thoughts, words, or actions that were hurtful to others or to your own body. Now is the time to take full responsibility for your health, work, and lifestyle and to be willing to make proper amends to correct any problems.

This is the strongest card of fate in the whole deck. Because the Saturn Period is also a karmic or 'fated' period, it triples the influence. Seeing this card coming, it is wise to take stock of your actions in the past and assume as much responsibility as you can for your deeds. It is especially important to make sure that your health and work habits are positive, honest, and healthful as you approach this period. Everything in your life that is out of balance will probably be brought into balance in a somewhat relentless and often extreme manner.

THE SIX OF SPADES IN THE URANUS PERIOD

This period will be marked by a lack of change in business, labor relations, a property deal, or your health, regardless of whether or not it was desired. It will take extra effort to initiate almost anything now, so you may feel like you are stuck in a rut. This card is very good for psychics or natural healers, as it bestows more of those gifts during this period. Your own intuition will be active and available to you if you choose to become aware of it.

This is such a powerful karmic influence that you may find that you have to face the consequences of one or more of your actions or words from the past. Things that are 'fated' often occur under the influence of the Six of Spades.

By tuning in to your most subtle thoughts and feelings now, you can make a strong connection to exactly what is your life's purpose, especially as it relates to your work and career.

THE SIX OF SPADES IN THE NEPTUNE PERIOD

During this period, you may have a long and monotonous journey, or a journey you had planned gets canceled or postponed. The steadying influence of the Six of Spades will usually counteract most proposed changes in location, work, or health now. This is an excellent influence for spiritual/intuitive studies, and you may have a keen appreciation of life and the mysteries of self. Your understanding of the laws of cause and effect will help you overcome situations of discord with others.

One of the possible benefits of this card in Neptune is that you could discover or deepen your life's purpose. All that is required is for you to tune in to your thoughts and feelings, especially when you are alone or meditating.

THE SIX OF SPADES IS YOUR PLUTO CARD

Health and work issues could take the spotlight for you this year as this heavy-duty 'karma card' brings you the results of your past actions, both good and bad. The Six of Spades card tends to create peace and balance in all things, and this may require the payment of past debts. If you have not been good to your body lately, now is the time you may be forced into making changes. The same goes for work and other lifestyle areas.

Another major objective for you this year will be having to contend with some sort of static situation in your work or health that perhaps you are wanting to be different. The Six of Spades is a strong influence of things in stasis, not changing. It can prevent travel, moves, changes in employment or health, so it is wise to have these areas in good condition before the year begins. It can indicate a year of trying to get a job or trying to change jobs and having to contend with a lack of success or change in that area. Your success this year will come from acknowledging the current situation and making compromises and adjustments to get the most out of what is already there.

Maintain balance at all costs. This is your key to success. This card can also indicate a less than desirable health condition that keeps reminding you of a need to change your health habits. Your Result Card will give you more information about this static situation or tell you who is involved in it.

One of the greatest potentials of this card is that you could actually discover or deepen your connection to an important and meaningful purpose in your life. This card's appearance in this important spot could be the signal of the time in your life when you find something of greater meaning to stand for.

AFFIRMATION:

I am learning to take responsibility for my health, my work, and life habits. I learn to make compromises. I am discovering my true life's purpose.

THE SIX OF SPADES IS YOUR RESULT CARD

Somehow connected to your Pluto Card, this year is the element of responsibility and compromise. The appearance of the Six of Spades suggests that one of your major goals for this year is associated with the payment of past obligations of some kind. These may be related to work, health, or almost any area of life. Rest assured that by your next birthday you will have realized the importance of being responsible for your actions and will have made considerable progress.

This card can also bring you a special gift by your next birthday. You could discover, by turning your attention within, a special purpose for your life, one that could inspire you to accomplish great things. This purpose could transform your life, giving it more meaningful direction.

AFFIRMATION:

By listening to my inner voice, I find my special purpose in life that will direct me to the highest occupation. I strengthen my sense of responsibility in all health and work matters.

THE SIX OF SPADES IS YOUR LONG-RANGE CARD

This will be a year with many possible levels of experience, all under the influence of the powerful Six of Spades. On a purely mundane level, the Six of Spades says that this will be a year of few, if any, changes in work, health, occupation, or place of residence. This can be good if you are in a good situation when the year begins. However, if you are unemployed when this year begins, you may have to contend with not having a new job for an entire year, so strong is the 'lack of change' influence of this card. There will probably be fewer opportunities for travel this year and no changes in residence.

On a deeper level, the Six of Spades has a strong 'balancing the scales' influence to it. It says that you will get exactly what you give this year, both in your work and in regards to your own health. If you are experiencing any health difficulties this year, they will most likely be the result of your not giving enough attention to your health. To improve your health under this influence, all you have to do is to put some constructive energy into loving your body and starting more healthful habits. On the work scene, you may find yourself involved in having to make compromises and adjustments, giving in a little or taking a little so that your entire work scene may run smoothly. Keeping a balance in all your affairs is a major theme this year.

Finally, the Six of Spades is the card of 'fate,' and 'destiny.' Many times when this card is present, we have major turning points that lead us to our ultimate destiny. If you take the time to tune in to your deepest thoughts and feelings, you may get an important message as to where you will go next and what you will do.

KEYWORDS:

A year of learning to be responsible for your work, health habits, and lifestyle. A year of keeping the peace and perhaps one of discovering a special and meaningful purpose for my life's work.

THE SIX OF SPADES IS YOUR ENVIRONMENT CARD

This is the card of 'fate' and if you pay attention, this could be a year of fateful events that lead you to your destiny in an important way. The highest meaning of this card would say that this is the year that you find out what truly your life's purpose is and when you set out to make a commitment to that purpose. On the other hand, the more mundane meaning of this card is that you will benefit from staying with the same job and finding ways to improve it.

THE SIX OF SPADES IS YOUR DISPLACEMENT CARD

This is likely to be a significant year, one that will have a powerful effect on your life, depending upon the current status of your life and the things you have done in your past. The Six of Spades is the strongest of all the karmic influences, one that promises that any outstanding debts will be settled and dealt with. These debts may be of many kinds, though the suit of Spades is primarily concerned with work and health. So, the first place to look for indications of what this card will mean to you are these areas. Have you maintained good work and health habits, or have you been leading a less than healthy lifestyle for quite some time? If the latter is true, you may expect some health difficulties this year, as all of these habits come to the surface and must be dealt with. The intensity of these health challenges will be proportional to your past habits and the length of time you have been doing them.

This card can also represent a repayment of negative karma from other past situations. Spades are associated with our will, which can translate into legal or other struggles with others. If you have been in a highly competitive or antagonistic involvement with anyone, this year will likely represent a time when these scores are settled for better or worse. Regardless of whether or not you think the outcome is fair, it will be.

This influence is especially fortunate for work and career. Many people ascend to great recognition and accomplishment while this card is present in this placement. This influence helps those in business and finance the most, promising great rewards and the opportunity for expansion. Any opportunities for expansion will likely lead to greater success.

An underlying theme of this card is that of finding our personal destiny or purpose. You will probably get some opportunities this year to fine-tune your direction in life and have the chance to discard any activities that are not contributing to you achieving your most heartfelt goals and desires.

Regardless of your personal situation, destined events are very likely to occur this year, ones that will change the course of your life in a significant way. As all of this is going on, practice fairness in all of your dealings, and you will be directed to the right path for you and your fulfillment.

Seven of Hearts

Learning unconditional love and non-attachment in relationships

The Basic Meaning of the Seven of Hearts

The Seven of Hearts indicates that whatever time this card appears could be marked by many challenges in love and feelings in your close relationships. The Seven of Hearts can manifest as betrayal by those we love. In any case, we will be tested to see just how attached we are to others being a certain way.

Seven, being a highly spiritual number, promises success in love if you try a new approach and adopt a more selfless or unattached attitude. If we can allow others to be who they are and not place so many demands upon them, we not only become more aware of their true personalities, but also we allow ourselves the freedom to be just who we are and experience just how it feels to be free of fear and attachment. Many high spiritual experiences have occurred while a seven was present.

THE SEVEN OF HEARTS IN THE MERCURY PERIOD

You are likely to have sudden and unexpected trouble or change in a friendship during this period. Jealousy and disruptions can arise unexpectedly and cause problems and disappointment. This will not be a long-lasting problem though; it will probably pass away as quickly as it arrives. Use tact and diplomacy in all your communications now to avoid arguments or misunderstandings. Drop your attachment to your ideas and people for best results.

Your other Mercury Card may indicate who or what is involved in the personal challenge indicated by this card. A powerful card, such as a Four, Eight or Ten, would help mitigate its challenges and bring a happy outcome to the situation as well. This is a spiritual love card and will bring success only by facing and letting go of fear and attachments.

THE SEVEN OF HEARTS IN THE VENUS PERIOD

An unfaithful friend or lover may be the cause of a considerable emotional disappointment during this period. Unreliable friends or associates can cause many problems. The major lesson is not to be so naive in your friendships. You may find that you are giving out your trust and friendships before knowing just who you are giving them to. Some may not be as they appear and do not deserve the trust you are bestowing upon them. See others as they truly are.

Your other Venus Card may tell you who or what the emotional or personal challenge is about. Also keep in mind that a strong or powerful other Venus Card, such as a Four, Eight or Ten, could mitigate the adversity of this card and bring about very positive results from a challenging situation.

THE SEVEN OF HEARTS IN THE MARS PERIOD

This period may bring a fearful and challenging legal or personal matter, perhaps associated with a man. Your own willfulness or arguing will only decrease your chances of success in the situations present. Look carefully at your expectations and attachments for the key to the present events. You will have much more success than you realize by acting upon the faith that you have nothing or no one to lose. Spiritual revelations are possible now as well.

Look to your other Mars Card to find out what or who is involved in the challenges that may arise during this period. Also keep in mind that a positive card, such as a Four, Eight, or Ten, would tell you that regardless of the challenges present, you are likely to have a happy and productive outcome to the situations that present themselves during this fifty-two-day period.

THE SEVEN OF HEARTS IN THE JUPITER PERIOD

It is possible that challenging situations may arise now connected to love and money. If you have mixed these two together and have some attachments to people or money, you may find yourself in a quandary. On the other hand, this blessed spiritual influence will make it much easier than usual to adopt a giving and selfless attitude in love and business. If you do, you stand the chance of experiencing more love and financial prosperity than you can imagine.

THE SEVEN OF HEARTS IN THE SATURN PERIOD

Jealousy, fearful attachments, and betrayal could be the cause of considerable emotional trauma during this period. This, in turn, could have a negative effect on your health. You may feel betrayed by someone, or situations have arisen that threaten your feeling of security in your personal relationships. Often, your other Saturn Card may be the Birth Card of someone who is a part of this scenario. You are being challenged now to practice non-attachment in your closest relationships and to overcome your fears of abandonment. You may feel as though you are being forced to make a sacrifice now, but if you apply your wisdom to the current situation, you could learn the value of real love.

Also, bear in mind that the difficulties or challenges indicated by this card could be offset by a strong card in the other position, for example, any of the Fours, Eights, or Tens.

THE SEVEN OF HEARTS IN THE URANUS PERIOD

Unexpected challenges with friends, associations, or co-workers may arise during this period. You could feel betrayed or abandoned by those in your circle of friends or acquaintances that you care for. You are now being challenged to drop your fears and attachments to others and let them be the individuals they are. Your other card for this period may be a person you are attached to. On the positive side, you are given an opportunity to experience the high side of unconditional love, which could result in a dramatic opening of your heart and mind. We often find ourselves counseling and helping others when this card is present.

This is a good influence for spiritual matters, learning new spiritual information, attending classes, etc. Also, keep in mind that a positive card, such as a Four, Eight, or Ten, in the other position of this period would offset any problematic situations that may arise and bring about good results overall.

THE SEVEN OF HEARTS IN THE NEPTUNE PERIOD

Though the influences present can bring a powerful opening of your heart and an experience of unconditional love, it most often brings challenges around personal attachments to someone or some cherished dreams. Perhaps you are planning a vacation and something goes wrong. The answers to your problems lie within. You have the power to look inside yourself and make meaningful evaluations. Challenge your own fantasies in the name of truth and love.

THE SEVEN OF HEARTS IS YOUR PLUTO CARD

This year you are likely to be challenged many times in the area of personal relationships. Either friends, family, or lovers will cause you to see areas where you hold expectations and attachments to others loving you in certain ways. At times, you may feel hurt or victimized by others, and you may be tempted to blame others for your hurt feelings. A deeper examination will reveal that you have set yourself up for these downfalls by placing unreasonable demands upon those you love and care for. You will learn to rise above this level of attachment this year to a new way of being in personal relationships that is more healthy and expansive than those in the past.

You may also have gotten involved in some sort of humanitarian work or counseling work where you give a lot to others, and this also may challenge you at times during the year. This is a year of developing a spiritual and unattached love for those in your life and to give both them and yourself the freedom to be who they are.

Look to your Result Card to find out who, specifically, may be involved in this raising of 'love consciousness' or to see what else is involved in it.

AFFIRMATION:

I am learning how to experience unconditional love for others, and in the process, I set myself free.

THE SEVEN OF HEARTS IS YOUR RESULT CARD

Though this year may seem to be full of problems from time to time, in actuality, you have taken on a very important challenge and work. This challenge is to love others unconditionally. This means you have to face your personal fears that have chained you to automatic reactions that are less than what you ultimately desire for yourself. This will not always be an easy process. You may feel betrayed or even abandoned by others in the process. By contacting the higher forces within yourself, you will emerge victorious from this important battle.

AFFIRMATION:

I create high spiritual and unattached love among those closest to me. I learn to release attachments and fears.

THE SEVEN OF HEARTS IS YOUR LONG-RANGE CARD

The Seven of Hearts indicates that this year could be marked by many challenges in love and feelings in your close relationships. Seven, being a highly spiritual number, promises success in love only by letting go of attachments, thinking less of your personal needs, and giving more of yourself. It may appear that your closest friends, family, or lovers are letting you down at various times throughout the year.

Look for the hidden lessons in these experiences. See now that you are being called upon to let go of petty attachments and adopt a larger viewpoint. Let your spiritual power rise up and conquer this area, and you will find that you are transformed into a much happier, fulfilled person. For those involved in spiritual work, this card signals much progress and success during this year. It could be a very successful year of giving of yourself, especially in such roles as counselor or personal helper.

KEYWORDS:

A year of learning to release fears and attachments concerning others and their love for us. I learn to trust.

THE SEVEN OF HEARTS IS YOUR ENVIRONMENT CARD

This could be the year that you have a real experience of unconditional love. As you allow others to be who they are, you also allow yourself to be yourself, and in this way, you will be able to experience a new sense of personal freedom. To be totally free means having no attachments to others and no worries about whether or not they love us. It also means having a knowing that there will always be enough love in our life, because it comes from within.

THE SEVEN OF HEARTS IS YOUR DISPLACEMENT CARD

This is likely to be a year in which you face some of your own emotional insecurity and learn to allow others in your life to have more freedom from your emotional manipulation. The Seven can bring a feeling of freedom from our fears of abandonment and betrayal and a true experience of spiritual and unconditional love. However, this only occurs after we recognize our fears and attachments and decide to make an effort toward letting go of our need to make those we love behave in a certain manner. You will be called upon to make this adjustment this year, and it will require some effort and determination in order to achieve a more loving way of being. This year is one of those that we call a 'spiritual cycle.' Things on the external level may seem to be difficult, and this would especially hold true in your personal relationships. That is not to say that all of your relationships will be difficult, but there will be one or more that will cause you to look deeper inside yourself for the answers to the challenges they present. This will be a year of letting go for you and one in which you are likely to make a sacrifice of some personal desires for something higher in nature, perhaps something that will benefit others in your life. Follow your inspiration, and be open to taking the higher path in your personal life. Though difficult at times, it will lead you to a place of more inner peace and of truly loving relationships.

Seven of Clubs

Dealing with our negativity, exposure to spiritual knowledge

The Basic Meaning of the Seven of Clubs

When the Seven of Clubs is present, you will either be exposed to spiritual knowledge, which is knowledge that leads one back to the self, or you will be challenged to let go of mental attitudes and beliefs that are keeping you trapped on lower levels of thought. The lowest side of this card is negative thinking. The highest side is mental and spiritual revelation, expanded consciousness. How it manifests for you will depend upon your ability to elevate your thinking.

THE SEVEN OF CLUBS IN THE MERCURY PERIOD

During this period, and this year to a lesser extent, you are being exposed to higher ways of thinking and will be given opportunities to transform negativity into revelation. Perhaps you have become attached to some plans or ideas that are being challenged. Maybe you notice how much you are worrying and want to change it. Now is the time to practice positive affirmations. You truly are what you think, and now you are given a chance to prove it.

Your other Mercury Card may tell you who or what you are learning to develop a more positive attitude about. In any case, a strong bottom card, such as a Four, Eight, or Ten, would help mitigate the negative aspects of this card, which can bring a lot of worry or frustration.

On the high side, this is a great influence for your acquiring some new information on the spiritual side of things. Keep on the look out for good books, tapes, and workshops that may open you up to a different side of life.

THE SEVEN OF CLUBS IN THE VENUS PERIOD

This period could bring challenges or obstacles to your most heart-felt desires. This could manifest as an argument with a woman or loved one. You may be the subject of gossip or have opposition to plans, especially related to love. You can transform any negative experiences now by elevating your attitudes and letting go of fear and attachments. Bear in mind that your own plans may not be the best for you, that something better is possible if your mind is open.

Your other Venus Card may tell you who or what the emotional or personal challenge is about. Also, keep in mind that a strong or powerful other Venus Card, such as a Four, Eight, or Ten, could mitigate the adversity of this card and bring about very positive results from a challenging situation.

THE SEVEN OF CLUBS IN THE MARS PERIOD

This is a strong influence for arguments, ones that bring on problems, worry, and pessimism. Your relationships with men in general could be a bit difficult during this period, but the solution to your problems lies within you, not in them. Opposition to your plans or desires can illicit anger and negativity in you at this time.

Caution is advised in all legal matters and affairs with men until you can take full responsibility for your attitudes and beliefs. Fear is often at the root of all anger and negative thinking. Elevate your mind now with positive affirmations, and expose yourself to sources of spiritual knowledge and inspiration to get the most good from this period.

Look to your other Mars Card to find out what or who is involved in the challenges that may arise during this period. Also, keep in mind that a positive card, such as a Four, Eight, or Ten, would tell

you that regardless of the challenges present, you are likely to have a happy and productive outcome to the situations that present themselves during this fifty-two-day period.

THE SEVEN OF CLUBS IN THE JUPITER PERIOD

Any challenges in business or finances during this period can be traced to negative attitudes or self-limiting plans and ideas. Now is the time to expand your thinking and elevate your thoughts for business and personal success. Exposure to any form of spiritual knowledge will be profitable in more ways than one and will help you attain the high states of realization associated with this card. Remember that thoughts are things and that you are who you think you are. This card can bring financial and spiritual rewards from the study of mystical knowledge or self-improvement subjects.

THE SEVEN OF CLUBS IN THE SATURN PERIOD

Negative attitudes, worry, and pessimism can affect your health at this time. In some cases, scandal or backbiting are involved. A positive attitude, patience, and mental discipline are a MUST in order to maintain your well-being. During this period, you will be faced squarely with the effects of your own negative attitudes and beliefs. Spiritual and mental discipline is the key to mastering not only yourself, but any problems on the external level.

Also, bear in mind that the difficulties or challenges indicated by this card could be offset by a strong card in the other Saturn position, for example, any of the Fours, Eights, or Tens.

THE SEVEN OF CLUBS IN THE URANUS PERIOD

This period could bring unexpected trouble or doubts related to work, a friend, or a real estate transaction. Perhaps some plans you have made were unexpectedly interrupted. Under this highly spiritual influence, you must be prepared to let go of your plans and adopt a positive attitude in spite of whatever circumstances present themselves. Then you may experience the 'higher mind' potential of this card, cosmic consciousness, and freedom from worry and concern.

This is a good influence for spiritual matters, learning new spiritual information, attending classes, etc. Also, keep in mind that a positive card, such as a Four, Eight, or Ten, in the other position of this period would offset any problematic situations that may arise and bring about good results overall.

THE SEVEN OF CLUBS IN THE NEPTUNE PERIOD

This is an influence of worrying over imaginary problems. Your confusion could stem from a heightened imagination, stimulated by Neptune. Strive for balance and common sense. Some cherished ideal may be thwarted or confused by events. Travel may have many disappointing experiences connected with it. However, if you apply the spiritual quality of this card by releasing fears and attachments to your plans, you could experience the higher consciousness of this card.

This is an excellent influence for the pursuit of spiritual knowledge—reading books, taking classes, etc. that will deepen your understanding of life and how you fit into it.

THE SEVEN OF CLUBS IS YOUR PLUTO CARD

This year you have taken on, or will be handed, a major challenge, which will bring your thinking up to a more positive and productive level. Whether by your own hand or forced upon you by events and circumstances, you will discover that your own thinking is the source of many of your problems and that you have the power to change them by changing your attitudes and thoughts. Attachments to old ways of looking at things will have to be let go of as you elevate yourself and your life by using your mind to create a better life.

Much of the knowledge to accomplish this goal may come through spiritual or uplifting books or classes. You may be exposed to many new ideas and concepts, and though you may see that these new ideas and concepts can help you, they will not always be easy to put into practice. However, this card guarantees that you have the power to make the necessary changes and be successful with this internal struggle. Your Result Card will either point to someone who will help you accomplish this goal or give you more information about what is involved in this new way of thinking.

AFFIRMATION:

I am enlightening my mind and transforming my negative thoughts into positive, higher levels of thinking.

The Seven of Clubs Is Your Result Card

The Seven of Clubs as the Result Card means you will learn to let go of self-defeating patterns of thinking and communicating. To overcome the challenges that you face this year, you will adopt positive attitudes or new sets of beliefs. You may be learning or sharing spiritual wisdom, or perhaps someone or something will remind you that 'As a man thinketh, so he is.' Your Pluto Card will give you more information about the new, positive, spiritual consciousness that you achieve.

AFFIRMATION:

I raise my consciousness to more positive, uplifting thoughts and beliefs. I spiritualize my thinking.

The Seven of Clubs Is Your Long-Range Card

This year you will be adopting some new and powerful ways of thinking that will change your life for the better and help you overcome any negative aspects of your thinking that are keeping you back. It is also likely that you will be sharing these new models for thinking with others. A realization that your own thought patterns are largely responsible for the success or failure in your life is prompting you to consciously adopt new patterns of thought and belief. You may be reading new books or taking workshops that reveal to you the science of positive affirmations. As you practice these affirmations, you will

want to share them with others, and much internal success can be had by doing just that. In practicing positive thinking and sharing that with others, it is likely that you will arrive at a new plateau of consciousness and have many mini-enlightenments as you go through this powerful year.

The Seven of Clubs is called the card of 'spiritual knowledge.' Any study of philosophies and ideas related to the higher mind or spiritual ways of thinking will bring you nothing but good this year.

KEYWORDS:

I am influenced by higher knowledge, and I am learning to transform negative thinking into enlightened mind power.

The Seven of Clubs Is Your Environment Card

This is a year that you could receive many benefits from exposure to 'spiritual knowledge.' Spiritual knowledge comprises any sort of information that leads us back to a deeper understanding of ourselves. So, you could take some workshops, read some new books, or meet new people who expose you to some of this knowledge. If so, open yourself up to receive. This information will be nothing less than a blessing in your life and a source of many good things.

The Seven of Clubs Is Your Displacement Card

Underlying all the different events and experiences of this year will be a subtle personal challenge that you will be facing and working on. This will likely be that of your learning to adopt a more positive attitude and a more positive expression of your ideas, feelings, etc. The Seven of Clubs represents a higher, spiritual mind. In its highest state, this card brings profound realizations about the true meanings of life along with a sense of unencumbered freedom from all of life's worries and fears. You might says that this is one of your goals this year, to achieve more of the high side of this card. In doing so, you may face negative patterns of thought and communications that are holding you back in an old habitually negative response to life. If you are interested in spiritual philosophy and concepts, this will be the year that you have to put these into solid practice.

This may seem like a difficult year in some respects, but it has a very good purpose as seen from a higher perspective. You are being prepared for a rebirth into a newer and much higher life than you have been living lately. After all, you are in the middle of one of the most significant cycles of your life, one which peaks next year as you reach the Pinnacle position. This year of mental house-cleaning will be just the right kind of preparation you need to fully experience the wonderful changes that are coming.

Seven of Diamonds

Financial challenges, learning appreciation for things valued

The Basic Meaning of the Seven of Diamonds

The Seven of Diamonds is one of the spiritual money cards. When it appears, we are always confronted with how attached we are to our money and given an opportunity to experience the real prosperity that comes with an attitude of gratitude.

Whether it is about money, plans to make money, or love, situations will present themselves that test our faith in the abundance of the universe. By realizing and then releasing our fears, we can transform our attachment into total fearlessness and personal freedom.

THE SEVEN OF DIAMONDS IN THE MERCURY PERIOD

This period could bring an unexpected expenditure or loss of money that leaves you feeling poor and afraid. Your own impulsiveness or extravagant spending may be at the root of this. This is not a good influence for speculation, gambling, or any get rich quick schemes. Whatever the specifics, situations during this period are encouraging you to drop your fears about money and adopt an abundance consciousness that will attract more money than you thought possible.

If you have a positive and powerful other Mercury Card, such as a Four, Eight, or Ten, the chances are that whatever problems you may encounter financially during this period will be overcome with ease. In other cases, this same bottom card could reveal who or what is involved in the challenges presented. Also keep in mind that things that happen in the Mercury period tend to be very short-lived and soon over.

THE SEVEN OF DIAMONDS IN THE VENUS PERIOD

A Seven of Diamonds in Venus means spending money on friends, lovers, or some lady friend or relative. A lot of money could be spent on luxury items or close friends. You are feeling very extravagant now, and this may be masking an emotional insecurity and desire to be loved. However, your true fears will be exposed now, and you will have to deal with your inner feelings of insecurity about money and love. Practice appreciation and affirmations to fill this inner void.

Your other Venus Card may tell you who or what the financial, emotional, or personal challenge is about. Also keep in mind that a strong or powerful other Venus Card, such as a Four, Eight, or Ten, could mitigate the adversity of this card and bring about very positive results from a challenging situation.

THE SEVEN OF DIAMONDS IN THE MARS PERIOD

This period will present a financial challenge from an investment, payment, or loss. This could have been as the result of a legal matter, an argument, gambling, or speculation. Your own aggressive nature and impatience could have played a major role in this. At the root of any money problems will be a fear of poverty and attachment to money plans. Take responsibility for your core attitudes, and you could turn this adversity into unexpected prosperity.

Look to your other Mars Card to find out what or who is involved in the challenges that may arise during this period. Also keep in mind that a positive card, such as a Four, Eight, or Ten, would tell you that regardless of the challenges present, you are likely to have a happy and productive outcome to the situations that present themselves during this fifty-two-day period.

THE SEVEN OF DIAMONDS IN THE JUPITER PERIOD

This card here is called the 'Millionaire's Card.' It often indicates a great deal of money being spent, but also a lot coming in to cover it as well. If you are feeling prosperous during this period, you could attract huge amounts of money. Of course, this will not occur if your prosperous thinking is only masking an inner fear of poverty and limited resources. But the chances are good for overcoming any fears about money and realizing the 'Lucky Seven' side of this card now. This card can also mean a large financial investment in your business or occupation for the purposes of expansion.

THE SEVEN OF DIAMONDS IN THE SATURN PERIOD

This card indicates a loss of money connected with the ill health of yourself, an associate, friend, or relative or a lack of funds as the cause of your own health problems. During this period, you will be faced squarely with your inner level of prosperity or poverty, and you may feel forced to contend with a fearful lack of funds. Through application of positive thinking and appreciation for what you have, you can turn this into financial success.

Also bear in mind that the difficulties or challenges indicated by this card could be offset by a strong card in the other position, for example, any of the Fours, Eights, or Tens.

THE SEVEN OF DIAMONDS IN THE URANUS PERIOD

This influence can bring an unexpected or unusual loss or outlay of money, or a situation with real estate, labor (employees), or speculation that leaves you feeling worried about money. You are given an opportunity now to experience an unfettered knowingness of prosperity and abundance if you choose. All you have to do is practice appreciation and follow your intuitive knowingness that you are safe and protected in the abundance of this magnificent universe.

This is a good influence for spiritual matters, learning new spiritual information, attending classes, etc. Also, keep in mind that a positive card, such as a Four, Eight, or Ten, in the other position of this period would offset any problematic situations that may arise and bring about good results overall.

THE SEVEN OF DIAMONDS IN THE NEPTUNE PERIOD

Unclarity and miscommunications could be the cause of situations that promote a general feeling of worry about money and finances during this period. At the same time, your chances of overcoming this fear are heightened by the spiritual position of this card. Rest assured that you can overcome any apparent lack of funds by practicing appreciation for what you have and realizing that your inner self is the source of all prosperity and wealth.

THE SEVEN OF DIAMONDS IS YOUR PLUTO CARD

Challenging financial situations could be a major theme for you this year. The time has come for you to take on more responsibility for your financial condition, but not from an external point of view. The mystical Seven of Diamonds says that prosperity can be attained through inner mastery.

Thoughts are things. If you are fearful about money and think about how much you don't have, you are attracting more poverty to you. Whatever form the financial challenges take this year, you can be sure that the roots of them are your attitudes and beliefs about money and prosperity and that the time has come to face yourself in this important area. Change your attitude, and you change the results, which in the case of the lucky Seven of Diamonds could result in a huge financial gain.

Your Result Card this year will further define the nature of your financial challenges this year or point to a person who is directly related to them.

AFFIRMATION:

I am learning how to create and maintain unlimited true abundance in my life by transforming my attitudes about possessions and money.

THE SEVEN OF DIAMONDS IS YOUR RESULT CARD

One of your major challenges this year will be to overcome worry or concern about money. If handled successfully, you may end up this year with more money than you ever have imagined. This may not be an easy task, as you may have to dismantle old attitudes and beliefs that tell you your financial status is controlled by forces outside of yourself. As you reclaim your power, your Pluto Card will be there to guide your way.

Success with the Seven of Diamonds requires that we carry on with our work and our life in spite of financial conditions that may be less than ideal. It also requires that we exhibit trust and faith that everything will be fine. The best tool at your disposal to get the highest and best manifestation from this powerful spiritual influence is gratitude.

AFFIRMATION:

I am learning to achieve fearlessness about my finances and to trust in the abundance of the universe.

THE SEVEN OF DIAMONDS IS YOUR LONG-RANGE CARD

During this year, you will learn some valuable lessons about money and its role in your life. Through some possibly challenging cir-

cumstances and situations, you will be confronted with your inner attitudes about money and your own level of inner prosperity. Are you feeling prosperous, or are you feeling impoverished? The Seven of Diamonds will put this inner state in front of you so you can see how your inner states are the source of your external reality. If you find yourself up against financial problems of one sort or another this year, ask yourself if you are in a state of fear or a state of relaxation about money and things in your life. This influence promises great material success once you adopt an inner attitude of prosperity and gratitude. You could have a direct and powerful experience of being provided for and taken care of by the universe under this auspicious spiritual influence.

This card has been called the 'millionaire's card,' so powerful is its effect when one has adopted the attitude of prosperity that it calls for.

KEYWORDS:

I am learning that prosperity is a state of mind and that gratitude attracts wealth. I appreciate all that I have.

THE SEVEN OF DIAMONDS IS YOUR ENVIRONMENT CARD

The Seven of Diamonds will never be anyone's Environment Card due to the fact that it is one of the Semi-Fixed Cards.

In a Weekly Reading, the Seven of Diamonds Environment Card will bring a sense of freedom around money issues and possibly some wonderful financial gains.

THE SEVEN OF DIAMONDS IS YOUR DISPLACEMENT CARD

The Seven of Diamonds will never be anyone's Displacement Card due to the fact that it is one of the Semi-Fixed Cards.

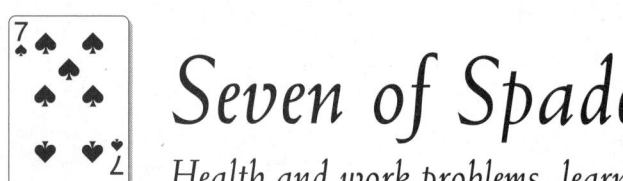

Seven of Spades

Health and work problems, learning to practice faith

The Basic Meaning of the Seven of Spades

The powerful Seven of Spades will challenge you to rise to higher levels of thinking, speaking, and acting. Its challenges will manifest mainly in the areas of work and health, areas where you are likely to be holding some negative patterns that need to be changed. If you are willing to take responsibility for your condition and practice positivity in spite of circumstances, you can realize the powerful spiritual potential of this card and attain new heights. In its highest form, this is the card of Faith.

THE SEVEN OF SPADES IN THE MERCURY PERIOD

This card can bring an illness connected with the head in some way, such as a headache or toothache, or in some cases, an accident of some kind. This period could also bring some trouble with your work or driving. The good news is that, because this is the Mercury period, this situation will probably be very quick and painless. Things happen quickly in Mercury and don't have a major impact on our life in general. Still, it would be a good idea to take a look at your work, thinking, and health habits now, and see if one or more of them may need upgrading to a more positive and healthful level. Exposure to spiritual wisdom will help you elevate yourself and may bring a profound realization of truth.

Your other Mercury Card may tell you who or what is involved in the challenge of this Seven of Spades. Also keep in mind that a strongly positive card, such as a Four, Eight, or Ten as the bottom card, could bring a very positive outcome to the situation at hand.

THE SEVEN OF SPADES IN THE VENUS PERIOD

This card can indicate illness connected with too much partying, a romantic involvement, or some lady friend. There could be an illness of a close friend, lover, or family member that presents challenges now as well. It is likely that whatever the specifics, your inner attitudes or habits are at the root of any personal difficulties you have. Now is the time to examine your fears about getting enough affection and practice letting others be as they are.

Your other Venus Card may tell you who or what the emotional or personal challenge is about. Also keep in mind that a strong or powerful other Venus Card, such as a four, eight or ten, could mitigate the adversity of this card and bring about very positive results from a challenging situation.

THE SEVEN OF SPADES IN THE MARS PERIOD

This period can bring illness caused by overdoing it in work or passion or trouble from some male. This can also represent difficulties in a legal matter. Indulging in negativity at this time will only make matters worse. This period may be marked by much arguing, conflict, and disappointment. This card represents a challenge, one which can best be met by a careful self-examination of negative attitudes and emotional habits.

Look to your other Mars Card to find out what or who is involved in the challenges that may arise during this period. Also keep in mind that a positive card, such as a Four, Eight, or Ten, would tell you that regardless of the challenges present, you are likely to have a happy and productive outcome to the situations that present themselves during this fifty-two-day period.

THE SEVEN OF SPADES IN THE JUPITER PERIOD

This period can bring on an illness related to worry about money or work, perhaps from overworking. You just might be overdoing things now, and fear may be the reason for it. This can also indicate money spent or time lost through illness. This card is a powerful spiritual influence, giving you more than the usual support to conquer your mundane problems through the application of faith, gratitude, wisdom, self-honesty, and discipline. Develop a positive mental attitude.

Any attempts to help others or to adopt a more sincere basis for your work could result in greater prosperity for you now. This powerful card of 'faith' could also bring the realization of many of life's deeper mysteries.

This is typically considered a difficult card to have in any position, but because it falls in Jupiter, it is much easier to manifest its higher spiritual benefits. However, those who are very attached to circumstances turning out a certain way or who are extremely materialistic by nature could still have some very difficult challenges when this card is present. It all depends upon the individual's point of view.

THE SEVEN OF SPADES IN THE SATURN PERIOD

This is one of the stronger indications of health problems of one kind or another. Negative attitudes or lifestyle habits can bring on illness and other difficulties during this period. The karmic nature of this period indicates that these problems are a result of deep-seated negativities or ways of living that are out of balance with a happy life. You will not be able to hold on to negative attitudes and thinking patterns without them affecting your health and work. You may be forced to do something about it. A positive attitude and healthy habits could go a long way towards healing yourself and others.

On a deep level, you could be confronting some of your deepest fears along with some of your deepest-seated negative beliefs about yourself or life in general. Though this may be a difficult period, you will come through it a much more free and happy person. It is a natural cleansing process that will rid you of impurities of one kind or another. Be open to the messages you are getting now, and all will turn out for the better.

Also bear in mind that the difficulties or challenges indicated by this card could be offset by a strong card in the other position, for example, any of the Fours, Eights, or Tens.

THE SEVEN OF SPADES IN THE URANUS PERIOD

Though you may not get full credit for your work now, do not let that become a source of problems on the job. This period may bring some kind of unexpected illness or trouble with one's job, maybe from overworking. You may suddenly be confronted with your own fears or negativity or bad habits that now need correcting. Success is highly possible now if you heed the call. Exposure to spiritual wisdom and people will be a great help and could add to your success.

This is a good influence for spiritual matters, learning new spiritual information, attending classes, etc. Also, keep in mind that a positive card, such as a Four, Eight, or Ten, in the other position of this period would offset any problematic situations that may arise and bring about good results overall.

THE SEVEN OF SPADES IN THE NEPTUNE PERIOD

This period could bring about either difficulties at work or illness related to travel, drugs, or something secret. Worry, unrealistic expectations, and other negative habits will likely be the cause of any difficulties during this period. However, the spiritual nature of this combination suggests that you could attain a high state of awareness and freedom of mind by being honest with yourself and looking within for the answers to the problems you now face.

The Seven of Spades Is Your Pluto Card

This powerful spiritual card will insist that you take an honest look at your work and health habits and root out any that are negative and creating negative results in your life. For this reason, this card is often associated with work and health problems. Obviously, you are ready to make some changes in your life to attain better health and lifestyle.

The Seven of Spades is one of the most powerful spiritual influences, which can also mean having the most problems on the material and mundane levels. If you have been harboring negative attitudes or patterns about your work or health, this powerful influence will cause you to face them squarely and experience, more than ever, the consequences of having them. Now, more than ever, you are the captain of your fate. To have the success you want in work and health though, you will have to make some changes in your behavior and in your whole approach to these areas.

The Seven of Spades is called the 'card of faith.' Success with this card requires rising to a new level of living that is beyond our normal fears and concerns. For those involved in spiritual work, this influence challenges you to move toward more success and make progress toward your work and personal goals. Your Result Card will either tell more about this challenge or point to a person with whom you need to adopt a more positive, unattached attitude.

Affirmation:

I am tapping into the source of God energy and transforming all the negativity in my life into fearlessness and appreciation. I am living faith.

The Seven of Spades Is Your Result Card

As part of this year's major challenge, represented by your Pluto Card, you will be working with negative patterns in yourself that may have been affecting your health or your ability to work with others effectively. The Seven of Spades will show you where there are areas to be upgraded, and it is certain that you will see them and do something about it. Achieving this new level of health or spirituality may not be easy, but you will surely do it before your next birthday.

Affirmation:

I complete this year with more positive health and work habits or create more spirituality in my work.

The Seven of Spades Is Your Long-Range Card

The Seven of Spades indicates that this could be a year of work and health difficulties or a card of success in spiritual work. This could be a year when you have to face squarely any negative attitudes or patterns that have been accumulating. Take this card as a spiritual challenge. Now is the time to take stock of your thoughts, words, and deeds and to see how they have created your world. Then it is possible to actualize this card's potential for spiritual success. The potential for inner development this year is enormous with this auspicious card present. Any problems you have this year have inner solutions. See yourself as the source of your success and good health, and take positive steps to create the work and health conditions you desire.

The Seven of Spades is also called the 'card of faith' and is one of the most potent of the spiritual cards. For this reason, the possibility of success and personal freedom are that much greater, provided one has listened to its message and learned to live and walk as one who is 'surrounded in the light.'

Keywords:

A year of adopting positive attitudes and habits related to work and health. Learning to create good health and life.

The Seven of Spades Is Your Environment Card

This could be a year when you experience personal freedom from any concerns about your health or your work. This is one of the most powerful of the spiritual cards, and as such, you could have some powerful and direct experiences of a higher nature. It is the card of faith and that of proceeding ahead in our life with what we know is our own true path with no concern for physical considerations or worries.

The Seven of Spades Is Your Displacement Card

Having the Seven of Spades as your Displacement Card brings both some blessings and some cautions. The blessing aspects of this placement guarantee a certain amount of success in your life overall. This is a year in which you will get some of your wishes fulfilled. You may be able to determine what these wishes will be by the other cards in your Yearly Spreads, especially the Jupiter and Result Cards.

On the other hand, your work and health habits may bring into focus a need for you to devote more of your energy into awareness of your lifestyle. It is a common experience to have either work or health problems under the influence of this powerful card. You may be called upon to adjust certain aspects of your lifestyle in order to be more healthy and happy. Challenges at work may also cause you to rethink your goals and plans. But remember that this is the card of faith. What you may be called upon to do this year is just to continue on, in spite of what is happening that may cause you to have doubts or hesitations. If your goals and dreams are really worthwhile, persist, and you will discover the magical quality of faith first hand.

Eight of Hearts

Emotional power and charm, success with people, especially the opposite sex

The Basic Meaning of the Eight of Hearts

The Eight of Hearts is a card of considerable emotional power, charm, and personal magnetism. This power could be used to bring you success in any activities that deal with groups of people such as acting or sales work. It is also an indicator of having healing energy, a 'spiritual force' gathering in you, a force you can use to better your life in many ways. When this card is present, this power is available to use at your discretion.

The Eight of Hearts will give you the power to get your way with people, both personally and professionally. It can bring you more social fun, better intimate relationships, or more success in your business.

THE EIGHT OF HEARTS IN THE MERCURY PERIOD

This period will bring an experience of sudden social success, perhaps at a party, group, or some educational function. You will have a certain charm that will make you the belle of the ball, at least for a while. This influence will not last for long, and you would do well to keep an eye on your own stubbornness in close relationships. Always getting your way may cause more harm than good when relating to loved ones at this time.

This is such a powerful and stabilizing influence that it will produce very good results during this period, even if your other Mercury Card is one of challenge or adversity.

THE EIGHT OF HEARTS IN THE VENUS PERIOD

During this period, you will have social success at the very least. Your charm and warm disposition could have very positive results in all of your relationships, both personally and professionally. This is called the 'Playboy Card,' and many who have this card in this position experience great romantic success both during this period and for the entire year to a lesser extent. Being in front of others is what you excel at most now, so pour it on. Just be careful that in all of this success you don't begin to think too much of yourself and bully your closest friends with unreasonable demands and expectations.

This is such a powerful and stabilizing influence that it will produce very good results during this period, even if your other Venus Card is one of challenge or adversity.

THE EIGHT OF HEARTS IN THE MARS PERIOD

The Eight of Hearts is a gift of charm and power among groups, especially where males predominate. Dynamic, aggressive charm will contribute to success in social and business endeavors during this period. Be careful that you do not overdo the social scene to the detriment of either your health or your work, as Mars energy can be very stimulating. Apply this gift to your work goals to get the most out of it.

The powerful and overcoming influence of this card is strong and will bring a happy and successful period for you, even if the indications of your other Mars Card are more challenging. Even if your other Mars card indicated a challenge or problem, this card guarantees that you will overcome it and that the result will be a positive one. A positive card in the other position will further strengthen the influence of this card and could tell you who

or what you will experience such success with during this fifty-two-day period.

THE EIGHT OF HEARTS IN THE JUPITER PERIOD

This auspicious influence brings to you a certain charm and social power that can be applied in all your business and personal areas for success. Through the cooperation of friends and associates, you can achieve much now, especially in any public-related endeavors. Huge financial successes are now possible through the cooperation of others. Also present with this influence is a certain amount of healing ability, which you can apply to yourself or others.

THE EIGHT OF HEARTS IN THE SATURN PERIOD

This card gives you the power to overcome illness and to heal or help others if you desire. A lot of charm and emotional power are present for you now, and this can be used successfully to further your career and financial goals. With the karmic influence of Saturn, you may find that your own power to get what you want emotionally leads you into some difficult relationships, ones that perhaps reflect your own immaturity in handling this power.

This card is such a strong influence that it will override any negative influences present during this period. Even if your other Saturn Card were one of challenge or problem, this card guarantees that you will have a successful outcome and an overcoming of difficulties.

THE EIGHT OF HEARTS IN THE URANUS PERIOD

Success in spiritual study and working with groups is highlighted now. The power and charm that you are now experiencing can be applied in your work or humanitarian endeavors with great success. You should find that you are successful wherever you direct this power during this period, though spiritually related activities are highlighted by the influence of Uranus. This is a card of cooperation among friends and co-workers.

Because of the power of this card, it is almost a guarantee that this will be a very successful and prosperous period. Even if your other Uranus Card were one of challenge or difficulty, this card's power will overcome it and have a successful outcome to the situations that arise.

THE EIGHT OF HEARTS IN THE NEPTUNE PERIOD

Rewards and good friends come through travel during this period. Overall, this should be a period of pleasant social experiences and friendships. You may find yourself devoting your healing powers to helping others during this period. Your own health should be good as well. Be careful that you are clearly understood by others now, as Neptune's influence can increase the likelihood of misunderstandings. Welcome any group situations. You are likely to shine.

You have the power now to achieve your dreams, especially where relationships are concerned. As long as you can get clear about exactly what it is that you wish to do, you are practically guaranteed to achieve it.

THE EIGHT OF HEARTS IS YOUR PLUTO CARD

This year you will be making changes in the way you approach or do things in order to have more success with the public or people in general. Perhaps you are involved in a business where you need more publicity or more contacts for success. Or, perhaps you have been somewhat reclusive for a while and want to just get out and meet people successfully, or you are learning public speaking. All professions that deal with the public are favored by this card, as long as you are willing to put forth the effort to get the success you want.

Another aspect of this card is that of developing charm and success in your romantic life. The Eight of Hearts is called the 'Playboy Card,' and for this reason, it may be that you are making some changes in your behavior in order to have more social and romantic success. Whatever the specifics of the challenges ahead of you this year, this card tells you that your success lies in focusing your attention on your goals and making a concerted effort in one direction. You must make a single-minded effort to harness all of your power in one direction. Then perhaps you will achieve your goals. Because this is the Pluto Card, it also tells you that this is something you probably haven't been doing lately and that it will take some changes in you in order to have this success.

Your Result Card will tell you more about this social, public, or romantic success you desire or point to someone who is directly involved in your getting it. This could also mean having to deal with someone in your life who is exhibiting a lot of personal and social power this year, someone that you find challenging at times.

Affirmation:

I create more success with people, in both personal and professional relationships, by learning how to focus my love energy.

The Eight of Hearts Is Your Result Card

An important aspect of the goals you have set for yourself this year is that of developing and using your charm and personal power with those around you. Developing this may not be easy, as it may require important changes in the way you communicate. It will, however, be well worth the effort. You will complete this year with people supporting your efforts to achieve your goals and dreams. You will also know that you can handle the public with ease.

Affirmation:

I develop power among my friends, associates, and the public. I accumulate personal love power this year.

The Eight of Hearts Is Your Long-Range Card

The Eight of Hearts tells you that you will have considerable emotional power at your disposal this year, which will bring you success in any activities that deal with groups of people such as acting, performing, or sales work. This is also an indicator of 'spiritual force' developing in you, a force that can be used to better your life. This

is a card of getting out to meet people in some way and getting into the limelight. This is a great year for promoting what you believe in and spreading your message. Just be careful that you don't hurt others as you use this power for your own success.

Probably the most fun aspect of this card is how it spices up your romantic and social life. This has been called the 'playboy card' and gives a lot of charm and charisma that you can use to get just about anything you want in these important areas.

Keywords:

I manifest love and personal power with those I love and work with. I increase my popularity and power through friends.

The Eight of Hearts Is Your Environment Card

If you have been waiting for a truly fun year, socially or romantically, this is it. The Eight of Hearts will bring many favorable experiences with people, and whether you use this love power and charm in your personal, social, or business life is entirely up to you. The fact is that you will have much better success than usual with people. So plunge ahead with assurance that you will get what you want. This is also a very good card for the healing of emotional wounds.

The Eight of Hearts Is Your Displacement Card

This card has the potential to make this one of the best years you have had in a while. While the year before this challenged you to develop a more spiritual and less attached approach to your personal relationships, this year will be sort of the reward for your efforts. Expect to have more than the usual amount of persuasiveness in your dealings with others and also to have many opportunities this year to enjoy the feeling of being popular in group situations. You may even want to plan a wonderful birthday party for yourself, inviting as many people as you can to celebrate it with you.

This year can bring especially good results for those who are seeking to rise up to higher levels of recognition in their work or careers. There is a chance of promotion to a higher level or of having your work become more recognized by the public. This would definitely be a year to advertise and promote yourself or your products on a larger scale as success is practically guaranteed. Your Jupiter, Saturn, and Uranus periods, in particular, should be filled with success in these areas.

This year is actually the beginning of a two-year mini-cycle of success in which you have some particularly good fortune. This good fortune always comes more to those who have a clear idea of what they want from life.

Eight of Clubs

Focus of the mind and plans brings more success and accomplishment

The Basic Meaning of the Eight of Clubs

The Eight of Clubs is the card of mental power, the ability to focus one's mind on a goal or objective and see it through to a successful conclusion. This power is usually applied to some mental or educational task. It bestows the power to overcome all problems by focusing one's thoughts, and it usually occurs when there is something that we need to learn or accomplish on the mental level.

The Eight of Clubs is one of the three 'fixed' cards. When it appears, we have the opportunity to fix our mind on certain goals and objectives. It is the card of focus of the mind. Out of that focus and concentration, success is assured.

THE EIGHT OF CLUBS IN THE MERCURY PERIOD

This card represents a rapid gaining of knowledge or power, or a rapid development of a situation you have been approaching. This could be a rapid education or a sudden opportunity to teach or speak or to acquire an education. This influence is one of overcoming any obstacles to success or current problems, especially related to communication. Success involving groups of people is also highlighted, as in teaching, speaking, or writing.

This is such a powerful and stabilizing influence that it will produce very good results during this period, even if your other Mercury Card is one of challenge or adversity.

THE EIGHT OF CLUBS IN THE VENUS PERIOD

The power of your mind can bring money and success during this period, especially with respect to women. This could mean advancement in female schools or with females. It can mean the development of psychic powers or the feminine side. This brings success particularly in association with groups of women of all kinds. You may be a salesperson or a teacher or a speaker, but regardless of your sex, you will find more success with women at this time.

This is such a powerful and stabilizing influence that it will produce very good results during this period, even if your other Venus Card is one of challenge or adversity.

THE EIGHT OF CLUBS IN THE MARS PERIOD

This influence brings success with males, and all things approached with aggressive mental strength. This could be advancement in a male school or male gatherings. A strong desire for knowledge or education could be present. This is an indicator of success in political arenas or in some connection with a legal matter. Ambition can take you far now but watch out for stubbornness, which may cause your personal relationships to suffer.

The powerful and overcoming influence of this card is strong and will bring a happy and successful period for you, even if the indications of your other Mars Card are more challenging. Even if your other Mars card indicated a challenge or problem, this card guarantees that you will overcome it and that the result will be a positive one. A positive card in the other position will further strengthen the influence of this card and could tell you who or what you will experience such success with during this fifty-two-day period.

THE EIGHT OF CLUBS IN THE JUPITER PERIOD

Your power of mind can bring you much success with money and business at this time. The proper application of education and knowledge will bring noticeable success with your business and people dealings. Your mental gifts are the source of your greatest benefits at this time. Success among groups of people is indicated, such as meetings or places where you speak or teach. You have more power than usual now. Use it wisely for popularity and profit.

This is probably one of the best influences for increasing your financial gains this year, so be sure to take advantage of it. It works especially well for those who have some business of their own. But even if you are employed by someone else, your mental power could bring you a promotion or some form of greater success.

THE EIGHT OF CLUBS IN THE SATURN PERIOD

This influence brings you the power to overcome illness or adversity through the application of knowledge. Through hard work and patience, you can accomplish a great deal now. This is a good time for constructive self-development. Under this influence you may experience some problems in relationships due to your own fixed opinions or ideas. Also, this is an unfavorable influence for gambling or speculative investments.

This card is such a strong influence that it will override any negative influences present during this period. Even if your other Saturn Card were one of challenge or problem, this card guarantees that you will have a successful outcome and an overcoming of difficulties.

THE EIGHT OF CLUBS IN THE URANUS PERIOD

During this period, you may have access to knowledge that brings power in labor relations or real estate deals. Meetings to deal with these areas are pegged for success at this time due to the power of your mind. Success is likely in any areas related to education, volunteer work, real estate, metaphysics, labor relations, high technology, or psychic development. You may have access to advanced or unusual knowledge that contributes to your career.

Because of the power of this card, it is almost a guarantee that this will be a very successful and prosperous period. Even if your other Uranus Card were one of challenge or difficulty, this card's power will overcome it and have a successful outcome to the situations that arise.

THE EIGHT OF CLUBS IN THE NEPTUNE PERIOD

Having some special knowledge of foreign or distant matters or matters related to travel could bring much success at this time. You also have the power to heal others through psychic sensitivity and application of acquired knowledge. This influence allows access to hidden information and a good deal of intuition. Your interest in metaphysical subjects and uncovering the mysteries of life could lead to much satisfaction during this period.

THE EIGHT OF CLUBS IS YOUR PLUTO CARD

The Eight of Clubs as the Pluto Card means this is a year of developing your mind power to concentrate on certain goals and aspirations. With this concentration will come more success in your life, but only after you have made the changes in yourself that will give you more of this focus of mind and will. You may desire success in one or more of the mental fields such as writing, learning, teaching, speaking, or communications.

Somehow, the success that you desire this year comes from a fixed and powerful mental state, perhaps by sticking with one or two important principles until they bear fruit. Others may see you as being stubborn or fixed at times, but inwardly, you sense that it takes this kind of single-mindedness to accomplish the success you desire. You will have to develop new habits to accomplish this goal, and the going will not always be easy. However, the influences are good, and you should accomplish all you set out to achieve. Combine the meaning of this mental 'power card' with your Result Card to get the whole picture of why this mental power and success is important to you or who is involved in the developing of it.

AFFIRMATION:

I create success that comes from a powerful mental state. I learn to focus my thoughts in order to achieve the impossible.

THE EIGHT OF CLUBS IS YOUR RESULT CARD

This powerful card promises success in almost any field, especially those involving the mind and communications. You may have to work hard to achieve this goal and may have to make changes in your life as well, but your success is practically guaranteed with the Eight of Clubs as a Result Card. If your Pluto Card is someone that you know, they may be directly involved in your success, perhaps even reflect back to you the power that you seek for yourself.

AFFIRMATION:

I create mental power and success. I overcome difficulties and reach my goals through a fixed and determined mind.

THE EIGHT OF CLUBS IS YOUR LONG-RANGE CARD

The Eight of Clubs brings you a great deal of mental power this year. This power can bring you success in any of the Mercury-ruled professions such as speaking, writing, or education. This power can also overcome most problems and obstacles that stand in the way of your goals. The only negative aspect of this influence could be a tendency towards mental stubbornness and fixed opinions that will tempt you to bully others. Set your goals high, and focus your mind on success.

Much of the success with this card comes with focusing the mind on definite objectives. By definition, this means excluding certain options in your life to put more energy into one main goal. As you progress through this year, you will experience firsthand the power comes from a one-pointed thrust of mental energy. Enjoy the success that it brings you.

KEYWORDS:

A year of mental power and accomplishment, especially in the mental or communications fields. I focus my energies for more success.

THE EIGHT OF CLUBS IS YOUR ENVIRONMENT CARD

Because the Eight of Clubs is one of the Fixed Cards, it will never appear as anyone's Environment Card.

THE EIGHT OF CLUBS IS YOUR DISPLACEMENT CARD

Because the Eight of Clubs is one of the Fixed Cards, it will never appear as anyone's Displacement Card.

Eight of Diamonds

Money to spend, financial power accumulated to make a major purchase

The Basic Meaning of the Eight of Diamonds

The Eight of Diamonds tells you that you will have a considerable amount of financial power. The power to make money is yours, and this is power that you probably want to use for some special purpose. Financial power can come from many avenues. You could earn the money or you could borrow the money, but one thing is for sure, in order to have this financial power, you will have to get very clear on how much money you want and what the purpose of having that money will be. You see, the Eight of Diamonds means focusing and concentrating our *values* and making choices about what is most important in our life and what is not. Through this kind of focus, money is always attracted to us in the amounts we need. This card usually occurs at a time when we want to make some major purchase.

THE EIGHT OF DIAMONDS IN THE MERCURY PERIOD

This card represents money coming in quickly or unexpectedly and a rapid gain of a desired financial object. This may have been motivated by impatience or may have been the result of your having some invaluable information or because of some short trip you take now. This is one of the few times when get rich quick schemes just might pay off. In any case, you will have quickly gained some financial power during this period.

This is such a powerful and stabilizing influence that it will produce very good results during this period, even if your other Mercury Card is one of challenge or adversity.

THE EIGHT OF DIAMONDS IN THE VENUS PERIOD

This can indicate a lot of money made in the arts, products for the home, beauty, or women. Your money power is strong now and is perhaps related to your friends, a lover or spouse, or some woman. You will prefer the company of well to do people, and money may be a consideration in all your friendships. Be careful that it doesn't become *the* most important thing. This is one of the best cards for money. You have the financial power to enjoy life at its best.

This is such a powerful and stabilizing influence that it will produce very good results during this period, even if your other Venus Card is one of challenge or adversity.

THE EIGHT OF DIAMONDS IN THE MARS PERIOD

This influence brings the financial resources to achieve your desired goals. This is a card of financial and commercial strength, possibly in some male-dominated organization, or it can mean a meeting of men for money considerations. This card can indicate the successful completion of a legal or tax-related matter or an inheritance. An aggressive pursuit of your financial goals now can pay off tremendously. You have the power to do it!

The powerful and overcoming influence of this card is strong and will bring a happy and successful period for you, even if the indications of your other Mars Card are more challenging. Even if your other Mars card indicated a challenge or problem, this card guarantees that you will overcome it and that the result will be a positive one. A positive card in the other position will further strengthen the influence of this card and could tell you who

or what you will experience such success with during this fifty-two-day period.

THE EIGHT OF DIAMONDS IN THE JUPITER PERIOD

This is a card of recognition and reward for efforts. A large sum of money could come into your life now, possibly making you affluent. Expansion of all business and financial dealings is favored by this auspicious influence. This influence brings such a focus on money that it might even be too much. Money is power, but it must be used wisely and for good purposes to bring inner satisfaction.

The Eight of Diamonds card usually shows up when there are important purchases to make. It usually brings in the money you need to buy something that you want. The extent of your financial success during this period will depend upon how well you are set up to take in large amounts of money. If you can find ways to increase the quantity of the goods and services you are providing, you can create more ways for this influence to pay off for you.

THE EIGHT OF DIAMONDS IN THE SATURN PERIOD

This card represents a large sum of money made through the illness, death, or loss of another (e.g., inheritance) or through hard work. Or the money could be connected somehow to death, hospitals, or healing. This can also mean a meeting of doctors. You may have to work hard under less than ideal conditions, but you can be successful—the money coming in now is proof of that. This card is one of overcoming illness or undesirable influences through patience and perseverance.

This card is such a strong influence that it will override any negative influences present during this period. Even if your other Saturn Card were one of challenge or problem, this card guarantees that you will have a successful outcome and an overcoming of difficulties.

THE EIGHT OF DIAMONDS IN THE URANUS PERIOD

With this influence, a sale of real estate could bring in a lot of money. This could also represent money made through employees, by using your gifts of intuition, or money made by or used for helping others in some humanitarian effort. In general, you will have a lot of financial power with this influence, and it may be either unusual in some way or be happening unexpectedly. You may also find money coming in from work with computers or advanced technologies of some sort, and this would be a good time to purchase any new high-tech items on your list.

Because of the power of this card, it is almost a guarantee that this will be a very successful and prosperous period. Even if your other Uranus Card were one of challenge or difficulty, this card's power will overcome it and have a successful outcome to the situations that arise.

THE EIGHT OF DIAMONDS IN THE NEPTUNE PERIOD

This indicates a large sum of money made related to travel or some distant business interests. This could very well be the fulfillment of your financial dreams or wishes. This financial power could be the result of an inheritance or some secret involvement. There may be some confusion or deception associated with it, so be cautious. This is an especially good card if you are in the healing profession or if you are in some way caring for others.

It is likely that there is something you have been wanting to purchase for a while, perhaps you have been dreaming about it all year. If so, you will have the money now to get it. Of course, you have to decide exactly what that is.

THE EIGHT OF DIAMONDS IS YOUR PLUTO CARD

This year, one of your main goals will be that of creating more money in your life. You are desiring to have the power that money represents, the power to make some purchases that are important to you. To acquire this power, you will have to change your behavior and possibly your attitudes about money.

This card indicates that you need a fixed and determined set of values. That is, you need to get perfectly clear about what you want and why you want it. Once you are clear about what you want, then you can devote yourself to a single-minded pursuit of those financial goals. This kind of dedication always brings success, but since this is the Pluto Card, it is likely that acquiring these qualities will be challenging at times and cause you to make some fundamental changes in the way you approach money, work, and finances. Your Result Card will tell you more about this financial power you seek or will point to a person in your life who is closely connected with it.

AFFIRMATION:

I create the financial prosperity to purchase the things that I want and deserve. I focus all my values into one powerful stream of 'wealth energy.'

THE EIGHT OF DIAMONDS IS YOUR RESULT CARD

As a result of meeting some of your major challenges and goals this year, you will be able to accumulate, earn, or borrow a large sum of money that you need for a specific purpose. Only you know your inner goals, but this card gives you a positive sign for financial success before year's end. Set your sites high this year and meet the challenge of your Pluto Card, knowing that in the end you will be successful.

By the time of your next birthday, you will have the finances you want to make a major and important purchase.

AFFIRMATION:

I create financial power. I accumulate money resources to achieve my goals. I end this year with financial success.

THE EIGHT OF DIAMONDS IS YOUR LONG-RANGE CARD

The Eight of Diamonds tells you that you will have a considerable amount of financial power this year. The power to make a lot of money is yours, and you should find that you have more money than usual. Meetings for financial gain are also represented by this card. Perhaps you have some definite goals this year related to things you want to purchase. The Eight of Diamonds promises that you will have the money you need, when you need it. Be careful in your money dealings not to bully others or to force others to go your way all the time. Though you may have the power to do this, you will create negative vibrations in others that will someday come back to you.

The Eight of Diamonds is also known as the fame or 'sun' card and thus has been found to show up during years when one rises up to some newfound prominence in one's work or profession. In most respects, this is a great card that will bring you much of what you need or want.

KEYWORDS:

A year of financial power and money to spend. Financial accumulation. I harness the power of my values to attract more money into my life.

THE EIGHT OF DIAMONDS IS YOUR ENVIRONMENT CARD

This could be the year in which you have the financial means to make some important purchases in your life. Whether it is to buy a new house, car, boat, or other items of importance, it is likely that there is something that you want to buy that you will have the means to acquire now. This is a very good omen for finances in general and for success in work or business. Be thankful for the blessings of prosperity that are now a part of your life.

THE EIGHT OF DIAMONDS IS YOUR DISPLACEMENT CARD

This year is one of the most auspicious years of your life, one in which you will make a big transition of some importance. When we displace the Eight of Diamonds, it is called the Pinnacle Year. This means that this year marks the end of a long cycle for you, perhaps seven to fifteen years, in which you have been climbing up a certain path in life, making some progress each year. Now you have reached the end of that journey, and the question remains as to where you will go next.

Many people reach a high point in their chosen profession during this auspicious year. They often reach the goals they were striving and working for or achieve great prominence or recognition. Those who have desires for fame or recognition often achieve it during this year. But for all people, this year marks a great turning point of some kind and the end of a particular mode of life that had been pursued for many years prior to this year. Expect some significant changes as a result.

Eight of Spades

Success and accomplishment in work and health, use of force and will power

The Basic Meaning of the Eight of Spades

The Eight of Spades is the most powerful card of physical and will power. When this card is present, you will find yourself experiencing more power over your health and work matters. Success is indicated by this card, along with the ability to overcome any obstacles that may appear in your way. Power comes from a focusing of our will, a narrowing down of the areas of our interest. Because of this, we often lose focus in less important areas while we gather force in one.

THE EIGHT OF SPADES IN THE MERCURY PERIOD

This period should bring a rapid accomplishment of some work or desired educational goal. The overcoming of obstacles in work or health is indicated. This indicates an instant or sudden success. You may just "fall into" a good job situation now. The only negative aspect of this period could be a tendency to use your power to bully others. If you balance this gift of power with wisdom, you could go very far now.

This is such a powerful and stabilizing influence that it will produce very good results during this period, even if your other Mercury Card is one of challenge or adversity.

THE EIGHT OF SPADES IN THE VENUS PERIOD

During this period, an active and productive social life will bring many rewards. Your job could bring in much money and social success now. This card can also represent groups of females meeting for work, community events, or just plain fun. This influence brings much power associated with women, friends, social occasions, and the home and family, as well as a strong desire to stand well in the community and have intelligent, well-to-do friends.

This is such a powerful and stabilizing influence that it will produce very good results during this period, even if your other Venus Card is one of challenge or adversity.

THE EIGHT OF SPADES IN THE MARS PERIOD

This period will bring you the ambition and drive to accomplish as much success as you like. Success in a legal matter or in dealing with groups or associations of men is especially favored. This is one of the most powerful combinations of energies you can find. You can achieve just about anything you desire at this time through your will and hard work. Just be careful that your abrupt manner doesn't put people off.

The powerful and overcoming influence of this card is strong and will bring a happy and successful period for you, even if the indications of your other Mars Card are more challenging. Even if your other Mars card indicated a challenge or problem, this card guarantees that you will overcome it and the result will be a positive one. A positive card in the other position will further strengthen the influence of this card and could tell you who or what you will experience such success with during this fifty-two-day period.

THE EIGHT OF SPADES IN THE JUPITER PERIOD

This is one of the strongest symbols of business and personal power and success. At this time, you will either expand your operations or make some invaluable connection with some large company that increases your own financial power appreciably. This is also one of the best signs of good health and recovery from any and all problems you may be facing. You can overcome all obstacles now through honest effort and integrity.

To take the fullest advantage of the opportunities presented by this card, you should find ways to expand your business interests. Someone on a fixed income may not experience the financial benefits of this card, since there is no way for them to increase the volume of goods or services that allows greater finances to manifest. However, if you have a business, this is the year to expand and to open up to more prosperity. You are in the midst of a cycle of prosperity.

THE EIGHT OF SPADES IN THE SATURN PERIOD

This period brings you the power to overcome illness and all work or business problems. Success in work and health will come through hard work, discipline, and patience. You may reach a high point of success now if you work for it. This is not a time when things come easily, and your work or health may have some restrictions or obligations associated with them. However, this card promises the overcoming of obstacles through consistent effort.

This card is such a strong influence that it will override any negative influences present during this period. Even if your other Saturn Card were one of challenge or problem, this card guarantees that you will have a successful outcome and an overcoming of difficulties.

THE EIGHT OF SPADES IN THE URANUS PERIOD

This period will be one of power and success within an organization or labor group, in real estate, humanitarian efforts, or some scientific work. You also have the power to overcome illness and most other obstacles present. Relations with employees will be beneficial now and all work with larger corporations or organizations should prove to be very successful. You can make some important and profitable connections during this period.

Because of the power of this card, it is almost a guarantee that this will be a very successful and prosperous period. Even if your other Uranus Card were one of challenge or difficulty, this card's power will overcome it and have a successful outcome to the situations that arise.

THE EIGHT OF SPADES IN THE NEPTUNE PERIOD

This period can bring success in the management of foreign or distant interests. This is also a good influence for travel of any kind, especially business-related. Just be careful with your emotions under this influence. If they are allowed to interfere in your business, you could suffer losses. Best to keep your personal feelings out of the way during this period and take advantage of the opportunity for the success that is offered by this card.

You have the power now to achieve your dreams. As long as you can get clear about exactly what it is that you wish to do, you are practically guaranteed to achieve it.

THE EIGHT OF SPADES IS YOUR PLUTO CARD

This year you have put before yourself a big challenge. This challenge may be related to work or health or just to having more strength of will in general. Whatever the case, you will have to make some positive changes in your life in order to achieve this goal, and it will not always be easy.

Perhaps your health hasn't been what you would like it to be lately and you want to begin a program of exercise and good diet to get back your strong constitution. Or perhaps you want more success in your work, perhaps even a promotion to a higher level of responsibility. Whatever your specific goals are for this year, inner power and determination are absolute requirements for your success. Your Result Card will further describe this power you seek or point to someone who is closely associated with it.

AFFIRMATION:

I create radiant health and success in my work through harnessing my unlimited will power and aligning my will with the will of the universe.

THE EIGHT OF SPADES IS YOUR RESULT CARD

As a result of contending with your Pluto Card this year, and largely associated with it, is the element of developing a strong willpower and determination that can help you overcome any obstacles in your path. The obstacles may be about work or health or simply about whatever your Pluto Card describes, but it is certain that you will accomplish this power and success by year's end. Don't forget this when the times get tough, as they inevitably do.

AFFIRMATION:

I create success in my work and health and other areas of my life. I develop the will power to overcome all problems.

THE EIGHT OF SPADES IS YOUR LONG-RANGE CARD

The Eight of Spades tells us that this year will find you experiencing more power and control over your health and work matters and more power in general. This power can be used to rise to a higher position at work, to improve your health or to have more success in any area of your life. The power and success indicated by this card must be properly applied and directed to get the best results. If you misuse this power to bully others or to impose your will upon them, you will create bad karma that will cause you problems in the future. Get your goals clear, and use this power wisely. You hold in your hand a magic wand. All you need to do to have anything you want is a little hard work and determination.

KEYWORDS:

A year of physical power and willpower that you can use to overcome any problems in work, health, or other areas.

THE EIGHT OF SPADES IS YOUR ENVIRONMENT CARD

The Eight of Spades gives you the power and determination to accomplish many good things this year. Through hard work and focus, many blessings will come your way. This card is a good omen for success in any legal matters or helpful in overcoming any sort of work or health problems. If you are willing to assert yourself and be powerful, there is little that you cannot achieve. You are protected this year in many ways, but don't forget to put in a little effort.

THE EIGHT OF SPADES IS YOUR DISPLACEMENT CARD

This is a year in which you will work hard and attain many results, if you have a direction for your efforts. You can also expect to overcome any problems that may arise, especially problems related to work or health. This is a good year to launch an exercise program or a new business. You have the power to make some real progress in your life. Take this opportunity to use this power. Put it to work, and you may surprise yourself with what you can do.

Power and its use in your life may become an issue this year that you need to address as well. The Eight of Spades is one of the most powerful cards in the deck, and often when we have that card, we may be tempted to abuse it or meet up with others who do so at our expense. Just how you use your power and whether or not you get into 'battles over control' with others could be the deciding factor on your success or failure during this interesting year ahead.

Nine of Hearts

The completion of some major relationship, giving counseling or help to others

The Basic Meaning of the Nine of Hearts

The Nine of Hearts can be a card of emotional disappointment and personal losses on the affectional level. However, this is the card of completions in love and of 'Universal Love.' Yes, the Nine of Hearts can signal the ending of one or more key relationships. If so, it is most likely that these relationships are no longer doing you any good. It is time for them to end, whether or not you realize this at the time they happen.

However, the Nine of Hearts can also represent our helping others by counseling them or in some way sharing our love and compassion with them. It means a giving of love in a more or less selfless manner.

THE NINE OF HEARTS IN THE MERCURY PERIOD

This period could harbor a sudden disappointment in someone, fortunately a disappointment that passes quickly also. You may have misjudged somebody in your haste to be friendly and liked. This same misjudgment could prove costly financially as well. Any heartache you feel now could help you to gain more maturity in relationships and to help you to see yourself and others as they truly are. This is also an unfavorable influence for gambling or any sort of speculation.

Look at your other Mercury Card to find out more about this emotional challenge or ending in your life. It may identify who or what is coming to an end in your life. It also may indicate what the outcome of the situation at hand is as it expresses itself in your life.

THE NINE OF HEARTS IN THE VENUS PERIOD

Disappointment in love, romance, and possibly finances are distinct possibilities at this time. You may find that there are many obstacles in the way of your emotional happiness, including lack of material resources. This is one of the stronger divorce cards, so the possibility of a painful separation is present. Remember that difficulties are in reality opportunities to learn about ourselves and to purify our own motivations. Selfless giving is a healer.

Your other Venus Card may tell you who or what the emotional or personal challenge or ending is about. Also keep in mind that a strong or powerful other Venus Card, such as a Four, Eight, or Ten, could mitigate the adversity of this card and bring about very positive results from a situation that may seem like a disappointment at the outset.

THE NINE OF HEARTS IN THE MARS PERIOD

Jealousies or misunderstandings between you and your loved one(s) are likely during this period. Caution is advised when relating to men during this time, in business and personally. You may be inclined to leave behind undesirable situations during this period and move on to greener pastures. Your own laziness combined with disappointment in others may prompt such an exit or make you impatient with the problems present. If you stick with it, you can overcome.

Look to your other Mars Card to find out what or who is involved in the challenges or endings that may arise during this period. Also, keep in mind that a positive card, such as a Four, Eight, or Ten, would tell you that regardless of the challenges present, you are likely to have a happy and productive outcome to the situations that present themselves during this fifty-two-day period.

THE NINE OF HEARTS IN THE JUPITER PERIOD

The Nine of Hearts in Jupiter is called the 'Wish Card.' Indeed, you may get one or more of your important wishes fulfilled during this period. However, this is also the card of endings in certain key relationships. Many have had divorces under this influence. If so, it is likely to be an easy parting or one in which the prosperity flows in your direction. There also could be some endings to relationships with others with whom you have had business or professional ties during this period. If so, let them go, as this is a good influence for completing things or relationships from the past.

If you are involved in spiritual work or helping or teaching others in some way, this card is an indicator of great success and could bring huge financial rewards as well. This is the card of the counselor and the giver of love. Any activities along these lines could be highly rewarding, both financially and to your inner self as well.

THE NINE OF HEARTS IN THE SATURN PERIOD

The likelihood of emotional problems causing ill health and other kinds of misfortune is present during this period. Personal relationships are challenging and disappointing, but contact with the public can be a source of fulfillment and joy. It may be that you are involved in a heavy karmic relationship now, one that was destined to teach you much about yourself and your love nature. In any case, one or more key relationships in your life have reached their place of completion and are now coming to an end. Letting go of personal attachments and relationships that are no longer serving any good purpose in your life will ultimately lead you to new and better relationships. This card can often represent a difficult divorce.

Also bear in mind that the difficulties or challenges indicated by this card could be offset by a strong card in the other position, for example any of the Fours, Eights, or Tens.

THE NINE OF HEARTS IN THE URANUS PERIOD

Unexpected circumstances can bring disappointments in work, in love, in romance, and with friends during this period. Jealousy and scandal may occur at work, and good friends may seem hard to come by during this Nine of Hearts Uranus period. Do not expect much from others now, and look to any sort of humanitarian work for inspiration and healing.

It is entirely possible that you have outgrown some of your friendships and that now is the time to let them go. See these endings as completions and let go willingly, if that is what is being called for by the situation. New and better relationships are just around the corner.

This is a good influence for spiritual matters, learning new spiritual information, attending classes, etc. Also, keep in mind that a positive card, such as a Four, Eight, or Ten, in the other position of this period would offset any problematic situations that may arise and bring about good results overall.

THE NINE OF HEARTS IN THE NEPTUNE PERIOD

This period could bring a disappointment regarding a journey or something at a distance. Your own inner conflict of freedom vs. companionship could contribute to misunderstandings and heartaches now. Neptune's glamour could also contribute to misunderstandings that make clear communications difficult, if not impossible. However, there is much potential for success in the area of helping others and realizing spiritual goals.

It is entirely possible that a longtime cherished relationship of yours could come to an end or be lost during this period. This could be something that you have been worrying about losing from time to time this year. If so, don't be afraid or disappointed. This ending is actually the best thing for you and everyone else in your life. Let it go, and many new and better things will soon come to replace it.

THE NINE OF HEARTS IS YOUR PLUTO CARD

This year you will likely have one or more of your most important relationships coming to an end. The time has come to let go of these and move on, and yet, it may not be easy to do. Either you are wanting it to end and that is a problem for you, or you don't want it to end and it is ending anyway. Personal attachments may be surfacing that make these endings very difficult. These endings could manifest as a divorce, either personally or professionally, or as the actual leaving or death of someone close to you. Even the death of a pet would qualify as a Nine of Hearts experience, especially if you had close bonds with the pet.

If these endings leave you disappointed in any way, it is likely that you are emotionally attached to someone. It is likely that you have an internal conflict about this. There are probably two parts inside yourself—one that wants an ending to one or more relationships and one that doesn't. If you can tune in to yourself, you may be able to resolve this inner conflict and reach a place of acceptance.

The universe is dictating that the endings must happen. If you change your perspective, you may discover that these endings are really the best thing for all concerned, and that includes you. Your Result Card will further describe these endings or tell you who it is that you will be ending it with.

AFFIRMATION:

I am letting go of relationships that were once good for me, but now have outlived their purpose in my life. I set myself free to move on to better relationships.

THE NINE OF HEARTS IS YOUR RESULT CARD

The net result of this year's efforts is likely to be the ending of one or more of your significant relationships. You may sense that these are coming to an end this year, and you may even want this, knowing that it will be for your own good. The Nine of Hearts means letting go of personal attachments to people. As you let go of certain people, you will be magically transformed to a higher level of awareness and

led to a new beginning in your personal relationships whereby you will attract new people who are much better for you in this new place that you have arrived at in your life. Your Pluto Card will tell you who or what is involved.

AFFIRMATION:

I release old relationships that are no longer serving my highest good. I learn to love without attachment.

THE NINE OF HEARTS IS YOUR LONG-RANGE CARD

It is likely that there will be one or more important emotional endings or losses in store for you this year. At the very least, you may be involved in a separation from a former lover or spouse. But this card can also indicate a death in the family or among your circle of friends. I have even seen this card appear when there was the death of a pet.

One or more of your relationships is coming to an end, and if you look deep inside yourself, you may discover that there are good reasons for the ending—that it will be good for you and for the other as well. This card often means disappointment, but that is the case only when we resist the ending. If you let go and let the universe take care of you, you could experience the heightened spiritual awareness and high consciousness that is also represented by this powerful card. Involvement in work that gives love to others, especially large groups of people, is slated for great success this year. You are a giver.

KEYWORDS:

I learn to let others go and to give love unconditionally. I complete some important relationships and let them go.

THE NINE OF HEARTS IS YOUR ENVIRONMENT CARD

Because the Nine of Hearts is one of the Semi-Fixed Cards, it will never appear as anyone's Environment or Displacement Card in the Yearly Spreads.

In a Weekly Reading, the Nine of Hearts will allow you to easily let go of certain relationships that are no longer good for you and bring benefits from counseling others in a compassionate way.

THE NINE OF HEARTS IS YOUR DISPLACEMENT CARD

Because the Nine of Hearts is one of the Semi-Fixed Cards, it will never appear as anyone's Environment or Displacement Card in the Yearly Spreads.

Nine of Clubs

Completion of plans, a mental disappointment, sharing knowledge with groups

The Basic Meaning of the Nine of Clubs

The Nine of Clubs literally means 'completion of plans or ideas.' When this card appears, it will signal a time when some ideas, ways of thinking or communicating, or some personal plans of yours are ready to end. If you choose to resist this ending, you will experience great disappointment by stubbornly holding on to things, ideas, or plans that are no longer useful or helpful to you. If it seems that things are going against you when this card is present, it is probably because you are resisting letting go of something, which in reality is no longer doing you any good.

On the positive side, you are ready to awaken to a new and higher way of thinking that will be better than you have imagined. The Nine of Clubs has been known to signal a time when powerful spiritual experiences may occur, such as universal consciousness, and it also indicates the success of any endeavors that involve spreading higher truths to the world.

THE NINE OF CLUBS IN THE MERCURY PERIOD

At this time, there could be something disappointing or some bad news that arises suddenly and passes away just as quickly. This could be a sudden antagonism to your wishes or plans by another. There will be some sudden and unexpected disappointment, but it will pass quickly. This influence could also represent a sudden interruption in your education, perhaps because of a family member.

Your other Mercury Card may tell you what thing or relationship in your life is coming to an end during this period. Nines usually mean that a cycle of life is coming to an end. Whether we feel like we are graduating or are disappointed because of the loss is entirely up to us.

THE NINE OF CLUBS IN THE VENUS PERIOD

This card is one of disappointment, either with friends or with someone you love dearly. Disloyal or uncooperative friends could be a source of much heartache. Your own personal plans and projects could be sacrificed as a result of the current situation. This influence can bring a delay or disruption of marriage plans or the betrayal of a mate or lover. Adopting a universal approach to love could bring success and happiness under this influence.

Your other Venus Card may tell you who or what the emotional or personal challenge or ending is about. Also keep in mind that a strong or powerful other Venus Card, such as a Four, Eight, or Ten, could mitigate the adversity of this card and bring about very positive results from a situation that may seem like a disappointment at the outset.

THE NINE OF CLUBS IN THE MARS PERIOD

This period could bring a troubling lawsuit or competition from some male. Relationships with males in particular are not good with this influence. You could even lose your job due to an argument or dispute with someone. This card can bring antagonism from others, especially if you are expressing a lot of aggression and impatience. Impatience may even cause you to change your line of work. Be careful about any gambling and speculation at this time.

Look to your other Mars Card to find out what or who is involved in the challenges or endings that may arise during this period. Also, keep in mind that a positive card, such as a Four, Eight, or Ten, would tell you that regardless of the challenges present, you are likely to have a happy and productive outcome to the situations that present themselves during this fifty-two-day period.

THE NINE OF CLUBS IN THE JUPITER PERIOD

This influence brings financial success through the spreading of knowledge or by doing some sort of spiritual teaching. It also suggests that this period will bring the culmination of a project or way of making money that was started some time ago. Though endings are often interpreted as losses, because this card falls in the Jupiter period, it is certain that this completion will bring you more of what you truly want out of life. Some of your best chances for success now lie in applying a universal and giving approach in your work while recognizing the power of your own mind.

Don't resist any endings or completions that may occur during this period. They will quickly bring you to a new beginning with much better things in store for you.

THE NINE OF CLUBS IN THE SATURN PERIOD

This period could see you experiencing much frustration and worry, and this state of mind could also affect your health. It is also possible that your worrying causes some business losses or even affects your health adversely. Any negative thoughts you have been holding about yourself or others could be at the root of your problems. There is healing potential now if you take responsibility for your mind and develop better attitudes and beliefs. Community or selfless service could also help.

This card indicates something important in your life coming to an end. Because this card falls in Saturn, you will probably resist and dislike this ending more than usual. For this reason, this may represent some personal challenge and learning opportunity for you, one that ultimately expands your view of yourself and your world.

Also bear in mind that the difficulties or challenges indicated by this card could be offset by a strong card in the other Saturn position, for example any of the Fours, Eights, or Tens.

THE NINE OF CLUBS IN THE URANUS PERIOD

Mental frustration and worry are definite possibilities now with some of the problems you may have with co-workers or labor groups. Also, there could be a disappointing real estate deal, and this is not a good time for real estate speculation. In addition, psychic experiments could prove to be disappointing. Do not expect much from others at this time, and adopt a more giving and universal approach in work and friendships to access the potential of this card.

The essential meaning of this card is the ending of some plan or mental occupation. This could represent the ending of a job or a way of thinking. This card only means that it is over. Whether it is experienced by you as a completion or a disappointment will be based upon your own attitudes about the thing that is ending.

This is a good influence for spiritual matters, learning new spiritual information, attending classes, etc. Also, keep in mind that a positive card, such as a Four, Eight, or Ten, in the other position of this period would offset any problematic situations that may arise and bring about good results overall.

THE NINE OF CLUBS IN THE NEPTUNE PERIOD

Vagueness in thinking and communicating can cause problems at this time. Stress clarity in all dealings. Also, there can be disappointments related to travel or an upset of some personal dream or ambition. This is not a good time for drugs or psychic experiments, as they may have ill side effects now. However, this is a very good influence for doing service in some sort of community project or spiritually based work.

It is entirely possible that a longtime cherished dream of yours could come to an end during this period. This could be something that you have been worrying about from time to time this year. If so, don't be afraid or disappointed. This ending is actually the best thing for you and everyone else in your life. Let it go, and many new and better things will soon come to replace it.

THE NINE OF CLUBS IS YOUR PLUTO CARD

This year could either be very uplifting and fulfilling, or it could be fraught with disappointment and painful endings. In one way or another, you will be challenged this year to let go of outworn concepts, ideas, and ways of thinking and communicating. You may even end a certain type of career or profession in preparation for starting something new. Any of these endings may be difficult for you to digest or allow. The more you resist the changes that are occurring, the more pain you will suffer. You will have to let go this year to make way for the new beginnings that will be occurring next year. This is graduation year. Isn't it funny how we sometimes resist leaving things?

In all likelihood, all these endings are good for you in many ways. This card tells us that you have reached a pinnacle and place of completion in one or more important areas of your life. This will be a year of tying up loose ends and saying goodbye to certain parts of yourself that are no longer helping you. However, our minds often have a hard time letting go.

On a more positive side, you could be developing and learning much in the way of spiritual knowledge. This education or sharing of ideas could prove an invaluable experience that broadens and enriches your perspective on life. Your Result Card will further clarify the areas in which you are having endings and more universality, or it may point to a person who is intimately involved in the broadening of your mind.

AFFIRMATION:

I am letting go of limiting concepts and ways of communicating and adopting more universal thinking.

THE NINE OF CLUBS IS YOUR RESULT CARD

Much of the challenge for you this year will be to let go of outworn ideas, projects, plans, or ways of communicating. This is a year of completions that may at times seem like disappointing endings. The Nine of Clubs says that you are completing a major chapter in your life and it is time to move on to greener pastures. Be open to spiritual wisdom in all forms, as this will help make change easier. Your Pluto Card will tell more about these endings or who is involved.

AFFIRMATION:

I complete projects this year and let go of the past. I broaden my understanding by releasing old ways of thinking.

THE NINE OF CLUBS IS YOUR LONG-RANGE CARD

The Nine of Clubs can be a card of mental disappointment and frustration, which is what sometimes happens when things in our life come to an end. However, you have the power to make this a 'graduation' year and a year of great fulfillment. This year you will be experiencing one or more important endings in your life. This could manifest as the loss or completion of a certain line of work or many people coming up against your plans to the extent that you have to abandon them. The universe is trying to tell you that it is time to let go of some cherished idea or plan and to move on. If you can see this and flow with the changes, you will discover that you are much better off for the ending.

The Nine of Clubs is the card of 'universal knowledge.' This means a mind that is able to perceive things beyond the boundaries of what we call reality. Thus, many have experienced some unique and powerful awakenings of the soul under the influence of this card. Positively applied, this card could reward you with universal knowledge and success in sharing it with others. Everything good about this card comes from surrender to universal will and letting go of our limited thinking.

KEYWORDS:

A year of some mental disappointments and endings of plans, or a year of important conclusions and endings, while gaining and sharing spiritual knowledge.

THE NINE OF CLUBS IS YOUR ENVIRONMENT CARD

Good fortune and blessings will come this year by letting go of the past, giving up outworn ideas and opinions, or even letting go of certain occupations that no longer serve a constructive purpose in your life. Though there may be some key endings in your life this year, rest assured that these will be relatively painless and full of wonderful blessings of many kinds. Also, you could have some major breakthroughs in your understanding of life by exposure to spiritual knowledge of some sort. This is a year when endings of various sorts will come easily and usher in a new period of greater success for you.

THE NINE OF CLUBS IS YOUR DISPLACEMENT CARD

This could be a year in which you experience some disappointments on a mental level. Plans you made may turn out differently than you expected, some projects you were working on come to an end in an unpleasant way, and you may even get into a feeling of overall depression about how the events in your life are turning out. In truth, there will be some important completions in your life, but they do not have to become a source of disappointment or depression. That is the challenge that is implied by this card—to let go of the past without feeling victimized by circumstances.

This is probably a key year for you, one in which you reach the end of a long journey, so to speak. To get the most out of it, try to see what areas of your life have really reached the end of their usefulness for you. This could be your work, since Clubs refer to mental occupations. But on a deeper level, there may be some beliefs, points of view, plans, and expectations that must be cleared out to make way for a larger, more healthy perspective on life that is wanting to come into your life. Look at the habitual ways you communicate, think, and interpret the events of your life for clues as to what needs clearing and releasing. The feeling of freedom and universal consciousness that comes after letting go of these negative patterns more than makes up for the trepidation we may have in giving them up. You are preparing for a brand new cycle that is just about to begin. Honor all the things that got you to where you are now as you let them go, and you will be rewarded with a bright new future.

Nine of Diamonds

Financial or job losses, charitable gifts, or the ending of a value system

The Basic Meaning of the Nine of Diamonds

The Nine of Diamonds is often associated with financial losses of one kind or another, but its true meaning is that of a completion in regards to some values we have been holding. For this reason, it could be an indicator of the ending of a certain kind of work that you have been doing for a long time or the ending of a certain pursuit. This could be the pursuit of some financial goal, some relationship, or some other 'thing' that is valued.

When money does seem to be lost under the Nine of Diamonds, keep in mind that this is just the preparation for a new cycle of incoming money. Sometimes we need to spend some money to stimulate more to come in.

In reality, the Nine of Diamonds represents the end of a certain thing that we once valued and accumulated. It is a graduation from one level of values to the next. If we can learn to let go, we can experience a feeling of freedom and exhilaration as we move to the next level in our personal development. Endings are only disappointments to those who are not conscious of what is really going on in their life and who have no faith in life or love.

THE NINE OF DIAMONDS IN THE MERCURY PERIOD

This influence brings an unexpected and sudden financial disappointment, one that passes quickly. There could be a loss of money connected with a short trip or a brother or sister. There could be a loss in a get rich quick scheme. This card can bring a lot of mental anxiety about financial problems or some huge outlay of money. In all probability, this loss is a result of your own extravagance or recklessness.

The ending that will occur during this period can bring a sense of freedom and expansion if you are able to just let go and move on. Your other Mercury Card will tell you more about the situation, perhaps identifying who or what you need to let go of.

THE NINE OF DIAMONDS IN THE VENUS PERIOD

This card indicates much money being spent on the home or luxury items. If you overdo it, you may not have much left for other needs. Relationship problems could arise now due to financial reasons. You could have a female friend with money problems. During this period, many of your financial problems may be related to your close relationships or your desire to live a lifestyle of luxury. Your extravagant spending may not sit well with others during this period.

Your other Venus Card may tell you who or what the emotional or personal challenge or ending is about. Also keep in mind that a strong or powerful other Venus Card, such as a Four, Eight, or Ten, could mitigate the adversity of this card and bring about very positive results from a situation that may seem like a disappointment at the outset.

THE NINE OF DIAMONDS IN THE MARS PERIOD

This influence brings a loss of money on speculation, legal matters, or in connection with a man. Aggressive business activities and speculation are not favored at this time and can bring losses. Be extra careful in what you do and say. Though you will be attracted to speculation and gambling during this period, your best returns come from long-term investments. This can also represent difficulties in collecting inheritance or in a tax or insurance matter.

Look to your other Mars Card to find out what or who is involved in the challenges or endings that may arise during this period. Also, keep in mind that a positive card, such as a Four, Eight, or Ten, would tell you that regardless of the challenges present, you are likely to have a happy and productive outcome to the situations that present themselves during this fifty-two-day period.

THE NINE OF DIAMONDS IN THE JUPITER PERIOD

Under Jupiter, this card can mean affluence. Spending or investing a large sum of money is indicated, which means you have to have money in order to spend it. A large sum of money can be both made and lost, all within this period. This card indicates extravagant tastes and poor judgment with money, which can cause financial loss to the point of discomfort. You might find much satisfaction, however, in matters that involve charity or other community service.

It is likely that a job or occupation could come to an end now, but if so, it will probably be one of the better endings you have had in your life. The end will be easy and perhaps financially protected. If you resist any endings that occur now, you are only depriving yourself of the wonderful changes that are moving you to a new and better stage of your life.

THE NINE OF DIAMONDS IN THE SATURN PERIOD

This card brings a disappointment in finances related to ill health or the death of someone. There could be trouble with an inheritance or money spent on health care or a funeral. Extravagance or speculation are bound to bring difficulties now. This is a heavy karmic influence, one that brings problems that are difficult to overcome. Any deviations from fairness or legitimate transactions will bring heavy consequences.

The essential meaning of this card is 'letting go of something valued.' This could be a job, a relationship, or some other thing or things that you have held dear for quite some time. Because this card falls in the Saturn position, this ending will most likely be resisted by you more than usual. In this case, this would be a personal challenge for you, one that has a specific lesson to teach you. Keep in mind that though Saturn is the teacher, he is also the helper. The lessons we learn under his influence always bring us more maturity, fairness, and the ability to have much greater success in our lives.

Also, bear in mind that the difficulties or challenges indicated by this card could be offset by a strong card in the other Saturn position, for example any of the Fours, Eights, or Tens.

THE NINE OF DIAMONDS IN THE URANUS PERIOD

This influence brings financial disappointment or loss in a real estate or labor-related area. This could mean the loss of your job or a loss connected with employees. Avoid all speculative and 'quick money' deals at this time. Long-term investments are okay, but one should be careful here too. This influence brings financial problems in the usual sense, but also promises great success for those who are giving of their time and resources to charitable causes.

The basic meaning of this card is the 'ending of something valued.' Something that you have wanted and worked for in the past has now outlived its usefulness in your life and is passing away. If you are conscious of this as the end of a cycle for you, you will be able to let go and move ahead, looking to the future for better things to come.

This is a good influence for spiritual matters, learning new spiritual information, attending classes, etc. Also, keep in mind that a positive card, such as a Four, Eight, or Ten, in the other position of this period would offset any problematic situations that may arise and bring about good results overall.

The Nine of Diamonds in the Neptune Period

This influence can bring a loss of money related to travel, foreign interests, drugs and alcohol, or deception. However, it is just as possible that this money could be money that is invested in your business or other financial instruments—money that will return to you later when your investments pay off. A trip now could prove to be much more expensive than you had planned and may not bring as much enjoyment. Even under the most favorable of circumstances, one should always be careful in all financially related dealings with this card present.

On the positive side, you could experience the completion of a financially related project that has been going for a long time. Its culmination may leave you feeling a bit lost or confused, but by the time your next birthday comes around, you'll be back in action, moving towards new goals and ideals. This is an excellent influence for giving money to the poor or helping others out financially with no expectation of repayment.

It is entirely possible that a long-time cherished dream or possession of yours could come to an end or be lost during this period. This could be something that you have been worrying about losing from time to time this year. If so, don't be afraid or disappointed. This ending is actually the best thing for you and everyone else in your life. Let it go, and many new and better things will soon come to replace it.

The Nine of Diamonds Is Your Pluto Card

During this year, you will find yourself often confronted with financial outlays of one kind or another, and these may truly tax your sense of prosperity and financial well-being. Whether you are investing this money for the future, giving it to charity, losing it on investments, paying it out on needed expenses, or having unexpected financial outlays such as cars breaking down, you will have to let go of some money this year. The only attitude that will help you retain peace of mind is that of letting go and having faith that you will be provided for by the universe. This year is a cycle of money going out. These are always followed by cycles of money coming back in.

This can also be a year when you complete your involvement with a certain type of work or money-making venture or occupation. Usually, when this card is Pluto, we tend to resist letting go of any means of support that has perhaps outlived its real meaning in our lives. Sometimes this card will signal a year when this job or occupation is taken away from us against our will. If we realize that the time has come to move on and simply accept the timing of things, we can flow with this on to something much better. Something new and better always follows a nine year.

Your Result Card will further clarify how this money will be spent or tell you who is involved in the financial outlays and completions.

Affirmation:

I am releasing myself from things, occupations, and people that were once good for me but have now outlived their purpose in my life. I set myself free to move on to higher and better things in my life.

The Nine of Diamonds Is Your Result Card

This powerful card of 'Universal Values' guarantees that by your next birthday you will be less attached to money and will have a new and broadened perspective about money that gives you more freedom and less concern than ever before. Somehow connected to your Pluto Card, you will learn and master the art of finances by the true knowledge of the nature of prosperity—that it follows cycles that go in and out and that only by flowing with it can we have peace of mind.

Affirmation:

I learn to release financial worries and to flow with the cycles of abundance in my life. I learn to give things away.

The Nine of Diamonds Is Your Long-Range Card

This could be a year of major financial outlays for you or one of repeated disappointments relating to your money condition unless and until you learn to let prosperity flow in your life without your personal obstruction. This card can actually bring you sudden wealth if you achieve the proper state of mind. There will be much money that needs to go out this year, because the Nine of Diamonds represents the time for this to happen. However, remember that money is like the tides once it goes out, it inevitably comes back in. If you don't obstruct the flow of energy by trying to control it, it will come back even better than before. Flow with it.

At the same time, this card tells us that there are many things in your life, be they possessions, jobs, money, or relationships, that have outlived their true usefulness to you. This is the year to complete these things and to prepare for a new beginning that will follow.

Keywords:

A year of much money going out, either for investments or expenditures. I learn to flow with the cycles of prosperity. I release those things that I once valued, but now have no real need for in my life.

The Nine of Diamonds Is Your Environment Card

Giving up things, people, or jobs that you once valued highly will bring many blessings and rewards this year. On some level, this is a year to let go of the past and prepare to move on to many new and better things. Usually, we are afraid to let go of things in our life, afraid that the loss will deprive us of something important and essential to our happiness. However, this year you are protected, and all completions will bring you greater fortune and happiness.

The Nine of Diamonds Is Your Displacement Card

This will be an important 'graduation' year for you in terms of your values or your job. If you are unaware that you have reached the end of a cycle and must move on, you could experience financial losses of many kinds, loss of your job, or disappointments related to losing things that you value in some way. However, you do not have to have these losses by any means. The truth is that something important in your value system has reached the end of its usefulness for you. This could mean your present line of work, something you collect or own, or simply your entire way of looking at life and the things that are important to you. This would be especially true if your Birth Card is a Diamond, since you would already tend to look upon everything in your life in terms of how much it is worth to you.

So, something is ending this year, and it is up to you as to whether this becomes a tragedy or a cause for celebration as you graduate from this level to move on to the next. How you handle this ending will determine your level of happiness this year. The best attitude is one of giving up and letting go, knowing that you are not losing anything that is actually good for you anymore. As a matter of fact, this year is the preparation for a new life just about to begin. This new life will be one that is more healthy and full of new and pleasant surprises for you. So, embrace the endings that occur this year with joy. You have come a long way to get where you are, and you will lose nothing that is truly yours.

Nine of Spades

Loss of job, poor health, death, major ending of some component of our lifestyle

The Basic Meaning of the Nine of Spades

The Nine of Spades can be a card of loss and disappointment. However, the true nature of the card reveals that its presence in your life for any period of time does not have to be a disaster. In actuality, the Nine of Spades represents making a completion of some importance. Whether this is the end of a certain occupation, way of life, or way of being with your health and body will depend upon the position of the card and the circumstances in your life at the time. But rest assured that some important aspect of your life is coming to an end when this potent card shows up.

This is also one of the death cards, and indeed, when this card shows up, there will be a death in your life of some kind. We go through many mini-deaths in the course of our lifetime, and just like the snake shedding its skin, arrive at a new and better place each time we do so. Therefore, the Nine of Spades is not a card to be feared, but instead, a card to be welcomed. It always has the ability to clear away all the unwanted and useless debris in our life and put us back on a new course where we are much more enlivened and satisfied.

THE NINE OF SPADES IN THE MERCURY PERIOD

This period may bring a sudden illness, accident, or trouble with work. This could be disappointing, but will probably not last long either. This could be a sudden loss of work or some unexpected bad news. This could also be a problem encountered on a short trip, such as an accident, or some trouble with a brother or sister. It is best to slow down now, take things at a safe pace until this period is over. Also, watch out for negative attitudes now.

Since all nines represent completions and endings, your other Mercury Card could indicate who or what in your life is now coming to an end. It also may indicate what the net result of your letting go is or give more background information about the ending.

THE NINE OF SPADES IN THE VENUS PERIOD

This influence can bring illness over a love relationship or a family-related disappointment. This could also be the illness of a close friend, marriage partner, or family member.

This card tells you that some major part of your lifestyle is coming to its fulfillment or completion. This could be a relationship or have something to do with your home or family. The ending of a relationship or friendship could cause much grief if you resist the completion that is scheduled for this period. This is an influence of difficulties in the home or in personal relationships, but only if we stubbornly hold on to people or things that are now passing out of our life. All these difficulties can be considered tests of emotional strength and maturity.

Your other Venus Card may tell you who or what the emotional or personal challenge or ending is about. Also, keep in mind that a strong or powerful other Venus Card, such as a Four, Eight, or Ten, could mitigate the adversity of this card and bring about very positive results from a situation that may seem like a disappointment at the outset.

THE NINE OF SPADES IN THE MARS PERIOD

This period could bring a difficult lawsuit or problems dealing with some man or group of males. A headstrong attitude or recklessness can bring troubles in work and health during this period. Illness can interfere with work also. Be wary of all associations with men, and try to settle difficulties out of court, as these are not favored by this influence. By

adopting a more universal (unselfish) attitude in these areas, you may find great success.

Look to your other Mars Card to find out what or who is involved in the challenges or endings that may arise during this period. Also, keep in mind that a positive card, such as a Four, Eight, or Ten, would tell you that regardless of the challenges present, you are likely to have a happy and productive outcome to the situations that present themselves during this fifty-two-day period.

THE NINE OF SPADES IN THE JUPITER PERIOD

During this period, you will likely experience a major completion or ending of a line of work or livelihood. This ending will in some way affect your basic lifestyle in an important way. It seems as though you have been doing a certain occupation for a long time, and now is the time to move on to something new. Don't resist these endings, as they are positively leading you to a new, more exciting, and more prosperous future. Even if you get fired, this will inevitably lead to something much better with this influence.

You are protected by Jupiter's blessings now, and all you need to do is take a close look at your situation to realize the good in what is happening. In truth, it was your desire to have this happen in the first place.

THE NINE OF SPADES IN THE SATURN PERIOD

This is a strong indicator of illness of you or a friend. This illness may be lingering and hard to diagnose and may interfere with work or other plans. Care should be taken in minding your health. This is one of the most difficult of influences, one that represents karmic debts to be repaid, that is, payments for things you had done in the past. Any negativity or bad habits now will only aggravate the situation.

This card can also indicate the ending of a job, relationship, or other important area in your life. Your other Saturn Card may tell you what will come to an end during this period. Because of Saturn's influence, it is likely that you will resist this ending more that you would in other circumstances. However, it will end anyway and ultimately will lead you to something better. This card usually indicates something in our lives that really is not good for us that has been hanging around much longer than it should. The death of this issue, regardless of what it is, usually comes hard in Saturn, but great healing always follows.

Also, bear in mind that the difficulties or challenges indicated by this card could be offset by a strong card in the other Saturn position, for example any of the Fours, Eights, or Tens.

THE NINE OF SPADES IN THE URANUS PERIOD

This influence can bring disappointments in work, labor relations, humanitarian efforts, or a real estate deal. Be cautious in any of these areas during this period. Many challenges may present themselves now, and overcoming these can lead to significant advancement. Aside from speculation, you may find that an intuitive insight can aid you in making decisions and helping others now.

On a deeper level, this card indicates that you are ready to move on to another line of work or a new lifestyle. This may be the time to let go of some of those things that you have had in the past to make way for the new that is coming. This is a card of completion and graduation. However, many of us resist letting go when the time comes. If you can let these things, whatever they are, fall away from you, you will find yourself feeling lighter, freer, and ready to embrace a new and exciting future.

This is a good influence for spiritual matters, learning new spiritual information, attending classes, etc. Also, keep in mind that a positive card, such as a Four, Eight, or Ten, in the other position of this period would offset any problematic situations that may arise and bring about good results overall.

THE NINE OF SPADES IN THE NEPTUNE PERIOD

This influence can bring an illness or accident related to the water, drugs, alcohol, or traveling. This could also be a disappointment related to a trip or distant affairs. The possibility of a hidden illness or disappointment is also present. Any association with travel or drugs or alcohol will be disappointing now. However, this card can represent a great fulfillment if one is involved in helping others in some humanitarian kind of work.

It is entirely possible that a long-time cherished dream or occupation of yours could come to an end or be lost during this period. This could be something that you have been worrying about losing from time to time this year. If so, don't be afraid or disappointed. This ending is actually the best thing for you and everyone else in your life. Let it go, and many new and better things will soon come to replace it.

THE NINE OF SPADES IS YOUR PLUTO CARD

This year you have one of the most challenging cards, the Nine of Spades. This card can signal a year of losses of many kinds. In many ways, this will be a year of completions and endings. You may lose your job or have to contend with lingering health problems that force you to change your habits. You could even lose someone you know, and this passing may not be easy for you to cope with.

For some people, transitions and changes of such a dramatic nature are very hard to deal with. An attitude that all is happening for a good reason will go a long way towards your getting through this year with sanity and peace of mind.

What is being called for this year is for you to let go of certain important parts of your lifestyle that are no longer good for you or those around you. Whether you can see it or not, you have reached a place of completion in these areas and need to move on. If you resist, it will seem like these endings are being forced upon you. See this as a year of completions as you prepare for a whole new chapter of life. The next year will be one of new beginnings leading you in an entirely new direction that is much better for you on all levels.

Your Result Card will tell you more about the challenges ahead for you this year, perhaps giving you clues as to which areas of your life are nearing completion. It may also point to someone that is directly involved in these endings.

AFFIRMATION:

I am transformed by the endings of relationships, jobs, or lifestyle habits that are occurring in my life this year. I release everything that has been holding me back, and in doing so, I set myself free.

THE NINE OF SPADES IS YOUR RESULT CARD

Somehow associated with your Pluto Card this year will be the element of 'ending.' This could be the death of someone you know, a job, or health habits that have created the problems you may now be experiencing. This letting go will certainly take you to a better place, a state of mind where you will be more free to live as you please. You are ending a major chapter in your life that will lead you to a new beginning that is just around the corner. In the process, there may be things that you have been doing for a long time that you will now let go of and stop doing. Let go and live.

AFFIRMATION:

I learn to let go of people, lifestyle habits, and jobs that have completed their purpose in my life. They are fulfilled and I am free to move on to new and better things.

THE NINE OF SPADES IS YOUR LONG-RANGE CARD

As the 'Nine of Nines,' the Nine of Spades is the strongest indicator of a year of important endings for you. You could end a line of work you have been doing for a long time or have to contend with health problems that cause you to make major changes in your lifestyle or habits. The Nine of Spades is often associated with work and health problems or disappointments, but this is only if we are unwilling to let go of the things, people, jobs, or habits that are now surely ending for us. This is a year of major completion. Whatever you are doing when you begin this year will likely be over by the time of your next birthday. There could be a death in the family or of someone you know or one of many conditions that will ultimately affect your lifestyle in an important way.

The Nine of Spades is also a strong indicator of spiritual work and could indicate much success in this area for you this year. Success applying universal principles is the key. This can mean letting go of things that are passing away and broadening of your life's goals to include some sort of humanitarian work. This will help you realize the success potential of this powerful card.

KEYWORDS:

A year of major endings and completions in your life. They can be related to health problems or deaths in the family.

THE NINE OF SPADES IS YOUR ENVIRONMENT CARD

This is likely to be a year when you are ending up a major cycle of your life, preparing for or entering into a new beginning for yourself. Endings represent phases completed and as such they can be cause for celebration and personal acknowledgment. Whether these completions relate to your work, health, or another important aspect of your lifestyle, now is the time to let go and prepare to move on to a new and much better phase of life.

THE NINE OF SPADES IS YOUR DISPLACEMENT CARD

This is likely to be a crucial year for you in which a major chapter of your life comes to an end. Some aspect of your life has reached its point of fulfillment and now must be swept away to make room for a new cycle of growth and opportunity. Be prepared and open to endings in most any area and you will be much less likely to suffer the disappointment and frustration generally associated with this card.

Often health matters come into play with this powerful card. If you have any negative habits that affect your health adversely, there is a very good chance that these habits will have to be cleared out this year. In many cases, it can be a matter of life or death—get rid of the bad habits or else. But for those who are aware of themselves, there will be no surprises, and the endings will be seen as the next stage in their evolutionary journey.

Another common manifestation of this card is loss of a job or the death of one or more people who are close to us. In any of these cases, regardless of how unfair they may seem to us at the time, whatever is lost was not really a part of us that was good for us any more. It is only our fear of the unknown that keeps us clinging on to jobs, relationships, and other things that we know inside are not good for us. We would rather suffer with the familiar than have to face an uncertain future. But when the Nine of Spades comes along, major housecleaning will occur. Just what areas of your life are affected, whether it be work, health, lifestyle, or relationships, will depend upon your personal circumstances. Life is an always-changing phenomena, and though we are attached to things the way they are, everything must evolve and grow eventually. This year marks an important graduation year for you. You have come a long way with things the way they are and have now progressed far enough that you are ready for a new future. All that remains is to clear out the old to make way for the new.

Ten of Hearts

Success with groups of people or the public, large gatherings of people, a wedding

The Basic Meaning of the Ten of Hearts

The Ten of Hearts literally means 'Ten Hearts.' Hearts represent people, so this card speaks about activities involving large numbers of people that you have a love connection with. It is sort of like the Ten of Clubs, but it will deal more with family, circles of friends, or with the audiences of musicians, artists, and other performers. In its highest manifestation, the Ten of Hearts brings much success with the public and groups of people.

To get the most out of this card, plan your advertising and promotional campaign when it is present. At the very least, this card represents a social occasion such as a party where you are well received and have a wonderful time. It can also represent a marriage or other large family gathering.

THE TEN OF HEARTS IN THE MERCURY PERIOD

This influence will bring sudden social success among some group of people or success in areas dealing with communication, publishing, and speaking. This could mean a party, such as a birthday party, or some other gathering where there are lots of people for you to impress with your wit and charm. This influence can be applied to business or financial success by scheduling advertising or promotions while this card is present.

THE TEN OF HEARTS IN THE VENUS PERIOD

This is a card of success in matters of the heart, either personal or social. Under this influence, you can have just about anything you want romantically or socially. This could mean a very successful love affair. Relationships with women will be better than usual now, and they could be the source of many good things in your life. Your desires for affection will be met, either in a one-on-one situation or in some sort of party or group situation.

THE TEN OF HEARTS IN THE MARS PERIOD

Relationships in all areas should be very successful under this influence, especially with men or groups of men. This could also translate as success in a lawsuit or legal matter. Aggressively pursuing friendships and relationships should bring you success and happiness under this influence, and this is certainly the time to take the active role in all social and personal situations. This is great influence for performers and artists and those dealing with the public.

THE TEN OF HEARTS IN THE JUPITER PERIOD

Successes, both personally and socially, can bring financial gains during this period. Apply your charm and magnetism now to your career for spectacular results. Friendships and partnerships will advance you along in your chosen field. If you are involved in selling, acting, or any business that involves groups of people, this is one of the best influences for social and financial success. Also, success in dealing with religious institutions is indicated.

THE TEN OF HEARTS IN THE SATURN PERIOD

If there are any difficulties present now, such as illness or other adversities, you have the power to overcome them. Help from friends is there if and when you need it. This card is a protective influence and a card of overcoming disappointments. Success in dealing with groups of people is also implied by this card, though you may have to work harder to achieve it. Your own popularity may in some way become a burden during this period.

THE TEN OF HEARTS IN THE URANUS PERIOD

This is a good influence for success in work and all things dealing with the public or charitable causes. This is also a good time for success and recognition related to spiritual studies. This could also translate as success in real estate related businesses or activities. The success you have now may happen unexpectedly, as things often do during one's Uranus period. This is a good card for psychic development or research.

You should have a great time during this period in any social occasions that you may attend, so go out there and get noticed!

THE TEN OF HEARTS IN THE NEPTUNE PERIOD

This period may bring success on a journey or from things connected to foreign places. If you are traveling, you will make many new friends and possibly business contacts during the trip. This is a strong indicator of success for actors, actresses, and other performers of the arts. You could also experience healing in the area of friendship and relationship with the public as a result of spiritual revelations.

THE TEN OF HEARTS IS YOUR PLUTO CARD

This year you see a need to get more involved with the public or with your circle of friends. There is something important for you in making contact with larger numbers of people, and this will be the year that you will make important changes in your life to accomplish just that. Maybe you are in a business that needs more public exposure, and you launch an advertising campaign. Or, just as likely, you have decided that you are tired of staying at home and want to get out and have more fun. The Ten of Hearts is just the influence to get you going. You may have to make some changes to accomplish this, and it may not be easy at first. But the rewards will be more than worth it.

The Ten of Hearts is also known as one of the performer cards. In the Pluto position, it can signal a year when one of your important goals is getting the attention of the public or having to deal with larger groups of people and getting them to like you. It has a lot to do with sharing the things you love with them. It is a successful card, so it is likely that you will have to really put in a lot of energy and determination to achieve these goals this year. As Pluto, these goals will cause you to make important changes in yourself.

Your Result Card will tell you more about this social or public exposure that you desire this year or point to someone who may be involved in it.

AFFIRMATION:

I am transformed by creating more social popularity and public exposure. I change myself to gain social influence.

THE TEN OF HEARTS IS YOUR RESULT CARD

The result of much of this year's activities and changes will be more power and recognition with the public or any large group of people. Perhaps you are wanting to be more socially active or need publicity for your business. In any case, this influence promises that though you may have to work hard for it, success in these areas is guaranteed by your next birthday. Your Pluto Card will tell more about this success or describe someone who is involved in it.

AFFIRMATION:

I achieve more social success and popularity or public exposure for my work or business. I create recognition.

THE TEN OF HEARTS IS YOUR LONG-RANGE CARD

The Ten of Hearts tells us that success, recognition, and popularity will come to you this year. Especially favored are activities dealing with the public or large groups. This recognition will play an important role in your life depending upon the other circumstances of your life. Perhaps you are in a business where you want more exposure and recognition. This is an excellent indication that you will meet with great success in those areas. This is one of the best cards for performers, because the Ten of Hearts indicates that large groups of people are favorably disposed towards you. In general, this is one of the best influences to have. It can overcome negative influences that may be present, and you might even become famous!

KEYWORDS:

I am surrounded by the love and admiration of people. I have success with groups and the public and enjoy much popularity.

THE TEN OF HEARTS IS YOUR ENVIRONMENT CARD

Your ability to get recognition from the public and to be well received in any large gathering of people will come to your aid this year and bring you greater success. With this in mind, this would be a good year to pursue any sort of artistic pursuit or to launch an advertising or promotion campaign for your business. This will also be a good year for family and social interactions, especially for parties and large social occasions.

THE TEN OF HEARTS IS YOUR DISPLACEMENT CARD

Social or family commitments, or work involving the public and large groups may take up a lot more of your time and energy than you planned this year. Expect to have to pay more attention to these areas and to have to put in more effort than expected to get them to go right. Likewise, if you are involved in a business, getting your products to market will take a lot of energy and determination. The Ten of Hearts represents groups of people, whether they are children, customers, fans, or people attending your wedding. One or more of these areas will be taxing your energies this year or require more of your attention in order to maintain good conditions and relationships.

Ten of Clubs

Success in the communications field or teaching, a lot on the mind

The Basic Meaning of the Ten of Clubs

The Ten of Clubs usually brings measurable success in one of the mind-related fields or endeavors. This could be publishing or teaching or other areas where large groups are benefiting from your talents and mental brilliance. Recognition for your talents and efforts are common when this card is present.

Essentially, the Ten of Clubs is the card of the 'teacher.' It means spreading knowledge or information to large groups of people. This is a great card for those in the publishing, radio, or television— businesses where much information is being distributed to large numbers.

THE TEN OF CLUBS IN THE MERCURY PERIOD

This card indicates a sudden or unexpected success, good news, or an opportunity to acquire some type of knowledge. This is a great card for things related to speaking, writing, teaching, or working with groups of people. Getting a good education and having some sort of instant acceptance or success in one or more of the mental fields is indicated. This may not be a long-lasting influence, but it could bring the acquisition of some desired goal.

THE TEN OF CLUBS IN THE VENUS PERIOD

Here we have some really good news or success with people or friends. Social activities with intellectual overtones are emphasized. Success with women. Having the right knowledge opens doors and makes many beneficial contacts and friends. This is a card of satisfaction and instant acceptance by others, perhaps dealing with intellectual pursuits. Friends, and women in particular, will be stimulating and fun.

THE TEN OF CLUBS IN THE MARS PERIOD

This influence brings success in most areas of life, especially related to education, speaking, writing, or teaching and in relation to men. Success comes through applying your understanding of human nature and common sense. This influence could indicate success in a legal matter or lawsuit or any matter that you are aggressively pursuing or that deals with groups of men such as fraternities or associations. You will be recognized now!

THE TEN OF CLUBS IN THE JUPITER PERIOD

This is a powerful indicator of a huge success in finances and business through application of knowledge. This success could be in any mind-related activity such as publishing, speaking, education or any of the communications fields. By applying your innate understanding of human nature, you can reap many rewards during this period. Money and business will be very good, and if you apply your mind, you could even make it better.

THE TEN OF CLUBS IN THE SATURN PERIOD

Overcoming undesirable influences is indicated by this card, especially through the application of wisdom and knowledge. Healing power, especially using natural methods, could be present for you now. Use it to heal yourself and others. By applying self-control, you can conquer many problems during this period. This card also brings success in any of the mind-related fields, such as publishing or teaching, if one is ready to work hard to get it.

Be ready for hard work. The success potential of this card is only accessed by those who are willing to put in a lot of effort in the process. As a matter of fact, this card often represents some project or task that is a lot of work.

THE TEN OF CLUBS IN THE URANUS PERIOD

This influence brings success and recognition in labor affairs, real estate deals, and any kind of teaching or writing. This is also a very good influence for humanitarian work or selfless service to your community. Psychic development or working with electronics and futuristic technology is also favored by this influence. Your intuition could be very strong now. Apply it in your work for success and understanding of yourself and others.

THE TEN OF CLUBS IN THE NEPTUNE PERIOD

This is a very good influence, one that brings much success and the realization of a dream. Travel can also be very rewarding at this time, as well as any business or interests that are foreign or distant from you in some way. This period may see you achieving success and recognition in the fields of writing, teaching, speaking, or learning, especially if it deals with helping or caring for others in some way.

THE TEN OF CLUBS IS YOUR PLUTO CARD

This year will bring much focus on your mind, how you use it, and how you go about sharing what you know with others. Perhaps you are involved in one of the mental fields such as publishing, writing, teaching, speaking, or communications. In this case, you may be attempting to get more success or recognition in that area. The Ten of Clubs always refers to reaching larger and larger groups of people, and it refers to knowledge passed on by you to them. Somehow, this is the goal and challenge for you this year.

To achieve your goals, you must institute some changes in the way you do things, and these changes may challenge you to be more than you have ever been before. In another vein, your mind may already be too powerful for you, and this is a year when you are learning to either harness its energies or to regain control over it so that you can sleep at night. Whatever the specifics, your relationship with your mind is in the spotlight. It can either be your ally or your enemy. Your Result Card will further describe your work with your mind and mental fields or describe someone associated with it.

AFFIRMATION:

I am challenged to use my mind to its full potential. I desire success in teaching or in other communications areas.

THE TEN OF CLUBS IS YOUR RESULT CARD

The Ten of Clubs promises that by your next birthday you will make some major accomplishment in terms of your work, especially work that involves communications or teaching or reaching a wide range of people. The Ten of Clubs is the card of the teacher who shares his or her knowledge with the world. This success will transform you. Your Pluto Card will tell you more about how you are going to bring information to the world or who will be a key element in your success.

I accomplish much success as a teacher or communicator. I harness my mind for recognition from the public.

THE TEN OF CLUBS IS YOUR LONG-RANGE CARD

The Ten of Clubs can bring measurable success and recognition in one of the mind-related fields or endeavors. This could be publishing or teaching or other areas where large groups are benefiting from your talent and brilliance. Recognition for your talents and efforts are forthcoming this year and will somehow touch upon all the areas of your life and take on a light of prominence in your affairs. However, if you don't have a productive and constructive outlet for your mind this year, the Ten of Clubs could indicate problems with stress and difficulty sleeping at night. Find a good outlet for the mental powers present. It could bring you a measure of success and recognition.

KEYWORDS:

A year of mental accomplishment and having a lot of ideas. I share my knowledge with a large number of people.

THE TEN OF CLUBS IS YOUR ENVIRONMENT CARD

This could be a year of great success for you, especially if you are involved in radio, television, teaching, publishing, writing, communications, or public speaking. You may have a lot on your mind and a lot of work to do, but your efforts will be well rewarded. All things having to do with knowledge and groups of people will bring blessings into your life. Broadcast your message for success.

THE TEN OF CLUBS IS YOUR DISPLACEMENT CARD

This is a very significant year in your life, one in which you begin a most significant cycle of change and evolution. The effects of this card will depend largely upon the current direction of your life, whether or not you are career or goal oriented, and just what you are striving for at this time, if anything. For those who have clear goals and directions, this year could bring a lot of success, actually a taste of even better things to come. All this year promises some progress along the lines of whatever is felt as important and meaningful.

Relationships in particular will go better than usual this year. You will have a certain power with people, as denoted by the King of Spades in your Venus period, that can bring you great success in all your relationships or with the public. In order to access this power, you must be willing to proclaim loud and clear just what you want from them. Success does not come to the meek and retiring under the influence of a King. Those involved in performing arts, advertising, or other jobs that deal with the public should notice unusually good success in these areas. Your charm is at an all-time high.

This year marks your 'final ascent to the pinnacle.' In some way, you are taking the last steps on a journey that began years ago. In three years, you will reach the pinnacle, your destination, and be ready to embark on a new journey. Take advantage of the next three years to enjoy yourself and to glean as much as possible from your current phase of life. All of that will soon change, and you will be glad you took the time to enjoy this most wonderful phase of your journey.

Ten of Diamonds

Dealing with or focusing on a very large sum of money

The Basic Meaning of the Ten of Diamonds

The Ten of Diamonds is a card of financial success and is considered to be the best money card to have in your yearly spread. Success in dealing with groups of people in some financial way is also indicated.

Essentially, the Ten of Diamonds means a large sum of money and infatuation or obsession with money. It doesn't always mean that you will receive large sums of money. Sometimes it can merely mean a preoccupation with finances. However, when the Ten of Diamonds falls in Jupiter or as the year's Result Card, the chances are much greater that a huge financial gain is forthcoming.

THE TEN OF DIAMONDS IN THE MERCURY PERIOD

This card indicates a sudden streak of financial success, perhaps in a speculative venture, related to a brother or sister, or while on a short trip. This is a sudden windfall of money that is possibly just as quickly spent. This is a very good indicator of financial success in the fields of education, writing, speaking, or teaching. You will be more money minded than usual, and this will contribute to your success and perhaps to your continuing education. Watch out for a preoccupation with money that could cause short-sightedness in other areas.

THE TEN OF DIAMONDS IN THE VENUS PERIOD

This card represents financial success connected to the arts, products for women or the home, some woman you know, or to your own lover or marriage. Any of these could be the source of a windfall of money. This could be great success for an artist. With this influence, you will choose to spend more time with friends and lovers that are well-to-do. Money will be a definite priority in your love relationships or marriage, perhaps too much.

THE TEN OF DIAMONDS IN THE MARS PERIOD

During this period, drive, ambition, and honest effort will bring great financial success. This success could be in a legal matter or related to men in some way. Resist the temptation to speculate at this time. Success comes with the right application of values and fairness. You have the ability to make a tremendous amount of money now, but it must be made with honest effort and honorable action. Deviations from higher values could bring trouble.

THE TEN OF DIAMONDS IN THE JUPITER PERIOD

This is one of the best possible indicators of success in business and money. Expansion of all financial and business interests will bring added success. This card represents large sums of money changing hands, usually into your hands. This could be as a result of an investment or from your business. Sound business sense and good luck are on your side, and you will prefer the company of successful and like-minded people now.

This card is arguably the best card possible for financial success. However, it will only bring success to those who are engaged in some enterprise that has the possibility of experiencing such a grand success. Don't make the mistake of telling someone without a job or on a fixed income that this card will bring them such great success. It just isn't going to happen.

THE TEN OF DIAMONDS IN THE SATURN PERIOD

This card brings financial success in matters relating to health or some older authority person in your life. There is the possibility of inheritance. With this money can come hard work and much responsibility. This card can also mean that your financial success is somewhat delayed due to the ill health of yourself or others. This is a card of financial success for doctors or those in the healing professions.

THE TEN OF DIAMONDS IN THE URANUS PERIOD

This card brings financial success from selling real estate or land (farms too), dealing with labor or employees, new technology, or in some humanitarian project. Money comes in from psychic work or some land-related business. This card can indicate money coming in unexpectedly or from some unusual source. This could be from a religious, psychic, or occult-related activity.

THE TEN OF DIAMONDS IN THE NEPTUNE PERIOD

This card indicates success and prosperity from travel, shipping, or foreign business interests. Also possible is money made through caring for others or related to drugs or alcohol, or from some hidden source. Success and enjoyment of travel and dealing with foreigners is indicated here. This might be a great time to take that business/pleasure trip overseas. Your greatest satisfaction comes through sharing your good fortune with others during this period.

THE TEN OF DIAMONDS IS YOUR PLUTO CARD

Financial matters are likely to take the spotlight this year. This year you will be dealing with a large sum of money, either directly or indirectly, and this will be a matter that causes a lot of change and personal growth for you. This could be your money or the money of someone else, but it will be important in your life. It might just be money that you use for work, or it could be an inheritance that is up for grabs. In some way, this large sum of money will challenge you. It may be that you have decided that you want to earn a lot of money this year. Your own business could be at the point where you desire a major expansion.

On a deeper level, the Ten of Diamonds tells us that you are wanting an expansion of your values. This is the year to expand both your self-worth and the boundaries of what you think you can earn or have as far as material things are concerned. Though it seems like an external matter, the real change is occurring within yourself. How much do you really think you are worth? How much will you allow yourself to have?

Whatever the case, you will have to make some changes in your life in order to have the success you want in this area, and at times, this will seem difficult. Your Result Card will give you more specifics about this money or tell you who, among those you know, is directly involved with it.

AFFIRMATION:

I desire a large sum of money. I am transformed by this desire or challenged by dealing with large sums of money.

THE TEN OF DIAMONDS IS YOUR RESULT CARD

The result of this year's major goals and challenges, represented by your Pluto Card, will somehow involve a large sum of money or financial success. You may actually achieve considerable prosperity as you expand your values to include the needs of those around you and your community or country. The further you expand your vision, the more you could make. This could represent taking your products and services to the public in a major way.

AFFIRMATION:

I create financial abundance or end up with a large sum of money this year. I expand my values.

THE TEN OF DIAMONDS IS YOUR LONG-RANGE CARD

This year you will be thinking about money a great deal. This is likely to be a large sum of money. However, this card doesn't guarantee that you will actually earn or get a large sum of money. You may be involved in some sort of affair where there is a large sum to deal with, but it may not necessarily be yours. This could be related to an estate, your work, a divorce, or any number of other reasons. In some cases, this card does indicate much money being made. This is not certain, but it is certain that you will be thinking about money a lot.

KEYWORDS:

A year of dealing with large sums of money or the concept of large sums of money. Possible huge financial success.

THE TEN OF DIAMONDS IS YOUR ENVIRONMENT CARD

Financial matters should proceed smoothly this year, and you should have a certain amount of financial protection as well. If there are circumstances where large sums of money are involved, these situations should resolve themselves in your favor. You may even feel protected by some large sum of money that is at your disposal. With such protection, you can safely proceed with business expansion or other financial deals designed to increase your wealth.

This is one of the most powerful of the wish cards. Expect one or more important things to turn out just as you would like them to. This is a year for you to collect some good karma from good deeds that you performed some time in your past.

THE TEN OF DIAMONDS IS YOUR DISPLACEMENT CARD

Having your card in this most auspicious position this year, is called being in the 'most blessed spot.' You are surrounded by the influence of Jupiter, the planet of spiritual and material blessings. Research has shown that people in this position usually receive whatever is their most heartfelt desire. Sometimes the wish that is fulfilled is of a more mundane nature, such as money or business success, and other times, it is of a more spiritual nature. The exact nature of your blessing will be determined by your approach to life and what it is that you find to be the most important.

People have made major breakthroughs in their life during this year, while others have had their prayers answered. It is not just some ordinary desire that is fulfilled, but instead something that is more personal and meaningful to the individual. You may be able to determine what it could be by asking yourself just what it is that you want most right now. But even after doing that, often the result is a mystery until it actually happens. The specific timing of the blessing is not definite either. All that is known is that it will occur sometime before your next birthday.

Ten of Spades

Success in work, health, and legal affairs, being a workaholic

The Basic Meaning of the Ten of Spades

The Ten of Spades is one of the best cards for success and satisfaction in your work and in health, though you may also expect to work very hard when it is present. Overcoming of all obstacles in work and health are the attributes of this card.

Like the Ten of Wands in the Tarot deck, your work may often seem to be a burden under this card's influence, or you may become obsessed with all the things that you have to do. This card can be a 'workaholic' kind of influence. However, if you have a list of specific goals and want to achieve them successfully, there is hardly a better card to have in your reading than this one.

The Ten of Spades in the Mercury Period

This period can bring a sudden success or a quick return for work done. This could be success in speculative deals, short trips, or in some Mercury-ruled pursuit. These would include education, writing, speaking, communications, publishing, or teaching. You have great mind power that you can use to get quick returns now, and you may receive much recognition during this period. A Ten of Spades in Mercury acts much in the same way as a Ten of Clubs, since Clubs and Mercury both deal with communications, education, and mental projects.

The Ten of Spades in the Venus Period

This is a card of success and happiness in love, home, money, work, health, and family. It is an influence that overcomes negativity and problems. This success may be connected to females in some way or to the arts and music. This is also a good influence for a working marriage or for working with large groups of people. Business expansion is favored, and you should have the resources to do this comfortably.

The Ten of Spades in the Mars Period

This influence promises great success through hard work and perseverance. This is also an indicator of radiant health and the ability to overcome problems, especially lawsuits and things dealing with men. If you apply ambition and effort during this period, you could have extraordinary results and overcome all problems. Relations or work with men are particularly favored by this influence.

The Ten of Spades in the Jupiter Period

This is one of the most powerful indicators of success in work and money enterprises. This influence favors expansion of business and dealings with powerful money people. Money may come through travel also. Honesty and integrity will pay off in a big way. Think BIG now. This is the time for you to expand your operations into what they could be. Politics, religion, and working with the public are favored, but you can flourish in other types of work as well.

The Ten of Spades in the Saturn Period

This influence promises success through hard work, possibly in the healing or medical fields. This influence also brings the ability to recover from illness and overcome problems through perseverance and determination. You may feel that you are paying a high price for success now, as work is harder than usual with many demands on your time and freedom. And yet, this is what you must do now, and it will bring you the success you want.

The Ten of Spades in the Uranus Period

This card represents success in organizations of labor, real estate, or other earth-related businesses. General success in work and the overcoming of work and health difficulties are suggested by this card. This success also applies in the areas of humanitarian work, futuristic technology, or in some unusual manner. This is an excellent influence and gives you a special gift of dealing with groups of people in a healing and positive way.

The Ten of Spades in the Neptune Period

This card brings a good measure of success, especially related to travel or distant interests. This could also be connected with your health, water, drugs or alcohol, or something secret or hidden. This success and recognition could be the fulfillment of a long cherished dream. Spiritual studies and ambitions are also favored at this time. The power of the Ten of Spades is such that the illusory nature of Neptune is overcome.

The Ten of Spades Is Your Pluto Card

This year you have decided on some level to accomplish a great deal. Whether this be in the realm of work or health, it is clear that you have decided to make a big change. Change is what is needed if you are to accomplish your goals and dreams. This change is likely to involve hard work, but hard work makes you stronger and more successful. The Ten of Spades often involves working with groups of people and either enlisting their help or teaching them. It is a successful card, but this year this success may cause you to make some radical changes in your life. It all depends on how you handle it.

It is likely that you will be in a situation in which you have to work much more than usual, and for some reason, this is creating some problems for you. This can be a workaholic card.

Your Result Card may tell you specifically what kind of success you desire this year or reveal someone you know who is an integral part of that success and hard work.

AFFIRMATION:

I am transformed by hard work, and my desire to achieve measurable success in all areas of my life.

The Ten of Spades Is Your Result Card

Though you may, at times, feel as though you are a workaholic this year, the end result will be that you have been very successful, especially if your work involves groups of people in some way. Your Pluto Card will give you specifics about where or with whom you desire this accomplishment, but your success is assured. The Pluto Card will also tell you about the changes you may have to make to achieve this success.

AFFIRMATION:

I create more success through hard work and determination this year. I create success with groups of people.

THE TEN OF SPADES IS YOUR LONG-RANGE CARD

The Ten of Spades is one of the best cards for success and satisfaction in your work and in health, though you can bet that you will have to work for it. With this powerful card present, it is advised that you make a list of all that you want to accomplish this year and get working. You will be successful. At times you will feel that all you do is work, work, work, but for most, the rewards will be more than worth the effort. Success related to groups is highlighted.

KEYWORDS:

A year of hard work and major accomplishment. Success with groups is assured. Make a wish list and be willing to work.

THE TEN OF SPADES IS YOUR ENVIRONMENT CARD

A willingness to work hard and take on extra projects will bring you unusually good success this year. This influence also can help to overcome health or work challenges that may be present. To get the most from this favorable card, make a list of goals and things that you wish to accomplish as you start the year. That list, combined with a willingness to do whatever it takes, can bring you great accomplishments in the areas you desire.

THE TEN OF SPADES IS YOUR DISPLACEMENT CARD

This will likely be a year of hard work for you and one in which you may have to make some difficult choices between your work and time spent at home and with family. When the Ten of Spades occurs, we have the opportunity to accomplish a great deal. However, we often take on so many projects that we feel weighted down by all the work we have to do, to the point that we begin to think that all we do is work, work, work. For those who are very goal-directed and career-oriented, this could be good. But even in these cases, it could be too much at times. Somehow, hard work and accomplishment of important goals are major themes this year, ones that will require more energy than you might have expected.

You will, however, receive many rewards for your efforts this year and achieve some of the dreams you have been wanting. Though you will likely work very hard for it, in the end, it will be worth the effort.

Jack of Hearts

Making personal sacrifices for a higher good, initiation into higher love

The Basic Meaning of the Jack of Hearts

The Jack of Hearts is known as the 'Christ Card,' or the 'Card of Spiritual Sacrifice.' Whenever it is present, you will feel and be encouraged to elevate your thinking, speaking and acting to a higher level. You may also decide to make some sort of personal sacrifice when this influence is present. This would likely be for the sake of someone younger than yourself, though it can take other forms. The period position will delineate the exact nature of the sacrifice you feel impelled to make.

In any case, this card does bring a strong dose of higher, spiritual love into our lives and will encourage us to do things from a higher motive than usual.

THE JACK OF HEARTS IN THE MERCURY PERIOD

During this period, you are given the gift of a creative mind that can come up with some great ideas about how to make some money quickly. You may find some quick returns from investments, selling something, or some other form of marketing or promotion. This would be a great time to do some market planning for your business or to try one of your get-rich-quick schemes. You may find that one of these will involve one of the communications fields.

This is a strong influence for involvement in learning about spiritual love. In other cases, it can represent giving up some of our own ideas or plans in order to help someone less fortunate than ourselves.

THE JACK OF HEARTS IN THE VENUS PERIOD

This card indicates putting aside your personal desires to help someone in the family. This could be a young friend, a lover, or a relative. This is always a card of sacrifice in love, usually for someone younger. You are inspired by a higher realization of truth to do something that is noble and brave. This card also gives you mastery of your emotions and affectional impulses, which can bring you more success in all your personal relationships.

THE JACK OF HEARTS IN THE MARS PERIOD

Under the influence of the Jack of Hearts, 'Sacrifice Card,' you could easily find yourself doing things that you don't usually do during this period. For example, you may decide to give up some cherished desire or passion for a higher reason or truth. For example, others who had this card have given up sex, legal battles, and other competitive goals, all in the name of following a higher wisdom. This card gives you mastery over your emotions and passions and encourages you to upgrade your actions towards higher and more selfless pursuits.

You may also find that there are one or more men of the Hearts suit for whom you feel some attraction or anger during this period.

THE JACK OF HEARTS IN THE JUPITER PERIOD

Under Jupiter the spiritual influence of the Jack of Hearts, 'Sacrifice Card,' can bring many blessings, but mostly when directed towards helping others or achieving spiritual goals. Direct your emotional power into selfless action for maximum success under this influence. You are being influenced by one of the highest forms of spiritual energy, and you could have many profound revelations as a result. Mastery of your emotions, personal relationships, and doing good for others all bring untold blessings during this special period of your year.

On a more mundane level, any men of the Hearts suit could be a source of financial and other blessings this year, especially those who are younger or involved in creative professions.

THE JACK OF HEARTS IN THE SATURN PERIOD

At this time, you could be feeling some limitation brought about by the illness or ill-fortune of someone close to you, usually a good-hearted young man. You could feel obliged to give up your personal desires to help this man, and yet you feel chained down or limited in some way. This influence usually indicates a time when difficult but necessary sacrifices have to be made. The other card in this same period may give you more details about what or who is involved.

Be on the lookout for men of the Hearts suit, especially those who are younger or who may be approaching you from either a romantic or creative point of view. These are likely to prove burdensome in some way during this period.

THE JACK OF HEARTS IN THE URANUS PERIOD

This is a beneficial influence for giving selflessly of yourself in your work or community/spiritual service. A strong spiritual influence is now present in your life, which could inspire you to act with higher integrity or encourage you to make some personal sacrifices. You may have decided to relinquish some part of your personal freedom or individuality or give up some acquaintances, all in the name of truth and the good of others.

Any Heart males you know may be acting strangely now, or leaving you feeling uncertain about their intentions or commitments. It would be best just to let them go their own way and maintain an open friendship.

THE JACK OF HEARTS IN THE NEPTUNE PERIOD

A very strong spiritual influence is present in your life during this period that could bring profound revelations and inspire you to higher levels of thought and action. Your dreams and cherished desires are undergoing a transformation to higher levels of truth and spirituality. This may prompt you to give up old patterns of thinking, desires, and ambitions and move towards helping others in a selfless way.

Any younger men of the Hearts suit that you meet during this period, and to a lesser extent, this entire year, are likely to be a little hard for you to see objectively. You could easily project your fantasies on them, romantic or otherwise. Therefore it is best not to make any important decisions related to them until after your next birthday.

THE JACK OF HEARTS IS YOUR PLUTO CARD

This year is likely to see you in a position of having to make some important sacrifices. These may be sacrifices of your time, resources, or goals in order to help someone else or for a higher, spiritual ideal. There is a powerful spiritual or religious influence present now that cannot be denied, even though you may find it difficult to do what you feel you are being called upon to do. The sacrifices represented by the Jack of Hearts are often related to someone younger, but they can be made just because you are following a higher principle or ideal too. You are learning important lessons this year and experiencing new ways of looking at life and love.

On the deepest levels, the Jack of Hearts Pluto card represents an initiation into higher forms of love. The highest form of love, represented by the Jack of Hearts, is that love that is selfless and willing to make sacrifices for the beloved. Your exposure to this higher love energy may be challenging at times, but the result will be a broadened understanding of the deeper aspects of love and truth.

Your Result Card will tell you more about the nature of this initiation into higher love or tell you who it is related to or who is involved in it.

AFFIRMATION:

Through my experiences, I am learning the true meaning and value of sacrifice. I transform my loving nature to a higher and more meaningful spiritual level.

THE JACK OF HEARTS IS YOUR RESULT CARD

The Jack of Hearts sacrifice card brings a strong spiritual influence into your life. You may learn the meaning of sacrifice by giving up personal desires to help someone, perhaps a younger person who you love very much. This may be challenging at times, though the result will be a broader perspective on life with a deep connection to your own spirituality. Your Pluto Card shows who you are making sacrifices for or gives more information about these sacrifices.

This card is also a powerful indicator that you could end up with some younger man of the Hearts suit by your next birthday. Whether this be a friend, lover, or family member, there is a strong indicator that the two of you will be joined in some meaningful way by year's end.

AFFIRMATION:

I make sacrifices this year for a higher spiritual purpose. I live my spirituality and follow my higher guidance.

THE JACK OF HEARTS IS YOUR LONG-RANGE CARD

This year you have a powerful spiritual influence in your life, the Jack of Hearts, which is also known as the 'sacrifice card.' What this means to you is that you are being called upon to make some personal sacrifices this year for something that will help others in some way. This may involve having to give up some personal goals and ambitions or simply having to give of your time and resources to help someone less fortunate. You are learning about sacrifice this year, its true meaning. The person or persons for whom you are making the sacrifice are usually younger than yourself.

However, sometimes the sacrifice is being made on principle alone. You are being called upon to take a higher role in your life. There is a powerful spiritual energy around you, and you may have some powerful revelations about your own spirituality. It is also possible that you will exhibit some of the personality traits of the Jack of Hearts this year, emotional stubbornness and emotional immaturity.

KEYWORDS:

I am surrounded by the Christ spirit. This encourages me to make personal sacrifices and elevates my actions this year.

THE JACK OF HEARTS IS YOUR ENVIRONMENT CARD

Because the Jack of Hearts is one of the Fixed Cards, it will never appear as the Environment or Displacement Card in anyone's Yearly Spread.

In a Weekly Reading, this card will bring benefits from sharing a spiritual kind of love with those around you. You may find that you are feeling inspired this week and elevated to a new level of love in your personal relationships.

THE JACK OF HEARTS IS YOUR DISPLACEMENT CARD

Because the Jack of Hearts is one of the Fixed Cards, it will never appear as the Environment or Displacement Card in anyone's Yearly Spread.

Jack of Clubs

Success using mental creativity, initiation into higher thought or spiritual knowledge

The Basic Meaning of the Jack of Clubs

The Jack of Clubs tells us that you will be dealing with some very creative and youthful energies. This is one of the most mentally creative cards in the deck and as such bestows a certain amount of success. This would apply especially to those involved in mental or communications-related occupations.

Sometimes when the Jack of Clubs is present, we are confronted with some new form of knowledge or information that has a transformative effect on our life. We could be lifted up to a new level of thinking by exposure to spiritual or some other form of knowledge or information.

Of course, the Jack of Clubs is also the Personality Card for all males of the Clubs suit, so this card could represent any Clubs male that you know playing a specific role in your life. In this regard, however, it is important to note that this would be that male operating out of the Jack side of his personality. The Jack of any suit is always romantic, creative, persuasive, and youthful, but also can be irresponsible, crafty, or downright dishonest. In this regard, the Jack of Clubs is no exception.

THE JACK OF CLUBS IN THE MERCURY PERIOD

This powerful creative card will give you the blessings of a quick, powerful, and very creative mind this period, and to a lesser extent, for the entire year. This power can be applied with great success to any project that involves writing or other creative mental pursuits. You may even get some ideas for projects that are far ahead of their time. This card can also represent an initiation into a new way or form of thinking or communicating.

THE JACK OF CLUBS IN THE VENUS PERIOD

This period could bring good relations with some bright and witty young man. For women, this could be a possible lover or suitor. This man could be very jealous and frivolous, so check his character before making any long-term commitments or plans. With this influence, you could have a desire to associate with those of intelligence and wit. You are also very witty, charming, and attractive now. Your creative energy is high and can be used successfully in many ways.

Creativity and charm will bring you a lot of success with people, especially the opposite sex, during this period. Use some of the ideas you get to further your success, both personally and professionally.

THE JACK OF CLUBS IN THE MARS PERIOD

This powerful mental card brings you success in any area where you can apply mental brilliance or creativity. This could be applied to writing, producing, or public speaking. This card can also represent an attorney or male associate that you are involved with in a legal matter. Under Mars, caution is advised in how you communicate. Though you may know that you are right, your impatience may prevent others from responding positively to what you say.

You may find that there are one or more men of the Clubs suit for whom you feel some attraction or anger during this period.

THE JACK OF CLUBS IN THE JUPITER PERIOD

During this period, you can expect great success in any or all of your creative mental pursuits. This could mean much success and money coming from writing, teaching, speaking, or other forms of creativity. Your mind is quick and bright and can be focused on ways to make money that become quite profitable for you. Your ability to sell your ideas or products is at an all-time high. Communicate these ideas, and expand the scope of your work in this favorable climate.

You will tend to receive good things from Club males this year, especially those who are younger or involved in a creative profession.

THE JACK OF CLUBS IN THE SATURN PERIOD

Creative projects may seem a burden during this period and to a lesser extent for the entire year. You will have to work harder to get ideas and to implement them, and the rewards seem less than usual for the efforts expended. In truth, this is a time of building for the future. Though your progress seems hampered, you are laying the foundation for future success. Be very careful when making verbal commitments, as they may return to haunt you if made casually with no intention of keeping them.

Be on the lookout for men of the Clubs suit, especially those who are younger or who may be approaching you from either a romantic or creative point of view. These are likely to prove burdensome in some way during this period. In some cases, this card can represent a doctor or physician who is underhanded or dishonest. Be cautious about placing your health into the hands of physicians during this period.

THE JACK OF CLUBS IN THE URANUS PERIOD

This is a powerful and productive influence for all mental pursuits, especially those where you need creative ideas. The ideas and inspirations you get now will be far ahead of their time and will lead you to further success. You may have some psychic experiences as your mind is attuned to very high vibrations now. If you know any males of the Clubs suit, they will be somewhat unpredictable this year. Give them the space and freedom they need.

Any Club males you know may be acting strangely now or leaving you feeling uncertain about their intentions or commitments. It would be best just to let them go their own way and maintain an open friendship.

THE JACK OF CLUBS IN THE NEPTUNE PERIOD

This is a highly creative and inspirational influence promising many gifts from your mind and intuitive ability. If you are involved in any work or project that requires creativity and inspiration, this is a time when you will excel. You could also excel at sales work now. Clubs men that you meet this period and this year are likely to be an enigma for you. Though they may seem to be everything you dreamed of, you may not be able to trust them totally.

Any younger men of the Clubs suit that you meet during this period, and to a lesser extent, this entire year, are likely to be a little hard for you to see objectively. You could easily project your fantasies on them, romantic or otherwise. Therefore, it is best not to make any important decisions related to them until after your next birthday.

THE JACK OF CLUBS IS YOUR PLUTO CARD

One of the major challenges for you this year is to develop the creativity to be successful in a mental field of interest, perhaps as a writer. The qualities of the Jack of Clubs are likely to have a direct role in your life this year, whether it is because you are acting as the Jack, trying to act as the Jack, or know someone who is acting as the Jack. It is even possible that all three are happening at the same time. These qualities revolve primarily around mental creativity, quick thinking, and quick talking. This is an excellent influence for those involved in sales or promotions, and it may be that this year you are trying to get more into this. Perhaps you are just wanting to get some better ideas about whatever work you are involved in.

Another aspect of the Jack of Clubs is that of being dishonest or less than truthful. For this reason, you may find events surfacing this year that relate to either your own dishonesty or that of others.

On a deeper level, the Jack of Clubs can represent an initiation into higher knowledge. So, for many with this card, there will be exposure to new ideas, forms of communications, or belief systems that cause a transformative effect on them. Some of these may even be spiritually based or have to do with personal development.

In any case, you will have to make a conscious effort to achieve your goal or to deal with these creative, youthful, and often immature energies of the Jack of Clubs. Your Result Card will tell you more about these energies or point to someone who is directly involved in this challenge.

AFFIRMATION:

I transform myself to become more mentally creative and successful this year. I begin a new and better life on an intellectual level.

THE JACK OF CLUBS IS YOUR RESULT CARD

As a result of, and connected to the challenges represented by your Pluto Card this year, you will achieve much more creativity and success in a mental field. This could mean success as a writer of some kind. In the process, you may be transformed by exposure to new forms of communication or information that advances your thinking into the current age of advanced technology. Be prepared to move ahead into unexplored areas of knowledge.

This card is also a powerful indicator that you could end up with some younger man of the Clubs suit by your next birthday. Whether this be a friend, lover, or family member, there is a strong indicator that the two of you will be joined in some meaningful way by year's end.

AFFIRMATION:

I achieve success as a writer or idea person in one of the mental fields. I revolutionize my thinking.

THE JACK OF CLUBS IS YOUR LONG-RANGE CARD

The Jack of Clubs tells us that you will be dealing with some very creative and youthful energies this year, either your own or those of an intellectually stimulating and, probably, younger man. This creativity can be channeled profitably and successfully into many endeavors, such as writing, sales work, or anywhere new and creative ideas are of value. You are really on a creative high this year and can expect good results from all forms of creative work. On the negative side, watch out for a tendency to be irresponsible and frivolous under this influence, and also, be watchful for others that play that role with you.

The Jack of Clubs has another important meaning for those who are interested in the spiritual side of life. If often represents an initiation into higher knowledge. This could mean that you are exposed to some new ideas or philosophies that could radically change the way you think about yourself or life. Your entire method of communicating could undergo a dramatic transformation as the year progresses.

KEYWORDS:

A year of heightened mental creativity and initiations into new forms of knowledge and ways of communicating.

THE JACK OF CLUBS IS YOUR ENVIRONMENT CARD

During this year, you could reap many rewards from the creative application of your mind and thinking ability. If you have been wanting new ideas, creative and enterprising ideas on how to better your life and work situation, this is the year when your wishes will be fulfilled. This is the time to express yourself and to let your wildest ideas come forth to be shared with others. Whether you are speaking or writing this year, you will be well received by others.

THE JACK OF CLUBS IS YOUR DISPLACEMENT CARD

Creative projects that you may be involved in this year could prove to be a burden at times and take more time and energy than you anticipated. Also, dealings with others who are less than honest could also prove challenging. It would be in your best interest to remain straightforward with all of your personal and business relationships this year and resist any temptations to get involved in anything dishonest or underhanded. Though this may actually be a successful year by most standards, these sorts of involvements may undermine your efforts or cause damage in other areas.

Men of the Clubs suit who are romantically involved may find this area of their life to be somewhat challenging this year, since the Jack of Clubs represents you when you are in love.

What is happening on a deeper level is that you are being called upon to rise up to a new level of communication, thinking, and perception, one that is based upon higher principles and more self-responsibility. In that light, you may be exposed to some new philosophies that challenge you to make some changes in your life along these lines. Contact with spiritual books, workshops, etc. will be helpful in this regard. Watch for a tendency towards stubbornness this year. A fixed mind has no room for new information or changes.

Jack of Diamonds

Financial success through salesmanship or creativity, initiation into higher values

The Basic Meaning of the Jack of Diamonds

The Jack of Diamonds is usually representing a younger, business-minded man who is creative. Often they are salesmen or promoters of some product or idea and always are involved in the world of business or finance. Either a person of this description will play a major role in your life when this card is present or you will be manifesting these qualities yourself.

For this reason, the Jack of Diamonds is considered to be a card of great financial success, especially success through promoting or selling or otherwise being very creative in your business.

On the other hand, if you know some man who is a Diamond Birth Card, this Jack could mean that he will be playing either a romantic, creative, or dishonest role in your life at the time this Jack appears.

On a spiritual level, this card often represents a time when we are lifted up to a new value level in our lives. This could occur through exposure to one of many things or people that inspire us to place acquisition and hoarding of things into their proper place in our lives. As such, our lives can be greatly improved during times when this card appears.

THE JACK OF DIAMONDS IN THE MERCURY PERIOD

During this period, you are given the gift of a creative mind that can come up with some great ideas about how to make some money quickly. You may find some quick returns from investments, selling something, or some other form of marketing or promotion. This would be a great time to do some market planning for your business or to try one of your get-rich-quick schemes. You may find that one of these will involve one of the communications fields.

You will find that you tend to get along very well with men of the Diamond suit this period. In a more general way, this card brings some good interactions with them for the entire year. Use this connection with them to open up new lines of communicating.

THE JACK OF DIAMONDS IN THE VENUS PERIOD

During this period, you have a powerful and financially creative influence that could help you attain more money. This influence is especially good for those who sell items of luxury, beauty, for the home, or any items to women. This is also a good influence for those in the arts. Use this influence to come up with better ways of marketing yourself or your products. Your creative energies are flowing, and this could cause the money to flow your way.

This card could also signal your involvement with some younger or romantic male of the Diamond suit. If so, the relationship will be congenial and pleasant. Just remember that Jacks do not always tell the truth. It could be fun though.

THE JACK OF DIAMONDS IN THE MARS PERIOD

This card can represent an attorney. You may be in competition with this person if you are a man. If you are a woman, you may have an attraction for him. He may also be a financial advisor or accountant. Besides these possibilities, this card gives you the ability to sell or market your ideas, products, or services with great success. This is the strongest of the financially creative influences. Used aggressively, this could reap huge returns.

You may also find that there are one or more men of the Diamonds suit for whom you feel some attraction or anger during this period.

THE JACK OF DIAMONDS IN THE JUPITER PERIOD

This period could be one in which your finances are helped considerably by using creative ideas for selling or marketing your products or services. Your creative and business abilities combine well now and could make you a lot of money. For those in the sales profession, this is one of the best influences. Diamonds men will be a great benefit in your life during this period and for the year. Let them show you more lucrative ways to make money.

THE JACK OF DIAMONDS IN THE SATURN PERIOD

This card can represent a businessman or associate with whom you have obligations or problems. This can be a karmic relationship, one that requires hard work and patience for success. It is necessary to regulate and balance your affairs at this time. Creative projects to make money may seem a burden to you, but this is a necessary part of establishing yourself and your future success. You will have success now, but you will need to work hard for it.

Be on the lookout for men of the Diamonds suit, especially those who are younger or who may be approaching you from either a romantic or creative point of view. These are likely to prove burdensome in some way during this period.

THE JACK OF DIAMONDS IN THE URANUS PERIOD

This card may represent a Diamonds man in your life who is involved perhaps in real estate, electronics, computers, or labor relations. He can be a very good friend as long as you don't have many expectations of how he should be. Otherwise he will leave you feeling uncertain. In any case, he is quite creative and innovative. All of his qualities are yours during this period and you will surely reap high financial returns if you apply them in your business.

Any Diamond males that you know may be acting strangely now or leaving you feeling uncertain about their intentions or commitments. It would be best just to let them go their own way and maintain an open friendship.

THE JACK OF DIAMONDS IN THE NEPTUNE PERIOD

This card can represent a traveling salesman or a young merchant you meet while traveling. If so, be careful not to place too much trust in him. There could be deception involved. Otherwise, this card promises some financial success for you by applying creativity and salesmanship to your current business or profession. If your current line of work demands some creative ideas to get things moving, now is the time to do just that.

Any younger men of the Diamonds suit that you meet during this period, and to a lesser extent, this entire year, are likely to be a little hard for you to see objectively. You could easily project your fantasies on them, romantic or otherwise. Therefore, it is best not to make any important decisions related to them until after your next birthday.

THE JACK OF DIAMONDS IS YOUR PLUTO CARD

This year you are wanting to be much more creative and successful in your business. Perhaps you are needing some good business ideas because things have gone stale lately. Or perhaps you are just desiring to make more money and need some good ideas and creative ways to generate more income. It will be a challenge for you, but your goal is in sight. To achieve this goal, you will have to make many changes in the ways you are doing things. You will also have to take full responsibility for the success or lack of success in your life.

The Jack of Diamonds is a member of the royal family, a leader, and you will have to assume creative leadership to achieve your goals this year. It is called the 'salesman's card,' and thus we usually get this card at times when we are either learning to promote ourselves and our products or when we actually do some selling for others. Along with all the Jacks comes the immature or dishonest aspects, and you may find yourself dealing with these aspects as well this year. Immaturity or shirking of responsibility will not get the results you want.

Your Result Card will further describe this need for creativity this year or tell you who is involved in this challenge you have set before yourself.

Affirmation:

I transform myself to become more financially creative and successful this year. I begin a new and better life in my relationship to money and prosperity.

The Jack of Diamonds Is Your Result Card

Somehow connected to your Pluto Card, and perhaps as a result of it, you are being transformed into a highly creative and successful money person. This could be in the role of a sales or marketing person or simply coming up with good ideas for your current business. You may not want to be the boss or take full responsibility for the business, but you will seek recognition and an outlet for your creative energies. Diversify, and you will multiply your rewards.

This card is also a powerful indicator that you could end up with some younger man of the Diamonds suit by your next birthday. Whether this be a friend, lover, or family member, there is a strong indicator that the two of you will be joined in some meaningful way by year's end.

Affirmation:

I become a successful sales person or creative financial and business person this year. I create money success.

The Jack of Diamonds Is Your Long-Range Card

This is the salesman's card and also the card of the successful entrepreneur. If these areas interest you, this is the year you could apply yourself to achieve much success and prosperity. You will have many opportunities to put these qualities to work in your life, and they could do a lot for your pocketbook. Actually, this creative energy can be applied to any work or business you are involved in with success, so think of ways you could use this. Everything involves selling of one sort or another. Watch a tendency to avoid taking responsibility or

to stretch the truth to suit your needs, which are other aspects often associated with this powerful card.

This card can mean that you get involved as a salesperson yourself at some point during this year. Your powers to promote things you believe in are at an all-time high. Use them for greater prosperity and happiness in your life.

The Jack of Diamonds has another important meaning for those who are interested in the spiritual side of life. It often represents an initiation into higher values. This could mean that you are exposed to some new ideas or philosophies that could radically change the things that you want out of life. This could, in turn, affect your job or occupation in a big way.

Keywords:

A year of financial success through application of creative ideas and salesmanship. I am initiated into higher values that bring more true happiness into my life.

The Jack of Diamonds Is Your Environment Card

This card guarantees financial success if you are ready to promote or sell your ideas, products, or services. Your ability to attract the right people and then to sway them to your side is enormous this year. Use this influence to increase sales or to simply come up with better ideas on how to make more money. As the 'salesman card,' the Jack of Diamonds will bring more success in sales, but almost all types of business and financial enterprises will benefit.

The Jack of Diamonds Is Your Displacement Card

Creative financial enterprises and dealings with fast-talking creative types could be a challenge for you this year, taking more of your time and energy than you had imagined. Before entering into any new finance-producing projects or partnerships, it would be wise to closely examine the deals, and those with whom you are making the deals. The Jack of Diamonds has the potential to represent dishonesty in business deals so you would want to be careful both of others who may be dishonest and of entering into deals that you know are dishonest yourself. Both are likely to prove troublesome in this influence.

Men of the Diamonds suit who are romantically involved may find this area of their life to be somewhat challenging this year since the Jack of Diamonds represents you when you are in love.

On a deeper level, you are being called upon to rise up to a new level of personal and professional values, one that is based upon the principles of abundance and honesty. It is fear of not having enough that often motivates us to cut corners and try to get something for nothing. But those sorts of actions always end up creating more poverty in the long run and reinforce our beliefs in the poverty itself. An attitude of abundance and of service to others always breeds more prosperity and well-being.

Jack of Spades

Success in the arts or in creative work, being ripped off by some thief or crook

The Basic Meaning of the Jack of Spades

The Jack of Spades is probably the most creative card in the entire deck. It is called the 'Actor Card,' the 'Card of the Thief,' and the 'Spiritual Initiate Card.' Just how it manifests in your life will depend a lot on what are your values and your occupation are.

In all cases, it is wise to safeguard your personal property when the Jack of Spades is present. Just be more careful than usual, because there is a strong potential for someone to either rip you off or in some other way do something dishonest.

Being such a creative force, the Jack of Spades can bring great success in any of the artistic pursuits. This is an energy that can be used to further one's success in many areas.

Finally, the Jack of Spades can represent an initiation into a higher lifestyle. For example, you might read a book that inspires you to start a regular plan of exercise. Because that book caused a positive change in your basic lifestyle, this would be considered to be a spiritual initiation. Of course, there are more profound spiritual initiations than a new exercise program, but keep in mind that the Jack of Spade's initiation will have a definite effect on what we do day in and day out.

THE JACK OF SPADES IN THE MERCURY PERIOD

During this period, you are given the gift of a creative mind that can come up with some great ideas that can help you in a multitude of ways. This gift can be artistic and so you may get some really good ideas for writing or illustrating something. Be cautious, though, with this card present, as it may indicate a theft incident related to driving, your car, or a short trip somewhere. Also, be on the alert for deceptive intentions from one or more of your siblings. Just be a little cautious and enjoy the creative aspects of this powerful card. You may actually read some books or be exposed to some new information that makes a positive change in your life.

THE JACK OF SPADES IN THE VENUS PERIOD

This is called the 'Actor's Card,' and it could see you having much success in one of the creative fields. At the same time, you should be aware of the possibility of theft around the home during this period. Keep a closer eye on your possessions. To get the most out of this influence, apply the creative potential into an artistic or sales profession. This is the most creative card in the deck and must be handled consciously to access its positive side.

Males of the Spades suit, especially those who are younger or coming at you in a romantic way, will be a lot of fun and you are bound to have pleasant interchanges with them now. Just remember that all Jacks can be dishonest from time to time. Not everything they say will be true.

THE JACK OF SPADES IN THE MARS PERIOD

Beware of dishonest dealings with men or legal involvements during this period. Don't be tempted to take shortcuts at the expense of honesty. If you get ripped off, the lessons you learn may not seem to be worth the price you paid for them. Be watchful of attorneys, especially because the ones you attract now are probably not very honest. You have a lot to lose if you or they are not working by the

book. Use this powerful influence to generate more creative ideas for your work or business.

You may also find that there are one or more men of the Spades suit for whom you feel some attraction or anger during this period.

THE JACK OF SPADES IN THE JUPITER PERIOD

This period will either see you have much financial success by using your creativity or by having an initiation into spirituality that could change your life. This is a highly spiritual influence that could bring you wisdom and alter your destiny, especially if this is the top card of the pair in Jupiter. On the other hand, your money-making interests will benefit greatly from any creative ideas that you implement now.

On a more mundane level, any men of the Spades suit could be a source of financial and other blessings this year, especially those who are younger or involved in creative professions.

THE JACK OF SPADES IN THE SATURN PERIOD

This card can represent difficulties through association with an incompetent physician. It would be wise not to put your trust in doctors during this period, or for the year to a lesser extent. There is also the possibility of being ripped off in some way, so it is advisable to watch over your personal possessions and beware of those who may be dishonest or disreputable. The other card during this period will give further details about this Jack of Spades influence.

Be on the lookout for men of the Spades suit, especially those who are younger or who may be approaching you from either a romantic or creative point of view. These are likely to prove burdensome in some way during this period.

THE JACK OF SPADES IN THE URANUS PERIOD

The 'Actor' or 'Rip-Off' Card's presence in your life this period warns you to be cautious in several areas. One is in real estate matters, and the other is in your work area with co-workers. Watch yourself and your belongings carefully. At the same time, your creativity is at an all-time high, and some of the ideas that you come up with could be well ahead of their time and successfully applied to your work or business for more gain.

On spiritual levels, this card could indicate your beginning a new lifestyle, one that is more in line with higher spiritual principles or philosophies. This is the card of initiation into a higher life.

Any Spade males you know may be acting strangely now or leaving you feeling uncertain about their intentions or commitments. It would be best just to let them go their own way and maintain an open friendship.

THE JACK OF SPADES IN THE NEPTUNE PERIOD

Though this card promises much creative power that could be applied to most any area for success, it is also a cautionary note to beware of deception and rip-off, especially in connection with a foreigner or man of the sea. Spiritually, this could be a very important time for you as inner revelations lead you to an initiation into higher levels. However, on the mundane level, beware of those who may appear to fulfill your dreams, but really do not.

Any younger men of the Spades suit that you meet during this period, and to a lesser extent this entire year, are likely to be a little hard for you to see objectively. You could easily project your fantasies on them, romantic or otherwise. Therefore, it is best not to make any important decisions related to them until after your next birthday.

THE JACK OF SPADES IS YOUR PLUTO CARD

As you can see by the keywords, the Jack of Spades has many different meanings and possible ways of expression. You should be on the alert for all of them because one or more is definitely present for you this year. With the Jack of Spades, one should always be cautioned about the possibility of being ripped off in some manner. Extra care should be taken in your affairs, relationships, and with the care and keeping of your belongings. However, this may be a year when you are making many efforts to develop your creativity, whether this be through one of the arts or just in general. The Jack of Spades is also called the 'Actor Card,' and it may signal a year when you are devoting a lot of your energy to being more successful in one of the creative arts or on the stage.

On another level, this year could bring you a new beginning in terms of your spiritual beliefs. You could join a new religion or spiritual group of some kind, and this may challenge you to change many areas of your life. Whatever the case, this is a powerful year for you with the Jack of Spades in such a prominent position. Your Result Card will further describe this major challenge or transformation this year or tell you who is involved in it.

AFFIRMATION:

I transform myself to higher levels of living and being. I become more creative and expressive, while at the same time learning the value of truth and honesty.

THE JACK OF SPADES IS YOUR RESULT CARD

This powerful card as your Result guarantees that by your next birthday you will be successful in the areas of acting, creative writing, or other creative pursuits, or that you will be exposed to a spiritual discipline that will alter most every area of your life. This could be a year of major transformation for you, one where you begin a entirely new lifestyle based on truth and higher wisdom. Even on a mundane level, success is yours, but especially in one of the creative areas.

This card is also a powerful indicator that you could end up with some younger man of the Spades suit by your next birthday. Whether this be a friend, lover, or family member, there is a strong indicator that the two of you will be joined in some meaningful way by year's end.

AFFIRMATION:

I create myself to be a successful artist, actor, or musician. I end up this year with a higher and healthier lifestyle.

THE JACK OF SPADES IS YOUR LONG-RANGE CARD

The Jack of Spades usually represents an industrious young man who may also be prone to dishonesty and illegal activities, so keep a close eye on him if you know one or run into one this year. The more spiritual ones are considered 'initiates' into the higher wisdom. In some way, this person will play a major role in your life this year and be one of the focuses of your attention. You may find yourself dealing with one or more people that are underhanded this year or find that you are guilty of dishonesty yourself. It would be advisable to be extra careful in all your affairs and not trust anyone without checking them out in detail. Also, watch your valuables, and keep your doors locked.

In a totally different sense, this may be a year when you are introduced to many new spiritual philosophies and concepts. You may even begin practicing a new ideology related to some new spiritual path that you have begun. Exposure to these new things may cause a significant change in your lifestyle, one that encourages you to do better things for your health and life in general.

KEYWORDS:

A year of success in creative fields such as acting or performing, a year of 'rip-offs' or of spiritual initiation.

THE JACK OF SPADES IS YOUR ENVIRONMENT CARD

This is an excellent influence for all creative endeavors and practically guarantees your success if you are involved in any of the creative pursuits. This includes acting, selling, music, painting, sculpting, designing, or any other creative job. However, this card can also represent a new beginning for you this year, an 'initiation' into a new lifestyle that is more healthy or more spiritual in nature. Any exposure to higher ways of living will be beneficial. You are likely to initiate some new things in your day-to-day schedule this year that will have a very positive effect on your well-being and lifestyle.

THE JACK OF SPADES IS YOUR DISPLACEMENT CARD

Creative projects and dealings with those who are less than honest are likely to be difficult this year, causing somewhat of a drain on your energies and more of your attention than you had planned. If you are an artist of any kind, your own work may require more of your attention now in order to maintain the level of success you are accustomed to. If you expect this up front, you can create more success in your work by the extra effort you must expend. This is a good year to fix your mind in one direction and to plan out your future success. Just don't be surprised if it takes more work than you planned for.

Dealings with those who are dishonest in nature could also prove to be a burden at times this year. It would be wise with this influence to safeguard your personal belongings, taking extra care to lock things up, etc. If you choose to take a dishonest path yourself, you may suffer the negative consequences of that choice, as all dishonest dealings are not favored by this influence for this year.

Men of the Spades suit who are romantically involved may find this area of their life to be somewhat challenging this year, since the Jack of Spades represents you when you are in love.

You are probably sensing that your lifestyle needs an overhaul, an upgrade to a new level. Perhaps you would like to include some exercise in your daily routine or some time meditating each day. Or perhaps you want to improve your diet or take some time each week for spiritual studies and practice. Whatever the case, there seems to be a need to rise up to a new living situation, one that is more healthy and positive in nature. Though that may prove to be challenging this year, it is within your reach if you are willing to put forth the effort and time.

Queen of Hearts

Marriage or childbirth, sensual and sexual pleasure

The Basic Meaning of the Queen of Hearts

The Queen of Hearts is a card with many significant meanings. On one hand, it represents 'the devoted mother,' and thus can indicate a time when a woman conceives or gives birth to a child. It also can be the indicator of marriage for a man or woman, especially as the Venus, Long-Range, or Result Card.

It is also the card of sexual enjoyment and romantic fantasy. You can bet that when it appears, one or more of these qualities will be present in your life.

The only negative manifestation of the Queen of Hearts may be a tendency towards laziness, fantasizing, or self-indulgence. It could cause someone to put on some weight or overdo it sexually or otherwise.

THE QUEEN OF HEARTS IN THE MERCURY PERIOD

Social charm is indicated by this card, and you might be using it to help friends or relatives now. Parties and social gatherings are favored by this influence, as well as communications with family members. Use this influence to clear up unresolved miscommunications. Marriages during this period are likely to have good communication, but they may not last very long. Overall, this should be an enjoyable romantic time.

THE QUEEN OF HEARTS IN THE VENUS PERIOD

This Queen of Hearts in Venus is a special and blessed combination of influences guaranteeing a period full of love and intimacy. This is one of the best signs for marriage or the birth or conception of a child. With this card present, a child born is likely to be a girl. Good relationships with women and enjoyment of sex and other pleasures are all strong possibilities during this period. Your charm and magnetism can be applied to any relationship with success.

THE QUEEN OF HEARTS IN THE MARS PERIOD

A marriage during this period would be one marked by a considerable amount of aggressiveness or sexual energy. You can achieve much now with the application of emotional and social power, and charm. A child conceived or born this year is likely to be a boy. This is a card of sexual enjoyment. However, if you are already married, this passion could turn into anger if not handled carefully. Do things with your loved one to channel this energy constructively.

You may also find that there are one or more women of the Hearts suit for whom you feel some attraction or anger during this period.

THE QUEEN OF HEARTS IN THE JUPITER PERIOD

Under this influence, a marriage or birth would be financially beneficial and blessed in many ways. Caution that this expansive influence doesn't cause you to overindulge in pleasures to the detriment of your health or weight. This influence promotes ease, comfort, and pleasure, as well as a good mixture of love and money. It also brings a spiritual quality to your personal relationships all year, causing them to glow with goodness and grace.

Another important meaning of this card is that your marriage partner is making more money this year. So, in a reverse sort of way, this card is a good indicator of financial success for your partner, whatever work they may be involved in. It also holds true for non-marriage relationships, but only when your partner helps to support you financially. This is one of the best influences for marriage and one of the best times of the year to get married.

Any and all women who have Birth Cards of the Hearts suit could be a financial or other blessing to you this year. Look to them for guidance and help.

THE QUEEN OF HEARTS IN THE SATURN PERIOD

A new marriage this year or period, or any kind of committed relationship is likely to be marked by karmic overtones. It is possible that the two of you have been brought together to settle old debts, even from previous lives. Likewise, a birth this year would likely have some challenges. Sexual and other forms of enjoyment will be limited or marked by burdens during this period, and to a lesser extent for the entire year. You are learning the responsibilities of love and romantic expression and perhaps how your sexual and romantic expression affects those around you. This can be a very healing experience that ultimately increases your chances of having a successful intimate relationship.

Be on the lookout for women of the Hearts suit, especially those who you are romantically involved with. These are likely to prove troublesome or burdensome in some way during this period.

THE QUEEN OF HEARTS IN THE URANUS PERIOD

This influence can bring an unexpected or unusual marriage or romantic encounter. Kinky sex is also indicated. Your romantic or marriage partner may seem a bit unpredictable now. This is the time to allow some freedom in your personal relationships and to let go of attachments. Perhaps you need a little space yourself. You can access high levels of being together if you give each other plenty of breathing room and the freedom to be yourselves. Create some space.

Any women of the Hearts suit may seem to be somewhat unpredictable during this period, and to a lesser extent for the entire year. To insure success in your relationships with them, it would be best to just step back and allow them to do or be whatever they need to. A good friendship comes from unconditional love and acceptance.

THE QUEEN OF HEARTS IN THE NEPTUNE PERIOD

This period is likely to bring a very romantic and idealistic intimate encounter. Sometimes it can bring a secret lover. However, all your personal relationships seem to take on a romantic glow that fulfills all your dreams. You have been dreaming about marriage this year, and now it may come true. If you are a female, you may also have been dreaming about having a child. Later, you will find out if you really want what you were dreaming about. Wait until after your birthday to make commitments or decisions.

Any women of the Hearts suit that you meet during this period, and to a lesser extent this entire year, are likely to be a little hard for you to see objectively. You could easily project your fantasies on them, romantic or otherwise. Therefore, it is best not to make any important decisions related to them until after your next birthday.

THE QUEEN OF HEARTS IS YOUR PLUTO CARD

The influence of this card depends upon your marriage status as you begin this year. If you are single, it is likely that just the concept of getting married is on your mind a lot and that you are choosing to take a close look at it with possibilities for the future. Perhaps you have never been married or you had a bad marriage before. Maybe you have met someone, often represented by the Result Card, that you would like to get married to. Whatever the case, it seems that getting married is something that you need time to think about and get used to before you do it. If you can examine your internal conflicts about it, it is possible that you could get married, if that is what you want. It is in your power.

If you are already married or in a committed relationship, this could be a very challenging year for you where you have to learn how much it takes to create a successful partnership.

This card could also mean challenges around the issue of motherhood, either with existing children or about a child yet to be born. The Queen of Hearts as the Pluto Card often occurs during the years when someone wants to have a baby. In some cases, the Result Card will be the Birth Card of the baby that will be born.

The last possible interpretation for this card is that of overindulgence in physical things. There have been people with this card in Pluto who are wrestling with their diet and trying to overcome eating disorders or weight matters. In these cases, this card indicates that something can be improved in these areas by exploring the 'broken dreams' of the individual. The disorder will often be linked to an attempt to escape from a situation that one doesn't want to face.

Your Result Card will further describe how marriage or birth is challenging you this year or tell you who is an integral part of that challenge.

AFFIRMATION:

I create love, happiness, and pleasure in my life in good measure and in balance with all of the other areas of my life.

THE QUEEN OF HEARTS IS YOUR RESULT CARD

This year you may either get married or have a child. The Pluto Card could be the Birth Card of the person you marry or the child that is born. If you are married or have children, you may be challenged by your marriage or your role as a mother. You must make changes in your behavior in order to maintain successful relationships. It is likely that you will succeed. Your Pluto Card points to someone involved in this challenge or gives specifics about it.

This card is also a powerful indicator that you could end up with some woman of the Hearts suit by your next birthday. Whether this be a friend, lover, or family member, there is a strong indicator that the two of you will be joined in some meaningful way by year's end.

AFFIRMATION:

I become married, a parent, or find a very compatible mate by my next birthday.

THE QUEEN OF HEARTS IS YOUR LONG-RANGE CARD

Either a Queen of Hearts person or marriage will be playing a major role in your life this year. Your focus is likely to be on love and relationships. If you are a single person, this card can indicate a marriage for you this year. At the very least, you can expect an intimate relationship that is very sensual and satisfying.

For married people, the Queen of Hearts tells us that your family and relationship with your spouse will assume a greater importance this year

than usual. This could be good or bad, depending on the other cards in your yearly spreads. The Queen of Hearts is also the card of motherhood, and so it is commonly found in the years when women either conceive or give birth. This card also gives great success in the arts or any business that deals with the public.

If your Birth Card happens to be a Heart and you are a female, the Queen of Hearts as your Long-Range Card could also mean a lot of focus on your role as a mother or a romantic partner for the year. For single women, this can often be a sign of new relationships coming into their life.

KEYWORDS:

A year of focus on marriage, the concept of marriage, the role as mother, the concept of birth or love of luxury and pleasure.

THE QUEEN OF HEARTS IS YOUR ENVIRONMENT CARD

This could be a year of pleasure and enjoyment, and success in personal and intimate relationships for you. If married, you will receive blessings from your marriage. Perhaps your spouse will make a lot more money this year or give you many gifts. Unmarried people could have a very fortunate marriage if they desired. At the very least, there is a good chance of meeting someone with whom you can have a very pleasurable sexual relationship. Women with children could receive good fortune from their role as a mother, and if you are a woman of the Hearts suit, you would have especially good luck in the areas of romance and motherhood.

Regardless of your situation, you will likely have a lot of enjoyment in the area of personal relationships.

THE QUEEN OF HEARTS IS YOUR DISPLACEMENT CARD

This card could have many different kinds of effects, most depending upon your personal situation. First of all, for those who are married, they will find their marriage requires much more of their attention than usual. At times throughout the year, you are likely to feel that it is a burden to you in some way because of the extra demands it is placing upon your time and energy. If you are a woman who has children, then this area will also have a burdening effect on you this year, again requiring more time and energy to manage effectively.

Those trying to have a baby may find this area difficult this year, and those who are single may find it difficult to find a sexual or romantic partner. In general, this is not such a good influence for pleasure, enjoyment, and romance.

If you happen to be a woman of the Hearts suit, your own personal life may be a source of challenges this year. This could include your role as a mother, wife, or romantic partner. For all others, dealings with Heart females in general, and anyone whose Birth or Planetary Ruling Card is the Queen of Hearts, could prove to be a drain on your energy and require more than the usual amount of your attention.

On the positive side, this card brings great success in legal matters and in any competitive enterprises or work that involves men or groups of men. You may even find that you achieve a certain amount of notoriety this year or more popularity among your peers. Your Venus and Mars periods, in particular, should be quite wonderful. This is especially true if you have a clear direction and goals that you wish to achieve.

Queen of Clubs

Service in the communications fields, good intuition and organizational ability

The Basic Meaning of the Queen of Clubs

The Queen of Clubs is a card of great intuition, good organizational ability, and the desire to serve and nurture others with some form of knowledge or information. Like the King of Clubs, she has much authority and power. However, her power comes more from the receptive side of her nature. She knows things before they happen and operates on a high mental vibration. She can be high strung and impatient.

When you get this card in your reading, it can bring success in any of the communications fields. It can help make you more receptive to your intuition and make you feel like serving others more. It is a successful card, much like the Eight or Ten of Clubs, but also present is the nurturing quality of the mother.

THE QUEEN OF CLUBS IN THE MERCURY PERIOD

This card represents an intelligent, quick-witted lady with whom you can communicate easily. This woman loves social life and people of intelligence but could be somewhat dominating. She could also possess some kind of unusual information. This card could represent you having the same qualities mentioned above. You must guard against an argumentative and impatient nature and use your sensitivity to help others to get the most out of this influence. This card is a symbol of great success for those involved in helping others with some form of knowledge or communications. It also bestows a keen intuitive nature that you can trust now for success.

THE QUEEN OF CLUBS IN THE VENUS PERIOD

This royal card bestows upon you several gifts during this period that you can use simply by being aware of their presence. First of all, your intuition will be much higher than normal. Many bits of information may seem to come to you about your family or work. Your mental power is also heightened. This power of mind can bring you success at work or with friends, especially females. You love others from a higher place now.

Overall, this is a card of success in work, but especially when performed in more of a nurturing way. Relationships with all Clubs women will be better this period, and to a lesser extent, for the entire year. There may be one or more of these Clubs females that play an important role during this time.

THE QUEEN OF CLUBS IN THE MARS PERIOD

This card represents an intelligent but aggressive and quick-tempered woman. For men, this woman could be an object of desire. For women, she may be an adversary. This woman will have a strong will and many masculine traits. If it is you who are displaying any of the above characteristics, you must be careful that you do not arouse too much resentment and animosity in others. Be especially careful in your dealings with women during this period.

You may also find that there are one or more women of the Clubs suit for whom you feel some attraction or anger during this period.

THE QUEEN OF CLUBS IN THE JUPITER PERIOD

Much success, both professionally and financially is possible this period by applying your intuition and organizational ability in your work. This powerful card of mind power and intuition will give you insights into better ways of making money, creative writing ability, organizing, and overall business acumen that will help you in many ways. Though you may find yourself a bit on the impatient side, the mental quickness you have will be worth it.

Any and all women who have Birth Cards of the Clubs suit could be a financial or other blessing to you this year. Look to them for guidance and help.

THE QUEEN OF CLUBS IN THE SATURN PERIOD

During this period, you will have to be careful of what you say and how you say it. Any impatience on your part could result in more problems than it's worth. Most Clubs women you meet or associate with will seem burdensome or difficult now, each perhaps with a different lesson to teach you. Any mental work you are involved in will seem more difficult, but the end result will be a more solid foundation on which you can build your future success.

Be on the lookout for women of the Clubs suit, especially those who you are romantically involved with. These are likely to prove troublesome or burdensome in some way during this period.

THE QUEEN OF CLUBS IN THE URANUS PERIOD

This is a very psychic and creative influence that bestows much success in almost any field where mind power, creativity, and intuition can be applied. Many ideas and bits of information will just seem to appear in your mind, and many of these could be very helpful in your work or personal life. You may seem more impatient than usual and should be careful while driving. But in general, this will be a productive and delightful period of mental success.

Any women of the Clubs suit may seem to be somewhat unpredictable during this period, and to a lesser extent, for the entire year. To insure success in your relationships with them, it would be best to just step back and allow them to do or be whatever they need to. A good friendship comes from unconditional love and acceptance.

THE QUEEN OF CLUBS IN THE NEPTUNE PERIOD

This is a very inspirational and intuitive influence that promises success in any of the mental fields. If you are doing any kind of work where organizational ability, creative ideas, or intuition play an important role, this period could be marked by much success. You may desire to play more of a service role during this time, and indeed much of the information that will come to you can be helpful to others. You walk with Mary, Mother of Jesus.

Any women of the Clubs suit that you meet during this period, and to a lesser extent this entire year, are likely to be a little hard for you to see objectively. You could easily project your fantasies on them, romantic or otherwise. Therefore, it is best not to make any important decisions related to them until after your next birthday.

THE QUEEN OF CLUBS IS YOUR PLUTO CARD

The Queen of Clubs, as your transformation card this year, tells us that being more intuitive or being in a position of helping others along mental lines will be something that causes you to make important changes in your life. Queens represent service and 'helpers.' Clubs relate to intuitive knowledge or mental occupations. You are challenged to assume a helping role while using your full mental capabilities and natural psychic ability to receive inner direction.

It is likely that you are somehow involved in either teaching, organizing, communications, or writing and that you desire more success in one of these areas. To be successful, you must make some changes in the way you have been doing things, and often these changes will seem difficult or burdensome. However, your goal is in sight, and you should be successful. Your Result Card will tell you what else or who else is involved with this mental power that you seek.

AFFIRMATION:

I am transformed in my service capacity that deals with knowledge and communications. I learn to love and nurture others by sharing my personal truth and intuitive messages.

THE QUEEN OF CLUBS IS YOUR RESULT CARD

In some way related to your Pluto Card this year, you will achieve a stronger connection to your inner source of guidance as well as success in areas where you use your mental abilities to serve others. This could be as a teacher, writer, publisher, or even a secretary, but it will be some communications-related field. On the spiritual side, this card could lift you to new heights of inspiration as direct lines to higher knowledge and guidance open up for you.

This card is also a powerful indicator that you could end up with some woman of the Clubs suit by your next birthday. Whether this be a friend, lover, or family member, there is a strong indicator that the two of you will be joined in some meaningful way by year's end.

AFFIRMATION:

I achieve more intuition and success applying my knowledge in a service capacity. I receive divine knowledge.

THE QUEEN OF CLUBS IS YOUR LONG-RANGE CARD

This is a year that you achieve a level of mastery in one of the information fields. Whether you are a school teacher, a secretary, or a public relations person, any Mercury-ruled profession or endeavor will benefit greatly by this powerful influence in your life. You could also find yourself in some capacity of service that is related to information in some way. Giving knowledge or information to others can take many forms. One of them is likely to be what you are involved

in to a great extent this year. At the same time, your natural intuitive abilities are higher than normal, and you may find that you can access hidden information for your benefit this year. You are standing in the 'royal court of knowledge' this year. Use this influence for success and accomplishment.

If your Birth Card happens to be a Club and you are a female, the Queen of Clubs as your Long-Range Card could also mean a lot of focus on your role as a mother or a romantic partner for the year. For single women, this can often be a sign of new relationships coming into their lives.

KEYWORDS:

A year of success in fields where I serve others with knowledge or information. I help nourish others with truth.

THE QUEEN OF CLUBS IS YOUR ENVIRONMENT CARD

The Queen of Clubs will bring many blessings into your life this year, especially along the lines of intuition, organizational ability, and work in any of the communications fields. This is a card of success through service and of sharing knowledge and information with others. If you are a Club female, you are also likely to have more success this year in the romantic or motherly departments of your life.

THE QUEEN OF CLUBS IS YOUR DISPLACEMENT CARD

If you are a female of the Clubs suit, your personal life this year, which includes any role you play as a mother, wife, or romantic partner, will be a source of burden at times and require additional effort in order to maintain. This doesn't have to be a source of major problems if you just put forth the necessary effort. It's just that it will take more time and energy than usual for this period.

For all others, organizational roles and projects will be time consuming and more difficult than usual. Any females of the Clubs suit could prove to be a burden at times, especially those who Birth or Planetary Ruling Card is the Queen of Clubs itself. If your job involves service to others through communications and organization, this would be an area where you must expend extra energy to be successful.

Queen of Diamonds

Financial success through nurturing and helping, being a successful businesswoman

The Basic Meaning of the Queen of Diamonds

The Queen of Diamonds represents a woman who likes to live and act extravagantly and who often spends beyond her means. Sometimes she is successfully engaged in her own business or in some business capacity. Service through money is her motto, and she often is generous, especially to those she loves. There may be such a woman (or man) in your life when this card is present, or you could find yourself playing out that role.

This card can bring much financial success if its creative aspect is applied in some business or financial pursuit that you may be involved in. The Queen of Diamonds is a masterful card when it comes to business and finance, especially promoting and marketing.

By the same token, watch out for a tendency to spend beyond your budget when this card appears. The Queen of Diamonds likes only the very best of everything, even if she cannot afford it.

THE QUEEN OF DIAMONDS IN THE MERCURY PERIOD

During this period, your mind is sharp, and you can have some good ideas about how to make more money for yourself. The Queen of Diamonds brings you a savvy about money that can be applied in any business for success. However, she also may stimulate you to suddenly go shopping and spend some money on a luxury item or two. Be aware so your desire to look good in front of others doesn't hurt your bank account. This is a good time to take classes on how to make money.

THE QUEEN OF DIAMONDS IN THE VENUS PERIOD

During this period, you have a heightened sense of how to successfully create more money in business. Use this ability in any line of work you do where you need a financial increase or a creative marketing plan. You will have your best success in businesses that involve items for the home or beauty or are related to the arts in some way. The Queen of Diamonds will also encourage you to go out and spend some money on items for the home, new clothes, or beauty products. Be careful to not spend beyond your budget.

Your relations with Diamond females should be very good during this period. There may be one or two of them that play an important role in your life now. That role is likely to be one that is pleasant and enjoyable for you.

THE QUEEN OF DIAMONDS IN THE MARS PERIOD

Success in businesses related to men is one of the keynotes for this card of financial mastery. Aggressive pursuit of your financial goals could bring in huge returns, and your sense of what sells has never been better. At the same time, it may be hard for you to slow down and control the urge to spend money impulsively on luxury items, the negative side of this card. Keep your impatience channeled into your work for the best results during this period.

You may also find that there are one or more women of the Diamonds suit for whom you feel some attraction or anger during this period.

THE QUEEN OF DIAMONDS IN THE JUPITER PERIOD

This powerful card of financial mastery can bring you huge returns if you apply her wisdom and business savvy to your current methods of making money. This is the time to expand your business and ways to make money and to develop new and better ways to market your products and services. Your timing is good, and your sense of generosity may encourage you to help others who are less fortunate than yourself. This could also add to the crown you are wearing now.

Any and all women who have Birth Cards of the Diamonds suit could be a financial or other blessing to you this year. Look to them for guidance and help.

THE QUEEN OF DIAMONDS IN THE SATURN PERIOD

Though you have better than usual business and sales ability during this period, your fears of poverty may hamper your efforts to obtain the finances you desire. Be careful during this period that you do not spend beyond your means on items you really cannot afford. These expenses could even affect your health, if not checked, as you are more prone than usual to worry about money. Use this time to work steadily at your business for more success later.

Be on the lookout for women of the Diamonds suit, especially those you are romantically involved with. These are likely to prove troublesome or burdensome in some way during this period.

THE QUEEN OF DIAMONDS IN THE URANUS PERIOD

This is an excellent influence for financial success in businesses involving either real estate or using your psychic gifts. Your business acumen is strong now. Use it to develop effective ways to market your products and services. Unexpected gains are possible. At the same time, watch a tendency to go out on impulsive spending sprees, the downside of this powerful card.

Any women of the Diamonds suit may seem to be somewhat unpredictable during this period, and to a lesser extent for the entire year. To insure success in your relationships with them, it would be best to just step back and allow them to do or be whatever they need to. A good friendship comes from unconditional love and acceptance.

THE QUEEN OF DIAMONDS IN THE NEPTUNE PERIOD

Your business sense is strong during this period, and it could help you to attain a financial goal that you have dreamt about. Or you may help others in need. This is a card of financial gains through successful sales and marketing. At the same time, watch for a tendency to spend money on luxury items that could deplete your resources and cause you to worry about money. Use your creativity in a positive direction to create the finances you have dreamed about.

Any women of the Diamonds suit that you meet during this period, and to a lesser extent this entire year, are likely to be a little hard for you to see objectively. You could easily project your fantasies on them, romantic or otherwise. Therefore, it is best not to make any important decisions related to them until after your next birthday.

THE QUEEN OF DIAMONDS IS YOUR PLUTO CARD

This year you are concerned about money in a big way. This powerful card tells that you will be transformed this year to somehow attain the prosperity you desire while not being swayed by the lure of money for its own sake. Either you find yourself overspending it and leaving yourself broke, or you are really wanting to have more success in all your business and financial enterprises.

The Queen of Diamonds is the card of the woman of expensive tastes, who loves the display of wealth and luxury. However, she often spends beyond her means. Her gift is that she has a great business head and knows how to successfully run a business. She can smell a good deal also. Consider that this year you are trying to adopt or simply deal with some of her characteristics in an important way. While you work hard to create more money, see if you are not also tempted by your own values. Major transformations may be in store for you during this process.

Your Result Card will tell you more about this challenge or point to someone who is directly involved in it.

AFFIRMATION:

I am transformed in my service capacity that deals with finances and business. I learn to love and nurture others by sharing higher values with them.

THE QUEEN OF DIAMONDS IS YOUR RESULT CARD

Somehow, as a result of some of this year's challenges, you will attain prosperity and success in business, while not allowing yourself to be lured into a false sense of values. The Queen of Diamonds is one who brings higher values to others, another important role you may end up playing before your next birthday. Expect challenges along the way, but ultimately, you will be successful in your business. For women, this could indicate starting your own business this year.

This card is also a powerful indicator that you could end up with some woman of the Diamonds suit by your next birthday. Whether this be a friend, lover, or family member, there is a strong indicator that the two of you will be joined in some meaningful way by year's end.

AFFIRMATION:

I create financial prosperity while maintaining a higher set of values, keeping money in its proper place in my life. I become successful in my business.

THE QUEEN OF DIAMONDS IS YOUR LONG-RANGE CARD

The Queen of Diamonds represents a woman who often spends beyond her means. Often she is successfully engaged in her own business or some business capacity. Service through money is her motto, and she is generous to those she loves. There may be such a woman (or man) in your life this year who comes into major focus. However, it also means that you will have some of the attributes of the Queen of Diamonds mentioned above. This influence can be very good for management of a business and financial success in almost any business or other endeavor. However, one should also be aware of the expensive tastes of the Queen of Diamonds, which accompany her business acumen. Inwardly, the Queen of Diamonds is one who gives others a higher and more spiritual set of values—another important role you may play this year.

If your Birth Card happens to be a Diamond and you are a female, the Queen of Diamonds as your Long-Range Card could also mean a lot of focus on your role as a mother or a romantic partner for the year. For single women, this can often be a sign of new relationships coming into their lives.

KEYWORDS:

A year of achieving financial success in business or in service to others. Making large purchases of luxury items.

THE QUEEN OF DIAMONDS IS YOUR ENVIRONMENT CARD

This is a year in which finances should improve, and you can have a lot of success in business-related activities. Your creative energies are high now, and you will get good ideas on how to improve your financial situation and better sell your products, services, or ideas. If you are a woman of the Diamond suit, benefits will come through romance and in your role as a mother or wife. Regardless of your Birth Card, you will tend to receive benefits from all Diamond women as well.

THE QUEEN OF DIAMONDS IS YOUR DISPLACEMENT CARD

This card is a caution in regards to overspending and being careless with your money. The Queen of Diamonds is the card which likes to look good by wearing the best clothes and purchasing only things of the highest quality. But, she often spends beyond her means, and though she may look like a million dollars, her actual financial status may not be what it seems. In this regard, it would be wise with this influence to govern your spending habits carefully and stay within some budget to insure your financial security.

Women involved in their own business may also find that they have to now pay closer attention to that business and that the chances of problems arising this year seems to have grown. It's not that there will be major problems, only that more effort will be required than usual.

Any women of the Diamonds suit will probably find that their personal lives require more of their time and energy this year than usual. This includes their roles as a wife, mother, or romantic partner. Any or all of these areas could be affected and become a burden at times. For all cards, involvements with anyone whose Birth or Planetary Ruling Card is the Queen of Diamonds may require this same additional effort.

On the positive side, this card often brings a very fortunate financial configuration that you can check for, the Seven of Diamonds in Jupiter. If you have this card this year, you have a special opportunity to experience true abundance, which could result in a windfall of money.

Queen of Spades
Organizational ability and hard work, self-mastery brings much success

The Basic Meaning of the Queen of Spades

The Queen of Spades is known as the card of 'self-mastery,' the one that sits in the position of highest accomplishment and recognition in what we call the 'Spiritual Spread.' Whenever this card appears, we are given a special opportunity to achieve much success in our external life by mastering ourselves within. This means creating more success by changing our inner thoughts, beliefs, and attitudes instead of trying to alter our external circumstances.

We rarely realize that it is not so much our efforts that create our successes and failures, but that it actually occurs based upon our inner attitudes and state of mind. The Queen of Spades teaches us that if we can master our inner state, we can master the universe and everything in it. Queens have their greatest power in the feminine, receptive mode. To truly receive, we must attain that state of mind in which we allow everything to come to us without hesitation. It usually requires some inner exploration to achieve this state, and this is something that most of us never do, because it is not taught as part of our culture. It is the spiritual aspirant who learns to master themselves instead of spending all their time trying to change external circumstances. And it is those aspirants who experience the real power of the feminine sides of their being, which the Queen of Spades represents. The Queen of Spades sits in the Sun position in the Spiritual Spread, which can be translated to mean the position of highest accomplishment in the spiritual sense. From this, we can infer that from the point of view of our soul and spirit, self-mastery is the highest quality we can aspire to and the one that deserves the highest recognition and reward.

The Queen of Spades is a hard-working woman card and a good manager as well, so we can also expect success in work and organizational ability whenever she appears in our spreads.

THE QUEEN OF SPADES IN THE MERCURY PERIOD

During this period, you will have the opportunity to experience 'Mastery of your Mind.' This translates as having control over your thoughts, which in turn controls the things you manifest in your life. Take responsibility for what you create in your world by realizing that the way you think determines how things show up in your life. Also during this period, you may find yourself working hard at some mental project. Your organizational skills are high now.

THE QUEEN OF SPADES IN THE VENUS PERIOD

During this period, you can expect better results with all your personal relationships, because you are going to be able to handle your feelings and emotions better. Romance will fall into its proper place in your life, as you develop your power to control your affections and emotions. Things will be running smoothly at home also, as you apply a firm, but wise hand to everyone and everything that comes up. Enjoy this time of 'Spiritual Self-Mastery.'

Relationships with any Spade females you know should be quite enjoyable during this period. As a matter of fact, there may be one or two of them that play an important role now, one that is either very romantic, friendly, or pleasant in some other way.

THE QUEEN OF SPADES IN THE MARS PERIOD

During this period, you can expect greater results from your work and the things that you are passionately pursuing, because now, you have control over yourself and your desires. This, in turn, will bring you more success in work and legal matters, as you develop patience and understanding that attracts success to you. You may have to work very hard now, but your organizational ability will help keep everything in its place and help keep you on the right track.

You may also find that there are one or more women of the Spades suit for whom you feel some attraction or anger during this period.

THE QUEEN OF SPADES IN THE JUPITER PERIOD

This is a powerful spiritual influence that will also have a powerful and beneficial influence on your business and money situation. Through mastery of yourself, you will be able to attract good luck into your life. This is the time to apply your organizational ability and to diligently work hard. Doing this could bring you more financial success than you realize. Finances should be running smoothly now and throughout this entire year to a lesser extent.

The power of this card is manifested when we make changes in our inner attitudes and beliefs. You could be amazed at just how much success you could have now without having to change anything in your world, except yourself. This card brings the realization that everything stems from within us and the power to demonstrate that truth in our lives in a tangible way.

Any and all women who have Birth Cards of the Spades suit could be a financial or other blessing to you this year. Look to them for guidance and help.

THE QUEEN OF SPADES IN THE SATURN PERIOD

This powerful card of self-mastery will give you what it takes to overcome any health problems or other difficulties that you may have been dealing with this year. By taking total responsibility for your health and your life, you will be in a position to make some changes that will have a positive impact. You may find that you have to work very hard now, but the rewards of better health and fewer problems will be worth it. You are learning secrets about how to improve your life from within, which is one of the highest spiritual achievements.

Be on the lookout for women of the Spades suit, especially those who you are romantically involved with. These are likely to prove troublesome or burdensome in some way during this period.

THE QUEEN OF SPADES IN THE URANUS PERIOD

This is a highly spiritual influence that could indicate a time when you have some profound experiences of awakening and self-realization. There are bound to be some interesting experiences during this period that lift you to new levels of understanding and awareness. On the practical side, you will find that your work and real estate concerns are going very well, as you work hard and apply this new understanding to the mundane situations in your life.

Any women of the Spades suit may seem to be somewhat unpredictable during this period, and to a lesser extent for the entire year. To insure success in your relationships with them, it would be best to just step back and allow them to do or be whatever they need to. A good friendship comes from unconditional love and acceptance.

THE QUEEN OF SPADES IN THE NEPTUNE PERIOD

Through meditation and inner reflection you could achieve some meaningful changes in your life. Your deepest dreams, the ones that are a major driving force in your life, are being uplifted to new levels. Expect some realizations that are profound and life-altering. On the mundane side, many areas of your life are going better now as you stop trying to change others and make changes in yourself that allow you to experience more joy and success.

Any women of the Spades suit that you meet during this period, and to a lesser extent, this entire year, are likely to be a little hard for you to see objectively. You could easily project your fantasies on them, romantic or otherwise. Therefore, it is best not to make any important decisions related to them until after your next birthday.

THE QUEEN OF SPADES IS YOUR PLUTO CARD

Somehow connected to your Result Card for this year, you are attempting to develop a sense of mastery from within, a greater level of organizational ability, or both. The Queen of Spades is a powerful card, and you are indeed asking for a lot. Self-mastery comes from inner knowledge and self-control. It comes from controlling one's thoughts, attitudes, beliefs, words, and actions guided by higher principles. It is knowing that you can have everything you want, not by changing the world, but by changing yourself.

The Queen of Spades can be a card of drudgery and hard labor. It would not be surprising if you found yourself having to work very hard this year and possibly doing work that you find somewhat distasteful or tedious. Spades are work, and the Queen uses her work as Karma Yoga, a tool to purify her thoughts and emotions.

This is the goal that you have set before yourself, and you must have good reasons for why you want this. Keep these reasons uppermost in your mind as you progress through the year. You no doubt will have to make some changes both within and outside of yourself to achieve this goal, and it will not always be easy. There also may be someone important, represented by your Result Card, that is part of this goal you are seeking. The Result Card may also give you more clues about what particular area of your life you desire to be more internally masterful about.

AFFIRMATION:

I develop my capacity to transform my life by changing my beliefs, thoughts, ideas, and concepts of the world. I become the master of my self.

THE QUEEN OF SPADES IS YOUR RESULT CARD

This powerful card of spiritual attainment guarantees that whatever the major challenges and changes of this year, represented by your Pluto Card, you will achieve success related to them and also success in any area of your life by going within for your answers and making fundamental changes in yourself. Though these changes may be very difficult at times, the end result will be well worth the efforts expended.

This card is also a powerful indicator that you could end up with some woman of the Spades suit by your next birthday. Whether this be a friend, lover, or family member, there is a strong indicator that the two of you will be joined in some meaningful way by year's end.

AFFIRMATION:

I become a master of myself and therefore a master of everything in my life. I share the value of service with others.

THE QUEEN OF SPADES IS YOUR LONG-RANGE CARD

The Queen of Spades is the card of 'self-mastery,' and many of those represented by this card have accomplished just that. They have an inner calm that speaks of knowledge and experience that can be successfully applied to any area. In any case, they are good business people with strong character. Their work is often a 'labor of the spirit,' meaning that they do it for more than just the material rewards it offers. The Queen of Spades is the second most powerful card in the deck,

and you are most fortunate to have her with you this year. This is a year when you can accomplish your dreams, but not by the usual approach. This year, all success comes from within you by mastering the causes of all your exterior events by mastery of yourself. By seeing that nothing happens in your life without your permission, you reclaim your power to create the world you desire without trying to change others.

This year you will have the qualities of the Queen of Spades at your disposal, and this could indeed be a year of mastery and accomplishment for you. Recognize the power that you have now, and apply it wherever you desire. Look within for your answers, and let that inner knowing help you in all your external endeavors.

If your Birth Card happens to be a Spade and you are a female, the Queen of Spades as your Long-Range Card could also mean a lot of focus on your role as a mother or a romantic partner for the year. For single women, this can often be a sign of new relationships coming into their lives.

KEYWORDS:

A year of hard work and spiritual 'self-mastery.' I master myself, and therefore, I master my entire life.

THE QUEEN OF SPADES IS YOUR ENVIRONMENT CARD

Blessings and good fortune this year will come through hard work, organization, and spiritual self-mastery. This is an important year when you could actually make some important inner changes that could alter the way you perceive your life and in turn, alter your destiny. In particular, you may find it relatively easy to achieve a measure of self-mastery this year that seems to attract everything you need without your having to work so hard for it. So, though this card indicates success through hard work, you can also benefit from going within and learning how to attract what you want to you without effort. For more information, read the Basic Meaning of the Queen of Spades.

If you are a Spades woman, benefits will come through your role as a mother, wife, or as a romantic partner. Everyone else will benefit from relationships with Spades women of all denominations.

THE QUEEN OF SPADES IS YOUR DISPLACEMENT CARD

You may find that you are caught up in a job or occupation that is somewhat tedious this year or that you are dealing with your own personal struggle in the drama of your life. The Queen of Spades tells us that you have a need this year to rise above the entire concept of struggle to a new life where you allow things to come to you more easily. It is our state of mind, beliefs, and attitudes that determine how our life is perceived, and many of us get ingrained in 'struggle mentality' as a matter of course. "You work hard, and then you die" is a familiar motto that governs the lives of millions of people today. If you feel that your life is just a continuous struggle in some areas, this year will give you the opportunity to examine your beliefs and attitudes so you may transform this into a life with more blessings and less effort.

The Queen of Spades requires inner work, not outer struggle. If we look within, we will see where we are the cause of the ups and downs of our life and be able to make some important changes that can bring greater success and more ease and comfort.

If you are a female of the Spades suit, this card could also represent some challenges for you in your role as a mother, wife, or romantic partner. One or more of these areas will require more of your attention this year or seem to be a burden at times.

On a positive note, you are in the middle of a very auspicious cycle in your life this year. Last year, you were in the pinnacle position and next year, you will be in the most blessed position. The inner work you do this year is a preparation for the blessings that will come next year. The more you can open yourself up to receive, the more you will benefit from this most important time in your life.

King of Hearts

Romantic or social success, becoming a father (men), finding a lover (women)

The Basic Meaning of the King of Hearts

The King of Hearts, being the highest card in the suit of love, rules through love, compassion, and wisdom. He has all the power and knowledge of love and knows how to use it, thus when this card appears, it gives you the opportunity to have more control over your feelings and romantic impulses. This will bring more success in all your personal relationships.

For men, this is also the card of the loving father and of sexual enjoyment. Thus, it can indicate the conception or birth of a child.

For ladies, the King of Hearts represents the perfect lover or companion, and so it often indicates having an enjoyable sexual relationship or in some cases, marriage.

But for all of us, the King of Hearts brings success in dealing with our own emotions, success with the public and in any of the artistic, fields and romantic success in one form or another.

THE KING OF HEARTS IN THE MERCURY PERIOD

This period could find you spending time with a man who is kind, intelligent, and a good influence. He may come in and out of your life quickly, but you will find him to be intellectually stimulating and friendly. You have a lot of emotional power and charm now that can help you meet new friends or bring you rewards in any business or work that involves dealing with people. Your ability to communicate in a loving manner can bring many rewards.

THE KING OF HEARTS IN THE VENUS PERIOD

This card brings emotional power, charm, and the ability to master your emotions and affections. This power can be used for success in any personal or professional relationship. For men, this card can indicate becoming a father sometime this year. It always brings success and harmony on the family level by exhibiting leadership abilities in love. You are the 'Master of Love' now and can get what you want from others. Use this power with wisdom.

There may be some male or males of the Hearts suit that play an important role in your life during the course of this period. The good news is that they will be a good influence to you, bringing you more pleasure and friendship. One of them may even be a romantic interest of yours. For women, this card often means a new romantic partner and one that is very fulfilling.

THE KING OF HEARTS IN THE MARS PERIOD

This card suggests a period when your passions are running high and where you have the ability to get what you want from others by aggressively using your charm and 'love power.' For men, this card can indicate becoming a father sometime this year, and if so, you are likely to have a boy. In addition to the charm and persuasiveness you have now, you may have a more mature attitude about your feelings that can be used for success in love and romance.

You may also find that there are one or more men of the Hearts suit for whom you feel some attraction or anger during this period.

THE KING OF HEARTS IN THE JUPITER PERIOD

Financial and other blessings will come as the result of your mastery over your own feelings and the ability to communicate with charm and grace with those in your business and home. You have much 'love power' at your disposal, see that you use it wisely. Your ability to handle others may astound you during this period. For men, this is a possible indication of the birth of a child this year. If so, it will be a blessed one.

Any men of the Hearts suit could be a source of financial and other blessings this year, especially those who are older or who are in a leadership role in their work.

THE KING OF HEARTS IN THE SATURN PERIOD

Through emotional self-control, wisdom, and healing power, you will be able to overcome any difficulties that may arise in this period, which is usually the most challenging of the year. Success with health matters, doctors, or other areas will be attributed to your emotional maturity. You are the 'loving father' now, and even though this responsibility may seem a burden, it promises ultimate success and increasing wisdom.

For women, this card could indicate difficulties from some man who is a romantic interest.

Be on the lookout for men of the Hearts suit, especially those who are older or who may be in positions of authority or responsibility. These are likely to prove troublesome or burdensome in some way during this period.

THE KING OF HEARTS IN THE URANUS PERIOD

Strong psychic power, hard work, and leadership in service to others can bring success during this period. Also, you may have the association of someone with these qualities which will be beneficial to you. Community or volunteer work is strongly benefited by this influence. Your love could produce some unexpected and satisfying results. Your own psychic powers will be at hand to help you in all that you do.

For men, this card can indicate the birth of a child or an unexpected pregnancy. It also represents success in their romantic love life.

Men, especially older men, of the Hearts suit will seem to be unpredictable during this period, and to a lesser extent for the entire year. You would do best not to place too many expectations on them while they are this sort of influence in your life.

THE KING OF HEARTS IN THE NEPTUNE PERIOD

This card brings a time when your charm and magnetism are at an all-time high and can be used for romantic or professional success. Especially favored are social or romantic occasions involving travel or vacations. For men, this can indicate a year when a child is born or conceived. For women, it may indicate meeting the lover of your dreams. You have considerable love and healing power now that you can use to help others or yourself.

Any men of the Hearts suit that you meet during this period, and to a lesser extent this entire year, are likely to be a little hard for you to see objectively. You could easily project your fantasies on them, romantic or otherwise. Therefore, it is best not to make any important decisions related to them until after your next birthday.

THE KING OF HEARTS IS YOUR PLUTO CARD

This year you are working on a heart and emotional level in a big way. Perhaps you are in a business that has a lot of people contacts, and you need more success in selling your ideas or in getting more cooperation. Just as likely, your role as a father has come into focus, and you have decided to put more energy into it. This is the 'Father Card' and can represent a year when you, as a man, may really want to become a father.

For ladies, this card can mean that you have a strong desire to meet a lover this year, someone who has almost ideal qualities such as being romantic, caring, and good in bed. The King of Hearts has been called the 'man that all women dream of' and the 'perfect lover.' In this case, the Result Card could be the Birth Card of a man that you will actually meet and be with by your next birthday.

On a deeper level, you may have decided to take a more mature and responsible role with your emotions. Perhaps you are doing therapy and working on cleaning up past debris that blocks your present happiness.

Whichever area of your life is being affected by this card, this goal you seek will take some determination from you. You will have to make some changes in yourself, and these may not always be easy. Your Result Card will further define this emotional power that you seek or tell you who is involved in it somehow.

AFFIRMATION:

I become the master of my emotions and through that, the master of all my relationships. I develop a 'Kingly' sort of love that expands my ability to accept and give loving help to others.

THE KING OF HEARTS IS YOUR RESULT CARD

The King of Hearts suggests that you are developing emotional and love power in conjunction with your Pluto Card this year. This card bestows charm and good communications, which is useful in people-oriented business. For this reason, this card can mean great success by year's end in any of the performing arts or in your romantic life.

To achieve more inner control and understanding of your emotions, or the success you desire, you must make changes inside yourself. The good news is that, even though it may be difficult, you will be successful.

This card is also a powerful indicator that you could end up with some man of the Hearts suit by your next birthday. Whether this be a friend, lover, or family member, there is a strong indicator that the two of you will be joined in some meaningful way by year's end.

If you are a man, this card may mean that you become a father sometime before your next birthday. If you are a female, this could mean finding the romantic partner of your dreams.

AFFIRMATION:

I create more power with people and my emotions. I create either being a father or being a more successful father.

THE KING OF HEARTS IS YOUR LONG-RANGE CARD

The King of Hearts rules through love. He has all the power and knowledge of love and knows how to use it. This powerful card bestows you with his power, and you can apply this to your personal and professional life this year to great success. This card is an indicator of success in the arts or in any business that deals with the public. Just remember not to abuse this power. Rule with love, and everything will turn out in your favor.

As someone with whom you may have an important involvement with this year, the King of Hearts is usually an older man, kind-hearted, and good tempered, who has considerable charm and emotional persuasiveness. The King of Hearts is a sign of strong feelings and power to influence others that can either help you achieve your goals or get you into trouble.

For women, the King of Hearts can mean having the lover or man of your dreams this year. It can be a sign of marriage as well. For men, the King of Hearts can indicate their role as a father and that this will be an important aspect of their life this year.

KEYWORDS:

I have mastery over my emotions. I have mastery in all my relationships this year. I am concentrating on my role as a father or romantic partner this year (men). I am focusing my attention on having a romantic partner this year (women).

THE KING OF HEARTS IS YOUR ENVIRONMENT CARD

This could be a very good year for personal relationships, as well as for mastering your own emotions. You have considerable charm and mastery with people, which could be applied in many ways for greater success. Since this is also called 'the father card,' men could benefit from fatherhood this year as well. For women, this card could indicate an ideal lover coming into your life, one that has many good things to share with you.

THE KING OF HEARTS IS YOUR DISPLACEMENT CARD

For men who are fathers, this card could indicate that you have to spend a lot more time and energy in this role than usual. Perhaps your child or children are having some problems of their own, and now you have to devote more of yourself to them to help them through. This is also an indicator for all men that their romantic life will have some challenges. The way that you handle your personal relationships will be up for review as some challenges appear in that area. I am not referring to really serious problems here, just ones that require more of your attention.

Males of the Hearts suit may also find that any roles they play as a leader or boss to others will likewise require more effort and expense this year.

Women will find that their romantic partners need more of them than usual or that it is more difficult to find a suitable romantic mate.

For both sexes, mastery of your emotions could be an issue that needs to be addressed this year. You are being called upon to take a more 'kingly' approach to your personal relationships, one in which you are less sensitive to others' actions and comments and where you take a more high-minded attitude in love and friendships.

King of Clubs

Becoming an authority in one of the communications fields, success and recognition

The Basic Meaning of the King of Clubs

The King of Clubs is the highest card in the suit of knowledge. It bestows mastery and success in any of the communications fields, especially in situations where we are able and willing to take a leadership position or assume responsibility. Remember that every King has a kingdom. If you are involved in one of the communications-related fields and are willing to stand up and take charge, there is no better card to indicate your success.

The King of Clubs is highly intuitive, can make fine mental distinctions, and will never do anything to compromise his or her integrity or inner truth. Keep these qualities in mind whenever this powerful card appears in your reading.

THE KING OF CLUBS IN THE MERCURY PERIOD

This powerful card of applied wisdom guarantees success in all your mental pursuits this period and this year. Your ability to distinguish the truth from illusion and to sort out the myriad of details seems amazing. You can apply the mind power of the "King of Knowledge" to any mental pursuit with success. You may even take a leadership role at work or in some mental pursuit that sets you apart from the crowd. Even your intuition is running high now.

THE KING OF CLUBS IN THE VENUS PERIOD

This card brings you much success at home and in personal relationships by exhibiting the King of Clubs mind power and remarkable ability to make distinctions. This mental power can be used in all areas of your life now, to clear away the clutter of unresolved relationship issues or family matters. You can also apply this power for more success in your work or business, especially if it relates to women, the arts, or entertainment in some way. Expect many positive results from the presence of this card of 'Mental Mastery' in your life.

THE KING OF CLUBS IN THE MARS PERIOD

During this period, you can expect much success in your life as a result of this card of 'Mastery of the Mind.' If you are involved in any legal matters, expect to come out on top. The same goes for situations involving men or groups of men. This influence gives you the ability to apply knowledge and wisdom to all your pursuits and guarantees success. Any of the mental fields are highlighted, especially those that you aggressively pursue.

You may also find that there are one or more men of the Clubs suit for whom you feel some attraction or anger during this period.

THE KING OF CLUBS IN THE JUPITER PERIOD

This period will be one of much success for you in your business or profession, especially if you are involved in one or more of the mental fields such as writing, speaking, teaching, or publishing. Your mental power is at an all-time high along with your ability to make informed and brilliant choices in your line of work. This is definitely the time to expand your scope of operation and to think big.

Any men of the Clubs suit could be a source of financial and other blessings this year, especially those who are older or who are in a leadership role in their work.

THE KING OF CLUBS IN THE SATURN PERIOD

Though the Saturn period is usually the most difficult, this powerful card's presence will guarantee that you will meet with some success by applying your mental power, maturity, and ability to make distinctions to situations at hand. The King of Clubs mind power can help solve health problems or any other difficulties that seem to place burdens on you now. Use it to heal yourself of any negative mental beliefs that may stand in the way of your happiness.

Be on the lookout for men of the Clubs suit, especially those who are older or who may be in positions of authority or responsibility. These are likely to prove troublesome or burdensome in some way during this period.

THE KING OF CLUBS IN THE URANUS PERIOD

The presence of this powerful card during this period gives you several important gifts that you can use to achieve more success and happiness in your life. First of all, you can expect success in any work in the mental fields. You can take a leadership position on the job and confidently make progress. Your intuition is also very active now. It will give you valuable insights into your work and those areas that will contribute to your success.

Men, especially older men, of the Clubs suit will seem to be unpredictable during this period, and to a lesser extent for the entire year. You would do best not to place too many expectations on them while they are this sort of influence in your life.

THE KING OF CLUBS IN THE NEPTUNE PERIOD

During this period, you can expect much success in any work that involves using your mind, intuition, or organizational ability. This would be an excellent time to expand the scope of your work and to realize some of your dreams along these lines. Your intuition is very high now, and you could receive valuable knowledge about your inner self that will guide you in better directions. Make fine distinctions in every area of your life, and you will progress rapidly.

Any men of the Clubs suit that you meet during this period, and to a lesser extent this entire year, are likely to be a little hard for you to see objectively. You could easily project your fantasies on them, romantic or otherwise. Therefore, it is best not to make any important decisions related to them until after your next birthday.

THE KING OF CLUBS IS YOUR PLUTO CARD

The King of Clubs will transform you this year through a desire on your part to achieve success in one or more of the mental fields such as writing, speaking, teaching, or publishing. You desire the kind of mind power that will put you in a leadership position in your field, and to achieve this, you must make some fundamental and important changes in yourself. It is likely that you must make some important distinctions about your life that will alter your path.

'Mental power that brings success' are the major keywords for the King of Clubs. Whether you are a writer, a teacher, a speaker, or working in any of the communications fields, it is certain that mental power, the ability to get and use the right information, is vital to your success this year. You will have to make some changes in the way you have been doing things in order to have this success, and it won't always be an easy task. However, this is the goal that you have set before yourself, and you must do it.

The King of Clubs, like all the Kings, is about becoming a leader and taking more responsibility in some mental field or endeavor. Perhaps you have the desire to rise up to a level where you are a recognized authority in some field or you want to take more of a leadership position in your job.

Be careful not to bully others this year as you develop this power. With power always comes the temptation to abuse it. Your Result Card will give you more information about this mental power and authority you seek or tell you who is directly involved in it.

AFFIRMATION:

I transform myself to become more responsible and clear in my communications, assuming a position of leadership and authority in some field that is important to me.

THE KING OF CLUBS IS YOUR RESULT CARD

Somehow connected to your Pluto Card this year, you will be transformed and take total responsibility for your life. Harnessing the power of your thoughts to create what you want can lead to major accomplishments in your work and an elevated position of leadership and responsibility. As soon as you are ready to step up and take the 'Crown,' it is yours. Rest assured that by your next birthday you will be wearing this 'Crown of Knowledge.'

This card is also a powerful indicator that you could end up with some man of the Clubs suit by your next birthday. Whether this be a friend, lover, or family member, there is a strong indicator that the two of you will be joined in some meaningful way by year's end.

AFFIRMATION:

I achieve mental power and success in a leadership position in my work. I take control of my mind and my life.

THE KING OF CLUBS IS YOUR LONG-RANGE CARD

This card means that you will be successful in many ways. Your mind power is strong, and success is yours in any of the mental fields such as teaching, writing, management, or communications. By applying what you know, there is no limit to what you can achieve this year. Any involvement with legal matters will be successful. Use this influence to take a leadership position in your area of expertise. Now is the time to take the initiative.

The King of Clubs is someone who wields much power and authority through their acquired or developed knowledge. This year may see you having much to do with such a person or displaying

and dealing with this side of your own personality. As a king, this person demands the respect of others and usually gets it. Often, they are found as the head of some business or establishment. In any case, they are people who live by their own truth and do not like interference from others. You will find yourself exhibiting some or all of these characteristics this year, and these can be applied to much success in your work. This can be especially good if your work involves writing, communications, publishing, teaching, or speaking. Any mental type of endeavor is bound to meet with success as a result of this influence.

KEYWORDS:

A year of much success in all areas where application of knowledge and mental discernment are concerned. I take a commanding role in some area of communication.

THE KING OF CLUBS IS YOUR ENVIRONMENT CARD

This is a year when you can take a leadership role in some form of knowledge and be recognized for your accomplishment. Perhaps you are studying a new subject you intend to master or have to learn for a new job. In any event, this card guarantees the ability to become a master at what you learn or do. You could be promoted to a higher position at work as well—a position that puts you in a more responsible place among your peers.

THE KING OF CLUBS IS YOUR DISPLACEMENT CARD

If you are involved in work that places you in a position of responsibility, this year may be more trying than usual. Also, if you are regarded as an authority in some area, especially in some area of information or communication, or if you run a business related to a communications field, you will find that more effort is required in this area as well. All in all, these are areas that insist on more of your attention, time, and energy this year.

For all people, this card could indicate a desire to become more knowledgeable in some area and that you must work hard this year in order to achieve this level of information. If you are going to school or reading books in this regard, you will have to devote more of yourself to the task than you may have imagined.

On the positive side, this card has a good career influence, one that often brings a special gift or bonus at the end of the year. You may achieve some recognition, a promotion, or greater influence by your next birthday.

King of Diamonds

Becoming successful in business, financial success through responsibility

The Basic Meaning of the King of Diamonds

The King of Diamonds can often represent a successful business man, one who runs his own business, or a financial man such as a banker or stockbroker. He is successful and has a strong sense of values that have made him the success he is. So, when this card appears, you could have some dealings with someone like this, or you could take on these qualities yourself.

The King of Diamonds often appears when we are ready to start our own business, and it promises great success if we do. It is the highest card in the suit of money and values and as such, bestows everything needed to make a success of some financial or business opportunity. When this card appears, don't let it go to waste. Find some way to be in business for yourself, and go for it.

THE KING OF DIAMONDS IN THE MERCURY PERIOD

During this period, you could see yourself attaining a quick but significant financial success by applying your savvy and quick thinking to some idea or business. You have a very good influence for success in most money-making ventures you are involved in, especially favored are those that are either "quick schemes" or those that involve education, cars, or short trips. Use your mind now. The ideas you get could be worth more than you think.

THE KING OF DIAMONDS IN THE VENUS PERIOD

This period will bring a considerable amount of financial success. This applies most if you are involved in a business or profession that involves women, the arts, or articles for the home or beauty. It is time to start your own business, if you are ready. This is also a good influence for artists or musicians that will encourage you to market yourself better and make more profitable business deals.

THE KING OF DIAMONDS IN THE MARS PERIOD

You can expect a certain amount of financial success during this period, especially if you have specific goals that you are aggressively pursuing. Legal matters will go your way, and you can do very well in your own business or by handling your own investments. You have the 'Master of Finance' in your life now. Use this influence to make more money or to start your own business. Success is assured, especially if this is the top card of the pair in the Mars period.

You may also find that there are one or more men of the Diamonds suit for whom you feel some attraction or anger during this period.

THE KING OF DIAMONDS IN THE JUPITER PERIOD

This is one of the best cards for money possible, especially if you are the owner of your own business or in a leadership position at your work. Look for huge returns. The more you can take matters into your own hands, the more you will make. This is the time to expand your business and other money-making activities as much as possible, and the returns could be substantial. Also, be open to the help or advice of any learned businessmen, especially Diamonds men.

Any men of the Diamonds suit could be a source of financial and other blessings this year, especially those who are older or who are in a leadership role in their work.

THE KING OF DIAMONDS IN THE SATURN PERIOD

Though financial success is attainable during this period, you may not feel that it is worth the amount of effort and difficulty in order to attain it. If you have your own business, this is especially true. See yourself laying the foundation for future successes. The problems you work with now will set the stage for more expansion and prosperity later. Any Diamonds men in your life may assume a teaching role with you, or they may become a burden.

Be on the lookout for men of the Diamonds suit, especially those who are older or may be in positions of authority or responsibility. These are likely to prove troublesome or burdensome in some way during this period.

THE KING OF DIAMONDS IN THE URANUS PERIOD

This card represents a real estate broker or tycoon who works hard for his success. He may also be successful in the computer or electronics industry or one who earns money with his psychic abilities. This person may be a friend, though you may feel uncertain about his comings and goings. The King of Diamonds also gives you a fair amount of business ability during this period, and that could bring in huge financial returns, especially if you are in one of the areas above.

Men, especially older men, of the Diamonds suit will seem to be unpredictable during this period, and to a lesser extent for the entire year. You would do best not to place too many expectations on them while they are this sort of influence in your life.

THE KING OF DIAMONDS IN THE NEPTUNE PERIOD

You could achieve some of your financial dreams during this period by applying the business know-how that the King of Diamonds brings into your life. Though this may represent someone you know or meet, remember that you also will have this ability to make more money by making the right moves in work or business. This is the time to start your own business, if you are ready, especially if it involves import or export, ships or things related to the sea.

Any men of the Diamonds suit that you meet during this period, and to a lesser extent this entire year, are likely to be a little hard for you to see objectively. You could easily project your fantasies on them, romantic or otherwise. Therefore, it is best not to make any important decisions related to them until after your next birthday.

THE KING OF DIAMONDS IS YOUR PLUTO CARD

One of your major goals this year will be to achieve more prosperity, probably by starting your own business or by taking a leadership position in some company. The King of Diamonds is the card of the successful business owner. He has full authority in the realm of finance and knows how to turn a profit in all that he does. He can be materialistic to a fault but knows what he does very well.

Somehow, you are either wanting to be more like him or are having to deal with someone like this that is very challenging for you. In either case, you are the one being challenged to deal with where you are at financially or in the realm of business experience and success. Perhaps you have been thinking about starting your own business for a while, and this is the year you pursue it.

This card can also mean that just the thought of starting your own business is a major topic for you that you need to get clear about somehow. Your Result Card will give more information about this or tell you who is involved with it.

AFFIRMATION:

I transform myself to become more financially successful by assuming a position of leadership and power in my business or job.

THE KING OF DIAMONDS IS YOUR RESULT CARD

This powerful money card guarantees more mastery of your finances by your next birthday. You may even end up owning your own business, which is highly favored by this card. 'Mastery of Values' are the key words for this card, so the effects of it run deeper than just external prosperity. You are learning to know what you want and how to respond to the values of others in a productive way. Your Pluto Card will tell more about this transformation into a 'master.'

This card is also a powerful indicator that you could end up with some older or successful man of the Diamonds suit by your next birthday. Whether this be a friend, lover, or family member, there is a strong indicator that the two of you will be joined in some meaningful way by year's end.

AFFIRMATION:

I end this year as the head of my own business or with more prosperity. I take a leadership role in my company.

THE KING OF DIAMONDS IS YOUR LONG-RANGE CARD

The King of Diamonds is a very powerful card for financial success that can be yours if you decide to start your own business or take a leadership position where you currently work. You are being given the gift of the 'know-how' that makes companies successful. This could be applied to marketing, sales, management or any business role with success but is especially powerful as the head of a business. Use this influence to launch your own enterprise.

This year you are more likely than ever to have success in your business and financial endeavors. The King of Diamonds bestows a lot of support in the areas of business and finance and practically guarantees that you will make more profitable decisions in these undertakings.

The focus is on business. Watch that money does not become the sole objective in your life, as other areas may suffer as a consequence.

Keep in mind that the financial success indicated by this card only comes to those who actually have their own business, or to those who are willing to take a leadership position at their job.

KEYWORDS:

A year of financial success and taking a leadership position in your business. Starting your own business.

THE KING OF DIAMONDS IS YOUR ENVIRONMENT CARD

This could be a very good year for you financially, especially if you have your own business. Benefits come from all occupations where you are calling the shots, especially those that are heavily financially oriented. This is one of the best times to start a new business of your own or to expand an existing business. You should also do well in any legal matters that arise this year, as you have the power to succeed in many areas.

THE KING OF DIAMONDS IS YOUR DISPLACEMENT CARD

For those who are involved in business, or those who are in a position of responsibility in any business or company, your role in these areas will require more of your time and energy this year if you wish to maintain good results and success. However, this is in many ways a fortunate influence, and you do have the power this year to achieve a lot of success if you are willing to put in for the necessary effort. Anyone with this card will have a certain amount of power this year, the power to overcome obstacles by focusing one's mind and will. Health matters should also improve this year unless other cards severely oppose this influence, which is unlikely. You have the power to really get things done, and this power can be applied to almost any area you choose.

If you are involved in business, you will be learning some lessons this year about how to be a successful business person. One of these lessons may be how to separate business from friendships so that you can keep a professional approach to all your business dealings. To others, you may appear ruthless or cold at times, but it is essential that you handle all your business affairs in a professional and businesslike manner to avoid potential problems.

King of Spades

Great success in work through taking on responsibility, fulfillment of goals

The Basic Meaning of the King of Spades

The King of Spades is the final and most powerful card in the deck, representing both mastery of one's environment and one's self. Whenever this card appears, you can bet that you will experience good fortune and results.

It is especially good for legal matters and business but can be applied to any area of life for success. It is truly the card of 'success in all things' but brings the most blessings to those who are ready and willing to take responsibility for their life and work and who can take a leadership position in their work. Remember this is a King we are talking about, and every King has a kingdom.

Be prepared to take a leadership role and to live by your own wisdom when this potent card appears. Success is yours for the taking, but you have to stand up and claim it.

THE KING OF SPADES IN THE MERCURY PERIOD

This period could find you spending time with a man who is powerful, intelligent, and a good influence. He may come in and out of your life quickly, but you will find him to be intellectually stimulating and helpful to you if you want to learn from him. You have a lot of mental power this year and could probably accomplish most anything you desire along educational lines. Focusing your mind on specific goals can bring many rewards.

This is such a powerful card that you are likely to get many of your wishes met during this period. This is especially true if you are in a position to be in charge and take command of some kind of work that you are doing. Leadership can pay off in phenomenal ways at this time. Take advantage of it.

THE KING OF SPADES IN THE VENUS PERIOD

During this period, you can expect much more success in your home and with all of your closest relationships due to the presence of the most powerful card in the deck. The wisdom of the King of Spades will help you make important distinctions in your emotions and affections that will guarantee your happiness and success. This is a period and a year for you to experience much happiness in relationships and with your family. Make a 'love wish list' and see what happens.

This is also a very good card for business success if your work involves the arts, beauty products, or working with people. You will find that you have a certain mastery with people now that can lead to great success.

THE KING OF SPADES IN THE MARS PERIOD

Any involvement with legal matters this year will turn out in your favor as the King of Spades rules over your Mars period. You can expect better relations with men and great success in any projects that you are passionately pursuing. As a matter of fact, this card guarantees success in every area of your life if you are willing to apply the wisdom he is bringing you now. If you are ready to take a leadership role in your work or business, now is the time.

You may also find that there are one or more men of the Spades suit for whom you feel some attraction or anger during this period.

THE KING OF SPADES IN THE JUPITER PERIOD

This is perhaps the best card there is for business success. If you are ready to take responsibility in your business, there is no limit to what you can achieve this period and this year. Trust your wisdom now, and be ready to expand your operations to take advantage of this auspicious influence. This is definitely the time to set goals and priorities. Much of what you define as a goal will happen just as you planned.

Any men of the Spades suit could be a source of financial and other blessings this year, especially those who are older or who are in a leadership role in their work.

NOTE: The immense financial benefits of this card will only manifest to those who have their own business or those who are in a position of leadership or management where there is the possibility of promotion. This card, which is probably the most fortunate card in the entire deck, only bestows its blessings upon those who are ready and willing to take full responsibility for their lives and their financial picture. It would not be wise to expect great financial benefits from this card if you are working for someone else doing menial labor or if you are on a fixed income or unemployed. However, it will still bring some good results in other areas of your life regardless of your situation.

THE KING OF SPADES IN THE SATURN PERIOD

Though Saturn is typically the most difficult time of the year, the presence of the King of Spades in this position this year promises that you will be able to overcome any difficulties that may arise, especially those relating to health or work. This powerful card also casts a favorable influence over your entire year, giving you better chances of success in every area of your life. For sure, your health will be good this year, mostly from taking matters into your own hands.

This is an especially good influence for progress and success in your career. Through hard work and the willingness to take responsibility, you can go far and receive some well-deserved recognition for your efforts.

Be on the lookout for men of the Spades suit, especially those who are older or who may be in positions of authority or responsibility. These are likely to prove troublesome or burdensome in some way during this period.

THE KING OF SPADES IN THE URANUS PERIOD

This powerful card guarantees success and accomplishment during this period. It is so powerful that you could simply decide what you want to accomplish, and it will be so. You will have to work for it, and you must be willing to look at yourself objectively and take whatever actions are necessary to accomplish your goals. However, success is assured. The Uranus influence brings especially good results in work, real estate, and group-related activities. Also, you may find success in computer or high-tech-related areas.

Men, especially older men, of the Spades suit will seem to be unpredictable during this period, and to a lesser extent for the entire year. You would do best not to place too many expectations on them while they are this sort of influence in your life.

THE KING OF SPADES IN THE NEPTUNE PERIOD

During this spiritual and dream-like period of the year, you now have the King of Spades, the most powerful card in the deck. With its presence now, you can accomplish most any task or goal that you set for yourself. These goals might have something to do with foreign interests, overseas travel, a vacation, spiritual development, or overcoming a drug or alcohol addiction. In any case, success is assured, as you are given the gift of wisdom and truth from the wisest card of all.

Any men of the Spades suit that you meet during this period, and to a lesser extent this entire year, are likely to be a little hard for you to see objectively. You could easily project your fantasies on them, romantic or otherwise. Therefore, it is best not to make any important decisions related to them until after your next birthday.

THE KING OF SPADES IS YOUR PLUTO CARD

The King of Spades suggests that one of your important goals this year is to accomplish a sense of mastery in your life, perhaps even a leadership position in your chosen line of work. The King of Spades is the last card in the deck, the most powerful and the most successful. He has the experience to do whatever he chooses well, and he is always successful. This is something you desire for yourself and are working on this year.

If you desire to have the success of the King of Spades, there are some things to consider about him that will help you. First of all, he is masterful at everything he does. He cares more for how well the job gets done than how much he is getting paid or what the final results of his work will be.

The King of Spades is a leader but does not brag about himself or abuse his leadership. He is both master of his work and master of himself. Should you wish to have more of his success, it would be wise to emulate some of his qualities this year. This will probably be a challenge for you, since the Pluto card usually represents qualities, people, or things that we don't have as we begin the year and ones that we have to make some important changes within ourselves to acquire.

Your Result Card, will tell you more about the mastery or leadership you seek or point to who is involved in this mastery in an important way.

AFFIRMATION:

I develop true power and authority in my life by being willing to master all that I do and take full responsibility for my own successes and failures.

THE KING OF SPADES IS YOUR RESULT CARD

As your Result Card, the King of Spades promises that you will attain the mastery you seek, not only in reference to your Pluto Card but in practically any area of your life you choose. The King of Spades is the most powerful card in the deck and represents taking a leadership position in whatever line of work you are involved. You may have to work hard to achieve this mastery and success, but it will be well worth the effort. Make a wish list, and be prepared to have all you desire.

This card is also a powerful indicator that you could end up with some man of the Spades suit by your next birthday. Whether this be a friend, lover, or family member, there is a strong indicator that the two of you will be joined in some meaningful way by year's end.

AFFIRMATION:

I attain a measurable amount of mastery this year that I can apply in any area of my life that I choose. I move into the role of leader and master of my destiny.

THE KING OF SPADES IS YOUR LONG-RANGE CARD

This is likely to be a hallmark year for you, one in which you can accomplish most anything you set your mind to. It is highly recommended that you set high goals for yourself this year to take advantage of this once, or at most twice, in a lifetime influence.

The King of Spades is considered the most powerful card in the deck as far as material mastery and accomplishment is concerned. All legal and work matters should go your way, and you can proceed with confidence in any direction you choose. To get the most from this influence, find an area where you can take responsibility, and assume the role of leader in some way. The sky is the limit. You can master new or existing situations, given the highest gift of mastery possible. Use it wisely.

It should be mentioned here that the power and success indicated by this card will only manifest itself to those who are ready and willing to also assume the responsibility that is implied here. For example, this could mean that you would have to be a leader of some sort or have your own business to get the most out of this powerful card.

KEYWORDS:

I am the master of my destiny and fate. Through application of knowledge and experience, I achieve anything this year.

THE KING OF SPADES IS YOUR ENVIRONMENT CARD

Because the King of Spades is one of the Fixed Cards, it will never appear as anyone's Environment or Displacement Card in their Yearly Spreads.

In a Weekly Reading, the King of Spades brings success in business and in all areas where one exerts authority and is willing to take responsibility. It is the most powerful card in the deck in a material sense.

THE KING OF SPADES IS YOUR DISPLACEMENT CARD

Because the King of Spades is one of the Fixed Cards, it will never appear as anyone's Environment or Displacement Card in their Yearly Spreads.

The Card Interpretation Keywords Table

	HEARTS	CLUBS	DIAMONDS	SPADES
ACE Desire, beginnings	New love, birth of child, desire for love, love affair	New idea, birth of new mental project, desire for knowledge	New financial project, desire for money, new money idea	Transformation, secrets, death and rebirth, desire for work
TWO Pairs of people, doing things	Love affair, union of lovers or friends	Discussing ideas, studying, or arguing	Business deals and meetings, financial arrangements	Working together, cooperating
THREE Indecision, creativity	Indecision or worry about love, a love triangle	Mental creativity or worry, the writer's card	Worry about money or making it from two sources, creativity	Physical stress, working two jobs at once
FOUR Stability, good supply	Marriage, satisfaction in love and family relationships	Mental peace and stability, strength of mind, stubbornness	Satisfaction in finances, ample finances, good values	Good health, recovery from health or work problems
FIVE Changes, travel, moves	Divorce, change of heart or feelings, a journey away from or to loved ones	Change of plans or change of mind, travel, move, restlessness	Business trip, change of values, money changing hands	Long distance travel or physical move, change of work or health
SIX Peace, karma	Love compromises, no change in relationships or karmic relationships	Intuition, psychic ability, compromises in communications, word karma	Repayment of financial obligations, no change in finances	Death or ill health (Saturn), karmic payback, unemployment
SEVEN Spiritual victory or challenge	Spiritual love, letting go of personal attachments	Spiritual knowledge, letting go of negative thinking patterns and beliefs	Abundance consciousness or letting go of money fears and worry	Work or health challenges, spiritual work, spiritual experiences
EIGHT Power, success	Social popularity, love power & charm, power with groups of people	Mental power to accomplish any task, success in mental fields	Money to spend, financial power, a sign of financial success	Good health, overcoming obstacles, success in work and health
NINE Endings, completions	Divorce, endings and completions in relationships, universal love	Ending, completions of plans, mental disappointment, universal knowledge	Money going out, financial loss or disappointment, money invested	Death (Saturn) or health problems, loss of job
TEN Success, a large amount	Success with the public or in the arts, many social commitments, party	The teacher, success in mental fields, too much on the mind	A large sum of money, not necessarily yours	Success through hard work, accomplishment
JACK Mastery of creativity	The Christ Card, sacrifices for a higher cause, emotional immaturity, stubborn	Mental creativity, success through creativity, stubborn and immature	The salesman, success in financial creativity, can be dishonest	The Spiritual Initiate or the rip-off card, a new philosophy of life
QUEEN Mastery and service	The mother card, childbirth for women, sexual or sensual indulgence, laziness	Mother Mary card, mental and intuitive success and mastery	Financial and business mastery, a spending spree or shopping trip	Self-mastery, hard working in a service capacity
KING Mastery and authority	The loving father card, emotional mastery, mastery with people	Mental mastery and authority and success	Mastery of business and finances	Mastery in any and all areas desired, authority and success in all areas

The Yearly Spreads

Ace of Hearts

AGE	MER	VEN	MAR	JUP	SAT	URA	NEP	LR	PLU/RES	ENV	DISP
0	A♦ J♠	Q♦ 9♠	5♥ 3♦	3♣ 6♠	3♠ K♣	9♥ 7♣	7♠	A♦	5♦/Q♠	A♥	A♥
1	9♦ 8♣	5♣ A♣	K♦ 2♦	J♦ 9♣	7♦ J♣	J♠ 3♣	3♣	Q♦	8♦/10♥	3♥	A♦
2	4♠ 3♠	8♣ 6♥	J♦ K♠	10♠ A♦	4♦ 9♠	8♦ 9♥	2♦	5♥	Q♣/3♦	Q♣	2♦
3	8♠ 6♠	3♠ 7♦	10♠ A♦	10♣ 3♥	K♠ J♦	Q♠ 3♦	2♥ K♠	3♠	8♦/6♦	10♦	6♣
4	Q♠ Q♣	10♦ J♣	K♦ Q♦	3♦ K♠	7♥ 3♥	5♠ 2♠	9♥	3♠	4♥/8♥	Q♠	8♦
5	5♥ 10♠	3♠ 8♦	3♦ Q♥	A♦ 6♣	9♠ K♦	Q♣ 2♦	2♦	9♥	J♣/9♠	8♦	K♣
6	6♠ 7♥	10♦ 2♣	A♦ 6♥	10♥ K♦	6♦ 3♦	10♠ 10♣	K♠ 6♦	7♠	J♠/A♣	7♣	2♠
7	5♠ Q♣	3♠ 9♣	Q♥ J♠	K♠ 6♦	10♣ A♦	2♦ 8♦	4♠	9♦	10♥/3♣	J♠	6♣
8	2♥ 7♥	A♦ 3♦	6♠ 10♦	8♥ 6♦	7♠ 10♣	7♣ 3♠	3♠	5♣	8♣/5♠	10♣	9♠
9	2♠ 6♣	7♥ 4♥	8♥ 5♠	J♠ 9♣	J♦ 2♣	8♣ 4♣	4♣	K♦	10♥/9♦	4♠	K♥
10	8♦ 9♥	Q♦ 7♣	4♦ 10♣	K♦ 4♣	Q♠ 8♥	6♣ K♠	J♠	J♦	10♦/5♣	4♥	2♣
11	A♦ 4♣	9♥ 9♦	K♦ 2♠	J♦ 4♥	6♥ 8♣	10♦ A♣	A♠	7♦	Q♣/8♠	10♠	A♣
12	7♦ 9♣	7♠ 5♣	J♥ J♦	3♦ 6♠	Q♠ Q♦	2♥ 10♦	10♦	J♠	6♣/K♥	Q♥	7♥
13	4♥ A♦	7♣ 5♦	3♦ J♣	5♥ K♥	10♥ J♥	K♠ 6♥	6♦ 10♥	3♣	2♥/3♠	9♣	8♥
14	Q♠ 3♣	4♠ J♣	K♦ 9♠	6♥ J♥	A♠ 3♦	10♣ 5♠	3♥	4♠	10♠/J♠	6♦	7♠
15	2♠ 9♥	6♠ 2♥	9♣ 2♣	5♠ 8♥	8♠ K♥	3♣ 6♥	6♥	8♣	7♥/10♣	3♠	K♦
16	7♠ A♠	9♥ K♣	5♣ 2♣	A♠ 10♠	4♦ 6♥	7♥ 4♥	2♣	J♦	Q♣/7♣	J♦	3♠
17	5♥ J♦	A♠ 8♣	A♦ A♠	10♦ 7♠	J♠ 3♠	Q♥ 7♥	7♥	10♠	9♦/9♠	J♣	5♦
18	Q♠ Q♣	10♣ K♥	9♣ 6♠	A♠ 9♠	5♦ 4♦	6♠ Q♦	Q♥	4♦	8♦/3♠	10♥	9♦
19	K♣ 7♥	10♦ 4♥	A♠ J♠	7♦ 4♦	3♦ 3♠	Q♣ 4♣	4♣	8♦	K♥/3♥	5♠	Q♦
20	4♠ 9♣	10♣ 3♠	7♣ Q♦	2♠ 4♦	J♥ 9♦	7♥ Q♥	Q♥	2♦	2♥/10♠	4♦	3♦
21	A♦ K♣	5♠ 4♠	5♦ 3♣	8♣ 3♠	2♦ 10♦	K♦ 8♦	8♠	8♠	6♥/J♣	5♥	6♥
22	4♦ J♥	3♣ 7♦	8♣ 9♦	K♥ 4♠	7♠ 10♣	K♣ 9♠	3♦	3♠	10♥/5♣	5♣	4♣
23	10♦ K♠	Q♥ 4♦	10♠ 9♣	9♥ 7♦	6♣ 5♠	J♥ 5♥	K♥	10♠	3♠/A♣	4♣	5♣
24	10♣ 7♥	2♠ 4♠	9♥ 7♦	K♦ A♣	J♠ A♦	5♦ 8♠	8♠	10♠	7♣/4♦	6♥	5♥

AGE	MER	VEN	MAR	JUP	SAT	URA	NEP	LR	PLU/RES	ENV	DISP
25	5♠ 6♣	Q♥ 3♥	5♣ A♠	10♥ 4♥	9♠ 9♥	7♥ 2♥	K♦	K♠	K♠/Q♠	3♦	4♦
26	J♥ 5♦	2♠ A♠	10♥ 4♦	2♥ 10♣	J♣ 4♥	10♠ A♦	8♦	Q♠	Q♠/6♥	Q♦	5♠
27	K♦ 7♠	4♣ 3♥	9♦ 3♣	Q♦ 2♣	10♣ 5♥	10♦ 4♠	10♠	2♥	6♣/7♦	9♦	10♥
28	4♥ Q♠	6♦ 9♠	10♥ 9♦	4♣ 7♦	A♦ A♠	6♠ 10♦	10♦	Q♠	5♣/3♦	5♦	J♠
29	2♠ Q♥	Q♠ 5♦	4♣ 8♣	J♦ A♣	Q♦ 10♥	5♣ 8♠	8♠	10♦	9♠/A♦	3♣	J♦
30	9♥ 7♥	K♥ 10♣	9♠ J♥	A♠ 8♠	Q♣ 2♣	Q♥ J♣	J♦	K♦	4♦/3♦	K♦	3♠
31	K♣ 5♣	Q♠ 5♠	A♠ 8♥	9♦ 8♠	7♠ 2♣	K♦ Q♥	Q♥	3♦	J♠/3♠	7♠	6♦
32	6♥ 4♠	2♥ K♠	4♣ 3♣	J♣ 5♠	10♠ 9♥	4♥ 5♦	K♦	7♥	2♠/8♣	8♥	9♣
33	8♠ Q♠	6♠ J♦	K♣ 8♥	A♠ 8♣	2♥ A♣	2♣ 5♣	A♦	5♠	4♥/9♣	7♥	Q♥
34	10♠ 2♠	6♦ 5♥	4♣ 4♦	5♠ Q♠	7♦ 9♠	10♣ Q♥	J♥	9♦	Q♣/Q♦	A♠	10♠
35	4♥ 2♠	3♣ J♠	5♣ Q♠	8♥ Q♦	5♦ 4♣	Q♣ K♥	2♦	5♥	K♣/K♠	2♣	4♥
36	4♠ 5♥	2♠ 7♦	8♥ A♣	K♥ 10♠	2♣ 10♣	J♣ Q♥	Q♥	3♠	4♦/7♠	K♥	4♠
37	6♣ 7♠	K♠ 5♠	6♠ 5♥	2♥ 4♥	2♠ J♦	10♦ 10♠	6♦ 2♠	3♦	J♣/Q♦	9♠	10♣
38	8♣ K♦	J♠ 10♥	Q♠ 7♠	10♠ 7♥	8♠ A♦	A♠ 6♠	6♠	A♦	9♠/5♠	6♠	J♠
39	5♣ 2♠	2♦ 3♥	10♠ 7♠	5♥ 5♠	3♦ 8♥	3♠ A♠	A♠	9♠	4♥/Q♠	2♠	7♠
40	K♠ 9♦	8♠ Q♦	A♣ 4♥	6♠ 2♦	7♠ 10♥	J♣ J♥	4♦ 7♣	Q♣	3♣/5♦	K♣	8♦
41	9♣ 5♣	4♠ 4♥	9♦ 8♥	7♠ 3♣	K♥ 6♣	Q♥ 7♠	7♠	2♦	J♦/2♣	8♠	Q♠
42	6♠ 4♦	6♣ J♥	8♠ 10♣	4♣ Q♣	10♥ 3♣	Q♦ 5♦	Q♥	6♠	9♥/10♦	6♠	10♦
43	4♠ 7♣	4♣ 9♠	4♣ 3♦	8♥ 9♣	7♠ J♦	9♥ 5♣	J♣	10♦	J♥/10♠	2♦	Q♣
44	A♣ 4♠	3♦ 10♦	4♥ 3♦	5♦ 9♣	6♥ 2♣	7♥ 8♥	8♥	A♦	7♦/10♥	A♦	3♥
45	A♦ J♠	Q♦ 9♠	5♥ 3♦	3♣ 6♠	3♠ K♣	7♦ 7♣	7♠	10♥	5♦/Q♠	A♥	A♥
46	9♣ 8♣	5♣ 2♥	K♦ 2♣	J♦ 9♠	9♥ J♣	J♠ 3♣	3♣	6♦	8♦/10♥	3♥	A♦
47	4♠ 3♠	8♣ 6♥	J♦ K♠	10♠ A♦	4♦ 9♠	8♦ 7♦	2♦	10♠	Q♣/3♦	Q♣	2♦
48	8♠ 6♠	3♠ 9♠	10♠ A♦	10♣ 3♥	K♠ J♦	Q♠ 3♦	A♠ K♠	K♠	8♦/6♦	10♦	6♣
49	Q♠ Q♣	10♦ J♣	K♦ Q♦	3♦ K♠	7♥ 3♥	5♠ 2♠	7♦	Q♠	4♥/8♥	Q♠	8♦

AGE	MER	VEN	MAR	JUP	SAT	URA	NEP	LR	PLU/RES	ENV	DISP
50	5♥	3♠	3♦	A♦	9♠	Q♣	2♦	3♠	J♣/9♣	8♦	K♣
	10♠	8♦	Q♥	6♣	K♦	2♦					
51	6♠	10♦	A♦	10♥	6♦	10♠	K♠	Q♥	J♠/2♥	7♣	2♠
	7♥	2♣	6♥	K♦	3♦	10♣	6♦				
52	5♠	3♠	Q♥	K♠	10♣	A♣	4♠	K♠	10♥/3♣	J♠	6♠
	Q♣	9♠	J♠	6♦	A♦	8♥					
53	A♣	A♦	6♠	8♥	7♠	7♣	3♠	10♣	8♣/5♣	10♠	9♠
	7♥	3♥	10♦	6♦	10♣	3♠					
54	2♠	7♥	8♥	J♠	J♦	8♣	4♣	2♥	10♥/9♦	4♠	K♥
	6♣	4♥	5♠	9♣	2♣	4♣					
55	8♠	Q♦	4♦	K♦	Q♠	6♣	J♠	4♠	10♦/5♣	4♥	2♣
	7♦	7♣	10♣	4♣	8♥	K♠					
56	A♦	7♥	K♦	J♥	6♥	10♦	2♥	2♥	Q♣/8♠	10♠	A♠
	4♣	9♦	2♠	4♥	8♣	2♥					
57	9♥	7♠	J♥	3♦	Q♠	A♣	10♦	A♦	6♣/K♥	Q♥	7♥
	9♣	5♠	J♦	6♠	Q♦	10♦					
58	4♥	7♠	3♦	5♥	10♥	K♠	6♦	6♠	A♣/3♠	9♣	8♥
	A♦	5♠	J♦	K♥	J♥	6♥	10♥				
59	Q♠	4♠	K♦	6♥	A♠	10♣	3♥	8♥	10♠/J♠	6♦	7♠
	3♣	J♠	9♠	J♥	3♦	5♠					
60	2♠	6♠	9♣	5♣	8♠	3♣	6♥	7♠	7♥/10♥	3♠	K♦
	7♦	A♣	2♣	8♥	K♥	6♥					
61	7♠	7♠	5♣	A♦	4♦	7♥	2♦	7♠	Q♣/7♣	J♦	3♣
	A♠	K♣	2♣	10♥	6♥	4♥					
62	5♥	A♠	A♦	10♦	J♠	Q♥	7♥	3♠	9♦/9♠	J♣	5♦
	J♦	8♠	2♥	7♣	3♣	7♥					
63	Q♠	10♣	9♠	A♠	5♦	6♠	Q♥	2♠	8♦/3♠	10♥	9♦
	Q♣	K♥	6♠	9♠	4♦	Q♦					
64	K♣	10♦	A♠	9♥	3♦	Q♣	4♣	7♥	K♥/3♥	5♠	Q♦
	7♥	4♥	J♠	4♦	3♣	4♣					
65	4♠	10♣	9♥	2♠	J♥	7♥	Q♥	8♥	A♣/10♠	4♦	3♦
	9♣	3♠	Q♦	4♦	9♦	Q♥					
66	A♦	5♠	5♦	8♣	2♣	K♦	2♠	J♠	6♥/J♣	5♥	6♥
	K♣	4♠	3♣	3♠	10♦	8♦					
67	4♦	3♣	8♠	K♥	7♠	K♣	3♦	J♦	10♥/5♣	5♠	4♣
	J♥	7♥	9♠	4♠	10♣	9♠					
68	10♦	Q♥	10♠	7♦	6♣	J♥	K♥	8♣	3♠/2♥	4♣	5♣
	K♠	4♦	9♣	9♥	5♠	5♥					
69	10♣	2♠	7♦	K♦	J♠	5♦	8♠	4♣	7♣/4♥	6♥	5♥
	7♥	4♠	9♥	2♥	A♦	8♠					
70	5♠	Q♥	5♠	10♥	9♠	7♥	K♦	8♦	K♠/Q♦	3♦	4♦
	6♣	3♥	A♠	4♥	7♦	A♣					
71	J♥	2♠	10♥	A♣	J♣	10♠	8♦	Q♦	Q♠/6♦	Q♦	5♠
	5♦	A♠	4♦	10♣	4♥	A♦					
72	K♦	4♠	9♦	Q♦	10♣	10♦	10♠	4♦	6♣/9♥	9♦	10♥
	7♥	3♥	3♣	2♣	5♥	4♠					
73	4♥	6♦	10♥	4♣	A♦	6♠	10♦	K♦	5♣/3♠	5♦	J♣
	Q♠	9♠	9♠	9♥	2♥	10♦					
74	2♠	Q♠	4♦	J♦	Q♦	5♣	8♠	Q♠	9♠/A♠	3♦	J♦
	Q♥	5♦	8♣	2♥	10♥	8♠					
75	7♦	K♥	9♠	A♠	Q♣	Q♥	J♦	6♠	4♦/3♦	K♦	3♠
	7♥	10♣	J♥	8♠	2♣	J♣					
76	K♣	Q♠	A♠	9♦	7♠	K♦	Q♥	J♠	J♠/3♠	7♠	6♦
	5♣	5♠	8♥	8♠	2♣	Q♥					
77	6♥	A♣	4♠	J♣	10♠	4♥	K♦	A♦	2♠/8♣	8♥	9♣
	4♠	K♠	3♠	5♣	7♦	5♦					
78	8♠	6♠	K♠	A♠	A♣	2♣	A♦	9♥	4♥/9♣	7♥	Q♥
	Q♠	J♦	8♥	8♠	2♥	5♣					
79	10♠	6♦	4♣	5♠	9♥	10♣	J♥	K♦	Q♣/Q♦	A♠	10♠
	2♠	5♥	4♦	Q♠	9♠	Q♥					
80	4♥	3♣	5♣	8♥	5♦	Q♣	2♦	J♥	K♣/K♠	2♣	4♥
	2♠	J♦	Q♠	Q♦	4♣	K♥					
81	4♠	2♠	8♥	K♥	2♣	J♣	Q♥	6♥	4♦/7♣	K♥	4♠
	5♥	9♥	2♥	10♠	10♣	Q♥					
82	6♣	K♠	6♠	A♣	2♠	10♦	6♦	10♦	J♣/Q♦	9♠	10♣
	7♠	5♠	5♥	4♦	J♦	10♠	2♠				
83	8♣	J♠	Q♣	10♠	8♠	A♠	6♠	A♣	9♠/5♣	6♠	J♠
	K♦	10♥	7♠	7♥	A♦	6♠					
84	5♣	2♦	10♠	5♥	3♦	3♣	A♠	7♦	4♥/Q♠	2♠	7♣
	2♠	3♥	7♠	5♠	8♥	A♠					
85	K♠	8♠	2♥	6♣	7♣	J♣	4♦	7♠	3♣/5♦	K♣	8♦
	9♦	Q♦	4♥	2♦	10♥	J♥	7♣				
86	9♣	4♦	9♥	7♠	K♥	Q♥	7♣	J♥	J♦/2♣	8♠	Q♠
	5♣	4♥	8♥	3♣	6♣	7♣					
87	6♠	6♣	8♠	4♣	10♥	Q♦	Q♥	3♦	7♦/10♦	6♠	10♦
	4♦	J♥	10♣	Q♣	3♣	5♦					
88	4♠	4♦	4♣	8♥	7♠	7♦	J♣	Q♠	J♥/10♠	2♦	Q♣
	7♣	9♠	3♦	9♦	J♦	5♣					
89	2♥	3♥	4♥	5♥	6♥	7♥	8♥	2♥	9♥/10♥	A♦	3♥
	4♠	10♦	3♦	9♣	2♣	8♥					
90	A♦	Q♦	5♥	3♣	3♠	9♥	7♣	10♦	5♦/Q♠	A♥	A♥
	J♠	9♠	3♦	6♠	K♣	7♠					
91	9♦	5♠	K♦	J♦	7♦	J♠	3♣	4♥	8♦/10♥	3♥	A♦
	8♣	A♣	2♠	9♣	J♣	3♣					
92	4♠	8♣	J♦	10♠	4♦	8♦	2♦	7♠	Q♣/3♥	Q♣	2♦
	3♠	6♥	K♠	A♦	9♠	9♥					
93	8♠	3♠	10♠	10♣	K♠	Q♠	2♥	3♦	8♦/6♦	10♦	6♣
	6♠	7♦	A♦	3♥	J♦	3♦	K♠				
94	Q♠	10♦	K♦	3♦	7♥	5♠	9♥	5♥	4♥/8♥	Q♠	8♣
	Q♣	J♠	Q♦	K♣	3♥	2♠					
95	5♥	3♠	3♦	A♦	9♠	Q♣	2♦	10♥	J♣/9♣	8♦	K♣
	10♠	8♦	Q♥	6♠	K♦	2♦					
96	6♠	10♦	A♦	10♥	6♦	10♠	K♠	K♠	J♠/A♣	7♠	2♠
	7♥	2♣	6♥	K♦	3♦	10♣	6♦				
97	5♠	3♠	Q♥	K♠	10♣	2♥	4♠	6♦	10♥/3♣	J♠	6♠
	Q♣	9♠	J♠	6♦	A♦	8♥					
98	2♥	A♦	6♠	8♥	7♠	7♣	3♠	Q♠	8♣/5♣	10♠	9♠
	7♥	3♥	10♦	6♦	10♣	3♠					
99	2♠	7♥	8♥	J♠	J♦	8♣	4♣	4♠	10♥/9♦	4♠	K♥
	6♣	4♥	5♠	9♣	2♣	4♣					

Two of Hearts

AGE	MER	VEN	MAR	JUP	SAT	URA	NEP	LR	PLU/RES ENV DISP
0	K♥	K♦	6♥	4♣	2♥	J♠	8♣	K♥	6♦/4♠
	A♠	Q♥	J♦	5♦	A♦	8♣			
1	10♦	Q♥	4♣	Q♦	2♣	A♠	9♥	K♦	4♦/J♥
	5♥	10♥	5♣	4♦	7♠	9♥			
2	6♠	8♥	Q♥	3♦	A♥	4♠	8♣	6♥	J♦/10♠
	K♥	6♦	10♥	K♦	3♥	8♣			
3	8♦	6♦	3♦	5♦	9♠	K♥	9♥	4♣	5♠/J♥
	4♣	4♦	6♥	Q♥	7♥	9♥			
4	K♣	A♠	5♦	9♥	Q♣	10♠	8♣	2♦	10♥/9♣
	6♠	J♦	4♦	8♥	10♦	8♣			
5	J♠	J♦	9♦	K♦	2♠	6♠	9♥	J♠	6♥/J♥
	3♦	5♣	Q♦	6♦	2♠	9♥			
6	6♠	K♥	K♦	3♣	Q♠	9♣	8♣	8♣	4♦/3♠
	K♣	10♥	5♠	A♠	8♦	8♣			
7	4♠	10♥	3♠	8♥	8♠	K♣	9♥	10♦	Q♦/J♥
	9♦	6♥	5♦	J♦	9♠	8♣			
8	A♦	6♠	8♥	7♠	7♠	3♠	8♣	Q♥	5♠/J♣
	6♣	4♦	6♥	K♥	J♠	8♣			
9	10♠	4♦	7♠	A♠	2♦	6♣	9♥	4♣	5♦/J♥
	3♣	Q♦	K♦	10♥	2♠	9♥			
10	3♥	K♣	A♠	7♥	10♣	J♣	8♣	Q♦	6♥/5♠
	A♦	5♣	Q♦	6♠	4♠	8♣			
11	9♣	5♣	7♥	K♥	A♥	A♦	9♥	2♣	K♦/J♥
	7♠	5♦	8♥	4♦	8♠	8♣			
12	10♦	6♣	K♥	2♣	4♥	5♠	8♣	A♠	Q♦/5♥
	3♥	6♥	5♦	K♣	10♠	8♣			
13	3♠	6♥	2♣	6♠	Q♣	3♥	9♥	9♥	8♦/J♥
	7♥	K♦	A♠	5♠	2♦	9♥			
14	8♦	A♦	6♠	9♠	Q♥	5♥	8♣	6♠	5♦/4♣
	10♦	Q♦	K♦	6♠	9♣	8♣			
15	J♣	Q♦	9♠	K♦	Q♠	10♦	9♥	8♥	A♠/J♥
	2♣	8♥	K♥	6♥	A♥	9♥			
16	J♠	3♥	K♣	2♠	6♦	4♣	8♣	Q♦	K♦/3♦
	8♦	5♦	8♥	A♦	3♠	8♣			
17	5♠	5♦	2♠	6♣	7♣	8♦	9♥	3♦	K♦/J♥
	9♠	A♠	6♠	Q♦	Q♣	9♥			
18	4♠	10♦	6♣	8♠	J♦	3♦	8♣	A♥	8♥/9♦
	J♠	K♦	A♠	3♥	J♣	8♣			
19	5♥	K♦	8♠	A♦	10♣	J♠	9♥	4♣	6♠/J♥
	2♠	K♥	K♣	5♦	Q♠	9♥			
20	10♠	8♣	A♦	2♦	10♥	9♦	8♣	8♣	A♠/3♣
	4♠	8♥	K♥	10♦	5♠	8♣			
21	4♣	8♥	2♦	3♥	4♥	4♠	9♥	8♦	K♣/J♥
	8♠	6♠	6♣	K♦	7♠	9♥			
22	9♥	J♠	3♥	A♥	4♦	3♠	8♣	6♦	K♥/7♠
	10♠	A♠	6♠	8♦	5♥	8♣			
23	3♦	A♠	A♥	10♦	Q♥	10♠	9♥	3♦	6♦/J♥
	2♦	K♣	A♦	8♥	10♣	9♥			
24	3♠	4♠	10♦	Q♣	5♦	7♠	8♣	5♦	6♠/7♥
	9♣	K♥	K♣	J♠	4♠	8♣			
25	9♦	K♦	Q♣	8♦	6♦	9♣	9♥	9♠	A♦/J♥
	A♥	6♣	3♥	A♠	4♥	9♥			
26	J♣	10♠	8♦	Q♠	6♥	7♥	8♣	K♦	K♣/2♣
	3♠	6♠	6♣	4♠	3♦	8♣			
27	3♣	6♠	Q♠	J♠	J♦	3♠	9♥	9♥	3♥/J♥
	Q♣	A♦	10♦	K♥	Q♥	9♥			
28	5♠	9♠	J♠	7♦	Q♦	2♠	8♣	K♣	6♣/9♠
	J♣	K♠	A♦	10♠	9♦	8♣			
29	7♠	K♣	7♣	4♠	10♥	J♣	9♥	A♠	10♦/J♥
	Q♠	3♥	8♦	6♠	6♦	9♥			
30	5♥	3♠	4♠	10♣	5♦	9♠	8♣	5♦	A♦/2♠
	5♠	6♠	3♥	9♣	3♦	8♣			
31	7♥	6♣	10♣	10♠	4♦	5♠	9♥	9♦	8♦/J♥
	7♠	10♦	J♠	K♣	J♦	9♥			
32	4♣	J♠	10♠	4♥	K♦	2♠	8♣	Q♣	3♥/8♣
	5♥	A♦	10♦	3♠	7♠	8♣			
33	2♣	A♦	4♥	9♣	5♠	5♥	9♥	10♠	J♠/J♥
	10♣	8♦	4♠	6♠	10♥	9♥			
34	3♦	5♠	9♣	Q♥	8♥	8♠	8♣	8♣	10♦/2♦
	4♣	3♥	8♦	J♣	7♥	8♣			
35	9♠	3♥	Q♥	3♠	6♥	4♣	9♥	J♠	4♠/J♥
	4♥	J♠	10♠	A♦	4♦	9♥			
36	9♦	5♥	3♠	6♦	A♠	2♦	8♣	J♦	8♦/A♦
	3♦	10♦	J♠	5♠	2♣	8♣			
37	2♠	10♦	6♦	J♣	Q♦	3♦	9♥	9♥	10♠/J♥
	Q♥	4♠	9♣	3♥	5♣	9♥			
38	3♠	4♣	J♣	J♦	K♥	A♥	8♣	K♦	J♠/Q♣
	9♦	8♦	4♠	5♥	9♠	8♣			
39	8♠	8♦	J♦	5♠	5♥	9♠	9♥	2♠	9♣/J♥
	6♦	10♠	3♠	10♦	6♥	9♥			
40	7♠	3♦	5♠	10♦	6♠	Q♣	8♣	6♠	4♠/Q♣
	3♣	J♠	10♠	4♠	2♠	8♣			
41	2♦	J♠	10♥	5♥	K♦	3♣	9♥	9♥	3♠/J♥
	J♦	9♣	J♣	8♦	Q♦	9♥			
42	7♥	9♦	5♥	4♦	K♣	Q♠	8♣	6♠	10♠/7♣
	7♠	4♠	9♣	3♦	8♠	8♣			
43	A♥	4♠	4♦	4♠	8♥	7♠	9♥	K♥	J♣/J♥
	10♦	3♠	5♠	J♠	5♦	9♥			
44	2♣	3♠	4♠	5♠	6♠	7♠	8♣	K♦	9♣/10♣
	7♥	10♠	3♠	9♦	2♦	8♣			
45	Q♣	10♠	5♣	3♦	A♠	7♥	9♥	3♣	5♠/J♥
	4♦	J♣	5♥	4♠	K♦	9♥			
46	9♠	7♠	3♦	6♥	A♦	10♣	8♣	Q♠	3♠/4♥
	2♠	9♣	J♦	3♣	A♥	8♣			
47	Q♥	9♣	6♥	9♦	K♥	2♣	9♥	9♣	5♥/J♥
	5♣	5♠	4♣	10♠	8♥	9♥			
48	2♠	7♥	9♦	Q♦	3♥	4♥	8♣	8♣	J♣/Q♥
	9♠	3♠	5♠	7♠	Q♣	8♣			
49	7♠	3♠	Q♦	3♣	6♠	9♠	9♥	4♠	4♣/J♥
	6♥	5♥	3♦	9♣	A♠	9♥			

AGE	MER	VEN	MAR	JUP	SAT	URA	NEP	LR	PLU/RES	ENV	DISP
50	8♠	2♣	3♣	5♦	10♦	Q♥	8♣	10♥	5♠/6♥		
	2♠	J♣	5♥	7♥	Q♠	8♣					
51	10♣	J♣	5♦	7♠	K♣	2♠	9♥	3♣	3♦/J♥		
	Q♦	4♣	9♦	3♠	K♥	9♥					
52	2♦	9♠	7♠	K♦	8♦	6♦	8♣	8♥	5♥/J♦		
	8♠	5♠	4♣	2♣	7♠	8♣					
53	4♥	5♠	K♦	7♥	6♣	8♠	9♥	8♠	9♦/J♦		
	5♦	3♦	3♣	J♣	6♠	9♥					
54	A♥	2♠	7♥	8♥	J♠	J♦	8♣	K♣	4♣/10♥		
	2♦	5♥	3♦	9♠	10♣	8♣					
55	Q♥	5♥	8♥	2♣	A♦	2♦	9♥	9♥	3♣/J♥		
	K♦	9♦	7♠	5♠	K♣	9♥					
56	Q♣	8♠	2♣	A♠	4♠	10♥	8♣	A♦	3♦/4♦		
	A♥	4♣	9♦	2♠	4♥	8♣					
57	6♦	4♣	A♠	9♠	3♥	A♥	9♥	6♠	7♠/J♥		
	8♥	3♣	7♥	5♥	6♣	9♥					
58	Q♠	2♦	9♠	K♥	10♠	4♦	8♣	8♥	9♦/5♣		
	Q♣	3♦	3♠	8♠	Q♥	8♣					
59	J♦	3♦	K♥	2♠	10♦	Q♣	9♥	7♠	7♥/J♥		
	A♠	7♠	2♣	4♣	A♦	9♥					
60	7♣	A♥	2♠	6♠	9♣	5♣	8♣	7♣	3♣/6♥		
	Q♠	9♦	7♠	2♦	6♦	8♣					
61	10♥	9♦	6♠	8♠	8♦	Q♠	9♥	3♠	2♣/J♥		
	K♥	7♥	9♠	3♦	3♥	9♥					
62	10♣	Q♣	8♠	K♣	3♠	6♥	8♣	8♣	7♠/Q♦		
	7♣	3♣	7♥	A♥	J♦	8♣					
63	4♦	3♣	K♣	2♦	J♠	7♠	9♥	10♠	9♠/J♥		
	6♠	2♣	2♠	9♠	10♦	9♥					
64	4♥	Q♠	2♦	6♣	J♣	Q♦	8♣	4♦	7♥/5♦		
	10♣	7♠	2♣	Q♣	10♥	8♣					
65	5♣	7♠	6♣	A♥	4♠	10♣	9♥	7♠	2♠/J♥		
	K♣	9♠	8♠	3♣	8♥	9♥					
66	Q♥	7♣	A♥	A♦	5♠	5♦	8♣	A♠	2♣/K♦		
	4♥	7♥	9♠	Q♠	4♦	8♣					
67	6♥	7♥	A♦	Q♣	10♠	4♥	9♥	2♦	8♠/J♥		
	6♣	2♠	2♦	7♠	J♠	9♥					
68	6♦	10♣	Q♣	3♥	5♥	K♦	8♣	6♣	9♠/8♥		
	Q♥	2♣	2♠	7♠	5♣	8♣					
69	Q♦	2♣	3♥	Q♠	9♣	Q♥	9♥	9♥	2♦/J♥		
	A♦	8♠	A♥	7♥	4♠	9♥					
70	J♦	4♥	Q♠	10♦	4♣	8♥	8♣	3♥	2♠/A♠		
	6♦	9♠	8♠	10♣	6♥	8♣					
71	5♥	9♠	10♦	7♣	3♠	6♦	9♥	K♣	A♥/J♥		
	3♥	2♦	Q♣	2♣	10♠	9♥					
72	10♥	Q♥	7♣	8♠	3♦	A♠	8♣	A♠	8♠/K♥		
	J♦	2♠	2♦	4♥	Q♦	8♣					
73	K♦	2♠	8♦	10♣	J♣	J♦	9♥	7♥	Q♣/J♥		
	10♦	A♥	Q♠	9♠	9♣	9♥					
74	4♦	6♦	10♣	J♠	9♦	K♥	8♣	10♠	2♦/6♦		
	10♥	8♠	A♥	Q♥	5♦	8♣					

AGE	MER	VEN	MAR	JUP	SAT	URA	NEP	LR	PLU/RES	ENV	DISP
75	8♥	8♠	J♠	4♥	5♠	10♥	9♥	J♣	Q♠/J♥		
	8♦	Q♣	7♣	2♠	3♠	9♥					
76	5♣	J♦	4♥	4♠	3♠	6♠	8♣	8♣	A♥/K♣		
	4♦	2♦	Q♣	6♦	K♦	8♥					
77	A♠	2♦	4♠	Q♥	5♥	4♦	9♥	9♣	7♣/J♥		
	J♠	Q♠	10♣	8♠	J♠	9♥					
78	6♥	10♥	Q♥	10♠	7♠	K♣	8♣	5♠	Q♣/6♣		
	5♣	A♥	Q♠	J♦	8♥	8♥					
79	K♥	A♥	10♠	6♦	4♠	5♣	9♥	7♥	10♣/J♥		
	4♠	7♣	4♥	2♦	5♠	9♥					
80	Q♦	4♦	6♦	9♣	7♥	6♠	8♣	K♥	Q♠/A♥		
	6♥	Q♣	7♣	10♥	A♠	8♥					
81	6♠	Q♣	9♣	J♦	3♦	6♥	9♥	A♥	4♥/J♥		
	10♠	10♣	Q♥	A♥	5♥	9♥					
82	5♦	5♣	J♦	3♠	2♣	A♦	8♣	A♦	7♣/3♥		
	Q♦	Q♠	10♣	4♦	K♥	8♣					
83	K♣	Q♠	3♠	10♥	9♠	Q♦	9♥	9♥	Q♥/J♥		
	9♣	4♥	6♦	Q♣	4♠	9♥					
84	K♦	6♥	10♥	J♠	9♠	3♥	8♣	10♦	10♣/10♦		
	5♦	7♣	4♥	5♣	6♠	8♥					
85	6♣	7♣	J♣	4♦	3♣	5♦	9♥	6♣	6♦/J♥		
	3♠	Q♥	J♦	Q♠	3♦	9♥					
86	8♥	Q♦	4♥	5♠	2♠	10♦	8♣	K♥	4♥/8♦		
	K♦	10♣	Q♥	6♥	K♣	8♣					
87	A♦	10♣	5♠	5♠	7♠	K♦	9♥	2♣	J♦/J♥		
	J♣	6♦	10♥	7♠	9♥	9♥					
88	A♠	5♦	5♣	5♥	8♠	8♦	8♣	4♥	Q♥/J♠		
	8♥	4♥	6♦	Q♦	6♣	8♣					
89	3♥	4♥	5♥	6♥	7♥	8♥	9♥	5♠	10♥/J♥		
	5♠	J♦	4♥	10♣	3♠	9♥					
90	K♥	K♦	6♥	4♣	2♥	J♠	8♣	8♣	6♦/4♠		
	A♠	Q♥	J♦	5♠	A♦	8♣					
91	10♦	Q♥	4♣	Q♦	2♠	A♠	9♥	3♠	4♦/J♥		
	5♥	10♥	5♣	4♥	7♠	9♥					
92	6♠	8♥	Q♦	3♦	A♥	4♠	8♣	6♥	J♦/10♠		
	K♥	6♦	10♥	K♦	3♥	8♣					
93	8♦	6♦	3♦	5♦	9♠	K♥	9♥	2♣	5♣/J♥		
	4♣	4♦	6♥	Q♥	7♥	9♥					
94	K♣	A♠	5♦	9♦	Q♣	10♠	8♣	6♠	10♥/9♣		
	6♠	J♦	4♦	8♥	10♦	8♣					
95	J♠	J♦	9♦	K♦	2♠	6♠	9♥	Q♣	6♥/J♥		
	3♦	5♣	Q♦	6♦	2♠	9♥					
96	6♣	K♥	K♦	3♣	Q♠	9♠	8♣	3♥	4♦/3♠		
	K♣	10♥	5♣	A♠	8♥	8♣					
97	4♠	10♥	3♣	8♥	8♠	K♣	9♥	9♥	Q♦/J♥		
	9♦	6♥	5♦	J♦	9♠	9♥					
98	A♦	6♠	8♥	7♠	7♠	3♠	8♣	8♦	5♣/J♣		
	6♣	4♦	6♥	K♥	J♠	8♣					
99	10♠	4♦	7♠	A♠	2♦	6♠	9♥	A♦	5♦/J♥		
	3♣	Q♦	K♦	10♥	2♠	9♥					

Three of Hearts

AGE	MER	VEN	MAR	JUP	SAT	URA	NEP	LR	PLU/RES	ENV	DISP
0	A♣	Q♣	10♠	5♣	3♦	A♠	7♥	A♣	7♦/5♠	3♥	3♥
	4♥	Q♠	Q♦	6♦	K♥	7♥					
1	A♥	9♦	5♣	K♦	J♦	7♦	J♠	Q♣	3♣/8♦	Q♣	A♥
	10♣	6♠	Q♦	2♠	8♠	J♠					
2	5♦	4♣	7♠	J♣	9♥	10♣	K♦	10♠	7♣/5♠	10♦	A♦
	8♣	2♥	K♥	6♦	10♥	K♦					
3	4♥	8♣	J♣	Q♥	5♦	7♠	A♦	5♣	10♦/Q♣	Q♠	2♦
	J♦	3♦	K♠	A♥	6♠	7♦					
4	6♣	J♦	Q♥	4♠	K♠	8♦	A♣	3♦	7♣/3♠	8♦	6♣
	2♠	9♥	A♥	Q♣	J♣	Q♦	K♠				
5	8♦	Q♠	7♠	Q♦	A♠	4♦	7♦	A♠	10♠/7♥	7♣	8♠
	10♦	10♥	9♦	K♠	Q♣	K♣					
6	5♣	J♦	Q♦	A♥	6♠	10♦	A♦	7♥	10♥/6♦	J♠	K♣
	Q♥	7♣	9♣	2♦	7♠	A♦					
7	2♠	Q♠	A♥	5♠	3♠	Q♥	K♠	A♥	10♣/2♥	10♣	2♠
	A♠	K♥	3♦	7♠	Q♦	4♠	3♠				
8	4♦	J♦	9♣	K♠	4♠	A♣	4♥	9♦	5♠/K♦	4♠	6♣
	10♦	6♦	10♣	3♠	A♥	7♥					
9	A♣	A♥	2♠	7♥	8♥	J♠	J♦	5♠	8♠/4♠	4♥	9♠
	A♠	Q♣	Q♠	3♠	4♠	J♦					
10	K♣	A♠	7♥	10♣	J♣	8♣	6♥	K♦	5♠/5♦	10♠	K♥
	2♦	10♠	4♦	6♦	K♥	6♥					
11	7♣	9♦	5♥	7♠	8♦	2♦	10♣	J♦	Q♠/4♣	Q♥	♣
	7♦	J♠	4♠	6♥	7♥	K♠					
12	A♥	7♦	7♠	J♥	3♦	Q♠	2♥	7♦	10♦/6♦	9♣	A♠
	6♥	5♦	K♣	10♠	8♣	2♥					
13	9♥	8♥	J♥	Q♦	8♦	A♣	Q♠	J♠	2♦/9♠	6♦	7♥
	6♦	4♣	J♣	2♠	9♦	Q♠					
14	10♠	J♠	Q♦	5♣	5♠	K♠	3♠	5♦	A♣/J♦	3♠	8♥
	A♥	3♣	J♣	9♠	J♥	3♦	5♠				
15	8♦	4♥	7♠	3♦	2♣	4♠	Q♠	4♣	Q♥/10♣	J♦	7♠
	K♦	10♥	6♠	J♥	Q♦	4♠					
16	K♣	2♠	6♦	4♣	8♣	K♦	3♦	7♠	A♠/5♠	♣	K♦
	7♦	A♣	K♥	7♥	9♠	3♦					
17	8♥	7♥	4♠	A♥	5♥	A♠	A♦	J♠	10♦/J♠	10♥	3♣
	2♣	8♠	K♥	5♠	3♦	10♠					
18	5♣	2♣	A♥	Q♠	10♣	9♣	A♠	9♥	5♦/6♠	5♠	5♦
	J♣	8♣	2♥	J♠	K♦	A♠					
19	8♦	4♠	6♦	2♣	3♣	2♠	9♣	10♣	7♣/J♦	4♦	9♦
	10♦	9♠	2♦	6♠	5♥	9♦					
20	8♠	Q♣	2♣	9♥	Q♦	10♦	6♥	K♦	9♠/Q♣	5♥	Q♦
	A♠	10♠	10♣	5♥	K♦	6♥					
21	4♥	4♠	9♥	K♣	J♥	A♠	4♣	4♥	A♣/Q♥	5♠	3♦
	6♦	J♠	9♠	5♥	5♦	9♠					
22	A♥	4♦	3♣	8♣	K♥	7♠	K♣	8♠	3♦/10♥	4♣	6♥
	8♠	6♥	K♦	J♦	Q♠	7♣					
23	5♥	K♦	8♠	9♠	8♥	8♠	Q♦	J♣	5♠/4♠	6♥	4♣
	J♥	A♠	5♦	4♥	4♠	6♠					
24	Q♠	9♠	Q♥	7♦	2♦	J♥	9♠	Q♥	J♦/2♥	3♦	5♠
	K♠	5♥	6♦	9♥	4♦	5♠					

AGE	MER	VEN	MAR	JUP	SAT	URA	NEP	LR	PLU/RES	ENV	DISP
25	4♠	K♣	7♦	7♠	10♣	3♣	6♠	5♥	J♠/10♠	Q♦	5♥
	A♠	4♥	9♥	2♥	A♥	6♣					
26	4♦	9♣	4♣	5♠	6♠	A♣	7♠	7♣	K♠/9♦	9♦	4♣
	2♦	Q♣	2♠	10♠	7♦	A♣					
27	J♥	K♣	5♠	A♣	10♥	Q♥	7♣	A♦	8♦/3♣	5♦	5♠
	3♣	2♠	5♥	4♠	10♠	A♥					
28	7♠	6♥	5♦	9♦	4♠	Q♠	Q♥	6♣	2♦/9♥	3♣	10♥
	J♠	Q♣	K♥	K♥	5♠	4♥					
29	10♠	3♠	5♠	6♥	A♥	2♠	Q♠	J♦	4♣/J♦	K♦	J♠
	8♦	6♥	6♦	9♥	2♥	Q♠					
30	K♣	8♦	6♥	J♣	9♦	4♣	6♠	Q♥	6♠/2♣	7♠	J♦
	9♣	3♣	8♠	2♦	5♠	6♣					
31	7♦	9♠	6♦	2♣	10♦	9♣	J♣	4♠	5♥/Q♦	8♥	3♠
	A♠	4♠	J♥	6♣	K♥	10♥					
32	8♠	8♦	2♣	5♦	8♥	7♠	9♣	K♠	10♣/J♦	7♥	6♦
	4♣	4♦	7♥	6♠	K♥	9♣					
33	3♦	A♣	6♥	10♥	Q♥	10♠	7♠	8♦	K♣/8♦	A♠	9♣
	4♥	K♠	K♦	4♣	7♦	3♣					
34	6♣	2♠	K♠	2♠	A♣	K♥	A♥	A♦	10♠/6♦	2♠	Q♥
	8♦	J♣	7♥	8♠	2♥	4♣					
35	Q♥	3♠	6♥	4♠	9♥	4♠	J♥	8♦	10♦/9♦	K♥	10♠
	K♣	5♠	5♥	8♠	6♠	9♠					
36	10♠	K♦	4♣	7♥	3♣	10♦	A♦	Q♠	8♠/K♣	9♠	4♥
	K♣	J♣	8♦	9♦	6♥	9♠					
37	4♥	K♣	7♥	9♠	K♥	10♥	9♣	7♠	5♥/J♠	6♠	4♠
	5♣	9♥	2♥	Q♥	4♠	9♣					
38	2♦	K♠	2♠	A♣	K♣	Q♠	3♠	Q♦	10♥/9♦	2♠	10♣
	8♥	4♦	5♠	10♠	J♣	Q♥	K♣				
39	8♣	10♣	10♦	Q♥	6♣	2♣	5♠	A♠	6♠/4♦	K♠	J♠
	7♠	5♠	8♥	A♣	A♥	2♠					
40	4♣	A♦	Q♥	5♣	Q♠	K♦	2♣	4♦	10♠/8♦	8♠	7♠
	K♣	Q♣	8♥	4♦	7♥	2♣					
41	K♠	6♣	2♥	2♦	J♠	10♥	5♥	7♣	K♦/3♣	6♣	8♣
	5♦	9♦	10♠	A♦	5♠	J♥	J♠				
42	6♣	6♥	5♦	8♥	9♠	9♠	J♠		J♣/K♥	2♦	Q♠
	4♣	10♠	7♥	K♦	2♦	♠					
43	2♠	2♦	6♣	6♥	5♠	9♠	9♣	J♦	7♦/Q♠	A♦	10♦
	5♥	J♥	4♠	10♦	K♦	3♣					
44	4♥	5♦	6♥	7♥	8♥	7♦	10♥	Q♥	J♥/Q♥	A♥	Q♣
	J♠	6♠	Q♦	5♦	J♣	4♠					
45	2♥	Q♣	10♠	5♣	3♦	A♠	7♥	A♥	9♥/5♠	3♥	3♥
	4♥	Q♠	Q♦	6♦	K♥	7♥					
46	A♥	9♦	5♣	K♦	J♦	9♥	J♠	6♠	3♣/8♦	Q♣	A♥
	10♣	6♠	Q♦	2♠	8♠	J♠					
47	5♦	4♣	7♠	J♣	7♦	10♣	K♦	10♠	7♣/5♠	10♦	A♦
	8♣	A♣	K♥	6♦	10♥	K♦					
48	4♥	8♦	J♣	Q♥	5♥	7♠	A♦	A♦	10♦/Q♣	Q♠	2♦
	J♦	3♦	K♠	A♥	6♠	9♥					
49	6♣	J♦	Q♥	4♠	K♠	8♦	2♥	2♠	7♣/3♠	8♦	6♣
	2♠	7♦	A♥	Q♣	J♣	Q♦	K♠				

AGE	MER	VEN	MAR	JUP	SAT	URA	NEP	LR	PLU/RES	ENV	DISP
50	8♦	Q♠	7♠	Q♦	A♠	4♦	9♥	Q♠	10♠/7♥	7♣	8♠
	10♦	10♥	9♦	K♠	Q♣	K♣					
51	5♣	J♦	Q♦	A♥	6♠	10♦	A♦	A♥	10♥/6♦	J♠	K♣
	Q♥	7♠	9♠	2♦	7♠	A♦					
52	2♠	Q♠	A♥	5♠	3♠	Q♥	K♠	5♠	10♠/A♠	10♣	2♠
	A♠	K♥	3♦	7♠	Q♦	4♠	3♠				
53	4♦	J♦	9♣	K♠	4♠	2♥	4♥	3♠	5♠/K♦	4♠	6♠
	10♦	6♦	10♣	3♠	A♥	7♥					
54	2♥	A♥	2♠	7♥	8♥	J♠	J♦	Q♥	8♠/4♣	4♥	9♠
	A♠	Q♠	Q♠	3♠	4♠	J♦					
55	K♣	A♠	7♥	10♣	J♣	8♣	6♥	K♠	5♠/5♦	10♠	K♥
	2♦	10♠	4♦	6♦	K♥	6♥					
56	7♣	9♦	5♥	7♠	8♦	2♦	10♣	4♦	Q♠/4♣	Q♥	2♠
	9♥	J♠	4♠	6♥	7♠	K♠					
57	A♥	9♥	7♠	J♥	3♦	Q♠	A♣	J♦	10♦/6♣	9♠	A♠
	6♥	5♦	K♣	10♠	8♣	A♣					
58	7♦	8♥	J♥	Q♦	8♦	2♥	Q♠	9♣	2♦/9♠	6♦	7♥
	6♦	4♣	J♣	2♠	9♦	Q♠					
59	10♠	J♠	Q♦	5♣	5♠	K♠	3♠	K♠	2♥/J♦	3♠	8♥
	A♥	3♣	J♣	9♠	J♥	3♦	5♠				
60	8♦	4♥	7♠	3♦	2♣	4♠	Q♣	4♠	Q♥/10♣	J♦	7♠
	K♦	10♥	6♠	J♥	Q♦	4♦					
61	K♣	2♠	6♦	4♣	8♣	K♦	3♦	A♣	A♠/5♠	J♣	K♦
	9♥	2♥	K♥	7♥	9♠	3♦					
62	8♥	9♥	4♣	A♥	5♥	A♠	A♦	4♥	10♦/J♠	10♥	3♠
	2♣	8♠	K♥	5♠	3♦	10♠					
63	5♣	2♣	A♥	Q♠	10♣	9♠	A♠	A♠	5♦/6♠	5♠	5♦
	J♣	8♣	A♠	J♠	K♦	A♠					
64	8♦	4♥	6♦	2♣	3♣	2♠	9♣	A♥	7♣/J♦	4♦	9♦
	10♦	9♠	2♦	6♠	5♥	9♦					
65	8♠	Q♠	2♠	7♦	Q♦	10♦	6♥	2♠	9♠/Q♣	5♥	Q♦
	A♠	10♠	10♣	5♥	K♦	6♥					
66	4♥	4♠	7♠	K♣	J♥	A♠	9♣	7♥	2♥/Q♥	5♠	3♦
	6♦	J♦	9♦	5♥	5♦	9♣					
67	A♥	4♦	3♣	8♠	K♥	7♠	K♣	8♥	3♦/10♥	4♣	6♥
	8♠	6♥	K♦	J♦	Q♠	7♣					
68	5♥	K♦	8♣	9♠	8♥	8♠	Q♦	J♠	5♠/4♣	6♥	4♣
	J♥	A♠	5♦	4♥	4♠	6♠					
69	Q♠	9♣	Q♥	9♥	2♦	J♥	9♠	J♦	J♦/A♣	3♦	5♣
	K♠	5♥	6♦	7♦	4♦	5♣					
70	4♠	K♣	9♥	7♠	10♣	3♠	6♣	K♣	J♠/10♠	Q♦	5♥
	A♠	4♥	7♦	A♣	A♥	6♣					
71	4♦	9♠	4♣	5♠	6♠	A♠	7♠	A♠	K♠/9♦	9♦	4♦
	2♦	Q♣	2♣	10♠	9♥	2♥					
72	J♥	K♣	5♠	2♥	10♥	Q♥	7♣	7♥	8♦/3♦	5♦	5♠
	3♣	2♣	5♥	4♠	10♠	A♥					
73	7♠	6♥	5♦	9♦	4♠	Q♠	Q♥	10♣	2♦/7♦	3♣	10♥
	J♠	Q♣	K♦	K♥	5♠	4♥					
74	10♠	3♠	5♠	6♥	A♥	2♠	Q♠	J♣	4♠/J♦	K♦	J♣
	8♦	6♠	6♦	7♦	A♣	Q♠					

AGE	MER	VEN	MAR	JUP	SAT	URA	NEP	LR	PLU/RES	ENV	DISP
75	K♣	8♦	6♥	J♣	9♦	4♣	6♣	8♣	6♠/2♣	7♠	J♦
	9♣	3♠	8♠	A♣	5♠	6♣					
76	9♥	9♠	6♦	2♣	10♦	9♣	J♣	6♥	5♥/Q♦	8♥	3♠
	A♠	4♠	J♥	6♣	K♥	10♥					
77	8♠	8♦	2♣	5♦	8♥	7♠	9♣	7♣	10♣/J♦	7♥	6♦
	4♣	4♦	7♥	6♣	K♥	9♣					
78	3♦	2♥	6♥	10♥	Q♥	10♠	7♠	9♦	K♣/8♣	A♠	9♣
	4♥	K♠	K♦	4♠	9♥	3♣					
79	6♣	2♠	K♠	2♣	2♥	K♥	A♥	5♥	10♠/6♦	2♣	Q♥
	8♦	J♣	7♥	8♣	A♣	4♣					
80	Q♥	3♠	6♥	4♣	7♦	4♠	J♥	7♠	10♦/9♦	K♥	10♠
	K♣	5♣	5♥	8♦	6♠	9♣					
81	10♠	K♦	4♣	7♥	3♠	10♠	A♦	8♦	8♠/K♠	9♠	4♥
	K♣	J♣	8♦	9♦	6♥	9♠					
82	4♦	K♣	7♥	9♠	K♥	10♥	9♣	2♣	5♥/J♠	6♠	4♠
	5♣	7♦	A♣	Q♥	4♠	9♣					
83	2♦	K♠	2♠	2♥	K♣	Q♠	3♠	10♣	10♥/9♦	2♠	10♣
	8♥	4♦	5♠	10♠	J♣	Q♥	K♣				
84	8♣	10♣	10♦	Q♥	6♣	2♣	2♠	A♥	6♠/4♦	K♠	J♠
	7♠	5♠	8♥	A♠	A♥	2♠					
85	4♣	A♦	Q♥	5♣	Q♦	K♦	2♣	7♦	10♠/8♦	8♠	7♣
	K♣	Q♣	8♥	4♦	7♥	2♣					
86	K♠	6♠	A♣	2♦	J♠	10♥	5♥	7♠	K♦/3♣	6♠	8♦
	5♦	9♠	10♠	A♦	5♠	J♥	J♠				
87	6♦	6♥	5♦	8♥	9♠	9♣	J♠	J♥	J♣/K♥	2♦	Q♠
	4♣	10♠	7♥	K♦	2♦	J♠					
88	2♠	2♦	6♣	6♥	5♠	9♦	9♣	3♦	9♥/Q♠	A♦	10♦
	5♥	J♥	4♠	10♠	K♦	3♠					
89	4♦	5♥	6♥	7♥	8♥	9♥	10♥	Q♠	J♥/Q♥	A♥	Q♣
	J♠	6♠	Q♦	5♦	J♣	4♣					
90	A♣	Q♣	10♠	5♣	3♦	A♠	7♥	2♥	7♦/5♠	3♥	3♥
	4♥	Q♠	Q♦	6♦	K♥	7♥					
91	A♥	9♦	5♣	K♦	J♦	7♦	J♠	9♥	3♣/8♦	Q♠	A♥
	10♣	6♠	Q♦	2♠	8♠	J♠					
92	5♦	4♣	7♠	J♣	9♥	10♣	K♦	8♥	7♣/5♠	10♦	A♦
	8♣	2♥	K♥	6♦	10♥	K♦					
93	4♥	8♣	J♣	Q♥	5♥	7♣	A♦	J♥	10♦/Q♣	Q♠	2♦
	J♦	3♦	K♠	A♥	6♠	7♦					
94	6♣	J♦	Q♥	4♠	K♠	8♦	A♣	Q♦	7♣/3♠	8♦	6♣
	2♠	9♥	A♥	Q♣	J♣	Q♦	K♠				
95	8♦	Q♠	7♠	Q♦	A♠	4♦	7♥	8♦	10♠/7♥	7♣	8♠
	10♦	10♥	9♦	K♠	Q♣	K♣					
96	5♣	J♦	Q♦	A♥	6♠	10♦	A♦	A♣	10♥/6♦	J♠	K♣
	Q♥	7♠	9♠	2♦	7♠	A♦					
97	2♠	Q♠	A♥	5♠	3♠	Q♥	K♠	Q♠	10♠/2♥	10♣	2♠
	A♠	K♥	3♦	7♠	Q♦	4♠	3♠				
98	4♦	J♦	9♣	K♠	4♠	A♣	4♥	10♠	5♠/K♦	4♠	6♠
	10♦	6♦	10♣	3♠	A♥	7♥					
99	A♣	A♥	2♠	7♥	8♥	J♠	J♦	J♠	8♣/4♣	4♥	9♠
	A♠	Q♣	Q♠	3♠	4♠	J♦					

Four of Hearts

AGE	MER	VEN	MAR	JUP	SAT	URA	NEP	LR	PLU/RES	ENV	DISP
0	4♦	2♠	8♥	6♣	6♠	Q♥	10♣	4♦	8♦/K♠	4♥	4♥
	Q♠	Q♦	6♦	K♥	7♥	3♥					
1	5♠	Q♠	6♣	3♥	A♥	9♦	5♣	2♠	K♦/J♦	10♠	4♠
	7♠	9♥	2♥	5♥	10♥	5♣					
2	J♠	K♠	10♦	A♣	Q♠	9♣	6♥	8♥	9♦/K♥	Q♥	10♣
	8♠	3♠	7♠	4♦	Q♦	5♥	Q♠				
3	8♣	J♠	Q♥	5♥	7♣	A♦	10♦	6♣	Q♣/3♣	9♣	J♠
	K♣	5♠	8♠	2♦	4♦	10♦					
4	8♥	10♣	5♥	7♠	2♠	2♠	A♦	6♠	4♦/6♦	6♦	7♣
	Q♠	10♠	8♠	3♠	6♠	A♦					
5	K♠	7♠	2♥	J♠	J♦	9♦	K♦	Q♥	2♠/6♠	3♠	8♦
	9♠	K♥	4♦	10♣	5♦	J♥	J♦				
6	4♠	7♥	9♠	8♠	3♥	5♣	J♦	10♣	Q♦/A♥	J♦	Q♠
	8♥	4♦	6♣	2♠	J♠	J♦					
7	10♦	J♠	7♣	7♥	5♥	K♥	5♠	5♠	7♦/9♣	J♣	10♣
	K♦	J♥	10♥	Q♥	2♠	6♠					
8	5♠	K♦	7♥	6♣	8♠	7♦	9♦	Q♠	J♥/5♥	10♥	Q♣
	J♦	Q♣	2♣	9♠	Q♦	8♥					
9	2♥	10♠	4♦	7♠	4♠	2♦	6♣	6♣	9♥/5♦	5♠	3♥
	5♠	9♠	2♣	4♣	A♥	6♣					
10	4♠	K♥	7♠	2♠	3♥	9♥	J♦	3♥	6♠/6♦	4♦	A♥
	J♣	Q♠	2♣	10♦	8♦	J♦					
11	9♠	8♥	K♣	Q♦	7♣	J♣	2♠	A♥	3♠/5♦	5♥	A♦
	8♣	A♣	A♥	4♣	9♦	2♠					
12	5♠	8♣	Q♦	5♥	K♦	3♠	10♣	9♦	Q♥/10♠	5♣	2♦
	3♦	A♠	K♠	4♠	Q♣	9♥					
13	7♣	3♦	5♥	10♥	K♠	6♦	2♥	5♣	3♠/6♦	4♣	6♣
	10♦	7♦	4♠	10♠	Q♦	2♣	K♠				
14	6♦	9♣	K♣	2♣	2♦	3♣	9♥	J♠	4♦/6♣	6♥	8♠
	Q♥	9♦	K♥	K♠	10♠	Q♠					
15	7♠	3♦	2♠	4♠	Q♣	Q♥	10♣	K♠	9♦/4♣	3♦	K♣
	5♥	3♠	5♠	J♠	K♣	10♣					
16	10♦	9♣	4♠	5♠	6♥	5♥	K♠	10♦	J♣/A♣	Q♦	2♠
	2♦	A♥	A♠	K♣	2♣	10♥	6♥				
17	3♦	3♦	5♠	K♠	10♥	2♥	5♠	A♣	5♦/2♠	9♦	6♠
	Q♥	4♦	J♣	6♥	4♠	6♣					
18	2♥	4♠	10♦	6♠	8♠	J♦	3♦	Q♠	8♣/8♥	5♦	9♠
	2♦	10♠	9♣	6♥	10♥	3♦					
19	Q♠	2♦	6♣	J♣	Q♦	8♠	7♥	9♣	5♦/9♠	3♣	K♥
	J♠	4♦	3♣	4♣	A♥	7♦					
20	3♠	K♥	K♦	K♣	6♦	J♠	J♣	6♥	9♣/8♥	K♦	2♣
	9♥	J♦	10♥	7♥	6♣	K♠					
21	4♠	9♥	K♣	J♥	A♠	9♠	A♣	8♠	Q♥/7♣	7♠	A♠
	7♥	9♠	Q♠	4♦	8♠	A♠					
22	7♦	8♠	J♥	2♣	6♦	2♥	9♣	J♣	J♠/3♥	8♥	7♥
	4♣	8♥	Q♦	10♦	K♥	9♣					
23	4♦	J♦	2♣	7♠	5♦	K♠	6♥	Q♥	2♥/3♣	7♥	8♥
	4♠	6♠	Q♦	3♥	J♥	A♠	5♦				
24	6♦	5♠	K♣	A♠	A♦	10♥	10♠	5♥	5♥/J♠	A♠	7♠
	2♠	9♦	Q♣	J♥	2♠	3♠					
25	Q♠	10♦	4♣	8♥	8♣	2♠	A♠	7♠	2♦/5♦	2♣	K♦
	9♥	2♥	A♥	6♣	3♥	A♠					
26	8♠	9♥	8♥	4♠	K♦	2♦	10♣	A♦	Q♥/J♦	K♥	3♣
	A♠	8♦	A♥	5♦	A♠	4♦					
27	7♠	A♥	4♠	9♣	J♣	5♠	2♦	10♦	9♠/Q♣	9♠	5♦
	Q♦	8♠	A♣	J♦	2♠	2♦					
28	6♦	10♥	4♣	A♦	6♠	10♦	5♠	8♥	3♠/3♦	6♠	9♦
	Q♥	3♥	J♠	Q♣	K♦	K♥					
29	8♦	9♣	A♦	7♦	2♣	Q♥	7♥	10♣	3♥/10♠	2♠	Q♦
	2♦	4♦	J♣	K♦	2♠	7♥					
30	5♠	10♥	7♦	Q♠	J♥	2♦	5♠	5♥	2♥/5♦	K♣	3♦
	4♣	3♦	K♥	K♦	9♠	5♣					
31	4♠	3♠	6♠	8♣	A♥	K♣	Q♠	7♠	A♠/9♦	8♠	6♥
	8♦	7♥	2♠	3♦	9♣	3♠					
32	K♦	2♠	8♣	3♥	8♠	8♦	2♠	2♣	5♦/8♥	6♣	4♣
	J♥	2♦	9♠	5♠	10♥	Q♣					
33	9♣	5♠	5♥	9♥	J♠	J♥	3♥	2♠	3♦/A♣	2♦	5♣
	K♠	K♦	4♣	7♦	3♣	7♠					
34	10♥	Q♠	9♥	K♣	J♠	6♠	7♠	A♦	J♦/4♦	A♦	5♥
	2♦	5♠	7♦	A♣	4♠	7♣					
35	3♣	5♠	8♥	5♦	Q♣	2♦	K♠	K♠	K♠/K♥	A♥	4♦
	J♠	10♠	A♦	4♦	9♥	2♥					
36	J♥	Q♠	5♦	2♥	9♠	5♥	3♠	7♠	6♦/A♣	3♥	5♠
	6♠	A♦	K♦	10♥	4♦	4♠					
37	K♣	7♥	9♠	K♥	10♥	9♣	5♥	2♥	J♠/7♦	Q♣	10♥
	J♦	10♠	2♠	A♥	7♠	5♠					
38	4♦	6♥	5♦	7♥	4♠	10♦	9♣	J♠	8♥/3♦	10♦	J♣
	6♦	Q♣	4♣	7♦	A♠	9♣					
39	Q♠	6♦	7♥	Q♦	K♥	8♥	7♣	J♦	Q♣/A♦	Q♠	J♦
	5♣	6♠	8♣	A♠	5♦	7♠					
40	9♥	3♥	4♠	A♦	Q♥	5♣	Q♦	9♠	K♦/2♣	8♦	3♠
	2♦	10♥	J♥	7♣	A♥	9♦					
41	8♦	6♦	A♠	9♠	8♠	K♣	5♣	K♦	J♣/3♦	7♠	6♦
	8♥	3♣	6♣	7♠	A♥	5♠					
42	A♠	2♥	7♥	9♦	5♥	4♦	K♠	4♠	Q♠/8♣	J♠	9♠
	5♠	K♠	2♠	8♥	9♥	6♠					
43	7♣	10♦	K♠	A♦	2♥	A♥	4♠	7♥	4♦/4♠	10♣	Q♥
	6♦	Q♦	6♠	8♣	A♣	8♥					
44	5♥	6♥	7♥	8♥	7♦	10♥	J♥	9♠	Q♥/K♥	4♠	10♠
	Q♠	7♠	K♦	6♦	Q♣	5♠					
45	4♦	2♠	8♥	6♣	6♠	Q♥	10♠	8♠	8♦/K♠	4♥	4♥
	Q♠	Q♦	6♦	K♥	7♥	3♥					
46	5♠	Q♠	6♣	3♥	A♥	9♦	5♣	3♥	K♦/J♦	10♠	4♠
	7♠	7♦	A♠	5♥	10♥	5♣					
47	J♠	K♠	10♦	2♥	Q♠	9♣	6♥	5♠	9♦/K♥	Q♥	10♣
	8♠	3♣	7♠	4♦	Q♦	5♥	Q♠				
48	8♣	J♣	Q♥	5♥	7♣	A♦	10♦	J♦	Q♣/3♣	9♣	J♠
	K♣	5♦	8♠	2♦	4♦	10♦					
49	8♥	10♣	5♥	7♠	2♣	2♠	A♦	10♦	4♦/6♦	6♦	7♣
	Q♠	10♠	8♠	3♣	6♠	A♦					

AGE	MER	VEN	MAR	JUP	SAT	URA	NEP	LR	PLU/RES	ENV	DISP
50	K♠	7♣	A♣	J♠	J♦	9♠	K♠	J♠	2♠/6♠	3♠	8♦
	9♠	K♥	4♦	10♣	5♦	J♥	J♦				
51	4♣	7♥	9♠	8♠	3♥	5♣	J♦	7♣	Q♦/A♥	J♦	Q♠
	8♥	4♦	6♣	2♠	J♠	J♦					
52	10♦	J♠	7♣	7♥	5♦	K♥	5♣	7♥	9♥/9♣	J♠	10♦
	K♦	J♥	10♥	Q♥	2♠	6♠					
53	5♠	K♦	7♥	6♣	8♠	9♥	9♦	5♦	J♥/5♦	10♥	Q♣
	J♦	Q♣	2♣	9♠	Q♦	8♥					
54	A♣	10♠	4♦	7♠	A♠	2♦	6♣	K♥	7♦/5♦	5♠	3♥
	5♠	9♣	2♣	4♣	A♥	6♣					
55	4♠	K♥	7♠	2♠	3♦	7♦	J♦	5♣	6♠/6♦	4♦	A♠
	J♣	Q♣	2♣	10♦	8♦	J♦					
56	9♠	8♥	K♣	Q♦	9♥	J♣	2♠	5♠	3♠/5♦	5♥	A♠
	8♣	2♥	A♥	4♣	9♦	2♠					
57	5♠	8♣	Q♦	5♥	K♦	3♠	10♣	K♦	Q♥/10♠	5♣	2♦
	3♦	A♠	K♠	4♠	Q♣	7♦					
58	7♣	3♦	5♥	10♦	K♠	6♦	A♣	7♥	3♠/6♥	4♣	6♣
	10♦	9♥	4♠	10♠	Q♦	2♣	K♠				
59	6♦	9♣	K♣	2♣	2♦	3♣	7♦	6♣	4♦/6♣	6♥	8♠
	Q♥	9♦	K♥	K♠	10♠	Q♠					
60	7♠	3♦	2♣	4♠	Q♣	Q♥	10♣	8♠	9♦/4♣	3♦	K♣
	5♥	3♠	5♣	J♠	K♣	10♣					
61	10♦	9♣	4♣	5♦	6♥	5♥	K♠	7♦	J♣/2♥	Q♦	2♠
	2♦	A♥	A♣	K♣	2♣	10♥	6♥				
62	3♣	3♦	5♣	K♠	10♥	A♣	5♠	9♦	5♦/2♠	9♦	6♠
	Q♥	4♣	J♣	6♦	4♠	6♣					
63	A♣	4♦	10♦	6♣	8♠	J♦	3♦	2♥	8♣/8♥	5♦	9♠
	2♦	10♠	9♣	6♥	10♥	3♦					
64	Q♠	2♦	6♣	J♣	Q♦	8♣	7♦	10♠	5♦/9♠	3♣	K♥
	J♠	4♦	3♣	4♣	A♥	7♥					
65	3♠	K♥	K♦	K♣	6♦	J♠	J♣	4♦	9♠/8♥	K♦	2♣
	7♦	J♦	10♥	7♦	6♣	K♠					
66	4♠	7♦	K♣	J♥	A♠	9♣	2♥	7♠	Q♥/7♣	7♠	A♣
	7♥	9♠	Q♠	4♦	8♣	2♥					
67	9♥	8♠	J♥	2♣	6♦	A♣	9♠	A♠	J♠/3♥	8♥	7♥
	4♣	8♥	Q♦	10♦	K♥	9♣					
68	4♦	J♦	2♣	7♠	5♦	K♠	6♥	2♦	A♣/3♦	7♥	8♥
	4♠	6♠	Q♦	3♥	J♥	A♠	5♦				
69	6♦	5♠	K♣	A♠	A♦	10♥	10♠	6♣	5♥/J♣	A♠	7♠
	2♠	9♦	Q♣	J♥	2♣	3♠					
70	Q♠	10♦	4♣	8♥	8♣	2♠	A♠	4♠	2♦/5♠	2♣	K♦
	7♦	A♣	A♥	6♣	3♥	A♠					
71	8♠	7♦	8♥	4♠	K♦	2♦	10♣	K♥	Q♥/J♦	K♥	3♣
	A♦	8♦	A♥	5♦	A♠	4♦					
72	7♠	A♦	4♠	9♣	J♣	5♣	2♦	7♠	9♠/Q♣	9♠	5♦
	Q♦	8♣	2♥	J♦	2♠	2♦					
73	6♦	10♥	4♣	A♦	6♠	10♦	5♣	2♠	3♠/3♦	6♠	9♦
	Q♥	3♦	J♠	Q♣	K♦	K♥					
74	8♦	9♣	A♦	9♥	2♣	Q♥	7♦	3♦	3♥/10♠	2♠	Q♦
	2♦	4♦	J♣	K♦	2♠	7♥					
75	5♠	10♥	9♥	Q♠	J♥	2♦	5♣	9♥	A♣/5♥	K♣	3♦
	4♣	3♦	K♥	K♦	9♠	5♣					
76	4♠	3♣	6♠	8♠	A♥	K♣	Q♠	J♦	A♠/9♦	8♠	6♥
	8♦	7♥	2♠	3♦	9♣	3♠					
77	K♦	2♠	8♣	3♥	8♠	8♦	2♣	9♠	5♦/8♥	6♣	4♣
	J♥	2♦	9♠	5♠	10♥	Q♣					
78	9♣	5♠	5♥	7♣	J♠	J♥	3♥	8♥	3♦/2♦	2♦	5♣
	K♠	K♦	4♣	9♥	3♣	7♠					
79	10♥	Q♠	7♦	K♠	J♣	6♠	7♣	K♣	J♦/4♦	A♦	5♥
	2♦	5♠	9♥	2♥	4♠	7♣					
80	3♣	5♠	8♥	5♦	Q♣	2♦	K♣	Q♦	K♠/K♥	A♥	4♦
	J♠	10♠	A♦	4♦	7♦	A♣					
81	J♥	Q♠	5♦	A♣	9♥	5♥	3♠	7♦	6♦/A♠	3♥	5♠
	6♠	A♦	K♦	10♥	4♦	4♠					
82	K♣	7♥	9♠	K♥	10♥	9♠	5♥	J♠	J♠/9♥	Q♣	10♥
	J♦	10♠	2♠	A♥	7♠	5♠					
83	4♦	6♥	5♦	7♥	4♠	10♦	9♣	2♠	8♥/3♦	10♦	J♣
	6♦	Q♣	4♣	9♥	2♥	9♣					
84	Q♠	6♦	7♥	Q♦	K♦	8♥	7♣	5♠	Q♣/A♦	Q♠	J♦
	5♣	6♠	8♣	2♥	5♦	7♠					
85	7♦	3♥	4♠	A♦	Q♥	5♠	Q♦	8♣	K♦/2♣	8♦	3♠
	2♦	10♥	J♥	7♠	A♥	9♦					
86	8♦	6♦	A♠	9♠	8♠	K♠	5♣	Q♦	J♣/3♦	7♠	6♦
	8♥	3♣	6♠	7♠	A♥	♣					
87	A♠	A♣	7♠	9♠	5♥	4♦	K♣	5♥	Q♠/8♠	J♠	9♠
	5♠	K♠	2♠	8♥	7♦	6♠					
88	7♣	10♦	K♠	A♠	A♣	A♥	4♠	K♦	4♦/4♣	10♣	Q♥
	6♦	Q♦	6♣	8♠	2♥	8♥					
89	5♥	6♥	7♥	8♥	9♥	10♥	J♥	3♠	Q♥/K♥	4♠	10♠
	Q♠	7♠	K♦	6♦	Q♣	5♣					
90	4♦	2♠	8♥	6♣	6♠	Q♥	10♣	10♣	8♦/K♠	4♥	4♥
	Q♠	Q♦	6♦	K♥	7♥	3♦					
91	5♠	Q♠	6♣	3♥	A♥	9♦	5♣	7♣	K♦/J♦	10♠	4♠
	7♠	9♥	2♥	5♥	10♥	5♠					
92	J♠	K♠	10♦	A♣	Q♠	9♣	6♥	3♦	9♦/K♥	Q♥	10♣
	8♠	3♣	7♠	4♦	Q♦	5♥	Q♠				
93	8♣	J♣	Q♥	5♥	7♣	A♦	10♦	5♥	Q♣/3♣	9♣	J♠
	K♣	5♦	8♠	2♦	4♠	10♦					
94	8♥	10♣	5♥	7♠	2♣	2♠	A♦	10♥	4♦/6♦	6♦	7♣
	Q♠	10♠	8♠	3♣	6♠	A♦					
95	K♠	7♣	2♥	J♠	J♦	9♠	K♦	K♠	2♠/6♠	3♠	8♦
	9♠	K♥	4♦	10♣	5♦	J♥	J♦				
96	4♣	7♥	9♠	8♠	3♥	5♣	J♦	6♦	Q♦/A♥	J♦	Q♠
	8♥	4♦	6♣	2♠	J♠	J♦					
97	10♦	J♠	7♠	7♥	5♦	K♥	5♣	2♥	7♦/9♣	J♣	10♦
	K♦	J♥	10♥	Q♥	2♠	6♠					
98	5♠	K♦	7♥	6♣	8♠	7♥	9♦	6♦	J♥/5♥	10♥	Q♣
	J♦	Q♣	2♣	9♠	Q♦	8♥					
99	2♥	10♠	4♦	7♠	A♠	2♦	6♣	9♣	9♥/5♦	5♠	3♥
	5♠	9♣	2♣	4♣	A♥	6♣					

Five of Hearts

AGE	MER	VEN	MAR	JUP	SAT	URA	NEP	LR	PLU/RES	ENV	DISP
0	3♣	3♠	9♥	7♣	5♦	Q♠	J♣	3♣	9♦/7♠	5♥	5♥
	4♠	K♦	7♦	A♣	4♦	J♣					
1	K♣	7♥	2♦	2♠	9♣	4♠	7♥	3♠	K♠/Q♣	5♣	4♦
	10♥	5♣	4♥	7♠	9♥	2♥					
2	J♥	3♠	2♠	2♥	6♠	8♥	Q♦	9♥	3♦/A♥	4♣	5♠
	Q♠	4♥	8♠	3♣	7♠	4♦					
3	7♣	A♦	10♦	Q♣	3♣	6♥	8♥	7♣	10♥/7♣	6♥	10♥
	9♦	5♣	8♦	10♠	6♣	K♦					
4	7♠	2♣	2♠	A♦	4♦	6♦	6♥	5♦	2♦/K♥	3♦	J♠
	3♦	9♣	A♠	7♦	A♠	6♥					
5	3♠	3♦	A♦	9♠	Q♣	2♦	J♣	Q♠	9♣/4♥	Q♦	J♦
	7♥	Q♠	8♣	A♣	2♠	J♣					
6	9♥	Q♥	A♠	4♥	4♣	7♥	9♠	J♣	8♠/3♥	9♦	3♠
	4♠	3♣	J♥	J♣	10♠	6♠					
7	J♦	3♦	4♥	10♦	J♠	7♣	7♥	K♠	5♦/K♥	5♦	6♦
	2♦	K♣	10♣	J♠	10♠	7♥					
8	A♥	2♥	A♦	6♠	8♥	7♠	7♣	7♥	3♠/8♣	3♣	9♠
	K♦	K♠	8♦	2♦	9♥	Q♠					
9	J♣	6♦	K♠	4♥	2♥	10♠	4♦	2♦	7♠/A♠	K♦	Q♥
	3♦	9♠	10♣	8♠	A♣	2♦					
10	8♥	2♣	A♦	2♦	7♦	3♣	J♥	2♠	4♣/Q♣	7♠	10♠
	3♠	6♣	8♠	3♦	9♣	7♥					
11	7♠	8♦	2♦	10♠	Q♠	4♣	5♠	9♠	J♦/K♠	8♥	4♥
	3♠	9♣	3♦	Q♣	A♦	Q♥					
12	K♦	3♠	10♣	Q♥	10♠	6♠	7♥	4♣	8♠/9♦	7♥	4♠
	6♣	7♦	A♣	8♥	3♣	7♥					
13	10♥	K♠	6♦	2♥	3♠	6♥	2♣	7♣	6♠/Q♣	A♠	10♣
	J♠	K♣	6♣	7♠	9♠	8♥	3♠				
14	8♠	5♦	4♣	8♥	J♣	4♥	6♦	J♥	9♣/K♣	2♣	J♠
	7♣	2♠	J♠	4♠	4♦	6♦					
15	2♠	5♠	8♥	6♣	3♥	8♠	4♥	3♠	7♠/3♦	K♥	7♠
	3♠	5♣	J♠	K♣	10♣	4♥					
16	K♠	J♣	A♣	10♥	9♦	6♠	8♠	2♠	8♦/Q♠	9♠	8♦
	10♦	Q♣	7♠	5♠	2♠	J♥	9♦				
17	A♠	A♦	10♦	J♠	Q♥	7♥	9♦	2♥	9♠/10♠	6♠	Q♠
	2♦	7♠	10♣	8♦	10♥	9♦					
18	6♦	10♥	J♣	A♦	2♠	Q♣	7♥	6♠	9♥/6♥	2♠	10♦
	8♠	J♥	3♣	4♣	8♦	Q♠					
19	K♦	8♠	A♦	10♣	J♠	9♥	9♠	8♥	J♥/8♦	K♣	Q♣
	9♦	9♣	3♥	10♦	9♠	2♦					
20	A♣	5♣	7♠	6♣	A♥	4♠	10♣	Q♦	7♦/2♠	8♠	3♥
	K♦	6♥	3♥	A♠	10♠	10♣					
21	4♦	Q♣	6♠	8♦	K♥	7♦	9♦	7♠	Q♠/3♦	6♣	A♦
	5♦	9♣	3♥	6♦	J♦	9♦					
22	10♦	2♦	7♣	9♠	9♥	5♦	8♦	A♦	Q♦/2♠	2♦	A♦
	8♣	2♥	10♠	A♣	6♠	8♦					
23	K♦	8♣	9♠	8♥	8♠	Q♦	5♠	10♦	4♣/5♠	A♦	2♦
	K♥	A♥	K♠	4♦	9♠	7♦					
24	J♣	K♥	8♥	3♠	K♠	3♦	A♠	Q♠	Q♦/2♣	A♥	6♠
	6♦	9♥	4♦	5♣	9♠	3♥	K♠				
25	3♣	6♥	7♠	3♥	4♠	K♣	7♠	3♣	7♠/10♠	3♥	8♠
	4♣	6♠	Q♣	K♠	5♣	3♠					
26	6♣	K♥	3♥	4♦	9♣	4♣	5♠	6♥	6♠/A♠	Q♣	K♣
	8♥	Q♦	7♥	10♥	7♣	5♠					
27	6♦	6♥	4♦	2♠	2♣	8♥	K♠	8♥	5♦/2♥	10♦	2♠
	4♠	10♠	A♥	7♣	3♥	3♣	2♣				
28	K♣	K♥	7♥	K♠	3♠	A♣	K♦	7♠	2♠/8♠	Q♠	6♠
	4♠	A♠	5♦	2♣	4♦	10♣					
29	A♣	4♦	6♦	10♣	J♠	9♦	K♥	2♣	8♣/2♦	8♦	9♠
	4♠	5♠	6♥	2♣	3♠	K♥					
30	3♠	4♠	10♣	5♦	9♠	8♠	A♦	2♠	2♠/10♦	7♣	K♥
	10♥	7♠	K♣	A♠	10♠	A♦					
31	Q♦	Q♣	8♠	7♣	3♦	10♥	5♠	A♦	6♥/2♦	J♠	2♠
	7♦	9♦	3♣	A♦	10♣	K♠					
32	4♦	7♦	7♠	J♦	A♥	6♥	2♥	4♦	4♣/J♣	10♣	A♠
	A♦	10♠	3♠	7♠	8♠	2♥					
33	9♥	J♠	J♥	3♥	3♦	A♠	6♥	6♦	10♥/Q♥	4♠	7♥
	A♠	2♦	9♠	6♦	Q♣	6♥					
34	7♠	9♦	3♥	6♣	2♠	K♠	2♣	6♥	A♣/K♥	4♥	8♥
	4♦	Q♠	9♠	Q♥	J♥	A♥	2♠				
35	3♦	K♦	7♣	A♥	4♥	3♣	5♠	3♠	8♥/5♦	10♠	7♠
	8♦	6♠	9♣	J♥	3♥	K♣					
36	3♠	6♥	A♠	2♠	8♣	8♣	A♥	3♦	4♠/2♠	Q♥	K♦
	7♦	A♣	10♠	10♣	Q♥	A♥					
37	J♠	7♥	2♦	4♦	8♠	4♠	5♠	A♦	4♣/9♦	9♣	3♠
	4♥	J♦	10♠	2♠	A♥	7♠					
38	6♣	4♥	4♦	6♥	5♦	7♥	4♠	9♠	10♦/9♠	6♦	5♦
	9♠	8♣	2♥	9♦	8♦	4♠					
39	3♦	3♠	A♠	4♥	Q♠	6♦	7♥	Q♠	Q♦/K♥	3♠	9♥
	4♣	Q♥	10♥	9♣	8♠	Q♣					
40	J♦	6♥	4♥	9♥	3♥	4♣	A♦	2♦	Q♥/5♠	J♦	Q♦
	4♠	7♠	5♦	8♠	8♦	A♠					
41	K♦	3♣	9♥	3♠	J♥	4♠	7♥	J♣	A♣/8♦	J♠	3♦
	A♠	K♥	Q♣	8♠	10♦	7♥					
42	4♦	K♣	Q♠	8♠	10♦	7♣	3♠	9♥	A♥/6♠	10♥	6♥
	J♦	A♦	8♦	K♥	6♥	Q♦					
43	8♣	8♦	8♣	Q♥	J♠	J♦	3♥	Q♥	2♠/2♦	5♠	4♠
	J♥	4♠	10♣	K♦	3♥	9♠					
44	6♥	7♠	8♥	7♦	10♥	J♥	Q♥	A♠	K♥/2♥	4♦	5♠
	K♠	8♠	A♠	9♥	K♣	6♠					
45	3♣	3♠	7♦	7♣	5♦	Q♠	J♠	4♥	9♦/7♠	5♥	5♥
	4♠	K♦	9♥	2♠	4♦	J♠					
46	K♣	7♥	2♦	2♠	9♣	4♠	7♠		K♠/Q♣	5♣	4♦
	10♥	5♣	4♥	7♠	7♣	A♠					
47	J♥	3♠	2♠	A♣	6♠	8♥	Q♦	7♥	3♦/A♥	4♣	5♠
	Q♠	4♥	8♠	3♣	7♠	4♦					
48	7♣	A♦	10♦	Q♣	3♣	6♥	8♥	9♠	10♥/9♥	6♥	10♥
	9♦	5♣	8♦	10♠	6♣	K♦					
49	7♠	2♣	2♠	A♦	4♦	6♦	6♥	J♦	2♦/K♥	3♦	J♠
	3♦	9♣	A♠	9♥	2♥	6♥					

AGE	MER	VEN	MAR	JUP	SAT	URA	NEP	LR	PLU/RES	ENV	DISP
50	3♠	3♦	A♦	9♠	Q♣	2♦	J♣	3♦	9♣/4♥	Q♦	J♦
	7♥	Q♠	8♣	2♥	2♠	J♣					
51	7♠	Q♥	A♠	4♥	4♣	7♥	9♠	4♥	8♠/3♥	9♦	3♠
	4♠	3♣	J♥	J♣	10♠	6♠					
52	J♦	3♦	4♥	10♦	J♠	7♣	7♥	10♦	5♦/K♥	5♦	6♦
	2♦	K♣	10♠	J♣	10♠	7♥					
53	A♥	A♣	A♦	6♠	8♥	7♠	7♣	J♠	3♠/8♣	3♠	9♠
	K♦	K♠	8♦	2♦	7♦	Q♠					
54	J♣	6♦	K♠	4♥	A♣	10♠	4♦	7♠	7♠/A♠	K♦	Q♥
	3♦	9♠	10♣	8♣	2♥	2♦					
55	8♥	2♣	A♦	2♦	9♥	3♣	J♥	7♠	4♣/Q♣	7♠	10♠
	3♠	6♣	8♠	3♦	9♣	7♥					
56	7♠	8♦	2♦	10♠	Q♠	4♣	5♠	A♥	J♦/K♠	8♥	4♥
	3♠	9♠	3♦	Q♣	A♦	Q♥					
57	K♦	3♠	10♣	Q♥	10♠	6♠	7♥	2♥	8♠/9♦	7♥	4♠
	6♣	9♥	2♥	8♥	3♣	7♥					
58	10♥	K♠	6♦	A♣	3♠	6♥	2♣	A♦	6♠/Q♣	A♠	10♣
	J♠	K♣	6♣	7♠	9♠	8♥	3♠				
59	8♣	5♦	4♣	8♥	J♣	4♥	6♦	6♠	9♣/K♣	2♣	J♠
	7♣	2♠	J♠	4♠	4♦	6♦					
60	2♦	5♠	8♥	6♣	3♥	8♦	4♥	8♥	7♠/3♦	K♥	7♣
	3♠	5♣	J♠	K♣	10♣	4♥					
61	K♠	J♣	2♥	10♥	9♦	6♠	8♠	7♠	8♦/Q♠	9♠	8♦
	10♦	Q♣	8♠	5♠	2♠	J♥	9♦				
62	A♠	A♦	10♦	J♠	Q♥	7♥	9♦	7♣	9♠/10♠	6♠	Q♠
	2♦	7♠	10♣	8♦	10♥	9♦					
63	6♦	10♥	J♣	A♦	2♠	Q♣	7♥	J♣	7♦/6♥	2♠	10♦
	8♠	J♥	3♠	4♣	8♦	Q♠					
64	K♦	8♠	A♦	10♣	J♠	7♦	6♠	6♦	J♥/8♥	K♣	Q♣
	9♦	9♣	3♥	10♦	9♠	2♦					
65	2♥	5♠	7♠	6♣	A♥	4♠	10♣	K♠	9♥/2♠	8♠	3♥
	K♦	6♥	3♥	A♠	10♠	10♣					
66	4♦	Q♣	6♠	8♦	K♥	9♥	9♦	4♥	Q♠/3♦	6♣	A♥
	5♦	9♣	3♥	6♦	J♦	9♦					
67	10♦	2♦	7♣	9♠	7♦	5♦	8♦	2♥	Q♦/2♠	2♦	A♦
	8♣	A♣	10♠	A♠	6♠	8♦					
68	K♦	8♠	9♠	8♥	8♠	Q♦	5♠	10♠	4♣/5♣	A♦	2♦
	K♥	A♥	K♠	4♦	9♣	9♥					
69	J♣	K♥	8♥	3♣	K♠	3♦	2♥	4♦	Q♦/2♣	A♥	6♣
	6♥	7♦	4♥	5♣	9♠	3♥	K♠				
70	3♦	6♥	7♣	3♥	4♠	K♣	9♥	8♥	7♠/10♣	3♥	8♠
	4♣	6♠	Q♣	K♠	5♠	3♠					
71	6♣	K♥	3♥	4♦	9♠	4♣	5♠	2♣	6♠/A♠	Q♣	K♣
	8♥	Q♦	6♥	10♥	7♠	5♠					
72	6♦	6♥	4♦	2♠	2♣	8♥	K♠	A♦	5♦/A♣	10♦	2♠
	4♦	10♠	A♥	7♣	3♥	3♣	2♠				
73	K♣	K♥	7♥	K♠	3♣	2♥	K♦	2♦	2♠/8♦	Q♠	6♠
	4♠	A♠	5♦	2♠	4♦	10♣					
74	2♥	4♦	6♦	10♣	J♠	9♦	K♥	7♦	8♠/2♦	8♦	9♠
	4♠	5♣	6♥	2♣	3♣	K♥					

AGE	MER	VEN	MAR	JUP	SAT	URA	NEP	LR	PLU/RES	ENV	DISP
75	3♠	4♠	10♣	5♦	9♠	8♣	A♦	3♠	2♠/10♦	7♣	K♥
	10♥	7♠	K♣	A♠	10♠	A♦					
76	Q♦	Q♣	8♠	7♣	3♦	10♥	5♦	J♥	6♥/2♦	J♠	2♣
	9♥	9♠	3♣	A♦	10♣	K♠					
77	4♦	9♥	7♠	J♥	A♥	6♥	A♣	7♠	4♣/J♣	10♠	A♠
	A♦	10♦	3♠	7♠	8♣	A♣					
78	7♦	J♠	J♥	3♥	3♦	2♥	6♥	8♦	10♥/Q♥	4♠	7♥
	A♠	2♦	9♠	6♦	Q♣	6♥					
79	7♠	9♥	3♥	6♣	2♠	K♠	2♣	2♦	2♥/K♥	4♥	8♥
	4♦	Q♠	9♠	Q♥	J♥	A♥	2♠				
80	3♦	K♦	7♠	A♥	4♥	3♣	5♣	10♣	8♥/5♦	10♠	7♠
	8♥	6♠	9♣	J♥	3♥	K♣					
81	3♠	6♦	A♣	2♦	8♣	8♦	A♥	Q♠	4♠/2♠	Q♥	K♦
	9♥	2♥	10♠	10♠	Q♥	A♥					
82	J♠	9♥	2♦	4♦	8♠	4♠	5♠	4♠	4♣/9♦	9♣	3♠
	4♥	J♦	10♠	2♠	A♥	6♥					
83	6♣	4♥	4♦	6♥	5♦	7♥	4♠	5♠	10♦/9♣	6♦	5♦
	9♠	8♣	A♠	9♦	8♦	4♠					
84	3♦	3♣	A♠	4♥	Q♠	6♦	7♥	K♦	Q♦/K♥	3♠	9♦
	4♣	Q♥	10♥	9♠	8♠	Q♣					
85	J♦	6♥	4♥	7♠	3♥	4♣	A♦	3♠	Q♥/5♣	J♦	Q♦
	4♠	7♠	5♦	8♠	8♦	A♦					
86	K♦	3♣	7♥	3♠	J♥	4♠	7♥	10♣	2♥/8♥	J♣	3♦
	A♠	K♥	Q♣	8♠	10♦	7♥					
87	4♦	K♣	Q♠	8♣	10♠	7♠	3♠	Q♥	A♥/6♠	10♥	6♥
	J♦	A♦	8♦	K♥	6♥	Q♦					
88	8♠	8♦	8♣	Q♥	J♠	J♦	3♥	10♠	2♠/2♦	5♠	4♣
	J♥	4♠	10♦	K♦	3♣	9♠					
89	6♥	7♥	8♥	9♥	10♥	J♥	Q♥	6♠	K♥/A♣	4♦	5♣
	K♠	8♠	A♠	7♦	K♣	6♣					
90	3♣	3♠	9♥	7♣	5♦	Q♠	J♣	7♥	9♦/7♠	5♥	5♥
	4♠	K♦	7♠	A♣	4♦	J♣					
91	K♣	7♥	2♦	2♠	9♣	4♠	7♣	10♥	K♠/Q♣	5♠	4♦
	10♥	5♣	4♥	7♠	9♥	2♥					
92	J♥	3♠	2♠	2♥	6♠	8♥	Q♦	K♠	3♦/A♥	4♣	5♠
	Q♠	4♥	8♠	3♣	7♠	4♦					
93	7♣	A♦	10♦	Q♣	3♣	6♥	8♥	6♦	10♥/7♦	6♥	10♥
	9♥	5♣	8♦	10♠	6♣	K♦					
94	7♠	2♣	2♠	A♦	4♦	6♦	6♥	2♥	2♦/K♥	3♦	J♣
	3♦	9♣	A♠	7♦	A♣	6♥					
95	3♠	3♦	A♦	9♠	Q♣	2♦	J♣	3♠	9♣/4♥	Q♦	J♦
	7♥	Q♠	8♠	A♣	2♠	J♣					
96	9♥	Q♥	A♠	4♥	4♣	7♥	9♠	6♥	8♠/3♥	9♦	3♠
	4♠	3♣	J♥	J♣	10♠	6♠					
97	J♦	3♦	4♥	10♦	J♠	7♣	7♥	2♠	5♦/K♥	5♦	6♦
	2♦	K♣	10♠	J♣	10♠	7♥					
98	A♥	2♥	A♦	6♠	8♥	7♠	7♠	8♠	3♠/8♣	3♠	9♠
	K♦	K♠	8♦	2♦	9♥	Q♠					
99	J♣	6♦	K♠	4♥	2♥	10♠	4♦	5♦	7♠/A♠	K♦	Q♥
	3♠	9♠	10♣	8♣	A♣	2♦					

Six of Hearts

AGE	MER	VEN	MAR	JUP	SAT	URA	NEP	LR	PLU/RES	ENV	DISP
0	4♣	2♦	J♠	8♣	6♦	4♠	10♥	4♣	10♦/8♣	6♥	6♥
	5♠	Q♣	10♣	2♠	9♦	3♣					
1	A♦	10♣	8♣	3♣	4♥	5♠	Q♠	2♦	6♣/3♥	3♦	4♣
	J♥	Q♥	7♣	7♥	8♥	J♦					
2	9♦	K♥	2♣	7♦	5♥	J♥	3♠	J♠	2♠/2♥	Q♦	5♣
	K♠	A♦	9♠	9♥	2♦	A♥					
3	8♥	10♥	7♠	4♠	7♠	J♠	4♦	8♣	K♦/A♠	9♦	5♥
	Q♥	7♥	9♥	2♠	4♠	4♦					
4	2♦	K♥	3♥	6♣	J♦	Q♥	4♠	6♦	K♠/8♦	5♦	4♦
	5♥	3♦	9♣	A♠	7♥	A♣					
5	J♥	10♥	6♣	A♣	8♠	2♣	3♣	4♣	5♦/10♦	3♣	5♠
	J♠	9♣	A♦	8♥	A♠	4♣					
6	4♠	Q♣	7♠	8♦	8♥	9♦	2♣	10♥	5♥/9♦	K♦	10♥
	K♦	3♦	10♣	6♦	A♥	7♥					
7	A♠	6♠	4♣	Q♣	4♠	J♠	9♦	A♦	3♥/2♠	7♠	J♣
	5♦	J♦	5♠	9♠	2♥						
8	10♥	5♣	Q♣	K♣	8♦	3♥	4♦	10♣	J♦/9♠	8♥	J♦
	K♥	J♠	8♣	2♥	6♣	4♦					
9	7♦	3♠	9♠	9♣	Q♦	K♥	K♣	8♠	A♦/Q♠	7♥	3♠
	Q♥	8♥	J♥	4♦	6♦	8♠					
10	5♠	5♦	9♣	7♠	4♥	4♠	K♥	3♠	7♠/2♠	A♠	6♦
	3♥	2♦	10♠	4♦	6♦	K♥					
11	10♦	A♣	Q♣	8♠	2♠	A♠	4♠	4♥	10♥/8♠	2♠	9♣
	7♥	K♣	10♣	3♥	7♥	J♠					
12	4♦	J♣	K♠	9♣	A♣	6♦	4♣	5♠	A♠/9♠	K♥	Q♥
	5♦	K♣	10♠	8♣	2♥	3♥					
13	2♣	6♠	Q♣	3♦	9♥	8♥	J♥	Q♠	Q♦/8♦	9♠	10♠
	10♥	A♥	A♦	5♦	J♥	K♥					
14	A♠	10♣	3♥	10♠	J♠	Q♦	5♠	9♦	5♠/K♠	6♠	4♥
	10♥	K♣	5♦	8♦	Q♣	3♠					
15	7♥	10♥	10♠	3♠	6♦	8♠	K♥	K♥	A♦/K♦	2♠	4♠
	A♥	9♥	2♥	2♣	8♥	K♦					
16	5♥	K♠	J♣	A♠	10♥	9♦	6♠	2♣	8♠/8♦	K♣	10♣
	4♥	2♦	A♥	A♠	K♣	2♣	10♥				
17	8♣	7♠	Q♦	2♣	4♦	9♣	J♣	7♦	J♦/2♦	8♠	J♠
	4♠	6♣	4♥	Q♥	4♠	J♣					
18	3♥	5♣	2♣	A♥	Q♠	10♣	9♣	5♥	A♠/5♦	6♣	7♠
	10♥	3♦	4♥	2♦	10♠	9♣					
19	K♠	4♦	2♥	5♥	K♦	8♠	A♦	J♥	10♣/J♠	2♦	8♦
	7♣	8♦	A♠	5♣	6♣	J♥	K♦				
20	9♠	Q♣	7♠	4♥	3♠	K♥	K♦	3♠	K♣/6♦	A♠	Q♠
	3♥	A♣	10♠	10♣	5♥	K♦					
21	J♣	5♥	4♦	Q♣	6♠	2♠	K♥	8♥	7♦/9♦	A♥	10♦
	A♦	J♥	8♥	Q♦	10♣	J♠					
22	7♥	A♦	Q♣	10♠	4♥	7♠	8♠	10♥	J♥/2♠	3♥	Q♣
	K♦	J♣	Q♠	7♣	K♣	3♥					
23	2♥	3♦	A♠	A♥	10♦	Q♥	10♠	7♦	9♥/6♠	Q♣	3♥
	7♥	9♦	Q♠	9♠	6♦	10♠					
24	4♣	8♦	A♥	10♠	2♠	9♥	K♦	4♠	J♠/5♦	10♦	A♥
	7♠	J♦	Q♠	J♣	5♠	K♦					
25	7♣	3♥	4♠	K♣	7♦	7♠	10♣	7♠	3♠/6♦	Q♠	A♦
	8♣	A♣	6♦	9♠	8♠	10♣					
26	7♥	8♣	K♣	2♠	A♦	3♣	5♣	J♠	Q♦/3♦	8♦	2♦
	2♠	10♦	K♠	4♣	J♥	9♥					
27	4♦	2♠	2♣	8♥	K♠	5♦	2♥	4♦	3♣/6♠	7♣	6♣
	J♣	7♦	4♣	3♦	K♣	Q♠	K♠				
28	5♦	9♠	4♠	Q♠	Q♥	2♦	9♦	2♦	A♠/10♠	J♠	8♠
	Q♦	8♠	8♦	K♠	3♦	10♥					
29	A♥	2♠	Q♠	4♣	J♦	Q♦	5♣	K♥	8♠/9♠	10♣	K♣
	2♣	3♣	K♥	5♠	4♠	5♣					
30	J♣	9♦	4♠	6♣	6♠	2♣	K♠	3♥	7♠/A♣	4♠	2♠
	Q♥	6♦	10♦	4♠	Q♠	8♥	6♠				
31	2♦	2♠	K♥	K♣	8♥	2♥	7♥	6♣	6♣/10♣	4♥	6♠
	Q♦	9♠	7♠	6♣	4♠	10♠					
32	2♥	4♣	J♣	10♠	4♥	K♦	2♠	J♦	8♣/3♥	10♠	9♠
	Q♥	3♦	9♦	6♠	8♥	2♠					
33	10♥	Q♥	10♠	7♠	K♣	8♣	Q♣	Q♥	6♣/7♣	Q♥	K♥
	5♥	A♠	2♦	9♠	6♦	Q♣					
34	3♣	8♦	A♦	4♠	5♦	5♥	7♠	4♠	9♦/3♦	9♠	2♣
	9♥	K♦	8♥	Q♣	10♠	K♠					
35	4♣	9♥	4♠	J♥	10♦	9♠	A♠	J♥	Q♦/4♦	6♦	A♠
	Q♣	7♣	10♥	A♠	8♣	A♣					
36	7♦	4♥	J♠	Q♠	5♦	2♥	9♦	10♥	5♥/3♠	3♠	7♥
	9♠	3♥	K♣	J♠	8♦	9♦					
37	A♠	K♦	Q♠	A♥	6♣	K♠	6♠	6♠	2♥/2♦	J♦	8♥
	4♣	J♠	K♣	3♠	J♥	10♦	6♣				
38	5♦	7♥	4♠	10♦	9♣	8♥	3♦	A♣	2♣/7♠	J♣	7♠
	10♣	8♠	J♦	J♥	Q♠	2♦					
39	10♥	J♣	9♠	3♥	8♠	10♣	10♦	8♠	Q♥/6♣	10♥	K♦
	9♥	2♥	6♦	10♠	3♠	10♦					
40	4♥	9♠	3♥	4♣	A♦	Q♥	5♠	2♠	Q♦/K♦	5♠	3♠
	9♣	5♠	6♦	6♣	10♦	A♠					
41	A♥	9♣	4♠	9♦	7♠	K♥	Q♥	3♣	7♣/J♦	4♦	5♦
	K♣	8♣	A♣	K♦	10♣	Q♥					
42	5♦	8♥	9♠	9♣	J♠	J♣	K♥	4♠	3♣/2♠	5♥	9♦
	Q♦	3♠	5♥	J♦	A♦	8♦					
43	5♠	9♦	9♠	7♦	Q♠	Q♦	Q♣	Q♣	3♠/3♦	5♣	Q♦
	Q♥	A♠	7♠	A♦	10♣	Q♠					
44	7♥	8♥	7♦	10♥	J♦	Q♥	K♥	7♠	2♥/2♣	4♣	3♦
	9♠	2♠	8♦	A♦	7♣	K♥					
45	4♣	2♦	J♠	8♣	6♦	4♠	10♥	8♦	10♦/8♠	6♥	6♥
	5♠	Q♣	10♠	2♠	9♦	3♣					
46	A♦	10♣	8♣	3♣	4♥	5♠	Q♠	8♥	6♣/3♥	3♦	4♣
	J♥	Q♥	7♣	7♥	8♥	J♦					
47	9♦	K♥	2♣	9♠	5♥	J♥	3♠	9♦	2♠/A♠	Q♦	5♣
	K♠	A♦	9♠	7♦	2♠	A♥					
48	8♥	10♥	9♥	4♠	7♠	J♠	4♦	2♠	K♦/A♠	9♦	5♥
	Q♥	7♥	7♠	A♠	4♠	4♦					
49	2♦	K♥	3♥	6♣	J♦	Q♥	4♠	A♠	K♠/8♦	5♦	4♦
	5♥	3♦	9♣	A♠	9♥	2♥					

AGE	MER	VEN	MAR	JUP	SAT	URA	NEP	LR	PLU/RES	ENV	DISP
50	J♥	10♥	6♣	2♥	8♠	2♣	3♣	6♠	5♦/10♦	3♣	5♠
	J♠	9♦	A♦	8♥	A♠	4♣					
51	4♠	Q♣	7♠	8♦	8♥	9♦	2♣	6♠	5♥/7♦	K♦	10♥
	K♦	3♦	10♠	6♦	A♥	7♥					
52	A♠	6♠	6♣	Q♠	4♣	J♣	9♦	Q♣	3♥/2♠	7♠	J♣
	5♦	J♦	9♠	7♦	A♣	9♦					
53	10♥	5♦	Q♣	K♣	8♦	3♥	4♦	4♣	J♦/9♣	8♥	J♦
	K♥	J♠	8♣	A♠	6♣	4♦					
54	9♠	3♠	9♠	9♣	Q♦	K♥	K♣	J♠	A♦/Q♠	7♥	3♠
	Q♥	8♥	J♥	4♦	6♦	8♠					
55	5♠	5♦	9♣	7♣	4♥	4♠	K♥	9♦	7♠/2♠	A♠	6♦
	3♥	2♦	10♠	4♦	6♦	K♥					
56	10♦	2♥	Q♣	8♠	2♣	A♠	4♠	10♥	10♥/8♣	2♣	9♠
	7♥	K♠	10♣	3♥	9♥	J♠					
57	4♦	J♣	K♣	9♣	2♥	6♦	4♣	5♦	A♠/9♠	K♥	Q♥
	5♦	K♣	10♠	8♣	A♣	3♥					
58	2♣	6♠	Q♣	3♥	7♦	8♥	J♥	Q♣	Q♦/8♦	9♠	10♠
	10♥	A♥	A♦	5♦	J♦	K♥					
59	A♠	10♣	3♥	10♠	J♠	Q♦	5♣	K♣	5♠/K♠	6♠	4♥
	10♥	K♣	5♦	8♦	Q♣	3♠					
60	7♥	10♥	10♠	3♣	6♦	8♠	K♥	8♦	A♦/K♦	2♠	4♠
	A♥	7♦	A♣	2♣	8♥	K♥					
61	5♥	K♠	J♣	2♥	10♥	9♦	6♠	3♥	8♠/8♦	K♣	10♣
	4♥	2♦	A♥	A♠	K♣	2♣	10♥				
62	8♣	7♠	Q♦	2♣	4♦	9♣	J♣	4♦	J♦/2♦	8♠	J♠
	4♠	6♠	4♥	Q♥	4♣	J♣					
63	3♥	5♣	2♠	A♥	Q♠	10♣	9♣	7♦	A♠/5♦	6♠	7♣
	10♥	3♦	4♥	2♦	10♠	9♣					
64	K♠	4♦	A♣	5♥	K♦	8♠	A♦	3♠	10♣/J♠	2♦	8♦
	7♣	8♦	A♠	5♣	6♣	J♥	K♦				
65	9♠	Q♣	7♠	4♥	3♠	K♥	K♦	9♠	K♣/6♦	A♦	Q♠
	3♥	A♠	10♠	10♣	5♥	K♦					
66	J♣	5♥	4♦	Q♣	6♣	8♦	K♥	9♣	9♥/9♦	A♥	10♠
	A♦	J♥	8♥	Q♦	10♣	J♠					
67	7♥	A♦	Q♣	10♠	4♥	9♥	8♠	Q♦	J♥/2♣	3♥	Q♠
	K♦	J♦	Q♠	7♣	K♣	3♥					
68	A♣	3♦	A♠	A♥	10♦	Q♥	10♠	K♥	7♦/6♣	Q♣	3♥
	7♥	9♦	Q♠	9♠	6♦	10♠					
69	4♣	8♦	A♥	10♣	2♠	7♦	K♦	K♣	J♠/5♦	10♦	A♥
	7♠	J♦	Q♠	J♣	5♠	K♦					
70	7♣	3♥	4♠	K♣	9♥	7♠	10♣	5♠	3♣/6♣	Q♠	A♦
	8♣	2♥	6♦	9♠	8♠	10♣					
71	7♥	4♣	K♠	2♣	A♦	3♣	5♣	5♦	Q♦/3♦	8♦	2♦
	2♠	10♥	K♠	4♣	J♦	7♥					
72	4♦	2♠	2♠	8♥	K♠	5♦	A♣	9♣	3♣/6♣	7♣	6♣
	J♣	9♥	4♣	3♦	K♣	Q♠	K♠				
73	5♦	9♠	4♠	Q♠	Q♥	2♦	7♦	7♣	A♠/10♠	J♠	8♠
	Q♦	8♠	8♦	K♠	3♦	10♥					
74	A♥	2♠	Q♠	4♣	J♦	Q♦	5♠	4♥	8♠/9♠	10♣	K♣
	2♠	3♣	K♥	5♥	4♠	5♣					
75	J♣	9♦	4♣	6♣	6♠	2♣	K♠	4♠	7♠/2♥	4♠	2♠
	Q♥	6♦	10♦	4♠	Q♠	8♥	6♠				
76	2♦	2♠	K♥	K♠	8♥	A♣	7♥	K♥	6♣/10♣	4♥	6♠
	Q♦	9♠	7♠	6♠	4♣	10♠					
77	A♣	4♣	J♣	10♠	4♥	K♦	2♠	10♦	8♣/3♥	10♠	9♠
	Q♥	3♦	9♦	6♠	8♥	2♠					
78	10♥	Q♥	10♠	7♠	K♠	8♣	Q♠	A♣	6♣/7♣	Q♥	K♥
	5♥	A♠	2♦	9♠	6♦	Q♣					
79	3♣	8♠	A♦	4♠	5♦	5♥	7♠	Q♠	9♦/3♥	9♣	2♣
	7♥	K♦	8♥	Q♣	10♠	K♠					
80	4♣	7♦	4♠	J♥	10♦	9♦	2♥	8♠	Q♦/4♦	6♦	A♠
	Q♣	7♠	10♥	A♠	8♣	2♥					
81	9♥	4♥	J♥	Q♠	5♦	A♣	9♦	2♣	5♥/3♠	3♠	7♥
	9♠	3♥	K♣	J♠	8♦	9♦					
82	A♠	A♦	Q♠	A♥	6♣	K♠	6♠	A♠	A♣/2♣	J♦	8♥
	4♣	J♠	K♣	3♠	J♥	10♦	6♠				
83	5♦	7♥	4♠	10♦	9♣	8♥	3♦	4♠	2♣/7♠	J♣	7♠
	10♣	8♠	J♦	J♥	Q♠	2♦					
84	10♥	J♠	9♠	3♥	8♣	10♣	10♦	4♦	Q♥/6♣	10♥	K♦
	7♦	A♣	6♦	10♠	3♠	10♦					
85	4♥	7♦	3♥	4♣	A♦	Q♥	5♣	J♣	Q♦/K♦	5♠	3♠
	9♣	5♠	6♦	6♣	10♦	A♠					
86	A♥	9♠	4♣	9♦	7♠	K♥	Q♥	K♠	7♣/J♦	4♦	5♦
	K♣	8♠	2♥	K♦	10♣	Q♥					
87	5♦	8♥	9♠	9♣	J♠	J♣	K♥	9♣	3♣/2♠	5♥	9♦
	Q♦	3♠	5♥	J♦	A♦	8♦					
88	5♠	9♦	9♣	9♥	Q♠	Q♦	Q♣	A♠	3♠/3♦	5♣	Q♦
	Q♥	A♠	7♠	A♦	10♠	Q♣					
89	7♥	8♥	9♥	10♥	J♥	Q♥	K♥	6♦	A♣/2♦	4♣	3♥
	9♠	2♠	8♦	A♦	7♣	K♥					
90	4♣	2♦	J♠	8♣	6♦	4♠	10♥	4♣	10♦/8♠	6♥	6♥
	5♠	Q♣	10♣	2♠	9♦	3♣					
91	A♦	10♣	8♠	3♠	4♥	5♠	Q♠	2♣	6♣/3♥	3♦	4♠
	J♥	Q♥	7♠	7♥	8♥	J♦					
92	9♦	K♥	2♠	7♦	5♥	J♥	3♠	6♠	2♠/2♥	Q♦	5♠
	K♠	A♦	9♠	9♥	2♦	A♥					
93	8♥	10♥	7♦	4♠	7♠	J♠	4♦	Q♠	K♦/A♠	9♦	5♥
	Q♥	7♥	9♥	2♥	4♣	4♦					
94	2♦	K♥	3♥	6♣	J♦	Q♥	4♠	3♥	K♠/8♦	5♦	4♦
	5♠	3♦	9♠	A♠	7♦	A♣					
95	J♥	10♥	6♣	A♣	8♠	2♣	3♠	9♥	5♦/10♦	3♠	5♠
	J♠	9♣	A♦	8♥	A♠	4♣					
96	4♠	Q♣	7♠	8♦	8♥	9♦	2♣	8♥	5♥/9♥	K♦	10♥
	K♦	3♦	10♣	6♦	A♥	7♥					
97	A♠	6♠	6♣	Q♣	4♣	J♣	9♦	J♥	3♥/2♠	7♠	J♣
	5♦	J♦	9♠	9♥	2♥	9♦					
98	10♥	5♦	Q♣	K♣	8♦	3♥	4♦	A♠	J♦/9♣	8♥	J♦
	K♥	J♠	8♣	2♥	6♣	4♦					
99	7♦	3♠	9♠	9♣	Q♦	K♥	K♣	10♣	A♦/Q♠	7♥	3♠
	Q♥	8♥	J♥	4♦	6♦	8♠					

Seven of Hearts

AGE	MER	VEN	MAR	JUP	SAT	URA	NEP	LR	PLU/RES	ENV	DISP
0	7♥	5♠	J♥	9♣	9♠	2♥	K♥	7♦	K♦/6♦	7♥	7♥
	3♥	4♥	Q♠	Q♦	6♦	K♥					
1	2♦	2♠	9♣	4♠	7♣	K♠	Q♣	5♠	2♥/10♦	A♠	8♥
	8♥	J♦	Q♠	6♥	J♥	Q♥	7♣				
2	9♠	6♣	10♥	Q♥	5♣	8♠	A♠	J♥	A♦/K♣	2♣	7♠
	J♣	8♦	3♦	J♥	9♣	J♠					
3	9♦	Q♦	3♥	4♥	8♣	J♣	Q♥	9♣	5♥/7♣	K♥	K♦
	9♥	2♥	4♣	4♦	6♥	Q♥					
4	5♠	9♥	4♥	8♥	10♣	5♦	7♠	9♠	2♣/2♦	9♠	3♣
	5♣	5♦	4♣	7♣	Q♥	2♦					
5	4♠	5♣	8♥	K♥	7♣	A♥	5♥	2♥	3♠/3♦	6♠	5♦
	Q♠	8♠	A♣	2♠	J♣	5♥					
6	9♠	8♠	3♥	5♣	J♦	Q♦	A♥	K♥	6♠/10♦	2♠	9♦
	2♣	6♥	K♦	3♦	10♣	6♦					
7	5♦	K♥	5♠	7♦	9♣	2♣	10♠	2♦	6♥/A♠	K♣	Q♦
	5♥	2♦	5♣	10♣	J♥	10♠					
8	6♠	8♠	7♥	9♦	J♥	5♥	A♥	2♠	2♥/A♦	8♠	3♦
	3♥	10♦	6♦	10♣	3♠	A♥					
9	8♥	J♠	J♦	8♣	4♣	10♥	9♦	9♣	Q♥/8♦	6♣	6♥
	5♦	10♠	J♣	10♦	K♥	6♠					
10	10♣	J♣	8♣	6♥	5♠	5♦	9♣	4♠	7♣/4♥	2♦	4♣
	J♥	5♥	3♠	6♣	8♠	3♦					
11	K♥	A♥	A♦	9♥	K♦	J♥	6♥	7♠	10♦/A♣	A♦	5♣
	K♠	10♣	3♥	7♦	J♠	4♠					
12	8♠	9♣	9♥	10♥	K♣	J♦	3♣	K♠	2♠/2♦	A♥	5♥
	5♥	6♣	7♣	A♣	8♥	3♣					
13	J♠	A♥	4♥	7♣	3♦	5♥	10♥	Q♣	K♠/6♦	3♥	4♦
	K♦	A♠	5♣	2♦	9♥	2♥					
14	J♥	9♦	7♣	2♥	8♦	A♦	6♠	9♠	9♠/Q♥	Q♣	5♠
	J♦	5♣	10♣	8♠	2♦	8♥					
15	10♥	10♠	8♣	6♦	8♠	K♥	A♦	6♠	K♦/7♦	10♦	10♥
	2♠	A♠	J♠	4♠	4♠	6♣					
16	2♦	Q♣	7♠	10♠	8♥	Q♦	K♥	10♥	4♥/10♦	Q♠	J♣
	9♠	3♣	3♥	7♦	A♣	K♥					
17	9♦	9♠	10♠	Q♠	6♦	4♥	3♣	Q♥	3♦/5♣	8♦	J♦
	A♥	J♦	8♠	A♣	7♣	3♣					
18	9♥	6♥	3♥	5♠	2♣	A♥	Q♠	5♠	10♣/9♣	7♣	3♠
	5♥	8♣	J♥	3♣	4♣	8♦					
19	5♦	9♠	5♣	3♠	5♠	10♥	A♥	8♠	K♣/10♦	J♠	6♦
	4♥	J♠	4♦	3♣	4♣	A♥					
20	Q♥	2♥	10♠	8♣	A♦	2♦	10♥	A♠	9♦/8♣	10♣	9♣
	6♣	K♠	J♣	4♥	9♥	J♦					
21	3♣	Q♦	K♠	5♣	2♥	4♠	8♥	9♠	2♦/3♦	4♠	Q♥
	9♠	Q♠	8♣	A♠	4♥						
22	A♦	Q♣	10♠	4♥	7♦	8♠	J♥	Q♦	2♣/6♦	4♥	10♠
	9♦	4♠	10♣	9♠	3♦	A♥					
23	2♦	J♠	4♥	4♦	J♦	2♠	7♠	3♥	5♦/K♠	10♠	4♥
	9♥	Q♠	9♠	6♦	10♠	6♥					
24	6♣	9♦	4♦	6♥	4♣	8♦	A♥	4♥	10♣/2♠	Q♥	4♠
	4♠	7♠	A♣	A♦	8♠	A♥					
25	K♦	K♠	Q♦	2♥	9♦	K♥	Q♣	8♠	8♦/6♦	9♠	10♣
	5♠	J♠	4♠	2♦	Q♠	A♦	9♦				
26	8♣	K♣	2♣	A♦	3♣	5♣	Q♦	J♣	3♦/J♠	6♦	J♠
	10♥	7♣	5♠	5♥	8♥	Q♦					
27	4♥	7♠	A♦	4♠	9♠	J♠	5♣	Q♥	2♦/9♠	3♠	7♣
	9♦	A♠	5♠	J♠	4♦	5♣					
28	K♠	3♣	A♠	K♦	2♠	8♦	10♣	5♠	J♣/J♦	J♦	8♦
	3♠	6♦	2♦	7♠	7♦	2♠					
29	3♥	10♠	3♠	5♠	6♥	A♥	2♠	9♥	Q♠/4♣	J♣	Q♠
	4♥	2♦	4♦	J♣	K♦	2♠					
30	Q♦	K♦	3♣	10♠	7♠	6♦	A♥	4♥	9♥/K♥	10♥	10♣
	10♣	J♥	8♠	2♣	J♣	J♦					
31	6♣	10♠	10♠	4♦	5♠	9♥	8♦	8♥	J♥/A♠	5♠	Q♣
	2♠	3♦	9♣	3♠	Q♠	4♥					
32	A♣	A♠	2♠	4♠	Q♥	5♥	4♦	10♣	7♦/7♣	4♦	3♥
	6♠	K♥	9♠	3♥	4♣	4♦					
33	8♥	6♣	4♠	J♣	10♦	7♦	2♠	5♥	J♦/9♠	5♥	A♥
	K♣	3♦	9♣	Q♦	5♦	2♠					
34	3♠	4♥	10♥	Q♠	9♥	K♣	J♠	7♠	6♠/7♣	5♠	A♦
	8♣	2♥	4♣	3♥	8♦	J♣					
35	6♣	8♣	Q♠	A♠	10♠	6♠	7♠	4♠	2♣/A♠	4♣	2♦
	10♦	Q♥	K♠	8♥	3♦	7♠					
36	3♣	10♠	A♦	8♠	K♠	9♠	A♣	5♠	6♠/Q♣	6♥	6♠
	Q♦	9♥	8♥	A♠	Q♠	9♣	K♠				
37	9♠	K♥	10♥	9♣	5♥	J♠	7♦	8♥	2♦/4♦	3♦	8♠
	2♣	8♦	6♦	K♠	A♠	9♦					
38	4♠	10♠	9♣	8♥	3♦	2♣	7♠	K♥	8♦/3♥	Q♦	K♣
	A♦	6♠	A♥	K♦	10♥	7♠					
39	Q♦	K♥	8♥	7♣	Q♣	A♦	K♠	K♣	K♣/2♥	9♦	2♠
	5♥	4♣	Q♥	10♥	9♣	8♠	Q♣				
40	J♠	10♦	A♥	K♠	8♠	A♠	6♠	A♥	7♣/J♠	5♦	6♠
	2♣	3♥	K♣	Q♣	8♥	4♦					
41	A♠	8♥	Q♦	4♦	5♠	2♠	10♦	5♥	8♣/4♥	3♣	9♠
	5♥	A♠	K♥	Q♣	8♠	10♦					
42	9♦	5♥	4♦	K♣	Q♠	8♠	10♠	9♠	7♣/3♣	K♦	K♥
	K♦	2♦	J♠	3♥	4♣	10♠					
43	6♠	6♦	10♣	10♥	9♠	K♦	K♣	8♠	K♥/4♥	7♠	2♣
	7♦	2♠	8♠	10♠	4♦	K♠					
44	8♥	7♦	10♥	J♥	Q♥	K♥	2♥	3♥	2♣/3♣	8♥	A♠
	10♠	3♠	9♦	2♦	8♣	2♥					
45	9♥	5♠	J♥	9♣	9♠	A♣	K♥	5♣	K♦/6♥	7♥	7♥
	3♥	4♥	Q♠	Q♦	6♦	K♥					
46	3♣	2♠	9♠	4♠	7♠	K♠	Q♣	J♦	A♣/10♦	A♠	8♥
	8♥	J♦	Q♠	6♥	J♥	Q♥	7♣				
47	9♠	6♣	10♥	Q♥	5♠	8♠	A♠	Q♣	A♦/K♣	2♣	7♠
	J♣	8♦	3♦	J♥	9♣	J♠					
48	9♦	Q♦	3♥	4♥	8♠	J♣	Q♥	A♥	5♥/7♣	K♥	K♦
	7♠	A♠	4♣	4♦	6♥	Q♥					
49	5♠	7♦	4♥	8♥	10♥	5♥	7♠	5♦	2♣/2♠	9♠	3♣
	5♣	5♦	4♣	7♣	Q♥	2♦					

AGE	MER	VEN	MAR	JUP	SAT	URA	NEP	LR	PLU/RES	ENV	DISP
50	4♠	5♣	8♥	K♥	K♣	A♥	5♥	K♥	3♠/3♦	6♠	5♦
	Q♠	8♣	2♥	2♠	J♣	5♥					
51	9♠	8♠	3♥	5♣	J♦	Q♥	A♥	5♣	6♠/10♦	2♠	9♦
	2♣	6♥	K♦	3♦	10♣	6♦					
52	5♦	K♥	5♣	9♥	9♠	2♣	10♠	7♦	6♥/A♠	K♣	Q♦
	5♥	2♦	K♣	10♣	J♣	10♠					
53	6♣	8♠	9♥	9♦	J♥	5♥	A♥	9♣	A♣/A♦	8♠	3♦
	3♥	10♦	6♦	10♣	3♠	A♥					
54	8♥	J♠	J♦	8♣	4♣	10♥	9♦	2♣	Q♥/8♦	6♣	6♥
	5♦	10♠	J♣	10♦	K♥	6♠					
55	10♣	J♣	8♣	6♥	5♠	5♦	9♣	10♠	7♣/4♥	2♦	4♣
	J♥	5♥	3♠	6♣	8♠	3♦					
56	K♥	A♥	A♦	7♦	K♦	J♥	6♥	6♣	10♦/2♥	A♦	5♣
	K♠	10♣	3♥	9♥	J♠	4♠					
57	8♠	9♦	7♦	10♥	K♣	J♥	3♣	8♠	2♠/2♦	A♥	5♥
	5♥	6♣	9♥	2♥	8♥	3♣					
58	J♠	A♥	4♥	7♣	3♦	5♥	10♥	7♦	K♠/6♥	3♥	4♦
	K♦	A♠	5♣	2♦	7♥	A♠					
59	J♥	9♦	7♣	A♣	8♦	A♦	6♠	9♦	9♠/Q♥	Q♣	5♠
	J♦	5♣	10♣	8♠	2♦	8♥					
60	10♥	10♠	3♠	6♦	8♠	K♥	A♦	J♥	K♦/9♥	10♦	10♥
	2♠	A♠	J♣	4♠	4♠	6♣					
61	2♦	Q♣	7♠	10♠	8♥	Q♦	K♥	5♥	4♥/10♦	Q♠	J♠
	9♠	3♦	3♥	9♥	2♥	K♥					
62	9♦	9♠	10♠	Q♠	6♦	4♥	3♣	A♥	3♦/5♣	8♦	J♠
	A♥	J♦	8♣	2♥	7♣	3♠					
63	7♦	6♥	3♥	5♣	2♠	A♥	Q♠	8♥	10♣/9♠	7♣	3♠
	5♥	8♠	J♥	3♣	4♣	8♦					
64	5♦	9♠	5♣	3♠	5♠	10♥	A♥	J♠	K♣/10♦	J♠	6♦
	4♥	J♠	4♦	3♣	4♣	A♥					
65	Q♥	A♣	10♠	8♦	A♦	2♦	10♥	J♦	9♦/8♣	10♣	9♣
	6♣	K♠	J♣	4♥	7♦	J♦					
66	3♣	Q♦	K♠	5♣	A♣	4♣	8♥	8♣	2♦/3♥	4♠	Q♥
	9♠	Q♠	4♦	8♣	2♥	4♥					
67	A♦	Q♣	10♠	4♥	9♥	8♠	J♥	4♣	2♣/6♦	4♥	10♠
	9♦	4♠	10♣	9♠	3♦	A♥					
68	2♦	J♣	4♥	4♣	J♦	2♣	7♠	10♥	5♦/K♠	10♠	4♥
	9♦	Q♠	9♣	6♦	10♠	6♥					
69	6♣	9♠	4♦	6♥	4♣	8♦	A♥	9♦	10♣/2♠	Q♥	4♠
	4♠	9♥	2♥	A♦	8♠	A♥					
70	K♦	K♠	Q♦	A♣	9♦	K♥	Q♣	10♠	8♦/6♦	9♣	10♣
	5♠	J♠	4♠	2♦	Q♠	A♦	9♦				
71	8♠	K♣	2♣	A♦	3♠	5♣	Q♦	J♣	3♦/J♠	6♦	J♠
	10♥	7♠	5♠	5♥	8♥	Q♦					
72	4♥	7♠	A♦	4♣	9♣	J♣	5♦	8♣	2♦/9♠	3♠	7♣
	9♦	A♠	5♠	J♠	4♦	5♠					
73	K♠	3♣	2♥	K♦	2♠	8♦	10♣	6♥	J♣/J♦	J♦	8♦
	3♠	6♦	2♦	7♠	7♣	J♥	2♠				
74	3♥	10♠	3♠	5♠	6♥	A♥	2♠	5♠	Q♠/4♣	J♣	Q♠
	4♥	2♦	4♦	J♣	K♦	2♠					
75	Q♦	K♦	3♣	10♠	7♥	6♦	A♥	5♦	7♦/K♥	10♥	10♦
	10♣	J♥	8♠	2♣	J♣	J♦					
76	6♣	10♣	10♠	4♦	5♠	7♦	8♦	9♣	J♥/A♦	5♠	Q♣
	2♠	3♦	9♣	3♠	Q♠	4♦					
77	2♥	A♠	2♦	4♠	Q♥	5♥	4♦	K♥	9♥/7♣	4♦	3♥
	6♠	K♥	9♣	3♥	4♣	4♦					
78	8♥	6♦	4♠	J♣	10♦	9♥	2♠	A♥	J♦/9♠	5♥	A♥
	K♣	3♦	9♣	Q♦	5♦	2♠					
79	3♠	4♥	10♥	Q♠	7♦	K♣	J♣	A♦	6♠/7♣	5♣	A♦
	8♣	A♣	4♣	3♥	8♦	J♣					
80	6♣	8♣	Q♠	A♦	10♣	6♠	7♠	9♥	2♣/A♠	4♣	2♦
	10♦	Q♥	K♠	8♥	3♦	9♥					
81	3♣	10♦	A♦	8♠	K♠	9♠	2♥	K♦	6♠/Q♣	6♥	6♣
	Q♦	7♦	8♥	A♠	Q♠	9♣	K♠				
82	9♠	K♥	10♥	9♣	5♥	J♠	9♥	J♥	2♦/4♣	3♦	8♠
	2♣	8♦	6♦	K♠	A♠	9♦					
83	4♠	10♠	9♣	8♥	3♦	2♣	7♠	6♥	8♦/3♥	Q♦	K♣
	A♦	6♠	A♥	K♦	10♥	7♠					
84	Q♦	K♥	8♥	7♣	Q♣	A♦	K♠	8♠	K♣/A♣	9♦	2♠
	5♥	4♣	Q♥	10♥	9♣	8♠	Q♣				
85	J♠	10♦	A♥	K♠	8♠	2♥	6♣	9♦	7♣/J♣	5♦	6♠
	2♣	3♥	K♣	Q♣	8♥	4♦					
86	2♥	8♥	Q♣	4♦	5♠	2♠	10♦	9♥	8♣/4♦	3♣	9♠
	5♥	A♠	K♥	Q♣	8♠	10♦					
87	9♦	5♥	4♦	K♣	Q♠	8♣	10♠	10♥	7♣/3♠	K♦	K♥
	K♦	2♦	J♠	3♥	4♣	10♠					
88	6♠	6♦	10♣	10♥	9♠	K♦	K♣	K♥	K♥/4♥	7♠	2♠
	9♥	2♠	8♠	10♠	4♦	K♠					
89	8♥	9♥	10♥	J♥	Q♥	K♥	A♣	J♦	2♣/3♣	8♥	A♠
	10♠	3♠	9♦	2♦	8♣	A♣					
90	7♠	5♠	J♥	9♣	9♠	2♥	K♥	3♠	K♦/6♥	7♥	7♥
	3♥	4♥	Q♠	Q♦	6♦	K♥					
91	2♦	2♠	9♣	4♠	7♠	K♠	Q♣	A♠	2♥/10♦	A♠	8♥
	8♥	J♦	Q♠	6♥	J♥	Q♥	7♠				
92	9♠	6♣	10♥	Q♠	5♠	8♠	A♠	A♥	A♦/K♠	2♣	7♠
	J♣	8♦	3♦	J♥	9♣	J♠					
93	9♦	Q♦	3♥	4♥	8♣	J♣	Q♥	4♦	5♥/7♣	K♥	K♦
	9♥	2♥	4♣	4♦	6♥	Q♥					
94	5♣	9♠	4♦	8♥	10♣	5♥	7♠	7♣	2♣/2♠	9♠	3♠
	5♣	5♠	4♣	7♠	Q♥	2♦					
95	4♠	5♣	8♥	K♥	K♣	A♥	5♥	3♦	3♠/3♦	6♠	5♦
	Q♠	8♣	A♣	2♠	J♣	5♥					
96	9♠	8♠	3♥	5♣	J♦	Q♦	A♥	5♥	6♠/10♦	2♠	9♦
	2♣	6♥	K♦	3♦	10♣	6♦					
97	5♦	K♥	5♣	7♦	9♣	2♣	10♠	10♥	6♥/A♠	K♣	Q♦
	5♥	2♦	K♣	10♣	J♣	10♠					
98	6♣	8♠	7♦	9♦	J♥	5♥	A♥	J♥	2♥/A♦	8♠	3♦
	3♥	10♦	6♦	10♣	3♠	A♥					
99	8♥	J♠	J♦	8♣	4♣	10♥	9♦	9♦	Q♥/8♦	6♣	6♥
	5♦	10♠	J♣	10♦	K♥	6♠					

Eight of Hearts

AGE	MER	VEN	MAR	JUP	SAT	URA	NEP	LR	PLU/RES	ENV	DISP
0	6♣ / 7♠	6♠ / 3♠	Q♥ / 10♠	10♠ / 4♠	8♦ / J♥	K♠ / 10♠	3♥ / 8♦	6♣	A♣/Q♠	8♥	8♥
1	K♥ / J♦	8♠ / Q♠	J♣ / 6♥	10♠ / J♥	5♥ / Q♥	K♠ / 7♣	7♥	6♠	2♦/2♠	7♥	7♠
2	Q♥ / 7♦	3♦ / A♣	A♥ / 5♣	4♠ / 5♠	8♣ / 4♣	J♦ / 10♠	10♠	Q♥	4♦/8♦	A♠	K♦
3	10♥ / 5♥	7♠ / 9♦	4♠ / 5♠	7♠ / 8♦	J♠ / 10♠	4♦ / 6♣	K♦	10♣	A♠/6♠	2♣	3♣
4	10♣ / 10♦	5♥ / 8♣	7♠ / 2♥	2♣ / 6♠	2♠ / J♦	A♠ / 4♦	4♦	8♦	6♦/6♥	K♥	5♦
5	K♥ / A♠	K♣ / 4♣	A♥ / 3♠	5♥ / 6♥	3♠ / J♠	3♦ / 9♠	A♦	K♠	9♠/Q♠	9♠	9♠
6	9♦ / 4♦	2♣ / 6♣	5♥ / 2♠	9♥ / J♠	Q♥ / J♦	A♠ / 4♥	4♥	3♥	4♣/7♥	6♠	Q♦
7	8♠ / A♥	K♣ / Q♣	9♥ / 9♣	Q♦ / J♠	J♥ / 6♦	4♠ / A♠	A♠	K♥	A♣/2♦	2♠	3♦
8	7♠ / 9♦	7♣ / 4♥	3♠ / J♦	8♣ / Q♣	5♠ / 2♣	J♣ / 9♠	Q♦	8♠	10♠/Q♠	K♣	6♥
9	J♠ / J♥	J♦ / 4♦	8♣ / 6♦	4♠ / 8♠	10♥ / K♣	9♦ / 6♥	Q♥	J♣	8♦/4♠	8♠	4♣
10	2♣ / K♠	A♦ / J♠	2♦ / A♥	7♦ / 9♥	3♣ / 7♣	J♥ / 10♣	4♣	10♠	Q♣/2♥	6♣	5♣
11	K♣ / 4♦	Q♦ / 8♠	7♦ / 9♥	J♣ / 2♥	2♠ / 7♠	3♠ / 5♦	5♦	5♥	6♠/6♣	2♠	5♥
12	7♣ / 3♣	A♦ / 7♥	4♠ / 5♥	8♠ / 6♣	6♥ / 7♦	4♦ / A♣	J♠	K♣	K♠/9♠	A♦	4♦
13	J♥ / 3♠	Q♦ / 5♥	8♦ / J♠	A♣ / K♣	Q♠ / 6♣	2♦ / 7♠	9♠	7♥	K♥/10♠	A♥	5♠
14	J♣ / 6♠	4♥ / 7♥	6♠ / J♦	9♣ / 5♣	K♠ / 10♣	2♣ / 8♠	2♦	Q♦	3♣/9♥	3♥	10♥
15	6♣ / K♥	3♥ / 6♥	8♠ / A♥	4♦ / 9♥	7♠ / 2♥	3♦ / 2♠	2♣	3♦	4♠/Q♠	Q♣	J♠
16	Q♦ / A♦	K♥ / 3♠	4♥ / 8♣	10♦ / 2♥	9♣ / 8♦	4♠ / 5♦	5♦	A♥	6♥/5♥	10♦	J♦
17	7♦ / 4♦	4♣ / K♣	A♥ / J♥	5♥ / 5♦	A♠ / 5♣	A♦ / Q♠	10♦	4♣	J♠/Q♥	Q♠	3♠
18	9♦ / 4♠	K♥ / 7♣	5♥ / 5♠	6♦ / 5♦	10♥ / 5♦	J♣ / A♠	A♦	8♣	2♠/Q♣	8♦	6♦
19	10♠ / 8♠	A♣ / K♠	4♥ / J♦	Q♠ / 4♠	2♦ / 7♦	6♠ / 3♠	J♣	J♦	Q♦/8♦	7♣	9♠
20	5♦ / K♥	3♦ / 10♦	K♠ / 5♠	5♥ / 8♣	A♣ / 2♥	5♣ / 4♠	7♠	10♠	6♣/A♥	J♠	Q♥
21	2♦ / Q♦	3♥ / 10♠	4♥ / J♠	4♠ / K♥	9♥ / 6♥	K♣ / A♦	J♥	10♥	A♠/9♣	10♣	10♠
22	6♣ / Q♦	J♦ / 10♦	4♠ / K♥	5♠ / 9♠	3♠ / 4♥	A♠ / 4♠	K♦	7♦	9♦/K♠	4♠	4♥
23	8♠ / 10♣	Q♦ / 9♥	5♠ / 2♥	4♣ / 2♦	5♠ / K♠	Q♠ / A♠	A♠	4♣	J♠/6♠	4♥	4♠
24	3♣ / 10♥	K♠ / 7♣	3♦ / 10♠	A♣ / 6♠	Q♦ / 10♦	2♣ / 2♦	3♥ / Q♦	7♠	Q♠/9♣	10♠	10♣

AGE	MER	VEN	MAR	JUP	SAT	URA	NEP	LR	PLU/RES	ENV	DISP
25	8♣ / J♣	2♠ / 8♦	A♠ / 10♥	2♦ / 4♠	5♠ / 7♠	5♥ / 3♦	3♦	J♠	6♥/7♠	Q♥	J♠
26	4♠ / Q♦	K♦ / 7♥	2♦ / 10♥	10♣ / 7♣	Q♥ / 5♠	J♦ / 5♥	5♥	4♦	6♣/K♥	9♣	7♣
27	K♠ / 6♦	5♦ / 9♣	2♥ / 6♣	3♠ / K♦	6♠ / 8♦	Q♠ / J♥	J♠ / 6♠	K♦	J♦/3♠	6♦	8♦
28	A♥ / 4♠	4♥ / 6♣	6♠ / 5♠	10♥ / J♦	4♣ / 3♣	A♦ / 6♠	6♠	10♣	10♦/5♣	3♠	Q♠
29	3♦ / J♠	3♣ / J♥	5♦ / K♣	4♥ / A♠	8♠ / J♦	9♣ / 3♠	A♦	5♥	7♦/2♣	J♦	10♦
30	8♠ / 6♠	J♠ / 6♥	4♥ / Q♥	5♠ / 6♦	10♥ / 10♦	7♦ / 4♠	Q♠	7♠	J♥/2♦	J♣	Q♠
31	2♥ / 8♠	7♥ / 2♣	6♣ / Q♥	10♣ / A♥	10♠ / 5♣	4♦ / 5♠	5♠	2♠	9♥/8♦	10♥	3♥
32	7♠ / 2♠	9♣ / 6♥	10♣ / Q♥	J♦ / 3♦	Q♣ / 9♥	9♥ / 6♠	6♠	2♠	3♠/K♥	5♠	A♥
33	6♦ / 8♣	4♠ / A♠	J♠ / 5♠	10♦ / A♥	7♦ / Q♠	2♠ / J♦	J♦	A♦	9♠/8♦	4♦	A♠
34	8♠ / Q♣	8♠ / 10♠	10♦ / K♠	2♦ / 7♠	J♠ / 6♥	9♠ / 9♥	K♦	4♦	A♠/7♥	5♥	2♦
35	5♦ / 3♦	Q♣ / 7♦	2♦ / 7♠	K♠ / 7♥	K♠ / 10♦	K♥ / Q♥	2♥ / K♠	K♥	9♠/3♥	5♠	6♣
36	K♥ / A♠	2♠ / Q♠	J♣ / 9♣	Q♥ / K♠	4♠ / 7♥	7♠ / Q♦	9♥	K♣	6♣/5♣	4♠	8♠
37	10♣ / 2♦	Q♣ / 9♠	Q♥ / A♦	7♠ / 3♣	6♥ / J♣	A♠ / K♦	K♦	A♥	Q♠/A♥	6♥	K♣
38	3♦ / 4♦	2♣ / 5♣	7♠ / 10♠	8♦ / J♣	3♥ / Q♥	2♦ / K♣	K♠ / 3♥	5♥	2♠/A♠	3♦	2♠
39	7♣ / A♠	Q♣ / A♥	A♠ / 2♠	K♠ / 3♥	K♣ / 7♠	2♥ / 5♠	8♠	3♠	8♦/J♦	Q♦	6♠
40	2♥ / 4♦	7♠ / 7♥	3♦ / 2♣	5♠ / 3♥	10♥ / K♣	6♠ / Q♣	Q♣	3♦	8♣/4♠	9♠	9♠
41	Q♦ / 3♣	4♦ / 6♣	5♠ / 7♣	2♠ / A♥	10♦ / 5♠	8♣ / 4♥	4♦	A♦	8♦/6♦	5♦	K♥
42	9♣ / 9♥	9♠ / 6♠	J♠ / K♣	J♣ / 4♥	K♥ / 5♠	3♠ / K♠	2♠	9♦	2♣/4♠	3♠	2♠
43	7♠ / 4♥	9♦ / 6♦	J♣ / Q♦	J♥ / 6♣	10♠ / 8♠	2♣ / A♣	A♣	2♣	A♠/5♦	K♦	A♠
44	7♦ / A♥	10♠ / 4♠	J♥ / 10♦	Q♥ / 3♦	K♦ / 9♣	2♥ / 2♣	2♣	5♥	3♣/4♣	7♠	7♦
45	6♣ / 7♠	6♠ / 3♠	Q♥ / 10♦	10♣ / 4♣	8♦ / J♥	K♠ / 10♠	3♥ / 8♦	9♥	2♥/Q♣	8♥	8♥
46	K♥ / J♦	8♠ / Q♠	J♣ / 6♥	10♠ / J♥	5♥ / Q♥	K♠ / 7♣	7♥	Q♥	2♦/2♠	7♥	7♠
47	Q♦ / 9♥	3♦ / 2♥	A♥ / 5♣	4♠ / 5♠	8♣ / 4♣	J♦ / 10♠	10♠	A♠	4♦/8♦	A♠	K♦
48	10♥ / 5♥	9♠ / 9♦	4♠ / 5♣	7♠ / 8♦	J♠ / 10♠	4♦ / 6♣	K♦	4♥	A♠/6♠	2♣	3♣
49	10♣ / 10♦	5♥ / 8♣	7♠ / A♣	2♣ / 6♠	2♠ / J♦	A♦ / 4♦	4♦	8♠	6♦/6♥	K♥	5♦

AGE	MER	VEN	MAR	JUP	SAT	URA	NEP	LR	PLU/RES	ENV	DISP
50	K♥	K♣	A♥	5♥	3♠	3♦	A♦	K♣	9♠/Q♣	9♠	9♦
	A♠	4♣	3♣	6♥	J♠	9♣					
51	9♥	2♣	5♥	7♦	Q♥	A♠	4♥	9♥	4♣/7♦	6♠	Q♦
	4♦	6♣	2♠	J♠	J♦	4♥					
52	8♠	K♣	7♥	Q♦	J♥	4♦	A♦	Q♦	2♥/2♦	2♠	3♦
	A♥	Q♣	9♣	J♠	6♦	A♦					
53	7♠	7♣	3♠	8♣	5♣	J♣	Q♦	J♥	10♠/Q♠	K♣	6♥
	9♦	4♥	J♦	Q♣	2♣	9♠					
54	J♠	J♦	8♣	4♣	10♥	9♦	Q♥	4♦	8♦/4♠	8♠	4♣
	J♥	4♦	6♦	8♠	K♣	6♥					
55	2♣	A♣	2♦	9♥	3♣	J♥	4♣	A♣	Q♠/A♣	6♠	5♣
	K♠	J♠	A♥	7♦	7♣	10♣					
56	K♣	Q♦	9♥	J♣	2♠	3♠	5♦	7♠	6♠/6♣	2♦	5♥
	4♦	8♠	7♦	A♣	7♠	5♦					
57	7♣	A♦	4♠	8♦	6♥	4♦	J♣	7♠	K♠/9♣	A♦	4♦
	3♣	7♦	5♥	6♣	9♥	2♥					
58	J♥	Q♦	8♦	2♥	Q♠	2♦	9♠	3♠	K♥/10♠	A♥	5♠
	3♠	5♥	J♠	K♣	6♣	7♠					
59	J♣	4♥	6♦	9♣	K♣	2♣	2♦	8♣	3♠/7♦	3♥	10♥
	6♠	7♥	J♦	5♣	10♣	8♠					
60	6♣	3♥	8♣	4♥	7♠	3♦	2♠	5♠	4♠/Q♣	Q♣	J♠
	K♥	6♥	A♥	7♦	A♣	2♣					
61	Q♦	K♥	4♥	10♦	9♣	4♠	5♦	J♣	6♥/5♥	10♦	J♠
	A♦	3♠	8♣	A♣	8♦	5♦					
62	9♥	4♣	A♥	5♥	A♠	A♦	10♦	Q♦	J♠/Q♥	Q♠	3♠
	4♦	K♣	J♥	5♦	5♣	Q♠					
63	9♦	K♥	5♥	6♦	10♥	J♣	A♦	J♠	2♠/Q♣	8♦	6♦
	4♠	7♣	5♠	5♦	5♣	A♦					
64	10♠	2♥	4♥	Q♠	2♦	6♠	J♣	J♦	Q♦/8♣	7♣	9♣
	8♠	K♠	J♦	4♠	9♥	3♠					
65	5♦	3♦	K♠	5♥	2♥	5♠	7♠	8♠	6♠/A♥	J♠	Q♥
	K♥	10♦	5♠	8♣	A♣	4♠					
66	2♦	3♥	4♥	4♠	7♦	K♣	J♥	4♣	A♠/9♣	10♣	10♠
	Q♦	10♣	J♠	K♥	6♥	A♦					
67	6♣	J♦	4♠	5♠	3♠	A♠	K♦	10♥	9♦/K♠	4♠	4♥
	Q♦	10♦	K♥	9♣	4♥	4♣					
68	8♠	Q♦	5♠	4♣	5♣	Q♠	A♦	9♠	J♠/6♠	4♥	4♠
	10♣	7♦	A♣	2♦	K♣	A♦					
69	3♣	K♠	3♦	2♥	Q♦	2♣	3♥	Q♥	Q♠/9♣	10♠	10♣
	10♥	7♠	10♦	6♣	10♦	2♦	Q♦				
70	8♣	2♠	A♣	2♦	5♦	5♥	3♦	2♣	6♥/7♣	Q♥	J♠
	J♣	8♦	10♥	4♦	7♠	3♦					
71	4♠	K♦	2♦	10♣	Q♥	J♣	5♦	A♠	6♣/K♥	9♣	7♣
	Q♦	7♥	10♥	7♣	5♠	5♥					
72	K♠	5♦	A♣	3♣	6♠	Q♠	J♠	2♦	J♦/3♠	6♦	8♦
	6♦	9♣	6♣	K♦	8♦	J♥	6♠				
73	A♥	4♥	6♦	10♦	4♣	A♦	6♠	7♦	10♦/5♣	3♠	Q♠
	4♠	6♣	5♠	J♦	3♣	6♠					
74	3♦	3♣	5♦	4♥	8♣	9♣	A♦	3♣	9♥/2♣	J♦	10♦
	J♠	J♥	K♣	A♠	J♦	3♠					

AGE	MER	VEN	MAR	JUP	SAT	URA	NEP	LR	PLU/RES	ENV	DISP
75	8♠	J♠	4♥	5♠	10♥	9♥	Q♠	J♥	J♥/2♦	J♣	Q♣
	6♠	6♥	Q♥	6♦	10♦	4♠					
76	A♣	7♥	6♣	10♣	10♠	4♦	5♠	4♣	7♦/8♦	10♥	3♥
	8♠	2♣	Q♥	A♥	5♣	5♠					
77	7♠	9♣	10♣	J♦	Q♣	7♦	6♠	K♣	3♠/K♥	5♠	A♥
	2♠	6♥	Q♥	3♦	9♦	6♠					
78	6♦	4♠	J♠	10♦	9♥	2♠	J♦	Q♦	9♠/8♦	4♦	A♦
	8♣	2♥	5♠	A♥	Q♠	J♦					
79	8♠	8♠	10♦	2♦	J♠	9♠	K♦	7♦	A♠/7♥	5♥	2♦
	Q♣	10♠	K♠	7♠	6♥	7♦					
80	5♦	Q♣	2♦	K♣	K♠	K♥	A♣	J♠	9♠/3♥	5♣	6♣
	3♦	9♥	7♠	7♥	10♦	Q♥	K♠				
81	K♥	2♣	J♠	Q♥	4♦	7♣	7♦	2♠	6♣/5♠	4♣	8♠
	A♠	Q♠	9♠	K♠	7♥	Q♦					
82	10♣	Q♣	Q♥	7♠	6♥	A♠	K♦	3♠	Q♠/A♥	6♥	K♣
	2♦	9♠	A♦	3♣	J♠	K♦					
83	3♦	2♣	7♠	8♠	3♥	2♦	K♠	5♦	2♠/2♥	3♦	2♠
	4♦	5♣	10♠	J♣	Q♥	K♣	3♥				
84	7♣	Q♣	A♦	K♠	K♣	A♣	8♠	7♠	8♦/J♦	Q♦	6♠
	A♠	A♥	2♠	3♥	7♠	5♠					
85	A♣	7♠	3♦	5♠	10♥	6♠	Q♣	A♦	8♣/4♠	9♦	9♠
	4♦	7♥	2♣	3♥	K♣	Q♣					
86	Q♦	4♦	5♠	2♠	10♦	8♠	4♦	4♠	8♦/6♦	5♦	K♥
	3♣	6♣	7♣	A♥	5♣	4♦					
87	9♠	9♠	J♠	J♣	K♥	3♣	2♠	8♦	2♣/4♠	3♣	2♣
	7♥	6♠	K♣	4♥	5♠	K♠					
88	7♠	7♥	J♣	J♥	10♠	2♠	2♥	6♥	A♠/5♦	K♦	A♠
	4♥	6♦	Q♦	6♣	8♣	2♥					
89	9♥	10♥	J♥	Q♥	K♥	A♠	2♠	4♦	3♣/4♣	7♠	7♥
	A♥	4♠	10♦	3♦	9♣	2♠					
90	6♠	6♠	Q♥	10♣	8♦	K♠	3♥	J♣	A♣/Q♣	8♥	8♦
	7♠	3♠	10♦	4♣	J♥	10♠	8♦				
91	K♥	8♠	J♣	10♠	5♥	K♣	7♥	J♥	2♦/2♠	7♥	7♠
	J♦	Q♠	6♥	J♥	Q♥	7♣					
92	Q♦	3♦	A♥	4♠	8♣	J♦	10♠	Q♦	4♦/8♦	A♠	K♦
	7♦	A♣	5♠	5♠	4♣	10♠					
93	10♥	7♦	4♠	7♠	J♠	4♦	K♦	8♦	A♠/6♠	2♣	3♣
	5♥	9♦	5♣	8♦	10♠	6♠					
94	10♣	5♦	7♠	2♣	2♠	A♦	4♦	A♣	6♦/6♥	K♥	5♦
	10♦	8♣	2♥	6♠	J♦	4♦					
95	K♥	K♣	A♥	5♥	3♠	3♦	A♦	Q♠	9♠/Q♣	9♠	9♦
	A♠	4♣	3♣	6♥	J♠	9♣					
96	9♥	2♣	5♥	9♥	Q♥	A♠	4♥	2♦	4♣/7♥	6♠	Q♦
	4♦	6♣	2♠	J♠	J♦	4♥					
97	8♠	K♣	9♥	Q♦	J♥	4♦	A♦	9♠	A♣/2♦	2♠	3♦
	A♥	Q♣	9♣	J♠	6♦	A♦					
98	7♠	7♣	3♠	8♣	5♣	J♣	Q♦	J♣	10♠/Q♠	K♣	6♥
	9♦	4♥	J♦	Q♣	2♣	9♠					
99	J♠	J♦	8♣	4♣	10♥	9♦	Q♥	4♥	8♦/4♠	8♠	4♣
	J♥	4♦	6♦	8♠	K♣	6♥					

Nine of Hearts

AGE	MER	VEN	MAR	JUP	SAT	URA	NEP	LR	PLU/RES	ENV	DISP
0	7♣	5♦	Q♠	J♣	9♦	7♠	2♣	7♣	K♠/J♦		
	8♠	2♦	9♣	5♣	K♠	6♣					
1	4♦	J♥	6♦	6♠	A♣	9♠	7♠	5♦	3♦/6♥		
	2♥	5♥	10♥	5♣	4♥	7♠					
2	10♣	K♦	7♣	5♠	3♣	7♥	9♠	Q♠	6♣/10♥		
	2♦	A♥	3♣	6♥	K♠	A♦					
3	5♣	J♥	J♦	K♠	A♣	2♠	7♥	J♣	9♦/Q♠		
	2♥	4♣	4♦	6♥	Q♥	7♥					
4	4♥	8♥	10♣	5♥	7♠	2♣	2♠	9♦	A♦/4♦		
	A♥	Q♣	J♣	Q♦	K♠	3♥					
5	6♥	J♥	10♥	6♣	A♣	8♠	2♣	7♠	3♣/5♦		
	2♥	3♦	5♣	Q♦	6♦	2♣					
6	Q♥	A♠	4♥	4♣	7♥	9♠	8♠	2♣	3♥/5♣		
	Q♣	Q♠	5♣	5♦	K♠	10♦					
7	Q♦	J♥	4♦	A♣	A♣	2♦	9♠	4♦	7♠/K♦		
	2♥	9♦	6♥	5♦	J♦	A♠					
8	6♥	K♥	Q♥	3♦	2♣	2♠	2♦	J♥	10♦/6♥		
	Q♠	7♣	5♥	K♦	K♣	8♦					
9	5♦	J♥	5♣	3♥	A♣	A♥	2♠	6♦	7♥/8♥		
	2♥	3♣	Q♦	K♦	10♥	2♠					
10	J♦	6♠	6♦	9♦	9♠	8♠	A♥	6♠	8♦/Q♦		
	7♣	10♣	4♣	8♥	K♠	J♠					
11	K♦	J♥	6♥	10♦	A♣	Q♣	8♠	A♣	2♣/A♠		
	2♥	7♣	5♦	8♥	4♦	8♠					
12	10♥	K♣	J♦	3♣	2♠	2♦	Q♣	9♠	J♠/5♦		
	10♣	4♥	3♦	A♠	K♠	4♠					
13	8♥	J♥	Q♦	8♦	A♣	Q♠	2♦	7♠	9♠/K♥		
	2♥	7♥	K♦	A♠	5♣	2♦					
14	4♦	6♣	10♥	7♠	8♠	A♥	Q♠	10♣	4♠/K♦		
	4♥	Q♥	9♦	K♥	K♠	10♠					
15	A♠	J♥	5♦	J♠	A♣	7♣	A♥	K♦	2♠/6♠		
	2♥	2♣	8♥	K♥	6♥	A♥					
16	5♣	A♥	4♦	7♥	2♦	Q♣	7♣	7♣	10♠/8♥		
	Q♥	6♦	3♣	6♠	K♠	9♣					
17	K♥	J♥	K♦	4♠	A♣	10♠	Q♣	5♠	8♠/K♣		
	2♥	9♠	A♠	6♠	Q♦	Q♣					
18	6♥	3♥	5♣	2♣	A♥	Q♠	10♣	3♠	9♣/A♠		
	6♦	J♦	7♠	K♣	K♠	3♠					
19	6♠	J♥	8♥	10♠	A♣	4♥	Q♠	7♠	2♦/6♠		
	2♥	2♠	K♥	K♣	5♦	Q♠					
20	Q♦	10♦	6♥	9♠	Q♣	7♣	4♥	9♠	3♠/K♥		
	J♦	10♥	7♠	6♣	K♠	J♠					
21	K♣	J♥	A♠	9♣	A♠	Q♥	7♣	5♠	A♥/A♣		
	2♥	8♠	6♠	6♣	K♦	7♣					
22	5♦	8♦	Q♦	2♠	Q♠	10♣	Q♥	J♥	J♣/6♠		
	10♥	4♦	2♣	A♦	K♠	5♠					
23	6♣	J♥	K♥	3♠	A♣	6♦	10♣	J♦	Q♣/3♥		
	2♥	2♦	K♣	A♦	8♥	10♣					
24	K♦	J♠	5♦	8♠	7♣	4♥	6♦	K♣	5♠/K♣		
	4♦	5♣	9♠	3♥	K♠	5♥					

AGE	MER	VEN	MAR	JUP	SAT	URA	NEP	LR	PLU/RES	ENV	DISP
25	A♦	J♥	6♠	J♣	A♣	J♦	4♥	A♣	Q♠/10♦		
	2♥	A♥	6♣	3♥	A♠	4♥					
26	8♦	4♠	K♦	2♦	10♣	Q♥	J♦	2♠	5♥/6♣		
	5♣	6♥	2♠	10♦	K♠	4♣					
27	3♥	J♥	K♣	5♠	A♣	10♥	Q♥	7♥	7♣/8♦		
	2♥	Q♣	A♦	10♦	K♥	Q♥					
28	A♠	10♠	8♥	A♥	4♥	6♦	10♥	4♥	4♣/A♦		
	6♥	Q♦	8♠	8♦	A♠	3♦					
29	10♦	J♥	6♣	5♥	A♣	4♦	6♦	8♥	10♣/J♠		
	2♥	Q♠	3♥	8♦	6♠	6♦					
30	K♥	9♣	A♠	Q♣	Q♥	J♦	4♦	10♣	3♦/3♥		
	Q♦	5♦	2♦	J♠	K♠	9♦					
31	8♦	J♥	A♦	4♠	A♣	5♠	J♦	5♥	4♥/4♠		
	2♥	7♠	10♦	J♠	K♣	J♦					
32	6♠	3♠	K♥	Q♠	6♦	10♥	5♣	7♠	9♦/10♦		
	5♦	K♦	A♥	4♠	K♠	3♣					
33	J♠	J♥	3♥	3♦	A♣	6♥	10♥	2♠	Q♥/10♠		
	2♥	10♣	8♦	4♠	6♣	10♥					
34	K♣	J♠	6♠	7♣	J♦	4♦	6♥	2♠	3♣/8♦		
	K♦	8♥	Q♣	10♠	K♠	7♠					
35	4♠	J♥	10♦	9♦	A♣	Q♦	4♦	6♥	6♦/9♣		
	2♥	4♥	J♠	10♠	A♦	4♦					
36	6♣	5♠	K♣	10♣	10♥	5♣	Q♦	J♥	7♠/J♣		
	8♥	A♠	Q♣	9♣	K♠	7♥					
37	10♠	J♥	8♦	3♣	A♣	5♦	5♣	10♥	J♦/3♠		
	2♥	Q♥	4♦	9♣	3♥	5♣					
38	A♦	5♥	6♣	4♥	4♦	6♥	5♦	6♣	7♥/4♠		
	A♠	K♥	7♣	3♠	K♠	2♣					
39	9♣	J♥	J♠	7♠	A♣	K♦	6♥	A♣	10♥/J♣		
	2♥	6♦	10♠	3♠	10♦	6♥					
40	3♥	4♣	A♦	Q♥	5♣	Q♦	K♦	8♠	2♣/10♠		
	K♥	6♠	10♣	J♣	K♠	9♠					
41	3♠	J♥	4♠	7♥	A♣	8♥	Q♦	2♣	4♦/5♠		
	2♥	J♦	9♠	J♣	8♦	Q♦					
42	10♦	3♦	3♥	6♦	6♥	5♦	8♥	Q♥	9♠/9♣		
	6♠	K♣	4♥	5♠	K♠	2♠					
43	J♣	J♥	10♠	2♣	A♣	A♠	5♦	A♣	5♣/5♥		
	2♥	10♥	3♠	5♠	J♠	5♦					
44	8♦	9♦	10♦	J♦	Q♦	K♦	A♠	4♥	2♠/3♠		
	K♦	6♠	Q♥	5♦	K♠	8♠					
45	5♠	J♥	9♣	9♠	A♣	K♥	K♦	4♣	6♥/4♣		
	2♥	4♦	J♣	5♥	4♠	K♦					
46	J♠	3♣	8♦	10♥	5♦	8♥	K♥	7♦	8♠/J♣		
	6♣	A♦	6♦	4♣	K♠	2♦					
47	5♥	J♥	3♠	2♠	A♣	6♠	8♥	9♣	Q♦/3♦		
	2♥	5♣	5♠	4♣	10♠	8♥					
48	4♠	7♠	J♠	4♦	K♦	A♠	6♠	8♠	2♦/5♠		
	A♦	3♥	J♦	3♦	K♠	A♥					
49	4♣	J♥	J♣	8♠	A♣	K♦	A♠	Q♦	5♦/9♦		
	2♥	6♥	5♥	3♦	9♣	A♠					

AGE	MER	VEN	MAR	JUP	SAT	URA	NEP	LR	PLU/RES	ENV	DISP
50	10♠	7♥	4♠	5♣	8♥	K♥	K♣	J♥	A♥/5♥		
	3♥	10♦	10♥	9♦	K♠	Q♣					
51	3♦	J♥	5♠	2♦	A♣	6♣	K♥	4♦	K♦/3♣		
	2♥	Q♦	4♣	9♦	3♠	K♥					
52	9♣	2♠	10♠	6♥	A♠	6♠	6♣	A♦	Q♣/4♣		
	10♦	8♦	4♦	3♣	K♠	Q♠					
53	9♣	J♥	5♥	A♥	A♣	A♦	6♠	A♣	8♥/7♠		
	2♥	5♦	3♦	3♣	J♣	6♠					
54	3♠	9♠	9♣	Q♦	K♥	K♣	A♦	2♦	Q♠/3♦		
	8♦	J♠	5♣	7♠	K♣	7♣					
55	3♣	J♥	4♣	Q♣	A♣	3♥	K♣	9♠	A♠/7♥		
	2♥	K♦	9♦	7♠	5♠	K♣					
56	J♥	2♠	3♠	5♦	6♠	6♣	3♥	6♦	7♣/9♦		
	J♠	4♠	6♥	7♥	K♠	10♣					
57	7♠	J♥	3♦	Q♠	A♣	10♦	6♣	K♥	K♥/2♣		
	2♥	8♥	3♣	7♥	5♥	6♣					
58	5♠	8♠	J♣	K♦	K♣	A♦	10♦	Q♥	10♣/3♣		
	4♠	10♠	Q♦	2♣	K♠	4♥					
59	7♥	J♥	9♦	7♠	A♣	8♦	A♦	3♦	6♠/9♠		
	2♥	A♠	7♠	2♣	4♣	A♦					
60	5♥	2♠	5♠	8♥	6♣	3♥	8♦	2♣	4♥/7♠		
	10♠	9♣	5♦	9♠	K♠	Q♥					
61	2♣	J♥	3♣	10♣	A♣	J♠	3♥	2♠	K♣/2♠		
	2♥	K♥	7♥	9♠	3♦	3♥					
62	4♣	A♥	5♥	A♠	A♦	10♦	J♠	2♦	Q♥/7♥		
	9♣	3♠	K♦	2♠	K♠	6♦					
63	9♠	J♥	7♠	4♥	A♣	4♠	10♦	5♦	6♣/8♠		
	2♥	6♠	2♣	2♠	9♦	10♦					
64	3♦	Q♣	4♣	K♥	3♥	8♦	4♠	J♥	6♦/2♣		
	3♠	J♣	8♥	8♠	K♠	J♦					
65	2♠	J♥	7♥	Q♥	A♣	10♠	8♦	5♠	A♦/2♦		
	2♥	K♣	9♠	8♠	3♣	8♦					
66	9♦	Q♠	3♦	6♠	10♦	J♠	10♠	3♥	J♦/9♠		
	J♣	5♠	A♠	2♦	K♠	10♥					
67	8♠	J♥	2♣	6♦	A♣	9♣	J♠	A♣	3♥/A♥		
	2♥	6♣	2♠	2♦	7♠	J♠					
68	3♣	7♣	9♦	K♣	8♦	4♠	9♣	A♥	10♥/2♠		
	5♠	5♥	K♥	A♥	K♠	4♦					
69	2♦	J♥	9♠	J♦	A♣	3♠	4♠	2♠	10♦/Q♣		
	2♥	A♦	8♠	A♥	7♥	4♠					
70	7♠	10♣	3♣	6♣	J♠	10♠	3♠	J♦	4♦/8♠		
	5♥	4♣	6♠	Q♣	K♠	5♣					
71	A♥	J♥	2♠	10♥	A♣	J♣	10♠	6♠	8♦/Q♠		
	2♥	3♥	2♦	Q♣	2♣	10♠					
72	7♥	4♥	7♠	A♦	4♠	9♣	J♣	6♦	5♣/2♦		
	4♣	3♦	K♣	Q♠	K♠	6♥					
73	Q♣	J♥	8♠	4♦	A♣	5♠	9♣	9♦	J♠/7♣		
	2♥	10♦	A♥	Q♠	9♠	9♠					
74	2♣	Q♥	7♥	3♥	10♠	3♠	5♠	9♠	6♥/A♥		
	3♦	9♦	6♣	7♣	K♠	Q♦					

AGE	MER	VEN	MAR	JUP	SAT	URA	NEP	LR	PLU/RES	ENV	DISP
75	Q♠	J♥	2♦	5♣	A♣	5♥	3♠	8♠	4♠/10♣		
	2♥	8♦	Q♣	7♣	2♠	3♠					
76	9♥	6♠	2♣	10♦	9♣	J♣	5♥	A♥	Q♦/Q♣		
	9♦	3♣	A♦	10♣	K♠	5♦					
77	7♣	J♥	A♥	6♥	A♣	4♣	J♣	K♦	10♠/4♥		
	2♥	J♠	Q♠	10♣	8♠	J♣					
78	2♠	J♥	9♠	8♦	3♠	5♠	4♣	J♥	5♦/Q♠		
	3♣	7♠	3♥	4♥	K♠	K♦					
79	10♣	J♥	Q♣	Q♦	A♣	3♦	5♠	6♥	9♣/Q♥		
	2♥	4♠	7♣	4♦	2♠	5♠					
80	8♠	10♥	2♠	J♠	J♣	5♥	3♦	10♦	K♦/7♣		
	7♠	7♥	10♦	Q♥	K♠	8♦					
81	4♥	J♥	Q♠	5♦	A♣	9♦	5♥	A♠	3♠/6♦		
	2♥	10♠	10♠	Q♥	A♥	5♥					
82	2♦	4♠	8♠	4♠	5♠	4♣	9♦	Q♣	8♥/10♣		
	7♥	2♣	8♦	6♦	K♠	A♠					
83	Q♥	J♥	7♣	K♦	A♣	3♣	4♠	8♠	J♣/J♦		
	2♥	9♣	4♥	6♦	Q♣	4♠					
84	A♥	5♠	2♦	10♠	5♥	3♦	3♣	10♥	A♠/4♥		
	2♣	9♠	J♠	J♦	K♠	K♥					
85	6♦	J♥	10♠	8♥	A♣	7♠	3♦	K♣	5♠/10♥		
	2♥	3♠	Q♥	J♦	Q♠	3♦					
86	Q♣	6♥	A♥	9♣	4♠	9♦	7♠	J♦	K♥/Q♠		
	9♠	2♠	4♠	10♥	K♠	6♠					
87	J♦	J♥	4♥	A♠	A♣	7♥	9♦	3♣	5♥/4♠		
	2♥	J♣	6♦	10♥	7♣	9♦					
88	Q♠	Q♦	Q♣	3♠	3♦	3♣	7♥	2♠	6♠/6♦		
	2♠	8♠	10♠	4♦	K♠	K♣					
89	10♥	J♥	Q♥	K♥	A♣	2♣	3♣	2♦	4♣/5♣		
	2♥	5♠	J♦	4♦	10♣	3♠					
90	7♣	5♥	Q♣	J♠	9♦	7♠	2♣	Q♣	K♣/J♦		
	8♠	2♦	9♣	5♣	K♠	6♠					
91	4♦	J♥	6♦	6♠	A♣	9♠	7♠	8♥	3♦/6♥		
	2♥	5♥	10♥	5♣	4♥	7♠					
92	10♣	K♦	7♠	5♠	3♣	7♥	9♠	J♥	6♣/10♥		
	2♦	A♥	3♠	6♥	K♠	A♦					
93	5♣	J♥	J♦	K♣	A♣	2♠	7♥	Q♦	9♦/Q♣		
	2♥	4♣	4♦	6♥	Q♥	7♥					
94	4♥	8♥	10♣	5♦	7♠	2♠	2♠	8♠	A♦/4♣		
	A♥	Q♣	J♣	Q♦	K♠	3♥					
95	6♥	J♥	10♥	6♣	A♣	8♠	2♣	A♠	3♣/5♦		
	2♥	3♦	5♠	Q♦	6♦	2♣					
96	Q♥	A♠	4♥	4♠	7♥	9♠	8♠	Q♠	3♥/5♣		
	Q♣	Q♠	5♠	5♠	K♠	10♠					
97	Q♦	J♥	4♦	A♦	A♣	2♦	9♠	2♦	7♠/K♦		
	2♥	9♦	6♥	5♦	J♦	9♠					
98	6♦	K♥	Q♥	3♦	2♠	2♠	2♦	4♦	10♦/6♥		
	Q♠	7♠	5♥	K♦	K♠	8♦					
99	5♦	J♥	5♠	3♥	A♣	A♥	2♠	6♠	7♥/8♥		
	2♥	3♣	Q♦	K♦	10♥	2♠					

Ten of Hearts

AGE	MER	VEN	MAR	JUP	SAT	URA	NEP	LR	PLU/RES	ENV	DISP
0	10♦	8♠	A♥	A♠	Q♦	5♥	3♣	10♦	3♠/9♦	10♥	10♥
	6♥	5♣	Q♣	10♠	2♠	9♦					
1	5♦	8♥	K♥	8♠	J♣	10♠	5♥	8♠	K♣/7♥	5♠	J♣
	5♣	4♥	7♠	9♥	2♥	5♥					
2	Q♥	5♣	8♠	A♠	A♦	K♣	6♦	A♥	4♥/J♠	4♦	J♦
	K♦	3♥	8♣	2♥	K♥	6♦					
3	7♥	4♠	7♠	J♠	4♦	K♦	A♠	A♦	6♠/2♦	5♥	3♠
	7♠	Q♦	J♥	6♦	10♣	2♣					
4	9♣	5♣	J♠	A♥	Q♠	10♦	K♦	Q♥	3♦/7♥	5♣	6♦
	K♣	9♠	8♦	6♥	10♣	K♦					
5	6♣	A♣	8♠	2♣	3♣	5♦	10♦	5♥	Q♥/8♣	4♣	9♣
	9♦	K♣	Q♣	K♣	7♦	3♥					
6	6♦	10♠	K♠	J♠	A♣	10♣	J♣	3♣	5♦/7♣	6♥	Q♥
	5♣	A♣	8♦	8♣	2♥	K♣					
7	3♣	8♥	8♠	K♣	9♥	Q♦	J♥	5♦	4♦/A♦	3♦	10♠
	Q♥	2♣	6♠	5♠	4♥	K♦					
8	5♦	Q♣	K♣	8♠	3♥	4♦	J♦	8♥	9♣/K♠	Q♦	4♥
	Q♥	A♠	5♣	A♦	8♠	4♠					
9	9♦	Q♥	8♦	4♠	10♣	2♣	K♦	K♥	6♠/6♥	9♦	4♠
	2♠	9♥	2♥	3♣	Q♦	K♦					
10	3♠	K♠	10♠	A♣	Q♥	5♥	8♥	8♠	2♣/A♦	5♦	10♣
	Q♠	9♠	2♠	5♦	A♠	3♣	Q♥				
11	8♣	3♦	4♦	3♣	6♦	J♠	10♠	J♣	4♥/9♠	3♣	J♠
	10♦	K♥	Q♠	7♠	J♠	10♠					
12	K♣	J♦	3♣	2♠	2♦	Q♣	J♠	10♠	5♦/5♣	K♦	7♠
	Q♥	5♠	Q♠	9♠	8♦	J♠					
13	K♠	6♦	2♥	3♠	6♥	2♣	6♠	5♥	Q♣/3♥	7♠	8♦
	A♥	A♦	5♦	J♦	K♥	J♥	6♥				
14	7♠	8♠	A♥	Q♠	4♠	K♦	6♥	Q♥	A♠/10♣	8♥	Q♠
	K♣	5♦	8♦	Q♣	3♠	6♥					
15	10♠	3♠	6♦	8♠	K♥	A♠	K♦	5♣	7♦/5♥	7♥	10♦
	6♠	J♥	Q♦	4♦	2♦	3♦					
16	9♦	6♠	8♠	8♦	Q♠	7♦	2♣	8♠	J♥/3♠	A♠	Q♣
	6♥	4♥	2♦	A♥	A♠	K♣					
17	2♥	5♠	5♦	2♠	6♠	7♠	8♦	A♠	9♥/K♥	2♣	3♥
	9♥	5♥	2♦	7♠	10♠	8♦					
18	J♣	A♦	2♠	Q♣	7♥	9♥	6♥	A♦	3♥/5♣	K♥	A♥
	3♦	4♥	2♦	10♠	9♦	6♥					
19	A♥	K♣	10♦	A♠	7♦	3♦	Q♣	K♣	4♣/K♥	9♠	A♦
	8♣	A♣	10♣	7♠	2♣	Q♣					
20	9♦	8♣	A♠	3♣	6♠	4♣	J♦	6♦	4♦/5♠	6♠	2♦
	7♥	6♣	K♠	J♠	4♥	9♥					
21	6♦	7♥	3♣	Q♦	K♠	5♠	2♥	7♦	4♣/8♥	2♠	6♠
	10♠	7♥	J♣	5♠	A♠	2♦	K♠				
22	5♣	5♥	10♣	2♦	7♥	9♠	9♥	4♠	5♦/8♦	K♣	8♠
	4♦	2♣	A♦	K♠	5♠	Q♥					
23	2♠	7♥	2♦	J♠	4♥	4♦	J♦	7♠	2♣/7♠	8♠	K♣
	3♣	4♣	K♦	3♠	10♦	J♦					
24	10♠	5♥	J♣	K♥	8♥	3♣	K♠	J♠	3♦/A♣	6♣	2♠
	7♣	10♣	6♠	10♦	2♦	Q♦	8♥				
25	9♠	7♥	K♦	K♠	Q♦	2♥	9♦	4♦	K♥/Q♣	2♦	6♠
	4♠	7♠	3♦	8♥	J♣	8♦					
26	2♥	J♣	10♠	8♦	Q♠	6♥	7♥	K♦	8♣/K♣	A♦	9♠
	7♣	5♠	5♥	8♥	Q♦	7♥					
27	Q♥	7♥	8♠	3♦	A♠	8♠	8♠	A♠	K♥/A♥	A♥	K♥
	3♠	5♥	9♠	7♠	10♣	8♠					
28	4♠	A♦	6♠	10♦	5♠	3♠	3♦	9♣	5♥/K♣	3♥	2♠
	9♥	6♥	Q♦	8♠	8♦	K♠					
29	J♣	9♥	10♦	J♥	6♣	5♥	A♣	5♠	4♦/6♦	Q♣	A♠
	8♠	A♥	Q♥	5♦	8♣	A♣					
30	7♦	Q♠	J♥	2♦	5♠	2♥	5♥	J♠	3♠/4♠	10♦	7♥
	7♠	K♣	A♠	10♠	A♦	5♥					
31	5♦	6♥	2♦	2♠	K♥	K♠	8♥	A♥	2♥/7♥	Q♠	8♥
	J♣	3♥	A♠	4♠	J♥	6♣	K♥				
32	5♠	9♥	10♦	6♠	J♠	Q♦	5♠	Q♠	3♣/3♦	8♦	7♠
	Q♣	2♠	4♥	J♥	2♦	9♠					
33	Q♥	10♠	7♠	K♠	8♣	Q♣	6♠	10♦	7♣/K♥	7♣	K♦
	9♥	2♥	10♣	8♦	4♠	6♣					
34	Q♠	9♥	K♣	J♠	6♠	7♣	J♦	K♦	4♦/6♦	A♠	3♣
	J♠	9♣	10♠	K♥	6♠	5♦					
35	2♠	J♠	J♣	5♥	3♦	K♦	7♣	6♣	A♥/4♥	10♣	5♦
	A♠	8♣	A♣	6♥	Q♣	7♣					
36	5♣	Q♦	7♠	J♠	3♥	10♠	K♦	A♣	4♣/7♥	4♠	9♣
	4♦	4♠	3♠	4♥	6♠	A♦					
37	9♣	5♥	J♠	7♦	2♦	4♦	8♠	8♠	4♠/5♠	4♥	Q♦
	7♣	5♦	3♦	6♠	Q♣	8♠					
38	9♦	Q♥	7♠	Q♥	J♥	7♠	K♦	2♣	2♥/3♣	10♠	3♦
	7♠	7♥	A♠	6♠	A♥	K♣					
39	J♣	9♠	3♥	8♣	10♥	10♦	Q♥	3♣	6♣/2♣	Q♥	6♥
	9♣	8♠	Q♣	7♥	5♥	4♠					
40	6♠	Q♣	8♠	4♠	Q♠	9♣	2♦	5♠	K♥/K♣	9♣	4♣
	J♥	7♣	A♥	9♦	Q♦	4♥					
41	5♥	K♦	3♣	9♥	3♠	J♥	4♠	10♦	7♥/A♣	6♦	5♣
	K♠	6♠	7♠	7♦	9♠	2♠					
42	Q♦	Q♥	9♥	10♦	3♦	3♥	6♦	6♦	6♥/5♦	3♠	5♥
	7♦	9♦	7♦	A♣	J♠	6♦					
43	9♠	K♦	K♣	K♥	4♥	7♠	10♦	10♠	K♠/A♦	J♦	4♦
	3♠	5♠	J♠	5♦	9♥	2♦					
44	J♥	Q♥	K♦	2♥	2♠	3♠	4♣	K♠	5♦/6♠	J♣	5♠
	3♥	J♠	6♠	Q♦	5♦	J♠					
45	10♦	8♠	A♥	A♠	Q♦	5♥	3♣	J♠	3♠/7♦	10♥	10♥
	6♥	5♣	Q♣	10♠	2♠	9♦					
46	5♦	8♥	K♥	8♠	J♣	10♠	5♥	A♣	K♣/7♥	5♠	J♠
	5♣	4♥	7♠	7♦	A♠	5♥					
47	Q♥	5♣	8♠	A♠	A♦	K♣	6♦	10♣	4♥/J♠	4♦	J♦
	K♦	3♥	8♣	A♠	K♥	6♦					
48	9♥	4♠	7♠	J♠	4♦	K♦	A♠	J♣	6♠/2♦	5♥	3♠
	7♠	Q♦	J♥	6♦	10♣	2♣					
49	9♣	5♣	J♠	A♥	Q♠	10♦	K♦	3♣	3♦/7♥	5♠	6♦
	K♣	9♠	8♦	6♦	10♣	K♦					

AGE	MER	VEN	MAR	JUP	SAT	URA	NEP	LR	PLU/RES	ENV	DISP
50	6♣	2♥	8♠	2♣	3♠	5♦	10♦	8♥	Q♥/8♣	4♣	9♣
	9♦	K♠	Q♣	K♣	9♥	3♥					
51	6♦	10♠	K♣	J♠	2♥	10♣	J♣	8♠	5♦/7♠	6♥	Q♥
	5♣	A♠	8♦	8♣	A♣	K♣					
52	3♣	8♥	8♠	K♣	7♥	Q♦	J♥	K♣	4♦/A♦	3♦	10♠
	Q♥	2♠	6♠	5♣	4♥	K♦					
53	5♦	Q♣	K♣	8♣	3♥	4♦	J♦	9♥	9♣/K♠	Q♦	4♥
	Q♥	A♠	5♣	A♦	8♠	4♠					
54	9♦	Q♥	8♣	4♠	10♣	2♣	K♦	Q♦	6♠/6♥	9♦	4♠
	2♠	7♦	A♣	3♣	Q♦	K♦					
55	3♠	K♠	10♠	2♥	Q♥	5♥	8♥	J♥	2♣/A♦	5♦	10♣
	Q♠	9♠	2♠	5♠	A♠	3♣	Q♥				
56	8♣	3♦	4♦	3♣	6♦	J♠	10♠	5♦	4♥/9♠	3♣	J♠
	10♦	K♥	Q♠	7♣	J♣	10♠					
57	K♣	J♦	3♣	2♠	2♦	Q♣	J♠	Q♣	5♦/5♣	K♦	7♣
	Q♥	5♠	Q♠	9♠	8♦	J♠					
58	K♠	6♦	A♣	3♠	6♥	2♣	6♠	K♣	Q♣/3♥	7♠	8♦
	A♥	A♦	5♦	J♦	K♥	J♥	6♥				
59	7♠	8♠	A♥	Q♠	4♠	K♦	6♥	8♦	A♠/10♣	8♥	Q♠
	K♣	5♦	8♦	Q♣	3♠	6♥					
60	10♠	3♠	6♦	8♠	K♥	A♠	K♦	3♥	9♥/5♦	7♥	10♦
	6♠	J♥	Q♦	4♣	Q♣	3♥					
61	9♦	6♠	8♠	8♦	Q♠	9♥	2♣	4♦	J♦/3♣	A♠	Q♣
	6♥	4♥	2♦	A♥	A♠	K♣					
62	A♣	5♠	5♦	2♠	6♣	7♠	8♦	J♦	7♦/K♥	2♣	3♥
	9♦	5♥	2♦	7♠	10♣	8♦					
63	J♣	A♦	2♠	Q♣	7♥	7♦	6♥	9♦	3♥/5♣	K♥	A♥
	3♦	4♥	2♦	10♠	9♣	6♥					
64	A♥	K♣	10♦	A♠	9♥	3♦	Q♣	Q♥	4♣/K♥	9♠	A♦
	8♣	2♥	10♣	7♠	2♣	Q♣					
65	9♦	8♣	A♠	3♠	6♠	4♠	J♦	8♦	4♦/5♠	6♠	2♦
	7♥	6♣	K♠	J♠	4♥	7♦					
66	6♦	7♥	3♣	Q♦	K♠	5♣	A♣	4♠	4♣/8♥	2♠	6♣
	10♠	9♥	J♣	5♠	A♠	2♦	K♠				
67	5♣	5♥	10♦	2♦	7♠	9♠	7♦	10♣	5♦/8♦	K♣	8♠
	4♦	2♣	A♦	K♠	5♠	Q♥					
68	2♠	7♥	2♦	J♣	4♥	4♦	J♦	2♣	2♣/7♠	8♠	K♣
	3♣	4♣	K♦	3♠	10♦	J♦					
69	10♠	5♥	J♣	K♥	8♥	3♣	K♠	K♦	3♦/2♥	6♣	2♣
	7♣	10♣	6♠	10♦	2♦	Q♦	8♥				
70	9♠	7♥	K♦	K♣	Q♦	A♠	9♦	3♠	K♥/Q♣	2♦	6♣
	4♦	7♠	3♦	8♥	J♣	8♦					
71	A♣	J♣	10♠	8♦	Q♠	6♥	7♦	K♠	8♣/K♣	A♦	9♣
	7♠	5♣	5♥	8♥	Q♦	7♥					
72	Q♥	7♣	8♦	3♦	A♠	8♣	8♠	10♠	K♥/A♥	A♥	K♥
	3♠	5♦	9♠	7♠	10♣	8♠					
73	4♣	A♦	6♠	10♦	5♠	3♠	3♦	A♣	5♥/K♣	3♥	2♣
	7♠	6♥	Q♦	8♠	8♦	K♠					
74	J♣	7♦	10♦	J♥	6♣	5♥	2♥	Q♥	4♦/6♥	Q♣	A♠
	8♠	A♥	Q♥	5♦	8♣	2♥					

AGE	MER	VEN	MAR	JUP	SAT	URA	NEP	LR	PLU/RES	ENV	DISP
75	9♥	Q♠	J♥	2♦	5♠	A♠	5♥	5♥	3♠/4♠	10♦	7♥
	7♠	K♣	A♠	10♠	A♦	5♥					
76	5♦	6♥	2♦	2♠	K♥	K♠	8♥	8♥	A♣/7♥	Q♠	8♥
	J♣	3♥	A♠	4♠	J♥	6♣	K♥				
77	5♣	9♦	10♦	6♣	J♠	Q♦	5♠	8♣	3♣/3♦	8♦	7♠
	Q♣	2♣	4♥	J♥	2♦	9♠					
78	Q♥	10♠	7♠	K♣	8♣	Q♠	6♣	3♦	7♣/K♦	7♠	K♣
	7♦	A♣	10♣	8♦	4♠	6♠					
79	Q♠	7♦	K♣	J♣	6♠	7♣	J♦	4♦	4♦/6♥	J♠	3♣
	J♠	9♣	10♠	K♥	6♣	5♦					
80	2♠	J♠	J♣	5♥	3♥	K♦	7♣	3♣	A♥/4♥	10♠	5♦
	A♠	8♣	2♥	6♥	Q♣	7♣					
81	5♣	Q♦	7♠	J♠	3♥	10♠	K♦	6♦	4♣/7♥	4♠	9♥
	4♦	4♠	3♠	4♥	6♠	A♦					
82	9♣	5♥	J♠	9♥	2♦	4♦	8♠	J♠	4♠/5♠	4♥	Q♦
	7♠	5♦	3♦	6♠	Q♣	8♠					
83	9♦	Q♦	9♥	Q♥	J♥	7♣	K♦	10♠	A♣/3♣	10♠	3♦
	7♠	7♥	A♦	6♠	A♥	K♦					
84	J♠	9♠	3♥	8♣	10♥	10♦	Q♥	K♣	6♠/2♣	Q♥	6♥
	9♣	8♠	Q♣	7♥	5♦	4♠					
85	6♠	Q♣	8♠	4♣	Q♠	9♠	2♠	J♦	K♥/K♣	9♣	4♠
	J♥	7♣	A♥	9♦	Q♦	4♥					
86	5♥	K♦	3♣	7♦	3♠	J♥	4♠	3♣	7♥/2♥	6♦	5♣
	K♠	6♠	7♠	9♥	9♣	2♠					
87	Q♦	Q♥	7♦	10♦	3♦	3♥	6♦	2♠	6♥/5♦	3♠	5♥
	7♣	9♦	9♥	2♥	J♣	6♦					
88	9♠	K♦	K♣	K♥	4♥	7♠	10♦	2♦	K♣/A♦	J♠	4♦
	3♠	5♠	J♠	5♦	7♠	A♣					
89	J♥	Q♥	K♥	A♣	2♠	3♠	4♣	Q♠	5♣/6♣	J♣	5♠
	3♥	J♠	6♠	Q♦	5♦	J♣					
90	10♦	8♠	A♥	A♦	Q♦	5♥	3♣	J♠	3♠/9♥	10♥	10♥
	6♥	5♠	Q♣	10♣	9♠	9♦					
91	5♦	8♥	K♥	8♠	J♣	10♠	5♥	K♠	K♣/7♥	5♠	J♣
	5♣	4♥	7♠	9♥	2♥	5♥					
92	Q♥	5♣	8♠	A♠	A♦	K♣	6♦	6♦	4♥/J♠	4♦	J♦
	K♦	3♥	8♣	2♥	K♥	6♦					
93	7♠	4♠	7♠	J♠	4♦	K♦	A♠	2♥	6♠/2♦	5♥	3♠
	7♣	Q♦	J♥	6♦	10♣	2♣					
94	9♣	5♣	J♠	A♥	Q♠	10♦	K♦	3♠	3♦/7♥	5♣	6♦
	K♣	9♠	8♦	6♦	10♣	K♦					
95	6♣	A♣	8♠	2♣	3♠	5♦	10♦	6♥	Q♥/8♣	4♣	9♣
	9♦	K♠	Q♣	K♣	7♦	3♥					
96	6♦	10♠	K♣	J♠	A♣	10♠	J♣	2♠	5♦/7♠	6♥	Q♥
	5♣	A♠	8♦	8♣	2♥	K♣					
97	3♣	8♥	8♠	K♣	9♥	Q♦	J♥	6♠	4♦/A♦	3♦	10♠
	Q♥	2♠	6♠	5♣	4♥	K♦					
98	5♦	Q♣	K♣	8♣	3♥	4♦	J♦	7♠	9♣/K♠	Q♦	4♥
	Q♥	A♠	5♣	A♦	8♠	4♠					
99	9♦	Q♥	8♠	4♠	10♣	2♣	K♦	8♠	6♠/6♥	9♦	4♠
	2♠	9♥	2♥	3♣	Q♦	K♦					

Jack of Hearts

AGE	MER	VEN	MAR	JUP	SAT	URA	NEP	LR	PLU/RES	ENV	DISP
0	9♣	9♠	2♥	K♥	K♦	6♥	4♠	9♣	2♦/J♠		
	10♠	8♦	8♥	7♠	3♠	10♦					
1	6♦	6♠	A♣	9♠	7♠	3♦	6♥	9♠	A♦/10♣		
	Q♥	7♣	7♥	8♥	J♦	Q♠					
2	3♠	2♠	2♥	6♠	8♥	Q♦	3♦	2♥	A♥/4♠		
	9♣	J♠	A♠	7♥	J♣	8♦					
3	J♦	K♠	A♣	2♠	7♥	9♦	Q♦	K♥	3♥/4♥		
	6♠	10♣	2♣	A♠	10♥	7♣					
4	J♣	8♠	2♥	K♣	A♠	5♦	9♦	K♦	Q♣/10♠		
	3♠	4♠	K♥	2♣	5♠	J♠					
5	10♥	6♣	A♣	8♠	2♣	3♣	5♦	6♥	10♦/Q♥		
	J♠	4♥	9♠	K♥	4♦	10♣					
6	5♠	2♦	2♥	6♣	K♥	K♦	3♣	4♣	Q♠/9♣		
	J♣	10♠	6♠	9♠	5♥	4♠					
7	4♠	A♦	A♣	2♦	9♠	7♠	K♦	6♦	8♦/6♦		
	10♥	Q♥	2♠	6♠	5♣	4♥					
8	5♥	A♥	2♥	A♦	6♠	8♥	7♠	6♠	7♣/3♠		
	5♠	9♣	K♠	2♠	4♣	10♠					
9	5♣	3♥	A♣	A♥	2♠	7♥	8♥	A♣	J♠/J♦		
	4♦	6♦	8♠	K♣	6♥	Q♥					
10	4♣	Q♣	2♥	3♥	K♣	A♠	7♥	9♠	10♣/J♣		
	5♥	3♠	6♣	8♠	3♦	9♣					
11	6♥	10♦	A♣	Q♣	8♠	2♣	A♠	7♠	4♠/10♥		
	5♣	J♦	2♣	6♣	Q♥	6♦					
12	3♦	Q♠	2♥	10♦	6♣	K♥	2♣	3♦	4♥/5♠		
	4♣	J♣	A♦	2♦	9♦	3♠					
13	Q♦	8♦	A♣	Q♠	2♠	9♠	K♥	6♦	10♠/4♦		
	6♥	10♥	A♥	A♦	5♦	J♦					
14	9♦	7♦	2♥	8♦	A♦	6♠	9♠	3♠	Q♥/5♥		
	3♦	5♠	3♥	A♥	3♣	J♣					
15	5♦	J♠	A♣	7♠	A♥	2♠	6♠	2♠	9♣/5♠		
	Q♦	4♦	Q♣	3♥	K♦	10♥					
16	3♣	10♣	2♥	J♠	3♥	K♣	2♠	2♥	6♦/4♠		
	9♦	5♥	10♦	Q♣	7♠	5♠					
17	K♦	4♠	A♣	10♦	Q♣	8♠	K♣	6♠	3♠/6♥		
	5♦	5♠	Q♠	10♦	8♥	4♦					
18	7♠	4♥	2♥	4♠	10♦	6♣	8♠	8♥	J♦/3♥		
	3♣	4♣	8♦	Q♠	7♥	5♥					
19	8♥	10♠	A♣	4♥	Q♠	2♦	6♣	Q♦	J♣/Q♠		
	K♦	6♥	7♠	8♦	A♠	5♠					
20	7♥	Q♥	2♥	10♠	8♦	A♦	2♠	3♦	10♥/9♦		
	7♠	3♦	J♠	7♥	2♣	4♣					
21	A♠	9♠	A♣	Q♥	7♠	A♥	A♦	J♦	5♠/5♦		
	8♥	Q♦	10♣	J♠	K♥	6♥					
22	2♣	6♦	2♥	9♣	J♠	3♥	A♥	K♣	4♦/3♣		
	7♥	9♦	4♠	10♠	9♠	3♦					
23	K♥	3♠	A♣	6♦	10♣	Q♣	3♥	A♣	5♥/K♦		
	A♠	5♦	4♥	4♠	6♠	Q♦					
24	9♠	J♦	2♥	3♠	4♠	10♦	Q♣	2♠	5♣/7♠		
	2♣	3♣	10♠	4♥	2♠	9♦					
25	6♠	J♠	A♠	J♦	4♥	Q♠	10♠	7♥	4♣/8♥		
	K♥	K♦	Q♥	10♠	K♣	5♦					
26	2♠	10♥	2♥	J♣	10♠	8♦	Q♠	9♠	6♥/7♥		
	9♠	7♠	9♣	Q♥	8♠	3♠					
27	K♣	5♠	A♣	10♥	Q♥	7♣	8♦	Q♠	3♦/A♠		
	6♠	8♥	6♦	9♣	6♠	K♦					
28	8♠	4♦	2♥	5♠	9♣	J♠	7♣	J♣	Q♦/2♣		
	2♠	7♥	3♠	6♦	2♦	7♠					
29	6♣	5♥	A♣	4♦	6♦	10♣	J♠	8♠	9♦/K♥		
	K♣	A♠	J♦	3♠	A♦	8♥					
30	2♦	5♣	2♥	5♥	3♠	4♠	10♣	2♥	5♦/9♠		
	8♠	2♣	J♣	J♦	A♥	7♥					
31	A♦	4♣	A♣	5♣	J♦	4♥	4♠	K♣	3♣/6♠		
	6♣	K♥	10♥	J♠	3♥	A♠					
32	A♥	6♥	2♥	4♠	J♣	10♠	4♥	A♠	K♦/2♠		
	2♦	9♠	5♠	10♥	Q♣	2♣					
33	3♥	3♦	A♣	6♥	10♥	Q♥	10♠	5♦	7♠/K♠		
	A♦	6♠	4♦	5♠	10♦	K♥					
34	Q♣	Q♦	2♥	3♦	5♠	9♣	Q♥	9♦	8♥/8♠		
	A♥	2♠	5♥	4♦	Q♠	9♠					
35	10♦	9♥	A♣	Q♦	4♦	6♦	9♣	10♥	7♥/6♣		
	3♥	K♣	5♣	5♥	8♦	6♠					
36	Q♠	5♥	2♥	9♠	5♥	3♠	6♦	6♣	A♠/2♦		
	Q♣	8♠	4♣	5♠	7♣	2♠					
37	8♦	3♣	A♣	5♦	5♣	J♦	3♠	A♣	2♣/A♦		
	10♦	6♣	6♥	4♣	J♠	K♣					
38	7♣	K♦	2♥	3♠	4♠	J♠	J♦	8♠	K♥/A♥		
	Q♠	2♦	3♠	6♥	10♣	8♠					
39	J♠	7♠	A♣	K♦	6♥	10♥	J♣	2♠	9♠/3♥		
	8♦	A♦	Q♦	3♦	4♠	6♣					
40	10♣	8♥	2♥	7♠	3♦	5♠	10♥	3♣	6♠/Q♠		
	7♣	A♥	9♦	Q♦	4♥	2♦					
41	4♠	7♥	A♣	8♥	Q♦	4♦	5♠	5♦	2♠/10♦		
	J♠	3♥	5♦	9♦	10♠	A♦					
42	4♥	A♠	2♥	7♥	9♦	5♥	4♦	5♠	K♣/Q♠		
	10♥	Q♣	3♣	5♦	Q♥	A♥					
43	10♠	2♣	A♣	A♠	5♦	5♣	5♥	2♦	8♠/8♦		
	4♠	10♦	K♦	3♣	9♣	3♥					
44	Q♥	K♦	2♥	2♣	3♠	4♠	5♣	2♥	6♣/7♠		
	4♥	Q♠	7♠	K♦	6♦	Q♣					
45	9♣	9♠	A♣	K♥	K♦	6♥	4♣	6♠	2♦/J♠		
	10♠	8♦	8♥	7♠	3♠	10♦					
46	6♦	6♠	2♥	9♠	7♠	3♦	6♥	K♥	A♦/10♣		
	Q♥	7♣	7♥	8♥	J♦	Q♠					
47	3♣	2♠	A♣	6♠	8♥	Q♦	3♦	K♦	A♥/4♠		
	9♣	J♠	A♠	7♥	J♣	8♦					
48	J♦	K♣	2♥	2♠	7♥	9♦	Q♦	3♣	3♥/4♥		
	6♦	10♣	2♣	A♠	10♥	7♣					
49	J♣	8♠	A♣	K♣	A♠	5♦	9♦	4♦	Q♣/10♠		
	3♠	4♠	K♥	2♣	5♠	J♠					

AGE	MER	VEN	MAR	JUP	SAT	URA	NEP	LR	PLU/RES ENV DISP
50	10♥	6♣	2♥	8♠	2♣	3♣	5♦	A♥	10♦/Q♥
	J♦	4♥	9♠	K♥	4♦	10♣			
51	5♠	2♦	A♣	6♣	K♥	K♦	3♣	A♣	Q♠/9♣
	J♣	10♠	6♠	9♠	5♥	4♠			
52	4♦	A♦	2♥	2♦	9♠	7♠	K♦	2♦	8♦/6♦
	10♥	Q♥	2♠	6♠	5♣	4♥			
53	5♥	A♥	A♣	A♦	6♠	8♥	7♠	9♠	7♣/3♠
	5♠	9♣	K♣	2♠	4♣	10♠			
54	5♣	3♥	2♥	A♥	2♠	7♥	8♥	7♠	J♠/J♦
	4♦	6♦	8♠	K♣	6♥	Q♥			
55	4♣	Q♠	A♣	3♥	K♣	A♠	7♥	K♦	10♣/J♣
	5♥	3♠	6♣	8♠	3♦	9♣			
56	6♥	10♠	2♥	Q♣	8♠	2♣	A♠	5♥	4♠/10♥
	5♣	J♦	2♦	6♣	Q♦	6♦			
57	3♦	Q♠	A♣	10♦	6♣	K♥	2♣	A♥	4♥/5♠
	4♣	J♣	A♦	2♦	9♠	3♠			
58	Q♦	8♦	2♥	Q♠	2♦	9♠	K♥	2♥	10♠/4♦
	6♥	10♥	A♥	A♦	5♦	J♦			
59	9♦	7♠	A♣	8♦	A♦	6♠	9♠	A♦	Q♥/5♥
	3♦	5♠	3♥	A♥	3♣	J♣			
60	5♦	J♠	2♥	7♣	A♥	2♠	6♠	6♠	9♣/5♣
	Q♦	4♦	Q♣	3♥	K♦	10♥			
61	3♣	10♣	A♣	J♠	3♥	K♣	2♠	8♥	6♦/4♣
	9♦	5♥	10♦	Q♣	7♠	5♠			
62	K♦	4♠	2♥	10♣	Q♣	8♠	K♣	7♠	3♠/6♥
	5♦	5♣	Q♠	10♦	8♥	4♦			
63	7♠	4♥	A♣	4♠	10♦	6♣	8♠	5♠	J♦/3♦
	3♦	4♣	8♦	Q♠	7♥	5♥			
64	8♥	10♠	2♥	4♥	Q♠	2♦	6♣	3♥	J♣/Q♦
	K♦	6♥	7♣	8♦	A♠	5♣			
65	7♥	Q♥	A♣	10♠	8♦	A♦	2♦	A♣	10♥/9♦
	7♠	3♦	J♠	7♣	2♣	4♣			
66	A♠	9♣	2♥	Q♥	7♣	A♥	A♦	A♥	5♠/5♦
	8♥	Q♦	10♠	J♠	K♥	6♥			
67	2♣	6♦	A♣	9♣	J♠	3♥	A♥	2♠	4♦/3♣
	7♥	9♦	4♠	10♣	9♠	3♦			
68	K♥	3♠	2♥	6♦	10♣	Q♣	3♥	7♥	5♥/K♦
	A♠	5♦	4♥	4♠	6♠	Q♦			
69	9♠	J♦	A♣	3♠	4♠	10♦	Q♣	8♥	5♣/7♠
	2♣	3♣	10♠	4♥	2♠	9♦			
70	6♠	J♣	2♥	J♦	4♥	Q♠	10♦	4♣	4♣/8♥
	K♥	K♦	Q♥	10♠	K♣	5♦			
71	2♠	10♥	A♣	J♣	10♠	8♦	Q♠	Q♣	6♥/7♥
	9♠	7♠	9♣	Q♥	8♠	3♠			
72	K♣	5♠	2♥	10♥	Q♥	7♣	8♦	2♥	3♦/A♠
	6♠	8♥	6♦	9♣	6♣	K♦			
73	8♠	4♦	A♣	5♠	9♣	J♥	7♣	3♥	Q♦/2♣
	2♠	7♥	3♠	6♦	2♦	7♠			
74	6♣	5♦	2♥	4♦	6♦	10♣	J♠	K♣	9♦/K♥
	K♣	A♠	J♦	3♠	A♦	8♥			
75	2♦	5♣	A♣	5♥	3♠	4♠	10♣	A♥	5♦/9♠
	8♠	2♣	J♣	J♦	A♥	7♥			
76	A♦	4♣	2♥	5♣	J♦	4♥	4♠	7♥	3♣/6♠
	6♣	K♥	10♥	J♣	3♥	A♠			
77	A♥	6♥	A♣	4♣	J♣	10♠	4♥	6♥	K♦/2♠
	2♦	9♠	5♠	10♥	Q♣	2♣			
78	3♥	3♦	2♥	6♥	10♥	Q♥	10♠	10♦	7♠/K♣
	A♦	6♠	4♦	5♠	10♦	K♥			
79	Q♣	Q♦	A♣	3♦	5♠	9♠	Q♥	A♣	8♥/8♠
	A♥	2♠	5♥	4♦	Q♠	9♠			
80	10♦	9♦	2♥	Q♦	4♦	6♦	9♣	Q♣	7♥/6♦
	3♥	K♣	5♣	5♥	8♦	6♠			
81	Q♠	5♦	A♣	9♦	5♥	3♠	6♦	8♠	A♠/2♦
	Q♣	8♠	4♣	5♣	7♣	2♠			
82	8♦	3♣	2♥	5♦	5♠	J♦	3♠	2♣	2♣/A♦
	10♦	6♣	6♥	4♦	J♠	K♣			
83	7♣	K♦	A♣	3♣	4♠	J♣	J♦	A♠	K♥/A♥
	Q♠	2♦	3♦	6♥	10♣	8♠			
84	J♠	7♠	2♥	K♦	6♥	10♥	J♣	3♦	9♠/3♦
	8♦	A♦	Q♦	3♦	4♠	6♣			
85	10♣	8♥	A♣	7♠	3♦	5♠	10♥	Q♠	6♠/Q♣
	7♣	A♥	9♦	Q♦	4♥	2♦			
86	4♣	7♥	2♥	8♥	Q♦	4♦	5♠	2♥	2♠/10♣
	J♠	3♥	5♦	9♦	10♠	A♦			
87	4♥	A♠	A♣	7♥	9♦	5♥	4♦	10♦	K♣/Q♠
	10♣	Q♣	3♣	5♦	Q♥	A♥			
88	10♠	2♣	2♥	A♠	5♦	5♣	5♥	6♣	8♠/8♦
	4♠	10♦	K♦	3♣	9♣	3♥			
89	Q♥	K♥	A♣	2♣	3♣	4♣	5♣	K♥	6♠/7♣
	4♥	Q♠	7♠	K♦	6♦	Q♣			
90	9♣	9♠	2♥	K♦	K♦	6♥	4♣	2♣	2♦/J♠
	10♠	8♦	8♥	7♠	3♠	10♦			
91	6♦	6♠	A♣	9♠	7♠	3♦	6♥	Q♦	A♦/10♣
	Q♥	7♠	7♥	8♥	J♦	Q♠			
92	3♠	2♠	2♥	6♠	8♥	Q♦	3♦	8♦	A♥/4♠
	9♣	J♠	A♠	7♥	J♣	8♦			
93	J♦	K♣	A♣	2♠	7♥	9♦	Q♦	A♣	3♥/4♦
	6♦	10♣	2♣	A♠	10♥	7♣			
94	J♣	8♠	2♥	K♣	A♠	5♦	9♦	Q♠	Q♣/10♠
	3♠	4♠	K♥	2♣	5♠	J♠			
95	10♥	6♣	A♣	8♠	2♣	3♣	5♦	2♦	10♦/Q♥
	J♦	4♥	9♠	K♥	4♦	10♣			
96	5♠	2♦	2♥	6♣	K♥	K♦	3♣	9♠	Q♠/9♣
	J♣	10♠	6♠	9♠	5♥	4♠			
97	4♦	A♦	A♣	2♦	9♠	7♠	K♦	K♥	8♦/6♦
	10♥	Q♥	2♠	6♠	5♣	4♥			
98	5♥	A♥	2♥	A♦	6♠	8♥	7♠	9♠	7♣/3♠
	5♠	9♣	K♣	2♠	4♣	10♠			
99	5♣	3♥	A♣	A♥	2♠	7♥	8♥	7♣	J♠/J♦
	4♦	6♦	8♠	K♣	6♥	Q♥			

Queen of Hearts

AGE	MER	VEN	MAR	JUP	SAT	URA	NEP	LR	PLU/RES	ENV	DISP
0	10♣	8♦	K♠	3♥	A♣	Q♣	10♠	10♣	5♦/3♦	Q♥	Q♥
	J♦	5♦	A♦	8♣	2♥	A♠					
1	4♣	Q♦	2♣	A♠	9♥	4♦	J♥	8♦	6♦/6♣	9♣	10♠
	7♠	7♥	8♥	J♦	Q♠	6♥					
2	5♣	8♠	A♠	A♦	K♣	6♦	4♥	K♠	J♠/K♠	6♦	4♥
	7♣	5♦	J♦	6♠	2♣	10♦					
3	5♥	7♣	A♦	10♦	Q♣	3♦	6♥	3♥	8♥/10♥	3♠	4♠
	7♥	9♥	2♥	4♣	4♦	6♥					
4	4♠	K♠	8♦	A♣	7♣	3♠	Q♦	A♣	3♣/6♦	J♦	10♣
	2♦	7♥	7♥	5♣	5♦	4♦	7♠				
5	8♣	5♠	6♦	4♣	3♦	3♥	8♦	Q♣	Q♣/7♠	J♣	J♠
	6♥	K♦	2♦	A♥	10♠	8♦					
6	A♠	4♥	4♣	7♥	9♠	8♠	3♥	10♠	5♣/J♦	10♥	7♣
	7♣	9♣	2♦	7♠	A♦	3♥					
7	K♠	10♣	2♥	4♠	10♥	3♣	8♥	4♣	8♠/K♠	5♠	8♠
	2♠	6♠	5♣	4♥	K♦	J♥	10♥				
8	3♦	2♣	2♠	2♦	10♦	6♥	10♥	Q♦	5♦/Q♣	4♦	Q♠
	A♠	5♣	A♦	8♠	4♠	10♥					
9	8♦	4♣	10♣	2♣	K♦	6♠	6♥	2♣	7♦/3♠	5♥	10♦
	8♥	J♥	4♦	6♦	8♠	K♣					
10	5♥	8♥	2♣	A♦	2♦	7♠	3♣	A♠	J♥/4♣	5♠	Q♣
	10♥	Q♠	9♠	2♠	5♦	A♠					
11	2♥	9♣	5♣	7♥	K♥	A♥	A♦	9♥	9♥/K♦	4♠	3♥
	5♥	3♠	9♠	3♦	Q♣	A♠					
12	10♠	6♠	7♥	8♠	9♦	9♥	10♥	4♦	K♣/J♦	6♥	A♥
	5♠	Q♠	9♠	8♦	J♠	10♥					
13	2♠	A♠	6♣	5♦	7♦	5♠	8♠	J♥	J♣/K♦	3♦	A♦
	8♣	A♣	Q♠	3♦	3♣	8♠					
14	5♥	8♣	5♦	4♣	8♥	J♣	4♥	5♣	6♦/9♣	Q♦	2♦
	9♦	K♥	K♠	10♠	Q♠	9♥					
15	10♣	9♦	4♣	4♦	K♣	J♦	2♥	8♠	J♣/Q♦	9♦	6♣
	8♦	7♦	10♠	9♣	5♦	9♠	K♠				
16	J♦	3♠	6♠	9♠	A♥	7♠	9♥	A♠	5♣/A♦	5♦	8♠
	6♦	3♣	6♠	K♠	9♣	7♣					
17	7♥	9♦	9♠	10♠	Q♣	6♦	4♥	A♦	3♣/3♦	3♠	K♣
	4♣	J♠	6♥	4♣	6♣	4♥					
18	8♠	3♠	10♠	K♦	Q♦	4♣	K♠	K♣	5♠/A♦	K♦	2♠
	A♥	Q♣	K♥	6♣	9♠	4♦	Q♦				
19	7♠	9♦	6♥	K♠	4♦	2♥	5♥	6♦	K♦/8♠	7♠	6♠
	6♦	3♣	5♠	Q♦	10♠	A♦					
20	2♥	10♠	8♦	A♣	2♦	10♥	9♦	4♥	8♠/A♠	8♥	9♠
	A♥	9♣	3♠	Q♣	4♦	9♦					
21	7♣	A♥	A♦	5♠	5♦	8♠	2♣	5♥	K♦/2♠	7♥	K♥
	4♠	5♣	7♠	3♦	Q♠	2♣					
22	J♣	6♠	8♥	6♣	J♦	4♠	5♠	7♣	3♠/A♠	A♠	2♣
	9♥	10♥	4♦	2♣	A♦	K♠					
23	10♠	9♥	6♠	J♥	K♥	3♠	A♣	A♦	6♦/10♣	2♣	A♠
	2♠	2♠	7♠	5♣	8♣	A♣					
24	7♦	2♦	J♥	9♠	J♦	2♥	3♠	10♦	4♠/10♦	K♦	7♥
	3♦	A♠	5♦	8♦	6♠	3♠					

AGE	MER	VEN	MAR	JUP	SAT	URA	NEP	LR	PLU/RES	ENV	DISP
25	5♣	10♥	9♠	7♥	K♦	K♠	Q♦	Q♣	2♥/9♦	9♠	8♥
	10♠	K♣	5♦	10♦	J♥	K♥	K♦				
26	J♥	5♥	6♣	K♥	3♥	4♦	9♣	3♣	4♣/5♠	6♠	7♠
	8♠	3♣	Q♠	J♥	9♠	7♠					
27	7♣	8♦	3♦	A♠	8♣	8♠	K♥	6♥	A♥/K♦	2♣	K♦
	9♥	2♥	Q♣	A♦	10♦	K♥					
28	2♦	9♥	A♠	10♠	8♥	A♥	4♥	4♠	6♦/10♥	K♣	3♣
	3♥	J♠	Q♣	K♦	K♥	5♣					
29	7♥	3♥	10♠	3♠	5♠	6♥	A♥	K♠	2♠/Q♠	8♠	5♦
	5♦	8♣	A♣	10♥	8♠	A♥					
30	J♦	4♦	3♦	3♥	K♣	8♦	6♥	8♦	J♣/9♦	6♠	9♦
	6♥	10♦	4♠	Q♠	8♥	6♠					
31	J♠	3♠	3♦	7♥	9♠	6♦	2♣	A♣	10♦/9♣	2♦	Q♦
	A♥	5♠	5♠	8♥	8♠	2♣					
32	5♥	4♦	7♥	7♣	J♥	A♥	6♥	7♣	2♥/4♣	A♦	3♦
	3♦	9♠	6♠	8♥	2♦	6♥					
33	10♠	7♠	K♣	8♣	Q♣	6♠	7♣	3♠	K♥/3♣	A♥	6♥
	J♠	2♣	8♠	9♦	3♠	J♣					
34	8♥	8♠	8♠	10♦	2♦	J♠	9♠	Q♦	K♦/A♠	3♥	4♣
	J♥	A♥	2♠	5♥	4♦	Q♠					
35	3♠	6♥	4♠	9♥	4♠	J♥	10♦	8♣	9♦/A♣	Q♠	5♠
	K♠	8♥	3♦	7♦	7♠	7♥					
36	4♦	7♣	9♥	6♠	5♠	K♣	10♣	5♠	10♥/5♣	10♦	5♥
	A♥	5♥	7♦	A♣	10♠	10♠					
37	7♠	6♥	A♠	K♦	Q♠	A♥	6♣	6♦	K♠/6♠	Q♠	4♦
	4♠	9♠	3♥	5♣	9♥	2♥					
38	J♥	7♠	K♦	2♥	3♣	4♠	J♥	4♠	J♦/K♥	8♦	5♠
	K♣	3♥	8♥	4♦	5♣	10♠					
39	6♣	2♣	2♠	6♠	4♦	3♠	4♣	10♣	4♠/7♦	7♣	10♥
	10♥	9♣	8♠	Q♣	7♥	5♥					
40	5♣	Q♦	K♦	2♣	10♠	8♦	3♠	3♥	A♠/9♦	J♠	J♣
	J♦	Q♠	3♦	7♦	A♣	3♠					
41	7♣	J♦	2♠	5♦	6♠	A♠	10♣	8♦	Q♠/3♥	10♣	J♦
	6♥	K♠	8♠	A♣	K♦	10♣					
42	9♥	10♦	3♦	3♥	6♦	6♥	5♦	A♠	8♥/9♠	4♠	3♠
	A♥	4♦	J♥	10♠	Q♣	3♣					
43	J♠	J♦	3♥	2♠	2♦	6♣	6♥	4♦	5♠/9♦	4♥	6♦
	A♠	7♠	A♦	10♣	Q♣	6♥					
44	K♥	2♥	2♣	3♠	4♣	5♠	6♣	4♠	7♠/8♣	10♠	9♣
	5♥	K♠	8♠	A♠	9♥	K♣					
45	10♣	8♦	K♠	3♥	2♥	Q♣	10♠	7♥	5♣/3♦	Q♥	Q♥
	J♦	5♦	A♦	8♣	A♣	A♠					
46	4♣	Q♦	2♣	A♠	7♠	4♦	J♥	9♠	6♦/6♣	9♣	10♠
	7♣	7♥	8♥	J♦	Q♠	6♥					
47	5♣	8♠	A♠	A♦	K♣	6♦	4♥	8♠	J♠/K♠	6♦	4♥
	7♣	5♦	J♦	6♠	2♣	10♦					
48	5♥	7♣	A♦	10♦	Q♣	3♠	6♥	3♥	8♥/10♥	3♠	4♠
	7♥	7♦	A♣	4♣	4♦	6♥					
49	4♠	K♠	8♦	2♥	7♠	3♠	Q♦	K♠	3♣/6♠	J♦	10♣
	2♦	7♠	7♥	5♣	5♦	4♣	7♠				

AGE	MER	VEN	MAR	JUP	SAT	URA	NEP	LR	PLU/RES	ENV	DISP
50	8♣	5♠	6♦	4♣	10♣	3♥	8♦	10♣	Q♠/7♠	J♠	J♠
	6♣	K♦	2♦	A♥	10♠	8♦					
51	A♠	4♥	4♣	7♥	9♠	8♠	3♥	2♥	5♣/J♦	10♥	7♣
	7♣	9♣	2♦	7♠	A♦	3♥					
52	K♠	10♣	A♣	4♠	10♥	3♣	8♥	4♠	8♠/K♣	5♠	8♦
	2♠	6♠	5♣	4♥	K♦	J♥	10♥				
53	3♦	2♣	2♠	2♦	10♦	6♥	10♥	10♥	5♦/Q♣	4♦	Q♠
	A♠	5♣	A♦	8♠	4♠	10♥					
54	8♦	4♠	10♣	2♣	K♦	6♠	6♥	3♣	9♥/3♠	5♥	10♦
	8♥	J♥	4♦	6♦	8♠	K♣					
55	5♥	8♥	2♣	A♣	2♦	9♥	3♠	8♥	J♥/4♣	5♣	Q♣
	10♥	Q♠	9♠	2♠	5♦	A♠					
56	A♣	9♠	5♣	7♥	K♥	A♥	A♦	3♦	7♦/K♦	4♣	3♥
	5♥	3♠	9♠	3♦	Q♣	A♦					
57	10♠	6♠	7♥	8♠	9♦	7♦	10♥	2♣	K♣/J♦	6♥	A♥
	5♠	Q♠	9♠	8♦	J♠	10♥					
58	2♠	A♠	6♣	5♦	9♥	5♠	8♠	2♠	J♣/K♦	3♦	A♦
	8♣	2♥	Q♠	3♦	3♠	8♠					
59	5♥	8♣	5♦	4♣	8♥	J♣	4♥	2♦	6♦/9♣	Q♦	2♦
	9♦	K♥	K♠	10♠	Q♠	7♦					
60	10♣	9♠	4♣	4♦	K♠	J♦	A♣	10♦	J♣/Q♦	9♦	6♣
	8♦	9♥	10♠	9♣	5♦	9♠	K♠				
61	J♦	3♠	6♣	9♠	A♥	7♠	7♦	6♥	5♣/A♦	5♦	8♠
	6♦	3♣	6♠	K♠	9♠	7♣					
62	7♥	9♦	9♠	10♠	Q♠	6♦	4♥	10♥	3♣/3♦	3♣	K♠
	4♣	J♣	6♥	4♠	6♠	4♥					
63	8♦	3♠	10♠	K♦	Q♦	4♣	K♠	8♦	5♠/2♥	K♦	2♠
	A♥	Q♣	K♥	6♣	9♠	4♦	Q♦				
64	7♠	9♦	6♥	K♠	4♦	A♣	5♥	4♠	K♦/8♠	7♠	6♠
	6♦	3♦	5♠	Q♦	10♠	A♦					
65	A♣	10♠	8♦	A♦	2♦	10♥	9♠	10♣	8♣/A♠	8♥	9♠
	A♥	9♣	3♠	Q♦	4♦	9♠					
66	7♣	A♥	A♦	5♠	5♦	8♣	2♣	2♣	K♦/2♠	7♥	K♥
	4♠	5♣	7♠	3♦	Q♣	2♣					
67	J♣	6♠	8♥	6♣	J♦	4♠	5♠	K♦	3♠/A♠	A♠	2♣
	7♦	10♥	4♦	2♣	A♦	K♠					
68	10♠	7♦	6♣	J♥	K♥	3♠	2♥	6♠	6♦/10♣	2♣	A♦
	2♣	2♠	7♣	5♣	8♣	2♥					
69	9♥	2♦	J♥	9♠	J♦	A♣	3♠	6♥	4♠/10♦	K♥	7♦
	3♦	A♠	5♦	8♦	6♠	3♠					
70	5♣	10♥	9♠	7♥	K♦	K♠	Q♦	5♥	A♣/9♦	9♠	8♥
	10♠	K♣	5♦	10♦	J♥	K♥	K♦				
71	J♦	5♥	6♣	K♥	3♥	4♦	9♣	8♥	4♣/5♠	6♠	7♠
	8♠	3♣	Q♣	J♥	9♠	7♠					
72	7♣	8♦	3♦	A♠	8♠	8♠	K♥	2♣	A♥/K♦	2♠	K♦
	7♦	A♣	Q♣	A♦	10♦	K♥					
73	2♦	7♦	A♠	10♠	8♥	A♥	4♥	A♦	6♦/10♥	K♣	3♠
	3♥	J♠	Q♣	K♦	K♥	5♠					
74	7♥	3♥	10♠	3♠	5♠	6♥	A♥	2♦	2♠/Q♠	8♠	5♦
	5♦	8♣	2♥	10♥	8♠	A♥					

AGE	MER	VEN	MAR	JUP	SAT	URA	NEP	LR	PLU/RES	ENV	DISP
75	J♦	4♦	3♦	3♥	K♣	8♦	6♥	7♦	J♣/9♦	6♠	9♦
	6♥	10♦	4♠	Q♠	8♥	6♠					
76	J♠	3♠	3♥	9♥	9♠	6♦	2♣	3♣	10♦/9♣	2♦	Q♦
	A♥	5♣	5♠	8♥	8♠	2♣					
77	5♥	4♦	9♥	7♣	J♥	A♥	6♥	2♥	A♣/4♣	A♦	3♦
	3♦	9♦	6♠	8♥	2♠	6♥					
78	10♠	7♠	K♣	8♣	Q♣	6♣	7♠	9♣	K♥/3♣	A♥	6♥
	J♠	2♣	8♠	9♦	3♠	J♣					
79	8♥	8♠	8♣	10♦	2♦	J♠	9♠	5♠	K♦/A♣	3♥	4♣
	J♥	A♥	2♠	5♥	4♦	Q♠					
80	3♠	6♥	4♣	7♥	4♠	J♥	10♦	7♥	9♦/2♥	Q♣	5♠
	K♠	8♥	3♦	9♥	7♠	7♥					
81	4♦	7♣	7♦	6♣	5♠	K♣	10♣	K♥	10♥/5♣	10♦	5♥
	A♥	5♥	9♥	2♥	10♠	10♣					
82	7♠	6♥	A♣	K♦	Q♠	A♥	6♣	A♥	K♠/6♠	Q♠	4♦
	4♠	9♣	3♥	5♠	7♠	A♣					
83	J♥	7♣	K♦	A♠	3♠	4♠	J♣	A♦	J♦/K♥	8♦	5♠
	K♣	3♥	8♥	4♦	5♠	10♠					
84	6♠	2♣	2♠	6♠	4♦	3♠	4♣	10♠	4♠/9♥	7♣	10♥
	10♥	9♣	8♠	Q♣	7♦	5♥					
85	5♠	Q♦	K♦	2♣	10♠	8♦	3♠	6♠	A♠/9♥	J♠	J♣
	J♦	Q♠	3♦	9♥	2♥	3♠					
86	7♠	J♦	2♠	5♦	6♠	A♠	10♣	7♥	Q♠/3♥	10♣	J♦
	6♥	K♣	8♠	2♥	K♦	10♣					
87	7♦	10♦	3♦	3♥	6♦	6♥	5♦	8♠	8♥/9♠	4♠	3♠
	A♥	4♦	J♥	10♣	Q♣	3♣					
88	J♠	J♦	3♥	2♠	2♦	6♣	6♥	9♥	5♠/9♦	4♥	6♦
	A♠	7♠	A♦	10♣	Q♣	6♥					
89	K♥	A♣	2♣	3♠	4♠	5♣	6♠	9♥	7♣/8♣	10♠	9♣
	5♥	K♠	8♠	A♠	7♠	K♣					
90	10♣	8♦	K♣	3♥	A♠	Q♣	10♠	10♥	5♣/3♦	Q♥	Q♥
	J♦	5♦	A♦	8♣	2♥	A♠					
91	4♣	Q♦	2♣	A♠	9♥	4♦	J♥	2♠	6♦/6♠	9♣	10♠
	7♣	7♥	8♥	J♦	Q♠	6♥					
92	5♣	8♠	A♣	A♦	K♣	6♦	4♥	A♠	J♠/K♣	6♦	4♥
	7♠	5♦	J♦	6♠	2♣	10♠					
93	5♥	7♣	A♦	10♦	Q♣	3♣	6♥	6♣	8♥/10♥	3♠	4♣
	7♥	9♥	2♥	4♣	4♦	6♥					
94	4♠	K♣	8♠	A♣	7♠	3♠	Q♦	5♦	3♣/6♠	J♦	10♠
	2♦	7♠	7♥	5♣	5♦	4♠	7♠				
95	8♣	5♠	6♦	4♣	10♣	3♥	8♦	7♦	Q♠/7♠	J♣	J♠
	6♣	K♦	2♦	A♥	10♠	8♦					
96	A♠	4♥	4♣	7♥	9♠	8♠	3♥	5♠	5♣/J♦	10♥	7♣
	7♣	9♣	2♦	7♠	A♦	3♥					
97	K♠	10♣	2♥	4♠	10♥	3♣	8♥	8♠	8♠/K♣	5♠	8♦
	2♠	6♠	5♣	4♥	K♦	J♥	10♥				
98	3♦	2♣	2♠	2♦	10♦	6♥	10♥	5♥	5♦/Q♣	4♦	Q♠
	A♠	5♣	A♦	8♠	4♠	10♥					
99	8♦	4♠	10♣	2♣	K♦	6♠	6♥	8♣	7♦/3♣	5♥	10♦
	8♥	J♥	4♦	6♦	8♠	K♣					

AGE	MER	VEN	MAR	JUP	SAT	URA	NEP	LR	PLU/RES	ENV	DISP
0	K♦	6♥	4♣	2♦	J♠	8♣	6♦	K♦	4♠/10♥	K♦	K♥
	7♥	3♥	4♥	Q♠	Q♦	6♦					
1	8♠	J♣	10♠	5♥	K♣	7♥	2♦	6♥	2♠/9♣	9♠	2♣
	7♦	6♣	A♦	6♦	4♣	K♠					
2	2♣	7♦	5♥	J♥	3♠	2♠	2♥	4♣	6♠/8♥	6♠	A♠
	6♦	10♥	K♦	3♥	8♣	2♥					
3	9♥	5♣	J♥	J♦	K♣	A♣	2♠	2♦	7♥/9♦	2♠	7♥
	Q♠	9♣	J♠	3♣	J♣	2♠					
4	3♥	6♣	J♦	Q♥	4♠	K♠	8♦	J♠	A♣/7♦	K♣	8♥
	2♣	5♠	J♠	9♦	J♥	3♠	4♠				
5	K♣	A♥	5♥	3♠	3♦	A♦	9♠	8♣	Q♣/2♦	8♠	7♠
	4♦	10♣	5♦	J♥	J♦	4♥					
6	K♦	3♣	Q♠	9♣	8♣	4♦	3♠	6♦	6♥/4♠	6♣	K♦
	7♦	A♣	Q♦	4♣	9♥	3♠					
7	5♣	7♦	9♣	2♣	10♠	6♥	A♠	8♠	6♠/6♣	2♦	3♣
	3♦	7♠	Q♦	4♣	3♠	3♥					
8	Q♥	3♦	2♣	2♠	2♦	10♦	6♥	J♣	10♥/5♦	A♦	5♦
	J♠	8♣	2♥	6♣	4♦	6♥					
9	K♣	A♦	Q♠	3♦	8♣	2♣	10♦	10♠	8♠/7♠	A♥	9♦
	6♠	9♦	7♥	5♦	10♠	J♣					
10	7♠	2♠	3♦	9♥	J♦	6♠	6♦	5♥	9♦/9♠	3♥	Q♦
	6♥	3♥	2♦	10♠	4♦	6♦					
11	A♥	A♦	9♥	K♦	J♥	6♥	10♦	K♣	A♠/Q♣	Q♣	3♦
	Q♠	7♣	J♣	10♠	10♥	10♦					
12	2♣	4♥	5♠	8♣	Q♦	5♥	K♦	7♥	3♠/10♣	10♦	6♥
	7♠	6♦	4♦	7♣	2♠	8♠					
13	10♠	4♦	8♣	9♦	5♣	7♠	J♦	2♦	4♠/9♣	Q♠	4♣
	J♥	6♥	10♥	A♥	A♦	5♦					
14	2♠	10♦	Q♣	7♦	7♥	J♥	9♦	2♣	7♣/2♥	8♦	5♣
	K♠	10♠	Q♠	9♥	4♥	Q♥					
15	A♦	K♦	7♦	5♥	2♦	5♠	8♥	7♦	6♣/3♥	7♣	5♥
	6♥	A♥	9♥	2♥	8♠						
16	4♥	10♦	9♣	4♣	5♦	6♥	5♥	5♥	K♠/J♦	J♣	4♦
	7♥	9♠	3♦	3♥	7♦	A♣					
17	J♥	K♦	4♠	A♣	10♣	Q♠	8♠	J♥	K♣/3♠	10♣	5♠
	5♠	3♦	10♠	A♦	3♥	2♣					
18	5♥	6♦	10♥	J♣	A♦	2♠	Q♣	3♠	7♥/9♥	4♠	10♥
	6♣	9♠	4♦	Q♦	Q♥	A♥					
19	3♥	8♦	4♣	6♦	2♣	3♠	2♠	2♠	9♣/7♣	4♥	J♣
	K♣	5♦	Q♠	9♥	K♥	2♠					
20	K♦	K♣	6♣	J♠	J♣	9♣	8♥	2♥	5♦/3♦	10♠	J♦
	10♦	5♠	8♠	2♥	4♠	8♥					
21	7♦	9♦	Q♠	3♦	6♠	10♦	J♠	9♥	10♠/J♦	Q♥	3♠
	6♥	A♦	J♥	8♥	Q♦	10♣					
22	7♠	K♣	3♦	10♥	5♣	5♥	10♦	5♣	2♦/7♣	9♣	6♦
	9♣	4♥	4♣	8♥	Q♦	10♦					
23	3♠	A♣	6♦	10♣	Q♣	5♥		J♥	K♦/8♣	6♦	9♣
	A♥	K♣	4♦	9♣	7♦	5♠					
24	8♥	3♣	K♠	3♦	A♠	Q♦	2♣	J♦	3♥/Q♠	3♠	Q♥
	K♣	J♠	4♣	8♣	2♥	9♣					
25	Q♣	8♦	6♥	9♣	9♥	A♣	J♥	K♣	6♠/J♣	J♦	10♠
	K♦	Q♥	10♠	K♣	5♦	10♦					
26	3♥	4♦	9♣	4♣	5♣	6♠	A♠	A♣	7♠/K♠	J♣	4♥
	K♦	J♠	K♣	J♣	6♦	9♦					
27	A♥	K♦	4♣	9♦	Q♦	10♣	10♦	2♠	10♠/6♣	10♥	4♠
	Q♥	9♥	2♥	Q♣	A♦	10♦					
28	7♥	K♠	3♣	A♣	K♦	2♠	8♦	3♥	10♣/J♣	5♠	10♣
	5♣	4♥	Q♥	3♥	J♠	Q♣	K♦				
29	8♣	2♦	6♠	Q♣	8♥	3♦	3♣	6♠	5♦/4♥	4♦	J♠
	5♥	4♠	5♣	6♥	2♣	3♣					
30	9♣	A♥	Q♣	Q♥	J♦	4♦	3♦	J♦	3♥/K♣	5♥	7♠
	K♦	9♠	5♣	4♥	4♣	3♦					
31	K♠	8♥	2♥	7♥	6♣	10♣	10♠	Q♥	4♣/5♠	5♣	8♦
	10♥	J♣	3♥	A♠	4♠	J♥	6♣				
32	Q♠	6♦	10♥	5♣	9♣	10♣	6♣	4♠	J♠/Q♦	4♣	Q♣
	9♣	3♥	4♣	4♦	7♥	6♣					
33	3♣	7♥	8♥	6♦	4♠	J♣	10♦	K♠	7♦/2♠	6♥	10♦
	10♠	J♥	A♦	6♠	4♦	5♠					
34	A♥	10♠	6♦	4♣	5♠	7♦	10♣	8♦	J♥/Q♣	3♦	Q♣
	6♣	5♠	J♦	10♥	J♠	9♣					
35	2♥	9♠	3♥	Q♥	3♠	6♥	4♣	K♣	9♥/4♠	Q♦	3♥
	A♥	2♠	J♥	Q♠	Q♦	4♣					
36	2♣	J♣	Q♥	4♦	7♠	9♥	6♣	A♥	5♠/K♣	9♦	A♥
	2♦	5♦	J♦	3♣	7♥	6♠					
37	10♥	9♣	5♥	J♠	7♦	2♦	4♦	5♥	8♠/4♠	5♦	A♦
	8♠	A♠	Q♦	Q♣	10♣	4♦					
38	A♥	8♠	J♠	Q♣	10♠	8♠	A♠	3♠	6♠/9♠	3♠	2♦
	7♣	3♠	K♠	2♣	5♦	9♥					
39	8♥	7♣	Q♣	A♦	K♠	K♣	2♥	3♦	8♠/8♦	K♦	6♣
	3♣	7♦	2♠	9♠	J♠	J♦	K♠				
40	K♣	2♠	5♥	J♦	6♥	4♦	9♥	A♦	3♥/4♣	7♠	8♣
	6♠	10♣	J♣	K♠	9♠	K♦					
41	Q♥	7♠	J♦	2♣	5♦	6♠	A♠	9♠	10♣/Q♠	8♥	K♣
	Q♣	8♠	10♦	7♥	5♥	A♠					
42	3♣	2♠	2♠	4♠	8♦	Q♠	K♠	K♦	2♦/A♣	7♥	2♠
	6♥	Q♦	3♠	5♥	J♦	A♦	8♦				
43	4♥	7♣	10♦	K♠	A♦	2♥	A♥	3♠	4♠/4♦	A♠	6♠
	6♠	Q♠	2♦	8♦	2♣	4♣					
44	2♦	2♣	3♣	4♣	5♣	6♣	7♣	Q♠	8♣/9♣	2♣	9♠
	6♥	9♠	2♣	8♦	A♦	7♣					
45	K♦	6♥	4♣	2♦	J♠	8♣	6♦	9♣	4♠/10♥	K♥	K♥
	7♥	3♥	4♥	Q♠	Q♦	6♦					
46	8♠	J♣	10♠	5♥	K♣	7♥	2♦	8♣	2♠/9♣	9♠	2♣
	9♥	6♣	A♦	6♦	4♣	K♠					
47	2♣	9♥	5♥	J♥	3♠	2♠	A♣	4♦	6♠/8♥	6♠	A♠
	6♦	10♥	K♦	3♥	8♣	A♣					
48	7♦	5♣	J♥	J♦	K♣	2♥	2♠	3♣	7♥/9♦	2♠	7♥
	Q♠	9♣	J♠	3♣	J♣	2♠					
49	3♥	6♣	J♦	Q♥	4♠	K♠	8♦	5♣	2♥/7♣	K♣	8♥
	2♣	5♠	J♠	9♦	J♥	3♠	4♠				

AGE	MER	VEN	MAR	JUP	SAT	URA	NEP	LR	PLU/RES	ENV	DISP
50	K♣	A♥	5♥	3♠	3♦	A♠	9♠	7♦	Q♣/2♦	8♠	7♠
	4♦	10♣	5♦	J♥	J♦	4♥					
51	K♦	3♣	Q♠	9♣	8♣	4♦	3♠	9♣	6♥/4♠	6♣	K♦
	9♥	2♥	Q♦	4♦	9♦	3♠					
52	5♣	9♥	9♠	2♣	10♠	6♥	A♠	2♣	6♠/6♣	2♦	3♣
	3♦	7♠	Q♦	4♠	3♠	3♥					
53	Q♥	3♦	2♠	2♠	2♦	10♦	6♥	10♠	10♥/5♦	A♦	5♦
	J♠	8♣	A♣	6♠	4♦	6♥					
54	K♣	A♦	Q♠	3♦	5♠	3♠	10♦	6♥	8♠/7♣	A♥	9♦
	6♠	9♦	7♥	5♦	10♠	J♣					
55	7♠	2♠	3♦	7♦	J♦	6♠	6♦	A♠	9♦/9♠	3♥	Q♦
	6♥	3♥	2♦	10♠	4♦	6♦					
56	A♥	A♣	7♥	K♦	J♥	6♥	10♦	Q♥	2♥/Q♣	Q♣	3♦
	Q♠	7♣	J♣	10♠	10♥	10♦					
57	2♣	4♥	5♠	8♣	Q♦	5♥	K♦	3♦	3♠/10♣	10♦	6♥
	7♠	6♦	4♦	7♠	2♠	8♠					
58	10♠	4♦	8♣	9♦	5♣	7♠	J♦	2♣	4♠/9♣	Q♠	4♣
	J♥	6♥	10♥	A♥	A♦	5♦					
59	2♠	10♦	Q♣	9♥	7♥	J♥	9♦	2♠	7♣/A♣	8♦	5♣
	K♠	10♠	Q♠	7♦	4♥	Q♥					
60	A♦	K♦	9♥	5♥	2♦	5♠	8♥	2♦	6♠/3♥	7♠	5♥
	6♥	A♥	7♦	A♣	2♣	8♥					
61	4♥	10♦	9♣	4♠	5♦	6♥	5♥	10♦	K♠/J♣	J♠	4♦
	7♥	9♠	3♦	3♥	9♥	2♥					
62	J♥	K♦	4♠	2♥	10♣	Q♣	8♠	6♥	K♣/3♠	10♣	5♠
	5♠	3♦	10♠	A♦	3♥	2♣					
63	5♥	6♦	10♠	J♣	A♦	2♠	Q♣	K♣	7♥/7♦	4♠	10♥
	6♣	9♠	4♦	Q♦	Q♥	A♥					
64	3♥	8♦	4♠	6♦	2♣	3♣	2♠	A♦	9♣/7♠	4♥	J♣
	K♣	5♦	Q♠	7♦	A♣	2♠					
65	K♦	K♣	6♦	J♠	J♣	9♣	8♥	Q♠	5♦/3♦	10♠	J♦
	10♦	5♠	8♣	A♣	4♠	8♥					
66	9♥	9♣	Q♠	3♦	6♠	10♦	J♠	3♦	10♠/J♦	Q♥	3♠
	6♥	A♦	J♥	8♥	Q♦	10♣					
67	7♠	K♣	3♦	10♥	5♠	5♥	10♦	5♠	2♦/7♣	9♣	6♦
	9♣	4♥	4♣	8♥	Q♦	10♦					
68	3♠	2♥	6♦	10♣	Q♣	3♥	5♥	3♣	K♦/8♣	6♦	9♣
	A♥	K♠	4♦	9♣	9♥	5♠					
69	8♥	3♣	K♠	3♦	2♥	Q♦	2♣	10♦	3♥/Q♠	3♠	Q♥
	K♣	J♣	4♣	8♣	A♣	9♣					
70	Q♣	8♦	6♦	9♣	7♦	A♦	J♥	7♠	6♠/J♣	J♦	10♣
	K♦	Q♥	10♠	K♣	5♦	10♦					
71	3♥	4♦	9♣	4♣	5♠	6♠	A♠	2♠	7♠/K♦	J♣	4♥
	K♦	J♠	K♣	J♣	6♦	9♦					
72	A♥	K♦	4♣	9♦	Q♦	10♣	10♦	3♦	10♠/6♣	10♥	4♠
	Q♥	7♦	A♣	Q♣	A♦	10♦					
73	7♥	K♠	3♣	2♥	K♦	2♠	8♦	9♥	10♣/J♣	5♠	10♣
	5♠	4♥	Q♥	3♥	J♠	Q♣	K♦				
74	8♣	2♦	6♠	Q♠	8♥	3♦	3♣	J♦	5♦/4♥	4♦	J♠
	5♥	4♠	5♠	6♥	2♣	3♣					
75	9♣	A♠	Q♣	Q♥	J♦	4♠	3♦	6♠	3♥/K♣	5♥	7♣
	K♦	9♠	5♣	4♦	4♠	3♦					
76	K♠	8♥	A♣	7♥	6♣	10♣	10♠	6♦	4♦/5♠	5♣	8♦
	10♥	J♣	3♥	A♠	4♠	J♥	6♣				
77	Q♠	6♦	10♥	5♣	9♦	10♦	6♣	A♥	J♠/Q♦	4♣	Q♠
	9♣	3♥	4♣	4♦	7♥	6♣					
78	3♣	7♥	8♥	6♦	4♠	J♣	10♦	A♦	9♥/2♠	6♥	10♦
	10♠	J♥	A♦	6♠	4♦	5♠					
79	A♥	10♠	6♦	4♣	5♠	9♥	10♣	9♥	J♥/Q♣	3♦	Q♣
	6♣	5♦	J♦	10♥	J♠	9♣					
80	A♣	9♠	3♥	Q♥	3♠	6♥	4♣	K♦	7♦/4♠	Q♦	3♥
	A♥	2♣	J♦	Q♣	Q♦	4♣					
81	2♣	J♣	Q♥	4♦	7♣	7♦	6♣	J♥	5♠/K♣	9♦	A♥
	2♦	5♦	J♦	3♣	7♠	6♣					
82	10♥	9♣	5♥	J♠	9♥	2♦	4♣	6♥	8♠/4♣	5♦	A♦
	8♣	2♥	Q♦	Q♠	10♠	4♦					
83	A♥	8♣	J♠	Q♣	10♠	8♠	A♠	10♦	6♠/9♠	3♣	2♦
	7♣	3♥	K♠	2♣	5♦	7♦					
84	8♥	7♣	Q♣	A♦	K♠	K♣	A♠	2♣	8♠/8♦	K♦	6♣
	3♣	9♥	2♣	9♠	J♠	J♦	K♠				
85	K♣	2♠	5♥	J♦	6♥	4♥	7♦	4♥	3♥/4♣	7♠	8♠
	6♠	10♣	J♣	K♠	9♠	K♦					
86	Q♥	7♣	J♦	2♣	5♥	6♠	A♠	5♠	10♣/Q♠	8♥	K♣
	Q♣	8♠	10♦	7♥	5♥	A♠					
87	3♠	2♠	2♣	4♠	8♦	Q♣	K♠	8♠	2♦/2♥	7♥	2♠
	6♥	Q♦	8♠	5♥	J♦	A♦	8♦				
88	4♥	7♣	10♦	K♠	A♦	A♣	A♥	Q♦	4♠/4♦	A♠	6♠
	6♠	Q♠	2♦	8♦	2♣	4♣					
89	A♣	2♣	3♠	4♣	5♠	6♣	7♠	5♥	8♠/9♣	2♣	9♠
	6♥	9♠	2♠	8♦	A♦	7♣					
90	K♦	6♥	4♣	2♦	J♠	8♣	6♦	K♦	4♠/10♥	K♥	K♥
	7♦	3♥	4♥	Q♠	Q♦	6♦					
91	8♠	J♣	10♠	5♥	K♣	7♥	2♦	10♠	2♠/9♣	9♠	2♣
	7♦	6♣	A♥	6♦	4♣	K♠					
92	2♣	7♦	5♥	J♥	3♠	2♠	2♥	4♦	6♠/8♥	6♠	A♠
	6♦	10♥	K♦	3♥	8♣	2♥					
93	9♥	5♣	J♥	J♦	K♠	A♣	2♠	8♠	7♥/9♦	2♠	7♥
	Q♠	9♣	J♠	3♣	J♣	2♠					
94	3♥	4♣	J♦	Q♥	4♠	K♣	8♦	9♦	A♠/7♣	K♣	8♥
	2♠	5♠	9♦	J♥	3♠	4♠					
95	K♣	A♥	5♥	3♠	3♦	A♦	9♠	5♣	Q♣/2♦	8♠	7♠
	4♦	10♣	5♦	J♥	J♦	4♥					
96	K♦	3♣	Q♠	9♣	8♣	4♦	3♠	7♠	6♥/4♠	6♣	K♦
	7♦	A♣	Q♦	4♦	9♦	3♠					
97	5♣	7♠	9♣	2♣	10♠	6♥	A♠	J♦	6♠/6♣	2♦	3♣
	3♦	7♠	Q♦	4♠	3♠	3♥					
98	Q♥	3♦	2♣	2♠	2♦	10♦	6♥	2♠	10♥/5♦	A♦	5♦
	J♠	8♣	2♦	6♠	4♦	6♥					
99	K♣	A♦	Q♠	3♦	5♠	3♣	10♦	10♦	8♠/7♣	A♥	9♦
	6♠	9♦	7♥	5♦	10♠	J♣					

Ace of Clubs

AGE	MER	VEN	MAR	JUP	SAT	URA	NEP	LR	PLU/RES ENV DISP
0	Q♣	10♠	5♠	3♦	A♠	7♥	7♦	Q♣	5♠/J♥
	4♦	J♠	5♥	4♠	K♦	7♦			
1	9♠	7♠	3♦	6♥	A♦	10♦	8♣	10♠	3♠/4♥
	2♣	9♣	J♠	3♠	A♥	8♠			
2	Q♣	9♣	6♥	9♦	K♦	2♣	7♦	5♠	5♥/J♥
	5♣	5♠	4♣	10♠	8♥	7♦			
3	2♠	7♥	9♦	Q♦	3♥	4♥	8♠	3♦	J♣/Q♥
	9♠	3♠	5♠	7♠	Q♣	8♠			
4	7♠	3♠	Q♦	3♣	6♠	9♠	7♦	A♠	4♣/J♥
	6♥	5♠	3♦	9♣	A♠	7♦			
5	8♠	2♣	3♠	5♦	10♦	Q♥	8♣	7♥	5♠/6♦
	2♠	J♣	5♥	7♥	Q♠	8♠			
6	10♣	J♠	5♦	7♠	K♠	2♠	7♦	7♦	3♦/J♥
	Q♦	4♣	9♠	3♠	K♥	7♦			
7	2♦	9♠	7♣	K♣	8♦	6♦	8♣	9♠	5♥/J♥
	8♠	5♠	4♣	2♣	7♠	8♣			
8	4♥	5♠	K♦	7♥	6♠	8♠	7♦	7♠	9♦/J♥
	5♦	3♦	3♣	J♣	6♠	7♦			
9	A♥	2♠	7♥	8♥	J♠	J♦	8♣	3♦	4♣/10♥
	2♦	5♠	3♦	9♠	10♣	8♠			
10	Q♥	5♥	8♥	2♣	A♦	2♦	7♦	6♥	3♣/J♥
	K♦	9♦	7♠	5♠	K♣	7♦			
11	Q♣	8♠	2♣	A♠	4♠	10♥	8♣	A♦	3♦/4♦
	A♥	4♣	9♦	2♠	4♥	8♠			
12	6♦	4♣	A♠	9♠	3♥	A♥	7♦	10♣	7♠/J♥
	8♥	3♣	7♥	5♦	6♣	7♦			
13	Q♠	2♦	9♠	K♥	10♠	4♦	8♣	8♣	9♦/5♠
	Q♣	3♦	3♣	8♠	Q♥	8♣			
14	J♦	3♦	K♥	2♠	10♦	Q♣	7♦	Q♠	7♥/J♥
	A♠	7♠	2♣	4♣	A♦	7♦			
15	7♣	A♥	2♠	6♠	9♠	5♠	8♣	9♠	3♣/6♦
	Q♣	9♦	7♠	2♦	6♠	8♠			
16	10♥	9♠	6♠	8♠	8♦	Q♠	7♦	6♥	6♣/J♥
	K♥	7♥	9♠	3♦	3♥	7♦			
17	10♣	Q♠	8♠	K♣	3♠	6♥	8♣	9♦	7♠/Q♦
	7♣	3♣	7♥	A♥	J♦	8♣			
18	4♦	3♠	K♣	2♦	J♠	7♣	7♦	K♥	9♠/J♥
	6♠	2♣	2♠	9♦	10♦	7♦			
19	4♥	Q♠	2♦	6♦	J♠	Q♦	8♣	2♦	7♥/5♦
	10♣	7♠	2♣	Q♣	10♥	8♠			
20	5♣	7♠	6♣	A♥	4♠	10♣	7♦	7♦	2♠/J♥
	K♣	9♠	8♠	3♣	8♦	7♦			
21	Q♥	7♠	A♥	A♦	5♠	5♦	8♣	2♠	2♣/K♦
	4♥	7♥	9♠	Q♠	4♦	8♣			
22	6♥	7♥	A♦	Q♣	10♠	4♥	7♦	7♥	8♠/J♥
	6♣	2♠	2♦	7♠	J♠	7♦			
23	6♦	10♣	Q♣	3♥	5♥	K♦	8♣	9♦	9♠/8♦
	Q♥	2♣	2♠	7♠	5♣	8♠			
24	Q♦	2♠	3♥	Q♠	9♣	Q♥	7♦	Q♦	2♦/J♥
	A♦	8♠	A♥	7♥	4♠	7♦			
25	J♠	4♥	Q♠	10♦	4♣	8♥	8♣	3♥	2♠/A♠
	6♦	9♠	8♠	10♣	6♥	8♣			
26	5♦	9♠	10♦	7♣	3♠	6♦	7♦	4♥	A♥/J♥
	3♥	2♦	Q♣	2♣	10♠	7♦			
27	10♠	Q♥	7♣	8♦	3♦	A♠	8♣	8♣	8♠/K♥
	J♦	2♠	2♦	4♥	Q♦	8♣			
28	K♦	2♠	8♦	10♣	J♣	J♦	7♦	7♠	Q♣/J♥
	10♦	A♥	Q♠	9♠	9♣	7♦			
29	4♦	6♦	10♣	J♠	9♦	K♥	8♣	3♠	2♦/6♠
	10♥	8♠	A♥	Q♥	5♦	8♣			
30	8♥	8♠	J♠	4♥	5♠	10♥	7♦	Q♦	Q♠/J♥
	8♦	Q♣	7♣	2♠	3♠	7♦			
31	5♣	J♦	4♥	4♠	3♠	6♠	8♣	3♠	A♥/K♣
	4♦	2♦	Q♣	6♦	K♦	8♣			
32	A♠	2♠	4♠	Q♥	5♥	4♦	7♦	6♠	7♣/J♥
	J♠	Q♠	10♣	8♠	J♣	7♦			
33	6♥	10♥	Q♥	10♠	7♠	K♣	8♣	9♠	Q♣/6♣
	5♣	A♥	Q♠	J♦	8♥	8♣			
34	K♥	A♥	10♠	6♦	4♣	5♣	7♦	7♦	10♣/J♥
	4♠	7♣	4♥	2♦	5♠	7♦			
35	Q♦	4♦	6♦	9♣	7♥	6♣	8♣	8♠	Q♠/A♦
	6♥	Q♣	7♣	10♥	A♠	8♣			
36	6♠	Q♣	9♣	J♦	3♠	6♥	7♦	2♣	4♥/J♥
	10♠	10♣	Q♥	A♥	5♥	7♦			
37	5♦	5♣	J♦	3♠	2♣	A♦	8♣	3♣	7♣/3♠
	Q♦	Q♠	10♣	4♦	K♥	8♣			
38	K♣	Q♠	3♠	10♥	9♦	Q♦	7♦	5♦	Q♥/J♥
	9♣	4♥	6♦	Q♣	4♣	7♦			
39	K♦	6♥	10♥	J♣	9♠	3♥	8♣	10♦	10♣/10♦
	5♦	7♣	4♥	5♣	6♠	8♣			
40	6♠	7♣	J♦	4♦	3♠	5♦	7♦	Q♥	6♦/J♥
	3♠	Q♥	J♦	Q♠	3♦	7♦			
41	8♥	Q♦	4♦	5♠	2♠	10♦	8♣	8♣	4♥/8♦
	K♦	10♣	Q♥	6♥	K♣	8♣			
42	A♦	10♣	5♠	5♠	7♠	K♦	7♦	10♣	J♦/J♥
	J♣	6♦	10♥	7♠	9♦	7♦			
43	A♠	5♦	5♠	5♥	8♠	8♦	8♣	J♣	Q♥/J♠
	8♥	4♥	6♦	Q♦	6♣	8♣			
44	3♥	4♥	5♥	6♦	7♥	8♥	7♦	5♦	10♥/J♥
	5♠	J♦	4♦	10♣	3♠	7♦			
45	K♥	K♦	6♥	4♣	2♦	J♠	8♣	7♠	6♦/4♠
	A♠	Q♥	J♦	5♦	A♦	8♣			
46	10♣	Q♥	4♣	Q♦	2♣	A♠	7♦	K♣	4♦/J♥
	5♥	10♥	5♣	4♥	7♠	7♦			
47	6♠	8♥	Q♦	3♦	A♥	4♠	8♣	2♠	J♦/10♠
	K♥	6♠	10♥	K♦	3♥	8♣			
48	8♦	6♦	3♦	5♦	9♠	K♥	7♦	7♦	5♣/J♥
	4♣	4♦	6♥	Q♥	7♥	7♦			
49	K♣	A♠	5♦	9♦	Q♣	10♠	8♣	2♦	10♥/9♣
	6♠	J♦	4♦	8♥	10♦	8♣			

AGE	MER	VEN	MAR	JUP	SAT	URA	NEP	LR	PLU/RES ENV DISP
50	J♠	J♦	9♦	K♦	2♠	6♠	7♦	9♠	6♥/J♥
	3♦	5♣	Q♦	6♦	2♣	7♦			
51	6♣	K♥	K♦	3♣	Q♠	9♣	8♣	7♠	4♦/3♠
	K♣	10♥	5♣	A♠	8♦	8♠			
52	4♠	10♥	3♣	8♥	8♠	K♣	7♦	K♦	Q♦/J♥
	9♦	6♥	5♦	J♦	9♠	7♦			
53	A♦	6♠	8♥	7♠	7♠	3♠	8♣	8♦	5♣/J♣
	6♠	4♦	6♥	K♥	J♠	8♣			
54	10♠	4♦	7♠	A♠	2♦	6♣	7♦	6♦	5♦/J♥
	3♣	Q♦	K♦	10♠	2♠	7♦			
55	3♥	K♣	A♠	7♥	10♣	J♠	8♣	8♠	6♥/5♠
	A♦	5♣	Q♦	6♠	4♠	8♣			
56	9♣	5♣	7♥	K♥	A♥	A♦	7♦	4♦	K♦/J♥
	7♠	5♦	8♥	4♦	8♠	7♦			
57	10♦	6♣	K♥	2♣	4♥	5♠	8♣	5♠	Q♦/5♥
	3♥	6♥	5♦	K♣	10♠	8♣			
58	3♠	6♥	2♣	6♠	Q♣	3♥	7♦	K♦	8♥/J♥
	7♥	K♦	A♠	5♠	2♦	7♦			
59	8♦	A♦	6♠	9♠	Q♥	5♥	8♣	7♦	5♦/4♣
	10♦	Q♦	K♦	6♠	9♠	8♦			
60	J♣	Q♦	9♠	K♣	Q♠	10♦	7♦	6♠	A♠/J♥
	2♣	8♥	K♥	6♥	A♥	7♦			
61	J♠	3♥	K♣	2♠	6♦	4♣	8♣	8♠	K♦/3♥
	8♦	5♦	8♥	A♦	3♠	8♣			
62	5♠	5♦	2♠	6♠	7♠	8♦	7♦	7♦	K♥/J♥
	9♠	A♠	6♠	Q♦	Q♣	7♦			
63	4♠	10♦	6♣	8♠	J♦	3♦	8♣	A♥	8♥/9♦
	J♠	K♦	A♠	3♥	J♣	8♣			
64	5♥	K♦	8♠	A♦	10♣	J♠	7♦	2♠	6♠/J♥
	2♠	K♥	K♣	5♦	Q♠	7♦			
65	10♠	8♦	A♦	2♦	10♥	9♦	8♣	7♥	A♠/3♣
	4♣	8♥	K♥	10♦	5♠	8♣			
66	4♣	8♥	2♦	3♥	4♥	4♠	7♦	8♥	K♣/J♥
	8♠	6♠	6♣	K♦	7♣	7♦			
67	9♣	J♠	3♥	A♥	4♦	3♣	8♣	J♠	K♥/7♠
	10♠	A♠	6♠	8♦	5♥	8♣			
68	3♦	A♠	A♥	10♦	Q♥	10♠	7♦	J♦	6♣/J♥
	2♦	K♣	A♦	8♥	10♣	7♦			
69	3♠	4♣	10♦	Q♣	5♣	7♠	8♣	8♣	6♠/7♦
	9♣	K♥	K♣	J♠	4♠	8♣			
70	9♦	K♥	Q♣	8♦	6♦	9♣	7♦	Q♥	A♦/J♥
	A♥	6♠	3♥	A♠	4♥	7♦			
71	J♣	10♠	8♦	Q♠	6♥	7♥	8♣	5♥	K♣/2♣
	3♠	6♠	6♣	4♠	3♦	8♣			
72	3♣	6♠	Q♠	J♠	J♦	3♠	7♦	8♥	3♥/J♥
	Q♣	A♦	10♦	K♥	Q♥	7♦			
73	5♠	9♣	J♠	7♣	Q♦	2♠	8♣	2♣	6♣/9♠
	J♣	K♣	A♦	10♠	9♦	8♣			
74	7♠	K♣	7♠	4♠	10♥	J♣	7♦	A♦	10♦/J♥
	Q♠	3♥	8♦	6♠	6♦	7♦			
75	5♥	3♠	4♠	10♣	5♦	9♠	8♣	2♦	A♦/2♠
	5♠	6♠	3♥	9♣	3♣	8♠			
76	7♥	6♠	10♣	10♠	4♠	5♠	7♦	7♦	8♦/J♥
	7♣	10♦	J♠	K♣	J♦	7♦			
77	4♣	J♣	10♠	4♥	K♦	2♠	8♣	Q♣	3♥/8♠
	5♥	A♦	10♦	3♠	7♠	8♣			
78	2♣	A♦	4♥	9♣	5♠	5♥	7♦	8♠	J♠/J♥
	10♣	8♦	4♠	6♣	10♥	7♦			
79	3♦	5♠	9♠	Q♥	8♥	8♠	8♣	2♠	10♦/2♦
	4♣	3♥	8♦	J♣	7♥	8♣			
80	9♠	3♥	Q♥	3♠	6♥	4♣	7♦	A♠	4♠/J♥
	4♥	J♠	10♠	A♦	4♦	7♦			
81	9♦	5♥	3♠	6♦	A♠	2♦	8♣	4♠	8♦/A♥
	3♦	10♦	J♠	5♠	2♣	8♣			
82	2♠	10♦	6♦	J♣	Q♦	3♠	7♦	10♥	10♠/J♥
	Q♥	4♠	9♠	3♥	5♠	7♦			
83	3♣	4♣	J♠	J♦	K♥	A♥	8♣	8♣	J♠/Q♣
	9♦	8♦	4♠	5♥	9♠	8♣			
84	8♠	8♦	J♦	5♠	5♦	9♠	7♦	6♦	9♣/J♥
	6♦	10♠	3♠	10♦	6♥	7♦			
85	7♠	3♦	5♠	10♥	6♠	Q♣	8♣	4♠	4♠/Q♠
	3♠	J♠	10♠	4♣	2♠	8♣			
86	2♦	J♠	10♥	5♥	K♦	3♣	7♦	A♠	3♠/J♥
	J♦	9♣	J♠	8♦	Q♦	7♦			
87	7♥	9♦	5♥	4♦	K♣	Q♠	8♣	9♠	10♠/7♣
	7♠	4♠	9♣	3♦	8♠	8♣			
88	A♥	4♠	4♦	4♣	8♥	7♠	7♦	3♥	J♣/J♥
	10♥	3♠	5♠	J♠	5♦	7♦			
89	2♣	3♠	4♠	5♣	6♠	7♠	8♣	A♥	9♣/10♣
	7♥	10♠	3♠	9♦	2♦	8♣			
90	Q♣	10♠	5♣	3♦	A♠	7♥	7♦	7♦	5♠/J♥
	4♦	J♣	5♥	4♠	K♦	7♦			
91	9♠	7♠	3♦	6♥	A♦	10♣	8♣	Q♠	3♠/4♥
	2♣	9♠	J♣	3♣	A♥	8♣			
92	Q♠	9♣	6♥	9♦	K♥	2♣	7♦	2♦	5♥/J♥
	5♣	5♠	4♠	10♠	8♥	7♦			
93	2♠	7♥	9♦	Q♦	3♥	4♥	8♣	9♠	J♣/Q♥
	9♠	3♠	5♠	7♦	Q♣	8♣			
94	7♣	3♠	Q♦	3♣	6♠	9♠	7♦	K♦	4♣/J♥
	6♥	5♥	3♦	9♣	A♠	7♦			
95	8♠	2♠	3♣	5♦	10♦	Q♥	8♣	10♠	5♠/6♦
	2♠	J♣	5♥	7♥	Q♠	8♣			
96	10♣	J♠	5♦	7♠	K♣	2♠	7♦	4♦	3♦/J♥
	Q♦	4♣	9♦	3♠	K♥	7♦			
97	2♦	9♠	7♠	K♦	8♦	6♦	8♣	8♣	5♥/J♥
	8♠	5♠	4♠	2♣	7♠	8♣			
98	4♥	5♠	K♦	7♥	6♠	8♠	7♦	J♦	9♦/J♥
	5♦	3♦	3♣	J♣	6♠	7♦			
99	A♥	2♠	7♥	8♥	J♠	J♦	8♣	3♦	4♣/10♥
	2♦	5♥	3♦	9♠	10♣	8♣			

♣ Two of Clubs

AGE	MER	VEN	MAR	JUP	SAT	URA	NEP	LR	PLU/RES	ENV	DISP
0	K♣	J♦	4♥	4♦	2♠	8♥	6♣	K♣	6♠/Q♥	2♠	2♣
	9♥	8♠	2♦	9♣	5♣	K♠					
1	A♠	9♥	4♦	J♥	6♦	6♠	A♣	J♦	9♠/7♠	K♥	A♠
	9♣	J♣	3♣	A♥	8♠	A♣					
2	7♦	5♥	J♥	3♠	2♠	2♥	6♠	4♥	8♥/Q♦	9♠	7♥
	10♦	Q♥	7♣	5♦	J♦	6♠					
3	A♥	8♠	3♠	10♠	10♣	K♠	Q♠	4♦	2♥/8♦	6♠	8♥
	A♠	10♥	7♣	Q♦	J♥	6♦	10♣				
4	2♠	A♦	4♥	6♦	6♥	2♦	K♥	2♠	3♥/6♣	2♠	7♠
	5♠	J♠	9♦	J♥	3♠	4♠					
5	3♣	5♦	10♦	Q♥	8♠	5♠	6♦	8♥	4♣/10♣	K♣	K♦
	9♥	2♥	3♦	5♣	Q♦	6♦					
6	5♥	9♥	Q♥	A♠	4♥	4♣	7♥	6♣	9♠/8♠	8♠	3♣
	6♥	K♦	3♦	10♣	6♦	A♥					
7	10♠	6♥	A♥	6♠	6♠	Q♣	4♣	A♠	J♣/9♦	6♣	5♦
	7♦	8♣	A♣	8♠	5♠	4♠					
8	2♠	2♦	10♦	6♥	10♥	5♣	Q♣	9♥	K♣/8♦	2♦	9♦
	9♠	Q♦	8♥	9♦	4♥	J♦					
9	K♦	6♠	6♥	7♦	3♠	9♠	9♣	4♦	Q♦/K♥	A♦	Q♦
	4♣	A♥	6♣	4♥	5♠	9♠					
10	A♦	2♦	7♦	3♣	J♥	4♣	Q♣	J♥	2♥/3♦	A♥	3♦
	10♦	8♦	J♦	4♥	J♣	Q♣					
11	A♠	4♠	10♣	8♠	3♦	4♦	3♣	6♦	6♦/J♠	3♥	6♥
	K♦	9♣	5♠	8♦	6♠	K♣					
12	4♥	5♠	8♣	Q♦	5♥	K♦	3♠	6♠	10♣/Q♥	Q♣	4♣
	J♥	4♣	J♠	A♠	2♦	9♥					
13	6♠	Q♣	3♥	9♥	8♥	J♥	Q♦	A♣	8♦/A♠	10♦	5♣
	K♠	4♥	10♦	7♦	4♠	10♠					
14	2♦	3♣	9♥	4♦	6♣	10♥	7♠	7♦	8♠/A♥	Q♠	5♥
	4♣	A♦	7♦	A♣	A♠	7♠					
15	4♠	Q♣	Q♥	10♠	9♦	4♣	4♦	5♥	K♠/J♦	8♠	4♦
	8♥	K♥	6♥	A♥	9♥	2♥					
16	J♥	3♣	10♣	2♥	J♠	3♥	K♣	J♥	2♠/6♦	7♣	5♠
	10♥	6♥	4♥	2♣	A♥	A♠					
17	4♦	9♣	J♣	J♦	2♦	6♠	3♥	3♠	8♥/7♦	J♠	10♥
	8♠	K♥	5♠	3♦	10♠	A♦					
18	A♥	Q♠	10♣	9♠	A♠	5♦	6♠	2♠	Q♥/8♦	10♣	J♣
	2♠	9♦	10♦	7♦	4♣	6♠					
19	3♣	2♠	9♣	7♠	J♦	Q♥	7♠	2♥	9♦/6♥	4♠	J♦
	Q♣	10♥	8♣	A♣	10♣	7♣					
20	9♥	Q♦	10♦	6♥	9♠	Q♣	7♣	6♠	4♥/3♠	4♥	3♠
	4♣	2♦	J♥	7♠	3♦	J♠					
21	K♦	2♠	6♥	J♣	5♥	4♦	Q♣	A♥	6♠/8♦	10♠	6♦
	Q♥	4♠	5♠	7♠	3♦	Q♣					
22	6♦	2♥	9♣	J♣	3♥	A♥	4♦	8♠	3♣/8♣	Q♥	9♣
	A♦	K♠	5♠	Q♥	9♥	10♥					
23	7♠	5♦	K♠	6♥	2♥	3♦	A♠	3♠	A♥/10♦	9♣	Q♥
	2♠	7♠	5♣	8♠	A♣	Q♥					
24	3♥	Q♠	9♣	Q♥	7♦	2♦	J♥	10♠	9♠/J♦	6♦	10♠
	3♣	10♠	4♥	2♠	9♦	Q♣					
25	A♥	5♠	Q♥	5♠	10♥	9♠	7♥	10♣	K♦/K♠	3♠	4♥
	3♣	7♣	2♠	J♦	9♣	Q♦					
26	A♦	3♣	5♠	Q♠	3♦	J♠	Q♣	K♠	4♥/8♠	J♦	4♠
	10♠	7♦	A♣	3♥	2♦	Q♣					
27	8♥	K♠	5♦	2♥	3♣	6♠	Q♠	Q♠	J♠/J♦	J♠	10♣
	5♥	4♠	10♠	A♥	7♠	3♥	3♣				
28	8♣	6♣	9♠	3♥	7♠	6♥	5♦	2♠	9♦/4♠	10♥	J♠
	4♦	10♣	5♥	4♣	A♠	5♦					
29	Q♥	7♥	3♥	10♠	3♠	5♠	6♥	A♦	A♥/2♠	5♠	7♠
	3♣	K♥	5♥	4♠	5♠	6♥					
30	K♠	7♠	A♣	8♥	8♠	J♠	4♥	4♦	5♠/10♥	4♦	8♦
	J♣	J♦	A♥	7♥	10♣	J♥	8♠				
31	10♦	9♣	J♠	5♥	Q♦	Q♣	8♠	6♦	7♣/3♦	5♥	Q♠
	Q♥	A♥	5♣	5♠	8♥	8♠					
32	5♦	8♥	7♠	9♣	10♣	J♦	Q♣	6♥	9♥/6♠	5♣	10♦
	4♥	J♥	2♥	9♠	5♠	10♥					
33	A♦	4♥	9♣	5♣	5♥	9♥	J♠	2♦	J♥/3♥	4♣	Q♣
	8♠	9♦	3♠	J♣	7♠	Q♥					
34	A♣	K♥	A♥	10♠	6♦	4♣	5♣	K♥	7♦/10♣	6♥	3♥
	A♦	6♠	3♠	10♦	3♦	5♠					
35	A♠	J♦	10♠	5♠	8♦	7♦	8♠	3♣	10♥/2♠	3♦	A♥
	6♣	9♦	3♠	5♦	K♦	8♠					
36	J♣	Q♥	4♦	7♣	9♥	6♣	5♠	5♦	K♣/10♣	Q♦	A♦
	8♣	2♥	3♦	10♦	J♠	5♠					
37	A♦	8♣	7♠	3♥	4♥	K♣	7♥	10♦	9♠/K♥	9♦	2♦
	8♦	6♥	K♠	A♠	9♦	7♥					
38	7♠	8♦	3♥	2♦	K♠	2♠	A♣	Q♥	K♣/Q♠	5♦	6♣
	5♦	9♥	A♠	K♥	7♠	3♠	K♠				
39	2♠	6♠	4♦	3♠	4♣	4♠	7♦	8♠	A♥/5♣	3♣	8♠
	9♠	J♠	J♦	K♠	K♥	3♣					
40	10♠	8♦	3♠	8♠	9♦	9♠	7♥	5♠	J♠/10♦	K♦	K♣
	3♥	K♣	Q♣	8♥	4♦	7♥					
41	5♦	6♠	A♠	10♣	Q♠	3♥	K♠	6♦	6♣/2♥	7♠	2♠
	4♣	3♦	6♠	4♦	3♠	2♦	Q♠				
42	4♥	8♦	Q♠	K♠	2♦	A♠	A♦	5♥	10♣/5♠	8♥	6♠
	9♠	10♦	6♠	Q♠	A♠	5♣					
43	A♣	A♠	5♦	5♣	5♥	8♠	8♦	9♥	8♣/Q♥	7♥	9♠
	4♣	K♥	6♠	Q♠	2♦	8♦					
44	3♠	4♣	5♠	6♣	7♣	8♠	9♣	Q♥	10♣/J♣	A♠	K♥
	8♥	A♥	4♠	10♦	3♦	9♣					
45	K♣	J♦	4♥	4♦	2♠	8♥	6♣	A♠	6♠/Q♥	2♣	2♣
	7♦	8♠	2♦	9♣	5♣	K♠					
46	A♠	7♦	4♦	J♥	6♦	6♠	2♥	4♦	9♠/7♠	K♥	A♠
	9♣	J♣	3♣	A♥	8♣	2♥					
47	9♥	5♥	J♥	3♠	2♠	A♣	6♠	4♣	8♥/Q♦	9♠	7♥
	10♦	Q♥	7♣	5♦	J♦	6♠					
48	A♥	8♠	3♠	10♠	10♣	K♠	Q♠	7♥	A♠/8♦	6♠	8♥
	A♠	10♥	7♣	Q♦	J♥	6♦	10♣				
49	2♠	A♦	4♦	6♦	6♥	2♦	K♥	10♠	3♥/6♣	2♠	7♠
	5♠	J♠	9♦	J♥	3♠	4♠					

AGE	MER	VEN	MAR	JUP	SAT	URA	NEP	LR	PLU/RES	ENV	DISP
50	3♣	5♦	10♦	Q♥	8♣	5♠	6♦	6♥	4♣/10♣	K♣	K♦
	7♦	A♣	3♦	5♣	Q♦	6♦					
51	5♥	7♦	Q♥	A♠	4♥	4♣	7♥	A♠	9♠/8♠	8♠	3♣
	6♥	K♦	3♦	10♣	6♦	A♥					
52	10♠	6♥	A♠	6♠	6♣	Q♣	4♣	6♠	J♣/9♦	6♠	5♦
	7♦	8♠	2♥	8♠	5♠	4♣					
53	2♠	2♦	10♦	6♥	10♥	5♦	Q♣	6♣	K♣/8♦	2♦	9♦
	9♠	Q♦	8♥	9♦	4♥	J♦					
54	K♦	6♠	6♥	9♥	3♠	9♠	9♣	Q♣	Q♦/K♥	A♠	Q♦
	4♣	A♥	6♣	4♥	5♠	9♠					
55	A♠	2♦	9♥	3♣	J♥	4♣	Q♣	4♣	A♣/3♥	A♥	3♦
	10♦	8♦	J♦	4♥	J♣	Q♣					
56	A♠	4♣	10♥	8♣	3♦	4♦	3♣	2♠	6♦/J♠	3♥	6♥
	K♠	9♣	5♠	8♦	6♠	K♣					
57	4♥	5♠	8♣	Q♦	5♥	K♦	3♠	2♦	10♣/Q♥	Q♣	4♣
	J♥	4♣	J♣	A♦	2♦	9♦					
58	6♠	Q♣	3♥	7♦	8♥	J♥	Q♦	10♦	8♦/2♥	10♦	5♣
	K♠	4♥	10♦	9♥	4♣	10♠					
59	2♦	3♠	7♦	4♦	6♣	10♥	7♠	6♥	8♠/A♥	Q♠	5♥
	4♣	A♦	9♥	2♥	A♠	7♠					
60	4♠	Q♣	Q♥	10♠	9♥	4♣	4♦	10♥	K♠/J♥	8♦	4♦
	8♥	K♦	6♥	A♥	7♦	A♣					
61	J♥	3♣	10♣	A♣	J♠	3♥	K♣	5♦	2♠/6♦	7♣	5♠
	10♥	6♥	4♥	2♦	A♥	A♠					
62	4♦	9♣	J♣	J♦	2♦	6♠	3♥	Q♣	8♥/9♥	J♠	10♥
	8♠	K♥	5♠	3♦	10♠	A♦					
63	A♥	Q♣	10♠	9♣	A♠	5♦	6♠	K♦	Q♥/8♦	10♣	J♣
	2♠	9♦	10♦	9♥	2♥	6♠					
64	3♣	2♠	9♣	7♣	J♦	Q♥	7♠	6♠	9♦/6♥	4♠	J♦
	Q♣	10♥	8♣	2♥	10♣	7♠					
65	7♦	Q♦	10♦	6♥	9♠	Q♣	7♠	6♥	4♥/3♣	4♥	3♠
	4♣	2♦	J♥	7♠	3♦	J♠					
66	K♦	2♠	6♥	J♣	5♥	4♦	Q♣	7♦	6♣/8♦	10♠	6♦
	Q♥	4♣	5♣	7♠	3♦	Q♣					
67	6♦	A♣	9♠	J♠	3♥	A♥	4♦	3♠	3♣/8♣	Q♥	9♣
	A♦	K♣	5♠	Q♥	7♦	10♥					
68	7♠	5♦	K♠	6♥	A♣	3♦	A♠	9♠	A♥/10♦	9♣	Q♥
	2♠	7♣	5♣	8♣	2♥	Q♦					
69	3♥	Q♠	9♣	Q♥	9♥	2♦	J♥	9♣	9♠/J♦	6♦	10♠
	3♣	10♠	4♥	2♠	9♥	Q♣					
70	A♥	5♣	Q♥	5♣	10♥	9♠	7♥	A♦	K♦/K♠	3♠	4♥
	3♣	7♣	2♠	J♦	9♣	Q♦					
71	A♦	3♣	5♣	Q♦	3♦	J♠	Q♣	2♦	4♥/8♠	J♦	4♠
	10♠	9♥	2♥	3♥	2♦	Q♣					
72	8♥	K♠	5♦	A♣	3♦	6♠	Q♠	7♦	J♠/J♦	J♣	10♣
	5♥	4♠	10♠	A♥	7♠	3♥	3♣				
73	8♣	6♣	9♠	3♥	7♠	6♥	5♦	3♣	9♦/4♠	10♥	J♠
	4♦	10♣	5♥	4♣	A♠	5♦					
74	Q♥	7♥	3♥	10♠	3♠	5♠	6♥	J♥	A♥/2♠	5♠	7♠
	3♣	K♥	5♥	4♠	5♠	6♥					
75	K♠	7♠	2♥	8♥	8♠	J♠	4♥	4♣	5♠/10♠	4♦	8♦
	J♣	J♦	A♥	7♥	10♣	J♥	8♠				
76	10♦	9♣	J♣	5♥	Q♦	Q♣	8♠	Q♣	7♣/3♦	5♥	Q♠
	Q♥	A♥	5♣	5♠	8♥	8♠					
77	5♦	8♥	7♠	9♣	10♣	J♦	Q♣	A♠	7♦/6♠	5♣	10♦
	4♥	J♥	2♦	9♠	5♠	10♥					
78	A♦	4♥	9♠	5♣	5♥	7♦	J♠	4♠	J♥/3♥	4♣	Q♣
	8♠	9♠	3♠	J♣	7♣	Q♥					
79	2♥	K♥	A♥	10♠	6♦	4♣	5♣	10♥	9♥/10♣	6♥	3♥
	A♦	6♠	3♠	10♦	3♦	5♠					
80	A♠	J♦	10♠	5♠	8♦	9♥	8♠	8♠	10♥/2♠	3♦	A♥
	6♣	9♦	3♠	5♦	K♦	8♠					
81	J♣	Q♥	4♦	7♣	7♦	6♣	5♠	3♦	K♣/10♣	Q♦	A♦
	8♣	A♣	3♦	10♦	J♠	5♠					
82	A♦	8♣	7♠	3♥	4♥	K♣	7♥	4♦	9♠/K♥	9♦	2♦
	8♦	6♦	K♠	A♠	9♦	9♥					
83	7♠	8♦	3♥	2♦	K♠	2♠	2♥	3♣	K♣/Q♠	5♦	6♣
	5♦	7♦	A♠	K♥	7♣	3♠	K♠				
84	2♠	6♠	4♦	3♠	4♣	4♠	9♥	4♦	A♥/5♣	3♣	8♠
	9♠	J♠	J♦	K♠	K♥	3♣					
85	10♠	8♦	3♠	A♠	9♥	9♠	7♥	5♠	J♠/10♦	K♦	K♣
	3♥	K♣	Q♣	8♥	4♦	7♥					
86	5♦	6♠	A♠	10♣	Q♠	3♥	K♣	8♠	6♣/A♣	7♠	2♠
	4♣	3♦	6♠	4♦	3♠	2♦	Q♣				
87	4♠	8♦	Q♣	K♠	2♦	2♥	A♦	Q♦	10♣/5♠	8♥	6♠
	9♠	10♦	6♣	Q♠	A♠	5♣					
88	2♥	A♠	5♦	5♣	5♥	8♠	8♦	5♥	8♣/Q♥	7♥	9♠
	4♣	K♥	6♠	Q♠	2♦	8♦					
89	3♣	4♣	5♠	6♣	7♣	8♣	9♣	K♦	10♣/J♣	A♠	K♥
	8♥	A♥	4♠	10♦	3♣	9♣					
90	K♣	J♦	4♦	4♦	2♠	8♥	6♣	3♣	6♠/Q♥	2♣	2♠
	9♥	8♠	2♦	9♣	5♣	K♠					
91	A♠	9♥	4♦	J♥	6♦	6♠	A♣	6♠	9♠/7♠	K♥	A♠
	9♠	J♣	3♣	A♥	8♣	A♣					
92	7♦	5♥	J♥	3♣	2♠	2♥	6♠	Q♣	8♥/Q♦	9♠	7♥
	10♦	Q♥	7♣	5♦	J♦	6♠					
93	A♥	8♠	3♠	10♠	10♣	K♠	Q♠	3♥	2♥/8♦	6♠	8♦
	A♠	10♥	7♣	Q♦	J♥	6♦	10♣				
94	2♠	A♦	4♦	6♦	6♥	2♦	K♥	9♥	3♥/6♣	2♠	7♣
	5♠	J♠	9♦	J♥	3♠	4♣					
95	3♣	5♦	10♦	Q♥	8♣	5♠	6♦	8♥	4♣/10♣	K♣	K♦
	9♥	2♥	3♦	5♣	Q♦	6♦					
96	5♥	9♥	Q♥	A♠	4♥	4♣	7♥	J♥	9♠/8♠	8♠	3♣
	6♥	K♦	3♦	10♣	6♦	A♥					
97	10♠	6♥	A♠	6♠	6♣	Q♣	4♣	Q♦	J♣/9♦	6♣	5♦
	7♣	8♠	A♣	8♣	5♠	4♣					
98	2♠	2♦	10♦	6♥	10♥	5♦	Q♣	2♦	K♣/8♦	2♦	9♦
	9♠	Q♦	8♥	9♦	4♥	J♦					
99	K♦	6♠	6♥	7♦	3♠	9♠	9♣	3♣	Q♦/K♥	A♦	Q♦
	4♣	A♥	6♣	4♥	5♠	9♣					

Three of Clubs

AGE	MER	VEN	MAR	JUP	SAT	URA	NEP	LR	PLU/RES	ENV	DISP
0	3♠	9♥	7♠	5♦	Q♠	J♣	9♦	3♠	7♠/2♣	3♣	3♣
	10♥	6♥	5♠	Q♣	10♠	2♠					
1	8♦	10♥	5♦	8♥	K♥	8♠	J♣	9♥	10♠/5♦	K♦	5♦
	A♥	8♣	A♣	2♣	9♣	J♠					
2	7♥	9♣	6♣	10♥	Q♥	5♠	8♠	7♠	A♠/A♦	7♠	9♦
	7♠	4♦	Q♦	5♥	Q♠	4♥					
3	6♥	8♥	10♠	7♦	4♠	7♠	J♠	5♦	4♦/K♦	8♥	Q♦
	J♠	2♠	K♥	Q♠	9♣	J♠					
4	6♠	9♣	7♠	4♣	J♥	J♣	8♠	Q♠	2♥/K♣	7♥	3♦
	6♣	A♦	4♥	Q♠	10♠	8♠					
5	5♦	10♦	Q♥	8♠	5♠	6♠	4♣	J♣	10♣/3♥	A♠	6♥
	6♥	J♠	9♣	A♦	8♥	A♠					
6	Q♠	9♣	8♠	4♦	3♠	6♥	4♠	9♣	Q♦/7♣	2♣	4♣
	J♥	J♣	10♠	6♠	9♠	5♥					
7	8♥	8♠	K♠	9♥	Q♦	J♥	4♦	8♦	A♠/A♣	K♥	5♠
	K♠	Q♣	6♠	7♦	10♦	8♠					
8	9♠	4♣	9♥	6♦	K♥	Q♥	3♦	10♥	2♣/2♠	9♠	5♥
	J♣	6♠	7♦	A♠	5♦	3♦					
9	10♦	8♠	7♣	Q♣	5♥	J♣	6♦	5♦	K♠/4♦	6♠	4♦
	Q♦	K♦	10♥	2♠	9♥	2♥					
10	J♥	4♣	Q♠	2♥	3♥	K♣	A♠	8♥	7♥/10♣	2♠	5♠
	Q♥	10♥	Q♠	9♠	2♠	5♦					
11	6♦	J♠	10♠	4♥	9♠	8♥	K♠	K♥	Q♦/7♦	K♠	10♥
	2♣	K♦	9♠	5♠	8♠	6♠					
12	2♠	2♦	Q♣	J♠	5♦	5♣	8♥	8♠	7♣/A♦	8♠	J♠
	7♥	5♥	6♣	7♦	A♣	8♥					
13	4♠	7♥	J♠	A♥	4♥	7♠	3♦	J♣	5♥/10♥	6♣	J♠
	8♠	Q♥	8♣	A♣	Q♣	3♦					
14	9♥	4♣	6♣	10♥	7♠	8♠	A♥	7♥	Q♠/4♠	2♦	3♠
	J♣	9♠	J♥	3♦	5♠	3♥					
15	6♥	7♥	10♥	10♠	3♠	6♦	8♠	9♠	K♥/A♠	A♦	6♦
	7♣	10♦	J♦	3♦	5♠	8♠					
16	10♣	2♥	J♠	3♥	K♠	2♠	6♦	6♠	4♣/8♠	A♥	9♣
	6♠	K♠	9♣	7♠	9♥	Q♥					
17	3♦	5♠	K♠	10♥	2♥	5♠	5♦	10♥	2♠/6♠	3♥	Q♥
	7♥	A♥	J♦	8♠	A♠	7♠					
18	K♣	2♦	J♠	7♠	7♥	9♠	J♥	Q♥	7♠/4♥	Q♣	10♠
	4♣	8♦	Q♠	7♥	5♥	8♠					
19	2♠	4♣	7♣	J♦	Q♥	7♠	9♦	5♣	6♥/K♠	10♦	4♥
	4♣	A♥	7♥	4♥	J♠	4♦					
20	6♠	4♣	J♦	4♦	5♠	3♥	8♠	8♠	Q♠/2♣	Q♠	4♠
	8♦	7♠	A♣	K♣	9♠	8♠					
21	Q♦	K♠	5♣	2♥	4♣	8♥	2♦	6♥	3♥/4♥	8♦	10♣
	3♠	10♦	8♦	2♠	A♥	K♣	4♣				
22	8♣	K♥	7♣	K♠	3♦	10♥	5♠	8♥	5♥/10♦	7♣	J♠
	6♦	Q♣	3♠	J♠	5♠	5♠					
23	7♥	9♦	K♣	8♦	4♠	9♣	10♥	10♥	2♠/7♥	J♠	7♠
	4♣	K♦	3♠	10♠	J♦	10♥					
24	K♠	3♦	A♣	Q♦	2♣	3♥	Q♠	7♦	9♣/Q♥	10♠	8♦
	10♠	4♥	2♠	9♦	Q♣	J♥	2♣				
25	6♣	J♠	10♠	3♠	4♦	8♠	2♣	4♣	A♥/5♦	4♠	Q♠
	7♣	2♠	J♦	9♣	Q♦	2♣					
26	5♣	Q♦	3♦	J♠	Q♣	4♥	8♠	7♠	9♥/8♦	4♥	10♦
	Q♠	J♥	9♠	7♠	9♣	Q♥					
27	6♠	Q♠	J♠	J♦	3♠	9♥	3♥	J♠	J♥/K♣	10♠	Q♣
	2♣	5♥	4♠	10♠	A♥	7♣					
28	A♣	K♦	2♠	8♦	10♣	J♠	J♦	6♠	7♦/Q♣	Q♥	3♥
	6♠	8♥	4♠	6♣	5♠	J♦					
29	5♦	4♥	8♠	9♠	A♦	7♠	2♠	9♠	Q♥/7♥	9♣	A♥
	K♥	5♥	4♠	5♣	6♥	2♣					
30	10♠	7♠	6♦	A♥	9♥	K♥	9♣	7♦	A♠//Q♣	6♦	A♦
	8♠	2♥	5♠	6♠	3♥	9♠					
31	6♠	8♠	A♥	K♠	Q♠	A♠	9♦	4♣	7♠/K♦	3♠	2♦
	A♦	10♣	K♠	5♦	5♥	7♦					
32	3♦	A♦	K♣	9♠	K♠	7♥	A♠	J♥	A♠/2♦	J♦	6♣
	5♠	9♥	5♦	K♦	A♥	4♠	K♠				
33	7♥	8♥	6♦	4♠	J♠	10♦	7♦	J♣	2♠/J♦	J♣	8♠
	7♠	3♥	4♥	K♠	K♦	4♠					
34	8♦	A♥	4♠	5♦	5♥	7♠	9♦	8♠	3♥/6♠	10♥	K♣
	K♣	A♠	8♠	Q♦	6♦	9♥					
35	5♣	8♥	5♦	Q♣	2♦	K♣	K♠	5♦	K♥/2♥	5♠	2♠
	J♣	5♠	10♠	6♦	4♠	9♠	2♦				
36	10♠	A♠	8♠	K♠	9♠	A♣	6♠	10♦	Q♠/9♣	4♦	6♠
	7♠	6♠	K♥	2♠	5♠	J♦					
37	A♣	5♦	5♣	J♦	3♠	2♣	A♦	Q♥	8♣/7♣	5♥	9♠
	J♣	K♦	8♥	2♦	9♠	A♦					
38	4♠	J♣	J♦	K♥	A♥	8♠	J♠	8♠	Q♣/10♠	5♣	K♥
	Q♦	2♠	10♦	6♣	5♠	J♠					
39	A♠	4♥	Q♠	6♦	7♥	Q♦	K♥	5♠	8♥/7♣	4♣	2♠
	7♦	2♣	9♠	J♠	J♦	K♠					
40	5♦	7♦	6♦	J♥	10♠	8♥	2♥	6♦	7♠/3♦	6♥	A♠
	J♠	10♠	4♣	2♠	8♠	2♥					
41	9♥	3♠	J♥	4♠	7♥	A♣	8♥	4♣	Q♦/4♦	3♦	7♥
	6♣	7♣	A♥	5♠	4♥	8♥					
42	2♠	2♣	4♠	8♠	Q♣	K♠	2♦	Q♠	A♠/A♦	Q♦	8♥
	5♦	Q♥	A♥	4♦	J♥	10♣	Q♣				
43	7♥	6♣	6♦	10♣	10♥	9♠	K♦	9♠	K♣/K♥	9♦	7♠
	9♣	3♥	5♥	J♥	4♠	10♦					
44	4♣	5♣	6♣	7♠	8♠	9♠	10♠	J♣	J♣/Q♣	5♦	K♦
	7♦	A♠	5♠	J♦	4♦	10♣					
45	3♠	7♦	7♣	5♦	Q♠	J♣	9♦	4♣	7♠/2♣	3♠	3♣
	10♥	6♥	5♠	Q♣	10♣	2♠					
46	8♦	10♥	5♦	8♥	K♥	8♠	J♠	3♠	10♠/5♥	K♦	5♦
	A♥	8♣	2♥	2♠	9♣	J♠					
47	7♥	9♠	6♣	10♥	Q♥	5♠	8♠	6♥	A♠/A♦	7♠	9♦
	7♠	4♦	Q♦	5♥	Q♠	4♥					
48	6♥	8♥	10♠	9♥	4♠	7♠	J♠	4♠	4♦/K♦	8♥	Q♦
	J♣	2♠	K♥	Q♠	9♣	J♠					
49	6♠	9♠	9♥	4♣	J♥	J♣	8♠	8♥	A♠/K♣	7♥	3♦
	6♣	A♦	4♥	Q♠	10♠	8♠					

AGE	MER	VEN	MAR	JUP	SAT	URA	NEP	LR	PLU/RES	ENV	DISP
50	5♦	10♦	Q♥	8♣	5♠	6♦	4♣	8♠	10♣/3♥	A♠	6♥
	6♥	J♠	9♣	A♦	8♥	A♠					
51	Q♠	9♣	8♣	4♦	3♠	6♥	4♣	K♣	Q♣/7♣	2♣	4♣
	J♥	J♣	10♠	6♠	9♠	5♥					
52	8♥	8♠	K♣	7♦	Q♦	J♥	4♦	9♥	A♦/2♥	K♥	5♣
	K♠	Q♠	6♣	9♥	10♦	8♠					
53	9♠	4♣	7♦	6♦	K♥	Q♥	3♣	Q♦	2♣/2♠	9♠	5♥
	J♣	6♠	9♥	2♥	5♦	3♦					
54	10♠	8♠	7♣	Q♣	5♥	J♣	6♦	J♥	K♠/4♥	6♠	4♣
	Q♦	K♦	10♥	2♠	7♦	A♣					
55	J♥	4♣	Q♣	A♣	3♥	K♣	A♠	4♦	7♥/10♣	2♠	5♠
	Q♥	10♥	Q♠	9♠	2♠	5♦					
56	6♦	J♠	10♠	4♥	9♠	8♠	K♣	9♠	Q♦/9♥	K♣	10♥
	2♣	K♦	9♣	5♠	8♦	6♠					
57	2♣	2♦	Q♣	J♠	5♦	5♠	8♥	4♣	7♣/A♦	8♠	J♣
	7♥	5♦	6♣	9♥	2♥	8♥					
58	4♣	7♥	J♠	A♥	4♥	7♣	3♦	9♥	5♥/10♥	6♣	J♦
	8♠	Q♥	8♣	2♥	Q♣	3♦					
59	7♦	4♦	6♣	10♥	7♠	8♠	A♥	6♦	Q♠/4♠	2♦	3♣
	J♠	9♠	J♥	3♦	5♠	3♥					
60	6♥	7♥	10♥	10♠	3♠	6♦	8♠	K♥	K♥/A♦	A♦	6♦
	7♣	10♦	J♦	3♦	5♠	8♠					
61	10♠	A♣	J♠	3♥	K♣	2♠	6♦	Q♥	4♣/8♣	A♥	9♣
	6♠	K♠	9♣	7♣	7♦	Q♥					
62	3♦	5♣	K♠	10♥	A♣	5♠	5♦	3♦	2♠/6♠	3♥	Q♥
	7♥	A♥	J♦	8♣	2♥	7♠					
63	K♣	2♦	J♠	7♠	9♥	9♠	J♥	10♦	7♠/4♦	Q♣	10♠
	4♣	8♦	Q♠	7♥	5♦	8♠					
64	2♠	9♣	7♣	J♦	Q♥	7♠	9♦	8♠	6♥/K♠	10♦	4♥
	4♣	A♥	7♥	4♥	J♠	4♦					
65	6♠	4♣	J♦	4♦	5♠	3♥	8♠	7♣	Q♠/2♣	Q♠	4♠
	8♠	9♥	2♥	K♣	9♠	8♠					
66	Q♦	K♠	5♣	A♣	4♠	8♥	2♦	Q♣	3♥/4♥	8♦	10♣
	3♠	10♦	8♦	2♠	A♥	K♣	4♣				
67	8♣	K♥	7♠	K♣	3♦	10♥	5♣	5♥	5♥/10♣	7♣	J♠
	6♦	Q♣	3♠	J♣	5♦	5♠					
68	7♣	9♦	K♣	8♦	4♠	9♣	10♥	J♣	2♠/7♥	J♠	7♣
	4♣	K♦	3♠	10♦	J♦	10♥					
69	K♠	3♣	2♥	Q♦	2♣	3♥	Q♠	6♦	9♣/Q♥	10♣	8♦
	10♠	4♥	2♠	9♥	Q♣	J♥	2♣				
70	6♣	J♠	10♠	3♠	4♦	8♠	2♦	J♥	A♥/5♠	4♠	Q♠
	7♣	2♠	J♦	9♣	Q♦	2♠					
71	5♣	Q♦	3♦	J♠	Q♣	4♥	8♠	4♣	7♦/8♥	4♥	10♦
	Q♠	J♥	9♠	7♠	9♠	Q♥					
72	6♠	Q♠	J♠	J♦	3♠	7♦	3♥	Q♣	J♥/K♣	10♠	Q♣
	2♣	5♥	4♠	10♠	A♥	7♣					
73	2♥	K♦	2♠	8♦	10♣	J♣	J♦	2♥	9♥/Q♣	Q♥	3♥
	6♠	8♥	4♠	6♠	5♠	J♦					
74	5♦	4♥	8♦	9♣	A♦	9♥	2♣	3♥	Q♥/7♥	9♣	A♥
	K♥	5♥	4♠	5♣	6♥	2♣					

AGE	MER	VEN	MAR	JUP	SAT	URA	NEP	LR	PLU/RES	ENV	DISP
75	10♠	7♣	6♦	A♥	7♦	K♥	9♣	K♣	A♠/Q♣	6♦	A♦
	8♣	A♣	5♠	6♣	3♥	9♣					
76	6♠	8♣	A♥	K♣	Q♠	A♠	9♦	A♠	7♠/K♦	3♠	2♦
	A♦	10♣	K♠	5♦	5♥	9♥					
77	3♦	A♦	K♣	9♠	K♠	7♥	2♥	6♦	A♠/2♦	J♦	6♣
	5♣	7♠	5♦	K♦	A♥	4♠	K♠				
78	7♥	8♥	6♦	4♠	J♣	10♦	9♥	J♠	2♠/J♦	J♣	8♠
	7♠	3♥	4♥	K♠	K♥	4♠					
79	8♦	A♦	4♠	5♦	5♥	7♠	9♦	10♠	3♥/6♣	10♥	K♣
	K♣	A♠	8♠	Q♦	6♦	9♦					
80	5♣	8♥	5♦	Q♣	2♦	K♣	K♠	4♥	K♥/A♣	5♠	2♠
	J♣	5♠	10♣	6♦	4♠	9♠	2♦				
81	10♦	A♦	8♠	K♣	9♠	2♥	6♠	9♠	Q♣/9♥	4♦	6♠
	7♠	6♣	K♥	2♦	5♦	J♦					
82	2♥	5♦	5♠	J♦	3♠	2♣	A♦	8♥	8♣/7♣	5♥	9♠
	J♣	K♦	8♥	2♦	9♠	A♦					
83	4♣	J♠	J♦	K♥	A♥	8♠	J♠	K♣	Q♣/10♠	5♣	K♥
	Q♦	2♠	10♥	6♣	5♠	J♠					
84	A♠	4♥	Q♠	6♦	7♥	Q♦	K♥	2♠	8♥/7♠	4♣	2♣
	9♥	2♣	9♠	J♠	J♦	K♠					
85	5♦	9♥	6♦	J♥	10♣	8♥	A♣	2♦	7♠/3♦	6♥	A♠
	J♠	10♠	4♣	2♠	8♣	A♣					
86	7♠	3♠	J♥	4♠	7♥	2♥	8♥	Q♣	Q♦/4♠	3♦	7♥
	6♣	7♣	A♥	5♠	4♥	8♥					
87	2♠	2♣	4♠	8♦	Q♣	K♠	2♦	J♠	2♥/A♦	Q♦	8♥
	5♦	Q♥	A♥	4♦	J♥	10♣	Q♣				
88	7♥	6♠	6♦	10♣	10♥	9♠	K♣	5♦	K♣/K♥	9♦	7♠
	9♣	3♥	5♥	J♥	4♠	10♦					
89	4♣	5♣	6♠	7♣	8♣	9♣	10♣	5♣	J♣/Q♣	5♦	K♦
	9♥	2♥	5♠	J♦	4♦	10♣					
90	3♠	9♥	7♣	5♦	Q♠	J♣	9♦	8♥	7♠/2♣	3♣	3♣
	10♥	6♥	5♠	Q♣	10♣	2♠					
91	8♦	10♥	5♠	8♥	K♥	8♠	J♣	4♣	10♠/5♥	K♦	5♠
	A♥	8♣	A♣	2♣	9♣	J♠					
92	7♥	9♠	6♠	10♥	Q♥	5♠	8♠	7♥	A♠/A♦	7♠	9♣
	7♠	4♦	Q♦	5♥	Q♠	4♦					
93	6♥	8♥	10♥	7♦	4♠	7♠	J♠	J♠	4♦/K♦	8♥	Q♦
	J♣	2♠	K♥	Q♠	9♣	J♠					
94	6♠	9♠	7♦	4♠	J♥	J♣	8♠	A♥	2♥/K♠	7♥	3♦
	6♣	A♦	4♥	Q♠	10♠	8♠					
95	5♦	10♦	Q♥	8♣	5♠	6♦	4♣	4♥	10♣/3♥	A♠	6♥
	6♥	J♠	9♣	A♦	8♥	A♠					
96	Q♠	9♣	8♣	4♦	3♠	6♥	4♣	7♣	Q♣/7♣	2♣	4♣
	J♥	J♣	10♠	6♠	9♠	5♥					
97	8♥	8♠	K♣	9♥	Q♦	J♥	4♦	3♦	A♦/A♣	K♥	5♣
	K♠	Q♠	6♣	7♦	10♦	8♦					
98	9♠	4♣	9♥	6♦	K♥	Q♥	3♦	9♥	2♣/2♠	9♠	5♥
	J♣	6♠	7♠	A♠	5♦	3♦					
99	10♠	8♠	7♣	Q♣	5♥	J♣	6♦	4♦	K♠/4♥	6♠	4♣
	Q♦	K♦	10♥	2♠	9♥	2♥					

Four of Clubs

AGE	MER	VEN	MAR	JUP	SAT	URA	NEP	LR	PLU/RES	ENV	DISP
0	2♦	J♠	8♣	6♦	4♠	10♥	10♦	2♦	8♣/A♥	4♣	4♣
	J♥	10♠	8♦	8♥	7♠	3♠					
1	Q♦	2♣	A♠	9♥	4♦	J♥	6♦	J♠	6♠/A♣	6♥	5♣
	K♠	2♦	K♥	7♦	6♠	A♦					
2	7♠	J♣	9♥	10♣	K♦	7♣	5♠	8♣	3♣/7♥	3♦	5♥
	10♠	8♥	7♦	A♣	5♠	5♠					
3	6♣	2♠	A♥	8♠	8♦	10♠	10♣	6♦	K♠/Q♠	Q♦	4♦
	4♦	6♥	Q♥	7♥	9♥	2♥					
4	J♥	J♣	8♠	2♥	K♣	A♠	5♦	4♠	9♦/Q♣	9♦	5♠
	7♣	Q♥	2♦	7♠	7♥	5♠					
5	10♣	3♥	8♦	Q♠	7♠	Q♦	A♠	10♥	4♦/7♦	5♦	10♥
	3♣	6♥	J♠	9♣	A♦	8♥					
6	7♥	9♠	8♠	3♥	5♠	J♦	Q♦	10♦	A♥/6♠	3♣	J♣
	9♦	3♠	K♥	7♦	A♣	Q♦					
7	J♣	9♠	3♥	2♠	Q♠	A♥	5♠	Q♦	3♠/Q♥	K♦	J♦
	2♣	7♠	8♠	A♣	8♠	5♠					
8	9♥	6♦	K♥	Q♥	3♦	2♣	2♠	2♣	2♦/10♦	7♠	3♠
	10♠	7♠	J♥	5♠	9♥	K♣					
9	10♥	9♦	Q♥	8♦	4♠	10♣	2♣	A♠	K♦/6♠	8♥	6♦
	A♥	6♣	4♥	5♦	9♦	2♣					
10	Q♣	2♥	3♥	K♣	A♠	7♥	10♣	9♥	J♣/8♣	7♥	9♣
	8♥	K♠	J♠	A♥	9♥	7♣					
11	5♠	J♦	K♠	Q♥	2♥	9♣	5♣	4♦	7♥/K♥	A♠	Q♥
	9♦	2♠	4♥	8♣	A♣	A♥					
12	A♠	9♠	3♥	A♥	7♦	7♠	J♥	J♥	3♦/Q♠	2♣	10♠
	J♣	A♦	2♦	9♥	3♠	2♣					
13	7♥	J♠	A♥	4♥	7♠	5♥		6♦	10♥/K♠	K♥	4♥
	J♣	2♣	9♠	Q♠	3♥	6♠					
14	8♥	J♣	4♥	6♦	9♣	K♣	2♣	7♠	2♦/3♣	9♠	4♠
	A♦	7♠	A♣	A♠	7♠	2♣					
15	4♦	K♠	J♦	2♥	J♣	Q♦	9♠	J♣	K♣/Q♠	6♠	10♣
	4♠	6♣	A♦	7♥	2♠	A♠	J♣				
16	8♣	K♦	3♦	A♠	5♠	Q♥	J♦	9♥	3♠/6♠	2♠	J♠
	10♣	8♠	4♠	10♠	5♣	J♦					
17	A♥	5♥	A♠	A♦	10♦	J♠	Q♥	10♣	7♥/9♦	K♠	7♠
	J♣	6♥	4♠	6♠	4♥	Q♥					
18	K♠	5♠	A♣	4♦	3♣	K♣	2♦	K♦	J♠/7♣	8♠	8♦
	8♠	Q♠	7♥	5♥	8♠	J♥	3♣				
19	K♥	3♥	8♦	4♠	6♠	2♣	3♣	7♣	2♠/9♣	6♣	Q♠
	A♥	7♥	4♥	J♠	4♦	3♣					
20	J♦	4♦	5♠	3♥	8♠	Q♠	2♣	5♠	9♥/Q♦	2♦	10♦
	2♦	J♥	7♠	3♦	J♠	7♠					
21	8♥	2♣	3♥	4♥	4♠	9♥	K♣	6♠	J♥/A♠	A♦	Q♣
	3♠	3♣	10♦	8♦	2♠	A♥					
22	A♣	6♥	7♥	A♦	Q♣	10♠	4♥	2♣	7♦/8♠	A♥	3♥
	8♥	Q♦	10♦	K♥	9♣	4♥					
23	5♣	Q♠	A♦	J♠	6♠	7♦	3♠	A♥	7♣/9♦	3♥	A♥
	K♦	3♠	10♦	J♦	10♥	3♣					
24	8♦	A♥	10♣	2♠	9♥	K♦	J♠	8♠	5♦/8♠	Q♣	A♦
	8♣	2♥	9♣	K♥	K♣	J♠					
25	8♥	8♣	2♠	A♠	2♦	5♠	5♥	3♠	3♦/6♥	10♦	2♦
	6♠	Q♣	K♠	5♠	3♠	7♦					
26	5♠	6♠	A♠	7♠	K♠	9♠	A♣	10♠	5♦/9♠	Q♠	6♣
	J♦	9♥	5♣	6♥	2♠	10♦	K♠				
27	9♦	Q♦	10♣	10♦	10♠	6♣	7♦	10♣	7♥/4♥	8♦	8♠
	3♦	K♣	Q♠	K♣	6♥	J♣					
28	A♦	6♠	10♦	5♠	3♠	3♦	5♥	J♥	K♠/K♥	7♣	K♣
	A♠	5♦	2♣	4♦	10♣	5♥					
29	J♦	Q♦	5♠	8♠	9♠	A♠	K♠	J♣	K♦/2♥	J♠	2♠
	10♠	9♣	Q♠	10♣	10♦	7♠	9♠				
30	6♠	6♠	2♣	K♠	7♠	A♠	8♥	8♠	8♠/J♠	10♣	6♠
	3♦	K♥	K♦	9♠	5♠	4♥					
31	A♣	5♠	J♦	4♥	4♠	3♠	6♠	2♥	8♣/A♥	4♠	9♠
	10♠	6♥	Q♦	9♠	7♠	6♠					
32	J♣	10♠	4♥	K♦	2♠	8♠	3♥	K♠	8♠/8♦	4♥	K♥
	4♦	7♥	6♠	K♥	9♠	3♥					
33	5♦	Q♠	2♠	10♣	9♠	4♦	K♦	A♠	Q♦/A♥	10♠	2♣
	7♦	3♣	7♠	3♦	4♥	K♠					
34	5♣	7♦	10♣	J♦	Q♠	Q♦	2♥	5♦	3♦/5♠	Q♥	A♠
	3♥	8♦	J♣	7♥	8♠	2♥					
35	9♥	4♠	J♥	10♦	9♦	A♣	Q♦	10♣	4♦/6♦	9♠	7♥
	K♥	A♥	2♠	J♦	Q♠	Q♦					
36	7♥	3♣	10♠	A♦	8♠	K♠	9♠	3♥	A♠/6♠	6♦	8♥
	5♣	7♠	2♠	6♦	J♥	Q♣	8♠				
37	9♦	8♥	10♣	Q♣	Q♥	7♠	6♥	8♦	A♠/K♦	3♠	7♠
	J♠	K♣	3♠	J♥	10♦	6♣					
38	J♣	J♦	K♥	A♥	8♣	J♠	Q♣	Q♠	10♠/8♠	J♦	K♦
	7♠	A♣	9♣	4♥	6♦	Q♠					
39	4♠	7♠	A♥	5♣	2♦	10♠	5♥	7♠	3♦/3♣	J♠	3♣
	Q♥	10♥	9♣	8♠	Q♣	7♥					
40	A♦	Q♥	5♣	Q♦	K♦	2♣	10♠	Q♦	8♦/3♠	10♥	5♦
	2♠	8♣	2♥	3♣	J♠	10♠					
41	9♦	7♠	K♥	Q♥	7♣	J♦	2♣	A♠	5♦/6♠	5♠	9♦
	3♦	6♥	4♦	3♠	2♦	Q♠					
42	10♥	Q♦	Q♥	9♥	10♦	3♦	3♥	7♦	6♦/6♥	4♦	Q♦
	10♠	7♥	K♦	2♦	J♠	3♥					
43	8♥	7♠	9♥	J♣	J♥	10♠	2♣	9♠	A♣/A♠	5♥	3♦
	K♥	6♠	Q♠	2♦	8♦	2♣					
44	5♣	6♠	7♠	3♣	9♠	10♠	J♠	8♠	Q♠/K♣	5♠	6♥
	10♥	3♥	J♠	6♠	Q♦	5♦					
45	2♦	J♠	8♣	6♦	4♠	10♥	10♦	3♥	8♠/A♥	4♣	4♣
	J♥	10♠	8♦	8♥	7♠	3♠					
46	Q♦	2♣	A♠	7♦	4♦	J♥	6♦	5♠	6♠/2♥	6♥	5♣
	K♠	2♦	K♥	9♥	6♣	A♦					
47	7♠	J♣	7♦	10♣	K♦	7♣	5♠	J♦	3♣/7♥	3♦	5♥
	10♠	8♥	9♥	2♥	5♣	5♠					
48	6♣	2♠	A♥	8♠	3♠	10♠	10♣	Q♦	K♠/Q♠	Q♦	4♦
	4♦	6♥	Q♥	7♥	7♦	A♠					
49	J♥	J♣	8♠	A♠	K♠	A♠	5♦	J♠	9♦/Q♣	9♦	5♠
	7♣	Q♥	2♦	7♠	7♥	5♣					

AGE	MER	VEN	MAR	JUP	SAT	URA	NEP	LR	PLU/RES	ENV	DISP
50	10♣	3♥	8♦	Q♠	7♠	Q♦	A♠	9♦	4♦/9♥	5♦	10♥
	3♣	6♥	J♠	9♠	A♦	8♥					
51	7♥	9♠	8♠	3♥	5♣	J♦	Q♠	3♥	A♥/6♠	3♣	J♣
	9♠	3♠	K♥	9♥	2♥	Q♦					
52	J♣	9♠	3♥	2♠	Q♠	A♥	5♠	2♠	3♠/Q♥	K♦	J♦
	2♣	7♠	8♠	2♥	8♠	5♠					
53	7♦	6♦	K♥	Q♥	3♦	2♣	2♠	Q♠	2♦/10♦	7♠	3♠
	10♠	7♠	J♥	5♠	9♣	K♣					
54	10♥	9♦	Q♥	8♠	4♠	10♠	2♣	A♥	K♦/6♠	8♥	6♦
	A♥	6♣	4♥	5♠	9♠	2♣					
55	Q♣	A♣	3♥	K♣	A♠	7♥	10♣	5♠	J♣/8♣	7♥	9♣
	8♥	K♠	J♠	A♥	7♦	7♣					
56	5♠	J♦	K♠	Q♥	A♣	9♣	5♣	9♥	7♥/K♥	A♠	Q♥
	9♦	2♠	4♥	8♣	2♥	A♥					
57	A♠	9♠	3♥	A♥	9♥	7♠	J♥	6♦	3♦/Q♠	2♣	10♠
	J♣	A♦	2♥	9♠	3♠	2♠					
58	7♥	J♠	A♥	4♥	7♣	3♠	5♥	K♥	10♥/K♠	K♥	4♥
	J♣	2♠	9♦	Q♠	3♥	6♦					
59	8♥	J♣	4♥	6♦	9♣	K♣	2♣	Q♥	2♦/3♣	9♠	4♠
	A♦	9♥	2♥	A♠	7♠	2♣					
60	4♦	K♠	J♦	A♣	J♣	Q♦	9♠	3♦	K♣/Q♠	6♠	10♣
	4♠	6♣	A♦	7♥	2♠	A♠	J♣				
61	8♣	K♦	3♦	A♠	5♠	Q♥	J♦	2♣	3♠/6♣	2♠	J♠
	10♣	8♠	4♠	10♠	5♣	J♦					
62	A♥	5♥	A♠	A♦	10♦	J♠	Q♥	2♠	7♥/9♦	K♣	7♣
	J♣	6♥	4♠	6♣	4♥	Q♥					
63	K♠	5♠	2♥	4♦	3♠	K♣	2♦	10♥	J♠/7♣	8♠	8♦
	8♦	Q♠	7♥	5♥	8♠	J♥	3♣				
64	K♥	3♥	8♦	4♠	6♦	2♣	3♣	9♦	2♠/9♣	6♠	Q♠
	A♥	7♥	4♥	J♠	4♦	3♣					
65	J♦	4♦	5♠	3♥	8♠	Q♠	2♣	Q♥	7♦/Q♦	2♦	10♦
	2♦	J♥	7♠	3♦	J♠	7♣					
66	8♥	2♦	3♥	4♥	4♠	7♦	K♣	8♦	J♥/A♠	A♦	Q♣
	3♣	3♠	10♦	8♦	2♠	A♥					
67	2♥	6♥	7♥	A♦	Q♣	10♠	4♥	4♠	9♥/8♠	A♥	3♥
	8♥	Q♦	10♦	K♥	9♣	4♥					
68	5♣	Q♠	A♦	J♠	6♠	9♥	3♣	10♣	7♣/9♦	3♥	A♥
	K♦	3♠	10♦	J♦	10♥	3♣					
69	8♦	A♥	10♣	8♠	7♦	K♦	J♠	2♣	5♦/8♠	Q♣	A♦
	8♣	A♠	9♣	K♥	K♣	4♣					
70	8♥	8♣	2♠	A♠	2♦	5♦	5♥	Q♣	3♦/6♥	10♦	2♦
	6♠	Q♣	K♠	5♣	3♠	9♥					
71	5♠	6♠	A♠	7♠	K♠	9♦	2♥	2♥	5♦/9♠	Q♠	6♣
	J♦	7♦	5♣	6♥	2♠	10♦	K♠				
72	9♦	Q♦	10♣	10♦	10♠	6♣	9♥	3♥	7♥/4♥	8♦	8♠
	3♦	K♣	Q♠	K♠	6♥	J♣					
73	A♦	6♠	10♦	5♠	3♠	3♦	5♥	K♣	K♣/K♥	7♠	K♣
	A♠	5♦	2♣	4♦	10♠	5♥					
74	J♦	Q♦	5♣	8♠	9♠	A♠	K♠	A♠	K♦/A♣	J♠	2♠
	10♠	9♣	Q♣	10♣	10♦	7♠	9♠				
75	6♣	6♠	2♣	K♠	7♠	2♥	8♥	7♥	8♠/J♠	10♣	6♠
	3♦	K♥	K♠	9♠	5♣	4♥					
76	2♥	5♣	J♠	4♥	4♠	3♣	6♠	10♣	8♣/A♥	4♠	9♠
	10♠	6♥	Q♠	9♠	7♠	6♠					
77	J♣	10♠	4♥	K♦	2♠	8♣	3♥	5♠	8♠/8♦	4♥	K♥
	4♦	7♥	6♣	K♥	9♣	3♥					
78	5♦	Q♠	2♦	10♣	9♦	4♦	K♦	J♦	Q♦/A♥	10♠	2♣
	9♥	3♣	7♠	3♥	4♥	K♠					
79	5♣	9♥	10♣	J♥	Q♣	Q♦	A♣	K♠	3♦/5♠	Q♥	A♠
	3♥	8♦	J♠	7♥	8♠	A♣					
80	7♦	4♠	J♥	10♦	9♦	2♥	Q♠	Q♥	4♦/6♦	9♣	7♥
	K♥	A♥	2♠	J♦	Q♠	Q♦					
81	7♥	3♠	10♦	A♠	8♠	K♠	9♠	2♥	2♥/6♠	6♦	8♥
	5♣	7♣	8♠	6♦	J♥	Q♣	8♠				
82	9♦	8♥	10♣	Q♣	Q♥	7♠	6♥	9♣	A♠/K♦	3♠	7♠
	J♠	K♣	3♠	J♥	10♦	6♣					
83	J♣	J♦	K♥	A♥	8♠	J♠	Q♣	5♠	10♠/8♠	J♦	K♦
	9♥	2♥	9♣	4♥	6♦	Q♠					
84	4♠	9♥	A♥	5♣	2♦	10♠	5♠	A♠	3♦/3♣	J♠	3♣
	Q♥	10♥	9♣	8♠	Q♣	7♥					
85	A♦	Q♥	5♣	Q♦	K♦	2♣	10♠	9♠	8♦/3♠	10♥	5♦
	2♠	8♣	A♣	3♣	J♣	10♠					
86	9♦	7♠	K♥	Q♥	7♠	J♦	2♣	3♥	5♦/6♠	5♠	9♣
	3♦	6♦	4♦	3♠	2♦	Q♠					
87	10♥	Q♦	Q♥	7♦	10♦	3♦	3♥	A♥	6♦/6♥	4♦	Q♦
	10♠	7♥	K♦	2♦	J♠	3♥					
88	8♥	7♠	7♦	J♣	J♥	10♠	2♣	7♦	2♥/A♠	5♥	3♦
	K♥	6♠	Q♠	2♦	8♦	2♣					
89	5♣	6♣	7♣	8♠	9♠	10♣	J♣	7♠	Q♠/K♣	5♠	6♥
	10♥	3♥	J♠	6♠	Q♦	5♦					
90	2♦	J♠	8♣	6♦	4♠	10♥	10♦	J♥	8♠/A♥	4♠	4♣
	J♥	10♠	8♦	8♥	7♠	3♠					
91	Q♦	2♠	A♠	9♥	4♦	J♥	6♦	7♥	6♠/A♣	6♥	5♣
	K♠	2♣	K♥	7♦	6♣	A♦					
92	7♠	J♣	9♥	10♣	K♦	7♠	5♠	J♠	3♣/7♥	3♦	5♥
	10♠	8♥	7♠	A♣	5♣	5♠					
93	6♣	2♣	A♥	8♠	3♠	10♠	10♣	A♥	K♠/Q♠	Q♦	4♦
	4♦	6♥	Q♥	7♥	9♥	2♥					
94	J♥	J♣	8♠	2♥	K♣	A♠	5♠	4♥	9♦/Q♠	9♠	5♠
	7♣	Q♥	2♦	7♠	7♥	5♣					
95	10♣	3♥	8♦	Q♠	7♠	Q♦	A♠	7♣	4♦/7♦	5♦	10♥
	3♣	6♥	J♠	9♠	A♦	8♥					
96	7♥	9♠	8♠	3♥	5♣	J♦	Q♦	3♦	A♥/6♠	3♣	J♣
	9♦	3♠	K♥	7♠	A♣	Q♦					
97	J♣	9♠	3♥	2♠	Q♠	A♥	5♠	5♥	3♠/Q♥	K♦	J♦
	2♣	7♣	8♣	A♣	8♠	5♠					
98	9♥	6♠	K♥	Q♥	3♦	2♣	2♠	8♥	2♦/10♦	7♠	3♠
	10♠	7♠	J♥	5♠	9♣	K♣					
99	10♥	9♦	Q♥	8♦	4♠	10♣	2♣	J♠	K♦/6♠	8♥	6♦
	A♥	6♣	4♥	5♠	9♣	2♣					

Five of Clubs

AGE	MER	VEN	MAR	JUP	SAT	URA	NEP	LR	PLU/RES	ENV	DISP
0	3♦	A♠	7♥	7♦	5♠	J♥	9♣	3♦	9♠/2♦	5♣	5♣
	K♠	6♣	2♣	9♥	8♠	2♦					
1	K♦	J♦	7♣	J♠	3♣	8♦	10♥	A♠	5♦/8♥	4♣	5♥
	4♠	7♠	9♥	2♥	5♥	10♥					
2	8♠	A♠	A♦	K♣	6♦	4♥	J♠	7♥	K♠/10♦	6♥	4♦
	5♠	4♣	10♠	8♥	7♦	A♣					
3	J♥	J♦	K♣	A♣	2♠	7♥	9♦	7♣	Q♦/3♦	3♦	5♠
	8♦	10♠	6♣	K♦	8♥	5♥					
4	J♠	A♥	Q♠	10♦	K♦	3♦	7♥	5♠	5♠/9♥	Q♦	10♥
	5♦	4♣	7♣	Q♥	2♦	7♠					
5	8♥	K♥	K♣	A♥	5♥	3♠	3♦	J♥	A♦/9♠	9♦	J♣
	Q♦	6♦	2♣	9♥	2♥	3♦					
6	J♦	Q♦	A♥	6♣	10♦	A♦	10♥	9♣	6♦/10♠	5♦	J♦
	A♠	8♦	8♣	2♥	K♣	10♥					
7	7♦	9♣	2♣	10♠	6♥	A♣	6♠	K♣	6♣/Q♣	3♣	3♠
	4♥	K♦	J♥	10♥	Q♥	2♠					
8	J♣	Q♦	10♠	Q♠	10♦	J♠	A♠	J♥	3♣/9♠	K♦	6♦
	A♦	8♠	4♠	10♥	Q♥	A♠					
9	3♥	A♠	A♥	2♠	7♥	8♥	J♠	7♥	J♦/8♦	7♠	9♣
	7♠	K♣	7♠	A♦	7♠	8♦					
10	10♥	3♠	K♣	10♠	A♣	Q♥	5♥	J♠	8♥/2♣	8♥	Q♥
	Q♦	6♠	4♠	8♣	2♥	A♦					
11	7♥	K♥	A♥	A♣	9♥	K♦	J♥	3♣	6♥/10♦	7♥	10♠
	J♦	2♦	6♣	Q♦	6♦	A♠					
12	8♥	7♠	A♦	4♠	8♦	6♥	4♦	8♦	J♣/K♣	A♠	4♥
	J♦	6♠	Q♦	10♦	A♥	9♣					
13	7♠	J♦	4♦	9♣	Q♥	2♠	A♠	10♥	6♣/5♦	2♣	4♣
	2♦	9♥	2♥	7♥	K♦	A♣					
14	5♠	K♠	3♠	A♣	J♦	3♦	K♥	8♠	2♠/10♦	K♥	10♣
	10♣	8♠	2♦	8♥	6♠	7♥	J♦				
15	8♣	3♣	6♥	7♥	10♥	10♠	3♠	A♠	6♦/8♠	9♠	J♠
	J♠	K♣	10♣	4♥	5♥	3♠					
16	A♦	4♦	7♥	2♦	Q♣	7♣	10♠	A♦	8♥/Q♣	6♠	7♣
	J♦	4♣	10♠	8♠	4♠	10♠					
17	K♠	10♥	2♥	5♠	5♦	2♠	6♣	K♣	7♣/8♦	2♠	8♦
	Q♠	10♦	8♥	4♦	K♣	J♥	5♦				
18	2♣	A♥	Q♠	10♣	9♣	A♠	5♦	6♦	6♠/Q♥	K♣	Q♠
	A♦	8♥	4♠	7♣	5♠	5♦					
19	3♠	5♠	10♥	A♥	K♣	10♦	A♠	4♥	7♦/3♦	8♠	10♦
	6♣	J♥	K♦	6♥	7♠	8♦					
20	7♠	6♣	A♥	4♠	10♣	7♦	2♠	J♠	J♥/7♥	6♣	Q♣
	5♦	6♦	Q♣	Q♠	6♠	A♦					
21	2♥	4♣	8♥	2♦	3♥	4♥	4♠	J♥	9♥/K♣	2♦	3♥
	7♠	3♦	Q♣	2♣	Q♥	4♠					
22	5♥	10♦	2♦	7♣	9♠	9♥	5♦	J♦	8♦/Q♦	A♦	A♥
	3♣	6♦	Q♣	3♠	J♣	5♦					
23	Q♠	A♦	J♠	6♠	7♦	3♣	7♣	K♣	9♦/K♠	A♥	A♦
	8♣	A♣	Q♦	2♣	7♣						
24	7♠	8♣	6♠	7♥	6♣	9♦	4♦	A♣	6♥/4♣	3♥	2♦
	9♠	3♥	K♠	5♥	6♦	9♥					
25	10♥	9♠	7♥	K♦	K♠	Q♦	2♥	2♠	9♦/K♥	Q♣	6♣
	3♠	7♠	5♥	4♣	6♠	Q♣	K♠				
26	Q♦	3♦	J♠	Q♠	4♥	8♠	9♥	7♥	8♥/4♠	10♦	8♠
	6♥	2♠	10♦	K♠	4♣	J♦					
27	2♦	9♠	Q♣	5♥	6♦	6♥	4♦	9♠	2♠/2♣	Q♠	K♣
	7♥	9♦	A♠	5♠	J♠	4♦					
28	3♠	3♦	5♥	K♣	K♥	7♥	K♠	J♠	3♣/A♣	8♦	2♠
	4♥	Q♥	3♦	J♠	Q♣	K♦	K♥				
29	8♠	9♠	A♠	K♣	K♦	2♥	7♠	A♥	K♣/7♣	7♣	6♠
	6♥	2♣	3♣	K♥	5♥	4♠					
30	2♥	5♥	3♠	4♣	10♣	5♥	9♠	Q♠	8♣/A♦	J♠	9♠
	4♥	4♣	3♦	K♦	K♠	9♠					
31	J♦	4♥	4♠	3♣	6♠	8♣	A♥	10♦	K♣/Q♠	10♣	K♥
	5♠	8♥	8♠	2♣	Q♥	A♥					
32	9♦	10♦	6♠	J♠	Q♦	5♠	3♣	K♦	3♦/A♦	4♠	2♣
	9♥	5♦	K♦	A♥	4♠	K♠					
33	5♥	9♥	J♠	J♥	3♥	3♦	A♣	3♦	6♥/10♥	4♥	A♠
	A♥	Q♠	J♦	8♥	8♣	A♣					
34	7♦	10♣	J♥	Q♣	Q♦	2♥	3♦	7♥	5♠/9♠	10♠	7♥
	2♣	A♦	6♠	3♠	10♦	3♦					
35	8♥	5♦	Q♣	2♦	K♣	K♠	K♥	8♥	2♥/9♠	Q♥	8♥
	5♥	8♦	6♠	9♣	J♥	3♥	K♣				
36	Q♦	7♠	J♠	3♥	10♠	K♦	4♣	K♥	7♥/3♣	9♠	7♠
	7♣	2♠	6♦	J♥	Q♣	8♠					
37	J♦	3♠	2♣	A♦	8♦	7♣	3♥	K♣	4♥/K♣	6♦	K♦
	9♥	2♥	Q♥	4♠	9♠	3♥					
38	10♣	9♥	A♦	5♥	6♠	4♥	4♦	A♥	6♥/5♦	3♠	3♠
	10♠	J♣	Q♥	K♠	3♥	8♥					
39	2♦	10♠	5♥	3♦	3♠	A♠	4♥	5♥	Q♠/6♦	J♦	5♦
	6♠	8♣	A♣	5♦	7♣	4♥					
40	Q♦	K♦	2♠	10♠	8♦	3♠	A♠	3♥	9♦/9♠	J♠	9♦
	6♥	9♣	5♠	6♦	6♣	10♦					
41	J♣	3♦	10♠	7♦	Q♣	6♥	A♥	3♦	9♣/4♠	10♥	Q♦
	4♥	8♥	3♣	6♣	7♠	A♥					
42	7♠	K♦	7♦	J♦	J♥	4♥	A♠	J♦	2♥/7♥	5♠	3♦
	2♣	9♠	10♦	6♠	Q♠	A♠					
43	5♥	8♠	8♦	8♣	Q♥	J♠	J♦	Q♦	3♥/2♠	4♦	6♥
	J♣	A♥	7♣	9♠	3♦	9♦					
44	6♠	7♠	8♠	9♣	10♦	J♣	Q♠	A♥	K♣/A♦	5♥	4♣
	J♥	4♦	Q♠	9♠	K♦	6♦					
45	3♦	A♠	7♥	9♥	5♠	J♥	9♣	6♠	9♠/A♣	5♣	5♠
	K♠	6♣	2♣	7♦	8♠	2♦					
46	K♦	J♦	9♥	J♠	3♣	8♦	10♥	10♠	5♦/8♥	4♣	5♥
	4♥	7♠	7♥	A♣	5♥	10♥					
47	8♠	A♠	A♦	K♣	6♦	4♥	J♠	A♦	K♠/10♦	6♥	4♦
	5♠	4♣	10♠	8♥	9♥	2♥					
48	J♦	J♦	K♣	2♥	2♠	7♥	9♦	10♥	Q♦/3♥	3♦	5♠
	8♦	10♠	6♣	K♦	8♥	5♥					
49	J♠	A♥	Q♠	10♦	K♦	3♦	7♥	7♦	5♠/7♦	Q♦	10♥
	5♦	4♣	7♣	Q♥	2♦	7♠					

Ages 50–74

AGE	MER	VEN	MAR	JUP	SAT	URA	NEP	LR	PLU/RES	ENV	DISP
50	8♥	K♥	K♣	A♥	5♥	3♠	3♦	9♣	A♦/9♠	9♦	J♣
	Q♦	6♦	2♣	7♦	A♣	3♦					
51	J♦	Q♦	A♥	6♠	10♦	A♦	10♥	2♣	6♦/10♠	5♦	J♦
	A♠	8♦	8♠	A♣	K♣	10♥					
52	9♥	9♣	2♠	10♠	6♥	A♠	6♠	10♠	6♣/Q♣	3♣	3♠
	4♥	K♦	J♥	10♥	Q♥	2♠					
53	J♣	Q♦	10♠	Q♠	10♣	J♠	A♠	6♥	3♣/9♠	K♦	6♦
	A♦	8♠	4♠	10♥	Q♥	A♠					
54	3♥	2♥	A♥	2♠	7♥	8♥	J♠	A♠	J♦/8♣	7♠	9♣
	7♠	K♠	7♠	A♦	9♥	8♦					
55	10♥	3♠	K♠	10♠	2♥	Q♥	5♥	6♠	8♥/2♣	8♥	Q♥
	Q♦	6♠	4♠	8♣	A♣	A♦					
56	7♥	K♥	A♥	A♦	7♥	K♦	J♥	J♣	6♥/10♦	7♥	10♠
	J♦	2♦	6♣	Q♦	6♥	A♠					
57	8♥	7♣	A♥	4♠	8♦	6♥	4♦	Q♦	J♣/K♠	A♠	4♥
	J♦	6♠	Q♦	10♦	A♥	9♣					
58	7♠	J♠	4♠	9♣	Q♥	2♠	A♠	10♠	6♣/5♦	2♣	4♠
	2♦	7♠	A♣	7♥	K♦	A♠					
59	5♠	K♠	3♠	2♥	J♦	3♦	K♥	Q♠	2♠/10♦	K♥	10♠
	10♣	8♠	2♦	8♥	6♠	7♥	J♦				
60	8♣	3♣	6♥	7♥	10♥	10♠	3♠	10♣	6♦/8♠	9♠	J♠
	J♠	K♣	10♣	4♥	5♥	3♠					
61	A♦	4♦	7♥	2♦	Q♣	7♣	10♠	J♠	8♥/Q♦	6♠	7♣
	J♦	4♣	10♣	8♠	4♠	10♠					
62	K♠	10♥	A♣	5♠	5♦	2♠	6♣	A♠	7♠/8♦	2♠	8♦
	Q♠	10♦	8♥	4♦	K♣	J♥	5♦				
63	2♣	A♥	Q♠	10♣	9♠	A♠	5♦	3♥	6♠/Q♥	K♣	Q♠
	A♦	8♥	4♠	7♠	5♠	5♦					
64	3♠	5♠	10♥	A♥	K♣	10♦	A♠	A♣	9♥/3♦	8♠	10♦
	6♣	J♥	K♦	6♥	7♠	8♦					
65	7♠	6♣	A♥	4♣	10♣	9♥	2♠	A♥	J♥/7♥	6♣	Q♣
	5♦	6♦	Q♣	Q♠	6♠	A♦					
66	A♣	4♣	8♥	2♦	3♥	4♥	4♠	2♠	7♦/K♣	2♦	3♥
	7♠	3♦	Q♣	2♣	Q♥	4♠					
67	5♥	10♦	2♦	7♠	9♠	7♦	5♦	7♥	8♦/Q♦	A♦	A♥
	3♣	6♦	Q♣	3♠	J♣	5♦					
68	Q♠	A♦	J♠	6♠	9♥	3♣	7♣	8♥	9♦/K♣	A♥	A♦
	8♣	2♥	Q♥	2♣	2♠	7♣					
69	7♠	8♣	6♠	7♥	6♣	9♥	4♦	J♠	6♥/4♣	3♥	2♦
	9♠	3♥	K♠	5♥	6♦	7♥					
70	10♥	9♠	7♥	K♦	K♠	Q♥	A♣	10♥	9♦/K♥	Q♣	6♣
	3♠	9♥	5♥	4♣	6♠	Q♣	K♠				
71	Q♦	3♦	J♠	Q♣	4♥	8♠	7♦	3♠	8♥/4♠	10♦	8♠
	6♥	2♠	10♦	4♣	J♦						
72	2♦	9♠	Q♣	5♥	6♦	6♥	4♦	K♠	2♠/2♣	Q♠	K♣
	7♥	9♦	A♠	5♠	J♠	4♦					
73	3♠	3♦	5♥	K♣	K♥	7♥	K♠	10♠	3♣/2♥	8♦	2♠
	4♥	Q♥	3♥	J♠	Q♣	K♦	K♥				
74	8♠	9♠	A♠	K♠	K♦	A♠	7♠	A♠	K♣/7♠	7♠	6♣
	6♥	2♣	3♣	K♥	5♥	4♠					

Ages 75–99

AGE	MER	VEN	MAR	JUP	SAT	URA	NEP	LR	PLU/RES	ENV	DISP
75	A♣	5♥	3♠	4♠	10♣	5♦	9♠	Q♥	8♣/A♦	J♠	9♠
	4♥	4♣	3♦	K♥	K♦	9♠					
76	J♦	4♥	4♠	3♣	6♠	8♣	A♥	5♦	K♣/Q♠	10♣	K♥
	5♠	8♥	8♠	2♣	Q♥	A♥					
77	9♦	10♦	6♣	J♠	Q♦	5♠	3♣	7♥	3♦/A♦	4♠	2♣
	7♦	5♦	K♦	A♥	4♠	K♠					
78	5♥	7♦	J♠	J♥	3♥	3♦	2♥	K♥	6♥/10♥	4♥	A♠
	A♥	Q♠	J♦	8♥	8♣	2♥					
79	9♥	10♣	J♥	Q♣	Q♦	A♠	3♦	A♥	5♠/9♣	10♠	7♥
	2♣	A♦	6♠	3♠	10♦	3♦					
80	8♥	5♦	Q♣	2♦	K♣	K♠	K♥	A♦	A♣/9♠	Q♥	8♥
	5♥	8♦	6♠	9♣	J♥	3♥	K♣				
81	Q♦	7♠	J♠	3♥	10♠	K♦	4♣	9♥	7♥/3♣	9♠	7♠
	7♣	2♠	6♦	J♥	Q♣	8♠					
82	J♦	3♠	2♣	A♠	8♠	7♠	3♥	K♦	4♥/K♣	6♦	K♥
	7♦	A♣	Q♥	4♠	9♠	3♥					
83	10♣	7♦	A♠	5♥	6♣	4♥	4♦	J♥	6♥/5♦	3♠	3♣
	10♠	J♣	Q♥	K♣	3♥	8♥					
84	2♦	10♠	5♥	3♦	3♣	A♠	4♥	8♥	Q♠/6♦	J♦	5♦
	6♠	8♣	2♥	5♦	7♠	4♥					
85	Q♦	K♦	2♠	10♠	8♦	3♠	A♠	7♣	9♦/9♠	J♠	9♦
	6♥	9♣	5♠	6♦	6♣	10♦					
86	J♣	3♦	10♠	9♥	Q♣	6♥	A♥	A♦	9♣/4♣	10♥	Q♦
	4♥	8♥	3♣	6♣	7♠	A♥					
87	7♠	K♦	9♥	J♦	J♥	4♥	A♠	4♠	A♣/7♥	5♠	3♦
	2♣	9♠	10♦	6♣	Q♠	A♠					
88	5♥	8♠	8♦	8♣	Q♥	J♠	J♦	8♦	3♥/2♣	4♦	6♥
	J♣	A♥	7♠	9♠	3♦	9♦					
89	6♣	7♣	8♣	9♣	10♣	J♣	Q♣	6♥	K♣/A♦	5♥	4♣
	J♥	4♥	Q♠	7♠	K♦	6♦					
90	3♦	A♠	7♥	7♦	5♠	J♥	9♣	4♦	9♠/2♥	5♣	5♣
	K♠	6♣	2♠	9♥	8♠	2♦					
91	K♦	J♦	7♦	J♠	3♣	8♦	10♥	7♠	5♦/8♥	4♣	5♥
	4♥	7♠	9♥	2♥	5♥	10♥					
92	8♠	A♥	A♦	K♣	6♦	4♥	J♠	J♦	K♠/10♦	6♥	4♦
	5♠	4♣	10♠	8♥	7♦	A♣					
93	J♥	J♦	K♣	A♣	2♠	7♥	9♦	4♠	Q♦/3♥	3♦	5♠
	8♦	10♠	6♣	K♦	8♥	5♥					
94	J♠	A♥	Q♠	10♦	K♦	3♦	7♥	9♣	5♠/9♥	Q♦	10♦
	5♦	4♣	7♠	Q♥	2♦	7♠					
95	8♥	K♥	K♣	A♥	5♥	3♠	3♦	Q♥	A♦/9♠	9♦	J♣
	Q♦	6♦	2♣	9♥	2♥	3♦					
96	J♦	Q♦	A♥	6♠	10♦	A♦	10♥	2♠	6♦/10♠	5♦	J♦
	A♠	8♦	8♣	2♥	K♣	10♥					
97	7♦	9♣	2♣	10♠	6♥	A♠	6♠	A♠	6♣/Q♣	3♣	3♠
	4♥	K♦	J♥	10♥	Q♥	2♠					
98	J♣	Q♦	10♠	Q♠	10♣	J♠	A♠	5♠	3♣/9♠	K♦	6♦
	A♦	8♠	4♠	10♥	Q♥	A♠					
99	3♥	A♣	A♥	2♠	7♥	8♥	J♠	K♠	J♦/8♣	7♠	9♣
	7♠	K♠	7♣	A♦	7♦	8♦					

Six of Clubs

AGE	MER	VEN	MAR	JUP	SAT	URA	NEP	LR	PLU/RES	ENV	DISP
0	6♠	Q♥	10♦	8♦	K♠	3♥	A♣	6♠	Q♣/10♠	6♦	6♣
	2♣	9♥	8♠	2♦	9♣	5♣	K♠				
1	3♥	A♥	9♦	5♣	K♦	J♦	7♦	Q♥	J♠/3♣	2♦	8♣
	A♦	6♦	4♣	K♣	2♦	K♥					
2	10♥	Q♥	5♣	8♠	A♠	A♦	K♣	10♣	6♦/4♥	A♦	K♣
	10♣	Q♣	4♠	2♠	9♦	K♣					
3	2♣	A♥	8♠	3♠	10♠	10♣	K♠	8♦	Q♠/2♥	A♥	2♠
	K♦	8♥	5♦	9♦	5♣	8♦	10♠				
4	J♦	Q♥	4♠	K♣	8♠	A♣	7♠	K♠	3♠/Q♦	3♥	6♠
	A♦	4♥	Q♠	10♠	8♠	3♣					
5	A♣	8♠	2♠	3♠	5♦	10♦	Q♥	3♥	8♣/5♠	Q♣	9♠
	K♦	2♦	A♥	10♠	8♦	Q♥					
6	K♥	K♦	3♣	Q♠	9♣	8♣	4♦	A♣	3♠/6♥	10♦	K♥
	2♠	J♠	J♦	4♥	8♥	4♦					
7	Q♣	4♣	J♣	9♦	3♥	2♣	Q♠	3♥	A♥/5♠	Q♠	2♣
	7♦	10♦	8♦	4♦	3♣	K♠					
8	8♠	7♠	9♣	J♥	5♥	A♥	2♥	A♥	A♦/6♠	8♦	A♠
	4♦	6♥	K♥	J♠	8♠	2♥					
9	9♥	5♠	J♥	5♠	3♥	A♣	A♥	9♦	2♠/7♥	7♣	7♥
	4♥	5♠	9♣	2♠	4♣	A♥					
10	J♠	10♦	5♣	10♥	3♠	K♠	10♠	5♠	A♦/Q♥	J♠	8♥
	8♠	3♦	9♣	7♥	J♥	5♥	3♠				
11	3♥	7♣	9♣	5♥	7♠	8♦	2♦	K♦	10♣/Q♠	10♣	7♠
	Q♥	6♦	A♠	J♥	5♣	J♦					
12	K♥	2♣	4♥	5♠	8♣	Q♦	5♥	J♦	K♦/3♠	4♠	K♦
	7♦	A♣	8♥	3♠	7♥	5♥					
13	5♦	7♣	5♠	8♠	J♣	K♦	K♣	7♦	A♦/10♣	4♥	3♣
	7♠	9♣	8♥	3♠	5♥	J♠					
14	10♥	7♠	8♠	A♥	Q♠	4♠	K♦	10♥	6♥/A♠	10♠	5♦
	9♣	8♣	2♥	10♦	Q♦	K♦					
15	3♥	8♠	4♥	7♠	3♦	2♣	4♠	Q♥	Q♣/Q♥	Q♥	9♦
	A♦	7♥	2♠	A♠	J♠	4♠					
16	9♠	A♥	7♠	9♥	5♣	A♠	4♦	5♣	7♥/2♦	9♣	Q♦
	K♦	J♠	Q♠	J♣	Q♦	4♦					
17	7♣	8♦	9♥	K♥	J♥	K♦	4♠	8♠	A♣/10♣	6♦	3♦
	4♥	Q♥	4♣	J♣	6♥	4♠					
18	8♠	J♦	3♦	8♣	8♥	9♣	K♥	A♠	5♥/6♦	3♠	6♥
	9♠	4♦	Q♦	Q♥	A♥	Q♣					
19	J♣	Q♦	8♠	7♥	5♦	9♠	5♠	A♦	3♠/5♠	J♦	4♣
	J♥	K♦	6♥	7♣	8♦	A♠					
20	A♥	4♠	10♣	7♦	2♠	J♥	7♠	K♣	Q♥/2♥	J♠	5♣
	K♠	J♣	4♥	9♥	J♦	10♥					
21	8♦	K♥	7♦	9♦	Q♠	3♦	6♠	2♣	10♦/J♠	10♥	5♥
	K♦	7♣	9♥	2♦	8♠	6♠					
22	J♦	4♠	5♠	3♠	A♠	K♦	9♠	A♥	K♠/4♣	5♠	4♦
	2♠	2♦	7♠	J♠	7♦	A♠					
23	J♥	K♥	3♠	A♠	6♦	10♣	Q♣	8♠	3♥/5♥	4♦	5♠
	3♦	7♠	J♣	8♦	J♦	8♠					
24	9♦	4♦	6♥	4♣	8♦	A♥	10♠	3♠	2♠/9♥	5♥	10♥
	10♦	2♦	Q♦	8♥	10♥	7♣					
25	J♠	10♠	3♠	4♦	8♠	2♠	A♥	10♠	5♠/Q♥	5♣	J♣
	3♥	A♠	4♥	9♥	2♥	A♥					
26	K♥	3♥	4♦	9♣	4♣	5♠	6♠	10♣	A♠/7♠	4♣	J♦
	4♠	3♦	8♣	2♥	3♠	6♠					
27	7♦	7♥	4♥	7♠	A♦	4♠	9♣	K♠	J♣/5♠	6♥	3♠
	K♦	8♦	J♥	6♠	8♥	6♦					
28	9♠	3♥	7♠	6♥	5♥	9♦	4♠	J♦	Q♠/Q♥	3♦	6♦
	5♠	J♦	3♣	6♠	8♥	4♠					
29	5♥	A♣	4♦	6♦	10♣	J♠	9♦	Q♥	K♥/8♣	Q♦	9♣
	7♣	K♠	Q♠	5♠	7♦	3♦					
30	6♠	2♣	K♠	7♠	A♣	8♥	8♠	4♦	J♠/4♥	9♦	Q♥
	3♥	9♣	3♣	8♣	2♥	5♠					
31	10♣	10♠	4♦	5♠	9♥	8♦	J♥	K♠	A♦/4♣	5♦	10♠
	K♥	10♥	J♣	3♥	A♠	4♠					
32	J♠	Q♦	5♠	3♠	3♦	A♦	K♣	8♦	9♠/K♣	3♣	4♥
	K♥	9♣	3♥	4♣	4♦	7♥					
33	7♣	K♥	3♣	7♥	8♥	6♦	4♠	A♣	J♣/10♣	K♦	4♠
	10♥	9♥	2♥	10♣	8♦	4♠					
34	2♠	K♠	2♣	A♠	K♥	A♥	10♠	7♠	6♦/4♣	7♠	10♣
	5♦	J♦	10♥	J♠	9♣	10♣	K♥				
35	8♣	Q♠	A♦	10♣	6♠	7♠	2♣	A♠	A♠/J♦	8♥	J♠
	9♦	3♠	5♦	K♦	8♠	2♣					
36	5♠	K♠	10♣	10♥	5♣	Q♦	7♠	8♠	J♠/3♥	7♥	7♣
	K♥	2♦	5♦	J♦	3♣	7♠					
37	K♠	6♠	2♥	2♠	10♦	6♦	J♣	2♣	Q♦/3♦	A♠	8♦
	6♥	4♣	J♠	K♣	3♠	J♥	10♦				
38	4♥	4♦	6♥	5♦	7♥	4♠	10♦	3♣	9♣/8♦	2♣	Q♠
	5♠	J♠	3♣	Q♦	2♠	10♦					
39	2♣	2♠	6♠	4♦	3♠	4♠	4♠	5♦	7♦/A♥	K♥	10♦
	J♣	J♥	8♦	A♦	Q♦	3♦					
40	7♣	J♠	4♦	5♣	5♦	7♦	6♦	10♦	J♥/10♠	9♠	Q♣
	10♦	A♠	5♣	6♥	9♣	5♠					
41	2♥	2♦	J♠	10♥	5♣	K♦	3♣	Q♥	9♥/3♠	6♠	3♥
	7♣	A♥	5♣	4♥	8♥	3♣					
42	8♠	4♣	10♥	Q♦	Q♥	9♥	10♦	K♥	3♦/3♥	2♠	A♥
	Q♠	A♣	5♣	2♣	9♣	10♦					
43	6♥	5♠	9♦	9♣	7♦	Q♠	Q♦	K♦	Q♣/3♠	K♠	A♦
	8♣	A♣	8♥	4♦	6♦	Q♦					
44	7♠	8♠	9♣	10♣	J♣	Q♣	K♣	3♣	A♦/2♦	8♠	2♦
	Q♥	5♥	K♠	8♠	A♠	9♥					
45	6♠	Q♥	10♣	8♦	K♠	3♥	2♥	Q♠	Q♣/10♠	6♣	6♠
	2♣	7♦	8♠	2♦	9♣	5♣	K♠				
46	3♥	A♥	9♦	5♣	K♦	J♦	9♥	9♣	J♠/3♣	2♦	8♣
	A♦	6♦	4♣	K♣	2♦	K♥					
47	10♥	Q♥	5♣	8♠	A♠	A♦	K♣	8♣	6♦/4♥	A♦	K♣
	10♣	Q♣	4♠	2♠	9♦	K♣					
48	2♣	A♥	8♠	3♠	10♠	10♣	K♠	4♦	Q♠/A♣	A♥	2♠
	K♦	8♥	5♦	9♦	5♣	8♦	10♠				
49	J♦	Q♥	4♠	K♣	8♠	2♥	7♠	Q♣	3♠/Q♦	3♥	6♠
	A♦	4♥	Q♠	10♠	8♠	3♣					

AGE	MER	VEN	MAR	JUP	SAT	URA	NEP	LR	PLU/RES	ENV	DISP
50	2♥	8♠	2♣	3♣	5♦	10♦	Q♥	4♣	8♣/5♦	Q♣	9♠
	K♦	2♦	A♥	10♠	8♦	Q♥					
51	K♥	K♦	3♣	Q♠	9♣	8♣	4♦	J♣	3♠/6♥	10♦	K♥
	2♠	J♠	J♦	4♥	8♥	4♦					
52	Q♣	4♣	J♣	9♦	3♥	2♠	Q♠	9♦	A♥/5♠	Q♠	2♣
	9♥	10♦	8♦	4♦	3♣	K♠					
53	8♠	9♥	9♦	J♥	5♥	A♥	A♣	3♥	A♦/6♠	8♦	A♠
	4♦	6♥	K♥	J♠	8♣	A♣					
54	7♦	5♦	J♥	5♣	3♥	2♥	A♥	2♠	2♠/7♥	7♣	7♥
	4♥	5♠	9♣	2♣	4♣	A♥					
55	J♠	10♦	5♣	10♥	3♣	K♠	10♠	Q♠	2♥/Q♥	J♠	8♥
	8♠	3♦	9♣	7♥	J♥	5♥	3♠				
56	3♥	7♠	9♦	5♥	7♠	8♦	2♦	8♠	10♣/Q♠	10♣	7♠
	Q♦	6♦	A♠	J♥	5♣	J♦					
57	K♥	2♣	4♥	5♠	8♣	Q♦	5♥	7♥	K♦/3♠	4♠	K♦
	9♥	2♥	8♥	3♣	7♥	5♥					
58	5♦	9♥	5♠	8♣	J♠	K♦	K♣	9♦	A♦/10♦	4♥	3♣
	7♠	9♠	8♥	3♠	5♥	J♠					
59	10♥	7♠	8♠	A♥	Q♠	4♠	K♦	J♥	6♥/A♠	10♠	5♦
	9♣	8♠	A♣	10♦	Q♦	K♠					
60	3♥	8♠	4♥	7♠	3♦	2♣	4♠	5♥	Q♣/Q♥	Q♥	9♦
	A♥	7♥	2♠	A♠	J♣	4♣					
61	9♠	A♥	7♠	7♦	5♣	A♦	4♦	A♥	7♥/2♦	9♣	Q♦
	K♦	J♠	Q♠	J♣	Q♦	4♦					
62	7♣	8♠	7♦	K♥	J♥	K♦	4♠	2♥	2♥/10♣	6♦	3♦
	4♥	Q♥	4♣	J♣	6♥	4♠					
63	8♠	J♦	3♦	8♣	8♥	9♦	K♥	9♥	5♥/6♦	3♠	6♥
	9♠	4♦	Q♦	Q♥	A♥	Q♣					
64	J♣	Q♦	8♠	7♥	5♦	9♠	5♣	5♦	3♠/5♠	J♦	4♣
	J♥	K♦	6♥	7♣	8♦	A♠					
65	A♥	4♠	10♣	9♥	2♠	J♥	7♥	J♥	Q♥/A♣	J♠	5♣
	K♠	A♣	4♥	7♦	J♦	10♥					
66	8♦	K♥	9♥	9♦	Q♠	3♦	6♠	5♣	10♦/J♠	10♥	5♥
	K♦	7♣	7♦	A♣	8♠	6♠					
67	J♦	4♠	5♠	3♠	A♠	K♦	9♦	3♥	K♠/4♣	5♠	4♦
	2♠	2♦	7♠	J♠	9♥	2♥					
68	J♥	K♥	3♠	2♥	6♦	10♠	Q♣	A♣	3♥/5♥	4♦	5♠
	3♦	7♠	J♣	8♦	J♠	8♠					
69	9♦	4♠	6♥	4♣	8♦	A♥	10♣	A♥	2♠/7♦	5♥	10♥
	10♦	2♦	Q♦	8♥	10♥	7♣					
70	J♠	10♠	3♠	4♦	8♠	2♣	A♥	J♠	5♠/Q♥	5♣	J♣
	3♥	A♠	4♥	7♦	A♣	A♥					
71	K♥	3♥	4♦	9♣	4♣	5♠	6♠	10♦	A♦/7♠	4♣	J♦
	4♠	3♦	8♣	A♣	3♠	6♠					
72	9♥	7♥	4♥	7♠	A♦	4♠	9♣	5♣	J♣/5♣	6♥	3♠
	K♦	8♣	J♥	6♠	8♥	6♦					
73	9♠	3♥	7♠	6♥	5♦	9♦	4♠	10♥	Q♠/Q♥	3♦	6♦
	5♠	J♦	3♣	6♠	8♥	4♠					
74	5♥	2♥	4♦	6♦	10♣	J♠	9♦	3♠	K♥/8♣	Q♦	9♣
	7♣	K♠	Q♦	5♠	9♥	3♦					
75	6♠	2♣	K♠	7♠	2♥	8♥	8♠	K♠	J♠/4♥	9♦	Q♥
	3♥	9♠	3♣	8♣	A♣	5♠					
76	10♣	10♠	4♦	5♠	7♦	8♦	J♥	10♠	A♦/4♣	5♦	10♠
	K♥	10♥	J♣	3♥	A♠	4♠					
77	J♠	Q♦	5♠	3♣	3♦	A♦	K♣	3♥	9♠/K♠	3♣	4♥
	K♥	9♣	3♥	4♠	4♦	7♥					
78	7♣	K♥	3♣	7♥	8♥	6♦	4♠	7♠	J♣/10♦	K♦	4♠
	10♥	7♠	A♣	10♣	8♦	4♠					
79	2♠	K♠	2♣	2♥	K♥	A♥	10♠	9♦	6♦/4♣	7♠	10♣
	5♦	J♦	10♥	J♠	9♣	10♣	K♥				
80	8♣	Q♠	A♦	10♣	6♠	7♠	2♣	5♥	A♠/J♦	8♥	J♠
	9♦	3♠	5♦	K♦	8♠	2♣					
81	5♠	K♣	10♣	10♥	5♣	Q♦	7♠	7♠	J♠/3♥	7♥	7♣
	K♥	2♣	5♦	J♦	3♣	7♠					
82	K♠	6♠	A♣	2♠	10♦	6♦	J♣	8♠	Q♦/3♦	A♠	8♦
	6♥	4♠	J♠	K♣	3♠	J♥	10♦				
83	4♥	4♦	6♥	5♦	7♥	4♠	10♦	2♦	9♣/8♥	2♣	Q♠
	5♠	J♠	3♣	Q♦	2♠	10♦					
84	2♣	2♠	6♠	4♦	3♠	4♣	4♠	K♥	9♥/A♥	K♥	10♠
	J♣	J♥	8♦	A♦	Q♦	3♦					
85	7♣	J♠	4♦	3♣	5♦	9♥	6♦	2♣	J♥/10♠	9♠	Q♣
	10♦	A♠	5♠	6♥	9♣	5♠					
86	A♣	2♦	J♠	10♥	5♥	K♦	3♣	4♥	7♦/3♠	6♠	3♥
	7♣	A♥	5♠	4♥	8♥	3♣					
87	8♠	4♣	10♥	Q♦	Q♥	7♦	10♠	5♠	3♦/3♥	2♠	A♥
	Q♠	A♣	5♣	2♣	9♠	10♦					
88	6♥	5♠	9♠	9♣	9♥	Q♠	Q♦	8♣	Q♣/3♠	K♣	A♥
	8♣	2♥	8♥	4♥	6♦	Q♦					
89	7♣	8♠	9♣	10♣	J♣	Q♣	K♣	Q♦	A♦/2♦	8♠	2♦
	Q♥	5♥	K♠	8♠	A♠	7♦					
90	6♠	Q♥	10♣	8♦	K♠	3♥	A♠	5♥	Q♣/10♠	6♣	6♠
	2♣	9♥	8♠	2♦	9♣	5♠	K♠				
91	3♥	A♥	9♠	5♣	K♦	J♣	7♦	5♦	J♠/3♣	2♦	8♠
	A♦	6♠	4♣	K♠	2♦	K♥					
92	10♥	Q♥	5♣	8♠	A♠	A♦	K♣	7♦	6♦/4♥	A♦	K♣
	10♣	Q♣	4♠	2♠	9♦	K♣					
93	2♣	A♥	8♠	3♠	10♠	10♣	K♠	5♠	Q♠/2♥	A♥	2♠
	K♦	8♥	5♥	9♠	5♣	8♦	10♠				
94	J♦	Q♥	4♠	K♠	8♦	A♣	7♠	8♠	3♠/Q♦	3♥	6♠
	A♦	4♥	Q♠	10♠	8♠	3♣					
95	A♣	8♠	2♣	3♣	5♦	10♦	Q♥	J♠	8♣/5♠	Q♣	9♠
	K♦	2♦	A♥	10♠	8♦	Q♥					
96	K♥	K♦	3♣	Q♠	9♣	8♣	4♦	K♦	3♠/6♥	10♦	K♥
	2♠	J♠	J♦	4♥	8♥	4♦					
97	Q♣	4♣	J♣	9♦	3♥	2♠	Q♠	K♣	A♥/5♠	Q♠	2♣
	7♣	10♦	8♦	4♦	3♣	K♠					
98	8♠	7♥	9♠	J♥	5♥	A♥	2♥	10♥	A♦/6♠	8♦	A♠
	4♦	6♥	K♥	J♠	8♣	2♥					
99	9♥	5♦	J♥	5♣	3♥	A♣	A♥	7♠	2♠/7♥	7♣	7♥
	4♥	5♠	9♣	2♣	4♣	A♥					

Seven of Clubs

AGE	MER	VEN	MAR	JUP	SAT	URA	NEP	LR	PLU/RES	ENV	DISP
0	5♦	Q♠	J♣	9♣	7♣	2♣	K♣	5♦	J♦/4♥	7♣	7♣
	A♥	J♠	9♠	3♦	6♠	K♣					
1	K♠	Q♣	2♥	10♦	Q♥	4♣	Q♦	Q♠	2♣/A♠	J♠	8♦
	7♥	8♥	J♦	Q♠	6♥	J♥	Q♥				
2	5♠	3♣	7♥	9♠	6♣	10♥	Q♥	J♣	5♣/8♠	10♣	Q♠
	5♦	J♦	6♠	2♣	10♦	Q♥					
3	A♦	10♦	Q♣	3♣	6♥	8♥	10♥	9♦	7♦/4♠	4♠	10♦
	Q♦	J♥	6♦	10♣	2♣	A♠					
4	3♠	Q♦	3♣	6♠	9♠	7♥	4♣	7♠	J♥/J♣	4♥	Q♣
	Q♥	2♦	7♠	7♥	5♣	5♦					
5	2♥	J♠	J♦	9♦	K♦	2♣	6♠	2♣	9♥/6♥	10♠	3♥
	3♣	4♣	7♠	5♠	8♠	6♣					
6	8♦	8♥	9♣	2♣	5♥	9♥	Q♥	K♣	A♠/4♥	Q♥	A♥
	9♣	2♦	7♠	A♦	3♥	Q♥					
7	7♥	5♦	K♥	5♣	7♦	9♣	2♣	K♠	10♠/6♥	9♣	A♦
	8♣	A♣	8♠	5♠	4♣	2♣					
8	3♠	8♣	5♣	J♣	Q♥	10♠	Q♠	Q♣	10♣/J♠	6♦	2♦
	5♥	K♦	K♠	8♦	2♥	9♥					
9	Q♣	5♥	J♣	8♠	K♠	4♥	2♥	2♥	10♠/4♦	3♠	6♣
	A♦	7♥	8♦	J♠	5♠	7♠	K♠				
10	4♥	4♠	K♥	7♠	2♠	3♦	9♥	10♦	J♦/6♠	J♦	8♠
	10♣	4♠	8♥	K♠	J♠	A♥					
11	9♦	5♥	7♠	8♦	2♦	10♣	Q♠	Q♥	4♣/5♠	J♣	K♣
	J♣	10♠	10♥	10♦	K♥	Q♠					
12	A♦	4♠	8♣	6♥	4♦	J♣	K♠	4♣	9♣/A♣	10♥	2♠
	2♠	8♠	K♦	K♥	7♠	4♦					
13	3♦	5♥	10♥	K♠	6♦	2♥	3♠	Q♦	6♥/2♣	5♠	6♠
	10♣	5♠	9♣	4♦	8♦	6♠					
14	2♥	8♣	A♦	6♠	9♠	Q♥	5♥	5♠	8♣/5♦	4♦	9♠
	2♠	J♠	4♠	4♦	6♦	5♥					
15	A♥	2♠	6♠	9♠	5♠	8♠	3♣	3♣	6♥/7♥	5♥	K♥
	10♦	J♦	3♣	5♠	8♠	3♠					
16	10♠	8♥	Q♦	K♥	4♥	10♦	9♣	7♥	4♠/5♣	5♣	2♠
	9♥	Q♥	6♦	3♣	6♠	K♠					
17	8♦	9♥	K♥	J♥	K♦	4♠	A♣	9♠	10♣/Q♣	4♠	A♠
	3♣	7♥	A♥	J♦	8♣	A♣					
18	7♦	9♠	J♥	7♠	4♥	2♥	4♠	6♣	10♦/6♣	6♥	7♥
	5♠	5♦	5♠	A♦	8♥	4♠					
19	J♦	Q♥	7♠	9♦	6♥	K♠	4♣	10♥	2♥/5♥	3♦	8♥
	8♦	A♠	5♣	5♣	J♥	K♦	6♥				
20	4♥	3♠	K♥	K♦	K♣	6♦	J♠	Q♥	J♣/9♠	Q♦	7♠
	2♣	4♣	2♦	J♥	7♠	3♦					
21	A♥	A♦	5♠	5♦	8♣	2♣	K♦	A♦	2♠/6♥	9♦	K
	9♥	2♥	8♠	6♠	6♣	K♦					
22	9♠	9♥	5♠	8♦	Q♦	2♠	Q♠	10♦	10♣/Q♥	5♦	3♣
	K♣	3♥	8♠	6♥	K♦	J♦					
23	9♦	K♣	8♠	4♠	9♠	10♥	2♠	K♠	7♥/2♣	3♣	5♦
	5♣	8♠	A♣	Q♥	2♣	2♠					
24	4♥	6♦	5♠	K♣	A♠	A♦	10♥	3♣	10♠/5♥	K♦	9♦
	10♣	6♠	10♦	2♦	Q♦	8♥					

AGE	MER	VEN	MAR	JUP	SAT	URA	NEP	LR	PLU/RES	ENV	DISP
25	3♥	4♠	K♣	7♦	7♠	10♣	3♣	6♥	6♣/J♠	7♠	Q♦
	2♠	J♦	9♣	Q♦	2♣	3♣					
26	3♠	6♦	7♦	A♥	J♥	2♠	10♥	8♥	2♥/J♣	8♥	3♦
	5♠	5♥	8♥	Q♦	7♥	10♦					
27	8♦	3♦	A♠	8♠	8♠	K♥	A♥	10♥	K♦/4♣	7♥	6♥
	3♥	3♣	2♠	5♥	4♠	10♠					
28	Q♦	2♣	8♣	6♠	9♠	3♥	7♠	3♠	6♥/5♦	A♠	4♣
	J♥	2♠	7♥	3♠	6♦	2♦					
29	4♠	10♥	J♣	9♥	10♦	J♥	6♣	Q♦	5♥/A♣	2♣	5♣
	K♠	Q♦	5♠	7♦	3♦	9♦					
30	6♦	A♥	9♥	K♥	9♣	A♠	Q♣	3♣	Q♥/J♦	K♥	5♥
	2♠	3♠	7♦	A♣	8♦	Q♣					
31	3♦	10♥	5♦	6♥	2♦	2♠	K♥	6♠	K♠/8♥	9♠	4♦
	10♦	J♠	K♣	J♦	9♥	2♥					
32	J♥	A♥	6♦	2♥	4♣	J♣	10♠	9♠	4♥/K♦	6♠	5♠
	A♠	K♣	Q♦	6♦	J♦	8♦					
33	K♥	3♣	7♥	8♥	6♦	4♠	J♣	7♦	10♦/7♦	2♠	10♥
	Q♥	J♠	2♣	8♠	9♦	3♠					
34	J♦	4♦	6♥	3♣	8♦	A♦	4♠	4♣	5♦/5♥	K♣	J♠
	4♥	2♦	5♠	7♦	A♣	4♠					
35	A♥	4♥	3♣	5♣	8♥	5♦	Q♣	2♥	2♦/K♣	8♠	J♦
	10♥	A♠	8♠	A♣	6♥	Q♣					
36	9♥	6♣	5♣	K♣	10♣	10♥	5♣	J♠	Q♦/7♠	6♣	3♠
	2♠	6♦	J♥	Q♣	8♠	4♣					
37	3♥	4♥	K♣	7♥	9♠	K♥	10♥	J♦	9♣/5♥	2♦	6♦
	5♦	3♦	6♠	Q♣	8♠	10♥					
38	K♦	2♥	3♣	4♣	J♣	J♦	K♥	9♦	A♥/8♣	A♦	9♣
	3♠	K♠	2♣	5♦	9♥	A♠					
39	Q♣	A♦	K♠	K♣	2♥	8♠	8♦	K♦	J♦/5♠	A♥	Q♥
	4♥	5♠	6♠	8♣	A♣	5♦					
40	J♣	4♦	3♠	5♦	7♦	6♦	J♥	2♠	10♣/8♥	3♥	10♠
	A♥	9♦	Q♦	4♦	2♦	10♥					
41	J♦	2♣	5♦	6♠	A♠	10♣	Q♠	6♠	3♥/K♠	Q♣	4♥
	A♥	5♣	4♥	8♠	3♣	6♣					
42	3♠	A♥	6♠	6♠	8♠	4♣	10♥	8♠	Q♦/Q♥	10♦	4♠
	9♥	7♦	A♣	J♠	6♦	10♥					
43	10♦	K♠	A♦	2♥	A♥	4♠	4♦	8♥	4♣/8♥	Q♠	10♣
	9♠	3♦	9♦	J♦	5♣	J♣	A♥				
44	8♣	9♣	10♣	J♣	Q♣	K♣	A♦	9♦	2♦/3♦	8♦	J♠
	K♥	6♥	9♠	2♠	8♦	A♦					
45	5♦	Q♠	J♣	9♦	7♠	2♣	K♣	2♣	J♦/4♥	7♠	7♣
	A♥	J♠	9♠	3♦	6♠	K♣					
46	K♠	Q♣	A♣	10♦	Q♥	4♣	Q♦	5♥	2♣/A♠	J♠	8♦
	7♥	8♥	J♦	Q♠	6♥	J♥	Q♥				
47	5♠	3♣	7♥	9♠	6♣	10♥	Q♥	9♥	5♣/8♠	10♣	Q♠
	5♦	J♦	6♠	2♣	10♦	Q♥					
48	A♦	10♦	Q♣	3♣	6♥	8♥	10♥	Q♥	9♥/4♣	4♠	10♦
	Q♦	J♥	6♦	10♣	2♣	A♠					
49	3♠	Q♦	3♣	6♠	9♠	9♥	4♣	7♥	J♥/J♣	4♥	Q♣
	Q♥	2♦	7♠	7♥	5♣	5♦					

AGE	MER	VEN	MAR	JUP	SAT	URA	NEP	LR	PLU/RES	ENV	DISP
50	A♣	J♠	J♦	9♥	K♦	2♠	6♠	5♦	7♦/6♥	10♠	3♥
	3♠	4♠	7♠	5♠	8♠	6♠					
51	8♦	8♥	9♦	2♣	5♥	7♠	Q♥	K♥	A♠/4♥	Q♥	A♥
	9♣	2♦	7♠	A♠	3♥	Q♥					
52	7♥	5♦	K♥	5♠	9♥	9♣	2♣	5♣	10♠/6♥	9♣	A♣
	8♣	2♥	8♠	5♠	4♠	2♠					
53	3♠	8♣	5♣	J♣	Q♦	10♠	Q♠	7♦	10♣/J♠	6♦	2♦
	5♥	K♦	K♠	8♠	2♦	7♦					
54	Q♣	5♥	J♣	6♦	K♠	4♥	A♣	9♣	10♠/4♦	3♠	6♣
	A♦	9♥	8♦	J♠	5♣	7♠	K♠				
55	4♥	4♠	K♥	7♠	2♠	3♦	7♦	2♣	J♦/6♠	J♦	8♠
	10♣	4♣	8♥	K♠	J♠	A♥					
56	9♦	5♥	7♠	8♠	2♦	10♠	Q♠	3♠	4♠/5♠	J♠	K♣
	J♣	10♠	10♥	10♦	K♥	Q♠					
57	A♦	4♠	8♠	6♥	4♦	J♣	K♠	8♣	9♣/2♥	10♥	2♠
	2♠	8♠	K♦	K♥	7♠	6♦	4♦				
58	3♦	5♥	10♥	K♠	6♥	A♣	3♠	5♣	6♥/2♣	5♠	6♠
	10♣	5♠	9♠	4♦	8♦	6♠					
59	A♣	8♦	A♦	6♠	9♠	Q♥	5♥	J♣	8♣/5♦	4♦	9♣
	2♠	J♠	4♠	4♠	6♠	5♥					
60	A♥	2♠	6♠	9♣	5♠	8♠	3♠	Q♦	6♥/7♦	5♥	K♥
	10♦	J♦	3♦	5♠	8♠	3♣					
61	10♠	8♥	Q♥	K♥	4♥	10♦	9♣	10♠	4♠/5♦	5♠	2♣
	7♦	Q♥	6♦	3♣	6♠	K♠					
62	8♦	7♦	K♥	J♥	K♦	4♠	2♥	Q♠	10♣/Q♣	4♣	A♣
	3♣	7♥	A♥	J♦	8♣	2♥					
63	9♥	9♠	J♥	7♠	4♥	A♣	4♠	Q♣	10♦/6♣	6♥	7♦
	5♠	5♦	5♣	A♠	8♥	4♠					
64	J♦	Q♥	7♠	9♦	6♥	K♠	4♠	5♥	A♣/5♥	3♦	8♥
	8♦	A♠	5♣	6♣	J♥	K♦	6♥				
65	4♥	3♠	K♥	K♦	K♣	6♦	J♠	J♣	J♠/9♣	Q♦	7♠
	2♣	4♣	2♦	J♥	7♠	3♦					
66	A♥	A♦	5♠	5♦	8♣	2♣	K♦	6♦	2♠/6♥	9♦	K♣
	7♦	A♣	8♠	6♠	6♣	K♦					
67	9♠	7♦	5♦	8♦	Q♥	2♠	Q♠	K♠	10♣/Q♥	5♦	3♣
	K♣	3♥	8♠	6♥	K♦	J♦					
68	9♦	K♠	8♦	4♠	9♣	10♥	2♠	4♥	7♥/2♦	3♣	5♦
	5♣	8♠	2♥	Q♥	2♣	2♠					
69	4♥	6♦	5♠	K♣	A♠	A♦	10♥	2♥	10♠/5♥	K♦	9♦
	10♣	6♣	10♦	2♣	Q♦	8♥					
70	3♥	4♠	K♣	9♥	7♠	10♣	3♠	4♥	6♦/J♠	7♠	Q♦
	2♠	J♦	9♣	Q♦	2♣	3♣					
71	3♠	6♦	9♥	A♥	J♥	2♠	10♥	4♠	A♣/J♠	8♥	3♦
	5♥	5♥	8♥	Q♦	7♥	10♥					
72	8♦	3♦	A♠	8♠	8♠	K♥	A♥	K♥	K♦/4♣	7♥	6♥
	3♥	3♣	2♠	5♥	4♠	10♠					
73	Q♦	2♣	8♣	6♠	9♠	3♥	7♠	7♠	6♥/5♦	A♠	4♠
	J♥	2♠	7♠	3♠	6♦	2♦					
74	4♠	10♥	J♣	7♦	10♦	J♥	6♠	2♠	5♥/2♥	2♠	5♣
	K♠	Q♦	5♠	9♥	3♦	9♦					
75	6♦	A♥	7♦	K♥	9♣	A♠	Q♣	3♦	Q♥/J♦	K♥	5♥
	2♠	3♠	9♥	2♥	8♦	Q♣					
76	3♦	10♥	5♦	6♥	2♦	2♠	K♥	9♥	K♠/8♥	9♠	4♦
	10♦	J♠	K♣	J♦	7♠	A♣					
77	J♥	A♥	6♥	A♣	4♠	J♣	10♠	9♦	4♥/K♦	6♠	5♠
	A♠	K♣	Q♦	6♦	J♥	8♦					
78	K♥	3♣	7♥	8♥	6♦	4♠	J♣	5♥	10♦/9♥	2♠	10♥
	Q♥	J♠	2♣	8♠	9♠	3♠					
79	J♥	4♦	6♥	3♣	8♦	A♦	4♠	7♠	5♦/5♥	K♣	J♣
	4♠	2♦	5♠	9♥	2♥	4♠					
80	A♥	4♥	3♣	5♠	8♥	5♦	Q♣	8♦	2♦/K♣	8♠	J♦
	10♥	A♠	8♣	2♥	6♥	Q♣					
81	7♦	6♣	5♠	K♣	10♣	10♥	5♣	2♦	Q♦/7♥	6♠	3♠
	2♠	6♦	J♥	Q♣	8♠	4♣					
82	3♥	4♥	K♣	7♥	9♠	K♥	10♥	10♣	9♣/5♥	2♦	6♦
	5♠	3♦	6♠	Q♣	8♠	10♥					
83	K♦	A♠	3♣	4♣	J♣	J♦	K♥	Q♠	A♥/8♣	A♦	9♣
	3♠	K♣	2♣	5♦	7♠	A♠					
84	Q♣	A♦	K♠	K♣	A♣	8♠	8♦	A♦	J♦/5♠	A♥	Q♥
	4♠	5♣	6♠	8♣	2♥	5♦					
85	J♣	4♦	3♣	5♦	9♥	6♦	J♥	4♠	10♣/8♦	3♥	10♠
	A♥	9♦	Q♦	4♥	2♦	10♥					
86	J♦	2♣	5♦	6♣	A♠	10♣	Q♠	8♦	3♥/K♠	Q♣	4♥
	A♥	5♣	4♥	8♥	3♣	6♣					
87	3♠	A♥	6♠	6♣	8♠	4♣	10♥	6♥	Q♦/Q♥	10♦	4♠
	9♦	9♥	2♥	J♣	6♥	10♥					
88	10♦	K♣	A♦	A♣	A♥	4♠	4♦	4♦	4♣/8♥	Q♣	10♣
	9♠	3♦	9♦	J♦	5♠	J♠	A♥				
89	8♣	9♣	10♣	J♣	Q♣	K♠	A♦	J♣	2♦/3♦	8♦	J♠
	K♥	6♥	9♠	2♠	8♠	A♦					
90	5♦	Q♠	J♣	9♦	7♠	2♣	K♣	K♠	J♦/4♥	7♠	7♣
	A♥	J♠	9♠	3♦	6♠	K♣					
91	K♠	Q♣	2♥	10♦	Q♥	4♣	Q♦	3♦	2♣/A♠	J♠	8♦
	7♥	8♥	J♦	Q♠	6♥	J♥	Q♥				
92	5♠	3♣	7♥	9♠	6♠	10♥	Q♥	5♥	5♣/8♠	10♣	Q♠
	5♦	J♦	6♠	2♠	10♦	Q♥					
93	A♦	10♦	Q♣	3♣	6♥	8♥	10♥	10♥	7♦/4♠	4♠	10♦
	Q♦	J♥	6♦	10♣	2♣	A♠					
94	3♠	Q♦	3♣	6♠	9♠	7♠	4♣	K♠	J♥/J♣	4♥	Q♣
	Q♥	2♦	7♠	7♥	5♣	5♦					
95	2♥	J♠	J♦	9♠	K♦	2♠	6♠	6♦	9♥/6♥	10♠	3♥
	3♠	4♠	7♠	5♠	8♠	6♠					
96	8♣	8♥	9♦	2♣	5♥	9♥	Q♥	2♥	A♠/4♥	Q♥	A♥
	9♣	2♦	7♠	A♠	3♥	Q♥					
97	7♥	5♦	K♥	5♣	7♥	9♣	2♣	3♠	10♣/6♥	9♣	A♣
	8♣	A♣	8♠	5♠	4♣	2♣					
98	3♣	8♣	5♣	J♣	Q♦	10♠	Q♠	2♥	10♣/J♠	6♦	2♦
	5♥	K♦	K♠	8♠	2♦	9♥					
99	Q♣	5♥	J♣	6♦	K♠	4♥	2♥	8♦	10♠/4♦	3♠	6♣
	A♦	7♦	8♦	J♠	5♣	7♠	K♠					

Eight of Clubs

AGE	MER	VEN	MAR	JUP	SAT	URA	NEP	LR	PLU/RES	ENV	DISP
0	6♦	4♠	10♥	10♦	8♠	A♥	A♥	6♦	Q♦/5♥		
	2♥	A♠	Q♥	J♦	5♦	A♠					
1	3♠	4♥	5♠	Q♠	6♠	3♥	A♥	4♠	9♦/5♣		
	A♣	2♣	9♠	J♣	3♣	A♥					
2	J♦	10♠	4♦	8♦	2♦	Q♣	3♥	10♥	5♦/4♣		
	2♥	K♥	6♦	10♥	K♦	3♥					
3	J♣	Q♥	5♥	7♣	A♦	10♦	Q♣	10♦	3♣/6♥		
	A♣	9♠	3♠	5♠	7♠	Q♣					
4	10♥	9♣	5♣	J♠	A♥	Q♠	10♦	8♠	K♦/3♦		
	2♥	6♠	J♦	4♦	8♥	10♦					
5	5♠	6♦	4♣	10♣	3♥	8♦	Q♠	A♥	7♠/Q♦		
	A♣	2♠	J♣	5♥	7♥	Q♠					
6	4♦	3♠	6♥	4♠	Q♣	7♣	8♦	A♠	8♥/9♦		
	2♥	K♣	10♥	5♣	A♠	8♦					
7	5♥	J♦	3♦	4♥	10♦	J♠	7♣	3♠	7♥/5♦		
	A♣	8♠	5♠	4♣	2♣	7♠					
8	5♣	J♣	Q♦	10♠	Q♠	10♣	J♠	4♥	A♠/3♣		
	2♥	6♣	4♦	6♥	K♥	J♠					
9	4♣	10♥	9♦	Q♥	8♦	4♠	10♣	5♠	2♣/K♦		
	A♣	2♦	5♥	3♦	9♠	10♣					
10	6♥	5♠	5♦	9♣	7♠	4♥	4♠	Q♠	K♥/7♠		
	2♥	A♦	5♣	Q♦	6♠	4♠					
11	3♦	4♠	3♣	6♦	J♠	10♠	4♥	6♣	9♠/8♥		
	A♣	A♥	4♣	9♦	2♠	4♥					
12	Q♦	5♥	K♠	3♠	10♣	Q♥	10♠	3♥	6♠/7♦		
	2♥	3♥	6♥	5♦	K♣	10♠					
13	9♦	5♣	7♠	J♦	4♠	9♣	Q♥	A♥	2♠/A♠		
	A♣	Q♣	3♠	3♣	8♠	Q♥					
14	5♦	4♣	8♥	J♣	4♥	6♦	9♣	J♦	K♣/2♣		
	2♥	10♦	Q♦	K♦	6♣	9♣					
15	3♣	6♥	7♥	10♥	10♠	3♠	6♦	10♠	8♠/K♥		
	A♣	Q♠	9♦	7♠	2♠	6♦					
16	K♦	3♦	A♠	5♠	Q♥	J♦	3♠	4♦	6♣/9♠		
	2♥	8♦	5♦	8♥	A♦	3♠					
17	7♠	Q♦	2♣	4♦	9♣	J♠	J♦	8♦	2♦/6♠		
	A♣	7♠	3♣	7♥	A♥	J♦					
18	8♥	9♦	K♥	5♦	6♦	10♥	J♣	2♦	A♦/2♣		
	2♥	J♠	K♦	A♣	3♥	J♣					
19	7♥	5♦	9♠	5♣	3♠	5♠	10♥	Q♣	A♥/K♣		
	A♣	10♣	7♠	2♣	Q♣	10♥					
20	A♠	3♦	6♠	4♣	J♦	4♦	5♠	3♥	3♥/8♠		
	2♥	4♠	8♥	K♥	10♦	5♠					
21	2♣	K♦	2♠	6♥	J♣	5♥	4♦	J♣	Q♣/6♠		
	A♣	4♥	7♥	9♠	Q♠	4♦					
22	K♥	7♠	K♣	3♦	10♥	5♣	5♥	Q♥	10♦/2♦		
	2♥	10♠	A♣	6♠	8♦	5♥					
23	9♠	8♥	8♣	Q♦	5♠	4♣	5♠	5♥	Q♠/A♣		
	A♣	Q♥	2♣	2♠	7♣	5♠					
24	6♠	7♥	6♦	9♦	4♦	6♥	4♣	7♠	8♦/A♥		
	2♥	9♣	K♥	K♣	J♠	4♣					

AGE	MER	VEN	MAR	JUP	SAT	URA	NEP	LR	PLU/RES	ENV	DISP
25	2♠	A♠	2♦	5♦	5♥	3♦	6♥	A♦	7♣/3♥		
	A♣	6♦	9♠	8♠	10♣	6♥					
26	K♣	2♣	A♠	3♣	5♣	Q♦	3♦	10♦	J♠/Q♣		
	2♥	3♠	6♠	6♠	4♠	3♦					
27	8♠	K♥	A♥	K♦	4♣	9♦	Q♦	Q♣	10♣/10♦		
	A♣	J♦	2♠	2♦	4♥	Q♦					
28	6♣	9♠	3♥	7♠	6♥	5♠	9♦	10♥	4♠/Q♠		
	2♥	J♣	K♣	A♦	10♠	9♦					
29	2♦	6♠	Q♣	8♥	3♦	3♣	5♦	9♣	4♥/8♦		
	A♣	10♥	8♠	A♥	Q♥	5♦					
30	A♦	2♠	10♦	7♥	Q♦	K♦	3♣	5♣	10♠/7♣		
	2♥	5♠	6♣	3♥	9♣	3♣					
31	A♥	K♣	Q♠	A♠	9♦	7♠	K♦	J♠	Q♥/J♠		
	A♣	4♦	2♣	Q♣	6♦	K♦					
32	3♥	8♠	8♣	2♣	5♦	8♥	7♠	A♥	9♣/10♠		
	2♥	5♥	A♦	10♦	3♠	7♠					
33	Q♣	6♠	7♣	K♥	3♣	7♥	8♥	Q♠	6♦/4♠		
	A♣	5♠	A♥	Q♠	J♦	8♥					
34	10♦	2♦	J♠	9♠	K♦	A♠	7♥	10♦	3♠/4♥		
	2♥	4♣	3♥	8♦	J♣	7♥					
35	Q♠	A♦	10♣	6♠	7♠	2♣	A♠	5♠	J♦/10♠		
	A♣	6♥	Q♣	7♣	10♥	A♠					
36	8♦	A♥	4♣	2♠	8♥	K♥	2♣	6♦	J♣/Q♥		
	2♥	3♦	10♦	J♠	5♠	2♣					
37	7♣	3♥	4♥	K♣	7♥	9♠	K♥	4♣	10♥/9♣		
	A♣	Q♦	Q♠	10♣	4♦	K♥					
38	J♠	Q♣	10♠	8♠	A♠	6♠	9♠	10♣	5♠/6♠		
	2♥	9♦	8♦	4♠	5♥	9♠					
39	10♣	10♦	Q♥	6♣	2♣	2♠	6♠	3♥	4♦/3♠		
	A♣	5♦	7♣	4♥	5♣	6♠					
40	4♠	Q♠	9♣	2♦	K♥	K♣	2♠	8♦	5♥/J♦		
	2♥	3♣	J♠	10♠	4♣	2♠					
41	4♥	8♦	6♦	A♦	9♠	8♠	K♣	Q♠	5♣/J♠		
	A♣	K♦	10♣	Q♥	6♥	K♣					
42	10♠	7♣	3♠	A♥	6♠	6♠	8♠	4♦	4♣/10♥		
	2♥	7♠	4♠	9♣	3♦	8♠					
43	Q♥	J♠	J♦	3♥	2♠	2♦	6♣	3♠	6♥/5♦		
	A♣	8♥	4♥	6♦	Q♦	6♣					
44	9♣	10♠	J♣	Q♣	K♣	A♦	2♦	6♥	3♦/4♦		
	2♥	7♥	10♠	3♠	9♦	2♦					
45	6♦	4♠	10♥	10♦	8♠	A♥	A♦	4♠	Q♦/5♥		
	A♣	A♠	Q♥	J♦	5♦	A♠					
46	3♠	4♥	5♠	Q♠	6♣	3♥	A♥	Q♣	9♦/5♣		
	2♥	2♣	9♠	J♣	3♠	A♥					
47	J♦	10♠	4♦	8♦	2♦	Q♣	3♥	7♣	5♦/4♣		
	A♣	K♥	6♦	10♥	K♦	3♥					
48	J♣	Q♥	5♥	7♣	A♦	10♦	Q♣	8♦	3♣/6♥		
	2♥	9♠	3♠	5♠	7♠	Q♣					
49	10♥	9♣	5♣	J♠	A♥	Q♠	10♦	5♥	K♦/3♦		
	A♣	6♠	J♦	4♦	8♥	10♦					

AGE	MER	VEN	MAR	JUP	SAT	URA	NEP	LR	PLU/RES ENV DISP
50	5♠	6♦	4♣	10♠	3♥	8♦	Q♠	J♦	7♠/Q♦
	2♥	2♠	J♣	5♥	7♥	Q♠			
51	4♦	3♠	6♥	4♣	Q♣	7♠	8♦	3♦	8♥/9♦
	A♣	K♣	10♥	5♣	A♠	8♦			
52	5♥	J♦	3♦	4♥	10♦	J♠	7♠	4♥	7♥/5♦
	2♥	8♠	5♠	4♣	2♣	7♣			
53	5♣	J♣	Q♦	10♠	Q♠	10♣	J♠	10♦	A♠/3♣
	A♣	6♠	4♦	6♥	K♥	J♠			
54	4♣	10♥	9♦	Q♥	8♦	4♠	10♣	J♠	2♣/K♦
	2♥	2♦	5♥	3♦	9♠	10♣			
55	6♥	5♠	5♦	9♣	7♦	4♥	4♠	7♣	K♥/7♠
	A♣	A♦	5♣	Q♦	6♠	4♠			
56	3♦	4♦	3♣	6♦	J♠	10♠	4♥	5♣	9♠/8♦
	2♥	A♥	4♣	9♦	2♠	4♥			
57	Q♦	5♥	K♦	3♠	10♣	Q♥	10♠	J♣	6♠/7♥
	A♣	3♥	6♥	5♦	K♣	10♠			
58	9♦	5♣	7♠	J♦	4♠	9♠	Q♥	Q♦	2♠/A♠
	2♥	Q♣	3♦	3♣	8♠	Q♥			
59	5♦	4♣	8♥	J♣	4♥	6♦	9♣	10♠	K♣/2♠
	A♣	10♦	Q♦	K♦	6♣	9♣			
60	3♣	6♥	7♥	10♥	10♠	3♠	6♦	Q♠	8♠/K♥
	2♥	Q♠	9♦	7♠	2♦	6♠			
61	K♦	3♦	A♠	5♠	Q♥	J♦	3♠	10♣	6♣/9♠
	A♣	8♦	5♦	8♥	A♦	3♠			
62	7♠	Q♦	2♣	4♦	9♣	J♣	J♦	J♠	2♦/6♠
	2♥	7♣	3♣	7♥	A♥	J♦			
63	8♥	9♦	K♥	5♥	6♦	10♥	J♣	4♣	A♦/2♠
	A♣	J♠	K♦	A♠	3♥	J♣			
64	7♥	5♦	9♣	5♣	3♠	5♠	10♥	10♥	A♥/K♣
	2♥	10♣	7♠	2♣	Q♣	10♥			
65	A♠	3♣	6♠	4♣	J♦	4♦	5♠	9♦	3♥/8♠
	A♣	4♠	8♥	K♥	10♦	5♠			
66	2♣	K♦	2♠	6♥	J♣	5♥	4♦	Q♥	Q♣/6♣
	2♥	4♥	7♥	9♠	Q♠	4♦			
67	K♥	7♠	K♣	3♦	10♥	5♠	5♥	8♦	10♦/2♦
	A♣	10♠	A♠	6♠	8♦	5♥			
68	9♠	8♥	8♠	Q♦	5♠	4♠	5♣	4♠	Q♠/A♦
	2♥	Q♥	2♣	2♠	7♣	5♠			
69	6♠	7♥	6♣	9♦	4♦	6♥	4♣	10♣	8♦/A♥
	A♣	9♣	K♥	K♣	J♠	4♠			
70	2♠	A♠	2♦	5♦	5♥	3♦	6♥	6♥	7♣/3♥
	2♥	6♦	9♠	8♠	10♣	6♥			
71	K♣	2♣	A♦	3♠	5♣	5♦	3♦	5♠	J♠/Q♣
	A♣	3♠	6♣	6♠	4♠	3♦			
72	8♠	K♥	A♥	K♦	4♣	9♠	Q♦	5♦	10♣/10♦
	2♥	J♦	2♠	2♦	4♥	Q♦			
73	6♣	9♠	3♥	7♠	6♥	5♦	9♠	9♣	4♦/Q♠
	A♣	J♠	K♣	A♦	10♠	9♦			
74	2♦	6♠	Q♣	8♥	3♦	3♣	5♦	7♣	4♥/8♦
	2♥	10♥	8♠	A♥	Q♥	5♦			

AGE	MER	VEN	MAR	JUP	SAT	URA	NEP	LR	PLU/RES ENV DISP
75	A♦	2♠	10♦	7♥	Q♦	K♦	3♣	4♥	10♠/7♣
	A♣	5♠	6♠	3♥	9♣	3♣			
76	A♥	K♣	Q♠	A♣	9♦	7♠	K♦	4♠	Q♥/J♠
	2♥	4♦	2♦	Q♣	6♦	K♦			
77	3♥	8♠	8♦	2♣	5♦	8♥	7♠	3♦	9♣/10♣
	A♣	5♥	A♦	10♦	3♠	7♠			
78	Q♣	6♦	7♣	K♥	3♣	7♥	8♥	4♦	6♦/4♠
	2♥	5♠	A♥	Q♠	J♦	8♥			
79	10♦	2♦	J♠	9♠	K♦	A♠	7♥	3♣	3♠/4♥
	A♣	4♣	3♥	8♦	J♣	7♥			
80	Q♠	A♦	10♣	6♠	7♠	2♣	A♠	6♦	J♦/10♠
	2♥	6♥	Q♣	7♣	10♥	A♠			
81	8♦	A♥	4♠	2♠	8♥	K♦	2♣	J♠	J♣/Q♥
	A♣	3♦	10♦	J♠	5♠	2♣			
82	7♣	3♥	4♥	K♣	7♥	9♠	K♥	10♠	10♥/9♣
	2♥	Q♦	Q♠	10♣	4♦	K♥			
83	J♠	Q♣	10♠	8♠	A♠	6♠	9♠	4♥	5♠/6♦
	A♣	9♦	8♦	4♠	5♥	9♠			
84	10♣	10♦	Q♥	6♣	2♣	2♠	6♠	Q♦	4♦/3♠
	2♥	5♦	7♠	4♥	5♣	6♠			
85	4♠	Q♠	9♣	2♦	K♥	K♣	2♠	5♥	5♥/J♦
	A♣	3♣	J♠	10♠	4♣	2♠			
86	4♥	8♦	6♦	A♦	9♠	8♠	K♣	K♦	5♠/J♣
	2♥	K♦	10♣	Q♥	6♥	K♣			
87	10♠	7♣	3♠	A♥	6♠	6♠	8♠	3♠	4♣/10♥
	A♣	7♠	4♠	9♠	3♦	8♠			
88	Q♥	J♠	J♦	3♥	2♠	2♦	6♣	10♣	6♥/5♠
	2♥	8♥	4♥	6♦	Q♦	6♠			
89	9♣	10♣	Q♣	Q♠	K♣	A♦	2♦	Q♥	3♦/4♦
	A♣	7♥	10♠	3♠	9♦	2♦			
90	6♦	4♠	10♥	10♦	8♠	A♥	A♦	10♠	Q♦/5♠
	2♥	A♠	Q♥	J♦	5♦	A♦			
91	3♠	4♥	5♠	Q♠	6♣	3♥	A♥	9♦	9♦/5♣
	A♣	2♣	9♣	J♠	3♣	A♥			
92	J♦	10♠	4♦	8♦	2♦	Q♣	3♥	5♣	5♦/4♣
	2♥	K♥	6♦	10♥	K♦	3♥			
93	J♣	Q♥	5♦	7♣	A♦	10♦	Q♣	7♠	3♣/6♥
	A♣	9♠	3♠	5♠	7♠	Q♣			
94	10♥	9♣	5♣	J♠	A♥	Q♠	10♦	J♦	K♦/3♣
	2♥	6♠	J♦	4♦	8♥	10♦			
95	5♠	6♦	4♣	10♣	3♥	8♦	Q♠	4♠	7♠/Q♠
	A♣	2♠	J♣	5♥	7♥	Q♠			
96	4♦	3♠	6♥	4♣	Q♣	7♣	8♦		8♥/9♦
	2♥	K♣	10♥	5♣	A♠	8♦			
97	5♥	J♦	3♦	4♥	10♦	J♠	7♣	Q♥	7♥/5♦
	A♣	8♠	5♠	4♣	2♣	7♠			
98	5♣	J♣	Q♦	10♠	Q♠	10♣	J♠	5♦	A♠/3♣
	2♥	6♣	4♦	6♥	K♥	J♠			
99	4♣	10♥	9♦	Q♥	8♦	4♠	10♣	4♦	2♣/K♦
	A♣	2♦	5♥	3♦	9♠	10♣			

The Yearly Spreads ♦ 291

Nine of Clubs

AGE	MER	VEN	MAR	JUP	SAT	URA	NEP	LR	PLU/RES	ENV	DISP
0	9♠	2♥	K♥	K♦	6♥	4♣	2♦	9♠	J♠/8♣	9♣	9♠
	5♣	K♠	6♣	2♣	9♥	8♠					
1	4♠	7♣	K♠	Q♣	2♥	10♦	Q♥	2♥	4♣/Q♦	6♦	Q♥
	J♣	3♣	A♥	8♣	A♣	2♣					
2	6♥	9♦	K♥	2♣	7♦	5♥	J♥	K♥	3♠/2♣	3♠	10♠
	J♠	A♠	7♥	J♣	8♦	3♦					
3	4♣	6♣	2♣	A♥	8♠	3♠	10♠	K♦	10♣/K♠	J♦	4♥
	J♠	3♣	J♣	2♠	K♥	Q♠					
4	5♠	J♠	A♥	Q♠	10♦	K♦	3♦	6♥	7♥/5♦	J♣	4♠
	A♠	7♦	A♣	6♥	5♦	3♦					
5	4♥	K♠	7♠	2♥	J♠	J♦	9♦	4♣	K♦/2♠	10♥	10♠
	A♦	8♥	A♠	4♣	3♠	6♥	J♠				
6	8♣	4♦	3♠	6♥	4♠	Q♣	7♠	2♦	8♦/8♥	5♠	J♠
	2♦	7♠	A♦	3♥	Q♥	7♣					
7	2♣	10♠	6♥	A♠	6♠	6♠	Q♠	4♠	4♣/J♣	4♦	7♠
	J♠	6♦	A♠	8♥	A♥	Q♣					
8	K♠	4♠	A♣	4♥	5♠	K♦	7♥	7♣	6♣/8♠	5♦	8♦
	K♣	2♠	4♣	10♠	7♠	J♥	5♠				
9	Q♦	K♥	K♣	A♦	Q♠	3♦	5♠	K♠	3♣/10♠	5♣	Q♠
	2♣	4♣	A♥	6♣	4♥	5♠					
10	7♣	4♥	4♠	K♥	7♠	2♠	3♦	Q♠	9♥/J♦	4♣	10♦
	7♥	J♥	5♥	3♠	6♣	8♠					
11	5♣	7♥	K♥	A♥	A♠	9♥	K♦	2♥	J♥/6♥	6♥	Q♣
	5♦	8♣	6♠	K♣	3♠	2♠					
12	A♣	6♦	4♠	A♠	9♠	3♥	A♥	10♦	7♦/7♠	3♦	3♥
	5♣	J♦	6♠	Q♦	10♦	A♥					
13	Q♥	2♠	A♠	6♣	5♦	7♦	5♠	Q♥	8♠/J♣	Q♦	A♥
	4♦	8♦	6♠	7♣	10♣	5♠					
14	K♣	2♣	2♦	3♣	9♥	4♦	6♠	6♥	10♥/7♠	9♦	A♦
	8♣	2♥	10♦	Q♦	K♦	6♣					
15	5♣	8♣	3♣	6♥	7♥	10♥	10♠	9♠	3♠/6♦	5♠	2♦
	5♦	9♠	K♠	Q♥	8♦	7♥					
16	4♠	5♦	6♥	5♥	K♠	J♣	A♣	K♥	10♥/9♣	3♣	6♣
	7♣	9♥	Q♥	6♦	3♣	6♠	K♠				
17	J♣	J♦	2♦	6♠	3♥	8♥	7♦	2♣	4♣/A♥	K♦	8♠
	3♠	K♦	2♠	K♣	6♦	J♠					
18	A♠	5♦	6♠	Q♥	8♦	3♠	10♠	7♦	K♦/Q♦	7♠	K♣
	6♥	10♠	3♦	4♥	2♦	10♠					
19	7♣	J♦	Q♥	7♠	9♦	6♥	K♠	5♥	4♦/2♥	8♥	2♠
	3♥	10♦	9♠	2♦	6♠	5♥	9♦				
20	8♥	5♦	3♦	K♠	5♥	A♣	5♠	J♥	7♠/6♣	7♥	6♠
	3♠	Q♦	4♦	9♦	Q♥	A♥					
21	A♣	Q♥	7♣	A♥	A♦	5♠	5♦	4♣	8♣/2♦	A♠	9♣
	3♥	6♦	J♦	9♦	5♥	5♦					
22	J♠	3♥	A♥	4♦	3♣	8♠	K♥	6♣	7♠/K♣	2♠	K♥
	4♥	4♣	8♥	Q♦	10♦	K♥					
23	10♥	2♠	7♥	2♦	J♣	4♥	4♦	2♣	J♦/2♣	K♥	2♣
	7♦	5♠	5♥	K♥	A♥	K♠					
24	Q♥	7♦	2♦	J♥	9♠	J♦	2♥	A♥	3♠/4♠	9♠	A♠
	K♥	K♣	J♠	4♣	8♣	2♥					
25	9♥	A♦	J♥	6♠	J♣	A♣	J♦	8♠	4♥/Q♠	6♠	7♥
	Q♦	2♣	3♣	7♠	2♠	J♦					
26	4♣	5♠	6♠	A♠	7♠	K♠	9♠	3♠	A♣/5♦	2♠	8♥
	Q♥	8♠	3♣	Q♠	J♥	9♠	7♠				
27	J♣	5♠	2♦	9♠	Q♣	5♥	6♦	10♠	6♥/4♦	K♣	7♠
	6♣	K♦	8♦	J♥	6♠	8♥					
28	J♠	7♣	Q♦	2♣	8♠	6♠	9♠	5♠	3♥/7♠	8♠	K♦
	7♠	A♥	10♠	A♥	Q♠	9♠					
29	A♦	7♦	2♣	Q♥	7♥	3♥	10♠	J♠	3♠/5♠	6♣	3♣
	Q♣	10♣	10♦	7♠	9♠	4♣					
30	A♠	Q♣	Q♥	J♦	4♦	3♦	3♥	A♥	K♣/8♦	2♦	5♦
	3♣	8♣	2♥	5♠	6♣	3♥					
31	J♣	5♥	Q♦	Q♣	8♠	7♣	3♦	Q♠	10♥/5♦	A♦	9♦
	3♠	Q♠	4♥	8♦	7♥	2♠					
32	10♣	J♦	Q♠	9♥	6♠	3♠	K♥	10♦	Q♠/6♦	A♥	Q♦
	3♥	4♣	4♦	7♥	6♣	K♥					
33	5♠	5♥	9♥	J♠	J♥	3♥	3♦	K♦	A♣/6♥	3♥	3♦
	Q♦	5♦	2♠	7♥	K♣	3♦					
34	Q♥	8♥	8♠	8♣	10♦	2♦	J♠	3♦	9♠/K♦	Q♣	6♥
	10♣	K♥	6♣	5♦	J♦	10♥					
35	7♥	6♣	8♣	Q♠	A♦	10♣	6♠	4♥	7♠/2♣	10♦	4♣
	J♥	3♥	K♣	5♠	5♥	8♦					
36	J♦	3♦	6♥	7♠	4♥	J♥	Q♠	K♠	5♦/2♥	Q♠	5♠
	K♠	7♥	Q♦	9♥	8♥	A♠					
37	5♥	J♠	7♦	2♦	4♦	8♠	4♠	7♣	5♠/4♣	8♦	5♥
	3♥	5♣	9♥	2♥	Q♥	4♠					
38	8♥	3♠	2♣	7♠	8♠	3♥	2♦	2♥	K♠/2♠	7♠	4♦
	4♥	6♦	Q♠	4♣	7♥	A♣					
39	J♥	J♠	7♠	A♣	K♠	6♥	10♥	J♠	J♣/9♠	J♠	5♠
	8♠	Q♣	7♥	5♥	4♣	Q♥					
40	2♠	K♥	K♠	2♠	5♥	J♦	6♥	J♦	4♥/9♥	10♣	10♥
	5♠	6♦	6♠	10♦	A♠	5♠					
41	4♣	9♦	7♠	K♥	Q♥	7♣	J♦	9♦	2♣/5♦	4♠	J♣
	J♣	8♦	Q♦	9♥	2♥	J♦					
42	J♠	J♣	K♥	3♣	2♠	2♠	4♠	8♣	8♦/Q♣	4♥	J♦
	3♦	8♠	8♣	2♥	7♠	4♣					
43	7♠	Q♠	Q♣	Q♣	3♠	3♦	3♣	4♦	7♥/6♠	10♠	3♠
	3♥	5♦	J♥	4♠	10♦	K♦					
44	10♣	J♦	Q♠	K♣	A♦	2♦	3♦	3♠	4♦/5♦	Q♥	6♦
	2♣	8♥	A♥	4♠	10♦	3♦					
45	9♠	A♣	K♥	K♦	6♥	4♣	2♦	6♥	J♠/8♦	9♣	9♠
	5♣	K♠	6♣	2♠	7♥	8♠					
46	4♠	7♣	K♠	Q♣	A♠	10♦	Q♥	4♠	4♣/Q♦	6♦	Q♥
	J♣	3♣	A♥	8♠	2♥	2♣					
47	6♥	9♦	K♥	2♠	9♥	5♥	J♦	Q♣	3♠/2♠	3♠	10♠
	J♠	A♠	7♥	J♣	8♦	3♦					
48	4♠	6♣	2♠	A♥	8♠	3♠	10♠	7♣	10♣/K♠	J♦	4♥
	J♠	3♣	J♣	2♠	K♥	Q♠					
49	5♣	J♠	A♥	Q♠	10♦	K♦	3♦	2♠	7♥/5♠	J♣	4♠
	A♠	9♥	2♥	6♥	5♥	3♦					

AGE	MER	VEN	MAR	JUP	SAT	URA	NEP	LR	PLU/RES	ENV	DISP
50	4♥	K♠	7♣	A♣	J♠	J♦	9♦	10♠	K♦/2♠	10♥	10♣
	A♦	8♥	A♠	4♣	3♣	6♥	J♠				
51	8♣	4♦	3♠	6♥	4♠	Q♣	7♣	6♥	8♦/8♥	5♠	J♠
	2♦	7♠	A♦	3♥	Q♥	7♣					
52	2♣	10♠	6♥	A♠	6♠	6♣	Q♣	A♠	4♣/J♣	4♦	7♣
	J♠	6♦	A♦	8♥	A♥	Q♣					
53	K♠	4♠	2♥	4♥	5♠	K♦	7♥	6♠	6♣/8♠	5♥	8♦
	K♣	2♠	4♣	10♠	7♠	J♥	5♠				
54	Q♦	K♥	K♣	A♦	Q♠	3♦	5♠	6♠	3♣/10♦	5♣	Q♠
	2♣	4♣	A♥	6♠	4♥	5♠					
55	7♣	4♥	4♠	K♥	7♠	2♠	3♦	Q♠	7♦/J♦	4♣	10♦
	7♥	J♥	5♥	3♠	6♣	8♠					
56	5♣	7♥	K♥	A♥	A♦	7♦	K♦	K♠	J♥/6♥	6♥	Q♣
	5♠	8♦	6♠	K♣	3♣	2♣					
57	2♥	6♦	4♣	A♠	9♠	3♦	A♥	4♠	9♥/7♠	3♦	3♥
	5♣	J♦	6♠	Q♦	10♦	A♥					
58	Q♥	2♠	A♠	6♣	5♦	9♥	5♠	A♣	8♠/J♣	Q♦	A♥
	4♦	8♦	6♠	7♣	10♣	5♠					
59	K♣	2♠	2♦	3♣	7♦	4♦	6♣	4♦	10♥/7♠	9♦	A♦
	8♠	A♠	10♦	Q♦	K♦	6♣					
60	5♣	8♠	3♣	6♥	7♥	10♥	10♠	5♠	3♠/6♦	5♦	2♦
	5♥	9♠	K♠	Q♥	8♦	9♥					
61	4♠	5♠	6♥	5♥	K♠	J♣	2♥	K♦	10♥/9♦	3♣	6♣
	7♣	7♦	Q♥	6♦	3♣	6♠	K♠				
62	J♣	J♦	2♦	6♠	3♥	8♥	9♥	7♠	4♣/A♥	K♦	8♠
	3♠	K♦	2♠	K♠	6♦	J♠					
63	A♠	5♦	6♠	Q♥	8♦	3♠	10♠	Q♦	K♦/Q♦	7♠	K♣
	6♥	10♥	3♦	4♦	2♦	10♠					
64	7♣	J♦	Q♥	7♠	9♦	6♥	K♠	K♥	4♦/A♣	8♥	2♠
	3♥	10♦	9♠	2♦	6♠	5♥	9♦				
65	8♥	5♦	3♦	K♠	5♥	2♦	5♣	K♣	7♠/6♣	7♥	6♠
	3♠	Q♦	4♦	9♦	Q♥	A♥					
66	2♥	Q♥	7♣	A♥	A♦	5♠	5♦	A♦	8♠/2♣	A♠	9♠
	3♥	6♦	J♦	9♦	5♥	5♦					
67	J♠	3♥	A♥	4♦	3♣	8♣	K♥	Q♠	7♠/K♣	2♣	K♥
	4♥	4♣	8♥	Q♦	10♦	K♥					
68	10♥	2♠	7♥	2♦	J♣	4♥	4♦	3♦	J♦/2♣	K♥	2♣
	9♥	5♠	5♥	K♥	A♥	K♠					
69	Q♥	9♥	2♦	J♥	9♠	J♦	A♣	5♠	3♦/4♠	9♠	A♠
	K♥	K♣	J♣	4♣	8♣	A♣					
70	7♦	A♦	J♥	6♠	J♣	2♥	J♦	7♣	4♥/Q♠	6♠	7♥
	Q♦	2♣	3♠	7♣	2♠	J♦					
71	4♣	5♠	6♠	A♠	7♠	K♠	9♦	4♥	2♥/5♦	2♠	8♥
	Q♥	8♠	3♣	Q♠	J♥	9♠	7♠				
72	J♣	5♠	2♦	9♠	Q♣	5♥	6♦	4♠	6♥/4♦	K♣	7♠
	6♠	K♦	8♦	J♥	6♠	8♥					
73	J♠	7♠	Q♦	2♣	8♠	6♠	9♠	K♥	3♥/7♠	8♠	K♦
	9♥	2♥	10♦	A♥	Q♠	9♠					
74	A♦	9♥	2♣	Q♥	7♥	3♥	10♠	7♠	3♠/5♠	6♠	3♣
	Q♣	10♣	10♦	7♠	9♠	4♣					
75	A♠	Q♣	Q♥	J♦	4♦	3♦	3♥	2♠	K♣/8♦	2♦	5♦
	3♣	8♠	A♣	5♠	6♣	3♥					
76	J♣	5♥	Q♦	Q♣	8♠	7♣	3♦	3♦	10♥/5♦	A♦	9♦
	3♠	Q♠	4♥	8♦	7♥	2♠					
77	10♣	J♦	Q♣	7♦	6♠	3♠	K♥	5♠	Q♠/6♦	A♥	Q♦
	3♦	4♣	4♦	7♥	6♣	K♥					
78	5♣	5♥	7♦	J♠	J♥	3♦	3♦	7♥	2♥/6♥	3♥	3♦
	Q♦	5♦	2♠	7♥	K♣	3♦					
79	Q♥	8♥	8♠	8♠	10♦	2♦	J♠	K♥	9♠/K♦	Q♣	6♥
	10♣	K♥	6♣	5♦	J♦	10♥					
80	7♥	6♠	8♣	Q♠	A♦	10♣	6♠	A♥	7♠/2♣	10♦	4♣
	J♥	3♥	K♣	5♠	5♥	8♦					
81	J♦	3♦	6♥	9♥	4♥	J♥	Q♠	A♦	5♦/A♣	Q♠	5♣
	K♠	7♥	Q♦	7♦	8♥	A♠					
82	5♥	J♠	9♦	2♦	4♦	8♠	4♠	9♥	5♠/4♣	8♦	5♥
	3♥	5♠	7♦	A♣	Q♥	4♣					
83	8♠	3♦	2♣	7♠	8♦	3♥	2♦	K♦	K♠/2♠	7♣	4♦
	4♥	6♦	Q♣	4♠	9♥	2♥					
84	J♥	J♠	7♠	2♥	K♦	6♥	10♥	A♠	J♣/9♠	J♠	5♠
	8♠	Q♣	7♥	5♦	4♣	Q♥					
85	2♦	K♥	K♣	2♠	5♥	J♦	6♥	6♠	4♥/7♦	10♠	10♥
	5♠	6♦	6♣	10♠	A♠	5♣					
86	4♣	9♦	7♠	K♥	Q♥	7♣	J♦	4♠	2♣/5♦	4♠	J♣
	J♠	8♦	Q♦	7♦	A♣	J♦					
87	J♠	J♣	K♥	3♣	2♠	2♠	4♠	A♠	8♦/Q♣	4♥	J♦
	3♦	8♠	8♣	A♣	7♠	4♠					
88	9♥	Q♠	Q♦	Q♣	3♠	3♦	3♣	9♠	7♥/6♠	10♠	3♠
	3♥	5♦	J♥	4♠	10♦	K♦					
89	10♣	J♠	Q♣	K♠	A♦	2♦	3♦	3♥	4♦/5♦	Q♥	6♦
	2♣	8♥	A♥	4♠	10♦	3♦					
90	9♠	2♥	K♥	K♦	6♥	4♣	2♦	A♥	J♠/8♦	9♣	9♠
	5♠	K♠	6♣	2♦	9♥	8♠					
91	4♠	7♠	K♠	Q♣	2♥	10♦	Q♥	Q♥	4♣/Q♦	6♦	Q♥
	J♣	3♠	A♥	8♣	A♣	2♣					
92	6♥	9♦	K♥	2♣	7♦	5♥	J♥	2♠	3♠/2♠	3♠	10♠
	J♠	A♠	7♥	J♠	8♦	3♦					
93	4♣	6♣	2♠	A♥	8♠	3♠	10♠	A♠	10♣/K♠	J♦	4♥
	J♠	3♣	J♣	2♠	K♥	Q♠					
94	5♠	A♥	A♥	Q♠	10♦	K♦	3♦	6♣	7♥/5♠	J♣	4♠
	A♠	7♦	A♣	6♥	5♥	3♦					
95	4♥	K♠	7♠	2♥	J♠	J♦	9♦	5♠	K♦/2♠	10♥	10♣
	A♦	8♥	A♠	4♣	3♣	6♥	J♠				
96	8♣	4♦	3♠	6♥	4♠	Q♣	7♣	7♦	8♦/8♥	5♠	J♠
	2♦	7♠	A♦	3♥	Q♥	7♣					
97	2♣	10♠	6♥	A♠	6♠	6♣	Q♣	5♠	4♣/J♣	4♦	7♣
	J♠	6♦	A♦	8♥	A♥	Q♣					
98	K♠	4♠	A♣	4♥	5♠	K♦	7♥	K♠	6♣/8♠	5♥	8♦
	K♣	2♠	4♣	10♠	7♠	J♥	5♠				
99	Q♦	K♥	K♣	A♦	Q♠	3♦	5♠	2♠	3♣/10♦	5♣	Q♠
	2♣	4♣	A♥	6♣	4♥	5♠					

Ten of Clubs

AGE	MER	VEN	MAR	JUP	SAT	URA	NEP	LR	PLU/RES	ENV	DISP
0	8♦	K♠	3♥	A♣	Q♣	10♠	5♣	8♦	3♦/A♠	10♠	10♣
	2♠	9♦	3♣	10♥	6♥	5♠	Q♣				
1	8♣	3♠	4♥	5♠	Q♠	6♣	3♥	K♠	A♥/9♦	4♠	J♠
	6♠	Q♦	2♠	8♠	J♣	3♥					
2	K♦	7♣	5♠	3♣	7♥	9♣	6♣	3♥	10♥/Q♥	4♥	7
	Q♣	4♠	2♠	9♦	K♣	6♣					
3	K♠	Q♠	2♥	8♣	6♦	3♦	5♦	A♠	9♠/K♥	10♠	8♣
	2♣	A♠	10♥	7♣	Q♦	J♥	6♦				
4	5♥	7♣	2♣	2♠	A♦	4♦	6♦	Q♣	6♥/2♦	Q♥	Q♠
	K♦	10♥	K♣	9♠	8♦	6♦					
5	3♥	8♦	Q♠	7♠	Q♦	A♠	4♦	10♠	7♦/10♠	9♣	10♦
	5♦	J♥	J♦	4♥	9♠	K♥					
6	J♣	5♦	7♠	K♣	2♠	7♥	3♦	5♣	J♥/5♠	6♥	Q♣
	6♦	A♥	7♥	2♣	6♥	K♥					
7	2♥	4♠	10♥	3♣	8♥	8♠	K♠	8♣	9♥/Q♦	3♠	3♥
	J♣	10♠	7♥	5♥	2♦	K♣					
8	J♠	A♠	3♠	9♠	4♣	9♥	6♦	3♠	K♥/Q♥	J♦	A♥
	3♠	A♥	7♥	3♥	10♦	6♦					
9	2♣	K♦	6♠	6♥	7♦	3♠	9♠	4♥	9♠/Q♦	J♣	A♦
	8♣	A♣	2♦	5♥	3♦	9♠					
10	J♣	8♣	6♥	5♠	5♦	9♠	7♣	5♠	4♥/4♠	10♥	2♦
	4♣	8♥	K♠	J♠	A♥	9♥					
11	Q♠	4♣	5♠	J♦	K♠	Q♥	2♥	Q♠	9♣/5♠	5♠	6♣
	3♥	7♠	J♣	4♠	6♥	7♥	K♠				
12	Q♥	10♠	6♠	7♥	8♠	9♦	9♥	6♣	10♥/K♣	4♦	8♠
	4♥	3♦	A♠	K♠	4♣	Q♣					
13	3♣	4♣	7♥	J♠	A♥	4♥	7♠	3♥	3♦/5♥	5♥	K♣
	5♠	9♣	4♦	8♦	6♠	7♠					
14	3♥	10♠	J♠	Q♦	5♣	5♠	K♠	K♦	3♠/A♣	5♠	2♠
	8♠	2♦	8♥	6♠	7♥	J♦	5♠				
15	9♦	4♣	4♦	K♠	J♦	2♥	J♣	7♣	Q♦/9♠	4♣	6♠
	4♥	5♥	3♣	5♠	J♠	K♣					
16	2♥	J♠	3♥	K♣	2♠	6♦	4♣	5♠	8♣/K♦	6♥	9♠
	8♠	4♣	10♠	5♣	J♦	4♣					
17	Q♣	8♠	K♣	3♠	6♥	8♣	7♠	3♣	Q♦/2♣	3♦	K♥
	8♦	10♥	9♣	5♥	2♦	7♠					
18	9♠	A♠	5♦	6♠	Q♥	8♦	3♠	7♥	10♠/K♦	Q♦	2♣
	9♥	6♦	J♦	7♠	K♣	K♠					
19	J♠	9♥	6♠	J♥	8♥	10♠	A♣	9♠	4♥/Q♠	9♦	A♠
	7♠	2♣	Q♣	10♥	8♣	A♣					
20	7♦	2♠	J♥	7♥	Q♥	2♥	10♠	6♣	8♣/A♦	5♦	7♥
	5♥	K♦	6♥	3♥	A♠	10♠					
21	10♥	6♦	7♥	3♣	Q♦	K♠	5♣	K♠	2♥/4♣	3♣	8♥
	J♠	K♥	6♥	A♦	J♥	8♥	Q♦				
22	Q♥	J♠	6♠	8♥	6♣	J♦	4♠	Q♠	5♠/3♠	K♦	7♠
	9♠	3♦	A♥	J♥	7♥	9♦					
23	Q♣	3♥	5♥	K♣	8♣	9♠	8♥	2♥	8♠/Q♦	7♠	K♦
	9♥	2♥	2♦	K♣	A♦	8♥					
24	2♠	9♥	K♣	J♠	5♦	8♠	7♠	8♦	4♥/6♦	8♥	3♣
	6♣	10♦	2♦	Q♦	8♥	10♥					

AGE	MER	VEN	MAR	JUP	SAT	URA	NEP	LR	PLU/RES	ENV	DISP
25	3♣	6♠	J♠	10♠	3♠	4♦	8♠	6♦	2♣/A♥	7♥	5♦
	6♥	8♠	A♣	6♦	9♠	8♠					
26	Q♥	J♦	5♥	6♣	K♥	3♥	4♦	3♦	9♣/4♣	A♠	9♦
	4♥	A♦	8♦	A♥	5♦	A♠					
27	10♦	10♠	6♣	7♦	7♥	4♥	7♠	5♦	A♦/4♠	2♣	Q♦
	8♠	10♥	3♠	5♦	9♠	7♠					
28	J♣	J♦	7♦	Q♣	J♥	8♠	4♦	5♥	2♥/5♠	K♥	3♦
	5♥	4♣	A♠	5♦	2♣	4♦					
29	J♠	9♦	K♥	8♣	2♦	6♠	Q♣	7♠	8♥/3♦	9♠	6♥
	10♦	7♠	9♠	4♣	10♠	9♣					
30	5♦	9♠	8♣	A♦	2♠	10♦	7♥	2♣	Q♦/K♦	6♠	4♣
	J♥	8♠	2♣	J♣	J♦	A♥					
31	10♠	4♦	5♠	9♥	8♦	J♥	A♦	2♠	4♣/A♣	2♠	5♣
	K♠	5♦	5♥	7♦	9♥	3♣					
32	J♦	Q♣	9♥	6♠	3♠	K♥	Q♠	A♦	6♦/10♥	K♣	5♥
	8♠	J♥	7♦	A♠	J♠	Q♠					
33	9♦	4♦	K♦	Q♦	A♥	8♠	6♠	4♦	K♠/A♠	8♠	4♦
	8♥	4♠	6♣	10♥	9♥	2♥					
34	J♥	Q♣	Q♦	2♥	3♦	5♠	9♠	6♦	Q♥/8♦	6♣	5♠
	K♥	6♣	5♦	J♦	10♥	J♠					
35	6♠	7♠	2♣	A♠	J♦	10♠	5♠	3♥	8♦/7♦	2♦	10♥
	6♦	4♠	9♠	2♦	3♠	J♣					
36	10♥	5♠	Q♦	7♠	J♠	3♥	10♠	8♦	K♦/4♣	A♦	J♣
	Q♥	A♥	5♥	7♦	A♣	10♠					
37	Q♣	Q♥	7♠	6♥	A♠	K♦	Q♠	Q♠	A♥/6♣	A♥	J♦
	4♦	K♥	8♠	A♣	Q♦	Q♠					
38	9♥	A♠	5♥	6♠	4♥	4♦	6♥	7♠	5♦/7♥	3♥	3♠
	8♠	J♦	J♥	Q♠	2♦	3♦					
39	10♦	Q♥	6♣	2♣	2♠	6♠	4♦	Q♦	3♠/4♣	Q♣	6♦
	K♦	9♦	K♣	Q♠	2♦	4♦					
40	8♥	2♥	7♣	3♦	5♠	10♥	6♠	A♠	Q♠/8♣	10♦	9♣
	J♣	K♠	9♠	K♦	9♥	K♥					
41	Q♠	3♥	K♠	6♣	2♥	2♦	J♠	4♦	10♥/5♥	Q♠	Q♥
	Q♥	6♥	K♣	8♣	A♣	K♦					
42	5♠	5♣	7♠	K♦	7♦	J♦	J♥	J♣	4♥/A♠	8♦	10♠
	Q♣	3♣	5♦	Q♥	A♥	4♦					
43	10♥	9♠	K♦	K♣	K♥	4♥	7♣	5♦	10♦/K♠	7♠	4♥
	Q♠	6♥	Q♥	A♠	7♠	A♦					
44	J♣	Q♣	K♣	A♦	2♦	3♦	4♦	7♠	5♦/6♦	J♠	4♠
	3♠	7♦	A♣	5♠	J♦	4♦					
45	8♦	K♠	3♥	2♥	Q♣	10♠	5♣	K♠	3♦/A♠	10♠	10♣
	2♠	9♦	3♣	10♥	6♥	5♠	Q♣				
46	8♣	3♠	4♥	5♠	Q♠	6♣	3♥	2♠	A♥/9♦	4♠	J♠
	6♠	Q♦	2♠	8♠	J♠	3♥					
47	K♦	7♣	5♠	3♣	7♥	9♣	6♣	7♥	10♥/Q♥	4♥	7♣
	Q♣	4♠	2♠	9♦	K♣	6♣					
48	K♠	Q♠	A♠	8♣	6♦	3♦	5♦	3♦	9♠/K♥	10♠	8♣
	2♠	A♠	10♥	7♣	Q♦	J♥	6♦				
49	5♥	7♠	2♣	2♠	A♦	4♦	6♦	2♥	6♥/2♦	Q♥	Q♠
	K♦	10♥	K♣	9♠	8♦	6♦					

AGE	MER	VEN	MAR	JUP	SAT	URA	NEP	LR	PLU/RES	ENV	DISP
50	3♥	8♦	Q♠	7♠	Q♦	A♠	4♦	4♠	9♥/10♠	9♣	10♦
	5♦	J♥	J♦	4♥	9♠	K♥					
51	J♣	5♦	7♠	K♣	2♠	9♥	3♦	10♥	J♥/5♦	6♦	Q♣
	6♦	A♥	7♥	2♣	6♥	K♦					
52	A♣	4♠	10♥	3♣	8♥	8♠	K♠	3♣	7♦/Q♦	3♠	3♥
	J♣	10♠	7♥	5♥	2♦	K♠					
53	J♠	A♠	3♣	9♠	4♣	7♦	6♦	8♥	K♥/Q♥	J♦	A♥
	3♠	A♥	7♥	3♥	10♦	6♦					
54	2♣	K♦	6♠	6♥	9♥	3♠	9♠	8♠	9♣/Q♦	J♣	A♦
	8♣	2♥	2♦	5♥	3♦	9♠					
55	J♣	8♣	6♥	5♠	5♦	9♣	7♥	K♣	4♥/4♣	10♥	2♦
	4♣	8♥	K♠	J♠	A♥	7♦					
56	Q♠	4♣	5♠	J♦	K♠	Q♥	A♠	J♠	9♣/5♣	5♠	6♣
	3♥	9♥	J♠	4♠	6♥	7♥	K♠				
57	Q♥	10♠	6♠	7♥	8♠	9♦	7♦	A♠	10♥/K♣	4♦	8♠
	4♥	3♦	A♠	K♠	4♠	Q♠					
58	3♣	4♣	7♥	J♠	A♥	4♥	7♣	3♣	3♦/5♦	5♥	K♣
	5♠	9♣	4♦	8♦	6♠	7♣					
59	3♥	10♠	J♠	Q♦	5♣	5♠	K♠	9♠	3♠/2♥	5♣	2♠
	8♠	2♦	8♥	6♠	7♥	J♦	5♣				
60	9♦	4♣	4♦	K♠	J♦	A♣	J♠	4♣	Q♦/9♠	4♣	6♠
	4♥	5♥	3♠	5♣	J♠	K♣					
61	A♣	J♠	3♥	K♣	2♠	6♦	4♣	9♥	8♣/K♦	6♥	9♠
	8♠	4♠	10♠	5♣	J♦	4♠					
62	Q♣	8♠	K♣	3♠	6♥	8♠	7♠	6♦	Q♦/2♣	3♦	K♥
	8♦	10♥	9♦	5♥	2♦	7♠					
63	9♣	A♠	5♦	6♠	Q♥	8♦	3♠	2♠	10♠/K♦	Q♦	2♣
	7♦	6♦	J♦	7♠	K♣	K♠					
64	J♠	7♦	6♠	J♥	8♥	10♠	2♥	K♦	4♥/Q♠	9♦	A♠
	7♠	2♣	Q♣	10♥	8♣	2♥					
65	9♥	2♠	J♥	7♥	Q♥	A♠	10♠	6♠	8♦/A♦	5♦	7♥
	5♥	K♦	6♥	3♥	A♠	10♠					
66	10♥	6♦	7♥	3♣	Q♦	K♠	5♠	6♥	A♣/4♣	3♣	8♥
	J♠	K♥	6♥	A♦	J♥	8♥	Q♦				
67	Q♥	J♣	6♠	8♥	6♣	J♦	4♠	7♦	5♠/3♠	K♦	7♠
	9♠	3♦	A♥	J♥	7♥	9♦					
68	Q♣	3♥	5♦	K♥	8♣	9♠	8♥	3♠	8♠/Q♦	7♠	K♥
	7♦	A♣	2♦	K♣	A♦	8♥					
69	2♠	7♦	K♦	J♠	5♦	8♠	7♣	9♠	4♥/6♦	8♥	3♣
	6♣	10♦	2♦	Q♦	8♥	10♥					
70	3♣	6♣	J♠	10♠	3♠	4♦	8♠	J♣	2♣/A♥	7♥	5♦
	6♥	8♣	2♥	6♦	9♠	8♠					
71	Q♥	J♥	5♥	6♣	K♥	3♥	4♦	8♠	9♣/4♣	A♠	9♦
	4♥	A♦	8♦	A♥	5♦	A♠					
72	10♦	10♠	6♣	9♥	7♥	4♥	7♠	6♥	A♦/4♣	2♣	Q♦
	8♠	10♥	3♠	5♦	9♠	7♠					
73	J♣	J♦	9♥	Q♣	J♥	8♠	4♦	5♠	A♣/5♠	K♥	3♦
	5♥	4♣	A♠	5♦	2♠	4♦					
74	J♠	9♦	K♥	8♣	2♦	6♠	Q♣	5♦	8♥/3♦	9♠	6♥
	10♦	7♠	9♠	4♣	10♠	9♣					
75	5♦	9♠	8♣	A♦	2♠	10♦	7♥	9♣	Q♦/K♦	6♠	4♣
	J♥	8♠	2♣	J♣	J♦	A♥					
76	10♠	4♦	5♠	7♦	8♦	J♥	A♦	7♣	4♣/2♥	2♠	5♣
	K♠	5♦	5♥	9♥	9♦	3♣					
77	J♦	Q♣	7♦	6♠	3♠	K♥	Q♠	Q♠	6♦/10♥	K♣	5♥
	8♠	J♣	9♥	2♥	J♠	Q♠					
78	9♦	4♦	K♦	Q♦	A♥	8♠	6♠	4♣	K♠/A♠	8♠	4♦
	8♦	4♠	6♣	10♥	7♦	A♣					
79	J♦	Q♣	Q♦	A♣	3♦	5♠	9♣	5♠	Q♥/8♥	6♠	5♠
	K♥	6♣	5♦	J♦	10♥	J♠					
80	6♠	7♠	2♣	A♠	J♦	10♠	5♠	J♦	8♦/9♥	2♦	10♥
	6♦	4♠	9♠	2♦	3♣	J♣					
81	10♥	5♣	Q♦	7♠	J♠	3♥	10♠	K♠	K♦/4♣	A♦	J♠
	Q♥	A♥	5♥	9♥	2♥	10♠					
82	Q♣	Q♥	7♠	6♥	A♠	K♦	Q♠	Q♥	A♥/6♣	A♥	J♦
	4♦	K♥	8♣	2♥	Q♦	Q♣					
83	7♦	A♦	5♥	6♣	4♥	4♦	6♥	2♥	5♦/7♥	3♥	3♠
	8♠	J♦	J♥	Q♠	2♦	3♦					
84	10♦	Q♥	6♣	2♣	2♠	6♠	4♦	Q♥	3♠/4♣	Q♣	6♦
	K♦	9♦	K♣	Q♠	2♦	4♦					
85	8♥	A♣	7♠	3♦	5♠	10♥	6♠	10♠	Q♣/8♣	10♦	9♣
	J♣	K♠	9♠	K♦	7♦	K♥					
86	Q♠	3♥	K♠	6♣	A♣	2♦	J♠	6♠	10♥/5♥	Q♠	Q♥
	Q♥	6♥	K♣	8♣	2♥	K♦					
87	5♠	5♣	7♠	K♦	9♥	J♦	J♥	7♥	4♥/A♠	8♦	10♠
	Q♣	3♣	5♦	Q♥	A♥	4♦					
88	10♥	9♠	K♦	K♠	K♥	4♥	7♠	8♠	10♦/K♠	7♣	4♥
	Q♣	6♥	Q♥	A♠	7♠	A♥					
89	J♣	Q♣	K♣	A♦	2♥	3♦	4♦	9♦	5♦/6♦	J♠	4♠
	3♣	9♥	2♥	5♠	J♦	4♦					
90	8♦	K♠	3♥	A♣	Q♠	10♠	5♠	9♥	3♦/A♠	10♣	10♣
	2♠	9♦	3♣	10♥	6♥	5♠	Q♣				
91	8♣	3♠	4♥	5♠	Q♠	6♣	3♥	3♣	A♥/9♦	4♠	J♠
	6♠	Q♦	2♠	8♠	J♠	3♥					
92	K♦	7♣	5♠	3♠	7♥	9♠	6♣	4♣	10♥/Q♥	4♥	7♠
	Q♣	4♠	2♠	9♦	K♣	6♠					
93	K♠	Q♠	2♥	8♦	6♦	3♦	5♦	7♥	9♠/K♥	10♠	8♦
	2♣	A♠	10♥	7♣	Q♦	J♥					
94	5♥	7♠	2♣	2♠	A♣	4♦	6♦	J♠	6♥/2♣	Q♥	Q♠
	K♦	10♥	K♣	9♠	8♦	6♦					
95	3♥	8♦	Q♠	7♠	Q♦	A♠	4♦	A♥	7♦/10♠	9♣	10♦
	5♦	J♥	J♦	4♥	9♠	K♥					
96	J♣	5♦	7♠	K♣	2♠	7♥	3♦	4♥	J♥/5♠	6♦	Q♣
	6♦	A♥	7♥	2♣	6♥	K♦					
97	2♥	4♠	10♥	3♣	8♥	8♠	K♣	7♠	9♥/Q♦	3♠	3♥
	J♣	10♠	7♥	5♥	2♦	K♣					
98	J♠	A♠	3♣	9♠	4♣	9♥	6♦	3♥	K♥/Q♥	J♦	A♥
	3♠	A♥	7♥	3♥	10♦	6♦					
99	2♣	K♦	6♠	6♥	7♥	3♠	9♠	10♠	9♣/Q♦	J♣	A♦
	8♣	A♣	2♦	5♥	3♦	9♠					

Jack of Clubs

AGE	MER	VEN	MAR	JUP	SAT	URA	NEP	LR	PLU/RES	ENV	DISP
0	9♦	7♠	2♣	K♣	J♦	4♥	4♦	9♦	2♠/8♥	J♣	J♠
	5♥	4♠	K♦	7♦	A♣	4♦					
1	10♦	5♥	K♣	7♥	2♦	2♠	9♣	7♠	4♠/7♣	10♥	J♦
	3♣	A♥	8♠	A♣	2♣	9♠					
2	9♥	10♣	K♦	7♣	5♠	3♣	7♥	2♣	9♠/6♣	5♠	3♣
	8♦	3♦	J♥	9♣	J♠	A♠					
3	Q♥	5♥	7♣	A♦	10♦	Q♣	3♣	K♣	6♥/8♥	4♦	6♦
	2♠	K♥	Q♠	9♣	J♠	3♣					
4	8♠	2♥	K♣	A♣	5♦	9♣	Q♣	J♦	10♠/8♣	5♥	9♣
	Q♦	K♠	3♥	2♠	9♥	A♥					
5	9♣	4♥	K♣	7♠	2♥	J♠	J♦	4♥	9♦/K♣	5♣	Q♥
	5♥	7♥	Q♠	8♣	A♣	2♠					
6	5♦	7♠	K♣	2♠	7♦	3♦	J♥	4♦	5♠/2♦	4♣	10♠
	10♠	6♠	9♠	5♥	4♠	3♣					
7	9♦	3♥	2♠	Q♠	A♥	5♠	3♠	10♠	Q♥/K♣	6♥	4♥
	10♠	7♥	5♦	2♦	K♣	10♣					
8	Q♦	10♠	Q♠	10♣	J♠	A♠	3♠	5♥	9♠/4♣	3♦	4♣
	6♠	7♦	A♣	5♦	3♦	3♣					
9	6♦	K♠	4♥	2♥	10♠	4♦	7♠	K♣	A♠/2♦	Q♦	10♣
	10♦	K♥	6♠	9♦	7♥	5♦	10♠				
10	8♦	6♥	5♠	5♦	9♣	7♣	4♥	7♥	4♠/K♥	9♦	J♠
	Q♣	2♣	10♠	8♦	J♦	4♥					
11	2♠	3♣	5♦	6♠	6♠	3♥	7♣	2♦	9♣/5♥	5♦	7♠
	10♠	10♥	10♦	K♥	Q♠	7♠					
12	K♠	9♣	A♣	6♦	4♣	A♠	9♣	2♠	3♥/A♥	3♣	8♠
	A♦	2♦	9♦	3♠	2♣	J♥	4♠				
13	K♦	K♣	A♦	10♦	10♣	3♠	4♠	9♠	7♥/J♠	K♦	Q♠
	2♠	9♦	Q♠	3♥	6♦	4♣					
14	4♥	6♥	9♣	K♣	2♣	2♦	3♠	9♥	9♥/4♦	7♠	10♦
	9♠	J♥	3♠	5♠	3♥	A♥					
15	Q♦	9♠	K♣	Q♠	10♦	9♥	A♠	10♣	J♥/5♦	8♥	Q♣
	4♣	4♠	6♣	A♦	7♥	2♠					
16	A♣	10♥	9♣	6♠	8♠	8♦	Q♠	K♦	7♦/2♣	7♥	3♥
	Q♦	4♦	6♣	K♦	J♠	Q♠					
17	J♦	2♦	6♠	3♥	8♥	7♦	4♠	7♠	A♥/5♦	A♠	A♥
	6♥	4♠	6♠	4♥	Q♥	4♠					
18	A♦	2♠	Q♣	7♥	9♥	6♥	3♥	5♠	5♣/2♣	2♣	A♦
	8♣	2♥	J♠	K♦	A♠	3♥					
19	Q♦	8♣	7♥	5♦	9♠	5♠	3♠	3♣	5♠/10♥	K♥	2♦
	8♥	8♠	K♠	J♦	4♠	7♦					
20	9♣	8♥	5♦	3♦	K♠	5♥	A♣	7♥	5♠/7♠	9♠	6♣
	4♥	9♥	J♦	10♥	7♥	6♣	K♠				
21	5♥	4♦	Q♣	6♣	8♦	K♥	7♦	Q♥	9♦/Q♠	6♠	8♠
	5♠	A♠	2♦	K♠	10♥	10♠					
22	6♠	8♥	6♣	J♦	4♠	5♠	3♠	5♥	A♥/K♦	2♠	K♣
	5♦	5♣	3♣	6♦	Q♣	3♠					
23	4♥	4♦	J♦	2♣	7♠	5♦	K♠	7♣	6♥/2♦	K♣	2♠
	8♦	J♠	8♠	Q♣	6♠	3♦	7♠				
24	K♥	8♦	3♣	K♠	3♦	A♣	Q♦	A♦	2♠/3♦	8♠	6♠
	5♠	K♦	6♥	7♠	J♦	Q♠					
25	A♣	J♦	4♥	Q♠	10♦	4♠	8♥	10♦	8♣/2♣	6♣	9♠
	8♦	10♥	4♦	7♠	3♦	8♥					
26	10♠	8♦	Q♠	6♥	7♥	8♠	K♣	Q♣	2♣/A♣	2♦	K♥
	6♦	9♦	K♥	K♦	J♠	K♣					
27	5♣	2♦	9♠	Q♣	5♥	6♦	6♥	3♣	4♦/2♣	A♦	2♣
	7♠	4♣	3♦	K♣	Q♠	K♠					
28	J♦	7♥	Q♣	J♥	8♠	4♦	2♥	8♠	5♠/9♣	A♥	A♠
	K♣	A♦	10♠	9♦	8♣	2♥					
29	9♥	10♦	J♥	6♠	5♥	A♣	4♦	2♥	6♦/10♣	3♥	7♥
	K♦	2♠	7♥	4♥	2♦	4♦					
30	9♦	4♣	6♠	6♠	2♠	K♣	7♠	K♣	A♣/8♥	Q♣	8♥
	J♦	A♥	7♥	10♣	J♥	8♠	2♣				
31	5♥	Q♦	Q♣	8♠	7♣	3♦	10♥	A♣	5♦/6♥	10♦	7♠
	3♥	A♠	4♠	J♥	6♣	K♥					
32	10♠	4♥	K♣	2♠	8♣	3♥	8♠	5♦	8♦/2♣	Q♠	K♦
	7♦	A♠	J♠	Q♠	10♣	8♠					
33	10♦	7♥	2♠	J♦	9♠	8♦	3♠	9♦	5♠/4♣	8♦	3♣
	7♣	Q♥	J♠	2♣	8♠	9♠					
34	6♠	7♠	J♥	4♦	6♥	3♣	8♦	Q♣	A♦/4♣	7♠	5♦
	7♥	8♣	2♥	4♣	3♥	8♦					
35	5♥	3♦	K♦	7♣	A♥	4♥	3♠	9♣	5♣/8♥	J♠	9♦
	5♠	10♣	6♦	4♠	9♠	2♦					
36	Q♥	4♦	7♠	9♥	6♣	5♠	K♣	4♥	10♣/10♥	10♣	Q♦
	8♦	9♦	6♥	9♠	3♥	K♣					
37	Q♦	3♦	9♥	10♠	J♥	8♦	3♣	K♠	A♣/5♦	4♠	3♦
	K♦	8♥	2♦	9♠	A♦	3♣					
38	J♦	K♥	A♥	8♣	J♠	Q♣	10♠	7♠	8♠/A♠	4♥	6♥
	Q♥	K♣	3♥	8♥	4♦	5♣					
39	9♠	3♦	8♠	10♣	10♦	Q♥	6♣	2♥	2♣/2♠	10♠	4♣
	J♥	8♦	A♦	Q♦	3♦	4♠					
40	4♦	3♣	5♦	7♦	6♦	J♥	10♠	J♠	8♥/2♦	Q♥	5♠
	K♠	9♠	K♦	9♥	K♦	6♠					
41	3♦	10♠	7♦	Q♣	6♥	A♥	9♣	J♦	4♣/9♥	9♣	5♥
	8♦	Q♦	9♥	2♥	J♦	9♣					
42	K♥	3♣	2♠	2♣	4♠	8♦	Q♣	5♦	K♠/2♦	6♦	4♦
	6♦	10♥	7♠	9♦	7♦	A♠					
43	J♥	10♠	2♣	A♣	A♠	5♦	5♣	7♠	5♥/8♠	3♠	5♠
	A♥	7♣	9♠	3♦	9♦	J♦					
44	Q♣	K♣	A♦	2♦	3♦	4♦	5♦	K♣	6♦/9♥	J♦	10♥
	4♣	10♥	3♥	J♠	6♠	Q♦					
45	9♦	7♠	2♣	K♣	J♦	4♥	4♦	2♠	2♠/8♥	J♣	J♠
	5♥	4♠	K♦	9♥	2♥	4♦					
46	10♠	5♥	K♣	7♥	2♦	2♠	9♣	7♠	4♠/7♣	10♥	J♦
	3♣	A♥	8♠	2♥	2♣	9♠					
47	7♦	10♣	K♦	7♣	5♠	3♣	7♥	3♦	9♠/6♣	5♠	3♣
	8♠	3♦	J♥	9♣	J♠	A♠					
48	Q♥	5♥	7♠	A♦	10♦	Q♣	3♣	J♥	6♥/8♥	4♦	6♦
	2♠	K♥	Q♠	9♣	J♠	3♣					
49	8♠	A♣	K♣	A♣	5♦	9♦	Q♣	9♦	10♠/8♣	5♥	9♣
	Q♦	K♠	3♥	2♠	7♦	A♥					

AGE	MER	VEN	MAR	JUP	SAT	URA	NEP	LR	PLU/RES	ENV	DISP
50	9♣	4♥	K♠	7♣	A♣	J♠	J♦	3♥	9♦/K♦	5♣	Q♥
	5♥	7♥	Q♠	8♠	2♥	2♠					
51	5♦	7♠	K♣	2♠	9♥	3♦	J♥	2♠	5♠/2♦	4♣	10♠
	10♠	6♠	9♠	5♥	4♣	3♠					
52	9♦	3♥	2♠	Q♠	A♥	5♠	3♠	Q♠	Q♥/K♠	6♥	4♥
	10♠	7♥	5♥	2♠	K♣	10♣					
53	Q♦	10♠	Q♠	10♣	J♠	A♠	3♣	A♥	9♠/4♣	3♦	4♠
	6♠	9♥	2♥	5♦	3♦	3♣					
54	6♦	K♠	4♥	A♣	10♠	4♦	7♠	5♠	A♠/2♦	Q♦	10♣
	10♦	K♥	6♠	9♦	7♥	5♦	10♠				
55	8♣	6♥	5♠	5♦	9♣	7♠	4♥	3♠	4♠/K♥	9♦	J♠
	Q♣	2♣	10♦	8♦	J♦	4♥					
56	2♠	3♠	5♦	6♠	6♣	3♥	7♠	Q♦	9♦/5♦	5♦	7♣
	10♠	10♥	10♦	K♥	Q♠	7♣					
57	K♠	9♣	2♥	6♦	4♣	A♠	9♠	10♠	3♥/A♥	3♣	8♦
	A♦	2♦	9♦	3♠	2♣	J♥	4♣				
58	K♦	K♣	A♦	10♦	10♣	3♣	4♣	Q♠	7♥/J♠	K♦	Q♠
	2♠	9♦	Q♠	3♥	6♦	4♣					
59	4♥	6♦	9♣	K♣	2♣	2♦	3♣	10♣	7♦/4♦	7♠	10♦
	9♠	J♥	3♦	5♠	3♥	A♥					
60	Q♦	9♠	K♣	Q♠	10♦	7♦	A♠	J♠	J♥/5♦	8♥	Q♣
	4♣	4♠	6♣	A♦	7♥	2♠					
61	2♥	10♥	9♦	6♠	8♠	8♦	Q♠	A♠	9♥/2♣	7♥	3♥
	Q♦	4♦	6♣	K♦	J♠	Q♠					
62	J♦	2♦	6♠	3♥	8♥	9♥	4♣	3♣	A♥/5♥	A♠	A♥
	6♥	4♠	6♣	4♥	Q♥	4♣					
63	A♦	2♠	Q♣	7♥	7♦	6♥	3♥	6♦	5♣/2♦	2♣	A♥
	8♣	A♣	J♠	K♦	A♠	3♥					
64	Q♦	8♣	7♥	5♦	9♠	5♣	3♠	K♠	5♠/10♥	K♥	2♦
	8♥	8♠	K♠	J♦	4♠	9♥					
65	9♣	8♥	5♠	3♦	K♠	5♥	2♥	4♥	5♣/7♠	9♠	6♠
	4♥	7♦	J♦	10♥	7♥	6♣	K♠				
66	5♥	4♦	Q♣	6♣	8♦	K♥	9♥	2♥	9♦/Q♠	6♠	8♠
	5♠	A♠	2♦	K♠	10♥	10♠					
67	6♠	8♥	6♣	J♦	4♠	5♠	3♠	10♠	A♠/K♦	2♠	K♣
	5♦	5♣	3♣	6♦	Q♣	3♠					
68	4♥	4♦	J♦	2♠	7♠	5♦	K♠	4♦	6♥/A♣	K♣	2♠
	8♦	J♠	8♠	Q♣	6♦	3♦	7♠				
69	K♥	8♥	3♣	K♠	3♦	2♥	Q♦	7♠	2♣/3♥	8♠	6♠
	5♠	K♦	6♥	7♠	J♦	Q♠					
70	2♥	J♦	4♥	Q♠	10♦	4♣	8♥	8♠	8♣/2♠	6♣	9♠
	8♦	10♥	4♦	7♠	3♦	8♥					
71	10♠	8♦	Q♠	6♥	7♥	8♣	K♣	6♥	2♣/A♦	2♦	K♥
	6♥	9♦	K♥	K♦	J♠	K♣					
72	5♣	2♦	9♠	Q♠	5♥	6♦	6♥	5♠	4♦/2♠	A♦	2♠
	9♥	4♣	3♦	K♣	Q♠	K♣					
73	J♦	9♥	Q♣	J♦	8♠	4♦	A♣	5♦	5♠/9♣	A♥	A♠
	K♣	A♦	10♠	9♦	8♠	A♣					
74	7♦	10♠	J♥	6♣	5♥	2♥	4♦	9♠	6♦/10♣	3♥	7♥
	K♦	2♠	7♥	4♥	2♦	4♦					
75	9♦	4♣	6♣	6♠	2♣	K♠	7♠	7♣	2♥/8♥	Q♣	8♥
	J♦	A♥	7♥	10♣	J♥	8♠	2♣				
76	5♥	Q♦	Q♣	8♠	7♠	3♦	10♥	4♥	5♦/6♥	10♦	7♠
	3♥	A♠	4♠	J♥	6♣	K♥					
77	10♠	4♥	K♦	2♠	8♣	3♥	8♠	2♠	8♦/2♣	Q♠	K♦
	9♥	2♥	J♠	Q♠	10♣	8♠					
78	10♦	9♥	2♠	J♦	9♠	8♦	3♠	3♠	5♠/4♣	8♦	3♠
	7♣	Q♥	J♠	2♣	8♠	9♦					
79	6♠	7♣	J♦	4♦	6♥	3♣	8♦	5♦	A♦/4♠	7♣	5♦
	7♥	8♣	A♣	4♣	3♥	8♦					
80	5♥	3♦	K♦	7♣	A♥	4♥	3♣	6♠	5♣/8♥	J♠	9♦
	5♠	10♣	6♦	4♠	9♠	2♦					
81	Q♥	4♦	7♣	7♦	6♣	5♠	K♣	6♣	10♣/10♥	10♣	Q♦
	8♦	9♦	6♥	9♠	3♥	K♣					
82	Q♦	3♦	7♥	10♠	J♥	8♦	3♠	3♥	2♥/5♦	4♠	3♦
	K♦	8♥	2♦	9♠	A♦	3♠					
83	J♦	K♥	A♥	8♣	9♠	Q♣	10♠	7♣	8♠/A♠	4♥	6♥
	Q♥	K♣	3♥	8♥	4♦	5♠					
84	9♠	3♥	8♣	10♣	10♦	Q♥	6♣	K♠	2♣/2♦	10♠	4♣
	J♥	8♦	A♦	Q♦	3♦	4♠					
85	4♦	3♣	5♠	9♥	6♦	J♥	10♣	9♠	8♥/A♠	Q♥	5♣
	K♠	9♠	K♦	7♦	K♥	6♠					
86	3♦	10♠	9♥	Q♣	6♥	A♥	9♠	A♠	4♣/9♦	9♣	5♥
	8♦	Q♦	7♠	A♣	J♦	9♣					
87	K♥	3♣	2♠	2♣	4♠	8♦	Q♣	6♦	K♠/2♦	6♦	4♦
	6♦	10♥	7♣	9♦	9♥	2♥					
88	J♥	10♠	2♣	2♥	A♠	5♦	5♠	4♣	5♥/8♠	3♠	5♠
	A♥	7♣	9♠	3♦	9♦	J♦					
89	Q♣	K♠	A♦	2♦	3♦	4♦	5♦	A♠	6♦/7♦	J♦	10♥
	4♣	10♥	3♥	J♠	6♠	Q♦					
90	9♦	7♠	2♣	K♣	J♦	4♥	4♦	9♠	2♠/8♥	J♣	J♠
	5♥	4♠	K♦	7♠	A♣	4♦					
91	10♠	5♥	K♣	7♥	2♦	2♠	9♣	K♦	4♠/7♠	10♥	J♦
	3♣	A♥	8♣	A♠	2♣	9♠					
92	9♥	10♣	K♦	7♠	5♠	3♣	7♥	K♠	9♠/6♠	5♠	3♠
	8♦	3♦	J♥	9♣	J♠	A♠					
93	Q♥	5♦	7♣	A♦	10♦	Q♣	3♣	A♦	6♥/8♥	4♦	6♦
	2♠	K♥	Q♠	9♣	J♠						
94	8♠	2♥	K♣	A♠	5♦	9♦	Q♣	10♦	10♠/8♣	5♥	9♣
	Q♦	K♠	3♥	2♠	9♥	A♦					
95	9♣	4♥	K♠	7♠	2♥	J♠	J♦	10♠	9♦/K♦	5♣	Q♥
	5♥	7♥	Q♠	8♣	A♣	2♠					
96	5♦	7♠	K♣	2♠	7♥	3♦	J♥	3♠	5♠/2♦	4♣	10♠
	10♠	6♠	9♠	5♥	4♣	3♣					
97	9♦	3♥	2♠	Q♠	A♥	5♠	3♠	4♣	Q♥/K♠	6♥	4♥
	10♠	7♥	5♥	2♦	K♣	10♣					
98	Q♦	10♠	Q♠	10♣	J♠	A♠	3♠	4♥	9♠/4♣	3♦	4♠
	6♠	7♠	A♣	5♦	3♦	3♠					
99	6♠	K♠	4♥	2♥	10♠	4♦	7♠	6♦	A♠/2♦	Q♦	10♣
	10♦	K♥	6♠	9♦	7♥	5♦	10♠				

Queen of Clubs

AGE	MER	VEN	MAR	JUP	SAT	URA	NEP	LR	PLU/RES	ENV	DISP
0	10♠	5♣	3♦	A♠	7♥	7♦	5♠	10♠	J♥/9♣	Q♣	Q♣
	10♣	2♠	9♦	3♣	10♥	6♥					
1	2♥	10♦	Q♥	4♣	Q♦	2♣	A♠	5♣	9♥/4♦	10♦	3♥
	10♠	8♦	9♦	3♣	9♠	A♠					
2	3♥	5♦	4♣	7♠	J♣	9♥	10♣	3♦	K♦/7♣	Q♠	A♥
	4♠	2♠	9♦	K♣	6♣	10♣					
3	3♣	6♥	8♥	10♥	7♦	4♠	7♠	A♠	J♠/4♦	8♦	A♦
	8♠	A♣	9♠	3♣	5♠	7♠					
4	10♠	8♣	10♥	9♣	5♠	J♠	A♥	7♥	Q♠/10♦	7♣	2♦
	J♣	Q♦	K♠	3♥	2♠	9♥					
5	2♦	J♣	9♣	4♥	K♠	7♣	2♥	7♥	J♠/J♥	J♠	6♣
	K♣	7♦	3♥	10♦	10♥	9♦	K♠				
6	7♣	8♦	8♥	9♣	2♣	5♥	9♥	5♠	Q♥/A♣	10♣	8♠
	Q♠	5♠	5♦	K♠	10♦	8♠					
7	4♣	J♠	9♣	3♥	2♠	Q♠	A♥	2♥	5♠/3♠	4♠	K♣
	9♣	J♠	6♦	A♥	8♥	A♥					
8	K♣	8♦	3♥	4♦	J♥	9♠	K♠	10♦	4♠/A♠	4♥	2♠
	2♣	9♠	Q♦	8♥	9♦	4♥	J♦				
9	5♥	J♣	6♦	K♠	4♥	2♥	10♠	Q♥	4♦/7♠	10♠	6♠
	Q♠	3♠	4♠	J♦	3♥	A♠					
10	2♥	3♥	K♣	A♠	7♥	10♣	J♠	4♣	8♠/6♥	Q♥	9♠
	2♣	10♦	8♦	J♦	4♥	J♣					
11	8♠	2♣	A♠	4♣	10♥	8♠	3♦	Q♦	4♦/3♣	9♣	K♥
	A♦	Q♥	5♥	3♠	9♠	3♦					
12	J♠	5♦	5♣	8♥	7♣	A♦	4♠	2♣	8♦/6♥	6♦	2♠
	9♥	10♣	4♥	3♦	A♠	K♠					
13	3♥	9♥	8♥	J♥	Q♦	8♦	A♣	A♠	Q♠/2♦	3♠	A♠
	3♦	3♣	8♠	Q♥	8♣	A♣					
14	7♥	7♥	J♥	9♦	7♣	2♥	8♠	3♥	A♦/6♠	J♦	7♥
	3♠	6♥	10♥	K♣	5♦	8♦					
15	Q♥	10♣	9♦	4♣	4♦	K♠	J♦	5♦	2♥/J♣	J♠	8♥
	3♥	K♦	10♥	6♠	J♥	Q♦	4♦				
16	7♣	10♠	8♥	Q♦	K♥	4♥	10♦	4♣	9♣/4♠	10♥	7♣
	7♠	5♠	2♠	J♥	9♦	5♥					
17	8♠	K♣	3♠	6♥	8♠	7♠	Q♦	7♠	2♣/4♦	5♠	K♦
	9♥	2♥	9♠	A♠	6♠	Q♦					
18	7♥	9♥	6♦	3♥	5♠	2♣	A♥	J♣	Q♠/10♦	4♦	3♠
	K♥	6♣	9♠	4♦	Q♦	Q♥					
19	4♣	K♥	3♥	8♦	4♠	6♦	2♣	9♥	3♣/2♠	5♥	5♦
	10♥	8♣	A♣	10♣	7♠	2♠					
20	7♣	4♥	3♠	K♥	K♠	K♣	6♦	10♠	J♠/J♣	5♣	9♦
	Q♠	6♠	A♦	2♠	5♣	5♦					
21	6♠	8♦	K♥	7♥	9♦	Q♠	3♦	3♣	6♠/10♦	4♣	Q♦
	2♣	Q♥	4♠	5♣	7♠	3♦					
22	10♠	4♥	7♦	8♠	J♥	2♣	6♦	6♥	2♥/9♣	6♥	3♦
	3♠	J♣	5♦	5♠	3♣	6♦					
23	3♥	5♥	K♦	8♠	9♠	8♥	8♠	8♥	Q♦/5♠	3♦	6♥
	6♣	3♦	7♠	J♣	8♦	J♠					
24	5♠	7♠	8♣	6♠	7♦	6♠	9♦	10♥	4♦/6♥	Q♦	4♣
	J♥	2♣	3♠	10♠	4♥	2♠					
25	8♦	6♦	9♣	9♥	A♦	J♥	6♠	7♦	J♣/A♣	9♦	5♣
	K♠	5♣	3♠	7♦	5♥	4♠					
26	4♥	8♠	9♥	8♥	4♠	K♦	2♠	4♠	10♣/Q♥	5♦	5♥
	2♣	10♠	7♦	A♣	3♥	2♦					
27	5♥	6♦	6♥	4♦	2♠	2♣	8♥	7♠	K♠/5♦	3♣	4♦
	A♦	10♦	K♥	Q♥	9♥	2♥					
28	J♥	8♠	4♦	2♦	5♠	9♣	J♠	10♠	7♣/Q♦	K♦	5♠
	K♦	K♥	5♠	4♦	Q♥	3♥					
29	8♥	3♦	3♠	5♦	4♥	8♦	9♣	8♣	A♦/7♦	7♠	10♥
	10♣	10♦	7♠	9♠	4♠	10♠					
30	Q♥	J♦	4♦	3♦	3♥	K♣	8♦	10♥	6♥/J♣	8♥	J♠
	7♣	2♠	3♠	7♦	A♣	8♦					
31	8♠	7♠	3♦	10♥	5♦	6♥	2♦	9♠	2♠/K♥	7♥	J♦
	6♦	K♦	8♣	A♣	4♦	2♦					
32	9♥	6♠	3♠	K♥	Q♠	6♦	10♥	5♣	5♣/9♦	A♠	3♠
	2♣	4♥	J♥	2♦	9♠	5♠					
33	6♣	7♣	K♥	3♣	7♥	8♥	6♠	J♠	4♠/J♥	2♣	6♦
	6♥	5♥	A♠	2♦	9♠	6♦					
34	Q♦	2♥	3♦	5♠	9♠	Q♥	8♥	A♥	8♠/8♣	K♥	9♣
	10♠	K♠	7♠	6♥	9♥	K♦					
35	2♦	K♣	K♠	K♥	2♥	9♠	3♥	2♦	Q♥/3♣	9♠	Q♥
	7♠	10♥	A♠	8♣	A♣	6♥					
36	9♣	J♠	3♦	6♥	7♦	4♥	J♥	J♣	Q♠/5♦	6♠	10♠
	8♠	4♠	5♠	7♣	2♠	6♦					
37	Q♥	7♠	6♥	A♠	K♦	Q♠	A♥	9♣	6♣/K♣	2♠	4♥
	8♠	10♥	7♣	5♦	3♦	6♠					
38	10♠	8♠	A♠	6♠	9♠	5♠	6♦	4♥	5♣/10♠	K♣	4♠
	4♣	7♠	A♠	9♣	4♥	6♦					
39	A♦	K♠	K♣	2♥	8♠	8♦	J♠	K♠	5♠/5♦	8♠	10♠
	7♥	5♥	4♣	Q♥	10♥	9♣	8♠				
40	8♣	4♠	Q♠	9♠	2♦	K♥	K♣	7♣	2♠/5♦	6♣	J♠
	8♥	4♦	7♥	2♣	3♥	K♠					
41	6♥	A♥	9♣	4♣	9♦	7♠	K♥	2♥	Q♥/7♣	2♦	7♣
	8♠	10♦	7♥	5♦	A♠	K♥					
42	K♠	2♦	A♣	A♦	10♣	5♠	5♠	7♠	7♠/K♦	A♦	8♦
	3♣	5♦	Q♥	A♥	4♦	J♥	10♣				
43	3♠	3♦	3♣	7♥	6♠	6♦	10♣	8♦	10♥/9♠	A♥	Q♠
	6♥	Q♥	A♠	7♠	A♦	10♣					
44	K♣	A♠	2♦	3♦	4♦	5♦	6♦	8♥	9♥/8♦	3♥	10♦
	5♣	J♦	4♦	Q♠	7♠	K♦					
45	10♠	5♣	3♦	A♠	7♥	9♥	5♠	9♦	J♥/9♣	Q♣	Q♣
	10♣	2♠	9♦	3♣	10♥	6♥					
46	A♣	10♦	Q♥	4♣	Q♦	2♣	A♠	2♠	7♦/4♦	10♦	3♥
	10♠	8♦	9♦	3♠	9♠	A♠					
47	3♥	5♦	4♣	7♠	J♣	7♦	10♠	5♥	K♦/7♣	Q♠	A♥
	4♠	2♠	9♦	K♣	6♣	10♣					
48	3♣	6♥	8♥	10♥	9♥	4♠	7♠	7♥	J♠/4♦	8♦	A♦
	8♠	2♥	9♠	3♣	5♠	7♠					
49	10♠	8♣	10♥	9♣	5♣	J♠	A♥	4♣	Q♠/10♦	7♣	2♦
	J♣	Q♦	K♠	3♥	2♠	7♦					

AGE	MER	VEN	MAR	JUP	SAT	URA	NEP	LR	PLU/RES	ENV	DISP
50	2♦	J♣	9♣	4♥	K♠	7♣	A♣	J♣	J♠/J♦	J♠	6♣
	K♣	9♥	3♥	10♦	10♥	9♦	K♠				
51	7♣	8♦	8♥	9♦	2♣	5♥	7♦	9♦	Q♥/A♠	10♣	8♠
	Q♠	5♣	5♦	K♠	10♦	8♠					
52	4♣	J♣	9♦	3♥	2♠	Q♠	A♥	3♥	5♠/3♣	4♠	K♣
	9♠	J♠	6♦	A♦	8♥	A♥					
53	K♣	8♣	3♥	4♦	J♦	9♣	K♠	2♠	4♠/2♥	4♥	2♠
	2♠	9♠	Q♦	8♥	9♦	4♥	J♦				
54	5♥	J♣	6♣	K♠	4♥	A♣	10♠	Q♠	4♦/7♠	10♠	6♠
	Q♠	3♠	4♠	J♦	3♥	A♠					
55	A♣	3♥	K♣	A♠	7♥	10♣	J♣	A♥	8♣/6♦	Q♥	9♠
	2♣	10♦	8♦	J♦	4♥	J♣					
56	8♠	2♣	A♠	4♠	10♥	8♣	3♦	K♣	4♦/3♣	9♣	K♥
	A♦	Q♥	5♥	3♠	9♠	3♦					
57	J♠	5♣	52♣	8♥	7♣	A♦	4♠	8♦	8♦/6♥	6♦	2♣
	7♦	10♣	4♥	3♦	A♠	K♠					
58	3♥	7♦	8♥	J♥	Q♦	8♦	2♥	3♥	Q♠/2♦	3♠	A♠
	3♦	3♣	8♠	Q♥	8♠	2♥					
59	9♥	7♥	J♥	9♦	7♣	A♣	8♦	4♦	A♦/6♠	J♦	7♥
	3♠	6♥	10♥	K♣	5♦	8♦					
60	Q♥	10♣	9♣	4♣	4♦	K♠	J♦	J♦	A♠/J♣	J♣	8♥
	3♥	K♦	10♥	6♠	J♥	Q♦	4♦				
61	7♣	10♠	8♥	Q♥	K♥	4♥	10♦	9♣	9♣/4♠	10♥	7♠
	7♠	5♠	2♠	J♥	9♠	5♥					
62	8♠	K♣	3♠	6♥	8♠	7♠	Q♦	K♠	2♣/4♦	5♠	K♦
	7♦	A♣	9♠	A♠	6♠	Q♦					
63	7♥	7♦	6♥	3♥	5♣	2♣	A♥	5♥	Q♠/10♣	4♦	3♣
	K♥	6♠	9♠	4♦	Q♦	Q♥					
64	4♣	K♥	3♥2	8♠	4♠	6♦	2♣	J♣	3♠/2♠	5♥	5♦
	10♥	8♣	2♥	10♣	7♠	2♣					
65	7♣	4♥	3♠	K♥	K♦	K♣	6♦	6♦	J♠/J♣	5♠	9♦
	Q♠	6♠	A♦	2♠	5♠	5♦					
66	6♣	8♦	K♥	9♥	9♦	Q♠	3♦	K♠	6♠/10♦	4♣	Q♦
	2♠	Q♥	4♠	5♠	7♠	3♦					
67	10♠	4♥	9♥	8♠	J♥	2♣	6♦	4♥	A♠/9♣	6♥	3♦
	3♠	J♣	5♦	5♠	3♣	6♦					
68	3♥	5♥	K♦	8♠	9♠	8♥	8♠	2♥	Q♦/5♠	3♦	6♥
	6♣	3♦	7♠	J♣	8♦	J♠					
69	5♥	7♠	8♣	6♠	7♥	6♣	9♦	10♠	4♦/6♥	Q♦	4♣
	J♥	2♣	3♠	10♠	4♥	2♠					
70	8♦	6♦	9♣	7♦	A♦	J♥	6♠	2♥	J♣/2♥	9♦	5♣
	K♠	5♣	3♠	9♥	5♥	4♣					
71	4♥	8♠	7♦	8♥	4♠	K♦	2♦	3♥	10♣/Q♥	5♦	5♥
	2♣	10♠	9♥	2♥	3♥	2♦					
72	5♥	6♦	6♥	4♦	2♠	2♣	8♥	K♠	K♠/5♦	3♣	4♦
	A♥	10♦	K♥	Q♥	7♦	A♣					
73	J♥	8♠	4♦	A♣	5♠	9♣	J♠	A♠	7♣/Q♦	K♦	5♠
	K♥	K♥	5♣	4♦	Q♥	3♥					
74	8♥	3♦	3♠	5♦	4♥	8♦	9♣	7♥	A♦/9♥	7♠	10♦
	10♣	10♦	7♠	9♠	4♣	10♠					
75	Q♥	J♣	4♦	3♦	3♥	K♣	8♦	10♠	6♥/J♣	8♥	J♣
	7♣	2♠	3♠	9♥	2♥	8♦					
76	8♠	7♣	3♦	10♥	5♦	6♥	2♦	J♣	2♠/K♥	7♥	J♦
	6♦	K♦	8♣	2♥	4♦	2♦					
77	7♦	6♠	3♠	K♥	Q♠	6♦	10♥	8♠	5♣/9♦	A♠	3♠
	2♣	4♥	J♥	2♦	9♠	5♠					
78	6♣	7♣	K♥	3♣	7♥	8♥	6♦	2♣	4♠/J♣	2♣	6♦
	6♥	5♥	A♠	2♦	9♠	6♦					
79	Q♦	A♣	3♦	5♠	9♣	Q♥	8♥	A♠	8♠/8♣	K♥	9♣
	10♠	K♠	7♠	6♥	7♦	K♦					
80	2♦	K♣	K♠	K♥	A♣	9♠	3♥	4♠	Q♥/3♠	9♠	Q♥
	7♣	10♥	8♠	8♣	2♥	6♥					
81	9♠	J♣	3♦	6♥	9♥	4♥	J♥	10♥	Q♠/5♦	6♠	10♠
	8♠	4♣	5♣	7♣	2♠	6♦					
82	Q♥	7♠	6♥	A♠	K♦	Q♠	A♥	8♣	6♣/K♠	2♠	4♥
	8♠	10♥	7♠	5♦	3♦	6♠					
83	10♠	8♠	A♠	6♠	9♠	5♠	6♦	3♦	5♣/10♣	K♣	4♠
	4♣	9♥	2♥	9♣	4♥	6♦					
84	A♦	K♠	K♣	A♠	8♠	8♦	J♦	J♠	5♠/5♦	8♠	10♣
	7♥	5♥	4♣	Q♥	10♥	9♣	8♠				
85	8♣	4♠	Q♠	9♣	2♦	·K♥	K♣	5♦	2♠/5♥	6♠	J♠
	8♥	4♦	7♥	2♣	3♥	K♣					
86	6♥	A♥	9♠	4♣	9♦	7♠	K♥	5♠	Q♥/7♣	2♦	7♠
	8♠	10♦	7♥	5♥	A♠	K♥					
87	K♠	2♦	2♥	A♦	10♣	5♠	5♠	8♥	7♠/K♦	A♦	8♦
	3♠	5♦	Q♥	A♥	4♦	J♥	10♣				
88	3♠	3♦	3♣	7♥	6♠	6♦	10♠	7♠	10♥/9♠	A♥	Q♠
	6♥	Q♥	A♠	7♠	A♦	10♣					
89	K♣	A♠	2♥	3♦	4♦	5♦	6♦	A♠	7♦/8♦	3♥	10♦
	5♣	J♥	4♥	Q♠	7♠	K♦					
90	10♠	5♣	3♦	A♠	7♥	7♠	5♠	4♠	J♥/9♣	Q♣	Q♠
	10♣	2♠	9♥	3♠	10♥	6♦					
91	2♥	10♦	Q♥	4♣	Q♦	2♣	A♠	3♥	9♥/4♦	10♦	3♥
	10♠	8♥	9♦	3♠	9♠	A♠					
92	3♥	5♦	4♠	7♠	J♣	9♥	10♠	9♥	K♦/7♣	Q♠	A♥
	4♠	2♠	9♦	K♣	6♠	10♣					
93	3♣	6♥	8♥	10♥	7♠	4♠	7♠	8♥	J♠/4♦	8♦	A♦
	8♣	A♣	9♠	3♠	5♠	7♠					
94	10♠	8♠	10♥	9♣	5♠	J♠	A♥	J♥	Q♠/10♦	7♣	2♦
	J♣	Q♦	4♣	3♥	2♠	9♥					
95	2♦	J♠	9♣	4♥	K♠	7♣	2♥	Q♦	J♠/J♦	J♠	6♣
	K♣	7♥	3♥	10♦	10♥	9♦	K♠				
96	7♣	8♦	8♥	9♦	2♣	5♥	9♥	8♦	Q♥/A♠	10♣	8♠
	Q♠	5♣	5♦	K♠	10♦	8♠					
97	4♣	J♣	9♦	3♥	2♠	Q♠	A♥	A♣	5♠/3♠	4♠	K♣
	9♣	J♣	6♦	A♦	8♥	A♥					
98	K♣	8♣	3♥	4♦	J♦	9♣	K♠	7♦	4♠/A♣	4♥	2♠
	2♣	9♠	Q♦	8♥	9♦	4♥	J♦				
99	5♥	J♣	6♦	K♠	4♥	2♥	10♠	7♦	4♦/7♠	10♠	6♠
	Q♠	3♠	4♠	J♦	3♥	A♠					

King of Clubs

AGE	MER	VEN	MAR	JUP	SAT	URA	NEP	LR	PLU/RES	ENV	DISP
0	J♦ 7♣	4♥ A♥	4♦ J♠	2♠ 9♠	8♥ 3♦	6♣ 6♠	6♠	J♦	Q♥/10♣	K♣	K♣
1	7♥ 5♦	2♦ K♠	2♣ 5♠	9♣ 3♦	4♠ 4♦	7♣ 10♦	K♠ 4♠	4♥	Q♣/2♥	8♠	2♠
2	6♦ 6♣	4♥ 10♣	J♠ Q♣	K♠ 4♠	10♦ 2♠	A♣ 9♦	Q♠	4♦	9♣/6♥	6♣	6♠
3	A♣ 5♦	2♠ 8♠	7♥ 2♦	9♦ 4♠	Q♦ 10♦	3♥ 4♥	4♥	2♠	8♠/J♣	2♦	9♠
4	A♠ 9♠	5♦ 8♦	9♦ 6♦	Q♣ 10♣	10♠ K♦	8♣ 10♥	10♥	8♥	9♠/5♠	A♦	K♣
5	A♥ 7♦	5♥ 3♥	3♠ 10♦	3♦ 10♥	A♦ 9♦	9♠ K♠	Q♣	6♣	2♦/J♣	A♥	2♣
6	2♠ 10♥	7♦ 5♣	3♦ A♠	J♥ 8♦	5♠ 8♠	2♦ 2♥	2♥	6♠	6♣/K♥	3♥	A♠
7	9♥ 10♣	Q♦ J♣	J♥ 10♠	4♦ 7♥	A♦ 5♥	A♣ 2♦	2♦	7♥	9♠/7♠	Q♣	7♥
8	8♦ 2♠	3♥ 4♣	4♦ 10♠	J♦ 7♠	9♣ J♥	K♠ 5♠	4♠ 9♣	2♦	A♠/4♥	10♦	8♥
9	A♦ 6♥	Q♠ Q♥	3♦ 8♥	5♣ J♦	3♣ 4♦	10♦ 6♦	8♠	2♠	7♣/Q♣	Q♠	7♠
10	A♠ 7♦	7♥ A♣	10♣ K♦	J♣ 9♥	8♣ 7♠	6♥ 5♠	5♠	9♣	5♦/9♣	8♦	K♦
11	Q♦ 3♣	7♦ 2♣	J♣ K♦	2♠ 9♠	3♠ 5♠	5♦ 8♦	6♠	4♠	6♣/3♥	7♣	3♣
12	J♦ 10♠	3♣ 8♣	2♠ 2♥	2♦ 3♥	Q♣ 6♥	J♠ 5♦	5♦	7♠	5♣/8♥	J♠	5♦
13	A♦ 6♣	10♦ 7♠	10♠ 9♠	3♣ 8♥	4♠ 3♠	7♦ 5♥	J♠	K♠	A♥/4♦	10♠	9♦
14	2♣ 5♦	2♦ 8♠	3♣ Q♣	9♥ 3♠	4♦ 6♥	6♣ 10♥	10♥	6♦	7♠/8♠	4♠	Q♦
15	Q♠ 10♣	10♦ 4♥	9♥ 5♥	A♠ 3♠	J♥ 5♠	5♦ J♠	J♠	4♥	A♣/7♠	4♥	3♦
16	2♠ 2♠	6♠ 10♥	4♣ 6♥	8♣ 4♥	K♦ 2♦	3♦ A♥	A♠	J♠	5♠/Q♥	10♠	6♥
17	3♠ J♥	6♥ 5♦	8♠ 5♠	7♠ Q♠	Q♦ 10♦	2♣ 8♥	4♦	K♠	9♠/J♣	Q♥	4♠
18	2♦ K♠	J♠ 3♠	7♣ 10♣	7♥ 9♥	9♠ 6♦	J♥ J♦	7♠	10♦	4♥/2♥	9♣	5♣
19	10♦ 5♦	A♠ Q♠	7♦ 9♥	3♦ 2♥	Q♣ 2♠	4♣ K♥	K♦	A♣	3♥/8♦	6♦	5♥
20	6♦ 9♠	J♠ 8♠	J♠ 3♠	9♣ 8♦	8♥ 7♥	5♦ A♣	3♦	Q♠	K♠/5♥	3♠	4♦
21	J♥ 4♣	A♠ 3♣	9♠ 3♠	A♣ 10♦	Q♥ 8♦	7♣ 2♠	A♥	A♠	A♦/5♠	J♦	5♠
22	3♦ 3♥	10♥ 8♠	5♣ 6♥	5♥ K♦	10♦ J♦	2♦ Q♠	7♣	2♠	9♠/9♥	J♣	10♥
23	8♦ A♦	4♠ 8♥	9♣ 10♣	10♥ 9♦	2♠ 2♥	7♥ 2♦	2♦	7♥	J♣/4♥	10♥	J♣
24	A♠ J♠	A♦ 4♣	10♥ 8♣	10♠ 2♥	5♥ 9♣	J♣ K♥	K♥	9♦	8♥/3♣	5♠	J♦

AGE	MER	VEN	MAR	JUP	SAT	URA	NEP	LR	PLU/RES	ENV	DISP
25	7♦ 5♦	7♠ 10♦	10♣ J♥	3♠ K♥	6♣ K♦	J♠ Q♥	10♠	Q♦	3♠/4♦	4♦	3♠
26	2♠ J♣	A♦ 6♦	3♣ 9♠	5♣ K♥	Q♦ K♦	3♦ J♠	J♠	3♥	Q♣/4♥	5♥	6♦
27	5♠ Q♠	A♣ K♠	10♥ 6♥	Q♥ J♣	7♠ 7♠	8♦ 4♣	3♦	4♥	A♠/8♣	5♠	9♣
28	K♥ A♦	7♥ 10♠	K♠ 9♦	3♣ 8♣	A♠ 2♥	K♦ J♣	2♠	A♠	8♦/10♣	4♣	Q♥
29	7♣ A♠	4♠ J♦	10♥ 3♠	J♠ A♦	9♥ 8♥	10♦ J♠	J♥	5♦	6♣/5♥	6♥	10♠
30	8♦ A♠	6♥ 10♠	J♣ A♦	9♦ 5♥	4♣ 10♥	6♣ 7♠	6♠	9♦	2♣/K♠	3♦	4♥
31	Q♠ J♦	A♠ 9♥	9♦ 2♥	7♠ 7♣	K♦ 10♦	Q♥ J♠	J♠	Q♣	3♠/3♥	Q♦	4♠
32	9♠ Q♦	K♠ 6♦	7♥ J♦	A♠ 8♦	A♠ 10♠	2♦ 7♣	4♠ A♠	10♠	Q♥/5♦	9♦	10♣
33	8♣ 3♦	Q♣ 9♣	6♣ Q♦	7♣ 5♦	K♥ 2♠	3♣ 7♥	7♥	8♣	8♥/6♦	5♦	J♠
34	J♣ A♠	6♠ 8♠	7♣ Q♦	J♦ 6♦	4♦ 9♦	6♥ 3♣	3♣	10♥	8♦/A♦	3♠	7♣
35	K♠ 5♣	K♥ 5♥	2♥ 8♠	9♠ 6♠	3♥ 9♣	Q♥ J♥	3♠ 3♥	A♥	6♥/4♣	K♦	8♣
36	10♣ J♣	10♥ 8♦	5♣ 9♥	Q♦ 6♥	7♠ 3♦	J♠	3♥	5♥	10♠/K♦	7♠	Q♠
37	7♥ 3♠	9♠ J♥	K♥ 10♦	10♥ 6♣	9♣ 6♥	5♥ 4♣	J♠	3♠	7♦/2♦	8♥	10♦
38	Q♠ 3♥	3♠ 8♥	10♥ 4♦	9♦ 5♣	Q♦ 10♠	7♦ J♣	Q♥	3♦	J♥/7♣	7♥	Q♣
39	2♥ Q♠	8♠ 2♦	8♦ 4♦	J♦ 10♠	5♠ K♦	5♦ 9♦	9♦	A♦	9♥/9♣	A♠	3♥
40	2♣ Q♣	5♥ 8♥	J♦ 4♦	6♦ 7♦	4♥ 2♣	9♥ 3♥	3♥	9♠	4♣/A♦	2♠	A♥
41	5♣ 8♣	J♠ A♠	3♦ K♦	10♠ 10♣	7♦ Q♥	Q♣ 6♥	6♥	Q♣	A♥/9♣	K♥	A♦
42	Q♠ 4♥	8♠ 5♠	10♣ K♣	7♣ 2♠	3♠ 8♥	A♥ 9♥	6♠	2♠	6♣/8♠	9♠	2♦
43	K♥ 7♥	4♥ 7♦	7♣ 2♠	10♦ 8♠	K♠ 10♠	A♦ 4♦	2♥ K♠	7♦	A♥/4♠	6♠	6♣
44	A♦ 6♣	2♦ Q♥	3♦ 5♦	4♦ K♠	5♦ 8♠	6♦ A♠	9♥	3♦	8♦/9♦	2♠	8♠
45	J♦ 7♣	4♥ A♥	4♦ J♠	2♠ 9♠	8♥ 3♦	6♣ 6♠	6♠	J♥	Q♥/10♣	K♣	K♣
46	7♥ 5♦	2♦ K♠	2♠ 5♠	9♣ 3♦	4♠ 4♦	7♣ 10♦	K♠ 4♠	5♠	Q♣/A♣	8♠	2♠
47	6♦ 6♣	4♥ 10♣	J♠ Q♣	K♠ 4♠	10♦ 2♠	2♥ 9♦	Q♠	2♦	9♣/6♥	6♣	6♠
48	2♥ 5♦	2♠ 8♠	7♥ 2♦	9♦ 4♠	Q♦ 10♦	3♥ 4♥	4♥	2♥	8♠/J♣	2♦	9♠
49	A♠ 9♠	5♦ 8♦	9♦ 6♦	Q♣ 10♣	10♠ K♦	8♣ 10♥	10♥	9♥	9♠/5♣	A♦	K♥

AGE	MER	VEN	MAR	JUP	SAT	URA	NEP	LR	PLU/RES	ENV	DISP
50	A♥	5♥	3♠	3♦	A♦	9♠	Q♣	Q♦	2♦/J♣	A♥	2♣
	9♥	3♥	10♦	10♥	9♦	K♠					
51	2♠	9♥	3♦	J♥	5♠	2♦	A♣	J♥	6♣/K♥	3♥	A♠
	10♥	5♣	A♠	8♦	8♠	A♣					
52	7♦	Q♦	J♥	4♦	A♦	2♥	2♦	4♦	9♠/7♠	Q♣	7♥
	10♣	J♣	10♠	7♥	5♥	2♦					
53	8♦	3♥	4♦	J♦	9♣	K♠	4♠	A♦	2♥/4♥	10♦	8♥
	2♠	4♣	10♠	7♠	J♥	5♠	9♣				
54	A♦	Q♠	3♦	5♠	3♣	10♦	8♠	A♣	7♣/Q♣	Q♠	7♥
	6♥	Q♥	8♥	J♥	4♦	6♦					
55	A♠	7♥	10♣	J♣	8♣	6♥	5♠	2♦	5♦/9♣	8♦	K♦
	9♥	2♥	K♦	9♦	7♠	5♠					
56	Q♦	9♥	J♣	2♠	3♠	5♦	6♠	8♦	6♣/3♥	7♣	3♣
	3♣	2♣	K♦	9♣	5♠	8♦					
57	J♦	3♣	2♠	2♦	Q♣	J♠	5♦	3♥	5♣/8♥	J♠	5♦
	10♠	8♣	A♣	3♥	6♥	5♦					
58	A♦	10♦	10♣	3♣	4♣	7♥	J♠	4♦	A♥/4♥	10♣	9♦
	6♣	7♠	9♠	8♥	3♠	5♥					
59	2♣	2♦	3♣	7♦	4♦	6♠	10♥	J♦	7♠/8♠	4♠	Q♦
	5♦	8♦	Q♣	3♠	6♥	10♥					
60	Q♠	10♦	7♦	A♠	J♥	5♦	J♠	9♣	2♥/7♣	4♥	3♦
	10♣	4♥	5♥	3♠	5♣	J♠					
61	2♠	6♦	4♣	8♣	K♦	3♦	A♠	K♠	5♠/Q♥	10♠	6♥
	2♣	10♥	6♥	4♥	2♦	A♥					
62	3♠	6♥	8♣	7♠	Q♦	2♠	4♦	4♠	9♣/J♣	Q♥	4♣
	J♥	5♦	5♣	Q♠	10♦	8♥					
63	2♦	J♠	7♣	9♥	9♠	J♥	7♠	A♦	4♥/A♣	9♣	5♣
	K♠	3♠	10♣	7♦	6♦	J♦					
64	10♦	A♠	9♥	3♦	Q♣	4♣	K♥	Q♠	3♥/8♦	6♦	5♥
	5♦	Q♠	7♦	A♣	2♠	K♥					
65	6♦	J♠	J♣	9♣	8♥	5♦	3♦	3♦	K♠/5♥	3♠	4♦
	9♠	8♠	3♣	8♦	9♥	2♥					
66	J♥	A♠	9♣	2♥	Q♥	7♣	A♥	5♠	A♦/5♠	J♦	5♠
	4♣	3♣	3♠	10♦	8♦	2♠					
67	3♦	10♥	5♣	5♥	10♦	2♦	7♣	3♠	9♠/7♦	J♣	10♥
	3♥	8♠	6♥	K♦	J♦	Q♠					
68	8♦	4♠	9♣	10♥	2♠	7♥	2♦	10♦	J♣/4♥	10♥	J♣
	A♦	8♥	10♣	7♦	A♣	2♦					
69	A♠	A♦	10♥	10♠	5♥	J♣	K♥	8♠	8♥/3♣	5♠	J♦
	J♠	4♣	8♣	A♣	9♣	K♥					
70	9♥	7♠	10♣	3♣	6♣	J♠	10♠	A♠	3♠/4♥	4♦	3♠
	5♦	10♦	J♥	K♥	K♦	Q♥					
71	2♣	A♦	3♣	5♣	Q♦	3♦	J♠	7♥	Q♣/4♥	5♥	6♦
	J♣	6♦	9♦	K♥	K♥	J♠					
72	5♠	2♥	10♥	Q♥	7♣	8♦	3♦	10♣	A♠/8♣	5♣	9♠
	Q♠	K♠	6♥	♣	9♥	4♣					
73	K♥	7♥	K♠	3♣	2♥	K♦	2♠	J♣	8♦/10♣	4♣	Q♥
	A♦	10♠	9♦	8♠	A♣	J♠					
74	7♣	4♠	10♥	J♣	7♦	10♦	J♥	8♠	6♣/5♥	6♥	10♠
	A♠	J♦	3♠	A♦	8♥	J♠					
75	8♦	6♥	J♣	9♦	4♣	6♠	6♠	6♥	2♣/K♠	3♦	4♥
	A♠	10♠	A♦	5♥	10♥	7♠					
76	Q♠	A♠	9♦	7♠	K♦	Q♥	J♠	5♠	3♠/3♥	Q♦	4♠
	J♦	7♦	A♣	7♠	10♦	J♠					
77	9♠	K♠	7♥	2♥	A♠	2♠	4♠	Q♦	Q♥/5♥	9♦	10♣
	Q♦	6♦	J♦	8♠	10♠	7♣	A♠				
78	8♣	Q♣	6♠	7♣	K♥	3♣	7♥	7♦	8♥/6♦	5♦	J♠
	3♦	9♣	Q♦	5♦	2♠	7♥					
79	J♣	6♠	7♠	J♦	4♦	6♥	3♣	J♣	8♦/A♦	3♠	7♣
	A♠	8♠	Q♦	6♦	9♦	3♣					
80	K♠	K♥	A♠	9♠	3♥	Q♥	3♠	2♠	6♥/4♣	K♦	8♦
	5♣	5♥	8♦	6♠	9♠	J♥	3♥				
81	10♣	10♥	5♣	Q♦	7♠	J♠	3♥	3♠	10♠/K♦	7♠	Q♠
	J♣	8♦	9♦	6♥	9♠	3♥					
82	7♥	9♠	K♥	10♥	9♣	5♥	J♠	5♦	9♥/2♦	8♥	10♦
	3♠	J♥	10♦	6♣	6♥	4♣					
83	Q♠	3♠	10♥	9♦	Q♦	9♥	Q♥	6♠	J♥/7♣	7♥	Q♣
	3♥	8♥	4♦	5♠	10♠	J♣					
84	A♣	8♠	8♦	J♦	5♠	5♦	9♦	J♦	7♦/9♣	A♠	3♥
	Q♠	2♦	4♦	10♣	K♦	9♦					
85	2♠	5♥	J♦	6♥	4♥	7♠	3♥	3♣	4♣/A♦	2♣	A♥
	Q♣	8♥	4♦	7♥	2♠	3♥					
86	5♣	J♣	3♦	10♠	9♥	Q♣	6♥	2♠	A♥/9♣	K♥	A♦
	8♣	2♥	K♦	10♠	Q♥	6♥					
87	Q♠	8♣	10♠	7♣	3♠	A♥	6♠	2♦	6♣	8♠	9♠
	2♦	4♥	5♠	K♠	2♠	8♥	7♦				
88	K♥	4♥	7♣	10♥	K♠	A♥	A♣	Q♣	A♥/4♣	6♠	6♣
	7♥	9♥	2♠	8♠	10♠	4♦	K♠				
89	A♦	2♦	3♦	4♦	5♦	6♦	7♦	J♠	8♦/9♦	2♠	8♠
	6♣	Q♥	5♥	K♠	8♠	A♠					
90	J♦	4♥	4♦	2♠	8♥	6♣	6♠	5♦	Q♥/10♣	K♣	K♠
	7♣	A♥	J♠	9♠	3♥	6♠					
91	7♥	2♦	2♠	9♣	4♠	7♠	K♠	A♦	Q♣/2♥	8♠	2♠
	5♦	K♦	5♠	3♦	4♦	10♠	4♠				
92	6♦	4♥	J♠	K♠	10♦	A♠	Q♠	10♦	9♣/6♥	6♣	6♠
	6♣	10♣	Q♣	4♠	2♠	9♦					
93	A♣	2♠	7♥	9♠	Q♦	3♥	4♥	10♣	8♣/J♣	2♦	9♠
	5♦	8♠	2♦	4♠	10♦	4♥					
94	A♣	5♥	9♦	Q♣	10♠	8♠	10♥	3♣	9♠/5♣	A♦	K♥
	9♠	8♦	6♦	10♣	K♦	10♥					
95	A♥	5♥	3♠	3♦	A♦	9♠	Q♣	4♣	2♦/J♣	A♥	2♣
	7♦	3♥	10♦	10♥	9♦	K♠					
96	2♠	7♥	3♦	J♥	5♠	2♦	2♥	7♥	6♣/K♥	3♥	A♠
	10♥	5♣	A♠	8♦	8♣	2♥					
97	9♥	Q♦	J♥	4♦	A♦	A♣	2♦	J♠	9♠/7♠	Q♣	7♥
	10♣	J♣	10♠	7♥	5♥	2♦					
98	8♦	3♥	4♦	J♦	9♣	K♠	4♠	2♣	A♣/4♥	10♦	8♥
	2♠	4♣	10♠	7♠	J♥	5♠	9♣				
99	A♦	Q♠	3♦	5♠	3♣	10♦	8♠	2♦	7♣/Q♣	Q♠	7♥
	6♥	Q♥	8♥	J♥	4♦	6♦					

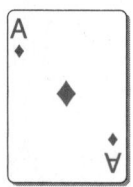

Ace of Diamonds

Age	Mer	Ven	Mar	Jup	Sat	Ura	Nep	LR	Plu/Res	Env	Disp
0	Q♦	5♥	3♣	3♠	9♥	7♣	5♦	Q♦	Q♠/J♣	A♦	A♦
	8♣	2♥	A♠	Q♥	J♦	5♦					
1	10♣	8♣	3♠	4♥	5♠	Q♠	6♣	5♥	3♥/A♥	A♥	2♦
	6♦	4♣	K♠	2♦	K♥	7♦					
2	K♣	6♦	4♥	J♠	K♠	10♦	A♣	3♣	Q♠/9♣	3♥	6♣
	9♠	9♥	2♦	A♥	3♠	6♥	K♠				
3	10♠	Q♣	3♣	6♥	8♥	10♥	7♦	3♠	4♠/7♠	Q♣	8♠
	3♥	J♦	3♦	K♠	A♥	6♠					
4	4♠	6♦	6♥	2♦	K♥	3♥	6♣	9♥	J♦/Q♥	10♦	K♠
	4♥	Q♠	10♠	8♠	3♣	6♠					
5	9♠	Q♣	2♦	J♣	9♣	4♥	K♠	7♣	7♣/2♥	Q♠	2♠
	8♥	A♠	4♣	3♣	6♥	J♠	9♣				
6	10♥	6♦	10♠	K♠	J♠	A♣	10♣	5♦	J♣/5♦	8♦	6♠
	3♥	Q♥	7♣	9♣	2♦	7♠					
7	A♣	2♦	9♠	7♠	K♦	8♦	6♦	10♣	8♠/5♥	7♠	9♠
	8♥	A♥	Q♣	9♠	J♠	6♦					
8	6♠	8♥	7♠	7♣	3♠	8♠	5♣	8♠	J♣/Q♦	J♠	K♥
	8♠	4♠	10♥	Q♥	A♠	5♣					
9	Q♠	3♦	5♠	3♣	10♦	8♠	7♠	3♠	Q♣/5♥	10♣	2♠
	7♦	8♦	J♠	5♣	7♠	K♠					
10	2♦	7♥	3♣	J♥	4♣	Q♣	2♥	4♥	3♥/K♣	4♠	A♠
	5♣	Q♦	6♠	4♠	8♣	2♥					
11	9♥	K♦	J♥	6♥	10♦	A♣	Q♣	5♠	8♠/2♣	4♥	7♥
	Q♥	5♥	3♠	9♠	3♦	Q♣					
12	4♠	8♦	6♥	4♦	J♣	K♠	9♣	Q♠	A♣/6♦	10♠	8♥
	2♦	9♦	3♠	2♣	J♥	4♠	J♣				
13	10♦	10♣	3♣	4♣	7♥	J♠	A♥	6♣	4♥/7♣	Q♥	7♠
	5♦	J♦	K♥	J♥	6♥	10♥					
14	6♠	9♠	Q♥	5♥	8♠	5♦	4♣	K♠	8♥/J♣	9♣	K♥
	7♦	A♣	A♠	7♠	2♠	4♠					
15	K♦	7♦	5♥	2♦	5♠	8♥	6♣	6♦	3♥/8♦	6♠	3♣
	7♥	2♠	A♠	J♠	4♠	4♠					
16	4♦	7♥	2♦	Q♣	7♣	10♠	8♥	4♥	Q♦/K♥	3♠	5♦
	3♠	8♣	2♥	8♦	5♦	8♥					
17	10♦	J♠	Q♥	7♥	9♥	9♠	10♠	J♠	Q♠/6♦	J♦	9♠
	3♥	2♣	8♠	K♥	5♠	3♦					
18	2♠	Q♣	7♥	9♥	6♥	3♥	5♣	K♠	2♣/A♥	J♠	Q♦
	8♥	4♠	7♠	5♠	5♦	5♣					
19	10♣	J♠	9♥	6♠	J♥	8♥	10♠	10♦	A♣/4♥	10♥	3♦
	Q♥	6♦	3♦	5♠	Q♦	10♠					
20	2♦	10♥	9♦	8♣	A♠	3♣	6♠	A♠	4♣/J♦	5♠	6♥
	2♠	5♣	5♦	6♣	Q♣	Q♠					
21	5♠	5♦	8♣	2♣	K♦	2♠	6♥	10♦	J♣/5♥	4♦	4♠
	J♥	8♥	Q♦	10♣	J♠	K♥					
22	Q♣	10♠	4♥	7♦	8♠	J♥	2♠	Q♣	6♦/2♥	5♥	5♣
	K♠	5♠	Q♥	9♥	10♥	4♦					
23	J♠	6♠	7♠	3♣	7♠	9♦	K♣	3♣	8♦/4♠	5♠	5♥
	8♥	10♠	9♥	2♦	2♦	K♠					
24	10♦	10♠	5♥	J♠	K♥	8♥	3♠	6♥	K♠/3♠	4♣	4♦
	8♠	A♥	7♥	4♠	7♠	A♣					

Age	Mer	Ven	Mar	Jup	Sat	Ura	Nep	LR	Plu/Res	Env	Disp
25	J♥	6♠	J♣	A♣	J♦	4♥	Q♠	8♥	10♦/4♣	6♥	5♠
	9♦	7♥	5♠	J♠	4♠	2♦					
26	3♣	5♠	Q♦	3♦	J♠	Q♣	4♥	10♥	8♠/9♦	3♦	10♥
	8♦	A♥	5♦	A♠	4♦	10♣					
27	4♠	9♣	J♣	5♣	2♦	9♠	Q♠	7♦	5♥/6♦	Q♦	J♣
	10♦	K♥	Q♥	9♥	2♥	Q♣					
28	6♠	10♦	5♠	3♠	3♦	5♥	K♠	4♦	K♥/7♥	9♦	J♦
	10♠	9♦	8♠	2♥	J♠	K♣					
29	7♦	2♣	Q♥	7♥	3♥	10♠	3♠	6♦	5♠/6♥	5♦	3♠
	8♥	J♠	J♥	K♠	A♠	J♦					
30	2♠	10♦	7♥	Q♦	K♦	3♠	10♠	6♥	7♣/6♦	3♣	6♦
	5♥	10♥	7♠	K♣	A♠	10♠					
31	4♣	A♠	5♣	J♦	4♥	4♠	3♠	2♦	6♠/8♠	K♦	9♣
	10♣	K♠	5♦	5♥	7♥	9♦					
32	K♣	9♠	K♠	7♥	A♠	A♠	2♦	K♥	4♠/Q♥	7♠	Q♥
	10♦	3♠	7♣	3♣	2♥	5♥					
33	4♥	9♠	5♠	5♥	9♥	J♠	J♥	3♥	3♥/3♦	8♥	10♠
	6♠	4♦	5♠	10♦	K♥	10♠					
34	4♠	5♦	5♥	7♠	9♥	3♥	6♣	6♣	2♠/K♠	7♥	4♥
	6♠	3♠	10♦	3♦	5♣	2♣					
35	10♠	6♠	7♠	2♣	A♠	J♦	10♠	9♠	5♠/8♦	A♠	4♠
	4♦	9♥	2♥	4♥	J♠	10♠					
36	8♠	K♠	9♠	A♣	6♠	Q♣	9♣	Q♣	J♦/3♦	2♣	10♠
	K♦	10♥	4♦	4♠	3♠	4♥	6♠				
37	8♣	7♣	3♥	4♦	K♣	7♥	9♠	2♦	K♥/10♥	K♥	J♠
	3♣	J♣	K♦	8♦	2♦	9♠					
38	5♥	6♠	4♥	4♦	6♥	5♦	7♥	J♣	4♠/10♦	9♠	7♣
	6♠	A♥	K♦	10♥	7♠	7♥					
39	K♠	K♣	2♥	8♠	8♦	J♥	5♠	9♣	5♦/9♦	6♠	8♦
	Q♦	3♦	4♣	6♣	J♣	J♥	8♦				
40	Q♥	5♣	Q♦	K♦	2♣	10♠	8♦	4♥	3♠/A♠	2♣	Q♠
	5♥	4♣	7♠	5♦	8♠	8♦					
41	9♠	8♠	K♣	5♠	J♠	3♦	10♠	K♠	7♦/Q♣	K♣	10♦
	5♠	J♥	J♠	3♥	5♦	9♠					
42	10♠	5♦	5♣	7♠	K♦	7♥	J♦	10♥	J♥/4♥	8♠	Q♠
	8♦	K♥	6♥	Q♦	3♠	5♥					
43	2♥	A♥	4♠	4♦	4♠	8♥	7♠	6♦	9♥/J♣	6♠	3♥
	10♣	Q♣	6♥	Q♥	A♠	7♠					
44	2♦	3♦	4♦	5♦	6♦	9♥	8♦	10♠	9♦/10♦	2♦	A♥
	7♣	K♥	6♥	9♠	2♠	8♦					
45	Q♦	5♥	3♣	3♠	7♥	7♠	5♦	K♠	Q♠/J♣	A♦	A♦
	8♣	A♠	A♠	Q♥	J♦	5♦					
46	10♠	8♣	3♠	4♥	5♠	Q♠	6♣	J♠	3♥/A♥	A♥	2♦
	6♦	4♣	K♠	2♦	K♥	7♥					
47	K♣	6♦	4♥	J♠	K♠	10♦	2♥	A♣	Q♠/9♣	3♥	6♣
	9♠	7♦	2♦	A♥	3♠	6♥	K♠				
48	10♦	Q♣	3♣	6♥	8♥	10♥	9♥	10♣	4♠/7♠	Q♣	8♠
	3♥	J♦	3♦	K♠	A♥	6♠					
49	4♦	6♦	6♥	2♦	K♥	3♥	6♣	A♠	J♦/Q♥	10♦	K♠
	4♥	Q♠	10♠	8♠	3♣	6♠					

AGE	MER	VEN	MAR	JUP	SAT	URA	NEP	LR	PLU/RES	ENV	DISP
50	9♠	Q♣	2♦	J♣	9♣	4♥	K♠	2♦	7♣/A♣	Q♠	2♠
	8♥	A♣	4♣	3♣	6♥	J♠	9♣				
51	10♥	6♦	10♠	K♠	J♠	2♥	10♣	9♠	J♣/5♦	8♦	6♠
	3♥	Q♥	7♣	9♣	2♦	7♠					
52	2♥	2♦	9♠	7♠	K♦	8♦	6♦	7♠	8♣/5♥	7♣	9♠
	8♥	A♥	Q♣	9♣	J♠	6♦					
53	6♠	8♥	7♠	7♣	3♠	8♣	5♣	K♦	J♣/Q♦	J♠	K♥
	8♠	4♠	10♥	Q♥	A♠	5♣					
54	Q♠	3♦	5♠	3♣	10♦	8♠	7♣	8♦	Q♣/5♥	10♣	2♣
	9♥	8♦	J♠	5♣	7♠	K♠					
55	2♦	9♥	3♣	J♥	4♣	Q♣	A♣	6♦	3♥/K♣	4♣	A♠
	5♣	Q♦	6♠	4♠	8♣	A♣					
56	7♦	K♦	J♥	6♥	10♣	2♥	Q♣	6♠	8♠/2♣	4♥	7♥
	Q♥	5♥	3♠	9♠	3♦	Q♣					
57	4♠	8♥	6♥	4♦	J♣	K♠	9♣	8♥	2♥/6♦	10♠	8♥
	2♦	9♥	3♠	2♣	J♥	4♣	J♣				
58	10♦	10♣	3♠	4♣	7♥	J♠	A♥	7♠	4♥/7♣	Q♥	7♠
	5♦	J♥	K♥	J♥	6♥	10♥					
59	6♠	9♣	Q♥	5♥	8♣	5♦	4♣	7♠	8♥/J♣	9♣	K♦
	9♥	2♥	A♠	7♠	2♣	4♣					
60	K♦	9♥	5♥	2♦	5♠	8♥	6♣	3♠	3♥/8♦	6♦	3♣
	7♠	2♠	A♠	J♣	4♣	4♠					
61	4♦	7♥	2♦	Q♣	7♣	10♠	8♥	8♣	Q♦/K♥	3♠	5♦
	3♠	8♠	A♣	8♦	5♦	8♥					
62	10♦	J♠	Q♥	7♥	9♥	9♠	10♠	5♣	Q♠/6♦	J♦	9♦
	3♥	2♣	8♠	K♥	5♠	3♦					
63	2♠	Q♣	7♥	7♦	6♥	3♥	5♣	Q♠	2♣/A♥	J♠	Q♦
	8♥	4♠	7♠	5♣	5♦	5♣					
64	10♣	J♠	7♦	6♠	J♥	8♥	10♠	3♦	2♥/4♥	10♥	3♦
	Q♥	6♦	3♦	5♠	Q♦	10♠					
65	2♦	10♥	9♣	8♣	A♠	3♣	6♠	5♠	4♣/J♦	5♠	6♥
	2♠	5♣	5♦	6♦	Q♣	Q♠					
66	5♠	5♦	8♣	2♣	K♦	2♠	6♥	3♣	J♣/5♥	4♦	4♣
	J♥	8♥	Q♦	10♣	J♠	K♥					
67	Q♣	10♠	4♥	9♥	8♠	J♥	2♣	10♦	6♦/A♣	5♥	5♣
	K♠	5♠	Q♥	7♦	10♥	4♦					
68	J♠	6♠	9♥	3♣	7♣	9♥	K♣	8♠	8♦/4♠	5♣	5♥
	8♥	10♣	7♥	A♣	2♦	K♣					
69	10♥	10♠	5♥	J♣	K♥	8♥	3♣	7♣	K♠/3♦	4♠	4♦
	8♠	A♥	7♥	4♠	9♥	2♥					
70	J♥	6♠	J♠	2♥	J♦	4♥	Q♣	2♦	10♦/4♣	6♥	5♠
	9♦	7♥	5♠	J♠	4♠	2♦					
71	3♣	Q♣	Q♦	3♦	J♠	Q♣	4♥	7♦	8♠/7♦	3♦	10♥
	8♦	A♥	5♦	A♠	4♦	10♣					
72	4♠	9♣	J♣	5♣	2♦	9♠	Q♣	3♣	5♥/6♦	Q♦	J♣
	10♦	K♥	Q♥	7♦	A♣	Q♣					
73	6♠	10♦	5♠	3♠	3♦	5♥	K♣	J♥	K♥/7♥	9♦	J♦
	10♠	9♦	8♠	J♠	J♠	K♣					
74	9♥	2♣	Q♥	7♥	3♥	10♠	3♣	4♣	5♠/6♥	5♦	3♠
	8♥	J♠	J♥	K♣	A♠	J♦					
75	2♠	10♦	7♥	Q♦	K♦	3♣	10♠	Q♣	7♣/6♦	3♣	6♦
	5♥	10♥	7♠	K♣	A♠	10♠					
76	4♣	2♥	5♣	J♦	4♥	4♠	3♣	2♥	6♠/8♣	K♦	9♣
	10♣	K♠	5♦	5♥	9♥	9♦					
77	K♣	9♠	K♣	7♥	2♥	A♠	2♦	9♥	4♠/Q♥	7♠	Q♥
	10♦	3♠	7♠	8♠	A♣	5♥					
78	4♥	9♣	5♠	5♥	7♦	J♠	J♥	K♦	3♥/3♦	8♥	10♠
	6♠	4♦	5♠	10♦	K♥	10♠					
79	4♠	5♦	5♥	7♠	9♦	3♥	6♣	J♥	2♠/K♠	7♥	4♥
	6♠	3♠	10♦	3♦	5♣	2♣					
80	10♣	6♠	7♠	2♣	A♠	J♦	10♠	6♥	5♠/8♦	A♠	4♠
	4♦	7♦	A♣	4♥	J♠	10♠					
81	8♠	K♠	9♠	2♥	6♠	Q♣	9♣	10♦	J♦/3♦	2♣	10♣
	K♦	10♥	4♦	4♠	3♠	4♥	6♠				
82	8♠	7♣	3♥	4♥	K♣	7♥	9♠	A♠	K♥/10♥	K♥	J♠
	3♠	J♣	K♦	8♥	2♦	9♠					
83	5♥	6♣	4♥	4♦	6♥	5♦	7♥	Q♣	4♠/10♦	9♠	7♣
	6♠	A♥	K♦	10♥	7♠	7♥					
84	K♠	K♣	A♠	8♠	8♦	J♦	5♠	4♠	5♦/9♦	6♠	8♦
	Q♦	3♦	4♠	6♠	J♣	J♥	8♦				
85	Q♥	5♣	Q♦	K♦	2♣	10♠	8♦	8♦	3♠/A♠	2♠	Q♠
	5♥	4♠	7♠	5♦	8♠	8♦					
86	9♠	8♠	K♣	9♣	J♠	3♦	10♠	6♥	9♥/Q♣	7♣	10♦
	5♠	J♥	J♠	3♥	5♠	9♠					
87	10♣	5♠	5♠	7♠	K♦	9♥	J♦	4♦	J♥/4♥	8♠	Q♣
	8♦	K♥	6♥	Q♦	3♠	5♥					
88	A♣	A♥	4♠	4♦	4♣	8♥	7♠	J♣	7♦/J♣	6♠	3♥
	10♣	Q♣	6♥	Q♥	A♠	7♠					
89	2♦	3♦	4♦	5♦	6♦	7♦	8♦	K♠	9♦/10♦	2♦	A♥
	7♣	K♥	6♥	9♠	2♠	8♦					
90	Q♦	5♦	3♠	3♠	9♥	7♠	5♦	9♠	Q♠/J♣	A♦	A♦
	8♣	2♥	A♠	Q♥	J♦	5♦					
91	10♣	8♠	3♠	4♥	5♠	Q♠	6♣	10♦	3♥/A♥	A♥	2♦
	6♦	4♣	K♠	2♦	K♥	7♦					
92	K♣	6♦	4♥	J♠	K♠	10♦	A♠	10♣	Q♠/9♣	3♥	6♠
	9♠	9♥	2♦	A♥	3♠	6♥	K♠				
93	10♦	Q♣	3♣	6♥	8♥	10♥	7♦	3♣	4♠/7♠	Q♣	8♠
	3♥	J♦	3♦	K♠	A♥	6♠					
94	4♦	6♦	6♥	2♦	K♥	3♥	6♣	4♣	J♦/Q♥	10♦	K♣
	4♥	Q♠	10♠	8♠	3♣	6♣					
95	9♠	Q♣	2♦	J♣	9♣	4♥	K♠	7♥	7♣/2♥	Q♠	2♠
	8♥	A♠	4♣	3♣	6♥	J♠	9♣				
96	10♥	6♦	10♠	K♠	J♠	A♣	10♠	J♠	J♣/5♦	8♦	6♠
	3♥	Q♥	7♣	9♣	2♦	7♠					
97	A♣	2♦	9♠	7♠	K♦	8♦	6♦	A♥	8♣/5♥	7♣	9♠
	8♥	A♥	Q♣	9♣	J♠	6♦					
98	6♠	8♥	7♠	7♣	3♠	8♣	5♣	6♠	J♣/Q♦	J♠	K♥
	8♠	4♠	10♥	Q♥	A♠	5♣					
99	Q♠	3♦	5♠	3♣	10♦	8♠	7♣	9♠	Q♣/5♥	10♣	2♣
	7♦	8♦	J♠	5♣	7♠	K♠					

Two of Diamonds

AGE	MER	VEN	MAR	JUP	SAT	URA	NEP	LR	PLU/RES	ENV	DISP
0	J♠ / 9♣	8♣ / 5♣	6♦ / K♠	4♠ / 6♣	10♥ / 2♣	10♦ / 9♥	8♠	J♠	A♥/A♦	2♦	2♦
1	2♠ / K♥	9♣ / 7♦	4♠ / 6♣	7♣ / A♦	K♠ / 6♦	Q♣ / 4♣	2♥	8♣	10♦/Q♥	A♦	6♣
							K♠				
2	Q♣ / A♥	3♥ / 3♣	5♦ / 6♥	4♣ / K♠	7♠ / A♦	J♣ / 9♠	9♥	6♦	10♣/K♦	A♥	8♠
3	5♠ / 4♠	9♣ / 10♦	4♣ / 4♥	6♠ / K♣	2♣ / 5♦	A♥ / 8♠	8♠	4♠	3♠/10♠	3♥	K♣
4	K♥ / 7♠	3♥ / 7♥	6♣ / 5♣	J♦ / 5♦	Q♥ / 4♣	4♠ / 7♣	K♠	10♥	8♦/A♣	Q♣	2♠
							Q♥				
5	J♣ / A♥	9♣ / 10♠	4♥ / 8♦	K♣ / Q♥	7♠ / 6♣	2♥ / K♦	J♠	10♦	J♦/9♦	10♦	6♣
6	2♥ / 7♠	6♣ / A♣	K♥ / 3♥	K♦ / Q♥	3♣ / 7♠	Q♠ / 9♣	9♣	8♠	8♣/4♦	Q♠	9♠
7	9♠ / K♣	7♠ / 10♣	K♦ / J♣	8♦ / 10♠	6♦ / 7♥	8♠ / 5♥	5♥	2♠	J♦/3♦	8♦	K♥
8	10♦ / 9♥	6♥ / Q♣	10♥ / 7♠	5♦ / 5♥	Q♣ / K♦	K♣ / K♠	8♦	9♠	3♥/4♦	7♣	2♣
9	6♣ / 5♥	9♥ / 3♦	5♦ / 9♠	J♥ / 10♣	5♠ / 8♠	3♥ / A♣	A♣	4♠	A♥/2♠	J♠	A♠
10	7♦ / 10♠	3♣ / 4♦	J♥ / 6♦	4♣ / K♥	Q♣ / 6♥	2♥ / 3♥	3♥	7♣	K♣/A♠	10♣	7♥
11	10♣ / 6♣	Q♠ / Q♦	4♣ / 6♦	5♠ / A♠	J♦ / J♥	K♠ / 5♣	Q♥	K♠	2♥/9♠	4♠	8♥
						J♦					J♦
12	Q♣ / 9♦	J♠ / 3♠	5♦ / 2♣	5♣ / J♥	8♥ / 4♣	7♣ / J♣	A♦	Q♣	4♠/8♦	4♥	7♠
13	9♠ / 9♥	K♥ / 2♥	10♠ / 7♥	4♦ / K♦	8♣ / A♠	9♠ / 5♣	5♣	2♥	7♠/J♦	10♠	K♦
14	3♣ / 8♥	9♥ / 6♣	4♦ / 7♥	6♣ / J♦	10♥ / 5♠	7♠ / 10♣	8♠	Q♣	A♥/Q♠	Q♥	3♣
15	5♠ / 6♦	8♥ / 8♣	6♣ / A♣	3♥ / Q♠	8♣ / 9♦	4♥ / 7♠	7♠	3♥	3♦/2♣	9♣	5♦
16	Q♣ / A♥	7♠ / A♠	10♠ / K♠	8♥ / 2♣	Q♦ / 10♥	K♥ / 6♥	4♥	5♠	10♦/9♣	6♦	9♦
17	6♠ / 7♠	3♥ / 10♣	8♥ / 8♦	7♦ / 10♥	4♣ / 9♦	A♥ / 5♥	5♥	4♠	A♠/A♦	3♠	Q♦
18	J♠ / 10♠	7♣ / 9♣	7♦ / 6♥	9♠ / 10♥	J♥ / 3♦	7♠ / 4♥	4♥	7♠	2♥/4♦	J♦	3♦
19	6♣ / 6♠	J♠ / 5♥	Q♦ / 9♦	8♠ / 9♣	7♥ / 3♥	5♦ / 10♦	9♠	J♠	5♣/3♠	J♣	6♥
20	10♥ / J♥	9♦ / 7♠	8♠ / 3♦	A♠ / J♠	3♣ / 7♣	6♠ / 2♣	4♠	9♥	J♦/4♦	10♥	4♣
21	3♥ / K♠	4♥ / 10♥	4♠ / 10♠	9♥ / 7♦	K♣ / J♠	J♥ / 5♠	A♠	5♠	9♣/A♣	5♠	5♠
22	7♣ / 7♠	9♠ / J♠	9♥ / 7♦	5♦ / A♣	8♠ / 6♠	Q♣ / 2♠	2♠	9♠	Q♠/10♣	4♦	5♥
23	J♠ / K♠	4♥ / A♦	4♦ / 8♦	J♦ / 10♣	7♥ / 9♦	2♥ / 2♥	5♦	4♠	K♠/6♥	5♥	4♦
24	J♥ / Q♦	9♠ / 8♥	J♦ / 10♥	2♥ / 7♣	3♠ / 10♠	4♠ / 6♣	10♦	6♠	Q♣/5♣	5♠	5♠
25	5♦ / Q♠	5♥ / A♥	3♦ / 9♦	6♥ / 7♥	7♣ / 5♠	3♥ / J♠	4♠	2♣	K♣/7♦	4♣	10♥
26	10♣ / Q♣	Q♥ / 2♣	J♦ / 10♠	5♥ / 7♦	6♣ / A♣	K♥ / 3♥	3♥	A♥	4♦/9♣	6♥	J♣
27	9♠ / 4♥	Q♣ / Q♦	5♥ / 8♠	6♦ / A♣	6♥ / J♦	4♦ / 2♠	2♠	8♠	2♣/8♥	3♦	J♦
28	9♥ / 7♠	A♠ / 7♠	10♠ / J♥	8♥ / 2♠	A♥ / 7♥	4♥ / 3♠	6♦	K♥	10♥/4♣	Q♦	3♠
29	6♠ / 4♦	Q♣ / J♣	8♥ / K♦	3♦ / 2♠	3♣ / 7♥	5♦ / 4♥	4♥	3♥	8♦/9♣	9♦	6♦
30	5♦ / J♠	2♥ / K♠	5♥ / 9♦	3♠ / 4♦	4♠ / 9♥	10♣ / Q♦	5♦	6♣	9♠/8♣	5♦	9♣
31	2♠ / Q♣	K♥ / 6♦	K♠ / K♦	8♥ / 8♣	2♥ / A♣	7♥ / 4♦	6♣	J♦	10♣/10♠	3♣	Q♥
32	4♠ / 9♠	Q♥ / 5♠	5♥ / 10♥	4♦ / Q♣	7♥ / 2♠	7♣ / 4♥	J♥	Q♥	A♥/6♥	K♦	10♠
33	10♣ / 9♠	9♥ / 6♦	4♦ / Q♣	K♦ / 6♥	Q♦ / 5♥	A♥ / A♠	8♠	4♠	6♠/K♠	7♠	4♥
34	J♠ / 5♠	9♠ / 7♦	K♦ / A♣	A♠ / 4♠	7♥ / 7♠	3♠ / 4♥	4♥	K♠	10♥/Q♠	8♥	4♠
35	K♣ / 3♣	K♠ / J♣	K♥ / 5♠	2♥ / 10♣	9♠ / 6♦	3♥ / 4♠	Q♥	J♣	3♠/6♥	7♥	10♣
						9♠					9♠
36	8♣ / 5♦	8♦ / J♦	A♥ / 3♣	4♠ / 7♠	2♠ / 6♠	8♥ / K♥	K♥	9♠	2♣/J♣	A♠	J♠
37	4♦ / 9♠	8♠ / A♦	4♠ / 3♠	5♠ / J♣	4♣ / K♦	9♦ / 8♥	8♥	4♥	10♣/Q♣	2♠	7♣
38	K♠ / 3♦	2♠ / 6♥	A♠ / 10♠	K♣ / 8♠	Q♠ / J♦	3♠ / J♥	10♥	K♠	9♦/Q♦	K♥	8♦
						Q♠					Q♠
39	10♠ / 4♦	5♥ / 10♣	3♦ / K♦	3♠ / 9♠	A♠ / K♣	4♥ / Q♠	Q♠	7♠	6♦/7♥	9♠	Q♠
40	K♥ / 10♥	K♣ / J♥	2♠ / 7♣	5♥ / A♥	J♦ / 9♦	6♥ / Q♦	4♥	2♥	9♥/3♥	6♠	10♦
41	J♠ / Q♠	10♥ / 2♠	5♥ / 4♣	K♦ / 3♦	3♣ / 6♦	9♥ / 4♦	3♠	J♠	J♥/4♠	2♠	Q♣
42	A♣ / J♠	A♦ / 3♥	10♠ / 4♣	5♠ / 10♠	5♣ / 7♥	7♠ / K♦	K♦	2♥	7♦/J♦	K♣	3♥
43	6♣ / 8♦	6♥ / 2♣	5♠ / 4♣	9♥ / K♥	9♠ / 6♠	7♦ / Q♠	Q♠	6♣	Q♦/Q♣	8♠	A♥
44	3♦ / 8♣	4♦ / 2♥	5♠ / 7♥	6♦ / 10♠	9♥ / 3♠	8♥ / 9♦	9♦	K♥	10♦/J♦	6♠	A♥
45	J♠ / 9♣	8♣ / 5♣	6♦ / K♠	4♠ / 6♣	10♥ / 2♣	10♦ / 7♦	8♠	K♦	A♥/A♦	2♦	2♦
46	2♠ / K♥	9♣ / 9♥	4♠ / 6♣	7♣ / A♦.	K♠ / 6♦	Q♣ / 4♣	A♣	3♣	10♦/Q♥	A♦	6♣
						K♠					
47	Q♣ / A♥	3♥ / 3♠	5♦ / 6♥	4♣ / K♠	7♠ / A♦	J♣ / 9♠	7♦	Q♠	10♣/K♦	A♥	8♠
48	5♠ / 4♠	9♣ / 10♦	4♠ / 4♥	6♠ / K♣	2♣ / 5♦	A♥ / 8♠	8♠	9♣	3♠/10♠	3♥	K♣
49	K♥ / 7♠	3♥ / 7♥	6♣ / 5♣	J♦ / 5♦	Q♥ / 4♣	4♠ / 7♣	K♠	9♠	8♦/2♥	Q♣	2♠
						Q♥					

AGE	MER	VEN	MAR	JUP	SAT	URA	NEP	LR	PLU/RES	ENV	DISP
50	J♣	9♣	4♥	K♠	7♣	A♠	J♠	7♠	J♦/9♦	10♦	6♠
	A♥	10♠	8♠	Q♥	6♠	K♦					
51	A♣	6♣	K♥	K♦	3♠	Q♠	9♣	K♦	8♣/4♦	Q♠	9♠
	7♠	A♦	3♥	Q♥	7♠	9♠					
52	9♠	7♠	K♦	8♦	6♦	8♠	5♥	8♦	J♦/3♦	8♦	K♥
	K♣	10♣	J♣	10♠	7♥	5♥					
53	10♥	6♥	10♥	5♦	Q♣	K♠	8♦	6♦	3♥/4♦	7♣	2♣
	7♦	Q♠	7♣	5♥	K♦	K♠					
54	6♣	7♦	5♦	J♥	5♣	3♥	2♥	8♣	A♥/2♠	J♠	A♠
	5♥	3♦	9♠	10♣	8♠	2♥					
55	9♥	3♣	J♥	4♣	Q♣	A♠	3♥	5♥	K♣/A♠	10♣	7♥
	10♠	4♦	6♦	K♥	6♥	3♥					
56	10♠	Q♠	4♣	5♠	J♦	K♠	Q♥	10♠	A♣/9♠	4♠	8♥
	6♣	Q♦	6♦	A♠	J♥	5♠	J♦				
57	Q♣	J♠	5♦	5♣	8♥	7♠	A♦	6♥	4♠/8♦	4♥	7♠
	9♦	3♠	2♠	J♥	4♣	J♣					
58	9♠	K♥	10♠	4♦	8♠	9♥	5♣	10♥	7♠/J♦	10♠	K♦
	7♦	A♣	7♥	K♦	A♠	5♠					
59	3♣	7♦	4♦	6♣	10♥	7♠	8♠	5♦	A♥/Q♠	Q♥	3♠
	8♥	6♠	7♥	J♦	5♠	10♣					
60	5♠	8♥	6♣	3♥	8♦	4♥	7♠	Q♣	3♦/2♠	9♣	5♦
	6♦	8♣	2♥	Q♠	9♦	7♠					
61	Q♣	7♣	10♠	8♥	Q♦	K♥	4♥	K♣	10♦/9♠	6♦	9♦
	A♥	A♠	K♣	2♣	10♥	6♥					
62	6♠	3♥	8♥	9♥	4♣	A♥	5♥	8♦	A♠/A♦	3♠	Q♦
	7♠	10♣	8♦	10♥	9♦	5♥					
63	J♠	7♥	9♥	9♠	J♥	7♠	4♥	6♣	A♣/4♠	J♦	3♦
	10♠	9♣	6♥	10♥	3♦	4♥					
64	6♣	J♣	Q♦	8♣	7♥	5♦	9♠	9♥	5♣/3♠	J♣	6♥
	6♠	5♥	9♦	9♣	3♥	10♦					
65	10♥	9♦	8♣	A♠	3♠	6♠	4♣	5♦	J♦/4♦	10♥	4♣
	J♥	7♠	3♦	J♠	7♠	2♠					
66	3♥	4♥	4♠	7♦	K♣	J♥	A♠	J♥	9♣/2♥	5♠	5♣
	K♠	10♥	10♠	9♥	J♣	5♠					
67	7♣	9♠	7♦	5♦	8♦	Q♦	2♠	5♣	Q♠/10♣	4♦	5♥
	7♠	J♠	9♥	2♥	6♣	2♠					
68	J♣	4♥	4♦	J♦	2♣	7♠	5♦	3♥	K♠/6♥	5♥	4♦
	K♣	A♦	8♥	10♣	7♥	A♣					
69	J♥	9♠	J♦	A♣	3♠	4♠	10♦	A♣	Q♣/5♠	5♠	5♠
	Q♦	8♥	10♥	7♣	10♣	6♠					
70	5♦	5♥	3♦	6♥	7♣	3♥	4♠	7♦	K♣/9♥	4♣	10♥
	Q♠	A♦	9♦	7♥	5♠	J♠					
71	10♣	Q♥	J♦	5♥	6♣	K♥	3♥	3♣	4♦/9♣	6♥	J♣
	Q♣	2♣	10♠	9♥	2♥	3♥					
72	9♠	Q♣	5♥	6♦	6♥	4♦	2♠	J♥	2♣/8♥	3♦	J♦
	4♥	Q♦	8♣	2♥	J♦	2♠					
73	7♦	A♠	10♠	8♥	A♥	4♦	6♦	4♣	10♥/4♣	Q♦	3♠
	7♠	7♠	J♥	2♠	7♥	3♠					
74	6♠	Q♣	8♥	3♦	3♣	5♦	4♥	Q♣	8♦/9♠	9♦	6♦
	4♦	J♣	K♦	2♠	7♥	4♥					
75	5♣	A♣	5♥	3♠	4♠	10♣	5♦	2♥	9♠/8♣	5♦	9♣
	J♠	K♠	9♦	4♦	7♦	Q♦					
76	2♠	K♥	K♠	8♥	A♣	7♥	6♣	3♥	10♣/10♠	3♣	Q♥
	Q♣	6♦	K♦	8♣	2♥	4♦					
77	4♠	Q♥	5♥	4♦	9♥	7♣	J♥	10♣	A♥/6♥	K♦	10♠
	9♠	5♠	10♥	Q♣	2♠	4♥					
78	10♣	9♦	4♦	K♦	Q♦	A♥	8♠	Q♠	6♠/K♠	7♠	4♥
	9♠	6♦	Q♣	6♥	5♥	A♠					
79	J♠	9♠	K♦	A♠	7♥	3♠	4♥	4♣	10♥/Q♠	8♥	4♠
	5♠	9♥	2♥	4♠	7♣	4♥					
80	K♣	K♠	K♥	A♣	9♠	3♥	Q♥	5♠	3♠/6♥	7♥	10♣
	3♣	J♣	5♠	10♣	6♦	4♠	9♠				
81	8♣	8♦	A♥	4♠	2♠	8♥	K♥	J♦	2♠/J♣	A♠	J♠
	5♦	J♦	3♣	7♠	6♣	K♥					
82	4♦	8♠	4♠	5♠	4♠	9♥		K♠	10♣/Q♣	2♣	7♠
	9♠	A♦	3♣	J♣	K♦	8♥					
83	K♠	2♠	2♥	K♣	Q♠	3♠	10♥	Q♥	9♦/Q♦	K♥	8♦
	3♦	6♥	10♣	8♠	J♦	J♥	Q♠				
84	10♠	5♥	3♦	3♠	A♠	4♥	Q♠	Q♣	6♦/7♥	9♠	A♠
	4♦	10♣	K♦	9♦	K♣	Q♠					
85	K♥	K♣	2♠	5♥	J♦	6♥	4♥	J♠	7♦/3♥	6♠	10♦
	10♥	J♥	7♣	A♥	9♦	Q♦					
86	J♠	10♥	5♥	K♦	3♣	7♥	3♠	5♦	J♥/4♠	2♠	Q♣
	Q♠	2♣	8♣	3♦	6♦	4♦					
87	2♥	A♦	10♣	5♠	5♣	7♠	K♦	5♣	9♥/J♦	K♣	3♥
	J♠	3♥	4♣	10♠	7♥	K♦					
88	6♣	6♥	5♠	9♠	9♣	9♥	Q♠	8♥	Q♦/Q♣	8♠	A♥
	8♦	2♣	4♠	K♥	6♠	Q♠					
89	3♦	4♦	5♦	6♦	7♦	8♦	9♦	7♣	10♦/J♦	6♠	A♣
	8♣	A♣	7♥	10♠	3♠	9♦					
90	J♠	8♣	6♦	4♠	10♥	10♦	8♠	A♦	A♥/A♦	2♦	2♦
	9♣	5♠	K♠	6♣	2♣	9♥					
91	2♠	9♣	4♠	7♠	K♠	Q♣	2♥	9♠	10♦/Q♥	A♦	6♣
	K♥	7♦	6♠	A♦	6♦	4♣	K♠				
92	Q♣	3♥	5♦	4♠	7♠	J♣	9♥	K♥	10♣/K♦	A♥	8♠
	A♥	3♠	6♥	K♠	A♦	9♠					
93	5♠	9♣	4♣	6♠	2♣	A♥	8♠	10♠	3♠/10♠	3♥	K♣
	4♠	10♦	4♥	K♣	5♦	8♠					
94	K♥	3♥	6♠	J♦	Q♥	4♠	K♠	4♦	8♦/A♣	Q♠	2♠
	7♠	7♥	5♣	5♦	4♠	7♠	Q♥				
95	J♣	9♣	4♥	K♠	7♣	2♥	J♠	8♣	J♦/9♦	10♦	6♠
	A♥	10♠	8♠	Q♥	6♠	K♦					
96	2♥	6♣	K♥	K♦	3♠	Q♠		9♠	8♣/4♦	Q♠	9♠
	7♠	A♦	3♥	Q♥	7♠	9♠					
97	9♠	7♠	K♦	8♦	6♦	8♣	5♥	5♠	J♦/3♦	8♦	K♥
	K♣	10♣	J♣	10♠	7♥	5♥					
98	10♦	6♥	10♥	5♦	Q♣	K♣	8♦	3♣	3♥/4♦	7♣	2♠
	9♥	Q♠	7♣	5♥	K♦	K♠					
99	6♣	9♥	5♦	J♥	5♠	3♥	A♣	9♥	A♥/2♠	J♠	A♠
	5♥	3♦	9♠	10♣	8♣	A♣					

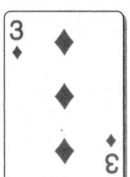

Three of Diamonds

AGE	MER	VEN	MAR	JUP	SAT	URA	NEP	LR	PLU/RES	ENV	DISP
0	A♠	7♥	7♦	5♠	J♥	9♠	9♠	A♠	2♥/K♥	3♦	3♦
	6♠	K♣	7♣	A♥	J♠	9♠					
1	6♥	A♦	10♣	8♠	3♠	4♥	5♠	7♥	Q♠/6♣	Q♦	6♥
	4♦	10♦	4♠	K♣	5♦	K♦					
2	A♥	4♠	8♣	J♦	10♠	4♦	8♦	7♦	2♦/Q♣	9♦	4♦
	J♥	9♣	J♠	A♠	7♥	J♣					
3	5♦	9♠	K♥	9♥	5♣	J♥	J♦	5♠	K♣/A♣	5♦	5♠
	K♠	A♥	6♠	7♦	A♦	3♥					
4	7♥	5♠	9♥	4♥	8♥	10♣	5♥	J♥	7♠/2♣	3♠	5♥
	9♣	A♠	7♦	A♣	6♥	5♥					
5	A♦	9♠	Q♣	2♦	J♣	9♠	4♥	9♣	K♠/7♣	K♦	4♦
	5♣	Q♦	6♦	2♣	9♥	2♥					
6	J♥	5♠	2♦	2♥	6♣	K♥	K♦	9♠	3♣/Q♠	7♠	5♠
	10♣	6♦	A♥	7♥	2♣	6♥					
7	4♥	10♦	J♠	7♣	7♥	5♦	K♥	6♥	5♣/7♦	8♥	10♥
	7♠	Q♦	4♠	3♠	3♥	A♠					
8	2♣	2♠	2♦	10♦	6♥	10♥	5♦	A♦	Q♠/K♣	7♥	J♣
	3♣	J♣	6♠	7♦	A♣	5♦					
9	5♠	3♣	10♦	8♠	7♣	Q♣	5♥	10♣	J♣/6♦	A♠	J♦
	9♠	10♣	8♠	A♣	2♦	5♥					
10	9♥	J♦	6♠	6♦	9♥	9♠	8♠	8♣	A♥/8♦	2♣	3♠
	9♣	7♥	J♥	5♦	3♠	6♣					
11	4♦	3♣	6♦	J♠	10♠	4♥	9♠	3♠	8♥/K♣	K♥	6♦
	Q♣	A♦	Q♥	5♥	3♠	9♣					
12	Q♠	2♥	10♦	6♣	K♥	2♣	4♥	4♥	5♠/8♣	9♠	9♣
	A♠	K♠	4♠	Q♠	9♥	10♣					
13	5♥	10♥	K♠	6♦	2♥	3♠	6♥	5♠	2♣/6♠	6♠	Q♥
	3♣	8♠	Q♥	8♣	A♣	Q♣					
14	K♥	2♠	10♦	Q♣	7♦	7♥	J♥	A♥	9♦/7♣	2♠	10♠
	5♠	3♥	A♥	3♠	J♣	9♠					
15	2♣	4♠	Q♣	Q♥	10♣	9♦	4♣	4♠	4♦/K♠	K♣	4♥
	5♠	8♠	3♣	7♠	10♦	J♦					
16	A♠	5♠	Q♥	J♦	3♠	6♠	9♠	8♣	A♥/7♠	8♠	4♠
	3♥	7♦	A♣	K♥	7♥	9♠					
17	5♣	K♠	10♥	2♥	5♠	5♦	2♠	J♦	6♣/7♠	6♠	10♣
	10♠	A♦	3♥	2♠	8♠	K♥	5♠				
18	8♣	8♥	9♦	K♥	5♥	6♦	10♥	10♠	J♣/A♦	2♦	J♠
	4♥	2♦	10♠	9♣	6♥	10♥					
19	Q♣	4♣	K♥	3♥	8♦	4♠	6♦	4♦	2♠/3♣	A♦	7♠
	5♠	Q♦	10♠	A♦	Q♥	6♦					
20	K♠	5♥	A♣	5♣	7♠	6♣	A♥	8♦	4♠/10♣	A♥	8♦
	J♠	7♣	2♣	4♣	2♦	J♥	7♠				
21	6♠	10♦	J♠	10♠	J♦	9♠	7♠	5♦	8♠/3♠	3♥	Q♠
	Q♣	2♣	Q♥	4♠	5♠	7♠					
22	10♥	5♣	5♥	10♦	2♦	7♣	9♠	9♠	9♥/5♦	Q♠	10♦
	A♥	J♥	7♥	9♦	4♠	10♠					
23	A♠	A♥	10♦	Q♥	10♠	9♠	6♣	K♥	J♥/K♥	10♦	Q♣
	7♠	J♣	8♦	J♠	8♠	Q♣					
24	A♣	Q♦	2♣	3♥	Q♠	9♣	Q♥	9♥	7♦/2♦	Q♠	3♥
	A♠	5♦	8♦	6♠	3♠	Q♥					
25	6♥	7♣	3♥	4♠	K♣	7♦	7♠	5♠	10♣/3♣	8♠	A♥
	8♥	J♣	8♦	10♥	4♦	7♠					
26	J♠	Q♣	4♥	8♠	9♥	8♥	4♠	J♥	K♦/2♦	7♣	A♦
	8♠	2♥	3♠	6♠	6♠	4♠					
27	A♠	8♣	8♠	K♥	A♥	K♦	4♣	J♦	9♦/Q♦	J♠	2♦
	K♣	Q♠	K♠	6♥	J♣	7♦					
28	5♥	K♣	K♥	7♥	K♠	3♠	A♣	7♥	K♦/2♠	10♣	6♣
	10♥	9♥	6♥	Q♦	8♠	8♦	K♠				
29	3♣	5♦	4♥	8♦	9♣	A♦	7♦	5♠	2♣/Q♥	4♠	8♠
	9♦	6♣	7♣	K♣	Q♦	5♠					
30	3♥	K♣	8♦	6♥	J♣	9♦	4♣	9♥	6♣/6♠	4♥	K♣
	K♥	K♦	9♠	5♣	4♥	4♣					
31	10♥	5♦	6♥	2♦	2♠	K♥	K♠	4♥	8♥/2♥	10♠	2♠
	9♣	3♠	Q♠	4♥	8♦	7♥	2♠				
32	A♦	K♠	9♠	K♣	7♥	A♠		8♥	2♦/4♠	Q♥	6♠
	9♠	6♠	8♥	2♠	6♥	Q♥					
33	A♣	6♥	10♥	Q♥	10♠	7♠	K♣	10♣	8♣/Q♣	9♠	9♠
	9♠	Q♦	5♦	2♠	7♥	K♣					
34	5♠	9♣	Q♥	8♥	8♠	8♣	10♦	5♥	2♦/J♠	6♦	K♥
	5♣	2♠	A♦	6♠	3♠	10♦					
35	K♦	7♣	A♥	4♥	3♠	5♠	8♥	A♦	5♦/Q♣	3♠	2♣
	7♦	7♠	7♥	10♦	Q♥	K♠					
36	6♥	7♣	4♥	J♥	Q♠	5♠	2♥	9♠	9♦/5♥	J♦	A♠
	10♦	J♠	5♠	2♣	8♣	2♥					
37	9♥	10♠	J♥	8♦	3♣	A♠	5♦	Q♣	5♣/J♦	J♠	7♥
	6♠	Q♣	8♠	10♥	7♣	5♦					
38	2♣	7♠	8♠	3♥	2♦	K♠	2♠	2♦	A♠/K♣	10♥	8♥
	6♥	10♣	8♠	J♦	J♥	Q♠	2♦				
39	3♣	A♠	4♥	Q♠	6♦	7♥	Q♦	J♣	K♥/8♦	5♠	7♠
	4♠	6♣	J♣	J♥	8♦	A♦					
40	5♠	10♥	6♠	Q♠	8♣	4♠	Q♠	9♠	9♣/2♦	4♦	K♦
	7♦	A♠	3♠	Q♥	J♦	Q♠					
41	10♠	7♦	Q♣	6♥	A♥	9♣	4♣	4♥	9♦/7♠	5♥	3♣
	6♦	4♠	3♠	2♦	Q♠	2♣					
42	3♥	6♦	6♥	5♦	8♥	9♠	9♠	J♥	J♠/J♣	5♠	5♦
	8♠	8♣	2♥	7♠	4♠	9♠					
43	3♣	7♥	6♠	6♦	10♣	10♥	9♠	5♠	K♦/K♣	4♠	9♦
	9♦	J♦	5♣	J♣	A♥	7♣					
44	4♠	5♦	6♦	9♥	8♦	9♦	10♦	2♦	J♦/Q♦	6♥	Q♦
	9♣	2♣	8♥	A♥	4♠	10♦					
45	A♠	7♥	9♥	5♠	J♥	9♣	9♠	2♥	A♣/K♥	3♦	3♦
	6♠	K♣	7♣	A♥	J♠	9♠					
46	6♥	A♦	10♣	8♠	3♠	4♥	5♠	6♠	Q♠/6♣	Q♦	6♥
	4♦	10♦	4♠	K♣	5♦	K♦					
47	A♥	4♠	8♣	J♦	10♠	4♦	8♦	K♥	2♦/Q♣	9♦	4♦
	J♥	9♣	J♠	A♠	7♥	J♣					
48	5♦	9♠	K♥	7♦	5♣	J♥	J♦	K♦	K♣/2♦	5♦	5♣
	K♠	A♥	6♠	9♥	A♦	3♥					
49	7♥	5♠	7♦	4♥	8♥	10♣	5♥	4♥	7♠/2♣	3♣	5♥
	9♣	A♠	9♥	2♥	6♥	5♥					

AGE	MER	VEN	MAR	JUP	SAT	URA	NEP	LR	PLU/RES	ENV	DISP
50	A♦	9♠	Q♣	2♦	J♣	9♣	4♥	10♦	K♠/7♣	K♦	4♦
	5♠	Q♦	6♦	2♣	7♦	A♣					
51	J♥	5♠	2♦	A♣	6♣	K♥	K♦	J♠	3♣/Q♠	7♠	5♠
	10♣	6♠	A♥	7♥	2♣	6♥					
52	4♥	10♦	J♠	7♠	7♥	5♦	K♥	7♣	5♠/9♥	8♥	10♥
	7♠	Q♦	4♠	3♠	3♥	A♠					
53	2♣	2♠	2♦	10♦	6♥	10♥	5♦	7♥	Q♣/K♣	7♥	J♣
	3♠	J♣	6♠	9♥	2♥	5♦					
54	5♠	3♣	10♦	8♠	7♣	Q♣	5♥	5♦	J♣/6♦	A♠	J♦
	9♠	10♣	8♠	2♥	2♦	5♥					
55	7♦	J♦	6♠	6♦	9♥	9♠	8♠	K♥	A♥/8♦	2♣	3♠
	9♣	7♥	J♥	5♥	3♠	6♠					
56	4♦	3♣	6♦	J♠	10♠	4♥	9♠	2♣	8♥/K♣	K♥	6♦
	Q♣	A♦	Q♥	5♥	3♠	9♠					
57	Q♠	A♠	10♦	6♣	K♥	2♣	4♥	2♠	5♠/8♣	9♠	9♣
	A♠	K♠	4♠	Q♣	7♦	10♣					
58	5♥	10♥	K♠	6♦	A♣	3♠	6♥	2♦	2♣/6♠	6♠	Q♥
	3♣	8♠	Q♥	8♣	2♥	Q♣					
59	K♥	2♠	10♦	Q♣	9♥	7♥	J♥	10♦	9♦/7♣	2♠	10♠
	5♠	3♥	A♥	3♣	J♠	9♠					
60	2♣	4♠	Q♣	Q♥	10♣	9♦	4♠	6♥	4♦/K♠	K♣	4♥
	5♠	8♠	3♣	7♣	10♦	J♦					
61	A♠	5♠	Q♥	J♦	3♠	6♣	9♠	10♥	A♥/7♠	8♠	4♠
	3♥	9♥	2♥	K♥	7♥	9♠					
62	5♣	K♠	10♥	A♣	5♠	5♦	2♠	5♦	6♠/7♣	6♠	10♣
	10♠	A♦	3♥	2♣	8♠	K♥	5♠				
63	8♣	8♥	9♦	K♥	5♥	6♦	10♥	5♠	J♠/A♦	2♦	J♠
	4♥	2♦	10♠	9♣	6♥	10♥					
64	Q♣	4♠	K♥	3♥	8♦	4♠	6♦	3♣	2♣/3♣	A♦	7♣
	5♠	Q♠	10♠	A♦	Q♥	6♦					
65	K♠	5♥	2♥	5♣	7♠	6♣	A♥	10♦	4♠/10♣	A♥	8♦
	J♠	7♣	2♠	4♣	2♦	J♥	7♠				
66	6♠	10♦	J♠	10♠	J♦	9♠	7♠	8♠	8♣/3♠	3♥	Q♠
	Q♣	2♣	Q♥	4♠	5♦	7♠					
67	10♥	5♣	5♥	10♦	2♦	7♠	5♣	7♣	7♦/5♦	Q♣	10♦
	A♥	J♥	7♥	9♦	4♠	10♣					
68	A♠	A♥	10♦	Q♥	10♠	7♦	6♣	Q♣	J♥/K♥	10♦	Q♣
	7♠	J♣	8♦	J♠	8♠	Q♣					
69	2♥	Q♦	2♣	3♥	Q♠	9♣	Q♥	5♠	9♥/2♦	Q♠	3♥
	A♠	5♦	8♠	6♠	3♠	Q♥					
70	6♥	7♣	3♥	4♠	K♠	9♥	7♠	9♥	10♣/3♣	8♦	A♥
	8♥	J♣	8♦	10♥	4♦	7♠					
71	J♠	Q♦	4♥	8♣	7♦	8♥	4♣	J♠	K♦/2♦	7♣	A♦
	8♣	A♠	8♠	6♠	6♣	4♠					
72	A♠	8♣	8♠	K♥	A♥	K♦	4♣	6♠	9♦/Q♦	J♠	2♦
	K♣	Q♠	K♠	6♥	J♣	9♥					
73	5♥	K♣	K♥	7♥	K♠	3♠	2♥	6♦	K♦/2♠	10♣	C♣
	10♥	7♦	6♥	Q♦	8♠	8♦	K♠				
74	3♣	5♦	4♥	8♦	9♣	A♦	9♥	9♦	2♣/Q♥	4♠	8♠
	9♦	6♠	7♣	K♠	Q♦	5♠					
75	3♥	K♣	8♦	6♥	J♣	9♦	4♣	9♠	6♣/6♠	4♥	K♣
	K♥	K♦	9♠	5♣	4♥	4♣					
76	10♥	5♦	6♥	2♦	2♠	K♥	K♠	8♠	8♥/A♣	10♠	2♠
	9♣	3♠	Q♠	4♥	8♦	7♥	2♠				
77	A♦	K♣	9♠	K♠	7♥	2♥	A♠	4♦	2♦/4♠	Q♥	6♠
	9♦	6♠	8♥	2♠	6♥	Q♥					
78	2♥	6♥	10♥	Q♥	10♠	7♠	K♣	3♠	8♣/Q♣	9♠	9♠
	9♠	Q♥	5♦	2♥	7♥	K♣					
79	5♠	9♠	Q♥	8♥	8♠	8♣	10♦	6♦	2♦/J♠	6♦	K♥
	5♣	2♠	A♦	6♠	3♠	10♦					
80	K♦	7♣	A♥	4♥	3♣	5♣	8♥	J♠	5♦/Q♣	3♠	2♣
	9♥	7♠	7♥	10♦	Q♥	K♠					
81	6♥	9♥	4♥	J♥	Q♠	5♦	A♣	10♠	9♣/5♥	J♦	A♠
	10♦	J♠	5♠	2♣	8♣	A♣					
82	7♦	10♠	J♥	8♦	3♣	2♥	5♦	4♥	5♣/J♦	J♣	7♥
	6♠	Q♣	8♠	10♥	7♣	5♦					
83	2♣	7♠	8♦	3♥	2♦	K♠	2♠	9♠	2♥/K♣	10♥	8♥
	6♥	10♣	8♠	J♦	J♥	Q♠	2♦				
84	3♣	A♠	4♥	Q♠	6♦	7♥	Q♦	Q♠	K♥/8♥	5♠	7♠
	4♠	6♣	J♠	J♥	8♠	A♦					
85	5♠	10♥	6♠	Q♣	8♣	4♠	Q♠	2♥	9♣/2♦	4♦	K♦
	9♥	2♥	3♠	Q♥	J♦	Q♠					
86	10♠	9♥	Q♣	6♥	A♥	9♣	4♣	10♦	9♦/7♠	5♥	3♣
	6♦	4♦	3♠	2♦	Q♣	2♠					
87	3♥	6♦	6♥	5♦	8♥	9♠	9♣	6♠	J♠/J♣	5♠	5♦
	8♠	8♣	A♠	7♠	4♠	9♣					
88	3♣	7♥	6♠	6♦	10♣	10♥	K♥		K♦/K♣	4♠	9♦
	9♠	J♣	5♣	J♠	A♥	7♠					
89	4♠	5♠	6♦	7♦	8♦	9♦	10♦	2♠	J♦/Q♦	6♦	Q♦
	9♠	2♠	8♥	A♥	4♠	10♦					
90	A♠	7♥	7♥	5♠	J♥	9♣	9♠	4♥	2♥/K♥	3♦	3♦
	6♠	K♣	7♠	A♥	J♠	9♠					
91	6♥	A♦	10♣	8♠	3♠	4♥	5♠	5♥	Q♠/6♣	Q♦	6♥
	4♦	10♦	4♠	K♣	5♦	K♦					
92	A♥	4♠	8♣	J♦	10♠	4♦	8♠	10♥	2♦/Q♣	9♠	4♣
	J♥	9♠	J♠	A♠	7♥	J♣					
93	5♦	9♠	K♥	9♥	5♣	J♥	J♦	K♠	K♣/A♣	5♦	5♣
	K♠	A♥	6♠	7♦	A♦	3♥					
94	7♥	5♠	9♥	4♥	8♥	10♣	5♥	6♦	7♠/2♣	3♠	5♥
	9♣	A♥	7♦	A♣	6♥	5♥					
95	A♦	9♠	Q♣	2♦	J♣	9♣	4♥	2♥	K♠/7♣	K♦	4♦
	5♣	Q♦	6♦	2♣	9♥	2♥					
96	J♥	5♠	2♦	2♥	6♣	K♥	K♦	3♠	3♣/Q♠	7♠	5♠
	10♣	6♠	A♥	7♥	2♣	6♥					
97	4♥	10♦	J♠	7♠	7♥	5♦	K♥	6♥	5♠/7♥	8♥	10♥
	7♠	Q♦	4♠	3♠	3♥	A♠					
98	2♣	2♠	2♦	10♦	6♥	10♥	5♦	K♥	Q♣/K♣	7♥	J♠
	3♠	J♣	6♠	7♦	A♠	5♦					
99	5♠	3♣	10♦	8♠	7♣	Q♣	5♥	2♠	J♣/6♦	A♠	J♦
	9♠	10♣	8♣	A♣	2♦	5♥					

Four of Diamonds

AGE	MER	VEN	MAR	JUP	SAT	URA	NEP	LR	PLU/RES	ENV	DISP
0	2♠	8♥	6♣	6♠	Q♥	10♣	8♦	2♠	K♠/3♥	4♦	4♦
	J♣	5♥	4♠	K♦	7♦	A♣					
1	J♥	6♦	6♠	A♣	9♠	7♠	3♦	8♥	6♥/A♦	5♥	5♠
	10♦	4♠	K♣	5♦	K♦	5♠					
2	8♦	2♦	Q♠	3♥	5♦	4♣	7♠	6♣	J♣/9♥	5♣	10♥
	Q♦	5♥	Q♠	4♥	8♠	3♣					
3	K♦	A♠	6♠	2♦	6♥	4♦	4♣	6♣	6♣/2♣	4♣	J♠
	6♥	Q♥	7♥	9♥	2♥	4♣					
4	6♦	6♥	2♦	K♥	3♥	6♠	J♦	Q♥	Q♥/4♠	6♥	J♦
	8♥	10♥	8♣	2♥	6♠	J♦					
5	7♦	10♠	7♥	4♠	5♣	8♥	K♥	10♣	K♣/A♥	3♦	3♠
	10♣	5♦	J♥	J♦	4♥	9♠					
6	3♠	6♥	4♠	Q♣	7♠	8♦	8♥	8♦	9♦/2♣	Q♦	6♦
	6♣	2♠	J♠	J♦	4♥	8♥					
7	A♥	A♣	2♠	9♠	7♠	K♦	8♦	J♥	6♦/8♣	9♦	9♠
	3♣	K♠	Q♠	6♣	7♦	10♦					
8	J♠	9♠	K♠	4♠	A♣	4♥	5♠	6♣	K♦/7♥	5♦	Q♥
	6♥	K♥	J♠	8♣	2♥	6♣					
9	7♠	A♥	2♦	6♣	9♠	5♦	J♥	6♠	5♣/3♦	3♣	10♠
	6♦	8♠	K♣	6♥	Q♥	8♥					
10	K♦	Q♠	6♣	J♠	10♦	5♣	10♥	A♣	3♠/K♠	K♦	4♥
	6♦	K♥	6♥	3♥	2♦	10♠					
11	3♣	6♦	J♠	10♠	4♥	9♠	8♥	9♠	K♣/Q♠	7♠	4♠
	8♠	9♥	2♥	7♠	5♦	8♥					
12	J♣	K♠	9♠	A♣	6♦	4♣	A♠	7♠	9♠/3♦	8♥	10♣
	7♥	2♠	8♠	K♦	K♥	7♠	6♦				
13	8♠	9♦	5♠	7♠	J♦	4♥	9♣	3♦	Q♥/2♠	7♥	J♠
	8♦	6♥	7♠	10♠	4♠	9♣					
14	6♣	10♥	7♠	8♠	A♥	Q♠	4♠	8♦	K♦/6♥	A♠	7♣
	6♦	5♥	7♣	2♠	J♠	4♠					
15	K♠	J♦	2♥	J♣	Q♦	9♠	K♣	2♦	Q♠/10♦	2♣	8♦
	Q♣	3♥	K♦	10♥	6♠	J♥	Q♦				
16	7♥	2♦	Q♠	7♠	10♠	8♥	Q♦	Q♣	K♥/4♥	K♥	Q♠
	6♣	K♥	J♠	Q♠	J♣	Q♦					
17	9♦	J♣	J♦	2♦	6♠	3♥	8♥	3♥	7♦/4♠	9♠	10♦
	K♣	J♥	5♦	5♠	Q♠	10♦					
18	3♣	K♠	2♦	J♠	7♠	7♦	9♠	5♦	J♥/7♠	6♠	Q♣
	Q♦	Q♥	A♥	Q♣	K♥	6♣					
19	2♥	5♥	K♦	8♠	A♦	10♣	J♠	4♠	9♥/6♠	2♠	3♥
	3♠	4♠	A♥	7♥	4♥	J♠					
20	5♠	3♥	8♠	Q♠	2♠	9♥	Q♦	7♠	10♦/6♥	K♣	A♥
	9♦	Q♥	A♥	9♣	3♠	Q♦					
21	Q♣	6♣	2♦	K♦	7♦	2♠	Q♠	K♦	3♦/6♣	8♠	A♦
	8♣	4♥	4♥	7♥	9♠	Q♠					
22	3♣	8♠	K♥	7♠	K♣	3♦	10♥	A♣	5♣/5♥	6♣	2♦
	2♠	A♦	K♠	5♠	Q♥	9♥					
23	J♦	2♠	7♠	5♦	5♠		2♥	6♠	3♦/A♦	2♠	6♠
	9♠	7♦	5♠	5♥	K♥	A♥	K♠				
24	6♥	4♣	8♠	A♥	10♣	2♠	9♠	2♦	K♦/J♠	A♦	8♠
	5♠	9♠	3♥	K♠	5♥	6♦					
25	8♠	2♠	A♥	5♠	Q♥	5♣	10♥	5♠	9♠/7♥	A♥	K♣
	7♠	3♦	8♥	J♣	8♦	10♥					
26	9♣	4♣	5♠	6♠	A♠	7♠	K♠	9♠	9♦/A♣	3♥	2♠
	10♣	4♥	A♦	8♦	A♥	5♦	A♠				
27	2♠	2♠	8♥	K♠	5♦	2♥	3♠	4♣	6♠/Q♠	Q♣	6♠
	5♠	7♥	9♦	A♠	5♠	J♠					
28	2♥	5♠	9♠	J♠	7♠	Q♦	2♠	6♦	8♣/6♣	10♦	9♠
	10♠	5♥	4♠	A♠	5♦	2♠					
29	6♦	10♣	J♠	9♦	K♥	8♠	2♦	6♥	6♠/Q♣	Q♠	K♥
	J♣	K♦	2♠	7♥	4♦	2♦					
30	3♦	3♥	K♣	8♦	6♥	J♠	9♦	2♦	4♣/6♣	8♦	2♣
	9♥	Q♦	5♦	2♦	J♠	K♠					
31	5♠	9♥	8♦	J♥	A♦	4♣	A♠	K♥	5♣/J♦	7♣	A♠
	2♦	Q♣	6♦	K♦	8♣	A♠					
32	7♦	7♣	J♠	A♥	6♥	2♥	4♣	3♥	J♣/10♠	A♠	7♥
	7♥	6♣	K♥	9♠	3♥	4♠					
33	K♦	Q♣	A♥	8♠	6♠	K♠	A♠	6♠	2♥/2♣	10♣	8♥
	5♠	10♦	K♥	10♠	J♥	A♦	6♠				
34	6♥	3♠	8♦	A♠	4♠	5♠	5♥	J♦	7♠/9♠	4♠	7♠
	Q♠	9♠	Q♥	J♥	A♥	2♠					
35	6♦	9♠	7♥	6♠	8♣	Q♠	A♦	7♦	10♣/6♠	4♥	K♦
	9♥	2♥	4♥	J♠	10♠	A♠					
36	7♣	9♥	6♠	5♠	K♣	10♣	10♥	10♠	5♣/Q♦	10♠	3♣
	4♠	3♠	4♥	6♠	A♦	K♦					
37	8♠	4♣	5♠	4♣	9♦	8♥	10♣	7♦	Q♣/Q♥	Q♥	5♦
	K♥	8♠	A♣	Q♦	Q♠	10♣					
38	6♥	5♦	7♥	4♠	10♥	9♣	8♥	4♠	3♦/2♣	9♠	9♥
	5♣	10♠	J♣	Q♥	K♠	3♥					
39	3♠	4♣	4♠	7♠	A♥	5♣	2♦	5♣	10♠/5♥	6♦	Q♦
	10♣	K♦	9♦	K♣	Q♠	2♦					
40	3♣	5♦	7♦	6♦	J♥	10♣	8♥	8♥	2♥/7♠	3♠	3♦
	7♥	2♣	3♥	K♣	Q♣	8♥					
41	5♠	2♠	10♦	8♣	4♥	8♦	6♦	K♥	A♦/9♠	J♦	6♥
	3♠	2♦	Q♠	2♣	4♣	3♦					
42	K♣	Q♠	8♣	10♠	7♠	3♠	A♥	3♠	6♠/6♣	J♠	4♠
	J♥	10♣	Q♣	3♠	5♦	Q♥					
43	4♣	8♥	7♠	9♥	J♣	J♥	10♠	6♥	2♣/A♣	10♥	5♣
	K♠	K♣	7♥	7♦	2♠	8♠					
44	5♦	6♦	9♥	8♦	9♦	10♦	J♦	4♠	Q♦/K♦	5♠	5♥
	10♣	3♦	7♦	A♠	5♠	J♦					
45	2♠	8♥	6♠	6♠	Q♥	10♣	8♦	Q♣	K♠/3♥	4♦	4♦
	J♣	5♥	4♠	K♦	9♥	2♥					
46	J♥	6♦	6♠	2♥	9♠	7♠	3♦	7♣	6♥/A♦	5♥	5♠
	10♦	4♠	K♣	5♦	K♦	5♠					
47	8♦	2♦	Q♣	3♥	5♦	4♣	7♠	8♦	J♣/7♦	5♣	10♥
	Q♦	5♥	Q♠	4♥	8♠	3♣					
48	K♦	A♠	6♣	2♦	5♠	9♠	4♠	8♥	6♣/2♣	4♣	J♠
	6♥	Q♥	7♥	7♠	A♠	4♠					
49	6♦	6♥	2♦	K♥	3♥	6♠	J♦	A♠	Q♥/4♠	6♥	J♦
	8♥	10♦	8♣	A♣	6♠	J♦					

AGE	MER	VEN	MAR	JUP	SAT	URA	NEP	LR	PLU/RES	ENV	DISP
50	9♥	10♠	7♥	4♠	5♣	8♥	K♥	A♣	K♣/A♥	3♦	3♠
	10♣	5♦	J♥	J♦	4♥	9♠					
51	3♠	6♥	4♠	Q♣	7♣	8♦	8♥	2♦	9♦/2♣	Q♦	6♦
	6♣	2♠	J♠	J♦	4♥	8♥					
52	A♦	2♥	2♦	9♠	7♠	K♦	8♦	9♠	6♦/8♣	9♦	9♣
	3♣	K♠	Q♠	6♣	9♥	10♦					
53	J♦	9♣	K♠	Q♣	2♥	4♥	5♠	7♠	K♦/7♥	5♦	Q♥
	6♥	K♥	J♠	8♣	A♣	6♠					
54	7♠	A♠	2♦	6♣	7♥	5♦	J♥	K♦	5♣/3♥	3♣	10♠
	6♦	8♠	K♣	6♥	Q♥	8♥					
55	K♦	Q♠	6♠	J♠	10♦	5♣	10♥	8♣	3♠/K♠	K♦	4♥
	6♦	K♥	6♥	3♥	2♦	10♠					
56	3♣	6♦	J♠	10♠	4♥	9♠	8♥	J♦	K♣/Q♦	7♠	4♠
	8♠	7♦	A♣	7♠	5♦	8♥					
57	J♣	K♠	9♣	2♥	6♦	4♣	A♠	9♠	9♠/3♥	8♥	10♣
	7♣	2♠	8♠	K♦	K♥	7♠	6♦				
58	8♠	9♣	5♣	7♠	J♦	4♠	9♣	K♠	Q♥/2♠	7♥	J♠
	8♦	6♠	7♣	10♣	5♠	9♣					
59	6♣	10♥	7♠	8♠	A♥	Q♠	4♠	4♠	K♦/6♥	A♠	7♣
	6♦	5♥	7♣	2♠	J♠	4♠					
60	K♠	J♦	A♣	J♠	Q♦	9♠	K♣	A♣	Q♠/10♦	2♣	8♦
	Q♣	3♥	K♦	10♥	6♠	J♥	Q♦				
61	7♥	2♦	Q♣	7♣	10♠	8♥	Q♦	4♥	K♥/4♥	K♥	Q♠
	6♣	K♦	J♠	Q♠	J♣	Q♦					
62	9♣	J♠	J♦	2♦	6♠	3♥	8♥	5♠	9♥/4♣	9♠	10♦
	K♣	J♥	5♦	5♣	Q♠	10♦					
63	3♣	K♣	2♦	J♣	7♠	9♥	9♠	7♠	J♥/7♠	6♠	Q♣
	Q♦	Q♥	A♥	Q♣	K♥	6♣					
64	A♠	5♥	K♦	8♠	A♦	10♣	J♠	A♠	7♦/6♠	2♠	3♥
	3♣	4♣	A♥	7♥	4♥	J♠					
65	5♠	3♥	8♠	Q♠	2♣	7♦	Q♦	2♦	10♦/6♥	K♣	A♥
	9♦	Q♥	A♥	9♣	3♠	Q♦					
66	Q♣	6♣	8♣	K♥	9♥	9♦	Q♠	6♣	3♦/6♠	8♠	A♦
	8♣	2♥	4♥	7♥	9♠	Q♠					
67	3♣	8♣	K♥	7♠	K♣	3♦	10♥	9♥	5♣/5♥	6♣	2♦
	2♣	A♦	K♠	5♠	Q♥	7♠					
68	J♦	2♣	7♠	5♦	K♠	6♥	A♣	5♠	3♦/A♠	2♦	6♣
	9♣	9♥	5♠	5♥	K♥	A♥	K♠				
69	6♥	4♣	8♠	A♥	10♣	2♠	7♦	J♥	K♦/J♠	A♦	8♠
	5♠	9♠	3♥	K♠	5♥	6♦					
70	8♠	2♣	A♥	5♠	Q♥	5♣	10♥	K♦	9♠/7♥	A♥	K♣
	7♠	3♦	8♥	J♣	8♦	10♥					
71	9♣	4♣	5♠	6♠	A♠	7♠	K♠	Q♠	9♦/2♥	3♥	2♠
	10♣	4♥	A♠	8♦	A♥	5♠	A♠				
72	2♠	2♣	8♥	K♠	5♦	A♣	3♣	6♠	6♠/Q♠	Q♣	6♠
	5♣	7♥	9♦	A♠	5♠	J♠					
73	A♣	5♠	9♠	J♠	7♠	Q♦	2♣	J♠	8♣/6♣	10♦	9♠
	10♣	5♥	4♠	A♠	5♦	2♣					
74	6♦	10♣	J♠	9♦	K♥	8♠	2♦	10♦	6♠/Q♣	Q♠	K♥
	J♣	K♦	2♠	7♥	4♥	2♦					

AGE	MER	VEN	MAR	JUP	SAT	URA	NEP	LR	PLU/RES	ENV	DISP
75	3♦	3♥	K♣	8♦	6♥	J♣	9♦	5♣	4♣/6♦	8♦	2♣
	7♥	Q♦	5♦	2♦	J♠	K♠					
76	5♠	7♥	8♦	J♥	A♦	4♣	2♥	10♥	5♣/J♦	7♣	A♠
	2♦	Q♣	6♦	K♦	8♣	2♥					
77	9♥	7♣	J♥	A♥	6♥	A♣	4♣	3♣	J♣/10♠	J♠	7♥
	7♥	6♣	K♥	9♠	3♥	4♣					
78	K♦	Q♦	A♥	8♠	6♠	K♠	A♠	6♦	A♣/2♣	10♠	8♥
	5♠	10♦	K♥	10♠	J♥	A♦	6♠				
79	6♥	3♣	8♦	A♦	4♠	5♦	5♥	J♠	7♠/9♦	4♠	7♠
	Q♠	9♠	Q♥	J♥	A♥	2♠					
80	6♦	9♣	7♥	6♣	8♣	Q♠	A♦	10♠	10♣/6♠	4♥	K♦
	7♠	A♣	4♥	J♠	10♠	A♦					
81	7♣	7♦	6♠	5♠	K♣	10♣	10♥	4♥	5♣/Q♦	10♠	3♣
	4♠	3♠	4♥	6♠	A♦	K♦					
82	8♠	4♣	5♠	4♣	9♦	8♥	10♣	9♠	Q♣/Q♥	Q♥	5♣
	K♥	8♣	2♥	Q♦	Q♠	10♣					
83	6♥	5♦	7♥	4♠	10♦	9♣	8♥	8♥	3♦/2♣	9♣	9♦
	5♠	10♠	J♣	Q♥	K♣	3♥					
84	3♠	4♣	4♣	9♥	A♥	5♣	2♦	J♣	10♠/5♥	6♦	Q♦
	10♣	K♦	9♠	K♣	Q♠	2♦					
85	3♣	5♦	9♥	6♦	J♥	10♣	8♥	K♠	A♣/7♠	3♠	3♦
	7♥	2♠	3♥	K♣	Q♣	8♥					
86	5♠	2♠	10♦	8♣	4♥	8♣	6♦	9♣	A♦/9♠	J♦	6♥
	3♠	2♦	Q♠	2♣	4♣	3♦					
87	K♣	Q♠	8♣	10♠	7♣	3♠	A♥	A♣	6♠/6♣	J♣	4♣
	J♥	10♣	Q♣	3♣	5♦	Q♥					
88	4♣	8♥	7♠	7♦	J♠	J♥	10♠	6♦	2♣/2♥	10♥	5♣
	K♠	K♣	7♥	9♥	2♠	8♠					
89	5♦	6♦	7♦	8♦	9♦	10♦	J♦	4♣	Q♦/K♦	5♠	5♥
	10♣	3♣	9♥	2♥	5♠	J♦					
90	2♠	8♥	6♣	6♠	Q♥	10♣	8♦	A♠	K♠/3♥	4♦	4♣
	J♣	5♥	4♠	K♦	7♦	A♣					
91	J♥	6♦	6♠	A♣	9♠	7♠	3♦	8♠	6♥/A♦	5♥	5♠
	10♦	4♣	K♣	5♦	K♦	5♠					
92	8♦	2♦	Q♣	3♥	5♦	4♣	7♠	9♦	J♣/9♥	5♣	10♥
	Q♦	5♥	Q♠	4♥	8♠	3♠					
93	K♦	A♠	6♠	2♦	5♠	9♣	4♣	5♠	6♣/2♠	4♣	J♣
	6♥	Q♥	7♥	9♥	2♥	4♣					
94	6♦	6♥	2♦	K♥	3♥	6♠	J♦	7♠	Q♥/4♠	6♥	J♦
	8♥	10♦	8♣	2♥	6♠	J♦					
95	7♦	10♠	7♥	4♠	5♣	8♥	K♥	J♠	K♣/A♥	3♦	3♠
	10♣	5♦	J♥	J♦	4♥	9♠					
96	3♠	6♥	4♠	Q♣	7♣	8♦	8♥	4♣	9♦/2♣	Q♦	6♦
	6♣	2♠	J♠	J♦	4♥	8♥					
97	A♦	A♣	2♦	9♠	7♠	K♦	8♦	9♠	6♦/8♣	9♦	9♣
	3♣	K♠	Q♠	6♣	7♦	10♦					
98	J♦	9♣	K♠	4♠	A♠	4♥	5♠	6♠	K♦/7♥	5♦	Q♥
	6♥	K♥	J♠	8♣	2♥	6♠					
99	7♠	A♠	2♦	6♣	9♥	5♦	J♥	10♥	5♣/3♥	3♣	10♠
	6♦	8♠	K♣	6♥	Q♥	8♥					

Five of Diamonds

AGE	MER	VEN	MAR	JUP	SAT	URA	NEP	LR	PLU/RES	ENV	DISP
0	Q♠	J♣	9♦	7♠	2♣	K♣	J♦	Q♠	4♥/4♦	5♦	5♦
	A♣	8♣	2♥	A♠	Q♥	J♦					
1	8♥	K♥	8♣	J♣	10♠	5♥	K♣	J♣	7♥/2♦	3♣	9♦
	K♦	5♣	3♦	4♦	10♦	4♠					
2	4♣	7♠	J♣	9♥	10♣	K♦	7♣	9♦	5♠/3♣	K♦	Q♦
	J♦	6♠	2♣	10♦	Q♥	7♣					
3	9♠	K♥	9♥	5♣	J♥	J♦	K♣	7♠	A♣/2♠	7♠	3♦
	8♠	2♥	4♠	10♦	4♥	K♣					
4	9♦	Q♣	10♠	8♣	10♥	9♣	5♣	2♣	J♠/A♥	8♥	6♥
	4♣	7♠	Q♥	2♦	7♠	7♥					
5	10♦	Q♥	8♣	5♣	6♦	4♣	10♣	K♣	3♥/8♦	7♥	4♣
	J♥	J♣	4♥	9♠	K♥	4♦					
6	7♠	K♣	2♣	7♠	3♦	J♥	5♠	J♦	2♦/2♥	A♠	5♣
	K♠	10♦	8♠	9♥	Q♣	Q♠					
7	K♥	5♣	7♦	9♣	2♣	10♠	6♥	8♥	A♠/6♠	2♣	5♥
	J♦	9♠	9♥	2♥	9♦	6♥					
8	Q♣	K♠	8♠	3♥	4♦	J♦	9♣	K♥	K♠/4♠	K♥	4♦
	3♠	3♣	J♣	6♠	7♦	A♣					
9	J♥	5♣	3♥	A♣	A♥	2♠	7♥	8♠	8♥/J♠	9♠	5♠
	10♠	J♣	10♦	K♥	6♠	9♦					
10	9♣	7♣	4♥	4♣	K♥	7♠	2♠	J♣	3♦/9♥	6♠	10♥
	A♠	3♣	Q♥	10♥	Q♠	9♠					
11	6♠	6♣	3♥	7♣	9♦	5♥	7♠	10♠	8♦/2♦	2♠	J♣
	8♥	4♦	8♠	9♦	2♥	7♠					
12	5♣	8♥	7♣	A♦	4♠	8♦	6♥	5♥	4♦/J♣	K♣	J♦
	K♣	10♠	8♠	2♥	3♥	6♥					
13	7♦	5♠	8♠	J♣	K♦	K♣	A♠	K♠	10♦/10♣	8♠	3♠
	J♥	K♥	J♥	6♥	10♥	A♥					
14	4♣	8♥	J♣	4♥	6♦	9♣	K♣	4♣	2♣/2♦	6♣	6♦
	8♦	Q♣	3♣	6♥	10♥	K♣					
15	J♠	A♣	7♣	A♥	2♠	6♠	9♣	7♠	5♣/8♣	2♦	9♣
	9♠	K♠	Q♥	8♦	7♦	10♠					
16	6♥	5♥	K♠	J♣	A♣	10♥	9♦	J♣	6♠/8♠	A♦	Q♥
	8♥	A♣	3♠	8♣	2♥	8♦					
17	2♠	6♣	7♣	8♦	9♥	K♥	J♥	9♥	K♦/4♠	A♥	10♠
	5♠	Q♠	10♦	8♥	4♦	K♣					
18	6♣	Q♥	8♦	3♠	10♠	K♦	Q♦	10♣	4♣/K♣	3♥	4♥
	5♠	A♦	8♥	4♣	7♣	J♣					
19	9♠	5♣	3♠	5♠	10♥	A♥	K♣	K♦	10♦/A♠	Q♣	4♠
	Q♠	9♥	2♥	2♠	K♥	K♣					
20	3♦	K♠	5♥	A♣	5♣	7♥	6♣	7♣	A♥/4♠	10♦	10♣
	6♦	Q♣	Q♠	6♠	A♦	2♠	5♣				
21	8♣	2♣	K♠	2♦	6♥	J♥	5♥	9♠	4♦/Q♣	Q♠	J♠
	9♣	3♥	9♣	J♦	9♠	5♥					
22	8♦	Q♣	2♠	Q♠	10♣	Q♥	J♣	K♥	6♠/8♥	8♦	7♠
	5♣	3♣	6♦	Q♣	3♠	J♣					
23	K♠	6♥	2♥	3♦	A♣	A♥	10♦	9♥	Q♥/10♠	7♠	8♦
	4♥	4♣	6♠	2♦	3♥	J♥	A♠				
24	8♠	7♣	4♥	6♣	5♠	K♣	A♠	5♣	A♦/10♥	J♠	Q♣
	8♦	6♠	3♠	Q♥	3♦	A♠					

AGE	MER	VEN	MAR	JUP	SAT	URA	NEP	LR	PLU/RES	ENV	DISP
25	5♥	3♦	6♥	7♣	3♥	4♠	K♣	J♥	7♦/7♠	10♣	10♦
	10♦	J♥	K♥	K♦	Q♥	10♠					
26	9♣	10♦	7♠	3♠	6♦	7♦	A♥	J♦	J♥/2♠	4♠	Q♣
	A♠	4♦	10♣	4♥	A♦	8♦					
27	2♠	3♣	6♠	Q♠	J♠	J♦	3♠	K♣	9♥/3♥	4♥	3♥
	9♠	7♠	10♣	8♠	10♥	3♠					
28	9♦	4♠	Q♠	Q♥	2♦	9♥	A♠	9♦	10♠/8♥	10♠	A♥
	2♣	4♦	10♣	5♥	4♠	A♠					
29	4♥	8♦	9♣	A♦	7♦	2♣	Q♥	Q♣	7♥/3♥	Q♥	A♦
	8♣	A♣	10♥	8♠	A♥	Q♥					
30	9♣	8♣	A♦	2♠	10♦	7♥	Q♦	10♠	K♦/3♣	9♣	2♦
	2♦	J♣	K♠	9♦	4♦	9♥					
31	6♥	2♦	2♠	K♥	K♠	8♥	2♥	8♣	7♥/6♣	6♦	6♣
	5♥	7♦	9♦	3♣	A♦	10♣	K♠				
32	8♥	7♣	9♣	10♣	J♦	Q♣	9♥	10♥	6♠/3♣	3♠	8♣
	K♦	A♥	4♠	K♠	3♣	5♣					
33	Q♠	2♦	10♣	9♣	4♦	K♦	Q♦	9♣	A♥/8♠	J♦	K♣
	2♠	7♥	K♣	3♦	9♣	Q♦					
34	5♥	7♠	9♦	3♥	6♣	2♠	K♠	5♣	2♣/A♣		2♠
	J♦	10♥	J♠	9♣	10♣	K♥	6♠				
35	Q♣	2♦	K♠	K♠	K♥	2♥	9♠	10♦	3♥/Q♥	10♥	6♠
	K♦	8♠	2♣	6♣	9♦	3♠					
36	2♥	9♣	5♥	3♠	6♦	A♠	2♦	Q♥	8♣/8♦	5♠	9♣
	J♦	3♣	7♠	6♣	K♥	2♠					
37	5♣	J♦	3♠	2♣	A♦	8♣	7♣	8♣	3♥/4♥	4♦	K♥
	3♦	6♠	Q♣	8♠	10♥	7♣					
38	7♥	4♠	10♦	9♣	8♥	3♦	2♣	5♠	7♠/8♥	5♥	2♣
	9♥	A♠	K♥	7♠	3♠	K♠					
39	9♦	9♥	9♣	J♥	J♠	7♠	A♣	6♠	K♦/6♥	5♠	A♠
	7♣	4♥	5♠	6♠	8♠	A♠					
40	7♠	6♦	J♥	10♣	8♥	2♥	7♠	4♠	3♦/5♠	4♠	7♥
	8♠	8♦	A♦	5♥	4♠	7♠					
41	6♠	A♠	10♣	Q♠	3♥	K♠	6♣	10♣	2♥/2♦	6♥	8♥
	9♦	10♠	A♦	5♠	J♥	J♠	3♥				
42	8♥	9♣	9♠	3♠	J♠	J♣	K♥	3♠	2♠/2♣	3♦	7♠
	Q♥	A♥	4♦	J♥	10♣	Q♣					
43	5♣	5♥	8♠	8♣	8♣	Q♥	J♠	K♣	J♦/3♥	Q♦	K♦
	9♥	2♥	10♥	3♠	5♠	J♠					
44	6♠	9♥	8♦	9♦	10♦	J♦	Q♦	2♠	K♦/A♠	9♠	3♣
	J♣	4♣	10♥	3♥	J♠	6♠					
45	Q♠	J♣	9♦	7♠	2♣	K♣	J♦	7♦	4♥/4♦	5♦	5♦
	A♦	8♠	A♣	A♠	Q♥	J♦					
46	8♥	K♥	8♣	J♣	10♠	5♥	K♣	3♦	7♥/2♦	3♠	9♦
	K♦	5♣	3♦	4♦	10♦	4♠					
47	4♣	7♠	J♣	7♠	10♣	K♦	7♣	J♥	5♠/3♣	K♦	Q♦
	J♦	6♠	2♣	10♦	Q♥	7♣					
48	9♠	K♥	7♥	5♣	J♥	J♦	K♣	5♠	2♥/2♠	7♠	3♦
	8♠	2♥	4♠	10♦	4♥	K♣					
49	9♦	Q♣	10♠	8♣	10♥	9♣	5♣	K♥	J♠/A♥	8♥	6♥
	4♣	7♣	Q♥	2♦	7♠	7♥					

AGE	MER	VEN	MAR	JUP	SAT	URA	NEP	LR	PLU/RES	ENV	DISP
50	10♦	Q♥	8♣	5♠	6♦	4♣	10♣	5♣	3♥/8♦	7♥	4♣
	J♥	J♦	4♥	9♠	K♥	4♦					
51	7♠	K♣	2♠	9♥	3♦	J♥	5♠	7♦	2♦/A♣	A♠	5♣
	K♠	10♦	8♠	7♦	Q♣	Q♠					
52	K♥	5♣	9♥	9♣	2♣	10♠	6♥	9♣	A♠/6♠	2♣	5♥
	J♦	9♠	7♦	A♣	9♦	6♥					
53	Q♣	K♠	8♦	3♥	4♦	J♦	9♠	2♣	K♠/4♠	K♥	4♦
	3♦	3♣	J♣	6♠	9♥	2♥					
54	J♥	5♣	3♥	2♥	A♥	2♠	7♥	10♠	8♥/J♠	9♠	5♣
	10♠	J♣	10♦	K♥	6♠	9♠					
55	9♣	7♣	4♥	4♠	K♥	7♠	2♠	6♥	3♦/7♦	6♠	10♥
	A♠	3♣	Q♥	10♥	Q♠	9♠					
56	6♠	6♣	3♥	7♣	9♦	5♥	7♠	Q♣	8♦/2♦	2♠	J♣
	8♥	4♦	8♠	7♦	A♣	7♠					
57	5♠	8♥	7♠	A♠	4♠	8♣	6♥	K♣	4♦/J♣	K♠	J♥
	K♣	10♠	8♣	A♠	3♥	6♥					
58	9♥	5♠	8♠	J♣	K♦	K♣	A♦	8♦	10♦/10♣	8♠	3♠
	J♦	K♥	J♥	6♥	10♥	A♥					
59	4♣	8♥	J♣	4♥	6♦	9♣	K♠	3♥	2♣/2♦	6♣	6♦
	8♦	Q♣	3♠	6♥	10♥	K♣					
60	J♠	2♥	7♣	A♥	2♠	6♠	9♣	4♦	5♣/8♣	2♦	9♣
	9♠	K♠	Q♥	8♦	9♥	10♠					
61	6♥	5♥	K♠	J♣	2♥	10♥	9♦	J♦	6♠/8♠	A♦	Q♥
	8♥	A♦	3♠	8♣	A♣	8♦					
62	2♠	6♣	7♣	8♦	7♦	K♥	J♥	9♣	K♦/4♠	A♥	10♠
	5♣	Q♠	10♦	8♥	4♦	K♣					
63	6♠	Q♥	8♦	3♠	10♠	K♦	Q♦	J♥	4♣/K♠	3♥	4♥
	5♣	A♦	8♥	4♠	7♣	5♠					
64	9♠	5♣	3♠	5♠	10♥	A♥	K♣	5♣	10♦/A♠	Q♣	4♠
	Q♠	7♦	A♣	2♠	K♥	K♣					
65	3♦	K♠	5♥	2♥	5♣	7♠	6♣	3♥	A♥/4♠	10♦	10♠
	6♦	Q♣	Q♠	6♠	A♦	2♠	5♣				
66	8♣	2♣	K♦	2♠	6♥	J♣	5♥	A♣	4♦/Q♣	Q♠	J♠
	9♣	3♥	6♦	J♦	9♦	5♥					
67	8♦	Q♦	2♠	Q♠	10♣	Q♥	J♣	A♥	6♠/8♥	8♦	7♣
	5♣	3♣	6♦	Q♣	3♠	J♣					
68	K♠	6♥	A♣	3♦	A♠	A♥	10♦	2♠	Q♥/10♣	7♣	8♦
	4♥	4♠	6♠	Q♦	3♥	J♥	A♠				
69	8♠	7♣	4♥	6♦	5♠	K♣	A♠	7♥	A♦/10♥	J♠	Q♠
	8♦	6♠	3♠	Q♥	3♦	A♠					
70	5♥	3♦	6♥	7♣	3♥	4♠	K♣	9♣	9♥/7♠	10♣	10♦
	10♦	J♥	K♥	K♦	Q♥	10♠					
71	9♠	10♦	7♣	3♠	6♦	9♥	A♥	7♠	J♥/2♠	4♠	Q♣
	A♠	4♦	10♣	4♥	A♦	8♦					
72	A♣	3♣	6♠	Q♠	J♠	J♦	3♠	4♥	7♦/3♦	4♥	3♥
	9♠	7♠	10♣	8♠	10♥	3♠					
73	9♦	4♠	Q♠	Q♥	2♦	7♦	A♠	4♠	10♠/8♥	10♠	A♥
	2♠	4♦	10♣	5♥	4♠	A♠					
74	4♥	8♦	9♣	A♦	9♥	2♣	Q♥	K♥	7♥/3♥	Q♥	A♦
	8♣	2♥	10♥	8♠	A♥	Q♥					

AGE	MER	VEN	MAR	JUP	SAT	URA	NEP	LR	PLU/RES	ENV	DISP
75	9♠	8♣	A♦	2♠	10♦	7♥	Q♦	7♠	K♦/3♣	9♣	2♦
	2♦	J♠	K♠	9♦	4♦	7♠					
76	6♥	2♦	2♠	K♥	K♣	8♥	A♣	2♠	7♥/6♣	6♦	6♣
	5♥	9♥	9♦	3♣	A♦	10♣	K♠				
77	8♥	7♣	9♣	10♣	J♦	Q♣	7♦	6♠	6♠/3♠	3♠	8♠
	K♦	A♥	4♠	K♠	3♣	5♣					
78	Q♠	2♦	10♣	9♦	4♦	K♦	Q♦	6♠	A♥/8♠	J♦	K♣
	2♠	7♥	K♣	3♦	9♣	Q♦					
79	5♥	7♣	9♦	3♦	6♣	2♠	K♠	3♥	2♣/2♥	J♣	2♠
	J♦	10♥	J♠	9♣	10♣	K♥	6♣				
80	Q♣	2♦	K♣	K♠	K♥	A♣	9♠	7♣	3♥/Q♥	10♥	6♠
	K♦	8♠	2♣	6♣	9♦	3♠					
81	A♦	9♦	5♥	3♠	6♦	A♠	2♦	9♦	8♣/8♦	5♠	9♠
	J♦	3♣	7♠	6♣	K♥	2♦					
82	5♣	J♦	3♠	2♠	A♦	8♣	7♠	5♥	3♥/4♥	4♦	K♥
	3♦	6♠	Q♣	8♠	10♥	7♣					
83	7♥	4♠	10♦	9♣	8♥	3♦	2♣	7♠	7♠/8♦	5♥	2♣
	7♦	A♠	K♥	7♠	3♠	K♠					
84	9♦	7♦	9♣	J♥	J♠	7♠	2♥	5♣	K♦/6♥	5♣	A♠
	7♣	4♥	5♠	6♠	8♠	2♥					
85	9♥	6♦	J♥	10♣	8♥	A♣	7♠	8♥	3♦/5♠	4♣	7♥
	8♠	8♦	A♦	5♥	4♠	7♠					
86	6♠	A♠	10♣	Q♠	3♥	K♠	6♣	7♠	A♣/2♦	6♥	8♥
	9♦	10♠	A♦	5♠	J♥	J♠	3♥				
87	8♥	9♠	9♣	J♠	J♠	K♥	3♣	A♦	2♠/2♣	3♦	7♠
	Q♥	A♥	4♦	J♥	10♣	Q♣					
88	5♣	5♥	8♠	8♦	8♣	Q♥	J♠	4♠	J♦/3♦	Q♦	K♦
	7♦	A♣	10♥	3♠	5♠	J♠					
89	6♦	7♦	8♠	9♦	10♠	J♦	Q♦	8♦	K♦/A♠	9♠	3♠
	J♣	4♣	10♥	3♥	9♠	6♠					
90	Q♠	J♣	9♦	7♠	2♣	K♠	J♦	6♥	4♥/4♦	5♠	5♦
	A♦	8♣	2♥	A♠	Q♥	J♦					
91	8♥	K♥	8♠	J♣	10♠	5♥	K♣	7♠	7♥/2♦	3♣	9♦
	K♦	5♠	3♦	4♦	10♦	4♠					
92	4♣	7♠	J♣	9♥	10♣	K♦	7♠	5♠	5♠/3♣	K♦	Q♦
	J♦	6♠	2♣	10♦	Q♥	7♠					
93	9♠	K♥	9♥	5♣	J♥	J♦	K♣	8♠	A♣/2♠	7♠	3♦
	8♠	2♦	4♠	10♦	4♥	K♣					
94	9♦	Q♣	10♠	8♣	10♥	9♣	5♣	J♣	J♠/A♥	8♥	6♥
	4♣	7♠	Q♥	2♦	7♠	7♥					
95	10♦	Q♥	8♣	5♠	6♦	4♣	10♣	K♦	3♥/8♦	7♥	4♣
	J♥	J♦	4♥	9♠	K♥	4♦					
96	7♠	K♣	2♠	7♦	3♦	J♥	5♠	K♣	2♦/2♥	A♠	5♣
	K♠	10♦	8♠	9♥	Q♣	Q♠					
97	K♥	5♣	7♦	9♣	2♣	10♠	6♥	A♦	A♠/6♠	2♣	5♥
	J♦	9♠	9♥	2♥	9♦	6♥					
98	Q♣	K♣	8♦	3♥	4♦	J♦	9♣	4♠	K♠/4♠	K♥	4♦
	3♦	3♣	J♣	6♠	7♦	A♠					
99	J♥	5♣	3♥	A♣	A♥	2♠	7♥	8♥	8♥/J♠	9♠	5♣
	10♠	J♣	10♦	K♥	6♠	9♦					

Six of Diamonds

AGE	MER	VEN	MAR	JUP	SAT	URA	NEP	LR	PLU/RES	ENV	DISP
0	4♠	10♥	10♦	8♠	A♥	A♠	Q♥	4♠	5♥/3♣	6♦	6♦
	K♥	7♥	3♥	4♥	Q♠	Q♦					
1	6♠	A♣	9♠	7♠	3♦	6♥	A♦	10♥	10♣/8♣	3♠	9♠
	4♣	K♠	2♦	K♥	7♦	6♣					
2	4♥	J♠	K♠	10♦	A♣	Q♠	9♣	10♦	6♥/9♦	J♦	Q♥
	10♥	K♦	3♥	8♣	2♥	K♥					
3	3♦	5♦	9♠	K♥	9♥	5♣	J♥	8♠	J♦/K♣	J♣	10♠
	10♣	2♣	A♠	10♥	7♠	Q♦					
4	6♥	2♦	K♥	3♥	6♣	J♦	Q♥	A♥	4♠/K♠	10♥	4♥
	10♣	K♦	10♥	K♣	9♠	8♦					
5	4♣	10♣	3♥	8♣	Q♠	7♠	Q♦	A♦	A♠/4♦	5♠	4♠
	2♠	9♥	2♥	3♦	5♣	Q♦					
6	10♠	K♠	J♠	A♣	10♣	J♠	5♦	Q♦	7♠/K♣	4♦	10♠
	A♥	7♥	2♣	6♥	K♦	3♦	10♣				
7	8♣	5♥	J♦	3♦	4♥	10♦	J♠	6♠	7♣/7♥	5♥	J♠
	A♦	8♥	A♥	Q♥	9♣	J♦					
8	K♥	Q♥	3♦	2♣	2♠	2♦	10♦	A♣	6♥/10♥	5♣	7♣
	10♣	3♠	A♥	7♥	3♥	10♦					
9	K♠	4♥	2♥	10♠	4♦	7♠	A♥	9♠	2♦/6♣	4♣	8♦
	8♠	K♣	6♥	Q♥	8♥	J♥	4♦				
10	9♦	9♠	8♠	A♥	8♦	Q♦	4♦	7♠	K♦/Q♠	6♥	Q♠
	K♥	6♥	3♥	2♦	10♠	4♦					
11	J♠	10♠	4♥	9♠	8♥	K♣	Q♦	3♦	7♦/J♣	3♦	10♠
	A♠	J♥	5♣	J♦	2♦	6♣					
12	4♣	A♠	9♠	3♥	A♥	7♦	7♠	6♥	J♥/3♦	Q♦	Q♣
	4♦	7♣	2♠	8♠	K♦	K♥					
13	2♥	3♠	6♥	2♣	6♠	Q♣	3♦	A♦	9♥/8♦	9♦	3♦
	4♣	J♣	2♠	9♦	Q♠	3♥					
14	9♣	K♠	2♣	2♦	3♠	9♥	4♦	4♥	6♣/10♥	5♦	A♥
	5♥	7♣	2♠	J♠	4♠	4♦					
15	8♠	K♥	A♦	K♦	7♦	5♥	2♦	J♠	5♠/8♥	3♣	A♦
	8♣	A♣	Q♠	9♦	7♠	2♦					
16	4♣	8♠	K♦	3♦	A♠	5♠	Q♥	K♠	J♦/3♠	K♦	2♦
	3♣	6♠	K♠	9♣	7♣	9♥					
17	4♥	3♣	3♥	5♠	K♠	10♥	2♥	10♦	5♠/5♦	7♠	6♣
	J♠	7♥	9♠	8♠	K♦	2♠	K♠				
18	10♥	J♣	A♦	2♠	Q♣	7♥	9♥	A♣	6♥/3♥	8♦	8♠
	J♦	7♠	K♣	K♠	3♠	10♣					
19	2♣	3♣	2♠	9♣	7♠	J♦	Q♥	Q♠	7♠/9♦	7♥	K♣
	3♦	5♠	Q♦	10♠	A♦	Q♥					
20	J♠	J♣	9♣	8♥	5♦	3♦	K♠	9♣	5♥/A♣	A♠	2♠
	Q♣	Q♠	6♠	A♦	2♠	5♣	5♦				
21	7♥	3♣	Q♦	K♠	5♣	2♥	4♦	3♦	8♥/2♦	2♣	6♣
	J♦	9♠	5♦	5♦	9♣	3♥					
22	2♥	9♣	J♠	3♥	A♥	4♦	3♣	5♦	8♣/K♥	K♥	9♣
	Q♣	3♠	J♣	5♦	5♠	3♠					
23	10♣	Q♣	3♥	5♥	K♣	8♣	9♠	9♠	8♥/8♠	9♠	K♥
	10♠	6♥	7♦	9♦	Q♠	9♠					
24	5♠	K♠	A♠	A♦	10♥	10♠	5♦	K♥	J♣/K♥	6♠	2♠
	9♥	4♦	5♣	9♠	3♥	K♠					
25	9♣	9♥	A♦	J♥	6♠	J♠	A♠	9♥	J♦/4♥	2♠	A♠
	9♠	8♠	10♣	6♥	8♠	A♠					
26	7♦	A♥	J♥	2♠	10♥	2♥	J♠	5♣	10♠/8♦	K♣	7♥
	9♦	K♥	K♦	J♠	K♣	J♠					
27	6♥	4♦	2♠	2♣	8♥	K♠	5♦	J♥	2♥/3♣	8♠	8♥
	9♣	6♠	K♦	8♦	J♥	6♠	8♥				
28	10♥	4♣	A♦	6♠	10♦	5♣	3♦	6♥	3♦/5♥	6♠	7♠
	2♦	7♠	7♠	J♥	2♠	7♥					
29	10♣	J♠	9♦	K♥	8♣	2♦	6♠	2♦	Q♣/8♥	2♦	K♦
	9♥	2♥	Q♠	3♥	8♦	6♠					
30	A♥	9♥	K♥	9♠	A♠	Q♣	Q♥	K♥	J♦/4♦	A♦	3♦
	10♦	4♠	Q♠	8♥	6♠	6♥					
31	2♣	10♦	9♣	J♣	5♥	Q♦	Q♠	3♥	8♠/7♣	A♥	5♦
	K♦	8♠	A♣	4♦	2♦	Q♣					
32	10♥	5♦	9♦	10♦	6♠	3♠	Q♦	6♣	5♠/3♣	3♥	9♦
	J♦	8♦	10♠	7♠	A♠	K♠					
33	4♠	J♣	10♦	7♦	2♠	J♦	9♠	J♦	8♦/3♠	Q♣	Q♦
	Q♣	6♥	5♥	A♠	2♦	9♠					
34	4♣	5♠	7♦	10♣	J♥	Q♣	Q♦	Q♥	2♥/3♦	10♦	3♦
	9♠	3♠	K♠	A♠	8♠	Q♦					
35	9♠	7♥	6♣	9♣	Q♠	A♦	10♣	4♠	6♠/7♠	Q♠	6♥
	4♠	9♠	2♦	2♣	J♣	5♠					
36	A♠	2♦	8♣	8♦	A♥	4♠	2♠	10♣	8♥/K♥	8♦	4♣
	J♥	Q♣	8♠	4♣	5♠	7♠					
37	J♣	Q♦	3♦	9♥	10♠	J♥	8♦	3♥	3♣/A♣	7♣	5♠
	K♠	A♠	9♦	7♦	7♥	2♠					
38	5♣	10♠	9♥	A♦	5♥	6♠	4♦	8♦	4♦/6♦	J♠	5♥
	Q♣	4♦	7♦	A♠	9♠	4♦					
39	7♥	Q♦	K♥	8♦	7♠	Q♣	A♦	Q♠	K♠/K♣	10♣	4♦
	10♠	3♠	10♦	6♥	9♥	2♥					
40	J♥	10♣	8♥	2♥	7♠	3♦	5♠	7♠	10♥/6♠	4♠	5♠
	6♣	10♦	A♠	5♣	6♥	9♠					
41	A♦	9♠	8♠	K♣	5♠	J♠	3♦	Q♦	10♠/7♦	4♥	10♥
	4♠	3♠	2♦	Q♠	2♠	4♣					
42	6♥	5♦	8♥	9♠	9♠	J♠		10♠	K♥/3♣	10♠	J♠
	10♥	7♠	9♦	7♠	A♣						
43	10♣	10♥	9♠	K♦	K♠	K♥	4♥	K♠	7♠/10♦	Q♥	J♦
	Q♦	6♣	8♠	A♣	8♥	4♦					
44	9♠	8♦	9♦	10♦	J♦	Q♦	K♦	J♠	A♠/2♠	9♣	3♠
	Q♣	5♠	J♦	4♦	Q♠	7♠					
45	4♠	10♥	10♦	8♠	A♥	A♦	Q♦	A♠	5♥/3♣	6♦	6♦
	K♥	7♥	3♥	4♥	Q♠	Q♦					
46	6♠	2♥	9♠	7♠	3♦	6♥	A♦	10♣	10♣/8♣	3♠	9♠
	4♣	K♠	2♦	K♥	9♥	6♣					
47	4♥	J♠	K♠	10♦	2♥	Q♠	9♣	J♣	6♥/9♦	J♦	Q♥
	10♥	K♦	3♥	8♣	A♠	K♥					
48	3♦	5♦	9♠	K♥	7♦	5♣	J♥	5♦	J♦/K♣	J♣	10♠
	10♣	2♣	A♠	10♥	7♠	Q♦					
49	6♥	2♦	K♥	3♥	6♣	J♦	Q♥	8♣	4♠/K♠	10♥	4♥
	10♣	K♦	10♥	K♣	9♠	8♦					

AGE	MER	VEN	MAR	JUP	SAT	URA	NEP	LR	PLU/RES	ENV	DISP
50	4♣	10♠	3♥	8♦	Q♠	7♠	Q♦	5♥	A♠/4♦	5♠	4♠
	2♠	7♠	A♣	3♦	5♣	Q♦					
51	10♠	K♠	J♠	2♥	10♣	J♣	5♦	J♦	7♠/K♣	4♦	10♣
	A♥	7♥	2♣	6♥	K♦	3♦	10♣				
52	8♣	5♥	J♠	3♦	4♥	10♦	J♠	3♦	7♣/7♥	5♥	J♠
	A♦	8♥	A♥	Q♣	9♣	J♠					
53	K♥	Q♥	3♦	2♣	2♠	2♦	10♦	4♥	6♥/10♥	5♣	7♣
	10♣	3♠	A♥	7♦	3♥	10♦					
54	K♠	4♥	A♣	10♠	4♦	7♠	A♠	10♦	2♦/6♣	4♠	8♦
	8♠	K♣	6♥	Q♥	8♥	J♥	4♦				
55	9♦	9♠	8♣	A♥	8♦	Q♦	4♦	J♠	K♦/Q♠	6♥	Q♠
	K♥	6♥	3♥	2♦	10♠	4♦					
56	J♠	10♠	4♥	9♣	8♥	K♣	Q♦	K♥	9♥/J♣	3♦	10♦
	A♠	J♥	5♣	J♦	2♦	6♣					
57	4♣	A♠	9♣	3♥	A♥	9♥	7♠	Q♥	J♥/3♦	Q♦	Q♣
	4♦	7♠	2♣	8♠	K♦	K♥					
58	A♣	3♠	6♥	2♣	6♠	Q♣	3♥	3♦	7♦/8♥	9♦	3♥
	4♠	J♣	2♠	9♦	Q♠	3♥					
59	9♣	K♣	2♠	2♦	3♠	7♥	4♦	2♣	6♣/10♥	5♦	A♥
	5♥	7♣	2♠	J♠	4♠	4♦					
60	8♠	K♥	A♦	K♦	9♥	5♦	2♦	2♠	5♠/8♥	3♣	A♦
	8♣	2♥	Q♠	9♦	7♠	2♦					
61	4♣	8♣	K♦	3♦	A♠	5♠	Q♥	2♦	J♦/3♠	K♦	2♦
	3♣	6♠	K♠	9♣	7♠	7♦					
62	4♥	3♣	3♦	5♣	K♠	10♥	A♣	10♦	5♠/5♦	7♠	6♣
	J♠	9♥	9♣	3♠	K♦	2♠	K♠				
63	10♥	J♣	A♣	2♣	Q♣	7♥	7♦	K♠	6♥/3♥	8♥	8♠
	J♦	7♠	K♣	K♣	3♠	10♣					
64	2♣	3♠	2♣	9♣	7♣	J♦	Q♥	4♦	7♠/9♦	7♥	K♣
	3♦	5♠	Q♦	10♠	A♦	Q♥					
65	J♠	J♣	9♠	8♥	5♦	3♦	K♠	2♥	5♦/2♥	A♠	2♠
	Q♣	Q♠	6♠	A♦	2♠	5♣	5♦				
66	7♥	3♣	Q♦	K♠	5♠	A♣	4♦	10♠	8♥/2♦	2♣	6♠
	J♦	9♣	5♥	5♦	9♣	3♥					
67	A♣	9♣	J♠	3♥	A♥	4♦	3♠	4♦	8♣/K♥	K♥	9♠
	Q♣	8♣	J♣	5♦	5♠	3♠					
68	10♣	Q♠	3♥	5♥	K♦	8♣	9♠	7♠	8♥/8♠	9♠	K♥
	10♠	6♥	7♥	9♦	Q♣	9♠					
69	5♠	K♣	A♠	A♦	10♥	10♠	5♥	A♠	J♠/K♥	6♠	2♣
	7♦	4♦	5♠	9♠	3♥	K♠					
70	9♣	7♦	A♦	J♥	6♠	J♣	2♥	9♦	J♦/4♥	2♠	A♠
	9♠	8♠	10♣	6♥	8♣	2♥					
71	9♥	A♥	J♥	2♠	10♥	A♣	J♠	9♠	10♠/8♦	K♣	7♥
	9♦	K♥	K♦	J♠	K♣	J♣					
72	6♥	4♦	2♠	2♣	8♥	K♠	5♦	8♠	A♣/3♣	8♠	8♥
	9♣	6♣	K♦	8♦	J♥	6♠	8♥				
73	10♥	4♣	A♦	6♠	10♦	5♠	3♠	A♥	3♦/5♥	6♠	7♠
	2♦	7♠	7♣	J♥	2♠	7♥					
74	10♣	J♠	9♦	K♥	8♠	2♦	6♠	8♦	Q♣/8♥	2♦	K♦
	7♦	A♣	Q♠	3♥	8♦	6♠					
75	A♥	7♠	K♥	9♣	A♠	Q♣	Q♥	Q♦	J♦/4♦	A♠	3♣
	10♦	4♠	Q♠	8♥	6♠	6♥					
76	2♣	10♦	9♣	J♣	5♥	Q♦	Q♣	4♦	8♠/7♣	A♥	5♦
	K♦	8♣	2♥	4♦	2♦	Q♣					
77	10♥	5♣	9♦	10♦	6♠	J♠	Q♦	J♠	5♠/3♣	3♥	9♦
	J♦	8♦	10♠	7♣	A♠	K♣					
78	4♠	J♣	10♦	9♥	2♠	J♦	9♠	10♠	8♦/3♠	Q♣	Q♦
	Q♣	6♥	5♠	A♠	2♦	9♠					
79	4♣	5♠	9♥	10♣	J♥	Q♣	Q♦	4♥	A♣/3♦	10♦	3♦
	9♦	3♣	K♣	A♠	8♠	Q♦					
80	9♣	7♥	6♣	8♣	Q♠	A♦	10♣	9♠	6♠/7♣	Q♠	6♥
	4♠	9♠	2♦	3♣	J♣	5♠					
81	A♠	2♦	8♣	8♦	A♥	4♠	2♠	8♥	8♥/K♥	8♦	4♣
	J♥	Q♣	8♠	4♣	5♠	7♠					
82	2♣	Q♦	3♦	7♦	10♠	J♥	8♦	K♣	3♠/2♥	7♠	5♣
	K♠	A♠	9♠	9♥	7♥	2♠					
83	5♣	10♣	7♠	A♦	5♥	6♣	4♥	Q♦	4♦/6♥	J♠	5♥
	Q♣	4♠	9♥	2♥	9♣	4♥					
84	7♥	Q♦	K♥	8♦	7♠	Q♣	A♦	4♠	K♠/K♣	10♠	4♦
	10♠	3♠	10♦	6♥	7♠	A♣					
85	J♥	10♠	8♥	A♣	7♥	3♦	5♠	A♠	10♥/6♠	4♠	5♠
	6♥	10♠	A♠	5♠	6♥	9♣					
86	A♦	9♠	8♠	K♣	5♠	J♣	3♦	9♠	10♠/9♥	4♥	10♥
	4♦	3♠	2♦	Q♠	2♣	4♠					
87	6♥	5♦	8♥	9♠	9♣	J♠	J♣	3♥	K♥/3♣	10♠	J♣
	10♥	7♣	9♦	9♥	2♥	J♣					
88	10♣	10♥	9♣	K♣	K♣	K♥	4♥	A♥	7♣/10♦	Q♥	J♦
	Q♦	6♣	8♠	2♥	8♥	4♥					
89	7♦	8♠	9♦	10♦	J♠	Q♦	K♦	7♠	A♠/2♠	9♣	3♠
	Q♣	5♠	J♥	4♥	Q♠	7♠					
90	4♠	10♥	10♦	8♠	A♥	A♦	Q♦	7♠	5♥/3♣	6♠	6♦
	K♥	7♥	3♦	4♥	Q♠	Q♦					
91	6♠	A♣	9♠	7♠	3♦	6♥	A♦	2♥	10♠/8♣	3♠	9♣
	4♣	K♠	2♠	K♥	7♦	6♣					
92	4♦	J♠	K♠	10♦	A♠	Q♠	9♣	3♠	6♥/9♦	J♦	Q♥
	10♥	K♠	3♥	8♣	2♥	K♥					
93	3♦	5♠	9♠	K♥	9♥	5♣	J♥	6♥	J♦/K♣	J♣	10♠
	10♣	2♠	A♠	10♥	7♣	Q♦					
94	6♥	2♦	K♥	3♦	6♣	J♦	Q♥	2♠	4♠/K♠	10♥	4♥
	10♣	K♦	10♥	K♣	9♠	8♦					
95	4♣	10♣	3♥	8♦	Q♠	7♠	Q♦	6♠	A♠/4♦	5♠	4♠
	2♣	9♥	2♥	3♦	5♠	Q♦					
96	10♠	K♠	J♠	A♠	10♣	J♠	5♦	Q♣	7♠/K♣	4♦	10♣
	A♥	7♥	2♣	6♥	K♦	3♦	10♣					
97	8♣	5♥	J♦	3♦	4♥	10♦	J♠	3♥	7♣/7♥	5♥	J♠
	A♦	8♥	A♥	Q♣	9♣	J♠					
98	K♥	Q♥	3♦	2♣	2♠	2♦	10♦	9♣	6♥/10♥	5♠	7♣
	10♣	3♠	A♥	7♦	3♥	10♦					
99	K♠	4♥	2♥	10♠	4♦	7♠	A♠	K♣	2♦/6♣	4♣	8♦
	8♠	K♣	6♥	Q♥	8♥	J♥	4♦					

Seven of Diamonds

AGE	MER	VEN	MAR	JUP	SAT	URA	NEP	LR	PLU/RES	ENV	DISP
0	5♠	J♥	9♣	9♠	2♥	K♥	K♦	5♠	6♥/4♣		
	A♦	4♦	J♣	5♥	4♠	K♦					
1	J♠	3♣	8♣	10♥	5♦	8♥	K♥	J♥	8♠/J♣		
	6♣	A♦	6♦	4♣	K♠	2♦					
2	5♥	J♥	3♠	2♠	2♥	6♠	8♥	9♣	Q♦/3♦		
	A♣	5♣	5♠	4♣	10♠	8♥					
3	4♠	7♠	J♠	4♦	K♦	A♠	6♠	9♣	2♦/5♠		
	A♦	3♥	3♦	3♦	K♠	A♥					
4	4♣	J♥	J♣	8♠	2♥	K♣	A♠	2♥	5♦/9♦		
	A♣	6♥	5♥	3♦	9♣	A♠					
5	10♠	7♥	4♠	5♣	8♥	K♥	K♣	K♥	A♥/5♥		
	3♥	10♦	10♥	9♣	K♠	Q♣					
6	3♦	J♥	5♠	2♣	2♥	6♠	K♥	K♦	K♦/3♣		
	A♣	Q♦	4♠	9♦	3♠	K♥					
7	9♣	2♣	10♠	6♥	A♠	6♠	6♣	J♠	Q♣/4♣		
	10♦	8♦	4♦	3♣	Q♠						
8	9♦	J♥	5♥	A♥	2♥	A♦	6♠	3♣	8♥/7♠		
	A♣	5♥	3♦	3♣	J♣	6♠					
9	3♠	9♠	9♣	Q♣	K♥	K♣	A♦	8♦	Q♠/3♦		
	8♦	J♠	5♠	7♦	K♠	7♣					
10	3♣	J♥	4♣	Q♣	2♥	3♥	K♣	10♥	A♠/7♥		
	A♣	K♦	9♦	7♣	5♠	K♣					
11	J♣	2♠	3♣	5♦	6♠	6♣	3♥	5♦	7♣/9♦		
	J♠	4♣	6♥	7♥	K♠	10♣					
12	7♠	J♥	3♦	Q♠	2♥	10♦	6♣	8♥	K♥/2♣		
	A♣	8♥	3♣	7♥	5♥	6♣					
13	5♠	8♠	J♣	K♦	K♣	A♦	10♦	K♥	10♣/3♣		
	4♠	10♠	Q♦	2♣	K♠	4♦					
14	7♥	J♥	9♦	7♣	2♥	8♦	A♦	5♥	6♠/9♠		
	A♣	A♠	7♠	2♣	4♠	A♦					
15	5♥	2♠	5♠	8♥	6♠	3♥	8♦	J♥	4♥/7♠		
	10♠	9♣	5♦	9♠	K♠	Q♥					
16	2♣	J♥	3♠	10♠	2♥	J♠	3♥	3♠	K♣/2♠		
	A♣	K♥	7♥	9♠	3♦	3♥					
17	4♣	A♥	5♥	A♠	A♦	10♦	J♠	2♠	Q♥/7♥		
	9♣	3♠	K♦	2♠	K♠	6♦					
18	9♠	J♥	7♠	4♥	2♥	4♠	10♦	2♥	6♣/8♠		
	A♣	6♠	2♣	2♠	9♦	10♦					
19	3♦	Q♣	4♣	K♥	3♥	8♦	4♠	6♠	6♦/2♣		
	3♠	J♣	8♥	8♠	K♠	J♦					
20	2♠	J♥	7♥	Q♥	2♥	10♠	8♦	8♥	A♦/2♦		
	A♣	K♣	9♠	3♣	3♠	8♦					
21	9♦	Q♣	3♦	6♠	10♦	J♠	10♠	4♣	J♦/9♠		
	J♣	A♠	A♣	2♦	K♠	10♥					
22	8♠	J♥	2♣	6♦	2♥	9♣	J♠	7♠	3♥/A♥		
	A♣	6♣	2♠	2♦	7♠	J♠					
23	3♣	7♠	9♣	K♣	8♥	4♠	9♣	J♠	10♥/2♠		
	5♠	5♥	K♥	A♥	K♠	4♦					
24	2♠	J♥	9♠	J♦	2♥	3♠	4♠	4♦	10♦/Q♣		
	A♣	A♦	8♠	A♥	7♥	4♠					
25	7♠	10♠	3♣	6♣	J♠	10♠	3♠	K♦	4♦/8♠		
	5♥	4♣	6♠	Q♣	K♠	5♣					
26	A♥	J♥	2♠	10♥	2♥	J♣	10♠	A♠	8♦/Q♠		
	A♣	3♥	2♦	Q♣	2♣	10♠					
27	7♥	4♥	7♠	A♦	4♠	9♣	J♣	6♠	5♣/2♦		
	4♣	3♦	K♠	Q♣	K♠	6♥					
28	Q♣	J♥	8♠	4♦	2♥	5♠	9♣	4♣	J♠/7♣		
	A♣	10♦	A♥	Q♠	9♠	9♣					
29	2♣	Q♥	7♥	3♥	10♠	3♠	5♠	J♥	6♥/A♥		
	3♦	9♦	6♣	7♣	K♠	Q♦					
30	Q♠	J♥	2♦	5♣	2♥	5♥	3♠	J♣	4♠/10♣		
	A♣	8♦	Q♠	7♣	2♠	3♠					
31	9♠	6♦	2♣	10♦	9♣	J♣	5♥	8♠	Q♦/Q♣		
	9♦	3♣	A♦	10♣	K♠	5♦					
32	7♣	J♥	A♥	6♥	2♥	4♣	J♣	2♥	10♠/4♥		
	A♣	A♠	Q♠	10♣	8♠	J♣					
33	2♠	J♥	9♠	8♦	3♠	5♠	4♣	K♣	5♦/Q♠		
	3♦	7♠	3♥	4♥	K♠	K♦					
34	10♣	J♥	Q♣	Q♦	2♥	3♠	5♠	A♠	9♣/Q♥		
	A♣	4♠	7♠	4♥	2♦	5♠					
35	8♠	10♥	2♠	J♠	J♣	5♥	3♦	10♠	K♦/7♣		
	7♠	7♥	10♦	Q♥	K♠	8♥					
36	4♥	J♥	Q♠	5♦	2♥	9♣	5♥	7♥	3♠/6♦		
	A♣	10♠	10♣	Q♥	A♥	5♥					
37	2♦	4♣	8♠	4♠	5♠	4♣	9♦	4♠	8♥/10♣		
	7♥	2♠	8♠	6♦	K♠	A♠					
38	Q♥	J♥	7♠	K♦	2♥	3♠	4♣	5♠	J♣/J♦		
	A♣	9♠	4♥	6♦	Q♠	4♣					
39	A♥	5♣	2♦	10♠	5♥	3♦	3♣	8♥	A♠/4♥		
	2♣	9♠	J♠	J♦	K♠	K♥					
40	6♦	J♥	10♣	8♥	2♥	7♠	3♦	K♥	5♠/10♥		
	A♣	3♠	Q♥	J♦	Q♠	3♦					
41	Q♣	6♥	A♥	9♣	4♣	9♦	7♠	K♣	K♥/Q♥		
	9♠	2♠	4♠	10♥	K♠	6♠					
42	J♦	J♥	4♥	A♠	2♥	7♥	9♦	3♦	5♥/4♦		
	A♣	J♣	6♦	10♥	7♠	9♦					
43	Q♠	Q♥	Q♣	3♠	3♦	3♣	7♥	J♥	6♠/6♦		
	2♠	8♠	10♠	4♦	K♠	K♣					
44	10♥	J♥	Q♥	K♥	2♥	2♣	3♠	5♠	4♣/5♣		
	A♣	5♠	J♦	4♦	10♣	3♠					
45	7♣	5♦	Q♠	J♣	9♥	7♠	2♣	2♦	K♣/J♦		
	8♠	2♦	9♣	5♠	K♠	6♠					
46	4♦	J♥	6♦	6♠	2♥	9♠	7♠	2♥	3♦/6♦		
	A♣	5♥	10♥	5♠	4♥	7♠					
47	10♣	K♦	7♠	5♠	3♣	7♥	9♠	6♣	6♣/10♥		
	2♦	A♥	3♠	6♥	K♠	A♦					
48	5♣	J♥	J♦	K♣	2♥	2♠	7♠	K♥	9♦/Q♦		
	A♣	4♠	4♦	6♥	Q♥	7♠					
49	4♥	8♥	10♣	5♥	7♠	2♣	2♠	9♣	A♦/4♣		
	A♥	Q♣	J♣	Q♦	K♠	3♥					

AGE	MER	VEN	MAR	JUP	SAT	URA	NEP	LR	PLU/RES ENV DISP
50	6♥	J♥	10♥	6♣	2♥	8♠	2♣	2♠		3♣/5♦
	A♣	3♦	5♣	Q♦	6♦	2♣			
51	Q♥	A♠	4♥	4♣	7♥	9♠	8♠	10♠		3♥/5♣
	Q♣	Q♠	5♠	5♦	K♠	10♦			
52	Q♦	J♥	4♦	A♦	2♥	2♦	9♠	6♥		7♠/K♦
	A♣	9♦	6♥	5♦	J♦	9♠			
53	6♦	K♥	Q♥	3♦	2♣	2♠	2♦	A♠		10♦/6♥
	Q♠	7♣	5♥	K♦	K♠	8♦			
54	5♦	J♥	5♠	3♥	2♥	A♥	2♠	6♠		7♥/8♥
	A♣	3♣	Q♦	K♦	10♥	2♠			
55	J♦	6♠	6♦	9♦	9♠	8♠	A♥	6♠		8♦/Q♦
	7♣	10♠	4♣	8♥	K♠	J♠			
56	K♦	J♥	6♥	10♦	2♥	Q♣	8♠	9♦		2♣/A♠
	A♣	7♠	5♦	8♥	4♦	8♠			
57	10♥	K♣	J♦	3♠	2♠	2♦	Q♣	J♥		J♠/5♦
	10♣	4♥	3♦	A♠	K♠	4♠			
58	8♥	J♥	Q♦	8♦	2♥	Q♠	2♦	5♥		9♠/K♥
	A♣	7♥	K♦	A♠	5♣	2♦			
59	4♦	6♠	10♥	7♦	8♠	A♥	Q♠	A♥		4♠/K♦
	4♥	Q♥	9♦	K♥	K♠	10♠			
60	A♠	J♥	5♦	J♠	2♥	7♣	A♥	2♥		2♠/6♠
	A♣	2♣	8♥	K♥	6♥	A♥			
61	5♣	A♦	4♦	7♥	2♦	Q♣	7♣	A♦		10♠/8♥
	Q♥	6♦	3♣	6♠	K♠	9♣			
62	K♥	J♥	K♦	4♠	2♥	10♣	Q♣	6♠		8♠/K♣
	A♣	9♠	A♠	6♠	Q♦	Q♣			
63	6♥	3♥	5♣	2♣	A♥	Q♠	10♣	3♠		9♣/A♠
	6♦	J♦	7♠	K♣	K♠	3♠			
64	6♠	J♥	8♥	10♠	2♥	4♥	Q♠	9♠		2♦/6♣
	A♣	2♠	K♥	K♠	5♦	Q♠			
65	Q♦	10♦	6♥	9♠	Q♣	7♣	4♥	9♠		3♠/K♥
	J♦	10♥	7♥	6♣	K♠	J♣			
66	K♣	J♥	A♠	9♣	2♥	Q♥	7♣	Q♦		A♥/A♦
	A♣	8♠	6♠	6♣	K♦	7♣			
67	5♦	8♠	Q♦	2♠	Q♠	10♣	Q♥	K♥		J♣/6♠
	10♥	4♦	2♣	A♦	K♠	5♠			
68	6♣	J♥	K♥	3♠	2♥	6♦	10♣	K♣		Q♣/3♥
	A♣	2♦	K♣	A♦	8♥	10♣			
69	K♦	J♠	5♦	8♠	7♥	4♥	6♦	A♠		5♠/K♣
	4♦	5♣	9♠	3♥	K♠	5♥			
70	A♦	J♥	6♠	J♣	2♥	J♦	4♥	3♠		Q♠/10♦
	A♣	A♥	6♣	3♥	A♠	4♥			
71	8♥	4♠	K♦	2♦	10♣	Q♥	J♦	J♥		5♥/6♠
	5♣	6♥	2♠	10♦	K♠	4♠			
72	3♥	J♥	K♣	5♠	2♥	10♥	Q♥	4♠		7♣/8♦
	A♣	Q♣	A♦	10♦	K♥	Q♥			
73	A♠	10♠	8♥	A♥	4♥	6♦	10♥	Q♣		4♣/A♦
	6♥	Q♦	8♠	8♦	K♠	3♦			
74	10♦	J♥	6♠	5♥	2♥	4♦	6♦	2♥		10♣/J♠
	A♣	Q♠	3♥	8♦	6♠	6♦			
75	K♥	9♠	A♠	Q♣	Q♥	J♦	4♠	3♥		3♦/3♥
	Q♦	5♦	2♦	J♠	K♠	9♦			
76	8♦	J♥	A♦	4♣	2♥	5♣	J♦	K♣		4♥/4♠
	A♣	7♥	10♦	J♠	K♣	J♦			
77	6♠	3♠	K♥	Q♠	6♦	10♥	5♣	J♣		9♦/10♦
	5♥	K♦	A♥	4♠	K♠	3♣			
78	J♠	J♥	3♥	3♦	2♥	6♥	10♥	2♠		Q♥/10♠
	A♣	10♣	8♦	4♠	6♣	10♥			
79	K♣	J♣	6♠	7♣	J♦	4♦	6♥	3♠		3♣/8♦
	K♦	8♥	Q♣	10♠	K♠	7♠			
80	4♠	J♥	10♦	9♦	2♥	Q♦	4♠	5♠		6♦/9♣
	A♣	4♥	J♠	10♠	A♦	4♦			
81	6♣	5♠	K♣	10♣	10♥	5♣	Q♦	6♠		7♠/J♠
	8♥	A♣	Q♠	9♣	K♠	7♥			
82	10♠	J♥	8♦	3♣	2♥	5♠	5♣	6♣		J♦/3♠
	A♣	Q♥	4♠	9♣	3♥	5♣			
83	A♦	5♥	6♣	4♥	4♦	6♥	5♦	3♥		7♥/4♠
	A♠	K♥	7♣	3♠	K♠	2♣			
84	9♣	J♥	J♠	7♠	2♥	K♦	6♥	7♠		10♥/J♣
	A♣	6♥	10♠	3♠	10♦	6♥			
85	3♥	4♣	A♦	Q♥	5♣	Q♦	K♦	J♥		2♣/10♠
	K♥	6♠	10♣	J♣	K♠	9♠			
86	3♠	J♥	4♠	7♥	2♥	8♥	Q♦	3♦		4♦/5♠
	A♣	J♦	9♣	J♠	8♦	Q♦			
87	10♦	3♦	3♥	6♦	6♥	5♦	8♥	Q♠		9♠/9♣
	6♠	K♣	4♥	5♠	K♠	2♠			
88	J♣	J♥	10♠	2♣	2♥	A♠	5♦	2♥		5♣/5♥
	A♣	10♥	3♠	5♠	J♠	5♦			
89	8♦	9♦	10♦	J♦	Q♠	K♦	A♠	10♦		2♠/3♠
	K♣	6♣	Q♥	5♥	K♠	8♠			
90	5♠	J♥	9♣	9♠	2♥	K♥	K♦	6♠		6♥/4♣
	A♣	4♦	J♣	5♠	4♠	K♦			
91	J♠	3♠	8♦	10♥	5♦	8♥	K♥	5♠		8♠/J♣
	6♣	A♦	6♦	4♣	K♠	2♦			
92	5♥	J♥	3♠	2♠	2♥	6♠	8♥	8♠		Q♦/3♦
	A♣	5♠	5♠	4♠	10♠	8♥			
93	4♠	7♠	J♠	4♦	K♦	A♠	6♠	J♣		2♦/5♠
	A♦	3♥	J♦	3♠	K♠	A♥			
94	4♠	J♥	J♣	8♠	2♥	K♣	A♠	K♦		5♦/9♣
	A♣	6♥	5♥	3♠	9♣	A♠			
95	10♠	7♥	4♠	5♠	8♥	K♥	K♣	K♣		A♥/5♥
	3♥	10♠	10♥	9♦	K♠	Q♣			
96	3♦	J♥	5♠	2♦	2♥	6♣	K♥	A♦		K♦/3♠
	A♣	Q♦	4♠	9♠	3♠	K♥			
97	9♣	2♠	10♠	6♥	A♥	6♠	6♠	10♦		Q♣/4♠
	10♦	8♦	4♦	3♣	K♠	Q♠			
98	9♦	J♥	5♥	A♥	2♥	A♦	6♠	7♥		8♥/7♠
	A♣	5♥	3♦	3♠	J♣	6♠			
99	3♠	9♠	9♣	Q♦	K♥	K♣	A♦	J♥		Q♠/3♦
	8♦	J♠	5♣	7♠	K♠	7♠			

Eight of Diamonds

AGE	MER	VEN	MAR	JUP	SAT	URA	NEP	LR	PLU/RES	ENV	DISP
0	K♠	3♥	A♣	Q♠	10♠	5♣	3♦	K♠	A♠/7♥	8♦	8♦
	8♥	7♠	3♠	10♦	4♣	J♥	10♠				
1	10♥	5♦	8♥	K♥	8♠	J♣	10♠	3♥	5♥/K♣	7♠	Q♠
	9♦	3♠	9♠	A♠	Q♣	10♠					
2	2♦	Q♣	3♥	5♦	4♣	7♠	J♣	A♣	9♥/10♣	J♠	10♦
	3♦	J♥	9♠	J♠	A♠	7♥					
3	6♦	3♦	5♦	9♠	K♥	9♥	5♣	Q♣	J♥/J♦	10♣	Q♣
	10♠	6♣	K♦	8♥	5♥	9♦					
4	A♣	7♦	3♠	Q♦	3♣	6♠	9♠	10♠	7♦/4♣	4♠	3♥
	6♥	10♣	K♦	10♥	K♣	9♠					
5	Q♠	7♠	Q♦	A♠	4♦	7♦	10♠	5♣	7♥/4♠	4♥	A♥
	Q♥	6♣	K♦	2♦	A♥	10♠					
6	8♥	9♦	2♣	5♦	9♥	Q♥	A♠	3♦	4♥/4♣	10♣	A♦
	8♣	2♥	K♣	10♥	5♠	A♠					
7	6♣	8♣	5♥	J♦	3♦	4♥	10♦	10♥	J♠/7♣	Q♥	2♦
	4♠	3♣	4♠	Q♠	6♥	7♦					
8	3♥	4♦	J♦	9♣	K♠	4♠	A♠	5♦	4♥/5♠	9♠	6♣
	2♦	9♥	Q♠	7♣	5♥	K♦	K♠				
9	4♠	10♣	2♣	K♦	6♠	6♥	7♦	8♥	3♠/9♠	6♦	8♠
	J♠	5♣	7♠	K♠	7♠	A♦					
10	Q♦	4♦	K♦	Q♠	6♣	J♠	10♦	K♥	5♣/10♥	3♠	K♠
	J♦	4♥	J♣	Q♣	2♣	10♦					
11	2♦	10♣	Q♠	4♣	5♠	J♦	K♠	8♠	Q♥/2♥	J♦	2♠
	6♠	K♣	3♠	2♠	K♦	9♣	5♠				
12	6♥	4♦	J♣	K♠	9♠	A♣	6♦	J♣	4♣/A♠	J♣	6♠
	J♠	10♥	Q♥	5♠	Q♠	9♠					
13	A♣	Q♠	2♦	9♠	K♥	10♠	4♦	10♠	8♠/9♦	10♥	9♠
	6♠	7♣	10♣	5♠	9♠	4♦					
14	A♦	6♠	9♠	Q♥	5♥	8♣	5♦	2♦	4♣/8♥	5♠	K♥
	Q♣	3♠	6♥	10♥	K♦						
15	4♥	7♠	3♦	2♣	4♠	Q♣	Q♥	Q♣	10♠/9♦	4♦	2♣
	7♦	10♠	9♠	5♦	9♠	K♣					
16	Q♠	7♦	2♣	J♥	3♠	10♠	2♥	3♥	J♠/3♥	5♥	A♠
	5♦	8♥	A♦	3♠	8♣	2♥					
17	9♥	K♥	J♥	K♦	4♠	A♠	10♣	5♦	Q♣/8♠	5♠	7♥
	10♥	9♦	5♥	2♦	7♠	10♣					
18	3♠	10♠	K♦	Q♦	4♣	K♠	5♠	4♠	A♣/4♦	4♣	8♥
	Q♠	7♦	5♥	8♠	J♥	3♣	4♣				
19	4♠	6♦	2♠	3♠	2♠	9♠	7♠	7♠	J♦/Q♥	6♥	7♠
	A♠	5♣	6♠	J♥	K♦	6♥					
20	A♦	2♦	10♥	9♦	8♠	A♠	3♣	J♣	6♠/4♣	3♦	K♦
	7♦	A♣	K♠	9♠	8♠	3♣					
21	K♥	7♦	9♦	Q♠	3♦	6♠	10♦	6♦	J♠/10♠	Q♦	3♣
	2♠	A♥	K♠	4♠	3♠						
22	Q♦	2♠	Q♠	10♣	Q♥	J♣	6♠	3♦	8♥/6♣	9♦	5♦
	5♥	8♣	2♥	10♠	A♠	6♠					
23	4♠	9♣	10♥	2♠	7♥	2♦	J♣	5♦	4♥/4♣	5♦	9♦
	J♠	8♣	Q♠	6♣	3♦	7♠					
24	A♥	10♣	2♠	9♥	K♦	J♠	5♦	9♠	8♠/7♣	3♣	Q♦
	6♠	3♠	Q♥	3♠	A♠	5♦					

AGE	MER	VEN	MAR	JUP	SAT	URA	NEP	LR	PLU/RES	ENV	DISP
25	6♦	9♣	9♥	A♦	J♥	6♠	J♣	K♥	A♣/J♦	K♦	3♦
	10♥	4♦	7♠	3♦	8♥	J♣					
26	Q♠	6♥	7♥	8♣	K♣	2♣	A♦	9♥	3♣/5♣	7♠	6♥
	A♥	5♦	A♠	4♦	10♣	4♥					
27	3♦	A♠	8♠	8♠	K♥	A♥	K♦	5♣	4♣/9♦	8♥	4♣
	J♥	6♠	8♥	6♦	9♣	6♠					
28	10♣	J♠	J♦	7♦	Q♣	J♥	8♠	A♣	4♦/2♥	7♥	5♣
	K♠	3♦	10♥	9♥	6♥	Q♦					
29	9♣	A♦	7♦	2♣	Q♥	7♥	3♥	7♣	10♠/3♠	A♠	5♥
	6♠	6♦	9♥	2♥	Q♠	3♥					
30	6♥	J♠	9♦	4♣	6♣	6♠	2♣	3♠	K♠/7♠	2♣	4♦
	Q♣	7♦	2♠	3♠	7♦	A♣					
31	J♥	A♦	4♣	A♣	5♠	J♦	4♥	Q♦	4♠/3♣	K♥	5♠
	7♥	2♠	3♦	9♠	3♠	Q♠					
32	2♠	5♦	8♥	7♠	9♠	10♣	J♦	3♣	Q♣/9♥	9♠	10♥
	10♠	7♠	A♠	K♠	Q♦	6♦					
33	3♠	5♠	4♣	5♦	Q♠	2♦	10♣	6♠	9♦/4♦	6♠	J♣
	4♠	6♣	10♥	9♥	2♥	10♣					
34	A♦	4♠	5♦	5♥	7♠	9♦	3♥	9♠	6♠/2♠	2♠	J♦
	J♣	7♥	8♠	2♥	4♣	3♥					
35	7♦	8♠	10♥	2♠	J♠	J♣	5♥	Q♠	3♦/K♦	K♣	3♠
	6♠	9♣	J♥	3♥	K♣	5♣					
36	A♥	4♣	2♠	8♥	K♥	2♣	J♣	7♠	Q♥/4♦	8♠	6♦
	9♦	6♥	9♠	3♥	K♣	J♣					
37	3♣	A♠	5♦	5♣	J♦	3♠	2♣	Q♦	A♦/8♣	6♠	9♣
	6♦	K♠	A♠	9♦	7♦	7♥					
38	3♥	2♦	K♠	2♠	A♠	K♠	Q♠	A♠	3♠/10♥	2♦	Q♥
	4♠	5♥	9♠	8♠	2♥	9♦					
39	J♦	5♠	5♦	9♦	9♥	9♣	J♥	4♦	J♠/7♠	A♦	10♠
	A♦	Q♦	3♦	4♠	6♣	J♠					
40	3♠	A♠	9♦	9♠	7♥	J♠	10♦	7♦	A♥/K♠	A♥	4♥
	A♦	5♥	4♠	7♠	5♦	8♠					
41	6♦	A♥	9♠	8♠	K♣	5♣	J♣	10♠	3♦/10♠	3♥	4♠
	Q♦	9♥	2♥	J♦	9♣	J♣					
42	Q♣	K♠	2♠	A♠	A♦	10♠	5♠	8♥	5♣/7♠	Q♣	10♠
	K♥	6♥	Q♦	3♠	5♥	J♦	A♦				
43	8♠	Q♥	J♠	J♦	3♥	2♠	2♦	9♠	6♣/6♥	10♦	J♠
	2♣	4♣	K♥	6♠	Q♠	2♦					
44	9♦	10♦	J♦	Q♦	K♦	A♠	2♠	2♣	3♠/4♠	Q♠	7♣
	A♦	7♣	K♥	6♥	9♠	2♠					
45	K♠	3♥	2♥	Q♣	10♠	5♣	3♦	5♥	A♠/7♥	8♦	8♦
	8♥	7♠	3♠	10♦	4♣	J♥	10♠				
46	10♥	5♦	8♥	K♥	8♠	J♣	10♠	9♥	5♥/K♣	7♠	Q♠
	9♦	3♠	9♠	A♠	Q♣	10♠					
47	2♦	Q♣	3♥	5♦	4♣	7♠	J♣	Q♥	7♦/10♣	J♠	10♦
	3♦	J♥	9♣	J♠	A♠	7♥					
48	6♦	3♦	5♦	9♠	K♥	7♥	5♣	A♠	J♥/J♦	10♠	Q♣
	10♠	6♣	K♦	8♥	5♥	9♦					
49	2♥	7♠	3♠	Q♦	3♠	6♠	9♠	6♦	9♥/4♠	4♠	3♥
	6♦	10♣	K♦	10♥	K♣	9♠					

Left table

AGE	MER	VEN	MAR	JUP	SAT	URA	NEP	LR	PLU/RES	ENV	DISP
50	Q♠	7♠	Q♦	A♠	4♦	9♥	10♠	8♣	7♥/4♠	4♥	A♥
	Q♥	6♣	K♦	2♦	A♥	10♠					
51	8♥	9♦	2♣	5♥	7♦	Q♥	A♠	5♥	4♥/4♣	10♠	A♦
	8♣	A♠	K♣	10♥	5♣	A♠					
52	6♦	8♣	5♥	J♦	3♦	4♦	10♦	J♦	J♠/7♣	Q♥	2♦
	4♦	3♣	K♠	Q♠	6♣	9♥					
53	3♥	4♦	J♦	9♣	K♠	4♠	2♥	3♦	4♥/5♠	9♣	6♣
	2♦	7♦	Q♠	7♣	5♥	K♦	K♠				
54	4♠	10♣	2♣	K♦	6♠	6♥	9♥	4♥	3♠/9♦	6♦	8♠
	J♠	5♣	7♠	K♠	7♣	A♥					
55	Q♦	4♦	K♦	Q♠	6♣	J♠	10♦	10♦	5♣/10♥	3♠	K♣
	J♦	4♥	J♣	Q♣	2♣	10♦					
56	2♦	10♣	Q♠	4♣	5♠	J♦	K♠	3♥	Q♥/A♣	J♦	2♠
	6♠	K♣	3♣	2♣	K♦	9♣	5♠				
57	6♥	4♦	J♣	K♠	9♣	2♥	6♦	4♦	4♣/A♠	J♠	6♠
	J♠	10♥	Q♥	5♠	Q♠	9♠					
58	2♥	Q♠	2♦	9♠	K♥	10♠	4♦	J♦	8♣/9♦	10♥	9♠
	6♠	7♣	10♣	5♠	9♣	4♦					
59	A♦	6♠	9♠	Q♥	5♥	8♣	5♦	9♣	4♣/8♥	5♠	K♥
	Q♣	3♠	6♥	10♥	K♣	5♦					
60	4♥	7♠	3♦	2♣	4♠	Q♣	Q♥	K♠	10♣/9♦	4♦	2♣
	9♥	10♠	9♣	5♦	9♠	K♠					
61	Q♠	9♥	2♣	J♥	3♣	10♠	A♣	4♠	J♠/3♥	5♥	A♠
	5♦	8♥	A♦	3♠	8♠	A♣					
62	7♦	K♥	J♥	K♦	4♠	2♥	10♣	A♣	Q♣/8♠	5♣	7♥
	10♥	9♦	5♥	2♦	7♠	10♣					
63	3♠	10♠	K♦	Q♦	4♣	K♠	5♠	4♠	2♥/4♦	4♣	8♥
	Q♠	7♥	5♥	8♠	J♥	3♣	4♣				
64	4♠	6♦	2♠	3♣	2♠	9♣	7♠	10♣	J♦/Q♥	6♥	7♠
	A♠	5♣	6♣	J♥	K♦	6♥					
65	A♦	2♦	10♥	9♠	8♣	A♠	3♠	2♣	6♠/4♣	3♦	K♦
	9♥	2♥	K♣	9♠	8♠	3♠					
66	K♥	9♥	9♦	Q♠	3♦	6♠	10♦	K♦	J♠/10♠	Q♦	3♣
	2♠	A♥	K♣	4♣	3♣	3♠					
67	Q♠	2♠	Q♠	10♣	Q♥	J♣	6♠	6♠	8♥/6♠	9♦	5♦
	5♥	8♣	A♣	10♠	A♠	6♠					
68	4♠	9♣	10♥	2♠	7♥	2♦	J♣	6♥	4♥/4♦	5♦	9♠
	J♠	8♠	Q♣	6♣	3♦	7♠					
69	A♥	10♣	2♠	7♦	K♦	J♠	5♦	7♦	8♠/7♣	3♣	Q♦
	6♠	3♠	Q♥	3♦	A♠	5♦					
70	6♦	9♣	7♦	A♦	J♥	6♠	J♣	Q♦	2♥/J♦	K♦	3♦
	10♥	4♦	7♠	3♦	8♥	J♣					
71	Q♠	6♥	7♥	8♣	K♣	2♣	A♦	4♦	3♣/5♦	7♠	6♥
	A♥	5♦	A♠	4♦	10♣	4♥					
72	3♦	A♠	8♣	8♠	K♥	A♥	K♦	K♦	4♣/9♦	8♥	4♣
	J♥	6♠	8♥	6♦	9♣	6♠					
73	10♣	J♣	J♦	9♥	Q♣	J♥	8♠	Q♠	4♦/A♣	7♥	5♠
	K♠	3♦	10♥	7♦	6♥	Q♦					
74	9♣	A♦	9♥	2♣	Q♥	7♥	3♥	6♠	10♠/3♠	A♠	5♥
	6♠	6♦	7♦	A♣	Q♠	3♥					

Right table

AGE	MER	VEN	MAR	JUP	SAT	URA	NEP	LR	PLU/RES	ENV	DISP
75	6♥	J♣	9♦	4♣	6♣	6♠	2♣	J♠	K♠/7♠	2♣	4♦
	Q♣	7♣	2♠	3♠	9♥	2♥					
76	J♥	A♦	4♣	2♥	5♣	J♦	4♥	10♦	4♠/3♣	K♥	5♠
	7♥	2♠	3♦	9♣	3♠	Q♠					
77	2♣	5♦	8♥	7♠	9♣	10♣	J♦	2♦	Q♣/7♦	9♠	10♥
	10♠	7♣	A♠	K♣	Q♦	6♦					
78	3♠	5♣	4♣	5♦	Q♠	2♦	10♣	10♠	9♦/4♣	6♠	J♣
	4♠	6♣	10♥	7♦	A♣	10♣					
79	A♦	4♣	5♦	5♥	7♠	9♦	3♥	Q♠	6♣/2♠	2♠	J♦
	J♣	7♥	8♣	A♣	4♣	3♥					
80	9♥	8♠	10♥	2♠	J♠	J♣	5♥	4♣	3♦/K♦	K♣	3♠
	6♠	9♣	J♥	3♥	K♣	5♠					
81	A♥	4♠	2♠	8♥	K♥	2♠	J♣	5♠	Q♥/4♦	8♠	6♦
	9♦	6♥	9♠	3♥	K♣	J♠					
82	3♣	2♥	5♦	5♠	J♦	3♠	2♠	J♦	A♦/8♣	6♠	9♣
	6♦	K♠	A♠	9♦	9♥	7♥					
83	3♥	2♠	K♠	2♠	2♥	K♣	Q♠	K♠	3♠/10♥	2♦	Q♥
	4♠	5♥	9♠	8♣	A♣	9♦					
84	J♦	5♠	5♦	9♦	7♦	9♣	J♥	6♥	J♠/7♠	A♦	10♠
	A♦	Q♦	3♦	4♠	6♣	J♣					
85	3♠	A♠	9♦	9♠	7♥	J♠	10♦	4♦	A♥/K♠	A♥	4♥
	A♦	5♥	4♠	7♠	5♦	8♠					
86	6♦	A♦	9♠	8♠	K♣	5♠	J♣	J♣	3♦/10♠	3♥	4♠
	Q♦	7♦	A♣	J♦	9♠	♣					
87	Q♣	K♠	2♦	2♥	A♦	10♣	5♠	K♣	5♣/7♠	Q♣	10♠
	K♥	6♥	Q♦	3♠	5♥	J♦	A♦				
88	8♣	Q♥	J♠	J♦	3♥	2♠	2♦	9♠	6♣/6♥	10♦	J♠
	2♣	4♠	K♥	6♠	Q♠	2♦					
89	9♠	10♦	J♦	Q♦	K♦	A♠	2♠	A♠	3♠/4♠	Q♠	7♠
	A♦	7♣	K♥	6♥	9♠	2♠					
90	K♠	3♥	A♠	Q♣	10♠	5♣	3♦	6♦	A♠/7♥	8♦	8♦
	8♥	7♠	3♠	10♦	4♣	J♥	10♠				
91	10♥	5♦	8♥	K♥	8♠	J♣	10♠	A♣	5♥/K♣	7♣	Q♠
	9♦	3♠	9♠	A♠	Q♣	10♠					
92	2♦	Q♣	3♥	5♦	4♣	7♠	J♣	Q♠	9♥/10♠	J♠	10♦
	3♦	J♥	9♣	J♠	A♠	7♥					
93	6♠	3♦	5♦	9♠	K♥	9♥	5♠	2♦	J♥/J♦	10♣	Q♣
	10♠	6♣	K♦	8♥	5♥	9♦					
94	A♣	7♣	3♠	Q♦	3♣	6♠	9♠	9♠	7♦/4♣	4♠	3♥
	6♦	10♣	K♦	10♥	K♣	9♠					
95	Q♠	7♠	Q♦	A♠	4♦	7♠	10♠	K♥	7♥/4♠	4♥	A♥
	Q♥	6♣	K♦	2♦	A♥	10♠					
96	8♥	9♦	2♣	5♥	9♥	Q♥	A♠	10♠	4♥/4♣	10♠	A♦
	8♣	2♥	K♣	10♥	5♣	A♠					
97	6♦	8♣	5♥	J♦	3♦	4♦	10♦	4♦	J♠/7♣	Q♥	2♦
	4♦	3♣	K♠	Q♠	6♣	7♦					
98	3♥	4♦	J♦	9♣	K♠	4♠	A♣	A♦	4♥/5♠	9♣	6♣
	2♦	9♥	Q♠	7♣	5♥	K♦	K♠				
99	4♠	10♣	2♣	K♦	6♠	6♥	7♥	6♠	3♠/9♦	6♦	8♠
	J♠	5♣	7♠	K♠	7♣	A♦					

Nine of Diamonds

AGE	MER	VEN	MAR	JUP	SAT	URA	NEP	LR	PLU/RES	ENV	DISP
0	7♠	2♣	K♣	J♦	4♥	4♠	2♠	7♠	8♥/6♣	9♣	9♦
	3♣	10♥	6♥	5♠	Q♣	10♣					
1	5♣	K♦	J♦	7♦	J♠	3♣	8♦	2♣	10♥/5♦	5♦	Q♣
	3♠	9♠	A♠	Q♣	10♠	8♦					
2	K♥	2♣	7♦	5♥	J♥	3♠	2♠	K♣	2♥/6♠	3♣	3♦
	K♣	6♣	10♣	Q♣	4♠	2♠					
3	Q♥	3♥	4♥	8♣	J♣	Q♥	5♦	J♦	7♣/A♦	K♦	6♥
	5♣	8♦	10♠	6♣	K♦	8♥					
4	Q♣	10♠	8♣	10♥	9♣	5♠	J♠	4♥	A♥/Q♠	7♠	4♣
	J♥	3♠	4♠	K♥	2♣	5♠					
5	K♦	2♠	6♠	9♥	6♥	J♥	10♥	4♦	6♣/A♠	8♥	5♣
	K♠	Q♣	K♣	7♦	3♥	10♦					
6	2♣	5♥	9♥	Q♥	A♠	4♥	4♣	2♠	7♥/9♠	7♥	5♦
	3♠	K♥	7♦	A♣	Q♦	4♣					
7	3♥	2♠	Q♠	A♥	5♠	3♠	Q♥	5♠	K♠/10♣	A♠	4♦
	6♥	5♦	J♦	9♠	9♥	2♥					
8	J♥	5♥	A♥	2♥	A♠	6♠	8♥	K♦	7♠/7♣	2♠	5♠
	4♥	J♦	Q♣	2♠	9♠	Q♦					
9	Q♥	8♦	4♠	10♣	2♠	K♦	6♠	J♦	6♥/7♦	K♥	10♥
	7♥	5♦	10♠	J♠	10♥	K♥					
10	9♠	8♠	A♥	8♦	Q♦	4♦	K♦	7♦	Q♠/6♠	9♠	J♠
	7♠	5♠	K♣	7♦	A♣	K♦					
11	5♥	7♠	8♦	2♦	10♣	Q♠	4♣	J♠	5♠/J♦	6♠	J♦
	2♠	4♥	8♣	A♠	A♥	4♣					
12	9♥	10♥	K♣	J♦	3♣	2♠	2♦	3♣	Q♣/J♠	2♠	3♠
	3♠	2♣	J♥	4♣	J♠	A♦					
13	5♣	7♠	J♦	4♠	9♣	Q♥	2♠	8♦	A♠/6♠	K♣	6♦
	Q♠	3♥	6♦	4♣	J♠	2♠					
14	7♠	2♥	8♦	A♦	6♠	9♠	Q♥	K♥	5♥/8♣	8♠	9♣
	K♥	K♠	10♠	Q♠	9♥	4♥					
15	4♣	4♦	K♠	J♦	2♥	J♣	Q♦	2♣	9♠/K♠	6♠	Q♥
	7♠	2♦	6♦	8♠	A♣	Q♠					
16	6♠	8♠	8♦	Q♠	7♦	2♣	J♥	7♦	3♣/10♠	2♦	10♠
	5♥	10♦	Q♣	7♠	5♠	2♠					
17	9♠	10♠	Q♠	6♦	4♥	3♣	3♦	5♥	5♣/K♠	A♠	4♥
	5♥	2♦	7♠	10♣	8♦	10♥					
18	K♥	5♥	6♦	10♥	J♣	A♦	8♠	J♥	Q♣/7♥	A♥	4♣
	10♦	7♦	A♣	6♠	2♠	2♠					
19	6♥	K♠	4♦	2♥	5♥	K♦	8♠	3♠	A♦/10♣	3♥	10♠
	9♣	3♥	10♦	9♠	2♦	6♠	5♥				
20	8♣	A♠	3♣	6♠	4♣	J♦	4♦	2♠	5♠/3♥	Q♣	J♠
	Q♥	A♥	9♣	3♠	Q♦	4♦					
21	Q♠	3♦	6♠	10♠	J♠	10♠	J♦	Q♦	9♠/7♠	10♦	7♠
	5♥	9♠	9♠	3♥	6♦	J♦					
22	K♠	4♦	A♣	6♥	7♥	A♦	Q♠	3♥	10♠/4♥	Q♠	8♦
	4♠	10♣	9♠	3♦	A♥	J♥	7♥				
23	K♣	8♦	4♠	9♠	10♥	2♠	7♥	4♥	2♦/J♠	8♦	Q♠
	Q♠	9♠	6♦	10♠	6♥	7♥					
24	4♦	6♥	4♣	8♦	A♥	10♣	2♠	8♠	9♥/K♦	7♣	10♦
	Q♣	J♥	2♠	3♣	10♠	4♥					

AGE	MER	VEN	MAR	JUP	SAT	URA	NEP	LR	PLU/RES	ENV	DISP
25	K♥	Q♣	8♦	6♦	9♠	9♥	A♠	J♣	J♥/6♦	J♠	Q♣
	7♥	5♠	J♠	4♠	2♠	Q♠					
26	A♣	5♦	9♠	10♦	7♠	3♠	6♦	Q♥	7♦/A♥	10♣	3♥
	K♥	K♦	J♠	K♣	J♠	6♦					
27	Q♦	10♣	10♦	10♠	6♣	7♦	7♥	5♥	4♥/7♠	4♠	A♥
	A♠	5♠	J♠	4♦	5♠	7♥					
28	4♠	Q♠	Q♥	2♦	9♥	A♠	10♠	Q♠	8♥/A♥	4♥	A♦
	8♣	2♥	J♠	K♣	A♦	10♠					
29	K♥	8♠	2♦	6♠	Q♣	8♥	3♦	10♠	3♣/5♦	10♠	2♦
	6♣	7♣	K♣	Q♦	5♠	7♥					
30	4♣	6♣	6♠	2♣	K♣	7♠	A♣	8♠	8♥/8♣	Q♥	6♣
	4♦	9♥	Q♦	5♦	2♦	J♠	K♠				
31	7♠	K♦	Q♥	J♠	3♠	3♥	7♦	10♥	9♠/6♦	9♣	8♠
	3♣	A♦	10♣	K♠	5♦	5♥					
32	10♦	6♠	J♠	Q♦	5♠	3♣	3♦	9♣	A♦/K♣	6♦	K♣
	6♠	8♥	2♠	6♥	Q♥	3♦					
33	4♠	K♦	Q♦	A♥	8♠	6♠	K♠	5♠	A♠/2♥	3♠	2♠
	3♠	J♣	7♣	Q♥	J♠	2♠	8♠				
34	3♥	6♠	2♠	K♠	2♠	A♠	K♥	J♠	A♥/10♠	J♦	6♠
	3♣	K♠	A♠	8♠	Q♦	6♦					
35	A♣	Q♦	4♦	6♦	9♣	7♥	6♣	K♦	8♣/Q♣	J♣	9♠
	3♠	5♦	K♦	8♠	2♣	6♠					
36	5♥	3♠	6♦	A♠	2♦	8♣	8♦	2♠	A♥/4♣	10♥	K♥
	6♥	9♠	3♥	K♣	J♣	8♦					
37	8♥	10♣	Q♣	Q♥	7♠	6♥	A♠	6♠	K♦/Q♠	5♠	2♣
	7♦	7♥	2♣	8♦	6♦	K♠					
38	Q♦	7♥	Q♥	J♥	7♠	K♦	2♥	9♥	3♣/4♠	4♦	A♠
	8♦	4♠	5♥	9♠	8♠	2♥					
39	9♥	9♣	J♥	J♠	7♠	A♠	K♦	6♥	6♥/10♥	5♥	7♥
	K♣	Q♠	2♦	4♦	10♣	K♦					
40	9♠	7♥	J♠	10♦	A♥	K♠	8♠	J♥	A♠/6♠	5♠	8♥
	Q♦	4♥	2♦	10♥	J♥	7♣	A♥				
41	7♠	K♥	Q♥	7♣	J♦	2♠	5♦	10♥	6♠/A♣	4♠	7♠
	10♠	A♦	5♠	J♥	J♠	3♥					
42	5♥	4♦	K♣	Q♠	8♠	10♠	7♠	2♣	3♠/A♥	6♥	K♦
	7♦	A♣	J♠	6♦	10♥	7♠					
43	9♠	7♦	Q♠	Q♦	Q♣	3♠	3♦	5♥	3♣/7♥	3♦	3♠
	J♦	5♣	J♠	A♥	7♣	9♠					
44	10♦	J♦	Q♦	K♦	A♠	2♠	3♠	9♥	4♠/5♠	Q♦	5♦
	2♦	8♣	2♥	7♥	10♠	3♠					
45	7♣	2♠	K♣	J♦	4♥	4♦	2♠	Q♥	8♥/6♦	9♦	9♣
	3♣	10♥	6♥	5♠	Q♣	10♣					
46	5♣	K♦	J♦	9♥	J♠	3♠	8♠	A♠	10♥/5♦	5♦	Q♦
	3♠	9♠	A♠	Q♣	10♠	8♦					
47	K♥	2♠	9♥	5♥	J♥	3♠	2♠	4♥	A♣/6♠	3♠	3♦
	K♣	6♣	10♣	Q♣	4♠	2♠					
48	Q♦	3♥	4♥	8♣	J♣	Q♥	5♦	4♣	7♣/A♦	K♦	6♥
	5♠	8♦	10♠	6♣	K♦	8♥					
49	Q♣	10♠	8♣	10♥	9♠	5♠	J♠	3♥	A♥/Q♠	7♠	4♣
	J♥	3♠	4♠	K♥	2♠	5♠					

AGE	MER	VEN	MAR	JUP	SAT	URA	NEP	LR	PLU/RES	ENV	DISP
50	K♦	2♠	6♠	7♦	6♥	J♥	10♥	2♠	6♣/2♥	8♥	5♣
	K♠	Q♣	K♣	9♥	3♥	10♦					
51	2♠	5♥	7♦	Q♥	A♠	4♥	4♣	Q♠	7♥/9♠	7♥	5♥
	3♠	K♥	9♥	2♥	Q♦	4♣					
52	3♥	2♠	Q♠	A♥	5♠	3♠	Q♥	A♥	K♠/10♣	A♠	4♦
	6♥	5♦	J♦	9♠	7♦	A♣					
53	J♥	5♥	A♥	A♣	A♦	6♠	8♥	5♠	7♠/7♣	2♣	5♠
	4♥	J♦	Q♣	2♠	9♠	Q♦					
54	Q♥	8♦	4♠	10♣	2♣	K♦	6♠	3♠	6♥/9♥	K♥	10♥
	7♠	5♦	10♠	J♣	10♦	K♥					
55	9♠	8♠	A♥	8♦	Q♦	4♦	K♦	Q♥	Q♠/6♣	9♠	J♣
	7♠	5♠	K♣	9♥	2♥	K♦					
56	5♥	7♠	8♠	2♦	10♣	Q♠	4♣	J♥	5♠/J♦	6♠	J♦
	2♠	4♥	8♠	2♥	A♥	4♣					
57	7♦	10♥	K♣	J♦	3♣	2♠	2♦	5♥	Q♣/J♠	2♠	3♠
	3♠	2♣	J♥	4♣	J♠	A♦					
58	5♠	7♠	J♦	4♠	9♣	Q♥	2♠	A♥	A♠/6♣	K♣	6♦
	Q♠	3♥	6♦	4♣	J♣	2♠					
59	7♣	A♣	8♦	A♦	6♠	9♠	Q♥	2♥	5♥/8♣	8♠	9♣
	K♥	K♠	10♠	Q♠	7♦	4♥					
60	4♣	4♦	K♠	J♦	A♣	J♣	Q♦	A♦	9♠/K♣	6♣	Q♥
	7♠	2♦	6♦	8♣	2♥	Q♠					
61	6♠	8♠	8♦	Q♠	9♥	2♣	J♥	6♠	3♣/10♣	2♦	10♠
	5♥	10♦	Q♣	7♠	5♠	2♠					
62	9♠	10♠	Q♠	6♦	4♥	3♣	3♦	8♥	5♣/K♠	A♦	4♥
	5♥	2♦	7♠	10♣	8♦	10♥					
63	K♥	5♥	6♦	10♥	J♣	A♦	2♠	Q♥	Q♣/7♥	A♥	4♠
	10♦	9♥	2♥	6♠	2♣	2♠					
64	6♥	K♠	4♦	A♣	5♥	K♦	8♠	8♦	A♦/10♣	3♥	10♣
	9♣	3♥	10♦	9♠	2♦	6♠	5♥				
65	8♣	A♠	3♣	6♠	4♣	J♦	4♦	4♣	5♠/3♥	Q♣	J♠
	Q♥	A♥	9♣	3♠	Q♦	4♦					
66	Q♠	3♦	6♠	10♦	J♠	10♠	J♦	10♣	9♠/7♠	10♦	7♣
	5♥	5♦	9♣	3♥	6♦	J♦					
67	K♠	4♣	2♥	6♥	7♥	A♦	Q♣	2♣	10♠/4♥	Q♠	8♦
	4♠	10♣	9♠	3♦	A♥	J♥	7♠				
68	K♣	8♦	4♠	9♣	10♥	2♠	7♥	K♦	2♦/J♣	8♦	Q♠
	Q♠	9♠	6♦	10♠	6♥	7♥					
69	4♦	6♥	4♣	8♦	A♥	10♣	2♠	6♠	7♦/K♦	7♠	10♦
	Q♣	J♥	2♣	3♣	10♠	4♥					
70	K♥	Q♣	8♣	6♦	9♣	7♦	A♦	9♠	J♥/6♠	J♠	Q♣
	7♥	5♠	J♠	4♠	2♦	Q♠					
71	2♥	5♦	9♣	10♦	7♠	3♠	6♦	8♠	9♥/A♥	10♣	3♥
	K♥	K♦	J♠	K♣	J♣	6♦					
72	Q♦	10♠	10♦	10♠	6♣	9♥	7♥	A♥	4♥/7♠	4♠	A♥
	A♠	5♠	J♠	4♦	5♣	7♥					
73	4♠	Q♠	Q♥	2♦	7♦	A♠	10♠	8♦	8♥/A♥	4♥	A♦
	8♣	A♣	J♠	K♣	A♦	10♠					
74	K♥	8♣	2♦	6♠	Q♣	8♥	3♦	Q♦	3♣/5♦	10♠	2♦
	6♣	7♣	K♠	Q♦	5♠	9♥					
75	4♣	6♣	6♠	2♣	K♠	7♠	2♥	4♦	8♥/8♠	Q♥	6♣
	4♦	7♦	Q♦	5♦	2♦	J♠	K♠				
76	7♠	K♦	Q♥	J♠	3♠	3♥	9♥	K♦	9♠/6♦	9♣	8♠
	3♣	A♦	10♠	K♠	5♦	5♥					
77	10♦	6♣	J♠	Q♦	5♠	3♣	3♦	5♥	A♦/K♣	6♦	K♣
	6♠	8♥	2♠	6♥	Q♥	3♦					
78	4♦	K♦	Q♦	A♥	8♠	6♠	K♠	7♠	A♠/A♣	3♠	2♠
	3♠	J♣	7♠	Q♥	J♠	2♣	8♠				
79	3♥	6♣	2♠	K♠	2♠	2♥	K♥	8♦	A♥/10♠	J♦	6♠
	3♣	K♣	A♠	8♠	Q♦	6♦					
80	2♥	Q♦	4♦	6♦	9♣	7♥	6♣	2♦	8♣/Q♠	J♣	9♠
	3♠	5♦	K♦	8♠	2♣	6♣					
81	5♥	3♠	6♦	A♠	2♦	8♣	8♦	10♣	A♥/4♠	10♥	K♥
	6♥	9♠	3♥	K♣	J♣	8♦					
82	8♥	10♣	Q♣	Q♥	7♠	6♥	A♠	Q♠	K♦/Q♣	5♠	2♠
	9♥	7♦	2♠	8♦	6♦	K♠					
83	Q♦	9♥	Q♥	J♥	7♣	K♦	A♣	4♠	3♣/4♣	4♦	A♠
	8♦	4♠	5♥	9♠	8♣	A♣					
84	7♦	9♠	J♥	J♠	7♠	2♥	K♦	9♥	6♥/10♥	5♥	7♥
	K♣	Q♠	2♦	4♦	10♣	K♦					
85	9♠	7♥	J♠	10♦	A♥	K♠	8♠	10♥	2♥/6♣	5♣	8♥
	Q♦	4♥	2♦	10♥	J♥	7♣	A♥				
86	7♠	K♥	Q♥	7♣	J♦	2♣	5♦	K♣	6♠/A♠	4♣	7♠
	10♠	A♦	5♠	J♥	J♠	3♥					
87	5♥	4♦	K♣	Q♠	8♣	10♠	7♣	J♦	3♠/A♥	6♥	K♦
	9♥	2♥	J♣	6♦	10♥	7♣					
88	9♣	9♥	Q♠	Q♦	Q♣	3♠	3♦	3♣	3♣/7♥	3♦	3♠
	J♦	5♣	J♠	A♥	7♣	9♠					
89	10♦	J♦	Q♦	K♦	A♠	2♠	3♠	Q♠	4♠/5♠	Q♦	5♦
	2♦	8♣	A♣	7♦	10♠	3♠					
90	7♠	2♠	K♣	J♦	4♥	4♦	2♠	2♦	8♥/6♣	9♦	9♦
	3♦	10♥	6♥	5♠	Q♣	10♣					
91	5♣	K♦	J♦	7♦	J♠	3♣	8♦	5♠	10♥/5♦	5♦	Q♦
	3♠	9♠	A♠	Q♣	10♠	8♦					
92	K♥	2♣	7♦	5♥	J♥	3♠	2♠	7♠	2♥/6♠	3♣	3♦
	K♣	6♣	10♣	Q♠	4♠	2♠					
93	Q♦	3♦	4♥	8♣	J♣	Q♥	5♥	J♦	7♣/A♦	K♦	6♥
	5♣	8♦	10♠	6♣	K♦	8♥					
94	Q♣	10♠	8♠	10♥	9♣	5♣	J♠	4♠	A♥/Q♠	7♠	4♠
	J♥	3♠	4♠	K♥	2♣	5♠					
95	K♦	2♠	6♠	9♥	6♥	J♥	10♥	9♣	6♣/A♣	8♥	5♣
	K♠	Q♣	K♣	7♦	3♥	10♦					
96	2♣	5♥	9♥	Q♥	A♠	4♥	4♣	Q♥	7♥/9♠	7♥	5♥
	3♠	K♥	7♦	A♠	Q♦	4♣					
97	3♥	2♠	Q♠	A♥	5♠	3♠	Q♥	2♠	K♠/10♣	A♠	4♦
	6♥	5♦	J♦	9♠	9♥	2♥					
98	J♥	5♥	A♥	2♥	A♦	6♠	8♥	7♠	7♠/7♣	2♣	5♠
	4♥	J♦	Q♣	2♠	9♠	Q♦					
99	Q♥	8♦	4♠	10♣	2♣	K♦	6♠	2♥	6♥/7♦	K♥	10♥
	7♥	5♦	10♠	J♣	10♦	K♥					

Ten of Diamonds

AGE	MER	VEN	MAR	JUP	SAT	URA	NEP	LR	PLU/RES	ENV	DISP
0	8♠	A♥	A♦	Q♦	5♥	3♣	3♠	8♠	9♥/7♣	10♦	10♦
	4♠	J♥	10♠	8♦	8♥	7♠					
1	Q♥	4♣	Q♦	2♣	A♠	9♥	4♦	A♥	J♥/6♦	Q♠	Q♣
	4♠	K♠	5♦	K♦	5♠	3♦					
2	A♣	Q♠	9♣	6♥	9♥	K♥	2♣	A♦	7♦/5♥	8♦	3♥
	Q♥	7♣	5♦	J♦	6♠	2♣					
3	Q♣	3♣	6♥	8♥	10♥	7♦	4♠	Q♥	7♠/J♠	7♣	A♥
	4♥	K♣	5♦	8♠	2♦	A♠					
4	K♦	3♣	7♥	5♠	9♥	4♥	8♥	5♥	10♠/5♥	J♠	A♦
	8♣	2♥	6♠	J♦	4♦	8♥					
5	Q♥	8♣	5♠	6♦	4♣	10♣	3♥	3♣	8♦/Q♠	10♣	2♦
	10♥	9♦	K♠	Q♠	K♣	7♦					
6	A♦	10♥	6♦	10♠	K♠	J♠	A♣	3♠	10♣/J♠	4♠	6♣
	8♠	9♥	Q♣	Q♠	5♠	5♦	K♠				
7	J♠	7♣	7♥	5♦	K♥	5♣	7♦	Q♥	9♣/2♣	4♥	8♠
	8♦	4♦	8♣	K♣	Q♠	3♣					
8	6♥	10♥	5♣	Q♣	K♣	8♦	3♥	4♣	4♦/J♦	10♠	K♣
	6♦	10♣	3♠	A♥	7♥	3♥					
9	8♠	7♣	Q♣	5♥	J♣	6♦	K♠	Q♦	4♥/2♥	Q♥	2♠
	K♥	6♠	9♦	7♥	5♦	10♠	J♣				
10	5♣	10♥	3♠	K♠	10♠	A♣	Q♥	2♣	5♥/8♥	9♣	6♠
	8♣	J♦	4♥	J♣	Q♣	2♣					
11	A♣	Q♠	8♣	2♣	A♠	4♠	10♥	A♠	8♠/3♦	6♦	9♠
	K♥	Q♠	7♠	J♣	10♠	10♥					
12	6♣	K♥	2♠	4♥	5♠	8♣	Q♦	9♥	5♥/K♦	3♠	K♥
	A♥	9♣	5♠	J♦	6♠	Q♦					
13	10♣	3♣	4♠	7♥	J♠	A♥	4♥	4♦	7♠/3♦	J♦	2♣
	7♦	4♠	10♠	Q♦	2♣	K♠					
14	Q♣	7♥	7♥	J♥	9♦	7♣	2♥	A♠	8♦/A♦	J♣	A♠
	Q♦	K♦	9♣	6♠	8♦	2♥					
15	9♥	A♠	J♥	5♦	J♠	A♠	7♣	Q♠	A♥/2♠	10♥	7♥
	J♦	3♦	5♠	8♠	3♣	7♣					
16	9♣	4♠	5♠	6♥	5♥	K♠	J♣	9♣	A♣/10♥	5♠	8♥
	Q♣	7♠	5♠	2♠	J♥	9♦	5♥				
17	J♠	Q♥	7♥	9♠	10♠	10♥	Q♠	6♥	6♦/4♥	4♦	7♠
	8♥	4♦	K♣	J♥	5♦	5♣					
18	6♣	8♠	J♦	3♦	8♣	8♥	9♦	9♦	K♥/5♥	5♥	K♦
	7♦	A♠	6♠	2♣	2♠	J♥					
19	A♠	7♦	3♦	Q♠	4♣	K♥	3♥	K♥	8♦/4♠	5♠	3♣
	9♠	2♦	6♠	5♥	9♦	9♣					
20	6♥	9♠	Q♣	7♠	4♥	3♠	K♥	2♣	K♦/K♠	4♠	5♦
	5♠	8♣	2♥	4♠	8♥	K♥					
21	J♠	10♠	J♦	9♠	7♠	8♠	3♠	Q♣	10♣/10♥	6♥	9♠
	8♦	8♠	A♥	K♠	4♠	3♠					
22	2♦	7♣	9♠	9♥	5♦	8♦	Q♦	3♣	2♠/Q♠	3♦	Q♦
	K♥	9♣	4♥	4♣	8♥	Q♦					
23	Q♥	10♠	9♠	6♦	J♥	K♥	3♠	6♥	A♠/6♦	Q♦	3♦
	J♦	10♠	3♣	4♣	K♣	3♠					
24	Q♣	5♣	7♠	8♣	6♠	7♥	6♠	8♥	9♦/4♦	9♦	6♥
	2♦	Q♣	8♥	10♥	7♣	10♣					
25	4♣	8♥	8♣	2♠	A♠	2♦	5♦	10♥	5♥/3♦	5♦	4♣
	J♥	K♥	K♦	Q♥	10♠	K♣					
26	7♣	3♣	6♦	7♦	A♥	J♥	2♠	7♦	10♥/2♥	3♣	5♣
	K♠	4♣	J♦	9♥	5♣	6♥					
27	10♠	6♣	7♦	7♥	4♥	7♠	A♦	4♠	4♠/9♣	K♦	5♥
	K♥	Q♥	9♥	2♥	Q♣	A♥					
28	5♠	3♣	3♦	5♥	K♣	K♥	7♥	K♦	K♠/3♣	7♠	4♦
	A♥	Q♥	9♣	9♣	7♦	A♣					
29	J♥	6♣	5♥	A♣	4♦	6♦	10♣	3♦	J♠/9♦	8♥	5♠
	7♠	9♣	4♣	10♠	9♣	Q♣					
30	7♥	Q♦	K♦	3♣	10♠	7♣	6♦	7♥	A♥/9♥	7♥	10♥
	4♠	Q♠	8♥	6♠	6♥	Q♥					
31	9♣	J♣	5♥	Q♦	Q♠	8♠	7♣	5♠	3♦/10♥	A♠	J♣
	J♠	K♠	J♥	9♥	2♥	7♠					
32	6♣	J♠	Q♦	5♠	3♣	3♦	A♦	9♥	K♣/9♠	2♣	J♦
	3♠	7♠	8♣	2♥	5♥	A♦					
33	7♦	2♠	J♦	9♠	8♦	3♠	5♠	4♥	4♣/5♦	K♥	3♠
	K♥	10♠	J♥	A♦	6♠	4♦					
34	2♦	J♠	9♠	K♠	4♠	7♥	3♠	8♥	4♥/10♥	9♠	6♦
	3♦	5♣	2♠	A♦	6♠	3♠					
35	9♦	A♣	Q♦	4♦	6♦	9♣	7♥	Q♥	6♣/8♣	6♠	9♣
	Q♥	K♠	8♥	3♦	7♦	7♠					
36	A♦	8♠	K♣	9♠	A♠	6♠	Q♣	8♠	9♣/J♦	2♠	Q♥
	J♠	5♠	2♣	8♣	2♥	3♦					
37	6♦	J♠	Q♦	3♦	9♥	10♠	J♥	5♠	8♦/3♣	K♣	10♠
	6♣	6♥	4♣	J♠	K♣	3♠					
38	9♠	8♥	3♦	2♣	7♠	8♠	3♥	6♦	2♦/K♠	8♠	4♥
	6♣	5♠	J♠	3♣	Q♦	2♠					
39	Q♥	6♣	2♣	2♠	6♣	4♦	3♠	4♣	4♣/4♠	6♣	4♠
	6♥	9♥	2♥	6♦	10♠	3♠					
40	A♥	K♠	8♠	A♣	6♣	7♠	J♦	10♣	4♦/3♣	2♦	10♣
	A♠	5♣	6♥	9♣	5♠	6♦	6♣				
41	8♣	4♥	8♦	6♦	A♦	9♠	8♠	3♥	K♣/5♣	A♦	J♠
	7♥	5♥	A♠	K♥	Q♣	8♠					
42	3♦	3♥	6♦	6♥	5♦	8♥	9♠	A♦	9♣/J♠	A♥	7♠
	6♣	Q♠	A♠	5♠	2♠	9♠					
43	K♠	A♦	2♥	A♥	4♠	4♦	4♣	10♥	8♥/7♠	3♥	8♦
	K♦	3♣	9♣	3♥	5♥	J♥	4♠				
44	J♦	Q♦	K♦	A♠	2♠	3♠	4♠	6♦	5♠/6♠	Q♣	Q♠
	3♦	9♣	2♣	8♥	A♥	4♠					
45	8♠	A♥	A♦	Q♦	5♥	3♣	3♠	10♠	7♦/7♣	10♦	10♦
	4♣	J♥	10♠	8♦	8♥	7♠					
46	Q♥	4♣	Q♦	2♣	A♠	7♥	4♦	K♠	J♥/6♦	Q♠	Q♣
	4♠	K♣	5♦	K♦	5♠	3♦					
47	2♦	Q♠	9♣	6♥	9♦	K♥	2♣	J♠	9♥/5♥	8♦	3♥
	Q♥	7♣	5♦	J♦	6♠	2♣					
48	Q♣	3♣	6♥	8♥	10♥	9♥	4♠	A♠	7♠/J♠	7♣	A♥
	4♥	K♣	5♦	8♠	2♦	4♠					
49	K♦	3♦	7♥	5♠	7♥	4♥	8♥	J♠	10♣/5♥	J♠	A♦
	8♣	A♣	6♠	J♦	4♦	8♥					

AGE	MER	VEN	MAR	JUP	SAT	URA	NEP	LR	PLU/RES	ENV	DISP
50	Q♥	8♣	5♠	6♦	4♣	10♣	3♥	7♣	8♦/Q♠	10♣	2♦
	10♥	9♦	K♠	Q♣	K♣	9♥					
51	A♠	10♥	6♦	10♠	K♠	J♠	2♥	7♥	10♣/J♣	4♠	6♣
	8♠	7♦	Q♣	Q♠	5♠	5♦	K♠				
52	J♠	7♣	7♥	5♦	K♥	5♣	9♥	5♦	9♣/2♣	4♥	8♠
	8♦	4♦	3♣	K♠	Q♠	6♣					
53	6♥	10♥	5♦	Q♣	K♣	8♦	3♥	K♥	4♦/J♦	10♠	K♣
	6♦	10♣	3♠	A♥	7♥	3♥					
54	8♠	7♣	Q♣	5♥	J♣	6♦	K♠	5♠	4♥/A♣	Q♥	2♠
	K♥	6♠	9♠	7♥	5♦	10♠	J♣				
55	5♣	10♥	3♠	K♠	10♠	2♥	Q♥	7♦	5♥/8♥	9♣	6♠
	8♦	J♦	4♥	J♣	Q♣	2♣					
56	2♥	Q♣	8♠	2♣	A♠	4♠	10♥	6♥	8♣/3♦	6♦	9♠
	K♥	Q♠	7♣	J♣	10♠	10♥					
57	6♣	K♥	2♣	4♥	5♠	8♣	Q♦	10♥	5♥/K♦	3♠	K♥
	A♥	9♣	5♣	J♦	6♠	Q♦					
58	10♠	3♣	4♣	7♥	J♠	A♥	4♥	5♦	7♣/3♦	J♦	2♣
	9♥	4♠	10♠	Q♦	2♣	K♠					
59	Q♣	9♥	7♥	J♥	9♦	7♣	A♣	Q♠	8♦/A♦	J♣	A♠
	Q♦	K♦	6♣	9♣	8♠	A♣					
60	7♦	A♠	J♥	5♦	J♠	2♥	7♣	K♣	A♥/2♠	10♥	7♥
	J♦	3♦	5♠	8♠	3♣	7♣					
61	9♣	4♠	5♦	6♦	5♥	K♠	J♣	8♦	2♥/10♥	5♠	8♥
	Q♣	7♠	5♠	2♠	J♥	9♦	5♥				
62	J♠	Q♥	7♥	9♦	9♠	10♠	Q♠	3♥	6♦/4♥	4♦	7♠
	8♥	4♦	K♣	J♥	5♦	5♣					
63	6♣	8♠	J♦	3♦	8♣	8♥	9♦	8♠	K♥/5♥	5♥	K♦
	9♥	2♥	6♠	2♣	2♠	9♦					
64	A♠	9♥	3♦	Q♣	4♣	K♥	3♥	7♣	8♦/4♠	5♠	3♣
	9♠	2♦	6♠	5♥	9♦	9♣					
65	6♥	9♠	Q♣	7♠	4♥	3♠	K♥	Q♠	K♦/K♣	4♣	5♦
	5♠	8♣	A♣	4♠	8♥	K♥					
66	J♠	10♠	J♦	9♠	7♠	8♠	3♠	5♥	10♣/10♥	6♥	9♦
	8♦	2♠	A♥	K♣	4♠	3♣					
67	2♦	7♠	9♠	7♦	5♦	8♦	Q♦	J♣	2♠/Q♠	3♦	Q♦
	K♥	9♠	4♥	4♠	8♥	Q♦					
68	Q♥	10♠	7♦	6♣	J♥	K♥	3♠	6♦	2♥/6♦	Q♦	3♦
	J♦	10♥	3♣	4♣	K♦	3♠					
69	Q♣	5♣	7♠	8♣	6♠	7♥	6♣	K♠	9♦/4♦	9♦	6♥
	2♦	Q♦	8♥	10♥	7♣	10♣					
70	4♠	8♥	8♣	2♠	A♠	2♦	5♦	5♠	5♥/3♦	5♦	4♣
	J♥	K♥	K♦	Q♥	10♠	K♣					
71	7♣	3♠	6♦	9♥	A♥	J♥	2♠	10♥	10♥/A♣	3♣	5♣
	K♠	4♣	J♦	7♦	5♣	6♥					
72	10♠	6♣	9♥	7♥	4♥	7♠	A♦	3♠	4♠/9♣	K♦	5♥
	K♥	Q♥	7♦	A♣	Q♣	A♦					
73	5♣	3♠	3♦	5♥	K♣	K♥	7♥	K♠	K♠/3♣	7♠	4♦
	A♥	Q♠	9♠	9♣	9♥	2♥					
74	J♥	6♣	5♥	2♥	4♦	6♦	10♣	10♠	J♠/9♦	8♥	5♠
	7♥	9♠	4♣	10♠	9♣	Q♣					
75	7♥	Q♣	K♣	3♣	10♠	7♣	6♦	A♣	A♥/7♦	7♥	10♥
	4♠	Q♠	8♥	6♠	6♥	Q♥					
76	9♠	J♣	5♥	Q♦	Q♣	8♠	7♣	Q♥	3♦/10♥	A♠	J♣
	J♠	K♣	J♠	7♦	A♠	7♠					
77	6♠	J♠	Q♦	5♠	3♣	3♦	A♦	A♣	K♣/9♠	2♣	J♦
	3♠	7♠	8♣	A♣	5♥	A♦					
78	9♥	2♠	J♦	9♠	8♦	3♠	5♠	Q♣	4♣/5♦	K♥	3♠
	K♥	10♠	J♥	A♦	6♠	4♦					
79	2♦	J♠	9♠	K♦	A♠	7♥	3♠	8♠	4♥/10♥	9♠	6♦
	3♦	5♣	2♠	A♦	6♠	3♠					
80	9♦	2♥	Q♦	4♦	6♦	9♣	7♥	2♣	6♣/8♣	6♠	9♣
	Q♥	K♠	8♥	3♦	9♥	7♠					
81	A♦	8♠	K♠	9♠	2♥	6♠	Q♣	A♠	9♣/J♦	2♠	Q♥
	J♠	5♠	2♣	8♠	A♣	3♦					
82	6♦	J♣	Q♦	3♦	7♦	10♠	J♥	4♠	8♦/3♣	K♣	10♠
	6♣	6♥	4♣	J♠	K♣	3♠					
83	9♣	8♥	3♦	2♣	7♠	8♦	3♥	10♥	2♦/K♠	8♠	4♥
	6♣	5♠	J♠	3♣	Q♦	2♠					
84	Q♥	6♠	2♣	2♠	6♠	4♦	3♠	6♠	4♣/4♠	6♣	4♠
	6♥	7♠	A♣	6♦	10♠	3♠					
85	A♥	K♠	8♠	2♥	6♣	7♣	J♣	K♥	4♦/3♣	2♦	10♣
	A♠	5♠	6♥	9♣	5♠	6♦	6♣				
86	8♠	4♥	8♦	6♦	A♥	9♠	8♠	2♣	K♣/5♣	A♦	J♠
	7♥	5♥	A♠	K♥	Q♣	8♠					
87	3♦	3♥	6♦	6♥	5♦	8♥	9♠	4♥	9♣/J♠	A♥	7♣
	6♣	Q♠	A♠	5♣	2♣	9♠					
88	K♠	A♦	A♣	A♥	4♠	4♦	4♣	5♠	8♥/7♠	3♥	8♦
	K♦	3♠	9♣	3♥	5♥	J♥	4♠				
89	J♦	Q♦	K♦	A♠	2♠	3♠	4♠	8♠	5♠/6♠	Q♣	Q♠
	3♦	9♣	2♣	8♥	A♥	4♠					
90	8♠	A♥	A♦	Q♦	5♥	3♣	3♠	Q♦	9♥/7♣	10♦	10♦
	4♣	J♥	10♠	8♦	8♥	7♠					
91	Q♥	4♣	Q♦	2♣	A♠	9♥	4♦	10♠	J♥/6♦	Q♠	Q♣
	4♠	K♣	5♦	K♠	5♠	3♦					
92	A♣	Q♠	9♣	6♥	9♠	K♥	2♣	3♠	7♦/5♦	8♦	3♥
	Q♥	7♠	5♦	J♦	6♠	2♣					
93	Q♣	3♣	6♥	8♥	10♥	7♠	4♠	4♠	7♠/J♠	7♣	A♥
	4♥	K♣	5♦	8♠	2♦	4♠					
94	K♦	3♦	7♥	5♠	9♥	4♦	8♥	7♥	10♣/5♥	J♠	A♦
	8♣	2♥	6♠	J♦	4♦	8♥					
95	Q♥	8♠	5♠	6♦	4♣	10♣	3♥	J♠	8♦/Q♠	10♣	2♦
	10♥	9♦	K♠	Q♣	K♣	7♦					
96	A♦	10♥	6♦	10♠	K♠	J♠	A♣	A♥	10♣/J♦	4♠	6♣
	8♠	9♦	Q♣	Q♠	5♠	5♦	K♣				
97	J♠	7♣	7♥	5♦	K♥	5♣	7♦	4♥	9♣/2♣	4♥	8♠
	8♦	4♦	3♣	K♠	Q♠	6♣					
98	6♥	10♥	5♦	Q♣	K♣	8♦	3♥	Q♣	4♦/J♦	10♠	K♣
	6♦	10♣	3♠	A♥	7♥	3♥					
99	8♠	7♣	Q♣	5♥	J♣	6♦	K♠	7♦	4♥/2♥	Q♥	2♠
	K♥	6♠	9♦	7♥	5♦	10♠	J♣				

Jack of Diamonds

AGE	MER	VEN	MAR	JUP	SAT	URA	NEP	LR	PLU/RES	ENV	DISP
0	4♥	4♦	2♠	8♥	6♠	6♠	Q♥	4♥	10♣/8♦	J♦	J♦
	5♦	A♦	8♣	2♥	A♠	Q♥					
1	7♦	J♠	3♣	8♦	10♥	5♦	8♥	4♦	K♥/8♠	J♣	3♠
	Q♠	6♥	J♥	Q♥	7♣	7♥					
2	10♠	4♦	8♦	2♦	J♣	3♥	5♦	2♠	4♣/7♠	10♥	6♦
	6♠	2♣	10♦	Q♥	7♣	5♦					
3	K♣	A♣	2♠	7♥	9♦	Q♦	3♥	8♥	4♥/8♣	5♠	9♣
	3♦	K♠	A♥	6♠	7♥	A♦					
4	Q♥	4♣	K♠	8♦	A♣	7♣	3♠	6♣	Q♦/3♣	4♦	Q♥
	4♦	8♥	10♦	8♣	2♥	6♠					
5	9♦	K♦	2♠	6♠	9♥	6♥	J♥	6♠	10♥/6♣	5♥	10♠
	4♥	9♠	K♥	4♦	10♣	5♦					
6	Q♦	A♥	6♠	10♦	A♦	10♥	6♦	Q♥	10♠/K♠	5♠	4♥
	4♥	8♥	4♦	6♠	2♠	J♠					
7	3♦	4♥	10♦	J♠	7♠	7♥	5♦	7♦	K♥/5♣	4♠	4♠
	9♠	9♥	2♦	9♦	6♥	5♦					
8	9♣	K♠	4♠	A♣	4♥	5♠	K♦	J♠	7♥/6♣	6♥	10♣
	Q♣	2♠	9♠	Q♦	8♥	9♦	4♥				
9	8♣	4♣	10♥	9♦	Q♥	8♦	A♠	3♣	10♠/2♣	3♦	J♠
	3♥	A♠	Q♣	Q♠	3♠	4♠					
10	6♠	6♦	9♦	9♠	8♠	A♥	8♦	8♦	Q♦/4♦	Q♦	7♣
	4♥	J♣	Q♣	2♣	10♦	8♦					
11	K♠	Q♥	2♥	9♣	5♠	7♥	K♥	10♥	A♥/A♦	9♦	8♦
	2♦	4♣	Q♦	6♦	A♠	J♥	5♣				
12	3♣	2♠	2♦	Q♣	J♠	5♦	5♠	5♦	8♥/7♣	5♦	Q♠
	6♠	Q♦	10♦	A♥	9♣	5♣					
13	4♠	9♣	Q♥	2♠	A♠	6♠	5♦	8♥	7♦/5♣	3♠	10♦
	K♥	J♥	6♥	10♥	A♥	A♦					
14	3♦	K♥	2♠	10♦	Q♣	7♦	7♥	10♠	J♥/9♦	K♦	Q♣
	5♣	10♣	8♠	2♦	8♥	6♠					
15	2♥	J♣	Q♦	9♣	K♣	Q♠	10♦	4♦	9♥/A♠	7♠	3♥
	3♦	5♠	8♠	7♣	3♣	10♦					
16	3♠	6♠	9♠	A♥	7♠	9♥	5♣	8♦	A♦/4♦	8♥	A♥
	4♣	10♣	8♠	4♠	10♠	5♣					
17	2♦	6♠	3♥	8♥	7♦	4♣	A♥	2♦	5♥/A♠	7♥	A♦
	8♣	A♣	7♣	3♠	7♥	A♦					
18	3♦	8♣	8♥	9♦	K♥	5♥	6♦	Q♣	10♥/J♣	A♠	2♦
	7♠	K♣	K♠	3♠	10♣	9♥					
19	Q♥	7♠	9♠	6♥	K♠	4♦	2♥	3♥	5♥/K♦	2♣	6♣
	4♠	7♠	3♠	J♣	8♥	8♠	K♠				
20	4♦	5♠	3♥	8♠	Q♠	2♠	9♥	5♦	Q♦/10♠	K♥	8♠
	10♥	7♥	6♣	K♠	J♠	4♥					
21	9♠	7♠	8♠	3♠	10♣	10♥	6♦	K♣	7♥/3♣	9♠	K♠
	9♦	5♥	5♦	9♣	3♥	6♦					
22	4♠	5♠	3♠	A♠	K♦	9♦	K♠	A♣	4♣/A♦	6♠	2♠
	Q♠	7♣	K♣	3♥	8♣	6♥	K♦				
23	2♣	7♠	5♦	K♠	6♥	2♥	3♦	2♠	A♠/A♥	2♠	6♠
	10♥	3♣	4♠	K♦	3♠	10♦					
24	2♥	3♠	4♠	10♦	Q♣	5♠	7♠	7♥	8♣/6♠	K♠	9♠
	Q♠	J♣	5♠	K♦	6♥	7♠					

AGE	MER	VEN	MAR	JUP	SAT	URA	NEP	LR	PLU/RES	ENV	DISP
25	4♥	Q♠	10♦	4♣	8♥	8♠	2♠	9♦	A♠/2♦	8♠	K♥
	9♣	Q♦	2♠	3♣	7♣	2♠					
26	5♥	6♠	K♥	3♥	4♦	9♣	4♣	Q♦	5♠/6♠	6♠	2♣
	9♥	5♠	6♥	2♠	10♦	K♠					
27	3♠	9♥	3♥	J♥	K♣	5♠	A♣	3♥	10♥/Q♥	2♦	A♠
	2♠	2♦	4♥	Q♦	8♠	A♣					
28	7♦	Q♣	J♥	8♠	4♦	2♥	5♠	Q♥	9♣/J♠	A♦	7♥
	3♣	6♠	8♥	4♣	6♠	5♠					
29	Q♦	5♣	8♠	9♠	A♠	K♠	K♦	4♠	2♥/7♠	A♥	8♥
	3♠	A♦	8♥	J♠	J♥	K♣	A♠				
30	4♦	3♦	3♥	K♣	8♦	6♥	J♣	K♠	9♥/4♣	3♥	7♠
	A♥	7♥	10♣	J♥	8♠	2♣					
31	4♥	4♠	3♠	6♠	8♠	A♥	K♣	8♦	Q♠/A♠	Q♠	K♦
	9♥	2♥	7♠	10♦	J♠	K♣					
32	Q♣	9♥	6♠	3♠	K♥	Q♠	6♦	A♣	10♥/5♣	10♦	3♣
	8♦	10♠	7♣	A♠	K♣	Q♦					
33	9♠	8♦	3♣	5♠	4♣	5♦	Q♠	7♣	2♦/10♣	Q♠	5♦
	8♥	8♣	A♣	5♣	A♥	Q♠					
34	4♦	6♥	3♠	8♦	A♦	4♠	5♦	3♠	5♥/7♠	8♦	9♦
	10♥	J♠	9♠	10♣	K♥	6♣					
35	10♠	5♠	8♦	7♠	8♠	10♥	2♠	9♦	J♠/J♣	7♣	Q♦
	Q♠	Q♦	4♠	K♥	A♥	2♠					
36	3♦	6♥	7♠	4♥	J♥	Q♠	5♠	K♦	2♥/9♦	J♠	3♦
	3♠	7♠	6♣	K♥	2♦	5♦					
37	3♠	2♣	A♦	8♣	7♣	3♥	4♦	2♠	K♣/7♥	10♣	6♥
	10♠	2♠	A♥	7♠	5♠	5♥					
38	K♥	A♥	8♠	J♠	Q♣	10♠	8♠	6♠	A♠/6♠	4♠	4♣
	J♥	Q♠	2♦	3♦	6♥	10♣					
39	5♠	5♦	9♠	9♥	9♣	J♥	J♠	9♥	7♠/A♣	4♥	5♠
	K♠	K♥	3♠	7♦	2♠	9♠					
40	6♥	4♥	9♥	3♥	4♣	A♦	Q♥	6♦	5♣/Q♦	10♠	5♥
	Q♠	3♦	7♠	A♣	3♠	Q♥					
41	2♣	5♦	6♠	A♠	10♣	Q♠	3♥	J♥	K♠/6♣	Q♥	4♦
	9♣	J♠	8♦	Q♦	9♥	2♥					
42	J♥	4♥	A♦	2♥	7♥	9♠	5♦	Q♦	4♦/K♠	9♠	3♠
	A♦	8♦	K♥	6♥	Q♦	3♠					
43	3♥	2♠	2♦	6♣	6♥	5♠	9♦	A♥	9♣/7♦	6♦	10♥
	5♣	A♥	7♣	9♠	3♦						
44	Q♦	K♦	A♠	2♠	3♠	4♠	5♠	6♠	6♠/7♠	3♠	J♣
	4♦	10♣	3♣	7♦	A♠	5♠					
45	4♥	4♦	2♠	8♥	6♠	6♠	Q♥	10♦	10♣/8♦	J♦	J♦
	5♦	A♦	8♣	A♣	A♠	Q♥					
46	9♥	J♠	3♣	8♦	10♥	5♦	8♥	A♦	K♥/8♠	J♣	3♠
	Q♠	6♥	J♥	Q♥	7♣	7♥					
47	10♠	4♦	8♦	2♦	Q♣	3♥	5♦	10♥	4♣/7♠	10♥	6♦
	6♠	2♣	10♦	Q♥	7♣	5♦					
48	K♣	2♥	2♠	7♥	9♦	Q♦	3♥	6♦	4♥/8♣	5♠	9♣
	3♦	K♠	A♥	6♠	9♥	A♦					
49	Q♥	4♠	K♠	8♦	2♥	7♣	3♠	3♦	Q♦/3♣	4♦	Q♥
	4♦	8♥	10♦	8♣	A♣	6♠					

AGE	MER	VEN	MAR	JUP	SAT	URA	NEP	LR	PLU/RES	ENV	DISP
50	9♦	K♦	2♠	6♠	7♦	6♥	J♥	4♥	10♥/6♣	5♥	10♠
	4♥	9♠	K♥	4♠	10♣	5♦					
51	Q♦	A♥	6♠	10♦	A♦	10♥	6♦	10♦	10♠/K♣	5♣	4♥
	4♥	8♥	4♦	6♣	2♠	J♠					
52	3♦	4♥	10♦	J♠	7♠	7♥	5♦	J♠	K♥/5♣	4♣	4♠
	9♠	7♦	A♣	9♦	6♥	5♦					
53	9♣	K♠	4♠	2♥	4♥	5♠	K♦	7♣	7♥/6♣	6♥	10♣
	Q♣	2♣	9♠	Q♦	8♥	9♦	4♥				
54	8♣	4♣	10♥	9♦	Q♥	8♠	4♠	7♥	10♣/2♣	3♦	J♠
	3♥	A♠	Q♣	Q♠	3♠	4♠					
55	6♠	6♦	9♠	9♠	8♠	A♥	8♦	5♦	Q♦/4♦	Q♦	7♠
	4♥	J♣	Q♣	2♣	10♦	8♦					
56	K♠	Q♥	A♣	9♣	5♠	7♥	K♥	9♣	A♥/A♦	9♦	8♦
	2♦	6♣	Q♦	6♦	A♠	J♥	5♣				
57	3♣	2♠	2♦	Q♣	J♠	5♦	5♣	K♠	8♥/7♣	5♦	Q♠
	6♠	Q♦	10♦	A♥	9♣	5♣					
58	4♠	9♣	Q♥	2♠	A♠	6♣	5♦	4♠	9♥/5♠	3♣	10♦
	K♥	J♥	6♥	10♥	A♥	A♦					
59	3♦	K♥	2♠	10♦	Q♣	9♥	7♥	A♣	J♥/9♦	K♦	Q♠
	5♣	10♣	8♠	2♦	8♥	6♠					
60	A♣	J♣	Q♦	9♠	K♣	Q♠	10♦	4♥	7♦/A♠	7♠	3♥
	3♦	5♠	8♠	3♣	7♠	10♦					
61	3♠	6♣	9♠	A♥	7♠	7♦	5♣	5♠	A♦/4♦	8♥	A♥
	4♣	10♣	8♠	4♠	10♠	5♣					
62	2♦	6♠	3♥	8♥	9♥	4♣	A♥	K♦	5♥/A♠	7♥	A♦
	8♣	2♥	7♣	3♠	7♥	A♥					
63	3♦	8♣	8♥	9♣	K♥	5♥	6♦	8♣	10♥/J♣	A♠	2♦
	7♠	K♣	K♠	3♠	10♣	7♦					
64	Q♥	7♠	9♦	6♥	K♠	4♦	A♣	4♣	5♥/K♦	2♣	6♣
	4♠	9♥	3♠	J♣	8♥	8♠	K♠				
65	4♦	5♠	3♥	8♠	Q♠	2♣	7♦	10♥	Q♦/10♦	K♥	8♠
	10♥	7♥	6♣	K♠	J♠	4♥					
66	9♠	7♠	8♠	3♠	10♣	10♥	6♦	9♦	7♥/3♣	9♠	K♣
	9♦	5♥	5♦	9♣	3♥	6♦					
67	4♠	5♠	3♠	A♠	K♦	9♦	K♠	Q♥	4♣/2♥	6♠	2♠
	Q♠	7♣	K♣	3♥	8♠	6♥	K♦				
68	2♣	7♠	5♦	K♠	6♥	A♣	3♦	8♦	A♠/A♥	2♠	6♠
	10♥	3♣	4♣	K♦	3♠	10♦					
69	A♣	3♠	4♠	10♦	Q♣	5♣	7♠	4♠	8♣/6♠	K♣	9♠
	Q♠	J♣	5♠	K♦	6♥	7♠					
70	4♥	Q♠	10♦	4♣	8♥	8♣	2♠	6♠	A♠/2♦	8♠	K♥
	9♣	Q♦	2♣	3♣	7♠	2♠					
71	5♥	6♣	K♥	3♥	4♦	9♣	4♣	6♦	5♠/6♠	6♣	2♣
	7♦	5♣	6♥	2♠	10♦	K♠					
72	3♠	7♦	3♥	J♥	K♣	5♠	2♥	9♦	10♥/Q♥	2♦	A♠
	2♠	2♦	4♥	Q♦	8♣	2♥					
73	9♥	Q♣	J♥	8♠	4♦	A♣	5♠	9♠	9♣/J♠	A♦	7♥
	3♣	6♠	8♥	4♠	6♠	5♠					
74	Q♦	5♣	8♠	9♠	A♠	K♠	K♦	8♠	A♣/7♠	A♥	8♥
	3♠	A♦	8♥	J♠	J♥	K♣	A♠				
75	4♦	3♦	3♥	K♣	8♦	6♥	J♣	A♥	9♦/4♣	3♥	7♠
	A♥	7♥	10♣	J♥	8♠	2♣					
76	4♥	4♣	3♣	6♠	8♣	A♥	K♣	8♦	Q♠/A♠	Q♣	K♦
	7♦	A♣	7♠	10♦	J♠	K♣					
77	Q♣	7♦	6♠	3♠	K♥	Q♠	6♦	K♠	10♥/5♣	10♦	3♣
	8♦	10♠	7♣	A♠	K♣	Q♦					
78	9♠	8♦	3♠	5♠	4♣	5♦	Q♠	Q♥	2♦/10♣	Q♠	5♦
	8♥	8♣	2♥	5♣	A♥	Q♠					
79	4♦	6♥	3♣	8♦	A♦	4♠	5♦	2♥	5♥/7♠	8♦	9♦
	10♥	J♠	9♣	10♣	K♥	6♠					
80	10♠	5♠	8♦	9♥	8♠	10♥	2♠	9♣	J♠/J♣	7♣	Q♦
	Q♣	Q♦	4♣	K♥	A♥	2♠					
81	3♦	6♥	9♥	4♥	J♥	Q♠	5♦	5♣	A♣/9♦	J♠	3♦
	3♣	7♠	6♣	K♥	2♦	5♦					
82	3♠	2♣	A♦	8♣	7♣	3♥	4♥	7♥	K♣/7♥	10♣	6♥
	10♠	2♠	A♥	7♠	5♠	5♥					
83	K♥	A♥	8♣	J♠	Q♣	10♠	8♠	K♥	A♠/6♠	4♠	4♣
	J♥	Q♣	2♦	3♦	6♥	10♣					
84	5♠	5♦	9♠	7♥	9♣	J♥	J♠	3♣	7♠/2♥	4♥	5♣
	K♠	K♥	3♣	9♥	2♣	9♠					
85	6♥	4♥	7♦	3♥	4♣	A♦	Q♥	2♠	5♣/Q♦	10♠	5♥
	Q♠	3♦	9♥	2♥	3♠	Q♥					
86	2♣	5♦	6♠	A♠	10♣	Q♠	3♥	2♦	K♠/6♣	Q♥	4♦
	9♣	J♣	8♦	Q♦	7♠	A♣					
87	J♥	4♥	A♠	A♣	7♥	9♦	5♥	Q♣	4♦/K♣	9♠	5♠
	A♦	8♦	K♥	6♥	Q♦	3♠					
88	3♥	2♠	2♦	6♣	6♥	5♠	9♦	J♠	9♣/9♥	6♦	10♥
	5♣	J♠	A♥	7♣	9♠	3♦					
89	Q♦	K♦	A♠	2♠	3♠	4♠	5♠	5♦	6♠/7♠	3♠	J♣
	4♦	10♣	3♣	9♥	2♥	5♠					
90	4♥	4♥	2♠	8♥	6♣	6♠	Q♥	5♣	10♣/8♦	J♦	J♥
	5♠	A♦	8♣	2♥	A♠	Q♥					
91	7♦	J♠	3♣	8♦	10♥	5♦	8♥	4♠	K♥/8♠	J♣	3♠
	Q♠	6♥	J♥	Q♥	7♣	7♥					
92	10♠	4♥	8♦	2♦	Q♣	3♥	5♦	9♣	4♣/7♠	10♥	6♦
	6♠	2♣	10♦	Q♥	7♠	5♦					
93	K♣	A♣	2♠	7♥	9♦	Q♠	3♥	Q♥	4♥/8♣	5♠	9♣
	3♦	K♠	A♥	6♠	7♦	A♦					
94	Q♥	4♠	K♠	8♦	A♣	7♠	3♠	2♠	Q♦/3♣	4♦	Q♥
	4♦	8♥	10♦	8♣	2♥	6♣					
95	9♦	K♦	2♠	6♠	9♥	6♥	J♥	A♠	10♥/6♣	5♥	10♠
	4♥	9♠	K♥	4♦	10♣	5♦					
96	Q♦	A♥	6♠	10♦	A♦	10♥	6♦	6♣	10♠/K♣	5♣	4♥
	4♥	8♥	4♦	6♣	2♠	J♠					
97	3♦	4♥	10♦	J♠	7♣	7♥	5♦	5♦	K♥/5♣	4♣	4♠
	9♠	9♥	2♥	9♦	6♥	5♦					
98	9♣	K♠	4♠	A♣	4♥	5♠	K♦	3♦	7♥/6♣	6♥	10♣
	Q♣	2♣	9♠	Q♦	8♥	9♦	4♥					
99	8♣	4♥	10♥	9♦	Q♥	8♠	4♠	K♥	10♣/2♣	3♦	J♠
	3♥	A♠	Q♣	Q♠	3♠	4♠					

Queen of Diamonds

AGE	MER	VEN	MAR	JUP	SAT	URA	NEP	LR	PLU/RES	ENV	DISP
0	5♥	3♣	3♠	9♥	7♣	5♦	Q♠	5♥	J♣/9♦	Q♦	Q♦
	6♦	K♥	7♥	3♥	4♥	Q♠					
1	2♣	A♠	9♥	4♦	J♥	6♦	6♠	3♣	A♣/9♠	9♦	3♦
	2♠	8♠	J♠	3♥	10♣	6♠					
2	3♦	A♥	4♠	8♣	J♦	10♠	4♦	3♠	8♦/2♦	5♦	6♥
	5♥	Q♠	4♥	8♠	3♣	7♠					
3	3♥	4♥	8♣	J♣	Q♥	5♥	7♣	9♥	A♦/10♦	3♣	4♣
	J♥	6♦	10♣	2♠	A♠	10♥					
4	3♣	6♠	9♠	7♦	4♣	J♥	J♣	7♠	8♠/2♥	K♦	5♣
	K♠	3♥	2♠	9♥	A♥	Q♣					
5	A♠	4♦	7♦	10♣	7♥	4♠	5♣	5♦	8♥/K♦	7♠	5♥
	6♦	2♣	9♥	2♥	3♦	5♣					
6	A♥	6♠	10♦	A♦	10♥	6♦	10♠	Q♠	K♠/J♠	8♥	4♦
	4♣	9♦	3♠	K♥	7♦	A♣					
7	J♥	4♦	A♠	A♣	2♦	9♠	7♠	2♣	K♦/8♦	7♥	5♠
	4♠	3♠	3♥	A♠	K♥	3♦					
8	10♠	Q♠	10♣	J♠	A♠	3♣	9♠	A♠	4♣/9♥	A♠	10♥
	8♥	9♦	4♥	J♦	Q♣	2♠					
9	K♥	K♣	A♦	Q♠	3♦	5♠	3♣	9♥	10♦/8♦	2♣	J♠
	K♦	10♥	2♠	9♥	2♥	3♣					
10	4♦	K♦	Q♣	6♣	J♠	10♦	5♣	4♦	10♥/3♣	K♥	J♦
	6♠	4♠	8♣	2♥	A♦	5♣					
11	7♦	J♣	2♣	3♠	5♦	6♠	6♣	J♥	3♥/7♣	9♠	3♠
	6♦	A♠	J♥	5♣	J♦	2♠					
12	5♥	K♦	3♣	10♣	Q♥	10♠	6♣	6♦	7♥/8♠	6♠	6♦
	10♦	A♥	9♣	5♣	J♦	6♠					
13	8♦	A♣	Q♠	2♦	9♠	K♥	10♠	6♠	4♦/8♠	2♠	9♠
	2♣	K♠	4♥	10♦	7♦	4♠					
14	5♣	5♠	K♠	3♠	A♣	J♦	3♦	3♦	K♥/2♠	K♣	Q♥
	K♦	6♣	9♣	8♣	2♥	10♦					
15	9♠	K♣	Q♠	10♠	9♥	A♠	J♥	A♥	5♦/J♠	8♠	10♠
	4♦	Q♣	3♥	K♦	10♥	6♠					
16	K♥	4♥	10♦	9♣	4♣	5♦	6♥	4♠	5♥/K♠	6♠	4♦
	4♦	6♣	K♦	J♠	Q♠	J♣					
17	2♠	4♦	9♣	J♣	J♦	2♦	6♠	8♠	3♥/8♥	2♦	4♠
	Q♣	9♥	2♥	9♠	A♠	6♠					
18	4♣	K♠	5♠	A♣	4♦	3♣	K♣	J♦	2♦/J♠	A♦	10♣
	Q♥	A♥	Q♣	K♥	6♣	9♠	4♦				
19	8♣	7♥	5♦	9♠	5♠	3♠	5♠	10♠	10♥/A♥	A♥	♠
	10♠	A♦	Q♥	6♦	3♦	5♠					
20	10♦	6♥	9♠	Q♣	7♣	4♥	3♠	4♦	K♥/K♦	3♥	7♠
	4♦	9♦	Q♥	A♥	9♣	3♠					
21	K♠	5♣	2♥	4♣	8♥	2♦	3♥	3♥	4♥/4♠	Q♣	8♦
	10♣	J♠	K♥	6♥	A♦	J♥	8♥				
22	2♠	Q♠	10♣	Q♥	J♣	6♠	8♥	4♥	6♣/J♦	10♦	Q♠
	10♦	K♥	9♣	4♥	4♣	8♥					
23	5♠	4♣	5♣	Q♠	A♣	J♠	6♠	8♠	7♦/3♣	Q♠	10♣
	3♥	J♥	A♠	5♦	4♥	4♠					
24	2♣	3♥	Q♠	9♣	Q♥	7♦	2♦	J♣	J♥/9♠	8♦	Q♣
	8♥	10♥	7♣	10♣	6♣	10♦					
25	2♥	9♦	K♥	Q♣	8♦	6♦	9♣	Q♥	9♥/A♦	7♣	3♥
	2♣	3♣	7♣	2♠	J♦	9♣					
26	3♦	J♠	Q♣	4♥	8♠	9♥	8♥	5♥	4♠/K♦	J♠	A♥
	7♥	10♥	7♣	5♠	5♥	8♥					
27	10♣	10♦	10♠	6♣	7♦	7♥	4♥	7♣	7♠/A♦	10♣	A♦
	8♣	A♣	J♦	2♠	2♦	4♥					
28	2♣	8♣	6♣	9♠	3♥	7♠	6♥	3♣	5♦/9♦	4♠	2♦
	8♠	8♦	K♠	3♦	10♥	9♥					
29	5♠	8♠	9♠	A♠	K♠	K♦	2♥	6♠	7♠/K♣	4♥	6♣
	5♠	7♦	3♥	9♦	6♣	7♣	K♠				
30	K♦	3♣	10♠	7♠	6♦	A♦	9♥	9♠	K♥/9♣	10♠	8♠
	5♦	2♦	J♠	K♠	9♦	4♦					
31	Q♣	8♠	7♠	3♦	10♥	5♦	6♥	7♠	2♦/2♦	Q♥	K♣
	9♠	7♠	6♠	4♠	10♠	6♥					
32	5♠	3♠	3♥	A♠	K♠	9♠	K♠	4♠	7♥/A♦	9♠	2♠
	6♦	J♠	8♠	10♠	7♠	A♠	K♣				
33	A♥	8♠	6♠	K♠	A♠	2♥	2♠	J♥	A♦/4♥	6♦	6♠
	5♦	2♠	7♥	K♣	3♦	9♠					
34	2♥	3♦	5♠	9♣	Q♥	8♥	8♠	J♣	8♣/10♦	3♠	9♠
	6♦	9♦	3♣	K♠	A♠	8♠					
35	4♦	6♦	9♣	7♥	6♣	8♣	Q♠	A♠	A♦/10♣	J♦	K♥
	4♣	K♥	A♥	2♠	J♦	Q♠					
36	7♠	J♠	3♥	10♠	K♦	4♣	7♥	4♦	3♣/10♦	J♣	2♣
	9♥	8♥	A♠	Q♠	9♣	K♠					
37	3♦	9♥	10♠	J♥	8♦	3♣	A♣	7♦	5♦/5♠	10♥	A♠
	Q♠	10♣	4♦	K♥	8♣	A♣					
38	7♦	Q♥	J♥	7♣	K♦	2♥	3♣	10♠	4♣/J♣	5♠	7♥
	2♠	10♦	6♣	5♠	J♠	3♣					
39	K♥	8♥	7♠	Q♣	A♠	K♠	K♣	7♥	2♥/8♠	4♦	8♥
	3♦	4♠	6♣	J♣	J♥	8♦	A♦				
40	K♦	2♣	10♠	8♦	3♠	A♠	9♦	4♠	9♠/7♥	5♥	7♠
	4♥	2♦	10♥	J♥	7♠	A♦					
41	4♦	5♠	2♠	10♦	8♠	4♥	8♠	5♣	6♦/A♠	5♣	K♦
	9♥	2♥	J♦	9♣	J♠	8♦					
42	Q♥	9♥	10♠	3♦	3♥	6♦	6♥	A♥	5♦/8♥	4♠	3♦
	3♠	5♥	J♦	A♦	8♦	K♥					
43	Q♠	3♣	3♦	3♣	7♥	6♠	6♦	6♠	10♣/10♥	6♥	5♦
	6♣	8♣	A♣	8♥	4♥	6♦					
44	K♦	A♠	2♠	3♠	4♠	5♠	6♠	10♦	7♠/8♠	3♦	9♣
	5♠	J♣	4♣	10♥	3♥	J♠					
45	5♥	3♣	3♠	7♦	7♣	5♦	Q♠	A♦	J♣/9♦	Q♦	Q♦
	6♦	K♥	7♥	3♥	4♥	Q♠					
46	2♣	A♠	7♥	4♦	J♥	6♦	6♠	10♥	2♥/9♣	9♦	3♦
	2♠	8♠	J♠	3♥	10♣	6♠					
47	3♦	A♥	4♠	8♣	J♦	10♠	4♦	6♦	8♦/2♦	5♦	6♥
	5♥	Q♠	4♥	8♠	3♣	7♠					
48	3♥	4♥	8♣	J♣	Q♥	5♥	7♣	10♠	A♦/10♦	3♣	4♣
	J♥	6♦	10♣	2♠	A♠	10♥					
49	3♣	6♠	9♠	9♥	4♣	J♥	J♣	J♥	8♠/A♦	K♦	5♣
	K♠	3♥	2♠	7♦	A♥	Q♣					

AGE	MER	VEN	MAR	JUP	SAT	URA	NEP	LR	PLU/RES	ENV	DISP
50	A♠	4♦	9♥	10♠	7♥	4♠	5♣	4♦	8♥/K♥	7♠	5♥
	6♦	2♣	7♦	A♣	3♦	5♣					
51	A♥	6♠	10♦	A♦	10♥	6♦	10♠	A♦	K♠/J♠	8♥	4♦
	4♣	9♦	3♠	K♥	9♥	2♥					
52	J♥	4♦	A♦	2♥	2♥	9♠	7♠	A♠	K♦/8♦	7♥	5♠
	4♠	3♠	3♥	A♠	K♥	3♦					
53	10♠	Q♠	10♣	J♠	A♠	3♠	9♠	2♦	4♣/7♦	A♠	10♥
	8♥	9♦	4♥	J♦	Q♣	2♣					
54	K♥	K♣	A♦	Q♠	3♦	5♠	3♠	9♠	10♦/8♠	2♣	J♣
	K♦	10♥	2♠	7♠	A♠	3♣					
55	4♦	K♦	Q♣	6♣	J♠	10♦	5♣	7♠	10♥/3♠	K♥	J♦
	6♠	4♠	8♣	A♣	A♦	5♣					
56	9♥	J♣	2♠	3♠	5♦	6♠	6♣	10♠	3♥/7♣	9♠	3♠
	6♦	A♠	J♥	5♣	J♦	2♦					
57	5♥	K♦	3♠	10♠	Q♥	10♠	6♠	Q♠	7♥/8♠	6♠	6♦
	10♦	A♥	9♠	5♣	J♦	6♠					
58	8♦	2♥	Q♠	2♦	9♠	K♥	10♠	10♠	4♦/8♣	2♠	9♣
	2♣	K♣	4♥	10♦	9♥	4♠					
59	5♣	5♠	K♠	3♠	2♥	J♦	3♦	J♠	K♥/2♠	K♣	Q♥
	K♦	6♠	9♣	8♣	A♣	10♦					
60	9♠	K♣	Q♠	10♦	7♦	A♠	J♥	A♠	5♦/J♠	8♠	10♠
	4♦	Q♠	3♥	K♦	10♥	6♠					
61	K♥	4♥	10♦	9♣	4♠	5♦	6♥	3♣	5♥/K♠	6♠	4♥
	4♦	6♣	K♦	J♠	Q♠	J♠					
62	2♣	4♦	9♣	J♣	J♦	2♦	6♠	9♠	3♥/8♥	2♦	4♠
	Q♣	7♠	A♣	9♠	A♠	6♠					
63	4♣	K♠	5♠	2♥	4♦	3♣	K♣	K♥	2♦/J♠	A♦	10♣
	Q♥	A♥	Q♣	K♥	6♣	9♠	4♦				
64	8♣	7♥	5♦	9♠	5♣	3♠	5♠	K♣	10♥/A♥	A♥	J♠
	10♠	A♦	Q♥	6♦	3♦	5♠					
65	10♦	6♥	9♠	Q♣	7♠	4♥	3♠	A♦	K♥/K♦	3♥	7♣
	4♦	9♦	Q♥	A♥	9♠	3♠					
66	K♠	5♠	A♣	4♣	8♥	2♦	3♥	Q♠	4♥/4♠	Q♣	8♦
	10♣	J♠	K♥	6♥	A♦	J♥	8♥				
67	2♠	Q♠	10♣	Q♥	J♣	6♠	8♥	3♦	6♣/J♦	10♦	Q♠
	10♦	K♥	9♣	4♥	4♣	8♥					
68	5♠	4♣	5♠	Q♠	A♦	J♠	6♠	5♠	9♥/3♣	Q♠	10♦
	3♥	J♥	A♠	5♦	4♥	4♠					
69	2♣	3♥	Q♠	9♣	Q♥	9♥	2♦	3♠	J♥/9♠	8♦	Q♣
	8♥	10♥	7♣	10♣	6♣	10♦					
70	A♣	9♥	K♥	Q♣	8♦	6♦	9♣	4♦	7♦/A♦	7♣	3♥
	2♣	3♠	7♠	2♠	J♦	9♣					
71	3♦	J♠	Q♣	4♥	8♠	7♥	8♥	K♦	4♠/K♦	J♠	A♥
	7♥	10♥	7♠	5♠	5♥	8♥					
72	10♣	10♠	10♠	6♣	9♥	7♥	4♥	Q♠	7♠/A♦	10♣	A♦
	8♣	2♥	J♦	2♠	2♦	4♥					
73	2♣	8♣	6♠	9♠	3♥	7♠	6♥	6♣	5♦/9♦	4♠	2♦
	8♠	8♣	K♠	3♦	10♥	7♦					
74	5♠	8♠	9♠	A♠	K♠	K♦	A♣	J♠	7♠/K♣	4♥	6♣
	5♠	9♥	3♦	9♦	6♠	7♣					
75	K♦	3♣	10♠	7♣	6♦	A♥	7♦	10♦	K♥/9♣	10♠	8♠
	5♦	2♦	J♠	K♠	9♦	4♦					
76	Q♣	8♠	7♣	3♦	10♥	5♣	6♥	5♣	2♦/2♠	Q♥	K♣
	9♠	7♠	6♠	4♣	10♠	6♥					
77	5♠	3♣	3♦	A♦	K♣	9♠	K♠	7♦	7♥/2♥	9♣	2♠
	6♦	J♦	8♦	10♠	7♣	A♠	K♣				
78	A♥	8♠	6♠	K♠	A♠	A♣	2♣	J♠	A♦/4♥	6♦	6♠
	5♦	2♠	7♥	K♣	3♦	9♠					
79	A♣	3♦	5♠	9♣	Q♥	8♥	8♠	2♣	8♣/10♦	3♠	9♠
	6♦	9♦	3♣	K♠	A♠	8♠					
80	4♦	6♦	9♣	7♥	6♠	8♣	Q♠	3♠	A♦/10♣	J♦	K♥
	4♣	K♥	A♥	2♠	J♦	Q♠					
81	7♠	J♠	3♥	10♠	K♦	4♣	7♥	5♦	3♣/10♦	J♣	2♣
	7♦	8♥	A♠	Q♠	9♣	K♠					
82	3♦	7♦	10♠	J♥	8♦	3♣	2♥	6♠	5♦/5♣	10♥	A♠
	Q♠	10♣	4♦	K♥	8♣	2♥					
83	9♥	Q♥	J♥	7♣	K♦	A♣	3♣	6♣	4♣/J♣	5♠	7♥
	2♠	10♦	6♣	5♠	J♠	3♣					
84	K♥	8♥	7♣	Q♣	A♦	K♣	K♠	5♥	A♣/8♠	4♦	8♥
	3♠	4♣	6♣	J♣	J♥	8♦	A♦				
85	K♦	2♣	10♠	8♦	3♠	A♠	9♦	K♦	9♠/7♥	5♥	7♠
	4♥	2♦	10♥	J♥	7♣	A♥					
86	4♦	5♠	2♠	10♦	8♠	4♥	8♠	3♠	6♦/A♦	5♣	K♦
	7♠	A♣	J♦	9♣	J♠	8♦					
87	Q♥	7♠	10♦	3♦	3♥	6♦	6♥	10♠	5♦/8♥	4♣	3♣
	3♠	5♥	J♦	A♦	8♦	K♥					
88	Q♣	3♠	3♦	3♠	7♥	6♠	6♦	Q♥	10♣/10♥	6♥	5♦
	6♣	8♠	2♥	8♥	4♥	6♦					
89	K♦	A♠	2♠	3♠	4♠	5♠	6♠	10♠	7♠/8♠	3♦	9♦
	5♦	J♣	4♣	10♥	3♥	J♠					
90	5♥	3♠	3♥	9♥	7♠	5♦	Q♠	6♠	J♣/9♦	Q♦	Q♠
	6♦	K♥	7♥	3♦	4♥	Q♠					
91	2♣	A♠	9♥	4♦	J♥	6♦	6♠	8♦	A♣/9♠	9♦	3♦
	2♠	8♠	J♠	3♥	10♣	6♠					
92	3♦	A♥	4♠	4♣	J♦	10♠	4♦	A♣	8♦/2♦	5♦	6♥
	5♥	Q♠	4♥	8♠	3♣	7♠					
93	3♥	4♥	8♣	J♣	Q♥	5♥	7♣	Q♠	A♦/10♦	3♣	4♣
	J♥	6♦	10♣	2♣	A♠	10♥					
94	3♠	6♠	9♣	7♠	4♠	J♥	J♣	2♦	8♠/2♥	K♦	5♣
	K♠	3♥	2♠	9♥	A♥	Q♣					
95	A♠	4♦	7♠	10♠	7♥	4♠	5♣	9♠	8♥/K♥	7♠	5♥
	6♦	2♣	9♥	2♥	3♦	5♣					
96	A♥	6♠	10♦	A♦	10♥	6♦	10♠	K♥	K♠/J♠	8♥	4♦
	4♣	9♦	3♠	K♥	7♠	A♣					
97	J♥	4♦	A♦	A♣	2♦	9♠	7♠	10♠	K♦/8♦	7♥	5♠
	4♠	3♠	3♥	A♠	K♥	3♦					
98	10♠	Q♠	10♣	J♠	A♠	3♠	9♠	5♠	4♣/9♥	A♠	10♥
	8♥	9♦	4♥	J♦	Q♣	2♣					
99	K♥	K♣	A♦	Q♠	3♦	5♠	3♣	5♠	10♦/8♠	2♣	J♣
	K♦	10♥	2♠	9♥	2♥	3♣					

King of Diamonds

AGE	MER	VEN	MAR	JUP	SAT	URA	NEP	LR	PLU/RES	ENV	DISP
0	6♥	4♣	2♦	J♠	8♣	6♦	4♠	6♥	10♥/10♦	K♦	K♦
	7♦	A♣	4♦	J♠	5♥	4♠					
1	J♦	7♦	J♠	3♣	8♦	10♥	5♦	4♣	8♥/K♥	7♠	3♣
	5♠	3♦	4♦	10♦	4♠	K♣					
2	7♣	5♠	3♠	7♥	9♠	6♣	10♥	2♦	Q♥/5♣	8♥	5♦
	3♥	8♣	2♥	K♥	6♦	10♥					
3	A♠	6♠	2♦	5♠	9♣	4♠	6♣	J♠	2♠/A♥	7♥	9♦
	8♥	5♥	9♦	5♣	8♦	10♠					
4	3♦	7♥	5♠	9♥	4♥	8♥	10♣	8♣	5♥/7♠	A♠	Q♦
	10♥	K♣	9♠	8♦	6♦	10♣					
5	2♠	6♠	9♥	6♥	J♥	10♥	6♣	6♦	A♠/8♠	2♠	3♦
	2♦	A♥	10♠	8♦	Q♥	6♣					
6	3♣	Q♠	9♣	8♣	4♦	3♠	6♥	4♠	4♠/Q♣	K♥	6♥
	3♦	10♣	6♦	A♥	7♥	2♠					
7	8♦	6♦	8♣	5♥	J♦	3♦	4♥	J♦	10♦/J♠	9♠	4♣
	J♥	10♥	Q♥	2♠	6♠	5♠					
8	7♥	6♣	8♠	7♥	9♦	J♥	5♥	7♠	A♥/2♥	6♠	5♣
	K♠	8♦	2♦	9♥	Q♠	7♠					
9	6♠	6♥	7♠	5♠	9♠	9♣	Q♦	J♠	K♥/K♣	2♠	5♥
	10♥	2♠	9♥	2♥	3♣	Q♦					
10	Q♠	6♣	J♠	10♦	5♠	10♥	3♠	3♣	K♠/10♠	K♣	4♦
	9♦	7♠	5♠	K♣	7♥	A♣					
11	J♥	6♥	10♦	A♣	Q♣	8♠	2♣	8♦	A♠/4♠	8♠	5♠
	9♣	5♠	8♦	6♠	K♣	3♠					
12	3♠	10♣	Q♥	10♠	6♣	7♥	8♠	10♥	9♦/9♥	6♣	10♥
	K♥	7♠	6♦	4♦	7♣	2♠					
13	K♣	A♦	10♦	10♣	3♣	4♣	7♥	5♦	J♠/A♥	2♦	J♣
	A♠	5♣	2♦	9♥	2♥	7♥					
14	6♥	A♠	10♣	3♥	10♠	J♠	Q♦	7♣	5♣/5♠	A♦	J♥
	6♣	9♣	8♣	2♥	10♦	Q♦					
15	7♠	5♥	2♠	5♠	8♥	6♣	3♥	5♠	8♦/4♦	A♥	3♠
	10♥	6♠	J♥	Q♦	4♦	Q♣					
16	3♦	A♠	5♠	Q♥	J♦	3♠	6♣	3♣	9♠/A♥	3♥	6♦
	J♠	Q♠	A♣	Q♦	4♦	6♣					
17	4♠	A♣	10♣	Q♠	8♠	K♣	3♠	7♥	6♥/8♣	Q♠	9♠
	2♠	K♠	6♦	J♠	7♥	9♠					
18	Q♦	4♣	K♠	5♠	A♣	4♦	3♠	9♠	K♣/2♦	10♦	Q♥
	A♠	3♥	J♣	8♣	2♥	J♠					
19	8♠	A♣	10♣	J♠	9♥	6♠	J♥	6♣	8♥/10♠	Q♠	10♠
	6♥	7♠	8♦	A♠	5♣	6♣					
20	K♣	6♦	J♠	J♣	9♠	8♥	5♦	10♥	3♦/K♠	8♦	4♥
	6♥	3♥	A♠	10♠	10♣	5♥					
21	2♠	6♥	J♠	5♥	4♦	Q♠	6♣	A♠	8♦/K♥	7♠	4♠
	7♣	9♥	2♥	8♠	6♠	6♠					
22	9♦	K♠	4♣	A♣	6♥	7♥	A♦	6♠	Q♣/10♠	J♠	10♣
	J♦	Q♠	7♠	K♣	3♥	8♠	6♥				
23	8♣	9♠	8♥	8♠	Q♦	5♠	4♣	2♦	5♣/Q♠	10♠	J♠
	3♠	10♦	J♦	10♥	3♠	4♣					
24	J♠	5♦	8♠	7♣	4♥	6♦	5♠	5♠	K♠/A♠	4♠	7♣
	6♥	7♠	J♦	Q♠	J♣	5♠					
25	K♠	Q♦	2♥	9♠	K♥	Q♠	8♦	9♣	6♦/9♣	4♥	8♦
	Q♥	10♠	K♣	5♦	10♦	J♥	K♥				
26	2♦	10♣	Q♥	J♦	5♥	6♣	K♥	4♣	3♥/4♦	10♠	Q♠
	J♠	K♣	J♠	6♦	9♦	K♥					
27	4♣	9♦	Q♦	10♣	10♦	10♠	6♣	6♣	7♦/7♥	Q♥	10♦
	8♦	J♥	6♠	8♥	6♦	9♣					
28	2♠	8♦	10♣	J♣	J♦	7♠	Q♣	3♦	J♥/8♠	9♠	Q♠
	K♥	5♣	4♥	Q♥	3♥	J♠					
29	2♥	7♠	K♣	7♠	4♠	10♥	J♣	7♥	9♥/10♦	6♦	3♥
	2♠	7♥	4♥	2♦	J♣						
30	3♠	10♠	7♠	6♦	A♥	9♥	K♥	5♠	9♣/A♠	3♠	A♥
	9♠	5♠	4♥	4♣	3♦	K♥					
31	Q♥	J♠	3♠	3♥	7♥	9♠	6♦	9♥	2♣/10♦	J♦	A♦
	8♣	A♠	4♦	2♦	Q♣	6♦					
32	2♠	8♣	3♥	8♠	8♦	2♠	5♦	4♥	8♥/7♠	J♣	2♦
	A♥	4♠	K♠	3♠	5♠	9♥					
33	Q♦	A♥	8♠	6♠	K♠	A♠	2♥	8♥	2♣/A♦	10♥	6♣
	4♠	7♥	4♣	7♠	3♥	4♥	K♠				
34	A♠	7♥	3♠	4♥	10♥	Q♠	9♥	10♣	K♥/J♣	5♠	8♠
	8♥	Q♠	10♠	K♠	7♠	6♥					
35	7♣	A♥	4♥	3♠	5♣	8♥	5♦	2♠	Q♣/2♦	4♦	K♠
	8♠	2♣	6♠	9♥	3♠	5♦					
36	4♣	7♥	3♠	10♦	A♦	8♠	K♠	6♠	9♠/A♣	5♥	2♠
	10♥	4♦	4♠	3♠	4♥	6♠	A♦				
37	Q♠	A♥	6♣	K♠	6♠	2♥	2♠	9♥	10♦/6♦	5♠	6♠
	8♥	2♦	9♠	A♦	3♣	J♣					
38	2♥	3♠	4♠	J♣	J♦	K♥	A♥	6♥	8♠/J♠	4♠	9♠
	10♥	7♠	7♥	A♦	6♠	A♥					
39	6♥	10♥	J♠	9♠	3♥	8♠	10♣	J♥	10♦/Q♥	6♥	K♥
	9♦	K♣	Q♠	2♦	4♦	10♣					
40	2♣	10♠	8♦	3♠	A♠	9♦	9♠	10♥	7♥/J♠	3♦	2♣
	9♥	K♥	6♠	10♣	J♣	K♠					
41	3♣	9♥	3♠	J♥	4♠	7♥	A♣	6♠	8♥/Q♦	Q♦	A♠
	10♣	Q♥	6♥	K♣	8♣	A♣					
42	7♦	J♦	J♥	4♥	A♠	2♥	7♥	3♠	9♦/5♥	9♦	7♥
	2♦	J♠	3♥	4♣	10♠	7♥					
43	K♣	K♥	4♥	7♠	10♦	K♠	A♥	Q♠	2♥/A♥	5♦	8♥
	3♣	9♣	3♥	5♥	J♥	4♠	10♦				
44	A♠	2♠	3♠	4♠	5♠	6♠	7♠	9♠	8♠/9♠	3♠	7♠
	6♦	Q♣	5♣	J♥	4♥	Q♠					
45	6♥	4♣	2♦	J♠	8♣	6♦	4♠	8♠	10♥/10♦	K♦	K♦
	9♥	2♥	4♦	J♣	5♥	4♠					
46	J♦	9♥	J♠	3♣	8♦	10♥	5♦	4♦	8♥/K♥	7♠	3♣
	5♠	3♦	4♦	10♦	4♠	K♠					
47	7♣	5♠	3♣	7♥	9♥	6♣	10♥	3♠	Q♥/5♣	8♥	5♦
	3♥	8♠	A♣	K♥	6♦	10♥					
48	A♠	6♠	2♦	5♠	9♠	4♠	6♠	6♥	2♠/A♥	7♥	9♦
	8♥	5♥	9♦	5♠	8♦	10♠					
49	3♦	7♥	5♠	7♦	4♥	8♥	10♣	8♦	5♥/7♠	A♠	Q♦
	10♥	K♣	9♠	8♦	6♦	10♣					

AGE	MER	VEN	MAR	JUP	SAT	URA	NEP	LR	PLU/RES	ENV	DISP
50	2♠	6♠	7♦	6♥	J♥	10♥	6♣	6♦	2♥/8♠	2♣	3♦
	2♦	A♥	10♠	8♦	Q♥	6♣					
51	3♣	Q♠	9♠	8♠	4♦	3♠	6♥	8♣	4♠/Q♣	K♥	6♥
	3♦	10♠	6♦	A♥	7♥	2♣					
52	8♠	6♦	8♣	5♥	J♦	3♦	4♥	5♥	10♦/J♠	9♠	4♣
	J♥	10♥	Q♥	2♠	6♠	5♣					
53	7♥	6♣	8♠	9♥	9♦	J♥	5♥	J♦	A♥/A♣	6♠	5♣
	K♠	8♦	2♦	7♦	Q♠	7♣					
54	6♠	6♥	9♥	3♠	9♠	9♣	Q♦	3♦	K♥/K♣	2♠	5♥
	10♥	2♠	7♥	A♣	3♣	Q♦					
55	Q♠	6♣	J♠	10♦	5♣	10♥	3♠	4♥	K♠/10♠	K♣	4♦
	9♦	7♠	5♠	K♣	9♥	2♥					
56	J♥	6♥	10♦	2♥	Q♣	8♠	2♣	7♥	A♠/4♠	8♠	5♠
	9♣	5♠	8♦	6♠	K♣	3♣					
57	3♠	10♣	Q♥	10♠	6♠	7♥	8♠	6♣	9♦/7♦	6♣	10♥
	K♥	7♠	6♦	4♦	7♣	2♠					
58	K♣	A♦	10♦	10♣	3♠	4♣	7♥	8♠	J♠/A♥	2♦	J♣
	A♠	5♣	2♦	7♦	A♣	7♥					
59	6♥	A♣	10♣	3♥	10♠	J♠	Q♦	7♦	5♣/5♠	A♦	J♦
	6♣	9♠	8♣	A♣	10♦	Q♦					
60	9♥	5♥	2♦	5♠	8♥	6♣	3♥	9♦	8♦/4♥	A♥	3♠
	10♥	6♠	J♥	Q♦	4♦	Q♣					
61	3♦	A♠	5♠	Q♥	J♦	3♠	6♣	J♥	9♠/A♥	3♥	6♦
	J♠	Q♠	J♣	Q♦	4♦	6♣					
62	4♠	2♥	10♣	Q♣	8♠	K♣	3♠	5♥	6♥/8♣	Q♣	9♣
	2♠	K♠	6♦	J♠	9♥	9♣					
63	Q♦	4♣	K♠	5♠	2♥	4♦	3♣	6♠	K♣/2♦	10♦	Q♥
	A♠	3♥	J♣	8♠	A♣	J♠					
64	8♠	A♦	10♣	J♠	7♦	6♠	J♥	6♥	8♥/10♠	Q♠	10♠
	6♥	7♣	8♦	A♠	5♣	6♣					
65	K♣	6♦	J♠	J♣	9♣	8♥	5♦	7♦	3♦/K♠	8♦	4♥
	6♥	3♥	A♠	10♠	10♣	5♥					
66	2♠	6♥	J♣	5♥	4♦	Q♣	6♠	3♠	8♦/K♥	7♣	4♠
	7♣	7♥	A♣	8♠	6♠	6♣					
67	9♦	K♠	4♠	2♥	6♥	7♥	A♦	9♠	Q♣/10♠	J♠	10♣
	J♦	Q♠	7♠	K♣	3♥	8♠	6♥				
68	8♣	9♠	8♥	8♠	Q♦	5♠	4♣	9♣	5♣/Q♠	10♣	J♠
	3♠	10♦	J♦	10♥	3♣	4♠					
69	J♠	5♦	8♠	7♣	4♥	6♦	5♠	Q♦	K♣/A♠	4♠	7♣
	6♥	7♠	J♦	Q♠	J♠	5♠					
70	K♠	Q♦	A♣	9♥	K♥	Q♣	8♦	Q♠	6♦/9♣	4♥	8♦
	Q♥	10♠	K♣	5♦	10♦	J♥	K♥				
71	2♦	10♣	Q♥	J♦	5♥	6♣	K♥	6♣	3♥/4♦	10♠	Q♠
	J♠	K♣	J♣	6♦	9♦	K♥					
72	4♣	9♦	Q♦	10♣	10♦	10♠	6♣	J♠	9♥/7♥	Q♥	10♦
	8♦	J♥	6♠	8♥	6♦	9♣					
73	2♠	8♦	10♣	J♣	J♦	9♦	Q♣	10♦	J♥/8♠	9♣	Q♠
	K♥	5♣	4♥	Q♥	3♥	J♠					
74	A♣	7♠	K♣	7♠	4♠	10♥	J♣	5♣	7♦/10♦	6♦	3♥
	2♠	7♥	4♥	2♦	4♦	J♣					
75	3♣	10♠	7♣	6♦	A♥	7♦	K♥	10♥	9♣/A♠	3♠	A♥
	9♠	5♠	4♥	4♣	3♦	K♥					
76	Q♥	J♠	3♠	3♥	9♥	9♠	6♦	3♠	2♣/10♦	J♦	A♠
	8♣	2♥	4♦	2♦	Q♣	6♦					
77	2♠	8♣	3♥	8♠	8♦	2♣	5♦	J♥	8♥/7♠	J♣	2♦
	A♥	4♠	K♠	3♣	5♣	7♥					
78	Q♦	A♥	8♠	6♠	K♠	A♠	A♣	6♥	2♣/A♦	10♥	6♣
	4♣	9♥	3♣	7♠	3♥	4♥	K♠				
79	A♠	7♥	3♠	4♥	10♥	Q♠	7♦	10♦	K♠/J♣	5♠	8♠
	8♥	Q♣	10♠	K♠	7♠	6♥					
80	7♣	A♥	4♥	3♠	5♠	8♥	5♦	A♣	Q♣/2♦	4♦	K♣
	8♠	2♣	6♠	9♦	3♠	5♦					
81	4♣	7♥	3♣	10♦	A♦	8♠	K♠	Q♣	9♠/2♥	5♥	2♣
	10♥	4♦	4♣	3♠	4♥	6♠	A♦				
82	Q♠	A♥	6♣	K♠	6♠	A♣	2♠	8♠	10♦/6♦	5♣	6♠
	8♥	2♦	9♠	A♦	3♣	J♣					
83	A♣	3♠	4♣	J♣	J♦	K♥	A♥	2♣	8♣/J♠	4♣	9♠
	10♥	7♠	7♥	A♦	6♠	A♥					
84	6♥	10♥	J♣	9♠	3♥	8♣	10♣	3♠	10♦/Q♥	6♥	K♥
	9♠	K♣	Q♠	2♦	4♦	10♣					
85	2♣	10♠	8♣	3♠	A♠	9♦	9♠	10♣	7♥/J♠	3♦	2♣
	7♠	K♥	6♠	10♣	J♣	K♠					
86	3♣	7♦	3♠	J♥	4♠	7♥	2♥	Q♥	8♥/Q♦	Q♦	A♠
	10♣	Q♥	6♥	K♣	8♠	2♥					
87	9♥	J♦	J♥	4♥	A♠	A♣	7♥	10♠	9♦/5♥	9♦	7♥
	2♦	J♠	3♥	4♣	10♠	7♥					
88	K♣	K♥	4♥	7♣	10♥	K♠	A♥	6♠	A♣/A♥	5♦	8♥
	3♣	9♠	3♥	5♥	J♥	4♠	10♦				
89	A♠	2♠	3♠	4♠	5♠	6♠	7♠	7♥	8♠/9♠	3♣	7♠
	6♦	Q♣	5♠	J♥	4♥	Q♠					
90	6♥	4♣	2♦	J♠	8♣	6♦	4♠	8♠	10♥/10♦	K♦	K♥
	7♦	A♣	4♦	J♣	5♥	4♠					
91	J♦	7♠	J♠	3♣	8♦	10♥	5♦	K♣	8♥/K♥	7♠	3♣
	5♠	3♦	4♦	10♦	4♠	K♣					
92	7♣	5♠	3♣	7♥	9♠	6♠	10♥	A♦	Q♥/5♣	8♥	5♦
	3♥	8♣	2♥	K♥	6♠	10♥					
93	A♠	6♠	2♣	5♠	9♣	4♣	6♣	10♦	2♣/A♥	7♥	9♦
	8♥	5♥	9♥	5♣	8♦	10♠					
94	3♦	7♥	5♠	9♥	4♥	8♥	10♠	10♣	5♥/7♠	A♠	Q♦
	10♥	K♣	9♠	8♦	6♦	10♣					
95	2♠	Q♠	9♥	6♥	J♥	10♥	6♠	3♠	A♣/8♠	2♣	3♦
	2♦	A♥	10♠	8♦	Q♥	6♣					
96	3♣	Q♠	9♠	8♣	4♦	3♠	6♥	4♣	4♠/Q♣	K♥	6♥
	3♦	10♣	6♦	A♥	7♥	2♣					
97	8♦	6♦	8♣	5♥	J♦	3♦	4♥	7♥	10♦/J♠	9♠	4♣
	J♥	10♥	Q♥	2♠	6♠	5♣					
98	7♥	6♣	8♠	7♥	9♦	J♥	5♥	6♥	A♥/2♥	6♠	5♣
	K♠	8♦	2♦	9♥	Q♠	7♣					
99	6♠	6♥	7♦	3♠	9♠	9♣	Q♦	A♠	K♥/K♣	2♠	5♥
	10♥	2♠	9♥	2♥	3♣	Q♦					

The Yearly Spreads ♦ 327

Ace of Spades

AGE	MER	VEN	MAR	JUP	SAT	URA	NEP	LR	PLU/RES	ENV	DISP
0	7♥	7♦	5♠	J♥	9♣	9♠	2♥	7♥	K♥/K♦	A♣	A♠
	Q♥	J♦	5♦	A♦	8♣	2♥					
1	9♥	4♦	J♥	6♦	6♠	A♣	9♠	7♦	7♠/3♦	2♣	7♥
	Q♣	10♠	8♦	9♦	3♠	9♠					
2	A♠	K♠	6♦	4♥	J♠	K♠	10♦	5♠	A♣/Q♠	K♥	8♥
	7♥	J♣	8♦	3♦	J♥	9♣	J♠				
3	6♠	2♦	5♠	9♣	4♣	6♣	2♣	J♥	A♥/8♠	9♠	7♣
	10♥	7♦	Q♦	J♥	6♦	10♣					
4	5♦	9♦	Q♠	10♠	8♠	10♥	9♣	9♣	5♣/J♠	6♠	K♦
	7♠	A♣	6♥	5♥	3♦	9♣					
5	4♦	7♦	10♠	7♥	4♠	5♠	8♥	9♠	K♥/K♣	2♠	3♠
	4♣	3♣	6♥	J♠	9♠	A♦					
6	4♥	4♣	7♥	9♠	8♠	3♥	5♣	2♥	J♦/Q♦	K♣	5♦
	8♦	8♣	2♥	K♣	10♥	5♣					
7	6♠	6♣	Q♣	4♣	J♣	9♠	3♥	9♥	2♠/Q♠	8♠	9♦
	K♥	3♦	7♠	Q♦	7♠	3♠					
8	3♣	9♠	4♣	9♥	6♦	K♥	Q♥	4♦	3♦/2♣	6♣	Q♦
	5♣	A♦	8♠	4♠	10♥	Q♥					
9	2♦	6♣	9♥	5♦	J♥	5♠	3♥	J♥	A♣/A♥	2♦	3♦
	Q♣	Q♠	3♠	4♠	J♦	3♥					
10	7♥	10♣	J♣	8♣	6♥	5♠	5♦	6♦	9♣/7♠	A♦	6♥
	3♠	Q♥	10♥	Q♠	9♠	2♠					
11	4♠	10♥	8♠	3♦	4♦	3♣	6♦	6♠	J♠/10♠	A♥	4♣
	J♥	5♣	J♦	2♦	6♣	Q♦					
12	9♠	3♥	A♥	7♦	7♠	J♥	3♦	A♣	Q♠/2♥	3♥	5♣
	K♠	4♠	Q♣	9♥	10♣	4♦					
13	6♣	5♦	7♦	5♠	8♠	J♣	K♦	9♠	K♣/A♦	Q♣	5♥
	5♣	2♦	9♥	2♥	7♥	K♦					
14	10♣	3♥	10♠	J♠	Q♦	5♣	5♠	A♠	K♠/3♠	10♦	4♦
	7♠	2♣	4♣	A♦	7♦	A♣					
15	J♥	5♦	J♠	A♣	7♠	A♥	2♠	K♣	6♠/9♣	Q♠	5♠
	J♠	4♣	4♠	6♠	A♦	7♥					
16	5♠	Q♥	J♦	3♠	6♠	9♠	A♥	6♦	7♠/9♥	8♦	10♥
	K♣	2♠	10♥	6♥	4♥	2♠					
17	A♦	10♦	J♠	Q♥	7♥	9♠	9♠	4♦	10♠/Q♠	7♣	J♠
	6♠	Q♦	Q♣	9♥	2♥	9♠					
18	5♦	6♣	Q♥	8♦	3♠	10♠	K♦	J♠	Q♦/4♣	J♠	J♦
	3♥	J♣	8♠	2♥	J♠	K♦					
19	7♦	3♦	Q♠	4♦	K♥	3♥	8♦	K♠	4♠/6♦	10♣	3♦
	5♣	6♣	J♥	K♦	6♥	Q♦					
20	3♣	6♠	4♣	J♦	4♦	5♠	3♥	10♦	8♠/Q♠	4♠	6♦
	10♠	10♣	5♥	K♦	6♥	3♥					
21	9♣	A♠	Q♥	7♣	A♥	A♦	5♠	6♠	5♦/8♠	4♥	9♣
	2♠	K♠	10♥	10♠	7♦	J♣					
22	K♦	9♦	K♠	4♠	A♣	6♥	7♥	2♦	A♦/Q♣	10♠	Q♥
	6♠	8♦	5♥	8♣	2♥	10♠					
23	A♥	10♦	Q♥	10♠	9♥	J♥	5♠		K♥/3♠	Q♥	10♠
	5♦	4♥	4♠	6♠	Q♦	3♥					
24	A♦	10♥	10♠	5♥	J♣	K♥	8♥	9♠	3♣/K♠	9♣	4♥
	5♦	8♠	6♠	3♠	Q♥	3♦					
25	2♦	5♦	5♥	3♦	6♥	7♣	3♥	4♦	4♠/K♣	6♦	4♠
	4♥	9♥	2♥	A♥	6♣	3♥					
26	7♠	K♠	9♠	A♣	5♦	9♠	10♦	6♣	7♣/3♠	3♠	10♣
	4♦	10♣	4♥	A♦	8♦	A♥	5♦				
27	8♠	8♠	K♥	A♥	K♦	4♣	9♦	2♣	Q♦/10♣	J♦	J♠
	5♠	J♠	4♦	5♠	7♥	9♦					
28	10♠	8♥	A♥	4♥	6♦	10♥	4♣	5♦	A♦/6♠	J♣	7♣
	5♦	2♣	4♦	10♣	5♥	4♣					
29	K♠	K♦	2♥	7♠	K♣	7♠	4♠	9♦	10♥/J♣	10♥	8♦
	J♦	3♠	A♦	8♥	J♠	J♥	K♣				
30	Q♣	Q♥	J♦	4♦	3♦	3♥	K♠	Q♣	8♦/6♥	5♠	Q♠
	10♠	A♦	5♥	10♥	7♠	K♣					
31	9♦	7♠	K♦	Q♥	J♠	3♠	3♥	10♠	7♦/9♠	4♦	10♦
	4♠	J♥	6♣	K♥	10♥	J♣					
32	2♦	4♠	Q♥	5♦	4♦	7♦	7♣	8♣	J♥/A♥	5♦	Q♣
	K♣	Q♦	6♦	J♦	8♦	10♠					
33	2♥	2♣	A♦	4♥	9♠	5♠	5♥	10♥	9♥/J♠	5♠	3♥
	2♦	9♠	6♦	Q♣	6♥	5♥					
34	7♥	3♠	4♥	10♥	Q♠	9♥	K♠	9♠	J♣/6♠	4♣	A♥
	8♠	Q♦	6♦	9♦	3♣	K♠					
35	J♦	10♠	5♠	8♦	7♦	8♠	10♥	4♦	2♠/J♦	6♥	A♥
	8♣	A♣	6♥	Q♣	7♣	10♥					
36	2♦	8♠	8♦	A♥	4♠	2♠	8♥	7♣	K♥/2♣	3♦	2♦
	Q♠	9♠	K♠	7♥	Q♦	9♥					
37	K♦	Q♠	A♥	6♣	K♠	6♠	2♥	10♠	2♠/10♦	Q♦	6♣
	9♦	7♦	7♥	2♣	8♦	6♥	K♠				
38	6♠	9♠	5♠	6♦	5♠	10♣	9♥	7♥	A♦/5♥	9♦	8♠
	K♥	7♣	3♠	K♠	2♣	5♦					
39	4♦	Q♠	6♦	7♥	Q♦	K♥	8♥	4♠	7♣/Q♣	5♦	K♣
	A♥	2♠	3♥	7♠	5♠	8♥					
40	9♦	9♠	7♥	J♠	10♦	A♥	K♠	5♠	8♠/A♣	3♣	2♠
	5♣	6♥	9♠	5♠	6♦	6♣	10♦				
41	10♣	Q♠	3♥	K♠	6♣	2♥	2♦	8♥	J♠/10♥	K♦	6♠
	K♥	Q♣	8♠	10♦	7♥	5♥					
42	2♥	7♥	9♠	5♦	4♦	K♣	Q♠	4♥	8♣/10♠	7♠	9♠
	5♣	2♣	9♠	10♦	6♠	Q♠					
43	5♦	5♣	5♥	8♠	8♦	8♣	Q♥	4♦	J♠/J♦	8♥	K♥
	7♠	A♦	10♣	Q♣	6♥	Q♥					
44	2♠	3♠	4♠	5♠	6♠	7♠	8♠	7♥	9♠/10♠	7♥	2♣
	9♥	K♣	6♠	Q♠	5♥	K♠					
45	7♥	9♥	5♠	J♥	9♣	9♠	A♣	9♠	K♥/K♦	A♠	A♠
	Q♥	J♦	5♦	A♦	8♣	A♣					
46	7♦	4♦	J♥	6♦	6♠	2♥	9♠	8♠	7♠/3♦	2♣	7♥
	Q♣	10♠	8♦	9♦	3♠	9♠					
47	A♦	K♠	6♦	4♥	J♠	K♠	10♦	3♥	2♥/Q♠	K♥	8♥
	7♥	J♣	8♦	3♦	J♥	9♣	J♠				
48	6♠	2♦	5♠	9♣	4♣	6♣	2♣	5♣	A♥/8♠	9♠	7♣
	10♥	7♦	Q♦	J♥	6♦	10♣					
49	5♦	9♦	Q♣	10♠	8♣	10♥	9♣	6♠	5♣/J♠	6♠	K♦
	9♥	2♥	6♥	5♥	3♦	9♣					

AGE	MER	VEN	MAR	JUP	SAT	URA	NEP	LR	PLU/RES	ENV	DISP
50	4♦	9♥	10♠	7♥	4♠	5♣	8♥	6♣	K♥/K♣	2♠	3♣
	4♣	3♣	6♥	J♠	9♣	A♦					
51	4♥	4♣	7♥	9♠	8♠	3♥	5♣	Q♣	J♦/Q♦	K♣	5♦
	8♦	8♠	A♣	K♠	10♥	5♣					
52	6♠	6♣	Q♣	4♣	J♠	9♥	3♥	4♣	2♠/Q♠	8♠	9♦
	K♥	3♦	7♠	Q♦	4♠	3♠					
53	3♣	9♠	4♣	7♦	6♦	K♥	Q♥	J♣	3♦/2♣	6♣	Q♦
	5♣	A♦	8♠	4♠	10♥	Q♥					
54	2♦	6♣	7♦	5♦	J♥	5♣	3♥	9♦	2♥/A♥	2♦	3♦
	Q♣	Q♠	3♠	4♠	J♦	3♥					
55	7♥	10♣	J♠	8♠	6♥	5♠	5♦	3♥	9♣/7♣	A♦	6♥
	3♠	Q♥	10♥	Q♠	9♠	2♠					
56	4♠	10♥	8♣	3♦	4♦	3♣	6♦	3♣	J♠/10♠	A♥	4♣
	J♥	5♣	J♦	2♦	6♣	Q♦					
57	9♠	3♥	A♥	9♥	7♠	J♥	3♦	9♠	Q♠/A♠	3♥	5♣
	K♠	4♠	Q♣	7♦	10♣	4♥					
58	6♣	5♦	9♥	5♠	8♠	J♣	K♦	4♣	K♣/A♦	Q♣	5♥
	5♦	2♦	7♠	A♣	7♥	K♦					
59	10♣	3♥	10♠	J♠	Q♦	5♣	5♠	9♥	K♠/3♠	10♦	4♦
	7♠	2♣	4♣	A♦	9♥	2♥					
60	J♥	5♦	J♠	2♥	7♣	A♥	2♠	6♦	6♠/9♣	Q♠	5♠
	J♣	4♣	4♠	6♣	A♦	7♥					
61	5♠	Q♥	J♦	3♠	6♣	9♠	A♥	K♥	7♠/7♦	8♦	10♥
	K♠	2♣	10♥	6♥	4♥	2♦					
62	A♦	10♦	J♠	Q♥	7♥	9♦	9♠	Q♥	10♠/Q♠	7♣	J♣
	6♠	Q♦	Q♣	7♦	A♣	9♠					
63	5♦	6♠	Q♥	8♦	3♠	10♠	K♦	2♠	Q♦/4♣	J♠	J♦
	3♥	J♣	8♣	A♣	J♠	K♦					
64	9♥	3♦	Q♣	4♣	K♥	3♥	8♦	6♣	4♠/6♦	10♠	3♠
	5♣	6♣	J♥	K♦	6♥	7♣					
65	3♣	6♠	4♣	J♦	4♦	5♠	3♥	9♥	8♠/Q♠	4♠	6♦
	10♠	10♣	5♥	K♦	6♥	3♥					
66	9♣	2♥	Q♥	7♣	A♥	A♦	5♠	5♦	5♦/8♣	4♥	9♣
	2♦	K♠	10♥	10♠	9♥	J♣					
67	K♦	9♠	K♠	4♣	2♥	6♥	7♦	J♥	A♦/Q♣	10♠	Q♥
	6♠	8♠	5♥	8♣	A♣	10♠					
68	A♥	10♣	Q♥	10♠	7♦	6♣	J♥	5♣	K♥/3♠	Q♥	10♠
	5♦	4♥	4♠	6♠	Q♦	3♥					
69	A♦	10♥	10♠	5♥	J♣	K♥	8♥	3♥	3♣/K♠	9♣	4♥
	5♦	8♣	6♠	3♠	Q♥	3♦					
70	2♦	5♦	5♥	3♦	6♥	7♣	3♥	7♥	4♠/K♣	6♦	4♠
	4♥	7♦	A♣	A♥	6♠	3♥					
71	7♠	K♠	9♦	2♥	5♦	9♠	10♦	10♣	7♣/3♠	3♠	10♣
	4♦	10♣	4♥	A♠	8♦	A♥	5♦				
72	8♣	8♠	K♥	A♥	K♦	4♣	9♦	J♣	Q♦/10♣	J♦	J♠
	5♠	J♠	4♦	5♣	7♥	9♦					
73	10♠	8♥	A♥	4♥	6♦	10♥	4♠	8♣	A♦/6♠	J♣	7♣
	5♦	2♣	4♦	10♠	5♥	4♠					
74	K♠	K♦	A♣	7♠	K♦	7♣	4♠	6♥	10♥/J♣	10♥	8♦
	J♦	3♠	A♦	8♥	J♠	J♥	K♣				

AGE	MER	VEN	MAR	JUP	SAT	URA	NEP	LR	PLU/RES	ENV	DISP
75	Q♣	Q♥	J♦	4♦	3♦	3♥	K♣	5♠	8♦/6♥	5♠	Q♠
	10♠	A♦	5♥	10♥	7♠	K♣					
76	9♦	7♠	K♦	Q♥	J♠	3♠	3♥	5♦	9♥/9♠	4♦	10♦
	4♠	J♥	6♣	K♥	10♥	J♣					
77	2♦	4♠	Q♥	5♥	4♦	9♥	7♣	4♠	J♥/A♥	5♥	Q♣
	K♣	Q♦	6♦	J♦	8♦	10♠					
78	A♣	2♠	A♦	4♥	9♠	5♠	5♥	10♥	7♦/J♠	5♠	3♥
	2♦	9♠	6♦	Q♣	6♥	5♥					
79	7♥	3♠	4♥	10♥	Q♠	7♦	K♣	8♠	J♣/6♠	4♣	A♥
	8♠	Q♦	6♦	9♦	3♣	K♣					
80	J♦	10♠	5♠	8♦	9♥	8♠	10♥	3♦	2♠/J♠	6♥	A♦
	8♣	2♥	6♥	Q♣	7♣	10♥					
81	2♦	8♣	8♦	A♥	4♠	2♠	8♥	4♦	K♥/2♣	3♦	2♦
	Q♠	9♣	K♠	7♥	Q♦	7♠					
82	K♦	Q♠	A♥	6♣	K♠	6♠	A♣	3♣	2♠/10♦	Q♦	6♣
	9♦	9♥	7♦	2♣	8♦	6♥	K♣				
83	6♠	9♠	5♠	6♦	5♠	10♣	7♦	6♣	A♦/5♥	9♦	8♠
	K♥	7♠	3♠	K♠	2♣	5♦					
84	4♥	Q♠	6♦	7♥	Q♦	K♥	8♥	9♠	7♣/Q♣	5♦	K♣
	A♥	2♠	3♥	7♠	5♠	8♥					
85	9♦	9♠	7♥	J♠	10♦	A♥	K♠	3♥	8♠/2♥	3♣	2♠
	5♣	6♥	9♠	5♠	6♦	6♣	10♦				
86	10♣	Q♠	3♥	K♠	6♠	A♣	2♦	A♥	J♠/10♥	K♦	6♠
	K♥	Q♣	8♠	10♦	7♥	5♥					
87	A♣	7♥	9♠	5♥	4♦	K♣	Q♠	7♦	8♣/10♠	7♠	9♠
	5♣	2♣	9♠	10♦	6♣	Q♠					
88	5♦	5♠	5♥	8♠	8♦	8♠	Q♥	7♠	J♠/J♦	8♥	K♥
	7♣	A♦	10♣	Q♣	6♥	Q♥					
89	2♠	3♠	4♠	5♠	6♠	7♠	8♠	J♥	9♠/10♠	7♥	2♣
	7♦	K♣	6♠	Q♥	5♥	K♠					
90	7♥	7♦	5♠	J♥	9♠	9♠	2♥	3♦	K♥/K♦	A♠	A♠
	Q♥	J♦	5♠	A♦	8♣	2♥					
91	9♥	4♦	J♥	6♦	6♠	A♣	9♠	6♠	7♠/3♦	2♣	7♥
	Q♣	10♠	8♦	9♦	3♠	9♠					
92	A♦	Q♣	6♠	4♥	J♠	K♠	10♠	5♦	A♣/Q♠	K♥	8♥
	7♥	J♣	8♠	3♦	J♥	9♣	J♠				
93	6♠	2♠	5♠	9♣	4♦	6♣	2♣	7♦	A♥/8♠	9♠	7♠
	10♥	7♣	Q♦	J♥	6♦	10♣					
94	5♦	9♦	Q♣	10♠	8♠	10♥	9♠	5♠	5♣/J♠	6♠	K♦
	7♥	A♠	6♥	5♥	3♦	9♠					
95	4♦	7♦	10♠	7♥	4♠	5♠	8♥	8♠	K♥/K♣	2♠	3♦
	4♣	3♣	6♥	J♠	9♣	A♦					
96	4♥	4♣	7♥	9♠	8♠	3♥	5♣	J♣	J♦/Q♦	K♣	5♦
	8♦	8♠	2♥	K♣	10♥	5♣					
97	6♠	6♣	Q♣	4♣	J♣	9♦	3♥	K♦	2♠/Q♠	8♠	9♦
	K♥	3♦	7♠	Q♦	4♠	3♠					
98	3♣	9♠	4♣	9♥	6♦	K♥	Q♥	J♣	3♦/2♣	6♣	Q♦
	5♣	A♦	8♠	4♠	10♥	Q♥					
99	2♦	6♣	9♥	5♦	J♥	5♠	3♥	3♥	A♣/A♥	2♦	3♦
	Q♣	Q♠	3♠	4♠	J♦	3♥					

Two of Spades

Age	Mer	Ven	Mar	Jup	Sat	Ura	Nep	LR	Plu/Res	Env	Disp
0	8♥	6♣	6♠	Q♥	10♣	8♦	K♠	8♥	3♥/A♣	2♠	2♠
	9♣	3♠	10♥	6♥	5♠	Q♣	10♣				
1	9♣	4♠	7♠	K♠	Q♣	2♥	10♦	6♣	Q♥/4♣	K♣	6♠
	8♠	J♠	3♥	10♠	6♠	Q♦					
2	2♥	6♠	8♥	Q♦	3♦	A♥	4♠	6♠	8♣/J♦	8♠	9♦
	9♦	K♣	6♣	10♣	Q♣	4♠					
3	7♥	9♠	Q♦	3♥	4♥	8♣	J♣	Q♥	Q♥/5♥	6♠	K♥
	K♥	Q♠	9♠	J♠	3♣	4♦					
4	A♦	4♦	6♦	6♥	2♦	K♥	3♥	10♣	6♣/J♦	2♦	2♣
	9♥	A♥	Q♣	J♣	Q♦	K♠					
5	6♠	9♥	6♥	J♥	10♥	6♣	A♣	8♦	8♠/2♣	A♦	A♠
	J♣	5♥	7♥	Q♠	8♦	A♣					
6	7♦	3♦	J♥	5♠	2♦	2♥	6♣	K♠	K♥/K♦	A♥	7♥
	J♠	J♦	4♥	8♥	4♦	6♣					
7	Q♠	A♥	5♠	3♠	Q♥	K♠	10♣	9♠	2♥/4♣	3♥	8♥
	6♠	5♠	4♥	K♦	J♥	10♥	Q♥				
8	2♦	10♦	6♥	10♥	5♦	Q♣	K♣	4♠	8♦/3♥	Q♣	7♠
	4♣	10♠	7♠	J♥	5♠	9♣					
9	7♥	8♥	J♠	J♦	8♠	4♠	10♥	7♠	9♦/Q♥	10♦	K♥
	9♥	2♥	3♣	Q♦	K♠	10♥					
10	3♦	9♥	J♦	6♠	6♥	9♠		K♠	8♠/A♥	Q♠	3♣
	5♦	A♠	3♣	Q♥	10♥	Q♠					
11	3♠	5♠	6♠	6♣	3♥	7♣	9♦	Q♣	5♥/7♠	8♦	5♠
	4♥	8♠	A♣	A♥	4♣	9♦					
12	2♦	Q♣	J♠	5♠	5♠	8♥	7♠	2♥	A♦/4♠	7♣	9♦
	8♠	K♦	K♥	7♠	6♦	4♦					
13	A♠	6♣	5♦	7♠	5♠	8♠	J♣	10♦	K♦/K♠	8♠	Q♦
	9♦	Q♠	3♥	6♦	4♣	J♠					
14	10♦	Q♣	7♦	7♥	J♥	9♦	7♣	2♥	2♥/8♣	10♣	3♦
	J♠	4♠	4♦	6♦	5♥	7♣					
15	6♠	9♣	5♣	8♣	3♠	6♥	7♥	6♠	10♥/10♠	4♠	6♥
	A♠	J♠	4♠	4♠	6♠	A♦					
16	6♦	4♣	8♣	K♦	3♦	A♠	5♠	8♥	Q♥/J♦	4♥	4♣
	J♥	9♦	5♥	10♦	Q♣	7♠					
17	6♣	7♠	3♣	9♥	K♥	J♥	K♦	Q♠	4♠/A♠	10♠	5♠
	K♠	6♦	J♠	7♥	9♠	3♠					
18	Q♣	7♥	9♥	6♥	3♥	5♣	2♣	3♦	A♥/Q♠	Q♥	5♥
	9♦	10♦	7♥	A♣	6♠	2♣					
19	9♣	7♠	J♦	Q♥	7♠	4♠	6♥	A♥	K♠/4♦	9♣	4♦
	K♥	K♣	5♦	Q♠	9♥	2♥					
20	J♥	7♥	Q♥	2♥	10♠	8♠	A♦	4♠	2♦/10♥	6♦	5♠
	5♣	5♦	6♦	Q♣	Q♠	6♠					
21	6♥	J♣	5♥	4♦	Q♣	6♠	8♦	7♥	K♥/7♠	3♠	10♥
	A♥	K♣	4♣	3♠	3♠	10♦					
22	Q♠	10♣	Q♥	J♣	6♠	8♥	6♣	9♦	J♦/4♠	J♦	J♣
	2♦	7♠	J♠	7♦	A♣	6♣					
23	7♥	2♦	J♣	4♥	4♦	J♦	2♣	Q♦	7♠/5♦	J♦	J♣
	7♠	5♠	8♣	A♣	Q♥	2♠					
24	9♥	K♦	A♠	5♦	8♠	7♣	4♥	3♥	6♦/5♠	10♥	3♠
	9♦	Q♣	J♥	2♣	3♣	10♠					
25	A♠	2♦	5♦	5♥	3♦	6♥	7♣	4♥	3♥/4♠	5♠	6♦
	J♣	9♣	Q♦	2♣	3♣	7♣					
26	10♥	2♥	J♠	10♠	8♦	Q♠	6♥	8♣	7♥/8♣	4♦	9♣
	10♦	K♠	4♣	J♦	9♥	5♣					
27	2♣	8♥	K♠	5♦	2♥	3♣	6♠	J♣	Q♠/J♠	5♥	Q♥
	2♦	4♥	Q♦	8♣	A♣	J♦					
28	8♦	10♣	J♣	J♦	7♦	Q♣	J♥	A♦	8♠/4♦	5♣	10♠
	7♥	3♠	6♦	2♦	7♠	7♣					
29	Q♠	4♣	J♦	Q♦	5♣	8♠	9♠	4♦	A♠/K♠	4♣	4♥
	7♥	4♥	2♦	4♦	J♣	K♦					
30	10♦	7♥	Q♦	K♦	3♣	10♠	7♦	6♦	6♦/A♥	6♥	4♠
	3♠	7♦	A♣	8♦	Q♣	7♠					
31	K♥	K♠	8♦	2♥	7♥	6♣	10♣	6♥	10♠/4♦	3♦	10♣
	3♦	9♣	3♠	Q♠	4♥	8♦	7♥				
32	8♣	3♥	8♠	8♦	2♣	5♦	8♥	2♦	7♠/9♣	Q♦	J♠
	6♥	Q♥	3♦	9♦	6♠	8♥					
33	J♦	9♠	8♠	3♠	5♠	4♣	5♦	K♥	Q♠/2♦	9♦	7♣
	7♥	K♣	3♦	9♣	Q♦	5♦					
34	K♠	2♣	A♣	K♥	A♥	10♠	6♦	3♥	4♣/5♣	5♦	8♦
	5♥	4♠	Q♣	9♠	Q♥	J♥	A♥				
35	J♠	J♣	5♥	3♦	K♦	7♣	A♥	6♠	4♥/3♣	3♣	Q♠
	J♦	Q♠	Q♦	4♣	K♥	A♥					
36	8♥	K♥	2♣	J♣	Q♥	4♣	7♠	9♥	9♥/6♣	K♦	10♦
	6♦	J♥	Q♣	8♠	4♣	5♣					
37	10♦	6♦	J♣	Q♦	3♦	9♥	10♠	6♥	J♥/8♦	7♠	Q♣
	A♥	7♠	5♠	5♥	4♥	J♦					
38	A♣	K♣	Q♠	3♠	10♥	9♦	Q♦	J♥	7♦/Q♥	8♥	3♥
	10♦	6♣	5♠	J♠	3♣	Q♦					
39	6♠	4♦	3♠	4♣	4♠	7♦	A♥	10♥	5♣/2♦	7♥	A♥
	3♥	7♠	5♠	8♥	A♠	A♥					
40	5♥	J♦	6♥	4♥	9♥	3♥	4♣	6♠	A♦/Q♥	A♠	A♦
	8♠	2♥	3♣	J♠	10♠	4♣					
41	10♦	8♣	4♥	8♣	6♥	A♠	9♠	A♣	8♠/K♣	2♣	2♦
	4♠	10♥	K♠	6♠	7♠	7♦					
42	2♣	4♠	8♦	Q♣	K♣	2♦	A♠	7♦	A♦/10♣	K♥	6♠
	8♥	9♦	6♠	K♣	4♥	5♠	K♣				
43	2♦	6♣	6♥	5♦	9♥	9♣	7♦	3♦	Q♠/Q♦	9♠	8♠
	8♠	10♠	4♦	K♣	K♣	7♥					
44	3♠	4♠	5♠	6♠	7♠	8♠	9♠	J♥	10♠/J♠	6♠	K♣
	8♠	A♦	7♣	K♥	6♥	9♠					
45	8♥	6♣	6♠	Q♥	10♣	8♦	K♠	5♠	3♥/2♥	2♠	2♠
	9♦	3♣	10♥	6♥	5♠	Q♣	10♣				
46	9♣	4♠	7♠	K♠	Q♣	A♠	10♦	2♣	Q♥/4♣	K♣	6♠
	8♠	J♠	3♥	10♠	6♠	Q♦					
47	A♣	6♠	8♥	Q♦	3♦	A♥	4♠	2♥	8♣/J♦	8♠	9♠
	9♦	K♣	6♣	10♣	Q♣	4♠					
48	7♥	9♠	Q♦	3♥	4♥	8♣	J♣	6♠	Q♥/5♥	6♣	K♥
	K♥	Q♠	9♠	J♠	3♣	J♣					
49	A♦	4♦	6♦	6♥	2♦	K♥	3♥	Q♠	6♣/J♦	2♦	2♣
	7♦	A♥	Q♣	J♣	Q♦	K♠					

AGE	MER	VEN	MAR	JUP	SAT	URA	NEP	LR	PLU/RES	ENV	DISP
50	6♠	7♥	6♥	J♥	10♥	6♠	2♥	A♥	8♠/2♣	A♦	A♠
	J♣	5♥	7♥	Q♠	8♣	2♥					
51	9♥	3♦	J♥	5♠	2♦	A♣	6♣	5♠	K♥/K♦	A♥	7♥
	J♠	J♦	4♥	8♥	4♦	6♣					
52	Q♠	A♥	5♠	3♠	Q♥	K♠	10♣	3♠	A♣/4♠	3♥	8♥
	6♠	5♣	4♥	K♦	J♥	10♥	Q♥				
53	2♦	10♦	6♥	10♥	5♦	Q♣	K♣	Q♥	8♦/3♥	Q♣	7♠
	4♣	10♠	7♠	J♥	5♠	9♣					
54	7♥	8♥	J♠	J♦	8♣	4♣	10♥	K♠	9♦/Q♥	10♦	K♦
	7♦	A♣	3♣	Q♦	K♦	10♥					
55	3♦	7♥	J♦	6♠	6♦	9♦	9♠	10♠	8♠/A♥	Q♠	3♣
	5♦	A♣	3♣	Q♥	10♥	Q♠					
56	3♠	5♦	6♠	6♣	3♥	7♣	9♦	2♦	5♥/7♠	8♦	5♦
	4♥	8♠	2♥	A♥	4♣	9♦					
57	2♦	Q♣	J♠	5♦	5♠	8♥	7♠	10♦	A♠/4♠	7♠	9♦
	8♠	K♥	K♥	7♠	6♦	4♦					
58	A♠	6♣	5♦	9♥	5♠	8♠	J♣	6♥	K♦/K♣	J♠	Q♦
	9♦	Q♠	3♥	6♦	4♣	J♣					
59	10♦	Q♣	9♥	7♥	J♥	9♦	7♣	10♥	A♣/8♦	10♣	3♦
	J♠	4♣	4♦	6♦	5♥	7♣					
60	6♠	9♣	5♣	8♣	3♣	6♥	7♥	5♦	10♥/10♠	4♠	6♥
	A♠	J♣	4♣	4♠	6♣	A♦					
61	6♦	4♣	8♣	K♦	3♦	A♣	5♠	Q♣	Q♥/J♦	4♥	4♣
	J♥	9♦	5♥	10♦	Q♣	7♠					
62	6♣	7♣	8♦	7♦	K♥	J♥	K♦	K♣	4♠/2♥	10♠	5♣
	K♠	6♦	J♠	9♥	9♣	3♠					
63	Q♣	7♥	7♦	6♥	3♥	5♣	2♣	7♥	A♥/Q♠	Q♥	5♥
	9♦	10♦	9♥	2♥	6♠	2♣					
64	9♣	7♣	J♦	Q♥	7♠	9♦	6♥	8♥	K♠/4♦	9♣	4♦
	K♥	K♣	5♦	Q♠	7♥	A♣					
65	J♥	7♥	Q♥	A♣	10♠	8♦	A♦	J♠	2♦/10♥	6♦	5♠
	5♣	5♦	6♦	Q♣	Q♠	6♠					
66	6♥	J♠	5♥	4♦	Q♣	6♣	8♦	J♦	K♥/9♥	3♠	10♥
	A♥	K♠	4♣	3♣	3♠	10♦					
67	Q♠	10♣	Q♥	J♣	6♠	8♥	6♠	8♣	J♦/4♠	J♦	J♣
	2♦	7♠	J♠	9♥	2♦	6♣					
68	7♥	2♦	J♠	4♥	4♦	J♦	2♣	4♣	7♠/5♦	J♣	J♦
	7♣	5♣	8♣	2♥	Q♥	2♣					
69	7♦	K♦	J♠	5♦	8♠	7♠	4♥	10♥	6♦/5♠	10♥	3♠
	9♦	Q♣	J♥	2♣	3♣	10♠					
70	A♠	2♦	5♦	5♥	3♦	6♥	7♣	3♦	3♥/4♠	5♠	6♦
	J♦	9♠	Q♦	2♣	3♣	7♣					
71	10♥	A♣	J♣	10♠	8♦	Q♠	6♥	9♥	7♥/8♣	4♦	9♣
	10♦	K♠	4♣	J♦	7♦	4♣					
72	2♣	8♥	K♠	5♦	A♣	3♣	6♠	J♦	Q♠/J♠	5♥	Q♥
	2♦	4♥	Q♦	8♣	2♥	J♦					
73	8♦	10♣	J♣	J♦	9♥	Q♣	J♥	6♠	8♠/4♦	4♣	10♠
	7♥	3♠	3♦	2♦	7♠	7♣					
74	Q♠	4♣	J♦	Q♦	5♣	8♠	9♠	6♦	A♠/K♠	4♣	4♥
	7♥	4♦	2♦	4♦	J♣	K♦					
75	10♦	7♥	Q♦	K♠	3♣	10♠	7♣	9♦	6♦/A♥	6♥	4♠
	3♠	9♥	2♥	8♦	Q♣	7♣					
76	K♥	K♠	8♥	A♣	7♥	6♣	10♣	9♠	10♠/4♦	3♦	10♣
	3♦	9♣	3♠	Q♠	4♥	8♦	7♥				
77	8♣	3♥	8♠	8♦	2♣	5♦	8♥	3♠	7♠/9♣	Q♦	J♠
	6♥	Q♥	3♦	9♦	6♠	8♥					
78	J♦	9♠	8♦	3♠	5♠	4♣	5♦	5♠	Q♠/2♦	9♦	7♣
	7♥	K♣	3♦	9♣	Q♦	5♦					
79	K♠	2♣	2♥	K♥	A♥	10♠	6♦	6♠	4♣/5♣	5♦	8♦
	5♥	4♦	Q♠	9♠	Q♥	J♥	A♥				
80	J♠	A♣	5♥	3♦	K♦	7♠	A♥	6♠	4♥/3♣	3♣	Q♠
	J♦	Q♠	Q♦	4♣	K♥	A♥					
81	8♥	K♥	2♣	J♣	Q♥	4♦	7♣	3♥	7♦/6♣	K♦	10♦
	6♦	J♥	Q♣	8♠	4♣	5♣					
82	10♦	6♦	J♣	Q♦	3♦	7♦	10♠	7♣	J♥/8♦	7♠	Q♣
	A♥	7♠	5♠	5♥	4♥	J♦					
83	2♥	K♣	Q♠	3♠	10♥	9♦	Q♦	9♥	9♥/Q♥	8♥	3♥
	10♦	6♣	5♠	J♠	3♣	Q♦					
84	6♠	4♦	3♠	4♠	4♠	9♥	A♥	2♦	5♣/2♦	7♥	A♥
	3♥	7♠	5♠	8♥	A♠	A♥					
85	5♥	J♦	6♥	4♥	7♦	3♥	4♣	Q♣	A♦/Q♥	A♠	A♦
	8♣	A♣	3♠	J♠	10♠	4♣					
86	10♦	8♣	4♥	8♦	6♦	A♥	9♣	J♠	8♠/K♣	2♣	2♦
	4♠	10♥	K♠	6♠	7♠	9♥					
87	2♠	4♣	8♦	Q♣	K♠	2♦	2♥	5♦	A♦/10♣	K♥	6♣
	8♥	7♦	6♠	K♣	4♥	5♠	K♠				
88	2♦	6♣	5♥	5♠	9♥	9♣	9♥	5♣	Q♠/Q♦	9♠	8♠
	8♠	10♠	4♦	K♠	K♣	7♥					
89	3♠	4♣	5♠	6♠	7♠	8♠	9♠	8♥	10♠/J♠	6♠	K♣
	8♠	A♦	7♠	K♥	6♥	9♠					
90	8♥	6♣	6♠	Q♥	10♠	8♣	K♠	7♠	3♥/A♣	2♠	2♠
	9♦	3♣	10♥	6♥	5♠	Q♣	10♣				
91	9♣	4♠	7♣	K♠	Q♣	2♥	10♦	A♠	Q♥/4♣	K♣	6♠
	8♠	J♠	3♥	10♣	6♠	Q♦					
92	2♥	6♠	8♥	Q♦	3♦	A♥	4♠	6♣	8♣/J♦	8♠	9♠
	9♦	K♠	6♠	10♣	Q♣	4♠					
93	7♥	9♦	Q♦	3♥	4♥	8♠	J♣	5♦	Q♥/5♥	6♣	K♥
	K♥	Q♠	9♣	J♠	3♣	J♣					
94	A♦	4♦	6♦	6♥	2♦	K♥	3♥	7♦	6♣/J♣	2♦	2♣
	9♥	A♥	Q♣	J♣	Q♦	K♠					
95	6♠	9♥	6♥	J♥	10♥	6♠	A♣	5♠	8♠/2♣	A♦	A♠
	J♣	5♥	7♥	Q♠	8♣	A♣					
96	7♦	3♦	J♥	5♠	2♦	2♥	6♣	8♠	K♥/K♦	A♥	7♥
	J♠	J♦	4♥	8♥	4♦	6♣					
97	Q♠	A♥	5♠	3♠	Q♥	K♠	10♣	J♦	2♥/4♠	3♥	8♥
	6♠	5♣	4♥	K♦	J♥	10♥	Q♥				
98	2♦	10♦	6♥	10♥	5♦	Q♣	K♣	10♦	8♦/3♥	Q♣	7♠
	4♣	10♠	7♠	J♥	5♠	9♣					
99	7♥	8♥	J♠	J♦	8♣	4♣	10♥	Q♠	9♦/Q♥	10♦	K♦
	9♥	2♥	3♣	Q♦	K♦	10♥					

3♠ Three of Spades

AGE	MER	VEN	MAR	JUP	SAT	URA	NEP	LR	PLU/RES	ENV	DISP
0	9♥	7♣	5♦	Q♠	J♣	9♦	7♠	9♥	2♣/K♣	3♠	3♠
	10♦	4♣	J♥	10♠	8♦	8♥					
1	4♥	5♠	Q♠	6♠	3♥	A♥	9♦	7♣	5♣/K♦	J♦	6♦
	9♠	A♠	Q♣	10♠	8♦	9♦					
2	2♠	2♥	6♠	8♥	Q♦	3♦	A♥	5♦	4♠/8♣	J♣	9♣
	6♥	K♣	A♥	9♠	9♥	2♣					
3	10♠	10♣	K♠	Q♠	2♥	8♦	6♦	Q♠	3♦/5♦	10♥	Q♥
	5♠	7♠	Q♣	8♣	A♣	9♠					
4	Q♦	3♣	6♠	9♠	7♥	4♣	J♥	J♣	J♣/8♠	5♠	10♠
	4♠	K♥	2♣	5♠	J♠	9♦					
5	3♦	A♥	9♠	Q♣	2♦	J♣	9♣	9♦	4♥/K♣	4♦	4♥
	4♠	7♣	5♠	8♠	6♠	7♦					
6	6♥	4♠	Q♣	7♣	8♦	8♥	9♦	7♠	2♣/5♦	5♥	4♠
	K♥	7♥	A♠	Q♦	4♣	9♦					
7	Q♥	K♠	10♠	2♥	4♠	10♥	3♣	4♥	8♥/8♠	5♠	10♣
	3♥	A♠	K♥	3♦	7♠	Q♦	4♠				
8	8♣	5♣	J♠	Q♠	10♠	Q♠	10♣	5♠	J♠/A♠	4♣	J♠
	A♥	7♥	3♥	10♠	6♦	10♣					
9	9♠	9♣	Q♦	K♥	K♣	A♦	Q♠	Q♠	3♦/5♠	6♥	7♠
	4♠	J♦	3♥	A♠	Q♣	Q♠					
10	K♠	10♠	A♣	Q♥	5♥	8♥	2♣	6♣	A♦/2♦	3♦	8♦
	6♠	8♠	3♦	9♣	7♥	J♥	5♥				
11	5♠	6♠	6♠	3♥	7♠	9♦	5♥	3♥	7♠/8♦	Q♦	Q♠
	9♠	3♣	Q♠	A♦	Q♥	5♥					
12	10♣	Q♥	10♠	6♠	7♥	8♠	9♦	A♥	9♥/10♥	9♦	10♦
	2♣	J♥	4♣	J♣	A♦	2♦					
13	6♥	2♣	6♠	Q♣	3♥	9♥	8♥	9♦	J♥/Q♦	5♦	Q♣
	5♥	J♠	K♣	6♠	7♥	9♠					
14	A♣	J♦	3♦	K♥	2♠	10♦	Q♣	2♠	7♦/7♥	3♣	3♥
	6♥	10♥	K♣	5♦	8♦	Q♣					
15	6♦	8♠	K♥	A♦	K♦	7♦	5♥	2♥	2♦/5♠	K♦	A♥
	5♣	J♠	K♣	10♠	4♥	5♥					
16	6♣	9♠	A♥	7♠	9♥	5♣	A♦	6♠	4♦/7♥	7♠	A♠
	8♣	2♥	8♦	5♦	8♥	A♦					
17	6♥	8♠	7♠	Q♦	2♣	4♦	9♣	8♥	J♣/J♦	8♥	2♦
	K♦	2♠	K♠	6♦	J♠	7♦					
18	10♠	K♦	Q♠	4♣	K♠	5♠	A♣	Q♦	4♦/3♣	7♥	6♣
	10♣	9♥	6♦	J♦	7♠	K♣	K♠				
19	5♠	10♥	A♥	K♣	10♦	A♦	7♦	3♦	3♦/Q♣	A♠	8♦
	J♣	8♥	8♠	K♠	J♦	4♠					
20	K♥	K♦	K♣	6♦	J♠	J♠	9♣	A♥	8♥/5♦	2♣	K♣
	Q♦	4♦	9♦	Q♥	A♥	9♣					
21	10♣	10♥	6♦	7♥	3♣	Q♦	K♠	10♠	5♣/2♦	K♥	2♠
	10♠	8♦	2♠	A♥	K♣	3♣					
22	A♠	K♦	9♠	K♠	4♣	A♣	6♥	10♣	7♥/A♦	9♠	6♠
	J♣	5♦	5♠	3♣	6♦	Q♣					
23	A♣	6♦	10♣	Q♠	3♥	5♥	K♦	K♠	8♣/9♠	6♠	9♠
	10♠	J♦	10♥	3♣	4♣	K♦					
24	4♠	10♣	Q♣	5♠	7♠	8♣	6♠	Q♠	7♥/6♦	2♠	K♥
	Q♥	3♦	A♠	5♦	8♦	6♠					
25	4♦	8♠	2♠	A♥	5♠	Q♥	5♣	2♥	10♥/9♠	K♣	2♣
	7♠	5♦	4♠	6♠	Q♣	K♠					
26	6♦	7♠	A♥	J♥	2♠	10♥	2♥	8♦	J♣/10♠	8♠	A♠
	6♠	6♣	4♠	3♦	8♣	2♥					
27	9♥	3♥	J♥	K♣	5♠	A♣	10♥	6♦	Q♥/7♣	6♠	7♥
	5♦	9♠	7♠	10♣	8♠	10♥					
28	3♦	5♥	K♣	K♥	7♥	K♠	3♣	Q♦	A♠/K♦	2♦	8♥
	6♦	2♦	7♠	7♣	J♥	2♠	7♥				
29	5♠	6♥	A♥	2♠	Q♠	4♣	J♦	3♣	Q♦/5♣	A♦	7♠
	A♦	8♥	J♠	J♥	K♠	A♠					
30	4♠	10♣	5♦	9♠	8♠	A♦	2♠	6♠	10♦/7♥	A♥	K♦
	7♦	A♣	8♦	Q♣	7♠	2♠					
31	3♥	7♥	9♠	6♦	2♣	10♦	9♣	9♠	J♣/5♥	3♥	3♣
	Q♠	4♥	8♦	7♥	2♠	3♦					
32	K♥	Q♠	6♦	10♥	5♠	9♥	10♦	7♦	6♣/J♠	Q♣	5♦
	7♠	8♠	2♥	5♥	A♦	10♦					
33	5♠	4♣	5♦	Q♠	2♦	10♣	9♦	4♣	4♦/K♦	10♦	9♦
	J♣	7♣	Q♥	J♠	2♠	8♠					
34	4♥	10♥	Q♠	9♥	K♣	J♣	6♠	J♥	7♣/J♦	Q♠	Q♦
	10♦	3♦	5♣	2♠	A♦	6♠					
35	6♥	4♣	9♥	4♠	J♥	10♦	9♦	3♦	A♣/Q♦	8♦	3♦
	5♦	K♦	8♠	2♣	6♠	9♦					
36	6♦	A♠	2♦	8♣	8♦	A♥	4♠	A♦	2♠/8♥	7♣	6♥
	4♦	6♠	A♦	K♦	10♥	4♦					
37	2♣	A♦	8♣	7♠	3♥	4♥	K♣	9♠	7♥/9♠	J♠	4♠
	J♥	10♦	6♣	6♥	4♣	J♠					
38	10♥	9♦	Q♦	7♦	Q♥	J♥	7♣	Q♣	K♦/2♥	10♣	5♣
	K♠	2♣	5♦	9♥	A♠	K♥					
39	4♣	4♣	7♦	A♥	5♣	2♦	10♠	2♦	5♥/3♦	4♠	5♥
	10♦	6♥	9♥	2♥	6♦	10♠					
40	A♠	9♦	9♠	7♥	J♠	10♦	A♥	J♣	K♠/8♠	4♥	4♦
	Q♥	J♦	Q♠	3♦	7♦	A♣					
41	J♥	4♠	7♥	A♣	8♥	Q♦	4♦	9♣	5♠/2♠	10♠	5♠
	2♦	Q♠	2♣	4♠	3♦	6♦					
42	A♥	6♠	6♠	8♠	4♣	10♥	Q♦	6♦	Q♥/9♥	Q♥	10♥
	5♥	J♦	A♠	8♦	K♥	6♦					
43	3♦	3♠	7♥	6♠	6♦	10♣	10♥	4♠	9♠/K♦	9♣	J♣
	5♠	J♠	5♦	9♥	2♦	10♥					
44	4♠	5♠	6♠	7♠	8♠	9♠	10♠	Q♣	J♠/Q♠	6♦	J♦
	9♦	2♦	8♣	2♥	7♥	10♠					
45	7♦	7♣	5♦	Q♠	J♣	9♦	7♠	7♣	2♣/K♣	3♠	3♠
	10♦	4♣	J♥	10♠	8♦	8♥					
46	4♥	5♠	Q♠	6♠	3♥	A♥	9♦	8♦	5♣/K♦	J♦	6♦
	9♠	A♠	Q♣	10♠	8♦	9♦					
47	2♠	A♠	6♠	8♥	Q♦	3♦	A♥	8♥	4♠/8♣	J♣	9♣
	6♥	K♣	A♦	9♠	7♥	2♦					
48	10♠	10♣	K♠	Q♠	A♣	8♦	6♦	9♦	3♦/5♦	10♥	Q♥
	5♠	7♠	Q♣	8♣	2♥	9♠					
49	Q♦	3♣	6♠	9♠	9♥	4♣	J♥	Q♥	J♣/8♠	5♠	10♠
	4♠	K♥	2♣	5♠	J♠	9♦					

AGE	MER	VEN	MAR	JUP	SAT	URA	NEP	LR	PLU/RES	ENV	DISP
50	3♦	A♦	9♠	Q♣	2♦	J♣	9♣	K♠	4♥/K♠	4♦	4♥
	4♠	7♠	5♠	8♠	6♠	7♣					
51	6♥	4♠	Q♣	7♣	8♦	8♥	9♦	10♣	2♣/5♥	5♥	4♠
	K♥	9♥	2♥	Q♦	4♣	9♦					
52	Q♥	K♠	10♠	A♣	4♠	10♥	3♣	2♥	8♥/8♠	5♣	10♣
	3♥	A♠	K♥	3♦	7♠	Q♦	4♠				
53	8♣	5♠	J♣	Q♦	10♠	Q♠	10♣	4♠	J♠/A♠	4♠	J♠
	A♥	7♠	3♥	10♦	6♦	10♣					
54	9♠	9♠	Q♦	K♥	K♣	A♦	Q♠	10♥	3♦/5♠	6♥	7♣
	4♠	J♦	3♥	A♠	Q♣	Q♠					
55	K♠	10♠	2♥	Q♥	5♦	8♥	2♣	3♣	A♦/2♦	3♦	8♦
	6♣	8♠	3♦	9♣	7♥	J♥	5♦				
56	5♦	6♠	6♣	3♥	7♠	9♠	5♥	8♠	7♠/8♦	Q♦	Q♠
	9♠	3♦	Q♣	A♦	Q♥	5♥					
57	10♣	Q♥	10♠	6♠	7♥	8♠	9♦	5♠	7♦/10♥	9♦	10♦
	2♠	J♥	4♣	J♣	A♦	2♦					
58	6♥	2♣	6♠	Q♣	3♥	7♠	8♥	J♣	J♥/Q♦	5♦	Q♣
	5♥	J♠	K♣	6♠	7♠	9♠					
59	2♥	J♦	3♦	K♥	2♠	10♦	Q♣	Q♦	9♥/7♥	3♣	3♥
	6♥	10♥	K♣	5♦	8♦	Q♣					
60	6♦	8♠	K♥	A♦	K♦	9♥	5♥	10♠	2♦/5♠	K♦	A♥
	5♣	J♠	K♣	10♣	4♥	5♥					
61	6♣	9♠	A♥	7♠	7♠	5♠	A♦	Q♠	4♦/7♥	7♠	A♦
	8♠	A♣	8♦	5♦	8♥	A♦					
62	6♥	8♣	7♠	Q♦	2♣	4♦	9♣	10♣	J♣/J♦	8♥	2♦
	K♦	2♠	K♠	6♦	J♠	9♥					
63	10♠	K♦	Q♦	4♣	K♠	5♠	2♦	9♠	4♦/3♣	7♥	6♣
	10♣	7♦	6♦	J♦	7♠	K♣	K♠				
64	5♠	10♥	A♥	K♣	10♦	A♠	9♥	9♣	3♦/Q♣	A♠	8♠
	J♣	8♥	8♠	K♠	J♦	4♠					
65	K♥	K♦	K♣	6♦	J♠	J♣	9♣	Q♦	8♥/5♦	2♣	K♣
	Q♦	4♦	9♦	Q♥	A♥	9♣					
66	10♣	10♥	6♦	7♥	3♣	Q♦	K♠	K♥	5♣/A♣	K♥	2♠
	10♦	8♠	2♠	A♥	K♣	4♣	3♣				
67	A♠	K♦	9♦	K♠	4♣	2♥	6♥	K♣	7♥/A♣	9♠	6♠
	J♣	5♦	5♣	3♣	6♦	Q♣					
68	2♥	6♦	10♣	Q♣	3♥	5♥	K♦	A♠	8♣/9♠	6♠	9♠
	10♦	J♦	10♥	3♣	4♣	K♦					
69	4♠	10♦	Q♣	4♠	7♠	8♠	6♠	Q♠	7♥/6♣	2♠	K♥
	Q♥	3♦	A♠	5♦	8♦	6♠					
70	4♦	8♠	2♣	A♥	5♠	Q♥	5♣	K♠	10♥/9♠	K♣	2♣
	9♥	5♥	4♣	6♠	Q♣	K♠					
71	6♦	9♥	A♥	J♥	2♠	10♥	A♣	10♠	J♣/10♠	8♠	A♠
	6♠	6♣	4♠	3♦	8♣	A♣					
72	7♦	3♥	J♥	K♣	5♠	2♥	10♥	A♣	Q♥/7♣	6♣	7♥
	5♦	9♠	7♠	10♣	8♠	10♥					
73	3♦	5♥	K♣	K♥	7♥	K♠	3♣	Q♥	2♥/K♦	2♦	8♥
	6♦	2♦	7♠	7♦	J♥	2♠	7♥				
74	5♠	6♥	A♥	2♠	Q♠	4♣	J♦	5♥	Q♦/5♣	A♦	7♠
	A♦	8♥	J♠	J♥	K♣	A♠					

AGE	MER	VEN	MAR	JUP	SAT	URA	NEP	LR	PLU/RES	ENV	DISP
75	4♠	10♣	5♦	9♠	8♣	A♦	2♠	8♥	10♦/7♥	A♥	K♦
	9♥	2♦	8♦	Q♣	7♣	2♠					
76	3♥	9♥	9♠	6♦	2♣	10♦	9♣	2♣	J♣/5♥	3♥	3♣
	Q♠	4♥	8♦	7♥	2♠	3♦					
77	K♥	Q♠	6♦	10♥	5♣	9♦	10♦	5♦	6♣/J♠	Q♣	5♦
	7♠	8♣	A♣	5♥	A♦	10♦					
78	5♠	4♣	5♦	Q♠	2♦	10♣	9♦	6♠	4♦/K♦	10♦	9♦
	J♣	7♠	Q♥	J♠	2♣	8♠					
79	4♦	10♥	Q♠	7♦	K♣	J♠	6♠	6♣	7♣/J♦	Q♠	Q♦
	10♦	3♦	5♠	2♣	A♦	6♠					
80	6♥	4♣	7♦	4♠	J♥	10♦	9♦	3♥	2♥/Q♦	8♦	3♦
	5♦	K♦	8♠	2♣	6♠	9♦					
81	6♦	A♠	2♦	8♣	8♦	A♥	4♠	7♠	2♠/8♥	7♣	6♥
	4♥	6♠	A♦	K♦	10♥	4♦					
82	2♣	A♦	8♠	7♣	3♥	4♥	K♣	9♦	7♥/9♠	J♠	4♣
	J♥	10♦	6♣	6♥	4♣	J♠					
83	10♥	9♦	Q♠	9♥	Q♥	J♥	7♣	5♥	K♦/A♣	10♣	5♣
	K♠	2♣	5♦	7♠	A♠	K♥					
84	4♣	4♠	9♥	A♥	5♠	2♦	10♠	10♠	5♥/3♦	4♠	5♥
	10♦	6♥	7♦	A♣	6♦	10♠					
85	A♠	9♦	9♠	7♥	J♠	10♦	A♥	Q♥	K♠/8♠	4♥	4♦
	Q♥	J♦	Q♠	3♦	9♥	2♥					
86	J♥	4♠	7♥	2♥	8♥	Q♦	4♦	10♠	5♠/2♠	10♠	5♠
	2♦	Q♠	2♣	4♣	3♦	6♦					
87	A♥	6♠	6♠	8♠	4♣	10♥	Q♦	6♠	Q♥/7♦	Q♥	10♥
	5♥	J♦	A♦	8♦	K♥	6♥					
88	3♦	4♣	7♦	6♠	6♦	10♣	10♥	7♥	9♠/K♠	9♣	J♠
	5♠	J♣	5♦	7♠	A♣	10♥					
89	4♠	5♠	6♠	7♠	8♠	9♠	10♠	8♠	J♠/Q♠	6♦	J♦
	9♦	2♦	8♠	A♣	7♥	10♠					
90	9♥	7♠	5♦	Q♠	J♣	9♦	7♠	9♦	2♣/K♠	3♠	3♠
	10♦	4♣	J♥	10♠	8♦	8♥					
91	4♥	5♠	Q♠	6♣	3♥	A♥	9♦	6♥	5♣/K♦	J♦	6♦
	9♠	A♠	Q♣	10♠	8♦	9♦					
92	2♠	2♥	6♠	8♥	Q♦	3♦	A♥	2♠	4♠/8♠	J♣	9♣
	6♥	K♠	A♦	9♠	9♥	2♦					
93	10♠	10♣	K♠	Q♠	2♥	8♦	6♦	6♠	3♦/5♦	10♥	Q♥
	5♠	7♠	Q♣	8♣	A♣	9♠					
94	Q♦	3♣	6♠	9♠	7♦	4♣	J♥	Q♠	J♣/8♠	5♠	10♠
	4♠	K♥	2♣	5♠	J♠	9♦					
95	3♦	A♦	9♠	Q♣	2♦	J♣	9♣	3♦	4♥/K♠	4♦	4♥
	4♠	7♠	5♠	8♠	6♠	7♣					
96	6♥	4♠	Q♣	7♣	8♦	8♥	9♦	9♦	2♣/5♥	5♥	4♠
	K♥	7♦	A♣	Q♦	4♣	9♦					
97	Q♥	K♠	10♣	2♥	4♠	10♥	3♣	8♥	8♥/8♠	5♣	10♣
	3♥	A♠	K♥	3♦	7♠	Q♦	4♠				
98	8♣	5♠	J♣	Q♦	10♠	Q♠	10♣	A♣	J♠/A♠	4♣	J♠
	A♥	7♠	3♥	10♦	6♦	10♣					
99	9♠	9♠	Q♦	K♥	K♣	A♦	Q♠	J♦	3♦/5♠	6♥	7♣
	4♠	J♦	3♥	A♠	Q♣	Q♠					

Four of Spades

AGE	MER	VEN	MAR	JUP	SAT	URA	NEP	LR	PLU/RES	ENV	DISP
0	10♥	10♦	8♠	A♥	A♦	Q♦	5♥	10♥	3♣/3♠	4♠	4♠
	K♦	7♦	A♣	4♦	J♣	5♥					
1	7♣	K♠	Q♠	2♥	10♦	Q♥	4♣	10♦	Q♦/2♣	4♥	10♣
	K♣	5♦	K♦	5♠	3♦	4♦	10♦				
2	8♠	J♦	10♠	4♦	8♦	2♦	Q♣	8♠	3♥/5♦	10♠	J♠
	2♠	9♦	K♣	6♣	10♣	Q♣					
3	7♠	J♠	4♦	K♦	A♠	6♠	2♦	A♥	5♠/9♠	Q♥	7♣
	10♦	4♥	K♣	5♦	8♠	2♦					
4	K♠	8♦	A♠	7♣	3♠	Q♦	3♣	A♦	6♠/9♠	9♣	8♦
	K♥	2♣	5♠	J♠	9♦	J♥	3♠				
5	5♣	8♥	K♥	K♠	A♥	5♥	3♠	Q♦	3♦/A♠	6♦	Q♠
	7♠	5♠	8♠	6♠	7♠	3♣					
6	Q♣	7♠	8♦	8♥	9♠	2♣	5♥	5♥	9♥/Q♥	3♠	10♦
	3♣	J♥	J♣	10♠	6♠	9♠					
7	10♥	3♠	8♥	8♠	K♣	9♥	Q♦	7♣	J♥/4♦	J♦	Q♣
	3♠	3♥	A♣	K♥	3♦	7♠					
8	A♣	4♥	5♠	K♦	7♥	6♥	8♠	K♠	7♦/9♦	J♣	3♥
	10♥	Q♥	A♠	5♣	A♦	8♠					
9	10♣	2♣	K♦	6♠	6♥	7♦	3♠	Q♠	9♠/9♣	10♥	A♥
	J♦	3♥	A♠	Q♣	Q♠	3♠					
10	K♥	7♠	2♠	3♦	9♥	J♦	6♠	2♥	6♦/9♦	5♠	A♥
	8♣	2♥	A♦	5♣	Q♦	6♠					
11	10♥	8♣	3♦	4♦	3♣	6♦	J♠	10♦	10♠/4♥	4♦	2♦
	6♥	7♥	K♠	10♣	3♥	7♦					
12	8♦	6♥	4♦	J♠	K♠	9♠	A♣	Q♥	6♦/4♣	5♥	6♣
	Q♣	9♥	10♣	4♥	3♦	A♠	K♠				
13	9♣	Q♥	2♠	A♠	6♣	5♥	7♦	4♣	5♠/8♠	5♣	8♠
	10♠	Q♦	2♣	K♠	4♥	10♦					
14	K♦	6♥	A♠	10♣	3♥	10♠	J♠	8♠	Q♦/5♣	4♣	K♣
	4♦	6♦	5♥	7♣	2♠	J♠					
15	Q♣	Q♥	10♠	9♦	4♣	4♦	K♠	J♠	J♦/2♥	6♥	2♠
	6♣	A♥	7♥	2♠	A♠	J♣	4♣				
16	5♦	6♥	5♥	K♠	J♣	A♣	10♥	10♠	9♣/6♠	3♦	6♠
	10♠	5♣	J♦	4♣	10♣	8♠					
17	A♥	10♠	Q♣	8♠	K♣	3♠	6♥	4♦	8♣/7♠	Q♦	9♠
	6♠	4♥	Q♥	4♦	J♣	6♥					
18	10♦	6♣	8♠	J♦	3♦	8♣	8♥	8♦	9♦/K♥	9♠	K♥
	7♣	5♠	5♦	5♣	A♦	8♥					
19	6♦	2♣	3♣	2♠	9♣	7♠	J♦	2♦	Q♥/7♠	5♦	2♠
	7♦	3♠	J♣	8♥	8♠	K♠					
20	10♣	7♣	2♠	J♥	7♥	Q♥	2♥	Q♣	10♠/8♦	3♣	A♠
	8♥	K♥	10♦	5♠	8♣	2♥					
21	9♥	K♠	J♥	A♠	9♠	A♣	Q♥	7♠	7♣/A♥	K♦	7♥
	5♠	7♠	3♦	Q♣	2♠	Q♥					
22	5♠	3♠	A♠	K♦	9♦	K♠	4♣	J♠	A♣/6♥	7♠	8♥
	10♣	9♠	3♦	A♥	J♥	7♥	9♦				
23	9♣	10♥	2♠	7♦	2♦	J♠	4♦		4♦/J♦	8♥	7♠
	6♠	Q♦	3♥	J♥	A♠	5♦					
24	10♦	Q♠	5♣	7♠	8♦	6♠	7♥	K♦	6♠/9♦	7♥	K♦
	7♦	A♠	A♦	8♠	A♥	7♥					
25	K♣	7♦	7♠	10♣	3♣	6♣	J♠	A♠	10♠/3♠	A♠	3♣
	2♦	Q♠	A♦	9♦	7♥	5♠					
26	K♦	2♦	10♠	Q♥	J♦	5♥	6♣	6♠	K♥/3♥	2♣	5♦
	3♦	8♠	2♥	3♠	6♠	6♣					
27	9♣	J♣	5♣	2♦	9♠	Q♣	5♥	2♦	6♦/6♥	K♥	9♦
	10♠	A♥	7♣	3♥	3♣	2♠					
28	Q♠	Q♥	2♦	9♥	A♠	10♠	8♥	K♣	A♥/4♦	9♠	Q♦
	6♣	5♠	J♦	3♣	6♠	8♥					
29	10♥	J♣	9♥	10♦	J♥	6♠	5♥	8♦	A♣/4♦	6♠	3♦
	5♣	6♥	2♣	3♣	K♥	5♥					
30	10♣	5♥	9♠	8♣	A♦	2♠	10♦	A♣	7♥/Q♦	2♠	6♥
	Q♠	8♥	6♠	6♥	Q♥	6♦					
31	3♣	6♠	8♠	A♥	K♣	Q♠	A♠	7♠	9♦/7♠	K♣	4♠
	J♥	6♣	K♥	10♥	J♣	3♥					
32	Q♥	5♥	4♦	7♦	7♠	J♥	A♥	3♠	6♥/2♥	8♠	5♣
	K♠	3♣	5♠	9♥	5♦	K♦					
33	J♣	10♦	7♦	2♠	J♦	9♠	8♦	Q♦	3♠/5♠	6♠	5♥
	6♣	10♥	9♥	2♥	10♣	8♦					
34	5♦	5♣	7♠	9♦	3♥	6♣	2♠	3♠	K♠/2♣	2♦	4♦
	7♠	4♥	2♦	5♠	7♥	A♣					
35	J♥	10♦	9♦	A♣	Q♦	4♦	6♦	5♠	9♣/7♥	A♦	5♠
	9♠	2♦	3♣	J♣	5♠	10♣					
36	2♠	8♥	K♥	2♣	J♣	Q♥	4♦	8♥	7♣/9♥	A♥	10♥
	3♠	4♥	6♠	A♦	K♦	10♥					
37	5♠	4♥	9♦	8♥	10♣	Q♣	Q♥	K♥	7♠/6♥	3♥	J♣
	9♣	3♥	5♣	9♥	2♥	Q♥					
38	10♦	9♣	8♥	3♦	2♣	7♠	8♦	K♣	3♥/2♦	Q♣	J♦
	5♥	9♠	8♠	2♥	9♦	8♦					
39	7♦	A♥	5♣	2♦	10♠	5♥	3♦	A♥	3♣/A♠	10♦	3♠
	6♣	J♣	J♥	8♦	A♦	Q♦					
40	Q♠	9♣	2♦	K♥	K♣	2♠	5♥	5♥	J♦/6♥	Q♠	6♦
	7♠	5♦	8♠	8♦	A♦	5♥					
41	7♥	A♣	8♥	Q♦	4♦	5♠	2♠	3♠	10♦/8♣	8♦	9♠
	10♥	K♠	6♠	7♠	7♦	9♠					
42	8♦	Q♣	K♠	2♦	A♠	A♦	10♠	Q♠	5♠/5♣	7♣	Q♥
	9♣	3♦	8♠	8♠	2♥	7♠					
43	4♦	4♣	8♥	7♠	9♥	J♣	J♥	7♠	10♠/2♣	J♠	10♠
	10♦	K♦	3♣	9♠	3♥	5♥					
44	5♠	6♣	7♠	8♠	9♠	10♠	J♠	8♦	Q♠/K♠	10♣	4♥
	10♦	3♦	9♣	2♠	8♥	A♥					
45	10♥	10♦	8♠	A♥	A♦	Q♦	5♥	8♥	3♣/3♠	4♠	4♠
	K♦	9♥	2♥	4♦	J♠	5♥					
46	7♠	K♠	Q♠	A♠	10♦	Q♥	4♣	9♦	Q♦/2♣	4♥	10♣
	K♣	5♦	K♦	5♠	3♦	4♦	10♦				
47	8♣	J♦	10♠	4♦	8♦	2♦	Q♣	2♣	3♥/5♦	10♠	J♠
	2♠	9♦	K♣	6♣	10♣	Q♣					
48	7♠	J♠	4♦	K♦	A♠	6♠	2♦	5♥	5♠/9♠	Q♥	7♣
	10♦	4♥	K♣	5♦	8♠	2♦					
49	K♠	8♦	2♥	7♠	3♠	Q♦	3♣	10♥	6♠/9♠	9♣	8♦
	K♥	2♣	5♠	J♠	9♦	J♥	3♠					

AGE	MER	VEN	MAR	JUP	SAT	URA	NEP	LR	PLU/RES	ENV	DISP
50	5♣	8♥	K♥	K♣	A♥	5♥	3♠	3♣	3♦/A♦	6♦	Q♠
	7♠	5♠	8♠	6♠	7♠	3♠					
51	Q♣	7♣	8♦	8♥	9♦	2♣	5♥	8♥	7♦/Q♥	3♠	10♦
	3♣	J♥	J♣	10♠	6♠	9♠					
52	10♥	3♣	8♥	8♠	K♣	7♦	Q♦	8♠	J♥/4♦	J♦	Q♣
	3♠	3♥	A♠	K♥	3♦	7♠					
53	2♥	4♥	5♠	K♦	7♥	6♣	8♠	K♣	9♥/9♦	J♣	3♥
	10♥	Q♥	A♠	5♣	A♦	8♠					
54	10♣	2♣	K♦	6♠	6♥	9♥	3♠	9♥	9♠/9♣	10♥	A♥
	J♠	3♥	A♠	Q♣	Q♠	3♠					
55	K♥	7♣	2♠	3♦	7♥	J♥	6♠	Q♦	6♦/9♦	5♠	A♦
	8♣	A♠	A♦	5♣	Q♦	6♠					
56	10♥	8♣	3♦	4♦	3♣	6♦	J♠	A♣	10♠/4♥	4♦	2♦
	6♥	7♥	K♠	10♣	3♥	9♥					
57	8♦	6♥	4♦	J♣	K♠	9♣	2♥	4♥	6♦/4♣	5♥	6♣
	Q♣	7♥	10♣	4♥	3♦	A♠	K♠				
58	9♣	Q♥	2♠	A♠	6♠	5♦	9♥	5♠	5♠/8♠	5♣	8♠
	10♠	Q♦	2♣	K♠	4♥	10♦					
59	K♦	6♥	A♠	10♣	3♥	10♠	J♠	K♦	Q♦/5♣	4♣	K♣
	4♦	6♦	5♥	7♣	2♠	J♠					
60	Q♣	Q♥	10♠	9♣	4♣	4♦	K♠	7♥	J♦/A♣	6♥	2♠
	6♣	A♦	7♥	2♠	A♠	J♣	4♣				
61	5♦	6♥	5♥	K♠	J♣	2♥	10♥	6♣	9♦/6♠	3♦	6♠
	10♠	5♣	J♦	4♣	10♣	8♠					
62	2♥	10♣	Q♣	8♠	K♣	3♠	6♥	8♠	8♣/7♠	Q♦	9♠
	6♠	4♥	Q♥	4♣	J♣	6♥					
63	10♦	6♣	8♠	J♦	3♦	8♠	8♥	10♣	9♦/K♥	9♦	K♥
	7♣	5♠	5♦	5♣	A♦	8♥					
64	6♦	2♣	3♣	2♠	9♠	7♣	J♦	2♣	Q♥/7♠	5♦	2♣
	9♥	3♠	J♣	8♥	8♠	K♠					
65	10♣	9♥	2♠	J♥	7♥	Q♥	A♣	K♦	10♠/8♦	3♣	A♠
	8♥	K♥	10♦	5♠	8♣	A♣					
66	7♦	K♣	J♥	A♠	9♣	2♥	Q♥	6♠	7♣/A♥	K♦	7♥
	5♣	7♠	3♦	Q♣	2♣	Q♥					
67	5♠	3♠	A♠	K♦	9♥	K♠	4♣	6♥	2♥/6♥	7♠	8♥
	10♣	9♠	3♦	A♥	J♥	7♥	9♦				
68	9♣	10♥	2♠	7♥	2♦	J♣	4♥	7♦	4♦/J♦	8♥	7♠
	6♠	Q♦	3♥	J♦	A♠	5♦					
69	10♦	Q♣	9♣	5♥	8♣	6♠	7♥	3♠	6♣/9♦	7♥	K♦
	9♥	2♥	A♦	8♠	A♥	7♥					
70	K♣	9♥	7♠	10♣	3♣	6♣	J♠	K♥	10♠/3♠	A♠	3♣
	2♦	Q♠	A♦	9♥	7♥	5♠					
71	K♦	2♦	10♣	Q♥	J♦	5♥	6♣	7♠	K♥/3♦	2♣	5♦
	3♦	8♣	A♣	3♠	6♠	6♠					
72	9♣	J♣	5♣	2♦	9♠	Q♣	5♥	2♠	6♦/6♥	K♥	9♦
	10♠	A♥	7♣	3♥	3♣	2♣					
73	Q♠	Q♥	2♦	7♥	A♠	10♠	8♥	3♦	A♥/4♥	9♠	Q♦
	6♠	5♠	J♦	3♣	6♠	8♥					
74	10♥	J♣	7♦	10♦	J♥	6♣	5♥	9♥	2♥/4♦	6♠	3♦
	5♣	6♥	2♣	3♣	K♠	5♥					

AGE	MER	VEN	MAR	JUP	SAT	URA	NEP	LR	PLU/RES	ENV	DISP
75	10♣	5♦	9♠	8♣	A♥	2♠	10♦	J♦	7♥/Q♦	2♠	6♥
	Q♠	8♥	6♠	6♥	Q♥	6♦					
76	3♣	6♠	8♠	A♥	K♠	Q♠	A♠	6♠	9♦/7♠	K♣	4♣
	J♥	6♣	K♥	10♥	J♣	3♥					
77	Q♥	5♥	4♦	9♥	7♣	J♥	A♥	10♥	6♥/A♣	8♠	5♣
	K♠	3♠	5♣	7♦	5♦	K♦					
78	J♣	10♦	9♥	2♠	J♦	9♠	8♦	8♠	3♠/5♠	6♣	5♥
	6♣	10♥	7♦	A♣	10♣	8♦					
79	5♦	5♥	7♠	9♠	3♥	6♣	2♠	3♦	K♠/2♣	2♦	4♦
	7♣	4♥	2♠	5♠	9♥	2♥					
80	J♥	10♦	9♦	2♥	Q♦	4♦	6♠	4♦	9♣/7♥	A♦	5♠
	9♠	2♦	3♣	J♣	5♠	10♣					
81	2♠	8♥	K♥	2♣	J♣	Q♥	4♦	3♠	7♣/7♦	A♥	10♥
	3♠	4♥	6♠	A♦	K♦	10♥					
82	5♠	4♣	9♦	8♥	10♣	Q♣	Q♥	6♦	7♣/6♥	3♥	J♣
	9♣	3♥	5♠	7♦	A♣	Q♥					
83	10♦	9♣	8♥	3♦	2♣	7♠	8♦	J♠	3♥/2♦	Q♣	J♦
	5♥	9♠	8♣	A♣	9♦	8♦					
84	9♥	A♥	5♣	2♦	10♠	5♥	3♦	8♦	3♣/A♣	10♦	3♠
	6♣	8♣	J♥	8♠	A♦	Q♦					
85	Q♠	9♣	2♦	K♥	K♣	2♠	5♥	6♥	J♦/6♥	Q♠	6♦
	7♠	5♦	8♠	8♦	A♦	5♥					
86	7♥	2♥	8♥	Q♦	4♦	5♠	2♠	4♦	10♦/8♣	8♦	9♣
	10♥	K♠	6♠	7♠	9♥	9♠					
87	8♦	Q♣	K♠	2♦	2♥	A♦	10♣	J♣	5♠/5♣	7♣	Q♥
	9♠	3♦	8♠	8♣	A♠	7♠					
88	4♦	4♣	8♥	7♠	7♦	J♣	J♥	K♠	10♠/2♣	J♠	10♠
	10♦	K♦	3♣	9♣	3♥	5♥					
89	5♠	6♠	7♠	8♠	9♠	10♠	J♠	9♣	Q♠/K♠	10♣	4♥
	10♦	3♦	9♣	2♣	8♥	A♥					
90	10♥	10♦	8♠	A♥	A♦	Q♦	5♥	A♣	3♣/3♠	4♠	4♠
	K♦	7♦	A♣	4♦	J♣	5♥					
91	7♣	K♠	Q♣	2♥	10♦	Q♥	4♣	9♣	Q♦/2♣	4♥	10♣
	K♣	5♦	K♦	5♣	3♦	4♦	10♦				
92	8♣	J♦	10♠	4♦	8♦	2♦	Q♣	Q♥	3♥/5♦	10♠	J♠
	2♠	9♦	K♣	6♣	10♣	Q♣					
93	7♠	J♥	4♦	K♦	A♠	6♠	2♦	2♠	5♠/9♣	Q♥	7♣
	10♦	4♥	K♣	5♦	8♠	2♦					
94	K♠	8♠	A♠	7♠	3♠	Q♦	3♠	A♠	6♠/9♦	9♣	8♦
	K♥	2♣	5♠	J♠	9♦	3♠					
95	5♣	8♥	K♥	K♣	A♥	5♥	3♠	6♣	3♦/A♦	6♦	Q♠
	7♠	5♠	8♠	6♠	7♣	3♠					
96	Q♣	7♣	8♦	8♥	9♦	2♣	5♦	5♦	9♥/Q♥	3♠	10♦
	3♣	J♥	J♣	10♠	6♠	9♠					
97	10♥	3♣	8♥	8♠	K♣	9♥	Q♦	7♦	J♥/4♦	J♦	Q♣
	3♠	3♥	A♠	K♥	3♦	7♠					
98	A♣	4♥	5♠	K♦	7♥	6♠	8♠	K♦	7♦/9♦	J♣	3♥
	10♥	Q♥	A♠	5♣	A♦	8♠					
99	10♣	2♣	K♦	6♠	6♥	7♠	3♠	6♥	9♠/9♣	10♥	A♥
	J♦	3♥	A♠	Q♣	Q♠	3♠					

Five of Spades

AGE	MER	VEN	MAR	JUP	SAT	URA	NEP	LR	PLU/RES	ENV	DISP
0	J♥	9♣	9♠	2♥	K♥	K♦	6♥	J♥	4♣/2♦	5♠	5♠
	Q♣	10♣	2♠	9♦	3♣	10♥					
1	Q♠	6♣	3♥	A♥	9♦	5♣	K♦	9♣	J♦/7♦	4♦	10♥
	3♦	4♦	10♦	4♠	K♣	5♦					
2	3♣	7♥	9♠	6♣	10♥	Q♥	5♣	9♠	8♠/A♠	5♥	J♣
	4♣	10♠	8♥	7♦	A♣	5♠					
3	9♣	4♣	6♣	2♣	A♥	8♠	3♠	2♥	10♠/10♣	5♠	J♦
	7♥	Q♣	8♠	A♠	9♠	3♠					
4	9♥	4♥	8♥	10♠	5♥	7♠	2♣	K♥	2♠/A♦	4♣	3♠
	J♠	9♠	J♥	3♠	4♠	K♥					
5	6♦	4♣	10♣	3♥	8♣	Q♠	7♠	K♦	Q♦/A♣	6♥	6♦
	8♠	6♣	7♣	3♠	4♠	7♠					
6	2♦	2♥	6♣	K♥	K♦	3♣	Q♠	6♥	9♣/8♠	3♦	9♣
	5♦	K♠	10♦	8♠	9♥	Q♣					
7	3♠	Q♥	K♠	10♣	2♥	4♠	10♥	Q♠	3♣/8♥	Q♦	Q♥
	4♠	2♣	7♠	8♣	A♣	8♠					
8	K♦	7♥	6♣	8♠	7♥	9♠	J♥	6♣	5♥/A♥	9♦	10♠
	9♣	K♣	2♠	4♣	10♠	7♠					
9	3♣	10♦	8♠	7♦	Q♣	5♥	J♠	3♥	6♦/K♣	5♦	4♥
	9♣	2♣	4♠	A♥	6♠	4♥					
10	5♦	9♣	7♠	4♥	4♠	K♥	7♠	A♥	2♠/3♦	3♣	4♠
	K♣	7♥	A♣	K♦	9♦	7♠					
11	J♦	K♠	Q♥	2♥	9♣	5♠	7♥	9♣	K♥/A♥	K♦	10♣
	8♦	6♠	K♠	3♣	2♣	K♦	9♣				
12	8♣	Q♦	5♥	K♦	3♠	10♣	Q♥	5♣	10♠/6♠	7♠	J♠
	Q♠	9♠	8♦	J♠	10♥	Q♥					
13	8♠	J♣	K♦	K♠	A♠	10♦	10♣	K♦	3♣/4♠	8♥	7♠
	9♣	4♦	8♦	6♠	7♣	10♣					
14	K♠	3♠	A♠	J♦	3♦	K♥	2♠	3♠	10♦/Q♣	7♥	8♦
	3♥	A♥	3♣	J♣	9♠	J♥	3♦				
15	8♥	6♣	3♥	8♦	4♥	7♠	3♠	7♥	2♣/4♠	A♠	Q♠
	8♠	3♣	7♣	10♦	J♦	3♦					
16	Q♥	J♦	3♠	6♠	9♠	A♥	7♠	9♠	9♥/5♠	2♣	10♦
	2♠	J♥	9♦	5♥	10♦	Q♣					
17	5♦	2♠	6♣	7♣	8♦	9♥	K♥	6♣	J♥/K♦	K♥	Q♣
	3♦	10♠	A♦	3♥	2♣	8♠					
18	A♣	4♦	3♠	K♣	2♦	J♠	7♣	10♥	7♦/9♠	9♠	3♥
	5♦	5♠	A♦	8♥	4♠	7♣					
19	10♥	A♥	K♣	10♦	A♠	7♠	3♦	Q♥	Q♣/4♣	6♠	A♥
	Q♦	10♠	A♦	Q♥	6♦	9♠					
20	3♥	8♠	Q♠	2♣	9♥	Q♦	10♦	5♣	6♥/9♠	2♠	A♥
	8♣	2♥	4♠	8♥	K♥	10♦					
21	5♦	8♣	2♣	K♦	2♠	6♥	J♣	9♣	5♥/4♦	K♣	2♦
	A♠	2♦	K♠	10♥	10♠	7♦					
22	3♠	A♠	K♦	9♣	K♠	4♣	A♣	4♣	6♥/7♥	8♠	6♣
	Q♥	9♥	10♠	4♦	2♣	A♦	K♠				
23	4♣	5♣	Q♠	A♣	J♠	6♠	7♦	7♣	3♣/7♠	6♠	8♠
	5♥	K♥	A♥	K♠	4♦	9♠					
24	K♣	A♠	A♦	10♥	10♠	5♥	J♠	2♠	K♥/8♠	2♦	K♣
	K♦	6♥	7♠	J♦	Q♠	J♣					
25	Q♥	5♣	10♥	9♠	7♥	K♦	K♠	A♥	Q♦/2♥	A♦	2♠
	J♠	4♠	2♦	Q♠	A♦	9♦	7♥				
26	6♠	A♠	7♠	K♠	9♦	A♣	5♦	8♠	9♠/10♦	A♥	6♠
	5♥	8♥	Q♦	7♥	10♥	7♣					
27	A♠	10♥	Q♥	7♣	8♦	3♦	A♠	3♠	8♣/8♠	3♥	9♠
	J♠	4♦	5♣	7♥	9♦	A♠					
28	9♣	J♠	7♣	Q♦	2♣	8♣	6♣	9♥	9♠/3♥	Q♣	K♥
	J♦	3♠	6♠	8♥	4♠	6♠					
29	6♥	A♥	2♠	Q♠	4♣	J♦	Q♦	4♥	5♣/8♠	10♦	2♣
	7♦	3♦	9♦	6♣	7♣	K♠					
30	10♥	7♦	Q♠	J♦	2♦	5♣	2♥	8♥	5♥/3♣	Q♠	A♣
	6♣	3♥	9♣	3♣	8♣	2♦					
31	9♥	8♦	J♥	A♦	4♣	A♣	5♣	10♣	J♦/4♥	8♦	7♥
	8♥	8♠	2♣	Q♥	A♥	5♣					
32	3♣	3♦	A♠	K♣	9♠	K♠	7♥	5♥	A♠/A♠	4♣	8♥
	10♥	Q♣	2♠	4♥	J♦	2♦	9♠				
33	4♣	5♦	Q♠	2♦	10♣	9♦	4♦	7♠	K♦/Q♦	J♠	7♠
	10♦	K♥	10♠	J♦	A♦	6♠					
34	9♣	Q♥	8♦	8♠	8♣	10♦	2♦	2♣	J♠/9♠	10♣	K♦
	7♦	A♣	4♠	7♠	4♥	2♦					
35	8♦	7♥	8♠	10♥	2♠	J♠	J♣	6♣	5♥/3♦	4♠	3♣
	10♣	6♥	4♠	9♠	2♦	3♣					
36	K♣	10♣	10♥	5♣	Q♣	7♠	J♠	4♣	3♥/10♠	4♥	5♦
	2♠	8♣	2♥	3♦	10♦	J♠					
37	4♣	9♦	8♥	10♣	Q♣	Q♥	7♠	10♣	6♥/A♣	10♠	9♦
	5♥	4♥	J♦	10♠	2♠	A♥					
38	6♦	5♣	10♣	9♥	A♦	5♥	6♠	3♥	4♥/4♦	Q♥	Q♦
	J♠	3♣	Q♦	2♠	10♦	6♣					
39	5♦	9♥	9♥	9♣	J♥	J♠	7♠	8♦	A♣/K♦	9♣	3♦
	8♥	A♠	A♥	2♠	3♥	7♠					
40	10♥	6♠	Q♣	8♣	4♣	Q♠	9♣	Q♠	2♦/K♥	6♦	6♥
	6♦	6♣	10♦	A♠	5♣	6♥					
41	2♠	10♦	8♣	4♥	8♣	6♦	A♦	7♠	9♠/8♠	3♠	4♠
	J♥	J♠	3♥	5♦	9♦	10♠					
42	5♣	7♠	K♦	7♥	J♦	J♥	4♥	2♦	A♠/2♥	J♦	5♠
	K♠	2♠	8♥	9♦	6♠	K♣					
43	9♠	9♠	7♦	Q♠	Q♦	Q♣	3♠	2♥	3♦/3♣	J♣	5♥
	J♠	5♦	9♥	2♥	10♥	3♠					
44	6♠	7♠	8♠	9♠	10♠	J♠	Q♠	A♣	K♠/A♥	10♥	4♦
	J♦	4♦	10♣	3♠	7♦	A♠					
45	J♥	9♣	9♠	A♠	K♥	K♦	6♥	K♥	4♣/2♦	5♠	5♠
	Q♣	10♣	2♠	9♦	3♣	10♥					
46	Q♠	6♣	3♥	A♥	9♦	5♣	K♦	K♦	J♦/9♥	4♦	10♥
	3♦	4♦	10♦	4♠	K♣	5♦					
47	3♣	7♥	9♠	6♣	10♥	Q♥	5♣	3♣	8♠/A♠	5♥	J♣
	4♣	10♠	8♥	9♥	2♥	5♣					
48	9♣	4♣	6♣	2♣	A♥	8♠	3♠	Q♠	10♠/10♣	5♣	J♦
	7♠	Q♦	8♣	2♥	9♠	3♠					
49	7♦	4♥	8♥	10♠	5♥	7♠	2♠	3♠	2♠/A♦	4♣	3♠
	J♠	9♦	J♥	3♠	4♠	K♥					

AGE	MER	VEN	MAR	JUP	SAT	URA	NEP	LR	PLU/RES	ENV	DISP
50	6♦	4♣	10♠	3♥	8♦	Q♠	7♠	Q♥	Q♦/A♠	6♥	6♦
	8♠	6♠	7♠	3♠	4♠	7♠					
51	2♦	A♣	6♣	K♥	K♦	3♣	Q♠	K♠	9♣/8♣	3♦	9♣
	5♦	K♠	10♦	8♠	7♦	Q♣					
52	3♠	Q♥	K♠	10♣	A♣	4♠	10♥	10♣	3♣/8♥	Q♦	Q♥
	4♣	2♣	7♠	8♣	2♥	8♠					
53	K♠	7♥	6♣	8♠	9♥	9♦	J♥	2♥	5♥/A♥	9♦	10♠
	9♠	K♠	2♠	4♣	10♠	7♠					
54	3♠	10♦	8♠	7♣	Q♣	5♥	J♣	4♠	6♦/K♠	5♦	4♥
	9♣	2♠	4♠	A♥	6♣	4♥					
55	5♦	9♣	7♠	4♥	4♠	K♥	7♠	10♥	2♠/3♦	3♣	4♠
	K♣	9♥	2♥	K♦	9♥	7♠					
56	J♠	K♠	Q♥	A♣	9♠	5♠	7♥	K♦	K♥/A♥	K♦	10♣
	8♦	6♠	K♣	3♣	2♣	K♦	9♣				
57	8♣	Q♠	5♥	K♦	3♠	10♣	Q♥	7♥	10♠/6♠	7♠	J♠
	Q♠	9♠	8♦	J♠	10♥	Q♥					
58	8♠	J♣	K♦	K♠	A♦	10♦	10♣	6♣	3♣/4♣	8♥	7♣
	9♣	4♦	8♦	6♠	7♣	10♣					
59	K♠	3♣	2♥	J♦	3♦	K♥	2♠	8♠	10♦/Q♣	7♥	8♦
	3♥	A♥	3♣	J♠	9♠	J♥	3♦				
60	8♥	6♣	3♥	8♦	4♥	7♠	3♦	7♦	2♣/4♠	A♠	Q♠
	8♠	3♣	7♠	10♦	J♦	3♦					
61	Q♥	J♦	3♠	6♣	9♠	A♥	7♠	9♦	7♦/5♣	2♣	10♦
	2♠	J♥	9♠	5♦	10♦	Q♣					
62	5♦	2♠	6♣	7♠	8♠	7♦	K♥	J♥	J♥/K♦	K♥	Q♣
	3♦	10♠	A♦	3♥	2♣	8♠					
63	2♥	4♦	3♣	K♣	2♦	J♠	7♠	3♣	9♥/9♠	9♠	3♥
	5♦	5♣	A♦	8♥	4♠	7♣					
64	10♥	A♥	K♣	10♠	A♠	9♥	3♦	10♦	Q♠/4♣	6♠	A♥
	Q♦	10♠	A♦	Q♥	6♦	3♦					
65	3♥	8♠	Q♠	2♣	7♦	Q♦	10♦	8♠	6♥/9♣	2♠	A♥
	8♣	A♠	4♠	8♥	K♥	10♦					
66	5♦	8♣	2♣	K♦	2♠	6♥	J♣	7♣	5♥/4♥	K♣	2♦
	A♠	2♦	K♠	10♥	10♠	9♥					
67	3♠	A♠	K♦	9♦	K♠	4♣	2♥	Q♣	6♥/7♥	8♠	6♣
	Q♥	7♦	10♠	4♦	2♣	A♦	K♠				
68	4♣	5♣	Q♠	A♦	J♠	6♠	9♥	5♥	3♣/7♣	6♣	8♠
	5♥	K♥	A♥	K♠	4♦	9♣					
69	K♣	A♠	A♦	10♥	10♠	5♥	J♣	J♠	K♥/8♥	2♦	K♣
	K♦	6♥	7♠	J♦	Q♠	J♠					
70	Q♥	5♣	10♦	9♠	7♥	K♦	K♠	5♦	Q♦/A♣	A♦	2♠
	J♠	4♠	2♦	Q♠	A♦	9♦	7♥				
71	6♠	A♣	7♠	K♠	9♦	2♥	5♦	9♠	9♠/10♦	A♥	6♠
	5♥	8♥	Q♦	7♥	10♥	7♣					
72	2♥	10♥	Q♥	7♠	8♦	3♦	A♠	7♣	8♠/8♠	3♥	9♠
	J♠	4♦	5♣	7♥	9♠	A♥					
73	9♣	J♠	7♠	Q♦	2♠	8♠	6♣	4♥	9♠/3♥	Q♣	K♥
	J♦	3♣	6♠	8♥	4♠	6♠					
74	6♥	A♥	2♠	Q♠	4♠	J♦	Q♦	4♠	5♣/8♠	10♦	2♣
	9♥	3♦	9♦	6♣	7♣	K♠					
75	10♥	9♥	Q♠	J♥	2♦	5♣	A♣	K♥	5♥/3♠	Q♠	A♠
	6♣	3♦	9♠	3♣	8♣	A♣					
76	7♦	8♣	J♥	A♦	4♣	2♥	5♣	7♠	J♦/4♥	8♦	7♥
	8♥	8♠	2♣	Q♥	A♥	5♠					
77	3♣	3♦	A♦	K♣	9♠	K♠	7♥	J♦	2♥/A♠	7♣	8♥
	10♥	Q♣	2♣	4♥	J♥	2♦	9♠				
78	4♣	5♦	Q♠	2♦	10♣	9♦	4♦	K♠	K♦/Q♦	J♠	7♠
	10♦	K♥	10♠	J♥	A♦	6♠					
79	9♣	Q♥	8♥	8♠	8♣	10♦	2♦	Q♥	J♠/9♠	10♣	K♦
	9♥	2♥	4♠	7♣	4♥	2♦					
80	8♦	9♥	8♠	10♥	2♠	J♠	♣	2♥	5♥/3♦	4♠	3♣
	10♣	6♥	4♠	9♠	2♦	3♣					
81	K♣	10♠	10♥	5♣	Q♦	7♠	J♠	9♠	3♥/10♠	4♥	5♦
	2♠	8♠	A♣	3♦	10♦	J♠					
82	4♠	9♦	8♥	10♣	Q♣	Q♥	7♠	5♣	6♥/A♠	10♠	9♦
	5♥	4♦	J♦	10♠	2♠	A♥					
83	6♦	5♣	10♣	7♦	A♠	5♥	6♣	7♥	4♥/4♦	Q♥	Q♠
	J♠	3♣	Q♦	2♠	10♦	6♠					
84	5♦	9♦	7♦	9♣	J♥	J♠	7♠	6♣	2♥/K♠	9♣	3♦
	8♥	A♠	A♥	2♠	3♥	7♠					
85	10♥	6♠	Q♣	8♣	4♠	Q♠	9♠	Q♦	2♦/K♥	6♠	6♥
	6♥	6♠	10♦	A♠	5♣	6♥					
86	2♠	10♦	8♠	4♥	8♦	6♠	A♦	5♥	9♠/8♠	3♠	4♣
	J♥	J♠	3♥	5♦	9♦	10♠					
87	5♣	7♠	K♦	9♥	J♦	J♥	4♥	K♦	A♠/A♣	J♦	5♠
	K♠	2♠	8♥	7♦	6♠	K♣					
88	9♦	9♣	9♥	Q♠	Q♦	Q♣	3♠	3♠	3♦/3♣	J♠	5♥
	J♠	5♦	7♦	A♣	10♥	3♠					
89	6♠	7♠	8♠	9♠	10♠	J♠	Q♠	10♣	K♠/A♥	10♥	4♦
	J♦	4♦	10♣	3♣	9♥	2♥					
90	J♥	9♣	9♠	2♠	K♥	K♦	6♥	Q♥	4♣/2♦	5♠	5♠
	Q♣	10♣	2♠	9♦	3♠	10♥					
91	Q♠	6♠	3♥	A♥	9♦	5♣	K♦	8♠	J♦/7♦	4♦	10♥
	3♦	4♦	10♦	4♠	K♠	5♦					
92	3♣	7♥	9♠	6♣	10♥	Q♥	5♣	J♣	8♠/A♣	5♥	J♠
	4♣	10♠	8♥	7♦	A♣	5♣					
93	9♣	4♣	6♣	2♣	A♥	8♠	3♠	K♦	10♠/10♣	5♣	J♦
	7♠	Q♣	8♠	A♣	9♠	3♠					
94	9♥	4♦	8♥	10♣	5♥	7♠	♣	K♣	2♠/A♦	4♠	3♠
	J♠	9♦	J♥	3♠	4♠	K♥					
95	6♠	4♣	10♣	3♥	8♦	Q♠	7♠	A♦	Q♦/A♠	6♥	6♦
	8♠	6♠	7♣	3♠	4♠	7♠					
96	2♦	2♥	6♣	K♥	K♦	3♣	Q♠	10♦	9♣/8♣	3♦	9♣
	5♦	K♠	10♦	8♠	9♥	Q♣					
97	3♠	Q♥	K♠	10♣	2♥	4♠	10♥	10♣	3♣/8♥	Q♦	Q♥
	4♣	2♣	7♠	8♣	A♣	8♠					
98	K♦	7♥	6♣	8♠	7♥	9♦	J♥	K♣	5♥/A♥	9♦	10♠
	9♠	K♣	2♠	4♣	10♠	7♠					
99	3♠	10♦	8♠	7♣	Q♣	5♥	J♣	3♠	6♦/K♠	5♦	4♥
	9♣	2♠	4♠	A♥	6♣	4♥					

Six of Spades

AGE	MER	VEN	MAR	JUP	SAT	URA	NEP	LR	PLU/RES	ENV	DISP
0	Q♥	10♣	8♣	K♠	3♥	A♣	Q♠	Q♥	10♠/5♣	6♠	6♠
	K♣	7♠	A♥	J♠	9♠	3♦					
1	A♣	9♠	7♠	3♦	6♥	A♦	10♣	10♣	8♣/3♠	2♠	9♠
	Q♦	2♠	8♠	J♠	3♥	10♣					
2	8♥	Q♦	3♦	A♥	4♠	8♣	J♦	8♦	10♠/4♦	K♣	K♥
	2♣	10♦	Q♥	7♦	5♦	J♦					
3	2♦	5♠	9♣	4♣	6♣	2♣	A♥	K♠	8♠/3♦	8♠	2♣
	7♠	A♦	3♥	J♦	3♦	K♠					
4	9♠	7♦	4♣	J♥	J♣	8♠	2♥	3♥	K♣/A♠	6♣	A♠
	J♦	4♦	8♥	10♦	8♣	2♥					
5	9♥	6♥	J♥	10♥	6♣	A♣	8♠	A♣	2♣/3♣	2♦	7♥
	7♣	3♣	4♠	7♠	5♠	8♠					
6	10♦	A♥	10♥	6♦	10♠	K♠	J♠	Q♣	A♦/10♣	A♦	8♥
	9♠	5♥	4♠	3♣	J♥	J♣	10♠				
7	6♣	Q♣	4♣	J♠	9♦	3♥	2♠	A♣	Q♠/A♥	A♥	7♠
	5♠	4♥	K♦	J♥	10♥	Q♥					
8	8♥	7♠	7♣	3♠	8♣	5♣	J♣	9♠	Q♦/10♠	3♥	K♦
	7♦	A♣	5♠	3♦	3♠	J♣					
9	6♥	7♦	3♠	9♠	5♣	Q♦	K♥	7♠	K♣/A♦	Q♣	3♠
	9♦	7♥	5♦	10♠	J♠	10♦					
10	6♦	9♠	9♠	8♠	A♥	8♦	Q♦	3♦	4♦/K♦	10♦	5♦
	4♠	8♣	2♥	A♦	5♣	Q♦					
11	6♣	3♥	7♣	9♣	5♥	7♠	8♦	6♥	2♦/10♣	Q♠	9♣
	K♣	3♣	2♣	K♦	9♣	5♠					
12	7♥	8♠	9♦	9♥	10♥	K♣	J♦	A♠	3♣/2♠	8♦	Q♦
	Q♦	10♠	A♥	9♣	5♣	J♦					
13	Q♣	3♥	9♥	8♥	J♥	Q♦	8♦	10♣	A♦/Q♠	7♣	3♦
	7♣	10♣	5♠	9♣	4♦	8♦					
14	9♠	Q♥	5♥	8♣	5♦	4♣	8♥	8♥	J♣/4♥	J♠	6♥
	7♥	J♦	5♣	10♣	8♠	2♦					
15	9♣	5♣	8♠	3♣	6♥	7♥	10♥	Q♦	10♠/3♠	10♣	4♣
	J♥	Q♦	4♦	Q♣	3♥	K♦					
16	8♠	8♣	Q♠	7♦	2♣	J♥	3♣	3♦	10♦/2♦	4♠	5♣
	K♠	9♣	7♣	9♥	Q♥	6♦					
17	3♥	8♥	7♣	4♣	A♥	5♥	A♠	A♥	A♦/10♦	4♥	5♥
	Q♦	Q♣	9♥	2♥	9♠	A♠					
18	Q♥	8♣	3♠	10♠	K♦	Q♦	4♣	4♠	K♠/5♠	10♠	4♦
	2♣	2♠	9♦	10♦	7♠	A♣					
19	J♥	8♥	10♠	A♠	4♥	Q♠	2♦	8♣	6♣/J♣	Q♥	5♠
	5♥	9♦	9♠	3♥	10♦	9♠					
20	4♣	J♦	4♦	5♠	3♥	8♠	Q♠	J♦	2♣/9♥	9♣	10♥
	A♦	2♠	5♣	5♦	6♦	Q♣					
21	10♦	J♠	10♠	J♦	9♠	7♠	8♠	2♦	3♠/10♣	6♦	J♣
	6♣	K♦	7♠	9♥	2♥	8♠					
22	8♥	6♣	J♦	4♣	5♠	3♠	A♠	5♠	K♦/9♦	3♠	J♦
	8♦	5♥	8♣	2♥	10♠	A♠					
23	7♦	3♣	9♥	9♦	K♣	8♦	4♠	5♣	9♣/10♦	J♦	3♠
	Q♦	3♥	J♥	A♠	5♦	4♥					
24	7♥	6♣	9♦	4♦	6♥	4♣	8♦	4♣	A♥/10♣	J♣	6♦
	3♠	Q♥	3♦	A♠	5♦	8♦					
25	J♣	A♠	J♦	4♥	Q♠	10♦	4♣	6♠	8♥/8♣	10♥	9♣
	Q♣	K♠	5♠	3♠	7♦	5♥					
26	A♠	7♠	K♠	9♦	A♣	5♦	9♠	2♣	10♦/7♣	5♠	Q♥
	6♣	4♠	3♦	8♣	2♥	3♠					
27	Q♠	J♠	J♦	3♠	9♥	3♥	J♥	A♥	K♣/5♠	4♦	10♠
	8♥	6♦	9♣	6♠	K♦	8♦					
28	10♦	5♠	3♠	3♦	5♥	K♣	K♥	9♠	7♥/K♠	5♥	4♥
	8♥	4♠	6♣	5♠	J♦	3♣					
29	Q♠	8♥	3♦	3♣	5♦	4♥	8♦	7♥	9♣/A♦	5♣	4♠
	6♦	9♥	2♥	Q♠	3♥	8♦					
30	2♣	K♠	7♠	A♣	8♥	8♠	J♠	4♣	4♥/5♠	4♣	10♠
	6♥	Q♥	6♦	10♦	4♠	Q♠	8♥				
31	8♣	A♥	K♣	Q♠	A♠	9♦	7♠	J♥	K♦/Q♥	6♥	J♠
	4♣	10♠	6♥	Q♦	9♠	7♠					
32	3♠	K♥	Q♠	6♦	10♥	5♠	9♦	J♣	10♦/6♣	3♦	7♣
	8♥	2♠	6♥	Q♥	3♦	9♦					
33	K♠	A♠	2♥	2♣	A♦	4♥	9♣	8♠	5♣/5♥	Q♦	8♦
	4♦	5♠	10♦	K♥	10♠	J♥	A♦				
34	7♣	J♦	4♦	6♥	3♣	8♦	A♦	2♥	4♠/5♦	9♦	Q♠
	3♠	10♠	3♦	5♦	2♣	A♦					
35	7♠	2♣	A♠	J♦	10♠	5♠	8♦	9♥	7♦/8♠	5♦	10♦
	9♣	J♥	3♥	K♣	5♠	5♥					
36	Q♣	9♣	J♦	3♦	6♥	7♥	4♥	6♥	J♥/Q♠	3♣	Q♣
	A♦	K♦	10♥	4♦	4♠	3♠					
37	2♥	2♠	10♦	6♦	J♣	Q♦	3♦	J♥	9♥/10♠	K♦	3♥
	Q♣	8♠	10♥	7♠	5♦	3♦					
38	9♠	5♠	6♦	5♠	10♠	9♥	A♦	10♥	5♥/6♣	7♠	A♥
	A♥	K♦	10♥	7♠	7♥	A♦					
39	4♦	3♠	4♣	4♠	7♠	A♥	5♣	6♣	2♦/10♠	8♥	A♦
	8♠	A♣	5♦	7♣	4♥	5♣					
40	Q♣	8♣	4♣	Q♠	9♣	2♦	K♥	A♣	K♣/2♠	7♥	2♦
	10♣	J♣	K♠	9♠	K♦	9♥					
41	A♠	10♣	Q♠	3♥	K♣	6♣	2♥	8♣	2♦/J♠	A♠	6♣
	7♠	7♦	9♠	2♠	4♠	10♥	K♠				
42	6♣	8♠	4♣	10♥	Q♦	Q♥	9♥	10♠	10♦/3♦	2♣	8♠
	K♣	4♥	5♠	K♠	2♠	8♥					
43	6♦	10♠	10♥	9♠	K♦	K♠	K♥	A♦	4♥/7♣	K♥	K♣
	Q♠	2♦	8♦	2♣	4♠	K♥					
44	7♠	8♠	9♠	10♠	J♠	Q♠	K♠	10♥	A♥/A♣	9♠	2♠
	Q♦	5♦	J♣	4♣	10♥	3♥	J♠				
45	Q♥	10♣	8♣	K♠	3♥	2♥	Q♣	6♠	10♠/5♣	6♠	6♠
	K♣	7♠	A♥	J♠	9♠	3♦					
46	2♥	9♠	7♠	3♦	6♥	A♦	10♣	10♠	8♣/3♠	2♠	9♠
	Q♦	2♠	8♠	J♠	3♥	10♣					
47	8♥	Q♦	3♦	A♥	4♠	8♣	J♦	K♠	10♠/4♦	K♣	K♥
	2♣	10♦	Q♥	7♦	5♦	J♦					
48	2♦	5♠	9♣	4♣	6♣	2♣	A♥	J♠	8♠/3♦	8♠	2♣
	9♥	A♦	3♥	J♦	3♦	K♠					
49	9♠	9♥	4♣	J♥	J♣	8♠	A♠	6♠	K♣/A♠	6♠	A♠
	J♦	4♦	8♥	10♦	8♣	A♣					

50	7♦	6♥	J♥	10♥	6♣	2♥	8♠	Q♣	2♣/3♣	2♦	7♥
	7♣	3♠	4♠	7♠	5♠	8♠					
51	10♦	A♦	10♥	6♦	10♠	K♠	J♠	4♣	2♥/10♣	A♦	8♥
	9♠	5♥	4♠	3♣	J♥	J♣	10♠				
52	6♣	Q♣	4♣	J♣	9♦	3♥	2♠	J♠	Q♠/A♥	A♥	7♠
	5♠	4♥	K♣	J♥	10♥	Q♥					
53	8♥	7♠	7♣	3♠	8♣	5♣	J♣	9♦	Q♦/10♠	3♥	K♦
	9♥	2♥	5♦	3♦	3♣	J♣					
54	6♥	9♥	3♠	9♣	9♠	Q♦	K♥	3♥	K♠/A♦	Q♣	3♣
	9♦	7♥	5♦	10♠	J♣	10♦					
55	6♦	9♦	9♠	8♠	A♥	8♦	Q♦	2♠	4♦/K♦	10♦	5♦
	4♣	8♠	A♣	A♦	5♠	Q♦					
56	6♣	3♥	7♣	9♦	5♥	7♠	8♦	8♥	2♦/10♣	Q♠	9♦
	K♣	3♣	2♠	K♦	9♣	5♠					
57	7♥	8♠	9♣	7♦	10♥	K♣	J♦	7♠	3♠/2♠	8♦	Q♦
	Q♦	10♦	A♥	9♠	5♠	J♦					
58	Q♣	3♥	7♦	8♥	J♥	Q♦	8♦	7♣	2♥/Q♠	7♣	3♦
	7♣	10♣	5♠	9♣	4♦	8♦					
59	9♠	Q♥	5♥	8♣	5♦	4♣	8♥	3♠	J♣/4♥	J♠	6♥
	7♣	J♦	8♣	5♠	8♠	2♦					
60	9♣	5♣	8♠	3♣	6♥	7♥	10♥	8♣	10♠/3♣	10♣	4♣
	J♥	Q♦	4♦	Q♣	3♥	K♦					
61	8♠	8♦	Q♠	9♥	2♣	J♥	3♣	5♣	10♣/A♣	4♠	5♣
	K♠	9♣	7♣	7♦	Q♥	6♦					
62	3♥	8♥	9♥	4♣	A♥	5♥	A♠	J♣	A♦/10♦	4♥	5♥
	Q♦	Q♣	7♦	A♣	9♠	A♠					
63	Q♥	8♦	3♠	10♠	K♦	Q♦	4♣	6♥	K♠/5♠	10♠	4♦
	2♣	2♠	9♥	10♦	9♥	2♥					
64	J♥	8♥	10♠	2♥	4♥	Q♠	2♦	7♦	6♣/J♣	Q♥	5♠
	5♥	9♦	9♠	3♥	10♦	9♠					
65	4♣	J♦	4♦	5♠	3♥	8♠	Q♠	3♠	2♣/7♦	9♠	10♥
	A♦	2♠	5♣	5♦	6♦	Q♣					
66	10♦	J♠	10♠	J♦	9♠	7♠	8♠	9♠	3♠/10♣	6♦	J♣
	6♣	K♦	7♠	7♥	A♣	8♠					
67	8♥	6♣	J♦	4♠	5♠	3♠	A♠	9♣	K♦/9♠	3♠	J♦
	8♦	5♥	8♠	A♣	10♠	A♠					
68	9♥	3♣	7♣	9♦	K♣	8♦	4♠	Q♦	9♣/10♥	J♦	3♠
	Q♦	3♥	J♥	A♣	5♦	4♥					
69	7♥	6♣	9♣	4♦	6♥	4♣	8♦	K♥	A♥/10♣	J♣	6♦
	3♠	Q♥	3♦	A♠	5♦	8♦					
70	J♣	2♥	J♦	4♥	Q♠	10♦	4♣	6♦	8♥/8♣	10♥	9♣
	Q♣	K♠	5♠	3♠	9♥	5♥					
71	A♠	7♠	K♠	9♦	2♥	5♦	9♠	9♦	10♦/7♣	5♠	Q♥
	6♣	4♠	3♦	8♠	A♣	3♠					
72	Q♠	J♠	J♦	3♠	7♦	3♥	J♥	9♠	K♣/5♠	4♦	10♠
	8♥	6♦	9♣	6♣	K♦	8♦					
73	10♦	5♠	3♠	3♦	5♥	K♣	K♥	8♠	7♥/K♠	5♥	4♥
	8♥	4♠	6♣	J♦	3♣						
74	Q♣	8♥	3♦	3♣	5♦	4♥	8♦	A♥	9♣/A♦	5♠	4♣
	6♦	7♦	A♣	Q♠	3♥	8♦					
75	2♣	K♠	7♠	2♥	8♥	8♠	J♠	8♦	4♥/5♠	4♣	10♣
	6♥	Q♥	6♦	10♠	4♠	Q♠	8♥				
76	8♣	A♥	K♣	Q♠	A♠	9♦	7♠	Q♦	K♦/Q♥	6♥	J♠
	4♣	10♠	6♥	Q♦	9♠	7♠					
77	3♠	K♥	Q♠	6♦	10♥	5♣	9♦	6♠	10♦/6♣	3♦	7♣
	8♥	2♠	6♥	Q♥	3♦	9♦					
78	K♠	A♠	A♣	2♣	A♦	4♥	9♣	3♥	5♦/5♥	Q♦	8♦
	4♦	5♠	10♦	K♥	10♠	J♥	A♦				
79	7♣	J♦	4♦	6♥	3♣	8♠	A♦	7♣	4♠/5♦	9♦	Q♠
	3♠	10♦	3♦	5♣	2♠	A♦					
80	7♠	2♣	A♠	J♦	10♠	5♦	8♦	9♦	9♥/8♠	5♦	10♦
	9♣	J♥	3♥	K♠	5♠	5♥					
81	Q♣	9♣	J♦	3♦	6♥	9♥	4♥	5♥	J♥/Q♠	3♠	Q♣
	A♦	K♦	10♥	4♦	4♠	3♠					
82	A♣	2♠	10♦	6♦	J♣	Q♦	3♦	7♠	7♦/10♠	K♦	3♥
	Q♣	8♠	10♥	7♣	5♦	3♦					
83	9♠	5♠	6♦	5♣	10♣	7♠	A♦	8♦	5♥/6♣	7♠	A♥
	A♥	K♦	10♥	7♠	7♥	A♦					
84	4♦	3♣	4♣	4♠	9♥	A♥	5♠	7♥	2♦/10♠	8♥	A♦
	8♠	2♥	5♦	7♠	4♥	5♠					
85	Q♣	8♣	4♠	Q♠	9♣	2♦	K♥	8♠	K♣/2♠	7♥	2♦
	10♣	J♠	K♠	9♠	K♦	7♦					
86	A♠	10♣	Q♠	3♥	K♠	6♣	A♠	9♦	2♦/J♠	A♠	6♣
	7♠	9♥	9♠	2♠	4♠	10♥	K♠				
87	6♣	8♠	4♣	10♥	Q♦	Q♥	7♦	9♥	10♦/3♦	2♣	8♠
	K♣	4♥	5♠	K♠	2♠	8♥					
88	6♦	10♣	10♥	9♠	K♦	K♣	K♥	10♥	4♥/7♣	K♥	K♣
	Q♠	2♠	8♦	2♣	4♣	K♥					
89	7♠	8♠	9♠	10♠	J♠	Q♠	K♠	K♣	A♥/2♥	9♠	2♠
	Q♦	5♦	J♣	4♣	10♥	3♥	J♠				
90	Q♥	10♣	8♦	K♠	3♥	A♠	Q♣	J♦	10♠/5♠	6♠	6♠
	K♣	7♣	A♥	J♠	9♠	3♦					
91	A♣	9♠	7♠	3♦	6♥	A♦	10♣	Q♣	8♣/3♠	2♠	9♠
	Q♦	2♠	8♠	J♠	3♥	10♣					
92	8♥	Q♦	3♥	A♥	4♠	8♠	J♠	3♥	10♠/4♦	K♣	K♥
	2♣	10♦	Q♥	7♣	5♦	J♦					
93	2♦	5♠	9♠	4♣	6♣	2♣	A♥	9♥	8♠/3♠	8♠	2♣
	7♦	A♦	3♥	J♦	3♦	K♠					
94	9♠	7♦	4♣	J♥	J♣	8♠	2♥	8♥	K♣/A♠	6♠	A♠
	J♦	4♦	8♥	10♦	8♣	2♥					
95	9♥	6♥	J♥	10♥	6♣	A♣	8♠	J♥	2♣/3♣	2♦	7♥
	7♣	3♠	4♠	7♣	5♠	8♠					
96	10♦	A♦	10♥	6♦	10♠	K♠	J♠	Q♦	A♣/10♣	A♦	8♥
	9♠	5♥	4♠	3♣	J♥	J♣	10♠				
97	6♣	Q♣	4♣	J♣	9♦	3♥	2♠	8♦	Q♠/A♥	A♥	7♠
	5♣	4♥	K♦	J♥	10♥	Q♥					
98	8♥	7♠	7♣	3♠	8♣	5♣	J♠	9♠	Q♦/10♠	3♥	K♦
	7♥	A♠	5♦	3♦	3♣	J♣					
99	6♥	7♥	3♠	9♠	9♣	Q♦	K♥	Q♥	K♣/A♦	Q♣	3♣
	9♦	7♥	5♦	10♠	J♣	10♦					

Seven of Spades

AGE	MER	VEN	MAR	JUP	SAT	URA	NEP	LR	PLU/RES	ENV	DISP
0	2♣ 3♠	K♣ 10♠	J♦ 4♣	4♥ J♥	4♦ 10♠	2♠ 8♦	8♥	2♠	6♠/6♣	7♠	7♠
1	3♦ 9♥	6♥ 2♥	A♦ 5♥	10♣ 10♥	8♣ 5♣	3♠ 4♥	4♥	K♣	5♠/Q♣	8♥`	K♦
2	J♣ 4♦	9♥ Q♦	10♦ 5♥	K♦ Q♠	7♣ 4♥	5♠ 8♠	3♣	J♦	7♥/9♠	7♥	3♣
3	J♠ Q♣	4♦ 8♠	K♦ A♣	A♣ 9♠	6♠ 3♠	2♦ 5♠	5♠	4♥	9♣/4♣	A♠	5♦
4	2♣ 7♥	2♠ 5♣	A♦ 5♦	4♦ 4♣	6♦ 7♣	6♥ Q♥	2♦	4♦	K♥/3♥	2♣	9♦
5	Q♦ 5♠	A♣ 8♣	4♦ 6♣	7♦ 7♣	10♣ 3♣	7♦ 4♠	4♠	2♠	5♣/8♦	K♥	Q♦
6	K♣ A♦	2♠ 3♥	7♣ Q♥	3♦ 7♠	J♥ 9♣	5♣ 2♦	2♦	8♥	2♥/6♣	9♠	3♦
7	K♦ Q♦	8♦ 4♠	6♦ 3♣	8♣ 3♥	5♥ A♠	J♦ K♥	3♦	3♦	4♥/10♦	6♠	6♥
8	7♣ J♥	3♠ 5♠	8♣ 9♣	5♣ K♣	J♣ 2♠	Q♦ 4♣	10♠	6♥	Q♠/10♣	2♠	4♣
9	A♠ K♠	2♦ 7♣	6♣ A♦	9♦ 7♦	5♦ 8♦	J♥ J♣	5♣	A♦	3♥/A♣	K♠	5♣
10	2♠ 5♠	3♦ K♣	9♥ 7♦	J♦ A♣	6♠ K♦	6♦ 9♦	9♣	10♣	9♠/8♠	8♠	5♦
11	8♦ 5♦	2♦ 8♥	10♣ 4♦	Q♠ 8♠	4♣ 9♥	5♠ 2♥	J♦	8♣	K♠/Q♥	6♣	4♦
12	J♥ 6♦	3♦ 4♦	Q♠ 7♣	2♥ 2♠	10♦ 8♠	6♣ K♦	K♥	3♠	2♣/4♥	2♦	5♠
13	J♦ 9♥	4♦ 8♥	9♣ 3♠	Q♥ 5♥	2♠ J♠	A♠ K♠	6♣	4♥	5♦/7♦	A♦	10♥
14	8♠ 2♣	A♥ 4♠	Q♠ A♦	4♦ 7♦	K♦ A♣	6♥ A♠	A♠	J♣	10♣/3♥	A♥	J♣
15	3♦ 2♦	2♣ 6♦	4♦ 8♣	Q♣ A♠	Q♥ Q♠	10♣ 9♦	9♦	9♥	4♣/4♦	3♥	J♦
16	9♥ 5♠	5♣ 2♠	A♦ J♥	4♦ 9♦	7♥ 5♥	2♦ 10♦	Q♣	10♣	7♣/10♠	3♠	
17	Q♣ 10♣	2♣ 8♦	4♦ 10♥	9♠ 9♦	J♠ 5♥	J♦ 2♦	2♦	K♦	6♠/3♥	10♦	6♦
18	4♥ K♣	2♥ K♠	4♠ 3♠	10♦ 10♣	6♣ 9♥	8♠ 6♦	J♦	7♠	3♦/8♣	Q♠	9♣
19	9♦ 2♣	6♥ Q♣	K♣ 10♥	4♦ 8♣	2♥ A♠	5♥ 10♣	K♦	5♠	8♠/A♦	8♦	Q♥
20	6♣ 3♦	A♥ J♠	4♠ 7♣	10♦ 2♠	7♦ 4♣	2♠ 2♦	J♥	3♣	7♥/Q♥	7♣	10♠
21	8♠ 3♦	3♠ Q♣	10♣ 2♣	10♥ Q♥	6♦ 4♠	7♥ 5♠	3♠	J♠	Q♦/K♠	J♠	4♥
22	K♣ J♠	3♦ 7♦	10♥ A♣	5♦ 6♣	5♥ 2♠	10♦ 2♦	2♦	4♦	7♣/9♠	10♣	4♦
23	5♦ J♣	K♠ 8♦	6♥ J♠	2♥ 8♠	3♦ Q♣	A♠ 3♦	A♥	K♦	10♦/Q♥	4♠	10♣
24	8♣ J♦	6♠ Q♠	7♥ J♣	6♣ 5♠	9♦ K♦	4♦ 6♥	6♥	A♠	4♣/8♦	4♥	J♠
25	10♣ 3♦	3♣ 8♥	6♣ J♣	J♠ 8♦	10♠ 10♥	3♠ 4♦	4♦	6♠	8♠/2♣	10♠	7♣
26	K♠ 9♠	9♠ Q♥	A♣ 8♠	5♠ 3♣	9♠ Q♠	10♦ J♥	7♣ 9♠	2♠	3♠/6♦	Q♥	8♦
27	A♦ 10♦	4♠ 8♠	9♣ 10♥	J♠ 3♠	5♠ 5♦	2♦ 9♠	9♠	5♠	Q♣/5♥	9♣	Q♠
28	6♥ 7♣	5♦ J♥	9♠ 2♠	4♠ 7♥	Q♠ 3♠	Q♥ 6♠	2♦	2♣	9♥/A♠	6♦	10♦
29	K♣ 9♠	7♠ 4♣	4♠ 10♠	10♥ 9♣	J♣ Q♣	9♥ 10♣	10♦	2♠	J♥/6♣	3♠	Q♣
30	A♠ K♠	8♥ A♠	8♠ 10♠	J♠ A♦	4♥ 5♥	5♠ 10♥	10♥	A♦	7♦/Q♠	J♦	3♥
31	K♦ 6♠	Q♥ 4♣	J♠ 10♠	3♠ 6♥	3♥ Q♦	7♦ 9♠	9♠	4♦	6♦/2♣	J♣	A♥
32	9♣ 8♣	10♠ 2♥	J♦ 5♥	Q♣ A♦	9♥ 10♦	6♠ 3♠	3♠	6♦	K♥/Q♠	10♥	A♦
33	K♣ 3♥	8♠ 4♥	Q♣ K♠	6♠ K♦	7♣ 4♠	K♥ 7♦	3♣	6♥	7♥/8♥	5♠	2♦
34	9♦ 6♥	3♥ 9♥	6♠ K♦	2♠ 8♥	K♠ Q♣	2♠ 10♠	A♠ K♠	2♦	K♥/A♥	4♦	6♠
35	2♣ 7♥	A♠ 10♦	J♦ Q♥	10♠ K♠	5♠ 8♥	8♦ 3♦	7♦	Q♦	8♠/10♥	5♥	8♠
36	J♠ 6♣	3♥ K♥	10♠ 2♦	K♠ 5♦	4♣ J♦	7♥ 3♣	3♣	A♠	10♦/A♦	5♠	K♣
37	6♥ 5♠	A♠ 5♥	K♦ 4♥	Q♠ J♦	A♥ 10♠	6♣ 2♠	K♠ A♥	4♦	6♠/2♥	4♣	2♠
38	8♦ 7♥	3♥ A♦	2♦ 6♠	K♠ A♥	2♠ K♦	A♠ 10♥	K♣	7♦	Q♠/3♣	6♥	6♠
39	A♣ 5♠	K♦ 8♥	6♥ A♠	10♥ A♥	J♣ 2♠	9♠ 3♥	3♥	10♠	8♣/10♠	3♦	9♠
40	3♦ 5♦	5♠ 8♠	10♥ 8♦	6♠ A♦	Q♣ 5♥	8♣ 4♠	4♠	7♥	Q♠/9♣	Q♦	K♥
41	K♥ 7♦	Q♥ 9♠	7♣ 2♠	J♦ 4♠	2♣ 10♥	5♦ K♠	6♠	4♠	A♠/10♣	9♦	2♣
42	K♦ 4♠	7♠ 9♠	J♦ 3♦	J♥ 8♠	4♥ 8♣	A♠ 2♥	2♠	K♣	7♥/9♦	5♦	A♠
43	9♥ A♦	J♣ 10♣	J♥ Q♣	10♠ 6♥	2♣ Q♥	A♣ A♠	A♠	2♠	5♦/5♣	3♣	7♥
44	8♠ K♦	9♠ 6♦	10♠ Q♣	J♠ 5♣	Q♠ J♥	K♠ 4♥	A♥ Q♠	7♦	A♣/3♥	K♦	8♦
45	2♣ 3♠	K♣ 10♦	J♦ 4♣	4♥ J♥	4♦ 10♠	2♠ 8♦	8♥	3♦	6♣/6♠	7♠	7♠
46	3♦ 7♦	6♥ A♣	A♦ 5♥	10♣ 10♥	8♣ 5♣	3♠ 4♥	4♥	J♥	5♠/Q♣	8♥	K♦
47	J♣ 4♦	7♦ Q♦	10♣ 5♥	K♦ Q♠	7♣ 4♥	5♠ 8♠	3♣	5♠	7♥/9♠	7♥	3♣
48	J♠ Q♣	4♦ 8♣	K♦ 2♥	A♣ 9♠	6♠ 3♠	2♦ 5♠	5♠		9♣/4♣	A♠	5♦
49	2♣ 7♥	2♠ 5♣	A♦ 5♦	4♦ 4♣	6♦ 7♣	6♥ Q♥	2♦	K♦	K♥/3♥	2♣	9♦

AGE	MER	VEN	MAR	JUP	SAT	URA	NEP	LR	PLU/RES	ENV	DISP
50	Q♦	A♠	4♦	9♥	10♠	7♥	4♠	8♦	5♣/8♥	K♥	Q♦
	5♠	8♠	6♠	7♠	3♠	4♠					
51	K♣	2♠	9♥	3♦	J♥	5♠	2♦	6♦	A♠/6♣	9♠	3♦
	A♦	3♥	Q♥	7♣	9♣	2♦					
52	K♦	8♦	6♦	8♣	5♥	J♦	3♦	8♣	4♥/10♦	6♠	6♥
	Q♦	4♠	3♠	3♥	A♠	K♥					
53	7♣	3♠	8♣	5♣	J♣	Q♦	10♠	5♥	Q♠/10♣	2♠	4♣
	J♥	5♠	9♣	K♣	2♠	4♣					
54	A♠	2♦	6♣	7♦	5♦	J♥	5♣	J♦	3♥/2♥	K♣	5♣
	K♠	7♣	A♦	9♥	8♦	J♠					
55	2♠	3♦	7♦	J♦	6♠	6♦	9♦	3♦	9♠/8♠	8♠	5♥
	5♠	K♣	9♥	2♥	K♦	9♦					
56	8♦	2♦	10♣	Q♠	4♣	5♠	J♦	7♠	K♠/Q♥	6♠	4♦
	5♠	8♥	4♦	8♠	7♦	A♣					
57	J♥	3♦	Q♠	A♣	10♦	6♣	K♥	3♠	2♠/4♥	2♦	5♠
	6♦	4♦	7♠	2♠	8♠	K♦					
58	J♦	4♠	9♠	Q♥	2♠	A♠	6♣	8♣	5♦/9♥	A♦	10♥
	9♠	8♥	3♠	5♥	J♠	K♣					
59	8♠	A♥	Q♠	4♠	K♦	6♥	A♠	5♠	10♣/3♥	A♥	J♣
	2♣	4♣	A♦	9♥	2♥	A♠					
60	3♦	2♣	4♠	Q♣	Q♥	10♠	9♦	J♠	4♣/4♦	3♥	J♦
	2♦	6♦	8♠	2♥	Q♠	9♦					
61	7♦	5♣	A♦	4♦	7♥	2♦	Q♣	Q♦	7♣/10♠	Q♣	3♠
	5♠	2♠	J♥	9♦	5♥	10♦					
62	Q♦	2♣	4♦	9♣	J♣	J♦	2♦	10♠	6♠/3♥	10♦	6♦
	10♣	8♦	10♥	9♦	5♥	2♦					
63	4♥	A♠	4♠	10♦	6♣	8♠	J♦	A♠	3♦/8♣	6♠	9♣
	K♣	K♠	3♣	10♣	7♦	6♦					
64	9♦	6♥	K♠	4♦	A♣	5♥	K♦	2♦	8♠/A♦	8♦	Q♥
	2♣	Q♣	10♥	8♣	2♥	10♣					
65	6♣	A♥	4♠	10♠	9♥	2♠	J♥	6♣	7♥/Q♥	7♠	10♠
	3♦	J♠	7♠	2♣	4♣	2♦					
66	8♠	3♠	10♣	10♥	6♦	7♥	3♣	9♥	Q♦/K♠	J♠	4♥
	3♦	Q♣	2♣	Q♥	4♠	5♣					
67	K♣	3♦	10♥	J♣	5♥	10♦	2♦	5♦	7♣/9♠	10♠	4♠
	J♠	9♥	2♥	6♣	2♠	2♦					
68	5♦	K♠	6♥	A♣	3♦	A♠	A♥	J♥	10♦/Q♥	4♠	10♣
	J♣	8♦	J♠	8♠	Q♣	6♠	3♦				
69	8♣	6♠	7♥	6♣	9♥	4♦	6♥	5♠	4♣/8♦	4♥	J♠
	J♦	Q♠	J♣	5♠	K♦	6♥					
70	10♣	3♣	6♣	J♠	10♠	3♠	4♦	2♠	8♠/2♣	10♠	7♣
	3♦	8♥	J♣	8♦	10♥	4♦					
71	K♠	9♦	2♥	5♦	9♠	10♦	7♣	3♦	3♠/6♦	Q♥	8♦
	9♣	Q♥	8♠	3♣	Q♠	J♥	9♠				
72	A♦	4♠	9♣	J♠	5♣	2♦	9♣	9♥	Q♣/5♥	9♣	Q♠
	10♣	8♠	10♥	3♠	5♦	9♠					
73	6♥	5♦	9♦	4♠	Q♠	Q♥	2♦	J♦	7♦/A♠	6♦	10♦
	7♣	J♥	2♠	7♥	3♠	6♦					
74	K♣	7♠	4♠	10♥	J♣	7♦	10♦	6♠	J♥/6♦	3♠	Q♣
	9♠	4♠	10♠	4♣	Q♣	10♦					
75	2♥	8♥	8♠	J♠	4♥	5♠	10♥	6♦	9♥/Q♠	J♦	3♥
	K♣	A♠	10♠	A♦	5♥	10♥					
76	K♦	Q♥	J♠	3♠	3♥	9♥	9♠	9♦	6♦/2♣	J♠	A♥
	6♠	4♣	10♠	6♥	Q♦	9♠					
77	9♣	10♣	J♦	Q♣	7♦	6♠	3♠	8♦	K♥/Q♠	10♥	A♦
	8♣	A♠	5♥	A♦	10♦	3♠					
78	K♣	8♣	Q♣	6♣	7♠	K♥	3♣	2♦	7♥/8♥	5♠	2♦
	3♥	4♥	K♠	K♦	4♣	9♥					
79	9♦	3♥	6♠	2♠	K♠	2♣	2♥	10♣	K♥/A♥	4♦	6♣
	6♥	7♦	K♦	8♥	Q♣	10♠	K♠				
80	2♣	A♠	J♦	10♠	5♠	8♦	9♥	Q♠	8♠/10♥	5♥	8♠
	7♥	10♦	Q♥	K♠	8♥	3♦					
81	J♠	3♥	10♠	K♦	4♣	7♥	3♣	4♣	10♦/A♦	5♠	K♣
	6♠	K♥	2♦	5♦	J♦	3♣					
82	6♥	A♠	K♦	Q♠	A♥	6♣	K♣	5♠	6♠/A♣	4♠	2♠
	5♠	5♥	4♥	J♦	10♠	2♠	A♥				
83	8♦	3♥	2♦	K♠	2♠	2♥	K♣	J♦	Q♠/3♠	6♥	6♠
	7♥	A♦	6♠	A♥	K♦	10♥					
84	2♥	K♦	6♥	10♥	J♣	9♠	3♥	J♥	8♣/10♣	3♦	9♠
	5♠	8♥	A♠	A♥	2♠	3♥					
85	3♦	5♠	10♥	6♠	Q♣	8♠	4♠	3♦	Q♠/9♣	Q♦	K♥
	5♦	8♠	8♦	A♦	5♥	4♠					
86	K♥	Q♥	7♣	J♦	2♣	5♠	6♠	Q♠	A♠/10♣	9♦	2♠
	9♥	9♠	2♠	4♠	10♥	K♠					
87	K♦	9♥	J♦	J♥	4♥	A♠	A♣	2♥	7♥/9♦	5♦	A♠
	4♠	4♣	3♦	8♠	8♣	A♣					
88	7♦	J♣	J♥	10♠	2♣	2♥	A♠	10♦	5♦/5♣	3♣	7♥
	A♦	10♣	Q♣	6♥	Q♥	A♠					
89	8♠	9♠	10♠	J♠	Q♠	K♠	A♥	6♣	2♥/3♥	K♦	8♥
	K♦	6♦	Q♣	5♠	J♥	4♥	Q♠				
90	2♣	K♣	J♦	4♥	4♦	2♠	8♥	K♥	6♣/6♦	7♠	7♠
	3♠	10♦	4♣	J♥	10♠	8♦					
91	3♦	6♥	A♥	10♣	8♣	3♠	4♥	J♦	5♠/Q♠	8♥	K♦
	9♥	2♥	5♥	10♥	5♣	4♥					
92	J♣	9♥	10♣	K♦	7♣	5♠	3♣	4♥	7♥/9♠	7♥	3♣
	4♦	Q♦	5♥	Q♠	4♥	8♠					
93	J♠	4♦	K♦	A♠	6♠	2♦	5♠	9♣	9♣/4♣	A♠	5♦
	Q♣	8♣	A♠	9♠	3♠	5♠					
94	2♣	2♠	A♦	4♦	6♦	6♥	2♦	Q♥	K♥/3♥	2♣	9♦
	7♥	5♠	5♦	4♣	7♠	Q♥					
95	Q♦	A♠	4♦	7♦	10♠	7♥	4♠	2♠	5♣/8♥	K♥	Q♦
	5♠	8♠	6♠	7♣	3♠	4♠					
96	K♣	2♠	7♥	3♦	J♥	5♠	2♦	A♠	2♥/6♣	9♠	3♦
	A♦	3♥	Q♥	7♣	9♣	2♦					
97	K♦	8♦	6♦	8♣	5♥	J♦	3♦	6♣	4♥/10♦	6♠	6♥
	Q♦	4♠	3♠	3♥	A♠	K♥					
98	7♣	3♠	8♣	5♣	J♣	Q♦	10♠	8♠	Q♠/10♣	2♠	4♣
	J♥	5♠	9♣	K♣	2♠	4♣					
99	A♠	2♦	6♣	9♥	5♦	J♥	5♣	A♥	3♥/A♣	K♣	5♣
	K♠	7♣	A♦	7♦	8♦	J♠					

Eight of Spades

Age	Mer	Ven	Mar	Jup	Sat	Ura	Nep	LR	Plu/Res	Env	Disp
0	A♥	A♦	Q♣	5♥	3♣	3♠	9♥	A♥	7♣/5♦	8♠	8♠
	2♦	9♠	5♣	K♠	6♣	2♣					
1	J♣	10♠	5♥	K♣	7♥	2♦	2♠	A♦	9♣/4♠	6♣	K♣
	J♠	3♥	10♠	6♠	Q♥	2♠					
2	A♠	A♦	K♣	6♦	4♥	J♠	K♠	Q♦	10♦/A♣	2♦	2♠
	3♣	7♠	4♦	Q♦	5♥	Q♠	4♥				
3	3♠	10♠	10♣	K♠	Q♠	2♥	8♦	5♥	6♦/3♦	A♦	6♠
	2♦	4♠	10♦	4♥	K♣	5♦					
4	2♥	K♣	A♠	5♦	9♦	Q♣	10♠	3♠	8♣/10♥	A♥	9♠
	3♠	6♠	A♦	4♥	Q♠	10♠					
5	2♣	3♣	5♦	10♦	Q♥	8♦	5♠	3♠	6♦/4♣	3♥	K♥
	6♠	7♠	3♠	4♦	7♥	5♠					
6	3♥	5♣	J♦	Q♦	A♥	6♠	10♦	9♥	A♦/10♥	Q♣	2♣
	9♥	Q♣	Q♠	5♠	5♥	K♠					
7	K♣	9♥	Q♦	J♥	4♦	A♦	A♠	J♠	2♦/9♠	10♦	A♠
	5♠	4♠	2♣	7♣	8♣	A♣					
8	7♦	9♥	J♥	5♥	A♥	2♥	A♦	10♠	6♠/8♥	Q♠	7♥
	4♥	10♥	Q♥	A♠	5♠	A♦					
9	7♣	Q♣	5♥	J♠	6♦	K♠	4♥	5♥	2♥/10♠	8♦	8♥
	K♣	6♥	Q♥	8♥	J♥	6♦					
10	A♥	8♣	Q♦	4♦	K♦	Q♠	6♣	K♠	J♠/10♦	7♣	7♠
	3♦	9♣	7♥	J♥	5♥	3♠					
11	2♣	A♠	4♠	10♥	8♣	3♥	4♦	7♥	3♣/6♦	J♠	K♦
	9♥	2♥	7♠	5♦	8♥	4♦					
12	9♦	9♥	10♥	K♣	J♦	3♣	2♠	2♦	2♦/Q♣	10♣	3♣
	K♦	K♥	7♠	6♦	4♦	7♣					
13	J♣	K♦	K♣	A♦	10♦	10♠	3♣	2♠	4♣/7♥	4♠	5♦
	Q♥	8♠	A♣	Q♣	3♦	3♠					
14	A♥	Q♠	4♠	K♦	6♥	A♠	10♣	A♠	3♥/10♠	4♥	9♦
	2♦	8♥	6♠	7♥	J♥	5♣					
15	K♥	A♦	K♦	7♥	5♥	2♦	5♠	A♦	8♥/6♦	10♠	Q♦
	3♣	7♥	10♦	J♠	3♥	5♠					
16	8♦	Q♠	7♦	2♣	J♥	3♣	10♠	K♣	2♥/J♠	Q♥	3♦
	4♠	10♠	5♣	J♣	4♥	10♣					
17	K♣	3♠	6♥	8♠	7♥	Q♦	2♠	6♥	4♦/9♠	9♠	6♥
	K♥	5♠	3♦	10♠	A♥	3♥					
18	J♦	3♥	8♣	8♥	9♦	K♥	5♥	4♥	6♦/10♥	6♦	4♣
	J♥	3♣	4♣	8♦	Q♠	7♥					
19	A♦	10♣	J♠	9♥	6♠	J♥	8♥	J♠	10♠/A♣	3♠	5♣
	K♠	J♦	4♠	7♦	3♠	J♠					
20	Q♠	2♣	9♥	Q♦	10♦	6♥	9♠	K♠	Q♣/7♠	J♦	5♥
	3♣	8♦	7♦	A♠	K♣	9♠					
21	3♠	10♣	10♥	6♦	7♥	3♣	Q♦	3♠	K♠/5♣	J♣	4♦
	6♠	6♣	K♦	7♣	9♥	2♥					
22	J♥	2♣	6♦	2♥	9♣	J♠	3♥	10♠	A♥/4♦	10♥	5♠
	6♥	K♦	J♦	Q♠	7♣	K♣					
23	Q♦	5♠	4♠	5♦	Q♠	A♦	J♠	10♠	6♠/7♦	5♠	10♦
	Q♣	6♠	3♦	7♠	J♠	8♥					
24	7♣	4♥	6♦	5♠	K♣	A♠	A♦	K♠	10♥/10♠	4♦	J♠
	A♥	7♥	4♠	7♦	A♣	A♦					

Age	Mer	Ven	Mar	Jup	Sat	Ura	Nep	LR	Plu/Res	Env	Disp
25	2♣	A♥	5♠	Q♥	5♣	10♥	9♠	Q♠	7♥/K♦	5♥	J♦
	10♣	6♥	8♠	A♣	6♦	9♠					
26	9♥	8♥	4♠	K♦	2♦	10♣	Q♥	2♥	J♦/5♥	5♣	3♠
	3♠	Q♠	J♥	9♠	7♠	9♣					
27	K♥	A♥	K♠	4♠	9♥	Q♦	10♣	8♠	10♦/10♠	4♣	6♦
	10♥	3♠	5♥	9♠	7♠	10♣					
28	4♦	2♥	5♠	9♣	J♠	7♣	Q♦	2♥	2♣/8♦	6♥	9♣
	8♦	K♠	3♦	10♥	9♥	6♥					
29	9♠	A♠	K♠	K♦	2♥	7♠	K♣	K♣	7♣/4♠	3♦	Q♥
	A♥	Q♥	5♦	8♣	A♣	10♥					
30	J♠	4♥	5♠	10♥	7♥	Q♠	J♥	A♠	2♦/5♣	Q♦	10♠
	2♣	J♣	J♦	A♥	7♥	10♣					
31	7♠	3♦	10♥	5♦	6♥	2♦	2♠	5♦	K♥/K♠	9♦	4♥
	2♣	Q♥	A♥	5♠	5♠	8♥					
32	8♦	2♠	5♦	8♥	7♠	9♣	10♣	9♦	J♦/Q♣	5♦	4♠
	J♣	7♦	A♣	J♠	Q♠	10♣					
33	6♠	K♠	A♠	2♥	2♣	A♦	4♥	Q♣	9♣/5♣	3♣	10♣
	9♥	3♠	J♣	7♣	Q♥	J♠	2♣				
34	8♣	10♦	2♠	J♥	9♠	K♠	A♠	10♠	7♥/3♠	K♦	J♠
	Q♦	6♥	9♠	3♠	K♠	A♠					
35	10♥	2♠	J♠	J♠	5♥	3♦	K♦	2♠	7♣/A♥	7♠	7♣
	2♣	6♣	9♠	3♠	5♦	K♦					
36	K♠	9♠	A♣	6♠	Q♣	9♣	J♦	3♣	3♦/6♥	8♥	8♦
	4♣	5♣	7♣	2♠	6♥	J♥	Q♣				
37	4♠	5♠	4♣	9♠	8♥	10♣	Q♣	5♦	Q♥/7♠	7♥	Q♠
	10♥	7♣	5♦	3♦	6♠	Q♣					
38	A♠	6♠	9♠	5♠	6♦	5♠	10♣	10♦	9♥/A♦	A♠	10♦
	J♦	J♥	Q♠	2♦	3♦	6♥					
39	8♦	J♦	5♠	5♦	9♥	9♥	9♣	Q♥	J♥/J♠	2♣	Q♣
	Q♣	7♥	5♥	4♣	Q♥	10♥					
40	A♦	6♠	7♠	J♠	4♦	3♠	5♦	8♣	7♦/6♦	K♥	3♥
	8♦	A♥	5♥	4♠	7♠	5♦					
41	K♣	5♣	J♣	3♦	10♠	7♣	Q♣	5♠	6♥/A♥	9♠	A♥
	10♦	7♥	5♥	A♠	K♥	Q♣					
42	4♣	10♥	Q♦	Q♥	9♥	10♣	3♦	3♥	3♥/6♦	6♠	A♦
	8♣	2♥	7♠	4♠	9♠	3♦					
43	8♦	8♣	Q♥	J♠	J♦	3♥	2♠	5♠	2♦/6♣	2♠	2♦
	10♠	4♦	K♠	K♣	7♥	7♦					
44	9♠	10♠	J♠	Q♠	K♠	A♥	A♣	J♦	3♥/4♥	K♣	6♠
	A♠	9♥	K♣	6♣	Q♥	5♥	K♠				
45	A♥	A♦	Q♣	5♥	3♣	3♠	7♥	Q♦	7♣/5♦	8♠	8♠
	2♦	9♠	5♣	K♠	6♣	2♣					
46	J♣	10♠	5♥	K♣	7♥	2♦	2♠	A♥	9♣/4♠	6♣	K♣
	J♠	3♥	10♣	6♠	Q♥	2♠					
47	A♠	A♦	K♣	6♦	4♥	J♠	K♠	6♠	10♦/2♥	2♦	2♠
	3♣	7♠	4♦	Q♦	5♥	Q♠	4♥				
48	3♠	10♠	10♣	K♠	Q♠	A♠	8♦	10♠	6♦/3♦	A♠	6♠
	2♦	4♠	10♦	4♥	K♣	5♦					
49	4♣	K♣	A♠	5♦	9♦	Q♣	10♠	K♣	8♣/10♥	A♥	9♠
	3♣	6♣	A♦	4♥	Q♠	10♠					

Age	Mer	Ven	Mar	Jup	Sat	Ura	Nep	LR	Plu/Res	Env	Disp
50	2♣	3♣	5♦	10♦	Q♥	8♣	5♠	9♥	6♦/4♣	3♥	K♥
	6♠	7♠	3♠	4♠	7♠	5♠					
51	3♥	5♣	J♦	Q♠	A♥	6♠	10♦	Q♦	A♦/10♥	Q♣	2♣
	7♦	Q♣	Q♠	5♠	5♦	K♠					
52	K♣	7♦	Q♦	J♥	4♦	A♦	2♥	J♥	2♦/9♠	10♦	A♠
	5♠	4♣	2♣	7♣	8♣	2♥					
53	9♥	9♣	J♥	5♥	A♥	A♣	A♦	4♦	6♠/8♥	Q♠	7♥
	4♠	10♥	Q♥	A♠	5♣	A♦					
54	7♣	Q♣	5♥	J♣	6♠	K♠	4♥	A♦	A♣/10♠	8♦	8♥
	K♣	6♥	Q♥	8♥	J♥	4♦	6♦				
55	A♥	8♦	Q♦	4♦	K♦	Q♠	6♣	A♣	J♠/10♦	7♦	7♠
	3♦	9♣	7♥	J♥	5♦	3♠					
56	2♣	A♣	4♠	10♥	8♣	3♦	4♦	7♦	3♣/6♦	J♠	K♦
	7♦	A♣	7♠	5♦	8♥	4♦					
57	9♦	7♦	10♥	K♣	J♦	3♣	2♠	9♦	2♦/Q♣	10♣	3♣
	K♦	K♥	7♠	6♦	4♦	7♣					
58	J♣	K♦	K♣	A♦	10♦	10♠	3♣	J♥	4♣/7♥	4♠	5♦
	Q♥	8♣	2♥	Q♠	3♦	3♠					
59	A♥	Q♠	4♣	K♦	6♥	A♠	10♣	5♥	3♥/10♠	4♥	9♦
	2♦	8♥	6♠	7♥	J♦	5♠					
60	K♥	A♦	K♠	9♥	5♥	2♦	5♠	A♥	8♥/6♣	10♠	Q♦
	3♣	7♠	10♠	J♦	3♦	5♠					
61	8♦	Q♠	9♥	2♣	J♥	3♣	10♣	2♥	A♣/J♠	Q♥	3♦
	4♠	10♠	5♣	J♦	4♣	10♣					
62	K♣	3♠	6♥	8♣	7♠	Q♦	2♣	A♦	4♦/9♣	9♣	6♥
	K♥	5♠	3♦	10♠	A♦	3♥					
63	J♦	3♦	8♣	8♥	9♦	K♥	5♥	7♣	6♦/10♥	6♦	4♣
	J♥	3♣	4♠	8♦	Q♠	7♥					
64	A♦	10♣	J♠	7♦	6♠	J♥	8♥	Q♣	10♠/2♥	3♠	5♣
	K♠	J♦	4♠	9♥	3♠	J♣					
65	Q♠	2♣	7♦	Q♦	10♦	6♥	9♠	5♥	Q♣/7♣	J♦	5♥
	3♣	8♦	9♥	2♥	K♠	9♠					
66	3♠	10♣	10♥	6♦	7♥	3♣	Q♦	J♣	K♠/5♣	J♣	4♦
	6♠	6♣	K♦	7♣	7♦	A♣					
67	J♥	2♣	6♦	A♣	9♣	J♠	3♥	6♦	A♥/4♦	10♥	5♠
	6♥	K♦	J♦	Q♠	7♣	K♣					
68	Q♦	5♠	4♣	5♠	Q♠	A♦	J♠	K♠	6♣/9♥	5♠	10♥
	Q♣	6♣	3♦	7♠	J♣	8♦					
69	7♣	4♥	6♠	5♠	K♣	A♠	A♦	4♥	10♥/10♠	4♦	J♣
	A♥	7♥	4♠	9♥	2♥	A♦					
70	2♣	A♥	5♠	Q♥	5♣	10♥	9♠	A♥	7♥/K♦	5♥	J♦
	10♣	6♥	8♠	2♥	6♦	9♠					
71	7♦	8♥	4♠	K♦	2♦	10♣	Q♥	8♦	J♦/5♥	5♣	3♠
	3♣	Q♠	J♥	9♠	7♠	9♣					
72	K♥	A♥	K♦	4♣	9♦	Q♦	10♣	Q♦	10♦/10♠	4♣	6♦
	10♥	3♠	5♦	9♠	7♠	10♣					
73	4♦	A♣	5♠	9♣	J♠	7♠	Q♦	4♦	2♣/8♣	6♥	9♣
	8♦	K♠	3♦	10♥	7♦	6♥					
74	9♠	A♠	K♠	K♦	A♣	7♠	K♣	K♦	7♣/4♠	3♦	Q♥
	A♥	Q♥	5♦	8♣	2♥	10♥					
75	J♠	4♥	5♠	10♦	9♥	Q♠	J♥	Q♠	2♦/5♣	Q♦	10♠
	2♣	J♣	J♦	A♥	7♥	10♣					
76	7♣	3♦	10♥	5♦	6♥	2♦	2♠	6♣	K♥/K♠	9♦	4♥
	2♣	Q♥	A♥	5♣	5♠	8♥					
77	8♦	2♣	5♦	8♥	7♠	9♣	10♣	2♣	J♦/Q♣	5♦	4♠
	J♣	9♥	2♥	J♠	Q♠	10♣					
78	6♠	K♠	A♠	A♣	2♣	A♦	4♥	A♠	9♣/5♣	3♣	10♣
	9♦	3♠	J♣	7♠	Q♥	J♠	2♣				
79	8♣	10♦	2♠	J♠	9♠	K♦	A♠	4♠	7♥/3♠	K♦	J♠
	Q♦	6♦	9♠	3♠	K♣	A♠					
80	10♥	2♠	J♠	J♣	5♥	3♦	K♦	10♥	7♣/A♥	7♠	7♣
	2♣	6♣	9♦	3♠	5♦	K♦					
81	K♠	9♠	2♥	6♠	Q♣	9♣	J♦	8♠	3♦/6♦	8♥	8♦
	4♣	5♠	7♣	2♠	6♦	J♥	Q♣				
82	4♠	5♠	4♣	9♦	8♥	10♣	Q♣	3♦	Q♥/7♠	7♥	Q♠
	10♥	7♠	5♦	3♦	6♠	Q♣					
83	A♠	6♠	9♠	5♠	6♠	5♠	10♣	4♦	7♦/A♦	A♠	10♦
	J♦	J♥	Q♠	2♠	3♦	6♥					
84	8♦	J♠	5♦	9♦	7♦	9♠		9♦	J♥/J♠	2♠	Q♣
	Q♣	7♥	5♦	4♠	Q♥	10♥					
85	2♥	6♣	7♠	J♣	4♦	3♣	5♦	9♥	9♥/6♦	K♥	3♥
	8♦	A♦	5♥	4♠	7♠	5♦					
86	K♣	5♣	J♠	3♦	10♠	9♥	Q♣	10♥	6♥/A♥	9♠	A♥
	10♦	7♥	5♥	A♠	K♥	Q♣					
87	4♣	10♥	Q♦	Q♥	7♥	10♠	3♠	K♣	3♥/6♦	6♠	A♦
	8♣	A♣	7♠	4♠	9♣	3♦					
88	8♦	8♣	Q♥	J♠	J♦	3♥	2♠	J♦	2♦/6♣	2♠	2♦
	10♠	4♦	K♠	K♣	7♥	9♥					
89	9♠	10♠	J♠	Q♠	K♠	A♥	2♥	3♣	3♥/4♥	K♣	6♣
	A♠	7♦	K♣	6♠	Q♥	5♥	K♠				
90	A♥	A♦	Q♦	5♠	3♠	3♠	9♥	2♠	7♣/5♦	8♠	8♠
	2♦	9♣	5♠	K♠	6♠	2♣					
91	J♣	10♠	5♥	K♣	7♥	2♠	2♠	J♣	9♣/4♠	6♠	K♣
	J♠	3♥	10♣	6♠	Q♦	2♠					
92	A♠	A♦	K♣	6♦	4♥	J♠	K♠	K♦	10♦/A♣	2♦	2♠
	3♣	7♠	4♦	Q♦	5♥	Q♠	4♥				
93	3♠	10♠	10♣	K♠	Q♠	2♥	8♦	K♣	6♦/3♦	A♦	6♠
	2♦	4♠	10♦	4♥	K♣	5♦					
94	2♥	K♣	A♠	5♦	9♦	Q♣	10♠	A♦	8♣/10♥	A♥	9♠
	3♣	6♣	A♦	4♥	Q♠	10♠					
95	2♣	3♣	5♦	10♦	Q♥	8♣	5♠	10♦	6♦/4♣	3♥	K♥
	6♠	7♣	3♠	4♠	7♠	5♠					
96	3♥	5♣	J♦	Q♦	A♥	6♠	10♦	10♣	A♦/10♥	Q♣	2♣
	9♥	Q♣	Q♠	5♠	5♦	K♠					
97	K♣	9♥	Q♦	J♥	4♦	A♦	A♠	3♣	2♦/9♠	10♦	A♠
	5♠	4♣	2♣	7♣	8♣	A♣					
98	7♦	9♣	J♥	5♥	A♥	2♥	A♦	A♥	6♠/8♥	Q♠	7♥
	4♠	10♥	Q♥	A♠	5♣	A♦					
99	7♣	Q♣	5♥	J♣	6♠	K♠	4♥	Q♠	2♥/10♠	8♦	8♥
	K♣	6♥	Q♥	8♥	J♥	4♦	6♦				

Nine of Spades

AGE	MER	VEN	MAR	JUP	SAT	URA	NEP	LR	PLU/RES	ENV	DISP
0	2♥	K♥	K♦	6♥	4♣	2♦	J♠	2♥	8♣/6♦	9♠	9♠
	3♦	6♠	K♣	7♣	A♥	J♠					
1	7♦	3♦	6♥	A♦	10♣	8♣	3♠	K♥	4♥/5♦	6♠	K♥
	A♠	Q♠	10♠	8♦	9♦	3♠					
2	6♠	10♥	Q♥	5♣	8♠	A♠	A♦	K♦	K♣/6♦	2♠	2♣
	9♥	2♦	A♥	3♠	6♥	K♠					
3	K♥	9♥	5♠	J♥	J♦	K♣	A♣	6♥	2♠/7♥	K♣	A♠
	3♠	5♠	7♠	Q♣	8♠	A♠					
4	7♦	4♣	J♥	J♣	8♠	2♥	K♣	4♣	A♠/5♦	8♠	7♥
	8♦	6♦	10♣	K♦	10♥	K♣					
5	Q♠	2♦	J♣	9♣	4♥	K♠	7♠	2♦	2♥/J♣	6♣	8♥
	K♥	4♦	10♣	5♦	J♥	J♦	4♥				
6	8♠	3♥	5♣	J♦	Q♦	A♥	6♠	J♠	10♦/A♦	2♦	7♠
	5♥	4♠	3♣	J♥	J♣	10♠					
7	7♠	K♦	8♦	6♦	8♠	5♥	J♦	7♠	3♦/4♦	A♦	K♦
	9♥	2♥	9♠	6♥	5♦	J♦					
8	4♣	9♥	6♦	K♥	Q♥	3♦	2♣	3♦	2♠/2♦	A♥	3♣
	Q♦	8♥	9♦	4♥	J♦	Q♣					
9	9♣	Q♦	K♥	K♣	A♦	Q♠	3♦	6♥	5♠/3♣	3♥	5♦
	10♥	8♣	A♣	2♦	5♥	3♦					
10	8♠	A♥	8♣	Q♦	4♦	K♦	Q♠	A♦	6♣/J♠	Q♣	9♠
	2♠	5♦	A♠	3♣	Q♥	10♥					
11	8♥	K♣	Q♦	7♦	J♣	2♠	3♠	10♣	5♦/6♠	10♦	Q♦
	3♦	Q♣	A♦	Q♥	5♥	3♠					
12	3♥	A♥	7♦	7♠	J♥	3♦	Q♠	8♣	2♥/10♦	Q♠	3♦
	8♦	J♠	10♥	Q♥	5♠	Q♠					
13	K♥	10♠	4♦	8♠	9♦	5♣	7♠	3♠	J♦/4♠	8♦	6♥
	8♥	3♠	5♥	J♠	K♣	6♠					
14	Q♥	5♥	8♣	5♦	4♣	8♥	J♠	6♣	4♥/6♦	7♣	4♣
	J♥	3♦	5♠	3♥	A♥	3♣					
15	K♣	Q♠	10♦	9♥	A♠	J♥	5♦	10♥	J♠/A♣	J♠	5♠
	K♠	Q♥	8♦	7♦	10♠	9♣					
16	A♥	7♠	9♥	5♣	A♠	4♦	7♥	Q♥	2♦/Q♣	10♠	5♥
	3♦	3♥	7♣	A♣	K♥	7♥					
17	10♠	Q♦	6♦	4♥	3♠	3♦	5♣	5♠	K♠/10♥	4♠	4♦
	A♥	6♠	Q♦	Q♣	9♥	2♥					
18	J♥	7♠	4♥	2♥	4♠	10♦	6♠	8♠	8♠/J♦	4♥	5♣
	4♦	Q♦	Q♥	A♥	Q♣	K♥					
19	5♣	3♠	5♠	10♥	A♥	K♣	10♦	A♠	A♠/7♦	10♠	10♥
	2♦	6♠	5♥	9♦	9♣	3♥					
20	Q♣	7♥	4♥	3♠	K♥	K♦	K♣	A♦	6♦/J♠	Q♥	J♣
	8♠	3♣	8♦	7♦	A♠	K♣					
21	7♠	8♠	3♠	10♣	10♥	6♦	7♥	K♥	3♣/Q♦	9♣	J♦
	Q♣	4♦	8♠	A♠	4♥	7♥					
22	9♥	5♦	8♦	Q♦	2♠	Q♠	10♣	9♥	Q♥/J♣	6♦	3♠
	3♦	A♥	J♥	7♥	9♦	4♠					
23	8♥	8♠	Q♦	5♠	4♣	5♦	Q♠	5♣	A♦/J♠	3♠	6♦
	6♦	10♠	6♥	7♥	9♦	Q♠					
24	J♦	2♥	3♠	4♠	10♦	Q♣	5♣	J♥	7♠/8♣	J♦	9♣
	3♥	K♠	5♥	6♦	9♥	4♦					
25	7♥	K♦	K♠	Q♦	2♥	9♦	K♥	J♦	Q♣/8♦	J♣	Q♥
	8♠	10♣	6♥	8♣	A♣	6♦					
26	10♦	7♣	3♠	6♦	7♠	A♥	J♥	K♣	2♠/10♥	10♥	10♠
	7♠	9♣	Q♥	8♠	3♣	Q♠					
27	Q♣	5♥	6♦	6♥	4♦	2♠	2♣	A♣	8♥/K♠	5♠	4♥
	7♠	10♣	8♠	10♥	3♠	5♠					
28	3♥	7♠	6♥	5♠	9♦	4♠	Q♠	7♦	Q♥/2♦	4♦	4♠
	9♣	7♦	A♣	10♦	A♥	Q♠					
29	A♠	K♠	K♦	2♥	7♠	K♠	7♠	4♠	4♠/10♥	5♥	10♣
	4♣	10♠	9♣	Q♣	10♣	10♦	7♠				
30	8♠	A♦	2♠	10♦	7♥	Q♠	K♦	J♥	3♣/10♠	5♠	J♠
	5♣	4♥	4♣	3♦	K♥	K♦					
31	6♦	2♣	10♦	9♣	J♠	5♦	Q♦	J♣	Q♣/8♠	4♣	7♣
	7♠	6♠	4♠	10♠	6♥	Q♠					
32	K♠	7♥	A♣	A♠	2♦	4♠	Q♥	8♠	5♥/4♦	6♥	8♦
	5♠	10♥	Q♣	2♣	4♥	J♥	2♦				
33	8♦	3♠	5♠	4♣	5♦	Q♠	2♦	2♥	10♣/9♦	3♦	Q♠
	6♦	Q♣	6♥	5♥	A♠	2♦					
34	K♦	A♠	7♥	3♠	4♥	10♥	Q♠	K♣	9♥/K♣	Q♦	10♦
	Q♥	J♥	A♥	2♠	5♥	4♦					
35	3♥	Q♥	3♠	6♥	4♣	9♥	4♠	Q♣	J♥/10♦	9♦	Q♣
	2♦	3♣	J♠	5♠	10♣	6♦					
36	A♣	6♠	Q♣	9♣	J♦	3♦	6♥	2♦	7♦/4♥	5♦	3♥
	3♥	K♣	J♠	8♦	9♦	6♥					
37	K♥	10♥	9♠	5♥	J♠	7♦	2♦	J♣	4♦/8♠	3♣	A♥
	A♦	3♣	J♠	K♦	8♥	2♦					
38	5♠	6♠	5♣	10♠	9♥	A♥	5♥	9♣	6♣/4♥	K♦	A♦
	8♣	2♥	9♦	8♦	4♠	5♥					
39	3♥	8♣	10♣	10♦	Q♥	6♠	2♣	4♥	2♠/6♠	7♠	2♦
	J♠	J♦	K♠	K♥	3♣	7♦					
40	7♥	J♠	10♦	A♥	K♠	8♠	A♠	K♠	6♣/7♣	8♥	6♣
	K♦	9♦	K♥	6♠	10♣	J♠	K♠				
41	8♠	K♣	5♣	J♣	3♦	10♠	7♦	7♣	Q♣/6♥	7♥	8♠
	2♠	4♠	10♥	K♣	6♠	4♥					
42	9♠	J♠	J♣	K♥	3♣	2♠	2♠	A♣	4♠/8♦	A♠	K♣
	10♦	6♣	Q♠	A♠	5♠	2♣					
43	K♦	K♣	K♥	4♥	7♣	10♦	K♠	3♥	A♦/2♥	2♣	2♠
	3♦	9♦	J♦	5♣	J♠	A♥	7♠				
44	10♠	J♠	Q♠	K♠	A♥	A♠	3♥	5♣	4♥/5♦	K♥	6♠
	2♠	8♦	A♦	7♣	K♥	6♥					
45	A♠	K♥	K♦	6♥	4♣	2♦	J♠	J♦	8♣/6♦	9♠	9♠
	3♦	6♠	K♣	7♣	A♥	J♠					
46	7♠	3♦	6♥	A♦	10♣	8♣	3♠	Q♦	4♥/5♠	6♠	K♥
	A♠	Q♣	10♠	8♦	9♦	3♠					
47	6♣	10♥	Q♥	5♣	8♠	A♠	A♦	A♥	K♣/6♦	2♠	2♣
	7♦	2♦	A♥	3♠	6♥	K♠					
48	K♥	7♠	5♣	J♥	J♦	K♣	2♥		2♠/7♥	K♣	A♠
	3♠	5♠	7♠	Q♣	8♣	2♥					
49	9♥	4♣	J♥	J♣	8♠	A♣	K♣	7♠	A♠/5♦	8♠	7♥
	8♦	6♦	10♣	K♦	10♥	K♣					

Age	Mer	Ven	Mar	Jup	Sat	Ura	Nep	LR	Plu/Res	Env	Disp
50	Q♣	2♦	J♣	9♠	4♥	K♠	7♣	K♦	A♠/J♣	6♣	8♥
	K♥	4♦	10♣	5♦	J♥	J♦		4♥			
51	8♠	3♥	5♣	J♦	Q♣	A♥	6♠	8♦	10♦/A♦	2♦	7♠
	5♥	4♠	3♣	J♥	J♣	10♠					
52	7♠	K♣	8♦	6♦	8♣	5♥	J♦	6♦	3♦/4♥	A♦	K♦
	7♣	A♣	9♦	6♥	5♦	J♦					
53	4♣	7♦	6♣	K♥	Q♥	3♦	2♣	8♣	2♠/2♦	A♥	3♣
	Q♦	8♥	9♦	4♥	J♦	Q♣					
54	9♣	Q♦	K♥	K♣	A♦	Q♠	3♦	5♥	5♠/3♣	3♥	5♦
	10♣	8♣	2♥	2♦	5♥	3♦					
55	8♠	A♥	8♦	Q♦	4♦	K♦	Q♠	J♦	6♣/J♠	Q♣	9♦
	2♠	5♦	A♠	3♣	Q♥	10♥					
56	8♥	K♣	Q♦	9♥	J♣	2♠	3♠	4♣	5♦/6♠	10♦	Q♦
	3♦	Q♣	A♦	Q♥	5♥	3♠					
57	3♥	A♥	9♥	7♠	J♥	3♦	Q♠	9♥	A♣/10♦	Q♠	3♦
	8♦	J♠	10♥	Q♥	5♠	Q♠					
58	K♥	10♠	4♦	8♠	9♥	5♣	7♠	6♦	J♦/4♠	8♦	6♥
	8♥	3♠	5♥	J♠	K♣	6♣					
59	Q♥	5♥	8♣	5♦	4♣	8♥	J♣	K♥	4♥/6♦	7♣	4♣
	J♥	3♦	5♠	3♥	A♥	3♣					
60	K♣	Q♠	10♦	7♦	A♠	J♥	5♦	Q♥	J♠/2♥	J♠	5♣
	K♠	Q♥	8♦	9♥	10♠	9♦					
61	A♥	7♠	7♦	5♣	A♦	4♦	7♥	3♦	2♦/Q♣	10♣	5♥
	3♦	3♥	9♥	2♥	K♥	7♥					
62	10♠	Q♠	6♦	4♥	3♣	3♦	5♠	2♣	K♠/10♥	4♠	4♦
	A♠	6♠	Q♦	Q♣	7♦	A♣					
63	J♥	7♠	4♥	A♣	4♠	10♦	6♠	9♣	8♠/J♦	4♥	5♠
	4♦	Q♦	Q♥	A♥	Q♣	K♥					
64	5♣	3♠	5♠	10♥	A♥	K♣	10♦	Q♦	A♠/9♥	10♠	10♥
	2♦	6♠	5♥	9♥	9♣	3♥					
65	Q♣	7♣	4♥	3♠	K♥	K♦	K♣	K♥	6♦/J♠	Q♥	J♣
	8♠	3♣	8♥	9♥	2♥	K♠					
66	7♠	8♠	3♠	10♣	10♥	6♦	7♥	K♠	3♣/Q♦	9♣	J♦
	Q♠	4♦	8♣	2♥	4♥	7♥					
67	7♦	5♦	8♦	Q♦	2♠	Q♠	10♣	A♦	Q♥/J♣	6♦	3♠
	3♦	A♥	J♥	7♥	9♦	4♠					
68	8♥	8♠	Q♦	5♠	4♠	5♣	Q♣	Q♠	A♦/J♠	3♠	6♦
	6♦	10♠	6♥	7♥	9♦	Q♠					
69	J♦	A♣	3♠	4♠	10♦	Q♣	5♠	3♦	7♠/8♣	J♦	9♣
	3♥	K♠	5♥	6♦	7♦	4♦					
70	7♥	K♦	K♠	Q♦	A♣	9♦	K♥	8♠	Q♣/8♦	J♣	Q♥
	8♠	10♣	6♥	8♣	2♥	6♦					
71	10♦	7♣	3♠	6♦	9♥	A♥	J♥	A♥	2♠/10♥	10♥	10♠
	7♠	9♣	Q♥	8♠	3♣	Q♠					
72	Q♣	5♥	6♦	6♥	4♦	2♠	2♣	8♦	8♥/K♠	5♠	4♥
	7♠	10♣	8♠	10♥	3♠	5♦					
73	3♥	7♠	6♥	5♦	9♦	4♠	Q♠	Q♦	Q♥/2♦	4♦	4♠
	9♣	9♥	2♥	10♦	A♥	Q♠					
74	A♠	K♠	K♦	4♣	7♠	K♣	7♣	4♦	4♠/10♦	5♥	10♣
	4♣	10♠	9♣	Q♣	10♣	10♦	7♠				

Age	Mer	Ven	Mar	Jup	Sat	Ura	Nep	LR	Plu/Res	Env	Disp
75	8♣	A♦	2♠	10♦	7♥	Q♦	K♦	K♦	3♣/10♠	5♣	J♠
	5♣	4♥	4♠	3♦	K♥	K♦					
76	6♦	2♣	10♦	9♣	J♣	5♥	Q♦	Q♠	Q♠/8♠	4♣	7♣
	7♠	6♠	4♣	10♠	6♥	Q♦					
77	K♠	7♥	2♥	A♠	2♦	4♠	Q♥	8♥	5♥/4♦	6♥	8♦
	5♠	10♥	Q♣	2♣	4♥	J♥	2♦				
78	8♦	3♠	5♠	4♣	5♦	Q♠	2♦	K♣	10♣/9♦	3♦	Q♠
	6♦	Q♣	6♥	5♥	A♠	2♦					
79	K♦	A♠	7♥	3♠	4♥	10♥	Q♠	Q♦	7♦/K♣	Q♦	10♦
	Q♥	J♥	A♥	2♠	5♥	4♦					
80	3♥	Q♥	3♠	6♥	4♣	7♥	4♠	7♦	J♥/10♦	9♦	Q♣
	2♠	3♣	J♣	5♠	10♣	6♦					
81	2♥	6♠	Q♣	9♣	J♦	3♦	6♥	J♣	9♥/4♥	5♦	3♥
	3♦	K♣	J♣	8♦	9♦	6♥					
82	K♥	10♥	9♣	5♥	J♠	9♥	2♦	2♠	4♦/8♠	3♣	A♥
	A♦	3♣	J♣	K♦	8♥	2♦					
83	5♠	6♦	5♣	10♣	7♥	A♦	5♥	3♠	6♣/4♥	K♦	A♦
	8♣	A♣	9♦	8♦	4♠	5♥					
84	3♥	8♣	10♣	10♦	Q♥	6♣	2♣	3♥	2♠/6♠	7♠	2♦
	J♠	J♦	K♠	K♥	3♣	9♥					
85	7♥	J♠	10♦	A♥	K♠	8♠	2♥	A♥	6♣/7♣	8♥	6♣
	K♦	7♦	K♥	6♠	10♣	J♣	K♠				
86	8♠	K♣	5♣	J♣	3♦	10♠	9♥	7♦	Q♣/6♥	7♥	8♠
	2♠	4♠	10♥	K♠	6♠	7♠					
87	9♣	J♠	J♣	K♥	3♠	2♠	2♠	7♠	4♠/8♦	A♠	K♣
	10♦	6♣	Q♠	A♠	5♣	2♣					
88	K♦	K♣	K♥	4♦	7♣	10♦	K♠	J♥	A♦/A♣	2♣	2♠
	3♦	9♦	J♦	5♣	J♣	A♥	7♣				
89	10♠	J♠	Q♠	K♠	A♥	2♥	3♥	3♦	4♥/5♥	K♥	6♠
	2♠	8♦	A♦	7♠	K♥	6♥					
90	2♥	K♥	K♦	6♥	4♣	2♦	J♠	Q♠	8♣/6♦	9♠	9♣
	3♦	6♠	K♣	7♠	A♥	J♠					
91	7♠	3♦	6♥	A♦	10♣	8♠	3♠	K♥	4♥/5♠	6♠	K♥
	A♠	Q♣	10♠	8♦	9♦	3♠					
92	6♣	10♥	Q♥	5♣	8♠	A♠	A♦	10♠	K♣/6♦	2♠	2♣
	9♥	2♦	A♥	3♠	6♥	K♠					
93	K♥	9♥	5♠	J♥	J♦	K♣	A♠	4♦	2♠/7♥	K♣	A♠
	3♠	5♠	7♠	Q♣	8♣	A♣					
94	7♠	4♣	J♥	J♣	8♠	2♥	K♣	8♠	A♣/5♦	8♠	7♥
	8♦	6♦	10♣	K♦	10♥	K♣					
95	Q♣	2♦	J♣	9♣	4♥	K♠	7♥	9♦	2♥/J♠	6♣	8♥
	K♥	4♦	10♠	5♦	J♥	J♦		4♥			
96	8♠	3♥	5♣	J♦	Q♦	A♥	6♠	5♣	10♦/A♦	2♦	7♠
	5♥	4♠	3♣	J♥	J♣	10♠					
97	7♠	K♦	8♦	6♦	8♣	5♥	J♦	7♠	3♦/4♥	A♦	K♦
	9♥	2♥	9♦	6♥	5♦	J♦					
98	4♣	9♥	6♦	K♥	Q♥	3♦	2♣	Q♥	2♠/2♦	A♥	3♣
	Q♦	8♥	9♦	4♥	J♦	Q♣					
99	9♣	Q♦	K♥	K♣	A♦	Q♠	3♦	5♥	5♠/3♣	3♥	5♦
	10♣	8♣	A♠	2♦	5♥	3♦					

Ten of Spades

AGE	MER	VEN	MAR	JUP	SAT	URA	NEP	LR	PLU/RES	ENV	DISP
0	5♣	3♦	A♠	7♥	7♦	5♠	J♥	5♠	9♣/9♠	10♠	10♠
	8♠	8♥	7♠	3♠	10♦	4♣					
1	5♥	K♣	7♥	2♦	2♠	9♠	4♠	3♦	7♣/K♠	Q♥	4♥
	8♠	9♥	3♠	9♠	A♠	Q♣					
2	4♦	8♦	2♣	Q♣	3♥	5♦	4♣	A♠	7♠/J♣	9♣	4♠
	8♥	7♦	A♣	5♠	5♣						
3	10♣	K♠	Q♠	2♥	8♠	6♠	3♦	7♥	5♦/9♠	6♦	10♣
	6♣	K♦	8♥	5♥	9♥	5♠	8♦				
4	8♠	10♥	9♣	5♠	J♠	A♥	Q♠	7♦	10♦/K♦	3♠	J♠
	8♠	3♣	6♠	A♦	4♥	Q♠					
5	7♥	4♠	5♣	8♥	K♥	K♣	A♥	5♠	5♥/3♠	J♦	7♣
	8♦	Q♥	6♠	K♦	2♦	A♥					
6	K♠	J♠	A♣	10♣	J♠	5♦	7♠	J♥	K♣//2♠	J♣	8♦
	6♠	9♣	5♥	4♠	3♣	J♥	J♣				
7	6♥	A♠	6♠	6♣	Q♣	4♠	J♣	5♥	9♦/3♥	10♥	Q♠
	7♥	5♥	2♦	K♣	10♣	J♣					
8	Q♠	10♣	J♠	A♠	3♠	9♠	4♣	K♣	9♥/6♦	5♠	10♦
	7♠	J♥	5♠	9♣	K♣	2♠					
9	4♦	7♠	A♣	2♦	6♠	9♥	5♠	7♥	J♥/5♣	4♦	Q♣
	J♣	10♦	K♥	6♠	9♥	7♥					
10	A♣	Q♥	5♥	8♥	2♣	A♦	2♦	2♦	7♦/3♣	5♥	3♥
	4♠	6♦	K♥	6♥	3♦	2♦					
11	4♥	9♠	8♥	K♣	Q♦	7♦	J♣	2♠	2♠/3♣	5♣	A♥
	10♥	10♦	K♥	Q♠	7♣	J♣					
12	6♠	7♥	8♠	9♦	9♥	10♥	K♣	9♣	J♦/3♣	4♣	A♦
	8♣	2♥	3♥	6♥	5♦	K♣					
13	4♦	8♣	9♦	5♠	7♠	J♦	4♠	4♣	9♣/Q♥	6♥	2♦
	Q♥	2♣	K♠	4♥	10♦	7♠					
14	J♠	Q♦	5♣	5♠	K♠	3♠	A♣	4♦	J♦/3♦	3♦	6♣
	Q♠	9♥	4♥	Q♥	9♦	K♥	K♠				
15	3♠	6♦	8♠	K♥	A♠	K♦	7♦	8♠	5♥/2♦	Q♦	8♠
	9♣	5♦	9♠	K♠	Q♥	8♦					
16	8♥	Q♠	K♥	4♥	10♥	9♣	4♠	2♦	5♦/6♦	9♦	K♣
	5♣	J♦	4♣	10♣	8♠	4♠					
17	Q♠	6♦	4♥	3♠	3♦	5♠	K♣	Q♣	10♥/2♥	5♦	2♠
	A♦	3♥	2♣	8♠	K♥	5♠	3♦				
18	K♦	Q♠	4♣	K♠	5♠	A♣	4♦	3♥	3♣/K♣	3♣	6♠
	9♣	6♥	10♥	3♦	4♥	2♦					
19	A♣	4♥	Q♠	2♦	6♠	J♣	Q♦	5♦	8♣/7♥	K♥	9♣
	A♦	Q♥	6♦	3♦	5♠	Q♦					
20	8♦	A♦	2♦	10♥	9♦	8♠	A♠	4♣	3♠/6♠	7♠	K♥
	10♠	5♥	K♦	6♥	3♥	A♠					
21	J♦	9♠	7♠	8♠	3♠	10♣	10♥	10♠	6♦/7♥	8♥	2♣
	7♦	J♣	5♠	A♠	2♦	K♠					
22	4♥	7♦	8♠	J♥	2♣	6♦	2♥	K♣	9♣/J♠	7♥	A♠
	A♠	6♠	8♦	5♥	8♣	2♥					
23	9♥	6♣	J♥	K♥	3♠	A♣	6♦	Q♣	10♣/Q♣	A♠	7♥
	6♥	7♥	9♦	Q♠	9♠	6♦					
24	5♥	J♣	K♥	8♥	3♣	K♠	3♦	2♥	A♠/Q♦	2♣	8♦
	4♥	2♠	9♦	Q♣	J♥	2♣	3♠				

AGE	MER	VEN	MAR	JUP	SAT	URA	NEP	LR	PLU/RES	ENV	DISP
25	3♠	4♦	8♠	2♣	A♥	5♠	Q♥	8♦	5♣/10♥	K♥	7♠
	K♣	5♦	10♦	J♥	K♥	K♦					
26	8♦	Q♠	6♥	7♥	8♣	K♠	2♣	6♦	A♦/3♣	9♠	K♠
	7♠	A♠	3♥	2♦	Q♣	2♣					
27	6♣	7♦	7♥	4♥	7♠	A♦	4♠	3♦	9♣/J♠	6♠	3♠
	A♥	7♣	3♥	3♠	2♠	5♥					
28	8♥	A♥	4♥	6♦	10♥	4♣	A♦	8♠	6♠/10♦	2♠	5♦
	9♦	8♣	2♥	J♣	K♣	A♠					
29	3♠	5♠	6♥	A♥	2♠	Q♠	4♣	10♥	J♦/Q♦	K♣	9♦
	9♦	Q♣	10♠	10♦	7♠	9♠					
30	7♣	6♦	A♥	9♥	K♥	9♣	A♠	9♣	Q♣/Q♥	8♠	Q♦
	A♦	5♥	10♥	7♠	K♣	A♠					
31	4♦	5♣	9♥	8♣	J♥	A♦	4♣	5♠	A♣/5♣	6♣	3♦
	6♥	Q♦	9♠	7♠	6♠	4♣					
32	4♥	K♦	2♠	8♣	3♥	8♠	8♦	J♠	2♣/5♦	2♦	6♥
	7♣	A♠	K♣	Q♦	6♦	J♦					
33	7♠	K♣	8♣	Q♣	6♣	7♠	K♥	A♥	3♣/7♥	A♦	4♣
	J♥	A♦	6♠	4♦	5♠	10♥					
34	6♦	4♣	5♠	7♦	10♣	J♥	Q♠	Q♦	Q♦/2♥	A♥	5♣
	K♠	7♠	6♥	9♥	K♦	8♦					
35	5♠	8♦	7♦	8♠	10♥	2♠	J♠	7♥	J♣/5♥	3♥	5♥
	A♦	4♦	9♥	2♥	4♥	J♠					
36	K♦	4♣	7♥	3♣	10♦	A♦	8♠	4♠	K♠/9♠	Q♣	4♦
	10♣	Q♥	A♥	5♥	7♦	A♣					
37	J♥	8♦	3♠	A♠	5♦	5♠	J♦	5♣	3♠/2♣	10♦	5♠
	2♠	A♥	7♠	5♠	5♥	4♥					
38	8♠	A♥	6♠	9♠	5♠	6♦	5♠	8♥	10♣/9♥	Q♠	10♥
	J♣	Q♥	K♣	3♥	8♥	4♦					
39	5♥	3♦	3♣	A♠	4♥	Q♠	6♠	K♥	7♥/Q♦	8♦	J♣
	3♠	10♦	6♥	9♥	2♥	6♦					
40	8♠	3♣	A♠	9♦	9♠	7♥	J♠	K♠	10♦/A♥	7♠	J♦
	4♣	2♠	8♠	2♥	3♣	J♠					
41	7♦	Q♣	6♥	A♥	9♣	4♣	9♣	A♥	7♠/K♥	J♠	3♠
	A♦	5♠	J♥	J♠	3♥	5♦					
42	7♣	3♠	A♥	6♠	6♣	8♠	4♣	K♠	10♥/Q♣	10♣	6♦
	7♥	K♦	2♦	J♠	3♥	4♣					
43	2♣	A♣	A♠	5♦	5♣	5♥	8♠	J♠	8♦/8♣	4♠	9♣
	4♦	K♠	K♣	7♥	7♦	2♠					
44	J♠	Q♠	K♠	A♥	A♣	3♥	4♥	A♠	5♥/6♦	4♥	Q♥
	3♠	9♦	2♦	8♣	2♥	7♥					
45	5♣	3♦	A♠	7♥	9♥	5♠	J♥	10♣	9♣/9♠	10♠	10♠
	8♦	8♥	7♠	3♠	10♦	4♣					
46	5♥	K♣	7♥	2♦	2♠	9♣	4♠	J♣	7♣/K♠	Q♥	4♥
	8♦	9♦	3♠	9♠	A♠	Q♣					
47	4♦	8♦	2♦	Q♣	3♥	5♦	4♣	5♦	7♠/J♣	9♠	4♠
	8♥	9♥	2♥	5♣	5♠	4♣					
48	10♣	K♠	Q♠	A♠	8♠	6♦	3♦	7♥	5♦/9♠	6♦	10♣
	6♣	K♦	8♥	5♥	9♥	5♣	8♦				
49	8♣	10♥	9♣	5♣	J♠	A♥	Q♠	6♥	10♦/K♦	3♠	J♠
	8♠	3♣	6♣	A♦	4♥	Q♠					

AGE	MER	VEN	MAR	JUP	SAT	URA	NEP	LR	PLU/RES	ENV	DISP
50	7♥	4♠	5♣	8♥	K♥	K♣	A♥	A♠	5♥/3♠	J♦	7♣
	8♠	Q♥	6♣	K♦	2♦	A♥					
51	K♠	J♠	2♥	10♣	J♣	5♦	7♠	6♠	K♣/2♠	J♣	8♦
	6♠	9♠	5♥	4♠	3♣	J♥	J♣				
52	6♥	A♣	6♠	6♣	Q♣	4♣	J♣	6♠	9♦/3♥	10♥	Q♠
	7♥	5♥	2♦	K♣	10♣	J♣					
53	Q♠	10♣	J♠	A♠	3♣	9♠	4♣	Q♣	7♦/6♦	5♠	10♦
	7♠	J♥	5♠	9♣	K♣	2♠					
54	4♦	7♠	A♣	2♦	6♣	7♦	5♦	4♣	J♥/5♣	4♦	Q♣
	J♣	10♦	K♥	6♠	9♦	7♥					
55	2♥	Q♥	5♥	8♥	2♣	A♦	2♦	J♣	9♥/3♣	5♥	3♥
	4♣	6♦	K♥	6♥	3♦	2♦					
56	4♥	9♠	8♥	K♣	Q♦	9♥	J♣	Q♠	2♠/3♠	5♣	A♥
	10♥	10♦	K♥	Q♠	7♣	J♣					
57	6♠	7♥	8♣	9♠	7♦	10♥	K♣	10♣	J♦/3♣	4♣	A♦
	8♣	A♣	3♥	6♥	5♦	K♣					
58	4♦	8♣	9♣	5♣	7♠	J♦	4♠	J♠	9♣/Q♥	6♥	2♦
	Q♦	2♣	K♠	4♥	10♦	9♥					
59	J♠	Q♥	5♣	5♠	K♠	3♣	2♥	A♠	J♦/3♦	3♦	6♣
	Q♠	7♦	4♥	Q♥	9♦	K♥	K♠				
60	3♠	6♥	8♠	K♥	A♦	K♦	9♥	3♣	5♥/2♦	Q♦	8♠
	9♣	5♥	9♠	K♠	Q♥	8♦					
61	8♥	Q♦	K♥	4♥	10♦	A♣	4♠	9♠	5♦/6♥	9♦	K♣
	5♣	J♦	4♠	10♣	8♠	4♠					
62	Q♠	6♦	4♥	3♣	3♦	5♣	K♠	4♣	10♥/A♣	5♦	2♠
	A♦	3♥	2♣	8♠	K♥	5♠	3♦				
63	K♦	Q♦	4♣	K♣	5♠	2♥	4♦	4♦	3♣/K♣	3♣	6♠
	9♣	6♥	10♣	3♦	4♥	2♦					
64	2♥	4♥	Q♠	2♦	6♣	J♣	Q♦	7♠	8♣/7♥	K♦	9♠
	A♦	Q♥	6♦	3♦	5♠	Q♦					
65	8♦	A♦	2♦	10♥	9♦	8♠	A♠	A♠	3♣/6♠	7♠	K♥
	10♣	5♥	K♦	6♥	3♥	A♠					
66	J♦	9♠	7♠	8♠	3♠	10♣	10♥	2♦	6♦/7♥	8♥	2♣
	9♥	J♣	5♠	A♠	2♦	K♠					
67	4♥	9♠	8♠	J♥	2♣	6♦	A♠	6♣	9♣/J♠	7♥	A♠
	A♠	6♠	8♦	5♥	8♣	A♣					
68	7♦	6♣	J♥	K♥	3♠	2♥	6♦	9♥	10♣/Q♣	A♠	7♥
	6♥	7♥	9♦	Q♠	9♠	6♦					
69	5♥	J♣	K♥	8♥	3♠	K♠	3♥	5♦	2♥/Q♦	2♣	8♥
	4♥	2♠	9♦	Q♣	J♥	2♣	3♣				
70	3♠	4♦	8♠	2♣	A♥	5♠	Q♥	A♣	5♣/10♥	K♥	7♠
	K♣	5♦	10♠	J♥	K♥	K♦					
71	8♦	Q♠	6♥	7♥	8♣	K♣	2♠	Q♥	A♦/3♣	9♠	K♦
	9♥	2♦	3♥	2♦	Q♣	2♣					
72	6♣	9♥	7♥	4♥	7♠	A♦	4♠	5♥	9♣/J♣	6♠	3♣
	A♥	7♣	3♥	3♣	2♣	5♥					
73	8♥	A♥	4♥	6♦	10♥	4♣	A♦	8♥	6♠/10♦	2♠	5♦
	9♦	8♣	4♣	5♣	K♠	A♦					
74	3♠	5♠	6♥	A♥	2♠	Q♠	4♣	2♠	J♦/Q♦	K♠	9♦
	9♠	Q♣	10♠	10♦	7♠	9♠					

AGE	MER	VEN	MAR	JUP	SAT	URA	NEP	LR	PLU/RES	ENV	DISP
75	7♣	6♦	A♥	7♥	K♥	9♣	A♠	A♦	Q♣/Q♥	8♠	Q♦
	A♦	5♥	10♥	7♠	K♣	A♠					
76	4♦	5♠	7♥	8♠	J♥	A♦	4♣	2♦	2♥/5♣	6♣	3♦
	6♥	Q♦	9♠	7♠	6♠	4♦					
77	4♥	K♦	2♠	8♣	3♥	8♠	8♦	4♥	2♣/5♦	2♦	6♥
	7♣	A♥	K♣	Q♦	6♦	J♦					
78	7♠	K♣	8♠	Q♣	6♣	7♣	K♥	9♠	3♣/7♥	A♦	4♣
	J♥	A♦	6♠	4♦	5♠	10♦					
79	6♦	4♣	5♠	9♥	10♣	J♥	Q♣	8♥	Q♦/A♣	A♥	5♣
	K♠	7♠	6♥	7♠	K♦	8♥					
80	5♠	8♦	9♥	8♠	10♥	2♠	J♥	K♠	4♣/5♦	3♥	5♥
	A♦	4♦	7♠	A♣	4♥	J♠					
81	K♦	4♣	7♥	3♣	10♦	A♦	8♠	Q♦	K♠/9♠	Q♣	4♦
	10♣	Q♥	A♥	5♥	9♥	2♥					
82	J♥	8♦	3♣	2♥	5♦	5♠	J♦	7♦	3♠/2♣	10♦	5♠
	2♠	A♥	7♠	5♠	5♥	4♥					
83	8♠	A♥	6♠	9♠	5♠	6♦	5♠	J♣	10♣/7♦	Q♠	10♥
	J♣	Q♥	K♣	3♥	8♥	4♦					
84	5♥	3♦	3♣	A♠	4♥	Q♠	6♦	6♠	7♥/Q♦	8♦	J♠
	3♠	10♦	6♥	7♦	A♣	6♦					
85	8♦	3♠	A♠	9♦	9♠	7♥	J♠	7♥	10♦/A♥	7♠	J♦
	4♣	2♠	8♠	A♣	3♣	J♠					
86	9♥	Q♣	6♥	A♥	9♣	4♣	9♠	8♠	7♠/K♥	J♠	3♠
	A♦	5♠	J♥	J♠	3♥	5♦					
87	7♣	3♠	A♥	6♠	6♣	8♠	4♣	9♦	10♥/Q♦	10♣	6♦
	7♥	K♦	2♦	J♠	3♥	4♣					
88	2♣	2♥	A♠	5♦	5♥	5♥	8♠	9♥	8♦/8♣	4♠	9♣
	4♦	K♠	A♣	7♥	9♥	2♠					
89	J♠	Q♠	K♠	A♥	2♥	3♥	4♥	10♥	5♥/6♥	4♥	Q♥
	3♠	9♦	2♠	8♣	A♣	7♥					
90	5♣	3♦	A♠	7♥	7♠	5♣	J♦	K♣	9♣/9♠	10♠	10♠
	8♦	8♥	7♠	3♠	10♦	4♣					
91	5♥	K♣	7♥	2♦	2♠	9♣	4♣	4♦	7♣/K♠	Q♥	4♥
	8♥	9♦	3♠	9♠	A♣	Q♣					
92	4♦	8♦	2♦	Q♣	3♥	5♦	4♣	8♣	7♠/J♥	5♣	4♦
	8♥	7♦	A♣	5♠	5♠	4♠					
93	10♣	K♠	Q♠	2♥	8♦	6♦	3♦	9♦	5♦/9♠	6♦	10♣
	6♣	K♦	8♥	5♥	9♦	5♣	8♦				
94	8♣	10♥	9♣	5♣	J♠	A♥	Q♠	5♦	10♦/K♦	3♠	J♠
	8♠	3♣	A♦	4♦	Q♠						
95	7♥	4♠	5♣	8♥	K♥	K♣	A♥	7♠	5♥/3♠	J♦	7♣
	8♠	Q♥	6♣	K♦	2♦	A♥					
96	K♠	J♠	A♣	10♣	J♣	5♦	7♠	J♦	K♣/2♠	J♣	8♦
	6♠	9♠	5♥	4♠	3♣	J♥	J♣				
97	6♥	A♣	6♠	6♣	Q♣	4♣	J♣	4♠	9♦/3♥	10♥	Q♠
	7♥	5♥	2♦	K♣	10♣	J♣					
98	Q♠	10♣	J♠	A♠	3♣	9♠	4♣	J♠	9♥/6♦	5♠	10♦
	7♠	J♥	5♠	9♣	K♣	2♠					
99	4♦	7♠	A♣	2♦	6♣	9♥	5♦	Q♦	J♥/5♣	4♦	Q♣
	J♣	10♦	K♥	6♠	9♦	7♥					

The Yearly Spreads ♦ 347

J♠ Jack of Spades

AGE	MER	VEN	MAR	JUP	SAT	URA	NEP	LR	PLU/RES	ENV	DISP
0	8♣	6♥	4♠	10♥	10♦	8♠	A♥	8♠	A♠/Q♦	J♠	J♠
	9♠	3♦	6♠	K♣	7♣	A♥					
1	3♣	8♦	10♥	5♦	8♥	K♥	8♠	6♦	J♣/10♠	10♣	7♣
	3♥	10♠	6♠	Q♦	2♠	8♠					
2	K♠	10♦	A♣	Q♠	9♠	6♥	9♦	4♠	K♥/2♣	4♠	8♦
	A♠	7♥	J♠	8♦	3♦	J♥	9♠				
3	4♦	K♦	A♠	6♠	2♦	5♠	9♣	10♥	4♣/6♣	4♥	Q♠
	3♣	J♠	2♠	K♥	Q♠	9♣					
4	A♥	Q♠	10♦	K♦	3♦	7♥	5♠	10♦	9♥/4♥	10♠	10♦
	9♦	J♥	3♠	4♠	K♥	2♣					
5	J♦	9♦	K♣	2♠	6♠	9♥	6♥	8♠	J♥/10♥	Q♥	Q♣
	9♣	A♦	8♥	A♠	4♣	3♣					
6	A♣	10♣	J♣	5♦	7♠	K♣	2♠	A♥	7♦/3♦	9♣	3♦
	J♦	4♥	8♥	4♦	6♠	2♠					
7	7♣	7♥	5♦	K♥	5♣	7♦	9♠	3♣	2♣/10♠	6♦	A♥
	6♦	A♠	8♥	A♥	Q♠	9♣					
8	A♠	3♠	9♠	4♠	9♥	6♦	K♥	8♦	Q♥/3♦	3♠	A♦
	8♠	2♥	6♠	4♦	6♥	K♥					
9	J♦	8♣	4♠	10♥	9♦	Q♥	8♦	10♥	4♠/10♠	J♦	2♦
	5♣	7♠	K♠	7♠	A♦	7♦					
10	10♦	5♣	10♥	3♠	K♠	10♠	A♣	5♦	Q♥/5♥	J♣	6♣
	A♥	9♥	7♣	10♣	4♠	8♥	K♠				
11	10♠	4♥	9♠	8♥	K♣	Q♦	7♦	8♥	J♣/2♠	10♥	8♠
	4♠	6♥	7♥	K♠	10♣	3♥					
12	5♦	5♣	8♥	7♣	A♦	4♠	8♦	K♥	6♥/4♦	5♠	K♣
	10♥	Q♥	5♠	Q♠	9♠	8♦					
13	A♥	4♥	7♠	3♦	5♥	10♥	K♠	8♠	6♦/2♥	4♦	4♠
	K♣	6♠	7♠	9♠	8♥	3♠	5♥				
14	Q♦	5♣	5♠	K♠	3♠	A♣	J♠	K♠	3♦/K♥	5♥	6♠
	4♠	4♦	6♦	5♥	7♣	2♠					
15	A♣	7♣	A♥	2♠	6♠	9♠	5♠	10♦	8♣/3♣	5♠	9♠
	K♣	10♣	4♥	5♥	3♠	5♣					
16	3♥	K♠	2♠	6♦	4♣	8♣	K♦	A♣	3♦/A♠	4♠	K♥
	Q♠	J♣	Q♦	4♦	6♣	K♦					
17	Q♥	7♥	9♦	9♠	10♠	Q♠	6♦	Q♣	4♥/3♣	6♦	2♣
	7♦	9♣	3♠	K♦	2♠	K♠					
18	7♣	7♦	9♠	J♥	7♠	4♥	2♥	9♣	4♠/10♦	3♦	A♠
	K♦	A♠	3♥	J♣	8♣	2♥					
19	9♥	6♠	J♥	8♥	10♠	A♣	4♥	6♥	Q♠/2♦	Q♦	7♥
	4♦	3♣	4♠	A♥	7♥	4♥					
20	J♣	9♣	8♠	5♦	3♦	K♠	5♥	9♦	A♣/5♠	9♦	8♥
	7♣	2♣	4♣	2♦	J♥	7♠	3♦				
21	10♠	J♦	9♠	7♠	8♠	3♠	10♠	4♦	10♥/6♦	5♦	7♠
	K♥	6♥	A♦	J♥	8♥	Q♠					
22	3♥	A♥	4♦	3♣	8♣	K♥	7♠	K♦	K♣/3♦	3♣	K♦
	7♦	A♣	6♣	2♠	2♦	7♠					
23	6♠	7♦	3♣	7♠	9♦	K♣	8♦	A♠	4♠/9♣	K♦	3♣
	8♠	Q♣	6♠	3♦	7♠	J♣					
24	5♦	8♠	7♣	4♥	6♦	5♠	K♣	6♠	A♠/A♦	7♠	5♦
	4♣	8♣	2♥	9♣	K♥	K♣					
25	10♠	3♠	4♦	8♠	2♣	A♥	5♠	2♦	Q♥/5♦	8♥	9♦
	4♠	2♦	Q♠	A♦	9♦	7♥					
26	Q♠	4♥	8♠	9♥	8♥	4♠	K♦	5♠	2♦/10♣	7♥	Q♦
	K♠	J♣	6♠	9♦	K♥	K♦					
27	J♦	3♠	9♥	3♥	J♥	K♣	5♠	9♣	A♣/10♥	A♠	3♦
	4♦	5♣	7♥	9♦	A♠	5♠					
28	7♣	Q♦	2♣	8♣	6♣	9♠	3♥	A♥	7♠/6♥	2♣	6♥
	Q♠	K♦	K♥	5♣	4♥	Q♥					
29	9♦	K♥	8♣	2♥	6♠	Q♣	8♥	Q♠	3♦/3♣	K♥	4♣
	J♥	K♣	A♠	J♦	3♠	A♦					
30	4♥	5♠	10♥	7♦	Q♠	J♥	2♦	10♦	5♣/2♥	9♠	5♣
	K♠	9♦	4♦	9♥	Q♦	5♦					
31	3♠	3♥	7♠	9♠	6♦	2♣	10♦	K♦	9♣/J♣	6♠	5♥
	K♣	J♥	9♥	2♥	7♣	10♦					
32	Q♦	5♠	3♣	3♦	A♦	K♣	9♠	3♦	K♠/7♥	2♠	4♦
	Q♠	10♣	8♠	J♣	7♦	A♣					
33	J♥	3♥	3♦	A♣	6♥	10♥	Q♥	7♥	10♠/7♠	K♣	5♠
	2♣	8♠	9♦	3♠	J♣	7♣					
34	9♠	K♦	A♠	7♥	3♠	4♥	10♥	5♠	Q♠/9♥	8♠	10♥
	9♣	10♣	K♥	6♠	5♦	J♦					
35	J♣	5♥	3♦	K♦	7♣	A♥	4♥	J♦	3♣/5♣	6♣	J♣
	10♠	A♦	4♦	9♥	2♥	4♥					
36	3♥	10♠	K♦	4♣	7♥	3♣	10♦	9♥	A♦/8♠	2♦	J♦
	5♠	2♣	8♣	2♥	3♦	10♦					
37	7♦	2♦	4♦	8♠	4♠	5♠	4♣	K♦	9♦/8♥	A♦	3♠
	K♣	3♠	J♥	10♦	6♣	6♥					
38	Q♣	10♠	8♠	A♠	6♠	9♠	5♠	2♠	6♦/5♠	A♥	6♦
	3♣	Q♦	2♠	10♦	6♣	5♠					
39	7♠	A♣	K♦	6♥	10♥	J♣	9♠	6♠	3♥/8♣	3♥	9♠
	J♦	K♠	K♥	3♣	7♦	2♣					
40	10♦	A♥	K♠	8♠	A♣	6♣	7♠	9♥	J♣/4♦	Q♣	Q♥
	10♠	4♣	2♠	8♣	2♥	3♣					
41	10♥	5♥	K♣	3♣	9♥	3♠	J♥	6♥	4♠/7♥	10♦	10♠
	3♥	5♦	9♦	10♠	A♦	5♠					
42	J♣	K♥	3♠	2♠	2♣	4♠	8♥	A♣	Q♣/K♠	Q♠	4♥
	3♥	4♣	10♠	7♥	K♦	2♦					
43	J♦	3♥	2♠	2♦	6♣	6♥	5♠	10♣	9♦/9♠	8♦	4♠
	5♦	9♥	2♥	10♥	3♠	5♠					
44	Q♠	K♠	A♥	A♣	3♥	4♥	5♥	J♣	6♥/7♦	7♣	10♦
	6♠	Q♦	5♦	J♣	4♠	10♥	3♥				
45	8♣	6♦	4♠	10♥	10♦	8♠	A♥	5♦	A♦/Q♦	J♠	J♠
	9♠	3♦	6♠	K♣	7♣	A♥					
46	3♣	8♦	10♥	5♦	8♥	K♥	8♠	7♠	J♣/10♠	10♣	7♣
	3♥	10♣	6♠	Q♦	2♠	8♠					
47	K♠	10♦	2♥	Q♠	9♣	6♥	9♦	K♣	K♥/2♣	4♠	8♦
	A♠	7♥	J♣	8♦	3♦	J♥	9♣				
48	4♦	K♦	A♠	6♠	2♦	5♠	9♣	2♠	4♣/6♣	4♥	Q♠
	3♣	J♠	2♠	K♥	Q♠	9♣					
49	A♥	Q♠	10♦	K♦	3♦	7♥	5♠	7♣	7♦/4♥	10♠	10♦
	9♦	J♥	3♠	4♠	K♥	2♣					

AGE	MER	VEN	MAR	JUP	SAT	URA	NEP	LR	PLU/RES	ENV	DISP
50	J♦	9♦	K♦	2♠	6♠	7♦	6♥	7♥	J♥/10♥	Q♥	Q♣
	9♣	A♣	8♥	A♠	4♣	3♣					
51	2♥	10♣	J♣	5♦	7♠	K♣	2♠	5♦	9♥/3♦	9♣	3♥
	J♦	4♥	8♥	4♦	6♠	2♠					
52	7♣	7♥	5♦	K♥	5♣	9♥	9♣	K♥	2♣/10♠	6♦	A♥
	6♦	A♦	8♥	A♥	Q♣	9♣					
53	A♠	3♣	9♠	4♣	7♦	6♦	K♥	5♣	Q♥/3♦	3♠	A♦
	8♣	A♣	6♠	4♦	6♥	K♥					
54	J♦	8♣	4♠	10♥	9♦	Q♥	8♦	7♦	4♠/10♣	J♦	2♦
	5♣	7♠	K♠	7♠	A♦	9♥					
55	10♦	5♣	10♥	3♠	K♠	10♠	2♥	9♣	Q♥/5♥	J♣	6♣
	A♥	7♦	7♣	10♣	4♣	8♥	K♠				
56	10♠	4♥	9♠	8♥	K♣	Q♦	9♥	A♠	J♣/2♠	10♥	8♠
	4♠	6♥	7♥	K♠	10♣	3♥					
57	5♦	5♣	8♥	7♣	A♦	4♠	8♦	3♣	6♥/4♦	5♠	K♣
	10♥	Q♥	5♠	Q♠	9♠	8♦					
58	A♥	4♥	7♣	3♦	5♥	10♥	K♠	9♠	6♦/A♣	4♦	2♠
	K♣	6♣	7♠	9♠	8♥	3♠	5♥				
59	Q♦	5♣	5♠	K♠	3♠	2♥	J♦	4♣	3♦/K♥	5♥	6♠
	4♠	4♦	6♦	5♦	7♣	2♠					
60	2♥	7♣	A♥	2♠	6♠	9♣	5♣	9♥	8♠/3♣	5♠	9♠
	K♣	10♣	4♥	5♥	3♠	5♣					
61	3♥	K♣	2♠	6♦	4♣	8♠	K♦	6♦	3♦/A♠	4♣	K♥
	Q♠	J♣	Q♦	4♦	6♠	K♦					
62	Q♥	7♥	9♦	9♠	10♠	Q♠	6♦	K♥	4♥/3♣	6♥	2♣
	9♥	9♣	3♠	K♦	2♠	K♠					
63	7♣	9♥	9♠	J♥	7♠	4♥	A♣	J♦	4♠/10♦	3♦	A♠
	K♦	A♠	3♥	J♣	8♣	A♣					
64	7♦	6♠	J♥	8♥	10♠	2♥	4♥	8♣	Q♠/2♦	Q♦	7♥
	4♦	3♣	4♠	A♥	7♥	4♥					
65	J♣	9♣	8♥	5♦	3♦	K♠	5♥	4♣	2♥/5♠	9♦	8♥
	7♣	2♣	4♠	2♦	J♥	7♠	3♦				
66	10♠	J♦	9♠	7♠	8♠	3♠	10♣	10♥	10♥/6♦	5♦	7♠
	K♥	6♥	A♦	J♥	8♥	Q♦					
67	3♥	A♥	4♦	3♣	8♣	K♥	7♠	9♦	K♣/3♦	3♠	K♦
	9♥	2♥	6♠	2♠	2♦	7♠					
68	6♠	9♥	3♣	7♠	9♠	K♣	8♦	Q♥	4♠/9♣	K♦	3♣
	8♠	Q♣	6♠	3♦	7♠	J♣					
69	5♦	8♠	7♣	4♦	6♦	5♠	K♣	8♦	A♠/A♦	7♠	5♦
	4♦	8♠	A♣	9♣	K♥	K♣					
70	10♠	3♠	4♦	8♠	2♣	A♥	5♠	10♦	Q♥/5♣	8♥	9♦
	4♠	2♦	Q♠	A♦	9♦	7♥					
71	Q♣	4♥	8♠	7♦	8♥	4♠	K♦	5♣	2♦/10♣	7♥	Q♦
	K♣	J♣	6♦	9♦	K♥	K♦					
72	J♦	3♠	7♦	3♥	J♥	K♣	5♠	10♥	2♥/10♥	A♠	3♦
	4♦	5♣	7♥	9♦	A♠	5♠					
73	7♣	Q♦	2♣	8♣	6♠	9♠	3♥	3♠	7♠/6♥	2♣	6♥
	Q♣	K♦	K♥	5♠	4♦	Q♥					
74	9♦	K♥	8♣	2♦	6♠	Q♣	8♥	K♠	3♦/3♣	K♥	4♣
	J♥	K♣	A♠	J♦	3♠	A♦					

AGE	MER	VEN	MAR	JUP	SAT	URA	NEP	LR	PLU/RES	ENV	DISP
75	4♥	5♠	10♥	9♥	Q♠	J♥	2♦	10♠	5♣/A♣	9♠	5♣
	K♠	9♦	4♦	7♦	Q♦	5♦					
76	3♠	3♥	9♥	9♠	6♦	2♣	10♦	A♣	9♣/J♣	6♠	5♥
	K♣	J♦	7♦	A♣	7♠	10♦					
77	Q♦	5♠	3♣	3♦	A♦	K♣	9♠	10♠	K♠/7♥	2♠	4♦
	Q♠	10♣	8♠	J♣	9♥	2♥					
78	J♥	3♥	3♦	2♥	6♥	10♥	Q♥	4♦	10♠/7♠	K♣	5♠
	2♣	8♠	9♦	3♠	J♣	7♣					
79	9♠	K♦	A♠	7♥	3♠	4♥	10♥	9♠	Q♠/7♦	8♠	10♥
	9♣	10♣	K♥	6♠	5♦	J♦					
80	J♣	5♥	3♦	K♦	7♠	A♥	4♥	8♥	3♣/5♣	6♣	J♠
	10♠	A♦	4♦	7♦	A♠	4♥					
81	3♥	10♠	K♦	4♣	7♥	3♣	10♦	K♠	A♦/8♠	2♦	J♦
	5♠	2♠	8♣	A♣	3♦	10♦					
82	9♥	2♦	4♦	8♠	4♠	5♠	4♣	Q♦	9♦/8♥	A♦	3♠
	K♣	3♠	J♥	10♦	6♣	6♥					
83	Q♣	10♠	8♠	A♠	6♠	9♠	5♠	7♦	6♦/5♣	A♥	6♦
	3♣	Q♦	10♦	6♣	5♠						
84	7♠	2♥	K♦	6♥	10♥	J♣	9♠	5♦	3♥/8♦	3♥	9♣
	J♦	K♠	K♥	3♣	9♥	2♣					
85	10♦	A♥	K♠	8♠	2♥	6♣	7♣	5♣	J♣/4♦	Q♠	Q♥
	10♠	4♦	2♠	8♣	A♣	3♣					
86	10♥	5♥	K♦	3♣	7♦	3♠	J♥	8♥	4♠/7♥	10♦	10♠
	3♥	5♦	9♠	10♠	A♦	5♠					
87	J♣	K♥	3♣	2♠	2♠	4♠	8♦	7♣	Q♣/K♠	Q♠	4♥
	3♥	4♣	10♠	7♥	K♦	2♦					
88	J♦	3♥	2♠	2♦	6♠	6♥	5♠	A♥	9♦/9♣	8♦	4♠
	5♦	7♦	A♣	10♥	3♠	5♠					
89	Q♠	K♠	A♥	2♥	3♥	4♥	5♥	4♠	6♥/7♥	7♣	10♣
	6♠	Q♦	5♦	J♣	4♣	10♥	3♥				
90	8♣	6♦	4♠	10♥	10♦	8♠	A♥	8♦	A♦/Q♦	J♠	J♠
	9♠	3♦	6♠	K♣	7♠	A♥					
91	3♣	8♠	10♥	5♦	8♥	K♥	8♠	A♥	J♣/10♠	10♣	7♣
	3♥	10♣	6♠	Q♦	2♠	8♠					
92	K♠	10♦	A♣	Q♠	9♣	6♥	9♦	4♥	K♥/2♣	4♠	8♦
	A♠	7♥	J♣	8♦	3♦	J♥	9♣				
93	4♦	K♦	A♣	6♠	2♦	5♠	9♣	7♣	4♦/6♣	4♥	Q♠
	3♣	J♣	2♠	K♥	Q♠	9♣					
94	A♥	Q♠	10♦	K♦	3♦	7♥	5♠	3♦	9♥/4♥	10♠	10♦
	9♥	J♥	3♠	4♠	K♥	2♠					
95	J♦	9♦	K♦	2♠	6♠	9♥	6♥	5♥	J♥/10♥	Q♥	Q♣
	9♣	A♣	8♥	A♠	4♣	3♣					
96	A♣	10♣	J♠	5♦	7♠	K♣	2♠	10♥	7♦/3♦	9♣	3♥
	J♦	4♥	8♥	4♦	6♠	2♠					
97	7♣	7♥	5♦	K♥	5♣	7♥	9♣	K♠	2♣/10♠	6♦	A♥
	6♦	A♦	8♥	A♥	Q♣	9♣					
98	A♠	3♣	9♠	4♣	9♥	6♦	K♥	Q♦	Q♥/3♦	3♠	A♦
	8♣	2♥	6♣	4♦	6♥	K♥					
99	J♦	8♣	4♠	10♥	9♦	Q♥	8♦	5♠	4♠/10♣	J♦	2♦
	5♣	7♠	K♠	7♣	A♦	7♦					

Queen of Spades

AGE	MER	VEN	MAR	JUP	SAT	URA	NEP	LR	PLU/RES	ENV	DISP
0	J♣	9♦	7♠	2♣	K♣	J♦	4♥	J♣	4♦/2♠	Q♠	Q♠
	Q♦	6♦	K♥	7♥	3♥	4♥					
1	6♣	3♥	A♥	9♦	5♣	K♣	J♦	9♦	7♦/J♠	8♦	10♦
	6♥	J♥	Q♥	7♣	7♥	8♥					
2	9♣	6♥	9♦	K♥	2♣	7♦	5♥	7♠	J♥/3♠	7♣	Q♣
	4♥	8♠	3♣	7♠	4♦	Q♦					
3	2♥	8♦	6♦	3♦	5♦	9♠	K♥	2♣	9♥/5♠	J♠	3♥
	9♣	J♠	3♠	J♣	2♠	K♥					
4	10♦	K♦	3♦	7♥	5♠	9♥	4♥	K♣	8♥/10♣	10♣	A♥
	10♠	8♠	3♠	6♣	A♦	4♥					
5	7♠	Q♦	A♠	4♦	7♦	10♠	7♥	J♦	4♠/5♣	4♠	A♥
	8♣	A♣	2♠	J♣	5♥	7♦					
6	9♣	8♠	4♦	3♠	6♥	4♠	Q♣	4♥	7♣/8♦	4♥	2♦
	5♠	5♦	K♣	10♦	8♠	9♥					
7	A♥	5♠	3♠	Q♥	K♠	10♣	2♥	6♠	4♠/10♥	10♠	6♣
	6♠	7♥	10♦	8♦	4♦	3♣	K♠				
8	10♣	J♠	A♠	3♦	9♠	4♠	9♥	3♥	6♦/K♥	Q♥	8♠
	7♣	5♥	K♦	K♠	8♦	2♦					
9	3♠	5♥	3♣	10♦	8♠	7♦	Q♣	A♥	5♥/J♣	9♠	K♣
	3♠	4♠	J♦	3♥	A♠	Q♣					
10	6♣	J♠	10♦	5♣	10♥	3♠	K♠	9♦	10♠/A♣	6♦	2♠
	9♠	2♣	5♦	A♠	3♣	Q♥	10♥				
11	4♣	5♠	J♦	K♠	Q♥	2♥	9♣	5♠	5♣/7♥	3♠	6♠
	7♠	J♣	10♠	10♥	10♦	K♥					
12	2♥	10♦	6♠	K♥	2♣	4♥	5♠	K♦	8♣/Q♦	J♦	9♠
	9♠	8♦	J♠	10♥	Q♥	5♠					
13	2♦	9♠	K♥	10♠	4♦	8♣	9♦	J♦	5♣/7♠	J♣	K♥
	3♥	6♦	4♣	J♣	2♠	9♦					
14	4♠	K♦	6♥	A♠	10♣	3♥	10♠	9♠	J♠/Q♠	10♥	2♣
	9♥	4♥	Q♥	9♦	K♥	K♠					
15	10♦	9♥	A♠	J♥	5♦	J♠	A♣	6♥	7♣/A♥	5♠	A♠
	9♦	7♠	2♦	6♦	8♣	A♣					
16	7♦	2♣	J♥	3♠	10♣	2♥	J♠	9♦	3♥/K♣	4♦	7♥
	J♣	Q♦	4♦	6♣	K♦	J♠					
17	6♦	4♥	3♣	3♦	5♣	K♠	10♥	K♦	2♥/5♣	5♥	8♥
	10♦	8♥	4♦	K♣	J♥	5♦	5♣				
18	10♣	9♣	A♠	5♦	6♠	Q♥	8♦	2♠	3♠/10♠	5♣	7♠
	7♥	5♥	8♠	J♥	3♠	4♣					
19	2♦	6♠	J♣	Q♥	8♣	7♥	5♦	7♦	9♠/5♣	4♣	K♦
	9♥	2♥	2♠	K♥	K♣	5♦					
20	2♣	9♥	Q♦	10♦	6♥	9♠	Q♣	5♥	7♣/4♥	6♥	3♣
	6♠	A♦	2♠	5♠	5♦	6♦					
21	3♦	6♠	10♦	J♠	10♠	J♦	9♠	2♥	7♠/8♠	3♦	5♦
	4♦	8♣	A♣	4♥	7♥	9♠					
22	10♣	Q♥	J♣	6♠	8♥	6♠	J♦	8♦	4♠/5♠	Q♦	9♦
	7♣	K♠	3♥	8♠	6♥	K♦					
23	A♦	J♠	6♠	7♦	3♣	7♠	9♦	6♦	K♣/8♦	9♦	Q♦
	9♠	6♦	10♠	6♥	7♥	9♦					
24	9♣	Q♥	7♦	2♦	J♥	9♠	J♦	3♦	2♥/3♠	5♦	3♦
	J♣	5♠	K♦	6♥	7♠	J♦					
25	10♦	4♣	8♥	8♣	2♠	A♠	2♦	5♦	5♦/5♥	3♣	6♥
	A♦	9♥	7♥	5♠	J♠	4♠					
26	6♥	7♥	8♠	K♣	2♠	A♦	3♣	9♠	5♣/Q♦	K♦	4♣
	J♥	9♠	7♠	9♣	Q♥	8♠					
27	J♠	J♦	3♠	9♥	3♥	J♥	K♣	K♥	5♠/A♣	7♠	5♣
	K♠	6♥	J♣	7♠	4♠	3♠					
28	Q♥	2♠	9♥	A♠	10♠	8♥	A♥	10♦	4♥/6♦	8♥	5♥
	9♠	9♣	7♦	A♣	10♦	A♥					
29	4♣	J♥	Q♠	5♣	8♠	9♠	A♠	K♦	K♠/K♦	7♥	4♦
	3♥	8♦	6♠	6♦	9♥	2♥					
30	J♥	2♠	5♣	2♥	5♥	3♠	4♠	3♦	10♣/5♦	A♠	5♠
	8♥	6♠	6♥	Q♥	6♦	10♦					
31	A♠	9♥	7♠	K♦	Q♥	J♠	3♠	7♥	3♥/7♦	2♣	10♥
	4♥	8♦	7♥	2♠	3♦	9♣					
32	6♦	10♥	5♠	9♦	10♦	6♠	J♠	5♠	Q♦/5♠	K♥	J♣
	10♣	8♠	J♠	7♦	A♣	J♠					
33	2♠	10♣	9♠	4♦	K♦	Q♦	A♥	9♥	8♠/6♠	9♠	J♦
	J♦	8♥	8♠	A♣	5♣	A♥					
34	9♥	K♣	J♠	6♠	7♠	J♦	4♦	4♥	6♥/3♣	6♠	3♠
	9♠	Q♥	J♦	A♥	2♠	5♥					
35	A♦	10♣	6♠	7♠	2♣	A♠	J♦	7♠	10♠/5♠	2♠	6♦
	Q♦	4♣	K♥	A♥	2♠	J♦					
36	5♦	2♥	9♠	5♥	3♠	6♦	A♠	Q♦	2♦/8♣	K♠	9♣
	9♣	K♠	7♥	Q♦	9♥	8♥					
37	A♥	6♣	K♠	6♠	2♥	2♠	10♦	A♠	6♦/J♣	8♠	Q♥
	10♣	4♦	K♥	8♠	A♣	Q♦					
38	3♣	10♥	9♦	Q♦	7♦	Q♥	J♥	4♦	7♣/K♦	6♣	10♠
	2♦	3♦	6♥	10♣	8♠	J♦					
39	6♦	7♥	Q♦	K♥	8♥	7♣	Q♣	7♦	A♦/K♠	2♦	4♥
	2♦	4♦	10♣	K♦	9♦	K♣					
40	9♣	2♦	K♥	K♣	2♠	5♥	J♦	10♠	6♥/4♥	A♦	4♠
	3♦	7♦	A♣	3♠	Q♥	J♦					
41	3♥	K♠	6♠	2♥	2♦	J♠	10♥	7♥	5♥/K♦	A♥	10♣
	2♣	4♣	3♦	6♦	4♦	3♠	2♦				
42	8♣	10♠	7♠	3♠	A♥	6♠	6♣	9♠	8♠/4♠	3♥	J♠
	A♠	5♣	2♠	9♠	10♦	6♠					
43	Q♦	Q♣	3♣	3♦	3♣	7♥	6♠	8♣	6♦/10♣	Q♣	7♣
	2♦	8♦	2♠	4♠	K♥	6♠					
44	K♠	A♥	A♠	3♥	4♥	5♥	6♥	4♦	7♥/8♥	10♦	8♦
	7♠	K♦	6♦	Q♣	5♠	J♥	4♥				
45	J♣	9♦	7♠	2♣	K♣	J♦	4♥	3♠	4♦/2♠	Q♠	Q♠
	Q♦	6♦	K♥	7♥	3♥	4♥					
46	6♣	3♥	A♥	9♦	5♣	K♦	J♦	6♥	9♥/J♣	8♦	10♦
	6♥	J♥	Q♥	7♣	7♥	8♥					
47	9♣	6♥	9♦	K♥	2♣	9♥	5♥	4♠	J♥/3♠	7♣	Q♣
	4♥	8♠	3♣	7♠	4♦	Q♦					
48	A♣	8♦	6♦	3♦	5♦	9♠	K♥	Q♣	7♦/5♠	J♠	3♥
	9♣	J♠	3♣	J♣	2♠	K♥					
49	10♦	K♦	3♦	7♥	5♠	7♦	4♥	A♥	8♥/10♣	10♣	A♥
	10♠	8♠	3♠	6♣	A♦	4♥					

The Yearly Spreads

AGE	MER	VEN	MAR	JUP	SAT	URA	NEP	LR	PLU/RES	ENV	DISP
50	7♠	Q♦	A♠	4♦	9♥	10♠	7♥	5♠	4♠/5♣	4♠	A♦
	8♣	2♥	2♠	J♣	5♥	7♥					
51	9♣	8♣	4♦	3♠	6♥	4♠	Q♣	3♠	7♣/8♦	4♥	2♦
	5♠	5♦	K♠	10♦	8♠	7♦					
52	A♥	5♠	3♠	Q♥	K♠	10♣	A♣	Q♥	4♠/10♥	10♠	6♣
	6♦	9♥	10♦	8♦	4♦	3♣	K♠				
53	10♣	J♠	A♠	3♣	9♠	4♣	7♦	K♠	6♦/K♥	Q♥	8♠
	7♣	5♥	K♦	K♠	8♦	2♦					
54	3♦	5♠	3♠	10♠	8♠	7♠	Q♣	10♣	5♥/J♣	9♣	K♣
	3♠	4♠	J♦	3♥	A♠	Q♣					
55	6♣	J♠	10♦	5♣	10♥	3♠	K♠	2♥	10♠/2♥	6♦	2♠
	9♠	2♣	5♦	A♠	3♣	Q♥	10♥				
56	4♣	5♠	J♦	K♣	Q♥	A♣	9♣	10♣	5♣/7♥	3♠	6♠
	7♣	J♣	10♠	10♥	10♦	K♥					
57	A♣	10♦	6♣	K♥	2♣	4♥	5♠	J♠	8♣/Q♦	J♦	9♠
	9♠	8♦	J♠	10♥	Q♥	5♠					
58	2♦	9♠	K♥	10♠	4♦	8♣	9♦	A♠	5♣/7♠	J♣	K♥
	3♥	6♦	4♣	J♠	2♠	9♦					
59	4♠	K♥	6♥	A♠	10♣	3♥	10♠	3♣	J♠/Q♠	10♥	2♣
	7♥	4♥	Q♥	9♦	K♥	K♣					
60	10♦	7♦	A♠	J♥	5♦	J♠	2♥	9♠	7♣/A♥	5♠	A♠
	9♦	7♠	2♦	6♦	8♣	2♥					
61	9♥	2♣	J♥	3♣	10♣	A♣	J♠	4♣	3♥/K♣	4♦	7♠
	J♣	Q♦	4♦	6♣	K♦	J♠					
62	6♦	4♥	3♣	3♦	5♣	K♣	10♥	9♥	A♣/5♠	5♥	8♥
	10♦	8♥	4♦	K♣	J♥	5♦	5♣				
63	10♣	9♣	A♠	5♦	6♠	Q♥	8♦	3♦	3♠/10♠	5♣	7♠
	7♥	5♦	8♠	J♥	3♣	4♠					
64	2♦	6♣	J♣	Q♦	8♠	7♥	5♦	5♠	9♠/5♣	4♠	K♦
	7♦	A♣	2♠	K♥	K♣	5♦					
65	2♣	7♦	Q♦	10♦	6♥	9♠	Q♣	3♣	7♣/4♥	6♥	3♣
	6♠	A♦	2♠	5♣	5♦	6♦					
66	3♦	6♠	10♠	J♠	10♠	J♦	9♠	10♦	7♠/8♠	3♦	5♦
	4♦	8♣	2♥	4♥	7♥	9♠					
67	10♣	Q♥	J♣	6♠	8♥	6♣	J♦	8♠	4♣/5♠	Q♦	9♦
	7♣	K♣	3♥	8♠	6♥	K♦					
68	A♦	J♠	6♠	9♥	3♣	7♠	9♦	7♣	K♣/8♦	9♦	Q♦
	9♠	6♦	10♠	6♥	7♥	9♦					
69	9♣	Q♥	9♥	2♦	J♥	9♠	J♦	Q♣	A♣/3♠	5♦	3♦
	J♠	5♠	K♦	6♥	7♠	J♦					
70	10♦	4♣	8♥	8♣	2♠	A♠	2♦	6♣	5♦/5♥	3♣	6♥
	A♦	9♦	7♥	5♠	J♠	4♠					
71	6♥	7♥	8♣	K♣	2♠	A♦	3♣	J♠	5♠/Q♦	K♦	4♠
	J♥	9♠	7♠	9♠	Q♥	8♠					
72	J♠	J♦	3♠	7♦	3♥	J♥	K♣	10♦	5♠/2♥	7♠	5♠
	K♠	6♥	J♣	9♥	4♣	3♦					
73	Q♥	2♦	7♠	A♠	10♠	8♥	A♥	5♣	4♥/6♦	8♥	5♥
	9♠	9♣	9♥	2♥	10♦	A♥					
74	4♣	J♦	Q♦	5♣	8♠	9♠	A♠	10♥	K♠/K♦	7♥	4♦
	3♥	8♦	6♠	6♦	7♦	A♣					

AGE	MER	VEN	MAR	JUP	SAT	URA	NEP	LR	PLU/RES	ENV	DISP
75	J♥	2♦	5♣	A♣	5♥	3♠	4♠	3♠	10♣/5♦	A♠	5♠
	8♥	6♠	6♥	Q♥	6♦	10♦					
76	A♠	9♦	7♠	K♦	Q♥	J♠	3♠	K♠	3♥/9♥	2♣	10♥
	4♥	8♦	7♥	2♠	3♦	9♣					
77	6♦	10♥	5♣	9♦	10♦	6♣	J♠	4♣	Q♦/5♠	K♥	J♣
	10♣	8♠	J♣	9♥	2♥	J♠					
78	2♦	10♣	9♦	4♦	K♦	Q♦	A♥	5♠	8♠/6♠	9♠	J♦
	J♦	8♥	8♠	2♥	5♣	A♥					
79	7♦	K♣	J♠	6♠	7♣	J♦	4♦	J♦	6♥/3♣	6♠	3♠
	9♠	Q♥	J♥	A♥	2♠	5♥					
80	A♦	10♣	6♠	7♠	2♠	A♠	J♠	K♠	10♠/5♠	2♠	6♦
	Q♦	4♣	K♥	A♥	2♠	J♦					
81	5♦	A♠	9♦	5♥	3♠	6♠	A♠	Q♥	2♦/8♣	K♣	9♣
	9♣	K♠	7♥	Q♦	7♦	8♥					
82	A♥	6♠	K♠	6♠	A♣	2♠	10♦	2♥	6♣/J♣	8♠	Q♥
	10♣	4♦	K♥	8♣	2♥	Q♦					
83	3♠	10♥	9♦	Q♦	9♥	Q♥	J♥	9♣	7♣/K♦	6♣	10♠
	2♦	3♦	6♥	10♠	8♠	J♦					
84	6♦	7♥	Q♦	K♥	8♥	7♠	Q♣	2♥	A♦/K♠	2♦	4♥
	2♠	4♦	10♣	K♦	9♠	K♠					
85	9♣	2♦	K♥	K♣	3♠	5♥	J♦	10♦	6♥/4♥	A♦	4♠
	3♦	9♥	2♥	3♠	Q♥	J♦					
86	3♥	K♠	6♣	A♠	2♠	J♠	10♥	6♣	5♥/K♦	A♥	10♠
	2♣	4♣	3♦	6♠	4♦	3♠	2♦				
87	8♣	10♠	7♣	3♠	A♥	6♠	6♣	K♥	8♠/4♣	3♥	J♠
	A♠	5♣	2♠	9♠	10♦	6♣					
88	Q♦	Q♣	3♠	3♦	3♠	7♥	6♠	2♣	6♦/10♣	Q♣	7♠
	2♠	8♦	2♣	4♣	K♥	6♠					
89	K♠	A♥	2♥	3♥	4♦	5♥	6♥	4♥	7♥/8♥	10♦	8♦
	7♠	K♦	6♠	Q♣	5♣	J♥	4♥				
90	J♣	9♦	7♠	2♣	K♣	J♦	4♦	5♠	4♦/2♠	Q♠	Q♠
	Q♦	6♦	K♥	7♥	3♦	4♥					
91	6♣	3♥	A♥	9♣	5♣	K♦	J♦	2♥	7♦/J♠	8♦	10♦
	6♥	J♥	Q♥	7♣	7♥	8♥					
92	9♣	6♥	9♣	K♣	2♣	7♠	5♥	9♠	J♥/3♣	Q♣	Q♦
	4♥	8♠	3♣	8♣	4♦	Q♠					
93	2♦	8♦	6♦	3♦	5♦	9♠	K♥	K♥	9♥/5♣	J♠	3♥
	9♣	J♠	3♣	J♣	2♠	K♥					
94	10♦	K♦	3♦	7♥	5♠	9♥	4♥	10♠	8♥/10♣	10♣	A♥
	10♠	8♠	3♣	6♣	A♦	4♥					
95	7♠	Q♦	A♠	4♦	7♦	10♠	7♥	4♠	4♠/5♣	4♠	A♦
	8♣	A♣	2♠	J♣	5♥	7♥					
96	9♣	8♣	4♦	3♠	6♥	4♠	Q♣	8♣	7♣/8♦	4♥	2♦
	5♠	5♦	K♠	10♦	8♠	9♥					
97	A♥	5♠	3♠	Q♥	K♠	10♣	2♥	9♦	4♠/10♥	10♠	6♣
	6♣	7♦	10♦	8♦	4♦	3♣	K♠				
98	10♣	J♠	A♠	3♣	9♠	4♣	9♥	4♠	6♦/K♥	Q♥	8♠
	7♣	5♥	K♦	K♠	8♦	2♦					
99	3♦	5♠	3♠	10♠	8♠	7♠	Q♣	K♦	5♥/J♣	9♣	K♣
	3♠	4♠	J♦	3♥	A♠	Q♣					

King of Spades

AGE	MER	VEN	MAR	JUP	SAT	URA	NEP	LR	PLU/RES	ENV	DISP
0	3♥	A♣	Q♣	10♠	5♣	3♦	A♠	3♥	7♥/7♦		
	6♣	2♣	9♥	8♠	2♦	9♣	5♣				
1	Q♣	2♥	10♦	Q♥	4♣	Q♦	2♣	A♣	A♠/9♥		
	2♦	K♥	7♦	6♣	A♦	6♦	4♣				
2	10♦	A♣	Q♠	9♣	6♥	9♦	K♥	Q♣	2♣/7♦		
	A♠	9♠	9♥	2♦	A♥	3♠	6♥				
3	Q♠	2♥	8♦	6♦	3♦	5♦	9♠	10♠	K♥/9♥		
	A♥	6♠	7♦	A♦	3♥	J♦	3♦				
4	8♦	A♣	7♣	3♠	Q♦	3♣	6♠	5♣	9♠/7♦		
	3♥	2♠	9♥	A♥	Q♣	J♣	Q♦				
5	7♣	2♥	J♠	J♦	9♦	K♦	2♠	3♦	6♠/9♥		
	Q♣	K♣	7♠	3♥	10♦	10♥	9♦				
6	J♠	A♣	10♣	J♣	5♦	7♠	K♣	A♠	2♠/7♦		
	10♦	8♠	9♥	Q♣	Q♠	5♣	5♦				
7	10♣	2♥	4♠	10♥	3♣	8♥	8♠	Q♣	K♣/9♥		
	Q♠	6♠	7♥	10♦	8♦	4♦	3♣				
8	4♠	A♣	4♥	5♠	K♣	7♥	6♣	2♥	8♠/7♦		
	8♦	2♦	9♥	Q♠	7♣	5♥	K♦				
9	4♥	2♥	10♠	4♦	7♠	A♠	2♦	10♦	6♣/9♥		
	7♣	A♦	7♦	8♦	J♠	5♣	7♠				
10	10♠	A♣	Q♥	5♥	8♥	2♣	A♦	Q♥	2♦/7♦		
	J♠	A♥	9♥	7♣	10♣	4♣	8♥				
11	Q♥	2♥	9♣	5♣	7♥	K♥	A♥	4♣	A♦/9♥		
	10♣	3♥	7♦	J♠	4♠	6♥	7♥				
12	9♣	A♣	6♦	4♣	A♠	9♠	3♥	Q♦	A♥/7♦		
	4♠	Q♣	9♥	10♣	4♥	3♦	A♠				
13	6♦	2♥	3♠	6♥	2♣	6♠	Q♣	2♣	3♥/9♥		
	4♥	10♦	7♦	4♠	10♠	Q♦	2♣				
14	3♠	A♣	J♦	3♦	K♥	2♠	10♦	10♦	Q♣/7♦		
	10♠	Q♥	9♥	4♥	Q♥	9♦	K♥				
15	J♦	2♥	J♣	Q♦	9♠	K♣	Q♠	A♣	10♦/9♥		
	Q♥	8♦	7♦	10♠	4♠	5♦	9♠				
16	J♣	A♣	10♥	9♦	6♠	8♠	8♦	Q♠	Q♠/7♦		
	9♣	7♣	9♥	Q♥	6♦	3♣	6♠				
17	10♥	2♥	5♠	5♦	2♠	6♠	7♠	9♠	8♦/9♥		
	6♦	J♠	7♦	9♣	3♠	K♦	2♠				
18	5♠	A♣	4♦	3♣	K♣	2♦	J♠	6♥	7♣/7♦		
	3♠	10♣	9♥	6♦	J♦	7♠	K♣				
19	4♦	2♥	5♥	K♦	8♠	A♦	10♠	9♦	J♠/9♥		
	J♦	4♠	7♦	3♠	J♠	8♥	8♠				
20	5♥	A♣	5♣	7♠	6♣	A♥	4♠	K♥	10♣/7♦		
	J♣	4♥	9♥	J♦	10♥	7♦	6♣				
21	5♣	2♥	4♣	8♥	2♦	3♥	4♥	Q♠	4♣/9♥		
	10♥	10♠	7♦	J♣	5♠	A♠	2♦				
22	4♣	A♣	6♥	7♥	A♦	Q♣	10♠	2♥	4♥/7♦		
	5♠	Q♥	9♥	10♥	4♦	2♣	A♦				
23	6♥	2♥	3♦	A♠	A♥	10♦	Q♥	8♦	10♠/9♥		
	4♦	9♣	7♦	5♠	5♥	K♥	A♥				
24	3♦	A♣	Q♦	2♣	3♥	Q♠	9♣	6♦	Q♥/7♦		
	5♥	6♦	9♥	4♦	5♣	9♠	3♥				
25	Q♦	2♥	9♦	K♥	Q♣	8♦	6♦	3♦	9♣/9♥		
	5♣	3♠	7♥	5♥	4♣	6♠	Q♣				
26	9♦	A♣	5♦	9♠	10♦	7♣	3♠	5♦	6♦/7♦		
	4♣	J♦	9♥	5♣	6♥	2♠	10♦				
27	5♦	2♥	3♣	6♠	Q♠	J♠	J♦	9♠	3♠/9♥		
	6♥	J♣	7♦	4♣	3♦	K♣	Q♠				
28	3♣	A♣	K♦	2♠	8♦	10♣	J♣	8♦	J♦/7♦		
	3♦	10♥	9♥	6♥	Q♦	8♠	8♦				
29	K♦	2♥	7♠	K♣	7♣	4♠	10♥	A♣	J♣/9♥		
	Q♦	5♠	7♥	3♦	9♦	6♣	7♣				
30	7♣	A♣	8♦	8♠	J♠	4♥	5♠	7♣	10♥/7♦		
	9♦	4♦	9♥	Q♦	5♦	2♦	J♠				
31	8♦	2♥	7♥	6♠	10♣	10♠	4♦	3♠	5♠/9♥		
	5♦	5♥	7♥	9♦	3♣	A♦	10♣				
32	7♥	A♣	A♠	2♦	4♠	Q♥	5♥	Q♦	4♦/7♦		
	3♣	5♠	9♥	5♦	K♦	A♥	4♠				
33	A♠	2♥	2♠	A♦	4♥	9♣	5♠	3♠	5♥/9♥		
	K♦	4♠	7♦	3♣	7♠	3♥	4♥				
34	2♣	A♣	K♥	A♥	10♠	6♦	4♣	6♠	5♣/7♦		
	7♠	6♥	9♥	K♦	8♥	Q♣	10♠				
35	K♥	2♥	9♠	3♥	Q♥	3♠	6♥	7♣	4♣/9♥		
	8♥	3♦	7♦	7♠	7♥	10♦	Q♥				
36	9♠	A♣	6♣	Q♣	9♣	J♦	3♦	2♥	6♥/7♦		
	7♥	Q♦	9♥	8♥	A♠	Q♠	9♣				
37	6♠	2♥	2♠	10♦	6♦	J♣	Q♦	J♠	3♦/9♥		
	A♠	9♦	7♦	7♥	2♣	8♦	6♦				
38	2♠	A♣	K♣	Q♠	3♠	10♥	9♦	J♦	Q♦/7♦		
	2♣	5♦	9♥	A♠	K♥	7♣	3♠				
39	K♣	2♥	8♠	8♦	J♦	5♠	5♦	9♥	9♦/9♥		
	K♥	3♥	7♦	2♣	9♠	J♠	J♦				
40	8♠	A♣	6♣	7♣	J♣	4♦	3♠	K♦	5♦/7♦		
	9♠	K♦	9♥	K♥	6♠	10♦	J♣				
41	6♣	2♥	2♦	J♠	10♥	5♥	K♦	2♠	3♣/9♥		
	6♠	7♠	7♦	9♠	2♠	4♠	10♥				
42	2♦	A♣	A♦	10♣	5♠	5♠	7♠	J♠	K♦/7♦		
	2♠	8♥	9♥	6♠	K♣	4♥	5♠				
43	A♦	2♥	A♥	4♣	4♦	4♠	8♥	A♣	7♠/9♥		
	K♣	7♥	7♦	2♠	8♠	10♠	4♦				
44	A♥	A♣	3♥	4♥	5♦	6♦	7♦	10♣	8♥/7♦		
	8♠	A♠	9♥	K♦	6♠	Q♥	5♦				
45	3♥	2♥	Q♣	10♠	5♠	3♦	A♠	J♠	7♥/9♥		
	6♣	2♣	7♦	8♠	2♦	9♣	5♠				
46	Q♣	A♣	10♦	Q♥	4♣	Q♦	2♣	5♦	A♠/7♦		
	2♦	K♥	9♥	6♣	A♦	6♦	4♣				
47	10♦	2♥	Q♠	9♣	6♥	9♦	K♥	7♠	2♣/9♥		
	A♦	9♠	7♦	2♦	A♥	3♠	6♥				
48	Q♠	A♣	8♦	6♦	3♦	5♦	9♠	K♣	K♥/7♦		
	A♥	6♠	9♥	A♦	3♥	J♦	3♦				
49	8♦	2♥	7♣	3♠	Q♦	3♣	6♠	10♣	9♠/9♥		
	3♥	2♠	7♦	A♥	Q♣	J♣	Q♦				

AGE	MER	VEN	MAR	JUP	SAT	URA	NEP	LR	PLU/RES	ENV	DISP
50	7♣	A♠	J♠	J♦	9♦	K♦	2♠	2♥	6♠/7♦		
	Q♣	K♣	9♥	3♥	10♦	10♥	9♦				
51	J♠	2♥	10♣	J♣	5♦	7♠	K♣	4♠	2♠/9♥		
	10♦	8♠	7♦	Q♣	Q♠	5♠	5♦				
52	10♣	A♠	4♠	10♥	3♣	8♥	8♠	10♥	K♣/7♦		
	Q♠	6♣	9♥	10♦	8♦	4♦	3♣				
53	4♠	2♥	4♥	5♠	K♦	7♥	6♣	3♣	8♠/9♥		
	8♦	2♦	7♦	Q♠	7♣	5♥	K♦				
54	4♥	A♣	10♠	4♦	7♠	A♠	2♦	8♥	6♣/7♦		
	7♣	A♦	9♥	8♦	J♠	5♣	7♠				
55	10♠	2♥	Q♥	5♥	8♥	2♣	A♦	8♠	2♦/9♥		
	J♠	A♥	7♦	7♠	10♣	4♦	8♥				
56	Q♥	A♣	9♣	5♣	7♥	K♥	A♥	4♠	A♦/7♦		
	10♣	3♥	9♥	J♠	4♠	6♥	7♥				
57	9♣	2♥	6♦	4♠	A♠	9♠	3♥	A♣	A♥/9♥		
	4♠	Q♣	7♦	10♣	4♥	3♦	A♠				
58	6♦	A♣	3♠	6♥	2♣	6♠	Q♣	4♥	3♥/7♦		
	4♥	10♦	9♥	4♠	10♠	Q♦	2♣				
59	3♠	2♥	J♦	3♦	K♥	2♠	10♦	5♠	Q♣/9♥		
	10♠	Q♠	7♦	4♥	Q♥	9♦	K♥				
60	J♦	A♣	J♣	Q♦	9♠	K♣	Q♠	K♦	10♦/7♦		
	Q♥	8♦	9♥	10♠	9♣	5♦	9♠				
61	J♣	2♥	10♥	9♦	6♠	8♠	8♦	7♥	Q♠/9♥		
	9♣	7♣	7♦	Q♥	6♦	3♣	6♠				
62	10♥	A♣	5♠	5♦	2♠	6♣	7♣	6♣	8♦/7♦		
	6♦	J♠	9♥	9♣	3♠	K♦	2♠				
63	5♠	2♥	4♦	3♣	K♣	2♦	J♠	4♥	7♣/9♥		
	3♠	10♣	7♦	6♦	J♦	7♠	K♣				
64	4♦	A♣	5♥	K♦	8♠	A♦	10♣	2♥	J♠/7♦		
	J♦	4♠	9♥	3♠	J♣	8♥	8♠				
65	5♥	2♥	5♣	7♠	6♣	A♥	4♠	10♠	10♣/9♥		
	J♣	4♥	7♦	J♦	10♥	7♥	6♣				
66	5♣	A♣	4♣	8♥	2♦	3♥	4♥	4♦	4♠/7♦		
	10♥	10♠	9♥	J♣	5♠	A♠	2♦				
67	4♣	2♥	6♥	7♥	A♦	Q♣	10♠	7♠	4♥/9♥		
	5♠	Q♥	7♦	10♥	4♦	2♣	A♦				
68	6♥	A♣	3♦	A♠	A♥	10♦	Q♥	A♠	10♠/7♦		
	4♦	9♣	9♥	5♠	5♥	K♥	A♥				
69	3♦	2♥	Q♦	2♣	3♥	Q♠	9♣	2♦	Q♥/9♥		
	5♥	6♦	7♦	4♦	5♣	9♠	3♥				
70	Q♦	A♣	9♣	K♥	Q♣	8♦	6♦	10♠	9♣/7♦		
	5♣	3♣	9♥	5♥	4♣	6♠	Q♣				
71	9♦	2♥	5♦	9♠	10♦	7♣	3♠	A♣	6♦/9♥		
	4♣	J♦	7♦	5♣	6♥	2♠	10♦				
72	5♦	A♣	3♣	6♠	Q♠	J♠	J♦	Q♥	3♠/7♦		
	6♥	J♣	9♥	4♣	3♦	K♣	Q♠				
73	3♣	2♥	K♦	2♠	8♦	10♣	J♣	5♦	J♦/9♥		
	3♦	10♥	7♦	6♥	Q♦	8♠	8♦				
74	K♦	A♣	7♠	K♣	7♠	4♠	10♥	8♥	J♣/7♦		
	Q♦	5♠	9♥	3♦	9♦	6♣	7♣				

AGE	MER	VEN	MAR	JUP	SAT	URA	NEP	LR	PLU/RES	ENV	DISP
75	7♠	2♥	8♥	8♠	J♠	4♥	5♠	2♣	10♥/9♥		
	9♦	4♦	7♥	Q♦	5♦	2♦	J♠				
76	8♥	A♣	7♥	6♣	10♣	10♠	4♦	A♦	5♠/7♦		
	5♦	5♥	9♥	9♦	3♣	A♦	10♣				
77	7♥	2♥	A♠	2♦	4♠	Q♥	5♥	Q♥	4♦/9♥		
	3♣	5♠	7♦	5♦	K♦	A♥	4♠				
78	A♠	A♣	2♣	A♦	4♥	9♣	5♠	2♥	5♥/7♦		
	K♦	4♠	9♥	3♣	7♠	3♥	4♥				
79	2♣	2♥	K♥	A♥	10♠	6♦	4♣	9♣	5♣/9♥		
	7♠	6♥	7♦	K♦	8♥	Q♣	10♠				
80	K♥	A♣	9♠	3♥	Q♥	3♠	6♥	5♠	4♣/7♦		
	8♥	3♦	9♥	7♠	7♥	10♦	Q♥				
81	9♠	2♥	6♠	Q♣	9♣	J♦	3♦	7♥	6♥/9♥		
	7♥	Q♦	7♦	8♥	A♠	Q♠	9♣				
82	6♠	A♣	2♠	10♦	6♦	J♣	Q♦	K♥	3♦/7♦		
	A♠	9♦	9♥	7♥	2♣	8♦	6♦				
83	2♠	2♥	K♣	Q♠	3♠	10♥	9♦	A♥	Q♦/9♥		
	2♣	5♦	7♦	A♠	K♥	7♣	3♠				
84	K♣	A♣	8♠	8♦	J♦	5♠	5♦	9♠	9♦/7♦		
	K♥	3♣	9♥	2♣	9♠	J♠	J♦				
85	8♠	2♥	6♣	7♣	J♣	4♦	3♣	A♠	5♦/9♥		
	9♠	K♥	7♦	K♥	6♠	10♣	J♣				
86	6♣	A♣	2♣	J♠	10♥	5♥	K♦	6♦	3♣/7♦		
	6♠	7♠	9♥	9♠	2♠	4♦	10♥				
87	2♦	2♥	A♦	10♣	5♠	5♣	7♠	4♣	K♦/9♥		
	2♠	8♥	7♦	6♠	K♣	4♥	5♠				
88	A♦	A♣	A♥	4♠	4♦	4♣	8♥	A♠	7♠/7♦		
	K♣	7♥	9♥	2♠	8♠	10♠	4♦				
89	A♥	2♥	3♥	4♥	5♥	6♥	7♥	9♠	8♥/9♥		
	8♠	A♠	7♦	K♣	6♣	Q♥	5♥				
90	3♥	A♣	Q♣	10♠	5♣	3♦	A♠	3♥	7♥/7♦		
	6♣	2♠	9♥	8♠	2♦	9♠	5♠				
91	Q♣	2♥	10♦	Q♥	4♣	Q♦	2♣	6♦	A♠/9♥		
	2♦	K♥	7♦	6♣	A♠	6♦	4♣				
92	10♦	A♣	Q♠	9♣	6♥	9♠	K♦	2♥	2♣/7♦		
	A♦	9♠	9♥	2♦	A♥	3♠	6♥				
93	Q♠	2♥	8♥	6♠	3♦	5♠	9♠	3♠	K♥/9♥		
	A♥	6♠	7♦	A♦	3♥	J♦	3♦				
94	8♠	A♣	7♣	3♠	Q♦	3♠	6♠	6♥	9♠/7♦		
	3♥	2♠	9♥	A♦	Q♣	J♣	Q♦				
95	7♣	2♥	J♠	J♦	9♦	K♦	2♠	2♣	6♠/9♥		
	Q♣	K♣	7♦	3♥	10♦	10♥	9♦				
96	J♠	A♣	10♣	J♣	5♦	7♠	K♣	6♠	2♠/7♦		
	10♦	8♠	9♥	Q♣	Q♠	5♠	5♦				
97	10♣	2♥	4♠	10♥	3♣	8♥	8♠	Q♣	K♠/9♥		
	Q♠	A♣	7♦	10♦	8♦	4♦	3♣				
98	4♠	A♣	4♥	5♠	K♦	7♥	6♣	3♠	8♠/7♦		
	8♦	2♦	9♥	Q♠	7♣	5♥	K♦				
99	4♥	2♥	10♠	4♦	7♠	A♠	2♦	A♠	6♣/9♥		
	7♣	A♦	7♦	8♦	J♠	5♣	7♠				

Appendix

Reading Worksheet

Name: __Jamie Jones__   Birthday: __3/29/65__   Birth Card: __7♣__   Ruling Card: __J♣__

Age for Reading: __27__   Personality Cards Used: __Q♣__

Planetary Periods	Mercury	Venus	Mars	Jupiter	Saturn	Uranus	Neptune
Period Dates	3/29/92	5/20/92	7/11/92	9/1/92	10/23/92	12/19/92	2/5/93

Birth Card		Mercury	Venus	Mars	Jupiter	Saturn	Uranus	Neptune
	Direct	8♦ Dad	3♦	A♠	8♣	8♠	K♥ John	A♥
	Vertical	3♥	3♣	2♣	5♥	4♠	10♠	A♥
Long-Range: 10♥ Pluto: K♦ Dad Result: 4♣ Environment: 7♥ Displacement: 6♥								

Planet Ruling Card		Mercury	Venus	Mars	Jupiter	Saturn	Uranus	Neptune
	Direct	5♣	2♦	9♠	Q♣	5♥	6♦	6♥
	Vertical	7♦	4♣	3♦	K♣ John	Q♠	K♠	6♥
Long-Range: 3♣ Pluto: 4♦ Result: 2♠ Environment: A♦ Displacement: 2♣								

Personality Card 1		Mercury	Venus	Mars	Jupiter	Saturn	Uranus	Neptune
	Direct	5♥	6♦	6♥	4♦	2♠	2♣ John	8♥
	Vertical	A♦	10♦	K♥	Q♥ Mom	9♥ EX	2♥	
Long-Range: 7♠ Boss Pluto: K♦ Boss Result: 5♦ Environment: 3♣ Displacement: 4♦								

Personality Card 2		Mercury	Venus	Mars	Jupiter	Saturn	Uranus	Neptune
	Direct							
	Vertical							
Long-Range: Pluto: Result: Environment: Displacement:								

NOTES

John 6/28 2♣, J♣, K♣   Boyfriend A♠, K♥ Karma Cards

Harry 9/1 7♣, J♣, K♣ - Boss

Ann 12/22 8♥, Q♥ - Mother

William 3/15 8♦, J♦, K♦ Father

Steve 9/28 9♥, J♥, K♥ Ex husband

Reading Worksheet

Name: _____   Birthday: _____   Birth Card: ____   Ruling Card: ____

Age for Reading: ____   Personality Cards Used: ____   ____

Planetary Periods	Mercury	Venus	Mars	Jupiter	Saturn	Uranus	Neptune
Period Dates							

Birth Card		Mercury	Venus	Mars	Jupiter	Saturn	Uranus	Neptune
	Direct							
	Vertical							

Long-Range: Pluto: Result: Environment: Displacement:

Planet Ruling Card		Mercury	Venus	Mars	Jupiter	Saturn	Uranus	Neptune
	Direct							
	Vertical							

Long-Range: Pluto: Result: Environment: Displacement:

Personality Card 1		Mercury	Venus	Mars	Jupiter	Saturn	Uranus	Neptune
	Direct							
	Vertical							

Long-Range: Pluto: Result: Environment: Displacement:

Personality Card 2		Mercury	Venus	Mars	Jupiter	Saturn	Uranus	Neptune
	Direct							
	Vertical							

Long-Range: Pluto: Result: Environment: Displacement:

NOTES

Reading Worksheet

Name: _____   Birthday: _____   Birth Card:_____   Ruling Card: _____

Age for Reading: _____   Personality Cards Used: _____   _____

Planetary Periods Period Dates	Mercury	Venus	Mars	Jupiter	Saturn	Uranus	Neptune

Birth Card		Mercury	Venus	Mars	Jupiter	Saturn	Uranus	Neptune
	Direct							
	Vertical							
Long-Range:		Pluto:		Result:		Environment:		Displacement:

Planet Ruling Card		Mercury	Venus	Mars	Jupiter	Saturn	Uranus	Neptune
	Direct							
	Vertical							
Long-Range:		Pluto:		Result:		Environment:		Displacement:

Personality Card 1		Mercury	Venus	Mars	Jupiter	Saturn	Uranus	Neptune
	Direct							
	Vertical							
Long-Range:		Pluto:		Result:		Environment:		Displacement:

Personality Card 2		Mercury	Venus	Mars	Jupiter	Saturn	Uranus	Neptune
	Direct							
	Vertical							
Long-Range:		Pluto:		Result:		Environment:		Displacement:

NOTES

The Powers Given to You by the Royal Court Cards

We now enter the domain of the castle where the royal family lives. Whenever you get one of these cards in your spreads, it is invariably describing someone you are in contact with. However, at the same time, each card has a personality trait or two, as well as its own mastery of a certain energy or quality. Any royal card in your spread will bring you some power or success in the area in which it sits. Though some of the cards have negative traits as well, it is not difficult to focus on the positive side of the influences present and get the most out of them. Look at each of the royal court cards as giving you a blessing and a sense of mastery. Dwell on this blessing and you will increase its power in your life for a period.

The Jacks have mastery over their suit and add their creative powers to that element.

The Jack of Hearts has mastery over the emotions and can sway people to his side.

The Jack of Clubs is a mental giant, full of creative ideas and versatility of thought.

The Jack of Diamonds is a master of business and entrepreneurship and generates creative ideas for making money.

The Jack of Spades has artistic ability and creativity that can be applied to almost any area.

The Queens also have mastery over their suit, but each prefers service and to serve from behind the scenes.

The Queen of Hearts is the loving mother card and knows how to love her family and children.

The Queen of Clubs feeds her children and the world knowledge. She is a mental intuitive genius.

The Queen of Diamonds is a business genius and is a philanthropist at heart. She can make lots of money.

The Queen of Spades has mastery over all things from an inner mastery of herself. She is the sun card in God's spread (The Natural Spread).

The Kings are born leaders and exhibit their mastery in positions of power, authority, and leadership.

The King of Hearts has mastered his or her emotions and knows the art of dealing with people effectively.

The King of Clubs is the mental ruler, can accomplish anything with his mind, and is also highly intuitive.

The King of Diamonds is the successful business owner and the master of money and finance.

The King of Spades is the master of anything he applies himself to, from a position of the highest power. He is the most powerful card in the entire deck.

When you get one of the cards in your spread, consider that you have these powers for yourself for that period of time.

Friends and Associates

Name	Birthday	Birth Card	Planetary Ruling Card	Personality Cards

Planetary Period Dates
January

Birthday	Card	Mercury	Venus	Mars	Jupiter	Saturn	Uranus	Neptune
1/1	K♠	1/1	2/22	4/15	6/6	7/28	9/18	11/9
1/2	Q♠	1/2	2/23	4/16	6/7	7/29	9/19	11/10
1/3	J♠	1/3	2/24	4/17	6/8	7/30	9/20	11/11
1/4	10♠	1/4	2/25	4/18	6/9	7/31	9/21	11/12
1/5	9♠	1/5	2/26	4/19	6/10	8/1	9/22	11/13
1/6	8♠	1/6	2/27	4/20	6/11	8/2	9/23	11/14
1/7	7♠	1/7	2/28	4/21	6/12	8/3	9/24	11/15
1/8	6♠	1/8	3/1	4/22	6/13	8/4	9/25	11/16
1/9	5♠	1/9	3/2	4/23	6/14	8/5	9/26	11/17
1/10	4♠	1/10	3/3	4/24	6/15	8/6	9/27	11/18
1/11	3♠	1/11	3/4	4/25	6/16	8/7	9/28	11/19
1/12	2♠	1/12	3/5	4/26	6/17	8/8	9/29	11/20
1/13	A♠	1/13	3/6	4/27	6/18	8/9	9/30	11/21
1/14	K♦	1/14	3/7	4/28	6/19	8/10	10/1	11/22
1/15	Q♦	1/15	3/8	4/29	6/20	8/11	10/2	11/23
1/16	J♦	1/16	3/9	4/30	6/21	8/12	10/3	11/24
1/17	10♦	1/17	3/10	5/1	6/22	8/13	10/4	11/25
1/18	9♦	1/18	3/11	5/2	6/23	8/14	10/5	11/26
1/19	8♦	1/19	3/12	5/3	6/24	8/15	10/6	11/27
1/20	7♦	1/20	3/13	5/4	6/25	8/16	10/7	11/28
1/21	6♦	1/21	3/14	5/5	6/26	8/17	10/8	11/29
1/22	5♦	1/22	3/15	5/6	6/27	8/18	10/9	11/30
1/23	4♦	1/23	3/16	5/7	6/28	8/19	10/10	12/1
1/24	3♦	1/24	3/17	5/8	6/29	8/20	10/11	12/2
1/25	2♦	1/25	3/18	5/9	6/30	8/21	10/12	12/3
1/26	A♦	1/26	3/19	5/10	7/1	8/22	10/13	12/4
1/27	K♣	1/27	3/20	5/11	7/2	8/23	10/14	12/5
1/28	Q♣	1/28	3/21	5/12	7/3	8/24	10/15	12/6
1/29	J♣	1/29	3/22	5/13	7/4	8/25	10/16	12/7
1/30	10♣	1/30	3/23	5/14	7/5	8/26	10/17	12/8
1/31	9♣	1/31	3/24	5/15	7/6	8/27	10/18	12/9

Planetary Period Dates
February

Birthday	Card	Mercury	Venus	Mars	Jupiter	Saturn	Uranus	Neptune
2/1	J♠	2/1	3/25	5/16	7/7	8/28	10/19	12/10
2/2	10♠	2/2	3/26	5/17	7/8	8/29	10/20	12/11
2/3	9♠	2/3	3/27	5/18	7/9	8/30	10/21	12/12
2/4	8♠	2/4	3/28	5/19	7/10	8/31	10/22	12/13
2/5	7♠	2/5	3/29	5/20	7/11	9/1	10/23	12/14
2/6	6♠	2/6	3/30	5/21	7/12	9/2	10/24	12/15
2/7	5♠	2/7	3/31	5/22	7/13	9/3	10/25	12/16
2/8	4♠	2/8	4/1	5/23	7/14	9/4	10/26	12/17
2/9	3♠	2/9	4/2	5/24	7/15	9/5	10/27	12/18
2/10	2♠	2/10	4/3	5/25	7/16	9/6	10/28	12/19
2/11	A♠	2/11	4/4	5/26	7/17	9/7	10/29	12/20
2/12	K♦	2/12	4/5	5/27	7/18	9/8	10/30	12/21
2/13	Q♦	2/13	4/6	5/28	7/19	9/9	10/31	12/22
2/14	J♦	2/14	4/7	5/29	7/20	9/10	11/1	12/23
2/15	10♦	2/15	4/8	5/30	7/21	9/11	11/2	12/24
2/16	9♦	2/16	4/9	5/31	7/22	9/12	11/3	12/25
2/17	8♦	2/17	4/10	6/1	7/23	9/13	11/4	12/26
2/18	7♦	2/18	4/11	6/2	7/24	9/14	11/5	12/27
2/19	6♦	2/19	4/12	6/3	7/25	9/15	11/6	12/28
2/20	5♦	2/20	4/13	6/4	7/26	9/16	11/7	12/29
2/21	4♦	2/21	4/14	6/5	7/27	9/17	11/8	12/30
2/22	3♦	2/22	4/15	6/6	7/28	9/18	11/9	1/1
2/23	2♦	2/23	4/16	6/7	7/29	9/19	11/10	1/2
2/24	A♦	2/24	4/17	6/8	7/30	9/20	11/11	1/3
2/25	K♣	2/25	4/18	6/9	7/31	9/21	11/12	1/4
2/26	Q♣	2/26	4/19	6/10	8/1	9/22	11/13	1/5
2/27	J♣	2/27	4/20	6/11	8/2	9/23	11/14	1/6
2/28	10♣	2/28	4/21	6/12	8/3	9/24	11/15	1/7
2/29	9♣	2/29	4/21	6/12	8/3	9/24	11/15	1/7

Planetary Period Dates
March

BIRTHDAY	CARD	MERCURY	VENUS	MARS	JUPITER	SATURN	URANUS	NEPTUNE
3/1	9♠	3/1	4/22	6/13	8/4	9/25	11/16	1/8
3/2	8♠	3/2	4/23	6/14	8/5	9/26	11/17	1/9
3/3	7♠	3/3	4/24	6/15	8/6	9/27	11/18	1/10
3/4	6♠	3/4	4/25	6/16	8/7	9/28	11/19	1/11
3/5	5♠	3/5	4/26	6/17	8/8	9/29	11/20	1/12
3/6	4♠	3/6	4/27	6/18	8/9	9/30	11/21	1/13
3/7	3♠	3/7	4/28	6/19	8/10	10/1	11/22	1/14
3/8	2♠	3/8	4/29	6/20	8/11	10/2	11/23	1/15
3/9	A♠	3/9	4/30	6/21	8/12	10/3	11/24	1/16
3/10	K♦	3/10	5/1	6/22	8/13	10/4	11/25	1/17
3/11	Q♦	3/11	5/2	6/23	8/14	10/5	11/26	1/18
3/12	J♦	3/12	5/3	6/24	8/15	10/6	11/27	1/19
3/13	10♦	3/13	5/4	6/25	8/16	10/7	11/28	1/20
3/14	9♦	3/14	5/5	6/26	8/17	10/8	11/29	1/21
3/15	8♦	3/15	5/6	6/27	8/18	10/9	11/30	1/22
3/16	7♦	3/16	5/7	6/28	8/19	10/10	12/1	1/23
3/17	6♦	3/17	5/8	6/29	8/20	10/11	12/2	1/24
3/18	5♦	3/18	5/9	6/30	8/21	10/12	12/3	1/25
3/19	4♦	3/19	5/10	7/1	8/22	10/13	12/4	1/26
3/20	3♦	3/20	5/11	7/2	8/23	10/14	12/5	1/27
3/21	2♦	3/21	5/12	7/3	8/24	10/15	12/6	1/28
3/22	A♦	3/22	5/13	7/4	8/25	10/16	12/7	1/29
3/23	K♣	3/23	5/14	7/5	8/26	10/17	12/8	1/30
3/24	Q♣	3/24	5/15	7/6	8/27	10/18	12/9	1/31
3/25	J♣	3/25	5/16	7/7	8/28	10/19	12/10	2/1
3/26	10♣	3/26	5/17	7/8	8/29	10/20	12/11	2/2
3/27	9♣	3/27	5/18	7/9	8/30	10/21	12/12	2/3
3/28	8♣	3/28	5/19	7/10	8/31	10/22	12/13	2/4
3/29	7♣	3/29	5/20	7/11	9/1	10/23	12/14	2/5
3/30	6♣	3/30	5/21	7/12	9/2	10/24	12/15	2/6
3/31	5♣	3/31	5/22	7/13	9/3	10/25	12/16	2/7

Planetary Period Dates
April

Birthday	Card	Mercury	Venus	Mars	Jupiter	Saturn	Uranus	Neptune
4/1	7♠	4/1	5/23	7/14	9/4	10/26	12/17	2/8
4/2	6♠	4/2	5/24	7/15	9/5	10/27	12/18	2/9
4/3	5♠	4/3	5/25	7/16	9/6	10/28	12/19	2/10
4/4	4♠	4/4	5/26	7/17	9/7	10/29	12/20	2/11
4/5	3♠	4/5	5/27	7/18	9/8	10/30	12/21	2/12
4/6	2♠	4/6	5/28	7/19	9/9	10/31	12/22	2/13
4/7	A♠	4/7	5/29	7/20	9/10	11/1	12/23	2/14
4/8	K♦	4/8	5/30	7/21	9/11	11/2	12/24	2/15
4/9	Q♦	4/9	5/31	7/22	9/12	11/3	12/25	2/16
4/10	J♦	4/10	6/1	7/23	9/13	11/4	12/26	2/17
4/11	10♦	4/11	6/2	7/24	9/14	11/5	12/27	2/18
4/12	9♦	4/12	6/3	7/25	9/15	11/6	12/28	2/19
4/13	8♦	4/13	6/4	7/26	9/16	11/7	12/29	2/20
4/14	7♦	4/14	6/5	7/27	9/17	11/8	12/30	2/21
4/15	6♦	4/15	6/6	7/28	9/18	11/9	1/1	2/22
4/16	5♦	4/16	6/7	7/29	9/19	11/10	1/2	2/23
4/17	4♦	4/17	6/8	7/30	9/20	11/11	1/3	2/24
4/18	3♦	4/18	6/9	7/31	9/21	11/12	1/4	2/25
4/19	2♦	4/19	6/10	8/1	9/22	11/13	1/5	2/26
4/20	A♦	4/20	6/11	8/2	9/23	11/14	1/6	2/27
4/21	K♣	4/21	6/12	8/3	9/24	11/15	1/7	2/28
4/22	Q♣	4/22	6/13	8/4	9/25	11/16	1/8	3/1
4/23	J♣	4/23	6/14	8/5	9/26	11/17	1/9	3/2
4/24	10♣	4/24	6/15	8/6	9/27	11/18	1/10	3/3
4/25	9♣	4/25	6/16	8/7	9/28	11/19	1/11	3/4
4/26	8♣	4/26	6/17	8/8	9/29	11/20	1/12	3/5
4/27	7♣	4/27	6/18	8/9	9/30	11/21	1/13	3/6
4/28	6♣	4/28	6/19	8/10	10/1	11/22	1/14	3/7
4/29	5♣	4/29	6/20	8/11	10/2	11/23	1/15	3/8
4/30	4♣	4/30	6/21	8/12	10/3	11/24	1/16	3/9

Planetary Period Dates
May

BIRTHDAY	CARD	MERCURY	VENUS	MARS	JUPITER	SATURN	URANUS	NEPTUNE
5/1	5♠	5/1	6/22	8/13	10/4	11/25	1/17	3/10
5/2	4♠	5/2	6/23	8/14	10/5	11/26	1/18	3/11
5/3	3♠	5/3	6/24	8/15	10/6	11/27	1/19	3/12
5/4	2♠	5/4	6/25	8/16	10/7	11/28	1/20	3/13
5/5	A♠	5/5	6/26	8/17	10/8	11/29	1/21	3/14
5/6	K♦	5/6	6/27	8/18	10/9	11/30	1/22	3/15
5/7	Q♦	5/7	6/28	8/19	10/10	12/1	1/23	3/16
5/8	J♦	5/8	6/29	8/20	10/11	12/2	1/24	3/17
5/9	10♦	5/9	6/30	8/21	10/12	12/3	1/25	3/18
5/10	9♦	5/10	7/1	8/22	10/13	12/4	1/26	3/19
5/11	8♦	5/11	7/2	8/23	10/14	12/5	1/27	3/20
5/12	7♦	5/12	7/3	8/24	10/15	12/6	1/28	3/21
5/13	6♦	5/13	7/4	8/25	10/16	12/7	1/29	3/22
5/14	5♦	5/14	7/5	8/26	10/17	12/8	1/30	3/23
5/15	4♦	5/15	7/6	8/27	10/18	12/9	1/31	3/24
5/16	3♦	5/16	7/7	8/28	10/19	12/10	2/1	3/25
5/17	2♦	5/17	7/8	8/29	10/20	12/11	2/2	3/26
5/18	A♦	5/18	7/9	8/30	10/21	12/12	2/3	3/27
5/19	K♣	5/19	7/10	8/31	10/22	12/13	2/4	3/28
5/20	Q♣	5/20	7/11	9/1	10/23	12/14	2/5	3/29
5/21	J♣	5/21	7/12	9/2	10/24	12/15	2/6	3/30
5/22	10♣	5/22	7/13	9/3	10/25	12/16	2/7	3/31
5/23	9♣	5/23	7/14	9/4	10/26	12/17	2/8	4/1
5/24	8♣	5/24	7/15	9/5	10/27	12/18	2/9	4/2
5/25	7♣	5/25	7/16	9/6	10/28	12/19	2/10	4/3
5/26	6♣	5/26	7/17	9/7	10/29	12/20	2/11	4/4
5/27	5♣	5/27	7/18	9/8	10/30	12/21	2/12	4/5
5/28	4♣	5/28	7/19	9/9	10/31	12/22	2/13	4/6
5/29	3♣	5/29	7/20	9/10	11/1	12/23	2/14	4/7
5/30	2♣	5/30	7/21	9/11	11/2	12/24	2/15	4/8
5/31	A♣	5/31	7/22	9/12	11/3	12/25	2/16	4/9

Planetary Period Dates
June

BIRTHDAY	CARD	MERCURY	VENUS	MARS	JUPITER	SATURN	URANUS	NEPTUNE
6/1	3♠	6/1	7/23	9/13	11/4	12/26	2/17	4/10
6/2	2♠	6/2	7/24	9/14	11/5	12/27	2/18	4/11
6/3	A♠	6/3	7/25	9/15	11/6	12/28	2/19	4/12
6/4	K♦	6/4	7/26	9/16	11/7	12/29	2/20	4/13
6/5	Q♦	6/5	7/27	9/17	11/8	12/30	2/21	4/14
6/6	J♦	6/6	7/28	9/18	11/9	1/1	2/22	4/15
6/7	10♦	6/7	7/29	9/19	11/10	1/2	2/23	4/16
6/8	9♦	6/8	7/30	9/20	11/11	1/3	2/24	4/17
6/9	8♦	6/9	7/31	9/21	11/12	1/4	2/25	4/18
6/10	7♦	6/10	8/1	9/22	11/13	1/5	2/26	4/19
6/11	6♦	6/11	8/2	9/23	11/14	1/6	2/27	4/20
6/12	5♦	6/12	8/3	9/24	11/15	1/7	2/28	4/21
6/13	4♦	6/13	8/4	9/25	11/16	1/8	3/1	4/22
6/14	3♦	6/14	8/5	9/26	11/17	1/9	3/2	4/23
6/15	2♦	6/15	8/6	9/27	11/18	1/10	3/3	4/24
6/16	A♦	6/16	8/7	9/28	11/19	1/11	3/4	4/25
6/17	K♣	6/17	8/8	9/29	11/20	1/12	3/5	4/26
6/18	Q♣	6/18	8/9	9/30	11/21	1/13	3/6	4/27
6/19	J♣	6/19	8/10	10/1	11/22	1/14	3/7	4/28
6/20	10♣	6/20	8/11	10/2	11/23	1/15	3/8	4/29
6/21	9♣	6/21	8/12	10/3	11/24	1/16	3/9	4/30
6/22	8♣	6/22	8/13	10/4	11/25	1/17	3/10	5/1
6/23	7♣	6/23	8/14	10/5	11/26	1/18	3/11	5/2
6/24	6♣	6/24	8/15	10/6	11/27	1/19	3/12	5/3
6/25	5♣	6/25	8/16	10/7	11/28	1/20	3/13	5/4
6/26	4♣	6/26	8/17	10/8	11/29	1/21	3/14	5/5
6/27	3♣	6/27	8/18	10/9	11/30	1/22	3/15	5/6
6/28	2♣	6/28	8/19	10/10	12/1	1/23	3/16	5/7
6/29	A♣	6/29	8/20	10/11	12/2	1/24	3/17	5/8
6/30	K♥	6/30	8/21	10/12	12/3	1/25	3/18	5/9

Planetary Period Dates
July

Birthday	Card	Mercury	Venus	Mars	Jupiter	Saturn	Uranus	Neptune
7/1	A♠	7/1	8/22	10/13	12/4	1/26	3/19	5/10
7/2	K♦	7/2	8/23	10/14	12/5	1/27	3/20	5/11
7/3	Q♦	7/3	8/24	10/15	12/6	1/28	3/21	5/12
7/4	J♦	7/4	8/25	10/16	12/7	1/29	3/22	5/13
7/5	10♦	7/5	8/26	10/17	12/8	1/30	3/23	5/14
7/6	9♦	7/6	8/27	10/18	12/9	1/31	3/24	5/15
7/7	8♦	7/7	8/28	10/19	12/10	2/1	3/25	5/16
7/8	7♦	7/8	8/29	10/20	12/11	2/2	3/26	5/17
7/9	6♦	7/9	8/30	10/21	12/12	2/3	3/27	5/18
7/10	5♦	7/10	8/31	10/22	12/13	2/4	3/28	5/19
7/11	4♦	7/11	9/1	10/23	12/14	2/5	3/29	5/20
7/12	3♦	7/12	9/2	10/24	12/15	2/6	3/30	5/21
7/13	2♦	7/13	9/3	10/25	12/16	2/7	3/31	5/22
7/14	A♦	7/14	9/4	10/26	12/17	2/8	4/1	5/23
7/15	K♣	7/15	9/5	10/27	12/18	2/9	4/2	5/24
7/16	Q♣	7/16	9/6	10/28	12/19	2/10	4/3	5/25
7/17	J♣	7/17	9/7	10/29	12/20	2/11	4/4	5/26
7/18	10♣	7/18	9/8	10/30	12/21	2/12	4/5	5/27
7/19	9♣	7/19	9/9	10/31	12/22	2/13	4/6	5/28
7/20	8♣	7/20	9/10	11/1	12/23	2/14	4/7	5/29
7/21	7♣	7/21	9/11	11/2	12/24	2/15	4/8	5/30
7/22	6♣	7/22	9/12	11/3	12/25	2/16	4/9	5/31
7/23	5♣	7/23	9/13	11/4	12/26	2/17	4/10	6/1
7/24	4♣	7/24	9/14	11/5	12/27	2/18	4/11	6/2
7/25	3♣	7/25	9/15	11/6	12/28	2/19	4/12	6/3
7/26	2♣	7/26	9/16	11/7	12/29	2/20	4/13	6/4
7/27	A♣	7/27	9/17	11/8	12/30	2/21	4/14	6/5
7/28	K♥	7/28	9/18	11/9	1/1	2/22	4/15	6/6
7/29	Q♥	7/29	9/19	11/10	1/2	2/23	4/16	6/7
7/30	J♥	7/30	9/20	11/11	1/3	2/24	4/17	6/8
7/31	10♥	7/31	9/21	11/12	1/4	2/25	4/18	6/9

Planetary Period Dates
August

Birthday	Card	Mercury	Venus	Mars	Jupiter	Saturn	Uranus	Neptune
8/1	Q♦	8/1	9/22	11/13	1/5	2/26	4/19	6/10
8/2	J♦	8/2	9/23	11/14	1/6	2/27	4/20	6/11
8/3	10♦	8/3	9/24	11/15	1/7	2/28	4/21	6/12
8/4	9♦	8/4	9/25	11/16	1/8	3/1	4/22	6/13
8/5	8♦	8/5	9/26	11/17	1/9	3/2	4/23	6/14
8/6	7♦	8/6	9/27	11/18	1/10	3/3	4/24	6/15
8/7	6♦	8/7	9/28	11/19	1/11	3/4	4/25	6/16
8/8	5♦	8/8	9/29	11/20	1/12	3/5	4/26	6/17
8/9	4♦	8/9	9/30	11/21	1/13	3/6	4/27	6/18
8/10	3♦	8/10	10/1	11/22	1/14	3/7	4/28	6/19
8/11	2♦	8/11	10/2	11/23	1/15	3/8	4/29	6/20
8/12	A♦	8/12	10/3	11/24	1/16	3/9	4/30	6/21
8/13	K♣	8/13	10/4	11/25	1/17	3/10	5/1	6/22
8/14	Q♣	8/14	10/5	11/26	1/18	3/11	5/2	6/23
8/15	J♣	8/15	10/6	11/27	1/19	3/12	5/3	6/24
8/16	10♣	8/16	10/7	11/28	1/20	3/13	5/4	6/25
8/17	9♣	8/17	10/8	11/29	1/21	3/14	5/5	6/26
8/18	8♣	8/18	10/9	11/30	1/22	3/15	5/6	6/27
8/19	7♣	8/19	10/10	12/1	1/23	3/16	5/7	6/28
8/20	6♣	8/20	10/11	12/2	1/24	3/17	5/8	6/29
8/21	5♣	8/21	10/12	12/3	1/25	3/18	5/9	6/30
8/22	4♣	8/22	10/13	12/4	1/26	3/19	5/10	7/1
8/23	3♣	8/23	10/14	12/5	1/27	3/20	5/11	7/2
8/24	2♣	8/24	10/15	12/6	1/28	3/21	5/12	7/3
8/25	A♣	8/25	10/16	12/7	1/29	3/22	5/13	7/4
8/26	K♥	8/26	10/17	12/8	1/30	3/23	5/14	7/5
8/27	Q♥	8/27	10/18	12/9	1/31	3/24	5/15	7/6
8/28	J♥	8/28	10/19	12/10	2/1	3/25	5/16	7/7
8/29	10♥	8/29	10/20	12/11	2/2	3/26	5/17	7/8
8/30	9♥	8/30	10/21	12/12	2/3	3/27	5/18	7/9
8/31	8♥	8/31	10/22	12/13	2/4	3/28	5/19	7/10

Planetary Period Dates
September

Birthday	Card	Mercury	Venus	Mars	Jupiter	Saturn	Uranus	Neptune
9/1	10♦	9/1	10/23	12/14	2/5	3/29	5/20	7/11
9/2	9♦	9/2	10/24	12/15	2/6	3/30	5/21	7/12
9/3	8♦	9/3	10/25	12/16	2/7	3/31	5/22	7/13
9/4	7♦	9/4	10/26	12/17	2/8	4/1	5/23	7/14
9/5	6♦	9/5	10/27	12/18	2/9	4/2	5/24	7/15
9/6	5♦	9/6	10/28	12/19	2/10	4/3	5/25	7/16
9/7	4♦	9/7	10/29	12/20	2/11	4/4	5/26	7/17
9/8	3♦	9/8	10/30	12/21	2/12	4/5	5/27	7/18
9/9	2♦	9/9	10/31	12/22	2/13	4/6	5/28	7/19
9/10	A♦	9/10	11/1	12/23	2/14	4/7	5/29	7/20
9/11	K♣	9/11	11/2	12/24	2/15	4/8	5/30	7/21
9/12	Q♣	9/12	11/3	12/25	2/16	4/9	5/31	7/22
9/13	J♣	9/13	11/4	12/26	2/17	4/10	6/1	7/23
9/14	10♣	9/14	11/5	12/27	2/18	4/11	6/2	7/24
9/15	9♣	9/15	11/6	12/28	2/19	4/12	6/3	7/25
9/16	8♣	9/16	11/7	12/29	2/20	4/13	6/4	7/26
9/17	7♣	9/17	11/8	12/30	2/21	4/14	6/5	7/27
9/18	6♣	9/18	11/9	1/1	2/22	4/15	6/6	7/28
9/19	5♣	9/19	11/10	1/2	2/23	4/16	6/7	7/29
9/20	4♣	9/20	11/11	1/3	2/24	4/17	6/8	7/30
9/21	3♣	9/21	11/12	1/4	2/25	4/18	6/9	7/31
9/22	2♣	9/22	11/13	1/5	2/26	4/19	6/10	8/1
9/23	A♣	9/23	11/14	1/6	2/27	4/20	6/11	8/2
9/24	K♥	9/24	11/15	1/7	2/28	4/21	6/12	8/3
9/25	Q♥	9/25	11/16	1/8	3/1	4/22	6/13	8/4
9/26	J♥	9/26	11/17	1/9	3/2	4/23	6/14	8/5
9/27	10♥	9/27	11/18	1/10	3/3	4/24	6/15	8/6
9/28	9♥	9/28	11/19	1/11	3/4	4/25	6/16	8/7
9/29	8♥	9/29	11/20	1/12	3/5	4/26	6/17	8/8
9/30	7♥	9/30	11/21	1/13	3/6	4/27	6/18	8/9

Planetary Period Dates
October

BIRTHDAY	CARD	MERCURY	VENUS	MARS	JUPITER	SATURN	URANUS	NEPTUNE
10/1	8♦	10/1	11/22	1/14	3/7	4/28	6/19	8/10
10/2	7♦	10/2	11/23	1/15	3/8	4/29	6/20	8/11
10/3	6♦	10/3	11/24	1/16	3/9	4/30	6/21	8/12
10/4	5♦	10/4	11/25	1/17	3/10	5/1	6/22	8/13
10/5	4♦	10/5	11/26	1/18	3/11	5/2	6/23	8/14
10/6	3♦	10/6	11/27	1/19	3/12	5/3	6/24	8/15
10/7	2♦	10/7	11/28	1/20	3/13	5/4	6/25	8/16
10/8	A♦	10/8	11/29	1/21	3/14	5/5	6/26	8/17
10/9	K♣	10/9	11/30	1/22	3/15	5/6	6/27	8/18
10/10	Q♣	10/10	12/1	1/23	3/16	5/7	6/28	8/19
10/11	J♣	10/11	12/2	1/24	3/17	5/8	6/29	8/20
10/12	10♣	10/12	12/3	1/25	3/18	5/9	6/30	8/21
10/13	9♣	10/13	12/4	1/26	3/19	5/10	7/1	8/22
10/14	8♣	10/14	12/5	1/27	3/20	5/11	7/2	8/23
10/15	7♣	10/15	12/6	1/28	3/21	5/12	7/3	8/24
10/16	6♣	10/16	12/7	1/29	3/22	5/13	7/4	8/25
10/17	5♣	10/17	12/8	1/30	3/23	5/14	7/5	8/26
10/18	4♣	10/18	12/9	1/31	3/24	5/15	7/6	8/27
10/19	3♣	10/19	12/10	2/1	3/25	5/16	7/7	8/28
10/20	2♣	10/20	12/11	2/2	3/26	5/17	7/8	8/29
10/21	A♣	10/21	12/12	2/3	3/27	5/18	7/9	8/30
10/22	K♥	10/22	12/13	2/4	3/28	5/19	7/10	8/31
10/23	Q♥	10/23	12/14	2/5	3/29	5/20	7/11	9/1
10/24	J♥	10/24	12/15	2/6	3/30	5/21	7/12	9/2
10/25	10♥	10/25	12/16	2/7	3/31	5/22	7/13	9/3
10/26	9♥	10/26	12/17	2/8	4/1	5/23	7/14	9/4
10/27	8♥	10/27	12/18	2/9	4/2	5/24	7/15	9/5
10/28	7♥	10/28	12/19	2/10	4/3	5/25	7/16	9/6
10/29	6♥	10/29	12/20	2/11	4/4	5/26	7/17	9/7
10/30	5♥	10/30	12/21	2/12	4/5	5/27	7/18	9/8
10/31	4♥	10/31	12/22	2/13	4/6	5/28	7/19	9/9

Planetary Period Dates
November

Birthday	Card	Mercury	Venus	Mars	Jupiter	Saturn	Uranus	Neptune
11/1	6♦	11/1	12/23	2/14	4/7	5/29	7/20	9/10
11/2	5♦	11/2	12/24	2/15	4/8	5/30	7/21	9/11
11/3	4♦	11/3	12/25	2/16	4/9	5/31	7/22	9/12
11/4	3♦	11/4	12/26	2/17	4/10	6/1	7/23	9/13
11/5	2♦	11/5	12/27	2/18	4/11	6/2	7/24	9/14
11/6	A♦	11/6	12/28	2/19	4/12	6/3	7/25	9/15
11/7	K♣	11/7	12/29	2/20	4/13	6/4	7/26	9/16
11/8	Q♣	11/8	12/30	2/21	4/14	6/5	7/27	9/17
11/9	J♣	11/9	1/1	2/22	4/15	6/6	7/28	9/18
11/10	10♣	11/10	1/2	2/23	4/16	6/7	7/29	9/19
11/11	9♣	11/11	1/3	2/24	4/17	6/8	7/30	9/20
11/12	8♣	11/12	1/4	2/25	4/18	6/9	7/31	9/21
11/13	7♣	11/13	1/5	2/26	4/19	6/10	8/1	9/22
11/14	6♣	11/14	1/6	2/27	4/20	6/11	8/2	9/23
11/15	5♣	11/15	1/7	2/28	4/21	6/12	8/3	9/24
11/16	4♣	11/16	1/8	3/1	4/22	6/13	8/4	9/25
11/17	3♣	11/17	1/9	3/2	4/23	6/14	8/5	9/26
11/18	2♣	11/18	1/10	3/3	4/24	6/15	8/6	9/27
11/19	A♣	11/19	1/11	3/4	4/25	6/16	8/7	9/28
11/20	K♥	11/20	1/12	3/5	4/26	6/17	8/8	9/29
11/21	Q♥	11/21	1/13	3/6	4/27	6/18	8/9	9/30
11/22	J♥	11/22	1/14	3/7	4/28	6/19	8/10	10/1
11/23	10♥	11/23	1/15	3/8	4/29	6/20	8/11	10/2
11/24	9♥	11/24	1/16	3/9	4/30	6/21	8/12	10/3
11/25	8♥	11/25	1/17	3/10	5/1	6/22	8/13	10/4
11/26	7♥	11/26	1/18	3/11	5/2	6/23	8/14	10/5
11/27	6♥	11/27	1/19	3/12	5/3	6/24	8/15	10/6
11/28	5♥	11/28	1/20	3/13	5/4	6/25	8/16	10/7
11/29	4♥	11/29	1/21	3/14	5/5	6/26	8/17	10/8
11/30	3♥	11/30	1/22	3/15	5/6	6/27	8/18	10/9

Planetary Period Dates
December

Birthday	Card	Mercury	Venus	Mars	Jupiter	Saturn	Uranus	Neptune
12/1	4♦	12/1	1/23	3/16	5/7	6/28	8/19	10/10
12/2	3♦	12/2	1/24	3/17	5/8	6/29	8/20	10/11
12/3	2♦	12/3	1/25	3/18	5/9	6/30	8/21	10/12
12/4	A♦	12/4	1/26	3/19	5/10	7/1	8/22	10/13
12/5	K♣	12/5	1/27	3/20	5/11	7/2	8/23	10/14
12/6	Q♣	12/6	1/28	3/21	5/12	7/3	8/24	10/15
12/7	J♣	12/7	1/29	3/22	5/13	7/4	8/25	10/16
12/8	10♣	12/8	1/30	3/23	5/14	7/5	8/26	10/17
12/9	9♣	12/9	1/31	3/24	5/15	7/6	8/27	10/18
12/10	8♣	12/10	2/1	3/25	5/16	7/7	8/28	10/19
12/11	7♣	12/11	2/2	3/26	5/17	7/8	8/29	10/20
12/12	6♣	12/12	2/3	3/27	5/18	7/9	8/30	10/21
12/13	5♣	12/13	2/4	3/28	5/19	7/10	8/31	10/22
12/14	4♣	12/14	2/5	3/29	5/20	7/11	9/1	10/23
12/15	3♣	12/15	2/6	3/30	5/21	7/12	9/2	10/24
12/16	2♣	12/16	2/7	3/31	5/22	7/13	9/3	10/25
12/17	A♣	12/17	2/8	4/1	5/23	7/14	9/4	10/26
12/18	K♥	12/18	2/9	4/2	5/24	7/15	9/5	10/27
12/19	Q♥	12/19	2/10	4/3	5/25	7/16	9/6	10/28
12/20	J♥	12/20	2/11	4/4	5/26	7/17	9/7	10/29
12/21	10♥	12/21	2/12	4/5	5/27	7/18	9/8	10/30
12/22	9♥	12/22	2/13	4/6	5/28	7/19	9/9	10/31
12/23	8♥	12/23	2/14	4/7	5/29	7/20	9/10	11/1
12/24	7♥	12/24	2/15	4/8	5/30	7/21	9/11	11/2
12/25	6♥	12/25	2/16	4/8	5/31	7/22	9/12	11/3
12/26	5♥	12/26	2/17	4/10	6/1	7/23	9/13	11/4
12/27	4♥	12/27	2/18	4/11	6/2	7/24	9/14	11/5
12/28	3♥	12/28	2/19	4/12	6/3	7/25	9/15	11/6
12/29	2♥	12/29	2/20	4/13	6/4	7/26	9/16	11/7
12/30	A♥	12/30	2/21	4/14	6/5	7/27	9/17	11/8
12/31	JOKER							

How to Do a One-Minute Reading

1. Find your Birth Card. Turn to the inside back cover of this book and find your birth date on the chart. The card listed in the first column (labeled "BC") is your Birth Card.

2. Find your Birth Card in the section titled The Yearly Spreads. Your two-page section will show your Birth Card at the top.

3. Find your current age in the left-hand column of these pages.

4. Follow the line of cards for your age to the right to the column marked "LR". The "LR" card listed here is your Long-Range Card, which will be a prominent influence in your life this year.

5. Find your Long-Range Card in the section titled The Card Interpretations. Within this section, find the interpretation labeled "[your Long-Range Card] Is Your Long-Range Card".

6. Read the interpretation of your Long-Range Card for this year. This card describes something that is of major importance to you during this entire year. Your Long-Range influence is just one small aspect of what is in store for you in *Cards of Your Destiny*. To begin doing full readings for yourself and for friends, turn to chapter two and follow the descriptions and instructions. Enjoy the mysteries revealed in the cards of your destiny!

PRODUCTS AND SERVICES BY ROBERT LEE CAMP
AND SEVEN THUNDERS PUBLISHING

Here we present a sampling of products and services that we offer readers on our website at www.7thunders.com. Come visit and enjoy free articles by Robert, a free Destiny E-Course, and free Destiny Readings! All the items listed here are found in the Products link at the top of every page.

Books

Cards of Your Destiny by Robert Lee Camp

392 pages, $27.99

This book is the other essential half of this system, where you can learn how to do amazingly accurate prediction readings for yourself or anyone you know. It shows you how to do yearly, fifty-two day, and weekly readings using the science of the cards. It includes the yearly spreads for every card in the deck, complete, step-by-step instructions, and a complete set of interpretations of every card in every one of ten possible positions. With this book, anyone can do readings for anyone else. You can even look in your past and see the cards for important events that have happened in your life.

Love Cards by Robert Lee Camp

400 pages, $27.99

Get a book for a friend. You can even have us mail it directly to them. Just send us their name, address, and birthday (for our records, if you know it) and we will send them a copy.

The Voice of the Seven Thunders Newsletter

6 issues per year, $12.00

Every two months, we publish our newsletter with articles on the cards, astrology, and other relevant topics. This is the best way to keep up on the latest discoveries made by Robert and others using this system.
SPECIAL! Send an email to themagi@7thunders.com to get your two free introductory issues.

Visions, Volumes I – IX

Ebooks downloaded after purchase
Prices vary from $12.95 - $14.95

Over twenty years of past articles on the cards, relationships, astrology, and spirituality by Robert Lee Camp. There is even a master volume that contains all nine for a special price. These books are all sold as PDFs.

***

Exploring the Little Book of the Seven Thunders by Robert Lee Camp

256 page, printed in color, $34.95

This is Robert Lee Camp's most recent book, the advanced book that was promised for many years. It will show you the roots of the system and how to read the cards in the ancient method that Robert was taught by his teacher. Once you begin using the ancient method, you will have much more information available to you. This book is better if you have read and understood *Cards of Your Destiny* and *Love Cards*. This new, updated version has over forty pages of more information and is perfect bound.

RECORDED LIVE WORKSHOPS WITH ROBERT LEE CAMP

The courses below are all recorded classes that Robert taught. Most come with handouts that you download. You watch these courses immediately after purchase in your web browser.

The Cards and Relationships

5 hours instruction $74.95

This five-hour live recorded class with Robert is where you will learn everything you need to know about how to use the cards in all of your relationship matters. Listen and follow along as Robert covers these topics:

- The many ways the Science of the Cards can help you with your relationships.
- What is attraction between couples and how does it operate? What connections are most responsible for it?
- The most important thing to consider when you are looking at two people's possibilities for a good relationship.
- How the relationship connections are derived.
- The important difference between Life Spread and Spiritual Spread connections.
- The number one most powerful sexual connection, and why.
- Who is marriageable, who isn't, and why? Which cards should never get married?
- How to do a relationship reading without using the Love Cards book.
- How to choose the best people for work, legal, health practitioners, and others that are non-intimate relationships.
- The importance of the Moon connection and how to spot these people quickly.
- When Saturn relationships are desired and beneficial.

These and many more topics are covered and many examples are covered as Robert interacts with the members of the class. This class will make you a master of choosing relationships.

The Intermediate Workshop
Six hours of instruction and handouts, $89.95
Also includes the yearly spreads for the fourteen people discussed in the class. This video workshop is all about learning how to use *The Cards of Your Destiny* book to make more accurate predictions. Learn the "Rules of Interpretation" that help you decide which cards in your yearly spreads are the most important. Learn how to find information in the yearly spreads on specific topics such as money, love, health, and travel. Watch Robert as he reviews all the elements of a yearly reading and how you can get the real messages that are there to be found. Hear questions and responses from the class and learn to interpret your cards better utilizing the latest discoveries.

***

The Advanced Card Training Course
Four hours of instruction and The Advanced Oracle Workbook (ebook format), $89.95
This original and ancient method of reading the cards is what you will encounter here. It is, by definition, more complex. But at the same time it offers you a wealth of information that is not available using the basic methods. This is the system as it was taught originally to Robert Lee Camp. His books took this complex method and simplified it to make it easier for everyone to use. But you can learn this ancient method now and have two to three times more information about anyone you are reading for.
 You will learn:

- How the Life Spread and Spiritual Spread are interconnected.
- How to create all of the 520 Yearly Spreads in the Cards of Your Destiny with only a deck of cards in your hand.
- How to Quadrate the deck to generate these yearly spreads and generate the Grand Solar Spreads
- How to locate and identify every card in the Yearly Spreads while looking at the Grand Solar Spreads, including the Environment, Displacement, Long Range, Pluto, etc.
- How to locate and use the Underlying Cards that give more meaning to each card in a Yearly Spread
- How to find the vertical Long Range Card, the Seven-Year Environment, Displacement, Pluto, and Result cards and how these become particularly important in certain years of life.
- How all the Auspicious Events listed in the Cards of Your Destiny book are identified in the Grand Solar Spreads
- The particular significance of the Critical Year, Rise to the Pinnacle, Pinnacle, and Most Blessed Years.
- Why the Fixed and Semi-Fixed cards are connected and why they are immune to many auspicious events.

Personal Readings and Computerized Reports

http://www.7thunders.com/products-services/destiny-reports/
Book of Destiny Yearly Report
35–45 pages in color, $24.95

These reports are great for personal use or for birthday presents. Every card in your yearly spreads is laid out and described in an organized manner. Includes your yearly Environment and Displacement Cards and reports on your Birthday Card as well as your Planetary Ruling Card or Personality Cards.

LOVER'S PROFILE REPORT

20–26 pages in color, $24.95

From our new version of Love Cards Reporter, this report takes you and someone close to you and does a complete analysis of your compatibility as taught in the book *Love Cards*. Includes the affirmations and in-depth analysis of each of the seven most significant connections between the partners of an intimate relationship. You will have to see these reports to really believe how great they are. They incorporate many advanced features to present an easy-to-read and very informative analysis of two people in love. You can also specify this as a **Friends and Family Report** or a **Business Associates Report**, which has completely different interpretations for those kinds of relationships.

A PERSONAL READING WITH ROBERT LEE CAMP

http://www.7thunders.com/personal-readings/personal-readings-with-robert/
60 minutes by phone, or in person, recorded, $300.00

Applying the Science of the Cards and astrology, my intent in giving you a reading is to open up the doors of your understanding of yourself. My readings are based upon the premise that you are the creator of your destiny. If I can reveal your power to you, along with the reasons why you have created your life to be the way it is right now, then you are free to make whatever changes you desire in your life and create a life that is closer to your ideals and dreams. I will do a complete analysis of both your Life Path Cards and your Astrological Natal Chart as you and I explore your deepest issues and reasons for being here on the planet. Includes the natal analysis, examination of your relationships, as well as the next one to three years of significant events. Once you know the cycles you are currently in, you can plan better for the future and take advantage of the influences.

Professional Destiny Software

http://www.7thunders.com/products-services/software/

We now have computer software for PCs and online software for all computers that do readings and create reports you can sell or share with others. The online versions, which are compatible with all computers that can browse the web, create Love Cards reports and Yearly Destiny Reports and are subscription based. Our desktop software for PCs only does the same but is a one-time purchase. People use the software for their personal use as well as a way to make money. How you use it is up to you.

- The Book of Destiny Professional for Windows 3.7 $399
- Love Cards Professional for Windows 3.0 $349
- The Book of Destiny 4.0 Web-based software $10-$35/month depending on which version
- Love Cards 4.0 Web-based software $10-$35/month depending on which version

Destiny Apps for iPhone and Android Phones and Devices

We have a basic app for cell phones that does daily, yearly, fifty-two-day and Birth Card readings. Just search in your app store for *My Destiny Cards*. These work on iPhones, iPads, and Android phones and tablets.

Free How to Read Your Destiny E-Course

Come to www.7thunders.com or www.e7thunders.com and sign up for our 17-day E-Course. This fun and educational course introduces you to all the concepts and methods found in the Destiny Cards system and includes some product specials as well.

Visit the Seven Thunders Publishing Website!

We have a host of information and resources for you to take advantage of on our website. The URL (address) is: http://www.7thunders.com

You can look up your Birth Card, download freeware software for Windows, find out about upcoming workshops and events with Robert Lee Camp as well as read many free articles by Robert. You can also send us email from the site and ask questions about the things you are learning from Robert's books. Come and take advantage of this free service to our readers and students!

Free Newsletter Subscription and Catalog!

_____Yes! I want my free subscription to *The Voice of the Seven Thunders* newsletter with articles by Robert Camp on the cards and other spiritual topics.

Name: _____ Your birthday: ____/____/_____
Address: _____ City: _____ State: ____ Zip: _____
Phone 1: (____) ____-_____ Phone 2: (____) ____-_____
Email Address: _____@_____

Send to the address on our website or email us at news@7thunders.com with your information.

Our current address:
Seven Thunders Publishing
6 Sunrise Valley
Leicester, NC 28748
(828) 236-0221
themagi@7thunders.com

Keep in mind that our address and phone numbers can change. Always check our website first to see what they are before contacting us.

Birth Card and Planetary Ruling Card Chart

January

	BC	PRC		BC	PRC
1	K♠	5♣	17	10♦	5♥
2	Q♠	K♣	18	9♦	4♥
3	J♠	10♦	19	8♦	10♠
4	10♠	7♦	20	7♦	2♥
5	9♠	4♣	21	6♦	A♥ or A♦*
6	8♠	3♣	22	5♦	K♣
7	7♠	4♦	23	4♦	10♣
8	6♠	3♥	24	3♦	9♣
9	5♠	K♥	25	2♦	10♦
10	4♠	A♦	26	A♦	7♣
11	3♠	J♣	27	K♣	6♣
12	2♠	10♣	28	Q♣	7♦
13	A♠	9♣	29	J♣	4♥
14	K♦	8♣	30	10♣	10♠
15	Q♦	7♣	31	9♣	4♣
16	J♦	6♣			

February

	BC	PRC		BC	PRC
1	J♠	8♠	16	9♦	4♦
2	10♠	5♠	17	8♦	5♣
3	9♠	2♦	18	7♦	K♥
4	8♠	3♠	19	6♦	A♥
5	7♠	2♠	20	5♦	K♣ or J♦*
6	6♠	A♣	21	4♦	8♦
7	5♠	K♦	22	3♦	9♠
8	4♠	Q♦	23	2♦	8♠
9	3♠	9♦	24	A♦	5♦
10	2♠	8♦	25	K♣	6♦
11	A♠	9♠	26	Q♣	5♠
12	K♦	6♦	27	J♣	4♦
13	Q♦	5♦	28	10♣	5♣
14	J♦	6♠	29	9♣	2♦
15	10♦	3♣			

March

	BC	PRC		BC	PRC
1	9♠	J♠	17	6♦	Q♦
2	8♠	9♥	18	5♦	J♦
3	7♠	8♥	19	4♦	8♦
4	6♠	Q♣	20	3♦	9♠ or 7♦*
5	5♠	6♥	21	2♦	8♠ or 6♦*
6	4♠	5♥	22	A♦	3♣
7	3♠	7♠	23	K♣	4♦
8	2♠	K♠	24	Q♣	3♦
9	A♠	2♥	25	J♣	2♦
10	K♦	4♦	26	10♣	3♦
11	Q♦	Q♠	27	9♣	K♥
12	J♦	Q♥	28	8♣	10♥
13	10♦	3♠	29	7♣	J♣
14	9♦	2♠	30	6♣	10♣
15	8♦	3♦	31	5♣	7♥
16	7♦	K♦			

April

	BC	PRC		BC	PRC
1	7♠	J♦	16	5♦	9♦
2	6♠	8♦	17	4♦	6♣
3	5♠	9♠	18	3♦	7♦
4	4♠	8♠	19	2♦	6♦
5	3♠	5♦	20	A♦	3♣ or 5♥*
6	2♠	6♠	21	K♣	4♦ or 4♥*
7	A♠	5♠	22	Q♣	5♣
8	K♦	2♦	23	J♣	7♠
9	Q♦	3♠	24	10♣	K♠
10	J♦	2♠	25	9♣	2♥
11	10♦	A♦	26	8♣	4♠
12	9♦	K♣	27	7♣	Q♠
13	8♦	A♣	28	6♣	Q♥
14	7♦	9♣	29	5♣	A♠
15	6♦	10♦	30	4♣	J♠

May

	BC	PRC		BC	PRC
1	5♠	9♣	17	2♦	8♣
2	4♠	10♦	18	A♦	5♥
3	3♠	7♣	19	K♣	4♥
4	2♠	6♣	20	Q♣	5♣ or 10♠*
5	A♠	7♦	21	J♣	7♠ or 9♦*
6	K♦	4♣	22	10♣	K♠ or 8♦*
7	Q♦	3♣	23	9♣	9♠
8	J♦	4♦	24	8♣	6♦
9	10♦	A♥	25	7♣	5♦
10	9♦	2♣	26	6♣	6♠
11	8♦	3♥	27	5♣	3♦
12	7♦	J♥	28	4♣	2♦
13	6♦	10♥	29	3♣	3♦
14	5♦	J♣	30	2♣	K♣
15	4♦	8♥	31	A♣	Q♣
16	3♦	7♥			

June

	BC	PRC		BC	PRC
1	3♠	9♥	16	A♦	Q♦
2	2♠	8♥	17	K♣	J♦
3	A♠	7♥	18	Q♣	10♠
4	K♦	6♥	19	J♣	9♦
5	Q♦	5♥	20	10♣	8♦
6	J♦	4♥	21	9♣	9♠
7	10♦	8♣	22	8♣	6♦ or J♠*
8	9♦	7♠	23	7♣	9♥
9	8♦	K♠	24	6♣	8♥
10	7♦	5♠	25	5♣	10♠
11	6♦	4♠	26	4♣	6♥
12	5♦	Q♠	27	3♣	5♥
13	4♦	2♠	28	2♣	7♠
14	3♦	A♠	29	A♣	3♥
15	2♦	J♠	30	K♥	2♥

* denotes cusp birth dates—see page 109 for full explanation.